A HISTORY OF

Christianity in Asia

VOLUME II

American Society of Missiology Series, No. 36

A HISTORY OF

Christianity in Asia

VOLUME II:

1500 to 1900

Samuel Hugh Moffett

ORBIS BOOKS

Maryknoll, New York 10545

Founded in 1970, Orbis Books endeavors to publish works that enlighten the mind, nourish the spirit, and challenge the conscience. The publishing arm of the Maryknoll Fathers and Brothers, Orbis seeks to explore the global dimensions of the Christian faith and mission, to invite dialogue with the diverse cultures and religious traditions, and to serve the cause of reconciliation and peace. The books published reflect the views of their authors and do not represent the official position of the Maryknoll Society. To obtain more information about Maryknoll and Orbis Books, please visit our website at www.maryknoll.org.

Library of Congress Cataloging-in-Publication Data

Moffett, Samuel H.
    A history of Christianity in Asia/ Samuel Hugh Moffett. Vol. 2.
      p. cm.
    Includes bibliographical references and index.
    Contents: v. 1 Beginnings to 1500. V. 2. 1500–1900.
    ISBN 1-57075-450-0
    1. Church history – Asia. I. Title.
BR1065.M63 1998
   275 – dc21
                                     97-49236

Contents

Part I: They Came by Sea: The Return of the West (1500–1800)

v

Part II: The Protestants Reach Asia (1600–1800)

Part III: "The Great Century" (1784–1860)

SECTION ONE:
PROTESTANTS AND CATHOLICS IN COMPETITION

Preface to the ASM Series

The purpose of the ASM (American Society of Missiology) series is to publish — without regard for disciplinary, national, or denominational boundaries — scholarly works of high quality and wide interest on missiological themes from the entire spectrum of scholarly pursuits relevant to Christian mission, which is always the focus of books in the series.

By *mission* is meant the effort to effect passage over the boundary between faith in Jesus Christ and its absence. In this understanding of mission, the basic functions of Christian proclamation, dialogue, witness, service, worship, liberation, and nurture are of special concern. And in that context questions arise, including, How does the transition from one cultural context to another influence the shape and interaction between these dynamic functions, especially in regard to the cultural and religious plurality that comprise the global context of Christian mission?

The promotion of scholarly dialogue among missiologists and among missiologists and scholars in other fields of inquiry may involve the publication of views that some missiologists cannot accept and with which members of the Editorial Committee do not agree. Manuscripts published in the series reflect the opinions of their authors and are not understood to represent the position of the American Society of Missiology or of the Editorial Committee. Selection is guided by such criteria as intrinsic worth, readability, and accessibility to a range of interested persons and not merely to experts or specialists.

The ASM Series, in collaboration with Orbis Books, seeks to publish scholarly works of high merit and wide interest on numerous aspects of missiology — the scholarly study of mission. Able presentations on new and creative approaches to the practice and understanding of mission will receive close attention.

The ASM Series Committee
JONATHAN J. BONK
ANGELYN DRIES, O.S.F.
SCOTT W. SUNQUIST

Preface

Meaning was built into life, in the beginning, by the Creator.
— Henry R. Luce (1898–1967)

I once was lost, but now I'm found; was blind, but now I see.
— John Newton (1779)

The future is as bright as all the promises of God.
— Adoniram Judson (1788–1850)

All the great religions of the world were born in Asia. Why is it that Christianity, which is larger and more universal than any one of them, spread more slowly in the land of its birth than on any other continent on earth?

Buddha was born in Asia, and most of the world's Buddhists live in Asia. Confucius was born in Asia, and most of the world's Confucianists live in Asia. Hinduism was born in Asia, and most of the world's Hindus live in Asia. Muhammad was born in Asia, and most of the world's Muslims live in Asia. Abraham was born in Asia, and the only Jewish nation in the world is in Asia.

Jesus Christ was born in Asia. But statistically at least, Asia is the least Christian continent in the world. Why? Why is it that if judged by the total reported number of members and adherents of the world's Christian churches, Latin America is 92.7 percent Christian, North America is 84.5 percent Christian, Oceania is 82.6 percent Christian, Europe is 76.5 percent Christian, Africa is 45.6 percent Christian, but Asia is at the most 8.5 percent Christian?[1]

Other questions, often asked, are just as important. Why should Christianity be expected to have any more adherents than that? Doesn't the continent already have enough great religions of its own? Are not its traditional majority religions best for Asia, and Christianity perhaps better for somewhere else? If the four hundred years of history in Asia that are the subject of this volume are any criteria for judgment, an answer to these questions will not be easy.

Fifty or so years ago at Yale, the story floated around the divinity school quadrangle that the professor of homiletics one day met the professor of church history, Roland Bainton, coming out of chapel. He said, "Roley, how can you know so much about church history and still be a Christian?" I do not know how Bainton answered him, but in all honesty it must be admitted that in Asia the missionary story of those four hundred years is a tumbled mixture of guns, greed, and amazing grace. It was the period of the greatest global, colonial occupation of conquered territory by Christian nations in history, and it was the period of greatest church expansion in history. It was not all bad, and it was not all good. But which word describes it better?

This volume does not pretend to have found a definitive answer to that question. It does, however, attempt to describe four centuries, from 1500 to 1900, of Christianity in Asia, both the good and the bad, in a way that may suggest an answer. But first a look back. Christianity came to Asia first by land, then by sea. For the first fifteen hundred years the land played the larger part in the shaping of the history of Christianity across Asia. Except in the case of Saint Thomas, who never fit comfortably into expected patterns and, it is said, came to India by sea, the gospel traveled by land. Jesus walked from Galilee to Judea, and rode into Jerusalem on a donkey. Addai's mission to Osrhoene in eastern Syria, which may have been "the first Christian kingdom," and the conversion of Tiridates, king of Armenia, which resulted in the first documented Christian kingdom a whole decade before Europe was converted Constantine — both were missions by land, not by sea. For centuries the dusty ribbon of the Old Silk Road tied Asia fitfully together along the longest, lowest, highest, hottest, and coldest highway in the world. In the seventh century it brought Alopen the Persian, first known Christian missionary to China, five thousand miles through mountain passes so cold that trees exploded as they passed.

It also brought Buddhists from India and Muslim Arab armies east across Central Asia to China, and it was on the same Old Silk Road in the other direction that the fierce Mongol horsemen of Genghis Khan rode west to invade Christian Europe. But at the same time, the thirteenth century, Mongol China welcomed the golden age of the Nestorians in Asia, the *pax Mongolica*, when Genghis Khan had a Christian daughter-in-law, and a Mongol Christian patriarch in Baghdad ruled an Asian church that stretched by land from Persia to the Pacific.

Volume 1 of this history ended on a melancholy note. That church, alas, almost disappeared after A.D. 1500, and the story suddenly changes.

Beginning about the year 1500 Asian history accelerates like a motion picture shifting from slow motion to fast, and it was the sea, not the land, that began to shape the change. Compare the slow waves of imperial rise and decline that moved across Asia between the time of Christ and the beginning of the sixteenth century — Roman, Persian, Indian, Chinese, Islamic, and Mongol — with the bewildering hurricanes that tore into the great continent in the next four hundred years.

It was the sea that carried the Portuguese to India and the Spaniards to the Philippines. It brought Xavier to Japan, Ricci to China, the Dutch to the Spice Islands of Indonesia, the British to India and China, the Moravians to South India, and Carey to Calcutta. They came to Asia in waves of a renewed and revived Christianity that was neither Nestorian nor unchallenged medieval Catholic. The first wave, it is true, was at first traditional Iberian Catholic for more than two hundred years. The second was Protestant, tentatively at first, in 1600, and then in strength in 1800.

They came by sea, those Western intruders. They came with missionaries, the salt of the earth, but their ships were heavier with guns than with missionaries, and the guns spoke louder than the missionaries. It was a tidal wave, and in a tidal wave no one notices the salt at first; the invaded are too busy desperately trying to escape the engulfing weight of the water. It is not surprising, therefore, that many have assumed that Western imperialism and Western missionaries came hand in hand, and that both were therefore to be condemned. But the history of colliding cultures is far more complex than that. The convergence of religions and empires is as multilayered as an artichoke, and we will do well in the following pages to peel the layers apart very carefully in order to distinguish where they clearly separate and where they adhere so closely as to seem indivisible.

Asia in its first fifteen hundred years had been a slow succession of dominating, intermittently clashing empires: Rome against Islam, the Mongols against India and Byzantium. After 1500 it more closely resembled the witches' cauldron in Macbeth, "bubble, bubble, toil and trouble," as four different Asias took shape out of the roiling vapor. We end this survey in 1900, but bear in mind that the continent is now usually divided into four sections: East Asia (the Far East), South Asia, West Asia (the Middle East), and Russian North Asia.

East Asia is still dominated by China's culture but not its politics. West Asia, for most of the last five hundred years, has been subject to two empires — strong Ottoman Turkey and weaker Persia — and to one religion, Islam, with two faces, Sunni and Shiite. South Asia centers still in Hindu India geographically, demographically, and statistically, though religiously its Hinduism is laced with strong, large pockets of Islam in Indonesia, Pakistan, and Bangladesh, and smaller enclaves of Buddhism in Burma (Myanmar), Ceylon (Sri Lanka), and Siam (Thailand). North Asia until very recently was Russia, for four hundred years an empire of Christian Orthodoxy, followed by almost one hundred years of communism, but now the farther south one moves in the west, the former Soviet Union is a collection of autonomous border states more Muslim than Christian. And the largest single religion in Asia is Islam.

Some clarification of terms and methods is needed here. What do I mean by "Asia," for example? Volume 1 sharpened its focus by concentrating mainly on the spread of Nestorian (that is, Syrian-Persian) Christianity as it spread across the continent. In that perspective Asia was arbitrarily limited roughly to Asia east of the Euphrates and south of Russia. In Volume 2 the focus has to widen, and the term "Asia" includes here everything from the Mediterranean to the Pacific, except for what the United Nations designates as Russia. To put it another way, this volume loosely follows the U.N. division of the continent into the four units described above, but excludes the whole northern cross-continental tier of the old Soviet Union, the new Russian Republic, which is sometimes called Eurasia.

The sixteenth century presented historians of Asia with another problem. Gutenberg introduced the Asian art of printing with movable metal type to Europe. It may have been invented in Korea as early as the thirteenth century. Whereas formerly the available sources of information had been too few, the art of printing added this new dimension of communication to our expanding world, and books have become too numerous to count, much less read. Every century since the sixteenth has been busy writing and printing about Asia. The problem is no longer lack of material but how to separate the wheat from the chaff.

Furthermore, the sheer size of Asia compounds the problem of describing Christianity as a movement of peoples and of the spirit, not merely a religious institution. The Asia of 1900 is not the Asia of the first century or even the sixteenth. In the first century Asia's population (excluding what is now Russia) was probably about 122 million in a world of 180 million; by 1500 it was about 277 million out of 425 million; and in 1900 almost a billion — 946 million — in a world population of 1.62 billion.[2] Note how dominant was Asia's part in the population explosion. The changing mix of cultures churned up on this one continent by such rapid growth makes continental generalizations dangerous and even country-by-country analysis difficult but necessary.

Another problem is periodization. History does not happen in decades or even centuries. I have used chronological periods as a convenience, not a cage, and where the flow of the narrative seems to be more important than chronological boundaries, I allow the periods to bend and blend and overlap at either end. So, though I divide this second volume of *A History of Christianity in Asia* roughly into three unequal parts — 1500–1800, 1800–1850 or 1860, and 1860–1900 — the momentum may cross decade and century datelines as well as area markers or ecclesiastical divisions.

The question of whether to use contemporary names and spellings of persons and places or those used during the period that this book deals with yields to no easy solutions. If one uses "Burma" instead of "Myanmar," "Ceylon" instead of "Sri Lanka," "Hong Kong" instead of "Xiangang," "Tzü Hsi" instead of "Cixi," or "Macao" instead of "Aomen," one runs the risk of appearing old fashioned and insensitive to legitimate postcolonial criticisms. In general, I use Pinyin transliterations of Chinese terms and contemporary names of places while putting their traditional names in parentheses. In the case of Macao and Hong Kong, however, I judge that the old conventions still seem to be observed by most English-language writers and use the old spellings myself. I am very grateful to Professors Michael Nai Chiu Poon of the Center for the Study of Christianity in Asia in Singapore and Lalsangkima Pachuau of United Theological College in Bangalore for their expert advice and comments. In another generation perfect consistency in such matters will be possible. I began working on this book when one set of standards was in place and complete it as another set is settling in. I have done the best I can to make room for the new and look forward to seeing the work of today's generation of well-trained Asian scholars, as they work through the period this volume deals with. They will have the advantage of knowing Asian languages and the ability to consult archival materials that were not available to me, and they will work out nomenclature standards in collaboration with their Asian peers.

I must once again express my indebtedness to the many monographs and secondary sources that lack of space forces me to acknowledge only in the footnotes. A survey of four hundred years of the history of the largest continent in the world can often do no more than point to the primary sources, but I will try to indicate the source of later citations. A part of this study was made possible by the generosity of the Pew Foundation's Glen Mead Trust through the Overseas Ministries Study Center in New Haven, Connecticut. The Henry Luce Foundation also assisted generously in seeing this work through to publication. The gracious librarians and unparalleled resources for church history in the Speer and Luce Libraries of Princeton Theological Seminary, and the gracious help of the staff in its archives, together with the invaluable collections of the Princeton University libraries, were the perfect supporting environment for the long journey. I wish to thank in a special way Joan LaFlamme, John Eagleson, Mary Ellen Eagleson, and Bob Land for their careful work in checking and correcting references and for editing the text. Thanks also to Loren Muehlius of Global Mapping International for designing the maps and to Image Club Graphics for the reproduction of Gerardus Mercator Jr.'s map of Asia. The work of Bill Burrows and Catherine Costello of Orbis Books was invaluable.

But the best and truest help of all was my wife, Eileen. Without her there would have been no first volume, and no second one, and no joy in the journey. But God is good, and before the journey ends there still may be time for a look at the critical hundred years of the twentieth century. There is always hope.

NOTES

1. See David B. Barrett et al., eds., *World Christian Encyclopedia*, 2nd ed. (New York: Oxford University Press, 2001), 13. The shifting boundaries of Russia confuse statistical comparisons of Asia and Europe in 1900 and 2000.

2. See the table in David B. Barrett, *World Christian Encyclopedia* (New York: Oxford University Press, 1982), 796.

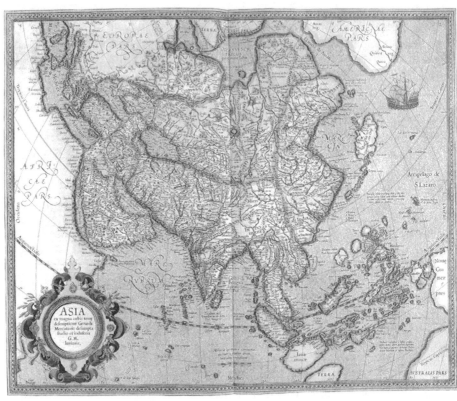

Asia as mapped and imagined by Europeans in the early seventeenth century, c. 1628.
The Latin inscription reads: Asia ex magna orbis terrae descriptione Gerardi Mercatoris
desumpta, studio et industria G. M. Junioris (Asia, based on the great map of the world
by Gerard Mercator, through the inquiries and efforts of Gerard Mercator, Junior).
Reproduced courtesy of Folger Institute.

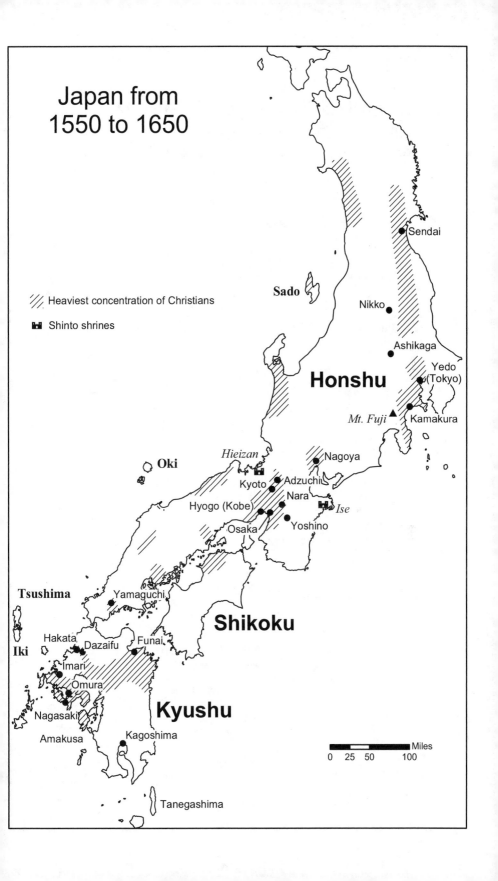

Japan from 1550 to 1650

//// Heaviest concentration of Christians

⛩ Shinto shrines

Sado

● Sendai

Nikko ●

● Ashikaga

Honshu

Yedo (Tokyo)

Mt. Fuji ▲ ● Kamakura

Hieizan

● Nagoya

Kyoto ● Adzuchi

Nara

Hyogo (Kobe) ● *Ise*

Osaka ● Yoshino

○ **Oki**

Tsushima

Yamaguchi ●

Shikoku

Hakata

Dazaifu Funai ●

Iki

Imari

Omura

Nagasaki

Kyushu

Amakusa Kagoshima ●

Tanegashima

Miles
0 25 50 100

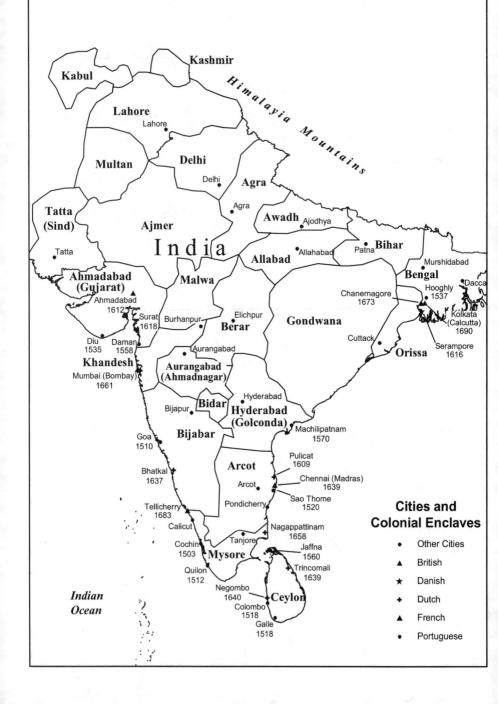

India and Ceylon in 1707

European Encroachments on India and Ceylon from the 16th to the Beginning of the 18th Centuries

Kabul

Kashmir

Himalayia Mountains

Lahore
Lahore

Multan

Delhi
Delhi

Agra
Agra

Tatta (Sind)
Tatta

Ajmer

Awadh
Ajodhya

I n d i a

Allabad
Allahabad

Patna • Bihar

Murshidabad

Bengal

Ahmadabad (Gujarat)
Ahmadabad 1612 ▲

Malwa

Chanernagore 1673

Hooghly • 1537

Dacca

Diu 1535

Daman 1558

Surat 1618

Burhanpur

Elichpur

Berar

Gondwana

Kolkata (Calcutta) 1690

Khandesh
Mumbai (Bombay) 1661

Aurangabad

Aurangabad (Ahmadnagar)

Cuttack

Orissa

Serampore 1616

Hyderabad

Bidar
Bijapur •

Hyderabad (Golconda)

Goa 1510

Bijabar

Machilipatnam 1570

Pulicat 1609

Arcot
Arcot •

Bhatkal 1637

Chennai (Madras) 1639

Tellicherry 1683

Pondicherry

Sao Thome 1520

Calicut

Nagappattinam 1658

Cochin 1503

Tanjore

Mysore

Jaffna 1560

Quilon 1512

Trincomali 1639

Negombo 1640

Indian Ocean

Colombo 1518

Ceylon

Galle 1518

Cities and Colonial Enclaves

- • Other Cities
- ▲ British
- ★ Danish
- + Dutch
- ▲ French
- • Portuguese

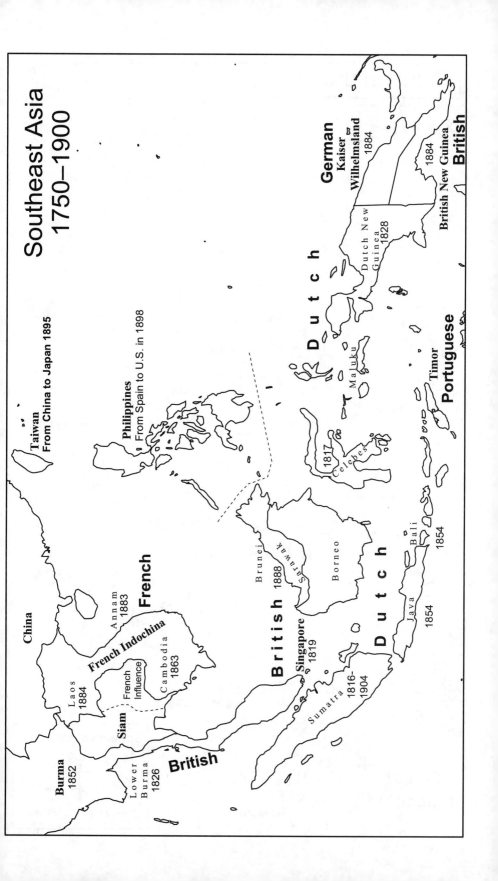

Southeast Asia
1750–1900

Taiwan
From China to Japan 1895

Philippines
From Spain to U.S. in 1898

China

French

Annam
1883

French Indochina

Laos
1884

Cambodia
1863

French
Influence

Siam

Burma
1852

Lower
Burma
1826

British

British

Singapore
1819

Brunei

Sarawak
1888

Borneo

Sumatra
1816–
1904

Dutch

Java
1854

Bali
1854

1817

Celebes

Dutch

Maluku

Timor
Portuguese

1854

German

Kaiser
Wilhelmsland
1884

Dutch New
Guinea
1828

British New Guinea
1884

British

The Korean Peninsula in 1900

Russia

Manchuko

Ch'ongjin

Kimch'aek

Kanggye

Hamhung
Hungnam

K o r e a

Wonsan

Sinuiju

P'yongyang

Namp'o

Kangnung

Ch'unch'on

Kaesong

Haeju

Seoul

Wonju
Chech'on

Ch'ungju

Andong
P'ohang

Ch'onan

Ch'ongju

Kyongju

Taejon

Taegu
Ulsan

Iri

Kimhae

Kunsan
Chonju

Masan
Pusan
Chinhae

Chinju

Kwangju

Sunch'on

Yosu

Mokp'o

Miles
0   25   50   75   100

Abbreviations and Acronyms of Journals, Annuals, and Organizations

ABCFM	American Board of Commissioners for Foreign Missions
AFH	*Archivum Franciscanum Historicum* (Rome)
AJT	*Asia Journal of Theology* (Bangalore, India)
APF	*Annals of the Propagation of the Faith* (Rome, Dublin)
ASJT	*Asiatic Society of Japan, Transactions* (Yokohama)
BER	*British Evangelical Review* (Carlisle, Cambria, U.K.)
BJRL	*Bulletin of the John Rylands Library* (Manchester)
CE	*The Catholic Encyclopedia* (New York, 1907, 1912)
ChF	*Ching Feng* (Hong Kong)
ChHB	*The Church at Home and Abroad* (Philadelphia)
ChM	*China's Millions* (Philadelphia); later, *East Asia's Millions*
ChMYB	*China Mission Year Book* (Shanghai, 1910–1938/1939)
CHR	*The Catholic Historical Review for the Study of the Church History of the United States* (Washington, D.C.)
ChRec	*The Chinese Recorder* (Shanghai and Foochow [Fuzhou])
ChRep	*The Chinese Repository* (Guangzhou)
CIM	China Inland Mission
CMIR	*Church Missionary Intelligencer and Record* (London)
CMS	Church Missionary Society
DTC	*Dictionnaire de Théologie Catholique* (Paris, 1903)
EAH	*Encyclopedia of Asian History* (New York: Scribner's, 1988)
EAPR	*East Asian Pastoral Review* (Manila/Quezon City)
EMQ	*Evangelical Missions Quarterly* (Wheaton, Illinois)
EM-Z	*Evangelische Missions — Zeitschrift* (Stuttgart)
ERel	*The Encyclopedia of Religion* (New York: Macmillan, 1987)
ERev	*The Edinburgh Review* (Edinburgh, Scotland)

FH   *Fides et Historia* (Grand Rapids, Michigan, Calvin College)

FM   *The Foreign Missionary* (New York)

GAL   *The Gospel in All Lands* (Baltimore)

IBMR   *International Bulletin of Missionary Research* (New Haven, Connecticut)

ICHR   *Indian Church History Review* (Bangalore)

IIASN   *International Association of Asian Studies Newsletter* (Leiden)

IM   *Immanuel: A Journal of Religious Thought and Research in Israel* (Jerusalem)

IndMD   *Indian Missions Directory.* Under various titles and publishers: Directory of Protestant Indian Christians; Year Book of Missions in India, Burma, and Ceylon; Directory of Christian Missions in I.B.C.; Directory of Churches in India and Pakistan, etc. (1900–)

IRM   *International Review of Mission* (Geneva)

ISPCK   India Society for Promoting Christian Knowledge

JA   *Journal Asiatique* (Paris)

JAS   *Journal of Asian Studies*

JCQ   *The Japan Christian Quarterly* (Tokyo)

KR   *The Korea Repository* (Seoul)

LMS   The London Missionary Society

MH   *The Missionary Herald* (Boston)

MIS   *Missiology* (Scottdale, Pennsylvania)

MN   *Monumenta Nipponica* (Tokyo)

MRW   *The Missionary Review of the World* (OS to 1887, Princeton, N.J.; NS New York, 1888–)

NAJT   *Northeast Asia Journal of Theology* (Tokyo)

NCE   *New Catholic Encyclopedia* (New York, 1967)

NRSM   *Nouvelle Revue de Science Missionaire* (Immensee, Switzerland). See also *NZM* (Uznach)

NZG   Netherlands Missionary Society (Nederlandsch Zendeling Genoorschap)

NZM   *Neue Zeitschrift für Missionswissenschaft* (Uznach)

NZV   Netherlands Missionary Union (Nederlandsche Zendings-Vereeniging)

OMS   Oriental Missionary Society

OW	*Operation World*, 1974–1993 (Grand Rapids, Michigan: Zondervan)
PIA	Protestants, Independents, and Anglicans
PS	*Philippine Studies* (Manila)
RBM	*Reformed Bulletin of Missions* (Philadelphia)
RHM	*Revue d'Histoire des Missions* (Paris)
RM	Rhenish Mission
SEAJT	*South East Asia Journal of Theology* (Singapore)
SPCK	Society for Promoting Christian Knowledge
SPG	Society for the Propagation of the Gospel in Foreign Parts
TRAS	*Transactions of the Royal Asiatic Society* (London)
TRASK	*Transactions of the Korea Branch of the Royal Asiatic Society* (Seoul)
UZV	Utrecht Missionary Society (Utrechtse Zendingsvereniging)
WM	*Women and Missions* (New York)
ZGK	Dutch Reformed Missionary Association (Nederlandsche Gereformeerde Zendingsvereeniging)
ZMR	*Zeitschrift für Missionswissenschaft und Religionswissenschaft* (Munster)

PART I

They Came by Sea: The Return of the West (1500–1800)

1500 A.D. 49 generations after Christ, the world is 19% Christians (92.6% of them white, 21% evangelized, printed scriptures available in 12 languages).
— David B. Barrett, *Cosmos, Chaos, and the Gospel*

Portugal had no window on the Mediterranean but was blessed by long navigable rivers and deep harbors opening oceanward... The Portuguese people, then, naturally faced outward, away from the classic centers of European civilization, westward toward the unfathomed ocean, and southward toward a continent that for Europeans was also unfathomed... around Africa and, it was hoped, to India... "for there was sea everywhere."
— Daniel J. Boorstin, *The Discoverers*

THE uneven flow of world dominance that from time immemorial has marked the tensions between Europe and Asia has swung like a pendulum back and forth, West to East, and East to West — Rome against Persia for seven hundred years, Muslims invading Europe for two hundred years, crusaders counterattacking Islam for two hundred years, Mongols bursting into Europe in the thirteenth century. Then suddenly in the last decade of the 1400s history paused and then began another momentous, abrupt reversal of its motion. In 1453 the capital of ancient Eastern Orthodox Christianity fell to the Turks, invading from the east. Less than fifty years later Christian Portugal opened its first beachhead in India. This was the West's answer to the invasion from Asia, not a land war against encroaching Turkey but, in Arnold Toynbee's vivid phrase, the encirclement of Islam "by conquering the Ocean."[1]

Two centuries after the disaster of the Crusades, the West returned to Asia. This time it was permanent. For the first time in the millennium and a half of the life of the church, the Christian faith, which had time and again been almost wiped out in Asia, came back to plant an enduring continental presence in the segment of the world where it had been born. It was the opening of a new age in church history, and it came by sea.[2]

NOTES

1. Arnold Toynbee, *The World and the West* (New York: Oxford University Press, 1953), 21.

2. For a brief treatment of the use of sea power on Western contacts in East Asia, see David (John) Wright, "Sea Power and Diplomacy in the Far East," *TRASK* (Seoul) 67 (1992): 1–19.

Chapter 1

India (1500–1700)

St. Thomas or St. Peter

At the time the Portuguese arrived in the Indian seas...the Vijayanagar Emperors [of South India] had [one thing] in common with them...Just as the presence of the Muslims in the Iberian peninsula and their Empire across the narrow Straits of Gibraltar constituted a standing menace to the Portuguese, the presence of the [Muslim] Bahmini Sultanates on the borders of Vijayanagar provided that State with the powerful motive of safeguarding Hindu religion and culture in South India and of upholding national independence...To both Portugal and Vijayanagar, Islam was the enemy.   — K. M. Panikkar, *Asia and Western Dominance*

ROUNDING Africa in search of the Orient at the beginning of the West's great age of discovery, European explorers first touched land in Asia on the same long stretch of southeast India's Malabar coast where Indian tradition locates the landing of the apostle Thomas some fifteen hundred years before.

In 1498 Vasco da Gama sailed into the port city of Calicut,[1] "where the pepper and ginger grew," ten months out of Lisbon, carrying the cross on his banner and a missionary on his ship. Along with the cross and the missionary, he carried cannon. Wisely he did not use the cannon, though he was received rather coldly by the city's ruler, who looked at the trade goods the foreigners had brought and dismissed them as far below Indian standards.[2]

Even when the Portuguese did unleash the cannon two years later, on their second expedition to the Malabar coast, this sixteenth-century wave of Western expansion was not a repetition of the Crusades. It was primarily a trade war, not a holy war. Da Gama went to India for pepper as much as for the pope. Portugal's dream was to find a sea route to India around Africa by which it could take away control of the immensely profitable spice trade from Venice and Genoa in the Mediterranean, and from the Turks and Arabs who blocked the way through the Middle East. By discovering the way around Africa, da Gama opened the door to the fabled riches of Asia.

Religion, however, played a significant role in the success of the enterprise. In the eyes of the Hindu rulers of southern India the Portuguese

3

came as non-Muslim allies against Muslim Mongol invaders expanding south out of Afghanistan into north India. As for the Portuguese, they remembered how recently the Moors had been driven from the Iberian peninsula, and all Europe was vividly aware of the Turkish counter-crusade that only a generation earlier had captured Christian Constantinople, invaded southern Italy, and was again advancing through the Balkans toward Vienna.

The whole world was changing, and few events in history have changed it so irreversibly as the opening of the sea route to India. The West had lost western Asia and seemed about to lose eastern Europe. Da Gama's arrival in Calicut heralded a third major turning point in Asian history. The first was the rise of Islam in the seventh century. The second was the short-lived emergence of the Mongols, whose *pax Mongolica*, violent though it was, gave to the greater part of thirteenth- and fourteenth-century Asia the one brief period of continental unity and identity it has ever achieved.

Around the year 1500 came a third turning point, the reentry of the West into global history. Some call it "the triumph of the West."[3] Others describe it as a disaster, an age of slavery and colonialism. Indian historian K. M. Panikkar names it "the Vasco da Gama Epoch of Asian History," "the final failure" of Western Christian mission activity in Asia.[4] None of those descriptions is quite true. For the West it was not all triumph, for Christian mission it was not a failure, and for Asia it was only briefly Portuguese. It was both triumph and tragedy. It was a tangled mixture of great successes and glaring failures, and whatever the world's final judgment may be upon that new age which dawned in Asia when the Portuguese landed with their cannon and their crosses, there is no denying the fact that for the Christian church it signaled the end of an age of despair and the beginnings of new hope.

The St. Thomas (Mar Thoma) Christians and the Portuguese

The first of da Gama's men to reach the town of Calicut after the landing was met by two Tunisian traders who asked him in Spanish what had brought him to India. He replied, "We have come to seek Christians and spices."[5]

Da Gama had in fact already found in Africa one man he identified as an "Indian Christian" and apparently used him as pilot for his twenty-three day run from the coast of Kenya across the Indian Ocean to the Malabar coast. It is extremely doubtful that the man really was a Christian, but whether he was or not,[6] it is clear from the commissions the explorers had received from the pope in Rome and from the kings of Portugal that they expected to find fellow Christians in India. Had not the Papal Bull of Nicholas V in 1455 commended Prince Henry the Navigator for his belief "that he could give God the best evidence of his submission, if by his effort the Ocean can be made navigable as far as India, which, it is said, is already subject to Christ"?[7]

At his first landing at Calicut, da Gama limited himself to trade, noting with some shock the number of Muslims in the predominantly Hindu town and mistaking a Hindu temple for a Christian church. A second Portuguese landing at Calicut, by Pedro Alvarez Cabral in 1501, with six ships and nineteen missionaries (including eight Franciscans), was both more religious and unfortunately more militant. When a riot in the town resulted in Portuguese deaths, including three of the Franciscan missionaries, Cabral unleashed his cannon. He savagely bombarded the city for two days, thereby alienating the city's Hindu ruler, the Muslim traders, and the entire population. It was an irreparable mistake. However it may have been provoked, and whatever immediate advantage the Portuguese may have gained from the brutal display of military power, the attack was long remembered bitterly in India.[8]

Not until Cabral sailed south to escape a counterattack from Calicut and found a welcome at Cranganore, a large and ancient center of Thomas Christians near Cochin, did Portuguese and Indian Christians make effective contact with each other. Politically and commercially as well as religiously, Cochin better suited the Portuguese than Calicut. The local rajah of Cochin was a rival of the Zamorin of Calicut and not at all sorry to hear of the attack in the north, Cochin was at the very center of Kerala's rich pepper fields, and the long-isolated Syrian Christians of St. Thomas (Mar Thoma) rejoiced at the arrival of fellow believers. As one of them wrote, about 1504, "The country of these Franks is called Portugal . . . and their king is called Emmanuel. May Emmanuel protect him!"[9]

Vasco da Gama returned in 1503 with a new title, admiral of the Indian Seas, and established Portugal's first fort in India at Cochin. With him this time were three Dominican missionaries, who built near the fort the first Catholic church in India, naming it for St. Bartholomew.[10] The Thomas Christians, it is said, met da Gama with all the enthusiasm of a religious minority anticipating the end of caste discrimination by Hindus and outright enmity by Muslims. An impressive delegation came to da Gama, bearing their "rod of justice," a red, silver-tipped staff that some regarded as the scepter of their own long-vanished royal family, and offered it to him as token of their loyalty to the great and Christian king of Portugal.[11]

Indian church historian G. M. Moraes estimates that there were then about a hundred thousand Thomas Christians along the Malabar Coast in what is now Kerala.[12] Politically the area was a maze of small principalities within the loosely controlled Vijayanagar Empire of south India. The strongest Christian communities, out of about fifty altogether, were in two of the empire's minor Hindu kingdoms, Cranganore (Kodungalor), Quilon (Kollam). One might also include Alangad (Mangate), where a stone St. Thomas cross was found.[13] Ecclesiastically the Indian Christians recognized the authority of the Nestorian patriarch in Mesopotamian Persia and were in fact in the process of restoring their own metropolitanate under that authority just as the Portuguese arrived. Their episcopate had lapsed, and in 1490 they had sent representatives to Patriarch Simon (Shimon V, A.D. 1472–1502), who responded with the appointment of two Persian (Syrian) bishops, Mar John and Mar Thomas. The two bishops "by the assistance of Christ our Lord reached [India] alive."[14] Simon's successor, Elias V, further strengthened the Thomas Christian hierarchy by sending a metropolitan, Yahbalaha, and two more bishops, George (renamed Mar Jacob) and Mar Denha. They arrived in 1503–1504 and reported back to the patriarch a stirring account, which still survives, of the Portuguese landings.[15]

India's Thomas (Syrian) Christians were neither as numerous nor as powerful as the arriving Westerners had hoped. They didn't control the all-important pepper trade, which was largely in the hands of Hindu rulers and Muslim traders, and they had no army. In the preceding centuries most had been displaced as traders and had moved into agriculture, their relatively high-caste social identity preventing them from soiling their hands by plowing, for which occupation they used low-caste Indian serfs. Nevertheless, the Portuguese were happy to discover that the St. Thomas people were indeed Indian Christians and possible allies, as they had hoped, and greeted them as brothers and sisters in the faith. Moreover, when the Portuguese drove out the Muslim traders from their territories, the Thomas Christians once again found employment as traders mediating between the Portuguese and the Hindus.[16]

The Portuguese missionaries soon discovered that the St. Thomas Syrian Christians of India were a different kind of Christian and began to describe the differences to Rome. The Indian Christians recognized the Nestorian patriarch in Persia, not the pope, as head of the church. Their liturgical language was Syriac, not Latin. Their priests married; the Roman priests were celibate. The St. Thomas churches had no images; the Portuguese Catholics considered this to indicate a lack of proper reverence to Christ, the Virgin Mary, and the saints. Attributing all this to ignorance rather than to faithfulness to the traditions of the ancient church of the East in which the Indian Christians had been raised, the Portuguese sometimes gently, sometimes rudely began to press the Indian Christian communities to conform to Western Catholic custom. Understandably, they met resistance.

The outstanding figure in the history of the Indian church in the first decades of the coming of the Portuguese was the Thomas Christian Mar Jacob, bishop of Malabar (d. ca. 1551). Mar Jacob was one of the "three pious monks," ordained by Nestorian Patriarch Elias in Mesopotamia in 1503 and sent to India, where in all probability he succeeded to the prestige if not the title of metropolitan of India.[17] Though proudly a Thomas Christian, he became the most effective clerical link between the Portuguese Roman Catholics and the Syrian Malabar churches, working closely with the Franciscans in the extremely difficult task of harmonizing the ancient indigenous rites and practices of the Indian Christians with the Roman rites of the Portuguese.[18]

It was Mar Jacob who secured the pepper trade of Cochin for the Portuguese. He was praised for the fact that the pepper produced by the Thomas Christians was the finest in the land. He also bravely objected when unscrupulous Portuguese traders were caught cheating the Indian Christians and appealed to the Portuguese king himself to persuade the Hindu ruler of Cochin to restore Christian civil rights, which had been taken from them when one or more Indian Christians were found guilty of breaking local Hindu religious laws. From the beginning Mar Jacob foresaw that the Thomas Christians, long isolated, must pursue better theological education for their clergy. He painstakingly made a copy of the Syriac psalter, and later a copy of the entire New Testament in Syriac. He was generously admiring of the thorough theological training of the Franciscan missionaries whom he encountered, and when the Franciscan "guardian" of the monastery in Cranganore, Vicente (Vincent) de Lagos, proposed the opening of a school in Cranganore, he apparently regarded it as no infringement on his own rights as bishop and welcomed it.[19] Though in the end he resided and died in the Franciscan monastery in Cochin, Mar Jacob remained the symbol of the ties of the indigenous Indian church to the apostleship of Thomas as preceding Peter, and to the Nestorian patriarch in Mesopotamia as the equal of the pope in Rome.[20] It was only after his death in 1551, which unfortunately coincided with a schism in the Nestorian patriarchate in Mesopotamia, that a combination of Nestorian divisions, Portuguese dominance, and an intensification of Roman Catholic missionary and ecclesiastical pressure shattered the organizational structures of the Thomas Christians.

On the Portuguese side, in the years before the coming of the Jesuits the Franciscans and Dominicans were most active. Franciscans gave India its first two resident Catholic bishops, Ferdinand Vaqueiro in 1532, and John d'Albuquerque (1537–1553).[21] The missionary witness of the Franciscan Vicente de Lagos stands out as the most significant serious and sustained effort of the foreign priests to work with the Thomas Christians in this early period. De Lagos came to India in 1538 with Bishop John d'Albuquerque and was assigned to Cranganore, where there were approximately sixty Christian centers. Though both praised and criticized for Latinizing the training of the St. Thomas clergy, Vicente de Lagos is best remembered as founder in 1540–1541 of the first seminary for the children of the Malabar Syrian Christians. Before long he had enrolled up to seventy students training for the Indian priesthood.[22]

Golden Goa and the Roman Catholics

In a sense the mid-Malabar coast from Cranganore through Cochin to Quilon, despite all Latinizing pressures, remained St. Thomas territory.[23] Goa, farther north, belonged to St. Peter. When the Portuguese fleet sailed up the coast from Kerala in 1510 to seize the island port of Goa from the Muslim Sultan of Bijapur, "Golden Goa" soon replaced Calicut as the principal base of Portuguese trading colonies on the whole west coast of India. The Portuguese advance was as irresistible ecclesiastically as militarily. Its strategy centered on creating small military and trading enclaves along the rim of South Asia and East Asia, not on territorial expansion. The principal centers were Cochin (1503), Goa (1510), Malacca (1511), Ormuz (1522), Macao (1557), and Nagasaki (1580). These also (except for Ormuz) became the major centers for the beginning of Catholic missions in Asia, and Goa became the largest diocese in the world geographically separated from Europe. Before the century was over, Roman Catholic missions had spread through the Asian seas from their hub in Goa as "the metropolitan see of the East," with missionary authority from the east coast to Africa and India to the Indian archipelago (Molucca), checked only in the end by the fleets of the Dutch and the British.[24] Even then Goa remained a Portuguese colony from 1510 to 1961.

For the first forty years after the arrival of the Portuguese, the only Catholic missionaries in that part of Asia were Franciscan. Eight Franciscans had come in 1500 with Cabral, and by 1518, as the numbers rose, they were made a commissariat and began to build a friary. Uncertain, perhaps, how best to relate to an already existing and very ancient hierarchy in India, the Portuguese were slow at first to organize a hierarchy of their own.[25] The first Catholic bishopric was not established until 1539, and then only as a suffragan see of Funchal (in the Atlantic Ocean!). A recent missionary arrival, the Franciscan John d'Albuquerque was its first bishop,[26] a fitting choice, since the only missionary priests were Franciscans, greatly helped by the brothers of the Misericordia (a service fraternity devoted to serving the poor, the hungry, and the crippled, and to burying the dead).[27] Their counterparts, the secular clergy, acted mainly as chaplains to the Portuguese. Another twenty years passed before Goa was elevated to an archbishopric with the unprecedentedly wide missionary jurisdiction mentioned above.

A side effect of the centralization of Catholic Church authority in Goa was a growing estrangement from the St. Thomas Christians farther south. Goa was at least two weeks' journey from the seat of the bishop of the St. Thomas Christians at Cranganore, and it was clear that even the friendly Franciscans in Cranganore and Cochin had not entirely won the confidence of those whose traditions stretched back to St. Thomas, not St. Peter. The Portuguese had established the first Christian hospital on the coast at Cochin in 1506, and a school for Christian children, which, to the surprise and not altogether to the liking of local Hindus, mixed both high-caste and low-caste boys together.[28] But Catholic institutions in the Cochin area declined after the removal of the Latin ecclesiastical headquarters to Goa. Unlike Goa to the north and the fishing villages of the Paravas farther south, both of which became strongly Roman Catholic, Kerala's Christians never quite ceased to be other than Thomas Christians, however much some of them might adapt to the ways and traditions of the incoming Portuguese clergy.

The Franciscans in Goa were mindful of the need for native Indian clergy in the Latin tradition. In 1518 Rome had opened the door to the training of an indigenous priesthood by a decree authorizing Lisbon to ordain morally and educationally suitable "Ethiopians, Indians, and Africans," but little came of it. Thus in 1532 Father Rodrigo de Serpa, head of the Franciscan order in Goa, complained that he was still being forbidden by Lisbon to admit local Goans for training as novices and was not allowed even to accept the sons of Portuguese fathers and Indian mothers (*mestiços*) who, he said, would be natural channels for the gospel to their Indian relatives on the mother's side.

It was another nine years before the vicar general of Goa, Michael Vaz, a fervent preacher not attached to any order, was able to persuade the authorities to open a seminary specifically for the religious training of East Asian and East African (not European or *mestiço*) young men. The Franciscans were charged with the task of opening the seminary. Later it was transferred to the Jesuit College of St. Paul, which also accepted Portuguese and Eurasians, but the student body remained principally Asiatic.[29] These were promising beginnings, but within a few years opposition hardened. A rector of the college was soon saying, "Without Portuguese priests we will achieve nothing." Only one Indian, notes Boxer, was ordained to the priesthood by the Jesuits, a Christian Brahmin in 1575.[30]

Francis Xavier and the Jesuits

The coming of the Jesuits forty years after the first Portuguese landings marked a second stage in the Latinizing of the Indian church. Their first and greatest representative was the famous Francis Xavier (1506–1552), whose whole life contradicts the unfortunate modern stereotype of Jesuit missions as a rigid, organization-centered, military-style spearhead of Western colonialism.[31] The genius of the early Jesuit missions was its spiritual base, born in a burning, personal, spiritual commitment to the overwhelming reality of a God who created the world not by accident but with a purpose. It caught fire as an explosion of mission to the world for which Christ died. Before the organization came the fire and the vision. Ignatius of Loyola (1491–1556), the founder of the Jesuits, wrote his *Spiritual Exercises* before he wrote his *Constitutions,* and the splendid order and organization of the latter was the child of the fire in the *Exercises.*[32] The first missions were spontaneous and personal. The missioners' personal vow of obedience to the pope, formulated in 1539, was rooted in mission: "I promise special obedience to the Sovereign Pontiff *as to the missions* in the manner specified in the Apostolic letters and in the Constitutions."[33]

Francis Xavier was a consummate example of the Jesuit ideal: fiery missionary spontaneity linked to uncompromising organizational obedience. He reached Goa in 1542, and, despite his rank as papal nuncio with special powers directly commissioned by both the pope in Rome and the king of Portugal,[34] he refused the fine lodgings prepared for him and chose to stay in a "poor little cottage" near the hospital.[35] He served in India for the next ten years, concentrating with genial, unpatronizing compassion on lepers, slaves, sinners, unbelievers, and the poorest of the poor.[36] One observer of Xavier's first years in India said, "You would have thought he had seen Christ with his [own] eyes in those poor, sick persons, and employed all his labor in serving Him."[37]

There were already about a hundred priests in Goa in 1542 when Xavier arrived, and most, save for the Franciscans, were poorly trained and not highly regarded.[38] By contrast, Xavier, with his street preaching, his faithful hospital and prison visits, his religious parades through the streets, his teaching of the catechism and the prayers (to which in gracious acknowledgment of Indian tradition he added the name of St. Thomas), and his fearless reproof of open sin won crowds of listeners and instant success.[39] For three and a half years he worked in Goa, the city that was the center for all Catholic missions in Portugal's expanding movement toward the Far East. He was restless in the small and foreign-dominated colonial enclave of Goa. He was gratified to see that the churches were growing — by the time he left India seven years later there were five thousand native Christians in Goa — but that, he pointed out, was all too few in comparison with the forty thousand who still remained pagan.[40]

He longed to reach out into Indian India. So when he was asked to consider an arduous major mission to the pearl fishers of Cape Comorin, about 450 miles to the south, he accepted without hesitation.

Some six years earlier, in the first mass movement of Indians into the Christian faith, the entire "outcaste" fishing villages of the Paravas, as they were called, had agreed to be baptized, thinking it was a fair price to pay for Portuguese protection against marauding Muslim fleets. Many more were added in the next few years, bringing the total number of baptized Christians up to perhaps as many as eighty thousand.[41]

Few of them, however, knew much about what baptism meant beyond the promise of physical safety from pirate attack.[42] When Xavier arrived and asked what they believed, they replied they did not know because they could not understand Portuguese. The children not yet baptized swarmed around him in such numbers that all he could do was ask the three seminarians who had come with him from Cochin to help him teach the boys and girls, and anyone one else not yet baptized, the sign of the cross, the Lord's Prayer, the Hail Mary, and parts of the creed, before baptizing them forthwith and proceeding to the next village to repeat the procedure.[43] "I began to understand that 'of such is the kingdom of heaven,'" he wrote, "and I am convinced that if there were anyone to instruct them in our holy faith, they would soon be good Christians."[44] His mission was to the very young, the poor, and the illiterate. At first he taught them orally, through his helpers, reading as best he could the Romanized transcriptions of prayers and catechisms in Tamil that they prepared for him. Then, as a second step, he had them begin to transpose the Romanized texts into the written Tamil language of the people, which they were to learn to read and memorize.[45] His methods were primitive, and his baptisms may have been hasty and shallow. Of the eighty thousand or so reportedly baptized Christians to whom he ministered on the coast, he says that he found only one man of high caste, a Brahman, who had become a Christian.[46] But Neill pays Xavier this high tribute: "He arrived to find an untutored mob, he left behind him a church in being." Before the century was out, there were sixteen large Christian village churches among the fisherfolk with a resident Jesuit missionary in each village.[47]

When he returned to Goa the next year, Xavier soon came to the conclusion that the Portuguese Christians in the trading posts were as great an obstacle to the spread of the gospel in India as any Indian superstitions or Hindu resistance to Christian evangelism. He was so shocked at the open immorality of the European traders and the cruelty and corruption of the Portuguese officials that at one point he wrote to the king in Lisbon: "Unless you threaten your officials with chains, prison and the confiscation of goods, and actually carry out your threats, all your commands for the furtherance of Christianity in India will be in vain."[48]

But Goa was only intermittently the center of his ten years in India. Firmly convinced that his commission from God and from his Society was for the evangelization of as much of Asia as he could reach, he ranged widely up and down the Malabar coast, around the Cape to what is now Madras, thence to Ceylon, and eventually as far as the "spice islands" of Molucca in Indonesia. Then, at the last, he left South Asia altogether to start a mission in Japan (1549–1552). Xavier died off the coast of China, still carrying around his neck a reminder of the Christians he had left behind in India: a holy relic (a bone perhaps), said to be of St. Thomas himself.[49]

Friction between Thomas Christians and the Missions

After the departure of Xavier and the death of Mar Jacob, relations between the Portuguese church in India and the old Syrian churches rapidly worsened. St. Thomas Christians describe what followed as the "suppression and disfigurement" of the native identity of the Malabar church.[50] They implied that the Portuguese converted by coercion, not by evangelism. How much the criticism is justified will always be debated, but few deny that it is at least partly true.[51]

In 1550 a new Portuguese rector of the Jesuit college in Goa arbitrarily dismissed all its Indian students, weakening the bonds between Indian Catholics and Catholic missionaries.[52] In 1553 a schism in Persian Kurdistan between rival patriarchs-elect broke the unity of the Nestorian church at its highest level. One of the rivals, Mar Sulaqa (or Sulaka) made submission to the pope in Rome, Julius III, and was ordained patriarch as a Uniate (a Roman Catholic permitted to follow a non-Latin liturgy, in this case Syriac). The other, Mar Denha, claimed the loyalty of traditional Nestorians. Thus began a division into two lines of succession, Uniates ("new line") and Nestorians ("old line").[53] The rivalry spread to India, much to the weakening of its Thomas Christians.

In 1556 two bishops, Joseph and Elias, arrived in Goa. Joseph was a brother of the new-line patriarch, John Sulaqa. Both had been appointed and sent to India by Sulaqa's successor, the Uniate (Catholic) patriarch, Mar Abdiso (or Abdisho), but their presence posed an immediate problem. On the one hand, though they were officially related as Uniates to Rome, Rome had already placed all of India under the jurisdiction of the bishop of Goa, not the Uniate patriarch in Mesopotamia. When Bishop Joseph began to show partiality toward the Thomas Christians and their Nestorian heritage, he was twice tried for heresy (or insubordination) and ordered back to Portugal.[54]

The Thomas Christians, left without a bishop (for there is no further mention of Bishop Elias in India), quite naturally asked their older mother church, Mesopotamia, for a replacement. This time it was the old-line Nestorian patriarch who responded, consecrating a Thomas Christian as Metropolitan Mar Abraham and sending him back to India. Remembering Bishop Joseph's treatment by the Portuguese, Mar Abraham eluded the authorities in Goa and went straight south to Thomas Christian territory. The Portuguese pursued and arrested him, but he escaped his captors and returned to Mesopotamia.[55] There, finally recognizing the futility of resisting Portuguese power, he made his peace with the new-line Patriarch Abdiso and with Rome, and returned to

India, outwardly and perhaps sincerely pro-Roman, but inwardly, insofar as he can be judged by his subsequent actions, determined to protect his Syrian Christian followers from a too rapid and insensitively enforced Latinization.[56]

Mar Abraham's stormy rule as the Syrian Metropolitan lasted for almost thirty years (1569–1597). He stubbornly refused to bow to Goa's claims to primacy. After all, he was surely the only Indian bishop ever consecrated three times, once by a Nestorian (old-line) patriarch, once by a Uniate Syrian (new-line, or Chaldaean) patriarch, and once by the pope in Rome. To protect his independence, he purposely avoided attending the Second (Roman) Council of Goa in 1575. He won support for a while from the Jesuits by helping them open and develop a seminary near Cochin, beginning in 1577, but thirteen years later he was again held insubordinate for refusing to ordain students from the seminary because they had been too Latinized, even though the Jesuits had allowed them the use of Syriac and the dress of their Syrian clergy. It was difficult for the old Nestorian, Mar Abraham, to walk the Roman way. But though charged with heresy, he was never brought to trial. He died in 1597, "the last Metropolitan of the undivided church of the Christians of St. Thomas," as Leslie W. Brown describes him.[57]

A further step in the aggravation of Indian sensibilities in the process of Westernizing the Christianity of the Thomas Christians was the establishment of the Inquisition in India in 1560. Enforcement of this distasteful form of religious control was placed in the hands of the new, and first, archbishop of Goa, who now carried a double title — bishop and grand inquisitor. Even Xavier, as observed above, in accordance with his Jesuit vow of absolute obedience, had earlier added his "profession" (acceptance) to the proclamation of the Inquisition as it was applied in Portugal and had written in 1546 that it would prove useful in India. It was his understanding, however, that it would be used only against new Christians (presumably converted Muslims, Hindus, or Jews) who renounced their faith and apostatized.[58] Nevertheless, the palace of the Inquisition in Goa represented an ever-present threat to leaders of the Thomas Christians, who might be targeted as heretics if they were tempted to stray from the orthodox Latin ways of Portuguese Christianity into their old traditional Syrian patterns. By 1572 Catholics numbered their membership at an estimated 280,000.[59]

The Synod of Diamper (1599)[60]

The Latinizing of the sixteenth-century Indian church reached its peak in 1599 at the Synod of Diamper (Udiyamperur) but never achieved its goal of a permanent union of all the St. Peter (Roman) and St. Thomas (Syrian) Christians of India. A young new archbishop, Alexis de Menezes, had arrived in Goa in 1595, determined to settle once and for all who ruled the Indian church: not the Syrian Nestorians of either stripe, not Indians, but Rome.[61] His appointment was clear — archbishop of Goa and primate of all India — with orders to force the Thomas Christians to renounce their errors and accept Roman jurisdiction under a loyal, thoroughly Roman bishop to be selected as the successor of Mar Abraham.

To this end Menezes approached the archdeacon of the Syrian church, who was not only the administrative leader of the Thomas Christian community but also, as custom decreed, their spiritual leader in the long intervals when no resident metropolitan, appointed by Baghdad, was in office in India.[62] However, the current archdeacon, Parambil George (known to the Portuguese as George of the Cross), while seeming to accept the appointment of a bishop by Rome, insisted that Thomas Christians could worship only under a Syrian bishop. The exasperated Menezes wrote, "They have taken an oath that if His Holiness sends them a Syrian Bishop, they will obey him; but if he is a Latin, they will take counsel."[63]

Disregarding the archdeacon's advice, the archbishop moved in three important steps straight toward his goal of bringing the Thomas Christians under Latin, not Syrian, rule. First, with a display of Portuguese pomp and power he influenced the Hindu rajah of Cochin to abandon his support of the rights of his Indian Christian subjects. Second, he seized the opportunity afforded by the absence of a Syrian Indian bishop and ordained close to ninety new Indian priests, requiring them to disavow any connection with the Nestorian patriarchate in Mesopotamia; he thereby created an ecclesiastical power base loyal to him personally. When Archdeacon George protested that this was an unwarranted violation of his own rights as vicar general of the St. Thomas Christians, and threatened to excommunicate anyone so ordained, Menezes proceeded to the third and final stage of his campaign, the calling of a general synod to legitimize the absolute authority of Rome over the Syrian community and thus make possible the appointment of a Latin bishop over it.[64]

The Synod of Diamper is the most controversial and most important single event in all the century and a half of the Portuguese period of Indian church history (roughly 1498 to 1653). It accomplished everything the Portuguese prelate could have wished — or so it seemed. A brief listing of some of its major decisions suffices to show how radical and thorough were the changes it imposed on St. Thomas Christianity.

The synod first made clear that there could not be two laws for the church in India — "one law of St. Thomas and another law of St. Peter" — but only one law, the law of Christ. Christ, moreover, has only one vicar who, the synod said, is "head of the whole Church on earth... and all who deny obedience to the said Roman Bishop... are transgressors of the Divine Commands, and cannot attain to Eternal Life."[65]

Accordingly, the synod renounced all "Nestorian heresies" in general, and the "heretical and schismatic" jurisdiction of the Syrian "patriarch of Babylon" in particular, though, in fact, the patriarch so slandered was, as even today's Catholics agree, "fully in communion with Rome."[66] Theodore of Mopsuestia, Diodorus of Tarsus, Narsai, and other greatly revered fathers of the Nestorian church were removed from the church calendar and prayers. Nestorian books were to be examined, burned if in grievous error, and corrected.[67]

Michael Geddes, in the preface to his seventeenth-century translation of de Gouvea's contemporary account, lists fifteen doctrines in which the Indian Christians differed with Rome, and which to him seemed to be proper Anglican. For example, the Malabar church condemns the pope's supremacy; denies transubstantiation; condemns images; denies purgatory, auricular confession, and extreme unction; and allows its priests to marry.[68]

All these were defects the synod proposed to correct. Whether or not the 153 Syrian priests and 650 laymen who attended the proceedings understood what was happening is not clear.[69] The synod was conducted in Portuguese, translated into Syriac, and parts may have been put into Malayalam, the local dialect, but probably not adequately, if at all. Nevertheless, at one point Menezes was unable to carry out his plan to take over and Latinize the Indo-Syrian church. The Thomas Christians won an important victory when they were allowed to continue to use their own Syriac liturgy in worship.

But Menezes had achieved his main purpose. He was now able to appoint a Latin bishop over the Syrian church and was wise enough to choose the irenic Jesuit Francis Roz for the post. The Latin victory, however, was short-lived. In the vivid phrases of Stephen Neill, Francis Roz was "installed in glory as the first Latin Bishop of the Serra and of the Thomas Christians, [but] it was not long before he discovered that he had inherited a crown of thorns."[70] Far from achieving its intended purpose of uniting Syrian and Roman Christianity in India, the fateful Synod of Diamper led instead to such division in the Indian churches that they still remain torn asunder to this day.

The first of the Thomas Christians' grievances was the discovery that they had lost status and identity. Their Syrian metropolitan (equal to an archbishop) had been taken from them, and in return they had been given only a bishop, and a Latin bishop at that, serving under Menezes, the Portuguese archbishop. In many ways Bishop Roz was admirably suited for the post; for example, he knew both Syriac and Malayalam. But the demotion and Latinization of their spiritual leader was an affront to the Syrian community's pride that not even the subsequent elevation of Roz to archbishop, in 1608, quite assuaged. The wound was further aggravated ten years later when Archdeacon George, the acknowledged Indian leader of the community, was charged with heresy and abruptly replaced with a foreigner.[71]

It was reported in 1622 that at least one-third of all the Thomas Christians supported the outranked Indian archdeacon against the powerful foreign archbishop.[72] Two-thirds of them, however, it should be noted, remained loyal to Rome. One small indication of the continuing vitality of the Latin strain in Indian Christianity is the report that about 1603 an Indian Brahmin, converted by the Jesuits, was one of a party of five Jesuit missioners who were sent to restore the persecuted Jesuit mission in Ethiopia.[73]

The Propaganda (or Propaganda Fide)

In that same period the papacy began to make some highly significant changes in Catholic mission policy. Aware of growing discontent with the dependency of its missions and churches upon the colonial powers in Asia and Latin America under the *padroado* (patronage) system, it sought means to regain for the church jurisdiction over the expansion of Christianity and to prevent expanding imperialism from riding roughshod over non-Western cultural patterns in growing national churches. To accomplish this the Vatican developed a two-pronged defense of its own religious and missionary rights against subordination to the state.

The first was the creation in 1622 of a new missionary agency that would be under direct Roman control. This was named the Sacred Congregation for the Propagation of the Faith, but is usually called simply the Propaganda or Propaganda Fide. The second was the revival of an ancient but long-lapsed pattern in the episcopate, the apostolic vicariate.

The Propaganda, as the direct missionary arm of the papacy, proceeded to open schools not only for missionaries but also for training native clergy. By providing a broader, more specifically Christian and less colonially Western structure for the advocacy of missions, it was able to operate as a counterbalance to imperial Portuguese and Spanish control of missions policy, particularly in Asia.[74]

The second change in structure was the appointment of apostolic vicars. In much the same way as the Propaganda was created as a Vatican balance on the home front to the rights of *padroado* granted to the kings of Portugal and Spain, apostolic vicars were sent to the mission field as a separate order of bishops, representatives of the pope with episcopal power independent of the powers of state-appointed diocesan bishops in the colonies under the *padroado* system.[75]

But neither of these far-reaching developments were yet of much influence in Asia. The first apostolic vicar in India, an Indian, did not reach India from Rome until forty years later. He was Matthew de Castro, son of a prominent Christian Brahmin family, and had been refused ordination as a priest by the Portuguese archbishop of Goa. Encouraged by the Carmelites, he went to Rome to plead his case and studied at the College of the Propaganda. He was ordained there about the year 1630. But upon his return to India he met continued resistance from the Portuguese and returned to Rome discouraged. Rome proceeded to consecrate him secretly in 1637 as bishop and apostolic vicar for that part of India which lay beyond the borders of Portuguese Goa, along with a missionary destined for Japan, planning to send both to Japan. The great Japanese persecutions prevented that, and finally, in 1638, de Castro returned again to his native India as its first apostolic vicar.[76]

Portugal not unnaturally resented his presence; the Portuguese hierarchy in Goa refused to recognize the Indian priests he ordained. Losing patience, Bishop de Castro returned to Rome about 1644 and was transferred to Africa as apostolic vicar of Ethiopia. But Ethiopia refused him entry; he got no farther than Cairo. Blocked at every turn by Portuguese hostility, Japanese persecution, or Ethiopian suspicion, this first attempt to build up an Indian clergy for India ended in melancholy failure. Returning for the last time to India, he was pursued by enmity and false charges, among them the unbelievable accusation that he had turned Muslim. He died in 1677, stripped of authority but clinging to his title as bishop and apostolic vicar.[77]

From India to Japan and from the Indonesian archipelago to the Philippines, Portuguese and Spanish power dominated missions for at least another century.

The Coonen (Koonan) Cross

In 1653 what had seemed to be the inevitable Romanizing of the St. Thomas Christian community met a dramatic obstacle. Rumblings of Indian discontent finally broke out into open revolt. The spark that ignited the explosion was the arrival in Mylapore (near Madras) of an unexpected Syrian bishop, Mar Atalla (or Ahatalla, known as Mar Ignatius), adding both political fuel and ecclesiastical confusion to the pent-up anger of the St. Thomas Christians against the Latins. The Portuguese, suspicious, arrested him at once and sent him to Cochin for questioning, but the Thomas Christians reacted with rejoicing; a Syrian bishop of their own had come. They thought that as a Syrian he would be Nestorian,[78] but he puzzled both the Indians and the Portuguese when he claimed he had been appointed patriarch of India and China by the pope in Rome. In fact he was neither Roman nor Nestorian. He was Syrian Orthodox, a Jacobite of the Monophysite Patriarchate of Antioch, ancient Christian rivals of the Nestorians in the Middle East. It appears that his story was at least partly true, and that he had indeed made submission to the pope on one of his journeys, but he had been appointed by neither pope nor monophysite patriarch to India.[79]

That made no difference to the new leader of the Indian Christian community, Archdeacon Thomas de Campo (Parambil Tumi).[80] To the archdeacon, a Syrian was a Syrian, and the Thomas Christians prepared to welcome Mar Atalla as their bishop. The Portuguese, however, suspecting trouble, did not land him at Cochin but carried him on to Goa. Rumors spread among the Syrians that their bishop had been kidnapped or killed. Some blamed the Jesuits, others the Portuguese military. Archbishop Garcia, the third and last Latin archbishop of an undivided St. Thomas episcopate,[81] refused an invitation to come down from Goa to explain what was happening, and the people rebelled.

On January 3, 1653, in a dramatic assembly that marks both the final division of the St. Thomas community and the restoration of Indian autonomy to the protesting (but not Protestant) St. Thomas churches of Kerala, the people gathered at a church near Cochin and, holding a long rope attached to the famous Coonen Cross, swore a solemn oath to abjure their loyalty to the Jesuits and to the foreign archbishop in Goa. A few months later, assembling again halfway between Cochin and Cranganore, they ordained twelve priests of their own and consecrated Archdeacon Thomas as their metropolitan, Mar Thomas I.[82] Though they still professed a qualified allegiance to the pope, provided he give them a genuine Syrian bishop, the revolt spread like wildfire. According to one estimate, only about twenty priests and perhaps four hundred to a thousand laymen remained loyal to Portuguese Archbishop Garcia.[83] That compares to a total Syrian Christian population in the 1650s of perhaps seventy thousand.[84]

The next fifty years present a confused and unedifying spectacle of Portuguese military decline, Christian dissension, and social and ecclesiastical divisions among the St. Thomas Christians of Kerala. Some measure of the confusion of these years in the later 1600s is shown by a brief glance at its major divisions. The Protestant Dutch captured Cranganore from the Catholic Portuguese in 1661 and took Cochin in 1663. They promptly expelled the European Catholic missioners. But though they were Protestant themselves, they favored the Latin-Syrian (pro-Roman) faction in the Malabar Syrian church over the Coonen Cross protesters. Pragmatically recognizing that the Catholics controlled the majority of city Christians, they accepted the Catholic Bishop Chandy as leader of the Indian Christians. The Calvinistic Dutch steadfastly refused, however, to recognize the authority of the Portuguese *padroado* over Indian Christians.[85]

The Catholics had their own divisions. For a time the premier Catholic archdiocese of India, Portuguese Goa, was vacant and had split into two city factions meeting separately.[86] Most tragic of all, the St. Thomas Syrian Christians were divided into three warring parties: Roman Catholic (Latin-Syrian), Jacobite (Antiochene–Syrian Orthodox), and Nestorian (East Syrian).

All sides, including Latin-Syrian Old Believers and Eastern Syrian New Believers[87] were racked by controversy. Resistance to Latinization and foreign control continued to trouble even the Syrians loyal to Rome. In an effort to win back the protesters, the pope had moved to remedy past mistakes and had replaced the Jesuits in Kerala who operated under the royal patronage of the Portuguese *padroado* with non-Portuguese Carmelites, mostly Italian, under the authority of the papal congregation of the Propaganda.[88] In Malabar the most important of these was an apostolic commissary assigned to Cochin, the Carmelite priest Jerome Sebastiani (known religiously as Joseph of St. Mary). But by the time Sebastiani reached Cochin, the Dutch were about to take the city and expel all foreign Catholic clergy. Just before he left in 1663, Sebastiani hastily consecrated as his successor the pro-Roman Archdeacon Chandy or Alexander Parambil (Alexander de Campo) as apostolic vicar of the Archdiocese of Angemali. At last the pro-Roman Latin St. Thomas Christians had the native Indian bishop they had longed for.[89]

But it was only a partial victory. The Portuguese Archbishop of Goa refused to recognize the new Indian apostolic vicar when he styled himself metropolitan of the whole of India, and once more friction arose between foreign and Indian priests. This was aggravated when Rome appointed a bishop of mixed Portuguese-Indian blood, Thomas de Castro of Goa, to succeed Bishop Chandy. It was a well-intentioned but culturally insensitive action that offended the Kerala Christians, in whom caste prejudice was as culturally embedded as among their Hindu neighbors.[90] Not until 1701 was Roman episcopal authority effectively reestablished in Kerala.[91]

The Drift from Nestorian to Jacobite Connections

The more serious and most damaging rivalry, however, was between the two groups of St. Thomas Christians, papal loyalists and independent East Syrian protesters. Both sides were now headed by Indian bishops, Alexander Chandy (Parambil) on the Latin or Roman side, and Thomas Parambil on the dissenting Nestorian East Syrian side. They were cousins from an old, aristocratic, priestly family who were all the more rigid rivals because of their close relationship.

The protesters' Bishop Thomas, originally an archdeacon and now a metropolitan, had been consecrated by his own priests and, perhaps sensing some doubts about the authenticity of his episcopacy, had apparently written to all the non-Roman Eastern patriarchs — Baghdad (Nestorian), Antioch (Jacobite), and Alexandria (Coptic) — asking any one of them to send him a bishop to confirm his title. He hoped at least one would be able to break through the religious blockade the Portuguese had thrown up against reinforcement of the Coonen Cross dissenters.

In 1665 one did, Mar Gregorios, a Jacobite Monophysite from Antioch. This was the beginning of a drift from Persian (Chaldaean) Nestorianism to Antiochene (Jacobite) Orthodoxy, a shift of jurisdictional loyalty of great historic and ecclesiastical significance, but one that in India evolved

almost unnoticed at first by the St. Thomas Christians, who had for centuries been isolated from the theological controversies of the West. It
seems likely that the newcomer, Mar Gregorios, was willing to reconse-
crate, or at least confirm, the "Coonen Cross" Indian metropolitan and
share episcopal functions. Syrian practices outlawed by the Synod of
Diamper were gradually reintroduced, such as the marriage of clergy.
Statues and crucifixes were removed from the sanctuaries. By the end
of the seventeenth century India's independent St. Thomas Christians
were not only non-Roman, they were also non-Nestorian. Almost unaware of the theological and ecclesiastical revolution this involved, they
had become Jacobite, that is, Syrian Orthodox, and remained so for about
a hundred years.[92]

A few years later, in 1708, when a Nestorian bishop belatedly arrived,
sent by the Patriarch Elias X in Mesopotamia to restore the Thomas
Christians to the Nestorian fold, he found few who would follow him,
although the Dutch preferred him to the Jacobite Orthodox Bishop
Mar Thomas IV. But Gabriel remained as a complicating factor in the
three-cornered mixture of Roman, Orthodox, and Nestorian jurisdictions
claiming the authority to speak for Christ on the Malabar coast in the
early 1700s.[93]

Though divided, the Malabar coast Christians were thoroughly Indian. Their Indian-style churches were spreading south along the whole
Kerala coast at intervals of not more than three to six miles. Both sides
at the time estimated the total number of Thomas Christians to be about
two hundred thousand.[94] Roman Catholic Syrian Christians probably
outnumbered the independent Syrians of Bishop Thomas about two to
one.[95] Not even the arrival of Dutch Protestant chaplains seemed to slow
the growth of the Catholics. As one Dutch historian noted, "What can
the zeal of a Reformed Preacher whom nobody can understand, do to
combat the bustle of the thousand Roman priests on this coast, who are
perfectly equipped with the necessary knowledge of the languages?"[96]

As for the non-Roman Syrian Christians, they were more and more
driven by the Portuguese into the mountains, where they were called
the people of the Serra.[97] One estimate of the relative strength of the
two parties of Malabar Christians, Roman and non-Roman Syrian, suggests that at the beginning of the nineteenth century, out of a total of
307,000 St. Thomas Syrian Christians along the southwestern Malabar
coast, 187,000 accepted the rule of Rome, while 120,000 followed the
titular rule of the Jacobite bishop of Antioch.[98]

Catholic Expansion beyond the Malabar Coast

Catholic growth in Portuguese India, ever since its first move north from
Kerala into Goa, had never been limited to the territory of the relatively

high-caste Syrian Thomas Christians. When Xavier, for example, traveled in the far south of the Indian subcontinent, he expanded Catholic outreach to the lower-caste people of the fishing villages of Cape Cormorin. On quite another social level was the pioneering work of another Jesuit, Robert de Nobili (1577–1656),[99] the aristocratic nephew of a cardinal. His family disapproved when at the age of twenty he joined the Jesuits and eight years later, in 1605, asked to be sent to India. His first assignment was to the poor but Christian fisherfolk of the Parava Coast where Xavier had been so successful. In 1606 he was transferred out of the area of Portuguese control into the independent Indian empire of Vijayanagar and became the pioneer to the Brahmins of Madurai (or Madura) in Tamil territory.[100]

The change at first depressed him. He was discouraged to find little evidence of effective mission. One of his fellow missionaries wrote in 1609: "Since the foundation of the mission, only fifteen natives have been baptized, and they are the dregs of society. Their conduct is so dishonorable that I have decided not to baptize any more."[101] De Nobili set about to rectify the situation and determined that the problem was a failure to recognize that the more sophisticated social life of Madurai would require a different missionary approach from that which had proved so effective among the fishing villages of the coast. So he began his new ministry by addressing the upper levels of the social scale. Noticing that Christians associated with the Portuguese were despised in this independently Indian territory, he made it known that he was Italian, and furthermore no low-class merchant or soldier but a member of the Roman aristocracy. He changed his black Jesuit cassock for the white dress of an Indian teacher and moved into a small house in the Brahmin section of town, living very simply and eating only vegetarian food. He became fluent in classical Tamil and would spend as many as twenty days in intense personal religious discussion with a single Brahmin. As he put it, in a Pauline turn of phrase, "I too will make myself Indian in order to save the Indians."[102]

Success followed with startling rapidity. In the four years from 1607 to 1611 he converted 108 high-caste Hindus, a class that had been most resistant to Portuguese missionary effort. Your customs, he told them, do not need to be changed; indeed, he followed them himself to the extent of not touching or even baptizing non-Brahmins. About thirty of his fellow European Jesuits were persuaded to follow his stringent example. One of them, Antony de Proenca, searched in vain for an ointment to change the color of his skin to look more Indian: "Just as we have changed our dress, language, food and habits . . . we may also change the color of our faces and become like those with whom we live."[103]

Not surprisingly, this drew criticism, particularly from the missionaries of other orders. De Nobili was even accused of turning Hindu. Much of the next ten years he had to spend defending his methods of adapting

the gospel to the life and customs of India, methods that were remarkably similar to those of his fellow Jesuit Matteo Ricci in China, as we
will see.

Both de Nobili and Ricci are celebrated in mission history for their
early experiments in "accommodation" in missionary outreach across
cultures. This is not without its limitations; it is particularly vulnerable
to misinterpretation and exaggeration by its opponents, as the Jesuits
discovered both in India and China. A crucial question, then as now,
is how to determine when adaptation to a non-Christian culture, if carried too far, as in syncretism, reverses its course and begins to distort
the Christian message it was designed to advance. But de Nobili was
no syncretist. His writings clearly show that however much he might
adapt to national and local customs, he was undeviating in his doctrinal orthodoxy. If a weakness must be found in him, it may well have
been, as a recent analysis suggests, that "he was too ready to preach
wisdom to the wise and too hesitant to preach a Gospel that must also
be 'folly to the wise.' "[104] Eventually, in 1623, Pope Gregory XV, on the
advice of Peter Lombard, cleared him of virtually all the charges against
him, stipulating only that he avoid even the appearance of idolatry and
superstition.[105]

Later, de Nobili himself took notice of problems raised by his strenuous and too-exclusive adaptation to one strand of India's culture, the
upper class. Without cutting off his effective contacts with the Brahmins,
he sought ways to soften the mission's discriminating attitude toward
the lower castes. He taught that all who believe and obey, whether high
or low, will be saved. He allowed high caste and low caste to worship
together in church, which was a more inclusive policy than even the Syrian Christians of the west coast were used to. Recognizing India's social
distinctions, however, he discreetly separated the upper castes from the
lower castes at worship by a balustrade. Moreover, for practical reasons
and to avoid giving offense, he saw to it that his colleagues worked
among the high caste by day and the low caste by night. When even this
caused riots, he brought in native missionaries of middle-caste status
who could work with all castes, including Brahmins.[106]

By 1700 this combination of social accommodation and doctrinal orthodoxy had produced a community of Christians in the Madurai area
second only in numbers to that of Portuguese Goa. De Nobili's successors in the mission, though rarely numbering more than seven or eight
at any one time, were baptizing 5,000 new converts annually and reported a total community of over 150,000.[107] Their very success brought
controversy. As in China after Ricci, so also in India the experiments
of de Nobili and his Jesuit successors in adapting Christian practice
and worship to national cultures, such as the caste barrier in India,
brought immediate criticism. A rising tide of opposition to the Malabar

Rites, as the accommodations were called, condemned them as caste discriminatory and religiously syncretistic. Papal censure followed in 1734, paralleling the contemporary disapproval of the Chinese Rites, which were finally prohibited in 1742.[108]

Mission to Muslims in North India

Thus far this brief survey of two centuries of Christianity in India (1500–1700) has dealt with only two of India's territorial divisions of the period, and mostly with the first one, Portuguese India. The other two were Indian South India and Moghul North India. Portuguese India was little more than a series of trading ports sprinkled along the shore, more closely on the east but leap-frogging up the west coast as far as Bengal. In those colonial beachheads the missionary encounter with Hinduism was overshadowed by the prickly meeting of two ancient forms of Christianity, European and Asiatic, which did not easily embrace and unite after so long a separation. The encounter of Christianity with the ancient native traditions of Hinduism in Indian South India was very different. It was the clash of a foreign, monotheistic faith with a non-Christian polytheism deeply rooted in Indian culture. North India was a different situation altogether. The North was Muslim. And Islam, though as foreign a religion to India as Christianity, not only built an empire there but was already shaping the culture of the north to its own Asian form of monotheism.

Earlier Muslim invasions of India, as far back as A.D. 1000, had been a succession of fierce but short-lived dynasties. But when the great Babur, a great-grandson of Tamerlane and grandfather of the builder of the Taj Mahal, marched south out of Afghanistan into North India in 1525, just as the Portuguese fleets were seizing the port cities along the coast of South India, he created a Muslim Indian empire that lasted for three hundred years (1526–1858) and accomplished something none of the Western conquerors — Portuguese, French, Dutch, or English — had been able to do. One short early episode in that history must be noted before we leave India: the story of the Jesuit mission to the Moghuls.

The third emperor, Akbar the Great, a grandson of Babur, was a very religious man and unusually tolerant, unlike Tamerlane. He was more like the ancestors on his father's side of the family who traced their lineage directly back to the great Genghis Khan. He came to the throne in 1556, and though most of his Muslim subjects were Sunni, he generously appointed a Shi'ite as his first prime minister. Then, to the surprise and delight of his Hindu subjects, he abolished the dreaded poll tax that Muslim rulers for almost a thousand years had traditionally levied against non-Muslims in Islamic Asia. In the same spirit of religious tolerance, when he heard that Jesuit missionaries in Bengal, which had recently been conquered by the Moghuls, rebuked some Christian merchants for cheating on their government taxes, he invited a Jesuit missionary to join the religious debates he loved to sponsor among the various faiths in his empire.[109] This led to a surprising invitation from Akbar to Jesuit headquarters in Goa asking for a mission to be sent to the imperial Moghul court.

Few missions to Muslim territory ever had such auspicious beginnings. Three Jesuit missionaries reached the emperor's court in 1579. They had impressive credentials. One was the son of a duke (Aquaviva). Another, Henrique, was a Persian convert from Islam — a risky choice in a culture with religious laws prescribing death for apostates. Akbar was most impressed by Aquaviva, perhaps feeling that his aristocratic lineage made him more acceptable as an emperor's companion. He even tolerated the Jesuits' blunt criticism of his imperially polygamous harem.[110]

Not all of his people were so tolerant. A rebellion sparked by more orthodox Muslim officials had to be crushed, but it forced the emperor to lessen the public favor he had shown toward the Jesuits. Nevertheless, though three separate Jesuit missions all called at the emperor's specific request — a second in 1590, and a third in 1594 led by a grandnephew of Francis Xavier — Akbar continued to allow public Christian preaching and public conversions.[111] By 1598 there were at least four Christian churches in his realm, at Agra and Lahore, and probably at Cambay and Thatta.[112]

But the motivation of some of the converts was questionable, and conversion was not what Akbar was seeking. He wanted peace among the religions, political peace. When no clear decision for any one clearly definable religion emerged from the debates, Akbar's enthusiasm for religious dialogue among Christians, Muslims, Hindus, and Jews ended, and he arbitrarily proposed a compromise of his own making — a featureless, mystic blend of all of them, to which he added some elements of Zoroastrianism. He called it divine monotheism. And he declared himself to be the infallible judge of whatever was true in any of them.[113]

Akbar died in 1605, and his unusual experiment in interfaith dialogue and organized religious pluralism died with him. He had offended all the religions, disappointed the Jesuit missionaries, and dangerously alienated his own Islamic people. A brave experiment in universal toleration it may have been, but a discouraging example. None of his successors showed the same measure of tolerance. Shah Jehan (1628–1658) built one of the most beautiful buildings in the world, the Taj Mahal, but persecuted Christians and demolished their churches. Shah Jehan's anti-Christian edict, prompted in part by a war against the Christian Portuguese invaders and in part by his own orthodox Muslim militancy, was published in 1632. He also prohibited further conversions of Muslims by Hindus. Nine years later, in 1641, he allowed Christians to rebuild their churches.[114] Jehan's son, Emperor Aurungzeb (1658–1707), was even more militantly Muslim. He ordered all Hindu schools and temples destroyed, executed the leader of the Sikhs, beheaded a Portuguese who had converted to Islam and reconverted back to Christianity, and in 1679, reversing the action of his great-great-grandfather Akbar, he reinstated the hated poll tax on all non-Muslims.[115]

By 1700, as the period of Portuguese expansion gave way before the advance of the Dutch and the British, little remained of the Portuguese Indian colonies outside Goa. But while the Portuguese empire was waning, the Catholic Church that had come with it in 1500, though unable to penetrate Muslim North India, had spread down the west coast south and east, around the edges of the whole subcontinent.

On the west coast, Goa and Kerala, Christian expansion was either linked principally to Portuguese colonial expansion, as in Goa and the Fisher coast, or to the strong preexisting communities of the St. Thomas Christians. In both, the Indian religious background was Hinduism, but converts from Hinduism apart from the supporting presence of the Portuguese or the Thomas communities were not numerous. On the east coast, as in Madurai, in proudly independent Indian royal territory, though there was no such indigenous or colonial Christian support there were surprisingly encouraging responses to Christian evangelism among all classes of Hindus.[116] But in the third portion of the huge subcontinent, North India, Christianity was barely visible and showed few signs of life. North India was Muslim. Its population may have been Hindu, but its rulers were the last of the conquering Mongols, descendants of Genghis Khan and Tamerlane, who had for a time considered Christianity but finally converted to Islam in Central Asia.

It is futile to expect agreement among the various estimates of the number of baptized Christians in India in the eighteenth century. About halfway through the 1700s the figures decline. Franciscan Indian historian Achilles Meersman marks "1750 or thereabouts" as "the beginning of the dark century in the history of Catholicism," a period that we describe in a later chapter. He reflects ruefully that after two centuries of uninterrupted missionary endeavor, there was a surprisingly small number of Catholics in India's two oldest Latin dioceses, the Archdiocese of Goa and the Diocese of Cochin, a combined area that covered the whole southwestern third of the subcontinent. He was even more saddened to note that almost all the converts were concentrated in areas of direct Portuguese control, and "little or no" or "comparatively small" progress had been made among the people under native rulers.[117] He estimated that there were about 400,000 Catholics in the two dioceses (excluding Ceylon).[118] Tamilnadu (southeastern India) had an estimated 200,000 Catholics, and Bombay another 100,000.[119] In all India the total number of Catholics in 1700 was estimated at no higher than 750,000,[120] and according to most reports had declined by 1750 and was still declining in 1800, as we shall see in chapter 8.[121]

Thus by 1800, India, which had once been the springboard from which Catholic missions in Asia swept out in a great circle along the islands of the Pacific to Japan first, and then into mighty China, was not yet ready to resume its role as the center and headquarters of Christian advance toward the east. Golden Goa was losing its luster. Catholics in Europe were engaged in the suppression of one their greatest missionary societies, the Jesuits. They would soon recover, but not before scattered little groups of Protestants leaped into the Christian missionary movement with an enthusiasm and energy that in the next hundred years would change the missionary map of the world.

NOTES

1. Calicut, in the southeast state of Kerala, is not to be confused with the better-known Calcutta in northeast India.

2. See Charles R. Boxer, *The Portuguese Seaborne Empire, 1415–1825* (London: Hutchinson, 1969), 34.

3. See J. M. Roberts, *The Triumph of the West* (Boston: Little, Brown, 1985).

4. K. M. Panikkar, *Asia and Western Dominance: A Survey of the Vasco da Gama Epoch of Asian History, 1498–1945* (London: George Allen & Unwin, 1953), 13–14, 16, 297, 328–31.

5. Boxer, *Portuguese Seaborne Empire*, 37.

6. Neill points out that the earliest Portuguese had difficulty distinguishing between Christians and Hindus among the Indians (Stephen Neill, *A History of Christianity in India*, vol. 1, *The Beginnings to A.D. 1707* [Cambridge: Cambridge University Press, 1984], 91ff. and 44 n. 12).

7. Quoted in Panikkar, *Asia and Western Dominance*, 26. On da Gama's "Indian Christians," see also A. Mathias Mundadan, *From the Beginning Up to the Middle of the Sixteenth Century*, vol. 1 of *History of Christianity in India* (Bangalore: Church History Association of India, 1984), 247ff.

8. See Neill, *A History of Christianity in India*, 1:92–93; G. M. Moraes, *A History of Christianity in India*, vol. 1 *From Early Times to St. Francis Xavier: A.D. 52–1542* (Bombay: Manaktalas, 1964), 126–127.

9. A. Mingana, "The Early Spread of Christianity in India," reprint from *BJRL* (Manchester) 10, no. 2 (July 1926): 41.

10. They may have chosen the name St. Bartholomew in deference to the Indian Christians' prior claim to St. Thomas or because of an early Western tradition attributing the first India mission to Bartholomew (see Samuel Hugh Moffett, *A History of Christianity in Asia*, vol. 1, *Beginnings to 1500* [Maryknoll, N.Y.: Orbis Books, 1998], 37–38; Neill, *A History of Christianity in India*, 1:113; and Moraes, *A History of Christianity in India*, 1:206ff.).

11. Mundadan, *From the Beginning Up to the Middle of the Sixteenth Century*, 265ff., citing Thome Lopes, *Navigatione verso l'India Orientali* (ca. 1603). Lopes, as an eyewitness, was one of the most reliable of the early Portuguese historians. For a critical Indian viewpoint on the early historians of this period, see Teotonio R. de Souza, "Spiritual Conquest of the East: A Critique of the Church Historiography of Portuguese Asia," *ICHR* 19 (June 1985): 10–24. There is no

proof that the Thomas Christians ever actually had a Christian king. See also Mundadan, *From the Beginning Up to the Middle of the Sixteenth Century*, 161ff.

12. Moraes, *A History of Christianity in India*, 1:175. See Georg Schurhammer, *Francis Xavier: His Life and His Times*, trans. M. J. Costelloe (Freiburg, 1955–; originally published as *Franz Xaver: sein Leben und seine Zeit*, 4 vols. [Rome: Jesuit Historical Institute, 1973– .], 2:485 n. 62). Neill prefers an estimate of about thirty-six thousand (*A History of Christianity in India*, 1:192).

13. For a detailed description, drawn from early Portuguese sources, of these principalities and the Thomas Christian communities, see Mundadan, *From the Beginning Up to the Middle of the Sixteenth Century*, 216ff. On the Christians, see especially 34, 232ff.

14. See Moffett, *A History of Christianity in Asia*, 1:502.

15. For the full letter, see Mingana, "The Early Spread of Christianity in India," 38ff.

16. V. Mathew Kurian, "Syrian Christians and the Political Economy of Kerala," *ICHR* 28 (December 1994): 98.

17. On Mar Jacob's ordination and trip to India, see Mingana, "The Early Spread of Christianity in India," 37–38. On his life, see Mundadan, *From the Beginning Up to the Middle of the Sixteenth Century*, 195ff., 286, 305–311, 327, 342–347; for more detail, see A. M. Mundadan, *The Arrival of the Portuguese in India and the Thomas Christians under Mar Jacob, 1498–1552* (Bangalore: Dharmaram College, 1967).

18. See the three letters of Mar Jacob in Georg Schurhammer, *Orientalia* (Rome: Institutum Historicum Societatis Iesu, 1963), 333–350.

19. Letter 2, in Schurhammer, *Orientalia*, 343–344. There is no evidence that Mar Jacob and Vicente actually worked together at the school, which tends to support Mundadan's suggestion that Vicente was too "Latin" even for the tolerant but traditionally Nestorian "Thomas" Indian Mar Jacob. Vicente's coworkers were two other Indian priests who had been trained, and "Latinized," in Portugal: Father George and Father Matthew (Dias). On the ups and downs of the college, see Mundadan, *From the Beginning Up to the Middle of the Sixteenth Century*, 323–343; and Georg Schurhammer, *The Malabar Church and Rome during the Early Portuguese Period and Before* (Trichinopoly, India, 1934).

20. See A. M. Mundadan, *Indian Christians: Search for Identity and Struggle for Autonomy* (Bangalore: Dharmaram College, 1984), 1–28. On differing interpretations of Mar Jacob's relationship with Rome, see especially Schurhammer, *Francis Xavier*, 3:593 n. 167.

21. Achilles Meersman, "Franciscan Bishops in India and Pakistan," *AFH* 72 (1979): 135–144.

22. On Father Vicente, see Mundadan, *From the Beginning Up to the Middle of the Sixteenth Century*, 318, 323–341; and Joseph Thekkedath, *From the Middle of the Sixteenth Century to the End of the Seventeenth Century*, vol. 2, *History of Christianity in India* (Bangalore: Church History Association of India, 1982), 34–35, 329ff.

23. For a contrary, minority view, see the booklet by Michael Arattukulam, *St. Francis Xavier on the Malabar Coast* (Alleppey, India, 1968). Arattukulam argues for a pre-Portuguese origin of Roman Catholic Syrian Christianity in Kerala.

24. On Portuguese expansion in Asia, see Boxer, *Portuguese Seaborne Empire*, esp. 46.

25. On the organization of Roman Catholicism and the Malabar churches, see Cardinal Eugene Tisserant, *Eastern Christianity in India: A History of the Syro-Malabar Church from the Earliest Time to the Present Day,* trans. E. R. Hambye (Westminster, Md.: Newman Press, 1957); M. D'Sa, *History of the Catholic Church in India,* 2 vols. (Bombay, 1910, 1924); Schurhammer, *The Malabar Church and Rome;* and Meersman, "Franciscan Bishops in India and Palestine." The best overall survey of Catholic mission organization in East Asia is P. A. Jann, *Die catholischen Missionen in Indien, China und Japan. Ihre Organisation und das portugiesische Patronat von 15 bis in 18 Jahrhundert* (Paderborn, 1915).

26. Before the establishment of the bishopric, a succession of three bishops sent out from Portugal served in Goa as "apostolic commissaries" with restricted episcopal powers and without territorial jurisdiction — and, it must be added, with very limited success (Meersman, "Franciscan Bishops in India and Pakistan," 135–144; cf. Neill, *A History of Christianity in India,* 1:115–116).

27. Neill quotes Father Gonzago, writing about 1587, as reporting, "all that has been done for forty years in the East Indies on behalf of the sick, the non-Christians, the catechumens, and the converts, rested on the shoulders of the Franciscans" (*A History of Christianity in India,* 1:121). On the *Misericordia,* see Mundadan, *From the Beginning Up to the Middle of the Sixteenth Century,* 455–459.

28. Mundadan, *From the Beginning Up to the Middle of the Sixteenth Century,* 367ff.

29. C. R. Boxer, "The Problem of the Native Clergy in the Portuguese and Spanish Empires from the Sixteenth to the Eighteenth Centuries," in *The Mission of the Church and the Propagation of the Faith,* ed. G. J. Cuming (Cambridge: Cambridge University Press, 1970), 86–90.

30. Boxer, "The Problem of the Native Clergy," 89, quoting Antonio Gomes.

31. The best reference on Francis Xavier, apart from his own letters, is Schurhammer, *Francis Xavier.* Volume 2 is titled *India, 1541–1545.* For a critical survey of the many early sources and biographies of Xavier, see Georg Schurhammer, *Xaveriana* (Lisbon: Centro de Estudos Historicos Ultramarinos, 1964), 90–114, 129–142; for a brief chronology, see 491–495. A highly readable biography is James Broderick, *St. Francis Xavier (1506–1552)* (New York: Pellegrini & Cudahy, 1952).

32. On Loyola's *Spiritual Exercises,* see Ignatius Iparaguirre, *Historia de la práctica de los Ejercicios Spirituales de San Ignacio Loyola,* 3 vols. (Bilbao and Rome: Institutum Historicum Societatis Jesu). Useful recent books include D. L. Fleming, *A Contemporary Reading of the Spiritual Exercises: A Companion to St. Ignatius's Text,* 2nd ed., rev. (St. Louis: Institute of Jesuit Sources, 1980); John Padberg, *Jesuit Spirituality* (Chicago: Loyola University Press, 1990); and the modern adaptation by Tad Dunne, *Spiritual Exercises for Today: A Contemporary Presentation of the Classic Spiritual Exercises of Ignatius Loyola* (San Francisco: Harper/San Francisco, 1990).

For the *Constitutions,* see G. E. Ganss, *The Constitutions of the Society of Jesus* (St. Louis: Institute of Jesuit Sources, 1970); Gaetan de Bernoville, *The Jesuits,* trans. Kathleen Balfe (London: Burns, Oates, and Washbourne, 1937), 69–123; and W. V. Bangert, *A History of the Society of Jesus,* 2nd ed., rev. (St. Louis: Institute of Jesuit Sources, 1986), 41–45, 50, 356, 374.

33. De Bernoville, *The Jesuits,* 146–147 n. 1 (italics added).

34. Schurhammer, *Francis Xavier,* 1:713ff.

35. Schurhammer, *Francis Xavier,* 2:153.

36. Xavier worked for three and a half years altogether as hospital chaplain, with interruptions for wider mission (Schurhammer, *Francis Xavier*, 2:218–224, 3:472).

37. Quoted without citation by Ken Newton, *Glimpses of India Church History* (Bombay: Gospel Literature Service, 1975), 18.

38. Schurhammer, *Francis Xavier*, 2:216.

39. Schurhammer, *Francis Xavier*, 2:218–224.

40. Schurhammer, *Francis Xavier*, 3:472 nn. 3, 4.

41. On the numbers baptized before Xavier's mission, see Schurhammer, *Francis Xavier*, 2:263 n. 487. Neill estimates a total of twenty thousand (*A History of Christianity in India*, 1:143 n. 33), which, though low, is higher than the figure of ten thousand he had cited in his *History of Christian Missions* (New York: Penguin, 1964), 149.

42. Moraes, *A History of Christianity in India*, 1:143–146.

43. See Neill, *A History of Christianity in India*, 2:453 n. 30.

44. Schurhammer, *Francis Xavier*, 2:301; see also 2:280, 290–359.

45. In the matter of texts used in mission, the methods of Xavier and Bishop Jacob, the Syrian Thomas Christian, provide an intriguing contrast. Jacob gave much time to copying texts from the Bible in Syriac but not apparently in the local vernacular, which was Malayalam; Xavier produced texts in the vernacular, in his case, Tamil, but only liturgical texts and creeds. In all his missionary work in Asia, reports Neill, it is probable that Xavier "never possessed a Bible or even a New Testament...[or] arranged for a single chapter of the Bible to be translated into Tamil or Malayalam" (Neill, *Francis Xavier*, 1:159). For a lively, detailed account of Xavier's mission on the Cape, see Broderick, *St. Francis Xavier (1506–1552)*, 130–156.

46. Neill, *A History of Christianity in India*, 1:144–147. Schurhammer gives additional information about one other Brahman to whom Xavier explained the gospel who may have been baptized later, in 1550 (Schurhammer, *Francis Xavier*, 1:356–359).

47. Neill, *A History of Christian Missions*, 1:150.

48. Rene Fulop-Miller, *The Jesuits: A History of the Society of Jesus* (New York: Capricorn Books, 1930; reprint, 1963), 202. Fulop-Miller adds, "He saw that a large part of his task would be to convert to Christianity, in the first place, the Christians who were living in India, and he had already learnt in Europe how hard it was to win Christians for Christ."

49. Mundadan, *From the Beginning Up to the Middle of the Sixteenth Century*, 425.

50. Placid Podipara, *The Malabar Christians* (Alleppey, India: Prakasam Publications, 1972), 4ff.; K. K. Kuruvilla, *A History of the Mar Thoma Church and Its Doctrines* (Madras: Christian Literature Society for India, 1951), 4ff.; G. M. Moraes, *A History of Christianity in India*, 1:222ff.; Mundadan, *From the Beginning Up to the Middle of the Sixteenth Century*, 348ff.

51. For a defense of Goa's missionary methods, see A. Brou, "Missions goanaises et conversions forcées?" *RHM* 13 (1936): 32–43.

52. Neill, *A History of Christianity in India*, 1:158.

53. See A. R. Vine, *The Nestorian Churches: A Concise History of Nestorian Christianity in Asia from the Persian Schism to the Modern Assyrians* (London: Independent

Press, 1937), 172ff. The subsequent tangled history of the schism is described in a later chapter.

54. See Tisserant, *Eastern Christianity in India,* 35–41; Mundadan, *Indian Christians,* 34–35.

55. On Mar Abraham's old-line patriarchal connection, see Leslie W. Brown, *The Indian Christians of St. Thomas: An Account of the Ancient Syrian Church of Malabar,* 2nd ed. (Cambridge: Cambridge University Press, 1982), 20ff., esp. 22 n. 2. Some Portuguese authorities relate Abraham's initial appointment to the new-line, pro-Roman Patriarch Abdiso (Ebed-Jesu), as does Cardinal Eugene Tisserant (*Eastern Christianity in India*). Stephen Neill, like Brown, accepts the likelihood of an initial independent, old-line connection (*A History of Christianity in India,* 1:204).

56. On the Latinization controversy from the Roman viewpoint, see Thomas Thayil, "The Origin of the Latin Christians of Kerala," in the *St. Thomas Christian Encyclopaedia of India,* 2 vols., ed. G. Menachery (Trichur, India: St. Thomas Christian Encyclopaedia of India, 1973, 1982), 2:61–65. Cf. Leslie W. Brown, *The Indian Christians of St. Thomas,* 20ff.

57. Joseph Wicki, "Early Jesuit Connections," in the *St. Thomas Christian Encyclopaedia of India,* 2:68–71; cf. Leslie W. Brown, *The Indian Christians of St. Thomas,* 26; see also Mundadan, *Indian Christians,* 36ff., and cf. Tisserant, *Eastern Christianity in India,* 42ff.

58. See Schurhammer, *Francis Xavier,* 2:385–386; Neill, *A History of Christianity in India,* 1:160.

59. Josef Franz Schütte, *Valignano's Mission Principles for Japan,* vol. 1, part 1, *The Problem (1573–1582),* trans. J. J. Coyne (St. Louis: Institute of Jesuit Sources, 1950), xvii.

60. The best contemporary source on the synod is Anthony de Gouvea, *Jornado de Arcebispo da Goa Dom Frey: A. de Menezes* (Coimbra, 1606), trans. into French by J.-B. de Glen as *Histoire orientale des grans progres de l'église Catholique et Romaine en la reduction des anciens chrestiens dits de S. Thomas* (Brussels, 1609).

61. See his letter to the Latin patriarch of Jerusalem, in Rome, in 1597: "I humbly suggest that he [the Latin bishop, preferably a Jesuit] be instructed to extinguish little by little the Syrian language...His priests should learn the Latin language, because the Syriac language is the channel through which all that heresy flows" (cited in M. K. Kuriakose, *History of Christianity in India: Source Materials,* Indian Theological Library, Serampore College [Madras: Christian Literature Society, 1982], 38–39).

62. See Jacob Kollaparambil, *The Archdeacon of All-India: An Historico-Juridical Study* (Rome: Lateran University, 1972).

63. Thekkedath, *From the Middle of the Sixteenth to the End of the Seventeenth Century,* 66. The primary source is G. Beltrami, *La Chiesa caldea nel secolo dell'Unione, Orientalia Christiana* 29, no. 83 (Rome, 1933), 121. See also J. N. Ogilvie, *The Apostles of India,* Baird Lectures (London: Hodder & Stoughton, 1915), 140.

64. The major source for all writers is the contemporary account by the Roman Catholic de Gouvea, *Jornado de Arcebispo da Goa Dom Frey: A. de Menezes,* and a few letters of the Jesuit Francis Roz, who became the Latin bishop of the St. Thomas Christians and was more sympathetic to the Indian side than de Gouvea (on the letters of Roz, see Tisserant, *Eastern Christianity in India,* 6 n. 2).

65. Michael Geddes, *The History of the Church of Malabar* (London: S. Smith and B. Walford, 1694), 112–113. The quotations here and below are from Geddes's 1694 translation (from the Portuguese into English) of the calling and decrees of Diamper (89–423).

66. E. Tisserant, "L'Eglise Nestorienne," in *DTC* 9:230, 263. The patriarch at the time was Simon IX Denha. As a result of the recent Nestorian schism, the Baghdad patriarchate had moved to improve its relationship with Rome. See also Thekkedath, *From the Middle of the Sixteenth to the End of the Seventeenth Century*, 66–67; Mundadan, *Indian Christians*, 45.

67. Geddes, *History of the Church of Malabar*, 112–116.

68. Geddes, *History of the Church of Malabar*, G4 (the paging is irregular: pages 1–109 are Geddes's summary of the history of the church of Malabar, bound with eleven pages irregularly numbered; the calling, acts, and decrees of the synod are numbered 89 to 443).

69. A letter of Father Roz, who became first Latin bishop of the Serra (the St. Thomas territory) admits that "not a single canon [of the synod] was discussed or altered" and that the people did not understand their meaning (Thekkedath, *From the Middle of the Sixteenth to the End of the Seventeenth Century*, 70).

70. Neill, *A History of Christianity in India*, 1:310.

71. See Tisserant, *Eastern Christianity in India*, 41, 70–75; and Thekkedath, *From the Middle of the Sixteenth to the End of the Seventeenth Century*, 75ff. Roz was named bishop of Angamali, an inland area near Cranganore.

72. Leslie W. Brown, *The Indian Christians of St. Thomas*, 95.

73. M. P. Harney, *The Jesuits in History* (New York: America Press, 1941), 220.

74. For a review of the bibliography on the Propaganda up to 1922, see Peter Guilday, "The Sacred Congregation de Propaganda Fide," *CHR* 6 (1920/1921): 478–494.

75. See Joseph Schmidlin, *Catholic Mission Theory*, trans. Matthias Braun (Techny, Ill.: Mission Press, 1931), 166–170.

76. The first five missionary apostolic vicars of this period were de Castro for India and the Franciscan François-Antoine Frascella for Japan, both in 1637; François Pallu of the Paris Missionary Society for Tonkin (now northern Vietnam) in 1639; Pierre de la Motte for Cochin China (southern Vietnam); and in 1660 Ignazio Cotolendi for China (including Korea). On de Castro see S. Delacroix, ed., *Histoire universelle des missions catholiques* (Paris: Librairie Grund, 1957), 2:132–138, 402, citing two theses: Theodore Ghesquière, *Matthieu de Castro, premier vicaire apostolique aux Indes: Une création de la Propaganda à ses débuts* (Louvain: Bureaux de la Revue, 1937); and *Matteo de Castro Mahalo*, by Carlo Cavallera.

77. On the apostolic vicars, see Dominic A. S. Theresa, "Vicars Apostolic and Missions under the Propaganda in the XVII and XVIII Centuries," in the *St. Thomas Christian Encyclopaedia of India*, 1:27ff.; and Delacroix, *Histoire universelle des missions catholiques*, 2:137–138. The seat of the apostolic vicariate in India was outside Goa in the Moghul Empire, and therefore beyond Portuguese control; after 1717 it was in Bombay, which was under British control.

78. A Nestorian bishop had been sent to India by the patriarch in Mesopotamia some time before the Synod of Diamper, perhaps in 1576, but he had been

captured and deported by the Portuguese (see Thekkedath, *History of India: From the Middle of the Sixteenth to the End of the Seventeenth Century*, 50–51).

79. For more on Mar Atalla, see Joseph Thekkedath, *The Troubled Days of Francis Garcia, S.J., Archbishop of Cranganore (1641–1659)* (Rome: Università Gregoriana, 1972), 50–59, 73–82. On the history of the Monophysites in Asia, see Moffett, *A History of Christianity in Asia*, 1:188–193, 243–247, 339–340.

80. Thomas de Campo (Parambil or Parampil) was a nephew of Archdeacon George of the Cross, who had been restored to influence in 1624 when the Portuguese realized that the appointment of a foreign archdeacon was a mistake (see Thekkedath, *The Troubled Days of Francis Garcia*, 21–40; and Leslie W. Brown, *The Indian Christians of St. Thomas*, 96–98). Cf. *St. Thomas Christian Encyclopaedia of India*, 2:49.

81. The succession of archbishops of the Serra (the St. Thomas Christian area of Malabar) in this period was Francis Roz (1608–1624), Stephen Britto (1624–1641), Francis Garcia (1641–1659), and after an interim, the Syro-Indian Alexander de Campo (Parambil) as Metropolitan of all India (1663–1687), and after another interim and over some objections the Portuguese Jesuit Archbishop John Rebeiro (1701–1709). The succession of archdeacons was George of the Cross (d. 1637), and Thomas de Campo (Parambil), who as Mar Thomas I, after 1653, became first of a new line of Syrian bishops of the non-Roman St. Thomas Christians. For a very Roman Catholic criticism of Thomas de Campo and his struggle against the Catholic Archbishop Garcia, see Thekkedath, *The Troubled Days of Francis Garcia*, 21–40; see also V. C. George, *The Church in India before and after the Synod of Diamper* (Alleppey, India: Prakasam Publications, 1977), 160–168.

82. See Thekkedath, *From the Middle of the Sixteenth to the End of the Seventeenth Century*, 93–94; Neill, *A History of Christianity in India*, 1:320–321; and Leslie W. Brown, *The Indian Christians of St. Thomas*, 100ff. The ordinations and consecration were irregular, though dubious letters allegedly from the abducted Mar Attala were produced as authorization.

83. Thekkedath gives the range at two hundred to one thousand laymen and fifteen to twenty-five Indian priests who followed the Portuguese (*The Troubled Days of Francis Garcia*, 61ff.); Tisserant mentions "400 Syrians who still remained loyal [to Rome]" (*Eastern Christianity in India*, 80).

84. There is no accord in the Portuguese records of those days. This figure represents merely a rough averaging of the growth, as of A.D. 1600, between the estimate thirty thousand Thomas Christians when the Portuguese arrived at the beginning of the sixteenth century, which was probably too low, and a high of between two hundred thousand to three hundred thousand Christians, Catholic and independent, as reported in the middle of the seventeenth century, which was probably too high. At the death of Portuguese Archbishop Garcia, only nine Thomas Christian churches recognized his authority. See Thekkedath, *The Troubled Days of Francis Garcia*, 148; Thekkedath, *From the Middle of the Sixteenth to the End of the Seventeenth Century*, 24–25; and Neill's remarks about the statistics in *A History of Christianity in India*, 1:326ff.

85. See Thekkedath, *The Troubled Days of Francis Garcia*, 150ff. This suggests that the Old Believers, as the Roman side of the Syrian church in Kerala came to call itself, had recovered rapidly both in numbers and in wealth after the Coonen Cross revolt, though most Christians, particularly in the fishing villages, were poor. On the social condition of the Christians on the Malabar coast, see

Thekkedath, *From the Middle of the Sixteenth to the End of the Seventeenth Century*, 120, 131ff.

86. Thekkedath, *From the Middle of the Sixteenth to the End of the Seventeenth Century*, 120.

87. New Believers and Old Believers are not to be confused with the pre-Diamper old-line Syrians and new-line pro-Romans. The pro-Romans were now "old party" (*pazhayakoon*), and the Syrians were "new party" (*puthenkoon*) (see George, *The Church in India before and after the Synod of Diamper*, 150ff.).

88. Tisserant, *Eastern Christianity in India*, 80–87.

89. On the commissaries and Sebastiani, see Thekkedath, *The Troubled Days of Francis Garcia*, 101–127, 151–159.

90. "It has to be said," writes a Christian Indian historian, "that the Syrian Christian community had become something like a caste... with all the exclusivism and narrowness attached to caste" (Thekkedath, *From the Middle of the Sixteenth to the End of the Seventeenth Century*, 140).

91. *St. Thomas Christian Encyclopaedia of India*, 1:32 (A. J. Panakkal); 2:53 (M. Vattakuzhy).

92. Thekkedath, *From the Middle of the Sixteenth to the End of the Seventeenth Century*, 101–103; and Tisserant, *Eastern Christianity in India*, 111–112. See also Indian Orthodox historian, David Daniel, *The Orthodox Church of India: History and Faith*, 2nd ed. (New Delhi: Rachel David, 1986), 125ff. Mar Gregorios died in 1671, and Mar Thomas I in 1673.

93. Tisserant, *Eastern Christianity in India*, 115–118.

94. Thekkedath, *From the Middle of the Sixteenth to the End of the Seventeenth Century*, 24 nn. 5, 6.

95. Neill, *A History of Christianity in India*, 1:326–327. Neill prefers an estimate of one hundred thousand Syrian Christians rather than two hundred thousand. This figure does not include the Goa territory, north of Kerala, which was almost completely Catholic but not Syrian.

96. Thekkedath, *From the Middle of the Sixteenth to the End of the Seventeenth Century*, 128–135.

97. K. V. Joseph, "The Vicissitudes of Syrian Christians in the Maritime Trade of Pre-Modern Kerala," *ICHR* 23 (1989): 141. Joseph cites a letter of J. C. Visscher, Dutch chaplain in Goa from 1711 to 1722.

98. Joseph Albert Lobley, *The Church and the Churches in Southern India: A Review of the Portuguese Missions* (Cambridge: Deighton, Bell, 1870), 100–101.

99. For insights into de Nobili's missionary innovations and mission theory, see introductory and commentary materials in Roberto de Nobili, *Preaching Wisdom to the Wise: Three Treatises by Roberto de Nobili, S.J., Missionary and Scholar in Seventeenth-Century South India*, ed. and trans. Anand Amaladass and Francis X. Clooney (St. Louis: Institute of Jesuit Sources, 2000).

100. On the Madurai mission, see J. Bertrand, *La Mission de Maduré d'après des documents inédits*, 4 vols. (Paris: Poussielgue-Rusand, 1847–1854), esp. vol. 2, *Fondation de la Mission*, and vol. 3, *Continuation de la Mission*.

101. Quoted by Thekkedath, *From the Middle of the Sixteenth to the End of the Seventeenth Century*, 211.

102. Bertrand, *La Mission du Maduré d'après des documents inédits*, 2:3, quoting a 1609 letter of A. Laerzio describing the work of de Nobili.

103. V. M. Gnanapragasam, "Interfaith Dialogue of Early Christian Missionaries in Tamil Nadu," *ICHR* 27, no. 2 (December 1993): 124–125.

104. De Nobili, *Preaching Wisdom to the Wise,* 42–48. The notes show how de Nobili's treatises — "Report on Indian Customs" in Latin; "Dialogue on Eternal Life" and "Inquiry into the Meaning of God" in Tamil — blend his Thomistic theological heritage into a careful adaptation to India's intellectual and religious culture. Clooney, one of the translators and annotators, concludes that de Nobili was right in taking seriously both human reason and the "reasonable strand" in Indian religion, but he was "too reasonable," too judgmental, too sympathetic, or "maybe tone deaf."

105. The papal brief *Romanae Sedis Antistes* [correcting the Latin], in Kuriakose, *History of Christianity in India,* 52–53.

106. Thekkedath, *From the Middle of the Sixteenth to the End of the Seventeenth Century,* 219ff., 260ff. The most notable of these catechists was a converted *yogi* (holy man) named Muthudaiyan, who as an ascetic could work with all classes. His main work was with the low castes. He is reported to have brought seven hundred of his former disciples to the faith, and before he died there were five thousand Christians in his hometown, where formerly there were none.

107. Harney, *The Jesuits in History,* 223.

108. On the Malabar Rites, see E. Amann, "Malabares (Rites)," *DTC* 9:1704–1746. The account in chap. 4 of this volume on the rites controversy in China describes the issues involved in more detail.

109. On Akbar, see Sri Ram Sharma, *The Religious Policy of the Mughal Emperors* (London: Asia Publishing House, 1962), 15–56. See also Kenneth Scott Latourette, *A History of the Expansion of Christianity,* 7 vols. (New York: Harper & Brothers, 1939), 3:257–258. On the historical background of the early Moghul empire, see R. C. Majumdar et al., *Advanced History of India* (London: Macmillan, 1946; reissued, New York: Macmillan, 1967), 425–526, esp. 452ff.

110. It is said, debatably but with considerable supporting evidence, that Akbar's wife was an Armenian Christian and was given a chapel of her own in which to worship (see Mesrovb Jacob Seth, *Armenians in India: From the Earliest Times to the Present Day* [New Delhi and Madras: Asian Educational Services, 1992], 151–166; this is a reprint of the 1937 edition).

111. Conversion had been tolerated for some time but was officially approved under written royal seal in 1601 (Thekkedath, *From the Middle of the Sixteenth to the End of the Seventeenth Century,* 430).

112. Sharma, *The Religious Policy of the Mughal Emperors,* 20 n. 52, citing Jesuit letters of 1597 and 1598.

113. See Sharma's discussion of Akbar's own religious faith and its critics (*The Religious Policy of the Mughal Emperors,* 39–49).

114. See Sharma, *The Religious Policy of the Mughal Emperors,* 88ff.

115. Sharma, *The Religious Policy of the Mughal Emperors,* 114, 131, 142–143.

116. For an indispensable Catholic survey of eighteenth-century Indian Christianity, see E. R. Hambye, *Eighteenth Century,* vol. 3 of *History of Christianity in India* (Bangalore: Church History Association of India, 1997).

117. A. Meersman, "Some Eighteenth-Century Statistics of the Archdiocese of Goa and the Diocese of Cochin," *ICHR* 2, no. 1 (June 1968): 116–117.

118. See Meersman, "Some Eighteenth-Century Statistics." He estimated that "by about the year 1750," there were 260,000 baptized Catholics in the Archdiocese of Goa, and 130,000 in the Diocese of Cochin, representing an area that stretched from Cranganore around the southern cape nearly to the diocese of Mylapore (Madras) and included 30,000 Catholics in Ceylon. Thus the total Catholic membership in southwest India may have been about 500,000, if we add 100,000 non-Catholic Syrian Thomas Christians. As noted earlier, two-thirds of the 300,000 Syrians had converted to Roman Catholicism, and one-third had begun to shift from Nestorianism to Syrian Jacobite Orthodoxy.

119. Hambye, *Eighteenth Century*, 485.

120. Thekkedath, *From the Middle of the Sixteenth to the End of the Seventeenth Century*, 482–484.

121. Cf. the more optimistic viewpoint of Hambye in *Eighteenth Century*, 482–487.

Chapter 2

The Buddhist Kingdoms of the South (1505–1800)

Portuguese Ceylon, Burma, Vietnam, Siam

One cannot deny that there are grounds for saying that oriental heathendom not only knew of, but even received from the Hebrews many observances, both genuine ones which they falsified, and false ones which they embraced and amplified . . . But it is one thing to say that they adopted many Hebrew usages and abused and profaned some dogmas of that holy law, and it is quite another thing to affirm that Buddum preached the law of Moses, because I do not see any ground for it, than that he inculcated the Commandments abbreviated but with the addition of two, not to drink wine, and not to kill any living thing . . . They think it a sin to kill an ant, but do not consider it a sinful thing to entertain inveterate hatred.

— Fernão de Queyroz (on Ceylon, ca. 1687),
citing a contemporary colleague in China

Buddhism is one of the three great missionary religions of world history — Buddhism, Christianity, and Islam. When India began to drive Buddhism out of its birthplace not long after the year 1000, that ancient faith had already planted deep missionary roots elsewhere in Asia. Whatever may have been the causes of its decline in India, the land of its birth — apparently a combination of absorption by Hinduism in the south, and conquest by Islam in the north — Buddhism was destined to spread for another full millennium and more throughout Asia. Today, six of Hindu India's closest neighbors are not Hindu but Buddhist: Ceylon (now Sri Lanka), Burma (now Myanmar), Siam (Thailand), Cambodia, Laos, and Vietnam.[1]

But like the other two missionary religions, Buddhism divided internally into different streams, for religious advance is often associated as much with divisive intellectual ferment as with organizational unity.[2] Divisions in Buddhism began to appear about five hundred years after the death of the Buddha. The most important schism, occurring about the time of Christ, split it into two diverging paths as it spread across Asia. One is called Hinayana (Lesser Vehicle) or Theravada Buddhism. It moved south and east from India to become the dominant religion in

Ceylon and Southeast Asia.[3] The other variant, developing a little later, is known as Mahayana (Great Vehicle) or Reformed Buddhism. It moved with missionary vigor north and east and became a powerful, but only intermittently dominant, religious influence in China, Korea, and Japan. In quite different forms it also shaped the Buddhist base of the religions of Tibet and Vietnam.[4]

Christianity, on the other hand, did not effectively reach these regions until the sixteenth century. Christian missionaries soon discovered that Buddhism, like the other high religions of Asia, was not to be as easily evangelized as the more primitive folk religions of the world. In South Asia, the Hinayana Buddhist countries are still as religiously Buddhist as India is Hindu, and as Pakistan, Indonesia, and Malaysia are Muslim.

So, as a corrective to many treatments of Christianity in Asia that tend quite naturally to center on the great Asian empires — India, China, and Japan — it must be pointed out that in proportion to population, church growth has been greater in the less dominant parts of the continent than in its empires. This chapter addresses the five larger Buddhist regions.

In the sixteenth century Buddhism, though exiled from greater India, still maintained its missionary momentum in the ring of smaller ethnic cultural contexts from Ceylon to Vietnam. All were then divided internally into changing clusters of smaller kingdoms, and all were shaken and shaped in different ways by the arrival of the Portuguese. But in two of them at least, Ceylon and Vietnam, whatever other more malignant aspects of the rolling colonizing wave may have been, one result was the planting of significant and permanent Christian communities. Elsewhere in the Southeast, Christian missions managed to post only a sprinkling of pioneer stations as the Portuguese came and left.

Portugal and the Buddhist Island of Ceylon (1505–1656)[5]

Ceylon's first shattering encounter with Western imperial advance was with an exploring party of Portuguese in 1505, just five years after Vasco da Gama "discovered" India. A priest was with them, and they may have thought they were the first Christians to reach the beautiful island, but if so, they were wrong. A sixth-century Nestorian explorer, Cosmas Indicopleustes, had found Christians there before Augustine of Canterbury converted the English or Columba evangelized the Scots. But a thousand years later, in the sixteenth century, no trace was left of that ancient Christian community, and Ceylon had forgotten it.[6]

At the first sight of the Westerners, startled courtiers told the king of Kotte,[7] largest of the island's kingdoms, that a boat of fair-skinned people had landed wearing "jackets of iron and hats of steel." They eat "bricks of stone and drink blood [bread and wine]," they said, "and the report of their cannon is louder than thunder."[8] Over the objections of Muslim traders who had hitherto enjoyed a monopoly of the Ceylon trade, the king of Kotte encouraged the armed and powerful Westerners to believe that he would favor giving them commercial access and a trading base, but no formal treaty was signed. The first Catholic priest to set foot on the island, Father Vicente, a Franciscan, came with the expedition, said Mass, and left with the others.[9]

No organized mission work was attempted, even after a second, larger Portuguese expedition in 1518 secured a trade treaty of "feudal vassalage" with the kingdom of Kotte. The expedition erected a fort and trading post at Colombo and left a chaplain to minister to the garrison.[10]

Beginnings of Christian Mission (1543–1551)

Twenty years later, in 1543, the Buddhist king Buvanaika Bahu VII (1521–1551), ruler of the kingdom of Kotte, sent an embassy bearing a golden image of his newborn grandson to ask King John III of Portugal to guarantee the baby's succession to the throne of Kotte.[11] In return for this, the embassy indicated it would welcome Christian missionaries to the island kingdom. Thus began the first Roman Catholic mission to Ceylon.

When the embassy arrived in Lisbon, King John was surprised and pleased. He agreed to the Ceylonese king's request to legitimize the succession of his grandson and rejoiced at what he thought was an open opportunity to convert the pagan ruler. So he placed a golden crown on the head of the solid gold effigy of the child, unaware of the ironies of the situation. The name of the infant whose future kingship this very Christian and missionary-minded king of Portugal had so trustingly confirmed was Dharmapala, which means protector of the doctrine of the Buddha.[12] And his grandfather, Buvanaika VII of Kotte, was in no way minded to become a Christian. When the great Xavier paid a brief visit to Ceylon the next year to confirm the Portuguese reports, he found the king amiable enough but unfortunately so given to unnatural vices and opium that he was obviously no candidate for the baptism that Xavier had been expecting him to accept.[13]

Ceylon at that time was a patchwork quilt of ten small kingdoms, mostly Buddhist except on the northern tip of the island where the population was ethnically Tamil and religiously Hindu. In the southwest center the kingdom of Kotte, famed for its golden Temple of Buddha's Tooth, claimed suzerainty over all the lesser kingdoms. But a division of Kotte between two royal princes in 1521 so weakened its rule that, despite the aid of Portugal in support of coastal Kotte's King Buvanaika VII, he was barely able to hold his own against insurrections and revolts in the plains and mountains, much less enforce his claim of sovereignty over the whole island. Throughout the first half of the sixteenth century civil strife tore the island apart and at times threatened to destroy Kotte itself.[14]

Adding to the political chaos of the times was a deterioration of the national religion, Buddhism. Ceylonese (Sinhalese) Buddhism had been weakening for centuries. Its discipline had declined, its hierarchy was disorganized, and its Hinayana doctrinal base had become diluted by the festivals and the worship of the lesser gods (*bodhisattva*) of Mahayana (northeastern Asian) Buddhism. Even in the strongly Buddhist southern parts of the island, creeping syncretism brought Buddhist worshipers into an increasing number of Hindu temples.[15]

The first group of Christian missionaries did not reach Ceylon until 1546. Six Franciscans, including their superior, John of Villa de Conde, came in a delayed answer to the Ceylonese king's request of 1543. With his approval they quickly built the first church on the island at Colombo. A bishop, Juan de Monterio, was appointed and the hierarchy established.[16] A false report spread quickly that a neighboring king in Kandy had been converted.[17] In Kotte, King Buvanaika Bahu VII was also reported to be about to become a Christian. He candidly admitted that he had thought about it, but that he was disappointed in the behavior of some of his subjects who had been baptized and was not about to do so himself. But when the king's attention was called to the fact that a number of Sinhalese had begun to convert from Buddhism to the new religion, his favor wavered. Approval was abruptly withdrawn and was replaced by an edict forbidding his subjects to embrace the Christian faith.[18] Not long thereafter he died, and, as promised by the Portuguese, his grandson, Dharmapala, succeeded him in 1551.

A Christian King, Church Growth, and Religious Reaction

The accession of Dharmapala, crowned in effigy in Lisbon in 1543 and educated in Ceylon by the Franciscans, might have ushered in an age of Christian expansion on the island like that which followed the conversion of the chiefs by the Spaniards in the Philippines at about the same period. But this was not to be. The Filipinos were animists; Kotte was Buddhist. And the little king of the golden effigy, Dharmapala, last king of Kotte, was no Constantine. He did manage to maintain nominal rule of his kingdom for the next forty-six years (1551–1597) and even accepted baptism in 1597–1598.[19] But it was the Portuguese, not the king of Kotte, who held together by force of arms what central power there was left on the island.

The abrupt change of rule from a Buddhist to a Christian king of Kotte in mid-sixteenth century Ceylon affected the progress of Christianity in two opposite ways. The first was negative. Dharmapala's grandfather, Buvanaika VII, had died under peculiar circumstances, shot apparently by the Portuguese while he was under their armed protection. It may have been an accident, as claimed, but many Ceylonese blamed it on the foreigners. Compounding the affront to Ceylonese national sensitivities, the Portuguese viceroy who had been sent to guarantee Dharmapala's succession, instead of building up the new young king's power and prestige, took advantage of the disorder, looted the palace, and robbed the royal family. Demonstrations brought open fighting to the streets of Colombo. The trading factory was razed.[20] The furor was harshly suppressed, but a few years later another shock upset the Ceylonese. About the year 1557 their teenage king, Dharmapala, protector of the doctrine of the Buddha, repudiated his Buddhist faith, as noted above. That might have been forgiven had he not, perhaps under colonial pressure, immediately and insensitively proceeded to turn over to the Franciscans the lands and revenues of Buddhist temples. The action was soon reversed, but the damage was done. Converts began to leave the church by the hundreds.[21]

On the positive side, it was also about the time of Dharmapala's accession in 1551 that a revival spread through the Catholic communities as they welcomed a king who was known to be friendly to the faith. While Portuguese colonial harshness was driving some away, a flurry of missionary activity brought new energy to the mission and a sharp rise in the number of new converts. Franciscans baptized three thousand people in Kotte in the first year of Dharmapala's accession. The next year they founded a training school for seventy Christian orphans in Colombo and other mission stations along the coast. Three years later, despite an outbreak of persecution in the south, the Franciscan superior, John of Villa de Conde, converted a whole tribe — a reported seventy thousand fisherfolk along with their chief on the coast north of Colombo. By the next year the public baptism of King Dharmapala spurred a surge of conversions among the nobility. The Franciscans could count twelve Catholic churches in the Colombo area alone ministering to a growing Christian community in that busy port city.[22]

Meanwhile, in the north, in Hindu Jaffna territory, whole areas were turning Christian in a movement that embraced both low-caste fisherfolk and the highest ranks of the nobility. A decade or so earlier, in 1544, the fisher caste of Careas on the island of Manar, hearing of Francis Xavier's mission among the fisher castes along the southern tip of India, had asked the great Jesuit to come and baptize them also. Unable to leave India, he sent a priest in his stead, who baptized about a thousand of them. Shortly thereafter a usurper to the Jaffna throne turned violently against the Portuguese and massacred approximately six hundred of the new converts among the fisher people. The island became known as the Isle of Martyrs.[23] When news of the massacre reached Colombo, even the Franciscan missioners joined the Portuguese community in urging a military conquest and occupation of the north. The Manar islanders, it was said, were ready to raise an army of ten thousand men to help.[24] The Portuguese, not at all unwilling to enlarge their territory, eventually did move north, but it took three invasions and almost half a century before they finally won control of the area, freeing Manar in 1560 and Jaffna in 1591.[25] Multiple conversions followed. One estimate, probably exaggerated, put the number of new converts in Jaffna in the first two years after the conquest at fifty thousand; in 1602, when parts of Jaffna were turned over to Jesuit missionaries, in the Franciscan half of the kingdom alone Christians were said to number seventy thousand.[26] Other sources report that the converts included "two queens, a princess and nearly the entire nobility of the kingdom of Jaffna."[27]

The Portuguese in Decline (1591–1656)

The final fall of Jaffna to the Portuguese in 1591 left Ceylon with only two major powers: one native, the kingdom of Kandy, and one foreign, Portugal. Dharmapala remained king of Kotte until his death in 1597, but his kingship was only nominal. His dying testament bequeathed his entire kingdom and his claimed sovereignty over all Ceylon to the king of Portugal. One proviso was allowed to the Ceylonese (Sinhalese): the country's laws and customs would remain Ceylonese save for a grant of religious liberty to Christians.[28]

But already Portugal's empire was in decline, as the Dutch expanded their power north and west from Indonesia along the coasts of Asia. Native rebellions flared throughout Ceylon in the 1580s and 1590s, and took on added intensity as the Dutch began to challenge Portuguese military supremacy. Atrocities committed on both sides aggravated the cruelty of the wars. A Portuguese force invaded Kandy and was defeated. The victorious king of Kandy took fifty of his Portuguese captives, mutilated them, and sent them back alive to Colombo "with one eye for each five." The Portuguese retaliated by fighting without mercy, sparing no male older than fourteen.[29]

A few decades earlier, about 1547, Franciscan evangelism had begun to spread beyond Kotte, the southern center of Portuguese rule, into the kingdom of Kandy in the interior and as far as Trincomalie on the island's eastern coast. A ruler of Kandy had welcomed some of the first Franciscans into his kingdom and granted them land for a church. Fearing Portuguese expansion, he made an unconvincing profession of conversion, which he soon retracted. His son was more sincerely baptized in 1550, but a revolt nearly wiped out the small Christian community in that kingdom and sent the royal family into exile under Portuguese protection. The exiled king died a Catholic in 1582, leaving an infant daughter, Dona Catharina, as heiress in exile to the throne of Kandy.[30]

During the next decade Kandy was sometimes allied with the Portuguese but more often with the invading Dutch. When the Dutch triumphed, Rajasinha II turned more anti-Dutch and pro-British,[31] making canny, intermittent use of guerrilla warfare to defend at least a nominal independence under the British into the second decade of the nineteenth century.[32] Kandy was the last Ceylonese kingdom to emerge from foreign rule.

As the Portuguese were driven from the island, and as the Protestant Dutch established control in the 1630s, there were reported to be 120 Roman Catholic missionaries on the island, a very small number indeed compared to the total number of Catholics in the missionary orders in the whole of Portuguese Asia as estimated three decades later (1,730 in 1663).[33] Maps of Ceylon at that period show 166 churches on the island.[34] But so great was the tumult of the constant warfare of the times that it is difficult to estimate the number of church members at the end of Portuguese rule. Franciscans reported fifty-two thousand baptized between 1600 and 1636, and in 1628 counted sixty thousand Catholics in the kingdom of Kotte alone; the Jesuits recorded thirty-seven thousand Christians in 1644.[35] The three areas where the Christian faith was most dominant were Jaffna in the north, Galle in the south, and Negombo just north of Colombo. Negombo, a once-Muslim trading port, became almost totally Christian after the Portuguese in 1626 ordered the Muslims driven out of Ceylon.[36]

Burma: Violence and Resistance (1554–1800)

As close to India on the east as Ceylon was on the south was what came to be known as Burma (now Myanmar). The territory was divided into several small Buddhist kingdoms north of Malacca. The people had been Buddhist since the eleventh century, but the peninsula was filling with proselytizing Muslim traders. The strongest of its kingdoms, Pegu, had temporarily unified most of the country in the mid-1500s only to face the first wave of another wave of intruders more lethal than the traders. Rapacious Portuguese adventurers, sea wolves little better than pirates, fought to replace Muslim traders from Moghal territory (now Bangladesh) who up to then had controlled the commerce of those regions.[37]

In 1548 Francis Xavier, then in India, asked in vain for missionaries to be sent into Burma and suggested that the four students from Pegu at the College of St. Paul in Goa would make excellent candidates for such work.[38] But the first missionary to enter the small Burmese kingdoms was the Franciscan Pierre Bomfer, who planted a short-lived mission in 1554. The Portuguese established a fort below Pegu in Lower Burma in 1600, but held it only thirteen years. During these years its commander, while aiding missionaries, so alienated the king of Pegu by his intrigues and deceptions that Burmese forces stormed the city, impaled the commander on a stake, and took captive a reported five thousand Burmese Christians and sixty Portuguese.[39] It is said that most of the Roman Catholics in that part of Burma today are descendants of those Portuguese captives.[40]

Repeated attempts to establish more permanent missions failed. In 1692, for example, the Paris Foreign Missions Society sent missionaries to Pegu. They were arrested, exposed in the sun to mosquitoes, sewn into sacks, and drowned in the river.[41] The Catholics tried again in 1722. An apostolic vicariate for Pegu, Ava, and Martaban won permission from the king for a resident mission at Ava of the order of Barnabites (Congregation of Clerks Regular of St. Paul). A friendly Armenian merchant built them a church there, but though they learned the language and translated a number of books of the Bible into Burmese, the Buddhist Burmese had proved to be solidly resistant to the gospel. The Catholic missionaries were forced out of the country by wars around 1800, having failed to reach beyond the Buddhist south into the animist tribes of the north[42] that later proved to be so responsive to the coming of the Protestants. Nevertheless, by 1800 there were two Catholic churches in Rangoon and about three thousand Roman Catholics.[43]

Alexander de Rhodes: Beginnings in Vietnam (Tonkin and Annam, 1583–1802)

Beyond Siam to the east a cluster of small kingdoms on the coast of the South China Sea managed for three hundred years to fight one another and at the same time fend off outside invaders and maintain a prickly independence from the ancient aggressor, China, in the north, and the newer imperial powers of Portugal, Spain, and France advancing from the west. Beginning in the 1860s, however, they began to be absorbed into the French colony of Indo-China.[44] Dominant among them in the seventeenth century were the two kingdoms of Tonkin in the north and Annam (or Cochin China, as Europeans referred to it) in the south; together, these form modern Vietnam.[45]

During those three hundred years the two kingdoms proved to be the most responsive territory in all of Southeast Asia for the preaching of the gospel and the rapid growth of the church. In the light of twentieth-century events, it is interesting to note that northern Vietnam (Tonkin) was then more receptive to Christian expansion than the south (Annam, or Cochin China).[46]

The first visits to the area had been made in the early 1500s by Dominicans from Malacca and Franciscans from the Philippines. The first church building was reportedly erected in 1583 in the Annamese capital, Hue (called Sinoa in the early reports).[47] But the pioneers in establishing a permanent work were the Jesuits, who first came as refugees from Japan in 1615, fleeing the great persecutions that were closing the door on the "Christian century" in that island empire.

Outstanding among these pioneers in courage and vision and wise missionary strategy was the incomparable Alexander de Rhodes (1591–1660), who came to Cochin China (Annam) and Tonkin by way of Macao in 1626. He ranks with the greatest of all the many notable seventeenth-century Jesuits in Asia. Born in southern France, he entered the Jesuit order when he was only eighteen and volunteered for Japan, sailing for Asia seven years later in 1619. Unable to enter Japan, he poured all the fervor of his mission into pioneering missionary evangelism along the Vietnam coast of the South China seas. He described it as "two kingdoms next door to China," a land of "gold, pepper, silk and sugar," but without wheat, wine, or oil.[48]

Rhodes paid tribute to an Italian Jesuit, François Buzomi, as "the true apostle to Cochin China," for Buzomi had preceded him by nine years and, as Rhodes admiringly reported, led twelve thousand pagans to the faith during twenty-four years of faithful evangelism in the turbulent country.[49] But it was Rhodes, arriving in 1624, who was the builder of the church. For twenty-one years, despite persecutions and banishments, which five times forced him to leave the field for various lengths of time, he laid firm foundations for two remarkable Christian communities [in Tonkin and Cochin China], which were "as flourishing as our society had seen in these new worlds." The planting of the church in Vietnam was one of the finest achievements of seventeenth-century Catholicism in Asia, a model of courage and Christian endurance for all Asia.

By 1625, only a year after his arrival, Rhodes was able to preach in the native language. He reported that though only one of the ten missionaries then in residence knew the language, they had reached all of the southern kingdom's provinces.[50] In 1640 the number of converts had reached thirty thousand in Cochin China (South Vietnam) alone.[51]

The numbers were even greater in Tonkin (North Vietnam), which Rhodes entered in 1627 as its first effective missionary,[52] baptizing forty-seven hundred in his first three years, including a sister of the king and seventeen of her near relatives. Tonkin, he said, was a land where Jesus Christ had not been known, a land with two kings, "one with only the name... the other with all the power"; and a culture with two laws that, if followed elsewhere, would improve society, even in Christian Europe. The first rule prohibited going to law against one's relatives, and the second prevented the appointment of a governor to the province in which he had been born.[53] It was in part this sensitivity to what was good in the native culture that contributed to Rhodes's success as a missionary, though it did not succeed in sheltering him from persecution. By 1639 there were approximately eighty-two thousand Christians and two hundred churches in Tonkin,[54] and by 1645 a reported three hundred thousand Christians.[55]

But more important than the numbers was the missionary strategy that was producing such results. From the beginning Rhodes noted with dismay that the foreign missionaries were still using interpreters. Seeing how it crippled their outreach, he set out to learn the local tongue and within six months was preaching in it with passion, often as many as four to six times a day.[56] He also produced an Annamite-Portuguese dictionary and a Latin-Annamite catechism for catechumens.[57]

Above and beyond his respect for native culture and his oft-repeated stress on the importance of learning the language of the people, Rhodes credited the rapidity of the spread of the Christian faith throughout the two kingdoms to the realization that until his Tonkinese and Annamite converts could be brought to take upon themselves the work of evangelizing their own people, his own efforts would be of limited value. Later, when he had been forced for the last time to leave Vietnam, he took with him back to Europe a personal commitment to persuade the missionary agencies of the church that their most urgent task in Christian missions abroad would be to develop a strategy for the training and ordination of an indigenous clergy.

Another important observation on Rhodes's missionary strategy is Peter Phan's conclusion in a comparison with Matteo Ricci's *True Meaning* and Rhodes's catechism in China. He writes, "Ricci's [format] is dialogue whereas de Rhodes's is continuous exposition. . . . " De Rhodes's "reliance is on divine revelation instead of only on pure reason." The comparison is limited.[58]

On his first visit to Tonkin, Rhodes had chosen three or four of his most promising converts for catechetical instruction and training as evangelists. The first, François, was a Tonkinese convert from a Buddhist temple. He was joined by three others, André, Ignace, and Antoine. All began their training by taking vows of chastity, obedience, and lifelong service in the church. Rhodes organized them into a close fellowship, a "seminary," as he called it, which functioned much like a missionary lay order; this Congregation of Catechists soon numbered one hundred pupils. The whole enterprise was supported by the Christian community, not by mission funds, because an important element in Rhodes's plan for the formation of a national clergy was the principle of self-support.[59]

He had scarcely embarked upon this ambitious program, however, when he was thrown out of the country by the same king who had been so friendly to him. The palace women and the Tonkinese concubines of the wealthier class had been offended by his Christian disapproval of multiple wives and had turned the court against him. Banished, Rhodes was forced to leave to his little band of lay evangelists the responsibility for the care of the Christian community and the expansion of the church. As for himself, he reluctantly spent the next ten years (1630 to 1640) in Macao as chaplain to the Chinese Christian community there, a task, he said, more difficult than mission to the Annamese, despite the freedom from persecution that Christians enjoyed in Portuguese Macao. The Chinese, he wrote, had too difficult a language and too great a sense of superiority to be willing to listen to foreigners.[60]

In 1640 he was allowed to return to Cochin China, only to find the church recovering with difficulty from a period of severe persecution. Continuing harassment forced him out of the country three times in the next two years, twice to Macao and once to the Philippines. But amid persecutions and banishments he discovered that he had found the secret of how to build a church to endure persistent, violent opposition: lay evangelism by committed native converts.

Returning from banishment once again in 1642, he found that he was the only priest left in the kingdom. So, hiding by day and working by night, he divided ten of the volunteer evangelists he had trained into two bands, one for the north, and one for the south. Expelled again, he rejoiced to find that the work continued in his absence as effectively, in many ways, as in his presence. The northern team, under Ignace and André, baptized 303 converts, and the southern team 293. Although they were laymen, baptism was too indispensable a sacrament to allow its postponement until the return of the priest.[61]

Rhodes longed to return to his catechists, "especially my brave Ignace," to whom he credited the continuing spread of the gospel. He was allowed back in 1644, and baptisms multiplied. In high circles the foreign priest was more effective than the catechists. He baptized an aunt of the king, naming her Marie. But among the common people numerical growth prospered under the lay evangelists. From the north came a report that in one district of Tonkin, as a result of the witness of a lay Christian named Simon, there were a thousand Christians awaiting baptism.[62]

The persecutions that brought the first martyrdoms to Cochin China began that same year. When Ignace was targeted for death by the authorities, his younger associate André sprang forward to offer his own life to save his superior and was publicly executed — stabbed twice front and back and then beheaded. Shortly thereafter thirty-five more Christians were martyred in a "great persecution." Ignace and Rhodes were both imprisoned, freed for a few months, and again imprisoned and sentenced to death. But by an order of the king Rhodes was freed on condition of immediate banishment, never to return. A few months later, three days after Rhodes reached Macao, the news reached him that two more of his beloved catechists, Ignace and Vincent, had been beheaded. The other seven were given a bloody warning: A finger was chopped off the hand of each as a grim reminder to Christians of the power of the state.[63]

The French Enter Vietnam (1664–1802)

These were the beginnings of the church in Vietnam. Its subsequent history, up to the encroachments of French colonization in 1858, was more of the same.[64] Intermittent persecutions could not prevent the spread and effective organization of the church.[65] When the papacy wisely loosened Catholic missions in Asia from the crippling effect of waning Portuguese colonial control, and in 1652 began to consider creating an episcopal rank of missionary bishops unfettered by imperial Portuguese *padroado* politics, one of the first names mentioned for such a crucial responsibility was that of Alexander of Rhodes.[66] Modestly he declined but was asked to recommend others.[67] Out of these events emerged a major realignment of Catholic missions in Asia: a hierarchy of missionary apostolic vicars under the authority of the Vatican's Congregation for the Propagation of the Faith and a new missionary agency, the Paris Society of Foreign Missions (La Société des Missions Etrangères de Paris).

On the political side, a complicating factor was the emergence of France to contest Portugal's monopoly of nationalist power over the Asian missions of the Catholic Church.[68] In Southeast Asia this culminated in what is called the Tonkin Synod of 1664, in which the newly arrived French bishops and priests gathered with nine indigenous priests in Siam to plan a grand missionary strategy for all Asia.[69] But even while they were meeting in the religiously tolerant Siamese capital across the mountains from Tonkin, a general persecution left hundreds of thousands of Tonkinese Christians without either priests or a bishop.

A foreshadowing of things to come, both good and bad, was the first effective entry two years later of the new French missionary society into Vietnam.[70] A French priest, Louis Deydier, managed to land in Tonkin disguised as an ordinary sailor and to inquire discreetly if any of the native catechists trained by Rhodes were left alive. Reporting success in making contact, he wrote back to Siam that the number of Christians since the banishment of the Jesuits had risen to eighty thousand Tonkinese, led by eight surviving catechists. Enthusiastically, Deydier proceeded to organize a secret seminary on a boat in the harbor to train the catechists for ordination, and within fourteen months, against all odds, he and the catechists had baptized a reported ten thousand people.[71]

Impressed by such reports, de la Motte Lambert, the apostolic vicar, resolved to visit Tonkin to ensure proper organization of the church. Upon arrival in 1669, he found the king friendly. He ordained seven of the Tonkinese catechists to the priesthood,[72] at the same time conferring minor orders on ten and the tonsure for twenty others. Two bishops were appointed for the church, Louis Deydier and J. de Bourges. Separate apostolic vicariates for Tonkin and Cochin China were created the same year.[73]

It is possible that the ordinations were premature. Some of the more critical foreign priests pointed out that the new priests did not even know enough Latin to conduct a valid mass.[74] Nevertheless, it was in Tonkin that the church grew most rapidly. By 1682, despite severe persecutions, two hundred thousand Christians were reported, with eleven native-born Tonkinese priests, seven European missionaries, and two French bishops.[75]

Cochin China, farther south, had a Christian community of about sixty thousand at that time, and a few years later, in 1687, the papacy endeavored to speed the development of a native clergy there, as in Tonkin, by nominating for apostolic vicar of Cochin China a priest whom it considered to be a native. But the man was half Portuguese, had no background in Cochin China, and displeased both the local clergy and the French missionaries alike, creating a problem that impeded the growth of the church there for the next thirty years.[76]

In fact, the next hundred years were a time of trial for all of Southeast Asia. Waves of persecution in Cochin China and Tonkin cut the number of Christians in those two areas almost in half. Cochin China (including Cambodia) dropped from eighty thousand in the 1650s to perhaps fifty thousand in the 1750s. The jewel of the Society's crown, Tonkin, fell from about four hundred thousand at its highest, a somewhat dubious estimate in the 1660s when the French apostolic vicars arrived, to two hundred thousand after the persecution of 1773.[77]

In the eighteenth century the Paris Foreign Missionary Society displaced the Jesuits as the primary agent of the church in Vietnam, both north and south. The education and training of native catechists improved, and in 1771 two of them, sent out to explore unreached fields, became the Catholic pioneers to Laos. There they found a few Tonkinese Christian refugees who had fled to the mountains seeking safety, some from the wars and some from their creditors.[78]

Inevitably, in Southeast Asia, as elsewhere, Christian missions were rarely free from the taint of Western imperialism once European political and commercial entrepreneurs discovered that the missionaries could be useful though not always willing allies for colonial ambitions. This was as true for the French as it had been for the missionaries of Portugal and Spain. The French monarchy added missionaries to its official embassies to native kings, and French trading companies freely borrowed money from the French missions. Missionaries, in turn, operating beyond the trading ports were willing to arrange trading concessions and settlements for the companies.[79] A significant example was how the French used the church as a tool in turning their dominant role in trade with the Vietnamese kingdoms into what became French Indo-China.

A key ecclesiastical figure in this entanglement of ecclesiastic with political and military expansion was Pigneau de Behaine, apostolic vicar of Cochin China at the end of the eighteenth century. He belonged to the Paris Missionary Society[80] and had come to the southeast about the time that a revolution of highland mountaineers had violently blocked the installation of the legitimate successor to the throne of Cochin China, a seventeen-year-old boy of the Nguyen family, and had sent him fleeing into Cambodia. The apostolic vicar, moved by the young man's plight, offered him refuge. Then, probably not unmindful of possible opportunities for future Christian mission in a Vietnam under a sovereign indebted to Catholic missions, the bishop went further. He held out the possibility of French military and political aid for the recovery of his throne to the young prince, who was, after all, the legitimate heir. In due course, having convinced Prince Nguyen of the advantages of foreign aid, he drafted a formal treaty of alliance between France and Cochin China and negotiated its acceptance by King Louis XVI. The date was 1787. In less than five years mighty France would send King Louis to the guillotine, while the throneless Cochin prince, with French aid, would retrieve his throne, unite Vietnam, and found a dynasty that, outlasting French colonialism, endured with fluctuating power until 1945. The prince, Nguyen Anh, was declared Emperor Gia Long in 1802.[81]

Siam (Thailand):
A Tenuous Base for Mission (1553–1769)

Less successful were the Catholic missions in Siam.[82] Between its great Buddhist rival Burma on the east and Vietnam to the west, Siam was initially no more open to the Christian evangelism than Burma. But its more pragmatic welcome of Western traders seemed at times to promise a measure of enlightened tolerance that might offer possibilities of a sheltered center for Catholic mission expansion in Southeast Asia.

The first Europeans reached its capital, Ayutthia, in 1533. There are vague reports of missions of the Catholic Church in Siam beginning perhaps in the 1550s if, as is implied, missionaries accompanied the earliest Portuguese embassies to the country.[83] But the earliest known missionaries to Siam were two Dominicans, Jeronimo da Cruz and Sebastião da Canto, who reached Ayutthia, the capital of old Siam, in 1567 after a two-months journey from Malacca. They were warmly received and learned Siamese very quickly, but Muslim agitators stirred up a protest and killed da Cruz, the first martyr in Thailand. Two replacements were sent from Malacca and witnessed bravely to their faith, but they were unable to win a single convert. Two years later, when Burma captured the Siamese capital, the missionaries were beheaded in their church by the invading Burmese.[84]

Catholic missions were again established in the country in the reign of King Songtham (1610–1628), who in opening up the country to foreign trade also granted permission for a missionary presence.[85] The first longer-lasting but often interrupted mission in Siam was that of the Jesuits. Their pioneer, Balthasar Sequiera, reached the capital in 1606 and maintained a tenuous presence for nearly three years.[86] But it was not until twenty years later, in 1626, that the Jesuits were able to establish reasonably permanent residence, if six years can be called permanent. A Spaniard, Pedro Morejon, nephew of the archbishop of Toledo, was head of the mission and brought with him a Japanese Jesuit, Romano Nixi, to minister to a considerable settlement of Christian Japanese refugees. These refugees had fled from the persecutions in their homeland and had settled in Ayutthia, where they had been allowed to build what is described as a beautiful church there. But Spanish pirate raids along the Siamese coast beginning in 1628 turned Siam against foreigners. In the next four years a combination of antiforeign distrust of Westerners and the denunciations of a resentful apostate Christian convert forced Nixi out of the country. The last of the Jesuits, Julion Marjico, the Italian head of the mission, was mistaken for a Spaniard, imprisoned, and poisoned in 1630. The mission was vacant for the next twenty-five years.[87]

A second Jesuit mission gave new life to the work in Siam (1655–1709). Appointed superior of the Jesuit mission, Thomas Valguarnera built up a church for the Portuguese community and a small school, grandly named the College of San Salvador.[88]

But the college, which was apparently principally for the education of the Portuguese community, was soon to be overshadowed by a more radical venture in Christian mission pioneered by the new French Catholic Society, the Paris Foreign Missionary Society founded in 1659. Its first three missionary bishops were de la Motte, Pallu, and Cotolendi, all three of whom were assigned to Asia as apostolic vicars in order to free them from dependence on the jealous Portuguese, who by right of *padroado* had hitherto dominated Catholic missions in Asia.[89] It was a critical time for Asian missions. Portuguese power was fading. The once-great flowering of the church in Japan had been crushed by the ferocity of the persecutions there. Jesuit missions in neighboring Tonkin and Cochin China were being expelled. Even the successful Catholic missions in China were feeling the first negative results of the rites controversies, which would set mission against mission and eventually drive them all out of the empire.

If colonial Portugal was failing, might France win the day for the church? To the new French bishops Siam seemed to be an ideal location to center just such an operation. Lambert de la Motte[90] reached Ayutthia in 1662 and was followed two years later by Bishop François Pallu.[91] They found a community of about two thousand Christians and eleven missionary priests, but they were not impressed. The missionaries — Jesuit, Franciscan, and Dominican — were uncoordinated, they thought, and tainted by their Portuguese connection. The Christians were mostly Portuguese and Eurasians who, like most expatriates in the trading ports of seventeenth-century Asia, were tepid and casual in their Christian faith.[92] Why, then, choose Siam as a base for outreach to Asia?

What made Ayutthia so attractive to the bishops was the spirit of religious toleration they found at the Siamese court under King Narai (1656–1688), so unlike the persecutions breaking out elsewhere in Asia. In that same year, 1664, the French bishops convened a synod at Ayutthia and petitioned the Vatican to make Siam an apostolic vicariate, independent of the Portuguese diocese of Malacca. The request was granted the next year but was not approved by the Vatican's missionary arm, the Congregation for the Propagation of the Faith, until 1669.[93]

In fact, it may well have been the lure of foreign trade and the presence of the energetic Jesuit superior, Father Thomas Valguarnera, who was also an engineer and architect, that, more than religious toleration, won the Buddhist king's favor for the Christian missions. So the Italian Valguarnera built forts and palaces for the king and a church for the Portuguese, while the French bishops built a seminary in 1665 to train Asian priests for Asia and the first hospital in 1669.

In the 1680s a colorful Greek adventurer, Constance Phaulkon, won the trust of King Narai of Siam (reigned 1657–1688) and rose to the high position of the king's personal advisor, in effect, minister of foreign affairs. Eager to advance French trade interests, he teamed with a Jesuit missionary, Gui Tachard, who was equally eager to evangelize the Thai people, and persuaded the king to propose a treaty to Louis XIV of France offering trade privileges and a military presence in Siam to the French. The missionaries rejoiced. It seemed as though the strictly Buddhist country was about to open to the Christian faith. But the Thai king fell ill; his suspicious government turned against Phaulkon; and the revolution of 1688 produced as Narai's successor the anti-Western King Phetraja (Bedra). Despite the internal turmoil, for the next 150 years Siam remained isolated but free.[94] As late as 1769, when a Burmese invasion forced the school to move into French territory, Siam remained the center for the development of an indigenous priesthood for Southeast Asian Catholic missions.[95]

Chronology of Buddhist South Asia (1500–1800)

1505	Portuguese claim Ceylon (Sri Lanka).
1511	Portuguese capture Malacca.
1540–1555	Reunification of Burma under Toungoo kings of Pegu (Ava, Prome, and so on, but not Arakan); invasion of Siam (1556–1569).
1543	Beginnings of Catholic mission in Ceylon.
1551	First Christian king of Kotte (Ceylon), Dharmapala, baptized 1597 or 1598.
1554	Temporary Franciscan mission in Burma.
1567	Dominican mission to Siam (Thailand).
1600	Pegu destroyed; Burma breaks into separate states again.
1615	Jesuits expelled from Japan, establish mission in Cochin China.
1627–1645	Alexander of Rhodes in Annam (Cochin China) and Tonkin.
1635	Burmese capital moved to Ava (near present Mandalay).

1641	Dutch capture Malacca from Portuguese; dominate East Indies.
1655–1709	Jesuit mission in Siam.
1656	Portuguese lose Ceylon to the Dutch.
1662	Paris Foreign Missionary Society enters Siam.
1664	Siam trade monopolized by Dutch; French military (1685); civil war (1688–1767).
	Synod held at Ayutthia, Siam, under de la Motte and French bishops.
1665	Seminary for Southeast Asia founded in Siam.
1669	Apostolic vicariate of Siam established under the Vatican's Congregation of Propaganda, not under Portuguese *padroado.*
1670	Synod of Tonkin establishes Church of Tonkin.
1673 (?)	Vietnam divides into Tonkin in the north and Annam (Cochin China) in the south; Annam drives out Champa in 1720 and controls much of Cambodia.
1767	Burma captures and rules Siam until 1782.
1780	Paris Foreign Missionary Society given charge of Annam, Cambodia, Siam, and western Tonkin.
1782	Bangkok dynasty of Thailand founded by Rama I (to present day).
1786	Annam (Cochin China)/Tonkin war ends in victory of Annam and the union of three regions (Tonkin in the north, Annam in center, and Cochin China in the south) under the Nguyen family (to 1945).

NOTES

1. What is now Vietnam has at various times been divided into separate small kingdoms, such as Tonkin, Annam, and Cochin China.

2. Christianity, for example, has its Catholic, Protestant, and Orthodox major divisions; Islam is divided into two major groups, Sunni and Shi'ite.

3. Theravada Buddhism survives as the only one of some eighteen earlier schools or sects into which the Buddhism of the pre-Christian era had divided; it takes somewhat different forms in different locations.

4. For a good summary of the immense literature on Buddhism, see the articles under "Buddhism" and "Theravada" in *ERel*, 2:335–497 and 14:469–479.

5. The basic documentary sources on the Portuguese period in Ceylon include P. E. Pieris and M. A. H. Fitzler, *Ceylon and Portugal*, part 1, *Kings and Christians 1539–1552, from the Original Documents at Lisbon* (Leipzig: Verlag der Asia Major, 1927); Georg Schurhammer and E. A. Voretzsch, *Ceylon zur des Konigs Bhuvaneka Bahu und Franz Xavers 1539–1552*, 2 vols. (Leipzig: Verlag der

Asia Major, 1928); and Ceylon sections of Antonio Da Silva Rego's multi-volume *Documentacāo para a historia das missões do Padroado portugues do Oriente* (Lisbon: Fundação Oriente, 1991); Fernão de Queyroz, *The Temporal and Spiritual Conquest of Ceylon* (3 vols., trans. S. G. Perera from the 1688 original [Colombo: A. C. Richards, Acting Government Printer, 1930]), is valuable for contemporary seventeenth-century narrative detail but is marred by uncritical embellishments and inaccuracies. Two important surveys are S. Gnana Prakasar, *A History of the Catholic Church in Ceylon*, vol. 1. *Period of Beginnings, 1505–1602* (Colombo: Catholic Union of Ceylon, 1924); and Tikiri Abeyasinghe, *Portuguese Rule in Ceylon, 1594–1612* (Colombo: University of Ceylon, 1966).

6. On Cosmas Indicopleustes, see Queyroz, *The Temporal and Spiritual Conquest of Ceylon*, 1:268–269.

7. The king at the time of the first landing was Parakrama Bahu VIII (ca. 1484–1513 or 1518), who was a predecessor of Buvanaika Bahu VII.

8. O. M. da Silva Cosme, *Fidalgos in the Kingdom of Kotte, Sri Lanka, 1505–1656: The Portuguese in Sri Lanka* (Colombo: Harwoods Publishers, 1990), 16; cf. L. E. Blaze, *A History of Ceylon* (Colombo: Christian Literature Society, 1900), 101.

9. The first trading concession was made in 1505, but it was extended and amplified in 1517–1518, when the fort at Colombo was built. A revolution in 1521 divided the kingdom under Parakrama VIII's three sons, of whom Buvanaika Bahu VII was the eldest (see Queyroz, *The Temporal and Spiritual Conquest of Ceylon*, 1:175–183). For more accurate details of the tangled history of this period, see Pieris and Fitzler, *Ceylon and Portugal*, 1–2; and H. W. Codrington, *A Short History of Ceylon*, rev. ed. (London: Macmillan, 1939), xviii, 90–99, and map on 131.

10. On these early expeditions, see also da Silva Cosme, *Fidalgos in the Kingdom of Kotte*, 1–27; cf. Simon G. Pereira, *Catholic Negombo: A Brief Sketch of the Catholic Church in Negombo under the Portuguese and the Dutch* (Colombo: Catholic Union of Ceylon, 1924), 4–5.

11. K. M. De Silva, *A History of Sri Lanka* (Delhi: Oxford University Press, 1981), 103–104. Transliteration of the name varies: Buvanaika, Bhuvanaika, Bhuwanaika, Boneca, and Bhuvaneka, for example.

12. Pieris and Fitzler, *Ceylon and Portugal*, 1:3, 49 (for the text of King John's Letter Patent), and 258–259. The letter transliterates Buvanaika as Buhanegua and refers to Dharmapala as Taomapala Pandarym. Dharmapala's baptismal name was John, and to the Portuguese his full name as king was Don João Perira Bandara. See also Schurhammer, *Francis Xavier*, 2:320, 371–372.

13. Schurhammer and Voretzsch, *Ceylon sur Zeit des Konigs Bhuvaneka Bahu und Franz Xavers*, 1:127, 194–196; 2:425–426, 495, 588; Schurhammer, *Francis Xavier*, 2:411–424.

14. See Chandra Richard de Silva, *Sri Lanka: A History* (New Delhi: Vikas Publishing House, 1987; reprint, 1994), 107–125.

15. De Silva, *Sri Lanka*, 102–103.

16. J. Emerson Tennent, *Christianity in Ceylon* (London: John Murray, 1850; reprint, New Delhi: Asian Educational Services, 1998), 10 n. 1.

17. Letters, Andre de Sousa, May 27, 1546, and Frey Antonio, November 25, 1546, in Pieris and Fitzler, *Ceylon and Portugal*, 1:130ff., 171–172. The king, or prince, is named here as Vikrama Bahu. Cf. Queyroz, often inaccurate, who mentions Franciscan missionaries in Kandy as early as 1544 and the building of a church in 1545 (he mistakenly writes 1515), and "in time" the conversion of a

king, Javira Astana (Jayavira Maha Asthana) (*The Temporal and Spiritual Conquest of Ceylon*, 1:258, 2:701–702).

18. Letter, king of Kotte, in Pieris and Fitzler, *Ceylon and Portugal*, 86–90. Civil war, which raged from about 1518 among the sons of Vijaya Bahu VII, Buvanaika's father, over the succession in Kotte, broke out at intervals throughout the reign of Buvanaika Bahu VII (1521–1551), who was supported by the Portuguese. See Queyroz, *The Temporal and Spiritual Conquest of Ceylon*, 1:195–299; Pieris and Fitzler, *Ceylon and Portugal*, 1:1–13. Cf. Latourette, *A History of the Expansion of Christianity*, 3:285–292; Marion A. Habig, *In Journeyings Often: Franciscan Pioneers in the Orient* (New York: Franciscan Institute, 1953), 204–206; Codrington, *A Short History of Ceylon*, xviii, 95ff.

19. Queyroz, *The Temporal and Spiritual Conquest of Ceylon*, 1:327.

20. Pieris and Fitzler, *Ceylon and Portugal*, 1:12–13, 270–271, 256–258, 283; see also Queyroz, 1:293–305.

21. Queyroz, *The Temporal and Spiritual Conquest of Ceylon*, 1:293–297, 299–300, 306–307, 330–332; de Silva, *Sri Lanka*, 111.

22. Queyroz, *The Temporal and Spiritual Conquest of Ceylon*, 1:327, 2:714; cf. Tennent, *Christianity in Ceylon*, 23 n. 1, 24–25; Habig, *In Journeyings Often*, 206.

23. A. J. B. Antoninus, cited in Robrecht Boudens, *The Catholic Church in Ceylon under Dutch Rule* (Rome: Officium Libri Catholici, 1957), 32; Perera, *Catholic Negombo*, 7–8.

24. See Schurhammer, *Francis Xavier*, 2:445–446, 460; 3:316–317, 325, 334.

25. Pieris and Fitzler, *Ceylon and Portugal*, 1:103–104, 126ff.; Codrington, *A Short History of Ceylon*, 103–104.

26. Queyroz, *The Temporal and Spiritual Conquest of Ceylon*, 2:656–666, 686. The zeal of the priests sometimes outstripped their integrity. One of the missionaries, eager to build a church in the Muslim section of Jaffna, set fire to the mosque and was able to persuade the defeated Hindu rajah to give him the ground for a new church. This occurred in 1614 (Queyroz, *The Temporal and Spiritual Conquest of Ceylon*, 2:666).

27. Paulo da Trinidade and Antonio da Silva Rego, cited in Boudens, *The Catholic Church in Ceylon under Dutch Rule*, 43 n. 32.

28. Codrington describes the extent of Dharmapala's royal claims, his vicissitudes, and the provisions of the transfer to Portuguese rule, but questions the claim that Portugal accepted the retention of Ceylonese customs (*A Short History of Ceylon*, 98, 101–107).

29. The Kandyan king was Vimala Dharma Surya I, also known as Konappu Bandara (1591–1604) (see Codrington, *A Short History of Ceylon*, 106, 110). On the tangled history of the kings and kingdoms, see da Silva Cosme, *Fidalgos in the Kingdom of Kotte, Sri Lanka, 1505–1656*, 30–41, 50–73, 93–97, 134–138, 167–171, 219ff., 233.

30. The ruler who welcomed the Franciscans to the interior was Jayavira Bandara, king of Kandy (1521–1551). His son, Karalliyade Bandara (1552–1581), who rebelled against him and seized Kandy in 1552, was converted about 1560 but was defeated by Rajasinha of Sitavaka in 1581 while fleeing to Portugal (see W. L. A. Don Peter, ed., *The Franciscans and Sri Lanka* (Colombo: Evangel Press, 1983), 143ff.; de Silva, *Sri Lanka*, 107–115; Pieris and Fitzler, *Ceylon and Portugal*, 1:4–6, 10, 54–56, 66–67, 175–186, 198–202, 236–237, 241; Codrington, *A Short History of Ceylon*, 93–101.

31. Codrington, *A Short History of Ceylon*, 108, 112, 116, 121. From 1647 to 1649 Kandy temporarily allied itself with the Portuguese against the Dutch.

32. Codrington, *A Short History of Ceylon*, 133ff., 174.

33. Boudens, *The Catholic Church in Ceylon under Dutch Rule*, 58 nn. 84, 85. The numbers in 1663 were Franciscans 560, Dominicans 250, Jesuits 660, Augustinians 220, Discalced Carmelites 40. These figures refer only to the members of the missionary orders, and only in Portuguese areas, not Spanish, such as the Philippines.

34. Boudens, *The Catholic Church in Ceylon under Dutch Rule*, maps follow 267.

35. Boudens, *The Catholic Church in Ceylon under Dutch Rule*, 34–39, 43, 49ff.

36. P. E. Pieris, *Ceylon, the Portuguese Era: Being a History of the Island for the Period 1505–1658*, 2 vols. (Colombo: Colombo Apothecaries Co., 1913), 2:358–359; Queyroz, *The Temporal and Spiritual Conquest of Ceylon*, 2:742–745.

37. Arthur P. Phayre, *History of Burma* (1883; reprint, London: Susil Gupta, 1967), 22, 124–125, 172ff. In its original form Buddhism had entered Burma as early as the third century B.C.

38. Schurhammer, *Francis Xavier*, 3:469; *CE*, s.v. "Burma."

39. Fernão Guerreiro, *Jahangir and the Jesuits with an Account of the Travels of Benedict Goes and the Mission to Pegu*, trans. C. H. Payne (London: George Routledge, 1930), 194–276, esp. 251.

40. Charles Henry Robinson, *History of Christian Missions* (New York: Charles Scribner's Sons, 1915), 151.

41. Robinson, *History of Christian Missions*. On the earlier mission of the Jesuits and Dominicans, see Schmidlin, *Catholic Mission Theory*, 309–310.

42. Latourette, *A History of the Expansion of Christianity*, 3:294.

43. Joseph Schmidlin, *Catholic Mission History* (Techny, Ill.: Mission Press, 1933), 309–310.

44. Cochin China was occupied by the French in the 1860s. Cambodia became a French protectorate in 1863, and Tonkin in 1883. In 1887 the three "countries" of Vietnam (Cochin China, Tonkin, and Annam), along with Cambodia, were united as French Indo-China. Laos was taken from Siam and added to Indo-China in 1893 (see Jan M. Pluvier, *A Handbook and Chart of Southeast Asian History* [Kuala Lumpur: Oxford University Press, 1967], 5–13). On the missions see Adrien Launay's volumes as the standard, *Histoire de la mission de Cochinchine, 1658–1923 documents historiques* 3 vols. (Paris: Missions étrangères de Paris, 2000) and *Histoire de la mission du Tonkin* (Paris: Missions étrangères de Paris, 2000).

45. Both Tonkin and Cochin China were ethnically Annamite and culturally Sinicized, as distinct from the earlier more Indianized cultures of Champa and Cambodia in the south. On the complicated variations in the names and territories of the Indo-Chinese kingdoms, see Patrick J. N. Tuck, *French Catholic Missionaries and the Politics of Imperialism in Vietnam, 1857–1914* (Liverpool: Liverpool University Press, 1987), 7–9.

46. Bangert, *A History of the Society of Jesus*, 249f. For a recent, comprehensive view of Alexander de Rhodes, see Phan, *Mission and Catechesis*.

47. Schmidlin, *Catholic Mission History*, 311–312.

48. Alexandre de Rhodes, *Voyages et missions du Père Alexandre de Rhodes de la Compagnie de Jesus en la Chine et autres royaumes de l'Orient* (1653, edited by S. Cramoisy; reprint, Paris: Julien, Lanier, 1854), 76, 78–79. In English, *Rhodes of Vietnam*, translated by S. Hertz (Westminster, Md.: Newman Press, 1966). Tonkin

(Hanoi) and Cochin China (Annam) became independent of China in the tenth century. In the fifteenth century Annam defeated Champa, making it first a vassal state, and by the seventeenth century completely absorbing it.

49. Rhodes, *Voyages et missions*, 82–85, 141–142.

50. Rhodes, *Voyages et missions*, 90–91.

51. Statistics do vary. Delacroix reports three hundred thousand Christians in the two kingdoms in 1645, with the number increasing by fifteen thousand annually (*Histoire universelle des missions catholiques*, 2:138).

52. Rhodes could well be called the apostle to Tonkin, for his predecessor there, Baldinotti, on a brief visit in 1626, could not speak a word of the language and his sole achievement was to baptize four infants on the point of death (Rhodes, *Voyages et missions*, 95–96).

53. Rhodes, *Voyages et missions*, 98ff., 108–113. The king in "name" was called *Bua*; the king with power, *Chua*. The *Chua* who welcomed Rhodes was Trinh-Trang, a man subject to alarming changes of mood — from curiosity to warm toleration to arbitrary banishment.

54. The numbers for Tonkin vary. J. Schmidlin gives the figure eighty-two thousand for 1639 (*Catholic Mission History*, 311–312); Bengert also quotes a figure of three hundred thousand for the whole Vietnam area in 1650 (270).

55. See G. Cussac's questions about these figures (in Delacroix, *Histoire universelle des missions catholiques*, 2:215).

56. Rhodes, *Voyages et missions*, 87–88, 114.

57. Rhodes, *Voyages et missions*, 86–89.

58. Peter C. Phan, *Mission and Catechesis: Alexandre de Rhodes and Inculturation in Seventeenth-Century Vietnam* (Maryknoll, N.Y.: Orbis Books, 1998), 121.

59. Rhodes, *Voyages et missions*, 123–125.

60. Rhodes, *Voyages et missions*, 126–127, 138.

61. Rhodes, *Voyages et missions*, 192–198.

62. Rhodes, *Voyages et missions*, 218.

63. Rhodes, *Voyages et missions*, 199–218, 235–255, 236–285, 300–335.

64. For more detail on Alexander of Rhodes's missionary methods, see Bernard-Maitre in Delacroix, *Histoire universelle des missions catholiques*, 2:63–69, and Phan, *Mission and Catechesis*.

65. In Tonkin there were persecutions in 1696, 1713, 1721, 1736, and 1773–1778; fully a quarter of the missionaries in Cochin China were put to death, and persecutions broke out again in from 1720 to 1726 and in 1773 (Delacroix, *Histoire universelle des missions catholiques*, 2:221).

66. Delacroix, *Histoire universelle des missions catholiques*, 2:139ff.

67. Adrien C. Launay, *Histoire générale de la Société des Missions-Etrangères*, 3 vols. (Paris: Tequi, 1894), 1:9; cf. Delacroix, *Histoire universelle des missions catholiques*, 2:140ff.

68. See Launay, *Histoire générale de la Société des Missions-Etrangères*, 1:114; Delacroix, *Histoire universelle des missions catholiques*, 2:216–217; Jean Guennou, *Missions Etrangères de Paris* (Paris: Sarment, Librairie Fayard, 1986), 17–26; and Surachai Chumsriphan, "The Great Role of Jean-Louis Vey, Apostolic Vicar of Siam (1875–1909) in the Church History of Thailand during the Reformation of King Rama V, the Great (1868–1910)" (PhD diss., Gregorian University, Rome, 1990), 64–69, 82–91.

69. See Guennou, *Missions Etrangères de Paris*, 119–129; Delacroix's mention of the "indigenous priests" as Tonkinese may refer to trained catechists (*Histoire universelle des missions catholiques*, 2:217).

70. French Jesuits, of course, like Alexander of Rhodes, had been working there for decades, but they where under the authority of the Portuguese *padroado*. One French father of the Paris Society, M. Chevreul, made a short visit to a port in Cochin China immediately after the Synod of 1664, were he found two Jesuits ministering to a community of three hundred Christians, mostly Japanese refugees from the great persecutions in that country (Guennou, *Missions Etrangères de Paris*, 136–137).

71. Launay, *Histoire générale de la Société des Missions-Etrangères*, 1:127ff.; Guennou, *Missions Etrangères de Paris*, 144ff. Numbers vary in the two texts. Launay gives thirty-five thousand for the total figure, but is uncertain; Guennou adds a qualifying footnote.

72. Their names were Martin Mat (aged sixty-six), Antoine Van Hoc (fifty-six), Philippe Nhum (fifty), Simeon Kien (sixty), Jacques Van Chu (forty-six), Léon Thu (forty-five), and Vite Van Tri (thirty) (Launay, *Histoire générale de la Société des Missions-Etrangères*, 1:140–141).

73. Schmidlin, *Catholic Mission History*, 310–312, 476 n. 5. The jurisdictions of the vicariates were curious. To Cochin China was given the administration of China's southern provinces; to Tonkin was given the central provinces; and administration of northern China was centered in Nanjing. This was partly due to rising friction between the papacy and the China missions over the rites issue in China.

74. The apostolic vicars had given them as candidates for priesthood a special dispensation excusing them from facility in Latin (Guennou, *Missions Etrangères de Paris*, 145–146; Delacroix, *Histoire universelle des missions catholiques*, 2:219).

75. Launay, *Histoire générale de la Société des Missions-Etrangères*, 1:286–287.

76. Guennou, *Missions Etrangères de Paris*, 254; Delacroix, *Histoire universelle des missions catholiques*, 2:219. Delacroix describes the man, Perez, as Siamese.

77. In Cochin China persecutions occurred in 1698, 1712, 1723, 1750; Tonkin was hit by persecutions in 1712, 1721, 1723, 1737, 1745, and 1773. Estimates of the number of Christians differ widely. On mid-seventeenth-century figures, Delacroix gives 80,000 for Cochin China and Cambodia (*Histoire universelle des missions catholiques* 2:386); Guennou quotes 400,000 for Tonkin alone in 1663, but qualifies the estimate (*Missions Etrangères de Paris*, 145 n. 110). On the later-eighteenth-century figures, Launay gives 35,000 Christians for Cochin China and Cambodia in 1755; 130,000 for Tonkin in 1786 (*Histoire générale de la Société des Missions-Etrangères*, 2:147). Delacroix gives 50,000 for Cochin China and Cambodia in 1765; 200,000 for Tonkin after the persecution of 1773 (*Histoire universelle des missions catholiques*, 2:386–387).

78. Launay, *Histoire générale de la Société des Missions-Etrangères*, 2:71–72.

79. Tuck, *French Catholic Missionaries and the Politics of Imperialism in Vietnam, 1857–1914*, 20.

80. Delacroix, *Histoire universelle des missions catholiques*, 2:222–226.

81. Delacroix, *Histoire universelle des missions catholiques*, 2:222–223; Pluvier, *A Handbook and Chart of Southeast Asian History*, 10. Though French government ministers had blocked execution of the treaty, its terms were carried out by French volunteer forces despite the overturn of the French monarchy.

82. Francis Xavier was apparently the first European to use "Siam" for what is now Thailand (in 1552). It has variously been called Sukhothai (thirteenth century), Ayutthaya or Ayuthiya (fourteenth to eighteenth centuries), and then Muang Thai, but it became Siam in European usage (1856–1939) (see Chumsriphan, "Jean-Louis Vey," 1–3, 73).

83. On earlier possible Catholic missions, see Chumsriphan, "Jean-Louis Vey," 36–37, 71–73. There are vague speculations that missionaries were attached to Portuguese diplomatic missions to Siam beginning in the early 1500s. The reported visit of a Christian trader and lay evangelist, de Pavia, to Siam in 1544 and his alleged conversion of a Thai king does not seem to be true; it is apparently based on a confusion of a Siam or Siao near Macassar with Siam (Thailand) (see Schurhammer, *Francis Xavier*, 2:522 n. 294).

84. Chumsriphan, "Jean-Louis Vey," 73–75. On earlier Christian contacts through Portuguese embassies, see 36–37.

85. Schmidlin, *Catholic Mission History*, 310.

86. Chumsriphan, "Jean-Louis Vey," 76–77.

87. Chumsriphan, "Jean-Louis Vey," 77ff.

88. Chumsriphan, "Jean-Louis Vey," 77–81. A biography of Thomas Valguarnera in Italian is cited by Chumsriphan: G. Gnolfo, *Un missionario assorino: Tomasso dei Conti Valguarnera, S.J.* (Catania: Sicilgraf, 1974). It describes his missionary method of inculturating the Christian message after the fashion of Ricci in China.

89. On the bitter feud between the apostolic vicars of the Vatican's Congregation for the Propagation of the Faith and the Portuguese crown's *padroado*, there is a vast amount of literature. See, for example, Adrien C. Launay, *Histoire de la mission de Siam 1662–1811* (Paris: Tequi, 1920); Chumsriphan, "Jean-Louis Vey," 82–91.

90. On Lambert de la Motte, see Guennou, *Missions Etrangères de Paris*, 58–59, 203–204, and on his missiology, 184–194.

91. On Pallu, see Guennou, *Missions Etrangères de Paris*, 47–50, 204–205, and on Pallu's missiology, 195–197.

92. Guennou, *Missions Etrangères de Paris*, 122–123, 135–136. See also Chumsriphan, "Jean-Louis Vey," 92, citing Launay.

93. Chumsriphan, "Jean-Louis Vey," 84–85, 93, citing Launay.

94. E. W. Hutchinson, *Adventurers in Siam in the Seventeenth Century* (London: Royal Asiatic Society, 1940); Chumsriphan, "Jean-Louis Vey," 45, 47.

95. Guennou, *Missions Etrangères de Paris*, 149–159; Chumsriphan, "Jean-Louis Vey," 94–96.

Chapter 3

The Muslim Kingdoms
of Southeast Asia (1500–1800)

Portuguese in Malaysia
and the Spice Islands (Indonesia)

The comparative study of the place of opposition in the shaping of Islam
through the Hegira to Medina, and of Christianity in the climax of the
Cross in Jerusalem, is deeply significant. For it is those two events, aris-
ing from situations partially comparable, that moulded so diversely and
decisively the resultant faiths of Islam and Christianity.
— *The Muslim World*, April 1954

RELIGION in South Asia has usually followed either navies or traders
along the great arc of the Malay peninsula and across into the Pacific
along the Indonesian archipelago. With the ships and the guns or the
goods came religions introducing new worldviews to basically tribal animist cultures. First Buddhism from India came to Burma as early as the
third century A.D., and mixed with Hinduism, went on to Sumatra and
Java. Southern Sumatra was the seat of a Mahayana Buddhist empire
from the seventh century to the twelfth century, but in Java first Hinduism and then Islam replaced Buddhism. A Hindu kingdom ruled East
Java and much of southern Sumatra from about 1300 to 1500.

Islam, the most effective and enduring missionary faith in Asia, first
entered South Asia from the north about 1200, finding beachheads along
the coast of Sumatra late in the thirteenth century. Early in the fifteenth
century an exiled Sumatran prince carried it farther, crossing the narrow straits of Malacca to establish a prosperous dynasty on the Malay
peninsula. Trade contacts with Islam increased, and the third king of
the dynasty converted to Islam in 1436, with an eye as much on Muslim
trade as on its religion. Malacca in 1511 was claimed as a fiefdom by
its larger and stronger Buddhist neighbor, Siam, but in practical politics
acknowledged only the overlordship of the Ming emperors and in religion was Sunni Islam. It became the base for uneven but increasingly
effective Muslim expansion along the coastal trading centers of the great
Indonesian archipelago and as far as the southern Philippines.[1]

Then came the West and the Christians. They came in four waves, Portuguese, Spanish, Dutch, and British. Portugal took Malacca from its Muslim kings in 1511, and Portuguese priests made that city a base second only to Goa for Asian missions north to Japan and China and south through the islands. Magellan's voyage around the world in 1521, the first to circumnavigate the globe, gave the Philippines to the Spanish. The Dutch brought the first Protestants beginning in 1596 and wrested Malacca from the Portuguese in 1641. They colonized and controlled the East Indies (Indonesia) for the next three centuries, although as Milton W. Meyer has observed, "Of all the European powers in Southeast Asia, [the Dutch] consolidated their holdings the fastest, ruled the longest, and departed the earliest."[2] The British did not greatly alter the balance of colonial power in the area until after 1800.

Malacca, Gateway to East Asia (1511–1663)

The fortress of Malacca, guarding the narrow strait between Malaysia and Sumatra, was the Gibraltar of Southeast Asia. It held the key to the sea lanes from the West to the South Pacific and the Far East. When it fell to the Portuguese in 1511, the churches of Lisbon celebrated the event as a triumph of Christianity over Islam. Because of its strategic location guarding the primary sea lane from the Indian Ocean to the China Seas, Malacca soon supplanted Goa as the springboard for missionary outreach into Asia beyond India.

But it was a poor model of a Catholic city. Portuguese imperialism had developed its own special brand of expansion. As Fitzgerald describes it, "They traded when they were still too weak to conquer, and sought to conquer when trade had given them a sufficient opportunity."[3] When Francis Xavier spent three months in Malacca in 1545, the city was known as the Sodom and Gomorrah of the East, as much because of its few hundred Portuguese colonists as because of its twenty thousand "pagan" and Muslim inhabitants.[4] But from that depraved city the missionaries — Franciscans, Dominicans, Jesuits, and Augustinians — fanned out to the islands of the East Indies. They were able to report that in Malacca and its closer islands eighteen monasteries had been established by 1549 and that sixty thousand Christians could be counted.[5] That was probably an exaggeration, but is an indication of the kind of energetic missionary zeal that began to sprinkle the Southeast with communities of Catholic Christians.

The Spice Islands (Indonesian Archipelago, 1511–1601)

Only after the Portuguese captured the fortress of Malacca from its Muslim rulers in 1511 did the Christian faith make any sustained impact in the Indonesian archipelago. Franciscan missionaries had visited Sumatra early in the fourteenth century, and the Portuguese established trading posts on Java soon thereafter that afforded bases for missionary activity. Catholic mission expansion on the two large islands was hindered, however, by three factors: (1) the spread of small Muslim kingdoms along the coasts of Sumatra and Java from the thirteenth to the early sixteenth centuries, (2) the increasing pressure of Dutch military and trading power centered after 1619 in Batavia (now Jakarta) on the northeastern tip of Java, and (3) the preference of the Portuguese for the more lucrative trade with the spice kingdoms in the islands to the north and east between Borneo and New Guinea rather than with the wet-rice kingdoms of Sumatra and Java.[6]

By 1534 Franciscans, Jesuits, Dominicans, and others had followed the Portuguese spice ships out of Malacca and established churches and missions in the Celebes (Macassar) and the Moluccas (which at that time centered in Ternate). From Malacca to Ternate was a difficult voyage of a month and a half or more. A decade later in 1545 an evangelistic-minded Portuguese trader, Antonio de Paiva,[7] brought back four students from the Celebes to the college in Goa for training as missionaries. He reported that two of the rajahs, the rulers of Supa and Siao, were baptized during his visit. Within a few years, it was reported that a number of other kings in the southwest Celebes had become Christians along with many of their people.[8] The rajah of Siao, however, died not long thereafter and was succeeded by an unconverted "pagan," probably Muslim.[9]

East of the Celebes were the Moluccas, the fabled Spice Islands which Columbus twenty years earlier had tried and failed to find in North America. The Portuguese found them in 1512. The great Jesuit, Xavier, spent fourteen months there in 1546 and 1547, and the story of that short interlude between his better-known missions in India and Japan is a microcosm of the bright hopes and failed achievement of Portuguese Christianity in the islands. The kings of Ternate had converted to Islam in 1460–1470, only about three generations earlier. Theirs was a small but rich island only five miles in circumference, but its kings claimed control of territories that extended as far as Amboina and the nutmeg island of Banda. This gave them a near monopoly over the trade in cloves, highly prized as a seasoning for Europe's luxury appetites. As Muslims, they began to style themselves as sultans, but their grasp for central control of the islands was bitterly contested by rival Muslim chieftains.

The coming of the black ships of the Portuguese, often considered a threat by the islanders, was welcomed in Ternate.[10] The Muslim sultan seized it as an opportunity to use the newcomers, though they were not Muslims, against his enemies and unite the islands under his own rule. With the traders had come a few Franciscan missionaries who seem to have been better regarded by the Muslim sultan than by the undisciplined Portuguese traders. The most effective evangelists seemed to have been the few devout Catholics among the Western merchants who took their faith seriously.[11]

If the sultan hoped for peace on the throne and prosperity for his kingdom through an alliance with the Portuguese, his hopes were never realized. He had reckoned without the contentious feuding that tore at his own many-wived royal family, the intensity of the ambitions and anger of his Muslim under-chieftains, and — most of all — the avarice and cruelty of his new Portuguese allies.

The Portuguese built their first fort in Ternate in 1522, the year the old sultan died. Four of his sons by various queens and concubines succeeded him in turbulent disorder, and a frustrated line of Portuguese captain-traders vacillated between supporting the sultanate and assuming authority themselves. The Portuguese were better traders than colonizers. Their military brutality antagonized the native people, and their arrogance ill fitted them to cope with the serpentine intrigues of local politics. Finally, they ceased trusting either their allies on the throne or their enemies in the hills and resorted to brute force against both. One after another the young sultans were seized and held hostage. The rebels outside were hunted down like animals. In one village the elders had their hands cut off while the village chief, his hands tied, was thrown to two fierce dogs. He ran into the sea trying to fend off the dogs with his teeth and drowned in the sight of all the helpless villagers.[12]

Tabarija, the First Christian King

In 1532, fourteen years before Xavier's arrival, the resident Portuguese captain suddenly arrested the teenage sultan, the second of the old sultan's sons to succeed him. They accused him of treachery and replaced him with his younger half-brother, Tabarija,[13] who was just fifteen. But before another year or more had passed (the chronology is difficult to determine), the next captain-trader seized Tabarija, threw him chained into prison, and placed his illegitimate thirteen-year-old half-brother, Hairun, on the throne of the Moluccas.[14] The Portuguese sent Tabarija off to Goa for trial. There, however, he was declared innocent; his title was restored, but not his throne. He was detained in Goa, legally not a hostage but yet not free to return to his islands either. Despite the arbitrariness of these proceedings, Tabarija became fascinated with Portuguese customs, dressed in Portuguese clothes, and in 1537, after long conversations about the Christian faith with his principal patron, the trader Jurdão de Freitas, he asked for Portuguese baptism as a Christian. He took the Portuguese name Dom Manuel. In gratitude he deeded one of his possessions, the important island of Amboina, over to de Freitas.[15]

As the first Christian king over any extended territory in the East Indies Tabarija deserved better treatment than he subsequently received.

He was neglected by the powerful Portuguese traders, who schemed to take over his lands; even the missionaries apparently failed to give him the systematic instruction in the faith he asked for. His stipend from the Portuguese government was often interrupted, and he sank into debt and immorality. Other Muslim rulers regarded his desperate situation as Allah's judgment upon him for turning Christian. Few of the more powerful chiefs were thereafter inclined to follow him into the Christian faith. In 1545, when at last he received permission to return to Ternate, it was too late. He died on the way, perhaps by poisoning, without ever recovering his kingdom. Tabarija did, however, bequeath sovereignty of the Moluccas in his will not to his usurping Muslim half-brother, Hairun, but to the king of Portugal.[16]

Francis Xavier in the Moluccas

Xavier had met Tabarija briefly in Goa in 1542 and was drawn to consider a mission to the Moluccas, but not until after Tabarija's death did he leave Malacca for the islands. His first stop was at mountainous Amboina, the island that Tabarija had given to his patron, de Freitas. Most of the people were "pagan," and though there were numerous Muslims also, he found that they were uninstructed and ignorant of their own faith. He was glad to find seven Christian communities on the island, which, though small, was seven times larger than the capital island of Ternate. Altogether there were some eight thousand Christians and three Christian chiefs.[17] But the last missionary priest had died leaving the Christians, wrote Xavier, like sheep without a shepherd. He spent six months there teaching, hearing confessions, and baptizing, relying on an interpreter, though he had taken great pains to learn some basic Malayan. If only the society could send a dozen more missionaries a year, the whole island would become Christian, he wrote to his colleagues in Europe.[18]

Proceeding northward to the Moluccan capital in Ternate, a voyage of from two to four weeks depending on the wind,[19] Xavier received a warm welcome from de Freitas, the new captain-trader of Ternate. Upon taking over command in 1544, de Freitas had deposed Tabarija's illegitimate half-brother who, though accepted as sultan, had been kept hostage in prison for five years, and sent him to Goa for trial. He prepared to welcome back to the throne Tabarija, the exiled sultan whom he had befriended and evangelized in India.

Tabarija's death on what was to have been his triumphal trip home to Ternate proved to be an irreparable setback to the Christianizing of the sultanate. De Freitas temporarily appointed Tabarija's mother, Niachile, a fervent Muslim and a shrewd political power in her own right, as regent. Gradually, however, de Freitas took control of the kingdom for himself and in so doing began to alienate his island allies. But he openly favored the propagation of the Christian faith, and for this the local priest and vicar of the capital was completely unfitted, having the reputation of being more interested in trade than in his parish, operating beyond the law in the former, and neglecting his duties to the latter. He had allowed the little Christian school on the island, started by de Freitas's predecessor, to die for lack of attention. So when Xavier arrived, promising a revival of Christian outreach, de Freitas offered him support. Xavier began at once to teach, putting the creed, the prayers, and the hymns into the native language so that all could understand. His greatest single accomplishment in the eyes of islanders and Portuguese alike, however, was the conversion of the queen mother, Niachile Pokaraga.[20]

But Xavier was never content to remain long in the ecclesiastical center. He gravitated always to the frontier. Within three months he left the capital to set out on a dangerous missionary journey north and east to the tip of the spider-shaped main Moluccan island of Halmahera and its northeastern neighbor, the island of Morotai.[21] The twenty-nine Christian communities there had been cut off for seven years from the Ternate Christians by a fierce Muslim rebellion against the Christianizing Portuguese and their hostage sultans. They were a primitive folk, and the Christians among them, evangelized some thirteen years earlier, numbered perhaps twenty thousand survivors of harsh persecution by Muslims and tribal religion believers alike.[22] The largest Christian centers were Tolo, with three thousand Christians, and Mamojo, whose Christian chiefs had been baptized in 1534. For three months Xavier traveled through the Christian villages, baptizing as many as two thousand children and promising to send more missionaries.[23]

Back in Ternate Xavier found everything turned upside down. "Freitas was no longer captain, and Niachile Pokaraga no longer queen of Ternate," as Schurhammer puts it.[24] A Portuguese ship had arrived unannounced, with an unexpected newly appointed captain-trader who brusquely ordered de Freitas arrested and announced that he had brought secretly on the ship with him the deposed sultan, the Muslim Hairun, to reclaim the throne from which de Freitas had dragged him not many months before in disgrace. Caught between two sets of rival political factions, two Portuguese captains, de Freitas and de Sousa, and two native claimants to power in the sultanate, Hairun and Niachile, mother of Tabarija, Xavier struggled to find a peaceful solution, fair to both sides, but in vain. De Freitas was carried to India to defend himself, and the Muslims reclaimed the throne. Somewhat surprisingly Hairun reserved his bitterness for de Freitas and treated Xavier cordially. He promised not to take reprisals against the Christians and even indicated a willingness to consider turning Christian himself, if this would not require giving up his large harem.[25] Four months later Xavier left Ternate never to return, no longer as optimistic as when he had arrived but not without hope.

Mission in the Islands after Xavier

Others came to continue Xavier's missionary labors and kept open the small school he had managed to start for the training of native priests.[26] Yet for the Portuguese and the Catholic fathers in the Spice Islands, time was running out. A native Muslim uprising drove the Portuguese from Ternate in 1574. The Dutch took Amboina in 1605 and received the submission of the Ternate sultanate in 1606. The future for Christianity in the islands for the next three centuries was Protestant.

Nevertheless, some Catholic beachheads endured. On the far southeastern islands the missions of the Dominicans flourished, beginning with the arrival of missionaries on Timor (1555), Flores (1562), and little Solor, which for a century became their "fortress of the faith," their largest Christian community in those islands. The mission on Flores reported twenty-seven thousand believers in eleven Christian communities; as many as fifty thousand Christians were baptized in their "fortress" on Solor. Both figures are undoubtedly exaggerated. By the end of the century the Dutch counted only 12,250 Catholics in the area, but though the larger group around the monastery fortress on Solor eventually disappeared in native uprisings and Dutch conquests, there was still a Catholic community on Flores as late as 1754.[27]

Beyond Flores and Solor, on the southeastern fringe of the archipelago, lay the island of Timor, famed throughout the Far East for its fragrant sandalwood. There the Dominicans established the most enduring Roman Catholic community in the islands, thanks in large part to the pioneering labors of the heroic apostle of Timor, Jacinto de Santo Antonio. Timor proved to be one of the few Catholic mission centers that was not uprooted or absorbed by Protestant missions when the Dutch swept the Portuguese out of the South Pacific in the middle of the seventeenth century (1655–1663).[28]

As the Dutch moved into the islands from the first trading base in Batavia in western Java, disrupting Portuguese sea lanes from India, and then took Malacca from the Portuguese in 1641, Timor shifted its trading base from Malacca to Macao, and many Malaccans, both Portuguese and Eurasian, moved to Macassar and Timor. But Macassar too fell to the Dutch in 1660, and little was left to Portugal by the Portuguese-Dutch treaty of 1663 but a tip of the island of Flores and tenuous, nominal control of Timor.[29] It was just enough, however, to ensure the survival of a direct line of organized Indonesian Catholicism for the next three hundred years.

The later history of the Dominican mission on Timor after the turn of the century is not particularly edifying. One viceroy early in the 1700s complained of the openly licentious freedom of the few remaining friars on the island. Churches were poorly maintained, and, with or without the knowledge of the indifferent missionaries, some of the "Christianized" tribes were still performing human sacrifices upon the death of a chief.[30] But the sense of identity with the church, however nominal, remained. To alter Boxer's conclusion slightly, after his somber recounting of the weaknesses of the missionaries and the follies of the colonials, he notes with some surprise that the islanders "never wholly threw off their allegiance" to "Crown or Cross" (Portugal or church), adding that "an influence which aroused such loyalty could not have been wholly bad."[31] The combination of nominal unity under the Portuguese and nominal Christianity under Christian chiefs and missionaries may partially explain the spirit of native independence that in the twentieth century led East Timor to resist absorption into either Islam or free Indonesia.

It would be presumptuous to estimate the number of Christians in the Indonesian islands by the year 1800, but according to what some have claimed, the number of Catholics and Protestants combined might lie between sixty-five thousand and two hundred thousand.[32]

NOTES

1. Brian Harrison, *South-East Asia: A Short History* (London: Macmillan, 1955), 50–57; Donald F. Lach and Carol Flaumenhaft, eds., *Asia on the Eve of Europe's Expansion* (Englewood Cliffs, N.J.: Prentice-Hall, 1965), 7–8, 81ff.

2. Milton W. Meyer, *Southeast Asia: A Brief History* (Totowa, N.J.: Littlefield, Adams, 1971), 69.

3. C. P. Fitzgerald, *A Concise History of East Asia* (New York: Frederick A. Praeger, 1966), 79.

4. Schurhammer, *Francis Xavier*, 21ff.

5. Schmidlin, *Catholic Mission History*, 308 n. 1.

6. The Portuguese lost Sumatra's pepper trade to the Dutch and British. On Java, Muslim influence expanded with the rise of the nominally Islamic Mataram kingdom, which came to control all of Central Java, but its Muslim identity was diluted by the animism of the hills and the cultural nationalism of the Javanese kings. Islam "survived only on Javanese royal terms" (*Encyclopaedia Britannica, Macropaedia*, 9:483).

7. A Portuguese captain and trader, de Paiva's knowledge of the Malay language, evangelistic forthrightness, and simple, layman's theology greatly impressed the local rulers. The small "kingdoms" that he evangelized were Macassar, Siao, Supa, and Alieta, all in the Celebes, but though many Christians were baptized, the faith had only a tenuous hold on the rulers, who wavered between Christianity and Islam (see Schurhammer, *Francis Xavier*, 2:520–531; 3:247–251, 468).

8. These "kings" were rulers of small territories, not much larger than clusters of villages. Supa and Siao were evangelized by the Franciscans, and Cion, Manado, and Sanguin by the Jesuits. On Paiva's visit, see Schurhammer, *Francis Xavier*, 2:520–531; see also Schmidlin, *Catholic Mission History*, 313.

9. Schurhammer, *Francis Xavier*, 3:47 n. 386. The "pagan" was his half-brother.

10. On the Portuguese occupation, see *A Treatise on the Moluccas (c. 1544), Probably the Preliminary Version of Antonio Galvão's Lost Historia das Moluccas*, ed. and trans. Hubert T. T. Jacobs (St. Louis: Jesuit Historical Institute, 1971).

11. Schmidlin, *Catholic Mission History*, 314.

12. For the chilling account of Portuguese brutality, see Schurhammer, *Francis Xavier*, 3:148.

13. On the troubled career of this first Christian king of the islands and his mother, Niachile Pokaraga, see Schurhammer (*Francis Xavier*, 2:249–256, 496; 3:38–42, 149ff., 157–159), whose well-documented account I follow.

14. The succession of Portuguese trader-captains of Ternate was Fonseca (1531–1533), de Ataide (1533–1536), Galvão (1536–1539), Jurdão de Freitas (1544–1546), B. de Sousa (1546–1549, 1550–1552). The sultans were Bayan Sirullah (reigned 1500–1522), and his four sons, Abu Hayat (1522–1529), Dayal (1529–1532, deposed by the Portuguese, but restored by Muslim chiefs in rebellion, 1532–1536), Tabarija (1532–1535, sultan in exile 1535–1545), Hairun (1535–1545, 1546–1570). The dates for the sultans are approximate. See Schurhammer, *Francis Xavier*, 2:694, 701–702.

15. Schurhammer, *Francis Xavier*, 2:249–256.

16. Schurhammer, *Francis Xavier*.

17. Schurhammer, *Francis Xavier*, 3:71–141, and a map marking the Christian communities, 3:66. The seven communities contained thirty villages and hamlets.

18. On Xavier's mission on Amboina, see Schurhammer, *Francis Xavier*, 3:52–141.

19. See the map of Xavier's travels in the Moluccas in Schurhammer, *Francis Xavier*, 3:144.

20. Niachile was mother of the Christian sultan Tabarija, not of Hairun who was the son of a Javanese concubine of the old sultan Bayan (see Schurhammer, *Francis Xavier*, 3:42, 159).

21. See the maps of Xavier's journeys in the Moluccas (Schurhammer, *Francis Xavier*, 3:144, 158).

22. On the Christians of Moro before Xavier, see Schurhammer, *Francis Xavier*, 3:160ff.

23. Schurhammer, *Francis Xavier*, 3:169–188. On the numbers of Christians and baptisms, see 177ff., 187 n. 255.

24. Schurhammer, *Francis Xavier*, 3:190.

25. Schurhammer, *Francis Xavier*, 3:191–200.

26. Schurhammer, *Francis Xavier*, 3:142–207.

27. The generous Dominican estimates are reported by Schmidlin, *Catholic Mission History*, 315, 500.

28. Charles R. Boxer, "Portuguese and Dutch Colonial Rivalry, 1641–1661," *Studia* 2 (Lisbon: Centro de Estudos Historicos Ultramarinos, July 1958), 12.

29. See Charles R. Boxer's lively descriptions of the Black Portuguese "uncrowned kings" of Timor and the struggles of the Portuguese governors and captains general from 1662 to 1770 (*Fidalgos in the Far East 1550–1770* [London and New York: Oxford University Press, 1968], 179–198).

30. Boxer, *Fidalgos in the Far East 1550–1770*, 197.

31. Boxer, *Fidalgos in the Far East 1550–1770*, 197–198.

32. See Latourette, *A History of the Expansion of Christianity*, 3:306.

Chapter 4

The "Christian Century" in Japan

> Among all the people of the Orient, they [the Japanese] are the most in-
> clined to the worship and veneration of divine things. This is not only to
> obtain temporal benefits such as long life, health, wealth, prosperity, chil-
> dren and other such things for which they ask their false gods but also
> even more to obtain with all their heart salvation in the next life. This
> they do even in their false and erroneous ways...They seem literally to be
> those people whom Isaias mentions in Chapter 18: "Go, ye swift angels to
> a waiting people." —João Rodrigues, circa A.D. 1627

CHRISTIANITY came to Japan in the middle of a stormy one-
hundred-years war that, as a Japanese poet put it, "destroy[ed] the law
of Buddha, and the law of kings."[1] Civil war convulsed the islands and
so changed the face of the nation that some say Japan has two histories,
one before the revolution of 1467, which led to the end of the dictatorship (shogunate) of the Ashikaga family, and one after 1600, when a
mighty battle determined the victor and restored unity under another
dictatorship, the Tokugawa shogunate.

Folded into that fiery, chaotic period and overlapping it in history
like counterpoint in music was a remarkable religious phenomenon, the
"Christian century" in Japan,[2] from 1549 to 1650, when, for a few fleet-
ing decades, it seemed that Christianity might mold the later history of
Japan much as a mixture of Shintoism, Buddhism, and to a lesser extent
Confucianism had shaped its earlier cultural history.[3]

One of the surprises hidden in any first reading of the history of that
Christian century is that there may have been a higher percentage of
Christians in the sixteenth century in Japan's population of about 20 million than there were at the close of the twentieth, when the population
is nearer 130 million. Another surprise is the extent of Japanese cooperation and patronage in the first decades of the Christian century. A
third surprise, which comes only after more reading, is how little the
Christian century affected the subsequent history of Japan.

Xavier, Jesuits, and Japanese Patronage (1551–1587)

The pioneer of the first Christian mission to Japan in 1549 was the great
Jesuit, Francis Xavier (1506–1552), who reached Japan in 1549.[4] But it

68

would be well to begin the story of his mission with an acknowledgment of the fact that at least some of the honor rightly due to the great Jesuit should probably be shared with an unlikely candidate for credit as a forerunner and catalyst of the mission, a Japanese fugitive from criminal justice named Anjiro (or Yajiro), who later styled himself simply Paul of Japan.[5] Those two, the Jesuit missionary from Portugal and the fugitive from Japan, opened up a whole new vision of Asian mission for the Society of Jesus. Strangely enough, it was the man from Japan who came to India looking for Xavier, not Xavier looking for Japan. The initiative was Japanese.

Anjiro, who was later baptized Paul of the Holy Faith, was from a good upper-class family in Kagoshima on the southern Japanese island of Kyushu. Caught in a youthful brawl and fleeing from a charge of manslaughter, probably accidental, he found refuge first in a Shingon Buddhist temple. He found no peace of mind or soul there, and boarded a Portuguese ship that was about to sail for Malacca. His mind was of a religious bent, and on the three-thousand-mile voyage south to the Malay archipelago he confided his sense of unforgiven sin in conversations with the ship's sympathetic Christian captain and decided to become a Christian. The captain told him that when he got to Malacca, he should ask a "holy priest" named Francis Xavier about these things. But when they reached Malacca Xavier had left for the East Indies (Indonesia), and Anjiro reluctantly took ship to return home to Japan. That might well have ended it all had not a storm forced his ship to make port in China, where by chance or by providence he met another Portuguese acquaintance and was persuaded to try again to find Xavier back in Malacca. This time, at last, he met the missionary, and there in Malacca (the Singapore of its day) the mission to Japan was born.

Xavier, who knew little more about Japan than that it was made up of "certain very large islands" that had been discovered about five years earlier, questioned Anjiro about the possibilities for Christian mission in Japan:

> I asked him whether if I went back with him to his country, the Japanese would become Christians, and he said that they would not do so until they had asked me many questions and had seen by the way I answered how much I knew. Most of all, they would want to see if I practiced what I preached and believed . . . then, after watching me for six months, the king, the nobility, and all other people of discretion would become Christians, for the Japanese, he said, are totally guided by the law of reason.[6]

Xavier added, "My mind seems to tell me that in less than two years either I or someone else from our Society will go to Japan, though the voyage is very dangerous."

In less than the two years he was on his way, with a remarkably international party of missionaries — Xavier and two fellow Jesuits (Cosme de Torres and a lay brother, Fernando), three Japanese (Anjiro and two companions), and a Chinese baptized Emmanuel (or Manuel). It took them six weeks for the first leg of the voyage, Cochin to Malacca, where the governor, a son of Vasco da Gama, gave them thirty measures of pepper to sell in Japan to build a church and enough money to support the company there for several years. No Portuguese ship was available for the seven-week-long journey by sea to Japan, and against all advice, they chose to sail instead on a Chinese junk manned by a captain and crew who looked so much like pirates to the Portuguese governor that he demanded the wife and son of the captain as hostages to guarantee the party's safety. The perceptive Anjiro privately noted with some satisfaction that, given the ill repute of Westerners in the China seas, it was providential that a Chinese and not the Portuguese would take Xavier to Japan.[7] Xavier spent only two years and three months in Japan (1549–1552), but in that short space of time he laid the foundations for the next two centuries of Catholic missions in Asia, and more particularly, of Jesuit missionary methods. The three pillars of the pattern were adaptation, fidelity, and discipline. The principle of adaptation, which Xavier only experimented with and left to his successors to develop, gave to the missioners the flexibility to accommodate their strategy to different social structures in a culturally pluralistic world. Fidelity to Catholic orthodoxy gave them a clear missionary theology that refused to dodge difficult questions, and their vow of absolute obedience to the pope gave them an organizational discipline second to none. It was a dynamic tension of motives and loyalties that often stretched the outer limits of unity and sorely tested the capacities of missionary stamina and ecclesiastical fellowship, but in the end it produced the greatest single missionary society the Christian church has ever known.

However, once Xavier moved beyond the circle of Anjiro's family and friends in Kagoshima, for whose benefit Anjiro memorized the entire gospel of Matthew in Portuguese and translated it into Japanese,[8] he discovered that effective accommodation to a culture requires accurate knowledge of the culture, and much of what he had been told about Japan was misinformation. For example, in India his first instinctive Christian inclination had plunged him primarily into work with the poor and the outcasts on the Fisher Coast. This, he must have noted, had brought him remarkable local success but failed to lead to any Christian impact on Indian society as a whole. So he resolved to change his strategy in Japan and begin at the other end of the social scale, with the emperor.[9] The result was disillusioning. No one had told him that the emperor was a powerless puppet. Even more depressing to him was the response of the powerful and militant Buddhist monks of the great monastery on Mount Hiei outside Kyoto. Despising his thin, black robe and apparent poverty, they refused to receive him.

Japan, in the middle of the sixteenth century, was not a cohesive empire but a constantly shifting, crazy-quilt pattern of about 214 largely independent dukedoms, each ruled by a feudal lord (daimyo), the more powerful of which had for centuries fought for political and military control of the emperor, the symbolic head of state.[10] In the twelfth century the ruling overlord (shogun) who controlled the emperor was the feudal ruler of Kamakura, whose family name was Hojo; in the fourteenth and fifteenth centuries the power of the shogunate passed into the hands of the Ashikaga family in Kyoto. But in 1550, when Xavier tried in vain to see the emperor, the Ashikaga shoguns were losing control and Japan was in political chaos. It was groping for centralized unity under a succession of three powerful warlords.

The first was Oda Nobunaga (1534–1582), the ruthless conqueror of half of Japan, who despised Buddhist priests but welcomed and protected the Jesuits and captured Kyoto from the Ashikaga shoguns in 1568. He was followed by a yet greater figure, Toyotomi Hideyoshi (1537–1598), low-born but brilliant and tenacious, who fought his way to control of virtually all the rest of Japan in less than twenty years, from 1582 to 1598. He too favored Christianity for the first five of those years (to 1587), then began to turn against it. But it was the third warlord, Tokugawa Ieyasu (1542–1616), who climaxed the restoration of national unity by establishing his long-lasting Tokugawa shogunate (1600–1868), and in the process finally drove the Christians out of Japan. Boxer quotes a Japanese saying: "Nobunaga mixed the dough, Hideyoshi baked the cake, but Ieyasu ate it."[11]

After his disappointments in Kyoto, Xavier turned his attention from the powerless emperor and the arrogant Buddhist priests to the real rulers of Japan, the daimyo. He forthwith adapted his style and approach from that of a self-effacing servant of the poor, which he much preferred, to that of an ambassador — an ambassador for Christ, for pope, and for the governor of India[12] — willing, like the apostle Paul, to "become all things to all men" for the glory of God.

Considerable success followed, a success built as much on his Western knowledge of astronomy[13] as on his respect for all that was good in Japanese culture and to a lesser extent in its religions, for he could be as bluntly honest in condemning Japanese culture as in acknowledging its virtues. Its three crippling blemishes, in Jesuit eyes, were idolatry, homosexuality, and abortion.[14] On the one hand, he could write of the Japanese, "They are the best [people] we have yet discovered; and it seems to me that, among unbelieving nations, there will not be another to surpass the Japanese." Not even Christians, he added, are so consistently opposed to theft.[15] But on the other hand, as far as their Buddhist religion was concerned, even at best it was inadequate. They had no doctrine either of creation or immortality, and they worshiped idols. Nevertheless, he was impressed by one wise old Zen abbot in

Kagoshima, who shared at least part of his criticisms of the temples. One day he asked the abbot what the monks were doing in their intense, motionless exercises in meditation. And with a characteristic Zen shock answer the abbot replied, "Counting what they've taken from the pilgrims, wondering how they can get better clothes, and dreaming about what they'll do in their leisure time. None of them is thinking of anything that makes any sense." Xavier was impressed, but he found little to admire in most Buddhist priests. To him, their two Buddhas, Sakyamuni and Amitabha, were "two demons."[16] The abbot, in turn, proved impossible to convince on the subjects of creation and immortality. Xavier later wrote to Loyola that any missionaries he might send in the future "should be well learned in philosophy, especially in dialectics, that they may be able to refute and convict the obstinate arguments of the Japanese."[17]

It was on the main Japanese island of Honshu, at the court of the Daimyo Ouchi Yoshitaka in Yamaguchi, that he had his greatest successes. He arrived, as an ambassador should, with rich presents: a musical clock with tones corresponding to the Japanese scale, spectacles, and an engraved musket, all of which immediately caught the attention of the court's scientifically inclined intellectuals. He also gave the daimyo a richly bound Bible, in Latin, of course. The daimyo, pleased, ordered that the Christians be given permission to preach publicly throughout his fiefdom. Even the Buddhist priests were pleased, apparently taking their cue from the fact the Xavier was unwittingly using a Shingon Buddhist name for God (*Dainichi*), the cosmic Vairocana Buddha and lord of light, as Anjiro had misleadingly translated it. Many of them believed that his religion was just one more of the many Buddhist sects of Asia. Xavier was horrified when he discovered what he had done and corrected the mistake by simply substituting for *Dainichi* the Latin word *Deus*. Then he sent his lay brother Fernandez, who was making great strides in learning Japanese, to shout along the streets, "Do not worship *Dainichi*."[18]

Within two months he had five hundred converts, including a few Buddhist priests. One great sticking point in the conversion of new inquirers, Xavier found, was the Christian doctrine of hell. "What about our ancestors?" they asked. In a long letter Xavier wrote in 1552 he describes their distressed reaction:

> [They were] greatly troubled and pained by a hateful and annoying scruple — that God did not appear to them merciful and good, because He had never made himself known to the Japanese before our arrival, especially if it were true that those who had not worshipped God as we preached were doomed to suffer everlasting punishment in hell.

Xavier's answer came straight from Saint Paul's Epistle to the Romans: Human reason, which is planted within us by God himself, "the Author of Nature," teaches us to do good and avoid evil, and insofar as anyone among our ancestors has followed faithfully that divine law in our hearts, God will treat that person justly, not unjustly. "The converts were so satisfied with this reasoning," he added, that "they received from us with a glad heart the sweet yoke of our Lord."[19]

He next received a most encouraging invitation from a feudal lord, Otomo Yoshishige of Bungo (now Oita), to preach in his territory. There on that southern island he planted what became the most effective radiating center of Jesuit outreach to other parts of Japan. Daimyo Yoshishige became the first of the higher Japanese nobility to convert to the Christian faith, but that was long after Xavier had left Japan in 1552. Shortly thereafter Xavier died off the coast of China waiting in vain for an opportunity to enter that great, closed land.

In his ten short years as a second "apostle to Asia" Xavier had planted the cross, it is said somewhat extravagantly, "in fifty-two different kingdoms, preached through nine thousand miles of territory, and baptized over one million persons."[20]

Leaving the pious exaggerations of others aside, it is instructive to observe what Xavier himself said had been the two greatest obstacles to his mission in Japan: first, misinterpretations of the Christian doctrines of God and life after death; second, "our greatest enemies are the *bonzes* [Buddhist priests] because we expose their falsehoods."[21]

And Anjiro? Xavier left him behind in Japan when he departed to try to enter China. Did that first Japanese to believe continue the work for which Xavier had brought him back — a "Japanese to evangelize Japan"? There is a mystery about Anjiro. The Christian faith never quite caught root in Anjiro's native province of Satsuma. In fact, only two years after Xavier's departure, the Christians in Kagoshima, whom Xavier had left in Anjiro's care, were described as "without a shepherd." Why? Had Anjiro failed? Accounts differ. Some reported that he had been driven out by persecution and was martyred in China. Others hint that it may have been not persecution but poverty, and not martyrdom but a failed attempt to support his family by returning to his military past and becoming involved in a plundering raid on the China coast that lost him his life.[22] But there is no denying that this first Japanese believer deserves to be remembered as the one who brought the first Christians to Japan and taught them how to respect his country and speak its language and introduce it to their Lord.

The Japan Mission after Xavier (1552–1579)

Xavier's departure left the Japan mission with only one priest, de Torres, and a lay brother. The next twenty-seven years before the arrival of another strong leader, Alessandro Valignano, sorely tested the fledgling mission. With its pioneer gone, his untried but brave disciples suddenly found themselves facing a mounting storm of religious persecution and civil upheaval. Not all the instances of persecution can be blamed on antiforeign xenophobia or Buddhist jealousy. There were times when the Christians were their own worst enemies, as when in Omura territory overzealous converts torched temples and overturned Buddhist images.[23]

The chief protector of the Christians in those early years was the daimyo of Yamaguchi who had so courteously welcomed Xavier. Unfortunately, shortly after Xavier left the daimyo was overthrown by rebels and forced to commit suicide. The missionaries were expelled. But when the rebels called on a neighboring daimyo family, that of the lord Otomo Yoshishige of Bungo, to supply a successor in Yamaguchi, he was glad to do so. Whether the rebels realized it or not, the daimyo of Bungo was also a friend of Xavier and promptly appointed his younger brother to the vacant fiefdom. So, for the next quarter of a century the ancient and powerful Otomo clan was a bulwark of support to the small but growing group of Christians in Japan.[24] In 1552, when Xavier left Japan, the number of Christians was estimated at somewhere between eight hundred and three thousand. In the next nineteen years, under de Torres, the number grew to about thirty thousand. It continued to grow even under the next superior, the dictatorial and somewhat racist Cabral, reaching more than a hundred thousand by 1581.[25]

The growth of the church in western Japan surprised even the missioners and could be attributed, at least in part, to three primary factors: a clear missionary theology, self-sacrificing work for the poor, and the realistic recognition of the need for winning the support of the daimyos. A contributing factor was undoubtedly the fact that this area was the base for all of Japan's rich overseas trade with Portugal, and the local rulers were therefore more inclined to welcome and protect a continuing foreign presence.

For all his openness toward adapting to Japanese ways, in the matter of theology Xavier had early recognized the peril of allowing Christianity to be confusingly identified as just another Buddhist sect and had begun to clarify the usage of theological terms in Japanese. Three years after he left, the mission completed a thorough revision of its preaching terminology to weed out inappropriate Buddhist expressions.[26] A new catechism was prepared and a few years later was put into Japanese by the first Japanese admitted to the Society, Brother Lourenco, a "half-blind minstrel and evangelist," who became the Society's most effective advocate in dialogue and argument with Buddhist priests, notably in the conversion of Prince Oin, superintendent of the Tendai sect. On another occasion, in a famous debate before the shogun Oda Nobunaga, he spectacularly confounded Nobunaga's most powerful religious advisor.[27] One of his most important converts was a samurai (a member of the warrior class but of lesser nobility than the ruling daimyo), Takayama Hida, whose son, Takayama Ukon, became "the greatest of the heroic figures of the Martyr Church of Japan."[28]

Christian compassion for the poor was another significant reason for the growth of the church. The pioneer in Japan was a wealthy, young Portuguese merchant, Luis d'Almeida. Greatly impressed by Loyola, he had come to Japan in 1554 to enter the mission. In literal obedience to Jesus' words to the rich young ruler (Luke 18:18ff.), he began to give away his entire fortune to the church and offer himself in service to the poor. In 1555 he founded an orphanage so that desperate mothers might have an alternative to infanticide. It was "the very first Christian institution of social action in Japan."[29] Then he opened a home for the homeless, and having had some acquaintance with surgical procedures, he went on to erect the first hospital in Japan to practice and teach surgery. In two years the number of Christians in Bungo (Oita) rose to two thousand.[30]

On the other side of the southern island, Kyushu, in Omura territory in 1562–1563, Almeida converted the first daimyo to become a Christian, Omura Sumitada.[31] This was to have momentous consequences. Within ten years of his conversion, which though genuine was not unmixed with desire for a part of the lucrative Portuguese trade, Sumitada announced his intention to make his whole small fiefdom a Christian province. In 1573 it was reported that twenty thousand had been baptized in only seven months.[32] Six years later, in what Boxer describes as an "unprecedented . . . cession of Japanese soil to foreigners," Omura Sumitada gave the Jesuits the whole little fishing village of Nagasaki (then Fukae) as a gift. It quickly supplanted Bungo as the heart and center of the Jesuit mission and coincidentally expanded to become the major trading port for all of Portugal's mutually profitable trade with Japan. By the year of Valignano's arrival, in 1579, nearly half of all the Christians in Japan were in Omura territory.[33]

The lesson was not lost upon the missioners. An unlikely combination of social compassion for the poor combined with an intentional effort to convert the nobles became the Jesuit pattern. One recent writer has realistically observed that whatever their motives may have been, "there were no better missionaries than the [Christian] feudal lords."[34]

Reforms of Valignano
in the Nobunaga Shogunate (1571–1582)

In the end, it was not the conversion of individual warlords that was to prove to be a primary political factor in the subsequent success or failure of the Japan mission. The 1560s were the years of the fall of the regional daimyo and the emergence of a new military dictatorship that led by the end of the century to the unification of Japan. Crucial to the progress of the church in this period of the Christian century was to be its relationship to the three unifiers.

The first unifier, as noted above, was Oda Nobunaga, a brutal, lean, young minor noble who fought his way against rival warlords and militant Buddhist monks to the control of central Japan in eleven bloody years, 1560–1571. Partly because the Buddhists openly warred against him, and partly because he was intensely curious about all that the Jesuits could tell him about the West, Nobunaga greatly favored the Christian missionaries and ruthlessly destroyed Buddhist temples. He was himself a nominal Buddhist of the Lotus (Hokke) sect, but he is reported to have said, when asked about his tolerance of Christianity, something like, "We already have eight principal religious sects, and the introduction of one more will do no harm."[35]

When Nobunaga's father-in-law accepted baptism, and two of his sons said they might soon do so also, some began to entertain hope that the great ruler himself might be converted.[36] It had been a not-uncommon phenomenon in the long, troubled history of Christianity in the East, this illusory expectation of the appearance of an Asiatic Constantine. Abgar of Edessa, Anoshaghzad of Seleucid Persia, Kuyuk Khan of Central Asia, and Arghun, ilkhan of Mongol Persia — all at one time or another were hailed as imminent converts. Now the sixteenth-century warlord of Japan, Oda Nobunaga, some believed, was on the brink of conversion.[37] But it remained wishful thinking. His "only god," summed up a later Jesuit historian, "was his own ambition."[38]

The climax of Nobunaga's rise to power was a savage assault on the Buddhist warrior-monasteries of Mount Hiei, near Kyoto, where in two September days in 1571 he plundered and burned what was left of the three thousand temples on the sacred hills, and in cold blood more like an animal hunt than a battle, massacred three thousand of the fighting monks and their followers, men, women, and children. Japanese Buddhism took several centuries to recover from the blows it received from its failed attempt to control by military power the unification of the country.[39]

Nobunaga opened to the Christians the capital city, Kyoto, which he captured in 1568, and closely befriended Luis Frois, the historian of the mission. When his more xenophobic followers objected, he retorted, "What can a single, unarmed foreigner do to harm so large a land [as our Japan]?"[40] This began a new phase of the Christian mission's relationship with government. Hitherto its protectors had almost always been only minor lords and those involved in foreign trade. Not long before he was assassinated, one of Oda Nobunaga's last favors to the missionaries was to welcome to Kyoto a man who, probably more than any other, including Xavier, shaped the Christianity of the Christian century in Japan, Alessandro Valignano.[41]

Valignano as "Missiologist"

The organizing genius of Jesuit missions in Asia was not Xavier the pioneer, but Alessandro Valignano (1539–1606), vicar general and visitor of the India mission (that is, head of all Jesuit missions in Asia). In this capacity he made three lengthy and immensely significant visits to Japan.[42] It was Valignano who reorganized the Japan mission, and, against considerable opposition both from within and without the mission, hammered out a basic Catholic approach to the central missionary problem of how to adapt Christianity to a bewilderingly alien culture without losing Christianity's own identity in the process.

One of the first problems Valignano faced upon his arrival was an embarrassing conflict of opinion with his deputy, the resident superior of the Japan mission, Francisco Cabral, an able and courageous man who had already had nine rough years of experience in the country.[43] The two men, both of them honest and strong willed, could not have been more diametrically opposed in their attitudes toward the Japanese people. Valignano arrived with an exceedingly high estimate of the Japanese. They were "white, courteous, and highly civilized, so much so that they surpass all the other known [pagan] races of the world."[44] Even after he had come to know them better, he was still amazed that "a people so utterly unlike ourselves should yet be so highly civilized."[45] But to the veteran Cabral, such an opinion could only be attributed to the inexperience and naivete of a new arrival. His own view, soured by numerous disappointments and by undisguised prejudice, was, "I have seen no other nation as conceited, covetous, inconstant and insincere as the Japanese."[46] His considered advice was that even the Japanese lay brothers in the Society were to be treated, in effect, as second-class members.[47] Fortunately for the mission, the views of his superior not surprisingly prevailed, and Cabral soon requested transfer.[48]

Valignano was neither inexperienced nor naive. With extraordinary energy and optimism, he spent the next two years of this, his first visit, in a strenuous series of consultations that completely reorganized the mission and laid down the basic principles of a policy of adaptation. Respect for the character of the Japanese people combined with his pleasure at the measurable signs of missionary success reported to him from the work of the missioners on the southern island of Kyushu convinced him that Japan could become the crown jewel of Jesuit missions in Asia.

But the underlying problem remained. Given the necessity of adaptation, or contextualization, as it would be called today, the question was, How? How Japanese should the message and the mission become? Valignano began, as Schütte points out, with the basic problem of fitting the missionaries into the Japanese social order.[49] The missioners must, of course, learn to eat Japanese food, and, in a land as etiquette conscious as Japan, it was also extremely important that they follow carefully the intricate Japanese rules of courtesy. Their clothes were to "conform to the poverty of the Order," which prescribed for Europeans a Jesuit black soutane (cassock), Japanese travel dress, and a Portuguese round black hat and for Japanese lay brothers blue kimonos.[50]

More difficult would be learning the language. Cabral had warned that the missionaries could never learn Japanese well enough to preach in it. Valignano was not so easily deterred. He insisted not only that the European priests learn Japanese, but that the Japanese initiates learn Latin.[51] Most important of all, the mission unanimously agreed to work for the training of a Japanese priesthood as "the sole, genuine remedy" to ensure that the future church in Japan would be a Japanese church. That much-desired goal, it was hoped, could be realized within ten years.[52] By the time he left Japan at the end of 1582, the Catholics had one college, one novitiate, two seminaries, and ten residences that functioned much like preparatory schools for training for the priesthood.[53] It was a good start. But it was twenty years, not ten, before the first Japanese Jesuits were ordained in 1601, and Japanese clergy never reached the number once anticipated.[54]

It is important to remember that the famous Jesuit principle of adaptation, which later in China stirred up such a storm of controversy, was never so uncritically transposed from cultural into theological accommodation as to imply doctrinal concessions toward a pluralism of religions. Respect for Japan's culture on the part of the Jesuits was never separated from a severe and forthright missionary theology which declared that the unbeliever is wholly and terribly lost. Xavier, for example, bluntly told his inquiring converts that neither their prayers nor their alms could save their families who died without Christ, though he softened the hard statement with a reminder that God is also merciful and condemns no one unjustly. And Valignano's catechism contains "an extraordinarily vivid and powerful" section on the resurrection of the dead and final judgment.[55] The missionary aim, in fact, as Drummond points out, was not accommodation to Japan's religions but their "total religious displacement."[56]

The second of Valignano's great tasks was to reorganize the structure and internal policies of the mission, which, for all its attempts at adaptation, remained essentially European. In its first two decades, up to 1570, there were never more than six priests. Valignano wrote home that he wanted "a hundred missionaries at once" and expected to have at least a thousand in Japan before he died.[57] At the end of his first visit in 1582 there were only twenty-eight priests, and when the persecutions began in earnest in 1614 there were still only sixty-two.[58] But assisting the priests as lay members of the mission was a class of Japanese helpers or apprentices (called *dojuku*), totaling about four times the number of priests. They "shave their head, renounce the world and promise to devote themselves to the service of the church" but were not preparing for the priesthood.[59] The number of Japanese Christians about the same time, 1582, was perhaps 150,000.[60]

On a related subject, the consultations decided that the unity of the Japanese church did not yet demand the appointment of a bishop, and to preserve that unity it would not be advisable for the time being, despite the shortage of personnel, to open the country to other orders.[61] The Jesuits remained the only Christian presence in Japan until 1593.

One problem that considerably disturbed the Jesuits was how closely they could allow themselves to be linked with the Portuguese silk trade. The general superior of the order in Portugal advised against any connection at all. But Valignano pointed out that to deprive the mission of the support the trade brought to the church would make it in effect wholly dependent upon the favor of the local warlords, most of whom were not Christians. Nevertheless, recognizing dangers in both involvements, the mission stipulated that neither relationship should be allowed to dominate the church.[62] This, of course, was a policy easier to describe than to implement. One suggestion was offered but rejected: investment by the church in rice lands. That would have given it some measure of financial independence, but it also would run the risk that the church would be seen as rich landowner and thus find it hard to remain spiritually relevant to the poor.[63]

Backlash: The Age of Persecution

LIMITED TOLERATION UNDER HIDEYOSHI (1584–1600)

When Nobunaga was killed in 1582, Valignano had just left Japan, taking with him as far as Goa an eye-catching embassy of four Japanese Christian youths of high-born families to be sent on to Europe as a spectacular demonstration of the global power of the gospel. The man who succeeded Nobunaga was his most brilliant general, a small, ugly, low-born peasant without a family name.[64] He would become the greatest military commander in Japanese history and the unifier of the nation, Toyotomi Hideyoshi.

Hideyoshi's first years of rule raised great hopes for the future of the Christian faith in Japan. His last years foreshadowed the great persecution. The whole period of some fifty years was a time of transient success in the church, overcast by four omens of impending disaster: the edict of 1587; the executions of 1597; the battle of Sekigahara in 1600, in which Ieyasu destroyed the power of the Christian daimyos; and the edict of 1614, which began an all-out war of extermination against the church. All but the last of these shocks, however, were succeeded by brief periods of unexpected religious toleration.

In the beginning Hideyoshi's court and army were filled with openly Christian advisors and generals. His personal physician, Manase Dosan, as well as his treasurer and one of his administrative secretaries were Christians, as were a number of the ladies of his court. Once, when Hideyoshi visited the Jesuit seminary in Osaka, he was in fine good humor and told its superior, de Cespedes, "You know that everything in your law contents me, and I find no other difficulty in it, except its prohibition of having more than one wife." Later, in a more serious vein, he confided to the Jesuit vice provincial Gaspar Coelho in the presence of Luis Frois that he might even order half of all Japan to turn Christian, presumably the western half, including the huge island of Kyushu, where a number of his most prominent daimyo and generals were located.[65] Two of the most famous, Takayama Ukon and Kuroda Yoshitaka, both Christians, helped him subdue a rebellion on Kyushu, leading their troops with crosses on their helmets and war banners.[66] Baptisms multiplied throughout Japan, and Christianity became what Murdoch describes as a "fashionable craze" at Hideyoshi's court.[67]

THE ANTI-CHRISTIAN EDICT OF 1587

Then overnight, so suddenly that it seemed that Hideyoshi might have been lulling the vice provincial into a feeling of false security, he stunned the church with a shocking succession of completely unexpected blows. The Jesuit leader, so recently wined and dined by the great general, was rudely awakened from sleep and charged with persecuting Buddhist priests, forcibly converting Japanese, and conniving with Portuguese traders in the business of enslaving overseas Japanese in the East Indies. At the same time, the most prominent Christian daimyo in the land, Takayama Ukon, who had just been richly rewarded for his part in the recovery of Kyushu, was stripped of his fiefdom and ordered into exile. The Christian priests, declared Hideyoshi, were as deceitful and treasonable as the Buddhist monks. The next day (July 25, 1587) he issued an edict of exile against all the missionaries. Only those foreigners engaged in commercial trade would be allowed to remain. Other sweeping anti-Christian notices followed. Jesuits who had not left within twenty days were to be executed. Mission property, especially in the great Christian centers of Nagasaki, Osaka, and Fukuoka (Hakata), was confiscated. All Japanese converts were ordered to recant.[68]

The most conspicuous victim of the edicts was Takayama Ukon (1553–1615), lord of Takatsuki castle, who had been one of Oda Nobunaga's most trusted generals. Nobunaga is reported to have said, "One thousand soldiers in Ukon's hands is worth more than ten thousand under anyone else."[69] But Takayama Ukon was then only an underlord, and when the daimyo revolted against Nobunaga, Ukon was faced with an agonizing choice: loyalty to his immediate superior or to his ultimate superior, the regent. In the ensuing struggle both factions sought to win Ukon to their side. The daimyo held Takayama's sister and his only son as hostages; Nobunaga seized the Jesuit missionaries and held them hostage. Takayama Ukon, whose utter honesty and selfless integrity baffled even his closest friends, finally decided that even if it meant loss of both castle and family, his final loyalty was neither to the daimyo nor to the regent but to God and that his Christian duty was to have no part in an unjust war. He then shaved his head as a sign that he was renouncing land and army for religious service and went unarmed to Nobunaga, ready to die, if necessary, with the hostage priests. In fact, however, the daimyo was defeated, and Nobunaga insisted on returning to Ukon his castle and his military rank. When Hideyoshi succeeded Nobunaga, Ukon took little part in any further wars but was so trusted that the new military dictator made him chief of his personal bodyguard.[70]

Now in 1587, when Hideyoshi so suddenly turned anti-Christian, Takayama Ukon, widely known by then as the most devout of all the Christian lords, found himself again forced to choose between his lands and his faith, and once again he disdained wealth and chose exile or death as preferable to apostasy. This time he was banished, penniless, into domestic exile, finding refuge with another great Christian general, Konishi Yukinaga.[71]

Then, as abruptly as the tempest had appeared, it blew away. Hideyoshi never enforced the edicts. The 120 or so foreign priests in Japan at the time prepared to depart or hide, but only three of them actually left the country. The Christian daimyos were not punished, except for Takayama Ukon, who was exiled again and deported with his whole family to the Philippines.[72]

Many reasons have been advanced for the extraordinary vacillations in Hideyoshi's attitude to the church in this period, but one important reason for his distrust of the Christians was undoubtedly his fear that the Jesuit mission was the vanguard of Portuguese imperialist expansion, which could threaten Japan. Perhaps equally responsible for his lack of zeal in implementing the edicts was the awareness that persecution of Christians could endanger Japan's trade with the West and invite military retaliation.

Whatever the reasons, the next ten or eleven years, from 1587 to 1598, were not the end of the mission, though the edicts did indeed mark the end of the period of euphoria. These years have been called "the period of restricted toleration."[73] Hideyoshi completed the unification of Japan, disregarded his own edict and, with one conspicuous exception, the Nagasaki martyrdoms of 1597, left the Christians relatively free to organize and expand the church. He welcomed Valignano back to Japan for a second visit in 1590, recognizing his diplomatic status but not his ecclesiastical authority as head of Jesuit missions in India, China, and Japan. With Valignano came the four young samurai of the 1583 embassy to Europe with rich presents, including an Arabian stallion and a printing press with the first movable metal type seen in Japan. News of their exciting welcome in Rome and Lisbon was a reminder to the court of the importance of good foreign relations. All four youths soon joined the Jesuit mission.[74] Valignano diplomatically assured the dictator that his priests would maintain a low profile and in return was given to understand that they would not further be harassed.

Valignano took with him for this extremely important audience with Hideyoshi the four young Japanese clothed in robes presented by the pope, and a young man whose language skills may have contributed more to preserving the fragile peace between the dictator and the Christians in those precarious years than any other single factor, but whose lack of tact and judgment in the end imperiled it. He was João Rodrigues (1561–1633), nicknamed the Interpreter. Rodrigues left Portugal when he was only fourteen to spend the next sixty years in Asia in the service of the Jesuits, including thirty-three in Japan. He reached Japan in 1577, after what Valignano once described as "the most arduous voyage known to man." The great three-masted Portuguese tradeships (eleven times as big as the *Mayflower*) carried as many as a thousand men, two hundred to four hundred of whom would usually die on a voyage that might take as long as two years with stops in India and Macao. One missionary complained mildly that he was packed into the bowels of the boat for three months with ten thousand head of live chickens. Rodrigues came apparently as a volunteer and almost immediately began the long process that led to his ordination nineteen years later. A brilliant linguist, he taught Latin to the Japanese initiates at the seminary in Kyushu and wrote the first grammar ever printed of the Japanese language (*Arte da Lingoa de Iapam* [1604–1608]).[75] But his greatest service was as the chief channel of communication between the mission and the Japanese feudal government of Hideyoshi and his successor, Ieyasu, and the mission.

For a few years the church expanded massively. In Hideyoshi's ill-ventured and unsuccessful invasions of Korea beginning in 1592, he relied heavily on the famous Christian general Konishi Yukinaga and his eighteen thousand Christian soldiers from Kyushu, who led the vanguard and captured the Korean capital.[76] In his domestic policy he favored other such stalwart Christian-sympathizing daimyos as Kuroda of Fukuoka, Asano of Wakayama, and Hosokawa Tadaoki of Tango and Buzen. The Hosokawa family was one of the most powerful of medieval Japan's feudal families. The daimyo's wife, Grace (Hosokawa Tamako Gratia, 1563–1600), sometimes referred to as the princess of Tango, was "a humanist-like scholar in her own right," an unusual reputation for a woman of the upper classes in that period. Converted by the Jesuits shortly before the impending exile of the missionaries, she had asked for baptism. In the confusion of the troubled times, and with no priest available, she was baptized in 1597 by her Christian lady-in-waiting, an active female catechist named Kiyohara Ito Maria. Three years later, in the anti-Christian backlash of 1600, she was martyred, one of the most illustrious women in the history of Christianity in Japan.[77] (Who would have dared predict that four hundred years later a Hosokawa of the same family would become prime minister of a Japan better known for its capitalists than for its almost forgotten aristocrats?)

In Central Japan also, around the capital, Christianity spread among the nobility: two sons of the governor of Kyoto, and a grandson and heir apparent of Oda Nobunaga.[78] Earlier, and most surprising of all, a son of the emperor was reported to have became a Christian with his entire family, though if true, which is unlikely, that would have been more culturally than politically significant in an age when military dictators (the shoguns) controlled the emperors.[79]

Among the lasting effects of these first five decades (1551–1597) of Japan's encounter with the West, not all were specifically religious, though the conduit was Christian and Portuguese and Jesuit. The medical initiatives already mentioned, such as surgery and the country's first hospital, gave the Christian faith a compassionate face. And its all-embracing concern for the disadvantaged and the poor in socially compartmentalized Japan balanced its obvious deference to the politically and intellectual elite.[80] Perhaps most effective of all was the introduction by the Catholic missionaries of writings on Western science and technology, which had an irresistible impact on both the intellectually inquiring and the politically or economically pragmatic. In this connection one of the most important gifts of the missionaries to Japanese culture was the printing press, which Valignano brought back with him in 1590 on his return from Europe with the delegation of scions of Japanese nobility. It eventually produced works not only on Christian subjects but numerous publications on Japanese and Latin grammar, a trilingual Japanese-Latin-Portuguese dictionary, and an anthology of Chinese and Japanese poetry.[81]

A significant omission, however, was that in all the hundred years of the Christian century in Japan, there is no mention by the missionaries in Japan of any printed translation of the Bible. Manuscripts of various portions of Scripture existed, including the first Japanese translations of the gospels as early as 1561, but the opportunity to publish and distribute even one full book of the gospels was apparently and unaccountably neglected.[82]

THE MARTYRDOMS OF 1597

Meanwhile, another missionary order had been allowed to enter Japan, the Franciscans in 1593.[83] They came from Spain, not Portugal, and from the Philippines, not India or Macao, and were welcomed by Hideyoshi as a politically useful counterbalance to Portuguese and Jesuit influence of which he was becoming suspicious. Despite the prohibitions of his 1587 edict, which were still technically in force, he promised the Franciscans land for a church and monastery in the capital, to which they added a hospital and soon expanded their extremely popular medical work to Osaka while preparing to open another in Nagasaki.[84] Their missionary strategy differed in emphasis from that of the Jesuits. The Franciscans worked mostly with the sick, the poor, and the neglected, whereas the Jesuits, though not neglecting the disadvantaged, had from the beginning directed their greatest efforts toward the more powerful upper classes, pointing out to the critical newcomers that it was only Jesuit success with the daimyos that had made Christian mission in Japan possible at all.

These differences unfortunately produced rivalry and led to animosity that exploded into mutual public recrimination with consequences that were to imperil the whole missionary enterprise.[85] The founder of the Franciscan Japan mission, Pedro Bautista Blasquez (1542–1597), was to become one of the martyrs of the persecution of 1597.[86]

The arrival of the first resident bishop in Japan, Pierre Martins (Martinez),[87] who reached Nagasaki in 1596, should have marked a significant step forward in strengthening the church and smoothing the relationships between the increasing number of missionary orders entering the country.[88] Instead, it only exacerbated ecclesiastical division.[89] Though he was a Jesuit, Martinez had already in Macao clashed with Valignano, the head of the Society's Asian missions, and in Japan he set out to arrogate to himself secular pomp and ecclesiastical power in ways that antagonized both the Jesuits and the Franciscans. He also managed to antagonize Japanese government officials by his discourtesy and insensitivity to national customs.[90] He lasted not much more than a year, and few were sorry when he left. His successor, Monsignor Luis de Cerqueira, also a Jesuit, was bishop of Japan for fifteen years (1598–1614). Though he was more mission-minded and irenic than Martinez, he was no more successful in reducing the interservice friction.[91] "Between Jesuits and Franciscans in Japan it was all but war to the knife," wrote Murdoch in 1903.[92] One of the results was another outbreak of persecution, the martyrdoms of 1597.

Even before Bishop Martinez left, the first shock fell. As though by design, Hideyoshi's central government struck first where Christianity was most deeply rooted and Portuguese trade most dominant, Nagasaki. Debate still rages over whether it was the rivalry of the two missionary orders, Franciscan and Jesuit,[93] or the expanding ambitions of the two Catholic empires, Portugal and Spain, which was primarily to blame for Hideyoshi's resurrection of the almost forgotten anti-Christian decrees of 1587. Japanese Buddhists had long warned him that the real threat to Japan was a combination of both factors, Western military aggression spearheaded by a Western missionary fifth column.[94] But there is no doubt that the affair of the *San Felipe* touched off the explosion.

This Spanish galleon, bound for Acapulco from Manila, had run aground on the Japanese island of Shikoku in 1596. It was loaded with guns, ammunition, seven missionaries, goods worth a king's ransom, and (if the report quickly carried to Hideyoshi were true, which it undoubtedly was not),[95] a fool of a pilot who threatened that if the Japanese seized the cargo, Spain would retaliate immediately with its irresistible, worldwide military might. It is difficult to believe the rumor being circulated at the same time that the pilot had also declared that Franciscan missionaries in Japan were preparing the way for just such a Spanish conquest as in Mexico, Peru, and the Philippines.

The truth of the affair will probably never be known,[96] but all Japan soon saw its tragic result. Hideyoshi angrily ordered the arrest of the meddling missionaries — six Franciscans and three Japanese Jesuits (who were probably seized by mistake) — and fifteen Japanese Christians from the Franciscan hospital in Kyoto. First, they bloodily mutilated one ear of each, then paraded them through the streets of Kyoto and sent them to Nagasaki for public crucifixion. The sentence read: "I have ordered these foreigners to be treated thus, because they have come from the Philippines to Japan, calling themselves ambassadors, although they were not so; because they have remained here for long without my permission; because in defiance of my prohibition they have built churches, preached their religion, and caused disorders."[97]

> In Nagasaki the twenty-six martyrs (two more had volunteered to join them on the way) were tied to a semicircle of crosses. The youngest — three boys only twelve, thirteen, and fifteen years old — raised their heads to sing a psalm, "O Children, Praise the Lord." Then all were mercifully pierced with lances to speed their deaths, and they died. Their bodies were left hanging there for nine months.[98]

Restoration Gives Way to Persecution: Ieyasu (1598–1614)

Less than a year after the martyrs' remains were at last removed, Hideyoshi himself died, the missionaries came out of hiding, the war with Korea ended, the Christian generals returned, and for another decade or more under Hideyoshi's eventual successor, Tokugawa Ieyasu, the church again found a measure of toleration and success. In the next two years Bishop Cerqueira wrote home that Jesuit baptisms alone numbered about seventy thousand. Meanwhile the Franciscans, returning, were allowed to extend Christian evangelism for the first time to what is now the Tokyo (then Edo) area; they built their first church there in 1599. Remembering the martyrdoms, they resolved to avoid mass baptisms and worked instead, as Luis Sotelo wrote to his superior in 1607, not for "quantity but quality."[99]

But a combination of adverse developments all too quickly tempered the growing optimism of the Christians. The first of these was the fall of the greatest of the Christian daimyos, the hero of the Korean War, Konishi Yukinaga, in whose territory church membership was growing explosively at the rate, briefly, of more than twenty-five thousand baptisms a year.[100] It now seems certain, as Richard Drummond has pointed out, that it was fear of the growing power of the Christian daimyos as a threat to Japanese national unity, and not alarm at the expanding Western imperialism of Spain and Portugal, that was the primary factor in the final prohibition of Christianity in Japan in 1614.[101]

In the civil war that broke out in 1600 between Ieyasu and the heirs of Hideyoshi, Konishi loyally defended the six-year-old son of his former commander, Hideyoshi, and was defeated. Ieyasu's victory proved to be a mighty step forward toward the final unification of Japan, but it was also a grim warning that loyalty to the emerging national government superseded all regional or religious loyalties. The captured Konishi, refusing to commit hara-kiri because he was a Christian, was beheaded. Christians feared countrywide reprisals, all the more so when his territory was turned over to his greatest rival, the Buddhist general Kato Kiyomasa, for a brutal persecution that would cut the number of Christians in that part of Japan in half.[102] All through the troubled history of the great continent come these sharp reminders of the power of the ruler to limit the progress of the church, one of the most painful lessons in the history of Asian Christianity. As though aware of this, Ieyasu forbade any further conversions of the daimyos by the missionaries. From 1600 to 1614, according to Jennes, only one ruling member of the nobility, the lord of Wakasa, was baptized. The sacrament was performed in secret.[103]

The First Protestants (1600)

Another influence that weakened the growth of Catholicism in Japan was the arrival of the first Protestants in 1600. They were not missionaries but rather sea traders from Holland and England, cutting away at the hitherto unchallenged supremacy of the Portuguese and Spanish on the high seas. The Dutch ("red-haired barbarians," the Japanese called them) were the ones who finally displaced the Portuguese in Japan, but the earliest and most influential of the Protestant arrivals was a shipwrecked English navigator, Will Adams, who walked the razor's edge of court intrigue to win the confidence of Ieyasu and pushed the Jesuit Rodrigues aside as court interpreter and principal trade negotiator for the shogun. In that capacity he steadily undermined the ruler's trust in Portuguese and Spanish traders and Catholic missionaries. "The significance of this event," writes Drummond, "is that an Englishman with apparently no missionary concern took the place of the linguistically most skilled Portuguese missionaries as confidant of the supreme ruler."[104]

The loss of the Japan trade monopoly by the Portuguese was a devastating blow to Catholic missions. It hurt them financially, for they had been accustomed to generous but irregular support from both Portuguese and Japanese sources that profited from the trade. Even more, it hurt them politically, for when Dutch victories removed Japan's fear of Iberian military expansion,[105] the Catholic missions lost their umbrella of imperial protection and were left vulnerable to the power of a Japanese state now unified under the Tokugawa shogunate. The squeeze began as early as the rout of the Spanish Armada by England in 1588. That overwhelming defeat speeded little Holland to eventual victory in its eighty-year war of independence against mighty Spain; this, in turn, allowed the Dutch to turn their attention from Spain to Portugal in the Far East. Boxer calls the sixteenth to seventeenth centuries' global struggle between Holland and Portugal, two small nations with imperial ambitions, the real First World War, more deserving of that name than the twentieth-century World War I in 1914. It was literally "waged in four continents and on seven seas," "a struggle for the spice trade of Asia, the slavery trade of West Africa, and for the sugar trade of Brazil. The final result was, on balance, a victory for the Dutch in Asia, a draw in West Africa, and a victory for Portugal in Brazil."[106]

The Dutch attack began far away from Japan in the Caribbean and in Brazil. It spread to Asia with the formation of the Dutch East Indies Company in 1602 and reached its climax with the capture from Portugal of the principal Spice Islands (Indonesia) in 1605, Formosa in 1624, Cochin on the Malabar Coast in 1633, Malacca, "the Singapore of the seventeenth century," in 1641, and Colombo on the island of Ceylon in 1658. In many of these places Dutch rule proved short and temporary. Only in the Dutch East Indies did it become a significant Protestant missionary presence, as we shall see. In Japan, though the Dutch managed to maintain a tiny trading toehold in Nagasaki for two hundred years, they brought no Protestant church. They only weakened the Catholic missions in Japan and hastened the so-called Christian century in Japan to its end.

The Great Persecution: The Beginning of the End

The year 1614 is often described as the beginning of the end of that early Japanese Christianity, but it might be more accurate to date the first tremors of impending disaster to 1612, when the Franciscan church in Ieyasu's capital at Tokyo (Edo) was destroyed and far to the southwest, the daimyo of Arima, whose family had long been famous as protectors of the Jesuits, was caught in a bribery scandal and executed. His son and successor, fearful of further reprisals, immediately apostatized and turned persecutor. He burned a number of Christians alive, trying to force them to recant, until massive Christian demonstrations by some thirty thousand Japanese memorializing the martyrs frightened him into desisting. The outpouring of public support for the Christians, however, only further increased the government's suspicions of them.[107]

It was then that Christians first began to lose hope in the new shogunate and to realize that government policy was changing from the earlier tolerance of Ieyasu to suspicion and distrust and, on the part of his son, Hidetada, undisguised antagonism. The old shogun had named his third son as shogun seven years earlier, in 1605. This important transition established a remarkable succession of fourteen of Ieyasu's blood descendants, who ruled as Tokugawa shoguns for the next 260 years.

Besides turning over the title to his son while still keeping control of the government, Ieyasu was distancing himself from the Christians and turning more and more toward the old Japanese religions. A neo-Confucian advisor, Hayashi Razan (1583–1657), pointed out to him the stabilizing social power of Confucianism in Chinese history.[108]

The unification of Japan produced a renewal of national pride and strengthened the ancient state religion, Shinto. The old shogun made a great show of reconstructing the nation's imperial shrine at Ise. Buddhism, too, which both of the early "unifiers" (Nobunaga and Hideyoshi) had fought to the death, experienced a revival. Ieyasu was himself a Buddhist of the Jodo (Pure Land) sect and was considerably influenced by a Zen Buddhist advisor, Soden (or Suden). Encouraged, a whole school of Buddhist scholars attacked Christians with renewed vigor in a considerable series of widely read accusations of treason and heresy.[109]

In January 1614 Ieyasu issued the infamous anti-Christian edict that marked the point of no return. In harsh, explicit language, he ordered the closure of all churches, the deportation of all missionaries, and prohibited all practice of Christianity by the Japanese whether in public or in secret.[110] The edict makes his reasons clear. Christianity, he charged, opposes all three of Japan's great religions: Buddhism, Shinto ("the gods"), and Confucianism ("benevolence and right doing"). It threatens Japan's possession of its own land, and it aims to overthrow the country's national government:

> The Christian band have come to Japan not only sending their merchant vessels to exchange commodities, but also longing to disseminate an evil law, to overthrow right doctrine, so they may change the government of the country, and obtain possession of the land.
>
> Japan is the country of gods and Buddha ... The principles of benevolence and right doing are held to be of prime importance ... Quickly cast out the evil law and spread our true Law more and more ... Let Heaven and the Four Seas hear this and obey.[111]

Buddhists rejoiced when there was added to the edict a series of instructions to their priests ordering them to see that everyone in the country was enrolled as a member of one or another of the Buddhist sects.[112] A special cause for Buddhist celebration was the defection from the Christian faith of Fabian Fukan (Fukansai Habian), who for more than twenty years had been an outstanding Japanese Jesuit, author (in 1605) of the best Christian exposé of the falsehood of Buddhism and Confucianism (*The Myote Dialogue*).[113] In many public debates he had invariably and spectacularly humiliated his Buddhist opponents. But about the year 1608 he disappeared. It was whispered that he had left the order under suspicion of scandal with "a devout woman who lived a common life in a House" next to the Jesuit center in Kyoto. He reappeared in 1620 and shockingly and publicly renounced his Christian faith. He proceeded to publish "the first anti-Christian book in Japan," turning on his former colleagues with all the venom of a discredited ally. The Jesuits, he wrote, "do not even consider the Japanese to be human."[114] That side of his attack was patently false, but his carefully written critique of his former faith became the touchstone for a wave of anti-Christian literature that added fire to the persecutions and inflamed a whole nation's xenophobic fear of foreigners and foreign religion for the next two hundred years.

By 1614, according to the most reliable estimates, the number of Japanese Christians had tripled in the thirty-five years since Valignano's first arrival in Japan. Church growth had been phenomenal.[115] There were only about 3,000 Christians when Xavier left Japan in 1551. In the next twenty years, under Torres, the number increased tenfold. In the next decade, under Cabral as superior, it quadrupled, which suggests that despite his stubborn and sometimes insensitive ways, Cabral's stern rule was no failure. At the time of the 1614 edict the baptized membership of the churches leaped from 100,000 or 120,000 to 300,000.[116]

But far more impressive than the numbers, in which there is always a large margin of error, were the courage and fidelity of Japanese Christians under the cruel, sustained pressures of persecution that now descended upon them.

The edict was issued in January, but the deportation of the missionaries was interrupted by lack of transportation and was further confused when the bishop of Japan, Luis Cerqueira, died and an unseemly dispute erupted among the waiting missionaries over who should succeed him. A diocesan commission of seven Japanese priests and three clerics "in minor orders" elected the Jesuit provincial Valentin Carvalho as interim apostolic administrator, but some dissident Franciscans and Dominicans objected and moved to transfer ecclesiastical authority over Japan from Macao to Manila by electing a Dominican to replace him. However, the head of the Dominican mission in Japan, Zumárraga, who had gone into hiding in hopes of martyrdom rather than deportation, was greatly disturbed at so public a division in the church when it most needed unity, and he ordered his rebellious missionaries to accept the Jesuit.[117]

Faithfulness to death as martyrs became an article of faith among the Japanese believers, and bystanders marveled at the calm with which they accepted torture and death without resistance or recantation. All year long their churches were burned, demolished, or closed. At the beginning of the year, of Jesuits alone there had been 121 members (62 priests, including 7 Japanese, and 59 brothers mostly Japanese), with another 245 Japanese seminarians and catechists. By the end of the year only a few were left.[118] The missionaries and many of their assistants, a total of ninety-five, had been deported to Macao and Manila in November, but a courageous band remained in hiding, including the brave Zumárraga, who achieved his wish and perished gloriously in the great martyrdom of 1622.[119]

As long as Ieyasu lived, however, the number of actual martyrdoms remained comparatively low. He advised torture to produce public apostasy rather than execution, which only gave the church more martyrs. But Ieyasu died in 1616, and his son Hidetada, who ruled alone for the next seven years, was more ruthless. The missionaries still in hiding were flushed out and decapitated. The famous Christian daimyos of Kyushu, unable to endure the pressure, turned persecutor to save their lives and families.[120] Martyrdoms climbed to approximately one hundred a year. Hidetada's hatred of Christians reached its peak in the "great martyrdom" of 1622 at Nagasaki. On a hill near that so-called Christian city, twenty-three martyrs, mostly Japanese, were slowly roasted to death on stakes; the wives and children of the Japanese were beheaded nearby.[121] An anti-Christian official noted during later martyrdoms that the Korean martyrs were particularly brave under torture, "especially the women."[122]

In describing the horrors of the next thirty years, during which the entire Christian population was systematically burned, strangled, starved, tortured, or driven underground, it is better to understate rather than exaggerate. The record needs no embellishment. The third shogun, Ieyasu's grandson Iemitsu (1623–1651), was more merciless than his grandfather and more brutal than his father. Under Ieyasu, noted one Japanese historian, the foreign missionaries were expelled but not one was killed; under Hidetada they were killed but not tortured; but the sadistic Iemitsu enjoyed watching to see whether their torture would end in recantation or death.[123]

Within three years an anti-Christian edict by the governor of Nagasaki stamped out almost all that was still visible of Christianity in Japan's most openly Christian city. Laures, discounting the exaggerations, speaks of at least 4,045 "well-documented martyrdoms" by 1651. If those not officially martyred but killed in the tragic Christian insurrection at Shimabara are included, he estimates that at least 13 percent of the whole Christian community gave up their lives for their faith.[124]

The tortures were fiendish. Some were killed by a gruesome dance of death in straw raincoats set afire while their hands were tied behind their backs.[125] Thousands of suspected Christians were flushed out of hiding and asked to step on metal plaques bearing the face of Christ. Those who refused faced imprisonment, loss of all property, and torture. Many apostatized. Shusaku Endo's novel *Silence* captures better than any history book the agony of the apostates in times when even the most devout wondered why God was silent while God's people suffered. His tragic figure Kichijiro prays in tears:

> Father, I betrayed you. I trampled on the picture of Christ...For a moment this foot was on his face..., the most beautiful face that any man can ever know...Even now that face is looking at me with eyes of pity..."Trample!" said those compassionate eyes. "Trample. Your foot...must suffer like all the feet that have stepped on this plaque. That pain alone is enough. I understand."
>
> "Lord, I resented your silence."
>
> "I was not silent. I suffered beside you."[126]

But many also chose to endure the pain without denying their Lord. After 1632, when neither burnings nor crucifixions nor immersion and suffocation in "the hot sulphur springs of Mount Unzen" produced enough apostates who could be paraded and humiliated to destroy the credibility of the Christian faith, a more ingenious form of torture was invented: "the pit." Its most notable success was the apostasy of the leader of the Jesuit mission, Christopher Ferreira, who dangled in bursting pain, suspended head downward in a pit of excrement, for six hours before signaling his submission. He was the first missionary to apostatize. Much later, no longer able to endure the shame, he is said to have recanted the denial of his faith.[127] Perhaps it was the example of those who endured to the end — like a young Japanese woman who suffered fourteen days of that twisting torment before she died — that explains the comparatively small proportion of apostates relative to the number of martyrs in the great persecutions.[128]

There were also, of course, mass defections of nominal Christians, especially when a Christian daimyo left the faith under political pressure. "Mass conversions were sometimes followed by mass desertions," a Catholic historian remarks.[129] But there is a difference between voluntary defection and apostasy under torture or threat of torture, and few periods of church history can record more instances of grace under pressure than the Christian century in Japan.

The farmers' revolt at Shimabara in 1637 is a picture of the age. There, in the "Christian province" (Arima) in the shadow of the sleeping volcano Mount Unzen, a fiendish religious persecution combining tax extortion, economic discontent, and torture of wives and daughters of the peasants led to a Christian farmers' revolt, pitting thirty-seven thousand embattled villagers[130] against an entire samurai army of a hundred thousand men. Not all were Christians, but they fought under banners with small red crosses, shouting "Jesus" and "Maria." Only when they ran out

of ammunition and had been starved out of the last of their food sup-
plies were they overrun and massacred — men, women, and children.
The victory was humiliating to the Japanese military, which was reluctant to credit mere peasants, and Christians at that, with such bravery.
The military tried to shift the reason for the unexpectedly stiff resistance to a more respectable enemy, the Portuguese, whom they accused
of fomenting and aiding the rebellion.[131]

Silence (1640–1800)

In the final anti-Christian edict known as the "closed country" statement of 1639, Japan cut all commercial and religious ties with Portugal
and declared the country off-limits to Portuguese on pain of death. So
ended ninety-five years of Portuguese influence in Japan. It was also the
virtual end of the Christian century in Japan. The revolt at Shimabara
was the final, bloody blow to a church that had been driven gradually
underground ever since its national prohibition by Ieyasu in 1614. Flare-
ups of persecution continued, such as the great persecution in Edo[132] and
the case of Ferreira. But by 1638 there survived in Japan only five hidden
priests, three Jesuits and two Franciscans. All had been seized and tortured until they either won their martyrdom or apostatized. The church
was left without sacraments, proper baptism, and leadership. Even when
a nonmissionary trade mission was sent to Japan in 1640 in an attempt to
at least restore trade between Japan and the Catholic West, its entire crew
was arrested, and sixty-one who refused to recant were beheaded.[133]

G. B. Sansom, writing about the clash of cultures in Japan, notes a
poignant contrast between the "strong current of affection and admiration for the Japanese people," which he finds in all the writings of the
missionaries in this period, and their ultimate fate:

> One cannot wonder at the affection that the missionaries felt for the people
> of Japan, since nowhere else in Asia were Christian propagandists able to
> gain such a ready hearing for the gospel from all classes, and nowhere were
> they more kindly treated. Yet nowhere were they more savagely repressed.
> This paradox is to be explained by the dual character of Japanese society,
> which combined a strong sense of social ethics with a great ruthlessness in
> the enforcement of law.[134]

Occasional outbreaks of violence against the hidden remnants occurred
in 1649, 1658, and 1667, but the last foreign missionary to enter Japan in
those silent, violent years was an Italian abbot, John-Baptist Sidotti, one
of the twelve members of the Rota in Rome (the papal supreme court).[135]
He was sent to Asia with de Tournon's mission concerning the rites
controversies in China, but fulfilled a lifelong dream by continuing on
to Japan, landing on Kyushu one dark night in 1708. It is worth noting
as a chronological reference point that this last of the Catholic fathers

in premodern Japan reached his goal in the same year that the first Protestant missionaries landed on the Asian continent in India.

Alone and unable even to speak intelligible Japanese, Sidotti came on his hopeless mission not as crusader but as a symbol of Christian unity with the persecuted, and perhaps as partial atonement for the apostasy of those whose spirit had proved tragically weaker than their flesh. He came prepared for martyrdom, but thanks to the good offices of his interrogator, a wise Japanese scholar named Arai Hakuseki (1657–1725), the founder of scientific historiography in Japan, he was not killed. Hakuseki, as chief Confucian advisor to the shogun was no friend of Christianity. As a religion, he considered Christianity inferior even to Buddhism. But he was much impressed with the tall priest and came to the pragmatic conclusion that, contrary to the Buddhist and nationalist propaganda of the times, the Christian missionaries had not been responsible for Portuguese and Spanish imperialist expansion and were no threat to Japanese sovereignty.[136] He was "the first Tokugawa statesman to reject the idea that Christian missionary expansion was inevitably a forerunner of European temporal conquest."[137] Nevertheless, he concluded, "once the doctrine begins to flourish," rebellion spreads, as it did in China, leading perhaps to the fall of the Ming dynasty. As for Sidotti, Hakuseki advised: send him home, or put him in prison for life, or kill him, "but the worst thing you could do is kill him."[138]

Sidotti died in prison some six years later.[139] The Tokugawa shoguns were satisfied that the church, too, was finally dead. But it survived longer than the shoguns. Before two centuries could pass, the last of the shoguns would discover that they were wrong. The resignation of Tokugawa Yoshinobu, fifteenth in direct descent from Tokugawa Ieyasu and described as "one of Meiji Japan's ablest nonentities,"[140] ended almost seven hundred years of feudal military government and at long last returned power to the emperor of Japan. Then, the long-hidden church, like the hidden fires of Mount Unzen brooding over the holocaust at Shimabara but not extinct, would burst into life again. One historian of Christianity in modern Japan, James Phillips, reminds us that about one-half of all the Catholics in Japan today are descendants of the hidden Christians of the years of silence.[141]

Chronology of Events

1500	Japanese expansionism curtailed by the West.
1514	Bishopric of Funchal created for all Portuguese overseas territories.
1533	Suffragan bishops of Angra, Cabo Verde, São Thome, and Goa separated from Funchal (Schütte, *Valignano's Mission Principles for Japan*, 1/1:110).

1542	Portuguese discover Japan.
1547	Xavier meets Anjiro in Malacca.
1548	Anjiro baptized in Goa.
1549	Xavier lands in Japan, with Anjiro.
1551	Xavier leaves Japan. Only priest de Torres; eight hundred converts.
1551	Ouchi Yoshishige, protector of Christians, defeated.
1552–1556	Only two priests in Japan.
1556–1562	Three priests in Japan.
1563	Conversion of Takayama Hida (Darius); his son Takayama Ukon (Justus) baptized.
1559	Oda Nobunaga (1534–1582), with Hideyoshi's help, becomes daimyo of Owari (Nagoya), east of Kyoto.
1560	Vilela builds chapel in Kyoto; protected by fourteenth Ashikaga shogun, Yoshitseru.
1562	Omura Sumitada converted, first Christian daimyo, baptized in 1563.
1563–1564	Takayama Hida (Dario), father of Ukon, converted.
1565	Shogun Yoshitseru killed; missionaries expelled from Kyoto; his brother appeals to Oda Nobunaga.
1568	Nobunaga, de facto shogun, unifies central Japan.
1569	Nobunaga's first meeting with a Jesuit priest, Luis Frois; turns against Buddhists who had supported his enemies. Francisco Cabral reaches Japan as regional superior of Malacca, Macao, and the Japan mission.
1570	Thirty thousand Christians in Japan. Nagasaki opened to foreign trade by Omura Sumitada.
1571	Nobunaga wars against Buddhists; destroys Mount Hiei monastery.
1578	Diocese of Macao given jurisdiction of Japan. Conversion of Otomo Yoshishige (Sorin), daimyo of Kyushu.
1579–1582	Valignano's first stay in Japan. First seminary opened (at Arima, Kyushu); another at Kyoto. Jesuits report 150,000 Christians in Japan.
1580	Omura Sumitada cedes Nagasaki to the Jesuits. First Japanese bishopric (Funai) moved to Nagasaki (1580–1581).
1582–1584	Hideyoshi (1537–1598), supported by Ieyasu, wrests control of Central Japan from Oda family.

1587	Five Christian daimyos in Japan.
1587–1598	"Period of Restricted Toleration." Hideyoshi issues anti-Christian, anti-Portuguese decree.
1588	Sixtus V creates Diocese of Funai (Bungo).
1590	Hideyoshi completes unification of Japan.
1590–1592	Valignano's second stay in Japan. Finds seventy Japanese novices in training. The first Japanese to visit Europe (1584–1586) return after eight and a half years; all join Jesuit order.
1592, 1597	Hideyoshi's generals invade Korea.
1593	Franciscans enter Japan, welcomed by Hideyoshi as Spanish alternative to Portuguese presence in Japan. Jesuit monopoly broken.
1595–1596	137 Jesuit missionaries (only 10 legally); 660 seminarians and catechists, and 300,000 Christians; 10 Christian daimyos.
1596	First resident bishop of Japan, Pierre Martinez.
1597	First executions of Christians, Nagasaki.
1598	Valignani returns, with second Jesuit bishop, Luis de Cerqueira. Hideyoshi dies.
1600	Ieyasu (1542–1616) defeats rivals; becomes ruler of Japan but not appointed shogun until 1603. Executes Christian daimyo Konishi for supporting Hideyoshi. First Dutch ship reaches Japan.
1601–1613	"Period of Toleration." *Daimyo* forbidden to convert. First Japanese Jesuits ordained; Rodrigues Tcuzzi becomes Ieyasu's advisor. Ieyasu legalizes three churches (Nagasaki, Kyoto, Osaka).
1602	First Dominicans arrive (Satsuma); Augustinians (Hirado).
1603	Ieyasu appointed shogun; makes Tokyo (Edo) his administrative center.
1608	William Adams, anti-Catholic English pilot (shipwrecked 1600), becomes commercial advisor for Ieyasu.
1609	Dutch open trading factory in Hirado. Jesuits report 220,000 Christians under their care in Japan.
1610	Sotelo (Franciscan) pioneers mission in North Japan; daimyo Date Masamune grants religious freedom in his territory.
1613	Portuguese monopoly of Japanese trade broken. Persecution in Edo.
1614	Christians in Japan reckoned at from three hundred thousand to five hundred thousand in population of about 20 million. Ieyasu issues edict of banishment. "Almost all churches razed or closed" (Jennes, *A History of the Catholic Church in Japan*, 120).

1616–1623	Hiteda Shogunate. Anti-Christian decree: foreign priests executed; foreign trade limited to Nagasaki and Hirado.
1620	First anti-Christian book in Japan (by Fabian Fukan, who had apostatized from the Jesuits).
1622	Great martyrdom of Nagasaki.
1623–1633	Iemitsu Shogunate (1623–1639).
1623	Ten years of persecution (1623–1633); mass defections; underground Christians.
1633	Christopher Ferreira (Jesuit's provincial) tortured; first missionary to apostatize.
1637–1638	Shimabara (former Arima "Christian province") rebellion.
1639–1854	Closing of the country; Portuguese trade ends, 1639.
1642	Rubino, visitor of the Far Eastern Missions, and four priests enter Japan; they are tortured and executed (Jennes, *A History of the Catholic Church in Japan*, 170).
1643	Ten European, Chinese, and Japanese missionaries land in disguise as samurai; they are captured, tortured; they apostatize but later recant apostasy.
1649, 1658, 1667	Mass martyrdoms.
1685	Last Portuguese attempt to restore relations with Japan fails.
1697	Last great martyrdom in Mino, thirty-five victims.
1708	Last missionary to enter Japan, Giovanni Battista Sidotti.

NOTES

1. Quoted in Mary Elizabeth Berry, *Hideyoshi* (Cambridge: Harvard University Press, 1982), 3.

2. The phrase "the Christian century" is widely used. See, for example, Charles R. Boxer, *The Christian Century in Japan, 1549–1650* (Berkeley and Los Angeles: University of California Press; London: Cambridge University Press, 1951), which is the best general survey of the period.

3. On the role of the religions in early Japanese history, see G. B. Sansom, *Japan: A Short Cultural History*, revised library edition (New York: D. Appleton-Century Co., 1931), esp. 51ff. on Shinto, 116ff. on Buddhism, and 111–116 on the lesser influence of Confucianism.

4. I adapt the chronological framework from Gordon D. Laman, "Our Nagasaki Legacy: An Examination of the Period of Persecution of Christianity and its Impact on Subsequent Christian Mission in Japan," *NAJT* 28/29 (March/September 1982): 94–141.

5. Anjiro's own account of himself in his sole surviving letter, a Spanish translation of the lost Portuguese original (Goa, November 29, 1548) is edited by Josef Wicki, in vol. 1 of the *Documenta Indica,* in *Monumenta Historica Societatis Iesu* (Rome: MHSI, 1948), vol. 1, sec. 2:332–341.

6. Xavier's January 20, 1548, letter is published (in Portuguese) in G. Schurhammer and J. Wicki, *Epistolae S. Francisci Xaverii* (Rome: MHSI, 1944), 1:391–392; and (in Latin) in *Monumenta Xaveriana* (Madrid: Typis Augustine Avriel, 1899–1900), 1:445–446.

7. Schurhammer, *Francis Xavier,* 4:9–10.

8. James Murdoch and Isoh Yamagata, *A History of Japan during the Century of Early Foreign Intercourse (1542–1651),* 3 vols. (Kobe, Japan: The Chronicle, 1903), 2:61.

9. Schurhammer, *Francis Xavier,* 4:20–21, 126.

10. The word "daimyo" is often translated "duke." The daimyos, of whom there were many, were not in any way equal in power, wealth, or extent of territory. An old but solid history of this period in Japan is Murdoch and Yamagata, *A History of Japan,* esp. 2:387ff., with map. A more up-to-date work is Sir George Bailey Sansom, *A History of Japan,* 3 vols. (Stanford, Calif.: Stanford University Press, 1958–1963), esp. 2:263–299, 346–351, 371–377, 404; 3:5, 7, 36–44, 168–169.

11. Boxer, *The Christian Century in Japan, 1549–1650,* 56.

12. Broderick, *St. Francis Xavier (1506–1552),* 428–431.

13. Murdoch and Yamagata, *A History of Japan,* 2:63.

14. For his conversations with the Zen abbot in Kagoshima and his letter to his colleague Torres, see Schurhammer, *Francis Xavier,* 4:72ff., 239–240; and Stephen Neill's concise summary in *History of Christian Missions,* 156.

15. Schurhammer, *Francis Xavier,* 4:82ff.

16. Paraphrasing George Bailey Sansom, *The Western World and Japan: A Study in the Interaction of European and Asiatic Cultures* (New York: Alfred A. Knopf, 1950), 117, 123.

17. Xavier, Letter 104, April 9, 1552, cited in Henry James Coleridge, *The Life and Letters of St. Francis Xavier,* 2 vols., 4th ed. (London: Burns & Oates, 1886; reprint 1921), 2:485.

18. Schurhammer, *Francis Xavier,* 4:223–226. See also P. Luis Frois, *Die Geschichte Japans (1549–1578). Nach der Handschrift der Ajudabibliotheck in Lissabon,* trans. and commentary by G. Schurhammer and E. A. Voretzsch (Leipzig: Verlag der Asia Major, 1926), 15.

19. Xavier, Letter 136, January 29, 1552, in Coleridge, *The Life and Letters of St. Francis Xavier,* 2:338–339.

20. As quoted by R. H. Glover, *The Progress of Worldwide Missions* (New York: Harper, 1952), 72.

21. Xavier, Letter 136, Cochin, January 29, 1552, in Coleridge, *The Life and Letters of St. Francis Xavier,* 2:331–350.

22. See Schurhammer, *Francis Xavier,* 4:129–130 n. 22, citing Alcaova in 1552, and Frois, the historian, who knew Anjiro personally.

23. As at Hirado in 1558. See Joseph Jennes, *A History of the Catholic Church in Japan, from Its Beginnings to the Early Meiji Era (1549–1873)* (Tokyo: Committee of the Apostolate, 1959; reprint, Oriens Institute for Religious Research, 1973), 14.

24. Otomo Yoshishige (later called Sorin), though a protector, did not convert to the Christian faith until about twenty-six years later, in 1578. His younger

brother, who became daimyo of Yamaguchi, took the name Ouchi Yoshitaka. See Murdoch and Yamagata, *A History of Japan*, 2:58ff.

25. These are the estimates of J. F. Schütte, discounting some of the more pious early exaggerations. See Schütte, *Valignano's Mission Principles for Japan*, 1/1:xvii, 199. Cf. Jennes, *A History of the Catholic Church in Japan*, 241; and Johannes Laures, *The Catholic Church in Japan: A Short History* (Tokyo and Rutland, Vt.: Charles Tuttle, 1954), 177–178. On Cabral's racial bias against the Japanese, see George Elison, *Deus Destroyed: The Image of Christianity in Early Modern Japan*, Harvard East Asian Monographs 141 (Cambridge, Mass.: Harvard University Press, 1988; reprint of 1973 edition), 16, 56.

26. Jennes, *A History of the Catholic Church in Japan*, 26–27. Examples of Japanese Buddhist terms no longer to be used in Catholic writings were *Hotoke* (Buddha) as a name for God; *Buppo* (law of Buddha) either for religion in general or for the law of God; and *So* (Buddhist priest) for Christian clergy. And a distinction was made between the Buddhist hell, which was not eternal, and the Christian concept of hell.

27. For a full report of the debate, see Frois, *Die Geschichte Japans (1549–1578)*, 377–385. Nobunaga at that time was already the most powerful man in Japan; his religious advisor was Nichijo Shonin. Lourenco also converted the governor of Kyoto and the former daimyo of Omi.

28. Johannes Laures, *Studies on Takayama Ukon*, in *Instituto Portugues de Hongkong, Secção de Historia* (Macau: Imprensa Nacional, 1955), esp. 9.

29. Elison, *Deus Destroyed*, 77.

30. Laures, *The Catholic Church in Japan*, 22ff.

31. Frois, *Die Geschichte Japans (1549–1578)*, 27, 58, 63; Laures, *The Catholic Church in Japan*, 22–24.

32. Reported by Francis Cabral, the vice provincial (quoted in Murdoch and Yamagata, *A History of Japan*, 1:86).

33. Murdoch and Yamagata, *A History of Japan*, 1:85–88; and Boxer, *The Christian Century in Japan, 1549–1650*, 100–102.

34. Elison, *Deus Destroyed*, 86.

35. Michael Cooper, *Rodrigues the Interpreter: An Early Jesuit in Japan and China* (New York: Weatherhill, 1974), 106. On Nobunaga's shogunate, see Sansom, *A History of Japan*, 2:273–310.

36. See Murdoch and Yamagata, *A History of Japan*, 2:172ff. Cf. Sansom, *A History of Japan*, 2:292ff.

37. Murdoch and Yamagata, *A History of Japan*, 2:171.

38. P. F. Xavier de Charlevoix (1682–1761), quoted in Murdoch and Yamagata, *A History of Japan*, 2:182.

39. On fanatical Buddhist militancy and its decline, see Sansom, *Japan: A Short Cultural History*, 375–376, 405ff., 477; and Boxer, *The Christian Century in Japan, 1549–1650*, 69–71, 159. The equally militant monks of the True Pure Land Sect, who had more popular support among the peasant class on their large landholdings, resisted until 1580. Christianity found the greatest religious resistance to conversion among Pure Land Buddhists (Sansom, *The Western World and Japan*, 132ff.).

40. Frois, *Die Geschichte Japans (1549–1578)*, 370. On his reception and interview with Nobunaga, see 372ff.

41. The name has usually been spelled Valignani, but Valignano is more accurate.

42. These visits were in 1579–1582, 1590–1592, and 1598–1603, the last as Visitor to Japan but not to the rest of Asia. The two essential sources on Valignano are Schütte, *Valignano's Mission Principles for Japan*; and Frois, *Die Geschichte Japans (1549–1578)*. An important recent analysis confirming papal support of Valignano's policies is by Andrew C. Ross, "Alessandro Valignano," in *MIS* 27, no. 4 (October 1999): 503–513.

43. On Cabral's views, and his fundamental differences with Valignano, see Schütte, *Valignano's Mission Principles for Japan*, 1/1:250–268, 376–378.

44. Boxer, *The Christian Century in Japan, 1549–1650*, 74, quoting from Valignano's "Japan Summary" of 1580. Comparing the Japanese with Africans or Indians, the Portuguese considered the Japanese to be white.

45. Broderick, *St. Francis Xavier (1506–1552)*, 363. The citation is imprecise and may be a paraphrase or summary. On the development of Valignano's estimate of the Japanese, see Schütte, *Valignano's Mission Principles for Japan*, 1/1:248, 271ff.

46. Elison, *Deus Destroyed*, 16, quoting Cabral who by then, in 1596, was Jesuit provincial of Goa.

47. Schütte, *Valignano's Mission Principles for Japan*, 1/1:243–246, quoting a letter from Cabral to J. Alvarez.

48. Cabral was succeeded as superior of the mission by Gaspar Coelho (see Schütte, *Valignano's Mission Principles for Japan*, 1/1:377ff.; 1/2:97, 126).

49. In 1581 Valignano wrote a manual of instructions for his missionaries in Japan (trans. J. F. Schütte, *Il Ceremoniale per i missionari del Giappone*, and summarized in Schütte, *Valignano's Mission Principles for Japan*, 1/2:155–190).

50. Schütte, *Valignano's Mission Principles for Japan*, 1/2:243ff.

51. Schütte, *Valignano's Mission Principles for Japan*, 1/2:250–251, 257, 336; 1/2:21, 51, 234.

52. Schütte, *Valignano's Mission Principles for Japan*, 1/2:224–226, 233, 243, 245.

53. Schütte, *Valignano's Mission Principles for Japan*, 1/2:276–277; Jennes, *A History of the Catholic Church in Japan*, 44–49. The two seminaries were at Arima (in northwestern Kyushu) and Azuchi (near Kyoto).

54. Jennes, *A History of the Catholic Church in Japan*, 105–106. The priests were Sebastian Kimura and Luis Niabara. A Japanese diocesan priest was ordained in 1604. Between 1601 and 1613 eight Japanese Jesuits and seven diocesan clergy were ordained.

55. Schütte has a long summary of the contents of the *Japanese Catechism (Catechismus Christianae Fidei)*, written in 1580, including an analysis of its treatment of Japanese religion (Schütte, *Valignano's Mission Principles for Japan*, 1/2:67–89).

56. Richard H. Drummond, *A History of Christianity in Japan* (Grand Rapids, Mich.: William B. Eerdmans, 1971), 59, 62.

57. Schütte, *Valignano's Mission Principles for Japan*, 1/2:117.

58. Jennes, *A History of the Catholic Church in Japan*, 13; and Joseph J. Spae, *Catholicism in Japan* (Tokyo: International Institute for the Study of Religions, 1963), 4.

59. See Jennes, *A History of the Catholic Church in Japan*, appendix A, 235–239.

60. Laures estimates the growth of the church as reaching 150,000 in 1582 (*The Catholic Church in Japan*, 177–178).

61. Laures, *The Catholic Church in Japan*, 216–223 and passim, 279ff.

62. Laures, *The Catholic Church in Japan*, 35ff., 304ff.

63. Valignano's recommendations regarding these problems are described in his reports and his general "Japan Summary" of 1583. They are analyzed in detail in J. F. Schütte, *Valignano's Mission Principles for Japan, 1/2, The Solution (1580–1582)*, 1/2:268–318, see n. 269. On the silk trade, see Schütte, *Valignano's Mission Principles for Japan*, 1/1:184–185; 1/2:256. On the financial predicament of the mission, see Schütte, *Valignano's Mission Principles for Japan*, 1/2:238, 304–310. On the bibliography of the reports and summaries, see Schütte, *Valignano's Mission Principles for Japan*, 1/1:401–428, esp. nos. 69, 79, 82, and 113. On the various editions, see Schütte, Index 1/2:376 and Boxer, *The Christian Century in Japan, 1549–1650*, 459 nn. 21, 22, 23.

64. He did not take the name by which he is known to history, Toyotomi Hideyoshi, until he became dictator (shogun) in 1585. See Berry, *Hideyoshi*, 6 n. 5.

65. Murdoch and Yanagata, *A History of Japan*, 2:213–218.

66. Jennes, *A History of the Catholic Church in Japan*, 57–58.

67. Murdoch and Yanagata, *A History of Japan*, 2:239.

68. Murdoch and Yanagata, *A History of Japan*, 2:240–243; Boxer, *The Christian Century in Japan, 1549–1650*, 145–149.

69. Laures, *Studies on Takayama Ukon*, 54.

70. On the Takayama family, and Ukon in particular, see Laures, *Studies on Takayama Ukon*. The Jesuits named him Justus, and called him Ucondono. See also Murdoch and Yanagata, *A History of Japan*, 2:168ff. At the time of the rebellion, Ukon was a vassal of Araki, daimyo of Settsu.

71. For the stormy life of Takayama Ukon, see Laures, *The Catholic Church in Japan*, 40–41, 55–59, 120, 150; Laures, *Studies on Takayama Ukon*, 13–16; and Murdoch and Yamagata, *A History of Japan*, 2:168–170.

72. Laures, *Studies on Takayama Ukon*, 19–20; Drummond, *A History of Christianity in Japan*, 79–81.

73. Jennes, *A History of the Catholic Church in Japan*, 62–85.

74. Jennes, *A History of the Catholic Church in Japan*, 64 n. 30.

75. On Rodrigues, see Cooper, *Rodrigues the Interpreter*; Michael Cooper, trans., *This Island of Japan: João Rodrigues' Account of Sixteenth-Century Japan* (Tokyo and New York: Kodansha, 1973).

76. Murdoch and Yamagata, *A History of Japan*, 2:317–324. Murdoch also notes that the early Jesuit historians tended to exaggerate the eminence of the Christian generals (Takayama, Konishi, and Kuroda), who in fact were outranked by a number of others, notably the Buddhist Kato Kiyosama, who was given Konishi's fief when the latter was executed for refusing to apostatize, and Mayeda Yasutoshi (Murdoch and Yamagata, *A History of Japan*, 2:226). But one of the most brilliant and eventually richest of them all, Gamo Ujisato, was later converted to the Christian faith by the indefatigable evangelist of the elite, Organtino Gnecchi (Murdoch and Yamagata, *A History of Japan*, 2:259, 442n.).

77. Johannes Laures, *Two Japanese Christian Heroes: Justo Takayama Ukon and Gracia Hosokawa Tamako* (Rutledge, Vt.: Bridgeway/Charles E. Tuttle, 1959), 69–196; Murdoch and Yamagata, *A History of Japan*, 2:275, 395n., 405–406; and Boxer, *The Christian Century in Japan, 1549–1650*, 152, 185, 338–339. Grace was the daughter of Akechi Mitsuhide, one of the great Nobunaga's generals and by popular

accounts that proto-shogun's assassin (Murdoch and Yamagata, *A History of Japan*, 2:137–141, 176–181).

78. On conversions among the elite, see Murdoch and Yamagata, *A History of Japan*, 2:274–278; Sansom, *History of Japan*, 2:350; and as a stated policy, see Boxer, *The Christian Century in Japan, 1549–1650*, 228–229, 232–233; and Laures, *The Catholic Church in Japan*, 61 n. 24, 88.

79. It is more probable that this unconfirmed rumor confuses an heir of the proto-shogun Oda Nobunaga, whom the Jesuits sometimes referred to as emperor, with a son of the real but puppet emperor (cf. Murdoch and Yamagata, *A History of Japan*, 2:237–238).

80. See below for a comparison of Jesuit and Franciscan missions in Japan on policy toward class distinctions.

81. Johannes Laures, *Kirishitan Bunko: A Manual of Books and Documents on the Early Christian Missions in Japan*, 3rd ed. (Tokyo: Sophia University, 1957), esp. 1–26 (on the printing press, the printers, and their techniques). See also Cooper, *Rodrigues the Interpreter*, 220–237, on the grammars and dictionaries; and Jennes, *A History of the Catholic Church in Japan*, 78–82, 121–124, on Bible translations and Christian books. Some early printings were in *romaji* (Japanese in Latin letters), while others were in Chinese characters with *hiragana* (cursive phonetic signs).

82. See Laures, *Kirishitan Bunko*, 26–116, esp. 98, which discusses a possible printing of the New Testament some time before 1613; and Jennes, *A History of the Catholic Church in Japan*, 78 n. 84. Among the unprinted manuscripts are a small psalter with extracts from the psalms, and a manuscript by the missionary Manuel Barreto, with readings from the gospels.

83. The best single survey of their work in this period is Thomas Uyttenbroeck, *Early Franciscans in Japan* (Himeji, Japan: Committee of the Apostolate, 1958).

84. Uyttenbroeck, *Early Franciscans in Japan*; Jennes, *A History of the Catholic Church in Japan*, 69ff.; Laures, *The Catholic Church in Japan*, 124–125.

85. See Boxer, *The Christian Century in Japan, 1549–1650*, 164–165, 230ff., 239ff.; and Cooper, *Rodrigues the Interpreter*, 126–132. See also Henri Bernard's section on different missionary methods in Mexico and Japan in *Les îles Philippines du grand archipel de la Chine* (Tientsin: La Procure de la Mission de Sienhsien, 1936), 111–127.

86. On Bautista, see Bernward Willeke, "Biographical Data on the Early Franciscans in Japan (1584–1640)," in *AFH* 83 (1990): 162–163, 165–166.

87. Uyttenbroeck, *Early Franciscans in Japan*; Jennes, *A History of the Catholic Church in Japan*, 65–66, 75, 78, 235–237.

88. Franciscans entered as an order in 1593; Dominicans and Augustinians in 1602 (Jennes, *A History of the Catholic Church in Japan*, 69–77, 109–114).

89. For a summary of the early history of the Japanese episcopate, see Jennes, *A History of the Catholic Church in Japan*, 235–236.

90. Cooper, *Rodrigues the Interpreter*, 110–119, 140–141; Jennes, *The Catholic Church in Japan*, 75–76; Frank Cary, *History of Christianity in Japan* (Tokyo: Kyo Bun Kwan, 1959), 1:122–123.

91. See his letter of 1603, in Cary, *History of Christianity in Japan*, 146–149.

92. Murdoch and Yamagata, *A History of Japan*, 2:490.

93. On the fierce rivalry in Japan between the mendicant orders, Franciscan and Dominican, and the Jesuits, Sansom remarks, "The patient tact of the Jesuits was outrivalled by the reckless ardour of the Franciscans" (A History of Japan, 2:373–374). For a more appreciative appraisal of the Franciscan mission, see Uyttenbroeck, Early Franciscans in Japan.

94. See Boxer, The Christian Century in Japan, 1549–1650, 166–170.

95. "The story of the indiscreet Spanish captain may be dismissed as fiction," writes G. B. Sansom (A History of Japan, 2:374). Sansom treats it as a later invention rising out of the quarrel between the Jesuits and the Franciscans.

96. For a critical review of the better sources concerning the San Felipe incident, see Boxer, The Christian Century in Japan, 1549–1650, 472–473 nn. 17–20. The Franciscan side of the argument is best represented by Uyttenbroeck (Early Franciscans in Japan, 17–20). On the Jesuit side most histories rely on the evidence of Bishop Pedro Martins, and Ruy Mendes de Figueiredo (translated in Boxer, The Christian Century in Japan, 1549–1650, app. 3); see also Cooper, Rodrigues the Interpreter, 128–162.

97. Murdoch and Yamagata, A History of Japan, 2:294–295.

98. Four of the twenty-six were Spaniards, one was Mexican, one was Indo-Portuguese, and twenty were Japanese. See Cooper, Rodrigues the Interpreter, 138–139; Latourette, A History of the Expansion of Christianity, 3:327–328; Jennes, A History of the Catholic Church in Japan, 76–77.

99. Jennes, A History of the Catholic Church in Japan, 103–104, citing the bishop's letter of January 12, 1603. On the reopening of the Franciscan Mission (1598–1614), see Uyttenbroeck, Early Franciscans in Japan, 34–79, 200; and Jennes, A History of the Catholic Church in Japan, 109ff.

100. Jennes, A History of the Catholic Church in Japan, 103; see also Cary, History of Christianity in Japan, 1:137ff.

101. See Drummond, A History of Christianity in Japan, 91–94.

102. Jennes, The Catholic Church in Japan, 88–89, 103.

103. Jennes, The Catholic Church in Japan, 102.

104. Drummond, A History of Christianity in Japan, 89–90; see also Boxer, The Christian Century in Japan, 1549–1650, 290ff.

105. The Dutch opened a trading factory in Hirado in 1609. The first English ship reached Japan in 1613. See Boxer, The Christian Century in Japan, 1549–1650, 308–314, 434; and Boxer, Portuguese Seaborne Empire, 106–127.

106. Boxer, Portuguese Seaborne Empire, 106ff. His pithy summary is on 110.

107. Boxer describes the Arima family as the "main prop and stay of Christianity in Japan" (The Christian Century in Japan, 1549–1650, 314–315). Its fiefdom was often described as Christian territory. L. Pagés, in his history of the martyrdoms, writes, "All the inhabitants of Arima were Christians" (Histoire de la religion chrétienne au Japon depuis 1598 jusqu'a 1651 [Paris: Charles Douniol, 1869], 1:273; for details of the Arima martyrdoms, see also 1:242ff.).

108. Sansom, Japan: A Short Cultural History, 501, 508; Jennes, A History of the Catholic Church in Japan, 98–99, citing Hans Müller, "Hai-Yaso, Anti-Jesus. Hayashi Razan's anti-christlicher Bericht über eine Konfuzianisch-Christliche Disputation aus dem Jahre 1606," in MN 2, no. 1 (1939): 268–275.

109. The most widely known of the anti-Christian Buddhist attacks is the apostate Jesuit Fabian Fukan's Deus Destroyed (1620), along with the Buddhist

monk Suzuki Shoshan's *Christians Countered* (ca. 1642) and the anonymous *Kirishitan monogatari* (ca. 1639) — all translated, annotated, and critically analyzed with thorough scholarship by George Elison in *Deus Destroyed*. Elison labels the *Kirishitan monogotari* as "propaganda at its worst." See also Boxer, *The Christian Century in Japan, 1549–1650,* 318; and Pagés, *Histoire de la religion chrétienne au Japon,* esp. 251ff., 371, 373.

110. Boxer, *The Christian Century in Japan, 1549–1650,* 317–318.

111. Quoted in Jennes, *A History of the Catholic Church in Japan,* 116ff. This was the final notice of prohibition, the last of a sequence of provisional bans and edicts in 1601, 1607, 1611, 1612, and 1613 (see Sansom, *Japan: A Short Cultural History,* 424).

112. See Jennes, *A History of the Catholic Church in Japan,* 97ff.: Pagés, *Histoire de la religion chrétienne au Japon depuis 1598 jusqu'a 1651,* esp. 1:155, 206–207, 250–251, 371–372. On the Buddhist addition to the edict, Boxer refers to Satow's translation of the edict in *ASJT* 6 (1878), 46–48 (see Boxer, *The Christian Century in Japan, 1549–1650,* 328–329 n. 6); and see Y. S. Kuno, *Japanese Expansion on the Asian Continent,* 2 vols. (Berkeley and Los Angeles: University of California Press, 1937–1940), 2:47–48.

113. See Elison, *Deus Destroyed,* 51–53, 141–142, 164–166, 171–184.

114. Elison, *Deus Destroyed,* 16, 154–159, 166–167, 184. For Elison's translation of "Deus Destroyed," see 257–291.

115. Schütte, *Valignano's Mission Principles for Japan,* 1:xviii, 198–203; 1/2:221, 277.

116. On the statistics, see Drummond, *A History of Christianity in Japan,* 57–58. Cf. Sansom, *The Western World and Japan,* 127.

117. Pagés, *Histoire de la religion chrétienne au Japon depuis 1598 jusqu'a 1651,* 1:257–258, 296, 315; 2:113–114; Jennes, *A History of the Catholic Church in Japan,* 119.

118. Jennes lists thirty-eight priests (eighteen Jesuits, seven Dominicans, seven Franciscans, one Augustinian, and five diocesan clergy) (*A History of the Catholic Church in Japan,* 120); see also Drummond, *A History of Christianity in Japan,* 105–106; and Sansom, *The Western World and Japan,* 174n.

119. Eighty-five Jesuits (including the vicar general Carvalho and forty-one priests) and four Franciscan priests, two Dominicans, two Augustinians, and two Japanese priests were deported (see Pagés, *Histoire de la religion chrétienne au Japon depuis 1598 jusqu'a 1651,* 1:280–281, 595).

120. Murdoch and Yamagata, *A History of Japan,* 2:617ff.; Laures, *The Catholic Church in Japan,* 169. Jennes lists the apostatizing daimyos as follows: Otomo Yoshimune (1589), So Yoshitomo of Tsushima (1600), Omura Yoshiaki (1604), Arima Harunobu (1612), and Arima Naozumi (1612); two, Yoshimune and Haronobu, died as Christians (*A History of the Catholic Church in Japan,* 244).

121. Pagés, *Histoire de la religion chrétienne au Japon depuis 1598 jusqu'a 1651,* 1:506–528.

122. Boxer, *The Christian Century in Japan, 1549–1650,* 337, 340.

123. Masaharu Anesaki, "Prosecution of Kirishitans after the Shimabara Insurrection," *MN* 1, no. 2 (1938): 296–297, cited by Jennes, *A History of the Catholic Church in Japan,* 138ff.

124. Laures, *The Catholic Church in Japan,* 178. Cf. Jennes, who reports that among the nonmissionary martyrs were "thirteen Koreans, several Chinese,

three Portuguese, one Spaniard and one Singhalese" (*The History of the Catholic Church in Japan*, 244–245).

125. For a print portraying similar torture (burning in rice bundles instead of at a stake), see Elison, *Deus Destroyed*, 358.

126. Shusaku Endo, *Silence* (Tokyo: Sophia University, 1969), 296–297.

127. Hubert Cieslik, "The Case of Christovão Ferreira," *MN* 29, no. 1 (1974): 1–54.

128. Jennes figures that up to 1614 there were, at the barest minimum, about 2,126 martyrs, but lists only 71 apostates (*A History of the Catholic Church in Japan*, 242–245).

129. Jennes, *A History of the Catholic Church in Japan*, 242.

130. Some estimates put the number lower, "20,000 to 37,000" (Boxer, *The Christian Century in Japan, 1549–1650*, 379).

131. One of the earliest accounts of the rebellion is a letter written by a Portuguese ship captain imprisoned nearby in 1638–1639. He was later burned alive (Pagés, *Histoire de la religion chrétienne au Japon depuis 1598 jusqu'a 1651*, 2:403–411). See also Boxer, *The Christian Century in Japan, 1549–1650*, 376–385; Murdoch and Yamagata, *A History of Japan*, 2:642–671; Cary, *History of Christianity in Japan*, 1:219–228. For a vivid, detailed description see Ivan Morris, *The Nobility of Failure* (New York: The Noonday Press, 1975), 143–170.

132. Hubert Cieslik, "The Great Martyrdom in Edo 1623," *MN* 10, no. 1/2 (1954): 1–44. In that one year 165 Christians were martyred.

133. See Jennes, *A History of the Catholic Church in Japan*, 146–148; Anesaki, "Prosecution of Kirishitans after the Shimabara Insurrection"; and Laures, *The Catholic Church in Japan*, 187.

134. Sansom, *The Western World and Japan*, 174.

135. See A. Brou, "L'Abbé Jean-Baptiste Sidotti," *RHM* 14 (1937): 367–379, 494–501.

136. See Arai Hakuseki, *Lessons from History: Arai Hakuseki's Tokushi Yoron*, trans. with commentary by Joyce Ackroyd (St. Lucia and New York: University of Queensland Press, 1982), esp. the introduction. See also Boxer, *The Christian Century in Japan, 1549–1650*, 397, 499 n. 10; and Jean-Pierre Lehmann, *The Roots of Modern Japan* (New York: St. Martin's Press, 1982), 39.

137. Boxer, *The Christian Century in Japan, 1549–1650*, 397.

138. Brou, "L'Abbé Jean-Baptiste Sidotti," 85. Brou describes in detail both the early interrogations (*RHM* 14:494ff.) and the meetings with Hakuseki (*RHM* 15:80–91). See Boxer, *The Christian Century in Japan, 1549–1650*, 499 n. 10; and Neil S. Fujita, *Japan's Encounter with Christianity: The Catholic Mission in Pre-Modern Japan* (New York: Paulist Press, 1991), 230–237.

139. See R. Tassinari, "The End of Padre Sidotti: Some New Discoveries," *MN* 5, no. 1 (1942): 246–253.

140. Tokugawa Yoshinobu (1837–1913) was disenfranchised in 1869. See *EAH* 119, crediting the "nonentity" phrase to H. Bolitho.

141. James M. Phillips, in a review of Elison's *Deus Destroyed*, in *Church History* 59 (1990): 246.

Chapter 5

Once More to China

"Missionaries and Mandarins"

Don Alvaro de Gama [son of Vasco da Gama], the Commandant of the city of Malacca, has violently opposed my going to China to preach the Gospel there, disregarded the formal authorization of the Viceroy of India which I presented to him, and has made it useless by his rebellious obstinacy...I am determined, as I told you, to go by sea to Siam, whence there is some expectation of being able to get to China...The devil has an unspeakable dread of the Society of Jesus entering China...But I am confident...that Jesus Christ, our Savior and Redeemer, will...disappoint...his wishes and mak[e] his vain hope void.

— Francis Xavier's last letter,
San Chan (Shang-Ch'uan) Island, November 1552[1]

THE great Xavier left Japan in 1552 determined to strike a blow for his Lord at the very center of the civilization of northern Asia, the Chinese empire, and to leave to his successors the work he had already begun on Asia's rim. But before the year was out he died on a small island within sight of the China coast near Guangzhou. The traditional dying words attributed to him, "O rock, rock, when wilt thou open to my Lord?" were not his, but though uttered by Valignano, the great organizer of Jesuit missions in Asia,[2] they were words from Xavier's heart. Lonely and half starved he died near the little grass-roofed chapel he had built on the island, still determined that China, the key to Asia, would be entered for Christ.

In some ways China presented a remarkably favorable opportunity for Christianity. Like pagan Europe in the first thousand years of Christian advance to the west, China despite an ancient cultural tradition had no securely established religion. It was ruled by what C. P. Fitzgerald has called "philosophic pagans, more interested in ethical doctrine than in religious beliefs" (Confucianism), and the common people were simple polytheists without the "theological prejudices" that had blocked the gospel in West Asia under Islam or South Asia under Hinduism.[3]

First Contacts in Macao

But it was no easy matter to enter China in the sixteenth century. The empire, reacting against the internationalism of the "pax mongolica,"[4] reverted to Chinese nationalism under a Chinese dynasty, the Ming, and a social structure that has been described as *bureaucratic* feudalism. In contrast to the expansive *military* feudalism of Europe in those years, it discouraged foreign adventuring.

Thirty years and more after Xavier's death his fellow Jesuits were able to fulfill the pioneer's dream of entering mighty China. The first step was the establishment of a beachhead on the south China coast by Portuguese traders, five years after Xavier died. They carved out for themselves a small colonial enclave, Macao, about sixty miles below the empire's major center for foreign trade Guangzhou (Canton).* This became the missionary center for Portuguese missions to China, and in fact to all of East Asia north of Malacca. Not until 1583, however, did the first Jesuits succeed in planting a base across the border in a little village east of Guangzhou. They were Michael Ruggieri and Francesco Pasio.[5]

They were only the forerunners of a remarkable trio that included Ruggieri as a minor partner and leaves Pasio as a footnote. The trio consisted of Matteo Ricci, Alessandro Valignano, and Michele Ruggieri, three Italians in Portuguese colonial territory, who spearheaded a missionary advance into China that forever changed the balance of religions in East Asia. Valignano was the master planner, the architect of the structure of Catholic missions for all of Northeast Asia. Ruggieri had made the first physical breakthrough into China. But it was Ricci who shaped the mission, reached the capital, and for the first time made Christianity a continuing, permanent presence in the empire.

It was the third historic breakthrough of Christianity into China. First had been Nestorianism from Persia in the Tang dynasty in the seventh century.[6] Second were the surviving Nestorians from Central Asia and the earliest Roman Catholics in thirteenth-century Mongol dynasty China.[7] Each time it had disappeared with the fall of the dynasty. But

---

*A word on the use of the Pinyin and Wade-Giles system of transliterating Chinese into Roman characters in this volume is necessary. The question of whether to use the modern Pinyin or the older Wade-Giles system of transliteration bedevils every historian. Wade-Giles is still used in Taiwan and by many traditionalists. Pinyin, however, is the standard for the People's Republic of China and has increasingly become de rigueur among scholars and the news media. I have been persuaded by my publisher that, even though most of my sources date from the era when Wade-Giles was standard, I should adopt Pinyin in this volume. My thanks to Dr. Michael Nai Chiu Poon of the Center for the Study of Christianity in Asia at Trinity Theological Seminary in Singapore for his assistance in making this transition. Accordingly, Chinese names and places below will generally be spelled according to Pinyin conventions. Notable exceptions are the retention of Hong Kong over its Pinyin equivalent, "Xiangang," and Macao over "Aomen," as that city has been known since 1999.

now once more Catholicism returned in the latter years of the Ming dynasty (1368–1644) to find that all traces of those earlier missions had been erased and forgotten.[8]

Valignano, as we have seen, was appointed head of Jesuit missions in the Far East in 1573 and reached India the next year.[9] There his study of the results of about seventy years of Catholic missions in that part of Asia brought him to three highly significant conclusions. The first was his judgment that Christianity's connections with Western colonial trade expansion were more a handicap than an aid to missionary evangelism. Not only in India, but also in Japan, China, and the East Indies[10] he began, very diplomatically and carefully, to wean the mission from too close a dependence on the Portuguese state and to guard against too much colonial interference in church affairs.

A second emphasis was equally liberating. He prohibited the members of his order from participating in the harsh procedures of the Inquisition's pursuit of heresy, which had been introduced into India in 1560.[11] But it was Valignano's third principle, cultural accommodation ("adaptation"), that became the distinguishing mark of Jesuit missions in Asia for most of the next two centuries, and nowhere so emphatically and with so many unforeseen consequences as in China.

In Macao (known since 1999 as Aomen), the tiny trading outpost that China, officially or not, had allowed Portugal to occupy near Guangzhou in return for promises to restrain the pirates on the China Sea, the Portuguese grew rich trading silver from Japan to China, and silk from China to Japan for more silver. Macao quickly became the Jesuit mission's beachhead for expansion into Northeast Asia. Already by 1565 they could count five thousand Chinese Christians in the city, although entry into China was forbidden.[12] Valignano was dismayed to find that his Portuguese missionaries were spending more time with the nine hundred Portuguese in the colony than with the Chinese population. They even insisted that their Chinese converts adopt Western dress and take European names. The Chinese language, they said, was impossible to learn and in consequence had become completely dependent on their interpreters. To reverse this crippling strategy, Valignano brought the Italian recruit, Ruggieri, into Macao with instructions to tie his missionary approach to the other end of the cultural context, the Chinese, not the Portuguese way of thinking. Begin with the Chinese language, he ordered.

Twice a year Portuguese traders were permitted into Guangzhou for the great trade fairs, and Ruggieri in 1580 attached himself to one of them. Though he was still knew very litte Chinese, his respect for Chinese customs proved to be the keys by which he broke through the barriers of distrust of foreigners that had turned the mainland into a "forbidden empire." He so pleased the authorities that they granted him exemption from the rule that forbade outsiders to remain overnight on

Chinese soil. On a second visit he was given a residence next to the embassy from Siam (Thailand). To a general of the army he gave a little present, an instrument unknown in China, a watch. It was a sensation.[13]

Matteo Ricci and the Entry into China (1583–1610)

In 1582 Ruggieri was joined by his confrere Matteo Ricci,[14] "a curly-bearded, blue-eyed man with a prodigious memory and a voice like a great bell."[15] Ricci, known as Li Ma-dou in Chinese, was destined to become, without doubt, the most famous missionary in all the long story of Christian missions in China. He went to Asia against his father's will. His father, in fact, had warned him against becoming "too religious," and tried to keep him from joining the Jesuits, but he reached India in 1572 and spent four years there teaching theology, before going on to tiny Goa, the Portuguese beachhead on the southern coast of China.[16]

Four times without success Ruggieri, first with Pasio and then with Ricci, sought to obtain permanent permission to reside in China. Then unexpectedly in 1583, just as they were about to give up hope, the viceroy, the very man who had repeatedly driven them out after Ruggieri's initial welcome, not only invited them to live in the county seat of Shaoqing (Chao-Ch'ing) near Guangzhou, but even offered to build them a chapel. Wisely, the two pioneers proceeded cautiously, perhaps remembering what had happened in Japan after the early Jesuit mass baptisms. Ruggieri wrote in 1584:

> We do not wish for now to baptize, even though there are several who seek it, in order to allow them to grow more in the knowledge and desire of things divine, and in order not to give occasion to the Demon if some would then leave the faith in these beginning [times].[17]

Though not the pioneer, Ricci soon became the leader of the work. He developed two main principles. First, make no secret of their faith but do not emphasize the missionary purpose. Second, try to win the attention of the Chinese by demonstrating a knowledge of things in which they show great interest, such as Western science and Western learning. To this end he taught mathematics and astronomy and prepared a famous map of the world, which for the first time astounded educated Chinese with the possibility that China might not be the only center of the world.[18] Most significant of all, he proved to be a master linguist. Within two years he had memorized extensive sections of the Chinese classics and could write hundreds of Chinese characters as called for, then from memory repeat the list backward.[19]

The effect of the second principle, using Western scientific knowledge as a means of entry into the culture of China, was to direct the mission's efforts toward the upper classes. This was no disparagement of the common people, for whom the missionaries had the highest respect. Ricci had written earlier, "The Chinese people are extraordinarily well-suited for the reception of the holy faith, far more than any other people; they are spiritually talented and significantly competent."[20] But as a matter of mission strategy he was forced to recognize the fact that with no protection by international treaties, foreigners could remain in China only so long as they maintained friendly relations with those who ruled.

The first convert of the two Jesuits, however, was a man of the very lowest class, a man abandoned by the side of the road and dying of an incurable disease. Compassion took precedence over strategy, and they took the man home, gave him a little hut near their own house, and told him that though there was no hope of curing the disease, they could save his soul. He was so grateful that he was happy to believe anything they told him, and died in peace shortly after his baptism.[21]

It is somewhat ironic, in the light of the missionaries' sensitivity to Chinese culture, that the next two baptisms in this Catholic reentry into the empire were by Father Francesco Cabral, the worthy but insensitive superior who had been transferred from Japan to Macao for his inability to adapt to Japanese customs.[22] He was invited in late 1584 by Ruggieri and Ricci, two champions of adaptation, to baptize two men. He proudly complied but wrongly described them as "the first to become Christians in China."[23]

By 1585, after two and a half years in China, the mission could still report only twenty converts. The general populace remained hostile, so hostile in fact that Ricci became persuaded that the only hope of establishing a stable mission in China was to win the favor and permission of the emperor in Beijing (formerly Peking). But Beijing was a thousand miles north. In 1588 Ruggieri was sent to Rome to see if an official embassy from Europe might not reach the court more quickly than missionaries struggling through unfriendly territory province by province from the south. Left in charge of the mission, and too impatient to wait for a delegation from Rome, Ricci began to push north, stage by stage, toward the distant emperor, Shenzong (1572–1620), the fourteenth and nearly the last of a long line of the famed Ming emperors who had ruled China for more than 250 years.[24]

Ricci took his first step toward Beijing in 1589 when an unfriendly viceroy drove him out of his village base near Guangzhou. Undaunted he moved to another town a little farther north[25] where he proceeded to build the second Catholic church in the country, choosing a Chinese style of architecture partly because it was cheaper, and partly to emphasize his conviction that Christianity was not bound by Western culture.[26] There also he was joined there by the first two Chinese lay-brothers to be admitted into the Jesuit order, Zhong Mingren, who had been given the name Sebastian Fernandez in Macao, and Hwang Ming-sha (Francesco Martinez), who was to become (in 1606) one of the earliest martyrs of the mission.[27] Even before he reached China, while still in India, Ricci had argued, against strenuous opposition from within his own Jesuit order, that the training of native converts for the priesthood "on a basis of equality with Europeans" was imperative for the future of the church in China.[28]

Six years later he took another step on his indefatigable journey toward the emperor in the north. So far the mission had been strictly limited to the one coastal province of Guangdong (Kwangtung). But in 1595 Ricci was for the first time allowed to establish a residence across a provincial border in the inland province of Kiangsi (Jiangxi). Nanchang, the province's capital, was halfway between Guangzhou and the old southern dynastic capital, Nanjing. It was about then that Ricci, following his principle of adaptation, determined that the Buddhist robes that Ruggieri had adopted as appropriate dress for foreign priests entering China were more a handicap than an advantage. The Confucian literati, from among whom high government officials and magistrates were chosen, despised the Buddhist priesthood as superstitious and uneducated. So in 1594 Ricci had asked and received permission from Macao to change the missionaries' dress to Confucian scholars' garb. Not long thereafter, in 1597, he was officially named superior of the China mission, which in fact if not in name he had been ever since Ruggieri's departure nine years earlier.[29]

It was a small mission with a big dream. The Jesuit mission in China, excluding Portuguese Macao, could count only seven members, three mission stations (one of which they were forced to abandon), and perhaps a hundred converts, but what was that in comparison with China's uncounted millions? The Jesuits thought there might be as many as 40 to 60 million Chinese.[30] To Europeans that was an enormous number, and they believed the missionaries were exaggerating. In fact they had underestimated by more than half. Modern statistics suggest there were at least 150 million people in China by the year 1600.[31]

Ricci quickly won a reputation in the intellectual circles of the city. Three years later a high official there received an invitation to the emperor's birthday celebrations at the capital and was persuaded to take with him this unusually gifted foreigner. After fifteen years in China, Ricci's dream of reaching the emperor's ear seemed at last about to be realized. But it was not yet to be. He did reach Beijing but returned disappointed. He found the throne almost completely insulated from unsettling outside contacts by a wall of eunuchs. His journal scathingly describes "these semi-men," the eunuchs, as "unlettered and barbarous, lacking shame and piety, utterly arrogant and very monsters of vice."[32] Though he failed to reach the emperor he was encouraged by one important accomplishment. He was allowed to move the Jesuit mission one step farther north, if not to Beijing the northern capital, at least to the southern capital, Nanjing.

Nanjing was halfway between Guangzhou and Beijing, and in some ways it was a more open intellectual and cultural center than the political capital, Beijing. Within two years Ricci reported that the number of converts there was growing at the rate of a hundred a year.[33] It was at Nanjing also that Ricci met and discipled the foremost Chinese convert of those first years of the mission, Paul Hsu (Xu Guangshi),[34] who for the next thirty years was to do more for the cause of Christianity in Ming dynasty China than any other Chinese of the century.

The Three Pillars of the Chinese Church

Paul Hsu (Xu Guangshi), with Michael Yang (Yang Tingyun) and Leon Li (Li Zhizao), was the first of what came to be called "the three pillars of the early Chinese church."[35] All three came from upper-class backgrounds, distinguished themselves in government service and intellectual studies, and were enormously influential both in the building up of Chinese Catholicism, and in introducing China to Western science and philosophy.

Xu Guangshi (d. 1633) first met Ricci in 1600. Less than four years later, thoroughly converted not so much by the impressive scientific learning of the missionaries but by how far their moral teachings surpassed his Confucianism and how superior their religion was to Buddhism, he asked to be baptized. Later he phrased his position in an elegant Chinese motto: "[Christianity] Supplements Confucianism and Displaces Buddhism (pu ru yi fo)."[36] One of his summaries of the Christian faith illustrates how he introduced Christianity to Confucianists: "According to [the Christians'] teachings, the service of Shangdi [God] is the fundamental principle; the protection of the body and the salvation of the soul are of utmost importance; loyalty, filial piety, compassion, and love are accomplishments; the reformation of errors and the practice of virtue are initial steps; repentance and the purification [of sin] are the prerequisites for personal improvement; the true felicity of celestial life is the glorious reward of doing good; and the eternal misery of hell is the recompense of doing evil."[37]

Academically Xu was a late bloomer. Four times he had failed in lower provincial examinations, and twice in the metropolitan examinations. Then he met Ricci, and after the second failure his new faith encouraged him to keep trying. Later he said that his failures must have been divinely arranged, for had he passed earlier he would never have met the Christian fathers and found salvation.[38]

At last in 1603 he passed his doctoral examinations and was persuaded by Ricci to sit for an even more prestigious degree, membership in the Imperial Academy (Han-lin) which each year admitted only twenty-four of the new literary doctors (jinshi).[39] That accomplished, he proceeded to rise even higher. Three years of further examinations brought him to the very highest rank of all, open only to the twelve highest ranking candidates each year.[40] Thereafter, his natural ability, intellectual reputation, and integrity of faith and character steadily won him promotion in government circles to a position of rank and influence that has been described as "second only to the emperor."[41] Working with Ricci to make Western mathematics, astronomy, hydraulics, and geography known in the empire, he was the first Chinese to translate European books into Chinese. Among Christians he was famed for his piety and discipline in the faith. After the death of Ricci in 1610 Paul Hsu became the acknowledged leader of the Chinese Christian community, protector of the missionaries, and a careful critic of overadaptation to Buddhist funeral rites, lest "the rules of Christianity" be violated.[42]

The case of Leon Li (Li Zhizao),[43] second of the "three pillars," is another reminder that the Jesuit policy of adaptation to national culture had its carefully recognized limits. Li was a native of Hangzhou from a military family. He was fascinated by Ricci's maps, for as a young scholar he had printed his own atlas which pictured the whole world as consisting almost entirely of China's fifteen provinces, and he was generously grateful to the foreign doctor for enlarging his scientific horizons in geography and mathematics. But Ricci's religious teachings and strict morality did not at first impress him. He was a Buddhist and held prominent positions in several well-known Buddhist organizations. He was also a "polygamist"[44] and could see no practical reason for the missionaries' insistence that Christians must give up their concubines. Ricci was soon able to convince him of the folly of Buddhist idolatry, but though convinced intellectually of the truth of Christianity, for years Li stubbornly declared he could see no practical reason for the requirement that if he wanted to be baptized he must have only one wife. Not until some ten years later, a few months before Ricci's death, did he gladden, to the great joy of his long-suffering wife who had already become a Christian, the hearts of the missionaries by asking for baptism. The next year he celebrated the occasion by building the first church in Nanjing for the fast-growing community there.[45]

Li was also the first scholar to receive, in 1625, a copy of a recently discovered inscription on a monument found near ancient Chang-an (Chang-an, now Xian), and recognize it for what it was: a reference to the presence of Christianity in China long before the coming of the Portuguese, and even before the Polos. He was ecstatic. "Who could have believed it?" he wrote. "Nine hundred and ninety years ago this doctrine was preached [here]." He had found an answer to the taunts of some of his fellow scholars in the academy about his apostasy to what they called a "strange, new, foreign" religion.[46]

The third of the "three pillars" was Michael Yang (Yang Tingyun),[47] the only one of the three not taught by Ricci. He was a scholar in Hangzhou deeply attracted to the Buddhism of the more intellectually stimulating Ch'an (Zen) school. He loved religious argument, and had founded his own "Truth Society" to promote the search for philosophical reality. Meeting the Jesuit missionary Lazzaro Cattaneo at the home of his relative, Li Zhizao, he was fascinated by his talk of the existence of God and invited him for nine days of intensive discussion on the subject. The stumbling point, for Yang, as for most Chinese intellectuals, was the doctrine of the incarnation of an infinite God in a human Christ. Equally difficult for upper-class inquirers were the moral requirements of the Christian faith. Like his relative, Li Zhizao, Yang had a second wife.

But once converted and baptized (in 1613), Yang wrote prodigiously in defense of the Christian faith and produced the most effective books which China had yet seen defending it against the attacks of the Buddhists. It is notable evidence of the measured care with which the Jesuits baptized converts in China, mindful of lessons learned from early mass baptisms in Japan, that Yang Tingyun's wife, though thankful of his return to monogamy, was not rushed to baptism for another two years, although most of his family quickly asked to be received with him.[48] The influence of such prominent converts in Hangzhou as Li Zhizao and Yang Tingyun soon made that provincial capital (of Zhejiang) the most conspicuously successful Christian community in China. It had already, a few years earlier in 1611, replaced Shanghai as the fifth major residential center for the Jesuit mission (after Ch'ao-chou in the south, Nanchang and Nanjing in the center, and Beijing in the north).

The Jesuits in Beijing to the Fall of the Ming Dynasty (1610–1644)

Meanwhile, Matteo Ricci had died in 1610 in Beijing. He died without once seeing the emperor whom he had believed he could persuade to open the empire to the gospel. But what he could not do through the emperor, he managed to accomplish in a limited way through the impact on the empire of his personal charm and sincere appreciation of Chinese culture, his maps, his books, and his disciples. His maps for the first time shocked China into an awareness of a world that was not flat and was at least as large and significant and in many ways better informed and stronger than China itself. One of his first books, *On Friendship* (1595), disarmed Confucian fears of the foreigner. His two most influential Chinese books were one on science and one on theology. The scientific treatise was a translation, with the aid of Paul Hsu in 1607, of Euclid's first six books. It revolutionized China's mathematics and astronomy. The other was a theological defense of Christianity and an apologetic directed primarily against the Buddhists, *The True Meaning of the Lord of Heaven* (*Tianzhu shi yi*, 1603).[49] In an attractively framed dialogue of questions and answers between a "Chinese scholar" and a "Western scholar," it sharply repudiated Buddhism, but left bridges open for exploration between Christianity and what he considered to be "original" Confucianism (not the then prevailing neo-Confucianism of the twelfth-century Confucian master Zhu Xi).

Ricci's *True Meaning of the Lord of Heaven* (*zhu xi*) has been called "the first attempt by a Catholic scholar to use a Chinese way of thinking to introduce Christianity to Chinese intellectuals."[50] J. S. Witek aptly summarizes his basic critique of the traditional Chinese religions thus: "The religion of Buddha was based on nothing, that of LaoTzu [Laozi, Taoism] on emptiness, and that of Confucius on the real [or on 'being']."[51] As we shall see in a later chapter, Ricci's *True Meaning* was also the first piece of Christian literature to reach Korea.

In so many ways Ricci had made such an impression in Beijing that upon his death he was buried by the imperial decree of an emperor who had never been allowed to see him, in a plot of land officially granted to the Jesuits near the West Wall.[52] It was the first sign of tacit government recognition and tolerance of a permanent foreign Christian presence in the capital. To Ricci, however, the Chinese converts were the most significant legacy of the Jesuit mission, not himself or any other of its missionaries. The best estimate of their number in 1610 when he died seems to be about twenty-five hundred. How disappointingly small, compared with China's population then of between 100 and 150 million.[53] But Ricci rejoiced. The growth of that little community of believers, from three Catholics in 1584, to about five hundred in 1603, and perhaps twenty-five hundred when he died in 1610, he described as "a very great miracle of God's Almighty hand" and "not inferior to that of any other ever accomplished from the time of the Apostles downwards."[54]

The Fall of the Ming Dynasty (1644)

On his deathbed Ricci appointed Nicholas Longobardi as his successor. It was a surprising choice. Writing much later, a French historian of the Beijing mission noted a sharp change of administrative tone in the mission after Ricci: "The harsh orthodoxy of Longobardi was very different from the excessive tolerance of Ricci."[55] But the comparison is unfair to both men. The new head of mission, while not directly opposing Ricci's highly successful missionary methods, was nevertheless lukewarm toward continuing his policy of accommodation to Chinese thought and culture. Disregarding the advice of the Christian mandarin, Xu Guangshi, who knew how thin a line the missionaries were walking in a country still largely opposed to foreigners, Longobardi promoted a more aggressive evangelistic confrontation with China's culture.[56]

Ricci's true successors were Adam Schall, a German, who did not reach Beijing until 1630,[57] and Schall's successor, Ferdinand Verbiest

(1623–1688), a Hollander from the Low Countries, who came to the capital thirty years later in 1660.[58] Eventually it was Ricci's earlier emphasis on science that again saved the mission. This time the instrument in the hands of the missionaries was not geography, but astronomy; not Ricci's maps of the world, but the Jesuits' knowledge of the sun and moon and stars.

Only a few months after Ricci's death, the Muslim mathematicians who were responsible for preparing the all-important Imperial Calendar made a mistake in their calculations of an eclipse, an unforgivable error at a court where the calendar was the regulator of protocol, the hinge of the people's deepest superstitions, controller of the rhythms of life, and China's symbol of central authority over all the earth. In all the Far East, one historian has noted, "a refusal to accept it was equivalent to a declaration of war."[59]

The high Christian mandarin, Paul Hsu (Xu Guangshi), Ricci's disciple, seized upon the error as an opportunity to suggest that the foreign missionary scholars in Beijing, whose scientific knowledge had already attracted favorable attention, be appointed to study and correct the old methods of calculation. The emperor agreed. Some Jesuits objected, fearing that secular scientific concerns were diluting the mission's primary goal of evangelism.[60] But the respected Chinese Christian's counsel prevailed, and along with his colleague, Leon Li (Li Zhizao), Schall was asked to assist two foreign priests[61] in a thorough reform of the Bureau of Mathematics [Astronomy]. Stung by its loss of face, the bureau fought back and scuttled the inquiry and the reforms.

The next few years saw the outbreak of a bitter reaction against the foreigners and the first general persecution of Christians in China. In 1616 a high official of the powerful Board of Rites in Nanjing launched an anti-Christian campaign against "all who profess to be adherents of the religion of the Lord of Heaven."[62] The entire mission in Nanjing was thrown into prison. Beijing in the north was at first not so negative, but the next year the emperor was pressured into signing an anti-Christian edict. Two of the priests who had been conspicuous for their part in exposing the errors of the court astronomers were forced into exile in Macao. Most of the others, discovering that many officials were more sympathetic to them than to their persecutors, found refuge in Chinese Christian homes. Only the two missionaries in Nanjing were cruelly treated; one was flogged, both were caged with metal chains and paraded, almost dead with wounds and sickness, all the thousand miles to Guangzhou where at last a sympathetic prefect released them and sent them with dignity on to exile in Macao.

However, in one historian's opinion, compared with the horrors of the martyrdoms occurring in Japan at the same time, the persecutors in Ming China "appear as almost paragons of civilized behaviour." Only four of the eighteen Jesuits then in China were expelled, not one was killed, and the work of the mission continued.[63]

The Chinese church prospered; the prestige and power of the Chinese court declined. Once again the threat of invasion by tribes beyond the Great Wall sent shock waves through the empire. In 1619 (Paul) Xu Guangshi offered to head a government mission to Korea to seek an alliance against the rising menace of marauding Manchus, and proposed to take a Jesuit missionary with him to explore possibilities for a Christian mission there. The offer, however, was declined, and he was appointed instead to train recruits for the Chinese army.[64]

The empire continued to crumble. Crushed internally by a failing tax system, military rebellion, and the corruptions of a eunuch-dominated court, the last Ming emperors watched helplessly while barbarians from the northeast in Manchuria broke through the Wall like their western relatives the Mongols four hundred years earlier, and closed in on Beijing.

The capital fell to the Manchus in 1644, and the last princes of the last Chinese dynasty to rule the empire fled south. One of them, Ming prince Kuei, who called himself the Yung-Li emperor, managed to establish a refugee court in Shaoqing, far to the south near Guangzhou, where the first of the China Jesuits, Ruggieri, had established his residence eighty years earlier, and where now two Jesuits still remained to minister to the last of the dynasty. The whole royal family began to turn Christian, including about fifty high-ranking women of the refugee court. Much of this was due to the encouragement and example of three influential Christian court officials, a eunuch (Pang Tienshou, known as Achilles), and two key palace attendants. The empress-dowager was baptized as Helen, the emperor's own mother as Marie, and his empress as Anne. The good Jesuit fathers regretted that the pretender, Yung-Li himself, did not accept baptism, but with his assurance that he would promise to raise his infant son as a Christian they rejoiced to baptize the potential heir to the throne, naming him Constantine in the tenuous hope that China, like Rome, by some miracle of Ming dynastic survival might have as its first Christian emperor a new Constantine.[65]

Christianity under the Manchu (Ch'ing, or Qing) Dynasty

The miracle never happened. Once more the church in Asia failed to produce a reigning monarch. As the Manchu armies closed in, the despairing pretender sent Michael Boym, one of the priests at his court, to Rome to beg for help. It was in vain.[66] Earlier in 1644 a ridiculously small Portuguese relief force had marched north from Macao to try to save the last real Ming emperor in Beijing, Zhangzhan, the Jesuits' friend. Politely but firmly they had been stopped in Nanjing and packed back to Macao. If there was no help for a real emperor, there would be no help from Europe for a pretender. Prince Yung-Li escaped into Burma with his baptized son, and a dubious tradition relates that a Ming general rescued the last of the Mings by boat and for a time eluded his pursuers at sea. But when all hope was lost, it was said that the general, loyal to the end, gathered the boy gently in his arms and leaped overboard. The less sentimental but more credible version of the end of the dynasty is that the pretender and his fourteen-year-old heir, Constantinus, were both executed in Burma by strangling in 1662.[67]

The Jesuits had prayed for a miracle and lost. They had even helped the imperial Ming army forge bronze cannons to hold off the invaders.[68] The greater miracle in the midst of what seemed to be total disaster was that for the first time in Chinese history, the fall of a protecting dynasty did not carry the church down with it. Seven hundred years earlier, the collapse of the Tang dynasty wiped out the church of the tenth century. Again, the end of the Mongol dynasty in the late fourteenth century saw the Chinese church disappear once more. But in the seventeenth century when the Manchus overthrew the Ming dynasty, although the Christians had been greatly favored by the fallen emperors, they did not vanish with them.

No one did more to accomplish this unexpectedly successful transition from one dynasty to the next than Adam Schall, a German Jesuit of noble Rhinelander lineage, who stayed resolutely at his post throughout the fall of Beijing, neither deserting his Chinese friends nor fleeing the incoming Manchu victors. He ordered some of the missionaries to seek refuge with the retreating Ming, but as the Manchus entered the capital he dressed in Chinese clothes and went boldly to the conquerors to ask permission to remain. In the course of his petition he managed diplomatically to remind the new conquerors, eager to establish their legitimacy to rule, of the importance of the imperial calendar as the symbol of peace and order in the realm, and pointed out that if vandals were allowed to destroy the invaluable astronomical instruments and mathematical calculations which the late emperor had entrusted to him for the preparation of the annual calendar, he could not be held responsible.[69]

Surprisingly, the request was granted, and even more surprisingly his value to the new rulers of China was immediately confirmed in highly dramatic fashion. It so happened that the year of the conquest, 1644, was also the year of an eclipse of the sun. The Manchus had entered the city in June. The eclipse was expected on September 1. The Bureau of the Calendar was required to calculate the exact hour. Three factions were at that moment jockeying for control of the powerful bureau: Muslim, traditional Chinese, and Christian. Ever since their success in the 1611 eclipse, the Christians had kept control. But that was under a vanquished dynasty. The Muslims and the Chinese mandarins, sensing an opportunity to displace them, rushed to present their calculations. The court asked Schall for his figures, and he obliged somewhat reluctantly, and even provided a telescope to reflect the eclipse on a piece of paper for all to see.[70] The result was a triumphant vindication of the accuracy of his methods, and by the end of the year he received imperial appointment not only as head of the Bureau of the Calendar but also as director of the entire Institute of Mathematics (Astronomy).[71]

The new Manchu emperor, Shunzhi, was only a boy of nine when he began his reign. He became genuinely fond of the old missionary. Schall relates a revealing incident:

> He once asked me, publicly, how it was that most government officials were so negligent in their administration of the affairs of the State ... I answered sincerely and promptly, "I think, your Majesty, that it is because of their desire to follow your example. They see you deal lightly with many affairs of great importance, as if you had little care for the Empire." Whereupon the emperor blushed and went out.[72]

The courtiers turned pale to see a commoner rebuke an emperor.

In the fourteen years between 1644, when he was appointed director of the Bureau of Astronomy, and 1658 Schall was promoted seven times, from mandarin fifth class to mandarin first class, first division, with right to wear the red button on his hat and the golden crane on the breast of his tunic. Dunne quotes de Rougemont as remarking, "I do not believe that since the foundation of the Chinese empire any foreigner has received so many marks of honor and kingly favor." Schall rose rapidly at the court.[73] That rise was not unnaturally followed by a strong resurgence of growth in the Chinese church. The whole capital was aware that he was the first Jesuit ever allowed to meet the emperor, and marveled at the familiarity with which the ruler even invited himself to dinner at the Christian foreigner's modest home. The skill of the Jesuits in so quickly winning the confidence and respect of the new Manchu rulers sent the numbers spiraling upward spectacularly. Schall's colleague, Martino Martini, caught in a more remote area, faced the entering conquerors with a red official-looking poster placed before his residence reading, "Here lives a doctor of the divine Law come from the Great West," and a table piled with European books, scientific instruments, and an image of Jesus. The Manchu horsemen were impressed and received him with honor.[74] These years were a golden period for China's Christians, particularly after 1650 when, upon the death of his uncle the regent, the young Manchu emperor, Shunzhi, became emperor in fact as well as in name.

Shunzhi favored the Jesuits with a gift of land, a church and a residence in the capital, and an annual subsidy from the imperial treasury. The dome of the Western-style church towered 150 feet high, highly visible on the whole north side of Beijing.[75] It was the first public church building in the capital of China since the time of John of Montecorvino in the Mongol dynasty. Heretofore Christians had worshiped in a small chapel in the Jesuit compound or in their homes.[76] Five years later the Dominicans were allowed to build a church at Fuzhou in Fujian province,[77] and in 1659 the Jesuits were allowed to build another church on the east side of Beijing. Even the emperor's mother, though a zealous Buddhist, warmed toward the Christians when she asked Schall for medical help for a sick "daughter" who was actually the emperor's intended bride. He said he would pray for her and recklessly added, "She will be well in four days." In four days the girl did recover; the empress dowager's faith in Buddhism waned, and her benefactions to the Christians increased.[78]

Just how many Christians there were in China at the end of the Ming dynasty in 1644 is not clear, but probably less than 100,000, though there were by then missionary residences in all of China's provinces except two in the far south, Kunming and Guizhou. Only six years later, in 1650 when the Jesuits built their first public church in Beijing, the Chinese Christian community in China is reported to have grown to 150,000. In the next fourteen years (1650–1664) it rose another 105,000 to 254,980, which, if the figures can be trusted, would mean a gain of 155,000 converts in only twenty years.[79]

Part of that rise in membership must be credited to the arrival of the new Catholic missionary orders. Up to the time of Ricci's death in 1610 only the Jesuits were allowed to reside in China proper, that is, outside Macao. The first Dominican, Thomas de Sierra, survived attacks by pirates to reach the mainland from Formosa (Taiwan) in 1630, and in 1633 probably the greatest, and also surely the most controversial, Dominican missionary to China, Juan de Baptista de Morales, joined him. With Morales came Antonio de Santa Maria (Anton Caballero), the first Franciscan to establish residence in China since the days of the Mongols three centuries earlier.[80]

Schall's last years were clouded by controversy with some of the newly arriving missionaries of other orders, and, after 1657, by a cooling of the emperor's favor.[81] Jealous Muslim astronomers and power-hungry eunuchs hurled charge after charge against the aging missionary. To the credit of his chief accuser, Yang Guangxian, however, it was neither jealousy nor ambition that in the old scholar's mind motivated the attack, but rather the firm conviction that Confucianism not Christianity was the only right foundation for Chinese civilization. Yang's criticisms of Schall are a revealing glimpse into how a Confucianist's inadequate knowledge of Christianity can be as dangerous in a Confucian-Christian encounter as Christian misinterpretations of Confucianism.[82]

Despite the attacks, for some years Schall's prestige protected him. However, when the emperor Shunzhi suddenly died in 1661, his opponents seized the opportunity of an interim reign by regents acting for the new nine-year-old emperor, Kangxi, to renew the assault. Suddenly in 1664, Schall, who had just suffered a paralyzing stroke, was arrested, and though too paralyzed to walk, was carried off to await trial. Three of his missionary associates were held in chains for six months. Incredibly, the sentence finally pronounced was death. Five Christians from the Bureau of Astronomy were publicly beheaded. Then, alarmed by the appearance of a comet in the skies, and a series of disasters that rocked the imperial palace with earthquake and fire and toppled the cross on the Christian church, in 1665 the troubled authorities released most of the accused. Schall never recovered. He died in Beijing the next summer.[83]

The Rites Controversy (1636–1692): Disunity in the Mission

By the time of Schall's death, a far greater threat to the progress of the faith than persecution had begun to throw a lengthening shadow across the Christian communities, both missionary and native. What came to be called "the rites controversy" struck at the very heart of a missionary strategy that had brought the Jesuits triumphantly into the inner corridors of Chinese imperial power but which now threatened to lose them the confidence of their own court of final appeal, the papacy.[84] It was their principle of cultural accommodation as developed by Ricci in China that triggered the attack. Later, "accommodation" was often termed "indigenization," and today more often as "contextualization."

At the heart of the controversy was the great debate about how much or how little a religious faith dares to adapt itself to terms and cultures shaped by other religions. That issue, of course, neither began nor ended in China. Its theological roots are as deep as the Christian doctrine of the incarnation. It has historical precedents stretching as far back as the Council of Jerusalem, described in the book of Acts, and Paul's arguments against the Judaizers, and Tertullian against Clement of Rome, and the Council of Elvira ca. A.D. 305, and Gregory the Great and his mission to England, and the Celtic Church against Rome at the Council of Whitby, and on and on clear up to the Puritans against the Establishment — an argument that was unsettling England at the same time as the rites controversy was troubling the church in China. In that great "middle empire" it dominated the history of Catholic missions for two centuries, from 1636 and the entry of new missionary orders into China, down to the Opium Wars and the edicts of toleration in the 1830s and 1840s.

The sad history of those two centuries can be divided into three periods and described as disunity in the missions (1636–1692), church against state (1692–1742), and the ruinous results (1742–1839). First, not long after the death of the greatly admired Ricci in 1610, the Jesuit-Portuguese monopoly of missions in China was challenged, as we have seen, by the arrival in 1633 of the first Spanish Franciscans and Dominicans. This added a whole new tangle of partisan loyalties — ecclesiastical, imperial, and cultural — to a difficult issue that the Jesuits had debated and hoped they had solved a generation earlier. Even the Jesuits, at first, were not of one mind about Ricci's methods. His successor, Longobardi, had warned of the dangers of promoting Christianity by painting it as a religion not much different from Confucianism (in *Traité sur quelques points de la religion des Chinois*, Latin original, ca. 1622; French translation, 1701). But he supported Ricci's toleration of attendance at Confucian ceremonial rites. The Society's consensus on accommodationism was not reached until 1628 at a celebrated Jesuit policy council, which brought the most concerned missionaries together with four of their best-known Chinese converts, including Paul Hsu ((Xu Guangshi)) and Leon Li (Li Zhizao).[85]

Since 1583 the Jesuits had been in complete control of the church's mission to China. It is not surprising that, as had happened in Japan in the 1590s, the arrival of missionaries under the authority of other orders, though stimulating the growth of the church, confused lines of ecclesiastic authority and sowed seeds of conflict between the two Catholic empires, Portugal and Spain, which had been the main pillars of Catholic expansion. In Japan, rivalries between the orders had led almost immediately to the executions in Yokohama. In China the fuse was longer, and the explosion was delayed, but in both countries the outbreak of quarrels within the missions and between their supporters in Europe wrought irreparable damage.

An important source of conflict lay in the area of competing colonial interests. Spaniards found it easy to oppose the Jesuits who had entered China under the authority of Portugal's rights of *padroado*, not Spain's. Portugal defended the Jesuits; Spain supported the Dominicans and Franciscans as they moved into China from the Philippines, which was Spanish ecclesiastical territory. Later, when the Paris Society of Foreign Missions (Société des Missions Etrangères de Paris) entered China, France too became involved.

The Franciscans, who had an ancient claim to China stretching back to John of Montecorvino's mission in Beijing in the thirteenth century, were the first to raise the issue and bring it to the attention of the authorities in Manila, and from there a Dominican, de Morales (a skilled but overconfident linguist and head of the Dominican order in China), carried the controversy to Rome.[86] Both the Franciscans and the Dominicans brought with them from the Philippines a severe missionary policy of eradication of non-Christian influences in the national culture, strongly supported by Spain's harsh philosophy of colonial rule.[87] Coming to China they looked with disdain and suspicion on the Jesuit practice of missionary accommodation to Chinese customs as a weak and unchristian compromise with "heathenism." But in seventeenth-century China, Western imperialism was not the decisive factor. The Portuguese had only dented China's coast, not conquered it. China was not South America, nor was it the Philippines. When foreign imperialism first met a ruling Chinese emperor, it was the Eastern ruler not the Western intruders who prevailed, but of that we shall speak later.

In China, missionary failure began from within, with missionary disunity. One of the first issues to divide the China missions was how to translate the word for "God" into Chinese. The Jesuits, following Ricci, had agreed in general, though some had reservations, that it would be fitting to adopt two titles from the Chinese classics: *Tianzhu*, which is literally "Lord of heaven," and *Shangdi*, which is literally "Emperor (or Lord) on high." Ricci had preferred *Tianzhu* (Lord of heaven) but saw nothing amiss with use of the other. His successor, Longobardi, assented to Lord of heaven, but advised against *Shangdi*. It may be worth noting that on this point the Tang dynasty Nestorians, in naming God on their monument, had avoided the whole argument by eschewing accommodation to a value-laden Chinese word for the deity. Their name for God was *Aloho*, a transliteration of the Syriac that was in turn derived from the Hebrew *Elohim* in Genesis. But in a companion phrase, they had described God also as "Lord of the universe," which is very close to the *Tianzhu* (Lord of heaven) of Ricci.[88] According to Gernet, the ancient Jewish colony in Kaifeng as early as 1489 and 1612 had adopted *Tianzhu* (Lord of heaven), and *Shangdi* (Lord on high) as translations of the Old Testament Yahweh (Jehovah), but of this the Jesuits were unaware.[89] They had also agreed on concessions toward Christian participation in certain secondary non-Christian Chinese customs, such as funeral ceremonies and reverence toward ancestors, distinguishing, as had Ricci, between reverence and worship.[90]

But the newcomers, the Dominicans and Franciscans, were shocked by the adaptations permitted. Some objected to the use of Chinese terms for God, reminding the Jesuits that their own great Xavier had tried and abandoned an equivalent attempt in Japan almost a century earlier.[91] They erroneously reported seeing a pagan "altar" to the emperor in the Beijing church, and leaped to the conclusion that the Jesuits were not only diluting the concept of God by the use of Chinese terms for God but were even allowing their converts to worship the emperor as a God. That report circulated misleadingly in Europe long before the Jesuits could point out that the supposed "altar" was only an honorific wooden inscription wishing "long life" for the emperor, whose generosity had made the building of the church possible.[92] Others simply criticized the Jesuits, especially Schall, for spending too much time adapting and too little on evangelism. Schall admitted the fault, and grieved that the emperor's orders were so demanding as to exclude anything else, including enough time to sleep.[93]

For most of the opponents of accommodation, however, the sticking point was the ceremonies.[94] "If that is permitted," wrote Anton Caballero, the Franciscan,[95] in 1659, "the missionaries will find themselves spared the most arduous part of their work and their worst problem, which is how to persuade converts to abandon the public cult of their idols."[96] The Jesuits were called liars and deceivers. It was said that they allowed Christian mandarins to perform Confucian rituals so long as they hid a crucifix in their robes and declared in their hearts that they were really worshiping the Christian God, not Confucius.[97]

The most important of the early public accusations submitted against the Jesuits to Rome was a formal presentation of seventeen charges, phrased as questions by the Dominican Juan Bautista de Morales in 1639, and carried by him to Rome in 1643. This event led directly to the first papal judgment against the Jesuits, the decree of Innocent X in 1645.[98] Five years later — not a long delay considering the distances involved — the Jesuits, stung by what they considered exaggerated and misleading reports of their missionary methods, appealed to the next pope, Alexander VII, who reviewed the matter and issued a contradictory decree in 1656 taking the side of the Jesuits.[99] This brought Morales again to the attack.

It is unnecessary to detail the swings of the pendulum favoring or condemning the Jesuit policy of adaptation to the national culture. The two apparently contrary papal decrees carefully straddling the issue increased the antagonisms of the missionary orders and encouraged further furious efforts to break the stalemate. One of the most passionate and persistent of the early opponents of Jesuit accommodationism was the Dominican Domingo Navarrete (1618–1686), who reached Macao in 1658, "fell in love with the Chinese," but by 1669 had begun to hate the Jesuits. "I fled from them and the stones they daily cast at me," he wrote.[100] In an effort at damage control and in answer to Morales, the pope in 1669 declared that both the anti-accommodation decree of 1645 and the pro-accommodation decree of 1656 were valid, each in its own way.

This decided nothing, of course, and perhaps was the best thing that could have happened to the church, for despite the swelling arguments that were tearing the missions apart, and even in the face of a persecution in 1664 that closed the Chinese churches and sent a sizeable group of missionaries to prison, including the highly respected Adam Schall, the Christian community continued to grow. Schall died in 1666 as a result of the harsh treatment. But a year later, the young emperor Kangxi took over the reins of government from his recalcitrant regents, and the fortunes of the church took a decided turn for the better.[101] In 1671 the missionaries were released and the churches were reopened.

One of the wisest positive aspects of Jesuit policy had been its announced emphasis on the training of a Chinese clergy.[102] Never as successful as was hoped, it had at least produced the first Chinese Catholic lay brothers, all Jesuits in the early years, but later in the other orders also. The ordination of a Chinese priesthood, however, which might have been expected as part of the same strategy, was inordinately delayed for nearly seventy years. In fact in 1606 the Jesuit director general in Rome explicitly forbade the ordination of native Chinese until by Christian experience they might prove the strength of their faith.[103] His undeclared justification for the delay was probably the fear that the required oath of celibacy was too much to ask of new converts in cultures where such restrictions were considered antisocial, and where the failures and weaknesses of Buddhist priests were common knowledge.

It was the Dominicans, not the Jesuits, who finally ordained the first Chinese Catholic priest. Luo Wenzao (Gregory Lopez) entered the Dominican order and was ordained in 1656 in Manila. His is the added and singular distinction of being the only Chinese bishop consecrated in China during all the 330 years of Catholic work from the time the Jesuits reopened Christian missions there in 1583 down to the twentieth century. The next Chinese Catholic bishop was not consecrated until 1926.[104] The first Indian Roman Catholic bishop was consecrated in 1923. The first Japanese in 1927, the first Annamese in 1933, the first Ceylonese the same year, and the first Korean in 1937. India had received Asian (Syro-Persian) St. Thomas bishops since 1500.[105] Moreover, because of tensions between the orders on the rites question, it was neither a Jesuit nor a Dominican but a Franciscan who in 1685 consecrated Father Lopez (Luo) as the first Chinese bishop. Bishop Luo (ca. 1610–1691) was given authority as apostolic vicar over all north China; the southern nine provinces were assigned to the French bishop and apostolic vicar François Pallu, a founder of the Paris Foreign Missions Society.[106] One of Bishop Luo's early acts was the ordination of three Chinese Catholic priests in 1688. An earlier Chinese ordination, but performed outside China, was that of the first Chinese Christian known to have reached Rome in this period, the Jesuit Cheng Wei-hsin (Emmanuel de Sequeira). Ordained in Rome in 1664, he did not return to China until 1671.[107]

Schall's successor at the Bureau of Astronomy, Ferdinand Verbiest (1671–1688) rose even higher in favor of the third Manchu emperor, Kangxi (1662–1723), at the court — higher even than Ricci at the Ming court, or Schall under the second Manchu emperor, Shunzhi. His influence became so great that he was able to correct the record of a whole month that had been wrongly inserted by Muslim astronomers in the sacred imperial calendar during his predecessor Schall's fall from favor. Verbiest was doubly important to the progress of the faith. His summary of Christian doctrine gave the church a systematic statement of the fundamentals of the faith, which had previously been lacking, and his favor with the court led to imperial edicts that possibly opened the way to a degree of unrestricted freedom of religious propagation that for a hundred years it had not yet been able to obtain.[108] So impressed was the emperor with what the Jesuits told him about the power of the pope that Kangxi wrote to the pontiff proposing a marriage to one of the pontiff's nieces![109] But religious freedom still had its limits. The emperor Kangxi's decree of toleration in 1671 granted the church a legal right to own land but no basic right to preach, and no withdrawal of the ban on Chinese becoming Christian.[110] Twenty years later in 1692 a decree of complete toleration was issued, three years too late for Verbiest to rejoice at the news (he died and was buried with high state honors in 1689).[111] In gratitude for all that the Jesuits had done for his country — from reform of the calendar to assistance in obtaining a treaty with Russia protecting the Chinese border[112] — Kangxi published the only unlimited edict of toleration[113] ever granted during this entire period of three hundred years of Christian missions in China from the entry of the Jesuits in 1683 down to the Opium Wars of the early to mid-nineteenth century.

The Catholic missionaries could now well look back at the first hundred years of their mission with well-earned satisfaction. There had never been more than a few score missionaries in China at any one time, yet the growth of the church had surprised not only the Vatican but the missionaries themselves. In 1607, shortly before the death of Ricci, Nicholas Trigault had estimated the number of Christians at only 700. Twenty years later Martini wrote of 13,000 in seven provinces. In another ten years he reported 40,000 in nine provinces, Fujian and Henan having been added, and by mid-century "more than 150,000." Another twenty years reportedly added more than 100,000 converted or baptized, a somewhat dubious total of 263,000 in 1672 as it reached its peak. Two hundred thousand might be more credible.[114] But even granting a certain amount of generosity in the calculations of the missionaries, the numbers represent an astonishing rise for an area so resistant to foreign intrusion as sixteenth- and seventeenth-century China.

Rowbotham marks 1692 as the climax of the church's prosperity in China. "As the discovery of the Nestorian tablet had proved the antiquity of the Christian faith, so the Edict of 1692 established its legality."[115] But if so, the next year was the beginning of its undoing.

The Controversy Continued (1693–1742): Church vs. State

When the Paris Foreign Missions Society joined the Dominicans in 1693 in denouncing the Jesuits to Rome for permitting pagan practices,[116] the conflict broke out beyond the boundaries of the Catholic Church. The Jesuits found a surprising ally in the Protestant philosopher Leibniz,[117] and a much more powerful friend in the emperor of China, Kangxi, protector and pupil of Verbiest. Confident of the emperor's approval, and perhaps unwisely ignoring the fact that they were asking a non-Christian ruler to pass judgment on church matters, the Jesuits appealed to Kangxi for a definitive statement as to whether the Chinese rites were religious in nature or merely civil observances. The emperor obliged with a public memorandum upholding the Jesuits against their opponents, and asking, in effect, how far-off Rome could know enough about Chinese customs to criticize them. He ruled that the honor that the Jesuits allowed their converts to pay in respect to Confucius was made only to him as a great teacher, and that the ceremonies to ancestors were memorial rites, not religious. He agreed with the Jesuit explanation that when Confucianists worship "Tian," they are not worshiping "the sky," but the Lord of heaven (Tianzhu) and all beneath it. This statement of Jesuit policy and the emperor's memorandum of approval were happily forwarded to Rome by the Jesuits in 1700.[118]

Rome was not so happy. Disturbed at the way the controversy was spreading, the pope recognized the need for tighter central control of the quarreling Catholic missionary orders and a quick end to the controversy. Yet how could he resolve tensions between semiautonomous field bodies and make judgments on strange cultures from half a world away in Rome, when the missions who were best informed on such matters could not themselves agree? His first step was to reorganize the church in China under a strengthened apostolic vicariate. Apostolic vicars, in this period, were titular bishops (that is, bishops without pastoral sees) responsible neither to the heads of the various missionary orders, nor to the bishops or archbishops appointed by Spain and Portugal, but only to the pope in Rome. It was an attempt to retrieve world mission out of the hands of European colonizers and diocesan churchmen and give it back to the papal organization specifically designed for mission, the Propaganda.[119]

As a second step, to ensure that theological orthodoxy would not be sacrificed in any accommodations made to non-Christian Chinese culture in the developing debate on rites, a decree from the Inquisition, confirmed by Clement XI in 1704, produced what was hoped could be an acceptable compromise. It approved the use of Tianzhu for "God," but disallowed Shangdi and Tian. More significantly it ruled against a number of aspects of the Jesuit policy of accommodation and forbade converts to "worship" at sacrifices to Confucius or the ancestors. Significantly, however, it did not forbid mere attendance, and allowed Christians to erect tablets to the ancestors if these bore only the names of the ancestors and did not include anything implying the presence of their spirits.[120]

The Mission of De Tournon (1704–1710)

Fully cognizant of the fact that this ruling would not resolve all the tensions in the missions, and fearful of offending the Chinese emperor,

Rome sent a high-level commission to China headed by a young noble-man of the House of Savoy, de Tournon,[121] to present the papal decree in as persuasive a way as possible, and win the assent and obedience of all concerned. For the next six years, 1704–1710, the legate fought bravely to complete the task, but his was an impossible mission. The Portuguese in Macao refused him recognition because he had no appointment from Lisbon. The Jesuits, knowing his instructions, blocked their converts from talking to him. The emperor, though courteous at first, was furious at bungling foreign intervention in what he considered a purely Chinese affair.

The momentous climax of the mission was a classic series of confrontations between Christians and non-Christians in the summer of 1706 on command by the Confucian emperor in a manner reminiscent of ancient religious debates in Asia, whether ordered by a Muslim Caliph in eighth-century Baghdad, or by a Shamanist Mongol Khan in thirteenth-century Tartary. The Jesuits' accusers were represented by de Tournon's advisor, Bishop Charles Maigrot of the Paris Society of Foreign Missions.[122] The choice of Maigrot to debate on issues of classical Chinese rites was a costly mistake. The feisty bishop was a stalwart defender of the faith, but neither a linguist nor a diplomat. With incredible discourtesy, from a Chinese point of view, he challenged the emperor's own interpretation of the ceremonies. Angrily asked to substantiate his claims, he proved himself unable apparently even to read Chinese and was publicly humiliated.[123] The emperor banished him from the realm, and shortly thereafter ordered de Tournon, too, out of the country. On his way out de Tournon issued his own edict, a threat of excommunication against all who refused obedience to the decree of 1704. When the Portuguese archbishop of Goa heard of this, he directed the bishop of Macao to pay no attention to a French-Italian ambassador who had no authority from Portugal. Ill, harassed, and completely frustrated, de Tournon ordered the Jesuit college in Macao to be closed, and wrote to a sympathetic priest, "The cause is ended, but not the error. The mission is destroyed before it could be reformed."[124]

Also detrimental to the Christian cause was the effect of the controversy outside the missions. Dissent and argument within the missions puzzled and angered Chinese Christians and threatened the safety and unity of the Chinese church. Gregory Lopez found his loyalty to his own order challenged by his sympathy with his fellow Chinese converts. His fellow Dominicans opposed Jesuits on the rites question, whereas most Chinese Christians — whether for convenience or by conviction it is impossible to say — favored accommodation to their own national customs. This was true particularly among the Christian government officials whose civil duties made it impossible to avoid attendance at Chinese ceremonies. For his defense of accommodation, the consecration of Lopez as bishop was delayed for thirty years.[125]

The controversy also worsened relations between the Chinese intellectuals for whom the Jesuit policy of accommodation had been
principally devised, and the missionaries who were most eager to win
their confidence.[126] Non-Christian Chinese intellectuals had hitherto
been surprisingly supportive of the introduction of Christianity. But the
increasingly aggressive criticisms of Jesuit policy by the other orders
revealed for the first time to the Confucian elite troubling differences
between the Christian faith and China's own religious traditions. These
scholars began to question the Jesuit claim that Chinese classical philosophy as interpreted by Christians was a return to all that was good
and true in the social moral fabric of original nonreligious Confucianism, to which Christianity was now adding an indispensable vitalizing
element: a transcendental, cosmic worldview far more accurate scientifically than the corruptions that twelfth-century neo-Confucianism (the
school of Zhu Xi, 1130–1200) had introduced into it.[127]

In defense of their own traditional neo-Confucian interpretation of the
classics, the Chinese scholars counterattacked by describing Christian
belief in the transcendental as a decline into the same kind of religious
superstitions that the scholarly class had always despised. Gernet quotes
one author who angrily but inaccurately wrote in 1643 or thereabouts,
"[Y]ou speak of one single Master of Heaven. What difference is there
between you and the Buddhists and Taoists? . . . You pretend to respect
Confucianism but in reality you are destroying it."[128]

Against this tide of turning sentiment, other Chinese Christian literati
loyally sprang to the defense of the Jesuits. One of the "three pillars of the
church," Yang Tingyun (Michael), wrote a famous Christian tract with
the intriguing title *The Owl and the Phoenix Do Not Sing Together*. It refutes
anti-Christian comparisons of Christian metaphysics to pagan superstition, but at times overeagerly reaches for an identification of Christianity
as a fulfillment and purification of ancient original Confucianism. Yang
had himself once been a zealous Buddhist, and knew from his own experience, he argued, that the Christian God, the *Shangdi* of the original
Confucianists, is in no way to be confused with the multiple gods and
spirits of the ignorant, credulous, pagan Chinese sects. If the despised
Buddhists sometimes seemed to Confucianists to resemble Christians,
he argued, it was only because they had borrowed and corrupted Christian ideas. Christianity was not a variant of Buddhism; Buddhism was
a corruption of Christianity.[129]

The rites controversy also became an ominous impediment to the
progress of Catholic missions in other parts of Asia. It not only set the
Catholic mission orders against each other, it frustrated the pope's efforts toward Catholic unity in world mission by accentuating rather than
resolving the rivalry between Europe's major Catholic colonial powers
(Portuguese and Spanish), to whom he had ceded rights of ecclesiastical

control of Catholic missions on the edges of colonial expansion. In terms of practical consequences in China, most damaging of all was the way it broke into the open an inevitable clash between Western and Chinese national pride which the Jesuit policy of accommodation had been expressly designed to soften. Animosities aroused in one area began to spread in all directions as, for different motives, the parties involved took different sides in the debate.

It took another papal constitution (*Ex illa die* of 1715)[130] to lay the severe foundations for a prohibition of accommodation to pagan rites. But an unsuccessful conciliatory papal mission led by Charles Mezzabarba in 1720–1721[131] only confused the issues with eight ambiguous "permissions." The conclusion came twenty years later with one final uncompromising roar from a papal bull, the *Ex quo singulari* of Benedict XIV, to end the debate ecclesiastically in 1742. After that all attempts at compromise, whether by the concessions to the Jesuits of Pope Alexander VII in 1656, or by the "permissions" of the legate Mezzabarba in 1721, were canceled. Only two small allowances were granted. *Tianzhu* would be allowed as a Chinese name for God, and civil ceremonies completely untainted by superstition would be allowed unless questioned and forbidden by higher ecclesiastical authority, episcopal or papal.[132]

It was a triumph for the Paris Society of Foreign Missions[133] and for the Dominicans. It was a traumatic defeat for the Jesuits and led directly, but not exclusively, to the dissolution of the Jesuit order by Clement XIV in 1773.[134] But which side really won, or whether all lost — China and the West, the missionary orders as well as the papacy, the pope and the emperor — are questions that are still being debated 250 years later.

Much can be said in defense of either side of the controversy. On the one hand, the papal position protected the integrity and purity and uniqueness of the Christian faith, all of which are fundamentally important to its very identity and survival. But on the other hand, the severity of the papal decree unavoidably stigmatized Christianity in China as foreign and un-Chinese, impeded its communication across cultural barriers, and brought persecution upon the Chinese churches and led to the breakup of the most successful missionary society that Catholics had ever had in China.[135]

The pope was the better theologian, and the Jesuits were better missionaries; the argument in missionary circles continues to this day. The popular edge in much missionary writing in the West leans toward a Jesuit style of accommodation, but the growing edge of church expansion in the third world is closer to the papal rejection of that view, for to converts who have come out of the old religions it is difficult to draw a line between what is called accommodation, and what is uncritically syncretistic.

Decline and Persecution (1742–1800)

In the year 1700 the Roman Catholic missions in China had reported about three hundred thousand Christians in China. A hundred years later, around 1800 there were probably only half as many. The number of priests had also dwindled, from about 117 (six of whom were Chinese in 1695), to about 111, but it was the shift in nationality that was significant, not the change in the numbers. In 1700, the number of European priests was 111, and only 6, apparently, were Chinese; but in 1800, the Europeans were only 31 and the Chinese priests about 80.[136]

Not all the decline can be blamed on the rites controversy by any means, but the sporadic persecutions that continued for the next hundred years were undoubtedly due in great measure to the loss of imperial favor which Christianity suffered as a result of the defeat of the Jesuits. No longer was the emperor thinking that a marriage with the niece of the pope might be a political advantage for him.[137] When the pope's ambassador De Tournon's failed negotiations with the Jesuits revealed Rome's intolerance of the Chinese rites, and Kangxi saw Clement XI's bull of 1715, the attraction had turned sour. Kangxi angrily wrote in its margin in red ink:

> This manifesto shows how narrow-minded Europeans speak about the high doctrine of China. And still none of the Europeans is versed in Chinese books. Most of what they say...makes people laugh. The author of this manifesto is like any other Bonze [Buddhist priest] or Taoist but none has ever gone as far as he. Henceforth no European missionary will be permitted to spread his Religion in China. Thus we shall avoid further trouble.[138]

The emperor's subsequent actions were milder than that first reaction. He demanded that all missionaries sign a statement of agreement with Ricci's defense of the rites or be banished but never followed up the edict with any widespread enforcement. The conspicuous deportation of the adamantly anti-rites Bishop Maigrot was more of an exception than the rule.[139]

Under Kangxi's successor, the emperor Yung-cheng who reigned from 1723 to 1736, the situation worsened, particularly in the coastal province of Fujian, which was Dominican territory, suggesting that Dominican opposition to the rites had not been forgiven. But the missionaries were not alone to blame for the sudden cooling toward foreign influences. Alarming intrusions of aggressive European traders who called themselves Christians but looted as ruthlessly along the coast as the Japanese pirates were beginning to reach the court and circulate through the provinces.[140] At any rate, in a nationalist reaction, churches were confiscated, priests were accused of lack of respect for Chinese customs, and even the Jesuits were no longer immune to punitive action. The only missionary actually executed in these attacks was a Jesuit, Juan Morao, sentenced to death, exiled to the far west, and strangled and killed in Turkestan.[141]

An edict in 1724 had ordered all missionaries to be isolated in the city of Guangzhou except those attached to the court. The emperor, Yung-cheng, officially declared that Christianity was a false religion, an enemy of the greatest of Confucian virtues, filial piety, and full of such "foolish teachings" as that God would become a man. The rites controversy was undoubtedly at the root of the persecutions, but other factors contributed, such as the opposition of an increasing number of conservative Confucianists to Christianity, and a struggle over the imperial succession in which some Christians of the royal clan may have been involved, though this is doubtful.[142] Except for the small group of missionaries still at the court, in the provinces churches were closed and priests driven into hiding. One determined missionary, to escape arrest, had himself carried in a coffin all the way from Guangzhou to Zhejiang, about a thousand miles.[143] A Dominican missionary, Dominique Parennin, one of the few still in Beijing in 1724, wrote of "the state of desolation to which this once flourishing mission has been reduced."[144]

Even the favored Jesuits in Beijing were never again to carry at the Chinese court the prestige once granted their predecessors. They were sometimes popular as painters and mathematicians and mechanics, sometimes unpopular, but always kept in their place as useful employees, not counselors, and especially not as missionaries.[145] According to Rowbotham, "Under the last of the Mings the Jesuits had been advisers; under Kangxi they were honored scholar-guests; under Qianlong they were merely servants of the crown."[146]

Yung-cheng died in 1736. His son, Ch'ien-lung (1736–1795), was one of China's greatest emperors, as famous in traditional China as his contemporary, George Washington, was in America. The Ch'ien-lung period marked the greatest extent of imperial territorial expansion in all the long history of the Celestial Empire. China moved into Burma, Nepal, and Tonkin (northern Vietnam) in the south, and west to Turkestan and up into the present Kazakhstan in Central Asia. Now, for the first time on a large scale, Chinese imperialism began to meet a European colonial expansion into Asia — Russian and British — far more threatening than the small dents the Portuguese had hammered into Chinese territory. There is no doubt that this was to become as important a contributing factor to the decline of Christianity in China in the latter part of the eighteenth century as the lingering memories of the rites controversy.

As a new emperor, Ch'ien-lung very early proved that he would be no trustworthy friend of the Christians, however much he might encourage and appreciate Jesuit artists like the versatile Castiglione and the muralist Gherardini, and the scientists at the Bureau of Astronomy.[147] Hitherto the capital city, Beijing, had usually been the safest city in China for Christians. In some respects it remained so. As long as there were western missionaries in charge of the empire's Bureau of Astronomy, as was indeed the fact for almost all the more than 150 years from 1669 to 1827, Christians at least had a voice at the top. But it was getting weaker.

In the first year of his reign Ch'ien-lung forbade his military banner-men to turn Christian. The next year, when a Chinese catechist was discovered baptizing infants in a Beijing orphanage he was arrested and tortured to produce evidence against the missionaries, and the capital erupted in demonstrations stirred up by the authorities against the foreigners and their converts.[148] Some ten years later the greatest persecution of all shattered the already wounded Christian communities, the persecution of 1746–1748. The emperor ordered a countrywide search for foreign priests. Before it was over, the missionaries had been driven into hiding or deported, churches were razed, and the number of apostasies of native converts saddened the missionaries even more than their own plight.[149] Seven missionaries including a bishop were executed, five Dominicans and two Jesuits. The bishop, Peter Sanz, apostolic vicar of Fujian, was publicly beheaded in 1749; the others were strangled.[150] In 1760 Ch'ien-lung declared a general amnesty to celebrate his conquest of Central Asia. The cruelty of the persecutions diminished, but harassment of Christians continued.

The Dissolution of the Jesuits (1773)

The next great shock came not from Beijing, but from Rome. When the news reached China in 1774 that a year earlier Pope Clement XIV had dissolved the whole Jesuit order, Christians in China were stunned. It was not unnaturally perceived as punishment for their stand in the rites controversy, and is still represented by some as such.[151] But that is an oversimplification. More overwhelmingly determinative in the pope's sudden decision was pressure in Europe from his major political allies, France and Spain.[152] Secularists of the Enlightenment like Voltaire, and sectarian Catholic movements like the Jansenists, had captured the high ground in European politics. The thunder of the French Revolution would soon be heard. Jesuits were the favored enemy, the popular scapegoat, not so much because of their stand on Chinese rites, but because of their highly disciplined and well-organized political power in Europe. As for their foreign mission policies, the Jesuits at that time were being criticized more for their missions in South America than in Asia.[153]

In China, however, the dissolution of the Society was one more devastating blow in a situation already out of control, though the Society's prior suppression by Portugal in the 1750s and Spain in the 1760s had been a forewarning of what was to come.[154] The loss of Jesuit mission organization brought confusion and a vacuum of authority to the very center of the Christian community's only remaining conduit of effective communication with the imperial government, the Jesuits in the court of Ch'ien-lung.[155] More persecution followed, especially in 1781 and 1784.

The successors to the Jesuits, the French Vincentians and the Paris Society of Foreign Missions, were in no way able to fill the vacuum, not even by an increasing number of ordinations of Chinese priests.[156] An unseemly dissension broke out as various missions and nations claimed the right of succession to the vacant episcopate of Beijing.[157] In 1793 Lord Macartney's famous embassy to the court at Peking seeking trade with China revealed to what shockingly low esteem the "barbarians of the west" had fallen since the days of the great Ricci and Schall and Verbiest. The mighty emperor Ch'ien-lung, who was then eighty-two years old, received the Englishman coldly and sent his famous answer to King George III:

> I set no value on objects strange and ingenious, and have no use for your country's manufactures...It behooves you, O King, to respect my sentiments and to display even greater devotion and loyalty in future, so that by perpetual submission to our throne, you may secure peace and prosperity for your country hereafter.[158]

At a time when the population of the empire was exploding, from 116 million in 1710 to 275 million in 1796,[159] Christian missions and the Chinese church were disintegrating. "We are not immortal," wrote the anguished head of the French Jesuits in the Beijing mission, referring to Spain's earlier expulsion of the Jesuits from Paraguay. "Beijing at last will fall, and will go the melancholy way of other missions."[160] Some were saying the church would never recover. They were wrong. But more hard times were ahead before better times returned.

NOTES

1. Coleridge, *The Life and Letters of St. Francis Xavier*, 2:565ff. I borrow the phrase "missionaries and Mandarins" from Arnold Rowbotham's excellent book *Missionary and Mandarin: The Jesuits at the Court of China* (Berkeley: University of California Press, 1942).

2. See Kenneth Scott Latourette, *A History of Christian Missions in China* (New York: Macmillan, 1929), 91.

3. Charles P. Fitzgerald, "Opposing Cultural Traditions, Barriers to Communication," in *Christian Missions in China: Evangelists of What?* ed. Jessie G. Lutz (Boston: D. C. Heath, 1965), 95.

4. On the "pax mongolica," see vol. 1 of this work, 397ff.

5. See M. Howard Rienstra, ed. and trans., *Jesuit Letters from China 1583–1584* (Minneapolis: University of Minnesota Press, 1986), 3–12.

6. See vol. 1 of this work, chap. 15.

7. See vol. 1 of this work, chap. 20.

8. See vol. 1 of this work, chap. 15, 288.

9. Chap. 1 of this volume.

10. His Jesuit "province" of Asia (the "East Indies"), which had been related to the reorganized bishopric of Goa (India) since 1542, was divided into two sections: India below the Ganges (i.e., India proper), and India beyond the Ganges (i.e., Malacca, the Moluccas, China, and Japan).

11. Schütte, *Valignano's Mission Principles for Japan*, 1/1:112–113.

12. Rowbotham, *Missionary and Mandarin*, 49–50.

13. Rienstra, *Jesuit Letters from China 1583–1584*, i–19. And see also George H. Dunne, *Generation of Giants: The First Jesuits in China* (London: Burns & Oates, and Notre Dame, Ind.: University of Notre Dame Press, 1962), 18–19.

14. The standard editions of Ricci's writings are contained in Pasquale M. D'Elia, ed., *Fonti Ricciane: Documenti originali concernenti Matteo Ricci e la storia delle prime relazioni tra l'Europa e la Cina (1579–1615)*, 3 vols. (Rome: Libreria dello Stato, 1942–1949), hereafter referred to as D'Elia, *Fonti Ricianne*); Pietro Tacchi-Venturi, ed., *Opere storiche del P. Matteo Ricci*, vol. 2: *Le Lettere dalla Cina, 1580–1610* (Macerata, Italy: F. Giorgetti, 1911–1913), hereafter Ricci (*Storiche*); and Ricci's *Diary*, translated into English from the Latin of Nicola Trigault by Louis J. Gallagher as *China in the Sixteenth Century: The Journals of Matthew Ricci: 1583–1610* (New York: Random House, 1953), hereafter Ricci (Gallagher), *Journals*.

15. A. E. Moule, "The First Arrival of the Jesuits at the Capital of China," *New China Review* 4 (1922): 455, translating *Jen-ho hsien chih*, chap. 22, fol. 21–22.

16. From Ricci (Gallagher), *Journals*, 134; see also Vincent Cronin, *The Wise Man from the West* (London: R. Hart-Davis, 1955); and Jonathan D. Spence, *The Memory Palace of Matteo Ricci* (New York: Viking Penguin, 1984).

17. Rienstra, *Letters from China*, 22.

18. Ricci (Gallagher), *Journals*, 270–273; P. J. Bettray, *Die Akkommodationsmethode des Matteo Ricci* (Rome: Gregorian University, 1955), 1–10.

19. Ricci (Gallagher), *Journals*, 277; cf. Spence, *The Memory Palace of Matteo Ricci*, 9.

20. Ricci letter of November 12, 1581, to Merkurian, in Ricci (*Storiche*) 2:402.

21. Ricci (Gallagher), *Journals*, 156–157.

22. See chap. 4 above. On Cabral in Goa, Macao, and extensively in Japan, see Schütte, *Valignano's Mission Principles for Japan*, 1/1:187–247, 376ff.

23. *Letter, F. Cabral*, December 1584 (Rienstra, in *Jesuit Letters*, 18).

24. Ming emperors are more often than not referred to by the title of their reign rather than by personal name. Hereafter I will follow the same convention (e.g., "Wanli," rather than "the Wanli emperor"). The same will be true of the following Qing (Manchu) dynasty. Ming emperors in the Jesuit period were: 12. Jiajing (1521–1566), 13. Longqing (1566–1572), 14. Wanli (1572–1620), 15. Taichang (1620), 16. Tianshi (1620–1627), and 17. Zhangzhan (1627–1644).

25. In Shaozhou (Ch'aochou).

26. On the mission's accommodation to Chinese architecture, see Bettray, *Die Akkommodationsmethode des Matteo Ricci*, 44–51.

27. D'Elia, *Fonti Ricciane*, 1:289–291, n. 3; Rowbotham, *Missionary and Mandarin*, 57; and Ricci (Gallagher), *Journals*, 228, 481ff. The names are transliterated in the Italian, Ciom (Chung)-Mimgen, and Hoam (Huang)-mimscia. The two Chinese lay-brothers had made their novitiate under Ricci in 1590.

28. See his letter of November 20, 1581, quoted in Dunne, *Generation of Giants*, 25, from *Storiche*, 2:20–21.

29. According to Latourette, *A History of Christian Missions in China*, 94, the superior of the mission since 1583 had been Duarte de Sande, whose poor health kept him from active work inside China and forced him to remain an absentee superior as rector of the college in Macao (from 1590).

30. *China in the Sixteenth Century: The Journals of Matthew Ricci: 1583–1610*, trans. Louis J. Gallagher (New York: Random House, 1953), 9.

31. The Jesuit estimates from that period are from Rada (60 million) and Mendoza (40 million), as noted in Donald F. Lach, *China in the Eyes of Europe: The Sixteenth Century* (Chicago: University of Chicago Press, 1965), 769, n. 208. For the modern reappraisal of that estimate, see Ping-ti Ho, *Studies on the Population of China, 1368–1953* (Cambridge, Mass.: Harvard University Press, 1959), 257ff.

32. Ricci (Gallagher), *Journals*, 343–344.

33. Ricci (Gallagher), *Journals*, 544.

34. Xu Guangshi (1562–1633) was baptized Paul Hsu. The Jesuits transliterated his Chinese name as Siucuamcchi. See the biographical sketches in D'Elia, *Fonti Ricciane*, 2:250ff.; and Arthur Hummel, ed., *Eminent Chinese of the Qing Period (1644–1912)* (Washington, D.C.: U.S. Government Printing Office, 1943), 1:316ff.

35. On the conversion of the "three pillars" see C. E. Ronan and Bonnie B. C. Oh, *East Meets West: The Jesuits in China, 1582–1773* (Chicago: Loyola University Press, 1988), 142–147. On Paul Hsu's theology and his position on Chinese religions and rites, see John D. Young, *Confucianism and Christianity: The First Encounter* (Hong Kong: Hong Kong University Press, 1983), 41–58.

36. Young, *Confucianism and Christianity*, 146.

37. Young, *Confucianism and Christianity*, 49.

38. *Ricci* (Gallagher), *Journals*, 429.

39. There is no exact parallel between the medieval doctor's degree and the *jinshi* of the Chinese academies, but the Jesuits considered them about equal.

40. D'Elia, *Fonti Ricianne*, 2:250–255, 308–309.

41. D'Elia, *Fonti Ricianne*, 2:251, n. 3, quoting Alfons Väth, *Johann Adam Schall von Bell, S.J., Missionar in China, Kaiserlicher Astronom und Ratbeger am Hofe von Peking, 1592–1666* (Cologne: J. P. Bachem, 1933), 103.

42. D'Elia, *Fonti Ricianne*, 2:361.

43. His name was transliterated by the missionaries as Licezao. See D'Elia, *Fonti Ricianne*, 2:168–171; and Hummel, *Eminent Chinese*, 1:452–454.

44. D'Elia, *Fonti Ricianne*, 178–179.

45. On the church and Christian community in Nanjing, see Ricci (Gallagher), *Journals*, 2:426–432.

46. From the French translation by Henri Havret, "La Stele Chretienne de Si-Ngan-Fou," in *Variétés Sinologiques* no. 12 (Shanghai: Imprimerie de la Mission Catholique, 1897), 86. The monument was, of course, the famous Nestorian Monument (see vol. 1, chap. 18 of this work).

47. On Michael Yang, see the biographical sketches in D'Elia, *Fonti Ricianne*, 3:13–14, 263 (where his name is spelled Iamttimiun); and in Hummel, 2:894–895.

48. Dunne, *Generation of Giants*, 114.

49. Matteo Ricci, *The True Meaning of the Lord of Heaven (T'ien-chu Shih-i)*, English translation, with Chinese text, by D. Lancashire and P. Hu Kuo-chen (St. Louis: Institute of Jesuit Sources, 1985).

50. Lancashire, introduction to Ricci's *True Meaning*, 47. For a helpful summary and analysis of the book, see Ralph Covell, *Confucius, the Buddha, and Christ:*

A History of the Gospel in Chinese (Maryknoll, N.Y.: Orbis Books, 1986), 45–56. He describes its purpose as intentionally "pre-evangelistic."

51. J. S. Witek, in Ronan and Oh, *East Meets West*, 69–70, basing his admittedly reductionist analysis on Ricci's seventh chapter of *The True Meaning of the Lord of Heaven*. See Ricci, *The True Meaning of the Lord of Heaven*, 389, 405.

52. See Trigault's account in Ricci (Gallagher), *Journals*, 566–594.

53. Estimates vary widely. See n. 30 above. Cf. Kenneth Scott Latourette, *The Chinese: Their History and Culture*, 2 vols. (New York: Macmillan, 1941), 2:8, 9; Ping-ti Ho, *Studies on the Population of China*, 257ff.

54. Figures of Catholic membership and the quotation are from Paschal M. D'Elia, *The Catholic Missions in China: A Short Sketch of the History* (Shanghai: Commercial Press, 1941), 39–40. D'Elia's source is Ricci's *Opere Storiche*, ed. P. T. Venturi, 2:253; 1:448.

55. A. Thomas, *Histoire de la mission de Pékin*, part 1: *Depuis les origines jusqu'a l'arrivée des Lazaristes* (Paris: Louis-Michaud, 1923), 86–88. Ricci appointed Longobardi as superior in 1610, but the new head of the mission made his base in Nanjing, leaving de Ursis in charge at Beijing. Not until 1625 did Longobardi come back to Beijing as superior, serving in that capacity until his death in 1654.

56. For a balanced judgment, see Latourette, *A History of Christian Missions in China*, 135; Rowbotham, *Missionary and Mandarin*, 132; and for a more sympathetic treatment of Longobardi, see Dunne, *Generation of Giants*, 109–112.

57. John Adam Schall von Bell (1592–1666), born in Germany, reached Macao nine years after Ricci's death, in 1630. His Chinese name was Tang Jo-wang (Tang Ruowang). The most comprehensive work on Schall is Väth, *Johann Adam Schall von Bell*. See also Rachel Attwater's well-written biography *Adam Schall: A Jesuit at the Court of China, 1592–1666* (London: Geoffrey Chapman, 1963); and Schall's own *Historica Relatio eorum quae contigerunt occasione concertationis Calendarii Sinica facta a R. P. Joanne Adamo Schall*, French trans. by P. Bornet, as *Lettres et Mémoires d'Adam Schall* (Tientsin: Hautes Études, 1942). Also Jonathan Spence, *The China Watchers: Western Advisers in China, 1620–1960* (New York and Harmondsworth, England: Penguin Books, 1980), 1–22.

58. Ferdinand Verbiest (1623–1688). *The Astronomia Europaea of Ferdinand Verbiest* (Dillingen, 1687). Latin text, Eng. trans., notes, commentary (Nettetal: Steyler Verlag, 1993).

59. Rowbotham, *Missionary and Mandarin*, 69.

60. Among them was the head of the mission in Japan, Carvalho, a refugee from the fierce persecutions there, who had been transferred to Macao in 1615.

61. The two foreign priests assisting Schall were Sebastiano de Ursis and Diego de Pantoia. Dunne, *Generation of Giants*, 115ff.

62. Incidents like the execution as a spy in Guangzhou of the lay-brother Huang Ming-sha, one of the two first Chinese Jesuits, in Guangzhou in 1606, and mob violence against the mission in Shaochou were local anti-Christian demonstrations, not countrywide. See Dunne, *Generation of Giants*, chap. 8, 128–145.

63. Dunne, *Generation of Giants*, 142–149. The remaining Jesuits included eight European priests and six Chinese lay-brothers. In 1621 alone the mission reported some 582 conversions, over half of them in Hangzhou.

64. See D'Elia, *Fonti Ricciane*, 151, n. 3; Dunne, *Generation of Giants*, 153.

65. The Ming crown prince's Chinese name was Chu Ts'u-hsuan (Tang-ting). See Robert Chabrié, *Michael Boym, Jésuite Polonais et la Fin des Ming en Chine*

(1646–1662) (Paris: P. Bossuet, 1933), 61–69, 82–83, 95–97, 196–202. See also D. E. Mungello, *Curious Land: Jesuit Accommodation and the Origins of Sinology* (Honolulu: University of Hawaii, 1985, 1989), 139.

66. Chabrié, *Michael Boym,* 111–167, 189ff.

67. Chabrié, *Michael Boym,* 198–202; cf. Dunne, *Generation of Giants,* 354.

68. See D'Elia, *Fonti Ricciane,* 151 n. 3; Dunne, *Generation of Giants,* 153; Rowbotham, *Missionary and Mandarin,* 73ff. As early as 1619 the influential Christian Kuang-ch'i (Paul) Hsu offered his services to head an embassy to Korea to ask for military help against the invading Manchus, and planned to take one of the Jesuit missionaries with him to explore the possibility of a Christian mission there.

69. Schall, *Lettres et Mémoires d'Adam Schall,* 142ff.

70. The first telescope in China had been brought in by the Jesuit Johann Terrenz Schreck (Terrentius, in Latin), a friend of Galileo, in 1618. See Bangert, *A History of the Society of Jesus,* 352.

71. Schall, *Lettres et Mémoires d'Adam Schall,* 146–154 and passim.

72. Schall, *Lettres et Mémoires d'Adam Schall,* 218.

73. Dunne, *Generation of Giants,* 349, citing Väth, *Johann Adam Schall von Bell,* 209 n. 67.

74. Mungello, *Curious Land,* 107.

75. Schall, *Lettres et Mémoires d'Adam Schall,* 318–328.

76. Abbé E. Huc, *Christianity in China, Tartary and Thibet* (New York: P. J. Kennedy, 1884), 2:329ff.

77. As early as 1582 the first Jesuit attempt to build a church in China, by Ruggieri in Shaoqing, was abandoned for lack of funds. He had planned a Western-style church building (Rowbotham, *Missionary and Mandarin,* 55).

78. Schall, *Lettres et Mémoires d'Adam Schall,* 202ff.

79. The estimates are from Leonard M. Outerbridge, *The Lost Churches of China* (Philadelphia: Westminster Press, 1952), 86, citing a PhD thesis by George Dunne. On the statistics, which vary, cf. Harney, *The Jesuits in History,* 230–231; Bangert, *A History of the Society of Jesus,* 242–243; and Latourette, *A History of Christian Missions in China,* 107. The numbers do not include Portuguese Macao.

80. Latourette, *A History of Christian Missions in China,* 109.

81. Schall, *Lettres et Mémoires d'Adam Schall,* 406ff.

82. Young, *Confucianism and Christianity,* 85–91.

83. Dunne, *Generation of Giants,* 360ff.; Attwater, *Adam Schall,* 143–156.

84. Literature on the rites controversy is immense, and the basic issues are still hotly debated. The primary documents of the first years include the Jesuit Alessandro Valignano's defense of the principle of missionary accommodation to Asiatic customs, *Apologia en la cual se responde a diversas calumnias contra los PP de la Compania del Japon y de la China* (1598); the Franciscan Antonio de Santa Maria's two *Informaciones* of 1636, reporting to the authorities in Manila on Jesuit practices in China; the Dominican Juan Baptista de Morales's letter of 1639 charging the Jesuits with twelve inappropriate practices; a letter to the pope by the Jesuit vice provincial Francisco Furtado in 1639; and later, of course, the decisive papal bulls on the subject, *Ex illa die* (1715) and *Ex quo singulari* (1742). Recent important studies include George Minamiki, *The Chinese Rites Controversy from Its Beginning to Modern Times* (Chicago: Loyola University Press, 1985); Mungello, *Curious Land;* and J. S. Cummins, *A Question of Rites: Friar Domingo Navarrete and the Jesuits* (Aldershot, U.K. and Rutland, Vt.: Scolar Press, 1993).

85. See Rowbotham, *Missionary and Mandarin*, 133–134, and Cummins, *A Question of Rites*, 60–62.

86. On the Franciscan Antonio de Santa Maria (Anton Caballero), see Jacques Gernan, *China and the Christian Impact* (Cambridge: Cambridge University Press, 1985), 10–11, 33, 69.

87. See below chap. 7.

88. See Antonio S. Rosso, *Apostolic Legations to China of the Eighteenth Century* (South Pasadena, Calif.: P. and Ione Perkins, 1948), 96ff. See P. Saeki, *The Nestorian Documents and Relics in China*, 2nd ed. (Tokyo: Maruzen, 1951), 162, 188; Young, *Confucianism and Christianity*, 28ff.; and Covell, *Confucius, the Buddha, and Christ*, 62ff.

89. Jacques Gernet, *China and the Christian Impact: A Conflict of Cultures*, trans. Janet Lloyd (Cambridge: Cambridge University Press, 1986), 253 n. 47.

90. D'Elia, *Fonti Ricciane*, 1:117–118. Ricci introduced his chapter on the Chinese religions in this collection with the statement, "One can confidently hope that in the mercy of God many of the ancient Chinese found salvation in the natural law, assisted as they must have been by that special help which, as the theologians teach, is denied to no one who does what he can toward salvation, according to the light of his conscience." Ricci (Gallagher), *Journals*, 93. But cf. carefully Romans 1.

91. See chap. 4 above.

92. Dunne, *Generation of Giants*, 247ff., citing *AFH* (Florence, 1908–) 8:583 n. 1.

93. Dunne, *Generation of Giants*, 246–251, which includes long excerpts of a letter from Adam Schall to Alexander de Rhodes, November 8, 1637.

94. It is difficult for Westerners to appreciate the pivotal place of "rites and ceremonies" in traditional Chinese culture. For a sensitive description of "the rites" as the quintessential bonding base of historical Chinese values, see the discussion of Jerry Dennerline's work on the twentieth-century Chinese historian and philosopher Qian Mu (Ch'ien Mu), in Jonathan Spence, *Chinese Roundabout: Essays in History and Culture* (New York and London: W. W. Norton, 1992), 156–160.

95. On Caballero, also known as Antoine de Saint Marie, see L. C. Goodrich and Fang Chaoying, *Dictionary of Ming Biography, 1368–1644*, 2 vols. (New York and London: Columbia University Press, 1976).

96. Gernet, *China and the Christian Impact*, 182.

97. Latourette, *A History of Christian Missions in China*, 136.

98. "Quaesta xvii a Father J. B. de Moralez, missionum sinarum procurate, proposita Romae 1643 S. Cong. de Prop. Fide" (Rome, 1645). For details from a Dominican perspective on Morales and his charges, see Benno M. Biermann, *Die Anfange der Neueren Dominikanermission in China* in *Missionswissenschaftliche Abhandlungen und Texte*, no. 10, ed. J. Schmidlin (Munster in Westfalen: Aschendorffschen Verlagsbuchhandlung, 1927), 35ff., 50–68; and Dunne, *Generation of Giants*, 270ff.

99. The decree of 1646 had included the reservation, "until it shall be decided otherwise." (Latourette, *A History of Christian Missions in China*, 137).

100. Cummins, *A Question of Rites*, esp. 3–5, 144–168, 191, 242ff. Navarrete's remark is quoted on 144.

101. See Rosso, *Apostolic Legations to China*, 122ff.

102. See Ricci's letter of 1581, even before he entered China, on the importance of a native clergy, in Dunne, *Generation of Giants*, 25; and the role of Nicholas Trigault in petitioning in 1621 for permission for the use of the Chinese language in the liturgy (Dunne, *Generation of Giants*, 162ff.).

103. Dunne, *Generation of Giants*, 162–182.

104. Kenneth Scott Latourette, *A History of Christian Missions in China* (New York: Macmillan, 1929), 122–124.

105. Neill, *History of Christian Missions*, 523.

106. See J. de Moidrey, *La hiérarchie catholique en China, en Corée et au Japon (1307–1914), Variétés Sinologiques*, no. 10 (Shanghai: L'Orphélinat de T'ou-se-we, 1914), 71–72, and map of the division of the vicariate in 1680, 249.

107. Gregory Lopez, titular bishop of Basileus and apostolic vicar of Nanjing with authority extending to Beijing, Shandong Henan, and Korea, was baptized by a Franciscan at age sixteen, was exiled to Macao and Manila in 1639, and returned to China where he joined the Dominican order. In 1656 he was ordained priest in Manila, the first Chinese to be received into that office. François Pallu, leader of the early French missionaries of the Paris Society of Foreign Missions in China, was so impressed with him that in 1659 he recommended Lopez to the pope for consecration as bishop. His appointment and consecration were delayed, the papal appointment until 1674, and because of opposition by the Dominicans to his position on the rites question, he did not receive consecration as bishop until 1685, and then not by the Dominican bishop but by the irenic Italian Franciscan, della Chiesa. See J. de Moidrey, *La hiérarchie catholique en Chine*, 22–24, 35. See also A. E. Moule, "The First Arrival of the Jesuits at the Capital of China," *New China Review* 4 (1922): 480–488; Launay, *Histoire générale de la Société des Missions-Etrangères*, 1:187; and Dunne, *Generation of Giants*, 174, 345.

108. Latourette, *A History of Christian Missions in China*, 116ff.; Rowbotham, *Missionary and Mandarin*, 103ff.

109. This letter is in the archives of the French Foreign Office, according to Fulop-Miller, *The Jesuits*, 253.

110. Latourette, *A History of Christian Missions in China*, 116.

111. Rosso, *Apostolic Legations to Peking*, 128–129. Latourette notes that teaching and baptizing were not explicitly granted, but the edict was so favorable that this would scarcely be denied by the local authorities (*A History of Christian Missions in China*, 126–127). Cf. Gernet's analysis of the edict (*China and the Christian Impact*, 137).

112. On the Russian treaty, see Joseph Sebes, *The Jesuits and the Sino-Russian Treaty of Nerchinsk: The Diary of Thomas Pereira, S.J.* (Rome: Institutum Historicum S.I., 1961). Verbiest's role, though not central, is noted on pp. 62, 67.

113. On the text of the decree, see Rowbotham, *Missionary and Mandarin*, 110; and Rosso, *Apostolic Legations*, 129 n. 25.

114. See the summary of the estimates in A. Thomas, *Histoire de la mission de Pékin*, part 2: *Depuis l'arrivée des Lazaristes jusqu'a la revolte des Boxeurs* (Paris: Louis-Michaud, 1923), 395–404.

115. Rowbotham, *Missionary and Mandarin*, 111.

116. In 1693 its apostolic vicar Charles Maigrot forbade Christians in his Fujian diocese to follow the Jesuit policy and actually removed two Jesuits who refused to obey him. See A. Thomas, *La Mission de Pékin*, 166–172; Launay, *Histoire générale de la Société des Missions-Etrangères*, 1:384–391.

117. Latourette, *A History of Christian Missions in China*, 140, citing Franz Rudolf Merkel, *G. W. von Leibniz und die China-Mission* (Leipzig: J. C. Hinrichs, 1920).

•118. See the Jesuit statement and the emperor's letter of approval in A. Thomas, *La Mission de Pékin*, 174–175; and in English, in Minamiki, *The Chinese Rites Controversy from Its Beginning to Modern Times*, 40–42.

119. See Schmidlin, *Catholic Mission Theory*, 163–170. The first apostolic vicariate in China had been created in 1658–1659, but the first *resident* apostolic vicars in the country were the French bishop Pallu, for Fujian province, and the Chinese bishop Luo Wenzao (Gregory Lopez), in 1685, for north China. In 1696 new vicariates were added to increase papal control of the wrangling China missions. See also de Moidrey, *La Hiérarchie Catholique*, 217–218, 228ff., 254–255.

120. Minamiki, *The Chinese Rites Controversy from Its Beginning to Modern Times*, 43–52; A. Thomas, *La Mission de Pékin*, 176; Dunne, *Generation of Giants*, 291–297. Thomas, though critical of both sides in the controversy, is generally biased against the Jesuits. Minamiki gives a more detailed analysis of the genuine papal attempt to reach a compromise, and defends the Jesuits.

121. On the de Tournon mission, see R. C. Jenkins, *The Jesuits in China and the Legation of Cardinal De Tournon* (London: David Nutt, 1894); and Rosso, *Apostolic Legations*, 149–186.

122. A. Thomas, *La Mission de Pékin*, 188–193.

123. The test was not entirely fair. He was suddenly asked to translate an inscription and stumbled badly over the characters. Better linguists than he have been similarly baffled, but a Ricci would have risen to the occasion. See Rowbotham, *Missionary and Mandarin*, 156 n. 9; Jenkins, *The Jesuits in China*, 28–29.

124. Rosso, *Apostolic Legations*, 169; Rowbotham, *Missionary and Mandarin*, 155ff.; Launay, *Histoire générale de la Société des Missions-Etrangères*, 1:469–477. For a vivid account of the legate's rough treatment by the Portuguese in Macao and high praise for de Tournon, see Jenkins, *The Jesuits in China*, 130–150. The quotation is from that book's title page.

125. De Moidrey, *La Hiérarchie Catholique*, 22–24, 35; Dunne, *Generation of Giants*, 174, 345.

126. A detailed analysis of negative reactions to Christianity in seventeenth-century China appears in Gernet, *China and the Christian Impact*.

127. See Young's analysis of Yang Guangxian's arguments (referred to above), *Confucianism and Christianity*, 85–96, 99–106. Also Gernet, *China and the Christian Impact*, 112–126, 181–192, 201–208.

128. Gernet, *China and the Christian Impact*, 107 n. 11, 12. See Gernet's full treatment of the growing gap between the missionaries and the literati, 105–213.

129. Gernet, *China and the Christian Impact*, 75–76, 114–115. The opponents of the Jesuits disputed the arguments of these Chinese defenders of the principle of accommodation, particularly Yang's, and dismissed them as unacceptable syncretism (Gernet, *China and the Christian Impact*, 32ff.).

130. See A. Thomas, *La Mission de Pékin*, 241–251, for a French translation of the bull.

131. See Minamiki, *The Chinese Rites Controversy from Its Beginning to Modern Times*, 62–66.

132. See the French translation of the 1715 bull (*Ex illa die*), in Thomas, *La Mission de Pékin*, 243–251, which was affirmed by the bull of 1742 (*Ex quo*

singulari); see Thomas, *La Mission de Pékin,* 365–374, and Minamiki, *The Chinese Rites Controversy from Its Beginning to Modern Times,* 58–76.

133. Launay, *Histoire générale de la Société des Missions-Etrangères,* 1:539–542.

134. Political pressures and growing nationalism in Europe were other major factors that forced the pope to dissolve the Society. The Jesuits were not restored until 1814.

135. A basic reference for original documents on the rites controversy is Robert Streit and Johannes Dindinger, *Bibliotheca Missionum,* 10 vols. (Munster and Aachen: Veröffentlichungen des Internationalen Instituts fur missionswissenschaft Forschung, 1916–1939), 5:728–779. A recent analysis favoring the Jesuit position describes it as a matter of "probability" and pragmatism, "a balanced halfway dialectic based on reasonable premises that were admissible by Catholic moral principles and made imperative in order to win a hearing for the Gospel" (Ronan and Oh, *East Meets West,* 48). In an analysis favoring the Jesuits' opponents, J. S. Cummins cites Jesuit errors in presenting "Catholicism as a revival of the primitive religion of China," which contrary to their claims had never known the Christian God, and which flung open the door to the absorption of Christianity by syncretism (J. S. Cummins, ed., *The Travels and Controversies of Friar Domingo Navarrete 1618–1686* [Cambridge University Press, 1962], 1:lxvii ff.).

136. For 1800 the number of Christians is estimated sometimes at 150,000, sometimes at 200,000. An estimate for 1810 places 31 European and 80 Chinese priests in China. Latourette, *A History of Missions in China,* 128–129, 158, 162, 174, 182.

137. Fulop-Miller, *The Jesuits,* 253–254.

138. D'Elia, *The Catholic Missions in China,* 53 n. 1. He quotes from a collection of Chinese documents published in facsimile by a Chinese scholar, Chen-yuan, *Documents Concerning Kanghsi and the Roman Legate* (Peiping: Ku-kung po-wu-yuan, 1932).

139. See the edict of banishment of Maigrot in A. Thomas, *La Mission de Pékin,* 196–197.

140. Wolfram Eberhard, *A History of China,* 3rd ed. (Berkeley and Los Angeles: University of California Press, 1971), 281–282.

141. Rowbotham, *Missionary and Mandarin,* 176–177.

142. Rowbotham, *Missionary and Mandarin,* 176ff.

143. Rowbotham, *Missionary and Mandarin,* 198.

144. Cited in John Parker, *Windows into China: The Jesuits and Their Books, 1580–1730* (Boston: Public Library of the City of Boston, 1978), 35.

145. See Rowbotham, *Missionary and Mandarin,* 180ff., 225–226; Joseph Krahl, *China Missions in Crisis: Bishop Laimbeckhoven and His Times, 1738–1787* (Rome: Gregorian University Press, 1964), 89.

146. Rowbotham, *Missionary and Mandarin,* 226.

147. Rowbotham, *Missionary and Mandarin,* 183–189.

148. A. Thomas, *La Mission dé Pekin,* 408–410; Latourette, *A History of Christian Missions in China,* 162.

149. Krahl, *China Missions in Crisis,* 50; Latourette, *A History of Missions in China,* 162ff.

150. Krahl, *China Missions in Crisis,* 49–77; Rowbotham, *Missionary and Mandarin,* 201–205.

151. By A. Thomas, for example, in 1923, in *La Mission de Pékin,* 431.

152. See Fredrik Nielsen, *The History of the Papacy in the XIXth Century,* 2 vols. (New York: E. P. Dutton, 1906), 1:56–87.

153. See Krahl, *China Missions in Crisis,* 127–135, 196–207, 209–245. Also *CE,* s.v. "Clement XIII," "Clement XIV."

154. Krahl, *China Mission in Crisis,* 127–135.

155. On the Beijing situation see A. Thomas, *La Mission de Pékin,* 1:432–453; Krahl, *China Missions in Crisis,* 223–288.

156. The Vincentians had a small seminary in Beijing, and the Portuguese seminary in Macao was still training Chinese priests in the early 1800s. A. Thomas, *La Mission de Pékin,* 2:24–25; Latourette, *A History of Christian Missions in China,* 174.

157. Krahl, *China Missions in Crisis,* 212–288.

158. George Macartney, *An Authentic Account of an Embassy from the King of Great Britain to the Emperor of China* (Philadelphia: Robert Campbell, 1799).

159. On China's population explosion, see Eberhard, *A History of China,* 274; and cf. Ho, *Studies on the Population of China,* 257ff.

160. Letter, François Bourgeois, Beijing, May 15, 1775, to the Abbé de Charvet, in *Lettres édifiantes et curieuses de Chine par des missionaires jésuites 1702–1776,* ed. J.-L. Vissière (Paris: Garnier-Flammarion, 1979), 501–502.

Chapter 6

Korea (1593–1800)

The Hermit Kingdom

The cold in Korea is very severe...All day long my limbs are half be-
numbed, and in the morning I can hardly move my hands to say mass, but
I keep myself in good health; thanks to God and the fruit that our Lord is
giving. I am cheerful and don't mind my work and the cold...Although
Hideyoshi sends food, so little reaches here that it is impossible to sustain
all with them...It is now two months since ships have come, and many
craft were lost.   —Letter of de Cespedes (1594/1595)[1]

De Cespedes and the Japanese Invasion

One of the unplanned and unexpected by-products of the Christian century in Japan was the first recorded introduction of Christianity into
the spiny peninsula of ancient Korea, which points like a bony finger
from the Asian mainland toward Japan.[2] The first Westerner known to
set foot on Korean soil was in all probability a Spanish Jesuit in 1593,
Gregorio de Cespedes (1551–1611). De Cespedes was accompanied by
a Japanese brother of the Jesuit order, Hankan, baptized Leon. Neither
Medina nor Cory mention the possibility that de Cespedes was not the
first European in Korea. "A certain Mari, a westerner," was shipwrecked
on Cheju-do eleven years earlier, in 1582, and sent on to China, according to the *Yak-p'o-chip* (the *Records* of Chong Tak whose pen name was
Yak-p'o). "Westerner" at that date in Korea did not necessarily denote
European, but the name and clothes hint of the Catholic priesthood; the
man is described as dressed in black, and it was Chong Tak who in 1582
led the annual Korean embassy to the Chinese court in Beijing, perhaps
taking Mari with him. At any rate it is possible that he was a Western
priest, and that Korea's first contact with Christianity and the West was
thus dignified by respect and courtesy, marred neither by the association
with an invading army, as with de Cespedes, nor by the indignities of
imprisonment, as with the shipwrecked Protestant, Hendrick Hamel, a
half-century later.[3] He came in troubled times and in unpropitious company as chaplain to the invading Japanese armies sent by Hideyoshi to
capture Korea as a stepping stone to the conquest of China. As a missionary in Japan for thirty-four years, from 1577 to his death, de Cespedes is
best known as superior of the Jesuit seminary in Osaka, where he was
noted for his fluency in Japanese, and for a visit the great Hideyoshi paid

him there in 1585. A few years later de Cespedes was called south to help encourage and disciple the converts of a mass movement toward Christianity that was spreading among the domains of the Christian daimyo in Kyushu, a difficult task for missionaries struggling with the language, but for which de Cespedes's linguistic ability made him singularly effective. His base was Nagasaki, the country's most important Christian center, and Arima.

When Hideyoshi in 1592 sent nine army divisions plunging across the straits to crush Korea, his most famous general, the leader of the vanguard, was Konishi Yukinaga, "the chivalrous Christian daimyo" as Baxter describes him, who fought his way spectacularly in twenty days from Pusan, the southern port city, three hundred miles north to the Korean capital, Seoul. In another two months he had captured the old northern capital, Pyongyang. Four out of Konishi's five brigade commanders were Christians, as were about eighteen thousand of his men.[4]

The invasion is often described as a race between Konishi's Christian division and the smaller army of his fierce rival, the aggressively Buddhist general Kato Kiyomasa, "the tiger of Korea," a race in which the invading Christians beat the Buddhists to the prize, the Korean capital, but it must be remembered that this was not a war of religion, but of Japanese imperialist expansion.[5]

Konishi's lightning strike to the north, incredibly successful though it was, had left his lifeline to Japan in the rear vulnerable to attack by a Korean admiral, Yi Sun-Shin, who was as much a genius of warfare on the sea as Konishi was on land. A Japanese historian ruefully remarks, "In the water the Japanese tiger was no match for the Korean shark,"[6] and Konishi was forced to fall back to a ring of fortresses along Korea's lower coast, where his soldiers faced a grim winter in 1593. Most of them were from warm Kyushu. One third of them had been killed. With his men short of food, shivering in the Korean cold and dispirited after a year and a half of military stalemate, the Christian general, Konishi, may well have decided to raise their sagging morale by sending for a priest "to come and console them in their exile." De Cespedes, with a Japanese brother of the Jesuit order, Leon Hankan, accompanying him, arrived on December 27, 1593.[7]

He was welcomed by the Christian troops, which included the flower of Kyushu samurai chivalry, and the Catholic lords of Arima, Hirado, Goto, Amakusa, and two sons of the Christian daimyo of Omura, lord of the region around Nagasaki. But the war was not going well. "Peace does not seem to be heading toward a conclusion," de Cespedes wrote. And again, "These Christians (i.e., the Japanese soldiers) are very poor and suffer from hunger, cold, illness and other inconveniences."[8] Three of the Japanese forts along the southern coast were commanded by Christians

(Konishi; his son-in-law, the son of the daimyo of Tsushima; and the daimyo of Buzen, Simon Kuroda), and these became de Cespedes's parish as he climbed the steep hills on which the forts were built, preaching constantly and baptizing a considerable number. But his stay in Korea was cut short when the bitter rivalry between Hideyoshi's two most successful generals, the Christian Konishi and the ardent Buddhist, Kato, caught de Cespedes in the middle and forced his return to Japan. The Buddhist threatened to report to Hideyoshi the questionable presence of a foreign priest spreading his doctrine among the troops.[9] How long de Cespedes was actually in Korea is uncertain, perhaps as little as a few months, perhaps as long as a year and a half.[10]

Of de Cespedes's later years in Japan little information is available. His work in Shimabara overwhelmed him with the growth of the church. He wrote in 1597 to a missionary in Mexico that his parish contained more than fifteen thousand Christians and he had only one priest as helper.[11] But on a more somber note he writes of the beginnings of persecution, and that twenty-six Catholics had been crucified in Nagasaki.[12] He concludes the letter with thanksgiving for their courage, and the hope that he too might be worthy of such a death: "Blessed be God our Lord that he thus has deigned in our time to irrigate his vineyard with the blood of so many of His servants...I beg of you to petition God for me the crown of martyrdom, if it is to be for the glory of His majesty."[13]

It is rather sad that this devout and faithful man was denied both the immediate honor for which he prayed — martyrdom — and another honor that he was too modest to claim and too limited by his extremely restricted circumstances in Korea to earn: that of being, though in a limited way, the first Christian missionary in Korea. He died in 1611 from apoplexy after thirty-four years in Japan. As far as we know, he met no Koreans in Korea. Dallet, an early historian of Korean Christianity, says flatly that the withdrawing Japanese troops "left no germs of the Christian faith behind," and that "de Cespedes saw no indigenous Koreans save the prisoners of war who were sent to Japan to be sold as slaves."[14] He was not the founder of the Korean church. He was not even a missionary to Korea. He was a chaplain to Japanese troops, and what he was called to do he did very well. That is all. There is no reference to him in Korean sources of that period.

There is, however, one illuminating, redeeming footnote that should be added to the story of this terrible invasion. When Seoul fell to the Japanese, one of the hostages taken was a twelve-year-old boy of aristocratic birth, who had apparently been voluntarily surrendered by his father to the Christian general, Konishi. Konishi sent him back to Japan asking that he not be treated as a captive but be given to the church. He was baptized in 1592 with the Christian name Vincent, and was enrolled in the Jesuit seminary.[15]

The boy's Korean name is given as Caoun — probably Kwon. He was only twelve years old when he was taken hostage. For a while the Jesuits dreamed that he might be the key to the return of Christianity to Korea, this time not with invaders, but as a returning prisoner of war. A small Korean community of Christian converts, composed mostly of those forcibly taken to Japan during the war, built a church in Nagasaki in 1610, "the first in the world put up by Korean Catholics."[16] In 1614, the year of Ieyasu's universal prohibition of Christianity in Japan, they sent him to Beijing, hoping he could make his way home across the Yalu River, but it was not to be. Vincent Kwon returned instead to Japan where in the persecutions of 1626–1627 he was arrested at Shimabara and burned at the stake in Nagasaki, one of Korea's earliest Christians, and one of the first Korean martyrs. The first Korean martyr, however, was not Vincent but a man known only by his Japanese name, Hachikan. He was baptized as Joaquin and beheaded four years later in 1613.[17]

Christian Influences from China

By the time of Vincent Kwon's martyrdom, the knowledge of the Christian faith was beginning to filter into closed Korea through contacts of the annual Korean embassy to Beijing with the Jesuit fathers in that city, at first perhaps by accident and later through the natural intellectual interest of scholars attached to the embassy in the ways and philosophy of the curious Westerners. The earliest mention by a Korean scholar of a Christian book is found in the writings of the Confucianist Yi Syu-Kwang who died in 1627. He gives a remarkably accurate summary of Matteo Ricci's famous *The True Meaning of the Lord of Heaven* (*T'ien-chu Shih-i*), and mentions also his *On Friendship*.[18]

Another more personal contact between Korea and the Christian faith occurred a few years later when the crown prince of Korea, So-hyun, was captured by the Manchus. So-hyun was declared heir to the throne during the reign of King Injo (reigned 1623–1649). Korea had sided with the Ming dynasty in its losing struggle against the invading Manchurians, and in 1644 the victorious Manchus (the Qing dynasty) brought the Korean prince as hostage to their court in captured Beijing. During his eight years as a hostage in Beijing the lonely young Korean was befriended by the great Jesuit, Adam Schall. A letter he wrote to the missionary is still extant. Note how his genuine appreciation of Schall's friendship and of European science is tempered with a cautious political hesitation about how the religious implications of his relationship with a missionary might play at home in Korea:

> Yesterday, looking at your unexpected gift of the image of our Divine Saviour, of the globe and the books on astronomy and other European sciences, I was moved by such extreme pleasure that I could hardly believe it

to be true ... Glancing through the books I noted that they bring us a doctrine which is quite new to us, and well fitted to improve our minds and develop our virtues. In our territories so cut off from intellectual matters, it has been quite unknown until now. The holy image possesses such majesty that, hanging on the wall, it calms the mind and drives out even the slightest thought of evil. As for the globe and the books on mathematics, they are of such great value that they are indispensable to our age ... It is true that we have books on the subject, but they are teeming with blunders and have not been revised for centuries. Once I have returned to the court I shall have them published for the use of our scholars.

We two come from different countries so distant from each other, yet ever since we met on foreign soil we have felt like brothers ... I should very much like to take these books and the holy image with me to my country, but when I consider that my subjects who know nothing about the cult of the divine may fall into the sin of sacrilege, I am full of anxiety. Let me therefore return the holy image to you that I may not be the occasion of sin in others by taking it with me.[19]

Upon his return to Korea, Prince So-hyun took the risk of taking with him five Chinese Catholic eunuchs and three Chinese Catholic court ladies. We shall never know what the home reaction to that might have been. It could, indeed, have been the beginnings of a Catholic mission in Korea but sixty days after he was received in audience by his father King Injo in 1645, the young crown prince died. His Catholic Chinese entourage was returned to China at once. But a connection at least had been made, and the French Order of the Blessed Sacrament was instructed by the bishop of Beijing to continue attempts to bring the gospel to Korea.[20]

The Dutch Come to Korea[21]

Through Western contacts with Japan also came a secondary brush of Christianity into Korea, less obviously and more peripherally Christian than the visit of de Cespedes or the discovery of Chinese Christian literature. This was the unplanned appearance in 1653 of a shipwrecked band of Dutch sailors and traders cast ashore by a storm on the island of Chejudo (Quelpart) as they neared their goal of Nagasaki, Japan. It would scarcely deserve mention in a broad survey like this were it not for the light the incident throws upon Korea's complete isolation from Western expansion in the seventeenth century and its blurred knowledge of a religion they had heard called *kirishitan* by the Japanese.

The twenty-six surviving Dutchmen were not very pious Protestants, but happily identified themselves as *kirishitan*. It was a mistake. What the Dutch did not know was that the word in Japan, and as understood by the Koreans, meant "Catholic," and that ever since the Tokugawa shogunate had outlawed Catholicism, a treaty between Japan and Korea stipulated that any Catholics seeking refuge or escape in Korea were to be sent at once back to Japan for execution.

Precisely such a disastrous end to a shipwreck on Korean soil had occurred about ten years earlier in 1644 when a Chinese ship bound for Guangzhou with some Catholics aboard ran aground on the Korean coast. When five of the fifty-two sailors aboard were found to be Catholics (*kirishitan*), they were dispatched to Japan and executed. As for the Dutchmen shipwrecked in 1653, eventually seven escaped and were returned to Holland; seven remained in Korea.[22]

Not for about another century and a half would Korea, "the Hermit Nation," slowly, painfully, and against violent resistance, be opened by its own people to a Christian presence, this time once again from China.[23]

NOTES

1. Letter of Gregorio de Cespedes (1594/1595). Ralph Cory, trans., "Some Notes on Father Gregorio de Cespedes, Korea's First European Visitor," *TRASK* 27 (1937): 44. Parts of this chapter appeared in different form in *The Korea Herald* as segments of a series on "Forerunners of Change" in Korea, March 4 and 11, 1973.

2. Efforts to trace Christianity in Korea back to contacts with Nestorianism in China in the seventh and eighth centuries fail for lack of either tradition or evidence. Cf. vol. 1 of this *History* (461–462) with the ambitious attempt to find Nestorian links in Oh Yun-Tae, *Hankuk Kitokyo Sa* (Church History of Korea), vol. 1, *On Nestorianism*. But it is important to note that as early as 1566 two Jesuits in Japan, Cosmo de Torres, superior of the mission, and Gaspar Vilela, had proposed a mission to Korea totally unconnected with any military invasion as a strategic move that might help to open the Chinese empire to the gospel (Juan Ruiz de Medina, *The Catholic Church in Korea: Its Origins 1566–1784*, trans. John Bridges [Rome: Istituto Storico, 1991], 36ff.).

3. Ruiz de Medina, *The Catholic Church in Korea*, 47–53; and Cory, "Some Notes on Father Gregorio de Cespedes," 1–55 (citing *Yak-p'o Chip*, vol. 3). See also Yu Song-yong, *Ching-bi-ro* (Hyon Am Press edition, 1969), 248.

4. Murdoch and Yamagata, *A History of Japan*, 2:317–320. See the entire chapter on "The Korean War," 2:302–359.

5. Konishi's and Kato's two divisions combined were only about one-fifth of the total Japanese land force (Murdoch and Yamagata, *A History of Japan*, 2:320) and few Koreans, if any, at the time were aware of the religious difference between two of the enemy generals.

6. Yoshi S. Kono, *Japanese Expansion on the Asian Continent*, vol. 1 (Berkeley: University of California Press, 1937), 1:153.

7. The date is disputed, but Cory's preference for 1593 is persuasive ("Some Notes on Father Gregorio de Cespedes," 9–10), as against 1594 (Dallet, Guzmán et al.), or 1597 (Henthorn). The place was probably the bay and fort at Ungch'on, near the naval port of Chinhae. See also Ruiz de Medina, *The Catholic Church in Korea*, 68 nn. 71, 72; and J. Laures, "Koreas Erste Berührung mit dem Christentum," *ZMR* 40 (1956): 177–189.

8. Quotations from the de Cespedes letters, here and below, are from Cory, "Some Notes on Father Gregory de Cespedes," 1–55.

9. Cory, "Some Notes on Father Gregorio de Cespedes," 17ff., citing Luis de Guzmán, *Historia de las Missiones* (Alcala, 1601; Tokyo: Yushodo, 1976), vol. 12, chap. 37.

10. Cory, "Some Notes on Father Gregorio de Cespedes," 20, argues better for the longer period than Steichen, who says de Cespedes after two months (*Les daimyos chrétiens ou un siècle de l'histoire et politique du Japon, 1549–1650* [Hong Kong, 1904]). Cory thinks de Cespedes may have returned to Korea in 1597.

11. The letter is translated in Cory, "Some Notes on Father Gregorio de Cespedes," app. 6:46–51.

12. See above chap. 4, for details of the 1597 martyrdoms.

13. Cory, "Some Notes on Father Gregorio de Cespedes," 50–51.

14. Ch. Dallet, *Histoire de l'église de Corée* (Paris: Librairie Victor Palmé, 1874), 1:4. There is, however, a reference to an unidentified samurai from Bungo among the Japanese troops who was so distressed at the sight of infants dying in abandoned villages that, though he could not save them, he stopped to baptize them "into heaven," about two hundred of them, according to the record. Ruiz de Medina, *The Catholic Church in Korea*, 74 nn. 1–4, devoutly describes this as "the birth of the Catholic Church in Korea," citing a 1595 letter of Luis Frois in the Japan/China section of the *Archivum Romanum Societatis Iesu*, 52 102v, in Rome.

15. On Vincent/Caoun, see Ruiz de Medina, *The Catholic Church in Korea*, 75, 94–97, 99–100, 111, 116, 127; Andreas Choi, *L'erection du premier vicariat apostolique et les origines du Catholicisme en Corée* (Schoneck-Beckenried, Switzerland: NRSM, 1961), 6. On other Christian contacts with Korea through Korean lay believers during the negotiations following the end of the invasion (1597–1604), see Ruiz de Medina, *The Catholic Church in Korea*, 86–90.

16. Ruiz de Medina, *The Catholic Church in Korea*, 88–90.

17. Ruiz de Medina, *The Catholic Church in Korea*, 91.

18. On Yi Syu-Kwang (Yi Siu-koang, 1563–1627), see Choi, *L'erection du premier vicariat apostolique*, 8, n. 1. The best translation of Ricci's *T'ien-chu Shih-i* is by Douglas Lancashire and Peter Hu Kuo-cen, *The True Meaning of the Lord of Heaven*.

19. Joseph Chang-Mun Kim and John Jae-sun Chung, eds., *Catholic Korea: Yesterday and Today* (Seoul: Catholic Korea Publishing Co., 1964), 21.

20. Kim and Chung, *Catholic Korea*, 22.

21. I borrow the phrase, and much that follows, from the title of the best account of this affair, Gary Ledyard's carefully annotated study *The Dutch Come to Korea*. On Dutch expansion in Asia see chap. 10 below.

22. Gary Ledyard, *The Dutch Come to Korea* (Seoul: Royal Asiatic Society, Korea Branch, 1971), 88.

23. See chap. 14, "The Catholic Century in Korea."

Chapter 7

The Spaniards in the Philippines (1521–1800)

You must exercise much care and vigilance to...effect what is proper for the colonization and pacification of the lands that are found. You will advise us...of the treatment of the natives of said lands, with whom you must be careful to use good faith and fulfil all that is promised — they must be treated most affectionately, both in order that they may be influenced to become good Christians, which is our principal desire, and that they may with good will serve us and be under our government, subjection, and friendship.   —Charles I of Spain (Charles V of Germany) Instructions to Magellan, April 6, 1519

TWO mistakes irreversibly changed the history of the world in the late 1400s and early 1500s. Every schoolchild knows about the first mistake. In 1492 Columbus sailed west across the blue Atlantic to find the Spice Islands of the East Indies for Spain, and discovered America instead. The Portuguese, however, with better navigators, sailed east around Africa and outraced Spain to the riches of the East Indies. A second mistake was made by the pope. To avoid conflict between these two important Catholic powers as they pushed their way around the earth searching for new worlds to conquer and new wealth to gain, the pope "sliced the world in two like an orange" as a current saying went, and in 1593 and 1595 divided its "unknown and heathen" portions between his two loyal empires, Spain and Portugal. He gave the Americas to Spain, he thought, and Asia to Portugal.

Magellan and the "Voyage around the World"

In 1519 a Portuguese explorer, Ferdinand Magellan (or Magãlhaes), after a quarrel with his own king, convinced the king of Spain that given the lack of more precise geographical knowledge, the rich Moluccas might actually be so far east of India as to lie on the Spanish side of the pope's line of demarcation rather than Portugal's, and was dispatched to probe westward beyond Columbus and beyond the Americas to find out.[1]

This was the famous first voyage around the world that has made the name of Magellan as familiar as that of Columbus. Actually Magellan did not quite circumnavigate the world, but his men and one of his ships did. What Magellan discovered was the Philippines, and though he was killed there in the islands, his discovery gave the Spanish crown its richest ecclesiastical prize in Asia, for the Philippine people "stand unique as the only large mass of Asiatics converted to Christianity in modern times." Arguable exceptions would be Korea, Indonesia, and India, but in none of these is the Christian population a majority, as is true of the Philippines.[2]

Magellan's missionary contribution to this is debatable. To his credit, he celebrated Easter 1521 with great ceremony on a small island off the coast of Leyte only two weeks after his first landfall to thank God for a safe arrival in the islands.[3] Moving on to Cebu, which was ruled by a more powerful chief named Humabon, Magellan sought to make sure that the natives fully understood the greater power of his own master, the king of Spain, and refused to pay port fees, but mindful of his orders from the king about "affectionate treatment of the natives," he offered peace and an exchange of gifts. The trading was all in favor of the Spaniards, ten pieces of Philippine gold for thirteen pieces of Spanish iron.[4] In the conversations that followed, Magellan, attentive to the evangelistic mandate contained in the instructions of Charles I — "that they may be influenced to become good Christians"[5] — spoke to the chief with the aid of interpreters about the power of his God, far greater than that of any local spirits. Within two weeks the chief asked for baptism. Probably more effective than any of the conversations, however evangelistic they may have been, was what appeared to the islanders to be a miracle. The chief's grandson had suffered for two years of an incurable fever. Magellan sent his chaplain to baptize the young man, and in a few days the young man was out of bed and walking. When word of the remarkable cure spread through the villages "over twenty-two hundred Indians" followed the chief's example and "were baptized and professed the name and faith of Christ."

But at that point Magellan turned more imperialist than missionary. Overconfident at the ease of his success, he persuaded his new convert that if he would only call his neighboring chiefs to believe also, he could, with Magellan's help, soon be premier chief of the whole area. "But will they come?" the chief asked. If they don't, Magellan boasted, his Spanish soldiers would compel them to come. At first, the response was gratifying. The chiefs did come, one by one, to profess allegiance — all but the premier chief, who refused. So, true to his promise, Magellan took forty (or sixty) of his men and crossed to the reluctant chief's island where he found himself facing an army of three thousand warriors. Undismayed and confident that his few armed Spaniards could defeat a hundred times their number of "Indians" he attacked and was killed by a thrust from a lance. The Spaniards retreated. The Cebu chief, Magellan's first "convert," was alarmed and fearing reprisal secretly recanted his new faith, negotiated an understanding with his former superior chief, and politely invited Magellan's surviving successor and his chief officers to a banquet. There his warriors fell upon them and slew them. The rest of the Spaniards fled, burning one of their three ships for lack of sailors to man it.[6]

This earliest encounter of Christianity and Philippine culture, with its unresolved mixture of superficial success and questionable methods, may have colored subsequent perceptions of the planting of Christianity in the islands. Harsh, ecclesiastically dominated Spanish rule in the Philippines is sometimes compared unfavorably with the more culture-sensitive Portuguese missions in Japan and China. But this ignores both the enduring nature of the church planted by the Spanish and the enlightened ministries of some of their first missions and missionaries.

The First Missions (1565–1578)[7]

The first Spanish missions proved to be not at all one-sidedly arrogant and violent, as their very first mission proved. In 1565, the first Catholic missionary to reach the islands, Andres de Urdaneta, landed with the Spanish expedition of 1565 on Cebu accompanied by four other Augustinian priests and a lay brother. This marks the beginning of established Catholic missions in the Philippines. Urdaneta was a former military captain and famous as a navigator. While still a layman he had reached Mindanao and the Moluccas on Spain's second expedition to the islands, in 1525, and for a while fought the Portuguese for control of the Moluccas. But though offered full military command of another expedition, he had wearied of the fightings and cruelties of the explorers and instead entered an Augustinian monastery in 1552. Only when a later expedition, named for its commander, Legaspi, asked Urdaneta to pilot a fleet from Mexico to the Far East, and granted him the additional title of "protector of the Indians," did he accept. His instructions specified his status as missionary, not a soldier, and allowed him to take five missionaries of his order to the Philippines with him. It was this Legaspi expedition that laid the critical necessary foundations for Spain's claim to the Philippines, and its success owed much to the wise counsel of Urdaneta and his Augustinians, who nevertheless continued to express very frankly their misgivings about Spain's right of conquest.[8] Throughout most of the first three centuries of Christianity in the islands the Augustinians were the dominant missionary force.

On the island of Cebu in the mid-Philippines pioneers began their work. The first convert of the Augustinians was a woman, a niece of the chief of Cebu, Rajah Tupas. She was baptized in 1565, and the Rajah himself three years later. Baptisms multiplied rapidly thereafter in a pattern that became familiar: when the chief accepted the faith, the village followed.[9]

Only slowly did the mission expand its outreach beyond Cebu. First it followed the colonizers to Panay in 1569 but with meager results — only three baptisms in two years, and those three were not of local Panayans. This was at a time when Catholic missions in the Moluccas could boast eighty thousand converts, and in Japan, thirty thousand.[10] Given such meager results in the Philippines, it is not surprising that in those early years Catholic missions tended to treat the islands as little more than a stepping stone to the great Asian continent beyond. Until the great persecutions of the shogunate in the seventeenth century closed Japan to Christian expansion the missionaries in the Philippines looked to Japan as an exciting model of missionary success, and to China, unreachable until the 1580s, as the key to the whole continent of Asia. But as the tribes of the Philippines began to respond to missionary preaching, the challenge of doors wide to evangelization all around them was a stimulus to increased concentration on the mission at hand.

It was their next move north to Manila in 1571 that established the permanent base both for colonists and missionaries and began to change the whole history and culture of the Philippines. There on the island of Luzon in the next year, 1572, the Augustinians baptized the first Tagalog chief to become Christian, Laya, "the Old Rajah of Manila." Shortly thereafter the neighboring chief of Tondo, Lakandula, also accepted baptism.[11] By 1594 the Augustinians already numbered thirty-five "houses" (residential missionary centers) throughout the islands.[12]

"The Golden Years" (1578–1609)

By the time Domingo de Salazar, a Dominican, reached the Philippines in 1581 as the first Catholic bishop of Manila,[13] Spanish governors had learned to regard the missionary friars with considerable though sometimes grudging respect. Manila had been constituted a bishopric under the archbishop of Mexico in 1578; it was made a metropolitanate with three dioceses in 1591. They could not help but notice the high esteem in which the Filipino people held the missionaries whose monastic vows kept them from seeking goods and properties for themselves.[14] The governors realized that they could not rule the colony without the missionaries, for during the first two hundred years of Spanish control there were never more than a few thousand colonists, clustered almost always around the large cities. It was the missionaries who came to know and work with the five hundred thousand Filipinos then living under Spanish rule.[15]

The new bishop quickly won a name among the Filipinos, Christians and pagans alike, for intervening on their behalf against Spanish tyranny and mistreatment of native laborers, protesting to the king himself about the floggings, underpayment, and outright theft by local Spanish mayors of the rice and gold that the workers produced.[16] Within a year of his arrival the good bishop bravely convened a synod (1582) to consider the prickly political question of whether in fact Spain actually had any legal right to rule the Philippines. Astonishingly, considering the usual generalizations about the inseparable tie between missions and colonialism, the synod concluded that Castile had neither the right of inheritance nor the exonerating excuse of a just war to defend its claims of jurisdiction over the native rulers of the islands. Not even the pope, the synod further declared, could grant Spain any rights over self-ruled territories other than the right to evangelize, though this startling pronouncement was somewhat inconsistently qualified by the synod's recognition of what J. G. Aragón describes as the "quasi-imperial authority" granted by God to the pope, and by the pope to the king of Spain. At least it did affirm the right of free evangelism and of spiritual authority over those natives who accepted baptism. In other words, Spain's only undebatable right in the Philippines was the right to preach the gospel and to defend and support the church. But, arguing further from this position, the synod somewhat dubiously accepted the conclusion that Spain had the legal obligation to overcome all that might hinder the spread of the gospel, including the opposition of unconverted native rulers.[17]

Salazar's most startling accusation against the colonists was that the Muslim chiefs of the southern islands were less oppressive of Filipino Christians than the Christian Spaniards who ruled from Manila. He wrote in 1583:

> They were better treated by the preachers of Mahoma than they have been by the preachers of Christ [i.e., the local Spanish authorities]...[for] what we preach to them...is accompanied with so much bad treatment and with so evil examples, they say "yes" with the mouth and "no" with the heart.[18]

Salazar is well named "the de las Casas of the Philippines."[19] Both were Dominicans and both championed the rights of the original inhabitants. It was largely in response to Salazar's efforts that Pope Gregory XIV in 1591 decreed an end to slavery in the Spanish-held islands.[20]

By the end of the century in the 1590s, there were four missionary orders operating in the Philippines: Augustinian (since 1565), Franciscan (since 1577), Jesuit (since 1581), and Dominican (since 1587). They reported a total in 1591 of 130 missionaries.[21] There were also about 20 "secular" priests under the authority of diocesan bishops and not in the missionary orders. A fifth order, the Augustinian Recollects, arrived in 1606. The first Dominican, Bishop de Salazar, had come in 1581, but as a bishop under royal appointment he was not technically responsible to the order as a missioner. The responsibility of the seculars was to minister only to Spaniards and non-Filipinos; the overwhelming responsibility of the regulars was mission to Filipinos.

By 1594 the number of missionaries belonging to the "regular" orders had risen to about 267 (thus not counting the Jesuits and secular priests), and the number of converts had risen even more spectacularly. In a report to the king, an earnest Augustinian, Francisco de Ortega, reported that about half of the 687,000 people in territory under Spanish control were now baptized and either well-instructed or at least under instruction. But he adds a heartfelt appeal for not less than 266 more missionaries to reach the other half, the unreached half.[22]

To avoid friction between the missions the Spanish crown soon divided up the entire territory of the islands for assignment among the missionary orders, each to its own area. The subsequent evangelizing of the various islands is largely the history of those religious bodies.[23] There were still, however, no Filipino priests, and apparently no books of the Bible had been translated into any of the tribal languages. But the archbishop's cathedral in Manila had been completed; two hospitals, one for Spaniards and one for Filipinos had been built; and the Jesuits had founded a promising school for the education of Filipino converts.[24] The missionaries had also spread out along the coastal plains and were even beginning to thrust up into the almost inaccessible mountainous interior. The fearless "apostle to the Igorots" Esteban Marin, an Augustinian, set off into the hills and for seventeen years worked among the headhunting, gold-mining forest tribes of northern Luzon. He was martyred in 1601 — tied to a tree, beheaded, and his body burned. Undeterred the Dominicans took over the mission to reach the headhunters, and reported the first Igorot convert, a "gold-mining chieftain" named Dogarat, baptized as Domingo, who proudly thereafter wore a gold rosary around his neck.[25]

The division of territory among the missionary orders proved beneficial. Augustinians, for example, were allotted much of northwest Luzon and most of the island of Cebu. Jesuits were given other parts of the Visayan islands and Muslim Mindanao; and Franciscans were given parts of southern Luzon.[26] They began to report mass conversions. Some claimed that by 1586 as many as 400,000 Filipinos were baptized Christians.[27] More credible is the estimate of modern Philippine church historian T. V. Sitoy Jr. that by 1591, out of a total population of nearly 700,000 in Spanish-held territory, half of them (382,000) had already been evangelized, and about a third had been baptized (250,000), and all this from a base of only 100 baptized Filipinos reported in 1569.[28]

It does not diminish the achievement of those pioneer friars to describe much of their work of evangelization as nominal. That would be true of the early history of Christian expansion in northern Europe as well. In fact, the alert friars in the Philippines recognized mistakes made in Catholic missions in Spanish America and took pains to avoid forced conversions or hasty confessions of faith. In principle at least, they insisted on examination for confirmation, and did not baptize infants without provision for nurture in faith and Christian life.[29]

Even discounting an inevitable amount of superficiality in their methods, what the missionaries accomplished in one generation, representing a scant thirty-five years of residence among tribes hitherto untouched by the gospel, has few parallels in any other period of church history, let alone the history of the church in Asia. And let the record show that in the Philippines, unlike Japan, the church endured as a visible, converting, culture-changing presence throughout the next four centuries and down to our own day.

By the first decade of the seventeenth century Catholic missions could credibly claim that almost all Filipinos in territory under Spanish control professed the Christian faith.[30] The exceptions were unreached tribes in the mountains and the solidly resistant Muslims of the far southern islands.

Setbacks and Friction in the Seventeenth and Eighteenth Centuries

The first half of the next century saw the beginnings of a loss in evangelistic momentum. Seventeenth-century Christianity in the islands began to show all the symptoms of what Phelan describes as a "second generation complex."[31] The zeal of first-generation converts did not automatically transfer to their children brought up from infancy as baptized Christians. Some of the weaknesses of the missions' earlier evangelistic methods, obscured at first by their more obvious successes, slowly became apparent: hasty catechetical instruction, inadequate elementary school education, failure to translate the Bible into native languages, and a woefully small supply of Filipino priests. On the other hand, the Catholic missionaries were the ones who produced almost all the best works on the Filipino language and its dialects — Tagalog, Ilocano, Pampango, Pangasinan, and Mindanao, for example.[32]

Among the foreign missionaries, too, pioneering enthusiasms began to dissolve in a sea of emerging problems. Their most intractable difficulty was a tangle of administrations and authorities flaring up into a three-sided rivalry between the church hierarchy, the missionary orders, and the colonial government.

The first area of irritation was in the relations of the hierarchy in Manila to the five missionary orders in the Philippines. History had given the latter an unusual measure of freedom from state and episcopal control, which irked both bishops and colonial governors. The archbishop of Manila and his bishops owed their appointment to the Spanish crown by right of the royal *patronato* (*padroado* in Portuguese), granted to King Ferdinand of Spain by Rome in the 1490s. They were directly responsible to Spain. The archiepiscopal province, in turn, was divided in 1595 into three episcopal sees, as proposed by the king and agreed to by the pope. But at the same time King Philip II partitioned the whole territory of the islands into four, and later five, distinct sections, giving each of the four missions rights of control over their own districts.[33] The Augustinian Recollects did not arrive until 1606. Manila was free territory for all; parts of Luzon and the Visayan islands (centering in Cebu) were Augustinian; Mindanao was Jesuit; the Franciscans and Dominicans were given strategic sections of Luzon.

Conflict of jurisdiction between the three dioceses on the one hand, and the five overlapping mission districts on the other, was inevitable, especially after Pope Adrian VI in 1622 awarded sweeping powers to the missionary orders, which in effect made bishops of the superiors of those orders in Spain's colonial possessions. They exercised all the functions of bishops save for that of consecration to the episcopate.[34] But the Council of Trent (1545–1563) had confusingly qualified this privilege with a decree that clergy in the orders (*regular* clergy), if they were engaged in pastoral duties, were as subject to the jurisdiction of the bishops as were the *secular* clergy, the parish priests.[35] It was a classic case of the perennial tension between churchmen and evangelists, between the demand for orderly church government and the indispensable need for freedom and flexibility in missionary outreach.[36]

Relations between the church and the colonial Spanish government also frayed, and as one historian writes, "soon degenerated into a bareknuckled contest for political power."[37] Governors in Manila resented the powerful influence of the missionary orders in the provinces and bristled at their criticisms of what the authorities considered to be necessary use of force against the native population to establish order. A royal chaplain-bishop in the islands in 1636 accused several of the orders of arrogant contempt of all authority but their own. "[They say] openly in their missions that they are kings and popes," he wrote, and "live without God, without king, and without law."[38] At least twice protesting archbishops were thrown into prison by governors general, and once missionary friars led a mob against a cruel governor general, killing both the governor and his son. The protests of the archbishops and missionary orders against the governors centered about mistreatment of Filipinos and interference in religious matters, but were sometimes motivated as much by ecclesiastical pride about trifles as by Christian compassion. The governors, often cruel and autocratic, responded with charges of clergy misconduct, illegal financial gain, or building church properties without license.[39]

Other sources of discontent were the internal disputes that boiled up between the missionaries in the orders and the secular priests appointed to settled parishes. As a general rule in Catholic missionary practice missionary priests were expected to move on to unreached areas after planting a church, turning over the new churches to the secular clergy for further organization and nurture. But when the archbishop of Manila in 1621 complained that the missionaries were holding on too long to their churches though parish priests were available, the friars in turn complained of episcopal intrusion into the freedom of the orders.[40] Pope Pius, defending the missionaries, is quoted as remarking to Philip II of Spain that he "opposed placing the reform of the orders in the hands of bishops...who had no experience in monastic [missionary] affairs."[41]

As though tensions between bishops and the missionary orders, and between governors and the orders were not enough, there was also rivalry between the orders themselves. A classic case was the Jesuit protest in 1658 against the elevation of the Dominican college of Santo Thomas to university rank instead of the Society's own college, San Ignacio. Solano went so far as to include a veiled accusation of heresy against the Dominicans in the matter of the immaculate conception of the Virgin Mary, though as the editor points out, that disputed doctrine, opposed by Thomas Aquinas, had not quite yet become officially orthodox.[42]

There were also disputes within some of the orders, and the period from 1593 into the 1630s was shamefully marked by ethical decline. Reform did not come easily in those fractious years. In 1619 a group of his own friars murdered their high-minded but tactless Spanish provincial of the Augustinian mission, Vicente de Sepúlveda, for exposing their misdeeds and pressing too hard for reforms.[43] This period of demoralization and disunity, from 1593 into the 1630s, split the Augustinians into two factions, Spanish and "creole" (i.e., those who had entered the order in the Far East or Mexico against those who had taken their vows in Spain). Sepúlveda's predecessor, Lorenzo de León, had been deposed for lack of discipline and for acting like a "public merchant."

But for two centuries, from shortly after colonization in the 1570s to 1800, a greater threat than internal rivalries boiled under the surface to hinder the expansion of the Christian faith. This was the simmering discontent of a people once free but now chafing under colonial rule. From time to time this undercurrent erupted into open revolt. Usually Spanish oppression triggered the outbreaks.[44] But in at least four or five cases, the protest was leveled squarely against the Christian church.

In 1621 a native priest, Tamblot, roused the people of Bohol against the Jesuit missionaries and called for a return to their native gods and ancestors. In that same year on the island of Leyte one of the first converted Filipino chiefs, Bankaw, who had warmly welcomed the first of the colonizers, Legaspi, to the islands fifty-six years earlier, apostatized in his old age and joined another priest of the old religions to return to the faith of his fathers. It took a flotilla of forty armed ships to defeat him. The Spanish beheaded him and posted his head on a stake as a warning to apostates. A third religious revolt occurred in 1663, led by a mystic and "sorcerer" named Tapar who went about in woman's clothes and roused his followers to form a new religion mingling Christian symbols and pagan rites. An Augustinian missionary who tried to recall them to the Catholic faith was run through with bamboo spears and killed, but the Spanish quickly quelled the rebellion.[45] The fiercest and longest revolt of all, that of Dagohoy in 1744, started with a minor incident in which a Jesuit curate refused burial in the church cemetery to a man killed in a duel. His brother, Francisco Dagohoy, exploded in anger, killed the Jesuit, and established an independent government in the mountains with twenty thousand followers who resisted Spanish arms for the next eighty-five years, until 1829.[46]

Somewhat different was a widespread series of agrarian revolts that troubled the islands in 1745 and 1746. Though economic in motivation, a common factor gave the movement an antichristian, antichurch coloring. Its basic protest was against the huge estates unilaterally granted by Spain to the missionary orders, and the refusal of the missionary friars even to allow Filipino tribesmen their traditional rights of fishing in the rivers, woodcutting in the forests, pasture for their water buffalo, and gathering of wild fruit. The protest was unsuccessful. Despite the recommendation of a royal auditor sent to examine the matter, the Spanish-dominated Manila courts overruled the claims of the native Filipinos against usurpation of their ancient lands, and the Catholic orders retained control.[47]

Efforts to Train a Filipino Clergy

Tensions induced by conflicts over land tenure are common in any expanding enterprise, secular or religious, and were probably not the most serious impediments to the development of Christianity in the Philippines. Far more damaging may well have been the Spanish missions' crippling lack of sustained attention to the training of a native priesthood. A comparison with contemporary Portuguese missions, particularly in Japan at that time, makes this clearly apparent. In 1580, Alessandro Valignano, supervisor of all missions in the Portuguese sphere of influence in Asia, laid down this operative indigenizing principle:

> It is necessary that there should be a bishop in Japan. But let him not be sent from Europe, a stranger both to the language and the customs... Consequently natives must be ordained either in Macao or in India. Let them be put to the test: we shall see whether one of them will be worthy of the episcopate.[48]

On his second trip to Japan in 1590, only forty years after the beginning of Catholic missions in Japan, Valignano was surprised and gratified to find seventy young Japanese novices in training for the priesthood, and ten or eleven years later, on his last trip in 1598–1603, he had the satisfaction of seeing the first two Japanese ordained as priests.[49]

In the Philippines, by contrast, it was eighty years after Magellan before the Spanish missions in 1601 began to open their colleges to Filipino candidates for ordination, and as late as 1725 Spanish missionary Father Gaspar de San Agustín, lamented the admission of natives to the priesthood on the grounds of their "scandalous incompetence."[50] But this should be balanced with the spirited answer to that same arrogant and critical Spaniard, San Agustín, by the Jesuit, Father Delgado, who refutes the criticisms and compares Filipino gentleness and ability with the "authority and arrogance that every Spaniard assumes upon his arrival in this country."[51]

The slower indigenizing of the priesthood in the Philippines may have been in part the consequence of the rivalry for power between the Spanish crown, the bishops, and the orders. The Portuguese king had no rights in Japan, and for the formative years there was only one mission in Japan, the Jesuits. On the other hand, the Philippines, uniquely in sixteenth- and early seventeenth-century Asia, was the West's only large colony. Elsewhere, until the Dutch entered the Indonesian archipelago, Western rule consisted only of small trading ports and beachheads. But Spain controlled all but a fraction of the Philippine islands for almost four hundred years. Its authority covered not only the colony but also the church and the missions by conquest and by papal grant, the *patronato real*, the right of patronage given by Pope Julius II to Ferdinand of Spain in 1508.[52] The crown therefore, rather naturally, preferred an uninterrupted line of ecclesiastical power from the Spanish kings to Spanish bishops to Spanish priests. Missing was any consistent emphasis on the development of a native clergy as an indispensable base for the transition from a Spanish missionary church to a Filipino church. Nor did the orders themselves move with any consistency to indigenize church leadership, perhaps fearing that only Spaniards could stand against Spaniards for the rights of the church.

An exception was the Jesuit pioneer, Alonso Sanchez, one of the first two Jesuits in the islands. He wrote in a 1589 letter to the Jesuit Father General, Aquaviva, of the pressing need for training indigenous leadership for the church: "Not only will [such schools] supply the colony as a whole with trusted interpreters, but some of them can serve as companions to our men on missionary expeditions; in fact many of them could be missionaries and catechists themselves."[53]

Heedless of his plea, at the second Council of Lima in 1591, the Catholic Church decreed, "Indians are not to receive any of the orders of the Church,"[54] a rule that by extension from South America applied also to the Philippines. This severe Spanish rule became a critical point of difference between the Spanish missions of the Americas and the Philippines, and the missions of the Portuguese and the Congregation of Propaganda in Asia, which were more mindful of the long-term necessity for the preparation of a native priesthood. India under the Portuguese, for example, had seminaries for training the priesthood from 1541 on, and Japan beginning in 1580. De la Costa gives three explanations for the retarding of the development of a national clergy in the Philippines: the primitive condition of society in the islands at that time compared with mainland Asia, the ecclesiastical establishment under *patronato,* and the arbitrary extension to the Philippines of Spanish colonial patterns in Latin America.[55]

Nevertheless, in this same critical period from the 1590s to the 1760s the Spanish in the Philippines laid down the foundations of what, next to the conversion of the people and the planting of churches, became Christianity's greatest contribution to the islands, a network of schools rising from the elementary classes in the villages to universities granting doctoral degrees. From these schools, though not without pain, an indigenous clergy eventually emerged to make the church Filipino.[56]

As early as 1583, the bishop of Manila, Domingo de Salazar, a Dominican and a forthright defender of Filipino native rights, had recommended to King Philip of Spain the founding of a school for the sons of Spanish colonists, and pending an answer from the king, asked the Jesuit missioners who had reached Manila with him in 1581 to begin preliminary instruction. But the father general of the Jesuits in Rome, Aquaviva, ruled that the Society's first task in the islands was not education for colonists but evangelization of the Filipinos, and the project was delayed. The establishment of the first Christian school of which there is mention in the records was apparently the accomplishment of a layman of the brotherhood of Santa Misericordia, a society for the charitable care of the poor. He opened a school for orphans in 1594.[57]

By then, the Manila Jesuits had persuaded their father general in Europe that the work of evangelism was progressing so well that an exception could be made for the islands and that it was time to begin regular institutional Christian education in the Philippines. In 1595 Aquaviva sent a cadre of nine Jesuits from Mexico to ensure the presence of enough missionaries for both evangelism and Christian education, and in that same year the first classes were held for the islands' first secondary school, the College of San Jose, which later, after some mergers and change of name, became the first university in the islands, the University of San Ignacio. The beginnings of San Jose in 1585 were preliminary lectures, not regular classes, which began only in 1595, becoming the Jesuit College of San Jose. It was still struggling to survive in 1601, when it was refinanced with a new foundation. About the year 1610 another Jesuit elementary school in Manila was elevated to secondary school rank as the College of Manila which about 1622 took the name of

the Society's founder Loyola as the College of San Ignacio, and eventually the University of San Ignacio.[58] By 1726 the Jesuits maintained four
colleges and a seminary.[59]

History was not kind to the Jesuit schools. The expulsion of the order
from the Philippines in 1768 left their schools as orphans. It was the Dominicans who stepped into the breach. Their secondary school in Manila,
established in 1611, had been raised to university rank in 1645 and became the most distinguished school in the islands, the University of
Santo Tomas. Between 1645 and 1768 Santo Tomas enrolled more than
fourteen thousand students of theology and philosophy.[60]

Schools for women were an afterthought of the Spanish rulers. A royal
decree in 1591 ordered the opening of a school and home for Spanish
girls, especially orphans "so that they may go out therefrom to be married and bear children."[61] All the more worthy of mention is a brave
woman with more compassion and less condescension, Ignacia del Es-
piritu Santo, a Chinese *mestiza*, founder of the first school specifically
organized for Filipino women in 1684.[62]

Most of these mission schools as they were raised to secondary- and
in a few cases to tertiary-level rank were originally intended for the
education of Spaniards, but by 1599 they were admitting students of
mixed parentage and by the 1650s were also permitting pure-blooded
Filipinos of prominent families to attend classes in a special category. The
secondary schools for male students were also primarily intended for the
education of Christian leadership, ordained and unordained, but at first
principally for those of Spanish birth and only peripherally for Filipinos.
This policy derived from the Spanish experience in the Americas where
Franciscans had founded a school for training native priests in Mexico in
1536. Its pattern could easily have been transferred to Manila, since the
Philippines was still ecclesiastically subject (until 1595) to the archbishop
of Mexico.[63]

In 1589 one of the first two Jesuit missioners in the Philippines, Alonso
Sanchez, argued persuasively for permission to open a school for Filipinos in the Mexican pattern. Even before permission was granted for
a building, he gathered a group of Tagalog boys for separate instruction near the recently founded College of Manila. But like the Mexican
schools, the school for native Filipinos soon failed, partly for lack of
funds and partly for the all-too-apparent poison of racist prejudice.[64]
Both in Mexico and the Philippines such failures only further confirmed
the impression generally held in all the early Spanish colonies that leadership in the church and in missionary outreach would be better left to
Spaniards. Government schools were even more harshly discriminatory
than the mission schools.[65]

It was left to a Frenchman, François Pallu, and an Italian, Jean Baptista Sidotti — almost by default — neither of whom intended to work
in the Philippines, to lay the permanent educational foundations for the

formation of an indigenous Filipino clergy. In this they were strongly supported and aided by the Spanish archbishop Diego Camacho (1697–1703). As Camacho put it in a letter to the king, "[Sidotti] prevailed where your Royal Orders and all my efforts failed."[66]

The accomplishment of the two outsiders, Pallu and Sidotti, was not without its obstacles. Not until early in the 1600s had any Filipino been raised to the priesthood, and not until halfway through the century was a second ordained. The first was Augustin Tabuyo, ordained by the Spanish archbishop of Manila, Miguel Garcia Serrano, in 1621. Serrano, an Augustinian, not only gave the Philippine priesthood its first Filipino, but "created a multi-racial clergy," temporary though it was, by ordaining a Japanese Jesuit, Miguel Magsunda, in 1622 and two Japanese Dominicans in 1625. The latter two, returning to Japan were, martyred in the great persecutions.[67] Whatever the archbishop's motives may have been — some say that ordination of Filipinos represented an attempt by the diocesan hierarchy to curb the ecclesiastical independence of the missionary orders[68] — it is welcome evidence that not all the Spanish were racially biased. But a measure of the opposition is the fact that only one more Filipino was ordained in the next seventy years, and he, Miguel Jeronimo, was admitted about 1655 but only to minor orders, serving as an interim parish priest.[69]

Most refreshing of all was the ministry of the Frenchman and the Italian. In 1672, François Pallu of France was stranded by a storm in Manila while on his way to China. He was later to be one of the most influential missionary statesmen of seventeenth-century Christianity in Asia, famous for two great achievements. He was the principal founder of the great Paris Missionary Society in 1663, the earliest Catholic order to devote itself entirely to missions to the completely unreached, and he was, after Valignano of India and Japan, one of the most persistent advocates of raising up a priesthood from within each foreign culture to evangelize their own countries and to lead in the formation of their own churches.[70]

Pallu had been appointed by the papal Congregation of Propaganda as apostolic vicar of Tonkin, Laos, and southwest China. On his way from Siam to China his ship was driven ashore in Manila. The Spanish authorities, suspicious of a missionary from Portuguese mission territory, took him off the China-bound ship, put him under house arrest, and ordered him sent back to Europe by way of Mexico. But while under house arrest in Manila, he took every opportunity to study the mission situation in the Philippines. He noted that regular priests of the orders were overworked and undermanned. He was not unaware of the governor's displeasure at the unchecked independence of the missionary orders. This only confirmed a conclusion to which he had already come from observations in Southeast Asia that the greatest need in all the Asian missions was a vigorous, well-trained body of native clergymen. Applied to the Philippine situation this would relieve the shortage of regular clergy, and at the same time produce a cadre of secular priests independent of the rule of the orders and more compatible with the bishops and the government.[71]

Upon his arrival in Mexico Pallu was received with honor, and he pressed his case before the authorities there and later in Spain. His labors were rewarded when in 1677 a decree from the king in council ordered the archbishop of Manila to provide seminaries and training for a Filipino priesthood. The Spanish archbishop was not pleased with this intrusion into his affairs, but the colonial attorney general in Manila endorsed the proposal with a vigorous letter to the king, shrewdly suggesting, among other things, that training fifty Filipino boys for the priesthood would probably cost the royal exchequer less than it spends on a comparable number of the "religious" (that is, those in the missionary orders). That argument is not the best rationale for indigenizing the clergy, and in this particular case proved ineffective. By 1700 there was still no diocesan seminary for training nationals.[72]

But just before the turn of the century the case for creating an indigenous priesthood received a vigorous Spanish champion in the person of Archbishop Diego Camacho, "heroic founder" of a permanent line of Filipino priests. Even before his arrival in Manila in 1697, while he was still in Mexico Camacho began his campaign to establish a theological seminary in which the training of native priests would be emphasized. He teamed with the Italian visitor Sidotti and lent his prestige and power to the founding in 1702 of the first seminary in the Philippines; even before the seminary could be established and recognized, he began to ordain Filipinos. The first so ordained was Brother Francisco Baluyot in 1698. The next year he elevated another Filipino to the priesthood, a Chinese mestizo, Joseph de Ocampo from a wealthy Chinese family. The number grew rapidly. The zealous Baluyot family alone sent four of their clan into service, including the first Filipino missionary, Brother Alfonzo Baluyot who was sent in 1703 to the mountain tribes on the northern tip of Luzon, "ministro y misionero apostolico de los montes del Abra de Vigan."[73]

The enthusiastic Camacho must, however, share the honor of establishing the first full-fledged seminary for Filipinos with the intrepid Italian Sidotti, whose extravagant hopes and exemplary faith eventually brought him all too soon to a martyr's grave in Japan. On his way to China in 1702 with the de Tournon mission, which tried and failed to settle the rites question there (as discussed previously in chap. 4), the unstoppable Sidotti busied himself with whatever was at hand. Judging Manila to be an advantageous site for a seminary, he began to collect funds and build one. Before he left with the group for China he had almost completed a building to house seventy-two seminarians, grandly designed as a training center for Asian priests from the entire rim of Asia — from the East Indies, Siam, and Malaysia to China and Japan. But Sidotti's whole missionary life was one of heroic failure. His Philippine seminary was torn down for lack of proper imperial Spanish permission;[74] the mission to China under de Tournon never solved the rites question; and his hopes of rescuing Japan from the tortures of the shogunate died with him in a martyr's prison.

Camacho's successor as archbishop was Francisco de la Cuesta (1704–1724), who arrived with a latent prejudice against native leadership and displaced Sidotti's projected seminary for non-Spaniards with an institution closed to *mestizos* and Filipinos. But further experience softened his racist stance. About the year 1710 he began to ordain Filipino clergy and appoint Filipino priests to the care of parishes.[75] By the middle of the century, in 1750, 142 of the islands' 569 parishes and missions were under the care of Filipino priests.[76] Eight years later, as a visible though temporary sign of the decline of Spain and the rise of a Filipino clergy, the Catholic hierarchy in Manila is said to have received its first Filipino archbishop (*ad interim*), Miguel Lino de Espeleta (1756–1759), who had served with distinction as bishop of Cebu. Two years later this native priest was given the unprecedented honor of elevation to the political rank of governor general of the islands (1759–1761).[77] For a short period, dissension between church and state ceased, at least at the top.

The honeymoon was soon over. As a result of the ecclesiastical turmoil following the banishment of the Jesuit order from all Spain's colonies in 1767, a belligerent anti-Jesuit bishop was sent to Manila as archbishop, Basilio Sancho. Instead of peace he brought the church near to disaster. Almost at once he roused the remaining missionary orders to fury by replacing missionary priests with native clergy. This increased his control of the church but threatened and weakened the orders. Besides, there were not enough native priests to fill the vacancies, and he began to ordain new ones with reckless speed. De la Costa relates a joke bandied about in the streets that "there were no oarsmen to be found for the coasting vessels, because the archbishop had ordained them all."[78] The result, as the hasty archbishop soon found to his sorrow, was an almost mortal blow to further ordinations of Filipinos. Untrained men were thrust too hurriedly into parish responsibilities; horror stories circulated of clerical inefficiency or worse; and the movement for an indigenous priesthood suffered irreparable harm. By the end of the century the number of Filipino priests and seminarians had risen to exceed that of the priests in the missionary orders, but the damage had been done and for most of the nineteenth century native priests still carried the stigma, though no longer deserved, of being inferior.[79]

In these same years of the eighteenth century, evangelization suffered a comparable loss of momentum, but paradoxically the cultural Christianizing of the islands never slackened. In 1621 the hierarchy reported half a million Filipinos under instruction; by 1750 there were more than a million.[80] It is probably true that one reason for the rapid growth was the simple spirit worship of their tribal worldview. They had never had an organized religious base for their culture other than the prevalent animism of other early Asian societies. But their civilization was not as primitive as it is sometimes portrayed. The first missionaries described the Filipinos as friendly, shrewd, skillful, and religious. They dressed in silk and cotton and wore impressive gold ornaments.[81] Tagalog culture had even developed a phonetic script, with the equivalent of three vowels and fourteen consonants.[82] But they were largely illiterate, and this the missions strove to rectify.

The first schools for the "Indians" (i.e., Filipinos), as we have seen, were started by the Jesuits and the Franciscans. Both orders kept their standards high, though not without difficulty.[83] At first a genuine effort was made to preach and teach in the native vernacular, but under pressure from the Spanish government, the colonial authorities sought to shift the emphasis to Spanish. The missionaries, however, were reluctant. To many of them, the vernacular was a gift from God, a bridge to the minds of the people, and far more effective for the education of the people. They did not exert themselves to force a foreign language on their pupils. Spanish was routinely taught in their higher schools, along with Latin in courses of training for the priesthood, but Spanish never became the language of the Philippine people. The greatest of the early linguists, the Dominican printer Francisco Blancas de San Jose, in his famous Tagalog grammar, printed in 1610, records his plea for a Pentecostal "fiery language" that he might more faithfully preach the gospel in the "unknown tongue" of the people.[84]

After more than three hundred years of Spanish rule only 10 percent of the people spoke Spanish.[85] But, as Latourette has pointed out, by the middle of the seventeenth century literacy was as widely spread in the Philippines as in Europe.[86] One reason was the advent of printing. The mission had established four printing presses and published works in native dialects, principally Tagalog, as well as bilingual dictionaries, grammars, and catechisms.[87] Christian schools and Christian literature, supported intermittently by the authorities and staffed largely by the missionary orders, became major forces in driving out more primitive religious beliefs and practices,[88] and an impressive majority of the population of the islands had professed the Christian faith.

One significant omission of the Catholic missions must be noted, however. Despite the great opportunity that their promotion of literacy presented, not until near the end of the nineteenth century, in 1873, three hundred years after the arrival of the first missionaries, did they give the people a translation of any extensive part of the Bible in their own language. Latin and Spanish, yes, but Filipino, no.[89]

Suppression of the Jesuits

The closing decades of the eighteenth century were somber years for Catholic missions in Asia. Japan was still enveloped in the anguished silence that followed the great persecution. In China the missions were closed by an imperious, suspicious Qing dynasty, which regretted it had ever favored them. The Dutch and English were sweeping Spanish and Portuguese shipping, the lifeline of the Catholic missions, out of South Pacific seas and the Indian Ocean. But the greatest shock of all was the suppression of the Society of Jesus and the expulsion of Jesuit missionaries from their fields, first by their own Catholic monarchs in Europe and finally by the pope himself.

In rapid succession within the space of eight years (1759–1767) the three pillars of the papacy, the "daughters of the church," Portugal, France, and Spain outlawed and exiled the Society from their borders and colonies, and in 1773 a "sick and nervous" Pope Clement XIV signed a decree (*Dominus ac Redemptor*) and dissolved the Jesuit order. It shook the world, not least of all Asia. Suddenly twenty-three men, spread across every continent from Europe to the Americas, were torn from their familiar spiritual home and left organizationally leaderless.[90]

For the next fifty years and more, Catholic world missions slid into a period of steep decline. The expulsion of the Jesuits in the Philippines was ordered by King Charles III of Spain. They left with Jesuit discipline, without protest. H. de la Silva describes the last scene: "A king of Spain had opened the door to them; a king of Spain now shut it in their faces." They left behind more than two hundred thousand Philippine Christians for whom they had been spiritually responsible.[91]

But whatever mistakes the Spanish missions may have made in the Philippines, no comparable mass penetration of an Asiatic culture by the Christian faith had ever before been achieved outside the continent's Greco-Roman-dominated western coast on the Mediterranean Sea. The "Christianization" of the Philippines matches in many respects the early spread of Christianity into the Roman Empire, but with this all-important difference; in second- and third-century Europe the expansion of the faith came from below without government support. In the Philippines, from the sixteenth to the eighteenth centuries, Christian expansion was always shadowed by the overwhelming military and political power of colonial Spain.

NOTES

1. Maximillianus Transylvanus, *De Moluccis Insulis* [1523], in *The Philippine Islands 1493–1803: Explorations by Early Navigators, Descriptions of the Islands and Their Peoples, Their History and Records of the Catholic Missions*, 55 vols., ed. Emma H. Blair and J. A. Robertson (Cleveland: A. H. Clark, 1903–1907), 1:309–310. This

letter to the cardinal of Salzburg is the earliest known account of Magellan's voyage. See also the editors' introduction, 23–28. The more official but somewhat unreliable record of the voyage is by Antonio Pigafetta, who accompanied Magellan, *First Voyage around the World,* Italian text and English trans. J. A. Robertson, in Blair and Robertson, *The Philippine Islands,* vols. 33, 34 (1906). Blair and Robertson's invaluable series will be often cited. Volume 53 is a bibliography and vols. 54 and 55 contain an extremely useful index.

2. Blair and Robertson, *The Philippine Islands,* 1:20.

3. Pigafetta, *First Voyage around the World,* 33:123ff.

4. Pigafetta, *First Voyage around the World,* 33:153.

5. See the quotation from the royal orders on the title page of this chapter above.

6. Pigafetta, *First Voyage around the World,* 33:137–187; Maximillianus (Blair and Robertson, *The Philippine Islands*), 1:323–328. See also the well-researched account of Magellan's expedition in the Philippines by T. Valentino Sitoy Jr., *A History of Christianity in the Philippines* (Quezon City, Philippines: New Day Publishers, 1985), 1:36–59; and the popular, colorful narrative by J. V. Braganza, *The Encounter: The Epic Story of the Christianization of the Philippines* (Manila: Catholic Trade School, 1965), 62–110.

7. Here I adapt J. L. Phelan's division of the early years into three periods, as in his *The Hispanization of the Philippines: Spanish Aims and Filipino Responses, 1565–1700* (Madison: University of Wisconsin Press, 1967), 70.

8. J. Gayo Aragón, "The Controversy over Justification of Spanish Rule in the Philippines," in *Studies in Philippine Church History,* ed. Gerald H. Anderson (Ithaca, N.Y.: Cornell University Press, 1969), 6 n. 17. For the May 28, 1560, letter from Urdaneta to the king, see R. Lopez and A. Felix Jr., *The Christianization of the Philippines: The Orders of Philip II and the Basic Reports and Letters of Legaspi, Urdaneta* (Manila: Historical Conservation Society, 1965), 253–254, and Blair and Robertson, *The Philippine Islands,* 2:33ff., 81, 161–168. See also the statement of the Augustinian provincial in Manila, Martin de Rada, June 21, 1574, and the dissenting opinion of a group of colonials (Lopez, *Christianization,* 347–353); and Sitoy, *History of Christianity in the Philippines,* 1:85ff., 130–138.

9. Not long thereafter she married one of the shipmen in the Spanish fleet, a Greek. Sitoy, *History of Christianity in the Philippines,* 1:134–135.

10. Sitoy, *History of Christianity in the Philippines,* 138ff., 148ff.

11. Sitoy, *History of Christianity in the Philippines,* 160–161, 170–171.

12. David Gutiérrez, *The Augustinians from the Protestant Reformation to the Peace of Westphalia 1518–1628* (Villanova, Pa.: Augustinian Historical Institute, Villanova University, 1979), 225.

13. Blair and Robertson, *The Philippine Islands,* 12:204.

14. So wrote Gov. de Sande in a 1577 report to Spain (Blair and Robertson, *The Philippine Islands,* 4:13). Franciscans had begun to arrive in 1577 (4:136–143). On the Dominicans, see 5:199–201.

15. Phelan, *The Hispanization of the Philippines,* 11.

16. Letter, Salazar to Philip II (1582), and his extensive 1583 report of "matters which require correction," in Blair and Robertson, *The Philippine Islands.* 5:188–191, 210–255.

17. For a concise summary of the synod's reasoning, and its aftermath, see Aragón, "The Controversy over Justification of Spanish Rule in the Philippines," 13–21.

18. Sitoy, *A History of Christianity in the Philippines*, 1:248, quoting from Bishop Domingo de Salazar, "Relacion de las cosas de las Filipinas" [1583], in Wenceslao E. Retana, *Archivo del Bibliofilo Filipino*, 5 vols. (Madrid, 1895–1905), 3:15–16.

19. *CE*, s.v. "Salazar." Las Casas was the famed defender of Indian rights in colonial Spanish America.

20. The text of the decree is in Blair and Robertson, *The Philippine Islands*, 8:70–72.

21. [Governor G. P. Dasmarinas to Philip II], "Account of the Encomiendas in the Philippinas Islands," May 31, 1591, translated in Blair and Robertson, *The Philippine Islands*, 8:96–141. Sitoy, *History of Christianity in the Philippines*, 343 n. 230, points out an error of addition in the original text's summary of statistics on 8:141, correcting 140 priests to 130. The total was 79 Augustinians, 9 Dominicans, and 42 Franciscans, plus 20 "secular" priests.

22. Francisco de Ortega, "Report concerning the Filipinas Islands" (1594), translated in Blair and Robertson, *The Philippine Islands*, 9:95–105. He reports the number of priests then in the islands as 188 regulars, not counting the Jesuits and the secular priests. His figures for converts and population are (as summarized in a chart by Sitoy, *History of Christianity in the Philippines*, 268): "Well-instructed," 204,264 (29.7 percent); "Having instruction," 138,728 (20.2 percent); "Never evangelized," 243,700 (35.5 percent); "In rebellion or hostile" 100,360 (14.6 percent). Total population in the Spanish "encomiendas" (land grants), 687,052.

23. For the histories, in Spanish, of the orders in the Philippines, see the bibliographical survey by Gerald H. Anderson in *Studies in Philippine Church History*, 391–397. On the missionary statistics, see Phelan, *The Hispanization of the Philippines*, 56.

24. Letters, Gov. Dasmarinas to Philip II, June 2, 1591, and June 20, 1593, and Letter, A. de Morga, July 6, 1596 (Blair and Robertson, *The Philippine Islands*, 8:144–146, 9:63, and 9:271–272). See Sitoy, *History of Christianity in the Philippines*, 1:263, for the estimate of the number of missionaries.

25. William Henry Scott, *The Discovery of the Igorots: Spanish Contacts with the Pagans of Northern Luzon* (Quezon City, Philippines: New Day Publishers, 1974), 14–23. See 1–39 for a detailed account of the first Spanish contacts with the tribesmen of northern Luzon, 1575–1625.

26. Miguel A. Bernad, *The Christianization of the Philippines: Problems and Perspectives* (Manila: Filipiniana Book Guild, 1972), 219–240; Sitoy, *History of Christianity in the Philippines*, 1:262–267. For the royal decree separating the orders into disconnected provinces, see Blair and Robertson, *The Philippine Islands*, 33:67ff. The number of missionaries increased from 13 Augustinians in 1576 to 103 (Augustinians and Franciscans) in 1586. By 1600 more than 450 missionaries of the orders had sailed for the Philippines by way of Mexico, though a great number died on the way, and perhaps just as many were held in Mexico for missionary work there to the expressed discontent of their overworked colleagues in Asia. See Latourette, *A History of the Expansion of Christianity*, 3:311; and Salazar's letter of June 27, 1588, in Blair and Robertson, *The Philippine Islands*, 7:72.

27. See the sixteenth-century historian Juan Gonzales de Mendoza, *Historia del gran Reyno de China* (Madrid, 1586), translated in part into English by James A. Robertson, in Blair and Robertson, *The Philippine Islands*, 6:83–153, see esp. 6:126, 148.

28. Sitoy, *History of Christianity in the Philippines*, 1:263–268. Sitoy gives the figures: 1569, 100 baptized; 1577, 10,000 or 12,000; 1591, 250,000. His figure for 1591 summarizes the 1594 report of the Augustinian Francisco Ortega (d. 1601), "A Report Concerning the Filipino Islands," in Blair and Robertson, *The Philippine Islands*, 9:103–104. Compare Phelan's statistics on the number of baptized converts: 1583, 100,000; 1586, 170,000; 1594, 286,000; 1612, 322,400; 1622, 500,000. Cf. Phelan, *The Hispanization of the Philippines*, 1:56.

29. See a letter of the Jesuit François Gonzalez, quoted at length by Pedro Chirino (*The Philippines in 1600* [Manila: Historical Conservation Society, 1969], 479–482), describing the bishop of Cebu's trip to Bohol about 1602. In twenty days the busy bishop confirmed three thousand Christians, and he reported four hundred new baptisms in the year. Chirino adds, "if there were no more it was because they did not dare to baptize in other towns until they could be sure of priests who would preserve them in the faith and in the Christian life." Phelan (*Hispanization of the Philippines*, 54–70) writes of baptism, catechetical instruction, confirmation, the sacraments, and moral discipline as the core of Catholic training for Philippine converts.

30. Phelan, *Hispanization of the Philippines*, 57.

31. Phelan, *Hispanization of the Philippines*, 57.

32. See Bernad, *The Christianization of the Philippines*, 255–260.

33. Bernad, *The Christianization of the Philippines*, 224–240.

34. See H. de la Costa, "Episcopal Jurisdiction in the Philippines during the Spanish Regime," in *Studies in Philippine Church History*, ed. Gerald H. Anderson (Ithaca, N.Y.: Cornell University Press, 1969), 48–49. De la Costa refers to Pastells, "Historia general," *Catalogo*, VI, ccxcv–cccvi, as a summary of the privileges granted to the orders engaged in missionary work.

35. De la Costa, "Episcopal Jurisdiction in the Philippines during the Spanish Regime," 48–54.

36. See the arguments from the missionary side by the Recollect Augustinian Diego de Santa Theresa in 1656–1666, translated in Blair and Robertson, *The Philippine Islands*, 36:149–172.

37. Peter G. Gowing, *Islands under the Cross: The Story of the Church in the Philippines* (Manila: National Council of Churches in the Philippines, 1967), 68. On friction between the religious orders and the king's rights of patronage, see W. E. Shiels, *King and Church: The Rise and Fall of the Patronato Real* (Chicago: Loyola University Press, 1961), 195ff. Religious orders reporting directly to the pope in Rome openly resented interference from the king in Spain.

38. Letter of Bishop Zamudio (Augustinian) to Philip IV, June 20, 1636, in Blair and Robertson, *The Philippine Islands*, 25:302.

39. Gregorio F. Zaide, *Philippine Political and Cultural History*, 2 vols. (Manila: Philippine Educational Co., 1949), 1:205–221. See also Bernad, *The Christianization of the Philippines*, 311–336.

40. Letter, Archbishop Serrano to Philip II, July 30, 1621, in Blair and Robertson, *The Philippine Islands*, 20:84–87. But see the counterargument, "Why the

Friars Are Not Subjected to Episcopal Visitation," by an anonymous missionary writing about 1666, in Blair and Robertson, *The Philippine Islands*, 36:264–276. H. de la Costa carefully reviews the issue, "Episcopal Jurisdiction in the Philippines during the Spanish Regime," 44–64.

41. Shiels, *King and Church*, 207.

42. See the memorial sent to the king by Miguel Solano (Blair and Robertson, *The Philippine Islands*, 36:74–86, esp. 84 n. 19). Disputes among the orders were numerous, as between Augustinians and Dominicans, for example (Blair and Robertson, *The Philippine Islands*, 38:237 n. 118).

43. Phelan, *Hispanization of the Philippines*, 35–37.

44. Zaide, in his *Philippine Political and Cultural History*, 343–367, traces four of the revolts to the people's desire for freedom (in 1574, 1588, 1643, and 1660–1661); and nine uprisings to protest Spanish tyrannical oppression (in 1596, 1621, 1630, 1639, 1649–1650, 1660–1661, 1744–1749, 1762–1763, and 1762–1764).

45. Blair and Robertson, *The Philippine Islands*, 38:87–94, 215–223, translating from C. Diaz, *Conquistas de las Islas Filipinas*, 172, and others.

46. Zaide, *Philippine Political and Cultural History*, 354–355.

47. See the response of King Fernando VI in 1751 to the auditors' report, translated in Blair and Robertson, *The Philippine Islands*, 48:27–36, with notes by a twentieth-century Filipino governor. Only after American occupation of the Philippines did these injustices begin to be conscientiously addressed (Zaide, *Philippine Political and Cultural History*, 1:357 n. 49).

48. A. Brou, "L'encyclique sur les missions," 593, cited in *Studies in Philippine Church History*, ed. Gerald H. Anderson, 76 n. 29, by H. de la Costa, "The Development of the Native Clergy in the Philippines." See also J. F. Schütte, *Valignano's Mission Principles for Japan*, 1:312 n. 138, citing a letter of Valignano in 1577.

49. Drummond, *A History of Christianity in Japan*, 68.

50. See "San Agustin's Letter on the Filipinos," in Blair and Robertson, *The Philippine Islands*, 40:183–295. See also de la Costa, "The Development of the Native Clergy in the Philippines," 87; and Luciano P. R. Santiago, *The Hidden Light: The First Filipino Priests* (Quezon City, Philippines: New Day Publishers, 1987).

51. Juan José Delgado, *Historia de Filipinas*, 297–302, trans. Blair and Robertson, *The Philippine Islands*, 40:283–295.

52. Shiels, *King and Church*, 109–113.

53. H. de la Costa, "Jesuit Education in the Philippines to 1768," *PS* 1 (1956): 130–131. The citation is from a 1589 letter to the Jesuit Father General Aquaviva.

54. H. de la Costa, "The Development of the Native Clergy in the Philippines," 75, citing A. Brou, "Notes sur les origines du clergé philippin," in *Revue d'histoire missionaire* 4 (1927): 544.

55. De la Costa, "The Development of the Native Clergy in the Philippines," 77–78.

56. For a survey of the beginnings of education in the islands as introduced by the missions in its early period, that is, up to the expulsion of the Jesuits in 1768, see Encarnacion Alzona, *A History of Education in the Philippines, 1565–1930* (Manila: University of the Philippines, 1932), chap. 2, 17–42.

57. *CE*, s.v. "Philippines."

58. De la Costa, "Jesuit Education," 1:128–130, 141–150. Cf. Alzona, *History of Education in the Philippines*, 24–27.

59. The Jesuit colleges were at Manila, Cavite, Cebu, and Iloilo, and San Jose seminary in Manila (Bangert, *History of the Society of Jesus*, 354).

60. See the account of the founding of Santo Tomas as a "college-seminary ... where the religious may instruct the novices and ... others ... who are sons of inhabitants of this city and the islands, and any other persons," in the report of Bernardo de Santa Catalina and others, April 28, 1611; English translation in Blair and Robertson, *The Philippine Islands*, 17:55ff., 154–171. The clauses quoted (159) seem to open the school to *mestizos* and Filipinos in addition to Spaniards. The enrollment figures are found in Blair and Robertson, *The Philippine Islands*, 37:11. See also Alzona, *Education in the Philippines*, 29–31; and H. de la Costa, *The Jesuits in the Philippines, 1581–1768* (Cambridge, Mass.: Harvard University Press, 1961), 408–411.

61. Alzona, *Philippine Education*, 32, citing S. de Mas, *Informe sobre el Estado de Filipinas en 1842* (1843). See Alzona's brief survey of other schools for women, 31–35.

62. *CE*, s.v. "Philippines."

63. De la Costa, "Jesuit Education," 1:138; and "The Development of the Native Clergy in the Philippines," 73–74; and de la Costa, *The Jesuits in the Philippines*, 172–173.

64. De la Costa, *Jesuits in the Philippines*, 72–73. This school eventually merged into the Jesuit University of San Ignacio, and students from the College of San Jose read for advanced degrees at the College of Manila (de la Costa, "Jesuit Education," 130–131, 136–137, 149).

65. De la Costa, *The Jesuits in the Philippines*, 172–173. For example, the Seminary of San Felipe de Austria in Manila specified in 1641 in its charter that "the collegiates must be of pure race and have no mixture of Moorish or Jewish blood to the fourth degree, and shall have no Negro or Bengal blood, or that of any similar nation, in their veins, or a fourth part of Filipino blood" (de la Costa, "The Development of the Native Clergy in the Philippines," 75).

66. Quoted by Santiago, *Hidden Light*, 39, and in "First Filipino Priests" in *PS* 31: 154.

67. Santiago, *Hidden Light*, 23–26, and in *PS* 31: 144ff., persuasively argues for Tabuyo's Filipino identity and credits him with a significant ministry among the Igorots. Serrano was created bishop of Manila in 1519. The Augustinians were noted as the most openly receptive to the formation of a native priesthood. In 1652, thirty-one years after Tabuyo's ordination, another Filipino was received into the order as a lay brother, and is described as a noted musician and composer.

68. See Santiago, *Hidden Light*, 26–27.

69. Santiago, *Hidden Light: The First Filipino Priests*, 26, 71.

70. Latourette, *A History of the Expansion of Christianity*, 3:35. For a more detailed account of Pallu's part in the founding of the Paris Missionary Society, and of his early commitment to the cause of indigenizing the priesthood in foreign cultures, see Launay, *Histoire générale de la Société des Missions-Etrangères*, 1:22–35; 36–75; and de la Costa, "The Development of the Native Clergy in the Philippines," 80ff.

71. Launay, *Histoire générale de la Société des Missions-Etrangères*, 1:39–41, 1:224ff., 233ff.; and de la Costa, "The Development of the Native Clergy in the Philippines," 80–81.

72. On Pallu's analysis of the Philippine situation, see de la Costa, "The Development of the Native Clergy in the Philippines," 80–84 nn. 36, 39, citing an Augustinian ms. of about 1718, and a collection of early documents (*Collección Pastells de Madrid*, XIV, 103v).

73. Santiago, *Hidden Light*, lists ten native priests ordained between 1699 and 1706; a second group of ten between 1707 and 1723. He credits Archbishop Camacho with the ordination of at least nine native priests, one deacon, and four Filipinos to minor orders ("First Filipino Priests," 32–68). He adds biographies of those first Filipino priests, 73–155, and a chronology, 157–175. On the missionary Alfonzo Baluyot, see 78–80.

74. For other reasons for its failure see Blair and Robertson, *The Philippine Islands*, 28:118ff., and de la Costa, "The Development of the Native Clergy in the Philippines," 85–86. Even the attempt to transfer the seminarians to the Catholic university, Santo Tomas, in 1714, was only partially successful.

75. Santiago lists nine Filipino priests so ordained by Cuesta, not counting one he had already ordained earlier "as an exception." "First Filipino Priests," in *PS* 31: 185.

76. De la Costa, "The Development of the Native Clergy in the Philippines," 87, citing Brou.

77. Zaide, *Philippine Political and Cultural History*, 355 n 44. On primary references to Espeleta (Lino de Espeleta), citing especially Montero y Vidal's *Historia de Filipinas*, 3 vols. (1887–1895) and Juan de la Concepción's fourteen-volume *Historia general de Philipinas (1788–1792)*, see Blair and Robertson, *The Philippine Islands*, 48:147–148, 190–192; and 49:178, and the list of archbishops of Manila from 1579 to 1903 in 51:298–317.

78. De la Costa, "The Development of the Native Clergy in the Philippines," 95.

79. De la Costa, "The Development of the Native Clergy in the Philippines," 96–99.

80. Latourette, *A History of the Expansion of Christianity*, 3:312.

81. The Jesuit Father Pedro Chirino's lengthy contemporary description of Christian work in the islands about 1600 is an important corrective to some of the more derogatory reports of the colonists. Chirino, *The Philippines in 1600*, esp. 238–243.

82. Vincente L. Rafael, *Contracting Colonialism: Translation and Christian Conversion in Tagalog Society under Early Spanish Rule* (Ithaca, N.Y.: Cornell University Press, 1988), 44.

83. Phelan, *Hispanization of the Philippines*, 58ff. Phelan rates the Jesuits highest in pedagogical method, and the Franciscans most effective for their primary schools.

84. Rafael, *Contracting Colonialism*, 26–29.

85. Phelan, *Hispanization of the Philippines*, 131–132. Phelan describes the Hispanization of the islands as "non-linguistic."

86. Latourette, *A History of the Expansion of Christianity*, 3:19.

87. Phelan, *Hispanization of the Philippines*, 51.

88. See Chirino's description of "idolatries and superstitions of the Filipinos," *The Philippines in 1600*, 296–305; and the more sociologically analytical summary of preconquest Filipino culture by Phelan, *The Hispanization of the Philippines*, 15–28.

89. Neill, *A History of Christian Missions*, 209.

90. For a concise summary of these tumultuous events, see Bangert, *History of the Society of Jesus*, 368–400.

91. De la Costa, *The Jesuits in the Philippines*, 581, 595. See also Gowing, *Islands under the Cross*, 71; and Zaide, *Philippine and Political Cultural History*, 20–23.

Chapter 8

Catholic Decline and Recovery (1792–1850)

The low state to which [the Christian religion in India] is now reduced, and the contempt in which it is held, cannot be surpassed. There is not at the present... more than a third of the Christians who were to be found in it eighty years ago, and this number diminishes every day by frequent apostasy... [W]ithin less than fifty years there will, I fear, remain no vestige of Christianity among the natives.

— Abbé J. A. Dubois
Letters on the State of Christianity in India, August 7, 1815

U NDER Gregory XVI (1831–1846) the papacy finally assumed the leadership of the entire missionary movement through the efforts of the Congregation for the Propagation of the Faith, and during this pontificate forty-four new mission bishoprics were established.[1]

A twentieth-century historian, Thomas Clancy, writing in the 1970s, singles out four periods as times of melancholy decline in Catholic church history:

There have only been four occasions in the history of the Church when the number of priests has declined steadily for more than a decade. The first such period was the Black Death in the fourteenth century. The second period was the Reformation. The third was the end of the eighteenth century and the start of the nineteenth. We are living in the fourth today.[2]

The dark side of his third period is traced in this chapter.

For two and a half centuries the Iberian wave of Western imperial conquest swept by sea around the edges of Asia, planting the Catholic faith from India to Japan and dominating the history of Christian expansion around the world. From da Gama's landing in India in 1498 to Antonio de Andrade's perilous penetration into snow-capped Tibet in 1624, and the Jesuit mission in Beijing up to 1774, the Roman Catholics were the pioneers.

Toward the end of the eighteenth century, though, Rome faltered. In 1773 the number of Roman Catholics in East and South Asia was nearing two to two and a half million; by the 1830s it had probably lost about half that number.[3] Two major shocks shook the Roman rock. The first, in 1773, was the dissolution of the Vatican's most effective missionary order, the Jesuits, as mentioned at the end of the last chapter.[4] The second was the anti-Christian, anti-imperial violence of the French Revolution (1789–1804). Only then did the paralyzing effect of the damage done to the church's missions become fully apparent.

Failure and Discouragement in India: Abbé Dubois

In 1792, the same year that William Carey published his famous call to Protestant global missions, a shy, modest French priest, Jean Antoine Dubois (c. 1770–1848),[5] left his beloved Paris still bleeding from the horrors of a revolution whose followers had turned from the pursuit of liberty to the execution of aristocrats, humiliation of clergy, and the ruin of the innocent.[6] He joined the Paris Missionary Society and sailed the same year to India with high hopes that however the West might for a time close its mind to the gospel, India, as yet untouched by the blight of antireligious fanaticism, might find in Christianity a purer religion than had been handed down to it by its ancient culture. He described his missionary purpose thus:

> I had no sooner arrived amongst the natives of India than I recognized the absolute necessity of gaining their confidence. Accordingly I made it my constant rule to live as they did. I adopted their style of clothing, and I studied their customs and methods of life in order to be exactly like them. I even went so far as to avoid any display of repugnance to the majority of their peculiar prejudices.[7]

Dubois's respect for their culture, his concern for the sick and the poor, and his linguistic skills quickly won him great affection. Mysore, the field of his labors, was a Hindu kingdom ruled by Tipu, a powerful Muslim Sultan, a relentless enemy of the British and an ally of the French. Tipu was tolerant toward the Hindu majority in his kingdom for good political reasons, but fell fiercely upon the defenseless Catholic minority and forced thousands of the French missionaries' converts to embrace Islam.[8] It is a measure of the regard in which the French Abbé Dubois was held that after the defeat of Tipu and his French allies, the victorious British Lieutenant Colonel Arthur Wellesley, who was soon to become much more famous as the Duke of Wellington, invited Dubois back to reconvert the apostates and reorganize the Catholic Church in Mysore.[9]

Though Dubois succeeded splendidly in reviving the church, the momentum of political and religious change in Indian missions was not moving in a Catholic direction. Already in the sixteenth century the tides of imperial power had turned against Catholic Portugal. The eighteenth century saw Catholic France attempt and fail to replace Portugal in India. Within little more than a hundred years after the defeat of the French at the battle of Plassey (1759), a Protestant queen, Victoria, was declared Empress of India (1877), English replaced Portuguese and French as the language of higher education, and the Anglican Church acquired the luster once given in Indian colonial society to Catholicism.

Perhaps the good Abbé never quite recovered from the spectacle of watching his flock so easily change their religion with each succeeding wave of conquest: under Sultan Tipu from Christian to Muslim, then back to Catholicism, and soon tempted toward Protestantism by the rise of Anglican and Presbyterian educational opportunities. He began to turn bitter.[10]

Fifteen years later, in 1815, Dubois was writing home that he had now lost hope for India. In deep depression he had come to the conclusion that further Christian missionary effort to reach Asia's 600 million pagans would be folly. The recent arrival of Protestant missions cheered him not a bit. He predicted with a touch of malice that their naive expectation that the translation of the "naked text of the Bible" into Asia's languages will only "accelerate the downfall of the tottering edifice of Christianity in India," and that William Carey's twenty-four translations of the Bible will in another twenty-four years not have produced "the conversion of twenty-four pagans."[11] In his view the age of evangelistic Christian missions in Asia had passed. The Hindus in particular, he declared, are beyond hope of conversion by further human effort, and all that remains is to pray for their "gratuitous election" by the mercy and inscrutable providence of God.[12]

How wrong he was — at least about Indian converts. Despite his dour predictions, within seventeen years of the death of William Carey, whose "twenty-four" translations the Abbé had so roundly disparaged, there were in 1851 not the "less than twenty-four converts" the discouraged priest had predicted but nearly four thousand times twenty-four Indian Protestant Christians.[13] Thirty years later in 1881 the number had risen to 417,000 Indian Protestants, including 129,000 communicants.

In 1823 Dubois had left India as he had once left France, discouraged, disillusioned, convinced that India was as hopeless a field for Christian mission as revolutionary, dechristianizing France. After thirty years of sensitive, conscientious missionary service in Mysore, he took a last look at India still thinking failure, as when a few years earlier he had written:

> I have made, with the assistance of a native missionary, in all two or three hundred converts... Two thirds were pariahs or outcasts... who, being without resource, turned Christians... I will declare it, with shame and confusion, that I do not remember any one who may be said to have embraced Christianity from conviction and through quite disinterested motives.[14]

What had gone wrong in the Catholic missions? Contrary to what he had written in the above statement, Dubois actually placed the greater part of the blame not on the converts for whom he felt much compassion, but on three underlying weaknesses of the eighteenth-century Catholic missionary movement itself, weaknesses that he identified as the principal causes for the failure of once-great Catholic missions. First was the almost fatal effect of the rites controversy, which set one mission against another and, when carried too far, alienated the gospel from the national culture. The second was a crippling shortage of missionary personnel resulting from the suppression of the Jesuits. The final and perhaps greatest obstacle, he thought, was the not unreasonable popular Indian identification of Christianity with "vile, contemptible" European invaders from the west, the Portuguese, the French, and the English.[15]

But whatever the causes, there is no doubt about the decline. When Abbé Dubois made his gloomy survey of the situation in east India in 1815 he noted that for at least seventy years, from about 1750, Catholics there in south and east India had been losing members until, by his time, they had been reduced to only a third of their former membership (from about 250,000, as he reckoned, to about 80,000), though he admitted that the situation on India's west coast might have been more encouraging.[16] Perhaps so, but not in the northwest where one Catholic historian describes the whole history of Catholics in the Bombay area during this period as a long, long "downhill slide from the windswept heights of spiritual fervor towards the quagmire lowlands of religious apathy."[17]

The total number of Catholics in India declined from about 1 million in 1700 to perhaps as low as 475,000 by 1800.[18]

Worldwide Catholic Decline

All in all, the latter part of the eighteenth century and the first decades of the nineteenth were a time of disaster for Catholic missions everywhere, not just in India. "At one of the great turning points in history the Jesuit presence in the world, so cogent and robust for over two centuries, was missing," a Jesuit historian has written.[19] A rising Protestant empire, Great Britain, was rapidly undermining what worldwide prestige the failing Iberian empires still retained. Moreover the revolution of 1789 tore from the church the support of its last remaining great power, France, and with France it lost into exile its most promising new missionary society, the Paris Foreign Missionary Society.[20]

The French actually seized and carried away Popes Pius VI (in 1798) and Pius VII (from 1809 to 1814) from Rome to imprisonment in France. In 1808 Pius VII resisted Napoleon's attempt to move "beyond the mountains" authority over all the missions of the church from Rome to "*ultramontane*" France. Napoleon tried to seize not only the pope, but also the substance of the entire papal missionary organization, the Congregation for the Propagation of the Faith.[21]

In this period the losses of missionary personnel after the abolition of the Jesuits were devastating. In a quarter of a century from 1792 to 1817 the great Paris Missionary Society was able to send to their missions in Asia only 12 new missionaries, 4 of them to India, of whom Abbé Dubois was one.[22] By 1822 only 27 of the Society's once-flourishing corps of active missionaries remained in East and South Asia.[23] The next year the discouraged Abbé himself left India. By then, in all the world outside Europe and North America there were said to be in 1822 only 270 active European priest-missionaries of the Roman Catholic Church.[24] In Burma, for example, after 130 years of heroic attempts to establish a Christian base, by 1827 only one priest was left, and a few years later the Italian Barnabite mission gave up the field, turning over to the papacy what was left.[25] In Siam, where a strong seminary at the capital, Ayutthia, had become the major center for Catholic expansion in the peninsula, the country had been so weakened by fierce, intermittent persecutions in the eighteenth century that in 1849 when all missionaries were expelled, little was left of their once-thriving foothold.[26]

Most of Asia remained closed to Catholic missionaries throughout the first half of the nineteenth century: Indonesia totally until 1808 and partially until 1850; China until 1842; Siam until 1860; Japan until 1883; and Korea until 1884.[27] Equally devastating was the loss in membership. The full measure of the decline had been foreshadowed by the first extensive statistical report of the state of Catholic missions, published in the year of the suppression of the Jesuits, 1773. Its tabulation of the estimated number of Christians then in Catholic mission areas is uneven but worth repeating (figures are approximate):

China — 5,000
Tonkin — 200,000
Cochin China, Siam, Burma — 3,000
India — 500,000 (225,000 in Goa)
Ceylon — 100,000
Syro-Chaldaean Catholics — 80,000
Other Asia areas — 100,000[28]
Philippines — 900,000[29]

Those figures, combined with other statistical estimates, suggest that between 1700 and 1800 the church in India alone had lost more than a million members, and at the turn of the century the losses were continuing.[30] The census was by Msgr. Borgia, who labored over it for eight years. Puzzling discrepancies in the figures are the apparent omission of the Philippines, which in 1750 reportedly had "more than a million" baptized members, and the estimate of five thousand Roman Catholics in China, which is far below other estimates, such as two hundred thousand in 1800.

More Persecution in China

China presented no less gloomy a picture for Catholicism than India at the turn of the century. Its great empire in 1792 was undergoing dramatic, and for the church, almost catastrophic change. In less than two decades, from 1796 to 1814, the country's population would explode from 275 million to 374 million.[31] But in that same period its Christian community would shrink with just as shocking a proportional decline. The decline from 1700 to 1800 was from about three hundred thousand to perhaps two hundred thousand.[32] The recession had begun years before with the debilitating divisiveness of the Chinese rites controversy from about 1628 to 1742, discussed in chapter 5. Even after their formal suppression, some former Jesuits were allowed by the Emperor Quianlong to remain in his service in Beijing, but the order was officially replaced in 1784 at the Chinese court by the Lazarists (known more popularly in English as the "Vincentians," after their founder, St. Vincent de Paul) a missionary society of secular priests. One of them, Nicolas-Joseph Raux, even attained the headship of the Bureau of Astronomy, and reported that there were still about five thousand Christians in the capital in 1793.[33] But the Catholic mission in Beijing never regained its former power and prestige.

A final imperial Chinese edict against Christianity in 1811 reduced the number of missionary scientists at the court to six Vincentians and "one aged ex-Jesuit" who died three years later.[34] About the same time two of Beijing's four famous Catholic churches were destroyed, and another, the great North Church, in 1827. The doors of the last remaining great church, the South Church, were sealed about ten years later. Its outer walls were demolished and its library was transferred to the Russian church for safe-keeping.[35] All through this period, persecution was intermittent but violent. Priests were hunted down and executed in the interior, an apostolic vicar in Chengtu, a Franciscan at Changsha, two Chinese priests in Sichuan. Even the Vincentians were expelled in 1834, and in 1838 in all of China there were left about forty European priests (thirty of whom had entered only after 1825) and about eighty Chinese priests, with a total Christian community of probably about two hundred thousand, a decline from about three hundred thousand in 1700, though the uncertainty of the estimates makes such a comparison risky.[36]

In an attempt to halt the decline, and compensate for the loss of missionary personnel and Chinese leadership, in 1773 Stefano Borgia, soon to become head of the Congregation for the Propagation of the Faith, the central control agency for all papal mission, made a daring proposal. He suggested the ordination of Chinese bishops. Unfortunately, he was ahead of his times. It took another hundred years for the church to act on the suggestion.[37]

Persecution breeds silence, but silence is not always a sign of defeat. All through the silent years, when it was almost impossible for foreign priests to enter the empire, Chinese priests from Macao slipped across unnoticed to minister quietly to the faithful, and Chinese priests were even able to keep alive the church in entire provinces, such as Sichuan (Szechwan) in far west China. Typical and heroic was the life of Andrew (André) Li (or Ly), who was trained in Macao and Siam, and ordained in 1725. In very difficult years of persecutions, he traveled widely to keep the faith alive from coastal Fujian province to Kunming in the far south, and finally far western Sichuan where, when the foreign priests were driven out, he survived imprisonments and became for six years the only priest in that huge province.[38]

Beginnings of Recovery and Revival

ATTEMPTS TO ENTER TIBET

As early as 1624 a Jesuit missionary, Antonio de Andrade (1580–1634), the first European to climb the white-topped mountain walls of the Himalayas and discover the source of the sacred Ganges, penetrated into mysterious Tibet as far as Tsaparang, a town clinging precariously to the side of one of the deep canyons of the upper Sutlej River. Traders from Kashmir sometimes described that bleak area as the icy cover of hell, "which lies just underneath." Surprisingly he was warmly welcomed by the Buddhist king.[39]

Andrade did not stay long, but when he left to return to India, the friendly ruler asked him to return. He gave him a written promise of protection from "the Moors" (Muslims), and with fine disregard for Christian/Buddhist differences, offered to make him "chief Lama" and build him a "House of Prayer" for the teaching of his holy law.[40] It was not an empty promise. The next year when he returned with two other missionaries, the ruler kept his promise and pulled down two of his own houses to give the Jesuits room for a church, a garden, and a home for the foreigners. The foundation stone of the first Christian church in Tibet was laid on Easter day, April 12, 1626.[41] Within the next year and a half the mission had expanded to another mountain station and a total of seven missionaries. The second station, Rudok, was two hundred kilometers north of Tsaparang, and east of Leh. A third station proposed for Utsang by Jesuits who had secured permission from the king at Shigatse, near Lhasa, proved impossible to open, but in attempting to open it, the two Jesuit missionaries, Stephen Cacella and John Cabral, became the first Europeans to penetrate into Bhutan.[42] The number of Tibetan Christians rose to about four hundred.[43] "It will be one of the most flourishing [missions] which the Society of Jesus possesses," wrote one of Andrade's colleague, dos Anjos.[44]

But once again high expectations for Christianity in Asia were followed by bitter disappointment. It was only a slippery toehold that the intrepid Jesuits had managed to create for their faith on the icy Tibetan slopes at the top of the world, and Christians did not survive there long. Andrade was recalled by the Society to Goa to become the head of all Jesuit mission work in Goa, Malabar, and Cochin. Shortly thereafter, in 1630, a revolution toppled the Jesuits' friend and protector from his throne. The king's own Buddhist lamas, angered by his toleration of the new religion, turned against him. A rival king in neighboring Ladakh was only too glad to come to their aid. The king of Tsaparang, protector of Christians, was taken prisoner, and many Christian converts were reduced to slavery and exile.

A missionary relief party attempted in vain to return to reestablish the mission in 1635. Two missioners remained briefly in Tsaparang but were imprisoned, then banished, and the mission was abandoned. A belated final Jesuit attempt was made in the early eighteenth century to revive Christian work in Tibet. Hippolyte Desideri (1684–1733) reached Lhasa in 1716 and left Tibet five years later without finding any evidence of a surviving Christian community.[45]

KOREA

Only in Korea were Catholic missionaries able to establish a new and permanent beachhead for the faith during these troubled times.[46] But for the whole century, Korean Christianity was forced to remain almost invisible, its survival shadowed by the anguish of its martyrs. Wave after wave of persecutions had driven underground the Catholic beachhead established in 1792, and in 1866 the last great persecution almost wiped it out. Korea was an example, though, of the fact that in Christian history, invisibility does not necessarily imply decline. Over and over again, troubled times have proved to be strengthening times for the church, and "the blood of the martyrs" paradoxically energizes it. Still the shadows are no less real and painful. For Catholics in Korea, revival to public prominence was delayed to the very last years of the nineteenth century.

INDOCHINA (VIETNAM)

If Korea appeared to be the only permanent new advance opened up by Catholic missions in this period of decline, thousands of miles farther south, Vietnam (that is, Tonkin, now northern Vietnam, and Annam, southern Vietnam) could at least give thanks for a few sustained periods of freedom of religion and church growth in the midst of general uncertainty. During the tolerant regime of the emperor Gia-long (Nguyen Anh, 1802–1820), who had finally united the entire peninsula in his empire of Annam, there were years when the churches flourished, the number of active indigenous clergy increased remarkably, and the number of Christians doubled, to a reported total of about four hundred thousand. There were seventy-four native priests reported in Tonkin about the year 1816, and a theological seminary; in the southern kingdom, Cochin China, there were eighteen native priests in about 1822.[47]

After the emperor's death, a series of virulent persecutions closed the country again to the Christian faith. Two apostolic vicars were beheaded; a priest who refused to betray hidden believers was strangled; another suffered the "death of a hundred wounds"; two more were strangled; and as late as 1857 a Spanish bishop, Msgr. Diaz, was beheaded. The times of fiercest persecution were from 1833 to 1840 and from 1847 to 1861, until French forces intervened, defeated the Annamese, and forced the cession of the southern provinces of Cochin China to the French Empire.[48]

THE MIDDLE EAST

In West Asia the Franciscans had not been deterred, even in the period of decline, from continuing Catholic witness among the Christian minorities of the Ottoman Empire, although they were having difficulty in their home base in Europe, where they were trying to recover a united approach to missionary expansion.[49] And in 1831 the Jesuits again entered Turkish Syria. They were treated well for a while by the Ottoman Empire for political reasons, until militant Syrian Muslims rose in bloody protest at the defiling presence of infidels in their midst. Thousands of Christians were massacred in Damascus, along with five French Jesuits.[50]

Recovery in Catholic Europe

Concurrent with such intermittent glimpses of renewed hope for Catholic missions in Asia, principally in Tonkin (northern Vietnam), Korea, and the Philippines, stirrings at the home base in Europe showed signs of a revival and restoration of the papacy. When the people's revolution in France failed as most revolutions do, it was succeeded by the rise of a military dictatorship under Napoleon. The revolution had been militantly atheistic; the dictatorship was no less secular but more pragmatic. Napoleon came to the conviction that, for the sake of social stability, "France needed a religion," provided it be one he could control.[51] So for about a decade and a half at the beginning of the nineteenth century he alternately cajoled and bullied the papacy and the church into a reluctant acceptance of his new order. In 1802 he offered Pope Pius VII French military protection for all the church's missions in China and the Middle East.[52] In 1809 he took the same pope captive to France.[53] In 1805, he allowed the reestablishment of the Paris Foreign Missionary Society, which the revolution had destroyed. In that year the Society, which at the beginning of the revolution had fifty-eight missionaries in the Far East, could count only twelve.[54] Four years later, displeased at the Society's refusal to place its assets and policies under government control,

Napoleon revoked its charter and once more dissolved its headquarters. It was not restored until after Waterloo. From 1804 until 1815 the Society was unable to send more than two missionaries to East Asia.[55]

Then, in what has been described as the "ultramontanist" reaction against revolutionary chaos and Napoleon's secular dictatorship, Catholic Christian Europe looked once again "over [ultra] the mountains" to Rome, and once more the papacy came to life. Count Joseph de Maistre set the stage for the recovery of just such a central, universal religious authority with his slogan: "No national character without religion...No Christianity without Catholicism, and no Catholicism without the Pope."[56]

By then the tide had already turned. A year before his defeat at Waterloo, Napoleon in desperation had allowed the pope to return to Rome, and after Napoleon's fall, one of the first acts of the liberated Pope Pius VII was to restore the papacy's old ally, the Society of Jesus.[57] So ended the suppression of the Jesuits who for a melancholy forty years (1773–1814) had been stripped of their world mission.[58] Other mission restorations followed in quick succession. In 1815 Louis XVIII, though not much of a believer himself, reestablished the Paris Foreign Missionary society and returned its missionary Seminary to its directors.[59] Two years later the pope reorganized the Vatican's own missionary arm, the Congregation for the Propagation of the Faith.[60]

It was in the pontificate of a great mission-minded pope, Gregory XVI (1831–1846), however, that a revitalized Roman Catholic Church returned with power and renewed unity to its worldwide missionary objectives. Gregory has been called "the great missionary pope of the nineteenth century."[61] During his reign "the losses of the Catholic Church in Europe were more than balanced by her gains in the rest of the world."[62]

Gregory came to the papacy with valuable experience as head of the Congregation for the Propagation of the Faith. He set about at once to reclaim authority for all the church's missions from Spain and Portugal, which for about three hundred years had controlled the churches in their colonies. In 1840 he sent out the first returning Jesuits, after their restoration, to Macao, the center of Catholic mission expansion to China, Korea, and hopefully Japan, but carefully used his own missionary bishops, the apostolic vicars, for independent advisory jurisdiction, and where necessary for controlling them. Despite all the criticisms he has received from modern historians, it is worth remembering that Gregory XVI saved the papacy, strongly supported the role of women in missions, and reversed decades of decline in Catholic world missions.[63]

By the end of his pontificate Gregory XVI had established a global missionary network of forty-four apostolic vicariates from India to China and Burma, Siam, and Indonesia and on around the world. These, like the central Congregation for the Propagation of the Faith (the Propaganda) operated directly under the authority of the pope.[64]

On the whole, the recovery described above was only gradual, but by the 1830s Catholic recovery was already spreading overseas to the mission field. In 1829, for example, the Jesuits had elected as their new general a Dutchman, Jan Roothaan, their youngest general in two hundred years, and the second after the restoration of the Society. One of his early acts (1833) was to issue a stirring call to the Society for missionary volunteers, and more than a thousand Jesuits responded.[65] His disciplined devotion to the strict Jesuit piety of Loyola's *Spiritual Exercises* inspired a new generation of volunteers, as three hundred years earlier the founder's challenge had sent Xavier and Ricci to Asia.[66] It was the beginning of a steady rise in missionary vocations. In another twenty years there were 975 Jesuits overseas — most of them, however, in the United States, which was then still a Catholic mission field.

Recovery in Asia

INDIA

In India, after the defeat of the French and the collapse of the Moghul Empire in 1761, all through the nineteenth century the dominant power was British, and in Christian circles, Anglican, but not numerically. The Catholic missionaries had a double handicap. They were not only European and non-Indian, but non-British and non-Protestant as well.[67] However, as a matter of practical fact, Portugal, not Britain, posed the greatest problem for Catholic missions. The Goanese, in the little Portuguese colony on the west coast, in 1794 claimed ecclesiastical jurisdiction over all India's Catholics and missions by their old rights of *padroado*. This tore India's Catholics apart in a bruising schism (1794–1812) that had long-lasting aftereffects. It set the Catholics and clergy of Portuguese Goa against the apostolic vicars appointed by the pope to represent Roman authority in British India.[68] The number of Catholic clergy in India declined sharply, and those who remained were criticized for replacing evangelism with internal bickering.[69]

The return of the Jesuits in 1831 brought a renewal of outreach, and by the middle of the nineteenth century Catholics could report more than twelve hundred conversions yearly on the Malabar coast, and an encouraging revival of training for the native priesthood at four seminaries.[70]

About the same time even the Portuguese archbishop of Goa, Manuel de S. Galdino, had come to the conclusion that Portuguese patronage (the *padroado*), with its crippling ties to a declining, secularizing empire, was sucking the life out of India's Catholic communities. Only strong action from Rome, he suggested, could save them from gradual extinction. Rescue came with the election in 1831 of the missionary-minded pope, Gregory XVI (1831–1846), who had been director of the papal missions of the Vatican (as distinct from the imperially controlled *padroado* missions of Portugal and Spain). Within four years, 1832 to 1836, he completely reorganized India's Catholic missions under Vatican-appointed apostolic vicars. It was none too soon. But it did retrieve Indian Catholicism from the control of a Portugal that had turned anticlerical, and prepared it to survive in an India turning British.

One last encouraging note remains to be added to what was for the most part a downturn in Roman Catholic missions at the end of the eighteenth and the beginning of the nineteenth centuries. Toward the end of this period, the good Abbé Dubois, whom we last saw returning to France in 1823 after thirty discouraging years in India, did not, it turns out, remain discouraged. Nor did he abandon his missionary vocation. Back in France, he became a director of the same Society under which he had served in Asia, and perhaps a little ruefully but with great Christian satisfaction he observed that while Catholic missions had often faltered, the day of Christian conversions in Asia was in no way past.[71]

CHINA

Catholic recovery in India was followed a few decades later by a turn for the better in China, but it may have been a recovery for the wrong reasons. It was foreign intervention, not Chinese initiative, that brought a respite from persecution. Foreign intervention in the form of political pressure from Catholic France after the First Opium War secured inclusion in the peace treaties of 1842–1844 of three edicts of toleration for Catholic missions and Christians.[72] Then, for the wrong reason — the Opium Wars — came the change. The coercive effect of the Opium Wars of the early 1840s and 1860s brought religious freedom for Christians again to China, but at a price that would become apparent only later. There was, to be sure, an encouraging surge in membership figures. At the beginning of the century there had been an estimated 300,000 Roman Catholics still in China. Many had fled into exile in Mongolia, but enough were left to assemble a synod in the far west, in Sichuan in 1803. Still, persecution and martyrdoms continued. An imperial decree in 1811 condemned to death any missionaries in control of the church.[73] But, by 1890, in the new climate, there were reported to be 500,000 Chinese Catholics, 369 foreign missionary priests, and 273 Chinese priests.[74]

The story of the Jesuits in China in those years is an example.[75] In 1773, the year of their dissolution, the Jesuits had three thousand missioners worldwide. Their Beijing mission in northern China had made history before it was expelled. After the last bishop of Nanjing, farther south, died under house arrest in 1838, no bishop of the Society was appointed to succeed him.[76] Jesuits did not return effectively to China until 1841, and then only to find themselves viewed as foreign intruders in the aftermath of the Opium Wars, increasingly unpopular because of "the unequal treaties" that placed foreign missionaries outside the jurisdiction of Chinese law and shielded them under the protection of the European powers.[77] Nevertheless, they proved to be remarkably successful, especially in the vicariate of Nanjing where by 1900 they counted 124,000 Catholics. It was their hope that from their strong base in Nanjing they could reopen Jesuit mission to Japan.[78]

So also with other Catholic missions. Thanks to those same unequal treaties, the French missions led by the Vincentians and the Paris Missionary Society, which had replaced the Jesuits, had been able to redouble their commitment to overseas missions.[79] Distribution throughout Europe of the popular missionary *Annals*, published by the reinvigorated papal board of missions, the Propaganda (the Congregation for the Propagation of the Faith), rose from less than 10,000 in the 1820s to more than 180,000 by the end of the 1850s.

There was a negative side, however, casting a shade over the recovery and growth of the church after the return of the missions. The reason was the lasting taint that in many Chinese eyes linked Christian missions with the invasions and unequal foreign treaties that ended the Opium Wars. An unexpected consequence to the limited new freedoms of religion granted by the treaties for a resumption of missionary outreach was a rise in anti-Christian riots and outbreaks of persecution. Quite different, however, were these from the massive state-led persecutions of the years of imperial edicts against Christianity. Now, because of the restrictions of the peace treaties, the government could no longer officially outlaw Christianity. The harassment and demonstrations of popular resentment had to be kept local, and whatever government support there may have been to the violence had to be hidden.[80] But the resentment was real, and the violence kept increasing to the end of the century.

THE PHILIPPINES

Almost alone in all of East and South Asia, the progress of Christianity in the Philippines was little disturbed by violence and the other developments we have been discussing. True, the British invaded and captured and looted Manila in 1742, and though British occupation was temporary, it shook the myth of Spanish invincibility and encouraged the rise of nationalist sentiment.[81] The expulsion of the Jesuits in 1768 was a more serious setback, particularly in the field of education, but Jesuits had not been ecclesiastically dominant there.[82] Their missions were given to the Franciscans and Augustinians, who were stretched thin but valiantly continued their outreach to the unevangelized.[83] At mid-century (about 1846) there were about 4 million Roman Catholics in the islands, and a million still unconverted pagans.[84] Even the failure of a program to ordain large numbers pf Filipino priests under the authority of diocesan bishops rather than missionary orders did not noticeably weaken the growth of the Christian faith in the islands.[85]

When Jesuits returned to the Philippines in 1859 after more than ninety years of expulsion, they immediately devoted their principal efforts to the evangelization of Mindanao, which was still predominantly Muslim. About the same time, a flood of priests from other orders driven out of Spain by the rise of anti-Catholic liberalism brought welcome recruits to the Philippine missions but proved to be a mixed blessing to the church. The arrival of the Spanish newcomers forced a number of Filipino priests from their parishes and aroused a sometimes violent protest among Filipino nationals. Some trace the rise of anti-Spanish nationalism in the latter half of the nineteenth century to this overflow of foreign priests.[86]

NOTES

1. Joseph A. Otto, *Grundung der Neuen Jesuitenmission durch General Pater Johann Philipp Roothaan* (Freiburg im Breisgau: Herder, 1939), 103, cited in H. Jedin and J. Dolan, eds. *History of the Church*, vol. 6, *The Church in the Age of Absolutism and Enlightenment* (New York: Crossroad, 1980), 204.

2. Thomas H. Clancy, *An Introduction to Jesuit Life: The Constitutions and History through 435 Years* (St. Louis: Institute of Jesuit Sources, 1976), 188.

3. See, for example, H. Jedin and J. Dolan, eds., *The History of the Church*, vol. 7, *The Church between Revolution and Restoration* (New York: Crossroad, 1980), 3–67, and passim; Arnulf Camps, *Studies in Asian Mission History, 1956–1998* (Leiden: Brill, 2000), 22–23; Latourette, *A History of the Expansion of Christianity*, 3:273, 312; 6:73, 216, 219, 225–226, 247, 251, 256; and Delacroix, *Histoire universelle des missions catholiques*, 3:27–28, 30–47.

4. They were officially withdrawn from China in 1774, though a few remained unofficially, and were reported as expelled from the Philippines the same year. Two Protestant rulers in continental Europe refused to suppress them, Catherine the Great of Russia and Frederick the Great of Prussia (Zaide, *Philippine Cultural and Political History*, 21).

5. Sources are meager on the life of Dubois. See Launay's classic, *Histoire générale de la Société des Missions-Etrangères*, 2:318, 383–386; 3:168ff.; and his more detailed *Histoire des missions de l'Inde: Pondichéry, Maissour, Coimbatour* (Paris: Charles Douniol, 1898), 1:191–204. See also the editor's introduction to Abbé Jean Antoine Dubois, *Hindu Manners, Customs, and Ceremonies*, trans. and ed. H. K. Beauchamp, 3rd ed. (Oxford: Clarendon Press, 1906).

6. See, for example, Michel Vovelle, *The Revolution against the Church: From Reason to the Supreme Being*, trans. Alan José (Columbus: Ohio State University Press, 1991).

7. Dubois, *Hindu Manners, Customs and Ceremonies*, ix.

8. Abbé Jean Antoine J. A. Dubois, *Letters on the State of Christianity in India in which the Conversion of the Hindoos Is Considered as Impracticable*, ed. Sharda Paul (New Delhi: Associated Publishing House reprint, 1977), letter 2:40–41. Of sixty thousand who were forced into apostasy, Dubois reckoned that twenty-two thousand repented and reconverted.

9. Dubois, *Hindu Manners,* editor's preface, xii. On Tipu, see R. C. Majumdar et al., *An Advanced History of India,* 685–688, 711–715. Tipu died bravely defending his capital in 1799.

10. Dubois, *Letters,* letter 2:41.

11. Dubois, *Letters,* letter 1 (August 1815), 14–23, especially 20 n. 1; and letter 2 (December 1815), 42.

12. Dubois, *Letters,* letter 1 (August 1815), 23–27.

13. In 1851 there were 91,092 Indian Protestant Christians (of whom 14,661 were communicant members). See the statistics in M. A. Sherring, *The History of Protestant Missions in India, 1706 to 1881,* 2nd rev. ed. (London: Religious Tract Society, 1884), 443.

14. Dubois, *Letters,* letter 3 (November 1816), 72.

15. Dubois, *Letters,* letter 1:6–7; letter 3:62–65.

16. Dubois, *Letters,* 4.

17. J. H. Gense, *The Church at the Gateway of India, 1720–1850* (Bombay: St. Xavier's College, 1960), 1–110.

18. See Latourette, *History of the Expansion of Christianity,* 3:265–273 (statistics on 273). Cf. Julius Richter, *A History of Missions in India,* trans S. H. Moore (New York: Fleming H. Revell, 1908), 92–95. Richter estimates 2 million nominal Roman Catholics in India in 1701 (*A History of Missions in India,* 92). Camps, *Studies in Asian Mission History,* 22, estimates that "toward the end of the eighteenth century" there were 1.5 to 2 million Catholics in Asia, Africa, and Latin America, excluding the Portuguese- and Spanish-speaking people of Latin America.

19. Bangert, *History of the Society of Jesus,* 430.

20. For the full history of the Society during the revolution see Launay, *Histoire générale de la Société des Missions-Etrangères,* 2:257–377.

21. See Jedin and Dolan, *History of the Church,* 7:46–50, 73ff., 190–191; and *CE,* s.v. "Pius VI," "Pius VII."

22. The other eight were assigned to China, Tonkin, Cochin China and Siam (Thailand). Jean-Claude Didelot, *Missions Etrangères de Paris* (Le Sarment, France: Fayard, 1986), 236.

23. Launay, *Histoire générale de la Société des Missions Etrangères,* 2:499; *Les ordres religieux: La Sociéte des Missions Etrangères* (Paris: Librairie Letouzey et Ané, 1923), 23. The statistics for the Society reported 5 missions (1 in India, 3 in Indo-China, 1 in China), 6 bishops, 27 missionaries, 120 (Launay) or 135 native priests, 400 evangelists ("catechists"), 11 seminaries with 250 students, and 300,000 or 370,000 (Launay) Christians.

24. Delacroix, *Histoire universelle des missions catholiques,* 3:169–170.

25. Latourette, *A History of the Expansion of Christianity,* 3:226.

26. Latourette, *A History of the Expansion of Christianity,* 6:242.

27. Delacroix, *Histoire universelle des missions catholiques,* 3:170.

28. Bernard de Vaulx, *Histoire des missions catholiques françaises* (Paris: Fayard, 1951), 121–122. See also Latourette, *A History of the Expansion of Christianity,* 3:273, 312, and *History of Christian Missions in China,* 182–183.

29. See Latourette, *A History of the Expansion of Christianity,* 3:312. If children under seven are added, "over a million." This figure for the Philippines is for the year 1750.

30. Latourette accurately notes the wide variations in Catholic membership figures for India in this period. Estimates for 1700 vary from 1.5 million to 2.5

million; for 1800, from 475,000 to 1.2 million. In either case the loss of membership in the century was more than 1 million Catholics (Latourette, *A History of the Expansion of Christianity*, 3:273).

31. Eberhard, *A History of China*, 274.

32. Latourette, *A History of Christian Missions in China*, 129. Latourette (129) reports estimates of about 300,000 Catholic Christians, possibly less, in 1705; 150,000 in 1793 (174), and "about 200,000 or 250,000 Roman Catholics in all China" in 1800 (183). Cf. Schmidlin's estimate of 300,000 for 1800 (Schmidlin, *Catholic Mission History*, 610).

33. Latourette, *A History of Christian Missions in China*, 168–169, 174; and *A History of the Expansion of Christianity*, 3:356.

34. Latourette, *A History of Christian Missions in China*, 177–178; and *A History of the Expansion of Christianity*, 3:356. The last French missionary expelled from the Beijing court was M. Lamiot in 1835 (A. Thomas, *La Mission de Pékin*, 2:124-125, 131–132).

35. A. Thomas, *La Mission de Pékin*, 2:92ff.

36. A. Thomas, *La Mission de Pékin*, 2:138–144; Latourette, *A History of Christian Missions in China*, 129, 178, 182; cf. Latourette, *A History of the Expansion of Christianity*, 3:356–358. In 1838 the Portuguese Vincentians reported forty thousand Christians in Jiongnan; twenty-five thousand in Beijing, and eighty thousand in Macao, Guangdong, and Guongxi; the French Vincentians estimated forty thousand. Catholic missions in China were reorganized in 1838, and the Jesuits reentered Nanjing as a vicariate in 1839 (Thomas, *La Mission de Pékin*, 2:139–140, 143).

37. Jedin and Dolan, *History of the Church*, 7:189–190.

38. See Adrien Launay, *Journal d'André Ly, Prêtre Chinois, Missionare et notaire apostolique, 1746–1763*, 2nd ed. (Hong Kong: Imprimerie de Nazareth, 1924).

39. On de Andrade and the mission in Tsaparang, see C. Wessels, *Early Jesuit Travellers in Central Asia, 1603–1721* (The Hague: Martinus Nijhoff, 1924), 43–93. Andrade was also the first to report to the West the words of the legendary, repetitive Buddhist prayer, "Om mani padme hum," sometimes translated, "O thou of the jewel and the lotus" (74, 264–265).

40. Wessels, *Jesuit Travellers*, 64–67.

41. Wessels, *Jesuit Travellers*, 70–71.

42. On the Tsaparang mission, see Wessel, *Jesuit Travellers*, 69–93, 120–161.

43. Wessels, *Jesuit Travellers*, 71–77.

44. Wessels, *Jesuit Travellers*, 73, 72 n. 2. Dos Anjos (Alain de la Beauchere) worked in Tibet from 1625 to at least 1633.

45. Wessels, *Jesuit Travellers*, 75–89. On unsuccessful attempts to identify the name of the Tsaparang king who had befriended the Christians, see 78ff.

46. Wessels, *Jesuit Travellers*, 205–272. Two Capuchins had reached Lhasa in 1707 and left in 1711 (208).

47. Launay, *Histoire générale de la Société des Missions Etrangères*, 2:386–393, 493–495; Cf. de Vaulx, *History of the Missions*, 124.

48. Launay, *Histoire générale de la Société des Missions Etrangères*, 2:525–573; 3:365–374.

49. Jedin and Dolan, *History of the Church*, 7:161, n. 28; 210.

50. Christopher Hollis, *The Jesuits: A History* (London: Macmillan, 1968), 237–240.

51. On Napoleon's dreams of control of the papacy, see Nielsen, *The History of the Papacy in the XIXth Century*, 1:329. On his church policy, see Launay, *Histoire générale de la Société des Missions Etrangères*, 2:377–380.

52. Launay, *Histoire générale de la Société des Missions Etrangères*, 2:354–355.

53. The pope was Pius VII. See Nielsen, *History of the Papacy in the XIXth Century*, 1:297ff., 310–321.

54. Launay, *Histoire générale de la Société des Missions Etrangères*, 2:377, 380–381.

55. Launay, *Histoire générale de la Société des Missions Etrangères*, 2:337–380, 422, 424ff.

56. Quoted by Josef L. Altholz, *The Churches in the Nineteenth Century* (Indianapolis and New York: Bobbs-Merrill, 1967).

57. Jean Lacouture, *Jesuits: A Multibiography*, trans. J. Leggatt (Washington, D.C.: Crosspoint, 1995), 334–335.

58. Bangert, *History of the Society of Jesus*, 428ff.

59. Launay, *Histoire générale de la Société des Missions Etrangères*, 2:523–524. See also Hollis, *The Jesuits*, 188.

60. *NCE*, s.v. "Propagation of the Faith."

61. The words are those of Georges Goyau, cited by Jedin and Dolan, *History of the Church*, 7:204.

62. *CE*, s.v. "Gregory XVI."

63. For Pope Gregory XVI's pertinent policies, see Claudia Carlen, ed., *The Papal Encyclicals*, vol. 1, 1740–1878, 5 vols. (London: Eyre & Spottiswoode, 1966); for English translations of his encyclicals: notably *Probe Nostis* (1840), 1:259–261, on missions. Less admired by Protestants was his *Inter Praecipuas* (1844), 1:267–271, against Bible societies. Most criticized by modern historians is his *Mirari Vos* (1832), 1:235–241, a strong condemnation of revolution and religious liberties, which at that time, however, was not an unnatural reaction to the refusal of his fiefdoms, the papal states, to acknowledge the sovereignty of the pope.

64. Otto, *Grundung der Neuen Jesuitenmission*, 103.

65. On Roothaan, see Otto, *Grundung der Neuen Jesuitenmission durch General Pater Johann Philipp Roothaan*, 104–193, 251–387, and passim.

66. Bangert, *History of the Society of Jesus*, 436–437.

67. Hollis, *The Jesuits*, 237–239.

68. On the Goa schism, and the controversy that dragged on for years after 1812, see Ernest R. Hull, *Bombay Mission History and the Padroado Question*, 2 vols. (Bombay: Examiner Press, 1927), 1:128ff.

69. Lobley, *Church and the Churches in Southern India*, 103ff.

70. The seminaries were at Verapoli, Quilon and Mangalore. Lobley, *Church and the Churches*, 104–106. For more extensive treatment of the Jesuits in India in this period see Otto, *Grundung der Jesuitenmission*, 254–343.

71. Launay, *Histoire générale de la Société des Missions Etrangères*, 3:168ff.

72. Latourette, *A History of Christian Missions in China*, 228–232.

73. Schmidlin, *Catholic Mission History*, 610–611.

74. Latourette, *A History of Christian Missions in China*, 329, 356; Schmidlin, *Catholic Mission History*, 610.

75. See Otto, *Grundung der Neuen Jesuitenmission*, 350–383.

76. Otto, *Gruandung der neuen Jesuitenmission*, 357ff.; Jedin and Dolan, *History of the Church*, 7:201.

77. Otto, *Gruandung der neuen Jesuitenmission*.

78. Schmidlin, *Catholic Mission History*, 616 n. 30. The Nanjing vicariate was among China's largest in extent of territory.

79. Clancy, *Introduction to Jesuit Life*, 191. The Paris Society sent six missionaries to the Far East in 1840, six in 1841, ten in 1844, twelve in 1845, eighteen in 1846, and twenty-four in 1847 (Launay, *Histoire générale de la Société des Missions Etrangères*, 3:104).

80. Latourette, *A History of Catholic Missions in China*, 346–356.

81. Zaide, *Philippine Political and Cultural History*, 2:1–25.

82. Jedin and Dolan, *History of the Church*, 6:324.

83. Schmidlin, *Catholic Mission History*, 635.

84. Schmidlin, *Catholic Mission History*, 634 n. 8.

85. Zaide, *Philippine Political and Cultural History*, 2:39–46.

86. De la Costa, "Episcopal Jurisdiction in the Philippines during the Spanish Regime," 63–84.

Chapter 9

West Asia under the Turks and Persians (1500–1800)

At long last [in 1820 C. J. Rich] revealed to the English-speaking races the astounding facts about the Assyrians, who still conversed in a language similar to that spoken by Jesus and the Apostles, and whose peculiar form of Christianity called for study and sympathy.   — A. S. Atiya

THE most substantial continental barrier separating Europe and Asia in 1500 was not geography but religion. It was Islam that forced the Portuguese, the Spanish, the Dutch, and the British to sail the long, long way around Africa to reach Asia in the world-changing years of what the West calls the Age of Discovery. After throwing the Crusaders out of Asia back into Europe in the thirteenth century, Islam ruled West Asia (the Middle East) for 150 years, guarding it carefully against further Western or Christian intrusion. Its two great Muslim empires, Ottoman Turkey (1300–1918) and Safavid Persia (1500–1736), were the formidable wall that blocked Europe from access to the fabled riches of the Orient, and the cement that sealed it tight was the ancient enmity between the Muslim and Christian religions.

Midway in the fifteenth century, beginning with the fall of Constantinople in 1454, Islam launched its own crusade, this time an Islamic holy war against Christian Europe. From their beachhead in Istanbul (Constantinople), where the southeastern tip of Europe faces Asia, the Turks moved north into the Balkans. But their initial success exposed a hidden weakness within the Islamic base. The two Muslim empires, Turkey and Persia, were themselves divided by a fissure in their one religion. Sunni Muslim Turkey and Shi'ite Muslim Persia were enemies — much as Europe's Christianity was soon to be divided Catholic against Protestant. In this crack in the fabric of Muslim unity lay one of the reasons for the continuing tenuous survival of Christianity in West Asia after the mass devastations of Tamerlane (d. 1405), which were described in the first volume of the present *History of Christianity in Asia*.[1]

The Nestorians on the Turko-Persian Borders

East of the Euphrates in the mountains of Kurdistan is where, in a historical sense, oriental Asia in this period begins. So it is there, in one of the two surviving pockets of the ancient Nestorians,[2] that we must now pick up the story of Christianity in western Asia.[3] These are the people who trace their theology to a fifth-century bishop north of Antioch, Theodore of Mopsuestia; their name, Nestorian, by which they are best known in the West, to a deposed fifth-century patriarch of Constantinople; and their roots to the first-century pioneers of Christianity outside the Roman Empire in Edessa.[4]

There at the beginning of the sixteenth century, a hundred years after the death of Tamerlane ("the Scourge of God"), and the disintegration of his empire under his feckless, quarreling descendants,[5] — scattered remnants of the once great church of the East, the Nestorians, were slowly but steadily being driven out of the cities into the mountains or the high river valleys on the border between Turkey and Persia (Iran). They lived in isolated villages within a region shaped roughly like an inverted triangle with its point in Mosul (ancient Nineveh), and its base running from Lake Van in Armenian Turkey to Lake Urmia in Iran.[6]

Despite their precarious situation the Nestorians had managed to maintain a line of patriarchs.[7] But where once two hundred years earlier a Mongol patriarch had ruled from his base in the capital of the Persian empire over a missionary church stretching from the Euphrates to China, by the year 1500 the missionaries were gone, and the patriarch was hiding in the mountains. The Nestorian Patriarch Simon V (1497?–1501) could probably count on the fingers of his two hands the number of village bishops who still recognized his authority. Nevertheless, one vestige of continental ecclesiastical order remained, one bright thread of mission to the world, as was mentioned at the end of volume 1 of this history.[8]

A decade earlier, in 1490, in an unexpected revival of its ancient Nestorian pan-Asian network, Simon V, or his predecessor Simon IV, had been surprised by the announcement that two Christian pilgrims had worked their way upstream on the Tigris River from Mosul and had reached his village, Gazarta.[9] They told him that they had come from the Malabar coast, three thousand perilous miles away, to ask for ordination by a bishop since no bishop was left in India. He complied with their request and sent them back. The timing was providential for the St. Thomas Christians in India. They would soon need all the organizational strength they could muster to meet the greatest challenge of their history. Within a decade the black ships of the Portuguese would appear off the India coast bringing a threat to their identity, not from Muslims or Hindus, but from within Christendom itself, shaking the very foundations of their ancient Nestorian heritage.

But history seems always to unfold in unforeseen ways. It so happened that the patriarchate in Mesopotamia was in graver danger than the Syrian Thomas Christians of India who came to it for ecclesiastical authentication. In the next three hundred years the Nestorians of the Middle East almost virtually disappeared, whereas in India the Syrian Christianity that traces itself to the apostle Thomas rather than to Peter grew larger and stronger, as we shall see.[10]

For a while in the early years of Persia's Safavid dynasty (1500–1732) after the fall of the Mongols, the Nestorians east of the Euphrates hoped against hope for better things. In contrast to the harsher Ottoman Turks west of the river whose Sultan Selim was slaughtering Shi'ite, Christian, and Jewish "heretics" by the thousands, the Safavids of Persia seemed to have a softer policy toward their religious minorities. Shah Isma'il (1500–1524), the founder of the dynasty, was reported by Western observers to be a friend of Christians. That may not have been the whole truth, but his treatment of the religious *dzimmis* (ghettos) followed the traditional Persian practice of granting semiautonomy to the various religious communities under their recognized religious leaders. Shah Abbas I a little later (1587–1628) went so far as to propose an alliance between Shi'ite Persia and the Christian West against the common enemy, Sunni Turkey. Nothing came of it, and Abbas I soon turned violently anti-Christian, but the Nestorians were encouraged; Roman Catholic missionaries, some of whom prematurely hailed the Shah as a potential convert, renewed their efforts to reestablish the missions in Persia destroyed by Tamerlane.[11]

Increasing Catholic missionary pressure, however well intentioned, tended to destabilize the organization of the Nestorian church without seemingly to do much to reform its spiritual weaknesses. Between 1500 and 1800 Ottoman and Persian rule of the Middle East, though only intermittently and locally rising to open persecution, was severe enough to force the Nestorians into a dangerous departure from their own canon law. In order to preserve the Christian integrity of patriarchal succession and protect it from intimidation and manipulation by non-Christian governments, they abandoned the traditional method of election through free and public vote by the bishops, and allowed the office to become hereditary. A dying patriarch would choose his successor from within his own family, usually a nephew or cousin since Nestorian bishops were celibate.[12] While this may have protected the office from usurpation by less than Christian outsiders, it narrowed the field of choice and paved the way for mediocrity. It also very soon produced a schism.

The Sixteenth-Century Nestorian Schism

In 1551 a revolt of bishops split the church in two. Patriarch Simon VII bar Mama, who had moved from Gazarta to another mountain retreat nearer to Mosul at Rabban Hormuzd (Hormizd), named his nephew to succeed

him. He was installed as Simon VIII Denha (1551–1558). But a party
of apparently three bishops, a number of clergy, and some of the most
prominent lay leaders rebelled in protest and elected a rival patriarch,
John Sulaqa, a monk from the monastery of Rabban Hormuzd, who took
the same name, Shimon (Simon) VIII, and with the aid of Franciscan
missionaries in the Mosul area in what is now Iraq was escorted to Rome
where he submitted loyalty to Pope Julius III and received recognition
as patriarch of the Chaldeans.[13]

For the next three hundred years, well into the nineteenth century, the
Nestorian community in Turkey and Persia was torn in loyalty between
these two lines of patriarchs. The "old line" of Shimon VII bar Mama
and his nephew claimed to represent the traditional ancient Nestorianism of the church of the East and the patriarchs of Seleucia-Ctesiphon.
The Sulaqa "new line" of the pro-Roman Shimon VIII claimed to be
equally Nestorian but more authentically canonical, and interpreted its
connection with the pope as a recognition of a wider ancient Christian
unity.

To anticipate a little, the painful story of this schism winds down to a
strange twisted ending. That could happen only in Mesopotamia (Iraq).
The pro-Roman Sulaqa line eventually turned independent Nestorian,
and the traditional Nestorian Simon VII bar Mama line did the exact
opposite and was absorbed into the fold of Rome as Uniate Chaldaean,
that is, recognizing the primacy of the pope but retaining the right to
use its own Syriac language in its liturgy and rites.

This outcome occurred gradually and very irregularly over the course
of the next two centuries.[14] The pro-Roman allegiance of the Sulaqa line
cooled first, reverting to a hereditary succession of patriarchates in 1600
and omitting the patriarchal vow of allegiance to Rome some time after
1670. About this time also, the old-line patriarchate moved its seat a
short distance across the border from Urmi in Azerbaijan to Kudshannis in Turkey, where it now claimed inheritance of the non-Catholic old
Nestorian line from which it had separated in 1551. The people approved.
They had never understood the necessity of a foreign, European connection anyway. Thus somewhat vaguely Rome lost its formal relationship
with the new-line Nestorians.

But meanwhile, the old-line successors of Shimon VII bar Mama, who
in 1551 had stood for Nestorian independence from Rome, had begun
about 1590 to explore the advantages of a Roman connection. The Franciscans in Jerusalem willingly permitted Nestorian envoys to participate
in Catholic communion mass in Jerusalem.[15] Moreover, Nestorians long
isolated in Persian Kurdistan, their mountain homeland, and cut off from
contact with Western Christians, may have begun to hear rumors of the
establishment of a Christian Portuguese trading post on the island of
Hormuz at the mouth of the Persian Gulf. As for the Vatican, puzzled by
confusing signals from the two rival Syrian Christian patriarchal lines,

Rome tried for a short while in the seventeenth century to recognize both Nestorian lines, giving to the successors of new-line Sulaqa the title "Patriarch of Oriental Assyria" and to those of old-line Simon bar Mama the title "Patriarch of Babylon."[16] In 1669 the old-line patriarch Elias X, who was only fourteen years old at the time but whose letter to Pope Clement IX was attested by three of his Nestorian metropolitans, asked the pope to establish a "college" at Rome to prepare young Nestorians for the priesthood. Despite years of negotiations for inter-communion between old-line patriarchs and Roman popes, it would be another century and a half before Rome in 1830 finally became convinced of the orthodoxy of at least one line of Nestorians and admitted what had once been the traditional Nestorian old-line church into full status as Uniate, or Chaldaean, Catholic, as it is known.[17]

The miracle is that Romanized "Chaldaeans" (Uniates) and Assyrian Nestorians alike, both still speaking a form of the Syriac language of the school of Nisibis and of the synods of their patriarchs Isaac and Dadyeshu and Mar Aba a millennium earlier, were still Christian in their precarious homeland among the mountains and by the rivers that water the Fertile Crescent.[18]

Decline of the Jacobite (Monophysite) Base on the Mediterranean Coast

When, at the end of the thirteenth century, the tolerant Mongol conquerors of western Asia began to turn Muslim, the ancient base of Jacobite (Monophysite) Orthodoxy centered in Antioch began to crumble. A century later the ruthless Tamerlane virtually wiped it out. His ravaging armies destroyed its monasteries, burned its books, and killed or drove its leaders into the caves and mountains. The Jacobite cathedral in Tekrit north of Baghdad was without a patriarch (*maphrian*) for twenty-five years until the conqueror neared death in 1404.[19] Then came the Turks to control and suffocate Christian recovery for another five centuries. By the nineteenth century there were probably only about two hundred thousand Jacobites left in churches loyal to the ancient patriarchate of Antioch.[20]

Catholic Missions in West Asia

Muslim disunity, Persians against Turks, combined with European eagerness to bypass and undermine the Turkish threat to Vienna, paved the way for a renewal of Roman Catholic missions in Persia, from which they had been expelled after the Crusades. First, the Portuguese took the island of Hormuz at the entrance of the Persian Gulf in 1507 as a trading base and turned it into what they hoped would become the key to Catholic penetration of the Persian Empire, just as Macao at the other end of Asia a few years later became a base for Catholic missions to the Chinese empire.

In the 1570s a group of Augustinians were sent to Hormuz as chaplains for the Portuguese military and trade community, and in 1582 King Philip of Spain and Portugal appointed their prior, Simon Morales, as his royal ambassador to the court of the Safavid Shahs of Persia. Morales, one of the "twelve apostles" of a new Augustinian missionary congregation named the Hermits of St. Augustine, had learned Persian. He was well received in Isfahan, and the order was able to establish a residential mission at the capital in 1602. Some of their farsighted proposals, such as to translate into Persian the Catholic missal and what seems to have been a ninth-century Persian translation of the four gospels, were misguidedly turned down, partly for fear of misuse of vernacular versions, and perhaps because the translated gospels were not based on the Vulgate.[21]

Other Catholic missions joined the Augustinians in Persia, most notably the Discalced (Barefoot) Carmelites in 1607 who followed the reforms of Teresa of Avila and John of the Cross, and endeared themselves to the people by their voluntary poverty and works of mercy. But the days of a Catholicism linked to Portuguese military power were at an end. In 1622 a combined force of Safavid and British troops stormed the great Portuguese fortress on Hormuz, the key to the Persian Gulf, and ended a hundred years of Portuguese trade supremacy between India and Europe. The arrival of the British also marked the beginning of the end of Catholic mission dominance in Asia. In the ensuing persecutions of Catholics five brave Persian converts of the Augustinians were martyred, choosing hideous tortures and death rather than apostasy, and the Augustinian missionaries were expelled.[22]

Next, in 1628, it was the French who sought to establish a Catholic presence in Persia to replace the Portuguese. But immediately they were face-to-face with steadily increasing difficulties. The very next year, in what Waterfield describes as "the edict which did more than any other single act to blight the chances of Christians in Persia," Shah Abbas I, "the Great," ended his long and until then rather enlightened reign (1587–1629) with one of the acts of cruelty that have besmirched his reputation ever since. The edict, vindictively retroactive, gave to Christians who would convert to Islam the right to confiscate all the property of their Christian relatives for seven generations back. This was later reduced to four years, but Abbas had already proved himself to be as cruel to his own family as to Christians. Paranoid fear that his sons were plotting against him led him to order his oldest son killed, and two other sons and a grandson blinded to prevent them from inheriting the throne.

Under the later Safavid Shahs (1666–1736) conditions in Persia degenerated into anarchy. Muslim religious persecution of the Christian minorities intensified, while the Christians, cracking under pressure, were sometimes their own worst enemies. Two Augustinians turned Muslim; the Armenians attacked the Catholic Carmelites; and the ambassador of Christian France, under no pressure of persecution whatever, arrived at the Persian capital in 1707 with a mistress whom he shamelessly described as "a present from the King of France to the Shah."[23]

Overall, in the 130 years from about 1650 to the end of the 1770s, Christianity was almost wiped out in Persia. Among the Georgians who, like the Armenians, had been displaced from north to south by the thousands, Christianity virtually disappeared. The Nestorians, already driven from the cities, grew more and more isolated, unschooled, and poverty stricken, though a Carmelite visitor in the mid-1650s found forty thousand families of Nestorians still surviving in the pockets in the Kurdistan hills near Lake Urmiah.[24]

Compounding the difficulties faced by the Catholic missions was the fact that conversion to Catholicism socially dislocated their converts from their ethnic and religious minority rights under the protection of the *dzimmi* (or *mellet, or millet*) system. Politically, Catholic converts were neither Greek Orthodox nor Armenian and thereby on both the Turkish and Persian sides of the border lost their protection as members of a *dzimmi*, the term for the local autonomy of a state-recognized religious minority under the umbrella of Islamic state control. For centuries this had been the only legal safeguard against extinction for unrecognized religious groups in Muslim lands. Whatever protection the Christian embassies of the West could offer Catholic converts, it was no substitute for official Muslim state recognition of equal citizenship, unless, as was not true in the Middle East, Western diplomatic pressure was clearly demonstrated as enforceable by the threat of effective military action. Such had not been the case in the Middle East since the fall of Constantinople, and would remain so until World War I.[25]

But as the Ottoman empire declined, and the Western powers — England, France, and Russia — began to use a combination of economic and military pressure against the weakening Asian empires of Turkey and Persia, Catholics began to revive as various Eastern communions left their ancient Asian traditions to accept the primacy of the pope as Uniate churches. The earliest of these was the Chaldaean Rite Uniate, headed by the Catholicos John Sulaqa, mentioned above, who made his submission to Rome in 1551.[26] The Melchite Patriarchate of Antioch is, since the schism of 1724, the minority Roman Catholic counterpart to the majority Jacobite Orthodox Patriarchate of Antioch. The latter secured the recognition of the Ottoman Sultanate.[27] A far larger Catholic communion in Syria and Lebanon is the Maronite Uniate, which, though submitting to the authority of Rome in 1182 "by an inspiration from heaven," received "uninterrupted" relationship with Rome only at the fifth Lateran

Council in 1512–1517.[28] An Armenian Rite Uniate, with a patriarchate centered in Lebanon, was established in 1742.[29]

Survival of the Armenian Church (1500–1800)

No ruler in either Safavid Persia or Ottoman Turkey was ever a Christian. And in those Muslim lands the Christian minority that suffered the most from Muslim intolerance and persecution was the Armenian, not the Eastern Orthodox, not the Nestorian, and not the converts of Catholic missions.

For more than a thousand years, ever since their king Tiridates was converted in the year 301, Armenians had been singularly united as a people by a Christian faith combined with national loyalty and ethnic identity.[30] They had the reputation of being the most warlike of the minorities in Old Rome's vast empire. Even when they lost their independence as a Christian kingdom, which happened intermittently,[31] they never lost their identity as Armenians or their faith as Christians. Not even Tamerlane the Terrible, the scourge of the world at the end of the 1300s, had been able to wipe them out.[32] With or without a king they held fast to their own language and worshiped God in their own Armenian tongue.

On the other hand, the Armenian Church has also had the reputation of being one of the most divided of the churches of the East. Over the centuries tensions within its hierarchy and the all-too-frequent schisms which resulted produced a vulnerably complex ecclesiastical structure with five separate Armenian patriarchates (or catholicates), and five recognized patriarchs, each of whom at one point or another has laid claim to supremacy.[33] Armenian historians refer to the three hundred years from 1500 to 1800 as the years of darkness.[34] The black shadows darkening those years were wars without and divisions within, tax penalties for the successful Christian, and outbreaks of violence against the visibly pious. Still, divided or not, Armenians kept the faith.

Unquestionably war was the cruelest factor. Three hundred years of never-ending war between two great empires, Ottoman Turkey and Safavid Persia, caught little Armenia between their ever-shifting boundaries and churned it into burning homes and battered refugees.

ARMENIANS UNDER THE TURKS

The Ottoman Empire of the Turks was the most powerful but least attractive of the four great Muslim empires that have ruled vast parts of Asia: Arab, Persian, Mongol, and Turk. Arabs, Persians, and even the Mongols in Moghul India produced great treasures of art, architecture, and poetry, but the Turks, as Julius Richter claims with some justification, produced wealth for the few and a "mailed fist" for the many.[35] Their triumphant advance westward out of Asia paralyzed Europe. In four centuries of Turkish conquest (1280–1683) it was the Turks who attacked and it was Europe that reeled back to the very edge of disaster. The fall of great Constantinople in 1453 led to the Turkish subjugation of the Balkans for five hundred years. Victorious Islam stormed to the very gates of Vienna, stabbed into the Ukraine, threatened Poland. Then abruptly the tide turned and for the next two centuries it was the Turks who retreated. In 1683 a mighty Ottoman army tried and failed for the second time to take Vienna and fled back in utter confusion toward Asia. Within thirty-five years the armies of Islam had been driven out of Hungary, Croatia, much of Serbia, and Transylvania.

But in the east, in Asia, the Turks were doing better. And ironically, Islamic victories against Christian Europe had at first seemed somewhat liberating for the Armenians in Turkish Asia Minor and Persia. To Turks the Armenians were infidels, and to Christian Orthodox Byzantine emperors they were heretics. But when the shrewd Turks turned to the problem of how best to govern their captured non-Muslim religious minorities, they used an ancient principle: divide and rule. They adopted the old Persian system of *millets* (or *dzimmis*), mentioned above — minority communities formed on the basis of religious connection.[36] The two largest Christian minorities were Greek and Armenian Christians. The Greek Orthodox was by far the larger, so the Sultan Mohammed (or Mehmet) II, "the Conqueror," almost immediately recognized the Greek Orthodox patriarch in 1453 as patriarch of conquered Constantinople, granting him authority as head of the Christian *dzimmi* over all Christians in Turkish-occupied Europe — Greek, Balkan, and by decree even Uniate Catholics at first. But very soon thereafter, as a balance, the wise sultan in 1461 created a second patriarchate of Constantinople and gave it to the Armenian bishop of Brusa, whom he brought to the capital as a patriarch with authority over all the other minorities in the empire. This greatly increased the power of the Armenian Church, for it brought under the control of an Armenian not only Armenians, but also Nestorians, Antiochene Jacobites, Copts, Georgians, and Ethiopians. The one exception was the Jewish community, which was placed under a presiding rabbi whose extent of authority was left ambiguous.[37]

ARMENIANS IN PERSIA AND INDIA

In Persia, the sultan's great enemy, Shah Abbas I, died in 1629, the same year he issued his anti-Christian edict. His reign had been a disaster for Christians. Waterfield reports that by one estimate, within twenty-five years "at least 50,000 Christians had apostatized in order to retain their patrimony." But not the Armenians. Few Armenians chose recantation as the way to survive.[38]

For a short few years after the death of Abbas I there appeared to be signs of better things. His successors, Shah Safi (1629–1642) and Abbas II (1642–1667), were weaker and indecisive, and the Persian Safavid dynasty began to deteriorate. As its power of enforcement declined, its toleration of non-Muslim religions increased. Taking advantage of this period of relative freedom, the Armenian hierarchy sensed an opportunity to mend their own internal divisions. The turn for the better was quickened by the evangelistic zeal of a reforming monk, Moses of Datev (d. 1632). He had won the respect of the church as the founder of "the Great Monastery" of Datev, which brought strict discipline back to Armenian monasticism, and of a seminary for the better training of priests. His character was so impressive that he was even able to persuade the Shah to grant exemptions from the confiscating taxes that were crippling the church.[39]

But in the confusion of ever-changing borders during the never-ending wars between Ottoman Turkey and Persia, Armenians found themselves churned again by warring armies and divided by shifting borders. Moses of Datev died within three years of becoming Catholicos of Echmiadzin, which was then in Persian territory. An attempt by his able successor in 1651 to unite the two patriarchates of Sis in Lesser Armenia, and Echmiadzin in the old Armenian homeland in eastern Turkey, produced better understanding but no union. Outside pressures not only from Muslim governments but also now from Rome threatened to rob the church of its Armenian identity and turn it Roman Catholic.[40]

Alexander of Rhodes, the renowned Jesuit pioneer of Cochin China and Tonkin, spent three months in Persia in 1647 and reported that Persia was much less repressive of Christians than neighboring Ottoman Turkey. He found Catholic missionaries of six different orders moving freely about the Persian Muslim capital, Isfahan, dressed in full clerical garb. Some Muslims, he wrote, even bring their very sick babies to the priests for Christian baptism. And at the Armenian enclave of New Julfa, which was almost a suburb of Isfahan, he was impressed by the way the fearless Armenians, though kept poor by overtaxation and social discrimination, crowded undeterred into their ornate churches.[41] Catholic missionary attempts to proselyte them and bring them into union with Rome met with no more success than their attempts to convert Muslims. No sooner had they established their Catholic mission in Isfahan than they discovered that some three thousand families of Armenian Christians, steadfastly loyal to their faith, were being repopulated there from the Turkish border, refugees from the scorched-earth policy by which the Safavids sought to delay Turkish attacks. In the decades of war that followed, thousands more Armenians were uprooted and brought in as refugees, perhaps as many as two hundred thousand.[42]

But if the Catholic missionaries had hoped these might be persuaded to join them in establishing a Christian Catholic base in Persia, they were to be disappointed.[43] Fiercely loyal to their Monophysite Armenian Orthodoxy,[44] wealthier than the Nestorians, and less foreign than the Catholics, they formed their own thriving minority community, an Armenian *dzimmi* in Persia but more independent of patriarchal control from either Constantinople or Echmiadzin. In fact, when government pressures tightened in the early eighteenth century, the Armenians simply relocated their trade center from Isfahan to India, where a thriving Armenian Christian trading community flourished under the Moghul dynasty of northern India. The great Moghul, Akbar, "the Marcus Aurelius of India" allowed the Armenians to build a church for their community at Agra as early as 1562.[45]

Most of the Armenians in India were traders seeking more freedom from the Muslim Moghul emperors than they were permitted in either Turkey or Persia. In India a surprising number rose to considerable status as diplomats, soldiers, and manufacturers of military instruments. The tombstone at Agra of Shah Nazar Khan, "the Armenian Krupp" (d. 1784), still bears the phrase, "He has kissed the feet of Jesus." Sarmad, the pen name of an eccentric Armenian mystic poet, concealed thinly concealed anti-Islamic sentiments in his immensely popular quatrains, which led to his execution under the Moghul Aurungzeb in 1659.[46]

But back in Persia, the religious tolerance of the Savafid Shahs had soon ended. In the 150 years from about 1650 up to the end of the 1700s, Christianity virtually disappeared among the Georgians, who like the Armenians had been displaced from north to south by the thousands. The Nestorians, already driven from the cities, grew more and more isolated, unschooled, and poverty stricken, though a Carmelite visitor in the mid-1650s found forty thousand families of Nestorians still surviving in pockets in the Kurdistan hills near Lake Urmiah. As for the Armenians, though perhaps least affected by the pressures of intolerance — their faith impressed even their tormentors — and their mercantile importance to the Persian economy somewhat shielded them from the worst of the persecutions — the Armenians were never free from the threats, violence, and relentless religious and economic pressures of Muslim Islam on both sides of the Turko-Persian border.[47]

Their villages were impoverished and their children largely illiterate, but they refused to lose either their identity or their faith. They were still Christians, they had their Armenian Bibles, and they were still speaking Armenian.

Christians in the Middle East at the End of the Eighteenth Century

It is difficult to close this chapter on anything but a melancholy note. One by one the Catholic missions had left Persia: the Augustinians in

1750, the Dominicans in 1764. But in the Ottoman Empire where they had established Uniate Patriarchates in Lebanon, Constantinople, and Jerusalem, small but still integrated Catholic communities survived. The Armenians on both sides of the Turko-Persian border were repressed and scattered but unintimidated and expanding as far east as India, where a humble Armenian cloth seller, Khojah Gregory, rose to be commander-in-chief of the Bengal army, and though never abandoning his Christian faith became for three short years (1760–1763) "virtual ruler of Bengal, Behar, and Orissa . . . the richest jewel in the diadem" of Muslim Moghul India.[48]

The Nestorians were irreconcilably split three ways, but surviving in their isolated villages in the Kurdish mountains. In 1800 there were three Nestorian patriarchs or near-patriarchs (catholici). First was Elias XIII Ishoyahb (1778–1804) of the old traditional Nestorian line. In the nineteenth century at Mosul where the Nestorian patriarch then resided, this line turned to Rome to become a Uniate church, and is known as the Chaldaean Church in Iran. A second patriarch was Simon XVI Jean (1780–1820), of the line which under John Sulaqa had turned Uniate in 1551 and then a hundred years later, as we have seen, confusingly turned back to independent Nestorianism. As the Assyrian Church of the East this second line now regarded itself as the only valid inheritor of the old name, "Nestorian." The third line, a separate uniate patriarchate on the upper Tigris, was decommissioned and absorbed into the Chaldaean Church (Catholic) at the turn of the century.[49]

They were divided and vulnerable, these Christian minorities. But when the first Protestant missionaries entered West Asia around 1820 they found a national Armenian Orthodox Church battered and troubled but still organized and self-governed; Nestorians lying low in the Kurdish mountains west of Lake Urmia, and Catholic Uniates loyal to Rome — all of them with their own liturgies, their own Bibles, and still speaking their own languages, but still divided as they worshiped separately the one God and Father of their one Lord, Jesus Christ.

A Chronology of West Asia (1405–1834)

1405   Death of Tamerlane.

1405–1500   Decline of the Timurids (Tamerlane's heirs) in Central Asia.

1407–1447   Temporary renaissance of Timurid power under Shah Rukh in Transoxiana and Persia.

1413   Muhammad I restores Ottoman Turkish power in West Asia.

1453   Ottoman Turks capture Constantinople (Istanbul). Golden age of the Ottomans (to 1566).

1500	Safavid dynasty (1500–1794) under Shah Isma'il restores Persian independence.
1503	Elias V, Nestorian patriarch on upper Tigris River, restores Nestorian succession for St. Thomas Christians in India.
1507	Portugal establishes trading base at Hormuz (until 1622).
1514	Ottomans defeat Safavids. Beginning of Turkish-Persian wars: Sunni Muslim against Shi'ite Muslims (1514–1823), and Armenian/Kurdish rivalry.
1520–1566	Sultan Suleyman the Magnificent of the Ottoman Empire takes Iraq from Safavids.
1551	Nestorian schism: Patriarch Shimon VII Bar-Mama dies; succession dispute: Shimon VIII Denha ("old line") traditional Nestorian vs. John Sulaqa ("new line" pro-Roman).
1603	Augustinians open convent in Isfahan.
1607	Traditional Nestorians (Elias VI) unite with Rome (Uniate).
1615	Ottomans allow Habsburgs (Austria) rights of protection of Christians in Ottoman empire.
1622	English drive Portuguese from Hormuz.
1624	Safavids (Abbas I) take Iraq except Mosul, Basra from Ottomans.
1638	Ottomans (Murat IV) retake Iraq from Iran, retain it to 1923.
1660?	Traditional Nestorians ("Elias line") break from Rome.
1667	Safavid decline begins.
1670–1692	Pro-Roman Nestorians ("Shim'un line") break permanently with Rome, claim "traditional" Nestorian succession.
1710	Beginning of Russian wars (of Peter the Great) against the Ottomans.
1722	Afghans defeat Safavids in Persia. Safavid puppets to 1773.
1827	Some Nestorians flee from Turks to Russia, accept Orthodoxy.
1830–1834	Traditional Nestorians ("Elias line") return to Rome as a Uniate church.

NOTES

1. See my *A History of Christianity in Asia*, 1:480–509. As in vol. 1 (*Beginnings to 1500*), the record of the next five hundred years will, with exceptions for important Christian minorities, concentrate on Asia east of the Euphrates so far as possible, leaving the Mediterranean coast and Asia Minor to the Greeks and Europeans who brought that area into the orbit of Western church histories.

2. The other surviving pocket of ancient Nestorianism was on the Malabar coast of South India. See chap. 1 above. On the use of the name "Nestorian," and its alternatives (Syrian, Chaldaean, Assyrian) from the eighteenth century to the present, see John Henry Joseph, *The Nestorians and Their Muslim Neighbors: A Study of Western Influence on Their Relations* (Princeton, N.J.: Princeton University Press, 1961), 3ff. Many whom Westerners call Nestorians are quick to point out that their "church of the East," as they proudly call themselves, antedates Nestorius by several centuries.

3. The tribulations of the larger Christian minorities of Asia Minor and the Mediterranean coast are surveyed in a later chapter.

4. See vol. 1 of this work, 47ff.

5. An exception to the decline of the Timurids was Tamerlane's fourth son, the brave and civilized Shah Rukh, who ruled from Herat (1405–1447). The last of the Timurids were driven from Herat by the Uzbeks in 1507. See René Grousset, *Empire of the Steppes,* trans. Naomi Walford (New Brunswick, N.J.: Rutgers University Press, 1970), 463–465.

6. Vine (*The Nestorian Churches,* 171) reports that the last mention of Nestorian churches in the major cities were Tabriz (1551), Baghdad (1553), Nisibis (1556), Arbela (Erbil, sixteenth century), and even remote Gazarta (Gezira or Bakerda, seventeenth century). See also A. S. Atiya, *A History of Eastern Christianity* (London: Methuen, 1968), 277ff.

7. The line of succession after the massacres of Tamerlane are obscure, but Tisserant's dates are usually credible: Elias IV, 1405–1437; Shimon (Simon) IV, d. 1497; Shimon V, 1497–1501; Elias V, 1502–1503; Shimon VI, 1504–1538; Shimon VII bar Mama, 1538–1551, and Simon VIII Denha 1551–1558. Alas, at this point schism separates the patriarchate into two disputing lines, "old" and "new." The old, traditional Nestorian line after Shimon VIII Denha takes the name Elias (Elija) from Elias VI (1538–1576) to Elias XIV (1879–1894). The protesting, pro-Roman line of the rival Shimon VIII Sulaqa, 1551–1555, takes the name Shimon — with the exception of his two immediate successors, Abdiso IV and Aitallah (Yabhallaha V) from Shimon IX (1617–1618) to Shimon XXI (1920–). See Tisserant, "Nestorienne," in *DTC* 11:262–263. Cf. George David Malech, *History of the Syrian Nation and the Old Evangelical-Apostolic Church of the East* (Minneapolis, 1910), 310, 315, 321, for variations in the dating.

8. See Moffett, *A History of Christianity in Asia,* 1:502–503.

9. Whether Simon IV or Simon V was the Patriarch Shimon who received the first envoys from the church in India is debatable. Tisserant, Adolphe d'Avril, and Malech all give different dates for the transition between the two Simons: Tisserant dates it at 1497, Malech at 1472, and d'Avril (*La Chaldée Chrétienne* [Paris: Bureaux de l'Oeuvre des Ecoles Orient, 1892], 10) at 1539. Gazarta (Gazara, Jesirah) is probably the modern Cisre in Turkey on the Tigris. Cf. n. 6 above for other alternative identifications.

10. Except for a small minority, Syrian Christianity, while clinging sturdily to its Syrian identity, did not retain the "Nestorian" connection. See chap. 1, "India: Pepper, Pope, and the Portuguese," in Moffett, *A History of Christianity in Asia,* vol. 1.

11. *Cambridge History of Iran,* 6:390ff., 635; and R. E. Waterfield, *Christians in Persia* (London: George Allen & Unwin, 1973), 58–65.

12. The change is attributed to Simon IV about the year 1450. Tisserant, "Nestorienne," in *DTC*, 11:228.

13. He submitted to the pope in 1553. W. van Gulik, "Die Konsistorialakten über die Begründung des uniert-chaldäischen Patriarchates von Mosul unter Papst Julius III," in *Oriens Christianus*, vol. 2 (Rome, 1904), 261–277. On the life of Sulaqa see 272ff. See also A. J. Arberry, ed., *Religion in the Middle East: Three Religions in Concord and Conflict*, vol. 1 (Cambridge: Cambridge University Press, 1969), 1:295.

14. On the tortuous history of the schism and the fluctuating relationships with Rome, I mainly follow Tisserant, "Nestorienne," in *DTC*, 11:228–243. He frequently cites, but does not always agree with, S. Giamil, *Genuinae relationes inter sedem Apostolicam et Assyriorum orientalis seu Chaldaeorum ecclesiam* (Rome: Ermanno Loescher, 1902). See also Adrian Fortescue, *Lesser Eastern Churches* (London: Catholic Truth Society, 1913), 101–103; and Atiya, *History of Eastern Christianity*, 278-279.

15. Tisserant, "Nestorienne," *DTC*, 11:233.

16. Tisserant, "Nestorienne," *DTC*, 11:231.

17. Space forbids note of a third line of schism (1681–1804), that of the metropolitans of Diarbekir upriver from Gazarta, who broke away from the old-line patriarch Elias VII and turned Uniate. See Tisserant, "Nestorienne," *DTC*, 11:238–239.

18. See Fortescue, *Lesser Eastern Churches*, 115.

19. See vol. 1 of this work, 486–487.

20. See statistics in Atiya, *History of Eastern Christianity*, 211 n. 1.

21. Waterfield, *Christians in Persia*, 58–65; and Roberto Gulbenkian, "The Translation of the Four Gospels into Persian," in *NRSM* 29 (1981): 27–37, 43–44, 61.

22. Waterfield, *Christians in Persia*, 68.

23. Waterfield, *Christians in Persia*, 71ff.

24. Waterfield, *Christians in Persia*, 71–72.

25. See H. A. R. Gibbs and J. H. Kramers, eds., "Nasara" = Christians, *Shorter Encyclopedia of Islam* (Leiden: Brill, 1953), 441.

26. See Donald Attwater, *The Christian Churches of the East*, vol. 1, *Churches in Communion with Rome*; vol. 2 *Churches Not in Communion with Rome* (Milwaukee: Bruce Publishing, 1947–48).

27. Attwater, *Christian Churches of the East*, 1:55–64.

28. Attwater, *Christian Churches of the East*, 1:158–168.

29. Attwater, *Christian Churches of the East*, 1:173–187.

30. On Armenian church history, see Leon Arpee, *A History of Armenian Christianity from the Beginning to Our Own Time* (New York: Armenian Missionary Association of America, 1946); Jean Mércérian, *Histoire et institutions de l'église arménienne: Evolution nationale et doctrinale spiritualité* (Beirut: Imprimerie Catholique, 1965); and Maghak'ia Ormanian, *The Church of Armenia: Her History, Doctrine, Rule, Discipline, Literature, and Existing Condition* (London: A. R. Mowbray, 1955).

31. Most of the territory of the early Armenian kingdom which had been under Persian protection was transferred to Byzantine rule in 519. It was taken again by Persia, and brought back again into the Eastern Roman Empire in the seventh century. Then, at the end of the seventh century it fell to the conquering

Arabs, and remained under Muslim rule (Turkish and Persian) into the twenti-eth century. There were periods of semi-independence, as in the ninth century with a Bagratid "prince of princes" recognized by the Caliphs of Baghdad, and again during the period of the Crusades when Byzantium recognized the in-dependence of the Christian kingdom of Lesser Armenia (Cilicia), on the south coast of Asia Minor, which lasted only until 1375.

32. When Tamerlane invaded Lesser Armenia in 1402, in just one of its cities, Sivas, he buried four thousand Armenian defenders alive. Arpee, *History of Armenian Christianity*, 206, and see 161–162, 189, 204ff.

33. The five patriarchates (or catholicates) are Echmiadzin (the traditional original home of the church, now in eastern Turkey); Constantinople (under the Ottoman Turks the most powerful center); Jerusalem (a titular patriarchate); Cili-cia or Sis (owing its catholicate/patriarchate to the short-lived kingdom of Lesser Armenia and the Crusades); and the tiny but historic catholicate of Aghthamar on Lake Van. See Ormanian, *The Church of Armenia*, 37–38, 56–57, 60–63, and 205–209.

34. From Tamerlane's death in 1404 to Shah Safir's edict in 1629 "literature and learning on Armenian soil were practically things of the past," states Leon Arpee, in his earlier book, *The Armenian Awakening: A History of the Armenian Church, 1820–1860* (Chicago and London: University of Chicago Press/T. Fisher Unwin, 1909), 14.

35. Julius Richter, *History of Protestant Missions in the Near East* (New York: Revell, 1910), 23.

36. On the *millet* (or *zimmi* in Persia) system of ordering religious minorities, see Arberry, ed., *Religion in the Middle East*, 1:255–256; 2:459–460, 547–548.

37. See Ormanian, *The Church of Armenia*, 60ff.; Arpee, *History of Armenian Christianity*, 226ff.; and Bernard Lewis, *The Jews of Islam* (Princeton, N.J.: Princeton University Press, 1984), 122–123, 124–128, 137–138.

38. Waterfield, *Christians in Persia*, 69–70; *Cambridge History of Iran*, 6:277. Some sources say that three of the princes were killed, and the survivor blinded. P. M. Sykes, *A History of Persia* (London: Macmillan, 1915), 267–268. On the bet-ter treatment of Armenians in Persia, see Vazken S. Ghougassian, *The Emergence of the Armenian Diocese of New Julfa in the Seventeenth Century* (Atlanta: Scholars Press, 1998), 56–59.

39. Moses of Datev (or Movse of Tathen) became patriarch as Moses III of Ech-miadzin. Arpee, *History of Armenian Christianity*, 217–222; Ormanian, *The Church of Armenia*, 64.

40. Arpee, *The Armenian Awakening*, 222–223.

41. [Alexander of Rhodes], *Voyages et missions du Père Alexandre de Rhodes* (Paris: Julien, Lanier, 1854), 403–414.

42. Ghougassian, *The Emergence of the Armenian Diocese of New Julfa in the Seventeenth Century*, 25ff.

43. Only a handful of the New Julfa Armenians became Catholic (Ghougas-sian, *The Emergence of the Armenian Diocese of New Julfa in the Seventeenth Century*, 197). The Armenian Catholic Church (Uniate), composed of those who accepted Rome's invitation to change ecclesiastical allegiance and were granted a Catholic patriarch with permission to use an Armenian liturgy, never achieved the num-ber of members hoped for. By the first decade of the 1900s before World War I, out

of a total of 3.5 million Armenian Christians, only 128,000 were Roman Catholic. Ormanian, *The Church of Armenia*, 209.

44. Armenian kings had been Christian since before Rome ever had a Christian emperor or Constantinople a patriarch. Some scholars prefer to call Armenian Orthodoxy Cyrillian, not Monophysite, but traditionally, like monophysitism (the theology of "one nature" in the person of Christ) it stresses the unity of the nature of Christ without denying that he was both divine and human. Since the "great schism" of the fifth century, this teaching has divided Armenian, Syrian Jacobite, and Egyptian Coptic churches (all Monophysite) from Roman Catholic, Greek Orthodox, and most Protestant churches, which are dyophysite ("two natures"). Over the centuries this technical theological differentiation has become more symbolic than practical. On Armenian creed and liturgy, see Ormanian, *The Church of Armenia*, 89–107.

45. Agra was not the only Armenian center in India. Seth — in *Armenians in India: From the Earliest Times to the Present Day*, x, 613 and passim — lists and describes sixteen or more different Armenian Christian communities in India during the seventeenth, eighteenth, and nineteenth centuries.

46. Seth, *Armenians in India*, 114–119, 167–194.

47. Ghougassian, *The Emergence of the Armenian Diocese of New Julfa in the Seventeenth Century*, 59–60. New Julfa, as a fief of the Queen Mother in the seventeenth century, was especially protected from Muslim harassment.

48. Seth, *Armenians in India*, 384–385, 615.

49. Donald Attwater, *The Catholic Eastern Churches* (Milwaukee: Bruce Publishing Co., 1935); Tisserant, "Nestorienne," *DTC* 11:263. The third line, at Diarbekir, demitted around the year 1781.

PART II

The Protestants Reach Asia (1600–1800)

Those who hold the truth have the means enough, knowledge enough, and opportunity enough, to evangelize the globe fifty times over.
— The Earl of Shaftesbury, 1860

It is a significant judgment upon nineteenth-century Christianity that its most striking successes were won outside the protected confines of Europe, in the open atmosphere of the new nations and the missions.
— Josef L. Altholz

THE year 1860 makes a good dividing point for the nineteenth century, although dividing history into compartments is never easy, and the neater the periodization is, the more inaccurate it becomes. A. T. Pierson, the influential editor of the *Missionary Review of the World*, looked back at the century in 1891 and chose the year 1858 as the beginning of a brave new period for the church around the world — at least for Protestants:

> Not one hundred years ago the world stood over against the Church like a gigantic fortress with doubled barred gates of steel...[But] within the past fifty years pagan, papal and heathen territory which a century ago defied the approach of Protestant missionaries now admits, if it does not welcome, the message of life...The year 1858 is the *annus mirabilis* of modern missions...No one year in history has been marked by changes more stupendous and momentous as affecting the evangelization of the world.[1]

Pierson was looking back nearly a half century later from his own chosen vantage point. In 1858, however, few would have considered the situation in Asia anything like one on the verge of "stupendous" and "momentous" change. Harvey Newcomb's quaint *A Cyclopedia of Missions*, published in 1858, painted Asia as huge, heathen, and polygamous — 48 percent Buddhist, 20 percent Hindu, 17 percent Muslim, and 7 percent Christian, with only twenty-eight thousand communicant Protestants on the whole continent. His estimate of the total number of Christians in Asia (Catholic, Orthodox, and Protestant), from the Mediterranean to the Pacific Islands, was 50 million in a continental population of 753 million.[2]

Whether the best periodization puts the beginning in 1858, 1860, or 1870, those few decades were indeed a time of decisive, worldwide change. In North America, the Civil War had ended. In Europe, English parliamentary reform advanced and Prussia became a major power. There was revolution in Spain and the birth of Italy as a united kingdom. In South Asia the British crown took India from the East India Company; England intervened in Persia; and France expanded into Indo-China. In East Asia, the 1860s saw the end of the shogunate and the revival of the empire in Japan, and in China the failure of the Taiping rebellion and the beginning of extraterritorial concessions to Western powers marked the deepening of opposition to Western colonialism in that important land.

As Toynbee observes, there was a difference between the encounters of the West and East in the sixteenth and the nineteenth centuries. In the sixteenth, the West presented itself as a "strange religion," Toynbee says, "and it failed. In the nineteenth century ... Western civilization presented itself primarily as a strange technology," and it succeeded.[3]

As the nineteenth century in missions in Asia drew to a close, three questions remained unsolved. Should Christian missions, in order to succeed, address the non-Christian world as an essential ingredient of Western civilization, inseparable from the West's desired technology, but therefore dangerously associated with its imperial expansion? If it did not do this, would it fail once more? And third, the classic question is repeated: How far and in what ways can the Christian faith adapt to cultures and civilizations informed by other religious and secular visions without losing its own identity?

NOTES

1. A. T. Pierson, "How Will the Church Meet the Crisis?" *GAL* 12, no. 12 (December 1891): 539–541.

2. Harvey Newcomb, *A Cyclopedia of Missions* (New York: Charles Scribner, 1858), 155–159. His statistics, based largely on board reports of twenty-nine Protestant missionary societies, should not be taken uncritically and are at times contradictory. Still, his eight hundred pages of text and tables are an important resource.

3. Toynbee, *The World and the West*, 54. See chap. 4 for the way this judgment is developed.

Chapter 10

The First Protestants

The Dutch Reach Indonesia, Formosa, and Ceylon

This is our duty everywhere, to make known among the nations the
greatness of God.   —John Calvin, Sermon on Isaiah 12:4–5

[Between 1550 and 1650] there was a change [in Reformed thought] to
remove business matters from religious supervision and to treat them as
if they were ethically indifferent.   —J. C. Riemersma (1967)

Wherever profit leads us, to every sea and shore, For love of gain the wide
world's harbors we explore.   —Vondel (1639)

Indonesia: Capitalist Traders, Calvinist Chaplains

On Christmas day in 1601 in the straits between Sumatra and Java five
small Dutch ships fearlessly engaged a fleet of thirty Portuguese vessels
which had been sent to drive the Dutch from a tiny Sumatran trading outpost at Bantam that guarded the principal sea route through
the Sunda Straits to the Spice Islands. "Trusting in the help of God
Almighty," as their officers recorded, the vastly outnumbered Dutch
drove back the Portuguese,[1] and thereby touched off a revolution in Asia
that was to have greater political, military, and economic consequences
in Asia than they could ever have imagined. It was the beginning of the
end of Portuguese expansion in Asia.

What those Dutchmen also could not have foreseen was how that
revolution would change the history of Christianity in South and East
Asia.[2] In this sense, it was a fourth revolution for Asia. The first great
change had been the rise of Islam in the seventh century. The second was
the Mongol conquest of Asia's heartland in the thirteenth century. The
third was the Roman Catholic reentry into Asia in the sixteenth century.
And now in the seventeenth century the Protestant Reformation began
to move out from Europe across the world. In Asia, its first wave was
Dutch.

When the Low Countries unexpectedly threw off the Spanish yoke
in the 1590s little Holland had surprised all Europe by blossoming suddenly into an empire. The Dutch sons of the Calvinistic wing of the
Protestant Reformation were natural sailors and hard fighters, and in

213

the islands of the East Indies and along the Asian coast from India to Japan they routed the Portuguese and built what quickly became the largest navy and "the greatest mercantile corporation in the world," the Dutch East India Company.[3]

In shocking succession, the Dutch seized a foothold in the Moluccas at Amboina (1605), and in Java established their main base at Batavia (now Jakarta) in 1619. From there they proceeded to expel the Portuguese from almost the entire Indonesian archipelago. Still expanding, the Dutch pushed the Portuguese out of Ceylon (Sri Lanka, 1638–1658), and though repelled from Portuguese Macao they occupied Formosa (Taiwan, 1624–1662) as a substitute center for trade with China. In 1641 the Dutch capture of Malacca cut the lifeline of Catholic missions between Goa and the Far East (1641), and in that same year they replaced the Portuguese in Nagasaki, Japan. Turning their attention again to South Asia, from 1658 to 1663 they drove the Portuguese out of India's famous Malabar coast, the home of the St. Thomas Indian Christians, rolling them back to their primary colonial stronghold in little Goa. In 1664 the Dutch even secured a monopoly of commercial trade with free Siam (Thailand).[4] All this in less than fifty years, while managing to keep the envious English from stealing into their territories. By 1677 the last fully independent Indonesian sultanate (Mataram) fell also to the Dutch advance and accepted the Company's authority.

The primary motive of the Dutch was trade, not the expansion of Christianity, unlike the great Catholic powers, Spain and Portugal, which recognized no sharp separation of church and state and always linked a zeal for evangelism with desire for profit, and territory under the power of the crown. In Republican Holland the state ceded virtually full sovereignty over its areas of control in Asia to a commercial company formed by the "seventeen gentlemen" who organized the Dutch East India Company. This made the Company virtually a government in itself,[5] and believing fervently in the separation of church and state, the Company was only too happy to give priority to its own business, trade.

Protestant historians somewhat ruefully compare the lack of Dutch colonial encouragement of missionary evangelism with the Christian zeal of imperial Spain and Portugal, and attribute to this difference, in part, the slow growth of Protestant Christianity in Asia during the first 250 years of the Reformation.[6] Catholic missions were explicitly state enterprises, state supported and state controlled, whereas Protestant missions in the South Pacific under the seventeenth-century Dutch were Company affairs, controlled neither by the government in Holland, nor even by the Dutch Reformed Church. The church was invited to nominate clergymen for service in Company territory, but they remained employees of a company structured and motivated for profit, not for the propagation of the gospel. If the Catholics were inescapably a part of Iberian imperialism, the Protestantism of the East Indies was no less linked to the commercial expansionism of the capitalist Dutch Calvinists. And however grievous were the mistakes and injustices of the Iberians, it must be admitted that in Asia the Catholic powers took their Christian responsibility for the eternal welfare of the souls of the colonized more seriously than either the Dutch or English governments.

Dutch sailors had often sailed to India and the East Indies on Portuguese ships, bringing back stories of the immense profits of the spice trade, and Dutch merchants thirsted to challenge the Portuguese for a share of it. Their successful war of independence against Spain and Spain's annexation of Portugal in 1580 gave them their opportunity. When Spain barred their ships from Lisbon, the hub of all trade with Asia, the hardy Dutch of the Low Country Protestant provinces (the Netherlands) thumbed their noses at the mighty Iberian empire and forged their own independent routes to the Far East under the orange colors of the House of Nassau.[7] As early as 1598, in one year five Dutch expeditions sailed for East Asia. Some of them carried Protestant lay instructors, called "Scripture-Readers" or visitors of the sick, to minister to the sailors and traders on those early, long voyages. They were apparently commissioned by the church *classis* (presbytery) in Amsterdam.[8] The next year, 1599, in what is sometimes described as "the beginning of Protestant world mission," the Dutch church broadened its responsibility by issuing a declaration reminding Hollanders trading with the Indies of their Christian responsibility "to teach the people living there in darkness the true Christian religion."[9] Whether that was indeed the beginning of Protestant missions is debatable,[10] but in any case it came very late. The Protestant Reformation was by then already almost a hundred years old.

In 1602 the Dutch government combined these earlier independent merchant enterprises into a national, private mercantile company, the Dutch East India Company, to which it granted not only a monopoly of trade in Asia, and the right to acquire and govern territory, but also transferred to that capitalist organization its own constitutional obligation to support the church and eradicate paganism.[11] Within a decade the Company controlled the appointment, employ, and assignments of all clergymen and schoolteachers in Dutch trading territories to "develop trade in the Indies to the profit of the great name of Christ and the salvation of the heathen."[12]

In practice, however, the Company subordinated its chartered religious responsibility for spreading the gospel and for "eradicating all false religion"[13] to the pursuit of commercial profit. It recognized local sovereignty as long as its profits were not endangered, and for the most part both local rulers and the Dutch prospered.

But the Company never gave more than nominal attention to its religious responsibilities. The "visitors of the sick" gave way to, but were not replaced by, officially ordained chaplains, and both "visitors" and chaplains were paid as company employees. In 1622 the Company financed the founding of a seminary ("Seminarium Indicum") at the University of Leiden for training the chaplains for the Indies, but when the trainees proved more interested in evangelizing the natives than in trade profits for the Company, it discontinued the subsidy and the school closed. The church in Holland while protesting its closing was not willing to undertake its financial support.[14]

Two factors diminished the missionary outreach of the Dutch in South Asia. The first was theological. Under the influence of a number of German theologians in the early 1600s, it became popular to weaken the biblical interpretation of Jesus' great missionary commission (Matt. 28:18–20; Mark 16:15–18; Luke 24:46–47; John 17:18–21; Acts 1:8) by concluding that the command was given only to the apostles, and that they in turn had already preached the gospel to all nations, and that the world had thus been given its chance to believe but had rejected it.[15]

The Dutch should have known better. Their own Reformed theologians had for years argued against this misleading interpretation of Scripture and church history. Adrianus Saravia of the University of Leiden bitingly observed in 1590 that the small band of the apostles could never have reached the whole world of their time with the gospel, and that therefore the missionary command of Christ has always been binding upon his church and will continue to be until the end of the world. He vehemently answered the dissent of an equally orthodox Calvinist, Theodore Beza of Geneva, who unfortunately took it upon himself to argue to the contrary.[16] In missions history, says Verkuyl, "the first Protestant drafts of a missiology arose in the Netherlands," and he cites a parade of seventeenth-century Dutch Calvinist theologians who argued in one way or another, like Gisbertus Voetius (1586–1676), that "the first goal of missions is the conversion of the heathen; the second, the planting of churches; and the highest, the glory of God."[17]

One of the clearest and most specific of seventeenth-century calls to a global Christian mission was that of the Pietist author Christian Scriver, writing sometime before 1693:

> When the soul reads that nineteen parts of the known world are occupied by heathens, six by Mohammedans, and only five by Christians, its heart heaves, tears start to its eyes, and it longs that it had a voice that might sound through all parts of the world to preach everywhere the Three-One God and Jesus Christ the crucified, and to fill all with His saving knowledge.[18]

But to the Company, more powerful than any theological arguments about missionary priorities was greed. Its single-minded pursuit of commercial profit ruled out all other considerations of conscience or duty, though most of the governors were aware of a somewhat subliminal responsibility to Christianize the heathen. The first chaplains were stationed in Amboina, which remained always one of the chief centers of Christianity in the islands. It had been a strong center of Roman Catholicism, but an anti-Portuguese reaction had already so greatly reduced the number of Christians that when the Dutch came they found the churches already destroyed. The Dutch simply removed the crosses, and what Christians were left gradually became Protestant, more by nominal acceptance of the religion of the new conquerors perhaps than by evangelization, for the Dutch chaplains were in general not noted for vigorous evangelizing. Nevertheless, by 1625 there were believers enough to form a Reformed presbytery (*classis*) of Amboina,[19] the first Protestant presbytery in Asia.

The Dutch attitude to Muslims is symptomatic of a general official indifference to religion despite lip-service recognition of the biblical mandate to preach the gospel to all peoples. The Company was more interested in trade, as one writer scathingly described it: "When the ruler is at the same time merchant . . . the pole-star [is] profit, and the lode-stone greed."[20] Muslim evangelism, mixing with ancient animism, by this time had converted most of the population in all the islands to Islam. To disturb this majority religiously would be to endanger cordial trading relations, so the Company though steadfastly Calvinist frowned on any too serious efforts to convert Muslims and sought rather military and economic profit by alliance with native sultans. Muslims on Amboina feared forcible conversion upon the arrival of the Dutch and were relieved when this did not happen.[21] In Ternate, once a stronghold of Portuguese Catholicism, the Company assented to a trade treaty that actually forbade the conversion of Muslims to Christianity; and on Java, where at Batavia the only official religion was by law declared to be Dutch Reformed, Dutch slaveholders objected if the chaplains attempted to convert their slaves.[22] The Company was content with the status quo, and was not interested in disturbing the peace by upsetting the prevailing religious beliefs of the people.

But where Christianity did not interfere with trade, particularly with non-Muslims, the Company was not at all reluctant to evangelize. It even commercialized the evangelists. It offered some of its not-too-conscientious chaplains a cash bonus for each convert. It bribed pagan rulers with special trade favors if they would consent to turn Christian.[23] As a result of the uneven mixture of pure and impure motives, honest and dishonest evangelism, the numbers of reported converts were impressive — 140,000 Protestants in Java and Amboina alone by 1800, and perhaps as many as 200,000 in the archipelago by 1800.[24] Impressive but hollow, for the suspicion is unavoidable that most were either nominal transfers from the Roman Catholicism of the earlier Portuguese missioners, or motivated more by politics and money than by the Spirit.

The first ordained clergyman resident in Batavia came in 1616, and within five years had gathered a congregation of only 31 members.[25] There were never more than about seventy-five of these Company chaplains in the archipelago at any one time, usually far fewer. Only a few could speak in anything but Dutch, and not many stayed more than five years. It was often difficult to find volunteers to minister in the other islands. Many preferred the easier life in the capital, Batavia, ministering to their fellow Dutch. When the Company was dissolved in 1798 there were only seven left.[26]

But underpaid and overcontrolled by the Company though they were, often ill and usually poorly trained, some remarkable men made their mark. A number learned Malay, the commercial language of the Indies, and in 1733–1734 produced a Malay translation of the entire Bible in a romanized alphabet. They built three schools to train native helpers. Their most outstanding missionary was perhaps Justus Heurnius, son of a professor in Leiden, who in 1618 wrote a book on the biblical mandate for world mission which applies to all Christians in all ages, and sailed to Java in 1624 to practice what he preached. For nine years he was the minister of the Batavia church, preaching plain Bible sermons and warning against the pursuit of riches. But then he felt called to reach out beyond the Dutch compounds to the tribes outside the walls. Batavia then allowed no Indonesians to live inside the city. He sailed to the outer islands and traveled extensively for the next five years from a base in Amboina, advocating a translation of the Bible into local languages, one of which he managed to learn. Not surprisingly he fell ill; Hollanders in those tropical islands rarely survived more than a few months. Reluctantly he returned to the Netherlands in 1638.[27]

Formosa (Taiwan): Gateway to China? (1642–1661)

Formosa (today known as Taiwan)[28] was seized by the Dutch in 1642 to protect the northern flank of their rich monopoly of trade in the Spice Islands, guard their sea route to Japan, and serve as a possible base for challenging Portuguese Macao for the China trade. It was a thinly populated, mountainous island, about 240 miles long, lying 100 miles off the China coast, between Japan and the Philippines.[29]

Though they occupied the "beautiful isle" for only thirty-five years (1626–1661)[30] the Dutch proved far more evangelistically energetic and successful there than in the richer Spice Islands of the East Indies. One reason was that the islanders were primitive animists with very little previous contact with any of the major organized religions.[31] Muslim expansion had not reached that far north, nor had the Chinese religions,

Confucianism and Buddhism, made an impact, for Formosa then was still outside the traditional bounds of Chinese empire. A tiny Spanish Catholic enclave planted for a short time in the north had never been able to expand and was soon driven out by the Hollanders. The Protestant Dutch were the first to enter into sustained evangelistic outreach among the people.

A second reason for the Protestant growth may well have been a difference between Dutch colonial policy in Formosa as compared with their methods in Indonesia. In the vast island chains of the South Pacific the Dutch were content to rule indirectly through semiautonomous native chiefs or sultans appointed as "regents." On smaller Formosa, however, where local society was less systematically organized,[32] Dutch control was direct and immediate,[33] and the influence of the new religion that they brought with them had more impact.

But by far the more important reason for the growth of the church was the character and faith of the missionaries themselves who, in Formosa, were farther from the Dutch East Indies Company's center at Batavia and less intimidated by its secularizing commercial and political power. They moved out quickly into the villages of the coastal interior from the base fort in Zeelandia (on the small inshore island of Tayouan)[34] on Formosa's southwest coast. They soon found out that the inhabitants of the countryside outside the villages were still fierce headhunters, and the missionaries were for a time forced to accept the protection of armed guards as they traveled.

Yet they took up residence in the villages, most of which were within one or two days travel from Zeelandia. There they recognized at once the importance of learning the native languages. They began to translate the Bible, and completed the gospels of Matthew and John.[35] They registered converts by the hundreds, most of whom, as they noticed, came from the non-Chinese tribal people on the island who then far outnumbered the more recently arrived Chinese.[36]

The first ordained missionary-chaplain,[37] Georgius Candidius, came to Formosa in 1627, and within a year and a half of his arrival had gathered together more than a hundred islanders eager to become Christians but not yet ready for baptism. Despite this early success, Candidius felt strongly that chaplains should promise to stay for at least ten years in order to learn the language of the natives, without which they would never be more than superficially effective. Also, contrary to the common accusation of racial prejudice leveled against Western missionaries in the colonial age, Candidius had high praise for the native ability of the tribal Formosans. He did not deny their reputation for savage intertribal wars and headhunting, but was impressed with the intellectual quickness of their minds and openness to new ways,[38] even advising that missionaries who came out unmarried should find and marry suitable Formosan women to render them more sensitive to the customs and needs of the people whom they hoped to win to the faith. He himself proposed to marry a Formosan woman if permitted, but was persuaded by the Company government not to be "too precipitate."[39] So great was his hope for a Christian future in Formosa that he wrote, probably in 1628, "I confidently believe that on this island of Formosa there may be established that which will become...the leading Christian community in all India [the East Indies]...there does not exist in all India a more tractable nation and one more willing to accept the Gospel."[40]

In some respects, however, his judgments were typically colonial, as when the large village in which he was living and preaching proposed that he accept a contest on the greater power he claimed for Christianity as against their old religions by making one house in the village a Christian house to let them see if in time it really prospered more than the others, and in great frustration he wondered if it would not be better to ask the Company government simply to order all the women and children to attend his instruction classes in the true faith. Fortunately the government refused, and four years later, without either a contest or a government order, it was happily reported that "all the inhabitants" of the village "have cast away their idols...and call upon one and the same almighty and true God."[41]

Candidius was soon joined by a Rotterdamer named Robert Junius, son of a Dutch father and a Scottish mother, who for the next fourteen years (1629–1643) laid the foundations of what, but for the loss of the island by the Dutch in 1662, might have proved to be the bastion of Protestantism in Asia.[42] An early account of an interview with Junius gives a glowing account of the spread of Christianity along the eastern coastal plains through seven villages north of Zeelandia and some twenty-three to the south. The work is quaintly titled, "Of the Conversion of five thousand nine hundred East Indians In the Isle Formosa neere China...,"[43] and must be tempered by the more realistic records of his own letters and those of his contemporaries on Formosa.[44] Upon arrival on the island, like most early Company chaplains he began preaching in Dutch to the mystification of the natives, but after two fruitless years, "moved with an exceeding desire of their Conversion...with great paines and diligence, in a short time...[he] learned the barbarous Language and rude Idiome of those Heathen."[45] By the time Junius left Formosa in 1643, there were over seventeen thousand Christian Formosans, of whom he had baptized more than fifty-four hundred adults in twenty-nine villages.[46] A presbytery had been formed, and in six villages north of Zeelandia Christian schools were flourishing, with about six hundred schoolchildren taught by eight Dutch and fifty-four native Christian schoolmasters. Instruction was in one of the five major Formosan tribal dialects (Sinkan),[47] into which Robert Junius had translated two *Catechisms,* and a *Formulary of Christianity* but the Dutch language was taught in the afternoon, for the bewildering variety of local dialects was causing the missionaries to consider using Dutch as a common language.[48] Two problems were noted however: some of the Dutch teachers were behaving scandalously ("one of them was decapitated on account of his misdeeds"); and the Formosan teachers were underpaid, forcing consideration of a proposal to reduce their number from forty-five to seventeen.[49]

The rapid growth of groups of Christians in the villages prompted the formation of another consistory (organized church session of elders and deacons) by dividing the original "consistory of Formosa" into two, the consistories of Tayouan (Zeelandia) and Soulang.[50] While still in Formosa Robert Junius had gathered about seventy boys, aged ten to thirteen, in a little school, teaching them in their own Sinkan language the Christian religion, writing the words in a Romanized alphabet. About sixty girls were taught in another class. In 1636 he pleaded for permission to take four or six of the most promising young men to Holland for ministerial training in his own house. "We believe," he wrote the governor in Zeelandia, "that such a native clergyman could effect more than all our Dutch ministers together could do."[51] Wisely perhaps, permission was refused to take them out of their own country. But this commendable concern for the development of an indigenous clergy was tarnished at one point with a compromising collaboration with colonialism. Native candidates for civil service under the Dutch were obliged to convert and accept the Christian sacraments before they were judged to be suitable for employment.[52]

By the time permission was granted in 1650 for the opening of a seminary in Formosa for the training of a native pastorate, Junius had long left the country. It was proposed to begin with thirty students, with Antonius Hambroek, one of Junius's most capable successors, as regent, but by the time the proposal worked its way through the complicated layers of bureaucratic authority in church and Company from Formosa to Java to Holland, Dutch rule in Formosa was nearing its end, and apparently the seminary never opened.[53] Instead of becoming the first regent of a Formosan seminary, Hambroek became the most prominent of the island's Christian martyrs.

The man who drove the Dutch out of Formosa to reclaim that island for Asia was no shining example of a liberator. He was the Chinese buccaneer Koxinga (Cheng Ch'eng-kung), son of a Chinese pirate and a Japanese mother, fiercely loyal to the fallen Ming dynasty, which he had faithfully served as an admiral until the victory of the Manchu Qing dynasty turned him into the scourge of the China seas. Needing a base for his sea-raiders he chose Formosa and attacked the small Dutch garrison at Zeelandia with twenty-five thousand men, first craftily protesting that he had no use for "such a small, grass-producing country as Formosa."[54] The siege was long, bloody, and terrifyingly cruel.

The most heroic death on the Dutch side was that of the brave Bible translator Antonius Hambroek, the man nominated as principal of the seminary which never opened, who was captured at his country station and paraded with his wife and several of his children in view of the besieged fort with the threat that all would be killed unless the Dutch immediately surrendered. When that failed, Koxinga sent Hambroek in to urge his countrymen to surrender. Instead, Hambroek urged them to stand fast even though that would mean not only his own death but that of his family and all other prisoners. Two of his daughters were in the fort, having escaped capture, but when the governor told him he need not go back, and urged him to stay with his daughters in safety, he refused and returned to face Koxinga with the news. He was beheaded publicly along with several other missionaries, including some of the women and children. One of Hambroek's daughters — a very sweet young girl, as a contemporary report described her — was seized by Koxinga for his harem when the fort fell.[55] Martyr or not — for technically he did not die for his Christian faith — Hambroek deserves honorable mention among the thirty-two ordained missionaries who preached, taught, and planted churches during the brief flowering of Protestantism on Formosa between 1627 and 1662.[56]

As for the Christian communities among the tribes, which had for a time numbered more than seventeen thousand recorded converts, none survived in organized form under the cruel anti-Christian persecutions of Koxinga and his son. Nor did the prospects for Christianity improve after the death of the latter in 1682. Formosa was then for the first time annexed into the Chinese empire where, unfortunately, the Qing dynasty's official toleration of Christianity was beginning to give way to harassment and soon to outright persecution. For the next two hundred years until Protestant missionaries again were able to enter the island, the church that had promised to become a model for the expansion of the faith in East Asia simply disappeared, leaving only a trace among a few who acknowledged to a visiting Catholic clergymen in 1715 that they remembered the words of the baptismal formula and believed in a God in three persons.[57]

The two hundred years following the defeat and expulsion of the Dutch were for Christianity in Formosa (Taiwan) the "years of silence," as in Japan after the expulsion of the Portuguese, except that in Formosa not even the silent Christians survived. And the next wave of the faith to reach the "Beautiful Isle," late in the nineteenth century, was English, not Dutch.

The Dutch Period in Ceylon (1656–1796)[58]

Three thousand miles south of Formosa was another beautiful island, Ceylon (Sri Lanka). It had been Portuguese for 150 years. By 1626 the

Portuguese had driven out their most troublesome trading rivals in the spice trade, the Muslims. But now halfway through the seventeenth century a far greater threat than land-based Muslim "pagans" appeared off the coasts of Ceylon: Dutch "heretics."

For most of the seventeenth century, the men of Holland, sons of the Calvinist wing of the Reformation, earned for their tiny kingdom a well-deserved reputation as "the chief seafaring nation in the world."[59] Dutch men-of-war based on the northern tip of Sumatra had been circling the rich island of Ceylon for a half a century, relentlessly subduing one Portuguese port after another before winning their greatest prize, Colombo, which surrendered in 1656. Two years later they took Jaffna in the north. With control of the southwest from Colombo south to the tip, and the Jaffna peninsula in the north, and the only two important ports on the east coast which they had won earlier, the Dutch thought they had conquered Ceylon. But they were still, in 1658, masters only of its coasts.

It was the lure of the cinnamon trade that had brought the Dutch to Ceylon, not zeal for evangelism. Unlike the Portuguese who had always linked imperial expansion with religious crusade, the profit-minded Dutch kept their ledgers more carefully than their churches. But they were implacably anti-Catholic, politically as well as religiously, for they suspected all Catholics of being pro-Portuguese. In 1638, in what has been called "the first blow against the Catholic Church in Ceylon," the Dutch negotiated a trade treaty with Kandy, binding its king to a promise to "exterminate" all papist monks and ecclesiastics in his domain.[60] Four years later one of the first acts of the victorious Dutch was to extend the outlawing of Roman Catholicism to all territory under their control:

> Within the territories of the Dutch East India company, no other religion will be exercised, much less taught or propagated, either secretly or publicly, than the Reformed Christian Religion as it is taught in the public Churches of the United Provinces [the Netherlands].[61]

In the same year the first Reformed (Presbyterian) clergyman was appointed for Ceylon, Antonius Hornhovius, but he died on the voyage from the Dutch East India Company's major base in Sumatra at Batavia. The first Protestant minister to reach the island was Johannes Stertemius, who landed the next year, 1643.[62]

Better known and more effective was the Reformed pioneer in northern Ceylon, Philip Baldaeus, who has been described as "the greatest missionary the Dutch Reformed Church sent to the island." He not only established a strong network of Reformed Christian communities in Jaffna, twenty-four in three years (1658–1661), but insisted that missionaries to Ceylon should use the language of the people; he also produced a widely used Tamil catechism. With great good sense he wrote: "The best and surest way to spread the religion is not to make the people learn Dutch — a long and tedious process likely to be very expensive. It is much more convenient for one man to learn the language of the whole people."[63] Unfortunately those who followed Baldaeus, with a few exceptions, were not so farsighted. Too often they relied more on coercive legislation than evangelistic communication. The results, as might have been expected, were counterproductive.

Few better examples of the futility of using civil legislation and penal laws as means of promoting Christian mission against other religions can be found than the 140 years of Dutch rule in Ceylon. All the odds were with the Dutch Protestants — government power, military control, commercial success, employment, social prestige. They began by rounding up Catholic priests and shipping them roughly off to India. At least one was beheaded on suspicion of conspiracy.[64] A proclamation in 1658 forbade on pain of death the concealment of Catholic priests in hiding.[65] Though that harsh penalty proved impossible to enforce, in 1715 public or private assemblies of Catholics were prohibited and priests were forbidden to baptize.[66] Catholics were driven underground; their priests took cover. Catholic mission reports from that period mention four periods of persecution in the forty years between 1689 and 1729: the first in Jaffna under the fiercely anti-Catholic Henry ven Rheede, who was the Dutch High Commissioner;[67] again in 1706 in Colombo and Negumbo;[68] in 1720 in Jaffna and Manar;[69] and the last in Colombo in 1729.[70] But such overt persecution was the exception rather than the rule.

In practice the missionary methods of the Dutch were more lenient than the rhetoric of their ever harsher edicts of prohibitions and penalties would imply.[71] By the 1740s Catholics could be sentenced to six years imprisonment for a first offense, and twenty-five years and banishment for a third. In fact, however, these laws proved so exasperatingly ineffective and counterproductive that in 1745 the Dutch finally admitted failure, and the Roman Catholic superior in Goa of the Goanese missionaries in Ceylon reported to the king of Portugal that the Catholic faith had gloriously triumphed "like beautiful roses among thorns."[72] Catholic growth continued.

The Buddhists fared better than the Catholics under Dutch Protestant law. One reason for Dutch anti-Catholic bitterness may have been the burning memory of a hundred years of brutal Spanish occupation of the Low Countries, which had ended in 1658, only ten years before Holland took Colombo from the Catholics. But the Dutch anti-Catholic persecution in Ceylon was inexcusable, however much allowance may be made in view of the standards of the turbulent, intolerant years of religious wars in sixteenth- and seventeenth-century Europe. The one redeeming feature was that it was ineffective. In fact, like so many persecutions in the history of the church, it not only stiffened the faith of the persecuted Catholics, it may well have ensured their survival.

A more immediate reason for the softer treatment of Buddhists, however, was the anxiety of the Dutch traders to let nothing interfere with their monopoly of the cinnamon trade. In the 1680s the Dutch governor, Van Pyl, bowed to pressure from the Dutch clergy and forbade idolatrous Buddhist ceremonies. A few years later the clergy demanded that the government forbid worship at the great Buddhist shrine of Kelaniya near Colombo, revered by Buddhists for the legend of the visit there by Lord Buddha himself. The Portuguese had unsuccessfully tried to replace the Buddhist tradition with a countertradition that it was the site of the burial of Adam and Eve.[73] The Dutch colonials simply compromised. For them the economic argument proved stronger than the theological. Fearing that the Buddhist kingdom of Kandy would retaliate against restrictions placed on local religious customs and could easily cut off the Dutch ports on the coast from the supply of cinnamon in the island's interior, the Company refused to interfere, and the restrictions against Buddhist practices were softened to apply only to nominal Christians found taking part in them. The clergy appealed the ruling to Holland. There the government feared a political backlash from its Protestant constituencies, and in 1592 overruled their colonial subordinates, restoring the restrictions against Buddhist ceremonies at the shrine. But about all the sanctions accomplished was to arouse public resentment.[74]

It must be remembered that the for the most part, Dutch Rule was largely effective only along the island's beautiful coasts. In the mountainous interior, beyond the reach of the Dutch navy, the "Lion King" Rajasinha II (1635–1687), ruler of the warrior kingdom of Kandy, remained as the last independent Ceylonese king. In square miles of land he was king of far more territory than the Dutch. He was the son of a Christian mother, Dona Catherina, daughter of the last king of a former king of a rival dynasty claiming the Kandy area. He himself was not Christian, professing to be a Buddhist though he was not above persecuting Buddhist monks whenever he suspected them of disloyalty. He had sided with the Dutch in their raids against the Portuguese, and joined them in outlawing Roman Catholicism where they had triumphed.[75] In return the Dutch had promised him the city of Colombo if and when it surrendered. But when they failed to keep the promise after the city's surrender, he turned against them. For the rest of his life he was a thorn in their side, demanding the return of ports and coastal areas that once had been his, blocking access to the rich cinnamon resources in the interior, raiding across their borders, and successfully keeping his kingdom independent.[76]

His son, a devout Buddhist, encouraged a revival of the old faith in Kandy. When the Buddhist revival began to spread into Dutch territory, the Protestant missionaries were scandalized that the Company, ignoring the edict of 1682 against Buddhist practices, as usual placed a higher priority on cinnamon from Kandy than on the conversion of Buddhists.[77]

The Kandy dynasty ruled the interior for another century and a quarter, keeping the kingdom at least nominally free and strongly Buddhist until 1815.[78]

In Dutch-occupied territory, meanwhile, for a good many years the Dutch Reformed missionaries felt no need to build churches: they simply confiscated Catholic churches and redesigned them into Reformed meeting-houses, using them for worship on the Sabbath and for schools during the week. The great Franciscan Church of St. Francis in Colombo became the official church of the Dutch East India Company in that city. The oldest remaining Protestant church structure in Ceylon is dated 1750, more than a century after the Dutch had evicted the Portuguese.[79]

Not surprisingly, the initial conversion of nominal Roman Catholics to the new Reformed version of the faith of the conquerors was rapid. In the north alone, in Jaffna in 1663, Protestants reported 65,000 converts in five years, opened a seminary, and by 1688 claimed a Protestant population of more than 180,000 in that province of 280,000 people.[80] The Tamil north was turning Protestant.

But in the Buddhist south, the Catholics were more tenacious about their faith. Some went underground, and many families, both Ceylonese and Portuguese, and a number of Catholic priests found refuge outside Dutch territorial control in the mountains of Kandy whose King, the same Rajasinha II who had once proscribed and persecuted Catholics, now granted them welcome asylum.[81]

The majority, however, remained in Dutch territory, some of them trading a nominal Catholicism for an equally nominal Protestantism. Others found the sober Calvinistic religion of the Dutch both rational and energizing. Still greater numbers never forsook their Catholic traditions. Instead they went underground, meeting in secret and surviving with the help of the brave, hidden priests of the Goanese Oratory of St. Philip Neri.[82] For the next hundred years or more the Indian priests of the Goanese Oratorians were in effect the only active Catholic missionary order in Ceylon. Outstanding among the Indian missionaries in the anti-Catholic territories of the Dutch was Joseph Vaz (1650–1711), born a Brahman near Goa, who "saved the Roman Catholic Church in Ceylon from extinction at the hands of the Calvinist Dutch."[83]

Vaz was ordained priest in 1676 and joined the Oratory of Goa at age thirty-five. Though born to the upper class in India's caste society, he was so eager for missionary work that he volunteered for missions among the poorest of the poor in the south, and there, hearing that the great island of Ceylon was forbidden territory for Catholics, he pleaded with his superior to allow him to sell himself as a slave to the Dutch "to go and redeem from the slavery of sin so many souls that lived captive under the heretics." That was unnecessary, but he did disguise himself as a beggar and secretly entered Ceylon as a missionary in 1687.[84]

For the next twenty-four years he labored there among the island's underground Catholics until his death in 1711. Driven by persecution out of Dutch-ruled Jaffna in the north, he made his more permanent base in the independent and more tolerant Ceylonese kingdom of Kandy, where he worked at first to revive the refugee Catholics who had fled there from the Dutch occupation, but soon began to slip back and forth, in disguise, through the jungles and across the border to minister to the scattered congregations in Dutch territory. So successful was he that other Oratorians were sent to join him, and finally the churches could no longer be kept hidden. Dutch efforts at repression proved dismally ineffectual despite their intermittent "priest hunts."[85]

In 1663 all but 2 of the 120 Catholic priests in Ceylon had been banished by the Dutch. In 1701, in the middle of the heroic mission of Father Vaz there were still only four missionaries. By 1717, seventy-five years after they were outlawed, Roman Catholic churches reportedly outnumbered the Dutch Reformed four to one (roughly four hundred Catholic churches to one hundred Reformed).[86]

THE CLOSING YEARS OF DUTCH RULE

The Dutch Reformed missionaries, however, also were not without their successes, and a heavy-handed hundred years of Dutch social and religious discrimination against the Catholics took its toll, despite the heroic efforts of Vaz and his colleagues. The Dutch Reformed Church divided the island into three districts, called consistories: Colombo in the center, Jaffna in the north, and Galle to the south. Each consistory met eight times a year. The church's Board of Education was in charge of all the schools, both secular and religious, and registered births, deaths and marriages. Responsibility for the poor was not neglected, and was placed under a board of deacons.[87]

Philip Baldaeus (1632–1672), the Dutch Reformed pioneer, described the methodical way in which the Dutch proposed to transform Catholics into proper Protestants. Catholics were required to attend Reformed services. All children were enrolled in schools that systematically were to teach the essentials of what was considered to be the purer new faith. Absentees from church and school were fined. A Dutch soldier was not allowed to marry a Ceylonese girl until she had professed Christian faith, and if after marriage she did not attend church services once a week, his army pay was forfeited.[88] The children of all slaves born of Protestant parents were given their freedom, but not so for Roman Catholics. Their children were slaves for life — a curiously counterproductive mission strategy indeed, as one historian has observed, since it gave "every slave-holder an interest in preventing the extension of Protestantism."[89] These regulations of disabilities imposed on the Catholics were often revised but never effectively removed, and were not entirely abolished until 1806, ten years after the island was taken from the Dutch by the British.[90]

Nevertheless, in 1796 when the Dutch were driven out by the British in much the same way as they, the Dutch, had replaced the Portuguese, though a realistic glance at the estimated numbers of both Roman Catholics and Dutch Reformed in the later eighteenth century suggests a decline in both branches of Christianity, Catholics still outnumbered Protestants. There may then have been as many as 342,000 Protestant adherents and somewhat more Roman Catholics, but such statistics distort the reality. It suggests too many baptisms and too few verifiable conversions. A letter from a Dutch consistory in 1730 reports a shocking mismatch in the ratio of baptisms to church members. There were, it said, 288,944 baptized Christians in Ceylon's native congregations, but only 505 professing church members,[91] a ratio of less than two-tenths of 1 percent.

A NOTE ON DUTCH AND PORTUGUESE COLONIALISM

K. M. Panikkar virtually equates colonialism and Christianity when he describes the arrival of the Portuguese in India as "the beginning of an Eighth Crusade," and dismisses Portuguese Catholic missions in Asia with the phrase, "to the Portuguese christianization was a state enterprise," profitable, exploitative, but fortunately temporary.[92] David Bosch has a better metaphor to describe the relationship. "The missionaries," he wrote, "were, by and large, a breed fundamentally different from their colonizing compatriots... They carried the odor of the colonial enterprise with them — much the way the stale smell of cigarette smoke clings to the clothes of a non-smoker coming out of a room full of smokers."[93]

There is a world of difference between a missionary like Xavier in India and the colonialist da Gama; between a Bishop Salazar in the Philippines and the Spanish landlords of the Philippine *encomiendas*; between the Jesuits in China and the British in the Opium Wars. But however careful the missionaries may have been to make the differences clear — and some did not even see the difference — a trace of the taint usually remained to be held against the missions in varying degrees in differing situations. For example, the judgment pronounced by Joseph Pattiasina on Portuguese missions in many ways fits the Dutch as well as the Portuguese in the islands of South Asia. He wrote, "In the left hand the invaders brought the sword and in the right hand, the cross, but when they encountered gold or spices, they dropped the cross and put the gold in their pocket."[94]

NOTES

1. Bernard H. M. Vlekke, *Nusantara: A History of the East Indian Archipelago* (Cambridge, Mass.: Harvard University Press, 1945), 302.

2. It is important to note that three East India companies were involved in this revolution: Portugal's *Estado da India*, and the British and Dutch companies. But Portugal's *Estado*, older and more religious but less successfully capitalist than the British and Dutch commercial ventures, was no military match for the two Protestant powers, and it barely survived the seventeenth century. The short-lived union of Portugal with Spain in 1580 explicitly excluded Portuguese territories from Spanish commercial control, and was of little military protection. See Niels Steensgaard, *The Asian Trade Revolution of the Seventeenth Century: The East India Companies and the Decline of the Caravan Trade* (Chicago and London: University of Chicago Press, 1974), 81–86.

3. C. R. Boxer, *Dutch Merchants and Mariners in Asia, 1602–1795* (London: Variorum Reprints, 1988), vii, I:82.

4. The dates here given mark the first Dutch trading centers, not the eventual establishment of territorial authority, which essentially begins with the "Statutes of Batavia" in 1642. For an outline of Dutch expansion see the chronology in Vlekke, *Nusantara*, 414ff.; and his more popularly written summary in *The Story of the Dutch East Indies* (Cambridge, Mass.: Harvard University Press, 1946), 64–131. For a more detailed map and chronology of the expansion, see Mohammad Ali Soedjatmoko, G. J. Resink, and G. McT. Kahn, eds., *An Introduction to Indonesian Historiography* (Ithaca, N.Y.: Cornell University Press, 1965), 358. The indispensable summarizing reference for Dutch missionary expansion in Asia is Latourette, *A History of the Expansion of Christianity*, 3:42–43, 288–292, 301–306, 333–334, 359–360.

5. Rita Smith Kipp, *The Early Years of a Dutch Colonial Mission: The Karo Field* (Ann Arbor: University of Michigan Press, 1990). She writes, "Far more than a mere trading company, the VOC [acronym for the Dutch name of the East India Co.] was for two centuries, roughly from 1600 to 1800, the effective government of the Europeans in the Indies." See also Amry Vandenbosch, *The Dutch East Indies: Its Government, Problems, and Politics* (Berkeley: University of California Press, 1941), 51–52.

6. Gustav Warneck's *Outline of a History of Protestant Missions from the Reformation to the Present Time*, trans. G. Robson (New York: Fleming H. Revell, 1903), 129, for example, describes Dutch colonial policy as blindly and actively supporting Muhammedanism, though this is more true of later rather than earlier policy. Cf. Vlekke, *Nusantara*, 132; and J. Verkuyl, *Contemporary Missiology* (Grand Rapids, Mich.: William B. Eerdmans, 1978), 22.

7. The southern, Catholic provinces were reabsorbed under Spanish sovereignty but eventually became Belgium.

8. Vlekke, *Nusantara*, 3:303.

9. Joh. Rauws, H. Kraemer, F. J. F. van Hasselt, and N. A. C. Slotemaker de Bruïne, *The Netherlands Indies* (London and New York: World Dominion Press, 1935), 33.

10. Calvin, for example, did not teach that the apostles had already taken the gospel to the whole world, and sent a mission to Brazil in 1555 which has sometimes been claimed as the "beginning of Protestant missions." However, that

mission was almost an instant failure. D. H.-W. Genischen, "Were the Reformers Indifferent to Missions?" in *Student World* (Geneva) 53, nos. 1, 2 (1960): 119ff.

11. In effect, the government transferred to the Company its constitutional obligation to aid the church and "eradicate false religion." Frank Cooley, "Altar and Throne" (PhD diss., Yale University, 1961), 347.

12. Quoted by R. C. Delavignette, *Christianity and Colonialism*, trans. J. R. Foster (New York: Hawthorn Books, 1964), 104. See also Rauws et al., *The Netherlands Indies*, 34.

13. Cooley, *Altar and Throne*, 347, 352–353; J. Richter, *Die Evangelische Mission in Niederlandisch-Indien. Fern- und Sudost-Asien, Australien, Amerika* (Gutersloh: C. Bertelsmann, 1931, 1932), 8–9; Vandenbosch, *The Dutch East Indies*, 39.

14. Warneck, *Outline of a History of Protestant Missions*, 44. See also a principal Dutch source on the Reformed Church in the Indies, Carel Wessel Theodorus Boetzelaer van Dubbledam, *De Gereformeerde Kerken in Nederland en de Zending in Oost-Indie in Dagen der Oost-Indishe Compagnie* (Utrecht: B. den Boer, 1906), 72–92, 166–174.

15. Some carried the argument into fantasy with claims that ancient Ethiopians had already carried the gospel to Brazil, and that long ago an unknown bearded missionary had preached to the ancestors of sixteenth-century Mexicans. See Warneck, *Outline of a History of Protestant Missions*, 25–31. See also D. H.-W. Genischen, "Were the Reformers Indifferent to Missions?" 119–127.

16. Adrianus Saravia, *De Diversis ministrorum evangelii gradibus, sic ut a Domino fuerunt instituti* (1590); Theodore Beza, *Ad tractationem de ministrorum evangelii gradibus ab Hadriano Saravia, Belga* (1592). See Warneck, *Outline of a History of Protestant Missions*, 20–22; and Gensichen, "Were the Reformers Indifferent to Missions?" 119–136.

17. Verkuyl, *Contemporary Missiology*, 18–22. Verkuyl gives brief summaries of the arguments of Saravia, J. Heurnius (who was a missionary in the East Indies), Voetius, and J. Hoornbeeck. Johannes Hoornbeeck (1617–1666), quite remarkably for that age of religious strife, unfavorably compared the missionary lethargy of his fellow Protestants with the zeal of the Roman Catholic Jesuits who go out, learn native languages, take medicine and healing to the sick, and preach and teach to the ends of the earth.

18. Christian Scriver, *Christlecher seelenschatz in predigten über die ganze evangelische* (Stuttgart: C. F. Elzel, 1841), quoted by Warneck, *Outline of a History of Protestant Missions*, 40. See also Johann Gerhard, *Loci Theologici*, 9 vols. (Tubingae: Sumtibus Io. Georgii Cottae, 1762–1787), xxiii, xxiv. The misconception that the worldwide missionary task had already been completed by the apostles was still prevalent as late as 1731. See Warneck, *Outline of a History of Protestant Missions*, 30 n. 2. Warneck's summary of seventeenth-century orthodox Protestantism on missions (22–31) points out that Gerhard, while repeating the historical error, nevertheless finds a continuing mandate for missionary outreach in the duties of the office of bishop as heir to the apostles.

19. Rauws et al., *The Netherlands Indies*, 32, 35. By 1700 the presbytery reported 1,232 students in 54 Christian schools. J. J. Van Klaveren, in *The Dutch Colonial System in the East Indies* (Rotterdam: D. Benedictus, 1953), 31, disparages Dutch evangelizing with the remark, "Had there not been a R.C. nucleus, no conversion by the Dutch had probably taken place." But his judgment is too severe. The

Catholic communities were already vanishing by the time the Dutch came, and Amboina was the center of much that was best in Dutch missions during the chaplaincy period.

20. Unattributed quotation in J. S. Furnivall, *Colonial Policy and Practice: A Comparative Study of Burma and Netherlands India* (Cambridge: Cambridge University Press, 1948), 519–520.

21. Klaveren, *Dutch Colonial System*, 54.

22. Rauws et al., *The Netherlands Indies*, 34. Slavery, incidentally, was not introduced to Indonesia by the colonists; it traces back to ancient Indonesia, long before even the coming of Islam (see Klaveren, *Dutch Colonial System*, 23–24).

23. The best treatment of early Dutch evangelization in the Indies, for those who read Dutch, is probably van Boetzelaer, *De Gereformeerde Kerken in Nederland en de Zending in Oost-Indie*. See also short summaries in Latourette, *A History of the Expansion of Christianity*, 3:303–306; Neill, *History of Christian Missions*, 223–224; and Richter, *Die evangelische Mission in Niederlandisch-Indien*, 1–12.

24. Richter, *Die Evangelische Mission in Niederlandisch-Indien*, 12; Warneck, *Outline of a History of Protestant Missions*, 46. The estimates for the archipelago vary from sixty-five thousand to two hundred thousand.

25. Rauws et al., *The Netherlands Indies*, 34.

26. Rauws et al., *The Netherlands Indies*, 33–37; Latourette, *A History of the Expansion of Christianity*, 3:305–306.

27. Verkuyl, *Contemporary Missiology*, 21; Richter, *Die Evangelische Mission in Niederlandisch-Indien*, 12 n. 1. On health and racial problems in Batavia, see Vlekke, *Story of the Dutch East Indies*, 102–107.

28. First named Formosa by the Portuguese who were the earliest Westerners to discover it in the sixteenth century. Its native people were not Chinese but probably of Malay-Polynesian origin. Significant Chinese migration from the mainland did not begin until the fourteenth century, and the island was not named Taiwan by the Chinese until 1612, nor was Chinese control firmly established until after 1683 under the Manchu dynasty. It was ceded to Japan as a result of the Sino-Japanese war in 1895, and recovered by the Chinese after World War II in 1945.

29. For a short time, fifteen years (1626–1641), Spaniards from the Philippines held a precarious beachhead on the northern tip of the island until driven off by the Dutch, who expelled the scanty Catholic presence established there by the Dominicans.

30. The Dutch established their first fortified position against the Spanish on the island in 1626, but did not control the entire island until 1642.

31. See the seventeenth-century account of Formosan religion by George Candidius in William Campbell's collection of letters and documents from this period, *Formosa under the Dutch, Described from Contemporary Records*, 2nd rev. enlarged ed., 2 vols. (London: Kegan Paul, Trench, Trubner, 1903), 1:22–25, 90ff., hereafter cited as Campbell, *Formosa under the Dutch* (with the name of his source given in parentheses).

32. Campbell, *Formosa under the Dutch* (Candidius), 1:15–16.

33. Furnivall, *Colonial Policy and Practice*, 20ff., 217–275 and passim.

34. This little islet of Tayouan (or Taiwan), later gave its name to the whole island of Formosa. On Zeelandia and Tayouan, see C. R. Boxer, "The Siege of

Fort Zeelandia . . . 1661–1662," in *Dutch Merchants*, 3:20–21; and map of Tayouan islet, 3:48.

35. Campbell, *Formosa under the Dutch* (here the source was his translation of the full text of Tayouan Church Minute-book, October 5, 1657).

36. The entire number of Chinese in Formosa at that time was perhaps about two hundred thousand, including some ten thousand on the little island around Zeelandia, and twenty-five thousand armed soldiers brought by Koxinga. Most of them had earlier immigrated with Dutch permission as rice and sugar cane farmers, merchants or laborers. Campbell, *Formosa under the Dutch*, 384; Boxer, *Dutch Merchants*, 3:20; Hollington Tong, *Christianity in Taiwan: A History* (Taipei: China Post, 1961), 6.

37. Two lay catechists, "Bible-Readers" were the first missionaries sent to Formosa, Michael Theodori in 1624 and Dirk Lauwrenzoon, but left little to record.

38. See Candidius's descriptions of the aboriginal tribes and their customs, in Campbell, *Formosa under the Dutch* (Candidius), 9–25, 89–93. "[T]he intellect of the people of Formosa is acute and their memories excellent; so much so that in one week I have been able to make them understand things which took me a whole fortnight to teach other Indians, and even persons belonging to our own nation" (89). This is a refreshing contrast to the judgment of the historian François Valentyn whose eighteenth-century *Oud en Nieuw Oost Indien* (1724–1726) has a very biased section on Formosa (6:33–93), as one sentence (from Campbell's translation) is enough to indicate: "the Formosans are a stupid, blind, and ridiculous heathen people." Campbell gives selections of Valentyn's description of Formosa and the Dutch mission. Campbell, *Formosa under the Dutch* (Valentyn), 1–9, 75–77.

39. Campbell, *Formosa under the Dutch* (Candidius), 92, 101 passim; quote from 104.

40. Campbell, *Formosa under the Dutch* (Candidius). "Memorandum from Rev. G. Candidius to Governor Nuyts," 89. He attributes the openness of the Formosans to their lack of a higher religion (Islamic or Chinese), and the absence of rulers of such religions who would oppose the entry of any other faith.

41. Campbell, *Formosa under the Dutch*, 95–96, 103, 105.

42. On Junius, see W. A. Ginsel, *De Gereformeerde Kerk op Formosa of de lotgevallen eener handelskerk onder de Oost-Indische-Compagnie 1627–1662* (Leiden: P. J. Mulder, 1931), 30–55. Campbell, *Formosa under the Dutch*, contains English translations of many of his letters, and the reports of his colleagues and the Dutch authorities on his work (116–197), as well as a prayer, sermon, and translations of his *Catechism*, and *Formulary of Christianity*, in the Formosan language, which in good seventeenth-century Calvinist terms proclaim trinitarian orthodoxy, condemn polytheism and idolatry and immorality, and teach salvation from sin through Christ alone; the authority of the Bible as the Word of God; and the meaning of the two sacraments, baptism and the Lord's supper, and of prayer (330–379).

43. Reprint, with appendices by William Campbell, as *An Account of Missionary Success in the Island of Formosa*, 2 vols. (London: Trubner, 1889).

44. Campbell, *An Account of Missionary Success in the Island of Formosa*, related by M. C. Sibellius (1650), 1:116–197.

45. Campbell, *An Account of Missionary Success in the Island of Formosa*, 1:32–33.

46. Campbell, *An Account of Missionary Success in the Island of Formosa*, 1:94–101. Almost all the converts came from the non-Chinese aboriginal natives, though there were a few Christians among the Chinese traders and laborers permitted by the Dutch to enter from the mainland. Campbell, *Formosa under the Dutch*, 201–202.

47. The many dialects of the island were not mutually understandable, although all presumably came from a Malay-Polynesian base, not from China. The missionaries reduced the spoken languages to written form in a Romanized alphabet. See examples in Campbell, *An Account of Missionary Success in the Island of Formosa*, 1:203–214.

48. The full texts are given in Campbell, *Formosa under the Dutch* (Junius), 336–379. See also in the same collection (from the Tayouan Minute Book, October 5, 1657), 306ff. On the dialect problem, see Campbell (Governor's letter, October 15, 1643), 197.

49. Campbell, *Formosa under the Dutch* (Letter, Formosa Consistory to Amsterdam presbytery, October 7, 1643; and Minute-Book of the Castle of Zeelandia, September 9, 1644), 192–193; 202. Cf. Campbell, *An Account of Missionary Success in the Island of Formosa*, 1:53, 58, 91. On occasional lapses of Dutch clerics and the consequent ecclesiastical censure for "debauchery" and for "bad conduct and drinking," see Campbell, *Formosa under the Dutch* (Zeelandia Gov. van der Burg, November 4, 1639), 158, 179.

50. Campbell, *Formosa under the Dutch* (Consistory of Formosa to Classis of Amsterdam, October 7, 1643), 192. The two consistories (sessions) often acted as one, more in the fashion of a presbytery (classis), though technically they were ecclesiastically subordinate to the presbytery of Amsterdam. It should also be remembered that by the charter of the Dutch East India Company they were also under the authority of the Company's Zeelandia governor and council, which in turn was responsible to Batavia, as Batavia was to the "seventeen gentlemen" in Amsterdam. See Campbell, *Formosa under the Dutch*, 540–541.

51. Campbell, *Formosa under the Dutch* (Junius), 142–147 and passim. The defect in his proposal was his expressed object to make them, in Holland, "Dutch in every respect" (146).

52. Tong, *Christianity in Taiwan*, 20.

53. Campbell, *Formosa under the Dutch*, 306–309, 314–315.

54. Campbell, *Formosa under the Dutch* (Koxinga), 404ff., translating Koxinga's letter in full. On the siege, see Boxer, "Siege of Fort Zeelandia," in *Dutch Merchants*, 3:16–48.

55. Day-Journal of Commander Caeuw, Zeelandia, October 21, 1661, as translated in Campbell, *Formosa under the Dutch*, 327. On Hambroek, see also 83–86, 299, 304, 307, 311, 314; and Ginsel, *De Gereformeerde Kerk op Formosa*, 126–133. Four or five other missionaries are known to have suffered the same fate as Hambroek, some by beheading, others by crucifixion.

56. Ginsel, *De Gereformeerde Kerk op Formosa*, 134. I add here two ministers (Hans Olhoff and Cornelius Copsma) not on his list but mentioned in his text.

57. The visitor was Father De Mailla, whose notes are translated in Campbell, *Formosa under the Dutch*, 504–516, esp. 510.

58. On the Dutch period in Ceylon see the principal original documents translated into English by V. Perniola, *The Catholic Church in Sri Lanka: The Dutch Period: Original Documents translated into English*, vol. 1: 1658–1711; vol. 2:

1712–1746; vol. 3: 1747–1795 (Dehiwala, Sri Lanka: Tisara Prakasakayo Ltd., 1983–1985), hereafter cited as Perniola, *Dutch Period*. The most careful analysis of the period is Boudens, *The Catholic Church in Ceylon under Dutch Rule*. See also P. E. Pieris, ed., *The Dutch Power in Ceylon (1602–1670)* (London: Curzon Press, 1929, new printing 1973); Tennent, *Christianity in Ceylon*, 37–77; and R. L. Brohier, *Links between Sri Lanka and the Netherlands* (Colombo: Netherlands Alumni Association of Sri Lanka, 1978).

59. Boxer, *Dutch Merchants*, 1:82.

60. Boudens, *The Catholic Church in Ceylon under Dutch Rule*, 63–64; P. E. Pieris, *Ceylon and the Hollanders, 1658 to 1796* (Tellippalai, Ceylon: American Ceylon Mission Press, 1918), 17–18.

61. This clause on religion is from the Old Statutes of Batavia (the Van Dieman Code), issued in 1642 by the Dutch East India Company through which the government in Holland administered Ceylon (Perniola, *Dutch Period*, 1:1).

62. Brohier, *Links between Sri Lanka and the Netherlands*, 99.

63. Cited in Boudens, *The Catholic Church in Ceylon under Dutch Rule*, 204. See also D. W. Ferguson, "Philippus Baldaeus and his Book on Ceylon," in *Ceylon Antiquary and Literary Register* (Colombo), 4 (1936): 304–310, 337–345, 386–394, 435–445.

64. Perniola, *Dutch Period*, 1:5 n. 3.

65. See the edicts of Van Goens, conqueror of Jaffna (1658) and later governor of Ceylon (1664–1675), in Perniola, *Dutch Period*, 1:3–8.

66. Tennent, *Christianity in Ceylon*, 42.

67. Perniola, *Dutch Period*, 1:55–56. Ven Rheede was Dutch high commissioner for Bengal, the Coromandel Coast, and Ceylon (1684–1691).

68. Perniola, *Dutch Period*, 1:361–384; cf. Perera, *Catholic Negombo*, 20–29.

69. Perniola, *Dutch Period*, 2:75–76.

70. Perniola, *Dutch Period*, 2:203–208, 214–217.

71. For a generous Anglican perspective on Dutch missionary methods see F. Lorenz Beven, ed., *A History of the Diocese of Colombo: A Centenary Volume* (Colombo: The Times of Ceylon, 1946), 370–371.

72. Report of Father Raphael dos Anjos, 1745, in Perniola, *Dutch Period*, 2:422–438; and the Catholic Mission of Ceylon Report, 1733 (2:256–261). See also the Dutch Edicts of 1715, 1733, and 1745; 2:252–254; 260; and 2:415–417.

73. Pieris, *Ceylon and the Hollanders*, 36–37.

74. Tennent, *Christianity in Ceylon*, 54–55.

75. See his treaty of 1638 (revised in 1649). The text is given in Perniola, *The Catholic Church in Sri Lanka*, 1:2. Rajasinha is sometimes transliterated Rajasimha.

76. Pieris, *Ceylon and the Hollanders*, 17, 21–22, 28–32.

77. Pieris, *Ceylon and the Hollanders*, 37.

78. Boudens, *The Catholic Church in Ceylon under Dutch Rule*, 63–64, 69; Pieris, *Ceylon and the Hollanders*, 37; and De Silva, *A History of Sri Lanka*, 133–143. See also Codrington, *Short History*, 133ff., 170–175.

79. Brohier, *Links between Sri Lanka and the Netherlands*, 100, 111.

80. Tennent, *Christianity in Ceylon*, 44; cf. 73–74 n. C.

81. Tennent, *Christianity in Ceylon*, 42–43, 73 n. B.

82. On the Goanese Oratory, founded in 1682, see Simon G. Perera, ed., *The Oratorian Mission in Ceylon: Historical Documents relating to the Life and Labours of the Venerable Father Joseph Vaz, His Companions and Successors* (Colombo: Caxton

Printing Works, 1936); and Perniola, *Dutch Period*, 1:xx, xxi, xxiii ff., 39 n. 1, 385 n. 2; 2:349–350, 385–386.

83. Boxer, "The Problem of the Native Clergy," 101–102.

84. Perniola, *Dutch Period*, 1:38–44.

85. On the remarkable life of Joseph Vaz, see "The Life and Virtues of Father J. Vaz," written by Francisco Vaz about 1722, and translated by Perniola in his *Dutch Period* 1:506–525 (with chronology added, 517–529). For contemporary letters by and about Vaz in chronological order beginning with 1687, see the same volume, 38, and passim. I was unable to consult Simon G. Perera, *Life of the Venerable Joseph Vaz* (Galle, Ceylon, 1953).

86. Tennent, *Christianity in Ceylon*, 51–53. An estimate of 424,000 Christians in 1722 was reported by Valentyn (63). But see below, p. 228, for a more trustworthy estimate in 1730.

87. See Boudens, *The Catholic Church in Ceylon under the Dutch*, 209–212.

88. Pieris, *Ceylon and the Hollanders*, 5–6. Readers of Dutch should check Philippus Baldaeus, *Afgoderye der Oost-Indische heydenen* (The Hague: M. Nijhoff, 1917).

89. Tennent, *Christianity in Ceylon*, 53–54.

90. For the text of the decree granting "liberty of conscience and the free exercise of worship" in all of British Ceylon, see Tennent, *Christianity in Ceylon*, 75–76.

91. Perniola, *Dutch Period*, 2:254 n. 1. Cf. a similar disproportion in membership figures for 1760, in Tennent, *Christianity in Ceylon*, 65 n. 1.

92. Panikkar, *Asia and Western Dominance*, 280, 313ff.

93. David Bosch, "The Biblical Roots of Christian Mission," in J. Phillips and R. Coote, eds., *Toward the Twenty-First Century in Mission* (Maryknoll, N.Y.: Orbis Books, 1992), 176.

94. Joseph M. Pattiasina, "An Observation of the Historical Background of the Moluccan Protestant Church and the Implications for Mission and Congregational Structures" (DMiss diss., Fuller Theological Seminary, 1987), 18.

Chapter 11

Eighteenth-Century India (1708–1792)

Danish Kings, German Pietists, and English Chaplains

Our [English] countrymen managed to work [in India] for the first eighty
years of the seventeenth century without building a church.

— J. W. Kaye, 1859

Amazing grace,
how sweet the sound
that saved a wretch like me...
— John Newton

The First English Chaplains

As with the Dutch in the East Indies, the emergence of English missions
in Asia began with the appointment of chaplains to a trading company.
In the case of the British, this was the East India Company, chartered
by Queen Elizabeth I in 1600. A year earlier in 1599 at the Synod of
Diamper the Portuguese had roughly stamped the imprint of their Latin
Christianity onto the Syrian Christianity of the Saint Thomas Christians
of Kerala. Now with the arrival of the British there came to India a third
form of Christianity, neither Syrian nor Catholic but Protestant.

We have already noted that the great Dutch East Indies Company, the
first to introduce Protestantism to South Asia, was somewhat reluctant to
allow any form of Christian mission to interfere with commercial profit.
Its smaller, but eventually more politically powerful British counterpart
was even more so. From the beginning the Dutch had at least made a
place in their company for a recognized chaplaincy that was expected
to minister not only to the Dutch trading communities but also to carry
the gospel to the natives. The British Company, however, made it clear
that its chaplains' duties were to the foreign community, mercantile and
military. It might allow and sometimes encourage its chaplains to engage
in voluntary service to the Indian communities, as in its early years,
but its first reaction to any outright Christian proclamation was always
cautious.[1]

One reason was the fear of offending the non-Christian population.
After 1640 as the acquisition of landholdings made the Company in effect the Christian rulers over those of other religions, for peace and order
if for no other reason a policy of religious toleration seemed mandatory,

236

and active promotion of the Christian religion might inflame opposition. But on the question of relations with the Roman Catholics, though they officially urged persuasion rather than persecution, they approved reasonable means to encourage the spread of Protestantism.[2] In 1698 they amended their charter just far enough to instruct the chaplains to learn Portuguese in order to teach the Company's slaves and servants about the Christian religion. But as for full-time missionaries, not chaplains, for the most part whether by indifference or on purpose the East India Company opposed and hindered the entrance of missionaries, who, not being under Company control, were considered a nuisance. By the end of the 1700s its policies had turned openly antimissionary.[3]

Thus it was a layman, Captain Best, not an ordained chaplain but an officer in British service, who became concerned about the spiritual welfare of a young Bengali Indian and brought him in 1614 for instruction in the faith to one of the early Anglican chaplains of the Company,[4] a preacher named Patrick Copeland. When the young man asked for baptism, the East India Company, alarmed at such an unexpected and unusual occurrence, advised that the new Christian could not be baptized in India but must be sent all the way to England for approval by the archbishop of Canterbury. That took almost two years but Copeland persevered and accompanied the young man to England. The archbishop approved, and the king himself, James VI of Scotland (James I of England), was pleased to give him the baptismal name of Peter.[5] Curiously, to his baptismal name the young man added the name Papa (or Pope). Nothing much else is known of him, but it seems that in 1616 shortly after his baptism, the Indian youth left with Mr. Copeland on a long missionary journey to colonial Virginia in America.[6] If true, that would make Peter Papa not only the first Indian Anglican, but also the pioneer in Asia of Protestant third-world missionary outreach.

But Protestants were slow in expanding their Christian missions globally. The number of English chaplains in India only very gradually increased. Unlike the Dutch, the East India Company did not begin to acquire ownership of land in India until after 1640, which discouraged permanent residence. Between 1667 and 1700 the Company had not more than eighteen chaplains in its employ.[7] It took more than another hundred years, almost two hundred years after the baptism of Peter Papa, before the British Parliament in 1813, pressed by a young reformer, William Wilberforce, forced the East India Company to abandon its antimissionary policies and grant "licenses of residence to people improperly refused them," in other words, to missionaries.[8]

The Danish-Halle Mission to Tranquebar (1706–1846)

Far from coming as allies of British imperial colonialism, therefore, the first organized Protestant missions in India were forced to seek a home outside British-controlled territory, and this they found in the small Indian trading enclaves established by one of the smallest countries in the West, Denmark. By and large, missionaries were not colonialists. As Lamin Sanneh has observed, colonialists expected the natives to learn English, or Spanish or Portuguese or Danish. The missionaries, on the other hand, chose to learn the languages of Asia, and translated the Bible into the people's vernacular.[9] The colonialists tried to keep the missionaries out, or when they could not control them, deported them. The missionaries just kept coming.

Ecclesiastically, too, the first organized Protestant missionaries came from the fringes, not the hierarchical centers of the West. When Frederick IV of Denmark was urged by his German Lutheran chaplain[10] to send a Danish missionary team to the Danish trading port in southeast India, he looked in vain for a Danish volunteer. The only willing volunteers he could find were from the Pietist periphery of German Lutheranism, for in 1704 organized Lutheranism, caught up in the post-Reformation Protestant reaction against foreign missions which we have described above,[11] was still thundering against the folly of trying to convert savages who had long ago heard the gospel and rejected it. More pressing and nearer home was the threat of the Catholic counterreformation.

By 1705 King Frederick had found his volunteers and sent off to India two young German Lutherans, fiery Bartholomaeus Ziegenbalg (1683– 1719) and his quieter companion, Heinrich Plutschau,[12] both of them former students of August Herman Francke at the university in Halle, which was becoming the center of the Pietist movement's startling missionary march around the world. They landed at Tranquebar in 1706, a date that competes with William Carey's arrival in India in 1792 as marking the beginning of modern Protestant missions.

Though personally dispatched by Denmark's king, the two Pietists found only a very cool welcome in the Danish colony, 150 miles south of Madras in the rice basket of South India and at the heart of the ancient culture of the Tamils. Undeterred the two men set about learning Tamil and within eight months Ziegenbalg was preaching extemporaneous sermons to the native population in its own language. Less than a year had passed before they performed their first baptisms, five slaves who spoke Portuguese, and within thirteen months they had formed and built a church, which they opened with a service in Tamil and Portuguese (not Danish). It was all too much for the Danish governor, who clapped the fiery Ziegenbalg into jail for four months of solitary confinement without benefit of visitors, pen, or paper.[13]

But when he was released, Ziegenbalg worked all the harder. By the end of 1709, the mission had been enlarged by the arrival of three new missionaries, and the Indian Christian community numbered more than 160. Non-Christians crowded the doors and the windows of the church to hear the missionaries preach in Tamil, Portuguese, or Danish.[14] Content with the progress of the mission in Tranquebar, Ziegenbalg resolved to leave the little Danish enclave, only about fifteen miles square, to reach the masses in the interior, despite warnings from his friends that the king of Tanjore did not allow white men in his domain and the people would kill him. His friends were wrong. The people welcomed the "young priest from Tranquebar who can preach in Tamil," as they called him. Though many asked to be baptized, he was slow to do so, requiring Bible study and training in the catechism, sometimes for a full year. Those he did baptize, said other missionaries, would "make the white Christians ashamed" for lack of similar Christian zeal and piety.[15]

In Tranquebar, Ziegebalg's colleague and successor came to the conclusion that the most fruitful field of Christian work for the future would be to begin with the children, win them for Christ and through them influence their parents. Though never abandoning this approach, a difficult experience with the first young boy he baptized led him to modify it. Instead of influencing his parents, the boy fell into degenerate ways as he grew older. This led Grundler to formulate the principle: "A missionary should preach to the heathen, not keep school for their children," for "A Christian school-life will be quickly produced by a Christian home-life."[16]

Ziegenbalg completed his Tamil translation of the New Testament in 1711, and when a printing press was sent from Denmark in 1712 the gospels and Acts were printed first and by 1715 the entire New Testament.[17] By 1716 the missionaries had opened a school to train native teachers. Ziegenbalg died in Tranquebar in 1719, leaving a church that had already been enlarged to accommodate the increase of its Tamil- and Portuguese-speaking Indian Christians from 35 (in 1707) to 428. In the Tamil congregation the ingrained cultural prejudice of members of the castes against the outcastes ("pariahs," as they were called in the colony) forced the missionaries to make concessions, and at Communion not only the men but caste women claimed precedence over even the male "pariahs."[18]

Ziegenbalg's last years had been marred by missionary friction as well. New recruits arrived, "stiff upholders of [Lutheran] orthodoxy" who never learned Tamil, but who immediately criticized the more flexible Pietists from Halle, for "unapostolic" missionary methods such as building churches and schools and their own houses instead of preaching on the road without gold or silver, shoes or staff or bag (as in Matt. 10:7–10). It was a grotesque blend of missionary inexperience and immature Bible interpretation, and it broke the veteran Ziegenbalg's heart. At least one of the newcomers repeated in a yet more radical form the old argument of scholastic seventeenth-century Protestantism that the Gentiles had already heard the gospel from the apostles. In Tranquebar, this faction argued, to be truly apostolic any resumption of a Christian world must start again with the "lost sheep of the house of Israel," the Jews.[19]

More new missionaries landed shortly after Ziegenbalg's death carrying a mandate from mission headquarters in Denmark that the methods of the Pietist pioneers must be abandoned. Ziegenbalg's faithful colleague, Grundler, obeyed in tears, but died within nine months. The new wave of missionaries, after Ziegenbalg and Grundler, were not all as misguided as the above example might suggest. For the most part they were men of talent and good intentions. One of their more commendable efforts was a brave but premature attempt to prohibit caste distinctions within the church. But when the experiment failed to break the cultural habits of a thousand years of social prejudice, in a desperate reaction to calm the uproar that had erupted, the missionaries were forced to swing too far the other way and allow even greater separation of castes than had the pioneers.[20]

But a most encouraging development at least partially offset the temporary missionary failures of the years between 1720 and 1798: the ordination of the first Indian Protestant ministers and catechists. As early as 1709, only three years after his arrival, Ziegenbalg had considered training one of his first converts for the ministry, but abandoned the venture when the candidate proved himself embarrassingly unfit.[21] It was, however, becoming increasingly obvious that as the church grew, the thin supply of foreign ministers would never be adequate to meet the opening opportunities. Besides, Europeans in Tranquebar were limited to the tiny coastal foreign colony, and were not welcome in the surrounding Indian kingdom of Tanjore (Thanjavur). Only the Indian converts could move freely across the border into Indian territory.

From England where Anglicans had early accepted a partial sponsorship of the Danish mission, the archbishop of Canterbury in 1727 urged upon the Danish missionaries the urgency of developing national leadership. "They have easier access to their countrymen and will find better opportunities for uniting them in their cause."[22] The missionaries discussed the advisability of training their catechists (converts employed as teachers in the Christian schools) to preach and administer the sacraments to isolated congregations that were beginning to spring up beyond the range of missionary itineration.[23]

Not until 1728 did the mission board in Denmark, with the king's permission, grant the missionaries power to ordain Lutheran Indian Christians. They at once selected three of the earliest catechists for intensive training, one of whom would be chosen for the ministry. The oldest, Schawrimutto, modestly withdrew himself from consideration in favor of the two younger teachers who were given five years of intensive instruction. Of these two, it was Aaron (1698–1745), born of pagan parents in a merchant caste family, educated under Schawrimutto and baptized in 1718, who was chosen as the first ordinand, in 1733. He had already proved himself as an able schoolmaster and indefatigable country evangelist.[24]

The other, Diogo, born of Roman Catholic parents and received into the Lutheran church in 1713, was not ordained until nine years later, for despite the promising beginning, the mission perceptibly lost its early enthusiasm for an indigenous clergy. Between 1733 and 1800 only six Indians were ordained.[25] The Christian community, meanwhile, had increased from 428 in 1719 to 3,766 in 1739.[26]

As if to compensate for the failure to develop an effective ordained Indian clergy, and without any forethought or preparation on the part of the missionaries, an alternative to missionary outreach by ordained Indians appeared in the unexpected, unplanned appearance in Tranquebar of a remarkable evangelistic-minded Christian layman, Rajanaikan, from across the Tanjore border. Rajanaikan was a low-caste Tamil and a low-ranking officer in the Tanjore army. His family was Roman Catholic. "We loved the holy Xavier very much," he wrote later, but he longed for more information about Jesus than he found in the books made available to him by the Catholics, and was so excited when he found a copy of Ziegenbalg's 1714 translation into Tamil of the first books of the New Testament that he began to copy it laboriously, verse by verse, onto palm leaves. This, in turn, led him to Tranquebar seeking more books, and there in 1728 he left the Tanjore army and joined the Evangelical Lutheran Church.[27]

Rajanaikan's return to Tanjore as a Lutheran catechist provoked one of the earliest confrontations in Asia between Catholics and Protestants on neutral ground, that is, where neither had the advantage of Portuguese, Danish, or Dutch colonial protection. The purple-robed, white-turbaned, Italian Jesuit, Constant Beschi, supervisor of a large Catholic constituency in Madurai and Tanjore numbering about 150,000, and a pioneer in the literary use of the Tamil vernacular,[28] shook with anger at the intrusion of "those swarming Lutherans" whom he saw descending upon the then-independent kingdom of Tanjore like low-caste locusts out of the book of Revelation. A Catholic mob attacked Rajanaikan's house, killing his father and wounding two of his brothers.[29] But the Lutherans kept coming and growing. In the next ten years Rajanaikan had tripled the number of Protestants in Tanjore.[30]

In fact, that pioneering missionary venture across the border into Indian territory was followed up by no "poor outcast Pariah" like the faithful Rajanaikan (whom not even the missionaries were able to ordain because of local caste prejudice).[31] Rajanaikan's most successful successor was a man who, with Ziegenbalg, ranks as the greatest of the German Pietist missionaries in India, trusted friend of rajahs and outcasts alike, "the brightest star in the constellation of the [Tranquebar mission],"[32] Christian Friedrich Schwartz (1726–1798). Schwartz reached Tranquebar in 1750 and spent the next half century in India until his death in

1798. Within four months of his arrival he was preaching in Tamil; in his second year there he baptized four hundred converts whom he had been instructing in the faith.

After fifteen years in Tranquebar Schwartz moved seventy-five miles east to Trichinopoly, a center of rising British power in India but the seat of a Muslim Nawab. For ministry to Muslims he learned not only Hindustani but also Persian, and as the Danish mission faltered for lack of home support, he was adopted by the British Society for the Propagation of Christian Knowledge. This gave the Tranquebar mission, the earliest of organized Protestant missions in Asia, a remarkable example of tripartite missionary cooperation. It was royal Danish in origin and control, largely German Pietist in personnel, with a mixture of independent German and English financial support. Perhaps the most notable ecumenical feature about it was that the Anglicans were willing to recognize Lutheran ordination and did not insist upon the reordination of Lutheran missionaries in their churches and under their support.[33]

The last twenty years of Schwartz's life (1778–1798) were spent back in Tanjore, where his honesty, good judgment, and his compassion for the poor and hungry, so impressed both the Hindu court and the English, who since the battle of Plassey in 1757 were fast becoming the real rulers of most of India, that the missionary was appointed to the Royal Advisory Council. As the rajah of Tanjore, Tulsi, lay dying, he tried to appoint Schwartz as guardian of his ten-year-old heir. "Padre," he said, "I trust you because you do not care for money." Schwartz gracefully declined, but eleven years later, in 1798, when Schwartz himself died, the young Hindu rajah ordered a marble monument erected to the memory of the missionary whom everyone trusted, and twenty-eight hundred members of the church he had founded mourned at his funeral.[34] The total number of Lutherans in Tranquebar and Tanjore by then had risen to close to twenty thousand. Of the fifty-seven missionaries who had served in the Danish mission between 1706 and 1846 when the mission was disbanded, forty-two had died in India, only fifteen returned to Europe.[35]

"Hidden Seed"[36]: The Moravians in India (1760–1803)

A second early expansion of eighteenth-century Protestant missionary outreach, after the Danish-Halle mission, was the worldwide explosion of Moravian missions. It began in 1732 and leaped with amazing speed across the seas. Like the Danish-Halle mission, the Moravians had their roots in German Pietism but found their ecclesiastical and missionary home outside organized Lutheranism in a movement of spiritual awakening in Saxony under Count von Zinzendorf. Calling themselves the Church of the United Brethren (*Unitas Fratrum*), they came to be better known as the Moravian Brethren.

Moravians have always tried to keep their priorities straight. Bishop John Amos Comenius (1592–1670), though he preferred educational reform to war, is said to have turned down an offer of the presidency of Harvard to lead his Brethren's Church through much of the tumultuous years of the Thirty Years Wars in Europe.[37] And their eighteenth-century leader, the pious nobleman Nicholas von Zinzendorf, taught them that to be born again was better than to be born into the nobility, and that a Christian missionary was a far higher calling than to be a count.

Moravian mission motivation was more biblical than systematically theological, but it was thoroughly centered in Christ as the only savior, and in the Holy Spirit, who converts, for as their missionaries were reminded, conversion is of God, not of human agents.[38] Moravian missions spread quickly into the Caribbean, Greenland, North America, South America, and as far south as South Africa, with enormous zeal and utter indifference to danger and hardship. "Within twenty years of the commencement of their mission," one historian observed, "the Moravian Brethren had started more missions than Anglicans and Protestants had started during the two preceding centuries."[39] But their first venture into Asia was a failure.

At Tranquebar, where the first group of fourteen Moravians landed in 1760, it might have been expected that their fellow German Pietists would welcome them, since the Danish king had offered them a base for work in the Nicobar Islands not far away, but such was not the case. Pietism was already waning in Europe under growing Protestant denominational rigidities, and the Danish mission treated the sectarians more as intruders than allies. Of all the leaders, missionary and Indian, in the Tranquebar church, the enthusiastic, unordained Tamil evangelist, Rajanaikan, found in the Moravians a kindred zeal and worked with them most closely. At times the Moravian missionaries in Tranquebar outnumbered the better-entrenched Danish mission there three to one.[40]

As in Germany, the Moravians did not attempt to plant new churches. Unobtrusively they contented themselves with the formation of small cells within the existing churches (*ecclesiola in ecclesiae*), seeking to enrich the spiritual life of the congregations through Bible study, prayer, and evangelism.

The goal that had brought them to India was to attempt a pioneering mission beyond Tranquebar to the unreached Nicobar Islands in the Bay of Bengal, but it foundered when eleven out of the twenty-four missionaries sent there died within twenty years and the surviving thirteen died soon after leaving the islands. They were more successful in establishing a mission in the northern Danish trading colony at Serampore, near Calcutta, in 1777 which lasted fifteen years, and produced translations of some devotional books and parts of the Bible into Bengali. But it too was abandoned on the very eve of William Carey's arrival in India in 1792 for lack of cooperation by the authorities.[41]

Discouraged by deaths and illnesses in their own community, and the denominational jealousy of the Lutherans, the last two missionaries of this "community of the lamb" departed quietly in 1803. They left no monument to themselves. Carey found little trace left of their work in Serampore.[42] It was enough for them that for forty-three years of sacrificial, uncomplaining service, they had themselves become "hidden seed" for an awakening in India that was soon to come.

The English "Evangelical Chaplains"

We have noted the indifference — an indifference that sometimes turned into hostility — on the part of the British East India Company toward Christian evangelism in its territories. In every way, for the first 150 years of the British trading company (1608–1757), India still seemed inhospitable soil for the Anglican Church in particular and for Protestants in general. The climate itself was demoralizing. In one year, a historian noted, "out of twelve hundred Europeans [in Calcutta, today Kolkata] there were four hundred funerals."[43] Despite the presence of chaplains, and perhaps because a few proved less than Christian, governors conspicuously avoided the church, and "irreligion and immorality" were rampant in the trading posts.[44] "It was of little use," wrote one observer, "to think of christianizing the people, until the English in India had begun in some measure to christianize themselves."[45] Interdenominational rivalry between Anglicans and Scots Presbyterians and Roman Catholics further poisoned the public reputation of the Christian faith. A Captain Hamilton reported that in Calcutta "all religions except the Presbyterian were tolerated."[46]

The pivotal year that turned the trading company into an empire, and began to improve the moral and religious situation in the trading posts, as well as expand the company's economic and military power throughout the subcontinent, was 1757, the year of Robert Clive's decisive victory over the French at Plassey. Within eight years this man who had begun as a lowly clerk in India combined in his own person both mercantile and political power over most of northeast (today more commonly called "eastern") India as the immensely rich executive officer of the Company there, and at the same time as the victorious British governor of Bengal, Bihar, and Orissa. He has been described as the founder of the empire of British India, and through his reorganization of the British East India Company he paved the way for the revitalization not only of the English chaplaincies but of Protestantism throughout India.

Under Clive, and his successor Hastings, both of whom combined outstanding achievements with significant character flaws, Calcutta replaced Tranquebar as the center of Protestant missionary expansion, with the Anglican Society for the Propagation of the Gospel cooperating in

partial support of missionaries from the Danish mission working in English zones of political and trade interest in India.[47] Within a year of
Clive's victory at Plassey, a Swedish Pietist, John Zachary Kiernander
(1710–1798), with two Indian assistants, was sent north from Tranquebar to Calcutta under this arrangement. They were warmly welcomed by
Clive himself. The city had lost its last two English chaplains in the massacre of the "Black Hole of Calcutta" two years earlier and Clive, eager
to organize and improve the province, saw advantages in the services of
Christian chaplains, two of whom had also arrived, and missionaries.[48]
Kiernander, a Swede trained at Halle and sent to India by the Anglican
Society for the Propagation of Christian Knowledge (SPCK), was more
missionary than chaplain. He began to convert Indian Catholic priests
as energetically as non-Christians, and reached out beyond the military
and mercantile elite in a ministry to Eurasians and Bengali, establishing
schools which included instruction in the Christian faith in the regular
curriculum. Then, having married a wealthy widow, and lamenting the
destruction of the old church and the failure of the both the Company
or the Anglicans to replace it, he built a new church at his own expense
on his own property, but designated it to the care of the SPCK. In good
Pietist fashion he called it "The House of Prayer."[49] Later it was entrusted
to the "evangelical chaplains" who being English preferred to call it the
"Old Mission Church." In the nineteenth century it became a center for
the work of the Church Missionary Society, founded in 1799, and has
been described as one of the great bastions of evangelicalism in India.[50]

But it was neither a Swedish Pietist, nor the English governors of the
Company nor Anglican bishops who did more to ignite a missionary
spirit among the India chaplains than a first-class athlete and uncom-
monly spiritual Anglican priest at Trinity Church, Cambridge, named
Charles Simeon (1759–1836). Simeon never set foot in India but was turning the religious atmosphere of that old university town upside down.
His biographer wrote that "no one . . . could be in the company of Simeon
long without having his attention drawn to India."[51]

It was his influence in large measure that sent out all three of the
best known "evangelical chaplains," as they have been called, David
Brown, Claudius Buchanan, and Henry Martyn.[52] They were the cutting
edge of a new breed of chaplains, spiritually warmed by the Wesleyan
revivals but remaining loyal ecclesiastically to the Anglican establishment, adding to their official duties of religious service to the British
communities, the fire and breadth of a missionary commitment to the
whole Indian nation.

The work of the latter two of this trio, Buchanan and Martyn, belong
almost entirely to the next century, the nineteenth. In the eighteenth
century, it was the first of the new chaplains, David Brown (1762–1812),
whose twenty-five years in Calcutta from 1787 to 1812 most stirred British India at the turn of the century. The sincerity and fervor of his

preaching in the Old Mission Church in Calcutta impressed both the English governor general in Bengal and his younger brother, Arthur Wellesley, then in the British India army but who will always be better known by the title he won later at Waterloo, the Duke of Wellington. At the other end of the social scale Brown preached to the poor, administered the army's school for orphans and opened a school for young Hindus. He was a chaplain with a missionary heart, calling repeatedly for mission beyond the Euro-centered chaplaincies. His letters home to England, to Charles Simeon and John Newton, the former slave-ship master who wrote "Amazing Grace," led to the formation of the great Church Missionary Society, which became the evangelical arm of worldwide Anglican missions.[53]

In 1800 Brown was appointed provost of the government's new College of Fort William in Calcutta, which he gladly accepted as his chance to reach the ruling Indian upper classes in Calcutta with a knowledge of the Christian faith. But it was a simple act of kindness to a new missionary who had come to Calcutta without experience or much in the way of organized support that may have been Brown's most significant contribution to the history of Christian missions. After a cool first encounter, he welcomed and found a place as a full professor at his new college for a Particular Baptist adrift in Anglican colonial territory, William Carey.[54]

All the above eighteenth-century Protestant pioneers in India — the Danish missioners, the German Pietists, the Moravians and the English chaplains, and the even earlier Dutch chaplains — are worthy of remembrance and admiration. They were the Protestant pioneers. However, from a different perspective in history they appear more as forerunners than world changers. In a sense they were the ones, too easily now forgotten, who raised the curtain for a whole new epoch of world Christian expansion that began — however difficult it may be to define just what was new about it — with the arrival of that singular latecomer to India in 1792, William Carey. That story must be reserved for another chapter and a new century, the nineteenth.

NOTES

1. The first suggestion for a more evangelistic approach came from the non-conformist Richard Baxter, who only asked for permission to send the chaplains Arabic translations of Grotius's *On the Truth of the Christian Religion* for distribution to non-Christians. The Company directors found diplomatic reasons to evade the offer. Frank D. Penny, *The Church in Madras, Being the History of the Ecclesiastical and Missionary Action of the East India Company in the Presidency of Madras in the Seventeenth and Eighteenth Centuries*, 3 vols. (London: Smith, Elder, 1904–1922), 1:35–36.

2. Penny, *The Church in Madras*, 1:71–72.

3. Sen K. P. Gupta, *The Christian Missionaries in Bengal, 1793–1833* (Calcutta: Firma K. L. Mukhopadhyay, 1971), 14–21; Penny, *The Church in Madras*, 1:95–98, 118–124, 496–499; Latourette, *A History of the Expansion of Christianity*, 3:177.

4. The earliest chaplains, from 1609 to 1614, were ordained and licensed preachers but not commissioned by the church and were employed by the Company usually only for one voyage of about three years. The first residential chaplain of the British East India Company was the Rev. William Leske, who reached Surat in 1614, stayed three years, and was abruptly removed for "unworthy conduct." See Penny, *The Church in Madras*, 1:3–10; Eyre Chatterton, *A History of the Church of England in India since the Early Days of the East India Company* (London: SPCK, 1924), 13.

5. Penny, *The Church in Madras*, 1:14–16; Chatterton, *A History of the Church of England in India*, 15–16; M. E. Gibbs, *The Anglican Church in India. 1600–1970* (Delhi: Indian Society for Promoting Christian Knowledge, 1972), 4.

6. Penny: *The Church in Madras*, 1: 14–16; Gibbs, *The Anglican Church in India*, 4. Peter Papa (or Pope) seems to have been in British employ in the English trading post at Masulipatam, north of Madras. One of the purposes of Copeland's voyage was to raise funds for a school and mission in Virginia, and members of the Company of Virginia attended Peter's baptism.

7. John William Kaye, *Christianity in India: An Historical Narrative* (London: Smith, Elder, 1859), 53; Robinson, *History of Christian Missions*, 79. For details see Chatterton, *A History of the Church of England in India*, 1–65. Chaplains were introduced in Surat (ca. 1614?), Madras (1647), and Calcutta (1678). The first permanent Anglican churches were built and consecrated in Madras (1680), Calcutta (1709), and Bombay (1718). Chatterton, *A History of the Church of England in India*, 28, 51–52, 70.

8. *Cambridge History of India*, 5:313; Richter, *A History of Missions in India*, 47–48. The Danes, too, like the English had chaplains in Tranquebar before 1706, but "they seem to have done nothing to spread the Christian faith outside the Danes and Germans" there, despite the title, "Danish Apostle of India," posthumously given to one of them, Jacob Worm, who died in 1691. Latourette, *A History of the Expansion of Christianity*, 3:278.

9. See Lamin Sanneh, *Translating the Message: The Missionary Impact on Culture* (Maryknoll, N.Y.: Orbis Books, 1989).

10. On the role of the chaplain, Dr. Lütkens, see A. H. Oussoren, *William Carey, Especially His Missionary Principles* (Leiden: Sijthoff's Uitgeversmaatschappij, 1945), 219ff.

11. Chaps. 10–11.

12. On these two pioneers, see W. Germann, *Ziegenbalg und Plutschau: Die Grundungsjahre der Trankebarschen Mission*, 2 parts (Erlangen: Andreas Deichert, 1868). A more recent collection of Ziegenbalg's hitherto unpublished letters confirms his very close connection with the Halle Pietist movement. Arno Lehmann, *Alte Briefe aus Indien: Unveroffentlichte Briefe von Bartolomaus Ziegenbalg 1706–1719* (Berlin: Evangelische Verlagsanstalt, 1957).

13. J. Ferd. Fenger, *History of the Tranquebar Mission*, an English translation of a German translation from the Danish original (Tranquebar, India: Evangelical Lutheran Mission Press, 1863), 21–43; Sherring, *The History of Protestant Missions in India*, 2; W. K. Lowther Clarke, *A History of the S.P.C.K.* (London: SPCK, 1959),

60–61. Fenger's *History of the Tranquebar Mission*, though published in 1863, was "worked out from the original [Danish]" sources.

14. Fenger, *History of the Tranquebar Mission*, 36–37, 48ff. Two years earlier there had been only thirty-five Indian Christians in the church.

15. Fenger, *History of the Tranquebar Mission*, 53–77.

16. Fenger, *History of the Tranquebar Mission*, 79.

17. Fenger, *History of the Tranquebar Mission*, 81–85. The "first printed matter ever printed in Tamil, the Apostles Creed," had already been produced, about 1713.

18. Richter, *A History of Missions in India*, 108. The term now most commonly used for "outcastes" is *dalit*.

19. As in Matt. 10:5ff. Presumably both religious Jews and the "lost sheep" of the "new Israel," the church — in other words, not pagans but the unbelievers within Christendom. This was the position of J. G. Bovingh, who reached Tranquebar the year Ziegenbalg died. Fenger, *History of the Tranquebar Mission*, 47–48, 115ff., 120–121. See also Richter, *A History of Missions in India*, 109–110.

20. Richter, *A History of Missions in India*, 110–111; Gibbs, *The Anglican Church in India*, 21–22.

21. Kanabadi Wathier, baptized as Frederick Christian in 1709, was a brilliant but unstable teacher and poet, who drifted first into the Roman Catholic Church to the dismay of the Protestants, then embarrassed the Catholics by returning to his pagan roots and was last heard of "as an idol-priest at a temple" near Cuddalore. Fenger, *History of the Tranquebar Mission*, 153–157.

22. Fenger, *History of the Tranquebar Mission*, 157–158.

23. Fenger, *History of the Tranquebar Mission*, 153–158.

24. On Aaron, see Fenger, *History of the Tranquebar Mission*, 162–173; P. J. Thomas, *100 Indian Witnesses to Jesus Christ* (Bombay: Bombay Tract and Book Society, 1974), 8–9; and Hambye, *Eighteenth Century*, 3:122, 128. Aaron was not a *dalit*, but of a *sudra* or "classified" caste.

25. Fenger, *History of the Tranquebar Mission*, 282–285, 323–324. The last one ordained before the end of the century was Sattianaden, ordained by C. F. Schwartz with his colleagues in 1790.

26. Richter, *A History of Missions in India*, 112. The total was composed of 299 "Portuguese" Indians, 1,021 Tamils, and 2,446 converts across the border in the Tanjore countryside.

27. See Fenger's account, *History of the Tranquebar Mission*, 174ff.

28. Apart from his militant anti-Protestant bias, Constantius Beschi was an outstanding missionary leader. He has been called "the father of Tamil prose," and produced the first grammar of spoken Tamil (see Ka Naa Subramanyam, *The Catholic Community in India* [Madras: Macmillan, 1970], ix).

29. On Beschi see Fenger, *History of the Tranquebar Mission*, 185–186; for a Catholic viewpoint, see Delacroix, *Histoire universelle des missions catholiques*, 2:211–212.

30. Neill, *A History of Christianity in India*, 1:43, citing A. Lehmann, *It Began in Tranquebar: The Story of the Tranquebar Mission* (Madras: Christian Literature Society, 1956), 140. Another early influential Indian layman in the Tranquebar area was Daniel Christian Pillae (b. 1770) who became a sub-judge in the Danish colonial government and a prolific translator of devotional Christian literature (P. J. Thomas, *100 Indian Witnesses*, 9–10).

31. Fenger, *History of the Tranquebar Mission*, 186.

32. Richter, *A History of Missions in India*, 116. On Schwartz see M. Justus, "Schwartz: A Missionary in Politics, 1750–1798," in *ICHR* 26, no. 1 (June 1992): 36–49.

33. Clarke, *A History of the S.P.C.K.*, 63–64, 68–72. Ever since 1731 Henry Newman, secretary of the S.P.C.K., had been urging cooperation between the Society and the Danish Mission in Tranquebar. In 1767 the Mission College in Copenhagen released Schwartz to the S.P.C.K.

34. Fenger, *History of the Tranquebar Mission*, 214–219, 22–23; Richter, *A History of Missions in India*, 120–123.

35. Richter, *A History of the Missions in India*, 127, citing James Hough, *The History of Christianity in India from the Commencement of the Christian Era*, vol. 3 (London: R. B. Seeley and W. Burnside, 1839–1860). In its first thirty years in India (1706–1736) the Danish mission had 3,517 converts; in its second thirty years (1736–1766) it reported 9,680 more. By 1800, the total number of converts over the ninety-four-year period since the beginning of the mission is estimated at between 40,000 and 50,000. Richter, *A History of the Missions in India*, 127, citing Hough, *History of Christianity in India*, vol. 3; and Sherring, *History of Protestantism in India, 1706–1882*, 27, 49–50. But the saddest statistical commentary of all on the later decline of the mission is that by 1850, four years after the dissolution of the mission, only 717 Christians remained in Tranquebar, and another 3,500 in the mission's surrounding Tamil centers from Tanjore to Madras (Sherring, *History of Protestantism in India, 1706–1882*, 51).

36. "The Hidden Seed" was the name the Moravians, spiritual heirs of John Huss, took for themselves in the early days of the persecutions of Protestants in the Hapsburg Austrian empire. See Adolf Vacovsky, "History of the 'hidden seed' (1620–1722)," in *Unitas Fratrum*, ed. M. P. Buijtenen et al. (Utrecht, the Netherlands: Riksarchief in Utrecht, 1975), 35–54.

37. See "The Moravian Church: Its History, Faith and Ministry" (Bethlehem, Pa.: Moravian Church in America, 1978), pamphlet.

38. See David Nii Anum Kpobi, *Mission in Chains: The Life, Theology and Ministry of the Ex-slave Jacobus E. J. Capitein, 1717–1747* (Zoetermeer, Netherlands: Uitgeverij Boekcentrum, 1993), 89–90.

39. Robinson, *History of Christian Missions*, 49–50.

40. Between 1760 and 1785 seventy Moravian missionaries were sent to Tranquebar. The total for the Danish mission from 1706 to 1813 was only fifty-four (Richter, *A History of Missions in India*, 125; Fenger, *History of the Tranquebar Mission*, 312–320).

41. Cf. Fenger, *History of the Tranquebar Mission*, 265–270, who writes from the perspective of the Danish mission, with Richter, *A History of Missions in India*, 124–125, 131, who treats the Moravians with appreciation.

42. Richter, *A History of Missions in India*, 131.

43. Chatterton, *A History of the Church of England in India*, 73.

44. Kaye, *Christianity in India*, 41–49, 110–112, 120–122. Chatterton, *A History of the Church of England in India*, 75.

45. Kaye, *Christianity in India*, 99.

46. Kaye, *Christianity in India*, 89 (apparently citing from Capt. Alexander Hamilton, *Journeys in the East Indies from 1688 to 1723*, which was not available to me).

47. Clarke, *History of the S.P.C.K.*, 61ff. Moravian missionaries were supported most notably in Cuddalore, Madras, and Calcutta in the early years.

48. Hough, *The History of Christianity in India*, 2:8ff. Two new chaplains, recently arrived, not only joined in the welcome to Kiernander but soon were so pleased with his expanding work that they asked the SPCK to send more missionaries. None being available the Society suggested he look to Tranquebar and the Moravians for reinforcements. The first missionary actually sent out by the Society was Abraham T. Clarke, in 1789. He was the first English clergyman missionary to India, as distinct from the chaplains of the Company (Hough, *History of Christianity in India*, 42).

49. On Kiernander's Calcutta ministry, see Hough, *Christianity in India*, 2:8– 41; 62–65; and Chatterton, *History*, 79–83. In eight years (1759 to 1766) he reported 189 converts (two-thirds from Roman Catholicism, including a number of priests), and from 1767 to 1776, 495 converts (pp. 17, 34). He also translated the catechism and portions of the Book of Common Prayer into Bengali (Hough, *History of Christianity in India*, 2:21).

50. Chatterton, *History of the Church of England in India*, 79–82. Kiernander, though sent by the Danish mission, had been supported in his work in the south outside Tranquebar by the Anglican Society for the Propagation of Christian Knowledge. For more on this early example of Protestant missionary ecumenicity between Danish Lutheranism, German Pietism, and the Anglicans, see Clarke, *A History of the S.P.C.K.*, 59–72.

51. Hugh Evan Hopkins, *Charles Simeon of Cambridge* (Grand Rapids, Mich.: William B. Eerdmans, 1977), 111.

52. Kaye, *Christianity in India*, 126.

53. David Brown has been called "the true father" of the Anglican Church Missionary Society, for it was his *Proposal for Establishing a Protestant Mission in Bengal and Bihar* in 1787 that was one of the triggers that produced the CMS in 1799. The same "Proposal" was a strong advocate for translating the Scriptures into the various languages of the peoples of Asia and sending missionaries to them (Chatterton, *History of the Church of England in India*, 111–113; and Charles Simeon, *Memorial Sketches of the Rev. David Brown, with a Selection of His Sermons Preached at Calcutta* [London: T. Cadell & W. Davies, 1816], xiii and passim).

54. On the ups and downs of Carey's relationship with Brown, see *The Journals and Letters of William Carey*, ed. Terry G. Carter (Macon, Ga.: Smyth & Helwys, 2000), 12, 82, 121, 139, 151, 177–178, 205–206, 211.

"The Great Century" (1784–1860)

SECTION ONE
PROTESTANTS AND CATHOLICS
IN COMPETITION

Chapter 12

A Fresh Start in India (1792–1860)

Carey and the Protestants

> If you want the Kingdom speeded, go out and speed it yourselves: only obedience rationalizes prayer: only missions can redeem your intercessions from insincerity.
> — William Carey

Carey: The Man and the Challenge

In the history of the global expansion of Protestant Christianity, the nineteenth century cannot properly be boxed into the one hundred years between 1800 and 1900. In a larger sense, it began in 1792. That was the year when a part-time shoemaker, part-time teacher, and weekend Baptist preacher named William Carey (1761–1834)[1] aroused the Protestants of Europe and North America out of some 250 years of preoccupation with their own problems and reminded them that there was a whole world out there that needed more than reformation. It needed compassion, evangelism, and conversion.

Some call him the "father of the modern missionary movement,"[2] but Carey would not have claimed the title. He must have known of John Calvin's attempt to send an evangelical mission to Brazil in 1555. He was aware and sometimes critical of the chaplains of the Dutch East India Company in the Indonesian archipelago in the 1660s. He knew of the first Lutherans sent to India in 1706, and was so much impressed by the Moravian missions in the West Indies and North America after 1732 that he borrowed from their pattern to form his own, though for lack of success and support they had abandoned their work in Serampore only

253

a year before Carey arrived.[3] He was also preceded in India by his own countrymen, the chaplains of the British East India Company.[4]

But for enduring global missionary impact, no rapid sequence of events in the history of Protestant missions can match what was accomplished in only thirteen months between May 1792 and June 1793. In that one year four incidents of great consequence, all involving William Carey, changed the history of modern missions: the publication of a book, the preaching of a sermon, the organization of a society, and the sending of a missionary.

It began with the publication of the book, Carey's *Enquiry*, a slim volume with a long title which forthrightly gets to the root of the matter: *An Enquiry into the Obligation of Christians to Use Means for the Conversion of the Heathens, in which the Religious State of the Different Nations of the World, the Success of Former Undertakings, and the Practicability of Further Undertakings Are Considered.*[5] In it Carey outlined the urgent necessity of finding a purpose and a strategy to reach out beyond the Western "Christendom" of his day in mission to the whole world. Its statistics on the numbers and location of Christians around the world at the end of the eighteenth century mark it as the first comprehensive statistical handbook of world missions ever compiled. Considering the state of demographic knowledge in Europe at that time, it is remarkable how accurate his estimates were. He told his fellow Christians that although Christ had commanded his church to take the gospel into all the world, and disciple all nations, in fact less than one-quarter of the people of the world had been reached with the gospel, 174 million Christians out of a world population of 731 million. Moreover, to the shame of Christendom, nearly all of those who had been reached were bottled up on one continent, Europe, with a marginal spillover into North America of about 3.5 million Christians in "the States of America." The Christians of the West, he warned, were doing very little to reach the other continents except for colonial Catholics in Latin America. As for Asia, in a total population of about 360 million, only two-tenths of 1 percent (about a hundred thousand) were Christians, ninety thousand of them Catholics in the Philippines.[6] Practical-minded preacher that he was, Carey followed up the cold statistics of the book with a passionate sermon to reach not just the minds of his fellow ministers, but their hearts as well. Many of them shared the common misapprehensions of the day that either the whole world had already been reached with the gospel by the apostles, or that the completion of the task must be left to the work of God. Carey belonged to a small band of nonconformist, extremely Calvinist Baptist churches on the fringe of Christian England. They took predestination even farther than Calvin.[7] At an earlier meeting of his area's Baptist ministers, when he proposed a debate on the subject of his forthcoming book — that is, the need for a direct global missionary response to reach non-Christians for Christ in the present age — it is said that one of the older ministers rebuked him, "Young man, sit down ... When God pleases to convert the heathen, He'll do it without consulting you or me."[8]

But Carey persisted; he was Calvinist but not hyper-Calvinist.[9] The turning point was a sermon he preached to the Baptist association of ministers at Nottingham, May 31, 1792. He took his text from Isaiah 54:2–3, and hammered home two simple points: begin with faith, but let faith be followed with action. "Expect great things from God"; and "Attempt great things for God." It was one of the most influential sermons ever preached. So stirred were the ministers that before they adjourned they had achieved the impossible; the little group of prickly, often divided, non-confirming Particular Baptists agreed to unite in the formation of a missionary society. Five months later it was done. They called it "The Particular Baptist Society for Propagating the Gospel among the Heathens."[10] Only fourteen of England's Baptist ministers were in its founding, and its total financial assets at the time added up to a promised pledge of only 13 pounds, 2 shillings, and 6 pence.[11]

But all this was mere promise and theory until June 1793 when Carey, rather than stay in England as founding president of a missionary society, sailed instead to India as a missionary. His father was incredulous. "Is William mad?" he said. His wife was equally disturbed. Poor Dorothy Carey, uncomfortably illiterate, burdened with the care of four children all under nine including a three-week-old baby, refused to go.[12] The man who had suggested India in the first place, John Thomas, a ship's surgeon who had spent some years in India as a zealous but improvident evangelist, almost scuttled the whole project by going bankrupt.[13] But Dorothy Carey changed her mind on condition that her sister go with her,[14] Thomas talked his way out of debt, and the little party set sail for India. Before he left, Carey entered into a covenant with his four closest friends and partners. As they later recalled it, it was as if Carey was about to enter a deep mine on a great venture, and was saying to the four who remained, "I will go down, if you will hold the rope."[15]

Carey in India: Opposition and Trials

The voyage to India took five tedious months,[16] but its difficulties and hardships were as nothing compared to the next seven tempestuous, unstable years in steamy, stormy Bengal. "The foundations of the mission work were laid in tears and anguish," as a later missionary wrote.[17] The first shocking disappointment was the meeting with Ram Basu, Mr. Thomas's teacher and early convert, only to discover that the man had again succumbed to temptation and fallen from grace.[18] A second shock was the refusal of the British colonial government to grant residence permits to the missionaries. In real history, contrary to much modern rhetoric, Christian mission and Western colonialism, though the relationship between the two was mixed, were as often as not opponents rather than collaborators.[19] In India the missions followed the empire, but they were fought by the empire's founders, the British East India Company. Such was the case in Calcutta as the party stepped ashore. The Careys, good Britishers though they were, were not welcome.[20] Driven out of Calcutta, and left almost penniless without permanent home, they found refuge first in a Catholic Portuguese settlement, and only when kind indigo planters sympathetically offered to employ the impoverished Carey as an assistant on their isolated plantations were they allowed temporary residence in British territory.

Those first years on a colonial plantation gave Carey firsthand contact with the exploited peasant laborers of the indigo trade and an enduring sympathy for India's rural poor that never left him. The experience laid the foundation for missionary protests that erupted a half-century later in the Indigo Question controversy.[21] Not until 1800 did the Careys find an abiding home and then not with their fellow Britishers, but in the little Danish colony at Serampore fifteen miles up the Hoogly River from Calcutta.

Most painful of all in those dark years of beginnings was the deterioration of Mrs. Carey's mental health. His dear wife, Dorothy, who only with great reluctance had left England, was never able to adjust to India and the rigors of missionary life. Three years after their arrival she began to lapse into severe mental and emotional instability. She embarrassed the mission and made a public shame of herself by repeatedly denouncing her bewildered husband as a "whoremonger," all without cause as everyone knew. Twice she even threatened his life.[22] "You must endeavor to consider it a disease," his warmhearted medical colleague, John Thomas wrote him to comfort him,[23] but Carey confided in his *Journal,* "This is . . . the Valley of the Shadow of Death."[24]

Serampore: The Trio and the Covenant

The arrival of four more missionaries in 1799 abruptly changed the future of the Baptist mission. When the English continued to prohibit residence to missionaries in Calcutta, the Baptist group moved upriver to the Danish colony of Serampore and, joined there by Carey, began to organize themselves for mission in ways that set a Protestant pattern for Christian expansion in Asia for the next hundred years.[25] Voluntary, independent, self-supporting "faith missions" became the dominant form of Protestant mission organization for much of what Latourette calls "the great century" of missions, the nineteenth.[26]

Carey had already outlined a tentative form of organization in 1796: a communal, self-supporting missionary settlement, living in "little straw houses" in subsistence poverty, and holding all things in common.[27] When this proved to be too ascetic and utopian an experiment for families with children as the community grew, in 1805 they revised it in the form by which it became famous, the Serampore Covenant.[28] The emphasis on subsistence communal living was retained but modified, and the emphasis shifted from *how* the missionaries lived to *what* they lived to accomplish and how their evangelistic goals might best be reached. The covenant's basic missionary principles are outlined in ten significant points:

1. The human soul is of inestimable value and is in mortal danger of eternal punishment. But Christ can and will save.

2. We must gain all the knowledge we can of the Indian mind and of the Indian religions.

3. We must not offend Indian sensibilities by vaunting our English ways and attacking theirs.

4. We must "watch [for] all opportunities of doing good," as in preaching, itinerating and talking to all who will listen.

5. The "great subject of our preaching" must be "Christ the Crucified."

6. We must do everything necessary to win the confidence of the people.

7. We must remember the importance of native leaders and building up the Christian lives of converts. We must value the work of female colleagues in their important work with women.

8. In all possible ways we must promote the development of Indian leadership and the formation of Indian churches led by Indian pastors.

9. We must labor with all our might in forwarding translations of the sacred scriptures in the language of Hindustan.

10. To be fit for these "unutterable important labors," we must be "instant in prayer and the cultivation of personal religion."[29]

These words they resolved to read publicly in all their stations three times a year to remind themselves that their highest priority must always be the salvation of those to whom they were sent, by the preaching of the Word, and that any temptation to personal worldly gain must be scrupulously avoided. Later, when Carey's fame as translator and scholar was bringing him what seemed to be the princely sum, first of 750, then 1,500, then 1,800 pounds a year as a professor in the government college, he faithfully kept only 50 pounds of it for himself, plus a small sum for proper clothes for college and government occasions, and turned over all the rest to the mission.[30]

Despite the emphasis on communal living, Carey was clearly the leader in the little missionary community, but not so much so as to obscure the fact that its strength derived from teamwork, not dictatorship. Eventually the mission was divided into six stations, but leadership focused on what came to be called the "Serampore Trio": Carey the pioneer and spokesman, Joshua Marshman (1768–1837) the schoolteacher, and William Ward the preacher, printer, and "radical reformer" turned practical administrator.[31] Carey was no dictator. He did not consider himself the most effective evangelist of the three. "In point of zeal," he once said with characteristic honesty, "[Marshman] is Luther, I am Erasmus."[32] Marshman was also the theologian. His defense of Christian orthodoxy in the 1820s against Ram Mohun Roy's brilliant but flawed critique of the doctrine of the deity of Jesus Christ was the first extensive intellectual debate between a Protestant missionary and a first-rate Indian mind. Theologians still argue which man won. Marshman's exegesis is at times questionable, but Roy, whom M. M. Thomas aptly describes as a "Protestant Hindu" not a Protestant Indian, slips into heresy when he argues for a dependent Jesus, neither eternally preexistent nor an equal in the trinity to God the Creator.[33]

In some respects the Serampore Trio was more like a quartet, with sturdy, cheerful Hannah Marshman, Marshman's wife, the "first woman missionary in India,"[34] who for forty-six years of a very happy marriage was "the equal of the three missionaries" of the trio. She was their aid and support "in the common home, in the schools, in the congregation, in the Native Christian families, and even . . . in purely Hindoo circles."[35] But the leader was Carey.

The First Converts

For the first seven years Carey not only had no abiding home, he had no Hindu converts.[36] His teacher, Ram Basu, of whom he and Dr. Thomas had once had great hopes, failed not once but many times and was never baptized. The first Hindu catechumen, Fakeer (or Fakira), was another disappointment. He had been working for a year in Thomas's sugar factory, listening to the preaching, when late in 1800 he asked for public baptism. His decision brought the mission to its feet singing the doxology. The baptism was arranged for the following Sunday, and he left, he said, to bring back his daughter in the country for the ceremony, but never returned. Carey feared he had deserted the faith, perhaps under great family pressure.[37]

Two weeks later, however, Carey was again exultant. On December 28, 1800, he baptized his first Hindu convert, Krishna Pal. The event was as disturbing a mixture of extreme joy and great pain as could be imagined. Carey, holding the Hindu with one hand and his own son Felix in the other, led them into the water while the missionaries sang a hymn. But behind them in the schoolhouse John Thomas was confined raving mad in a straitjacket, and Carey's wife, Dorothy, was lying deranged in a house on the other side. George Smith describes the scene: "When Carey led [Krishna and Felix] into the river . . . the ravings of Dr. Thomas in the schoolhouse on one side, and of Mrs. Carey on the other, mingled with the strains of the Bengali hymn of praise."[38]

Other baptisms soon followed: Krishna's wife and sister-in-law, and early the next year, the first Bengali of the writer class to join the Baptists, Petumbar Singh, who became a schoolmaster and the mission's first native preacher.[39] And in 1802 a nineteen-year-old Krishna Prasad described by the early Protestants as "the first Brahman who had bowed his neck to the Gospel in all India up to this time," gave up his friends and his caste to be baptized.[40] Krishna Prasad's marriage later to Krishna Pal's daughter was the first Indian Christian marriage celebrated at Serampore.[41] Another Brahman convert, Narapot Singh, baptized by Carey, changed his name to Narapot Christian and became one of the most effective early evangelists of the London Missionary Society among upper-class Indians.[42]

But it would be misleading to characterize these Brahman conversions as a breakthrough into the upper classes. Some of those described as Brahmans were on the lowest fringes of the somewhat higher castes. They were carpenters, like Krishna Pal, the first convert, or distillers like Gokul, who joined him in renouncing caste. They were, as one careful historian has reported, "distillers, washermen, fishermen, weavers and oilmen" and even beggars. They had indeed bravely renounced caste distinctions, which gave them some qualified measure of social status, and endured the wrath of their social peers, but they were also prone to internal feuds and jealousies within the Christian community, and their occasional moral lapses frustrated the missionaries.[43]

Nevertheless, by 1805, when the Serampore missionaries drew up their "Form of Agreement," they had already begun to recognize one all-important fact of the missionary strategy that was to shape the future of Protestantism in Asia: the indispensable role of native evangelists. They put it this way:

> It is only by means of native preachers that we can hope for the universal spread of the gospel through this immense continent. Europeans are too few, and their subsistence costs too much, for us ever to hope that they can possibly be the instruments of the universal diffusion of the word amongst so many millions of souls.[44]

Even so, the numbers of conversions were disappointing, and there were few volunteers among the converts for the formation of an Indian ministry. This was particularly true in the northeast in Bengal, and not only in the Baptist mission. According to an 1851 report, all the missionary societies in Lower Bengal (excluding Krishnagar) reported only 1,266 converts in the forty years of Protestant missions between 1793 and 1833, the year before Carey died.[45] It did not improve in the next decade. After forty years in India and the East Indies, one Baptist veteran, William Robinson of Dacca (Dakha), wrote, in 1847: "There is, dear Christian friends, something which causes great distress both to myself and, I believe, to everyone in the mission: it is the fear, the almost certainty, that we are laboring in vain."[46]

Translation, Social Reform, and Education for India

More than any other single person, Carey contributed to the establishment of a fundamental characteristic of Protestant Christian expansion that was to distinguish it from Catholic missionary methods for the next two hundred years, a single-minded determination to put the Bible into the language of the common people as quickly as possible. In his little cobbler's shop in England he had placed a Bible before a leather-stitched globe of the world: that was his call to mission.[47] He took naturally to languages, beginning by teaching himself Latin at age twelve, soon moving on to Greek, and as a preacher in Leicester he spent Mondays translating various texts from different languages.[48] On the voyage to India, with the help of Mr. Thomas, he translated much of the book of Genesis into Bengali, and within three years of his arrival in India he had produced a first draft in Bengali of the entire New Testament and parts of the Old Testament.[49]

Before his death in 1834 Carey, who by trial and error soon learned the importance of working through a team of native-speaking Indian assistants, had produced and published translations of the entire Bible in five languages, the complete New Testament in eighteen languages, and parts of the New Testament in several more, "for a total of thirty-four languages."[50] They were far from perfect translations and for the most part suffered the usual fate of first translations, soon being superseded by more graceful, accurate renderings into the vernacular.[51] "Serampore Bengali" is how some Indian critics described Carey's use of their language. Others now more generously admit that India owes to Carey and the Serampore Press the birth of modern Bengali literature,[52] much as modern German once owed a debt to Luther and French to Calvin. All in all, Carey's work, says one recent mission historian, was "perhaps the most remarkable individual achievement in the history of Bible translation."[53]

Next to evangelism and Bible translation in scale of importance to the Serampore Baptists were the moral and social imperatives of the Christian faith, particularly as they concerned widow-burning, abortion, and infanticide. His early experiences in self-supporting "tent-making ministry" as manager of an indigo plantation opened his eyes to the oppressed "indigo ryots" (peasant laborers) and championing of their rights led to his dismissal, but it was missionary protest that eventually led to the 1860 India Commission and reform.[54]

As early as 1803 Carey was also pioneering a careful investigation and protest against the grisly Hindu practice of *sati,* the forcible burning of surviving widows on the funeral pyres of their deceased husbands. His first sight of it was in 1799, and unable to stop the atrocity, he fled in horror from the scene. But for the next thirty years he crusaded against the atrocious practice. The British government general, timidly reluctant to interfere in what it euphemistically identified as "the religious opinions and prejudices of the natives," postponed action.[55] But when the edict of prohibition was finally passed in 1829 and sent to him for an official translation, it is said that: "Springing to his feet and throwing off his black coat, [Carey] cried, 'No church for me today!...If I delay an hour to translate and publish this, many a widow's life may be sacrificed.' By evening the task was finished."[56]

An equally significant contribution to India's social future was the role of the English Baptists in breaking through India's sharp cultural barriers against education for Indian women. As early as 1800 Hannah Marshman, wife of Joshua Marshman of the Serampore Trio, opened a short-lived school for girls in Calcutta.[57] The English Baptists were keenly aware of the need. William Ward, the third member of the Serampore Trio, in 1818 wrote of the "unfeeling" and "barbarous custom" of denying to all Indian females, at least in Bengal, even the beginnings of an opening to literacy:

> The most direful calamities are denounced against the woman who shall dare to aspire to the dangerous pre-eminence of being able to read and write. Not a single female seminary exists among the Hindoos; and possibly not twenty females blest with the common rudiments of even Hindoo learning, are to be found among [20] million.[58]

Three years later, in 1821, thanks to Ward's moving descriptions of the plight of Indian women, a remarkably determined English woman reached Calcutta, Miss Mary Ann Cooke (later Mrs. Isaac Wilson), and was received by the Church Missionary Society, Anglican. "A Henry Martyn...in female form," said the bishop of Miss Cooke.[59] Throwing herself against the walls of prejudice which permeated the traditional Hindu treatment of women, in less than six months she had persuaded a few dubious Calcutta parents that their daughters, too, could learn to read. Within a year she had built up a network of eight little schools for girls, the first girls' schools in North India, and their mothers "with one voice cried out (smiting themselves with their right hand) 'O what a pearl of a woman is this!'" In another year there were twenty-two schools and four hundred girls.[60]

The Serampore Baptists, meanwhile, whose pioneer William Ward had touched off the movement, had year by year been opening similar girls' schools. By 1826 they had twelve with three hundred pupils. In that year the recently formed Ladies' Society for Female Education in Calcutta and Vicinity reported a total of thirty schools and an enrollment of six hundred girls, and prepared to open a central school for women's education in the city.[61] Mrs. Wilson rejoiced that the prejudices against teaching females were fading away, but wistfully observed that if more Christian teachers were available and there could be less reliance on non-Christian instructors, how much greater would be the progress.[62]

In Serampore, during the final years of Carey's life, an unfortunate and wounding but not altogether unfriendly rift separated the Serampore group of missionaries from the Baptist Missionary Society in England. The India group had become self-supporting; the home society nevertheless felt responsible for how they used the funds they raised. When Serampore, in effect, insisted that the missionaries in the field were better placed to know how to use money, most of which they had raised themselves, the Baptist Missionary Society withdrew further support of the Serampore pioneers. Carey did not live to see the wounds healed and unity restored. For ten years, 1827 to 1837, Serampore operated as an independent mission until a reunion was negotiated four years after his death.[63]

The story is told that Alexander Duff, later famed as a great missionary educator himself, shortly after his arrival in Calcutta in 1830 made sure to visit the aging Dr. Carey of Serampore. As he left, Carey called him back. "Mr. Duff," he said, "you have been speaking about Dr. Carey, Dr. Carey. When I am gone, say nothing about Dr. Carey — speak about Dr. Carey's Savior."[64]

Carey deserves his reputation as the foremost missionary of the first three and a half centuries of Protestant Christianity. He did not work alone, but more than any other single figure he contributed to the rise of the modern Protestant missionary movement. He gave the movement its major early pattern of organization for mission: the voluntary society unattached to a larger church establishment. He laid the foundations for global translation of the Bible into the vernacular languages of the modern world. His was one of the earliest brave examples of a successful Christian protest against caste barriers in India. To Carey, the very preaching of the gospel carried with it the power to "break the bonds of . . . Hindu caste." His was not the first voluntary society, nor the first Bible translations, nor the first protests against caste. But it was Serampore, not its forerunners, which for the next century became the acclaimed and acknowledged model, often modified, but never forgotten.[65]

Within seven years of Carey's death in 1834, the number of converts in what was by then called the General Baptist Mission (English), had risen to 791. That was not much to boast of in a total Indian population nearing 50 million. A more encouraging statistic was that the number of Indian preachers had surpassed the number of foreign missionaries, forty-three to thirty-one.[66] In fact, the unestablished, independent-minded Baptists, joined by vigorous American missions during the next century, had by 1900 drawn very nearly level with their more officially privileged comrades of the established church of India's empress, Queen Victoria, in the number of reported adherents (207,000 Anglicans to 197,000 Baptists).[67]

The Serampore Trio, all Baptists, would be pleased to know that today at the end of the twentieth century there are more Baptists in India than in England.[68]

The Charter of 1813:
Freedom for Christian Missions in India

Ever since the arrival of Carey in 1793, Protestant missionaries in British India ironically had found themselves as often as not more severely opposed by the Protestant ruling establishment of the East India Company than by non-Christian rajahs of surrounding native kingdoms. Toward the end of the eighteenth century, the Company successfully thwarted a whole series of attempts by missionaries to enter India. A wealthy Scot, Robert Haldane, funded a mission to Benares complete with printing press and teachers, but was not even allowed to leave England for India.[69] The first missionary whom the London Missionary Society (founded in 1795) sent to India (1798) was made so unwelcome by his fellow Britishers in Calcutta that, like the Serampore Baptists, he settled in a nearby European trading center, Dutch Chinsurah. When the first missionaries of the newly formed American Board of Commissioners for Foreign Missions landed in Calcutta in 1812 (not the best year for Americans to appear unannounced on British soil), they were promptly deported, along with three English missionaries. Of the eight expelled missionaries, one managed to relocate in Burma, the great Adoniram Judson (of whom we shall hear more later); another in Java; one returned to America; and the remaining five were shipped back to England where the Company brazenly demanded payment for their passage.[70]

But one year later, in 1813, everything began to change. In that year, the East India Company, which every twenty years was required to submit its charter to Parliament for review and renewal, found itself facing a storm of public condemnation of its antimissionary policies. Leadership in the fight for freedom of religious witness in the colonies came from the rise of English evangelicalism,[71] fueled by the Wesleyan revivals of the last half of the eighteenth century.[72] Seven years earlier, William Wilberforce, a strong supporter of Anglican foreign missions, and nephew of a loyal Methodist aunt, had led the abolitionists in Parliament to victory and the end of the slave trade in Britain. Now, he renewed efforts to free Christian missions in the British trading colonies from repression by the East India Company. A Baptist minister, Robert Hall, aided the cause with a stirring "Address to the Public" that won wide circulation.[73] Its point was blunt:

> That the most complete toleration should be extended to the various modes of belief prevailing in those remote dependencies of our empire... is readily admitted. But for a Christian nation to give decided preference to polytheism

and idolatry by prohibiting the dissemination of a purer faith, and thus employ its powers in suppressing the truth...is repugnant...We have no example in the history of the world of such a conduct; *we have no precedent of a people prohibiting the propagation of their own faith.*[74]

The power of Hall's logic and rhetoric combined with the parliamentary skill of Wilberforce carried the day. The new charter not only expressly ordered the creation of an Anglican church structure in India (a bishop and three archdeacons), but also that liberty of residence and freedom of preaching be granted to those going to India to introduce "useful knowledge" and "religious and moral improvement" — in other words, freedom of entry and residence for all missionaries.[75]

Until the next revision of the charter in 1833 this "edict of toleration" was effective only for areas of British control largely in East India, and there only for English and the Scottish missionaries, excluding Americans with whom the crown had so recently been at war. Nevertheless a rapidly increasing number of missionaries poured through the halfway-opened door.

The Baptists of Serampore, of course, were already accepted ever since the appointment of Carey in 1801 to the "Oxford of the East," Lord Wellesley's short-lived College of Fort William.[76] Thanks to Carey's growing fame, and despite a lamentable sixteen-year rift (1818–1834) between the pioneers and junior arrivals,[77] the Baptist mission continued its advance.

The incandescent Henry Martyn, brilliant Cambridge linguist and the best known of the evangelical Anglican chaplains, reached India in 1806. Twelve short years later he was dead. But already he had translated the Bible into Urdu (for northeast India), and had completed the New Testament in such graceful Persian that the Shah, receiving a copy while Martyn was dying, praised its style as "most befitting sacred books...an easy and simple diction."[78]

The Church Missionary Society (CMS) landed its first missionary to India in Calcutta in 1807, representing the evangelical wing of Anglicanism and sent twenty-eight missionaries to India between 1815 and 1833; by 1820 the London Missionary Society had eight missionaries in Bengal.[79]

For the future organization and structure of the church in British India, however, the most notable result of the charter of 1813 was the arrival in 1814 of the first Anglican bishop in India, Thomas Middleton, described as "a moderate high churchman" whose moderation was nevertheless too high church for the Presbyterian Scots in Calcutta, and too dismissive of his low-church Anglican brethren of the Church Missionary Society, refusing even to ordain them or their converts.[80] Not so the second bishop, Reginald Heber, who was a gentle, irenic man, loved for befriending the CMS missionaries and being willing to ordain their catechist Abdul Masih, converted by Henry Martyn, as the first Indian Anglican priest.[81] Heber is probably best remembered for hymns that still live and lift the spirit — "Holy, Holy, Holy," "Brightest and Best of the Sons of the Morning," and "From Greenland's Icy Mountains," the last of which was for more than a century the missionary anthem of the English-speaking world.

Alexander Duff and Christian Education for India

Four years before the death of Carey, a man reached India who was to accomplish for Christian education in India very much what Carey had done for missionary motive and methods and Bible translation. He was a tall, ruddy Highlander named Alexander Duff (1806–1882)[82] who so imprinted his influence on India that Julius Richter, the historian of missions in India, calls the first forty years of the century (1792–1833) "the age of Carey," but gives the next quarter of a century (1830–1857) the name "the age of Alexander Duff."[83]

With the appointment of Alexander Duff in 1829 the General Assembly of the Church of Scotland began to atone for some 270 years of neglect of the emphatic opening sentence of its 1560 Confession of Faith: "And this glaid tydingis of the kyngdome will be preacheit through the haill warld for a witness unto all natiouns, and then sall the end cum."[84] The reawakening came to Scotland under the powerful evangelical preaching of Thomas Chalmers (1780–1847), mathematician, theologian, and social reformer whose zeal for higher education influenced Duff's whole approach to missions in India. Within one year of Duff's arrival in Calcutta he had established a Christian college designed to challenge the best thinkers in Hinduism with the intellectual and social inadequacies of their own ancient faith, and with the equally ancient but ever revitalizing, more complete truth of the Christian religion. Like the Jesuit de Nobili, two hundred years earlier,[85] he aimed his mission directly at the upper-class, educated Brahmins.

The almost immediate result was an explosion of ardent enthusiasm and virulent opposition. Duff, writes one biographer, was soon "the best known, best hated and best loved man in Calcutta." His earliest Indian supporter was a highly respected intellectual critic of popular Hinduism, Ram Mohun Roy, "the Erasmus of India," a man who was intensely affected by his study of the New Testament but could never quite make the transforming move from respect for a miracle-working, divine Christ, to acceptance of him as the only savior.[86] This was a pattern of response to be repeated thousands of times in the subsequent history of the engagement between evangelistic Christianity and the Hindu intellectual elite. But it was Roy who defended the new young missionary from his Hindu critics and when merchants refused to sell him property for his college, offered him rental of a hall used by his own Hindu disciples. Roy even brought Duff his first upper-class Brahmin students.[87]

His own fellow missionaries were as critical of Duff as the militant Hindus. They berated him for turning missions upside down. Evangelism must come first, and translating the Bible into the vernacular, they said. But here was Duff teaching English to unconverted Hindus. It is true that he was teaching the Bible, but also secular Western studies like economics. Only Carey, among the traditionalists, gave Duff his blessing. At any rate, the school became enormously popular. Hundreds of applicants had to be turned away, and Duff blunted the criticism that he was not evangelizing but only making Englishmen out of Indians by adding courses in vernacular Bengali and taking the unprecedented step of moving his quarters from the European section of the city into an Indian neighborhood.[88]

Hindu opposition continued, however, at one point growing so intense that when reports spread that the Christian was defiling his Hindu upper-caste students by placing Bibles in their hands and asking them to read the Christian Scriptures, and that students of the nearby Hindu College were visiting his home for lectures on Christianity, suddenly one morning out of three hundred students only five showed up in class.[89] They soon returned, but the far more serious problem was the roar of outrage in the Hindu community when in the last half of the year 1832, three of an elite group of reformist-minded Hindu students in Duff's formidably intellectual lectures given weekly in his home began to ask for baptism. They were Mohesh Chunder Ghose, a student at the Hindu College, and Krishna Mohun Banerjea, a Brahmin of the Brahmins (Koolin class). Both of them, in time, were ordained into the Anglican Church. The third, Gopinath Nundi, was immediately cast out by his wealthy family.[90]

The witness of the new converts when they gave their public testimonies of faith did much to soften the criticisms of Duff's fellow missionaries against his innovations in missionary education. The Christian Calvinist foundations on which the sturdy Scot built his college became clear when Ghose, for example, exclaimed:

> A twelvemonth ago I was an atheist, a materialist, a physical necessitarian; and what am I now? A baptized Christian!...I was the most miserable of the miserable; and what am I now?...the happiest of the happy. What a change!...I became a Christian in spite of myself...Surely this must have been what the Bible calls "grace," free grace, sovereign grace, and if ever there was an election of grace surely I am one.[91]

Three years later, in 1835 Duff's success and influence were major factors in the adoption of English as the medium of higher education for the government schools of all India, a policy not without dangers of denationalizing the students. However, it must be said that the teaching of English offered some liberation from India's crippling multiplicity of languages and at least a partial softening of caste barriers, particularly in the study of medicine. Duff, in fact, was one of the founders of

India's first modern hospital, the Medical College in Calcutta. He was not, however, unmindful of the masses. For all his emphasis on English in higher education as indispensable for intellectual and economic progress in a nineteenth century so pregnant with startling changes for ancient Asia, he was well aware that the heart of India would be reached only through the vernacular. For Christian primary schools he championed the local languages — in Bengal, of course, Bengali — and introduced the Christian Vernacular Education Society into Calcutta.[92]

The year of the Disruption in Scotland, 1843, was a disaster for Scottish missions. The issue was governmental right of patronage in church appointments and ordinations. The Scottish ecclesiastical establishment bowed to the rights of government. The dissenters insisted on the prior rights of presbyteries in church appointment and left the national church to form the Free Church of Scotland. In India, where the issue brought back bad memories of the antimissionary policies of the East India Company government, the entire Scottish mission, including Alexander Duff, seceded from the established church, giving up its residences, schools, and churches. Indefatigable, they simply moved out and began all over again. They built up new Christian colleges in Calcutta, Bombay (today, Mumbai), and Madras (today, Chennai), and ironically, the new colleges prospered, while the old ones languished.[93]

As a consequence missionary interest declined for a time in the established Church of Scotland. It was the Free Church Presbyterians who for the rest of the century became what a German historian of Indian missions has described as "the 'educational' mission *par excellence*" of India.[94] The Protestant mission colleges were the revolutionary foundation stones that transformed the nation's whole program of higher education.[95]

When Duff returned from India for three and a half years in 1850 to help organize the missions of the newly formed Free Church of Scotland, he was unexpectedly elected to "the highest ecclesiastical seat in Scotland," that of moderator. He was the first missionary moderator of a Scottish General Assembly in three hundred years since its organization in 1560.[96] (Twelve years later, in 1863 when he left India for the last time, again he was given an unusual honor, election as professor to the first appointed chair of missions in any European university, at New College of the University of Edinburgh.[97])

Church Growth: Indian Protestantism in Mid-Century

By 1851, some sixty years after the arrival of William Carey, the first all-India census of Protestant missions gave the earliest generally reliable numerical measurements of Protestant progress on the subcontinent. It reported a total of 91,092 converts, of whom 14,681 adults had reached the stage of full communicant membership, in 267 churches, with 21

ordained Indian Christian ministers or evangelists. The number of ordained Protestant missionaries had reached 339, working under 19 large
missionary societies and a few smaller ones. Almost a third of the missionaries were Anglican, with Congregationalists and Baptists next in
number.[98] More than half (56 percent) of all the converts were, interestingly enough, not from Bengal, which captured the greatest missionary
attention outside India, but from Madras Presidency, including the far
south.

Ten years later, in 1861, at the close of this first extended half of
the nineteenth century, the number of Indian Protestant Christians had
reached 138,731, a growth (in India) of 52 percent. At least three-fourths
of the new converts in that period came from the lower castes or from
aboriginal tribes.[99] The two decades from 1840 to 1860 mark the beginnings of what later became mass movements of *dalits* ("outcasts" from
Hinduism), and non-Hindu tribal animists, into those segments of the
Christian faith that did not discriminate against them.[100]

Another reason for growth was a rising emphasis on the ordination of
Indian pastors and evangelists, for membership growth without corresponding growth in national Christian leadership is a fragile, vulnerable
phenomenon. The first Anglican Tamil pastor,[101] John Devasagaiyam
(1786–1864), an evangelist working with the Church Missionary Society, was ordained in 1830 by Bishop Turner, fourth bishop of Calcutta.
The importance of an Indian ministry was noted by Bishop George J. T.
Spencer of Madras, who described Devasagaiyam as "an excellent specimen of a native parish priest, such as India must possess by hundreds
and thousands before it can be fully evangelized...We [missionaries]
must contentedly bear the burden and heat of the day, but the harvest
will be gathered by the native clergy."[102] Bishop J. T. Spencer, a great
grandson of the Duke of Marlborough, so emphasized the role of Indian
clergy that in his nine years in India (1838–1847), he pressed the foundation of a diocesan school in Madras for the training of Indian evangelists,
teachers, and priests.[103]

A third reason, possibly, for the greater growth in the south was
the fact that there the newer English missions — the Church Missionary Society (CMS), the London Missionary Society (LMS), and the
Society for the Propagation of the Gospel (SPG) — inherited the evangelical foundations laid down a century earlier by the German-Danish
evangelicals of Tranquebar. The first Indian Anglican ordained in the
south, Devasagaiyam, was born in Tranquebar and was in all probability
brought up under the teaching of the Lutheran pietists of that pioneering
Protestant missionary enclave there.[104]

In fact, by the time of Carey's death, the Anglican missionary societies, not the Baptists, were fast becoming the leading edge for Protestant
missions in India. The relationship between the low-church CMS, which
preferred to keep bishops at a distance and emphasized lay leadership

and evangelism, and the high-church SPG, strong on bishops and liturgy, was not always easy,[105] but the balance between the two proved remarkably successful. To oversimplify — the CMS planted churches; the bishops and the SPG organized the church.

The process of achieving that balance, however, was stormy. In the frictions that developed, the Church Missionary Society lost its greatest missionary in India, Charles T. E. Rhenius, a Lutheran minister and a gifted linguist in Tamil, and an indefatigable evangelist. For fifteen years (1820–1835) he had worked happily in the Society, and with surprisingly successful results. Nevertheless, when the Anglican episcopate demanded powers of oversight and submission of all the Society's ordained workers, Rhenius refused and joined, interestingly enough, not the Lutherans but the Plymouth Brethren[106] — an early indication of a trend toward independent missions that had begun with Carey and was to accelerate throughout the rest of the century.

It was the bishops, however, who brought discipline and order into the Anglican missionary movement. They were a remarkable line of men in their own right: authority-conscious Thomas Fanshaw Middleton; gentle Reginald Heber, better remembered now, perhaps, for the hymns he wrote than as a bishop; and evangelical Daniel Wilson, who learned how to share in mission with less formal but more exuberant missionary laymen.[107] By mid-century the Anglicans in India were by far the largest of the Protestant communions, and second only to the far more numerous Roman Catholics.

Numbers are not the most definitive sign of success in mission, but they are the most measurable indication of progress. In 1862 there were reported to be 725,746 Roman Catholics and 138,731 "native Christians" in the Protestant denominations, of whom in the latter at least three-fourths were from the lower castes, which had begun to enter the churches in large groups in protest against the Hindu caste system.[108] In the larger Protestant denominational groups, the number of Indian Christians in 1861–1862 was reported as follows:[109]

Anglicans (CMS and SPG)	50,500
Independent (LMS and ABCFM)	34,700
European (mostly Lutheran)	10,800
Baptists	7,700
Total Protestant Community	138,731

In reporting on Protestant church growth in this period, it must be remembered that though percentage growth was smaller in Roman Catholicism, Catholic membership was far higher as noted above — more than five Catholics to every Protestant.[110]

Chronology (1792–1859)[111]

1789	The French Revolution.
1791	John Wesley dies.
1792	William Carey (1761–1834) publishes *An Enquiry*.
	Estimated world population: 731 million (of which, 57 percent "heathen"; 18 percent Muslim, 14 percent Roman Catholic; 6 percent Protestant; 4 percent Orthodox. Christian total of world population is 24 percent; 1 percent Jewish).
	Particular Baptist Missionary Society founded in London.
	Denmark becomes first nation to abolish the slave trade.
1793	Louis XVI executed in France.
	Agha Mohammed founds Kajar dynasty in Persia.
1795	London Missionary Society founded.
	Dutch surrender Ceylon to British.
	Catholic Ceylonese number 67,000 despite 140-year ban.
1796	Population of China: estimated to be 275 million.
	Beijing edict outlaws import of opium into China.
1797	Netherlands Missionary Society founded.
	Marquis Wellesley (1760–1842) appointed governor general of India.
1798	French capture Rome; Pius VI leaves for Valence.
	Church Missionary Society founded.
1800	World is estimated to be 23.1 percent Christian (86.5 percent of whom are white); 27.2 percent evangelized; printed Scriptures available in 67 languages.
	1,070,000 Roman Catholic mission converts estimated worldwide: 500,000 in India; 300,000 in Indochina; 200,000 in China; 5,000 in Burma; 2,300 in Siam.
	100 Protestant missionaries worldwide.
1801	342,000 Protestants in Ceylon (most turn Buddhist by 1830).
	Persecution of Roman Catholics in Korea; James Chu, first foreign missionary martyred, along with 300 Korean Christians.
1802	320,000 Roman Catholics estimated in Indochina; 3 European bishops, 15 missionary priests, 119 native priests.
1803	Arthur Wellesley (Duke of Wellington) wins Second Mahratta War.

1804	Pope Pius VII attends crowning of Napoleon emperor in Paris.
	British & Foreign Bible Society founded.
1807	England prohibits slave trade.
	Robert Morrison (1782–1834), first Protestant missionary to China.
1808	U.S. prohibits import of slaves from Africa.
	Napoleon abolishes the Inquisition in Spain and Italy.
1809	Napoleon annexes papal states; Pius VII taken prisoner.
1810	U.S. population: 7,239,881.
	China Christians estimated at 215,000, with 6 bishops, 2 coadjutors, 23 missionaries, 80 native agents.
	William Carey proposes regional ecumenical missionary conference.
	American Board of Commissioners for Foreign Missions founded.
1811	British occupy Java.
	William Martin undertakes translation of Bible into Persian.
	Anti-Christian edict in China (will be renewed in 1857).
1812	Napoleon's Grand Army retreats from Moscow.
	Baptist Union of Great Britain formed.
1813	British East India Company loses its trade monopoly.
	Methodist Missionary Society formed.
	Adoniram Judson (1788–1850) reaches Burma.
1814	First Anglican bishop in India.
	Pius VII returns to Rome; reestablishes Jesuits; restores Inquisition.
1815	World is estimated to be 23.2 percent Christian; 30.3 evangelized; printed Scriptures available in eighty-six languages.
	Battle of Waterloo.
	Basel Missionary Society founded.
1816	Java restored to Dutch.
1817	Lutheran and Reformed churches in Prussia form Evangelical Union.
1818	Morrison's translation of Bible into Chinese.
1819	British establish settlement at Singapore.

1820	Jesuits driven out of Rome.
1821	U.S. population: 9.6 million.
	Minh Mang ("Nero of Indochina") begins brutal persecution.
1823	Leo XII elected pope.
1824	First Burmese War (to 1826). Rangoon captured by British.
1825	Bombay Missionary Union promotes ecumenical mission unity.
	Church of Scotland mission (Presbyterian) organized.
1826	Russia declares war on Persia (takes Armenia in 1827).
1828	Russia declares war on Turkey (war lasts to 1829).
	Karl Gützlaff (1803–1851), Lutheran, begins work in Indonesia, Siam, China.
	Ram Mohun Rai (1772–1833) begins semi-Protestant Hindu reform movement in Calcutta.
1830	Alexander Duff (1806–1878) reaches India.
	Duff's college in Calcutta opens.
1831	Egypt takes Syria from Ottoman Empire.
	Massacre of Nestorians by Kurds (also 1843, 1846).
	First Protestant mission (ABCFM) to Iran (Nestorians).
1833	Britain abolishes slavery.
	Parliament directs East India Company
1834	Deaths of Carey in India; Morrison in China.
	Spanish Inquisition suppressed.
	British East India Company loses China monopoly.
1837	Queen Victoria ascends throne of England.
1838	Revivals under ABCFM among Armenians in Turkey.
1839	First Opium War (to 1842) between Britain and China.
1839	Persecution in Korea (to 1846): 81 martyrs including apostolic vicar and first Korean priest, Andrew Kim.
1841	U.S. population, 17 million; Great Britain, 18.5 million. Britain claims sovereignty over Hong Kong.
	First university degrees granted women in United States.
	Edinburgh Medical Missionary Society founded.
	Henry Venn (of CMS) proposes "Three-Self" missionary method.

1842	Treaty of Nanjing ends First Opium War.
	Japanese translates Life of Jesus (Dutch), arrested, suicide.
1843	SS *Great Britain* is first propeller-driven ship to cross Atlantic.
	Samuel F. B. Morse begins first telegraph line (from Washington to Baltimore).
	Taiping Rebellion (to 1862), of Hong Xiuquan.
	20,000 Nestorians massacred by Kurds.
	Roman Catholic schism in Goa (1843–1886); 600 untrained Indians ordained.
1844	YMCA founded in London.
	China and U.S. sign first treaty of peace, amity, and commerce.
	Nestorian revival in Urumiah (ABCFM).
	Karl Marx, "Religion is the ... opium of the people."
	Bahaism founded by Bab al-Din (1819–1850), as "one worldwide faith."
1845	Anglo-Sikh War begins; Sikhs surrender, 1849.
	Tranquebar sold by Denmark to British East India Company
	Southern Baptists begin work in China.
	Gossner Mission (Berlin, 1842) begins work in India.
	Fifteen-year massacre of Maronites by Druzes in Lebanon.
1847	Latin patriarchate of Jerusalem restored.
	Macarius Glukharev (1792–1847), "apostle to the Altai."
	Fifth major persecution of Catholics in Annam ('51, '56, '84).
1848	Year of European Revolutions. *Communist Manifesto* published by Marx and Engels. Proudhon predicts end of all religion by 1970.
	Nasr-ed-Din made shah of Persia.
1849	Britain annexes Punjab.
	Charles Finney's evangelistic campaigns, in England. Evangelical Alliance of India formed.
	Thailand orders all foreign missionaries deported.
1850	World estimated to be 27.4 percent Christian (82.5 percent of whom are white); 38.1 percent evangelized; printed Scriptures in 205 languages.
1850	Ramakrishna (G. Chatterji), Hindu mystic, claims seeing Jesus after studying Christianity.

Orthodox mission in Siberia to Tunguz, Yakuts, and Samoyed.

First detailed study of India missions by A. Sutton in Orissa.

1851   Indochina persecution; edict of Tu Duc.

Population of India estimated to be 150 million; among whom 14,661 are Protestant communicants, 91,092 adherents, 339 ordained missionaries, 19 mission societies.

1854   First Union Missionary Convention, in New York City, led by A. Duff.

Indonesia: Dutch form single Protestant church, state controlled (Church of the Indies).

1855   First ecumenical foreign missionary conferences: North India, 1855–1863; South India, 1858–1900; All-India, 1873–1902; China, 1877–1907 (in Shanghai); Japan, 1872–1900.

1857   D. L. Moody (1837–1899) organizes mass evangelistic meetings.

1858   Over 1 million Roman Catholics estimated in India; 100,000 Protestants.

Hindu Church of the Lord Jesus, first of more than 150 subsequent attempts at indigenous Hindu-Christianity.

Britain declares religious freedom and impartiality for all.

China/Russian treaty grants Orthodox freedom to evangelize.

1859   Second Evangelical Awakening in England begins.

NOTES

1. A valuable source of primary material is Carter, *The Journal and Selected Letters of William Carey*. Most useful among the vast number of biographies: J. C. Marshman, *The Life and Times of Carey, Marshman and Ward: Embracing the History of the Serampore Mission*, 2 vols. (London: Longman, Brown, Green, Longmans, & Roberts, 1859); George Smith, *The Life of William Carey D.D., Shoemaker and Missionary* (London: John Murray, 1885); S. Pearce Carey, *William Carey*, 8th ed., rev. and enlarged (London: Carey Press, 1934); Eustace Carey, *Memoir of William Carey* (Boston: Gould, Kendall & Lincoln, 1836). For important perspectives on the Carey legacy from Indian writers, see the Carey bicentennial edition of the *ICHR* 27, no. 1 (June 1993). And on Carey's mission methods, Oussoren, *William Carey*. On his personal life, see Mary Drewery, *William Carey, Shoemaker and Missionary* (London: Hodder & Stoughton, 1978). A critical evaluation of Carey is by A. Christopher Smith, "A Tale of Many Models: The Missiological Significance of the Serampore Trio," *MIS* 20, no. 4 (October 1992): 479–500.

2. Carey indeed in many ways deserves the title, but the addition of the word "Protestant" would make the description more accurate, lest the heirs of the Reformation do injustice to the global missions of the Catholic Counter-Reformation as traced in earlier chapters of this volume.

3. Oussoren, *William Carey*, 250–268. The only significant Hindu convert of the Moravians was Ganesa Das who became Persian interpreter and translator for the British Supreme Court at Calcutta (Richter, *A History of Missions in India*, 129ff.).

4. The Church of England's Society for the Propagation of the Gospel in Foreign Parts, founded in 1698, did not organize itself for mission to Asia before 1818, though it supported the work of the earlier Danish mission in India. Its first missionaries, professors for the Bishop's College near Calcutta, reached India in 1821. Further SPG missions in Asia were Ceylon, 1840; Borneo, 1848; the Straits Settlements, 1856; Burma, 1859; China, 1863; Japan, 1873; Korea, 1889; Manchuria, 1892; and Western Asia (temporarily) in 1842. See C. F. Pascoe, *Two Hundred Years of the S.P.G.: An Historical Account of the Society for the Propagation of the Gospel in Foreign Parts 1701–1900 (Based on a Digest of the Society's Records)* (London: SPG, 1901), 468ff., 474.

5. William Carey, *An Enquiry into the Obligations of Christians to Use Means for the Conversion of the Heathens* (Leicester: Ann Ireland, 1792); facsimile reprints London: Hodder & Stoughton, 1891; Henderson & Spalding, 1934; Carey Kingsgate Press, 1961.

6. Carey, *An Enquiry*, 38–66. The number of Christians in the world he estimated at 100 million Catholics, 44 million Protestants, and 30 million Orthodox ("Greek and Armenian"). Non-Christians were perhaps 7 million Jews, and 420 million in "pagan darkness" (62). A sampling of his statistics for Asia are most pertinent for this survey. The total population of Asia, excluding the South Pacific islands, he thought, was about 360 million (46–52). China's 60 million people he describes as pagan; "Great Tartary's" 40 million in North China and Central Asia are Muslim and pagan; so also are India's 50 million "beyond the Ganges," and "Indostan's" 110 million in south India. Persia and Turkey have a population of 20 million each. Japan's islands are given a population of about 15 million; and the Indonesian archipelago including Borneo about 17 million. The Dutch, he noted, have twenty-five churches in Amboin with about 7,500 Christians, and on other smaller islands a few thousand Christians (46–49). The Philippines' 370,000 people he describes as pagan and Muslim, with about 90,000 "papists."

7. On the hyper-Calvinism of the more conservative Particular Baptists, see George Smith, *Life of William Carey*, 47. Calvin was content to leave the resolution of apparent conflict between the concepts of predestination and human free will to the mystery of the divine will, accepting both as taught in Scripture.

8. The meeting was in 1786. The authenticity of the remark is debated, but is not out of character, and is attested by the only then living survivor of those present at the meeting, Morris of Clipstone. See Carey, *Memoir of William Carey*, 35–36; George Smith, *Life of William Carey*, 31–32; S. Pearce Carey, *William Carey*, 54.

9. The influence toward a more moderate predestinarian theology came from his fellow Baptist and lifetime supporter, the Rev. Andrew Fuller, a man of great "native common sense." See George Smith, *Life of William Carey*, 30, 46ff.

10. The text of the organizing resolution is given by George Smith, *Life of William Carey*, 51–52.

11. The total was really 14 pounds (guineas), for a guinea and a half had previously been contributed. The financial statement is in S. Pearce Carey, *William Carey*, 93ff.

12. On the reasons for her refusal, see James R. Beck, *Dorothy Carey: The Tragic and Untold Story of Mrs. William Carey* (Grand Rapids, Mich.: Baker Book House, 1992), 69–76. On her illiteracy (15ff.), and a photostat of her marriage license with her name signed with the mark (x), 128 b. Beck rightly disputes some of the more adverse comments made about her, as in George Smith, *Life of William Carey* (1885 ed.), 23, 180.

13. On Thomas see C. B. Lewis, *The Life of John Thomas, Surgeon of the Earl of Oxford, East Indiaman, and First Baptist Missionary to Bengal* (London: Macmillan, 1873): his earlier problems, 107ff.; his debts, 234ff., 253, 285–286; Carey's disappointment with him, but continuing loyalty, 254ff., 275ff.

14. E. Carey, *Memoir*, 63–64. It was a last-minute, emotional appeal by John Thomas that persuaded her, reluctantly, to leave England.

15. S. Pearce Carey, *William Carey*, 117–118. The "four who remained" were Ryland, Sutcliff, Fuller, and Pearce, and the "rope" metaphor was actually Fuller's.

16. Carey's own account of the voyage is in E. Carey, *Memoir of William Carey*, 76–84.

17. Lewis, *John Thomas*, 278.

18. On Ram Basu see Lewis, *John Thomas*, 111–112, 177, 194–195, 229ff., 248, 294, 319; and S. Pearce Carey, *William Carey*, 172–173. Ram was forever postponing baptism and in 1796 was found guilty of adultery with a young widow, and of the murder of the baby then born to them. He was dismissed from Mudnabatty, and Carey was forced to close the little school he had started for Indian children in 1794 using Ram as guide to the Indian teacher (Oussoren, *William Carey*, 63, 65).

19. For Serampore's taint of colonialism, see the arguments of J. S. Dharmaraj, "Serampore Missions and Colonial Connections," in *ICHR* 26 (June 1992): 21–35; and his longer treatment, Jacob S. Dharmaraj, *Colonialism and Christian Mission* (Delhi: Society for Promoting Christian Knowledge, 1993), which though one-sided should be read. But cf. the even, balanced judgment of E. Daniel Potts, *British Baptist Missionaries in India 1793–1837: The History of Serampore and its Missions* (Cambridge: Cambridge University Press, 1967); and Justus's favorable comments on a missionary "imperialist," the Moravian C. F. Schwartz ("Schwartz," 36–49). Dharmaraj cites Carey's remunerative positions, first as indigo planter paying his workers 2.5 to 4 rupees a month, which he left as soon as possible; and then as professor at a thousand rupees a month in a university training British colonial administrators. His salary, however, he used to support the mission. Self-supporting mission precedents trace back as far as the apostle Paul. Dharmaraj also notes the mission's acknowledged acceptance of government assistance after 1813. The criticisms are somewhat anachronistic. Early nineteenth-century Indian reformers also were, on the whole, highly approving of government support of programs designed for educational, medical, and social improvement, however much they criticized British colonialism. See the writings of Ram Mohun Roy and Babu Krishna Mohun Banerjea, for example.

20. On the early encouragement of missionaries by the Company, and its later hostility after 1757 and until 1813, see Marshman, *The Life and Times of*

Carey, Marshman and Ward, 1:38–50, 72ff., 225–226. The Company had erected the first church in Calcutta (Anglican) in 1709.

21. Abhijit Dutta, *Christian Missionaries on the Indigo Question in Bengal 1855–1860* (Calcutta: Minerva Associates, 1989), citing Sunil Kuma Chatterjee. Carey's advocacy of peasant (*ruot*) rights lowered profits to the displeasure of the planters.

22. Beck, *Dorothy Carey.* On Mrs. Carey's "retreat from reality," see especially 107–125 for analysis and sympathetic insight into her difficulties.

23. Lewis, *John Thomas,* 277–278.

24. *Journal,* February 3, 1795, quoted in E. Carey, *Memoir,* 146.

25. The best overall surveys and analyses of the early years of the Baptist Mission and its base in Serampore are Potts, *British Baptist Missionaries in India 1793–1837*; Brian Stanley, *The History of the Baptist Foreign Missionary Society 1792–1992* (Edinburgh: T & T Clark, 1992), 36–67, 140–149; and A. Christopher Smith, "A Tale of Many Models," 479–500.

26. Latourette, *A History of the Expansion of Christianity,* vols. 4–6. On the independence of the Serampore mission from the home denomination, and even from the missions Society, see Oussoren, *William Carey,* 142; S. Pearce Carey, *William Carey,* 365ff. On the principle of a self-supporting, subsistence-level mission, see Marshman's letter of April 1804 (Marshman, *The Life and Times of Carey, Marshman and Ward,* 1:195–196).

27. The text of his proposal is given in Beck, *Dorothy Carey,* 197–198. See also Oussoren, *William Carey,* 65–66.

28. For the full text of this very important document see *Form of Agreement* (Serampore: Brethren's Press 1805, reprinted Calcutta, 1874), and reproduced in George Smith, *Life of William Carey,* app. I, "The Bond of the Missionary Brotherhood of Serampore," 441–450, and by Oussoren, *William Carey,* 274–284.

29. S. H. Moffett in *Latin America Evangelist* (January–March 1992): 16.

30. Oussoren, *William Carey,* 79.

31. See A. Christopher Smith, "William Ward, Radical Reform, and Missions in the 1790s," *American Baptist Quarterly* 10, no. 3 (September 1991): 218–244. The social activist element in the Baptist mission at Serampore was at times a matter of some anxiety to its Mission Society in England, and even to William Carey whose concern for the poor was more pastoral and nonpolitical than radical. Smith quotes a Carey letter, "Bless God we are all as cold as ice in a political sense except Bro. Fountain." Ward, whose background included antislavery passion, married Fountain's widow (238–239).

32. Quoted by A. Christopher Smith, "A Tale of Many Models," 480–500. Quotation on 484.

33. On the Marshman/Roy controversy see M. M. Thomas, *The Acknowledged Christ of the Indian Renaissance* (London: SCM, 1969), 1–37. The principal primary sources are: Joshua Marshman, *A Defense of the Deity and Atonement of Jesus Christ . . .* (London, 1822); and Rammohun (or Ram Mohun Roy), *Collected Works of Raja Rammohun Roy* (Allahabad, 1906).

34. S. K. Chatterjee [Saral Kumar Chatterji], *Hannah Marshman: The First Woman Missionary in India* (Hooghly, India: S. S. Chatterjee, 1987).

35. George Smith, *Life of William Carey,* 127. The Serampore Covenant emphasized the importance of the missionary wives, observing, "We see that in primitive times the Apostles were very much assisted in their great work by

several pious females," and insisting that the women should learn the native language as well as the men (Smith, *Life of William Carey,* 279). On Hannah Marshman, see the many references in Marshman, *The Life and Times of Carey, Marshman and Ward,* 2:106.

36. The first convert of the two Baptists, Carey and Thomas, was Ignatius Fernandez of Portuguese descent in Macao, who had been trained there for the priesthood. But in Bengal he gave up his training to become a clerk and well-to-do cloth merchant. A copy of a Portuguese Bible given him by a Hindu turned him against image worship, and upon meeting John Thomas he was soon, in 1796, led into the Protestant faith, eventually becoming an "honorary" Baptist missionary (S. Pearce Carey, *William Carey,* 174–175).

37. Carey, letters, November 2, 22, December 18, 1800, in E. Carey, *Memoir,* 283–284, 285, 292; S. Pearce Carey, *William Carey,* 205.

38. George Smith, *Life of William Carey,* 135–136.

39. George Smith, *Life of William Carey,* 137–141.

40. George Smith, *Life of William Carey,* 139–140. The good Baptists did not mention much earlier Brahman baptisms by Roman Catholic missionaries, and Smith dismisses as apparently failed an early baptism of a Brahman by Kiernander, the East India Company's chaplain.

41. Neill, *History of Christianity in India: 1707–1858,* 198.

42. George Gogerly, *The Pioneers: A Narrative of Facts Connected with Early Christian Missions in Bengal, Chiefly Relating to the Operations of the London Missionary Society* (London: John Snow, 1871), 207–211.

43. Gupta, *The Christian Missionaries in Bengal,* 143–167.

44. "Form of Agreement," 1805, reproduced in George Smith, *Life of William Carey,* app. I.

45. Gupta, *Christian Missionaries in Bengal,* 142–143.

46. Quoted by Stanley, *History of the Baptist Foreign Missionary Society,* 140.

47. On his Bible study habits, see E. Carey, *Memoir,* 5, 12; S. Pearce Carey, *William Carey,* 35, 37–38, 48.

48. Marshman, *The Life and Times of Carey, Marshman and Ward,* 1:2–3, 12, 60; George Smith, *Life of William Carey,* 23–24.

49. On Carey as a translator in India, see William A. Smalley, *Translation as Mission: Bible Translation in the Modern Missionary Movement* (Macon, Ga.: Mercer University Press, 1991), 40–52.

50. Smalley, *Translation as Mission,* 46–47. By 1832, Smalley adds, the Serampore Press had published 212,000 volumes in forty languages. Depending on definitions, the number varies. Stanley, for example, lists six complete Bibles: Bengali, Oriya, Hindi, Marathi, Sanskrit, and Assamese (Stanley, *History of the Baptist Foreign Missionary Society,* 49 n. 56). On the sometimes understated indispensable work of the non-Christian Indian teachers assisting the missionaries in the work of translation, see Potts, *British Baptist Missionaries in India 1793–1837,* 81–82.

51. See the summary of criticisms and praise for Carey's translations in Potts, *British Baptist Missionaries,* 83–89.

52. Gupta, *The Christian Missionaries in Bengal,* 88–96, 189. But Sen Gupta balances his praise with criticism. He also writes, "It is very difficult to accept Ingham's view...that the missionary translations contributed in any way 'to

the establishment of structural unity among the vernacular and to their uniform development.'" (Cf. 96 and 189.)

53. Stanley, *History of the Baptist Missionary Society*, 49.

54. See Dutta, *Christian Missionaries on the Indigo Question in Bengal*, 1ff. and passim.

55. Catholic Portugal had prohibited *suttee* as early as 1510 in its Indian enclave at Goa (Edward Thompson, *Suttee: A Historical and Philosophical Enquiry into the Hindu Rite of Widow-Burning* [London: George Allen & Unwin, 1928], 56–81). On the Serampore Mission and *suttee*, see S. Pearce Carey, *William Carey*, 176, 209–210, 336–337, 361–363; and William Ward, *A View of the History, Literature, and Mythology of the Hindoos Including a Minute Description of Their Manners and Customs*, 2 vols. (Serampore, India: Mission Press, 1815, 1818), 1:62, 204, 206.

56. Thompson, *Suttee*, 78, citing F. Deaville Walker, *William Carey: Missionary Pioneer and Statesman* (London: Student Christian Movement, 1926), 310.

57. The school may have been for Portuguese-Indian girls. See Gupta, *The Christian Missionaries in Bengal*, 108–112. Note his reference to an early defense of education for females by a Hindu scholar, Gaur Mohan Vidyalankar, in 1822. See also Potts, *British Baptist Missionaries*, 123–125.

58. Ward, *History, Literature, and Mythology among the Hindoos*, 1:202–203.

59. Eugene Stock, *The History of the Church Missionary Society: Its Environment, Its Men and Its Work*, 5 vols. (London: Church Missionary Society, 1899, 1916), 1:317. After the death of her husband in 1828 she left the Anglican communion for the Plymouth Brethren.

60. Miss Cooke (Mrs. Wilson) was sent to India by the British and Foreign Bible Society, but was transferred to the Church Missionary Society of the Anglicans. Priscilla Chapman, *Hindoo Female Education* (London: Seeley and Burnside, 1839), 3, 75–81; Stock, *The History of the Church Missionary Society*, 1:199–200, 283, 317; 2:161–162, 3:138; William Canton, *A History of the British and Foreign Bible Society*, 5 vols. (London: John Murray, 1904, 1910), 2:100. Cf. Sherring, *History of Protestant Missions in India 1706–1882*, which contains slight differences in the statistics.

61. Sherring, *Protestant Missions*, 85–86; Chapman, *Female Hindoo Education*, 85ff.

62. Chapman, *Hindoo Female Education*, 89–97.

63. Marshman, *The Life and Times of Carey, Marshman and Ward*, 2:329–397, 508–514, 520–526; and George Smith, *Life of William Carey*, 359–375; 393–395. For a longer perspective, see also the recently published Stanley, *The History of the Baptist Missionary Society*, 57–67.

64. George Smith, *Life of William Carey*, 422, citing *William Carey* by James Culross (1881). In his *Life of Alexander Duff* (1:105), Smith does not include the anecdote from Culross.

65. Before Carey, the Danish missionaries, with the exception of Benjamin Schultze and Pohle, were not inclined to raise objections to caste distinctions. On Carey and caste, see Marshman, *The Life and Times of Carey, Marshman and Ward*, 1:155–156. Anglican missions, until Bishop Daniel Wilson in 1832, two years before Carey's death, tended to agree with their own converts that caste was more a social than religious issue, and after Wilson's attempts to prohibit it, returned to limited tolerance as in Bishop Spencer's advice: as a civil or social distinction, "touch it not"; but as "a badge of religious or moral superiority...Away with it

down with it, even to the ground" (Penny, *The Church in Madras,* 3:52). The non-Anglican Protestant missions, however, almost all followed Carey, and at one of the first interdenominational missionary conferences, Madras, 1848, agreed in principle to prohibit baptism to any who refused to break caste. See Richter, *A History of Missions in India,* 168–173; and Rufus Anderson, *History of the Missions of the American Board of Commissioners for Foreign Missions in India* (Boston: Congregational Publishing House, 1875), 211, 226, 289–290.

66. F. A. Cox, *History of the Baptist Missionary Society from 1792 to 1842 to Which Is Added a Sketch of the General Baptist Mission,* 2 vols. (London: T. Ward and G. & J. Dyer, 1842), 1:394, 40. The statistics, for Calcutta and North India, report churches in forty stations, and about 100 inquirers in addition to the 791 members. The mission in India also operated seventy-four day schools with 2,738 scholars. It is not clear whether the eleven "female missionaries" reported are included among the thirty-one missionaries listed. Indian preachers named are: Shujaat Ali, Gunga Narayan Sil, Ram Hari in Calcutta; Harish Chandra in Howrah; Jacob in Lakhyantipur; Sonatan, Sonatan Jr., and Karadhan in Beerhboom; Nayansukh, Haridas, and Sudin in Monghyr; Kashi in Patna; Devigir in Delhi; Ramdhan in Jessore; Chand, Ramjiban, and Moses in Dacca; and Peter in Dinagepore. On India's population of about 50 million (in 1857), see Marshman, *The Life and Times of Carey, Marshman and Ward,* 1:231.

67. See the statistic in Pascoe, *Two Hundred Years of S.P.G.,* 471. Queen Victoria was crowned empress of India in 1877.

68. Roger E. Hedlund, "Carey: A Missiologist before Time," in *ICHR* 27, no. 1 (June 1993), 40, n. 20.

69. Alexander Haldane, *Memoirs of the Lives of Robert Haldane of Airthrey and His Brother James Alexander Haldane* (New York: Robert Carter, 1853), 94–118, 195–196. Haldane, later a zealous lay preacher, was one of the first Scottish Presbyterians to enroll as a supporting member of the London Missionary Society.

70. Richter, *A History of Missions in India,* 144–145; Sherring, *History of Protestant Missions in India,* 58, 69, 76–78.

71. Literature on the social and political impact of the evangelicals is immense. A fairly recent text is K. E. Heasman, *Evangelicals in Action: An Appraisal of Their Social Work in the Victorian Era* (London: G. Bles, 1962).

72. John Wesley died in 1791, still an Anglican but the "father of the Methodist Church."

73. Robert Hall, *An Address to the Public on the Renewal of the Charter of the East India Company* (London: Josiah Conder, 1813).

74. Hall, *An Address to the Public,* 4–5 (italics mine).

75. The "missionary clause" is in resolution no. 13 of the 1813 charter. On the charter controversy, see Penny, *The Church in Madras,* 2:1–50; Arthur Mayhew, *Christianity and the Government of India: An Examination of the Christian Forces at Work in the Administration of India, 1600–1920* (London: Faber & Gwyer, 1929), 89–103; and Neill, *India,* 2:151–155.

76. Wellesley was the older brother of Arthur Wellesley, later to be the Duke of Wellington.

77. See S. P. Carey, *William Carey,* 359–371; Marshman, *The Life and Times of Carey, Marshman and Ward,* 2:509–514; Walker, *William Carey,* 298–301, 304.

78. The primary source is *Journal and Letters of the Rev. Henry Martyn*, ed. S. Wilberforce, 1st American ed. (New York: M. W. Dodd, 1851). Two excellent biographies are: George Smith, *Henry Martyn, Saint and Scholar* (London: Religious Tract Society, 1892), and Constance E. Padwick, *Henry Martyn, Confessor of the Faith* (London: Student Christian Movement, and New York: George H. Doran, 1922). The quotation is from Padwick, 285.

79. A longer list of early notable Protestant missions would include the great Baptist Mission, reestablished in 1834 on the foundations of the earlier work of The Serampore Trio from which the Society had begun to separate itself in 1818, with final separation in 1827, and reunion in 1834; and the Basle Evangelical Society (Basle Mission) beginning in 1834 in Mangalore, halfway between Goa and Cochin on India's west coast, and spreading rapidly throughout India.

80. The first six missionary bishops for Anglican India (Calcutta), were Thomas Fanshaw Middleton (1815–1822); Reginald Heber (1823–1826); two brief episcopates, John Thomas James (1827–1829) and John Turner (1829–1831); and Daniel Turner (1832–1858) whose title was raised to the rank of metropolitan of India in 1833 when two suffragan bishops were appointed (for Bombay and Madras). See Chatterton, *History of the Church of England in India*, 123–183, and Neill, *India*, 2:261–275.

81. Abdul Masih (whose pre-Christian name was Sheikh Salih) was a Muslim convert of Henry Martyn, the evangelical British chaplain. He was, says Neill, "probably the leading Indian Christian of his time" (*India*, 2:340). Baptized by David Brown, another of the evangelical chaplains, he assisted Daniel Corrie, also a chaplain, and later became reader and catechist for the CMS. Excerpts from Masih's *Journal* and letters, translated by Corrie, are the most important source for his life and work. See *The Missionary Register* (London, 1816), 20–31, 335–338, 375–377; (1818), 451. On Daniel Corrie who became Bishop Heber's archdeacon and later the first bishop of Madras, see Chatterton, *Church of England in India*, 119–120, 191–193; Neill, *India*, 340–341; and Penny, *The Church in Madras*, 2:174, 353–355.

82. Duff was appointed in 1829, reaching Calcutta in 1830. The two best biographies are George Smith, *The Life of Alexander Duff*, 2 vols. (London: Hodder & Stoughton, 1879; 3rd ed. abridged and revised, 1899); the two-volume 1879 edition has more detail than the 1899 edition; and William Paton, *Alexander Duff, Pioneer of Missionary Education* (New York: H. Doran; London: Student Christian Movement, 1923).

83. Richter, *A History of Missions in India*, 128, 173.

84. The earliest Scottish missionary society, The Society in Scotland for Propagating Christian Knowledge, chartered in 1709, sent some small funds, including grants to Serampore, but not personnel overseas (see Stock, *History of the Church Missionary Society*, 1:27).

85. See chap. 1.

86. The best treatment of Rom Mohun Roy (or Rommohun Roy), founder of Brahmo Samaj, an Indianized unitarianism, and his love/hate relationship with the missionaries and their Christian faith, is by Potts, *British Baptist Missionaries*, 226–243. Potts characterizes Roy as the "brahmin reformer and Hindu Protestant." The basic source in English is Kalidas Nag and Debhyoti Burman, eds., *The English Works of Raja Rommohun Roy*, 7 parts (Calcutta: Sadharan Brahmo Samaj, 1945–1958), See also Richter, *A History of Missions in India*, 367ff.

87. George Smith, *Alexander Duff*, 59ff.

88. George Smith, *Alexander Duff*, 66–67.

89. George Smith, *Alexander Duff*, 78–79; Paton, *Alexander Duff*, 79.

90. George Smith, *Alexander Duff*, 85–87. Smith quotes from their testimony of faith some striking tributes to the evangelical centrality of Duff's kind of Christian education. From Ghose, "When I first came to your lectures, it was not instruction I wanted. Instruction was the pretext, a secret desire to expose what I reckoned your irrational and superstitious follies the reality. At last, against my feelings, I was obliged to admit the truth of Christianity . . . In spite of myself I became a Christian." And Banerjea, "I understood not aright the doctrine of the atonement . . . And as the Bible pointed unequivocally to it, I strove to persuade myself . . . not to believe in the sacred volume . . . till God, by the influence of His Holy Spirit, was graciously pleased to open my soul to discern its sinfulness and guilt, and the suitableness of the great salvation which centered upon the atoning death of a *Divine* Redeemer."

91. George Smith, *Alexander Duff*, 85–86.

92. George Smith, *Alexander Duff*, 98–107.

93. Only one, in Calcutta, survived with any effectiveness, as the "General Assembly's Institution." See Richter, *A History of Missions in India*, 193.

94. Richter, *A History of Missions in India*, 183–184 (emphasis his), 319 n. 2. Duff's Scottish colleagues became almost as celebrated as he: John A. Anderson (1805–1855), evangelist, educator, and first Church of Scotland missionary in South India; later, William Miller (1838–1923) at the Christian College of Madras, and pioneer in interdenominational cooperation; John Wilson (1804–1875) in Bombay (founder of the college later named for him, Wilson College); and Stephen Hislop at Nagpur in Central India.

95. See the list of Protestant colleges in Richter, *A History of Missions in India*, 318 n. 2. Among other well-known colleges founded in this "age of the mission school" were two started by the Church Missionary Society, St. John's College at Agra, and Robert Noble's college at Masulipatam in Telugu territory.

96. George Smith, *Life of Alexander Duff*, 258.

97. Only Princeton Theological Seminary in the United States had an earlier professorship of missions, 1836–1838. The Edinburgh position was called the Missionary Professorship of Evangelistic Theology, and included lectureships in Glasgow and Aberdeen Universities. See George Smith, *Life of Alexander Duff*, 2:416–423.

98. Converts usually became communicant members of the church only after a year or more of evidence of a Christian life and knowledge of the Bible and basic Christian doctrine. Two-thirds of all the Protestant missionaries in India belonged to the six largest mission societies: Church Missionary Society (CMS, Anglican evangelical), 64; London Missionary Society (LMS, largely Congregational/English Presbyterian), 49; Society for the Propagation of the Gospel (Anglican high church), 35; Baptist, 30; Basle Mission (Lutheran), 23; and American Board of Commissioners for Foreign Missions (ABCFM, American Congregational/Presbyterian), 22. See Richter's figures and analysis of the census in his *History of the Missions in India*, 201, 408.

99. Decennial Missionary Conference, India, *Report of the First Decennial General Missionary Conference, Allahabad, 1872–1873* (London and Madras: Seeley,

Jackson & Halliday, 1873), 518; 476–484. In 1861 there were 479 Protestant missionaries, 97 ordained Indian "agents," and 25,000 communicant members. In comparisons of India statistics of this period, care must be taken to subtract figures for Burma and Ceylon, which are often included.

100. Terminology defining the "low castes" in Hinduism varies widely. The preferred term for what were once called outcastes, untouchables, depressed classes, *harijans*, or "scheduled castes" now seems to be "Dalit," which means " 'broken' or 'oppressed.' " See John C. B. Webster's admirable historical study, *A History of the Dalit Christians in India* (San Francisco: Mellen Research University Press, 1992), i–iii.

101. Bishop Heber had ordained in Calcutta a Ceylonese, Christian David; and Abdul Masih, who had received Lutheran ordination, was given Anglican orders by Heber in 1825 (Stock, *History of the Church Missionary Society*, 1:191 n.).

102. Penny, *The Church in Madras*, 3:406. Devasagaiyam (or Devasagayam) received his orders as a priest from Bishop Corries in Madras in 1836. He had been ordained deacon by Bishop Turner of Calcutta in 1830, and worked for forty-four years under the CMS in the Tinnevelly district (see 3:405–446).

103. On Spencer, see Penny, *The Church in Madras*, 2:45–65; and Hans Cnattingius, *Bishops and Societies: A Study of Anglican Colonial and Missionary Expansion 1698–1850* (London: SPCK, 1952), 211ff. Under various names the new "college," which was at first called by the bishop's name, "Spencer" (later the S.P.G. Theological College), well served the high-church mission society (SPG), but was viewed as too clergy-bound and ecclesiastically "correct" by the more evangelical Anglican society, the CMS. The latter started its own school for training the native clergy and in fact eventually produced more Indian priests than the SPG. In 1824 it reported only two "native missionaries," but by 1851 the number had increased to eleven ordained and many more unordained evangelists (Penny, 2:280–281, 430ff.; Stock, *History of the Church Missionary Society*, 1:244, 318–331; *Report of the First Decennial General Missionary Conference, Allahabad, 1872–73*, 521). On relations within the Anglican Church between SPG and CMS, see Henry Venn's famous "Remarks on the Constitution and Practice of the Church Missionary Society . . ." (184), summarized and analyzed in Stock, *History of the Church Missionary Society*, 71, 384–399; and Cnattingius, *Bishops and Societies*, 57–71, 160–174.

104. See Pascoe, *Two Hundred Years of the S.P.G.*, 501ff., 531ff. What seemed a beginning of a mass movement began after persecutions in 1841; by 1843 there were thirty-five thousand inquirers and converts in the SPG and CMS missions in the Tinnevelly district alone, such a movement as had "never yet taken place in India," was the report (536–537). The Lutheran pietist mission in Tranquebar had long been supported by and was working with the English societies; in 1845 that Danish trading colony was bought outright by the British East India Company.

105. On the Church Missionary Society see Cnattingius, *Bishops and Societies*, 159–185, 220ff.; and Stock, *History of the Church Missionary Society*, 1:328–330; 2:375, 520. On the Society for the Propagation of the Gospel, see Cnattingius, *Bishops and Societies*, 139ff.

106. The work of Rhenius for the CMS and of Ringeltaube for the London Missionary Society between 1820 and 1835 is described by Richter as "the crown and rejoicing of Protestant missions." (See Richter, *A History of Missions in India*,

158; Stock, *History of the Church Missionary Society,* 1:90, 185, 202, 283, 300, 320–322.) Rhenius is known as Charles Theophilus Ewald Rhenius in English, and as Karl Gottlieb Ewald Rhenius in German. See also Neill, *History of Christianity in India 1707–1858,* 218–222.

107. On the bishops see Chatterton, *A History of the Church of England in India;* on Middleton (1815–1822), 123–129; on Heber (1823–1826), 130–143; and on Daniel Wilson (1832–1858), 155–183.

108. *Report of the First Decennial General Missionary Conference, Allahabad, 1872–73,* 476–477.

109. *Report of the First Decennial General Missionary Conference, Allahabad,* 521–522. For a Catholic statistical table, see 533.

110. On Catholicism in India, 1773 to 1850, see chap. 8 above, "Catholic Decline and Recovery."

111. Sources on secular dates: David Barrett, *Cosmos, Chaos and Gospel: A Chronology of World Evangelization* (Birmingham, Ala.: New Hope Press, 1987); Bernard Grun, *The Timetables of History* (New York: Simon & Schuster, 1972, 1987); William L. Langer, *An Encyclopedia of World History,* rev. ed. (Boston: Houghton Mifflin, 1948); and others.

Chapter 13

The Door to China Opens Again
(1807–1860)

What, then, do the Chinese require from Europe?
— Not the arts of reading and printing; not merely general education;
not what is so much harped on by some philanthropists — civilization: they
require that only which St. Paul deemed supremely excellent, and which it
is the sole object of the Missionary Society to communicate — they require
the knowledge of Christ.   — Robert Morrison (1824)

It is desirable that the men of this great and glorious Middle Kingdom...
should not boast vainly of their own country's being the land of propriety
and righteousness as well as of fine literature. [They should] humbly cast
aside their prejudices regarding the country in which Christianity originated and instead consider that the God of Heaven created us as human
beings. Everyone who is human ought to know the saving doctrines of the
Bible.   — Liang Fa (1832)

IN the fourth year of the reign of Jiaqing, emperor of China — the
year A.D. 1800 by the western calendar — the "celestial monarch" issued an edict on religion. He had inherited from his father, the great
Qianlong, more land and more people than any ruler in all of China's
long history.[1] But he was troubled by a rising tide of rebellion in the
land. A confirmed Confucianist like his father, he blamed the social un-
rest on wrong-thinking religion — hence the edict that he claimed to
have written himself and titled, "Discourse on Heretical Religions."[2] Its
basic premise is that incitement to rebellion is "heresy" in any religion.
Even Confucianism could accept traditional Buddhism and Taoism as
being of some useful social service so long as they respected the throne.
But insurrectionary semi-Buddhist and Taoist sects, like the White Lotus Society which had risen in rebellion in West China, were another
matter. Against such, the empire must show no mercy. Appropriate punishment, said the "Discourse," would be "the scouring with sand," a
delicate Chinese phrase for torture and obliteration.
     What about Christians? The dynasty had already learned from the
rites controversy of the preceding century[3] how easily guilt by association could be attached to China's small Christian minority, if for no

other reason than it had foreign connections. The fifth emperor's edict of 1800 only reaffirmed prohibitions and harassments that had already effectively closed China's doors to Christian missions for 150 years, on the suspicion that Christians owed a higher obedience to Rome than to a Chinese emperor.

As a result, the fifth Manchu emperor's China in 1800 contained more Chinese and fewer Christians proportionate to the population than in any of the dynasties of the distant past under which Christianity had once flourished — the Tang in the eighth century, the Mongol (Yuan) in the thirteenth, and even his own dynasty in the Jesuit period of the seventeenth century. Louvet's estimate is 800,000 Chinese Christians in 1700, and only 187,000 in 1800.[4] The door seemed to be closed. Until 1842 it was legally impossible for missionaries to be residents in China.[5] Their only recourse was to seek local employment in another category, involuntary tent-making missionaries, as it were, after the pattern of the apostle Paul.

But in one sense the door into China for Christian mission had always been open. It was just not often entered. Alopen found it open in A.D. 635 and entered it with the Nestorians to establish Christian churches in the empire of the Tang dynasty.[6] Seven hundred years later Marco Polo and the Franciscan, John of Montecorvino, reached China to find Nestorian Christians there, even at the court of the Mongol emperors in thirteenth-century Beijing.[7] Two and a half centuries passed, and the Jesuit fathers had all but forgotten those earlier missions when they pushed the door open once more in 1583.[8]

Two centuries later, it was the Protestants' turn to penetrate the officially closed empire. There were Catholics still there, but they had survived only with difficulty.[9] What the new arrivals accomplished in little more than the next one hundred years has given the period from 1792 to 1914 the name of "the great century" of Protestant missions — first in India with William Carey, then with Robert Morrison in China, and on across the whole continent of Asia.[10]

Robert Morrison and China (1807–1834)

Robert Morrison (1782–1834), a Presbyterian Scot born in England, sailed for China in 1807 as a missionary of the London Missionary Society. His call to the mission field came to him when he was twenty-one years old studying for the ministry. Reading again Christ's command to "Go into all the world and preach the gospel," and shocked to find that thousands upon thousands outside his own small "corner" of the world had never heard the gospel preached, he asked the Missionary Society to send him "where the difficulties were greatest, and most insurmountable."[11] A prayer he wrote in 1803 says it best, "O Lord . . . Perhaps one part of the field is more difficult than another. I am equally unfit for any . . . but through thee strengthening me, 'I can do all things.' "[12]

This confidence was characteristic of his life as a missionary through thirty more years of dogged perseverance against a multitude of difficulties. First was the determined opposition of the British East India Company, still commercially and imperially antimissionary after a hundred years of British trade expansion in the Orient.[13] The Company blocked his passage to China on a British ship. Morrison was not so easily to be stopped. He went instead by way of America, 80 days to New York, and 113 days from there to Guangzhou (Canton). His widow later told how when his New York host took him to arrange for the voyage, the shipowner looked up with a skeptical smile. "And so, Mr. Morrison, you really expect that you will make an impression on the idolatry of the great Chinese empire?" And Morrison answered, "No, Sir. I expect God will."[14]

Imperial China, however, proved to be a far more formidable opponent to the missionary than colonial England. A decade earlier, in 1793, the great Emperor Quianlong (1736–1796) had politely but firmly dismissed a British trading embassy with ill-concealed disdain as coming from a land of barbarians. The emperor not only forbade trading concessions but pointedly warned King George III's ambassador, Lord Macartney, that no propagation of "the English religion" in China would be permitted.[15] Technically and legally missionary activity was forbidden in the empire. A scattering of Roman Catholic missionaries remained, most visibly in Beijing, where at last two severe persecutions, in 1805 and 1811, virtually ended two hundred years of the famous Catholic mission connection at the imperial court. Two of the four Catholic churches in the Beijing were destroyed, and only seven European priests were able to remain.[16] Latourette remarks, "The wonder is, not that Christianity was persecuted, but that it was allowed to exist at all."[17]

Nevertheless in the south when Morrison reached Guangzhou in 1807 he found three Chinese Roman Catholic priests itinerating around the province.[18] But it was illegal to spread the Christian faith; the penalty was strangulation.[19] So Morrison spent his first two years living like a fugitive, adopting Chinese clothes, avoiding the public eye, and going so far as to wear a false pigtail in order to look as Chinese as possible. Before long, however, he gave up the pretense as ineffectual and misleading but still kept a very low profile.[20]

In 1809 his situation considerably improved when the East India Company took notice of his rapidly increasing knowledge of the language. Two Chinese Roman Catholics had been secretly helping him.[21] The result was an appointment as translator for the very company that had tried to keep him out of China three years earlier,[22] and his presence in China seemed secure. But not for long.

In 1812 a shocking anti-imperial edict from Beijing threatened to cancel out whatever had been gained. Even his attempts to continue the study of the language were surrounded by danger. It was forbidden on pain of death for a Chinese to teach the language to a foreigner. At least one of his Chinese teachers, it is said, carried a small portion of poison with him, prepared to commit suicide rather than be tortured for breaking the law.[23] The new laws were not uniformly enforced, but unlike the situation in India, where within thirty years of the arrival of the first Protestant pioneers resident missionaries were freely preaching in all major parts of the country, in China not until 1843, six years after Morrison's death, was there even a partial lifting of the prohibitions, and that only as the result of foreign military intervention, the Opium War, 1839–1842. It was still sixteen more years after that before Guangzhou, where he had labored all his missionary life, could be opened in 1859 as a permanent mission station of the London Missionary Society.[24]

But first we must outline the pioneering achievements of Morrison himself on the mainland. Very early he made a highly significant and difficult decision that shaped his missionary strategy for the rest of his life. Should he preach and teach, or begin by concentrating whatever time and energy might be allowed him on a translation of the Bible into Chinese? He chose translation, because, as he put it, public evangelizing would soon bring deportation and leave the people without the continuing witness of the Word of God.[25]

The subsequent history of missions in the Far East attests that it was the right choice. Morrison's Chinese Bible, both Old and New Testaments, though probably not the first translation of the Bible into Chinese,[26] was the first published translation of the complete Scriptures into the written language of a fourth of the population of the globe.[27] In its impact on Asian Christianity it eclipsed all earlier Bible translations. The 1668 Malay translation of the gospel of Matthew,[28] Ziegenbalg's 1714 translation of the New Testament into Tamil, even William Carey's first translations into a number of Indian languages — none of these had the long-term, abiding influence in Asia of Morrison's Chinese Bible.[29] He completed the massive work in manuscript in 1819 with the aid of his colleague, William C. Milne, and acknowledging great help from a Chinese manuscript found in the British Museum in which "some pious missionary of the Romish Church," name unknown, had translated substantial parts of the New Testament from the book of Acts to the epistle to Philemon. To Morrison's first complete translation of the Bible into Chinese, and to the manuscript of his Chinese grammar (1815) and the manuscript of his Chinese-English dictionary (1821–1822), subsequent generations of missionaries were indebted for a hundred years.[30]

It was perhaps inevitable that there were some criticisms of his concentration on translations. What about evangelism? Where were the conversions? It was a time when missionaries from the same Society were sending glowing reports back to England of thousands of converts in the islands of the South Pacific, of cannibals baptized, and island kings bowing the knee to the King of Kings.[31] By contrast, it was seven years before Morrison could report the baptism of his first Chinese convert, Tsae A-Ko, the earnest young son of a second concubine.[32] In the first twenty-five years of the China mission there were only ten Chinese Christians baptized.[33]

But it would be a mistake to disparage the solid foundations for future growth laid down by Morrison, his colleagues, and the pioneers of the many Protestant societies who entered the door to China that he had opened.

The Ultra-Ganges Mission

On the edge of an empire so embittered by the rites controversy's rejection of its culture that it still opposed teaching the Chinese language to foreigners, Morrison's precarious early years led him to consider other means of bringing the Christian faith into China than by frontal attempts to insert foreign missionaries through China's only open port, Guangzhou. As early as September 1807 he warned against too visible a foreign Christian presence in Guangzhou and suggested instead the formation of a team of lay missionaries — a medical man, an astronomer, and a watch-maker — stationed outside China, but prepared to enter the empire when it might become possible.[34]

In 1809 again he wrote from Guangzhou to the directors of the London Missionary Society suggesting a "stepping stone" approach. Since for the foreseeable future China would be closed tight against the public entry of missionaries, why not establish a string of missionary bases along xenophobic China's southern frontiers on the southern coasts of Asia? There, in a great arc from Siam to Malaysia, Singapore, and down across the Indonesian archipelago to Amboina (Ambon),[35] the missionaries could learn Chinese in peace in Chinese communities outside China free from imperial prohibitions, and could translate and print the Bible, establish schools for the Chinese, and even train Chinese evangelists to return to their own homeland with the gospel. His first suggestion for such a base was the island of Penang (then Prince of Wales Island) on the Malay coast.[36] The Society responded favorably with the formation of what it called "the Ultra-Ganges Mission," that is, a mission to Asia beyond India. Its most important base proved to be Malacca, where the mission was finally provisionally organized in 1817, consisting at first of only two missionaries, William Milne[37] and the newly arrived Dr. Walter Henry Medhurst (1796–1857).[38]

Malacca was not unfamiliar ground for Christian missions. The Portuguese had occupied the city in 1511. The great Francis Xavier had used it as launching ground for his historic mission to Japan in 1549. The Protestant Dutch had taken it from the Portuguese in 1641; the English seized it from the Dutch in 1795. Moreover, by the providence of God, thought Milne, only a little more than a year before he arrived in Asia, the English Parliament, prodded by the evangelicals of the Wesley revivals, had forced an amendment to the charter of the East India Company that in effect reproved its previous long lapses into antimissionary policies and ensured freedom for the propagation of the Christian religion wherever British rule extended.[39]

Thus, because entry to China was so difficult, William Milne, the first missionary sent to help Morrison by the London Missionary Society, ended up not in China but in Malacca. He reached the Far East in 1813, and after a year-long unsuccessful search for permanent residence, first in Catholic Macao, and then with Morrison in Guangzhou, settled in English Malacca where four years later he helped form the Ultra-Ganges mission. His first confrontations with the Chinese language had been daunting. He wrote, almost in despair, "To acquire the Chinese [language] is a work for men with bodies of brass, lungs of steel, heads of oak, . . . eyes of eagles, hearts of apostles, memories of angels, and lives of Methusaleh!"[40]

Milne was not granted Methusaleh's 969 years, nor a body of brass and lungs of steel; after only nine years as a missionary in Asia he died, weak and emaciated, his lungs riddled with tuberculosis. He was only thirty-seven years old.[41] Yet in those few short years he had managed to contribute important sections to the most significant translation and printing of the Chinese Bible in all the previous twelve hundred years of China missions.[42] For the LMS he had surveyed missionary prospects in Southeast Asia from Guangzhou to Java. He had opened the first Protestant free school for the Chinese, published issues of the first Protestant periodical in Chinese, and with Morrison established the famous Anglo-Chinese College in Malacca, the first organized Protestant institution to begin to train Chinese evangelists for China.[43] His Chinese tract, *The Two Friends*, was the most effective and most widely distributed single piece of Christian literature in China in the nineteenth century (perhaps as many as 2 million copies in seventeen editions, and still used in the twentieth century).[44]

He also seems to merit the distinction of being the first writer to denounce the opium trade as the "curse of China and the disgrace of the East India Company," and it was he who encouraged Morrison to do the same in Guangzhou. Let it be noted that China missionaries, sometimes too quickly declared guilty of association with that despicable trade, were in fact the first to "raise the cry, 'No Opium.' "[45]

On November 3, 1816, Milne performed one of the most significant acts of his whole short ministry on the edge of China. On that day he baptized Liang Fa, a young Cantonese who was in mission employ as a printer. Liang had come with Milne to Malacca the year before, quite willing to listen to the missionaries and work for them, but he was neither persuaded enough nor courageous enough to take the step of public profession of the Christian faith. Milne never pressed him, but was rewarded for his patience and rejoiced when of his own volition Liang asked for baptism. Milne did not live long enough to know how much he had contributed to the future of organized Protestant Christianity in China. He did not know that some five years later the young man would be ordained by Morrison in Guangzhou as the first ordained Chinese Protestant evangelist to his own people.[46]

Liang Fa[47] and the Beginnings of Indigenous Evangelism

Three or four years before the Protestant pioneer, Morrison, landed in Guangzhou, a teenaged Hakka[48] boy was forced by family poverty to seek a better life in the big city about seventy miles away. There Liang Fa (or Liang A-Fa)[49] met Morrison's colleague William Milne, who discovered that the young man had already memorized the basic Confucian classics and had acquired some experience as a carver of wooden printing blocks for the printing of Chinese books. As mentioned above, Milne hired him for the Christian printing project that Morrison and he proposed to set up in Malaya and took him to Malacca in 1815.

Liang enjoyed the work there, but reacted against enforced Bible reading, preferring for a time the arguments of a friendly Buddhist priest. But the Bible readings and Milne's daily prayers had their effect. His Confucian background had given him a sense of the importance of moral integrity but no assurance of his power to attain it either in his own life or in the culture of his own heritage. Confucianism had not freed him from "licentious thoughts," and Buddhist chanting of the sutras was impotent against what he came to believe was the agonizing power of evil and sin not only in his own heart but in the obvious corruptions of the Chinese culture which he saw all around him. His immediate recourse was to turn to the Christian faith of his new foreign friends, and to the moral and spiritual power for which he had been seeking and now found in a renewed study of the New Testament. In 1816, after long discussions with Milne, he asked for and received baptism "in the name of the adorable Trinity."[50] Liang Fa had become, as Milne wrote, "no longer a servant, but more than a servant, a brother beloved."[51]

This conversion experience, together with copious quotations from Morrison's and Milne's Chinese translations of the Bible, was the basic background for what proved to be Liang's most influential literary work, "Good Words to Admonish the Age" (*quan shi liang yan*). It has been called "the most complete statement of Protestant doctrine by a Chinese during the first half of the nineteenth century." Basing his philosophic argument on a strong statement of Christian monotheism couched in terms of filial devotion to the one, true God and therefore calculated to catch the attention of Confucianists, he severely criticized his own Chinese Confucian culture — and even more unsparingly Buddhism, Taoism, and spirit-worship — for a moral, philosophic, and religious self-ishness that lacked concern for social welfare and compassion for the poor.[52] But it is important to remember, with Bohr, that "Liang turned to Christianity not to repudiate the ideals of his own Chinese moral tradition but to achieve them."[53] John K. Fairbank describes this influential work as "a case study in Sinification — how a Chinese convert found in Protestantism what he had been seeking in China."[54]

By 1819 Liang was back in Guangzhou distributing Christian literature and already beginning to itinerate in the province outside the city. This was the first important breakthrough by Protestants into the immediate interior surrounding the ports, territory still closed to free access by foreign missionaries. In 1824 Morrison ordained him as an evangelist, and he was looked upon both by the British and American missionaries as a Chinese colleague and advance representative in outreach to the countryside.[55] Liang Fa's improved knowledge of the classics made him a sharp conversationalist with non-Christians. When a listener objected to talk of Jesus' miracles and asked if he had seen them, Liang answered, "No, but they are related in the Sacred Books." The man scornfully quoted Mencius, "It would be better to have no books than to believe every book," and the evangelist aptly replied with another quotation from Mencius, "A good man may be deceived by a distorted representation of facts, but cannot be deluded so as to believe things absolutely absurd."[56]

But evangelism was interrupted by government persecution, and for some four or more years Liang was in exile in Malacca. In 1839 he returned and soon had baptized four new believers and was leading Sunday worship for a congregation of twelve believers.[57] But events were moving fast toward war between Britain and China. By a strange coincidence, John R. Morrison, the son of Liang's old patron, Robert Morrison, had been appointed British representative in Guangzhou. Liang called on the younger Morrison to plead for peace between England and China, and in great distress, pleaded with him to make every effort to avoid a clash between the two powers. If England goes to war with China, he said, the Chinese will no longer listen to the missionaries or read their Bible. But it was too late. War broke out, and he eased his sorrow by visiting patients in the Hog Lane hospital of the American missionary, Dr. Peter Parker. After the war he was officially appointed hospital chaplain. Within three and a half years his records showed that he had preached the gospel to fifteen thousand people there in the hospital chapel. He lamented, though, how few had been converted, and at his own expense he built a chapel attached to his own home, beginning with a congregation of about eight people.[58] He was still serving as a hospital evangelist in 1855, this time as the evangelistic partner of the British medical missionary, Dr. Benjamin Hobson of the LMS, son-in-law of Robert Morrison. After his funeral "in the little church of the Hospital of Merciful Love," fifteen people asked for Christian baptism.[59]

There was another breakthrough directly attributable to this often lonely pioneer Chinese Protestant evangelist, a matter of which even he was not aware. From the beginning he had taken the initiative not only in preparing the blocks for printing the tracts in Chinese, but also in writing them. For his first attempt he chose a selection of Scripture passages he thought would catch the attention of Chinese readers, and had carved the woodblocks himself and printed off two hundred copies before the police caught wind of it, destroyed the blocks and tracts, and cast him into prison. Morrison managed to secure his release, but not until Liang had been bloodily beaten with large bamboo staves.[60]

The evangelist was irrepressible. He printed another, much longer tract, a five-hundred-page work in nine small volumes in 1832, which became his most famous work, "Good Words," noted above, and in 1834 was out distributing it to some of the 11,600 candidates at the prestigious national examinations for aspiring candidates for offices in government service. A copy, either then or later, fell into the hands of a disappointed unsuccessful candidate, Hong Xiuquan (1813–1864).[61] Out of the seed of biblical teaching and imagery planted by that tract and wildly distorted in Hong's fevered mind would come the visions and concepts that turned Hong, the disappointed scholar, into an angry, charismatic rebel. In the 1850s his Taiping rebellion came within a few miles of toppling the Qing (Ch'ing) dynasty from its throne a whole half-century before its time.[62]

But more about that later. The rebellion was only one of a series of shocks that rocked the empire throughout the last sixty years of the nineteenth century. Liang Fa died in 1855.

The Growth of Protestant Missions to the Chinese (1817–1840)

Though Milne was soon joined by others who undertook work among the Muslim Malay majority in Malacca,[63] the focus remained fixed on reaching the Chinese community as a bridge to the still forbidden empire. And the motive was urgently evangelistic. Walter Henry Medhurst, the London Missionary Society printer who joined Milne in Malacca in 1817 and in 1835 surveyed prospects in China for the mission after the death of Morrison, wrote forcibly on the mission's foremost challenge:

> Three hundred and sixty millions of human beings huddled together in one country, under the sway of one despotic monarch, influenced by the same delusive philosophy, and bowing down to the same absurd superstition. One

third of the human race, and one half of the heathen world . . . ; one million of whom are every month dropping into eternity, untaught, unsanctified, and, as far as we know — unsaved.[64]

The most ambitious step toward the evangelization of that forbidden empire was Morrison's imaginative project of a Christian school to bring together under a Christian framework European and Chinese students for joint education in Eastern and Western science and culture, for better mutual understanding, and preeminently for Christian worship and instruction with a view to training for evangelism. Launched in 1818 and opened in Malacca in 1820 with Milne as its principal, it continued for twenty-two years before moving to Hong Kong, but never quite lived up to expectations. It moved to Hong Kong in 1842, adding some theological courses for training evangelists. One of its students was Liang Junde, son of Morrison's first convert, Liang Fa.[65]

Other Protestant missions soon followed the example of the London Missionary Society and began to feel their way toward a mission that would penetrate the wall of separation China had built around itself against foreigners. An American counterpart of the LMS, the American Board of Commissioners for Foreign Missions (ABCFM), independent and interdenominational, had been organized in 1811 upon the initiative, surprisingly, not of church leaders but of students. In 1829 it sent two young men to China, David Abeel[66] and Elijah C. Bridgman, who reached Guangzhou in 1830. Bridgman began language study at once, and managed to open a small school for Chinese boys, install a printing press, and begin publication of the most widely read periodical about China — religious or secular — in the first half of the nineteenth century, *Chinese Repository.*[67]

Then arrived a young man of whom it has been said, "He opened China at the point of a lancet," the first medical missionary fully assigned to work for Chinese in China, Dr. Peter Parker (1804–1888). He joined Bridgman in 1834, fresh from Yale where he had studied both theology and medicine.[68] The versatile Parker proved to be one of the most effective missionaries among the early pioneers. During his twenty-three years in China (1834–1857) his medical skill opened doors closed to evangelists, established the first mission hospital, the Ophthalmic Hospital in Guangzhou,[69] and a Medical Missionary Society to coordinate on a nationwide basis the healing witness of the Christian gospel.[70] In 1844, Parker's national reputation as a friend of the Chinese moved the American government to appoint him secretary of the United States legation and eventually U.S. Commissioner to the Chinese Empire, the highest American diplomatic office in the land. His home board, The American Board of Commissioners for Foreign Missions, adhering to its policy forbidding missionaries to engage in government employment, terminated his service, but Parker never stopped being a missionary. In his new position, he promptly used his powers to prohibit the slave trade in Chinese coolies by Americans on American ships, and helped negotiate the notable treaty of 1858 between the United States and China that finally guaranteed freedom of Christian missionary work in the empire.[71]

In Ningbo, about one hundred miles straight south of Shanghai across the Hangzhou (Hangchow) Bay, the Presbyterians opened another hospital and a boys' school in 1844–1845, just after British victory in the first Anglo-Chinese (or "Opium") War. The hospitals and the school — tiny, unimpressive symbols of healing and enlightenment — were the almost unnoticed beginnings of Protestant medical and educational missions in China, which were so greatly to influence the history of the next hundred years.[72] They were also examples of the spreading influence of the new American missions at a time when French and British imperialism was dominant in the nineteenth-century encounter of China with the West, the arrival of the American missions presented a somewhat less threatening face than their European counterparts.

Gützlaff, a Continental European Protestant Pioneer

One European mission in China seemed to pose no imperialist threat. Whatever its history had been in earlier centuries in South Asia,[73] the Netherlands Missionary Society, despite its reputation in Indonesia, represented too small a country to be dangerous. But its pioneer in China, the impatient, indefatigable Karl Friedrich Augustus Gützlaff (1803–1851), a Lutheran, proved to be one of the most gifted and controversial Protestant figures on the China coast for much of the first half of the nineteenth century.[74] Gützlaff reached Southeast Asia in 1827, learned Chinese in Java and Bangkok, and made three important voyages along the Chinese coast from 1831 to 1833, in the course of which he became the first Protestant missionary to set foot on the soil of the fast-closed kingdom of Korea.[75]

Out of his observations in the China trading ports he visited came a word of hope to the increasing number of mission societies eager to enter China but blocked by its closed borders. There were three doors already open or beginning to open, he pointed out. The empire's ports of international trade afforded at least temporary, partial access; the country was also open to the "silent evangelism" of Christian publications in Chinese carried by ship; and in larger areas surrounding the ports Chinese evangelists were already successfully itinerating in the countryside, preaching and distributing Christian printed materials.[76] Faithful to his own advice, Gützlaff wrote untiringly in Chinese. One listing of his published Chinese books and treatises contains sixty-one different titles.[77]

Less successful, but no less important was Gützlaff's experiment with the organization of a band of native Chinese evangelists and colporteurs, beginning in 1844. This was after he had left the Netherlands Missionary Society to work as an independent missionary in the new British colony of Hong Kong. It was a brilliant concept. His "Christian Union" of native Chinese, as he called it, unfettered by the handicap of foreign birth and appearance, would cross the border and fan out across the mainland into all of China's unreached "Eighteen Provinces," excluding only Gangsu in the far west, preaching, distributing Bibles, and organizing in each province their own Christian Unions. Thus the whole untouched empire would be reached for Christ.[78] He wrote, "China can only be converted through Chinese. To reach this goal the nation itself has to be stirred and the [gospel] has to be given to it as a graceful gift of God, but not as a present of foreigners or as a teaching of foreign countries."[79]

But it was an idea whose time had not yet come. The heartbreak of Gützlaff's missionary life was the collapse of the Union. Unfortunately, since he could not go with the colporteurs to observe and advise, some abused their responsibility and once out of sight not only made a profit by selling the literature instead of distributing it, but also falsified reports of their travel and contacts.[80] This has been called Gützlaff's great failure: putting too much of his trust in Chinese converts. However, his failure, if failure it was, was not in trusting the Chinese converts, but in trusting the wrong ones. In fact the unexpected success of the work of the Basel mission in China among Hakka of southern China was largely due to former discredited members of Gützlaff's China Union.

The Hakka were a Han Chinese people speaking a minority language, not just a dialect, unintelligible to other Chinese. This had isolated them from the Chinese mainstream, which held them in disdain and subjected them to social discrimination and poverty. But as a result, they proved to be all the more receptive to the liberating message of the Christian faith. The apostle to the Hakka was Jiang Jioren (Kong Jin), himself a Hakka, and one of the guilty colporteurs who had deceived Gützlaff. The pioneer Basel mission pioneer to China, Theodor Hamberg, who in Gützlaff's absence was directing the Chinese Union, with great wisdom sensed that not all the counterfeit colporteurs were irredeemable. Jiang and a number of others sincerely repented, confessed, and proved their conversion by their deeds. Jiang Jioren, with another faithful evangelist, laid the foundations of the rise of Hakka Christianity, which spread beyond the borders of his own village in the Hakka heartland, about 250 miles northeast of Guangzhou, throughout the province, and into Hong Kong and across to Formosa (Taiwan).

Even more unusual, for China at that time, was the contribution of Jiang Jioren's wife, Ye Huansha, who broke the barriers against female education, learned Chinese characters, romanized the Hakka language, and translated Chinese tracts into Hakka. The opposition of Jiang's family and the hatred of his home village to such a feminist contravention of tradition melted, first in his own family, then among his relatives, and soon doors began to open to the new ways of the new religion through his wife's relatives in another village.[81]

Gützlaff has also been criticized unfairly for traveling on the opium ships, which were often the only means of transportation up the rivers and along the China coast. They were the freighters of their day and travel on them was often inescapable. He is more vulnerable to the accusation of complicity in the first Opium War (1841–1842) as translator and negotiator for the British commander-in-chief, a task that inevitably involved the communication of reports from the invaders' Chinese spies. He even drew up the plans for the victorious advance to Nanjing that ended the war. There is no question that he saw in a British victory a decisive opening for the Christianizing of China. What he did not foresee was how his use of questionable means toward that end would affect Chinese reaction not only to foreign armies but to foreign missionaries as well.[82]

The Opium Wars (1839–1844, 1856–1860)

Midway in the century two wars between the empire and Western powers broke China's control of its own borders, destroyed its myth of world supremacy, and brought to an end its centuries-old policy of deliberate isolation from unwanted outside contacts. When the British East India Company lost its monopoly of the opium trade with China in 1834, Britain's demand for free trade on the basis of diplomatic equality threw China into economic chaos and political demoralization.[83] Free trade meant enormous profits for Britain in a drug traffic that China, commendably, was trying to stamp out with edict after edict against the supply of opium on Western ships from South Asia.[84] In one fifteen-year period between 1820 and 1835, just before outbreak of war between England and China, as a result of the shameful and illegal trade the number of opium addicts in China leaped from 366,000 to 2,040,000.[85]

Out of this clash between Britain's demand for free trade and China's struggle to stem the tidal wave of smuggled drugs came the first Opium War (1834–1842), in which Chinese war-junks and port batteries proved no match for the British gunboats. The Treaty of Nanjing in 1842, however, not only opened up China for opium, incongruously it also opened the coast for missionaries. Five of China's major ports — Guangzhou (Canton), Xiamen (Amoy), Fuzhou (Foochow), Ningbo (Ningpo), and Shanghai — became treaty ports, not only open to foreigners, but with special privileges granted to foreigners. And an apparently useless island, Hong Kong, was ceded outright to the British, who knew a natural port when they saw one. Foreigners at last were legally permitted to study Chinese, and could build houses, schools, and churches in the open ports.[86]

A second Opium War fourteen years later added to China's humiliation (1856–1860). It brought France to join Great Britain after the execution and torture of a French priest in the inland southern province of Guongxi, where the Taiping rebellion had originated. The resulting treaties of 1858 to 1860 marked a significant enlargement of foreigners' extraterritorial rights in China. For the first time foreigners could legally travel outside the treaty ports, and additional ports were opened.[87] Most important of all to the Christian missions were the clauses guaranteeing freedom of worship and protection of Christians, both foreign and Chinese, anywhere in the empire.[88]

The Taiping Rebellion (1851–1864)[89]

About five years before the outbreak of the first Opium War,[90] the ambitious scholar Hong Xiuquan, during his failed attempt to pass the all-important government examinations, had received a copy of Liang Fa's book *Good Words*, as noted above. Mentally depressed by his failure, he may only have glanced at it. But his mind was filled with strange, disturbing visions. An old man with a golden beard appeared to him, gave him a sword, and commanded him to destroy the demons. Then a younger man, whom Hong calls "elder brother," berates Confucius for not teaching "the true doctrine." Confucius flees, and the "elder brother" orders Hong to pursue him, bind him, and have him whipped.[91]

In 1843 Hong tried the examinations again and failed again. But this time his attention was called once more to the tracts of Liang Fa, which he had laid aside for seven or more years. To his amazement they now suddenly seemed to make sense of his strange visions. The old man with the gold beard, could that be Jehovah (Liang's *shen ye he hua*)? The younger man, Hong's "elder brother," was he not Jesus Christ? From that time on, his life was changed and so was the course of Chinese history.[92] He baptized himself and began to convert some fellow schoolmasters, who removed the Confucian tablets from their schoolrooms and formed themselves into a "God Worshipers Society," devout, praying, and speaking in tongues.[93] They were Hakka people, from the sizeable Hakka minority in China's southern provinces, and Hong, also a Hakka, was accepted as their leader and teacher.

In 1847, he spent two months in Guangzhou in the home of an American Southern Baptist missionary, Issachar Jacoz Roberts (1802–1871),[94] but left unsatisfied when Roberts told him he was not ready for genuine baptism.[95] Nevertheless, the instruction he had received there further filled Hong's mind with Bible passages and images, which he pulled together the next year in an account of his conversion and call.[96] In it he tells how the God of the Christians, the Heavenly Father, and his eldest son, Christ the Savior, had appointed him, Hong, as the "Taiping (Great Peace) Son of Heaven" to exterminate the depraved and preserve the upright,[97] to cleanse China from its sins, to expose the errors of Confucius,[98] to drive out the demons of Buddhism,[99] and to hurl the usurping Manchu emperor from his throne in Beijing.[100]

With astonishing speed Hong proceeded to form and discipline an army that marched north, routing the empire's Manchu troops and capturing the old southern capital, Nanjing, in 1853. There he established his own "Heavenly Capital," his New Jerusalem and "paradise on earth"[101] in Nanjing, with himself as its heaven-born "True Lord." All people were to worship God and destroy their idols.[102] A steady stream of edicts and publications poured from the Taiping press. They represent a more explicit but much less orthodox pattern of the Christianity that he thought he had learned from Liang Fa's *Good Words,* and from the brief period of instruction with the Baptist missionary, Roberts, in Guangzhou. The Taiping government did indeed quickly print, all in one year, 1853, various portions of the Bible, culminating in *The Holy Book of the Old Testament* (containing six of the Old Testament Books, Genesis to Joshua), and *The Holy Book of the Former Testament* (containing all the books of the New Testament).[103]

Observers were astonished; missionaries prematurely rejoiced. But further examination, as by the American missionary, W. H. Medhurst (1796–1857), of the ABCFM,[104] produced disquieting information. The Taiping insurgents in 1852 had added a third book to the canon, *The Book of Heaven-Commanded Edicts.* Moreover, Hong Xiuquan had written copious, bizarre annotations on portions of the Old Testament and New Testament texts as his own authoritative interpretation of the Scriptures.[105] The result was theological anarchy, an explosive mix of Bible truth, Chinese mythological fantasy, and imperial egocentricity. It was pseudo-Christianity. An example is his doctrine of the Trinity, found in his annotations on the First Epistle of John, and the book of Revelation:

> There is only one Supreme God. Christ is the First Son of God. The Son was born of the Father, originally one and only one body. But the Father is the Father; the Son, the Son; one in two and two in one. As to the Holy Spirit or the Eastern King, Almighty God issued an edict appointing him to be the Spirit. The Eastern King is a beloved Son of God, and, together with the Great Elder Brother [Jesus] and Myself was born of the same Mother...The Father knows...that the people on earth mistakenly think that Christ is God...I Myself ascended to the High Heaven, saw the Heavenly Father, the Heavenly Mother, the Great Elder Brother and the Heavenly Sister-in-Law many times.[106]

And further, "I Myself was the Sun; My Wife, the Moon."[107]

Equally alarming were reports that began to circulate about excessive disciplines demanded of the rebel armies. All must memorize the Ten Commandments; if they fail to do so within three weeks, "cut off their heads." If they are noisy during worship, "cut off their heads." If any are caught in adultery, "cut off their heads." If any smoke tobacco, or fail to attend the preaching services, on the first violation, the punishment will be a hundred lashes, on the second, a thousand lashes, and on the third, "cut off their heads."[108]

But discipline did not win the war; it was foreign intervention assisting a Confucian counterattack[109] against the pseudo-Christian Taiping that, in 1864, finally rescued the Qing (Ch'ing) dynasty from destruction. There is dramatic irony in the fact that a Christian British general, "Chinese" Gordon, was instrumental in saving the non-Christian Manchu empire from a Chinese "Christian" claimant to the throne by destroying the myth of Taiping military invincibility. The other irony is that the Confucian counterattack against Taiping anti-Confucianism failed to save Confucianism from decline and an eventual "dying fall" that had begun with the planting of the poison seed of the worldview of the Taiping rebels.[110] However distorted their Christianity may have been, it was thoroughly transcendental and ultra-Chinese, an opening wedge for disturbing knowledge brought from beyond the seas, but spread by Chinese themselves. For Christianity, however, that religious seed though disavowed in its Taiping form by Protestants and Catholics alike, was not poison but a catalyst for coming change.[111]

NOTES

1. I use the reign titles of Chinese emperors, as is customary. More technically correct would be to refer to his period as the Jiaqing reign of Renzhong (1796–1820); and to his father's as the Quianlong reign of Hung Li (1736–1795).

2. The text is translated in J. J. M. De Groot, *Sectarianism and Religious Persecution in China: A Page in the History of Religions*, 2 vols. in 1 (Amsterdam: J. Müller, 1903), 378–382.

3. On the rites controversy (1645–1742), see chap. 5.

4. L.-E. Louvet, *Les missions catholiques au XIXme siècle* (Lille: Société de Saint Augustin, 1898), 25. Cf. Latourette, *A History of Christian Missions in China*, 129, 174, who estimates that in 1700, there were 300,000 Christians, "possibly very much less"; in 1783, 150,000. Cf. Schmidlin, *Catholic Mission History*, 610, who gives a generous estimate of 300,000 for the number of Chinese Christians in 1800.

5. Latourette, *History of Christian Missions in China*, 229ff.; Beatrice Leung Ka-Lun and John D. Young, eds., *Christianity in China: Foundations for Dialogue* (Hong Kong: University of Hong Kong, 1993), 37.

6. See vol. 1 of this work, chap. 15, 287–323.

7. See vol. 1 of this work, chap. 20, 442–469.

8. See vol. 1 of this work, 288.

9. See above chaps. 8 and 9.

10. The phrase is Latourette's.

11. Elizabeth Morrison, *Memoirs of the Life and Labours of Robert Morrison*, 2 vols. (London: Longman, Orme, Brown, Green and Longman, 1839), 1:50–51, 65.

12. The phrase is from St. Paul, Phil. 4:13. E. Morrison, *Memoirs of the Life and Labours of Robert Morrison*, 51. For samples of Morrison's own theology and motivation, see Robert Morrison, *The Knowledge of Christ Supremely Excellent: The Means and Duty of Diffusing It among All Nations* (London: Francis Westley, 1825); and *A Parting Memorial: consisting of Miscellaneous Discourses . . . , with Remarks on Missions* (London: W. Simpkins & R. Marshall, 1826).

13. Throughout the history of the Company there were notable exceptions to its antimissionary attitudes. To mention only a few of the supporters of missions in the Company, there were Elihu Yale, president at Madras (1687–1692), who, incidentally, made enough of a fortune in India to endow later the beginnings of Yale University in the American colonies; Gov.-General Lord Wellesley; Charles Grant (in India, 1768–1790), a powerful member of the Company's court of directors in India, and a strongly evangelical, Calvinistic Anglican; and John Shore (later Lord Teignmouth), the principal advisor to the Gov. General Lord Cornwallis. It should also be remembered that the evangelical chaplains, especially David Brown, Claudius Buchanan, and Henry Martyn, were all Company employees.

14. E. Morrison, *Memoirs of the Life and Labours of Robert Morrison*, 1:136, citing the *New York Observer* (see microfilm 3438:1; 3–230).

15. Latourette, *A History of Christian Missions in China*, 160 n. 5.

16. Latourette, *A History of Christian Missions in China*, 174–180. Of the seven priests remaining, six were Vincentians, one "an aged Jesuit" (178).

17. Latourette, *A History of Christian Missions in China*, 180.

18. Morrison, Letter, November 4, 1807, in E. Morrison, *Memoirs of the Life and Labours of Robert Morrison*, 1:165–166.

19. The prohibition of Christianity, previously somewhat ambiguous, was sharpened by edicts in 1814, 1826, and 1836. See Robert Morrison, "Respecting the Disposition and Policy of This Government toward Christianity," *ChRep* 6 (June 1837): 49–54.

20. William Milne, *A Retrospect of the First Ten Years of the Protestant Mission to China* (Malacca: Anglo-Chinese Press, 1820), 64ff.

21. In Guangzhou the Roman Catholics were friendly, but the Portuguese hierarchy in Macao forbade their people to help Morrison with the language (E. Morrison, *Memoirs of the Life and Labours of Robert Morrison*, 1:288).

22. E. Morrison, *Memoirs of the Life and Labours of Robert Morrison*, 1:159, 163–164, 244.

23. At first, there seemed to be no specific prohibition against Bible translation, but the government became more and more hostile to such foreign influences until the harsh 1812 anti-imperial edict made the printing of Christian books in Chinese a capital crime. Morrison, letter from Guangzhou, April 2, 1812, in E. Morrison, *Memoirs of the Life and Labours of Robert Morrison*, 1:334ff. See also Milne, *A Retrospect of the First Ten Years of the Protestant Mission to China*, 74. Cf. E. Nida, ed., *The Book of a Thousand Tongues*, rev. ed. (New York: United Bible Societies, 1972), 71. See also E. Morrison, *Memoirs of the Life and Labours of Robert Morrison*, 1:288–289, on government hostility.

24. Norman Goodall, *A History of the London Missionary Society 1859–1945* (London and New York: Oxford University Press, 1954), 145.

25. Morrison, Letter, December 6, 1807, in E. Morrison, *Memoirs of the Life and Labours of Robert Morrison*, 1:181.

26. Morrison himself had used a manuscript in the British Museum of a Chinese translation by an unknown Catholic of at least parts of the Bible, and there are other references as early as 1696 to translations of portions, and perhaps of both Old and New Testament, but none were published. See Arnold Foster, *Christian Progress in China* (London: Religious Tract Society, 1889), 36–40, citing Alexander Wylie, "The Bible in China," in *The Bible Society Monthly Reporter,* August 1882.

27. Morrison's Chinese translation was published in 1823; an 1822 version from the Serampore group, principally Marshman and Lassar, was flawed and not circulated but influenced New Testament translations by Goddard (1853) and Lord (1872). But to Morrison's magisterial translation, all subsequent Protestant translations directly or indirectly derive: Medhurst, Gützlaff, Bridgman and J. Morrison (1835), Gützlaff (1840), a "Delegates" version (1855), Bridgman and Culbertson (1863), the Pekin Committee N.T. (1870), Schereschewsky's O.T. (1875), Griffith John (1883), Blodget and Burdon N.T. (1889), and the Union Version authorized by the Shanghai Conference in 1890 but published after the turn of the century. All such translations must be credited with making significant improvements on the original. For a chart, see J. Campbell Gibson, *Mission Problems and Mission Methods in South China* (New York: Fleming H. Revell, 1901), 208.

28. Nida, *The Book of a Thousand Tongues,* 484; Smalley, *Translation as Mission,* 21.

29. For a careful summary of the history of early publication of Bible translations into literary Chinese (High Wenli, or Wenyen), see Nida, *The Book of a Thousand Tongues,* 70–72. Manuscript translations of portions date back to seventh-century Nestorians and thirteenth-century Franciscans in Mongolia. In 1615 the Jesuits in Beijing obtained permission for a Bible translation but produced no published Bible. Joshua Marshman's attempt at a translation in Serampore, India, was published in 1822, a year before Morrison's, but proved to be unusable.

30. Two letters of Morrison from Guangzhou, December 4, 1809, and November 25, 1819, in E. Morrison, *Memoirs of the Life and Labours of Robert Morrison,* 1:233, 265, 268; 2:2–11. The manuscript referred to was in the British Museum, and was copied for Morrison by the London Missionary Society. It contained a translation of the New Testament books from Acts through Philemon, which Morrison corrected and adapted. Milne's contribution was the translation of Job and the historical books of the Old Testament.

31. Letter, William Milne to Robert Morrison, from Malacca, November 26, 1819, in E. Morrison, *Memoirs of the Life and Labours of Robert Morrison,* 2:12–14. The Society speaks of the years 1820–1850 as years of triumph in the Pacific.

32. On Tsae A-Ko, see E. Morrison, *Memoirs of the Life and Labours of Robert Morrison,* 1:408–410. The date was July 10, 1814. See also Robert Philip, *The Life and Opinions of the Rev. William Milne, D.D., Missionary to China, Illustrated by Biographical Annals of Asiatic Missions from Primitive to Protestant Times* (Philadelphia: Herman Hooker, 1840), 147–151; and George Hunter McNeur, *China's First Preacher, Liang A-Fa 1789–1855* (Shanghai: Kwang Hsueh Publishing House, Oxford University Press, China Agency, 1934), 21–22.

33. E. Morrison, *Memoirs of the Life and Labours of Robert Morrison,* 1:409; Latourette, *History of China Missions,* 212–213.

34. Morrison, Letter, September 27, 1807, in E. Morrison, *Memoirs of the Life and Labours of Robert Morrison*, 1:170–171.

35. Latourette, *A History of Christian Missions in China*, 212–213; Henry Northcott, *Glorious Company: One Hundred and Fifty Years Life and Work of the London Missionary Society 1795–1945* (London: Livingstone Press, 1945), 28, 77.

36. E. Morrison, *Memoirs of the Life and Labours of Robert Morrison*, 273, quoting at some length from Morrison's December 4, 1809, letter to the directors.

37. Philip, *The Life and Opinions of the Rev. William Milne*, 250–251. William Milne, raised and educated by his mother after his father died when the boy was six, left the Church of Scotland for a "more evangelical" Congregational church near Aberdeen and served under the largely Congregational London Missionary Society. Two primary sources for Milne are: Milne, *A Retrospect of the First Ten Years of the Protestant Mission to China*; and his letters, collected and edited by Philip, *The Life and Opinions of the Rev. William Milne*. Morrison joined Milne briefly in Macao to draw up the organizing regulations (E. Morrison, *Memoirs of the Life and Labours of Robert Morrison*, 1:512–515).

38. On Medhurst, who reached China in 1817 as a printer, and moved to Shanghai in 1843 to begin, with others, a new Chinese version of the Bible in Mandarin, see Latourette, *A History of Christian Missions in China*, 213, 247, 262, 269, 337, 430.

39. Milne, *A Retrospect of the First Ten Years of the Protestant Mission to China*. On the 1813 amendment to the charter, made even more explicit by another amendment in 1833, see chap. 5 above. But note Milne's later sharp opposition to the same East India Company's opium policy referred to above.

40. Written in Guangzhou in 1814. Philip, *The Life and Opinions of the Rev. William Milne*, 129.

41. Philip, *The Life and Opinions of the Rev. William Milne*, 309.

42. A not sufficiently recognized contribution of the Protestant printing of the Bible was its pioneering role in the printing of the Chinese language, the replacement of traditional Chinese xylography by typography. See Jean-Pierre Drège, "Les aventures de la typographie et les missionnaires protestants en Chine au XIXe siècle," in *JA* 30 (1992): 279–309. The pioneers in the development of typography were Marshman in India, who was impatient with his attempts at block-printing of Chinese works, and in China, Morrison, Milne, Liang Fa (Liang A-Fa), and W. H. Medhurst, who began to champion movable metal type over block-printing. Samuel Dyer (1804–1843) made an important contribution to Bible publishing in inventing and perfecting movable Chinese metal type to replace the traditional wood blocks in the printing of the Scriptures. He designed punches of type for the five thousand most common Chinese characters, reducing considerably the cost of printing. See Evan Davies, *Memoir of the Rev. Samuel Dyer, Sixteen Years Missionary to the Chinese* (London: J. Snow, 1846); and Alexander Wylie, Memorials of Protestant Missionaries to the Chinese: Giving a List of Their Publications and Obituary Notices (Shanghai: American Presbyterian Mission, 1867), 51–53. See W. H. Medhurst, *China: Its State and Prospects* (Boston: Crocker & Brewster, 1838), 552–565. It should be noted, however, that the earliest use of movable metal type was Asiatic, not Western, and traceable to Korea in 1403 (and possibly a century earlier), rather than to Gutenberg in 1440. See Melvin P. McGovern, *Specimen Pages of Korean Moveable Type* (Los Angeles: Dawson's Book Shop, 1966), frontispiece and 13–14.

43. Philip, *The Life and Opinions of the Rev. William Milne,* 159–167, 249 (on language translation); 166–714 (on relocation in Malacca); 172–177 (on the free school); 181–184 (on the Chinese periodical); and 213–217, 249 (on the printing press).

44. Daniel H. Bays, "Christian Tracts: The Two Friends," in *Christianity in China: Early Protestant Missionary Writings,* ed. Suzanne Wilson Barnett and John King Fairbank (Cambridge, Mass.: Harvard University Press, 1985), 19–34.

45. See Milne, *A Retrospect of the First Ten Years of the Protestant Mission to China,* 318; Philip, *The Life and Opinions of the Rev. William Milne,* 428ff.

46. On Liang Fa see Philip, *The Life and Opinions of the Rev. William Milne,* 206–212; Medhurst, *China: Its State and Prospects,* 270–282; and McNeur, *China's First Preacher,* 23–30.

47. Liang Fa was born about 1794 and died in 1855. The earliest account of his life is by Elijah C. Bridgman, "Brief Memoir of the Evangelist Leang A-Fa," in *MH* 30 (October 1834): 353–357. A fine biography by McNeur is the most complete source, *China's First Preacher.* Cf. Alexander Wylie, under Leang Kung-Fa in *Memorials of Protestant Missionaries to the Chinese,* 21–25.

48. The Hakka were originally from North China, part of a centuries-old (twelfth-century?) flight of refugees into the southern provinces, notably Guangdong and Guongxi.

49. Liang Fa was his name in Cantonese, but he was a Hakka. The missionaries used Liang (or Leang) Fa (or Fah). His move to Guangzhou was probably in 1804, but could have been in 1803 (McNeur, *China's First Preacher,* 10). See also P. Richard Bohr, "Liang Fa's Quest for Moral Power," in *Christianity in China: Early Protestant Missionary Writings,* ed. Suzanne Wilson Barnett and John King Fairbank (Cambridge, Mass.: Harvard University Press, 1985), 36–37.

50. Bridgman, "Brief Memoir of the Evangelist Leang A-Fa," 354–356; Philip, *The Life and Opinions of the Rev. William Milne,* 206–209; McNeur, *China's First Preacher,* 14–15, 23–30; Bohr, "Liang Fa's Quest for Moral Power," 36–40. Liang's criticisms of China's religious and popular culture were scathing, as Bohr notes: "In Liang's view the Chinese worship of 'lifeless images' sacrificed moral purity to pragmatic utility. In particular he charged that Confucians prayed only for success in examinations. The Taoists were obsessed with seeking immortality he believed, while the Buddhists quested selfishly after entrance into the Western Paradise. Further the populace engaged in geomancy, fortune telling, communicating with ghosts, and working spells for protection, wealth and sons. In Liang's view, all this bespoke a lack of serious commitment to the Chinese religious tradition and inhibited faith in God's compassionate governance. In fact, it was responsible for the violence, sexual license, gambling, and opium addiction for which Canton was infamous." Bohr (41, nn. 20, 21), citing Liang's tract, "Good Words to Admonish the Age."

51. McNeur, *China's First Preacher,* 29.

52. See Wylie's summary of the contents of "Good Words," which was not published until 1832, *Memorials of Protestant Missionaries to the Chinese,* 23–24; and Bohr's extended analysis, "Leang Fa's Quest," 40–46; and Daniel Philip Corr, " 'The Field Is the World': Proclaiming, Translating, and Serving by the American Board of Commissioners for Foreign Missions" (PhD diss., Fuller Theological Seminary, 1993), 166–168, 181–185, 194.

53. Bohr, "Leang Fa's Quest," 36.

54. Fairbank, "Introduction," in Barnett and Fairbank, *Christianity in China*, 15.

55. McNeur, *China's First Preacher*, 40–46; Philip, *The Life and Opinions of the Rev. William Milne*, 206–209. On his "dangerous inland mission[s]," see McNeur, *China's First Preacher*, 54–66. See also D. P. Corr, "The Field Is the World," 162–164; Marshman, *China: Its State and Prospects*, 273, 274; E. Morrison, *Memoirs of the Life and Labours of Richard Morrison*, 1:426, 512ff.; 2:224–226; and Latourette, *A History of Christian Missions in China*, 214, 223–224.

56. Cited by Morrison's colleague Medhurst in *China: Its State and Prospects*, 271. On A-Fah as evangelist, see also 271–282.

57. McNeur, *China's First Preacher*, 88.

58. McNeur, *China's First Preacher*, 86–87, 100–103.

59. McNeur, *China's First Preacher*, 103–116.

60. Bridgman, "Leang A-Fa," 35–36. This was probably in 1820.

61. The date is often given as 1833 or 1834 in early contemporary reports (Meadows, Mackie, Boardman, and in Liang Fa's biographer McNeur); but 1836 is preferred. See Franz Michael, with Chung-li Chang, *The Taiping Rebellion: History and Documents*, 3 vols. (Seattle and London: University of Washington Press, 1966–1971), 1:24 n. 10; and *The Cambridge History of China*, 10:75–79. See Thomas Taylor Meadows, *The Chinese and Their Rebellions* (London: Smith, Elder, 1856), 75–79.

62. Latourette, *A History of Christian Missions in China*, 282–302.

63. C. H. Thompsen, a German originally from Lower Saxony, arrived for this work in the fall of 1815, and opened a short-lived Malay and English School. Philip, *The Life and Opinions of the Rev. William Milne*, 197–198, 202–203.

64. Medhurst, *China: Its State and Prospects*, 71.

65. On the Anglo-Chinese College in Malacca, not to be confused with the school of the same name in Shanghai later, see Latourette, *A History of Christian Missions in China*, 214–215. See also Leung Ka-Lun and Young, *Christianity in China*, 37–38.

66. Abeel was technically under the American Seaman's Friend Society, sent as a chaplain to American sailors in the China seas. See David Abeel, *Journal of a Residence in China and the Neighboring Countries, from 1829 to 1833* (New York: Leavitt, Lord, 1834). He soon returned to America as a powerful champion of the urgency of foreign missions (381–390); and of women in mission. His was a forceful influence in the formation of the first of the Women's Mission Boards, the Society for Promoting Female Education in the East (391–392). On women in mission, see particularly, Abeel, *The Missionary Convention at Jerusalem: Or an Exhibition of the Claims of the World to the Gospel* (New York: John S. Taylor, 1838), 186–192. On Abeel, see also Murray Rubinstein, *The Origins of the Anglo-American Missionary Movement in China 1807–1840* (Lanham, Md.: Scarecrow Press, 1996), 238–247; and Latourette, *A History of Christian Missions in China*, 218 n. 40.

67. On Bridgman, see Eliza J. Bridgman, ed., *The Life and Labors of Elijah Coleman Bridgman* (New York, 1864). *ChRep* was published from 1832 to 1851, and was succeeded, nearly twenty years later by *The China Recorder* (Foochow), in 1870.

68. George B. Stevens, *The Life, Letters and Journals of the Rev. and Hon. Peter Parker, M.D.* (Boston and Chicago: Congregational Publishing Society, 1896), 56–78, 182.

69. Peter Parker, "Report: The Ophthalmic Hospital in Canton," *ChRep* (1837/1838): 4:461–473; 6:34–40, 433–445.

70. Stevens, *The Life, Letters and Journals of the Rev. and Hon. Peter Parker, M.D.,* 118–131; 132–140.

71. Stevens, *The Life, Letters and Journals of the Rev. and Hon. Peter Parker, M.D.,* 249ff., 279ff., and esp. 306–314; see also G. H. Anderson et al., eds., *Mission Legacies: Biographical Studies of Leaders of the Modern Missionary Movement* (Maryknoll, N.Y.: Orbis Books, 1994), 549.

72. Robert E. Speer, *A Missionary Pioneer in the Far East: Divie Bethune McCartee* (New York: Fleming H. Revell, 1922), 75–91.

73. See chaps. 4 and 10 in vol. 1 on the Dutch in Indonesia.

74. The standard sources on Gützlaff are both by Herman Schlyter: the biography, *Karl Gützlaff als Missionar in China* (Lund: C. W. K. Gleerup, 1946), and his later extensive and thorough examination of Gützlaff's reports and relations with his home bases in the West, *Der China-Missionar Karl Gützlaff und Seine Heimatbasis* (Lund: C. W. K. Gleerup, 1976). See also Adriaan Goslinga, *Dr. Karl Gützlaff en het Nederlandsche Protestantisme in het midden der vorige eevw* (The Hague: Boekencentrum n.v., 1941).

75. See Karl Gützlaff, *The Journal of Three Voyages along the Coast of China, in 1831, 1832, and 1833, With Notices of Korea, and the Loo-Choo Islands* (London: Fr. Westley and A. H. Davis, 1834).

76. Cf. Abeel, *Journal of a Residence in China,* 140 n.

77. Wylie, *Memorials of Protestant Missionaries to the Chinese,* 54–66. He also published two in Japanese and one in Siamese (Thai).

78. Schlyter, *Karl Gützlaff als Missionar in China,* 157–204, 216-224; *Der China-Missionar,* 17–18, 70–71, 134ff.; and *Geschichte der Missionen in China von den altesten Zeiten bis auf Gützlaff, herausgegeben von dem Pommerschen Hauptverein für Evangel: Missionen in China* (Stettin, 1850), 72.

79. Cited by Rudolf G. Wagner, *Reenacting the Heavenly Vision: The Role of Religion in the Taiping Rebellion* (Berkeley: University of California Press, 1982), 13. Cf. Karl Gützlaff, copy of a ms. apparently written in his own hand, September 7, 1849, in New College, Edinburgh, Center for the Study of Christianity in the Non-Western World.

80. Schlyter, *Karl Gützlaff,* 225ff.; G. E. Burkhardt, *Die Evangelische Mission in China und Japan. Zweite Auflage, ganzlich ungearbeiter und bis auf die Gegenwart fortgeführt von Dr. K. Grundemann* (Biefeld and Leipzig, 1880), 183–186; Latourette, *A History of Christian Missions in China,* 253–254.

81. For the Hakka story, I am indebted to Jessie G. and Rolland Ray Lutz, "The Invisible China Missionaries: The Basel Mission's Chinese Evangelists, 1847–1866," in *Mission Studies 24* 12, no. 2 (1995): 204–227. The retraining and instruction in the faith of these evangelists salvaged from the Christian Union devolved not so much on Gützlaff but on the Basel mission pioneers, Theodore Hamberg (to whom Jiang owed his conviction of sin and conversion) and Heinrich Bender.

82. See John Nicolson, "The Reverend Charles Gützlaff, The Opium War and General Gough," in *MIS* 13 (July 1985): 353–361.

83. For the opinions of advocates of free trade and opium, see "Edicts," in *ChRep* 6 (1837–1838): 40–44, 524–527, 528–544. For spirited condemnation of the opium traffic, see *ChRep* 5 (1836–1837): 297–305 (by archdeacon Dealtry of

Calcutta) and 5:367–370, 391–418. See J. K. Fairbank, *China: A New History* (Cambridge, Mass.: Harvard University Press, 1992), 198ff., for a succinct summary of the background of the Opium Wars.

84. On the Chinese anti-opium edicts, see "Edicts of the Chinese Government against the Illicit Trade in Opium," *ChRep* 6 (November 1837): 341–351.

85. *ChRep* 6 (October 1837): 302–303.

86. Latourette, *A History of Christian Missions in China*, 229.

87. Newchwang in Manchuria, Chefoo on the Yellow Sea, two on Formosa, and Swatow, Kiungchow, and Nanjing.

88. Russia and the United States joined in negotiating the treaties, but not in the war. See Latourette's discussion of the toleration clauses that were most explicit in the Russian and American versions of the treaties (Latourette, *A History of Christian Missions in China*, 274–281).

89. The major reference work is Franz H. Michael, with Chung-li Chang, *The Taiping Rebellion*. On its religious roots, see Philip L. Wickeri, "Christianity and the Taiping Rebellion: An Historical and Theological Study" (MDiv thesis, Princeton Theological Seminary 1974); Theodore Hamberg, *The Visions of Hung-Siu-tshuen and Origin of the Kwangsi Insurrection* (New York: Praeger Reprint, 1969; from original, Hong Kong, 1854); Joseph R. Levenson, "Confucian China and Taiping 'Heaven': Political Implications of Clashing Religious Concepts," *Comparative Studies in Society and History* 4 (July 1962): 436–453; and Covell, *Confucius, the Buddha, and Christ.*

90. On the date, probably in 1834, not 1836, see John Foster, "The Christian Origins of the Taiping Rebellion," *IRM* 40 (1951): 158 n. 1. Cf. Hamberg, *The Visions of Hung-siu-tshuen,* revised as *The Chinese Rebel Chief, Hung-Siu-Tshuen, and the Origin of the Insurrection in China* (London, 1855), which implies 1836 as the date.

91. Michael, *The Taiping Rebellion*, 2:54, 57. Cf. J. C. Cheng, *Chinese Sources for the Taiping Rebellion, 1850–1864* (Hong Kong: Hong Kong University Press, 1963), 7–9.

92. In 1848 Hong specifically credited Liang Fa's "Good Words to Admonish the Age" as the source of his interpretations (Michael, *The Taiping Rebellion*, 2:63–64). Comparisons of his esoteric interpretations with the Chinese evangelist's Bible-based text show how far he distorted Liang's teachings. Cf. Foster, "The Christian Origins of the Taiping Rebellion," 156–167.

93. Meadows, *The Chinese and Their Rebellions*, 81–85; Michael, *The Taiping Rebellion*, 1:28–42.

94. On Roberts and Hong Xiuquan, see Margaret M. Coughlin, "Strangers in the House: J. Lewis Shuck and Issachar Roberts, First American Baptist Missionaries to China" (PhD diss., University of Virginia, 1972), 254–280. Coughlin notes that Roberts died in Macao of leprosy, "perhaps contracted from the small congregation of lepers he had gathered in Macao in 1837, who constituted, he believed, the first Protestant church on Chinese soil" (140). But see Latourette, *A History of Christian Missions in China*, 248, who says of the Presbyterian church organized in Ningbo in 1845, "possibly the first Protestant church ["organized"] on Chinese soil." The two statements are not necessarily contradictory.

95. Coughlin, "Strangers in the House," 256–261. Also on Roberts, one of the first group of China missionaries appointed by the newly formed Southern Baptist Board of Foreign Missions, see Wylie, *Memorials of Protestant Missionaries to the Chinese*, 94–97, and Baker J. Cauthen et al., *Advance: A History of Southern*

Baptist Foreign Missions (Nashville: Broadman Press, 1970), 77–80, 106. See also T. T. Meadows, *The Chinese and Their Rebellions*, 87–88. Later Hong invited Roberts to his court at Nanjing, but Roberts was unable to go. Seven years later he did reach Nanjing, and though he stayed with the Taiping for fifteen months, the missionary and the Taiping found themselves often at odds (Michael, *The Taiping Rebellion*, 2:509–510).

96. On the visions and his later interpretation, see "The Taiping Heavenly Chronicle," written in 1848, published in Chinese in 1862, and in English translation in Michael, *The Taiping Rebellion*, 2:51–76. It was the first "Imperial Declaration" of Hong's proposed new dynasty.

97. Michael, *The Taiping Rebellion*, 2:53ff.

98. Michael, *The Taiping Rebellion*, 1:8; 2:57.

99. On the movement's anti-Buddhist position, see Michael, *The Taiping Rebellion*, 2:56, 149.

100. On Hong's rejection of Manchu rule and claim to the throne, see Michael, *The Taiping Rebellion*, 1:62ff.; 2:78, 144ff.

101. Cheng, *Chinese Sources for the Taiping Rebellion*, 91.

102. Cheng, *Chinese Sources for the Taiping Rebellion*, 64, 91, quoting in full the "Joint Proclamation by the Eastern and Western Kings," Hong Xiuquan's principal generals.

103. Cheng, *Chinese Sources for the Taiping Rebellion*, 81. The title "Former" was used instead of "New" to allow the addition of a third scripture to the Taiping canon, Hong's *The Book of Heaven-Commanded Edicts* (1852). The biblical portions were based largely on Gützlaff's translations, not Morrison's. See Wylie, *Memorials of Protestant Missionaries to the Chinese*, 62–63.

104. W. H. Medhurst, *Pamphlets Issued by the Chinese Insurgents in Nanking* (Shanghai, 1853), cited by Cheng, *Chinese Sources for the Taiping Rebellion*, 81, 146. Ten copies of "The Book of Heaven-Commanded Edicts" have survived. See listing by Cheng, *Chinese Sources for the Taiping Rebellion*, 151–152, also 41, 143 n. 10.

105. Cheng, *Chinese Sources for the Taiping Rebellion*, 82–91; Michael, *The Taiping Rebellion*, 2:226–237.

106. Cheng, *Chinese Sources for the Taiping Rebellion*, 88–89.

107. Cheng, *Chinese Sources for the Taiping Rebellion*, 89.

108. Michael, *The Taiping Rebellion*, "Rules of Conduct," 2:575–582. The list of offenses and punishment, which is variously reported, was probably issued at Nanjing, between 1853 and 1855.

109. The effective Chinese commander of the counterattack was Tseng Kuo-fan (Zeng Guofan), a scholar-statesman and strong Confucian, belatedly appointed in the 1860s by the Qing (Ch'ing) dynasty's Empress Dowager, the famed Tz'u Hsi (Cixi). See Fairbank, *China: A New History*, 212–213.

110. See Joseph R. Levenson's convincing arguments on this point in *Confucian China and Its Modern Fate: A Trilogy* (Berkeley and Los Angeles: University of California Press, 1968), 87–118.

111. Communist historians, of course, using the rebellion as an inspiring example of social revolt, minimized the religious elements, and Western secular historians have displayed a not too dissimilar bias. A refreshing exception is Fairbank, *China: A New History*, 206–212. On the historiography of the rebellion, see Wickeri, "Christianity and the Taiping Rebellion."

Chapter 14

The Catholic Century in Korea (1784–1886)

The Martyrs

All the nations of the universe have received the grace of redemption, all the earth is full of bishops and priests. Why should only this small corner of the earth which we occupy be deprived of the benefits of redemption?
— Yi Seung-Hun, 1789

The Korean Initiative

In Korea it was the Koreans themselves, not foreign missionaries, who first brought the Christian faith to their own people from across its guarded borders. This was true of the planting of the church by Catholics, and then, almost a hundred years later, by Protestants. In both cases the route of entry for the new faith was by way of China.

Every year it was the custom of the Korean kingdom to send two embassies to the imperial court in Beijing, a journey then of about three months. Its purpose was as much for trade as for the symbolic Confucian gesture of respect from king to emperor. The winter embassy of 1783, which reached Beijing early in 1784, included a young scholar, Lee Seung-Hun,[1] the son of its third-ranking ambassador. Lee had been asked by a friend to contact the foreign priests and bring back more information about their religion to a small group of Confucian scholars[2] who were intensely interested in foreign books on religion and mathematics that had found their way into Korea from the Jesuits in China.[3]

Apparently the religion more than the mathematics was what interested the twenty-seven-year-old Lee, for when he presented himself to Jean-Joseph de Grammont, formerly of the dissolved Jesuit mission in Beijing but still a priest and mathematician at the court, Lee immediately asked for baptism. After a period of questioning, and with the permission of his father, he was baptized, the first baptized Korean in Korea. He was given the name Peter (Pierre), and presented with Catholic books and devotional objects to take back to Korea, in the hope that he might be "the first stone ['Peter'] of the Korean church."[4]

Upon his return Peter Lee Seung-Hun and his friend, Lee Pyok,[5] who had commissioned him to contact the missionaries in Beijing, threw themselves so enthusiastically into the study and practice of their new-found faith that within a few months they reported a thousand followers asking for baptism. Untrained and ignorant of ecclesiastic rules, since they had no priest available, Lee Seung-Hun first baptized Lee Pyok as "John-Baptist," and then they proceeded to baptize others. They chose leaders and "ordained" them as priests, commissioning them to hold mass and administer the sacraments. Sunday worship was a problem. It is said that they knew weekly worship was mandatory, but what day of their Korean lunar calendar was the Western Sunday? They decided that every seventh day of their own calendar would do just as well even though it might fall on the West's Wednesday or Thursday as often as on Sunday.[6]

Within a year, as the movement spread, a Confucian reaction to this invasion of a foreign religion triggered an abrasive persecution. Ten Catholics were martyred. Shockingly, the two leaders, Lee Seung-Hun and Lee Pyok, recanted under intense family pressure and withdrew from the community.[7] But the example of the martyrs strengthened the little Catholic community and brought back to Christian leadership Lee Seung-Hun who, like the apostle Peter for whom he had been named, repented in anguish for his betrayal of his Lord.[8] At great risk Lee reestablished letter communication with Beijing, apologizing for the errors that, as he had discovered from further reading of the books, they had committed: the self-ordinations, the baptisms, and the masses. He pleaded for forgiveness for his own apostasy, and concluded with a plaintive plea to the Beijing missionaries to find a way to bring the blessings of the sacraments to Korea: "the whole world is full of bishops and priests...Why should only this small corner of the earth which we occupy be excluded from the benefits of redemption?"[9]

These letters of 1789 and 1790 shocked the missionary community. How could the faith be spreading so rapidly in Korea without missionaries? But also how could they not help but rejoice at word of a growing Catholic church in a forbidden land? So though they were scandalized by descriptions of a mass without a priest, and priests without ordination, the replies from Beijing were congratulatory and conciliatory. The bishop, de Gouvea, praised the zeal of the evangelists in the face of persecution, and agreed to recognize their baptisms as valid "lay baptisms." In no uncertain terms, however, he condemned the uncanonical masses and the ordination of priests without bishops.[10]

Further correspondence between Seoul and Beijing, written on silk and carried by secret couriers, brought information from the bishop that shocked the Korean Catholics much as the earlier letters had shaken the Beijing missionaries. The question was about ancestor worship, so basic in Korea's family-centered society. The ruling from Beijing was short and blunt. Ancestor worship was idolatry and could not be permitted.[11] What other answer could the bishop, de Gouvea, a Franciscan, give? To permit the converted to worship their ancestors would be disobedience to Rome, and the whole Franciscan order might face the same fate as the Jesuits in China who had been suppressed by the pope on this very issue less than twenty years earlier. Since 1742, in fact, a papal bull prohibiting ancestor worship had decisively ended the rites controversy in China and led to the dissolution of the famous Jesuit mission at the court in Beijing.[12]

The same controversy now almost destroyed the vulnerable little Catholic beachhead in Korea, planted only five years earlier. No sooner did Korean Catholics begin to obey the foreign bishop in China and not their Korean families than another persecution more terrible than the first produced a second wave of exiles and executions. There were three kinds of executions: one for ordinary criminals, another for the military, and the most extreme for rebellion and *lèse majesté*. For that third form, the ears were pierced with arrows, the body was then beheaded and quartered.[13] One of the first victims was Paul Yun Chi-ch'ung, who had in obedience to his faith destroyed his ancestor tablets. For him Christian truth was more absolute than Confucian morality, and the tablets were a superstition. But for his accusers, family loyalty and traditional Confucian morality was more important to society than truth. Because of his noble birth, when he was executed in 1791 his body was not quartered.[14]

In this persecution, sad to say, once again the church's leader, Lee Seung-Hun, apostatized.[15] He was the pioneer and leader of the first Catholic mission to Korea, but not the "rock" the priests had hoped for when they baptized him "Peter" in Beijing. Nevertheless, not even the obstacle of a papal edict which offended Korea's cultural tradition, nor the defection of the fledgling church's first Korean leader, could smother the missionary zeal of the Beijing hierarchy or the faith of the hard-pressed Korean Catholics. Despite or because of the martyrdoms, in the next five years the number of converts quadrupled, from one thousand in 1790 to four thousand in 1795.[16] And in Beijing, Bishop de Gouvea, Franciscan and missionary to the core, had already set in motion the search for a way to introduce a foreign missionary into forbidden Korea.[17]

The Founding of the Catholic Church in Korea (1792–1801)

Despite fleeting contacts, there was still no surviving Christian presence in the forbidden Hermit Kingdom. Not until some forty years after the Dutch shipwreck was the Christian faith finally and permanently established in the forbidden Hermit Kingdom, and it was not a missionary who opened the way. A young Korean Confucian scholar of philosophy and mathematics, Seung-Heun Lee (Yi Seung-hun, 1756–1801),[18] was persuaded to join the annual Korean embassy to the Chinese court in Beijing. It would be easy for him to go; his father had been named "third ambassador" in the embassy.

For some years a group of Korean scholars, including Chung Yak-jong, younger brother of the famous Confucianist Ta-san (Chung Yak-yong), had rediscovered the Chinese writings of the seventeenth-century Jesuits in Beijing. Greatly interested, they asked Lee Seung-Hoon to make contact with the foreign scholars at the Chinese court and bring back more information. The twenty-seven-year-old Korean reached the Chinese capital in 1784 and found some ex-Jesuit French priests still living at the old North Church. He asked if they could give him some books on mathematics and inquired about their unusual new religion. The unexpected result was his conversion. He asked for baptism but the priests hesitated, not sure that he knew what baptism meant. After some further lessons, however, and with the rather surprising approval of his father, he was baptized by the former Jesuit, Jean-Joseph de Grammont, who happened to be a mathematician himself. When he returned to his homeland, baptized as Pierre Lee, he brought to his friends books, crosses, and the Christian faith. He was the first known Korean Christian in Korea.[19]

Yi Seung-Hun found a warm reception from his Confucian friends upon his return. With his closest associate, Yi Piek,[20] he began to gather together a little Catholic community, and unaware of the ancient customs of the church that reserved the right of baptism to ordained priests, began to baptize converts as he had been baptized. A more serious transgression of church law was his decision in 1786 to allow the community's leaders, all laymen of course, to perform the sacrament of the mass. Yet by 1789, without priests, without the Bible, but with the passion of a new faith, the Korean Catholic community numbered about a thousand Christians.[21]

The government soon heard about this penetration of foreign ideas into the "Hermit Kingdom," as self-isolated Korea came to be called. Its quick response was a wave of intense persecution. More than four hundred Korean Christians were publicly executed for their faith in the first ten years of organized Korean Catholicism (1784–1794).[22] But Yi Seung-hun was not among the martyrs. Under intense pressure both from his family and the government, he gradually disassociated himself from the little Christian community, first in 1785, and finally under further interrogation in 1791.[23]

News of the new little Catholic community springing up in the closed land of Korea alarmed not only the Korean government. It astonished the Catholic clergy in Beijing. Obviously delighted to hear of the amazing growth of the gospel against all odds, they were nevertheless dismayed to hear of disturbing departures from accepted Catholic practice in the community, such as uninstructed converts baptizing inquirers and holding masses without benefit of priests and clergy.[24] To correct their errors and to bring them orthodox instruction in the faith, the bishop of Beijing, Msgr. de Gouvea (d. 1808), a Portuguese Franciscan,[25] sent a missionary to Korea, a Chinese priest named James Chou Wen-Mo, who crossed the border late in 1794 and reached Seoul on January 5, 1795.[26] Five years later he was dead. He arrived on the verge of what Catholic historians call "the first great persecution," and after five terrible years of desperate attempts to elude capture, the young Chinese priest gave himself up to the authorities in a futile effort to save the lives of his Korean believers. He was beheaded in 1801.[27] Thus the first foreign missionary to Korea,[28] and one of its earliest martyrs, was no Westerner, but, like the Koreans, Asiatic.

In 1801, then, the future loomed dark for Christianity in Korea. It was like a premature baby, born but immediately orphaned, with little apparent chance of survival. Its principal leaders had been martyred or had recanted. Ahead lay a century of storm and persecution. The nineteenth century, the "great century of missions" as it was called, did not look to be so great in Korea. But, as always, Christian history is full of surprises.[29]

The First Foreign Missionary and the Persecution of 1801

It would be three or four years, however, before the bishop found the right foreigner. James Chou was a forty-two-year-old Chinese priest, not a Westerner, chosen because he knew the culture and looked like a Korean. He left Beijing in February 1794, reaching Seoul in January 1795 where on Easter Sunday he celebrated the first valid mass held in Korea for Korean Christians. His Chinese name (Chou Wen-Mo) became in Korean Chou Moon-Mo.[30] For six years he ministered to the Catholic community, at first openly, but when after only six months an informer posing as a convert betrayed him, he spent the rest of his short life in Korea desperately eluding the nationwide search ordered by the king. At times, converts posed in his stead, wearing a Chinese queue to throw the gendarmes off the priest's trail; many hid him in cellars and secret rooms, and were tortured and died rather than reveal his presence. But the church kept growing, from four thousand when he had arrived, to ten thousand in five years.[31] But at last, in 1801, Father James Chou, unwilling that any more of his followers should die on his account, surrendered himself to the authorities. "I am a Catholic," he said. "I have heard of the . . . killing of many innocent people, and I wish to join the ranks of death." Two months later he was executed.[32]

This was the first nationwide persecution of Christians. At least two hundred gave up their lives for their Lord, and about four hundred were banished into exile.[33] Two examples of martyrdom stand out in the record. The first was Columba Kang Wan-Suk, a wealthy widow, and apparently at that time, "the only convert among the families of the nobility."[34] For several years she had hidden in her home, James Chou from his pursuers. He appointed her as a catechist, the first Korean woman ever granted that responsibility. It was a work for which she proved to be uniquely valuable, for unlike her male colleagues she was able to witness to her faith openly under the protection of a clause in Korean law at that time which forbade the punishment of noblewomen. In the end, however, even that did not save her from martyrdom. She was forty-one when she was tortured, her legs tied together at foot and knee and pried apart until the long bones curved in an arc, and then when she refused to recant, was beheaded.[35]

Even more startling to the nation was the witness of another martyr of 1801, a symbol of the attraction of the Christian message to Koreans at the most elite intellectual level. In the original group of Confucian scholars who in the 1770s sent Lee Seung-Hun to Beijing were three brothers, all philosophers, of the nationally respected Chung (Chong, Tjyeng) family. The eldest, Chung Yak-Chong, baptized as Augustine in 1897, helped to form the first Catholic laymen's society (the *Myong-do-hwei*). He was the theologian of the early Catholic community. His book, *Principles of the Christian Faith*, was as important culturally as theologically, for it was the first Christian book printed in Korea in the indigenous Korean alphabet (*hankul*), making it accessible to the common people outside the educated elite.[36] Augustine Chung Yak-Chong's younger brother, Chung Yak-Yong (known as Ta-San), was nationally famous as an advisor to the king, author of more than fifty books, and a leader of one of the most influential of the Confucian schools of thought, a branch of the Southern (Nam-in) Confucianists, which was friendly to the new ideas filtering into the country from the West, and therefore keenly interested in Roman Catholicism. But Ta-San never presented himself for baptism, and though always friendly and sometimes imprisoned for being so, he never apparently formally joined the church.[37]

Sixty-Five Years of Persecution

The nineteenth century was "the Catholic century" in Korea, but it was also the century of the great persecutions, wave after wave — in 1801, 1815, 1827, 1839, 1846, and finally the cruelest of all in 1866–1867.[38] The record of suffering and death in those years is sometimes tragic, sometimes triumphant. As was noted above, the first leaders of the proto-Catholic community at the end of the eighteenth century were persecuted into apostasy; the first foreign missionary, a Chinese, was martyred in 1801. The first two Western missionaries to penetrate the Hermit Kingdom, Pierre-Philibert Maubant and Jacques-Honoré Chastan, died as martyrs in the persecution of 1839, beheaded on the sands of the Han River, along with the first resident apostolic vicar, Bishop Laurent Imbert.[39] The first ordained Korean priest, Andrew Kim Tae-Kon, won his martyrdom in the persecution of 1846, his ears first pierced with arrows, his head slashed off in a kind of warrior's dance by the sabers of twelve soldiers, and not falling until the eighth stroke.[40]

In early 1846 there were said to be some six thousand Catholics in Korea. That year seventy-five Korean Christians and the three European missionaries were martyred, but providentially the persecution was short. Under the tranquil reign of King Ch'ol-jong (1850–1863) which followed, toleration was restored. The first Catholic seminary in Korea was founded about 1857 south of Seoul with some ten seminarians,[41] but it was only the calm before the storm. Six years later the storm came close to wiping the Christian faith out of the land.

The Great Persecution of 1866–1867 and Catholic Survival

In 1866 the greatest of all the nineteenth-century Korea persecutions broke with fury upon the long-suffering Catholics of Korea. It occurred in the reign of King Ko-jong (1864–1907), who had come to the throne as a twelve-year-old boy. Later the king would prove to be surprisingly progressive in his sympathies,[42] but in 1866 he was still powerless under the regency of his strongly nationalistic father, the Taewongun. In domestic matters the Taewongun was strongly nationalistic, in foreign affairs reactionary. The regent's wife was increasingly attracted to the Christian faith, but the mother of the queen, the queen regent, came from a bitterly anti-Christian family heavily involved in the persecution of 1839.[43] In the tangled political scene of the late Yi dynasty, little Korea was caught between the competing rivalries of the great powers that hemmed in Korea from all sides — China, Japan, Russia, and farther away, the expanding West. The most immediate pressures in 1866 were from China, Korea's traditional superpower; Japan was just beginning to flex its colonialist muscle. The king's father was generally pro-Chinese; the king's wife, the strong-minded and exceedingly able Queen Min, was pro-Japanese but only in the sense of favoring Japan as a balance to complete dependence on declining China. There were to be times when the king would come to prefer the West as a less threatening alternative than alliance with either China or Japan.

An ominous internal problem also threatened both the stability of the government and the safety of the Catholic mission. Rebels in the southern provinces raised the banner of a sectarian movement called *Tonghak* (Eastern Doctrine) to oppose the government for its corruption, and the Christians for their "western heresy."[44]

As the persecution broke, there were nine Catholic missionaries in Korea, a French bishop, Siméon-François Berneaux,[45] and twelve other European missionaries, including four French priests who had just arrived. All were still vulnerable to outbreaks of persecution, but for two decades or more they had been able to move freely in their duties about the country. By 1863 there were Roman Catholics in all of Korea's provinces, and the total Catholic community was said to number twenty-three thousand believers.[46]

It was the threat of French and Russian encroachment into Korea, however, that set off the persecutions in early 1866, with the slogan: "Death to the Western Barbarians! Death to all Christians!"[47] In January Russian ships demanded trading and residential rights on the northeast Korean coast south of Siberia. Some prominent Korean Catholics with government connections suggested that the only hope against further Russian pressure would be an alliance with France which the French missionaries could arrange, and without consulting the bishop so informed the prince regent (the Taewongun). It was a foolish mistake, and only reinforced the suspicion that the missionaries might actually be forerunners of French expansion. At the same time a false report from the Korean embassy in Beijing arrived with news that the Chinese were ordering death for all foreigners in China.[48]

In Korea the killings began in February. "In less than ten years," vowed the regent, the Taewongun, "I will annihilate every vestige of this religion."[49] Among the first seized was Bishop Berneux with three other French priests. One of them, upon arrest, and knowing that others had already died, said, "I came to this country to save souls. I shall die with joy."[50] Three other French priests, including Father Ridel who was later to become apostolic vicar, managed to escape to China, where the story of the executions so angered the French that they mounted an unsuccessful expeditionary naval attack on the Korean port nearest the Korean capital. That only further spread the angry flames of the persecution.[51]

The Catholic Church in Korea never really recovered from the Great Persecution, though again it did survive. Nine of the ten French priests had been martyred. The Catholic printing press was destroyed. The total number of Korean martyrs is uncertain but has been estimated at eight thousand — five hundred of them in Seoul alone in September 1868.[52] That represented a loss of a quarter of the entire Korean Catholic community, not counting those who died of starvation and exhaustion while hiding from their hunters in the hills.

Brighter days came with the retirement of the regent in 1873 and the accession to power of his son, King Kojong. The new king's reign ushered in decades of comparative freedom of religion, shadowed by increasing Japanese domination of the peninsula, beginning with the opening of three ports to Japanese traders in 1875, and a formal Treaty of Amity in 1876, which for the first time in five hundred years ended the "closed-door policy" of Korea, the Hermit Kingdom. One of King Kojong's early acts, in 1875, was an edict prohibiting the execution of Catholics without prior royal consent.[53]

The next year, ten years after the terrible persecutions of the Taewongun, Felix Clair Ridel, sixth bishop of the Korean vicariate, who was one of the three priests who barely escaped with their lives in 1866, returned at last to Seoul with two other French priests.[54] Not quite trusting the edict of toleration, they entered the city in disguise, a habit widely followed by the priests for years thereafter.

Their fears were justified. Early in 1878 the bishop was arrested, but times had changed. Expecting death, he was only expelled, never to return to Korea. Not so fortunate were the Korean Catholics who accompanied him to the border. They were arrested and, to avoid bad publicity as the country gradually opened to foreign trade, they were starved to death in prison.[55]

Then the barriers that had barred contact with the West began to fall. Korea's first treaty with a Western nation was signed with the United States in 1882, followed that same year by similar treaties with Great Britain and Germany. Confucian protests against foreign religions prevented the inclusion of clauses of religious toleration, but the king leaned to the view that the best way to eliminate Christianity, if that was desired, would be faithfulness to the Confucian proprieties, not persecution, and the treaty with Britain added a clause granting to foreigners the right "to practice their religion in freedom."[56]

By the time a treaty with the French was signed in 1886, for the first time, after 102 years of Catholicism in Korea, the French Catholic missionaries were at liberty to travel freely in all areas open to trade. There were then (in 1884) one bishop, the seventh apostolic vicar Father Blanc,[57] with nine foreign priests in Korea, and a community of some 12,500 believers. Up to 1885, because of the persecutions, most Korean candidates for the priesthood had been sent to Penang on the Malaysian peninsula for seminary training, but in 1885 the church established its first continuing theological seminary in Korea, which moved two years later to the capital, Seoul.[58]

Up to that point, only two Koreans had been ordained to the priesthood, Andrew Kim (1821–1846) and Thomas Choi (d. 1861).[59] A great step forward in the Koreanizing of the church was the ordination of ten new Korean Catholic priests in 1896, 112 years after the baptism of the pioneer Catholic Korean, Peter Lee Seung-Hun in Beijing, and fifty-one years after the ordination of the first Korean priest, Andrew Kim Tae-Kon.[60] About the same time work began on a great Gothic cathedral, of red brick, in the very heart of the capital where once had stood the home of the first martyr "who on Korean soil gave his life to Christ."[61]

But for the Roman Catholics in Korea, it was almost too late. A new wind was already blowing across the Korea peninsula. The Protestants had landed with Bible in hand and an enthusiasm for evangelism that was destined to change Korea in a way that few could have imagined during the hundred years of terror so recently ended.[62]

NOTES

1. Lee Seung-Hun's family name is variously transliterated as Lee, Yi, I, Rhee, or Ni. See Choi, *L'erection du premier vicariat apostolique*, 17 n. 1; and Dallet, *Histoire de l'église de Corée*, 1:16–17. His given name also has a variety of easily recognizable variations (Choi, for example, spells it Seung-houn; Dallet as Seng-houn-i).

2. The nucleus of the group, since about 1799, were Chung Yak-Chon (1754–1816), older brother of the more famous Chung Yak-Yong (1762–1836, better known as Ta-San), and of the martyr Augustine Chung Yak-Jong (1760–1801); and two brothers-in-law of the older Chung, Lee Pyok and Peter Lee Sung-Heun. A later leader of the group was Paul Yun Chi-ch'ung, a cousin of Chung Yak-Chon. See Donald L. Baker, "The Martyrdom of Paul Yun: Western Religion and Eastern Ritual in 18th Century Korea," *TRASK* 54 (1979): 33–58.

3. In the first mention of Roman Catholicism by a Korean scholar, Lee Su-Kwang (1563–1628) wrote a summary of Ricci's *The True Meaning of the Lord of Heaven (T'ien-chu Shih-i)*. See Choi, *L'erection du premier vicariat apostolique*, 8, 33; Dallet, *Histoire de l'église de Corée*, 1:11, 15; and Kim and Chung, *Catholic Korea*, 22.

4. Dallet, *Histoire de l'église de Corée*, 1:17–20; Choi, *L'erection du premier vicariat apostolique*, 18–21.

5. Lee Pyok (Lee Tok-jo) became the primary evangelist in forming a proto-Christian community out of his fellow scholars and their friends, a circle which included members of the famous Confucian family of Chung Yak-Yong (Ta San), mentioned above (Choi, *L'erection du premier vicariat apostolique*, 32–33, 41–42, 47, 53–54). Choi transliterates the name Chung as Tjyeng.

6. Choi, *L'erection du premier vicariat apostolique*, 1:23, 25–27; Kim and Chung, *Catholic Korea*, 26–27. Choi corrects some mistakes in other histories: no one was made bishop, though Lee Seung-Hun was the acknowledged leader and Lee Pyok the ablest evangelist.

7. Choi, *L'erection du premier vicariat apostolique*, 23–26.

8. Dallet, *Histoire de l'église de Corée*, 1:30. But Dallet is in error when he reports that Francis-Xavier Kwen replaced Lee Seung-Hun as leader with the title of bishop. Cf. Choi, *L'erection du premier vicariat apostolique*, 27.

9. See Lee Seung-Hun's letter of 1789, French translation in Choi, *L'erection du premier vicariat apostolique*, 90–93. See also the letter of Hiuen-chen, later martyred (Augustin Ryu Hang-kom or Niou Hang-kem?), undated (1786?), to Lee Seung-Hun, calling his attention to the ecclesiastical errors committed. Choi, *L'erection du premier vicariat apostolique*, 27, 94–97; Kim and Chung, *Catholic Korea*, 28, 64.

10. Choi, *L'erection du premier vicariat apostolique*, 29–31; Baker, "Martyrdom of Paul Yun," 43–44; Kim and Chung, *Catholic Korea*, 27–30; Dallet, *Histoire de l'église de Corée*, 26–32.

11. On the connotations of the prohibition of ancestor worship in Korea, see Baker, "Martyrdom of Paul Yun," 44–55.

12. See chap. 5. The Jesuits were suppressed in 1773.

13. Paul Chi-ch'ung Yun (Ioun) had carried the secret letters to and from Beijing. See Baker, "Martyrdom of Paul Yun," 48–58; Dallet, *Histoire de l'église*

de Corée, 1:37–56; Kim and Chung, *Catholic Korea*, 31–46. On the methods of torture, see Chang-Seok Thaddaeus Kim, *Lives of 103 Martyr Saints of Korea* (Seoul: Catholic Publishing House, 1984), 116–119.

14. Dallet, *Histoire de l'église de Corée*, 1:37–55; Baker, "Martyrdom of Paul Yun," 48–58; Kim and Chung, *Catholic Korea*, 31–42.

15. On Lee Seung-Hun's apostasy, and execution in 1801 despite his second recantation of the faith, see Dallet, *Histoire de l'église de Corée*, 1:59, 82–83, 121–122; and Choi, *L'erection du premier vicariat apostolique*, 45–46. On the persecution of 1791, Dallet, 1:37–56; Choi, 39ff.

16. Choi, *L'erection du premier vicariat apostolique*, 31, citing a letter of Bishop de Gouvea, August 15, 1797. See also Dallet, *Histoire de l'église de Corée*, 1:67.

17. Choi, *L'erection du premier vicariat apostolique*, 31, 34–35; and (in Latin), a letter from Bishop de Gouvea to Rome, October 6, 1790, Choi, 99–103.

18. Lee's surname is variously transliterated as Yi, Ri, or Ni. His given names appear as Seung-hun, Sung-heun, Sung-hoon, etc.

19. The best book on these early Catholic beginnings in Korea is Choi, *L'erection du premier vicariat apostolique*. On Yi Seung-Hun, see 17–33, 45–46, 90–99. Cf. Dallet, *Histoire de l'église de Corée*, the earliest Western treatment of the period; and Kim and Chung, *Catholic Korea*, 18–124, for more detail.

20. On Yi Piek (or Lee Pyok, baptized Jean-Baptiste), see Choi, *L'erection du premier vicariat apostolique*, 18, 22–23, 32; and Kim and Chung, *Catholic Korea*, 23, 25–27.

21. Choi, *L'erection du premier vicariat apostolique*, 25, 93 (1789 letter of Yi Seung-Hun).

22. For detailed accounts of the martyrdoms, see Kim and Chung, *Catholic Korea*, 27, 31–46. For grisly descriptions of Korean torture — the plank, dislocation of bones, crushing of the knee, sawing the legs, etc., see Ch. Dallet, *Traditional Korea*, English translation of ethnographic introduction to 1874 French text of Dallet's *Histoire* (New Haven, Conn.: Human Relations Area Files, 1954), 67–72.

23. Choi, *L'erection du premier vicariat apostolique*, 24ff., 31, 45–46. It is sad to relate that the two principal pioneers of the faith in Korea, Yi or Lee, Seung-hun (Pierre), and his closest associate, Li Pyok (or Piek), who baptized Jean-Baptiste, both finally apostatized while so many of their converts chose martyrdom rather than deny their Lord. Their high social standing made them particularly vulnerable to political pressure and most resistant to Catholic condemnation of ancestor worship. See also Yi Seung-Houn's letter of 1789 in Kim and Chung, *Catholic Korea*, 28–31.

24. Choi, *L'erection du premier vicariat apostolique*, 90–99 (letters between Yi Seung-Hun and the missionaries in Beijing, ca. 1786, and 1790). English translation of Yi's second letter is in Kim and Chung, *Catholic Korea*, 228–229.

25. For biographical details on Gouvea, see Choi, *L'erection du premier vicariat apostolique*, 20 n. 6. His name in Chinese was Tang Ya-li-chan.

26. Choi, *L'erection du premier vicariat apostolique*, 48–49. The Chinese priest James Chou Wen-Mo was known in Korean as Chou Moon-Mo, in French as Jacques Tsiou, and in Portuguese as Jacques Vellozo (see 48 n. 6); Kim and Chung, *Catholic Korea*, 46–49; A. Thomas, *Histoire de la mission de Pékin*, Part 2, 71–73.

27. Choi, *L'erection du premier vicariat apostolique*, 49–54.

28. De Cespedes, the sixteenth-century Jesuit who came briefly to Korea as chaplain to invading Japanese troops, is better described as a missionary "in" Korea, not a missionary "to" Korea.

29. For the story of the nineteenth-century persecutions, see below, chap. 24.

30. The Beijing missionaries called him by his baptismal name, Jacques Vellozo. See Lak-Geoon George Paik (Paek Nak-Jun), *The History of Protestant Missions in Korea, 1832–1910* (Seoul: Yonsei University, 1987), 34 n. 34; Choi, *L'erection du premier vicariat apostolique*, 48 n. 6; and Kim and Chung, *Catholic Korea*, 47ff.

31. Kim and Chung, *Catholic Korea*, 48–49.

32. Kim and Chung, *Catholic Korea*, 56–57; cf. Dallet, *Histoire de l'église de Corée*, 70–81, 141–148.

33. Kim and Chung, *Catholic Korea*, 92 n. 1.

34. That claim is made by Kim and Chung, *Catholic Korea*, 55, 62–63; Dallet, *Histoire de l'église de Corée*, 1:157–159. Her husband was of the lower nobility (*yang-ban*). Cf. Dallet, *Histoire de l'église de Corée*, 74. Choi, *L'erection du premier vicariat apostolique*.

35. On Columba Kang, see Dallet, who transliterates her name as Colombe Kang Oan-siouk, *Histoire de l'église de Corée*, 74ff., 157–159; Kim and Chung, *Catholic Korea*, 55, 62–63.

36. Cf. Dallet, *Histoire de l'église de Corée*, 1:14, 117–121 and passim; cf. Kim and Chung, *Catholic Korea*, 50, 59. Augustine Chung was beheaded on April 8, 1801, still refusing to recant or reveal the whereabouts of the missionary James Chou. Executed with him was the unrepentant apostate, his one-time leader, Peter Seung-Hun Lee.

37. As noted elsewhere Chung is variously transliterated Chong or Tjyeng. On Chung Ta-san, see Gregory Henderson, "Chong Ta-san: A Study in Korea's Intellectual History," *JAS* 16 (1957): 3; and Choi, *L'erection du premier vicariat apostolique*, 41–42. Of the two divisions of Confucian "Southerners" (Nam-in), the pro-Western, pro-Catholic faction was called the *Choi*, or *Sinam* group; the anti-Western faction was the *Hong* or *Piek-nam* group. The whole range of seventeenth- and eighteenth-century Confucian scholars particularly interested in Western ideas is often described by the term *Silhak-p'a* (Practical Knowledge School).

38. For a record of the principal martyrs, see Chang-Seok Thaddaeus Kim, *Lives of 103 Martyr Saints of Korea*.

39. Kim and Chung, *Catholic Korea*, 161–165; cf. Dallet, *Histoire de l'église de Corée*, 1:182–185.

40. Kim and Chung, *Catholic Korea*, 213–217. Cf. Dallet, *Histoire de l'église de Corée*, 2:319–320; Chang-Seok Thaddeus Kim, *Lives of 103 Martyr Saints of Korea*, 23–25.

41. Kim and Chung, *Catholic Korea*, 222–230.

42. See Martina Deuchler, *Confucian Gentlemen and Barbarian Envoys* (Seattle and London: University of Washington Press, 1977), 32–33, 48–49, 90–92, and passim; and James B. Palais, *Confucian Statecraft and Korean Institutions: Yu Hyong-won and the Late Choson Dynasty* (Seattle and London: University of Washington Press, 1996).

43. *APF* 30, no. 175 (January 1867): 12.

44. On the anti-government and anti-Christian elements in the Tonghak movement, see Paik, *The History of Protestant Missions in Korea*, 171–173, 259–260; and Benjamin B. Weems, *Reform, Rebellion, and the Heavenly Way* (Tucson: University of Arizona Press, 1964).

45. On Bishop Berneux see *KR* (March 1898): 83–91.

46. *APF* 30:6; Kim and Chung, *Catholic Korea*, 231–232.

47. Kim and Chung, *Catholic Korea*, 234–236.

48. Kim and Chung, *Catholic Korea*, 234ff.

49. See *APF* 30:114 and 31:325.

50. This was the statement of Father Fretenières (Kim and Chung, *Catholic Korea*, 245).

51. The leader of the two expeditions was Rear Admiral Roze. See *APF* 30 no. 175 (January 1867): 126–127, 196–200; cf. Kim and Chung, *Catholic Korea*, 271–287.

52. An estimate of two thousand in 1868 was raised to eight thousand in 1870. Cf. *APF* 30:114 and 31:325.

53. Kim and Chung, *Catholic Korea*, 299.

54. Kim and Chung, *Catholic Korea*, 298–299.

55. Kim and Chung, *Catholic Korea*, 300, 311.

56. George S. McCune and Horace H. Underwood, "The Korean Shrine Question: A Debate," *Presbyterian Tribune* 58 (January 20, 1938).

57. The succession of apostolic vicars of Korea: Bruguière (1831–1835), who was unable to cross the border into Korea; Imbert (1837–1839), martyred; Ferréol (1843–1853); Berneux (1854–1866), martyred; Ridel (1870–1884), escaped the massacre of 1866; Blanc (1884–1890); Mutel (1890–1933).

Choi, *L'erection du premier vicariat apostolique*, 72–87.

58. Kim and Chung, *Catholic Korea*, 313–314. A second seminary was established in Taegu (or Taeku) in 1914.

59. Andrew Kim was born in 1821, ordained priest in 1845 near Shanghai, and martyred in 1846 (See Dallet, *Histoire de l'église de Corée*, 1:280–321; 2:308–321); and Thomas Yang-op Choi (Ch'oe) was ordained in 1849 in Shanghai and died in Korea in 1861 (see Kim and Chung, *Catholic Korea*, 224–225).

60. On Father Andrew Kim, see Kim and Chung, *Catholic Korea*, 197–216.

61. The proto-martyr, Kim Pom-u, one of the first converts of the pioneer Peter Seung-Hun Lee, had died in exile after torture in 1785, only a year after Lee returned from his conversion in Beijing to plant a Korean Catholic community (see Dallet, *Histoire de l'église de Corée*, 1:26–27).

62. For Protestant beginnings in Korea, see chap. 24 below.

Chapter 15

Burma (1813–1850)

Protestant Pioneers and Disrupted Catholics

> The future is as bright as the promises of God.
> — Adoniram Judson

Adoniram Judson and Baptist Beginnings (1813–1824)

Until he was twenty-five years old Adoniram Judson (1788–1850),[1] who became one of the first two ordained Protestant missionaries sent overseas from North America,[2] seemed remarkably unable to stay on course for more than a few years at a time. The son of a stern, devout New England Congregational minister, he turned rebelliously agnostic at college. He graduated from what is now Brown University at the head of the class of 1807, a proud and dissident Deist. Two years later he was a believer again, back in his father's faith and thinking of becoming a minister. He went to seminary and joined an earnest little group of mission-minded students at Andover who called themselves the Brethren. His conversion, however, was not sudden. It was as rational as it was emotional. He wrote to his fiancée, "I am persuaded that the chief reason why we do not enjoy religion is, that we do not try to enjoy it."[3]

It was the students there at Andover, not the organizational leadership of the church, who ignited the fire that gave America its first organized foreign missionary society. Passionately eager to serve abroad, and convinced that "Asia, with its idolatrous myriads, was the most important field in the world for missionary effort,"[4] but finding no mission board to send them, they appeared before their Congregational Church's General Association to appeal for support for their missionary intentions. Impressed as much by the polite behavior of the four young men as by their obvious sincerity, their knowledge of European mission societies, and deep sense of purpose, the elders of the association voted, in 1810, to form "a Board of Commissioners for Foreign Missions," to which the word "American" was later added.[5]

The Judsons and the Newells sailed for Calcutta in early 1812, the first missionaries from North America to Asia. They had been advised to try to locate their mission in Burma, but to inquire first in India how feasible such a mission might be. On the long sea voyage, Judson found himself making another startling change in his career. He turned Baptist. Knowing that in India he would be dependent on the advice of William Carey and his Serampore Baptists, Judson thought it might be wise to prepare himself for anticipated questions on the subject of baptism. Congregationalists sprinkled; Baptists immersed. Congregationalists baptized infants; Baptists did not. So Judson turned to study the Bible's teaching on the subject, and, for practice, asked his wife Ann to defend the Baptist view while he upheld their own long-held position. Mrs. Judson did not like the assignment but must have been a strong debater, for by the time they reached India, though she was still unconvinced, the Bible study combined with Ann's arguments had led her husband to a sincere belief that the Baptists were right and that Scripture was not pedobaptist. Ann herself, however, was not convinced. Only after more reading on the subject in Calcutta did she finally change her mind. As she wrote to a friend, "Thus, my dear Nancy, we are confirmed Baptists, not because we wished to be, but because truth compelled us to be." A few months later they asked the Serampore English missionaries to baptize them by immersion.[6] Then a more immediate problem beset them. They were ordered out of India by the British East India Company, to whom American missionaries were even less welcome than British. They were baptized in September; already in June the United States had declared war on England.

It was another difficult year before the Judsons finally reached their originally intended destination, Burma.[7] India had never been an easy field for the Serampore British Baptists, but they warned the Judsons that Burma would be even more difficult and dangerous. William Carey's son, Felix, had tried with others since 1807 to establish a British Baptist mission in Rangoon, and failed. One missionary of the London Missionary Society had already died there, and Felix Carey, despairing of missionary success, had taken a post with the government. The Catholics, though they had been intermittently active since the sixteenth century, were strictly limited by law to work only with descendants of the early Portuguese traders in a small Burmo-Portuguese community. Buddhist Burma, Judson was told, was impermeable to Christian evangelism.[8]

Four years passed before Judson dared even to hold semipublic services. At first he had tried adapting to Burmese customs by wearing a yellow robe to mark himself as a teacher of religion, but soon changed to white to show he was not a Buddhist. Then he gave up the whole attempt as artificial and accepted the fact that no matter how much he changed his clothes, no Burmese would identify him as anything but a foreigner.[9] But he was aware of the importance of some accommodations to Burmese customs and built a *zayat*, the customary bamboo and thatch reception shelter, on the street near his home as a reception room and meeting place for Burmese men. Fifteen men came to his first public meeting in April 1819. He was encouraged but observed that he suspected that they had probably come more out of curiosity than anything else. Their attention wandered, and they soon seemed uninterested.[10] Two months later, by a lotus pond and under the unseeing eyes of a large image of Buddha, he baptized his first Burmese convert, Maung Naw (or Nau),[11] a thirty-five-year-old timber worker. That baptism has been called "the beginning of the Protestant Church in Burma."[12]

It was not, however, typical of the subsequent history of Protestantism in Burma. For Maung Naw was Burmese, yet by and large, Burmese Christianity, whether Protestant or Catholic, grew not among the majority Burmese Buddhists of the cities and coasts, but among the animist tribes of the hills — the Karen, the Kachin, the Chin, the Losu, the head-hunting Wa, and, to a lesser extent, the Shan (ethnic Thai) along the eastern coast who like the Burmese were Buddhist.

By 1820, after seventeen years of American Baptist missionary work, Judson reported only ten Burmese converts.[13] Nevertheless, there was much to encourage him. He had written a grammar of the language that is still in use today, and had begun to translate the Bible.[14] His remarkable wife, Ann Hasseltine Judson, was even more fluent in the spoken, conversational language of the people than her more academically literate husband, and made friends everywhere, with the kind wife of the viceroy of Rangoon as quickly as with illiterate workers and women.[15] Moreover a printing press had been sent from Serampore, and a missionary printer, George Hough, whose arrival from America with his wife doubled the size of the mission, produced, in 1817, the first printed materials in Burmese ever printed in Burma, including eight hundred copies of Judson's translation of the *Gospel of Matthew*.[16]

Driving Judson's persistence toward a complete translation of the Bible was the slow but steady growth of the Burmese church.[17] Within less than six months of the first baptism two more Burmese were converted, and within another year, by 1820 the number of converts had increased to ten, the tenth being the first Burmese woman to receive a Baptist baptism, Ma Min Lay, later to pioneer with Ann Judson in founding the first coeducational school in Burma. The chronicler of the Burma church, Maung Shwe Wa, concludes this part of the story: "So was born the church in Rangoon — logger and fisherman, the poor and the rich, men and women. One travelled the whole pathway to Christ in three days; another took two years. But once they had decided for Christ they were his for all time."[18]

One of the most important of those early disciples was a teacher, U Shwe Ngong, leader of an influential group of intellectuals, dissatisfied with Buddhism, who were attracted to the new faith. He was a Deist skeptic, to whose mind the preaching of Judson, once a college skeptic himself, was singularly challenging, but he assured Judson that after consideration he was ready to believe in God, and Jesus Christ and the atonement. Judson, instead of welcoming him to the faith, pressed him further, asking if he believed what he had read in the Gospel of Matthew, that Jesus the Son of God died on the cross. He shook his head. "Ah, you have caught me now. I believe that he suffered death, but I cannot admit that he suffered the shameful death of the cross." Not long thereafter he came back to tell Judson, "I have been trusting in my own reason, not the word of God...I now believe the crucifixion of Christ because it is contained in Scripture."[19]

The essence of Judson's preaching was a combination of conviction of the truth and rationality of the Christian faith, a firm belief in the authority of the Bible, and a determination to make Christianity relevant to the Burmese mind without violating the integrity of Christian truth, or, as he put it, "to preach the Gospel, not Anti-Buddhism."[20] By 1823, ten years after his arrival, Judson could take pride that the membership of the little church had grown to eighteen, and that he had finally finished the first draft of his translation of the entire text of the New Testament in Burmese.[21]

One other highly significant event in this opening decade of the mission work in Burma was the arrival near the end of 1821 of Burma's first medical missionary, Dr. Jonathan Price. Not all his skill could save his own wife, who died within five months in the heat and pollution of the tropics, but it was his ability to restore sight to the blind by cataract operations that caught the attention of the king and gave Judson his first effective audience at the royal court. But it was Dr. Price in whom the king was interested. Judson was virtually ignored as only an interpreter. Not until after repeated visits did the king finally look at Judson and ask, "And you in black, what are you? A medical man, too?" "No, a teacher of religion," said Judson, and for the first time Judson was able to answer royal questions about his converts and the Christian faith. Much depended on his answers. He feared instant disapproval, perhaps banishment. But he answered wisely and honestly, admitting that even some Burmese had become Christian, and was elated that the king showed no sign of displeasure.[22] To Judson, the arrival of Dr. Price was a sign of a promising new means of winning the attention of the nation and assuring the people of the good intentions of the missionaries. His elation was short-lived. Within two years the optimistic missionary and the good doctor were both in prison facing death.

The First Anglo-Burmese War (1824–1826)

Two irreconcilable hungers triggered the Anglo-Burmese War of 1824: Burma's insatiable greed for more territory, and Britain's unslaked hunger for more trade. Burma threatened Assam and Bengal; Britain responded by attacking and absorbing two Burmese provinces into her India holdings to broaden her trade routes to East Asia. The war was a rough interruption of the Baptists' missionary work. English-speaking Americans were too easily confused with the enemy and suspected of spying.

Judson and Price were violently arrested. Officers led by an official executioner burst into the Judson home, threw Mr. Judson to the ground before the eyes of his wife, bound him with torture thongs, and dragged him off to the infamous, vermin-ridden "death prison" of Ava. Twelve agonizing months later he and Dr. Price, along with a small group of surviving Western prisoners, were marched overland, barefoot and sick, for six more months of misery in a primitive village prison near Mandalay. Of the sepoy British prisoners of war imprisoned with them, all but one died. The sufferings and brutalities of those twenty long months and days in prison, half-starved, iron-fettered, sometimes trussed and suspended by his mangled feet with only head and shoulders touching the ground, is described in unexaggerated detail by his wife, Ann, shortly after his release.[23] The heroic Ann, however, was perhaps the greater model of supreme courage. Heedless of all threats against herself, left alone as the only Western woman in an absolute and anti-Christian monarchy at war with the West, beset with raving fevers and nursing a tiny baby her husband had not yet seen, she wore herself to death rushing from office to office in desperate attempts to keep her husband alive and win his freedom.[24]

The collapse of Burma's armies brought Judson out of prison, but his release was not complete freedom. For several months in 1826 after the surrender, Burma pressed Judson into its service as a translator for the peace negotiations. Some have used Judson's acceptance of a role in the treaty negotiations as evidence of complicity in imperialism, but it should be noted that he first acted on behalf of the defeated Burmese as translator, not for the Western victors. Only later did he help the British in the same capacity but in the hope, a vain hope as it proved, that he might be able to secure a clause in the treaty guaranteeing freedom of religion.[25]

The Rise of the Burma Baptist Church (1826–1860)

The end of the war should have been a time of rejoicing for the mission. As soon as Ann and her husband were released by the Burmese, Mrs. Judson wrote that one good result of the war could be that terms of the treaty which ceded Burmese provinces to the British might provide opportunity to expand the witness of the mission into hitherto unreached parts of the country.[26] But a few months later Ann was dead, a victim of the long, dreadful months of disease, death, stress, and loneliness that had been hers for twenty-one months. She died alone. Her husband was already out exploring in one of the ceded provinces, Tenasserim. And it was in the wild hills of that newly British province of

Tenasserim that the first signs of rapid growth in Protestant Christianity in Burma began. The statistics are startling. Within a few years of the end of the war, Baptist church membership doubled on an average of every eight years for the thirty-two years between 1834 and 1866.[27]

Three significant factors had a part, though not the only part, in such growth. Most of the growth was in British-ruled territory, not in the Burmese-ruled kingdom. It may be also be significant that after an Anglo-Burma war, the missionaries were American, not British. But probably the most telling factor was religion. Most of the growth came from among the animist tribes, not from the major population group, the Buddhist Burmese.

"The Karen Apostle" and Expanding Growth (1827–1860)

The nation was Burmese; its lost province was British; and the missionaries were American, but the "apostle" of that first numerically significant evangelistic breakthrough in Burma was neither British nor American nor Burman. He was a Karen, Ko Tha Byu,[28] though credit is rightly due also to the three missionary pioneers to the Karen, George and Sarah Boardman, and Adoniram Judson.

The Karen were a primitive, hunted minority group of ancient Burmo-Tibetan ancestry scattered in the forests and jungles of the Salween River and in the hills along the southeast coast.[29] Judson was the first missionary to make contact with them about 1827 when he ransomed and freed a debt-slave from one of his early converts. The freed slave, Ko Tha Byu, was an illiterate, surly man who spoke almost no Burmese and was reputed to be not only a thief but a murderer who admitted killing at least thirty men, but could not remember exactly how many more.[30]

In 1828 the former Karen bandit, "whose rough, undisciplined genius, energy and zeal for Christ" had caught the notice of the missionaries, was sent south with a new missionary couple, the Boardmans, into the territory of the strongly animistic, non-Buddhist Karen. There, he was no sooner baptized[31] than he set off into the jungle alone to preach to his fellow tribespeople. Astonishingly, he found them strangely prepared for his preaching. Their ancient oral traditions, handed down for centuries, contained such startling echoes of the Old Testament that some scholars conjecture a linkage with Jewish communities (or possibly even Nestorians) before their migrations from western China into Burma perhaps as early as the twelfth century.[32]

The core of what they called their "Tradition of the Elders" was a belief in an unchangeable, eternal, all-powerful God, creator of heaven and earth, of man, and of woman formed from a rib taken from the man. They believed in humanity's temptation by a devil, and its fall, and that some day a messiah would come to its rescue. They lived in expectation of a prophecy that white foreigners would bring them a sacred parchment roll.[33] While the Boardmans and Ko Tha Byu were penetrating the jungles to the south, Adoniram Judson shook off a paralyzing year-long siege of depression that overcame him after the death of his wife, Ann,[34] and set out alone on long canoe trips up the Salween into the tiger-infested jungles to evangelize the northern Karen.[35] Between trips he worked untiringly at his lifelong goal of translating the whole Bible into the Burmese language. When he finished it at last in 1834, he had been laboring on it for twenty-four years. It was printed and published in 1835.[36]

Judson lived for fifteen more years of work in and for Burma. He lived to approve and welcome the first single women missionaries to Burma. A general rule of the mission had hitherto prevented such appointments. It was, said Judson, "probably a good" rule, "but our minds should not be closed" to making exceptions.[37] The first two "exceptions" were extraordinarily exceptional. Miss Sarah Cummings arrived in 1832. Miss Cummings proved her mettle at once, choosing to work alone with Karen evangelists in the malaria-ridden Salween River valley north of Moulmein, but within two years she died of fever.[38] A second single woman, Eleanor Macomber, after five years of mission to the Ojibway Indians in Michigan, joined the mission in faraway Burma in 1835. Alone, with the help of Karen evangelistic assistants, she planted a church in a remote Karen village and nurtured it to the point where it could be placed under the care of an ordained missionary. She lived five years, and died of jungle fever.[39]

Judson kept on and on. He lived to see the evangelization of the once wild and turbulent tribesmen swell into a mass movement that was one of the most impressive monuments of the history of Christian expansion in Asia. In 1828 only 1 Karen had been baptized. By 1831 the little church in Tavoy numbered 110 members, mostly Karen. When Ko Tha Byu died in 1840 there were 1,270 Karen Christians, and in 1841 it was reported that 3,000 had been baptized in the previous five years alone. By 1856 the number of reported baptized believers among the Karens had reached 11,878 and would keep rising for more than the next 150 years.[40]

Judson died in 1850, halfway through the first century of Protestantism in Burma. In that year the statistics reported a total of 48 missionaries and wives in the Baptist mission, 114 native preachers and assistants, 74 organized churches, a total baptized membership of 7,904, 12 schools (including a theological seminary), and 5 million pages of Christian literature in the Burmese languages printed and distributed.[41] Few have suffered more personal grief, depression, trials, and tribulations, and few have been able to survive with a more indomitable hope.[42]

Between 1824 and 1836 the number of missionaries in Burma had increased from 3 to more than 50.[43] An attempt was made to reach the Chin tribal groups in the mangrove swamps and jungles of Burma's steamy upper west coast Arakan, but after seventeen deaths in twenty-one years of cholera, malaria, and two hundred inches of rain annually, the attempt to reach that part of Burma with foreign missionaries had to be abandoned.[44]

Between the two Anglo-Burma wars (1826–1852), the American Baptist mission established a remarkable network of Christian schools in the British provinces of Burma, prompting one English writer to note that though the British had conquered Burma militarily, later generations of the Burmese may well be saying, "our American teachers were conquerors of ignorance, and dispelled the darkness from which the English never strove to rescue us."[45] By 1852 there were twelve central schools in the three city centers, and fifteen self-supporting village schools.[46] Of particular importance for the development of Burmese leadership in the church was the establishment in 1836 of a Central Theological School for both Burmans and Karens, which was eventually located in Moulmein.[47]

The First Baptist Missionary Convention (1853)

At the close of the second Anglo-Burman War, and three years after the death of Judson, Great Britain added to its former area of control all of Lower Burma (the Irrawaddy and Salween Deltas, including the great cities of Rangoon and Bassein), and the Baptist Mission held its first Missionary Convention (1853). The ostensible reason for the meeting was to consider the missionary consequences of the Burmese cession of all Lower Burma to Great Britain. This included the great cities of Rangoon and Bassein, and almost doubled the territory opened to Christian evangelism by British recognition of freedom of religion in its Burmese provinces. It also forced a rethinking of the mission's whole strategy after nearly half a century of its existence.

Twenty missionaries, six "national assistants," and a deputation of two Baptist ministers from the missionary board in America (the Missionary Union) attended the convention.[48] There were then eleven native Burmese pastors and more than 120 lay Baptist preachers connected with the mission. Among their most important decisions was a call for still more such national leaders so that "were every missionary withdrawn, they would possess within themselves . . . the ability to continue as witnesses of Christ." They also stressed the need for medical work and dispensaries to authenticate the evangelistic witness in a non-Christian culture. "Teamwork between doctor and preacher" was to be encouraged. A third emphasis, much discussed, was the place of the network of Christian schools already successfully planted. Here the emphasis was a shift from missionary leadership (except in teacher training and the seminary) to self-support and national leadership.[49]

One unexpected and lamented result of the conference was the first schism in the mission. Five of the leading missionaries to the Karen people left the mission in a dispute over some of the policies adopted, which seemed more suited to settled areas than the tribal frontier.[50] A second complaint was against increasing control of mission policy from distant America, which meant less flexibility for decision making on the field. An example had recently occurred, as recounted by the historian Maung Shwe Wa. Faced with a desperate famine situation and people dying in the streets, J. C. Vinton, missionary to the Karen, abruptly cut through mission red tape. He had received no funds from America for more than a year. His school supply of rice, shared with the starving, was exhausted. So against regulations he went straight to the rice merchants on his own personal guarantee. "I'll pay you as soon as I can," he said. And to his surprise they said, "Mr. Vinton, take all the rice you want. Your word is all the security we need." He was one of those who left the mission, yet his action so impressed the people that in later days they would still crowd around him. "This is the man who saved our lives," they would say. "His religion is the one we want."[51]

Both the issues — unified mission policy and local authority to make decisions — ran counter to Baptist tradition against centralization. The reaction was perhaps inevitable, for though conventions solve some problems, they usually raise others. Nevertheless, it was in Vinton's Karen territory around Rangoon that within two years a fourth Karen Home Missionary Society was organized which, added to three others east and west, now gave the Karen a national network of self-supporting, Karen-led missions to their own people. By 1856 there were forty-two Karen churches with over two thousand members, thirty-nine Karen preachers, and thirty-six village schools.[52]

The Judson era in Burma missions was over. Total statistics for the Baptists in all Burma in 1854 were 63 missionaries (including wives), 154 Burmese preachers and assistants, and 8,836 members. New problems arose, but when had it ever been otherwise in Asia? And like the old pioneer, Judson's successors also believed that "the future is as bright as the promises of God."[53]

Catholics in Burma

Catholic missionaries first entered Burma long before the Protestant, in 1554. Not until 1613, however, was there a permanent mission presence, with churches in Ava, Sirian, and three hundred Roman Catholic believers in Rangoon. But growth was so disrupted by wars between Burma and Siam in the next two centuries that as they entered the nineteenth century, a total membership of five thousand in 1800 had fallen to about three thousand in 1832. So great was the discouragement about the unhappy situation that two apostolic vicars who were sent out in 1830 gave up in despair and returned to Europe.[54]

Then at about mid-century came the Catholic recovery. In Burma the Congregation for Propagation of the Faith finally in 1857 turned missional responsibility for the whole peninsula over to the Foreign Mission Society of Paris. By 1870 there had been enough progress to allow a reorganization into two vicariates and one prefecture: British Burma in the south, the ancient Burmese kingdom in the north, and tribal Burma on the Chinese border and south and east along the long Siamese border.[55] But unlike Ceylon where Dutch and British Protestant occupation failed to present a serious challenge to prior Catholic expansion, in Burma the opposite was true. As British control widened in the first half of the nineteenth century, Protestant growth, chiefly Baptist, made the greater advances.[56] Since 1800, by about mid-century Roman Catholics had increased their membership by only about a thousand, from five thousand to about six thousand; Protestants had grown from nothing to about eighty-seven hundred.[57] But Catholics too were on the verge of a recovery, and their future would be encouraging though less spectacular than that of the Baptist successors of Adoniram Judson.

By 1896, in a hundred years Catholic membership had grown from about five thousand in 1800 to fifty thousand, ten times that number. In a total population of about 9 million this was nothing to boast about perhaps. But in Asia it was nothing to be ashamed of, either. Very significantly, the number of Burmese priests (thirteen) compared to foreign missionary priests (sixty-two) was growing at a considerably faster rate. Add 325 Catholic churches and chapels, and 191 schools with 5,000 pupils,[58] and the future for Roman Catholics in Burma was no less bright than Judson's claim for his much-admired model of a nineteenth-century Protestant mission.

NOTES

1. The most thorough biography of Judson is still by the then president of Brown University, Francis Wayland, *A Memoir of the Life and Labors of the Rev. Adoniram Judson, D.D.*, 2 vols. (Boston: Phillips, Sampson, and Co., 1853). An important recent monograph with bibliography is William H. Brackney's "The Legacy of Adoniram Judson," *IBMR* 22, no. 1 (July 1998): 122–127.

2. The Rev. William Newell and his wife sailed on the same ship to India. Not allowed to reside in India, Judson went to Burma, Newell to Ceylon. See Robert Torbet, *Venture of Faith: The Story of the American Baptist Foreign Missionary Society and the Woman's American Baptist Foreign Missionary Society 1814–1954* (Philadelphia: Judson Press, 1955), 19ff.

3. Wayland, *A Memoir of the Life and Labors of the Rev. Adoniram Judson, D.D.*, 1:27–28, 32.

4. Wayland, *A Memoir of the Life and Labors of the Rev. Adoniram Judson, D.D.*, 1:44.

5. Wayland, *A Memoir of the Life and Labors of the Rev. Adoniram Judson, D.D.*, 1:48–61. The four young men were Adoniram Judson Jr. (who had drawn up their

written request), Samuel Nott Jr., Samuel J. Mills, and Samuel Newell. See also Joseph Tracy, *History of the American Board of Commissioners for Foreign Missions,* 2nd ed. (New York: M. W. Dodd, 1842), 22–28; also Rufus Anderson, *History of the Missions of the American Board of Commissioners.*

6. See the letters from both Judsons quoted in Wayland, *A Memoir of the Life and Labors of the Rev. Adoniram Judson, D.D.,* 1:95–110; and Edward Judson, *The Life of Adoniram Judson* (New York: A. D. F. Randolph, 1883), 36–44. The change in their theology of baptism led to their resignation from the Congregational Mission Board, the ABCFM, and eventually to the formation of the American Baptist Missionary Society. It is interesting to note, however, that it was not the Judsons but their American missionary colleagues, Hall, Nott, and Rice, who felt that the issue of re-baptism would make a separation into denominational missions imperative. See Stacy R. Warburton's readable and well-documented *Eastward! The Story of Adoniram Judson* (New York: Round Table Press, 1937), 52ff.

7. The best book on the history of the Baptist mission is Maung Shwe Wa, *Burma Baptist Chronicle,* ed. Genevieve Sowards and Edward Sowards (Rangoon: Burma Baptist Convention, 1963), which is particularly valuable because its perspective is that of the national church, not the mission.

8. For Judson's first feeling of depression on reaching Rangoon, see Wayland, *A Memoir of the Life and Labors of the Rev. Adoniram Judson, D.D.,* 1:120–121; and his later realization of the difficulty of evangelizing Buddhists (2:416). Judson had been told the population of Burma was then 18 million, about equal to that of the United States, but later estimates suggest only about 8 million (1:30). The Roman Catholics, after two hundred years of missionary attempts to establish permanent work among the Burmese, could only report in 1800 a total Christian community of less than five thousand, almost all of mixed Portuguese descent and therefore treated as foreigners (G. E. Harvey, *History of Burma* [New York and London: Longmans, Green and Co., 1925], 345–346). For Judson's own descriptions of Burmese Buddhism, see Wayland, *A Memoir of the Life and Labors of the Rev. Adoniram Judson, D.D.,* 1:138–141, 407ff. His estimate of the number of Buddhists in the world was 400 million out of a world population of nine hundred thousand compared to 250 million Christians, 140 million Muslims, and 100 million Hindus (2:410).

9. Alexander McLeish, *Burma: Christian Progress to the Invasion* (London and New York: World Dominion Press, 1942), 21. Later, Mrs. Ann Judson did adopt Burmese dress, particularly for visits with upper-class women (Wayland, *A Memoir of the Life and Labors of the Rev. Adoniram Judson, D.D.,* 1:310).

10. James D. Knowles, *Memoir of Mrs. Ann H. Judson, late Missionary to Burmah,* 2nd ed. (Boston: Lincoln & Edmands, 1829), 143–146.

11. A confusion in Burmese names is caused by the prefixes *Maung, Ko,* and *U.* "Maung" literally denotes younger brother; "Ko" was formerly used of those somewhat older, and "U" (which means uncle) is a title of respect. Usage is changing, but in the sources the same man may be first called Maung Nu, and later Ko Nu, or U Nu.

12. The date was June 27, 1819. Judson, *The Life of Adoniram Judson,* 132, citing his father's Journal entry of that date. See also Francis Wayland, *A Memoir of the Life and Labors of the Rev. Adoniram Judson, D.D.,* 1:216–224; and Mrs. Macleod

Wylie, *The Gospel in Burmah* (London: W. H. Dalton, 1859), 23–24; and Maung Shwe Wa, *Burma Baptist Chronicle,* 16–19.

13. McLeish, *Christian Progress in Burma,* 21.

14. Maung Shwe Wa, *Burma Baptist Chronicle,* 8ff.

15. Knowles, *Memoir of Mrs. Ann H. Judson,* 110, 112, 120, 124–125; Maung Shwe Wa, *Burma Baptist Chronicle,* 7; and see Helen G. Trager, *Burma through Alien Eyes* (New York: Frederick A. Praeger, 1966), 125–130, who sometimes overstresses negative foreign reactions to Burma.

16. The others were two pamphlets, *A View of the Christian Religion* and a catechism (Maung Shwe Wa, *Burma Baptist Chronicle,* 9–10).

17. On his persistence in giving priority to translation, see his letter of January 5, 1839, in Wayland, *A Memoir of the Life and Labors of the Rev. Adoniram Judson, D.D.,* 2:128–129.

18. See Maung Shwe Wa, *Burma Baptist Chronicle,* 19–31, 33, quotation on 31.

19. Maung Shwe Wa, *Burma Baptist Chronicle,* 22–25. The citations are on 24–25.

20. Wayland, *A Memoir of the Life and Labors of the Rev. Adoniram Judson, D.D.,* 2:126.

21. Judson, *The Life of Adoniram Judson,* 105–112, 127–132; Maung Shwe Wa *Burma Baptist Chronicle,* 12, 32–40.

22. Judson, *The Life of Adoniram Judson,* 198–199, citing Judson's "Journal" entry for October 1, 1822.

23. Ann Judson, letter, Rangoon, May 26, 1826. This famous and earliest account of the imprisonment of Judson was printed in full in Knowles, *Memoir of Mrs. Ann H. Judson,* 227–260. It launched the Judsons into an instant fame that they had never sought. See also Judson's own matter-of-fact deposition to the British commissioner, in Wayland, *A Memoir of the Life and Labors of the Rev. Adoniram Judson, D.D.,* 2:422–447. See also 1:338–393.

24. Wayland, *A Memoir of the Life and Labors of the Rev. Adoniram Judson, D.D.,* 1:358–366, 373–374, 378ff., 388, 394, 396ff. See also Ethel Daniels Hubbard's *Ann of Ava* (New York: Missionary Education Movement, 1913), a popular biography of Ann Hasseltine, the first Mrs. Judson, which dramatizes the story without distorting the facts.

25. Ann Judson, letter, May 26, 1826, in Knowles, *Memoir of Mrs. Ann H. Judson,* 252–259; Wylie, *The Gospel in Burmah,* 37; Wayland, *A Memoir of the Life and Labors of the Rev. Adoniram Judson, D.D.,* 1:389–391, 411ff.; Maung Shwe Wa, *Burma Baptist Chronicle,* 169–170; Helen Trager, *Burma through Alien Eyes,* 173 n. 116.

26. Ann Judson, letter, British Camp, Yandabo, February 25, 1826, and of April 26 from Rangoon, in Knowles, *Memoir of Mrs. Judson,* 226–227, 262–263. She died October 24, 1826.

27. Maung Shwe Wa, *Burma Baptist Chronicle,* 266, and chart (267).

28. The only biography of Ko Tha Byu is Francis Mason, *The Karen Apostle, or, Memoir of Ko Tha-Byu, the First Karen Convert,* rev. ed. (Boston: Gould, Kendall and Lincoln, 1847).

29. H. P. Cochrane, *Among the Burmans: A Record of Fifteen Years* (New York: Fleming H. Revell, 1904, citing the census of 1901), 101. For statistics of the other major tribes see Cochrane, *Among the Burmans,* 95, 103, 108; Burmese numbered 6.5 million (89).

30. Mason, *The Karen Apostle,* 11–12.

31. Ko Tha Byu's baptism by Mr. Boardman in 1828 was in Tavoy ([Mrs.] Emily Chubbock Judson, *Memoir of Sarah B[oardman] Judson, Member of the American Mission to Burmah* [New York: L. Colby, 1849], 76).

32. The authenticity of this ancient story as a tradition is confirmed by the fact that it has been found not only among the Karen, but also, with variations, among the Kachins, Was, Akhas, Lisus, and even the Mizo and Naga tribes of northeastern India. See Herman G. Tegenfeldt, *A Century of Growth: The Kachin Baptist Church of Burma* (Pasadena, Calif.: William Carey Library, 1974), 46; John Stuart, *Burma through the Centuries* (London: Kegan, Paul, Trench, Trubner, 1925), 5ff.; Harvey, *History of Burma*, 3.

33. Excerpts from the "Traditions" are given in Mason, *The Karen Apostle*, 97–104. See also Stuart, *Burma through the Centuries*, 6–7.

34. On his "dark night of the soul," see Judson, *The Life of Adoniram Judson*, 302ff. He built a hut in the woods "away from the haunts of men...and the desolation around me accords with the desolate state of my own mind" (308, citing Judson's letter of October 24, 1828). And again, "God is to me the great Unknown. I believe in Him, but I find Him not" (letter, October 24, 1829).

35. Maung Shwe Wa, *Burma Baptist Chronicle*, 89–101. Judson's colleague, Jonathan Wade, had already baptized the first northern Karen in 1831, and had reduced the Sgaw Karen language to writing (36, 64–65, 80–81).

36. Judson, *The Life of Adoniram Judson*, 376–395. For a more extensive survey of the Baptist mission's printing and publications up to 1852, see Maung Shwe Wa, *Burma Baptist Chronicle*, 123–126. In this period, 1831–1835, Judson also married again. His second wife was Mrs. Sarah Boardman, who had for three years after the death of her husband worked alone with the Karen in the south. On his Burmese Bible translation, see Judson, *The Life of Adoniram Judson*, 404–416.

37. Adoniram Judson's letter of April 18, 1837, cited by Wayland, *A Memoir of the Life and Labors of the Rev. Adoniram Judson, D.D.*, 2:115–116.

38. See J. Clement, *Memoir of Adoniram Judson: His Life and Missionary Labors* (Auburn, N.Y.: Derby and Miller, 1851), 220–221.

39. Daniel C. Eddy, *Christian Heroines* (Boston: Estes and Lauriat, 1881), 133–162.

40. For 1828, Maung Shwe Wa, *Burma Baptist Chronicle*, 68; for 1840, Mason, *The Karen Apostle*, 75; for 1836–1841, Emily C. Judson, *Sarah B. Judson*, 155–156, and Wylie, *The Gospel in Burmah*, 107; for 1856, Latourette, *A History of the Expansion of Christianity*, 6:231. It is important to remember that Baptist membership figures are for baptized, communicant members only, and should be doubled for comparison with most Protestant and Catholic denominations which include baptized infants, and sometimes adherents and inquirers as well.

41. Maung Shwe Wa, *Burma Baptist Chronicle*, 135.

42. See the note at the end of this chapter on his famous reply when questioned by an inquirer in Boston about the future of the work in precarious Burma.

43. Including missionary wives. Trager, *Burma Through Alien Eyes*, 25, citing Knowles, *Memoir of Ann Judson*, 357–359.

44. Maung Shwe Wa, *Burma Baptist Chronicle*, 110; Barrett et al. eds., *World Christian Encyclopedia*, 2001, 202.

45. Maung Shwe Wa, *Burma Baptist Chronicle*, citing the *Calcutta Review*, 1847, 139–145.

46. Maung Shwe Wa, *Burma Baptist Chronicle*, 115–123.

47. The seminary functioned primarily as a Bible school, and after 1850 separated into two parts, a center in the city for Burmans, and village centers for Karens in the stations (Maung Shwe Wa, *Burma Baptist Chronicle*, 123).

48. The Burmese members, who did not attend every meeting, were Sayas Dway, Oung Moo, Shway Doke, Zu Thee, Shway A, and Avung (Maung Shwe Wa, *Burma Baptist Chronicle*, 144).

49. Maung Shwe Wa, *Burma Baptist Chronicle*, 145–147.

50. Maung Shwe Wa, *Burma Baptist Chronicle*, 151–152.

51. Maung Shwe Wa, *Burma Baptist Chronicle*, 160–164.

52. Maung Shwe Wa, *Burma Baptist Chronicle*, 164. The earlier Karen Home Mission Societies were organized in Tavoy (1830), Sandoway (1851), and Bassein (1853) (70, 113, 175). See also Judson's "new system of evangelism," which involved using five or six native assistants with whom he met every morning to pray, plan, and report, and then sent out through the whole Moulmein area (Maung Shwe Wa, *Burma Baptist Chronicle*, 127).

53. This oft-repeated quotation attributed to Judson is probably a not unreasonable paraphrase of his reply to a questioner in Boston who asked, "Do you think the prospects bright for the speedy conversion of the heathen?" To which his prompt reply was "As bright as the promises of God" (Wayland, *A Memoir of the Life and Labors of the Rev. Adoniram Judson, D.D.*, 2:381). Cf. a similar sentiment in another statement by Judson (2:417).

54. Louvet, *Les missions catholiques au XIXme siècle*, 151–152; Schmidlin, *Catholic Mission History*, 309–310.

55. Louvet, *Les missions catholiques au XIXme siècle*, 155.

56. Latourette, *A History of the Expansion of Christianity*, 6:225ff.

57. On Catholic growth in Burma, see Louvet, *Les missions catholiques au XIXme siècle*, 152; cf. Latourette, *A History of the Expansion of Christianity*, 6:225–227. On Protestant growth, cf. Newcomb, *A Cyclopedia of Missions*, 214; and Latourette, *A History of the Expansion of Christianity*, 6:232. The statistics fall within a date range from 1854 to 1862.

58. Louvet, *Les missions catholiques au XIXme siècle*, 152.

Chapter 16

Ceylon under British Rule
(1796–1860)

> You are to permit liberty of conscience and free exercise of religious worship to all persons who inhabit...the settlement, provided that they be contented with a quiet and peaceable enjoyment of the same.
> — British Government Directive (1798)[1]

Transition: Dutch to British, Reformed to Anglican

The British took Ceylon from the Dutch in 1796 after nearly a century and a half of Dutch rule, much as the Dutch had driven out the Portuguese after a century and a half of the earlier Iberian occupation of that beautiful island.[2] The Dutch were ill prepared to defend their distant possession. Still reeling at home from the shock of the revolution in neighboring France they might have lost more than one island, but were fortunate to be able to retreat eastward across the Indian Ocean to their larger holdings in the islands of Indonesia. So Britain added Ceylon to its Indian territories and ruled it for the next 150 years. Not until 1948 was the island granted its own freedom and emerged at last from foreign control as the independent country of Sri Lanka. Ecclesiastically this might seem to represent a transition from Reformed to Anglican predominance, save for one fact that became increasingly clear: most Ceylonese were still Buddhist, and even of the Christians most had never except nominally lost their Catholic heritage.

Ceylon's four centuries under three different colonial flags present three different exposures of its people's native culture to the expansion of Christianity in South Asia. These have been rather unfairly described by some in negative terms as a Portuguese period of colonial aggression, a Dutch period of indifference and harassment, and a British period of moderate imperialism.[3] A more positive and fairer generalization would be 110 years of Portuguese imperial patronage and Catholic evangelization (1546–1656), 150 years of Dutch Protestant neglect and commercial exploitation (1642–1796), and 150 years of British religious toleration, Western education, and benign but self-interested economic improvement (1796–1948).

Comparisons are odious, but it is difficult to avoid making an unsettling observation about the church statistics of those four centuries of colonialism in Ceylon. Portuguese Catholics, Dutch Reformed, and British Anglicans governed the island in succession, each for more than a hundred years. Portuguese rule is usually described as the most cruel and intolerant. But the hard fact is that according to the statistics, a Catholic combination of colonial aggression and evangelism proved more effective than either the Dutch Reformed pattern of commercial pressure, religious harassment, and emphasis on education, or the British attitude of benign imperialism and understated evangelism. At the end of the colonial period, as we shall see, it was neither Protestantism nor Anglicanism but the Roman Catholicism of the Portuguese conquistadors and friars that had taken root and grown within the Sinhalese (Ceylonese) culture as the more effective Christian counterpart to the island's native Buddhism.

Sir James Tennent, writing on Christianity in Ceylon in 1850, hailed the British displacement of the Dutch as a window of opportunity for a whole new approach to the spread of the gospel by Christian missions. The Portuguese, he said, with some venom but not without a measure of truth, had used "artifice and corrupt inducement" to win unbelievers to the church; the Dutch employed "alternate bribery and persecution"; but now at last under the fair-minded British, "for the first time a legitimate field was offered…, and a fair and unbiased trial has been given to the efficacy of truth and simplicity…, unaided by the favor and uninfluenced by the frowns of authority."[4]

Moving out from captured Colombo, by 1805 the British controlled the Ceylonese coastlands, and in the next ten years finally subdued the fierce and bloody resistance of the landlocked highlanders of the kingdom of Kandy in 1815. From that time on the essential shape of British administration of the island did not greatly change. It was religiously tolerant, humanitarian, and focused on commerce and trade. In 1806 The British administration removed the restrictions on Roman Catholicism. In 1844 it abolished slavery, twenty years before Lincoln's proclamation of emancipation in 1863.[5] In 1853 it disassociated itself from governmental administration of Buddhist affairs.[6] In trade matters, it supported the island's growing colonial plantation economy through the fall of the cinnamon trade to a coffee period, followed by a tea trade cycle, and finally the years of rubber.[7] In the process the British brought Ceylon from feudalism into modern statehood, granting it independence in 1948.

From its beginnings in 1796 Britain adopted a milder religious policy than the Dutch toward both Catholics and Buddhists. As early as 1798, shortly after the government of the island was transferred from military to civilian administration under the British East India Company, a Company directive ordered that though members of the Church of England were to be given preference in the administration, "you are to permit liberty of conscience and free exercise of religious worship to all persons who inhabit and frequent the settlement, provided that they be contented with a quiet and peaceable enjoyment of the same."[8] This applied to all religions: Catholic, Protestant, Buddhist, and Hindu. Eight years later, the edict of 1806, mentioned above, further enlarged the parameters of religious freedom for Catholics, granting them "unmolested profession and exercise of their religion." Surprisingly, this left Catholics in Ceylon more free from restraint than Catholics in England.[9] Equally surprising, the government as late as 1807 still recognized the "Presbyterian religion" of the Dutch Reformed Church as the "ecclesiastical establishment of the colony."[10] As for Buddhists, the treaty of 1815 with the Buddhist kingdom of Kandy, which ended its effective independence, guaranteed support to its national religion with the clause, "The religion of the Buddhoo is declared inviolate and is to be maintained and protected."[11]

Catholic Survival and Schism

It was the Catholics who at first seemed best able to take advantage of their newly granted freedom of religion. They still had in place an effective missionary organization, the Indian missionaries of the Goanese Oratory, which years of Dutch harassment had failed to destroy. Unfortunately internal problems arose within the Catholic hierarchical structure that for the next half century kept them from capitalizing on their release from legal handicaps. One problem was a crippling shortage of missionary personnel. British toleration was not followed up by a surge of Catholic missionary reinforcements. In 1826 there were "only 12 priests to care for perhaps 60,000 Catholics"; in 1832, only 14; by 1871 61 for 173,000 Catholics.[12]

A second reason advanced for Catholic inertia in this period was strife among the missionary orders. To some degree the division was racial, a falling-out between Indian missionaries of the Goanese Oratory and European priests now permitted by the British to return to the island. The Goanese Oratory, a missionary order of indigenous Goanese priests, had saved the church from extinction under Dutch oppression. They had been left as virtually the only intact Catholic mission in Ceylon, highly respected for their willing acceptance of poverty and persecution. They resented the return of Western priests, returning in easy times to criticize those whom in hard times had left them to face the persecutors alone. The new arrivals, in turn, were embarrassed to have to report a sharp and tragic decline of morale, missionary zeal, and lifestyle among the Goanese priests. Affluent, lazy, and spiritually indifferent — that is how the new Italian apostolic vicar, Orazio Bettacchini, described them. Another Italian, Stephen Semeria, who succeeded Bettacchini, chided them for being content merely to take care of Christians, "Are we never to occupy ourselves with the conversion of the pagans?" Where was the glorying in poverty and the missionary fervor of their Goanese pioneers, Vaz and Gonsalves, in the old days under the Dutch?[13]

A third criticism was that the Goanese had, on the one hand, too easily adapted to native religious customs, but, on the other hand, had failed to train native Ceylonese clergy,[14] a complaint that the Goanese felt was insufferably European and insensitive to Ceylonese ways of life. Ceylon's Catholicism had been partially shielded by the Dutch occupation from the bitter debates of the rites controversies in Portuguese mission territories concerning the limits of adaptation to non-Christian ceremonies. The returning Western priests, on the other hand, were all too aware of the fate of the Great Jesuit Missions and the consequences of disobedience to the sharp rulings of the Vatican on native religious rites.[15]

The friction between the two was one of the major causes of what came to be known as the Goanese schism, a rare breakdown in the organizational unity that is one of the prides of the Roman Church. It was largely an issue of ecclesiastical authority, the Vatican against Portuguese *padroado*, with a disturbing tincture, seemingly, of racial prejudice, between Indian Goanese and European priests. In 1849 it split Ceylon's Catholic missions in two. A Goanese Oratorian, Miguel Filippo Mascarenhas, accused of drunkenness, repudiated the authority of the apostolic vicar of the newly erected vicariate in Jaffna. When the European bishop, Orazio Bettacchini, asked him not too politely to leave the mission, the Goan roused his people to demonstrate against the foreign priests. Other Goanese priests joined in. The movement spread. An incident was reported in which local Catholics tried to steal the key to a European priest's house to give it to a Goanese. At a higher level it spread to a break with the archbishopric of Goa, which threatened to separate the throne of Portugal from the Vatican over the troubling question of Portuguese control of missions in its territories under the rights of *padroado*. Though partially quieted by a compromise concordat between Lisbon and Rome, neither side was completely satisfied, and a small Goanese remnant remained separated and in schism until as late as about 1940.[16] The Catholic community did, however, continue to grow despite the ecclesiastical tensions. From 40,000 members in 1780, the number of reported Catholics increased from 66,000 in 1809 to a dubious high of 185,000 reported in 1832.[17]

Protestant Missions: Recession and Reinforcements (1795–1860)

Meanwhile, the Dutch Reformed churches, which had once numbered nearly three hundred thousand adherents, were fast declining. Too many of the thousands reported were only nominally Christian. In 1757 they reported only ninety thousand members, and at the end of the eighteenth century they had almost disappeared.[18] According to observers, except for two churches, one in Colombo and one in Galle, they had either returned to Catholicism or reverted to Buddhism.[19] As one missionary wrote, "One hundred thousand of those who are called Christians because they are baptized, need not go back to heathenism for they never have been anything but worshippers of Buddha."[20] And when Anglican baptism replaced Dutch Reformed baptism as the *pro forma* sign of a Christian, the Reformed congregations evaporated.

On the other hand, as the British took Ceylon and the Dutch Protestants withdrew, English-speaking Protestant missionary societies anticipated a providential opportunity for expansion, and there was in fact, at first, a temporary surge in membership in the non–Roman Catholic churches. New Protestant missionary societies entered the island. Only the losers, the Dutch and their Reformed churches, suffered serious decline and eventually virtual elimination. But the Protestants[21] were never able to mount more than a temporary challenge to Catholicism for possession of the minds and hearts of the island's Christians, and never did either of those two branches of the Christian faith, Catholic or Protestant, come near to replacing the basic Buddhist religious foundations of Ceylonese culture and society.[22]

The first civilian governors of Ceylon under the East India Company were all tolerant Anglicans, but Anglicans were slow to send missionaries. They were content at first with chaplains appointed by the Company for service primarily to the colonial traders and military.[23] Other Protestant societies, mindful of the Company's antimissionary attitude in India toward Carey's Baptists, were also slow to see Ceylon as a field of missionary opportunity.[24] As late as 1813, seventeen years after the British had begun to rule (and after the East India Company's policy was officially changed from prejudice to toleration), there were on the whole island of Ceylon only five ordained Protestant clergymen — three government chaplains and two German Reformed missionaries temporarily attached to the London Missionary Society.[25]

The first Protestant missionary efforts were some fitful and usually impermanent ventures by the London Missionary Society beginning in 1804.[26] In 1812 Carey's Baptists tried for forty years and more to transplant to Burma the enthusiasm and pioneering methods of the Serampore pioneers, but found themselves crippled by lack of personnel.[27] The next year the enterprising pioneer missionary society of a new nation abuilding across the Atlantic, the American Board of Commissioners for Foreign Missions, landed a missionary scout in Colombo to prepare for a permanent mission to Jaffna in the north, but not until 1816 did its first group of American missionaries reach the island.[28]

The first sustained organization of a Protestant mission in Ceylon, church-supported as distinct from Company-salaried, was that of the

English Wesleyans. Led by John Wesley's close friend, the indefatigable Methodist pioneer Thomas Coke, a party of four Methodist missionaries reached the port of Galle in 1814. Toward the end of his life Coke had felt an irresistible call to the mission field. He wrote, "I am now dead to Europe and alive for India. God himself has said to me, 'Go to Ceylon'...I had rather be set naked on the coast of Ceylon, without clothes and without a friend, than not go there." So he went. He never reached his destination. He died on the long voyage out, obedient "even unto death."[29]

His shipmates, undeterred, pressed on to establish the most vigorous and successful of the earliest Protestant missions in Ceylon. Arriving in the southern port of Galle, the Methodists were warmly greeted by an Anglican chaplain who told them to their surprise that the governor, anticipating their arrival, had suggested that they begin at once to establish schools to teach English as an opening for the preaching of the gospel. More than that, the governor offered to pay them a handsome monthly stipend for each school they opened.[30] Being dissidents in England, the Methodists hesitated at the government connection, but were prevailed upon to accept. Within little more than a year they had established mission schools for both Tamil- and Sinhalese-speaking Ceylonese, and while teaching English diligently studied the native languages for themselves. In an amazingly short time they had reached out beyond the schools to talk with the village Buddhist monks, to such effect that within six months, one of their number, Benjamin Clough (1791–1853), using interpreters, converted and baptized the abbot of a Buddhist temple. Clough described him as "the Chief Priest in this whole Island except one." The man renounced his priesthood and his Buddhist name, Sri Dharma Pandita Thero, to become Petrus Panditasekara, thereby willingly forfeiting his considerable wealth and large freehold estates. Clough was so impressed that he wrote, "[He] will be capable of doing as much good among the natives as fifty European Missionaries."[31]

Buddhist Reaction and Revival[32]

Reaction in Buddhist southern Ceylon to the defection of some of their best-known leaders was curiously muted at first. It puzzled the missionaries that the priests welcomed them hospitably and did not argue when missionary preachers in the villages characterized the religion of their temples as false, godless, hopelessly nihilistic, and fatally tainted with devil worship. The strident rhetoric was not unseemly for the world of that day. Missionary preaching in the days of the Wesley revivals was spontaneous, enthusiastic, confrontational, and thoroughly evangelistic. One historian describes that first half-century of Protestant missions in Ceylon as passing through two stages. The first generation (to 1830), arrived like Clough with little knowledge of Buddhism, but absolutely convinced that any religion without Christ was without the truth. They preached salvation in Christ alone, open to all but effective only in Jesus Christ. A second wave (1830–1870), however, wisely began to study Sinhalese Buddhism. Methodists like Daniel Gogerly and Robert Spence Hardy, without in any way losing their evangelical fervor or surrendering the exclusive claims of their faith, were led to moderate their language. Intensive study of the Pali Buddhist Scriptures softened their continuing criticisms with a commendable measure of compassion and respect.[33] Gogerly, for example, admitted to great appreciation of the historic Buddha and of Buddhist morals as described in its sacred texts, but he could only describe the Buddhism as he saw it practiced on the island as "this wretched system . . . this stronghold of Satan."[34]

But unknown to, or ignored by, missionaries and colonialists alike, ever since the middle of the previous century the Theravada (Hinayana) Buddhism of Ceylon had been experiencing an internal revolution, a renaissance of its national faith. Reform and reorganization of the whole Buddhist ecclesiastical superstructure had begun as early as 1750 in the then still independent inland kingdom of Kandy with assistance from Buddhist Siam. The remaking of the ecclesiastical structure grew slowly for the next hundred years, though not without opposition and schisms between inland and coastal monks.[35]

The first sign given to the missionaries of this Buddhist renaissance was a reaction in the late 1820s against the printing and distribution of Christian tracts and posters, like "Why I Am Not a Buddhist," by the Methodist Robert Clough. This was followed by the planting of new Buddhist schools in the villages, and the printing of tracts and books by Buddhist monks defending Buddhism at first politely but with rising anti-Christian vehemence.[36]

In that same period there were few visible signs of Christian progress. The population of Ceylon in 1831 was about 951,000, of whom 20,000 were slaves.[37] Seven years later in 1838, when Methodists prepared to celebrate the twenty-fifth anniversary of their mission in Ceylon, on the whole island they could count only 572 Ceylonese Methodist church members.[38] The American Board missionaries in the north were no more successful: 492 church members in twenty-three years (1816–1839), and most of them were pupils in the mission schools.[39] The financial depression of 1837 in the United States had forced the American mission to close many of its schools and reduce the number of scholars in training at the seminary from 151 to 100. "The heathen [had] triumphed," lamented the mission's report.[40] But the controversy had not ended.

Protestant Advances in Education and Cooperation

Gogerly, the English Methodist, was still convinced of an eventual Christian triumph. "Buddhism in Ceylon," he declared in 1839, "is on the wane."[41] One reason for his confidence was the increasing success of the missions' schools, Methodist, Anglican, and even the American Board Mission, which quickly recovered from its financial setback of 1837. Evangelistic results had been meager. But in their school systems the missions could claim to be making a distinct, highly visible impact on the whole of life in the island, which they were accomplishing in close ecumenical cooperation between most of the Protestant missions. The Methodist motto had been John Wesley's "Friends of all and enemies of none," and ever since 1819 the three Protestant missions in the north (English Methodist, Anglican CMS, and American Congregational) had vowed together to cooperate.[42] From the beginning the mission policies of the American Board (ABCFM) had been irenic and interdenominational, founded as it was by Congregationalists, Presbyterians, and at first, Baptists. Its stated policy abroad was a two-pronged intention to prevent conflict and rivalry, first by preaching to those not yet reached by other Protestant agencies, and second by strict care to avoid interference with the affairs of the other missions.[43]

In 1832 Ceylon's Protestant missions reported 235 schools, and 90 government schools, compared with the 118 schools that the Catholics reported five years later.[44] By mid-century, the principal of one of Ceylon's government schools, commenting on the moral and spiritual influence of the mission school in the national life of the island, estimated that it exceeded by four times the numbers reached by the church services.[45] In Southern Ceylon Methodists reported 81 schools in 1838,[46] and though the Methodists had only five British missionaries on the island, they had already appointed nine Ceylonese as "assistant missionaries."[47]

As might be expected, however, in a British colonial setting the major role in non–Roman Catholic missions in Ceylon for the next century and a half was played by the Anglicans, though only after a very slow start. Anglicanism replaced Dutch Calvinism as the established religion, not so much by law, but as perceived in the eyes of the people, since that was the religion of the government. It appointed its first chaplain for the military garrison late in 1799.[48] Two years later, in 1801, the first church-supported Anglican missionary came briefly to Ceylon, the Indian evangelist Christian David, who had been trained by the great Moravian missionary of Tranquebar, C. F. Schwartz. Speaking fluent Tamil, David came to explore Ceylon as a prospective field for mission, and later returned for years of effective church planting in Jaffna.[49]

But the Anglicans, despite the prestige of their government connections, had little success to report in their first forty years on the island. When Ceylon was erected into a separate Bishopric of Colombo in 1843, the first bishop, Dr. James Chapman, gloomily reported ruined churches in the towns, and the whole west coast from Jaffna to Galle "entirely destitute of [Anglican] clergymen." Outside Colombo there were only three "consecrated churches." "Wherever one goes," he wrote, "it is the same; Brahma, Vishnu, Siva, Mohomet and Buddha, each can number his thousands; Christians are counted only by units." How could Christian England after fifty years of rule have done so little for the spiritual improvement of the people? Even the Dutch had done better, he said.[50]

Undaunted the good bishop threw himself into the work of church renewal. In his sixteen years as missionary bishop of Ceylon, the hard-working Chapman gave Anglicans a fresh start. It is true that as an Anglo-Catholic, a "Puseyite," he had difficulty cooperating with the more Protestant mission societies, English Wesleyan and American, and his relationship was sometimes strained even with his fellow Anglicans in Ceylon, the missionaries of the "low church" Church Missionary Society. But his zeal in reawakening the organizational morale and spiritual life of his churches was outstanding. He promoted the founding in 1851 of the first Anglican college, St. Thomas', with a divinity school for training clergy. He encouraged the development of an indigenous clergy. Ten years later he could report that the number of Anglican missionaries in Ceylon had tripled, and that more than half of them were either Tamil or Ceylonese.[51] Two native Anglican clergymen, the first in Ceylon, had been ordained, Cornelius Jayesinha and Abraham Gunasekara in 1839, and a third, Cornelius Sennanayaka, by Bishop Chapman in 1846.[52]

Ceylon at Mid-Century

Nevertheless, as the century turned at midpoint,[53] these few bright patches could not hide an overall sense of failure. What had turned the bright prospects of the early conversions from Buddhism into disappointment? The most powerful factor was probably the Buddhist revival in southern Ceylon, mentioned above, which had begun slowly but, after twenty-five years of gradual reaction against foreign teachings, became more and more vehemently anti-Christian. It had begun as a response to missionary criticism of their national religion. Negative missionary reactions to Buddhism may well have been almost unconsciously automatic, as when in the earliest years, many of them arrived with a stereotype in their minds of "heathenism" as "a steel barrier" raised against the gospel, blocking the missionaries from friendly discourse with what they considered to be the godless, hopeless, nihilistic religion of the Buddhists.[54]

Against this enemy, the missionaries reasoned, war must be waged on two fronts: first, to expose once and for all the false science of Buddhism's view of this world, replacing it with the new sciences of the West; and second, to counter the hopelessness of its view of life after death, the world-to-come, with an invitation to accept the good news of the promises of the eternal God in Jesus Christ.[55] Only on the first front, the educational, were the Protestant missions more than marginally successful. Buddhist reaction and revival blunted the Protestant advance on the second front, the evangelistic.

The new missions on the island, mostly American and British, Methodist, Anglican, and Congregational/Presbyterian, were never even to match their feared rivals, the Catholics, in numbers. Protestant presence was influential, thanks to their schools and to their acknowledged relationship to the religion of the established colonial government. But the South Indian Mission Conference of Protestants in India, meeting in 1858, reported that the total number of Protestant communicants in Ceylon (including Anglicans) was only 3,700, in a population of about 2 million.[56] Even allowing for a calculation of two or three times as many adherents and inquirers, this was the handful of Protestants who, with perhaps 185,000 Roman Catholics, would face in the next half century a rising tide of a Buddhist revival preparing to reassert that ancient faith's challenge for the hearts and minds of the people of Sri Lanka.

NOTES

1. Robrecht Boudens, *Catholic Missionaries in a British Colony: Successes and Failures in Ceylon 1796–1893* (Immensee and Uznach, Switzerland: NRSM, 1979), 25; on Christianity in Ceylon under British rule, see Boudens, *Catholic Missionaries in a British Colony*; Tennent, *Christianity in Ceylon*, 77–345; and Beven, *A History of the Diocese of Colombo*.

2. See chap. 2 above. The Portuguese dated their rule from their first landing in 1505, but did not effectively rule until after 1540.

3. See Tennent, *Christianity in Ceylon*, 77–78.

4. Tennent, *Christianity in Ceylon*, 77.

5. De Silva, *A History of Sri Lanka*, 172–173.

6. De Silva, *A History of Sri Lanka*, 177.

7. See Reginald L. Rajapakse, "Christian Missions, Theosophy and Trade: A History of American Relations with Ceylon 1815–1915" (PhD diss., University of Pennsylvania, 1973), 13–19. Cinnamon to coffee (1830), to tea (1880s), rubber (1910s).

8. Boudens, *Catholic Missionaries in a British Colony*, 25.

9. Boudens, *Catholic Missionaries in a British Colony*, 28–30. Boudens notes occasional examples of failure to implement the promised freedoms.

10. Tennent, *Christianity in Ceylon*, 78–79.

11. W. J. T. Small, ed., *A History of the Methodist Church in Ceylon 1814–1964* (Colombo: Wesley Press, 1964), 164–165.

12. According to figures collected in R. L. Stirrat, *Power and Religiosity in a Post-Colonial Setting: Sinhala Catholics in Contemporary Sri Lanka* (Cambridge: Cambridge University Press, 1992), 15, by 1911, there were "233 priests, 122 brothers and 512 sisters to serve a Catholic population of almost 340,000," citing D. J. B. Kuruppu, *The Pearl of the Indian Ocean: A Handbook of Ceylon* (Colombo: Catholic Messenger Press, 1924), 51.

13. Boudens, *Catholic Missionaries in a British Colony*, 39–45, 54–58, 165–166. Bettacchini reached Ceylon in 1842, was made apostolic vicar of the north in 1845, and died in 1857. Semeria succeeded Bettacchini as coadjutor with right of succession in 1856. On Gonsalves, see an account of his life in Perniola, *Dutch Period*, 2:321–356. Celibacy, admittedly, was one of the great stumbling blocks to the recruitment of Ceylonese as candidates for the ministry. And see in this volume chap. 10 above.

14. Boudens, *Catholic Missionaries in a British Colony*, 39.

15. On the rites controversy, see chap. 5 above.

16. On the schism, see Boudens, *Catholic Missionaries in a British Colony*, 58–64, 88–90.

17. The statistics are murky. For example, Boudens suggests that the 185,000 reported in 1832 may have been a mistake for 85,000. For various estimates, see Boudens, *Catholic Missionaries in a British Colony*, 30; and compare with less reliable figures in Tennent, *Christianity in Ceylon*, 63ff. Dutch Reformed statistics are even less firm, particularly after 1760. Reports estimate 94,681 Protestant Christians in 1757 and 40,000 Catholics in 1780 (Perniola, *Dutch Period*, 3:124, 356).

18. On the decline of the Dutch Reformed churches, see Tennent, *Christianity in Ceylon*, 100–105; Boudens, *Catholic Church in Ceylon*, 206ff.; Pieris, *Ceylon and the Hollanders*, 87–91. They reported only two Dutch clergymen in Colombo, but membership of the Dutch Reformed Church outnumbered that of the Scottish Presbyterians, 2000 to only 40 or 50 (Tennent, *Christianity in Ceylon*, 103, 106).

19. Tennent, *Christianity in Ceylon*, 81–90. Cordiner's optimistic estimate, which Tennent quotes, is untenable.

20. Richard Lovett, *The History of the London Missionary Society, 1795–1895*, 2 vols. (London: Henry Frowde, 1899), 2:20.

21. I for the most part use the term "Protestants" to refer also to Anglicans, with apologies to high-church Anglicans.

22. See Richard Fox Young and J. P. V. I. Somaratna, *Vain Debates: The Buddhist-Christian Controversies of Nineteenth-Century Ceylon* (Vienna: Institute of Indiology, University of Vienna, 1996); and Elizabeth J. Harris, "A Case of Distortion: The Evangelical Missionary Interpretation of Buddhism in 19th Century Sri Lanka," in *Dialogue* (Ecumenical Institute for Study and Dialogue, Colombo) 21 (1994); and de Silva, *Sri Lanka*, 180–182.

23. Tennent, *Christianity in Ceylon*, 79–80.

24. See chap. 10 above.

25. Lovett, *The History of the London Missionary Society*, 2:20–21. The records also note the assistance of six Anglican "proponents" (licensed lay-preachers).

26. The London Missionary Society landed a brief mission in Ceylon in 1804. It disappeared in 1818 (Lovett, *The History of the London Missionary Society*, 2:20–21).

27. Tennent, *Christianity in Ceylon*, 282–293. After more than thirty years of preaching, only two hundred Ceylonese church members could be reported, but the Baptist pioneer, Chater, was the first to produce a Sinhalese grammar as an aid toward a translation of the Bible.

28. Joseph Tracy, *History of the American Missions to the Heathen, from Their Commencement to the Present Time* (Worcester, Mass.: Spooner & Howland, 1840), passim, 38, 41–42, 54–55, 58–62; Rufus Anderson, *History of the Missions of the*

American Board of Commissioners, 129–193. Even before the Americans, the London Missionary Society supported two German pastors of former Dutch churches in Colombo (1804–1818), and the English Baptists expanding out of Serampore in India opened intermittent work in Ceylon beginning in 1812. See also Latourette, *A History of the Expansion of Christianity*, 6:221–226.

29. On the Methodists, see Small, *A History of the Methodist Church in Ceylon*; and John N. Hollister, *The Centenary of the Methodist Church in Southern Asia* (Lucknow, India: Lucknow Publishing House, Methodist Church in Southern Asia, 1956). The quotation is from Small, *A History of the Methodist Church in Ceylon*, 21ff. On Thomas Coke, with bibliography, see *BJRL* 2, no. 2 (Summer 1994): 206–307.

30. Small, *A History of the Methodist Church in Ceylon*, 25–26.

31. Small, *A History of the Methodist Church in Ceylon*, 29–31. Not all the missionaries approved of so quick a conversion. Some thought him only half-converted, but he died a practicing, witnessing believer in 1844. On early important converts, such as Petrus Panditta Sekara (whose Buddhist name was Sree Dharma Panditta Tirrunancy), and George Nadoris de Silva (Kapugama Dhamakkhandha), a popular chief monk who was baptized but later disappointed his sponsors by "notorious" political actions that were no credit to his Christian profession; see Young and Somaratna, *Vain Debates*, 53–57.

32. On the roots of the nineteenth-century Buddhist revival, see Young and Somaratna, *Vain Debates*, 33–111; and Harris, "A Case of Distortion," 171–200. See also Rajapakse, "Christian Missions, Theosophy and Trade"; Small, *A History of the Methodist Church in Ceylon*, 156–162; and Michael M. Ames, "Westernization or Modernization: The Case of Sinhalese Buddhism," *Social Compass* 20 (1973): 139–170.

33. Harris, "A Case of Distortion," 19–27; and Young and Somaratna, *Vain Debates*, 42–43, 44, 59–63.

34. Cited by Kitsiri Malalgoda, "Buddhist-Christian Confrontation, 1800–1880," *Social Compass* 20 (1973): 181. For a partial collection of Gogerly's writings see Daniel John Gogerly, *Ceylon Buddhism: Being the Collected Writings of Daniel John Gogerly*, ed. A. S. Bishop (Colombo: Wesleyan Methodist Book Room, 1908), especially "An Introductory Sketch of Buddhism," 1–14. Though the tone is more irenic than in some of his earlier writings, Gogerly decries the infiltration of demon worship and interprets the doctrine of Nirvana as "a complete and final cessation of existence," not as in Brahminism as "an absorption into a Superior Being."

35. Kitsiri Malalgoda, *Buddhism in Sinhalese Society, 1750–1900: A Study of Religious Revival and Change* (Berkeley: University of California Press, 1976), 62–176.

36. Small, *History of the Methodist Church in Ceylon*, 74–77; Young and Somaratna, *Vain Debates*, 50, 67–88.

37. Tracy, *History of the American Missions to the Heathen*, 59.

38. Small, *History of the Methodist Church in Ceylon*, 51.

39. R. Anderson, *History of the Missions of the American Board of Foreign Missions*, 180. See also Tracy, *History of the American Missions to the Heathen*, 296–297.

40. Tracy, *History of the American Missions*, 280–282.

41. Small, *History of the Methodist Church in Ceylon*, 76–77.

42. Small, *History of the Methodist Church in Ceylon*, 81–82, 144, 162–163.

43. Tracy, *History of the American Missions to the Heathen*, 294–295.

44. Small, *History of the Methodist Church in Ceylon*, 111.

45. Small, *History of the Methodist Church in Ceylon*, 177.

46. Small, *History of the Methodist Church in Ceylon*, 44, cf. 177.

47. Small, *History of the Methodist Church in Ceylon*, 51.

48. Beven, *History of the Diocese of Colombo*, 9–10; Harold de Soysa, ed., *The Church of Ceylon: Her Faith and Mission* (Colombo: Daily News Press for the Church of Ceylon, 1945), 122–123; and Tennent, *Christianity in Ceylon*, 79–80. On the Anglicans in Ceylon see also Pascoe, *Two Hundred Years of the S.P.G.*, 660–681; and statistics as of 1900, 732–733, 925–926; and Stock, *History of the Church Missionary Society*, 1:215–218.

49. David, a native of Malabar, trained in Tranquebar, had unsuccessfully sought Lutheran ordination in India, and was sent by the Anglican Society for the Propagation of Christian Knowledge to Ceylon from Tanjore as an unordained preacher (called "a proponent" by the Anglicans in Ceylon), authorized to administer the sacraments, but not as a priest. Later, though refused Anglican ordination by Bishop Middleton of Calcutta (1814–1823), he was ordained by his successor, Bishop Heber (1823–1826). See Cnattingius, *Bishops and Societies*, 90–91, 134–135; Boudens, *Catholic Missionaries in a British Colony*, 33; and Bevens, *History of the Diocese of Colombo*, 23–25.

50. Pascoe, *Two Hundred Years of the S.P.G.*, 661.

51. Pascoe, *Two Hundred Years of the S.P.G.*, 663; and see Beven, *History of the Diocese of Colombo*, 68–87, 131–135.

52. Stock, *History of the Church Missionary Society*, 1:332.

53. Richard F. Young marks 1848 as a pivotal year in Buddhist reaction, responding to the publication of Gogerly's major critique of Buddhism, *Kristiyani Prajnapti* (Christian Institutes). See Young and Somaratna, *Vain Debates*, 45, 79ff.

54. Harris, "A Case of Distortion," 19–20; Small, *A History of the Methodist Church in Ceylon*, 156ff.

55. Harris, "A Case of Distortion," 19–20; Small, *A History of the Methodist Church in Ceylon*, 156ff.

56. *Proceedings of the South India Missionary Conference, Ootacamund, 1858* (Madras: SPCK, 1858), table 5, reports: 3,700 communicant Protestants and a total of 15,457 adherents (Anglican CMS & SPG 9,000, Methodists 5,595, ABCFM 421, Baptists 441). Ceylon's population in 1871 was estimated at 2.4 million (Zeylanicus, *Ceylon between Orient and Occident* [London: Elek Books, 1971], 9). Compare these figures with those for Ceylon in Newcomb, *A Cyclopedia of Missions*, 242–243. He reports 3,101 communicants and 12,976 students in the Protestant and Anglican schools.

Chapter 17

Southeast Asia from Thailand to Vietnam (1800–1860)

For twenty-six years [King Mongkut] had been in the Buddhist priest-hood...He had studied English...and in his quest for knowledge had come into contact with the American missionaries who were most sympathetic...little realizing how royally he would later make return for every service rendered. As a mendicant priest he went among his own people and learned their actual condition and needs. No king ever had a better training for the responsibilities placed upon him.
—G. B. McFarland, 1928[1]

P ROTESTANT entry into Southeast Asia was, in a way, a by-product of its missionary strategy to reach the great Chinese empire with the gospel. China, as Morrison had discovered, was closed against any direct attempts to replant Christian missions on Chinese soil. Ever since the rites controversy had infuriated the emperor against foreign intrusion into Chinese affairs in the eighteenth century, the interdiction of Roman Catholic missions, though never quite completely enforced, had prevented open proclamation of the Christian faith. The last renewal of such a prohibition occurred in 1811, four years after Morrison's arrival in Guangzhou, and we have noted how China's antiforeignism had already led his mission board, the London Missionary Society, to form a subsidiary Ultra-Ganges Mission as a stepping-stone approach to mission to the Chinese until the day when the door to the mainland might reopen.[2]

We now resume the circled route that led Protestants beyond India and Burma around China's southern borders from Siam to the East Indies.

Siam (1800–1860)

Siam, as it was known to the West until 1939, or Thailand as it is known today,[3] is the only country in South Asia that never lost its independence to the imperialisms of the West — hence the modern name Thailand, which means "land of the free." And Siam, in direct contrast to its no less Buddhist neighbor, Burma, is also noteworthy as one of the most tolerant but at the same time most resistant nations in Asia toward the introduction of Christianity. About the middle of the nineteenth century, a ten-year veteran of the Siam mission wrote, "there is scarcely any other field in which modern missions have been established where the introduction of the gospel has met with so little opposition as in Siam proper...It is equally just to say that there is scarcely any other field which has been so barren of results."[4]

This confirms the observation of a British diplomat a few years earlier, in 1857, that after almost thirty years of faithful missionary effort, "It is doubtful whether there are ten professing Protestant Christians among the Siamese."[5] But so stated, the facts are not as negative as they sound. The early missionary witness was not a failure, but most of its first visible effects were among the Chinese in Siam, not the Siamese.

FIRST PROTESTANT CONTACTS

A very brave woman who never set foot in Siam made the first Protestant missionary contact with Siam. In 1817 Ann Hasseltine Judson (Mrs. Adoniram Judson) befriended a troubled group of Siamese prisoners of war in Burma and began to study their language. She translated her husband's Burmese *Catechism* and the Gospel of Matthew into the Thai language, arranging to have the *Catechism* printed by the Baptists in Serampore on a crude press with a font of Siamese type. That *Catechism*, and even the press itself, eventually found its way to Bangkok to prepare the way for the gospel in Siamese.[6]

The first Protestant missionaries actually to enter Siam, however, were the peripatetic German, Karl Gützlaff, who had turned independent after leaving the Netherlands Missionary Society, and the Rev. Jacob Tomlin of the London Missionary Society. Parenthetically it should be noted that Gützlaff was a doctor of medicine, though he does not seem to have practiced medicine and is far better known as an evangelist and linguist.[7] Even so, as was so often the case in the history of Protestant missions, a doctor was the pioneer. Both men were welcomed by the Roman Catholic Portuguese consul in Bangkok in 1828, and within six months had translated the four gospels and the Gospel of Matthew into Siamese, but neither stayed long in Siam. Before moving on in 1831 to some twenty more years of work along the China coast Gützlaff did manage to sketch out a rough Siamese translation of the entire Bible, and baptized one convert, Boon Tee, a Chinese, who lamentably fell victim to opium addiction and left the faith.[8] Another early but temporary arrival was David Abeel, in 1831, a missionary of the American Board of Commissioners for Foreign Missions (ABCFM), the first American missionary to Siam.[9]

Of more long-lasting significance was the work of the pioneer practicing missionary doctor in Siam, the Rev. Dan Beach Bradley, M.D. (1804–1873), a Presbyterian but serving, like Abeel, under the ABCFM, who reached Bangkok in 1835 and gave the rest of his life, thirty-eight years, in mission to the Siamese. He performed the first surgical operation in the country and gave the first successful vaccinations for smallpox, using virus carried by a sailing ship that took nine months to reach Bangkok from America. He helped to introduce printing, publishing Siam's first newspaper, and it was on his press that the first Royal Decree against opium was printed. He had "the eye of a scientist and the ear of a journalist," writes Bradley's biographer.[10] But the doughty Congregational medical pioneer, Bradley, left the ABCFM in 1848 to work as an independent, self-supporting missionary loosely attached to a new board, the American Missionary Association (AMA). After years of outstanding service as physician, translator, ordained minister, editor, and trusted counselor to all the missions, he died in Bangkok in 1873, still bravely insisting on self-support and dependent on no mission.[11] It is a tribute to the pivotal role of medical missions to the expansion of Christianity that in Siam, thanks to Dr. Bradley and the missionary physicians who followed him, American missionaries are to this day still called "moh" (medical doctor).[12]

Two years before Dr. Bradley, a Baptist couple, Rev. John Taylor Jones and his wife, became the first long-term resident Protestant missionaries in Siam, and she has the added distinction of being the first American woman missionary there. They landed in 1833, and before the year was out Jones had baptized three converts, all Chinese. Two years later William Dean, who reached Bangkok in 1835, organized the first Protestant church in Siam, a Baptist church for Chinese with eleven members. That same year both Dean and Taylor almost lost their lives in a small boat near Singapore. Malay pirates attacked them, speared them, robbed them, and threw Jones into the shark-infested sea, then left them to die. Dean, exhausted and bleeding, managed to pull Jones back into the boat, and a passing fishing boat rescued them.[13]

Compared to China, Siam was relatively tolerant to the new arrivals, but not even a fair amount of Siamese tolerance made the propagation of the Christian faith easy in that thoroughly Buddhist land. Both the Congregational and Baptist missions were short-lived. After fifteen years with minimum results, the pioneering American Board of Commissioners for Foreign Missions (largely Congregational) transferred its attention and personnel to China in 1849.[14] In 1869 the American Baptists, who had sent the first long-term resident American missionaries to Siam, virtually suspended mission to the native Siamese after thirty-six years of effort, in order to concentrate their limited resources and personnel on their more successful work with the Chinese in Siam. At that point their Chinese converts numbered 149.[15]

The most successful Protestants in the country proved to be the persevering American Presbyterians, though at first they seemed destined for an even shorter history than the earlier Congregational and Baptist missions.[16] The Presbyterian Board of Foreign Missions, newly formed in

America, appointed as its first missionaries to Siam Mr. and Mrs. William Buell, who reached Bangkok in 1840 and were joyfully welcomed by the twenty-four Congregational and Baptist missionaries then on the field. But in three years Mrs. Buell's ill health, probably polio, forced them to return home. Permanent Presbyterian work did not begin until 1847 with the arrival, after an eight-month journey from New York, of an evangelistic couple, the Stephen Mattoons, and a medical missionary, the gifted, strong-willed Dr. Samuel R. House. These three, it has been said, really began Presbyterian mission in Siam.[17] Two years later, in 1849, the Presbyterians organized their first church, which in its first year consisted of five American missionaries and one Chinese who was a transfer from the Congregationalist mission (ABCFM) as it was preparing to close its work in Siam.[18]

It was the Presbyterians who stayed as the other missions began to leave. The three pioneers, Mr. and Mrs. Mattoon and Dr. S. R. House,[19] were a well-balanced team. The Mattoons were evangelistic and capable educators, and Mr. Mattoon was also an able administrator. Dr. House, the physician, had been licensed to preach by his presbytery in America before coming to Siam. The Siamese called him "the man with the gentle heart," though a few of his fellow missionaries at times found him a little prickly.[20] No one questioned, however, his healing skills, undeniable courage, and passion for evangelistic outreach. He was the first to dare to use ether in Siam — perhaps the first in Asia — recognizing its value as an anaesthetic while its use was not yet fully approved even in the West. He was an innovative, fearless man. Once, while he was on his way through thick jungle to deliver money to the mission hospital in the north, he was gored in the stomach by an elephant but refused to send for help and operated on himself, stuffing his intestines back inside the gaping wound. He realized his chances for life were slim but refused to send for help, but did send a note that if he failed to recover, he would send the mission money on to the hospital by the four Siamese men traveling with him.[21]

A NEW KING AND A NEW ERA (1851–1860)

In that monolithically Buddhist country an invitation to consider a change of religion, however kindly it was made, was a threat to the national identity. To a real Thai, it was apparently unthinkable. In 1851, however, a new king ascended to the Siamese throne. The first decade of Mongkut's reign (1851–1860) marks the end of the day of difficult beginnings and the heady prospect of an open door for Christian missions. Unlike Rama III,[22] his suspicious, ardently pro-Buddhist, antiforeign predecessor, Mongkut, the fourth king of the Chakri dynasty,[23] was progressive, spoke English, and within four months of his accession permitted the missionaries for the first time to lease land and build homes. In August 1851, he went even further. In an unprecedented gesture, he threw open his palace to the women of the three American missions (Presbyterian, Baptist, and independent), inviting them to teach English to the women of the court. This happy state of affairs continued for the next three years.[24]

In all the missions the primary thrust for the first twenty-seven years of Protestant presence in Siam had been on Christian witness to the Chinese community, which was found to be more open to evangelism than the resistant Buddhist Siamese. Mongkut reigned for seventeen years and the missionaries rejoiced. Compared to the stone wall of resistance earlier encountered, moderate though the results were they were enough to produce an encouraging expansion of Christian missions in the country. Under the benevolent, inquiring eye of King Mongkut (later popularly known in the West as the king in *Anna and the King of Siam*), the attention of the missions broadened beyond evangelism of the Chinese to include careful attempts to find how best to bring a Christian witness to the native Siamese in so thoroughly Buddhist a land.

When Great Britain and the United States in 1855 and 1856 secured treaties of friendship and commerce with Siam, another liberating step was taken toward widening the door to Christian missions. The first two American consuls were missionaries, Stephen Mattoon, a Presbyterian (1856–1859), followed by Mr. Chandler of the Baptist mission.[25]

Then the persevering Presbyterians, after working for fifteen years with few volunteers and little success, decided it was time to give the little church they had started in 1849 a proper organizational structure. They formed a presbytery.[26] It was a remarkable and perhaps premature act of faith, for they still had not a single Siamese convert. But "to organize still unborn churches" in 1858 they organized their presbytery, a presbytery composed of four ordained missionaries, all of them Americans, "to govern still unborn churches." They named it the Presbytery of Siam.[27]

Premature or not, they had reason for some optimism. Working with them was "the first outstanding Protestant convert" to Christianity in Siam. He was not Siamese, but neither was he American. He was Chinese, the teacher Kieng Qua-Sean (Ki-eng Qua-Wean), who was baptized by the Congregationalists in 1844, and was seconded to the Presbyterians when the American Board of Commissioners for Foreign Missions (ABCFM) transferred its mission from Siam to China two years later. Kieng founded a little school for the sons of Chinese families that eventually developed under several names into what is now Bangkok Christian College. He died that same year, but the Christian family he left behind — his wife, daughters, and sons-in-law — within two generations became the backbone of Siamese Protestant leadership in the development of the Church of Christ in Siam, as we shall see.[28]

Growth, however, remained agonizingly slow. Siam never saw the kind of spectacular success achieved by the Baptists among the tribes in neighboring Burma. In 1859, the Baptists in Bangkok reported an attendance of between 150 and 200 at Sunday services. In 1861 they separated their Bangkok church into two congregations, one for Chinese, and a smaller one for the fourteen Siamese who had by then been converted. But total baptized membership was never more than 41 during the first three decades of the mission, and in the next thirty years, when the Baptist mission finally closed, it had never risen above 500.[29]

The first missions had either left or were losing hope. The Presbyterians had organized their first church but it was an all-missionary church, "a church without a convert," and formed their first presbytery, but it was a presbytery without churches. Not until ten years after the first church, and one year after the founding of the presbytery, were they able to celebrate the baptism of their first Siamese convert, Nai Chune a teacher in the Chinese teacher Kieng's little school. So few Siamese (Thai) had been converted up to that time that when Nai Chune applied for baptism they found it difficult to believe that he was sincere, and asked him to wait a few weeks. Only when the young man's persistence finally persuaded them that, in their own words, "the miracle of converting grace had actually been wrought even in a Siamese," did they baptize him the next year, 1859.[30]

BIBLE TRANSLATION AND DISTRIBUTION

One possible reason for the slow growth of the Siamese church may have been a failure of sustained attention to Bible translation and distribution. Translation into the national and tribal languages of the people has been an immensely important distinguishing difference between the two waves of Western expansion into Asia after 1500: colonialist conquest and missionary expansion.[31] Until recently it has also been a significant mark of contrasting priorities in Roman Catholic and Protestant mission policy. With Protestants, access to the Bible through translations was a supreme practical obligation. For Roman Catholics, the first priority was to establish the church. Yet in Siam, it took the Protestants almost a hundred years to publish a complete Bible in the Thai language.

Not that they failed to approach the task, they just did not finish it. Karl Gützlaff, who entered Siam as the first Protestant missionary in 1828, made a rough translation of the whole Bible into Siamese by 1830. It was too imperfect to publish.[32] But the pioneer Baptist, John Taylor Jones, proved to be a highly skilled linguist widely known for his near-perfect fluency in Siamese. He made Bible translation his life priority. First he produced a Siamese dictionary, and with the help of Chinese converts who already had the Bible in Chinese he translated all the New Testament except Hebrews and Revelation by 1839. His final New Testament was published in 1843–1844,[33] first in Siamese, then later (after 1891) into Lao (northern Thai), which though closely related linguistically to Siamese used completely different written characters.[34] Incidentally, it was the missionary printing of Bible portions into Lao that first made writing more readable for the Thai themselves by separating the printed words instead of running them all together without spacing.[35] But the complete Siamese New Testament was not published until 1843, and the complete Bible not until as late as 1893,[36] sixty-six years after Gützlaff's first trial translations.

WOMEN'S WORK FOR WOMEN

Although Protestants in Siam lagged in church growth and were slow to finish a complete Bible translation, there were signs here and there of encouragement for the struggling missions. Among them was a growing appreciation of the indispensable role of women in missions. To the women, Siam owes the first Christian approach to the secluded women's quarters of the upper classes — zenana mission, as it was termed in India[37] — and its first schools for girls.

As early as 1848 Mrs. Mattoon had already started a little Presbyterian boarding school for small boys and girls. Four years later she started a day school for boys in a Peguan village near Bangkok, which within months merged with a boarding school for boys which her assistant, the Chinese teacher Kang, was just organizing under the Presbyterian Mission as its first regularly organized day school.[38] Turning from coeducational classes to concentrate on a school for boys was not surprising, considering Siam's traditional gender-separated culture. But this mission school was unusual. It was Christian, and education in Siam was almost impenetrably Buddhist. Even more glaringly unusual was the fact that the founder of its originating schools not only was non-Buddhist but a woman. The acting head of the new school had been her assistant. Mrs. Mattoon, who started the two little schools out of which this one grew, was indeed an unusual woman. The Siamese described her best as "always trying to make a better world for poor people."[39]

If the first result of the merger of her two schools seemed at first to turn Christian education back to the boys, it had not entirely forsaken the promises of its beginnings. In 1859 the Presbyterian school admitted its first girl student.[40] Meanwhile, two years earlier the widow of the pioneer Baptist John Taylor Jones had opened a boarding school for girls in Bangkok, which within a year had sixty-six pupils, mostly Chinese, studying many subjects but with special emphasis on Bible and the Christian religion.[41]

Five years later the Presbyterians received into membership their first Siamese woman convert, Esther, daughter of a Siamese astrologer, who had been adopted by the Mattoons and had gathered a little class of Siamese children to teach them to read Siamese. She later married the first ordained Siamese elder, Nai Naa. Earlier on a trip to America with the Mattoons she had received some training as a nurse, and became famous as Siam's first trained midwife, honored by the royal family service in the birth and care of a future queen.[42] Esther also joined her husband, Nai Naa, in translating *Pilgrim's Progress* into Chinese. Years later, shortly before she died in 1928 at the age of eighty-five, she said, "I am going to where John Bunyan is; I am going home. Put the pictures of Father and Mother Mattoon in my coffin."[43]

Progress in the South

At times it almost seemed that the missionaries might make a breakthrough into the Siamese culture similar to their progress in work with the Chinese communities. In 1841 the Baptists baptized six Chinese and one Siamese, which encouraged them to start a class in theology for training preachers, but it was still conducted in Chinese because of the lack of sufficient Siamese converts. In 1853 they were briefly cheered by the conversion and baptism of eight Siamese in one year.[44] But only sixteen years later, in 1869, after a sudden increase of forty-five Chinese converts, "a number equal to all that had been baptized during the preceding thirty years," the mission suspended its work among the Siamese to concentrate on the expanding Chinese groups.[45]

Presbyterians did not act quite so drastically. With them too it was the Chinese who most readily responded. The primary figure in this was Mrs. Mattoon's young assistant to whom the Presbyterians turned for leadership of the two boys' schools mentioned above, and who organized them into a school for the sons of the Chinese community. Kang (spelled variously) Qua-Sean (baptized in 1844, d. 1859) has been called "the first outstanding Protestant convert in Siam."[46] When he died in 1859, his successor, Kru Keo, was Siamese, and the language was changed to Thai with great consequences for its eventual growth. It was the first in a long line of mission schools that began to make changes in the country's models for education. Later, changing its name several times, the school evolved into what is now called Bangkok Christian College.[47]

Those were the days of small beginnings, the period of the pioneers, but a beginning nonetheless. By early 1860, despite an exodus of missions to more productive fields, there were seventeen Protestant missionaries still at work in Siam,[48] and three little churches, two of which were Baptist, and one Presbyterian.[49] In the remaining forty years of "the great century of missions," church growth in Siam would still be modest. But it would be progress enough to be called by Protestants "The Period of Expansion."[50]

Malaysia and Singapore (1800–1860)

Malacca (Melaka), far down the Malay Peninsula about halfway between the modern Malay capital, Kuala Lumpur, in the north and independent

Singapore in the south, was the early center of Malay culture and history. Though captured in 1511 and dominated by Catholic Portugal for about 130 years (1511–1641), and by Protestant Holland for another 154 years (1641–1795), it remained principally Muslim, a center for the expansion of Islam in Southeast Asia, and only to a limited extent for short periods a base for Christian mission in Asia. But to the frustration of both Muslim and Christian evangelists, most Malays even in 1800 were neither pure Muslims nor Christians but Hindu-Buddhist or animist with only an overlay of the "new" religions.[51] The best of the Catholic missionaries had to admit that Malacca's Catholics were "not very Christian."

THE PROTESTANTS

When the Protestant Dutch snatched the rich trading post from the Portuguese and tried hard to suppress Catholicism, Malacca's Catholics remained surprisingly Catholic. Thanks to the Dutch, "the first translation of any portion of Scripture printed in a non-European language" was the Gospel of Matthew in High Malay.[52] But seventy years later, in 1712, there were still six times as many Catholics as Protestants in Malacca, and when European home politics brought Portugal and Holland together in an alliance, the Dutch virtually gave up their efforts to suppress and replace the old faith with the Reformation.[53]

Moreover, by the end of the nineteenth century, Malacca had already lost its preeminence in the trade and politics of Southeast Asia. Portugal was in steep decline as Great Britain and France expanded their colonial holdings and the Dutch retreated to their more lucrative spice islands of the Indonesian archipelago. Stamford Raffles, England's ambitious, trail-breaking colonialist, landed on a tiny, undeveloped island south of Malacca in 1819. It was named Singapore.[54]

With the English colonists came the Anglican Church. In Malaysia the Church of England remained for almost two hundred years primarily a chaplain church ministering to the white, English-speaking communities. The first recorded Anglican service was a marriage service by a visiting chaplain in 1799.[55] The first resident Anglican chaplain was Robert Hutchings in 1814. He took his post under the British East Indies Company at Penang (a large Malay island farther north, near where Malaysia meets the southern tip of Thailand). Penang was the site of an early British trading settlement in 1786, three decades before Raffles settled in Singapore. Hutchings built an impressive church there, the Church of St. George the Martyr, and learned the Malay language. He even published a Dutch Malay version of the Bible into a local script. He seemed inexhaustible. He organized a Bible Society and founded the Penang Free School, which one history describes as one of the most famous schools in Malaysia.[56]

Had his successors been as actively missionary outside the foreign community, and as less tied to Britain's colonialist bureaucracy as Robert

Hutchings, the Church of England might still be the most vital Protestant presence in greater Malaysia. It is a continuing prestigious presence, but it has been outevangelized by others, notably a branch of the former China Inland Mission (Overseas Missionary Fellowship), and American Methodists.[57] However, since these and other missions did not enter the territory until after 1860, we shall note their contributions in a later chapter.

One important player in the first half century of Protestant work in the Malay peninsula was no missionary, and not even a Christian. The case of Munshi ("teacher") Abdullah is the epitome of the mixed measure of hope and frustration that characterizes most Christian efforts to penetrate the wall of Muslim resistance to any other religion than Islam. Abdullah (Abdullah bin Abdul Kadir, 1797–1854) was born a Tamil of Yemeni Arab ancestry near Malacca. "He had the pride of the Arab, the perseverance and subtility of the Hindu."[58] A precocious linguist, he was noticed and employed by Sir James Raffles, whom he later helped as copyist of manuscripts and occasional translator in the founding and development of Singapore.[59] When William Milne settled in Malacca in 1813[60] as the first resident Protestant missionary and started a Bible class for local children, Abdullah saw a chance to add English to his knowledge of languages and joined it. Against his father's orders he urged Malay children to attend it. He proved so proficient that Milne made him his language teacher in Malay. For the next almost forty years Abdullah was the indispensable Malay assistant to the Christian missionaries, both English in Malacca and American in Singapore, translating Bible portions and tracts, working with the mission press on publications, and organizing the Malay section of Milne's Anglo-Chinese College library in Malacca. His own writings in the Malay language made him famous, a major factor in stabilizing and purifying the written Malaysian.[61]

But he never converted to the Christian faith. In fact he died in 1854 on a pilgrimage to Mecca, the dream every pious Muslim longs to fulfill in his lifetime. Malaysia is a repetition of the story of Christian missions in any Muslim land: great hopes, sympathetic openings, yet so rare and difficult the closure to final commitment. Abdullah writes movingly of his friend the missionary, William Milne: "To the pair of us [Abdullah and his wife] he was just like a father . . . a gracious person, one who knows how to win the affections of men and how to appreciate their feelings. Such a person I call good."[62] But not even Milne could persuade him to become a Christian.

THE CATHOLICS

The survival of the Catholic Church in Malaysia under 130 years of Protestant Dutch rule in Malacca (1641–1795 and briefly again in 1814–1824) was heroic. The Dutch destroyed or confiscated as military barracks all but one of Malacca's nineteen Catholic churches. So when the British pushed out the Dutch and announced a policy of freedom for all religions the Catholics rejoiced.[63] But to the Catholic majority in this period, in Malaysia as well as elsewhere, the centuries-long rivalry between the Vatican and Portugal for control of Roman Catholic missions was probably more of a hindrance to growth than the irritating intrusion of Protestant missionaries. It pitted the Propaganda Fide and apostolic vicariates of the pope against the continuing rights of *padroado* granted Portugal in the fifteenth century and the diocesan bishops and "secular" priests appointed by Portugal in its territories.[64]

In Malaysia the diocese of Malacca (Melaka) was merged into that of Portuguese Goa in 1818, and thence, successively into that of Burma and Siam, but in 1841 Pope Gregory XVI placed the whole mission under the Paris Missionary Society as the apostolic vicariate of the Malay peninsula. Tension continued, and in 1846 a complicated compromise placed it under Portuguese Macao while remaining French.[65] Under the French mission, the old seminary in Thailand dating back to 1665 was moved to Penang in Malaysia and reorganized in 1807–1810 around a cadre of Chinese seminarians brought from the Chinese mainland. It became the major Catholic college for Southeast Asia. A request from three hundred Catholics in Singapore brought an opening for Catholic missions in that British enclave in 1830.[66] An indication of the growing importance of the Chinese Christian community in Malaysia was a tragic event in Singapore in 1851. About five hundred Chinese, most of whom were Catholics, were killed by a fanatically anti-Christian, antiforeign Chinese secret society, the Hong Brotherhood.[67]

By that time, increasing expansion of the British Empire in Asia had changed the religious as well as the political equations of the area.[68] Under British colonial tolerance, churches were built and filled with Catholic worshipers; in 1838 Penang reported four thousand, Malakka two thousand, Singapore five hundred.[69] By contrast Protestant growth was static and limited in this period (1800–1860) to Anglicans and Scottish Presbyterians witnessing and ministering mostly to the white, colonial community,[70] as we have noted.

Malaysia Chronology

1511	Portuguese seize Malacca.
1606	Johore Malays (from North Sumatra) gain foothold, force conversion to Islam.
1629	First translation of a Bible portion into a non-European language in the modern period: the Gospel of Matthew into High Malay.
1641	Dutch replace the Portuguese.
1795	English replace Dutch and Johore Sultan; reinstate Dutch 1814.

| 1824 | Reclaimed by English; Malacca, Penang, and Singapore united as "Straits Settlements" colony; gradually include all Malay states as colony or protectorates (Perak, Selangor, Negri, Sembilan, Pahang, Kedah, Johnore, etc.). |
| 1954 | Independence as Malaysia. |

Vietnam (1800–1860)

When France in 1787 began to acquire control of portions of what they would eventually name French Indo-China, the territory now called Vietnam[71] was still recovering from recent persecutions, of the considerable number of Catholics in the population — perhaps as many as 310,000 in 1800.[72] The turn of the century seemed to promise a new era of advance under the friendly emperor of Annam, Gia-long. Its first thirty years were quiet, but not without intermittent persecution, and church membership did not grow.[73] Then, unexpectedly, the thirty quiet years were followed by thirty years of anti-Christian pressure, outright persecutions and a tragic number of martyrdoms.

Gia-long died in 1820;[74] his successor, Minh-men, was no friend of Christians. Edicts in 1825 and 1826 condemned the foreign faith as undermining national traditions and refused entry to any more missionaries. The full storm broke in 1833 with persecutions reminiscent of the seventeenth-century persecutions in Japan. All Christians were ordered to renounce their faith and trample on the cross. Church buildings were torn down. A missionary was executed. More martyrdoms followed. About ten missionaries and hundreds of faithful Vietnamese Catholics gave their lives rather than apostatize. But once more the blood of the martyrs was the seed. Catholic membership, by 1840, instead of declining had added a hundred thousand new adherents to the rolls.[75]

The persecuting king, Minh-men, died early in 1841. Persecution relaxed, but intermittent imprisonment and torture of foreign priests and Annamese Christians still continued in "the dungeons of Hué," the Annam capital. Two missionaries, newly arrived in Tonkin, Simeon-François Berneux and Galy, were seized along with seven native believers, including two nuns. They were caged and chained with bonds almost too heavy to carry, then taken by cart for trial before the magistrates. The initial questioning was surprisingly gentle, but they were warned that when they were sent on to the royal city "even innocent people under torture are compelled to acknowledge their guilt." It was all too true. More torture in the dungeons followed — two years of beatings, flogging, occasional relaxation but never ending demands for recantation of the foreign faith. Berneux prayed for martyrdom. His prayer was not granted in Annam, but it was strangely answered more than twenty years later. Along with other missionary priests Berneux was released in 1843 by the timely arrival of a French man-of-war.[76] His next assignment was as apostolic vicar "to a land more dangerous than Annam, Corea." There after ten hard years the brave bishop perished with other martyrs in the great Korean persecution of 1866.[77]

With the arrival of the French, persecution in Indochina waned but did not entirely cease. A general amnesty in 1847 brought the captives out of prison and the church grew. In ten years, from 1839 to 1849 the number of vicariates increased from three to six; the number of bishops from one to ten; churches and "colleges" were built. In one vicariate alone the number of Vietnamese priests had mounted from 38 to 65, and the number of Catholics from 100,000 to 130,000.[78]

Intermittent local harassment continued. In 1851 suddenly a foreign priest was executed, and when another's head was cut off the next year, alarm spread through the churches. When a French naval vessel appeared in 1857 antiforeign feeling exploded, not just against the French but against Christians in general. Wisely or not Pellerin, the apostolic vicar of northern Cochin China, hastened to France to ask for government help.[79] Napoleon III sent a naval expedition, and Spain added a contribution on behalf of Spanish Dominican missions in the territory. The war lasted five years (1856–1862).[80]

In those years five thousand Christians were reported killed, and forty thousand lost homes and livelihood. Msgr. Retort, the apostolic vicar of the northern kingdom, Tonkin, who had survived twenty-four years in the country, went into hiding and died of exposure and fatigue. Two other apostolic vicars, Msgr. Diaz of central Tonkin, and Bishop Melchior, were publicly executed. Royal anti-Christian edicts in 1860 and 1861 added fury to the persecution.[81] Only French victory in 1862 and the final peace treaty of 1874 with its promise of freedom of religion ended the long story of half a century of death, martyrdom, suffering, and endurance that laid the foundations for a Catholic future in Vietnam.[82]

NOTES

1. George Bradley McFarland, ed., *Historical Sketch of Protestant Missions in Siam, 1828–1928* (Bangkok: Bangkok Times Press, 1928), 44–45.

2. See chap. 13.

3. As an effective nation-state Siam dates its beginnings to 1772–1775 and the defeat of invading Burma by the founder of the present Chakri dynasty. In 1939, after a transition from absolute to constitutional monarchy in 1932, the name was changed to Thailand. We follow that chronology in referring to it: Siam until 1939, and then Thailand.

4. N. A. McDonald, *Siam: Its Government, Manners, Customs &c.* (Philadelphia: Alfred Martin, 1871), 173.

5. Sir John Bowring, *The Kingdom and People of Siam with a Narrative of the Mission to that Country in 1855,* 2 vols. (London: John W. Parker, 1857), 1:335.

6. Letter of Ann Hasseltine Judson, April 29, 1819, in Knowles, *Memoir of Ann H. Judson,* 181–182. The press, taken to Bangkok in 1835 by Dr. Dan Beach Bradley, became the first printing press in Siam. Cf. McFarland, *Historical Sketch of Protestant Missions in Siam,* 16. On Ann Judson, see chap. 15 above.

7. McFarland, *Historical Sketch of Protestant Missions in Siam,* 3–5, 195. On Gützlaff in China see above chap. 13.

8. Kenneth E. Wells, *History of Protestant Work in Thailand, 1828–1958* (Bangkok: Church of Christ in Thailand, 1958), 5–7. Tomlin had gone first to Singapore in 1827, then to Bangkok.

9. Lovett, *The History of the London Missionary Society,* 2:437, 439. Tomlin went first to Singapore in 1827, then to Bangkok. Tracy, *History of the American Board of Commissioners for Foreign Missions,* 247. Abeel served for less than a year in Siam.

10. William L. Bradley, *Siam Then: The Foreign Colony in Bangkok before and after Anna* (Pasadena, Calif.: William Carey Library, 1981). Written dramatically in the first person as though by Dr. Bradley, this unusual biography is carefully based on Dr. Bradley's private journal and records, as well as on many other primary sources as annotated (192–196). On surgery, 24ff.; on vaccination, 57–62; on his conversion to homeopathic medicine, 85–86; on opium, 36, 48; on printing, 48; on the AMA, 50, 74, 75, 83, and 88ff. See also McFarland, *Historical Sketch of Protestant Missions in Siam,* 8, 12–18, 23–26, 195–196; and Mary Backus, ed., *Siam and Laos: As Seen by Our American Missionaries* (Philadelphia: Presbyterian Board of Publications, 1884), 357.

11. McFarland, *Historical Sketch of Protestant Missions in Siam,* 12–26, 34, 41, 50, 74–75, 83, 88ff., and passim.

12. Rong Syamananda, *A History of Thailand,* 3rd ed. (Bangkok: Chulalongkorn University, 1977), 115.

13. See McFarland, *Historical Sketch of Protestant Missions in Siam,* 27–31, 344–353, reprinting an extract, "Missionary Sketches," by S. F. Smith, 5th ed., 1887; and on the pirate attack, Wells, *History of Protestant Work in Thailand,* 16–20; and Torbet, *Venture of Faith,* 52–53.

14. On the ABCFM in Siam see McFarland, *Historical Sketch of Protestant Missions in Siam,* 10–26.

15. The last Baptist missionary of this period left Siam in 1893; the Baptist mission officially closed in 1927. McFarland, *Historical Sketch of Protestant Missions in Siam,* 27–34, 344–351; Herbert Swanson, *Krischak Muang Nua: A Study in Northern Thai Church History* (Bangkok: Chuan Printing Press, 1984), 3–5; Torbet, *Venture of Faith,* 52ff., 77–73, 538; and Wells, *History of Protestant Work in Thailand,* 13, 21.

16. McFarland, *Historical Sketch of Protestant Missions in Siam,* 34, 41; on Bradley, *Siam Then,* 12–26, 124–135, 169–179.

17. McFarland, *Historical Sketch of Protestant Missions in Siam,* 36–37.

18. McFarland, *Historical Sketch of Protestant Missions in Siam,* 41.

19. See his biography by George H. Feltus, *Samuel Reynolds House of Siam, Pioneer Medical Missionary* (New York: Fleming H. Revell, 1924).

20. On contributions to medical pioneering, scientific interests, and extensive church planting, see Wells, *History of Protestant Work in Thailand,* 23, 29–32; and McFarland, *Historical Sketch of Protestant Missions in Siam,* 39–42. On the controversies, see Bradley, *Siam Then,* 124–235, 169–179. Dr. Bradley, the independent medical missionary, originally a Presbyterian but under the Congregational

ABCFM and soon independent, with whom House had his differences, was as often as House the center of controversy.

21. A copy of House's letter, March 2, 1868, is printed as appendix IX by McFarland in *Historical Sketch of Protestant Missions in Siam*, 358–359.

22. Syamananda, *History of Thailand*, 101, 107.

23. Siam became a modern nation-state, debatably either in 1767 with King Taksin, or in 1782 with the founding of the present Chakri dynasty whose kings in the first century of Protestant missions were P'ra Nang Klao (Rama III, 1824–1851), who was reactionary; Mongkut (Rama IV, 1851–1868), who was just the opposite, and the great Chulalongkorn (Rama V, 1868–1910).

24. The three women were Mrs. S. Mattoon (Presbyterian), Mrs. D. B. Bradley (independent), and Mrs. J. T. Jones (Baptist). See McFarland, *Historical Sketch of Protestant Missions in Siam*, 45.

25. Portugal had a consul in Bangkok since 1820 (McFarland, *Historical Sketch of Protestant Missions in Siam*, 49).

26. In Presbyterian church order, a presbytery functions something like a bishop, but with less control, as a higher judicatory body over the congregations in its territory. Siam therefore then had one presbytery with only one congregation.

27. Cf. Swanson, *Krischak Muak Nua*, 5. Cf. McFarland, *Historical Sketch of Protestant Missions in Siam*, 50, where a typographical error reads the date as 1878 instead of the correct 1858.

28. On Ki-eng Qua Wean, see McFarland, *Historical Sketch of Protestant Missions in Siam*, 17, 21, 41, 60, 287ff.; and Wells, *History of Protestant Work in Thailand*, 25. On his descendants, see McFarland, 288–295.

29. The number of Baptists reported in 1863 was 41 (13 Chinese and 28 Siamese), and the peak was 500 Baptists in 1882. Eleven years later the mission sold its property and left the field. On the Baptist mission in Thailand, see McFarland, *Historical Sketch of Protestant Missions in Siam*, 344–353. Cf. Wells, *History of Protestant Work in Thailand*, 16–21.

30. See Backus, *Siam and Laos*, 180–181, 407–408. Cf. McFarland, *Historical Sketch of Protestant Missions in Siam*, 50. When the Chinese teacher, Kieng Qua-Sean, died the same year Nai Chune was baptized, Nai Chune took his place as head of the school (Wells, *History of Protestant Work in Thailand*, 27).

31. For a thorough discussion of the same issue in Africa, see Sanneh, *Translating the Message*.

32. See above chap. 16; Wells, *History of Protestant Work in Thailand*, 6–7; and McFarland, *Historical Sketch of Protestant Missions in Siam*, 334–337.

33. The American Baptist Mission brought in a second press in 1836 (McFarland, *Historical Sketch of Protestant Missions in Siam*, 16, 29, 38, 344–348, 378). The first printed publication in Siam was produced on the old wood and stone press of the American Board by the Rev. Charles of the ABCFM in 1836. His eight-page tract included the Ten Commandments (Wells, *History of Protestant Work in Thailand*, 9).

34. Wells, *History of Protestant Work in Thailand*, 84–85; Daniel McGilvary, *A Half Century among the Siamese and the Lao* (New York: Fleming H. Revell, 1912), 222–223.

35. McFarland, *Historical Sketch of Protestant Missions in Siam*, 124–125, 250.

36. McFarland, *Historical Sketch of Protestant Missions in Siam*, 253ff.

37. It may even have been the first example of *zenana* mission not only in Siam but in all Asia, as Dr. Samuel House claimed in his chapter in Backus, *Siam and Laos*, 372.

38. McFarland, *Historical Sketch of Protestant Missions in Siam*, 45; Wells, *History of Protestant Work in Thailand*, 25.

39. Mrs. Mattoon's grandson, Norman Mattoon Thomas, was equally remarkable and tenacious — America's perennial socialist candidate for the presidency of the United States from 1928 to 1948. Her husband Stephen spoke Thai "like a native," according to Townsend Harris of Japan, and was the first U.S. Consul in Siam (1856), at the same time fretting because it distracted him from his "higher calling" as a missionary. Lucy Starling, *Dawn over Temple Roofs* (New York: World Horizons, 1960), 92–93; and Syamananda, *History of Thailand*. Cf. McFarland, *Historical Sketch of Protestant Missions in Siam*, 45–46, 69; and Wells, *History of Protestant Work in Thailand*, 25.

40. McFarland, *Historical Sketch of Protestant Missions in Siam*, 60.

41. McFarland, *Historical Sketch of Protestant Missions in Siam*, 349. Jones died in 1851, and later his widow married the Rev. J. S. Smith.

42. Esther had cared for Queen Rambaibarni as a baby (Wells, *History of Protestant Work in Thailand*, 27; McFarland, *Historical Sketch of Protestant Missions in Siam*, 45–46).

43. Quoted by Wells, *History of Protestant Work in Thailand*, 28.

44. McFarland, *Historical Sketch of Protestant Missions in Siam*, 349.

45. McFarland, *Historical Sketch of Protestant Missions in Siam*, 347–349. By 1863 the Baptist church had been divided into two sections, one for Chinese, one for Siamese, the latter at that time outnumbering the Chinese twenty-eight to thirteen, but from then on the momentum shifted sharply to the Chinese.

46. K-eng Qua-Sean was born in Xiamen, where he practiced Eastern medicine. He was converted under the teaching of ABCFM missionaries in 1844 on a visit to Bangkok. See S. S. Nuam Sresthidor, "Outstanding Men and Women of Siam," in McFarland, *Historical Sketch of Protestant Missions in Siam*, 288–289; and Wells, *History of Protestant Work in Thailand*, 25.

47. McFarland, *Historical Sketch of Protestant Missions in Siam*, 60–61, 211. The school for Chinese boys started in 1852/53; merged with Mrs. Mattoon's school in 1853; moved to Samray as the Samray School in 1862; merged with the Bangkok Christian High School in 1888; and in 1892 took the name Samray Boys' Christian High School; in 1900 the name was changed to Bangkok Christian College.

48. Listed in McFarland, *Historical Sketch of Protestant Missions in Siam*, 317–319. Two were independent (the D. B. Bradleys); eight American Baptist (the William Deans, J. H. Chandlers, S. J. Smiths, and R. Telfords), and seven American Presbyterian (the S. Mattoons, S. R. Houses, J. Wilsons, and Daniel McGilvary).

49. McFarland, *Historical Sketch of Protestant Missions in Siam*, 31, 41.

50. The years 1860–1900 in Siam follow in chap. 27.

51. *EAH*, s.v. "Malaysia," 2:472.

52. Kilgour, in an appendix to Rauws et al., *The Netherlands Indies*, 171. The 1629 volume was printed in Dutch and Malay parallel columns. If not the first in any non-European language, it was at least the first known to have been printed for an evangelistic purpose.

53. Robert Hunt, Lee Kam Hing, and John Roxborogh, eds., *Christianity in Malaysia: A Denominational History* (Selangor Darul Ehsan, Malaysia: Pelanduk Publications, 1992), 5–9.

54. The British moved south into Malaysia, the French north into Indo-China. Stamford Raffles, active in Java, had been appointed "agent to the Governor General with the Malay States" in 1818. A hundred years earlier a Sultan of Johore had offered the island of Singapore as a personal present to an English trade explorer, Alexander Hamilton, who turned it down as of little use to him for private purposes, though he noted prophetically that it might make a good place for a trading colony some day (Brian Harrison, *South-East Asia: A Short History* [London: Macmillan, 1955], 144, 164, 174–177).

55. Hunt, Hing, and Roxborogh, *Christianity in Malaysia*, 35–36.

56. Hunt, Hing, and Roxborogh, *Christianity in Malaysia*, 37.

57. Hunt, Hing, and Roxborogh, *Christianity in Malaysia*, 35–42, 47.

58. Munshi Abdullah, *The Hikayat Abdullah*, trans. and annotated by A. H. Hill, vol. 28, pt. 3 of the *Journal of the Malayan Branch of the Royal Asiatic Society* (Singapore: Malay Publishing House, 1955), 10–11. Abdullah's father was *khatib* of the village mosque, an Arab trader/missionary who worked for a while as captain of a Dutch trading ship along the Malay and Java coasts.

59. Abdullah, *The Hikayat Abdullah*, 15–16, 18ff.

60. See chap. 13 above, on the Ultra-Ganges Mission.

61. Abdullah, *The Hikayat Abdullah*, 17–18, 21–26.

62. Abdullah, *The Hikayat Abdullah*, 117–118.

63. Felix George Lee, *The Catholic Church in Malaya* (Singapore: Eastern Universities Press, 1963), 44.

64. See Mary Just, *Immortal Fire: A Journey through the Centuries with the Missionary Great* (St. Louis: Herder, 1951). This internal struggle remained a thorn in the flesh to Catholic missions in Asia until 1950.

65. Hunt, Hing, and Roxborogh, *Christianity in Malaysia*, 10 and 31 n. 35. An 1886 concordat between the Vatican and Portugal assigned all Catholics at Malacca or in Singapore Island and belonging to the old Portuguese Diocese of Malacca to the care of the bishop of Portuguese Macao.

66. Lee, *Catholic Church in Malaysia*, 47–48.

67. Lee, *Catholic Church in Malaysia*, 46–47; Hunt, Hing, and Roxborogh, *Christianity in Malaysia*, 10–13.

68. British control became dominant in 1874 in Malaysia.

69. Lee, *Catholic Church in Malaysia*, 48.

70. Hunt, Hing, and Roxborogh, *Christianity in Malaysia*, 38, 79.

71. Before partition in 1683 the whole country now known as Vietnam was called Annam. From 1883 to 1887 it was divided into three parts: the north was Tonkin ("Eastern Capital"), with its capital at Hanoi; the center was Annam ("Southern Peace"), with its throne at Hué; and the south was Cochin China, with its capital at Saigon. France, which had begun to control the area in 1802, unified the three units as its colony of Indochina in 1887. A convenient short history is Meyer's *Southeast Asia*.

72. Indo-China (Cochin China, and West and East Tonkin) in 1800 reported 15 missionaries, 119 native priests, and 310,000 Roman Catholics (Latourette, *A History of the Expansion of Christianity*, 6:247, citing Descamps, *Histoire génerale comparée des missions*).

73. For details of persecutions even under the generally friendly monarch Gia-long, see John R. Shortland, *The Persecutions of Annam: A History of Christianity in Cochin China and Tongkin* (London: Burns & Oates, 1875), 132–150.

74. On the Nguyen emperor, Gia-long, see *EAH*, 1:507–508.

75. The number in 1800 had been 310,000; it was still just about the same in 1830, but by 1840 during the persecutions it had climbed to a reported 420,000 Catholics, 29 missionaries (a decrease), and 144 native priests. See Shortland, *The Persecutions of Annam*, 154–206. Cf. Louis-Eugène Louvet, *La Cochinchine religieuse*, 2 vols. (Paris: E. Leroux, 1885), 2:63–69, 75, 84–85, 86–94, 173ff.

76. Shortland, *The Persecutions of Annam*, 206–262.

77. Kim and Chung, *Catholic Korea*, 245–248.

78. Shortland, *The Persecutions of Annam*, 263–267.

79. Latourette, *A History of the Expansion of Christianity*, 6:249, citing Louvet, *La Cochinchine religieuse*, 2:223–224.

80. Meyer, *Southeast Asia*, 56–57.

81. Latourette, *A History of the Expansion of Christianity*, 6:250. See Shortland, *The Persecutions of Annam*, 263–268. Shortland is valuable for rich detail but borders on hagiography.

82. Shortland quotes the texts in the 1874 treaty guaranteeing freedom of religion for Catholics, restoration of property, and right of assembly and free access for missionaries and Annamist priests. Shortland, *The Persecutions of Annam*, 428–429.

Chapter 18

Indonesia (1800–1860)

The virtues that made the Netherlands the most ardently-worked plot of land in Europe — thrift, care, cleanliness and attention to detail — were lost in the sprawling plenitude of the East Indies... In the land of the islands... [the Dutch] were conspicuously out of place. The tall blond invader strode among the small brown people like someone from another world. — Bruce Grant, 1967[1]

IN 1833 two Congregational missionaries of the American Board of Commissioners of Foreign Missions (ABCFM), Munson and Lyman, ventured on a trip of inquiry into the high mountains and dense forests of northeastern Sumatra. They never returned. Captured by a fierce tribal group, called Bataks, they were butchered; some accounts even say they were eaten by their captors.[2] It was not until 1861, almost thirty years later, that effective missionary outreach finally penetrated into Batak territory. In the next century, though, the Batak Protestant community would become one of the fastest-growing churches in Southeast Asia.[3]

Dutch Colonialism

Why was the Christian mission in the Indonesian archipelago such a volatile mixture of peril and progress? Part of the answer lies in the nature of Protestant Holland's attitude toward its most lucrative colonial possession. "With the Indies," wrote one historian, "Holland was the world's third or fourth colonial power; without them, it would be a cold little country on the North Sea."[4] No wonder then that Holland fought so long and so tenaciously to win control of the fertile "spice islands" of the South Pacific. It took the Dutch more than three hundred years to complete the colonizing of the three thousand isles — from 1596 when the first Dutch ships appeared off the west coast of Sumatra and Java to drive out the Portuguese,[5] to 1906 when Holland finally "pacified" the last of the 250 rulers of the smaller islands, Bali.

Then, for the first time in history, the islands were unified in what is now Indonesia. Colonization gave Indonesia its national identity, but for three centuries it denied the islands their freedom. Bruce Grant points to the immense irony of it all: "It is as if the invader, having laboriously established the outline of his territorial possessions in the East Indies, provided the people for the first time with a definite area by which to assert the rights to national independence."[6]

The Dutch form of colonization was occupation of acquired territory by settlers, as in South Africa, not by absentee landlords as in much of the rest of Asia. In 1914 on the eve of World War I, out of a total population of 40 million there was a sizable group of 250,000 Dutch settlers who were still largely in control of the Dutch East Indies.[7] Moreover, for the first two hundred years of expanding Dutch rule, Dutch colonial policy favored the settlers, the traders, and the native rulers, not the missionaries. One historian, Bentley-Taylor, argues:

> It has often been asserted that the Christian gospel has been foisted upon eastern races by imperialistic western powers as part of their colonial policy. Of this the Dutch certainly cannot be accused in Java; it was their deliberate plan to keep Christianity to themselves and to withhold it from the peoples of the land they had conquered ... The dismal fact has to be recorded that the history of the Church in Java only began in the 19th century.[8]

But Java was not quite typical. We must temper that picture of what seemed to be Dutch missionary failure in Java,[9] with a brief look back at some of the nineteenth-century bright spots of mission history in the islands. Java was not only the center of colonial occupation, but also the island of greatest Muslim, not Christian, missionary success. Indeed, Islam was as significant a factor contributing to the slow pace of Christian expansion as was trade-centered obstructionism of the Dutch colonials. At one point, for fear of offending the Muslim majority, the government went so far as to prohibit the distribution of a translation of the New Testament into Javanese.[10] In the islands outside Java occurred the most vigorous movements into the Christian faith — Sumatra to the west, the Celebes (Sulawesi) and the Moluccas to the north, and to the far southeast the Little Sundas (Flores and Timor). Shortly after the turn of the century, in 1906, the proportion was 26,000 Christians on Java to 434,000 on the Outer Islands.[11]

The Conversion of the Bataks

If, as Tertullian says, "the blood of the martyrs is the seed of the church," one of the most dramatic evidences of the truth of his oft-quoted observation occurred in the fatal mission to the Batak tribes, noted above. Samuel Munson and Henry Lyman, recent graduates of Amherst and Andover Newton Seminary, landed on Sumatra, the fifth-largest island in the world, in 1833. Barely a year later they were killed.[12] They had been sent by the American Board of Commissioners to follow up on the failure of earlier attempts to reach the Batak tribals of the interior.[13] They made their first and only trip into the hills in the summer of 1834 with a police runner as guard, a cook, and ten porters. On leaving Munson wrote home, "We go well provided and guarded at every point. Our only danger is that our faith in God will not be strong enough." A week later the policeman and the porters returned alone and in distress. A band of two hundred Bataks had suddenly surrounded them, killed the foreigners, while the rest ran for their lives. The cook's arm was cut off as he fled.[14]

From that tragedy emerged one of the largest indigenous churches in all of Asia, and the largest single Protestant denomination in the islands, the Batak Christian Protestant Church.[15] Seventy-five years later, the fiercely independent Bataks, whose fathers had murdered the first missionaries they saw, erected a monument at the site of the murder, with an inscription, "The blood of the martyrs is the seed of the Church."[16] The seed had been planted, but it was a missionary born the year of the murder of the two martyrs who would bring that seed to its amazing growth. His name was Nommensen, and he landed in the islands in 1862, as we shall see in a later chapter.

The Dutch Reformed Churches of the Islands

It would be a mistake to allow the good news of the sudden growth of Batak Christianity, in territory so recently and so rapidly brought under Dutch control, to obscure the fact that by far the larger proportion of the population of the islands remained in regions long controlled by the Dutch and in churches growing under the nurture of the Dutch missionary societies. This was in spite of the fact that control of the church in the colonies by an imperial state proved, particularly in Dutch Indonesia, to be a very mixed blessing.

Sometimes the obstruction took the form of well-meaning but arbitrary attempts at long-distance control of mission policy by the government in Holland. An early example in 1820 was the sudden decree of King William I of the Netherlands, when the Indies in 1816 were made a crown colony, that all Protestant churches in the islands must unite in one state church, his own Reformed Church. Under the comfortably loose policies of the Dutch East Indies Company, which paid more attention to trade than to religion, the Protestant church of the islands had agreeably been open to missionaries of different nationalities and confessions. With three thousand islands in the archipelago, there seemed to be room enough for everybody — Reformed, Congregational, Lutheran, and Mennonite. But a restrictive union under the denominational name "reformed" irked the German and Dutch Lutherans. Even the Dutch Reformed were not too pleased with such arbitrary state interference in ecclesiastical matters. The result was a delaying action that blocked the premature union for almost a quarter of a century. Finally, in 1854 the Lutheran Church of Batavia accepted a compromise and joined the united church.[17]

Until the middle of the nineteenth century only two Protestant missionary societies were successfully active in the islands, the Netherlands Missionary Society (NZG, 1797), and the Rhenish Mission (RM, 1828), a German Pietist blend of Calvinists and Lutherans, mentioned above in connection with its famously successful evangelization of the Bataks. Both were orthodox, evangelistic, independent of state control, and intentionally interdenominational.[18]

First and most prominent of the societies was the Netherlands Missionary Society (known in Dutch abbreviation as the NZG). Like its English prototype, the London Missionary Society, it had been formed in 1797–1798 not only free of the trade-obsessed Dutch East Indies Company, which until its dissolution in 1798 had ruled the islands under the crown, but free even from control by its home church, the Dutch Reformed Church.[19] However, as missionary vision at home in Holland waned in the midst of theological controversies, and mission support weakened in the Dutch churches in the early 1800s, the Netherlands Missionary Society became more and more financially and organizationally related to the state church of the islands, the Protestant Church in the Dutch East Indies.[20]

Then out of some refreshing nineteenth-century revivals in Holland arose a renewal of missionary enthusiasm, a reaction against state control of Dutch missions, and a criticism of the chilling secularizing effects that dependence on the government was exerting on the motivating energies and theological convictions that were basic to missionary commitment. In mid-century, 1858–1861, three new Dutch missionary societies were formed, less inclusive, less political, more evangelistic and incisively theological: the Netherlands Missionary Union (NZV), the Utrecht Missionary Society (UZV) and the Dutch Reformed Missionary Association (ZGK).[21]

Joseph Kam in the Moluccas

This new surge of missionary outreach in the last half of the century was borne upon waves stirred earlier by the labors of a pioneer of the old NZG in the first half of the century. He was Joseph Carel Kam (1769–1833), the "apostle to the Moluccas," as he has been called.[22] Kam had come in 1813 during a brief interlude of British control of the islands. He chose to come, therefore, at first not under the NZG, but under the auspices of the famous English mission, the London Missionary Society, which had been urgently advised by their China pioneer, Robert Morrison, to take advantage of Joseph Kam's availability as an opportunity to bring new life into the declining Dutch mission in Java.[23]

When Kam arrived, he found only one Dutch preacher left in the northern islands. The failure of the Dutch East Indies Company in the 1790s had left Holland's Protestant missions, which for two hundred years had been controlled by the Company and the state, completely disorganized. For twenty years he gave himself to the islands, not once returning to his homeland in Holland. But as a Hollander himself, when the islands were given back to the Dutch, he moved from the London Missionary Society to work through the colonial government and the NZG.[24] His ministry brought renewed energy and life into the islands' churches. Evangelistic conversions of pagans and even Muslims[25] began to spread through the archipelago. He traveled thousands of miles through the three thousand islands, often in a schooner that he built himself, evangelizing, preaching sound Calvinistic doctrine to neglected nominal Christians, and arguing with William Carey's son Jabez who was introducing Baptist baptism.[26] He trained national leaders for the church in his own home, which later developed into the first seminary and became known as the "School for the Training of Native Teachers" in 1885.

In his missionary practice, Kam was resourcefully innovative in adapting native culture patterns to Christian use. He organized flute orchestras to bring native sounds and rhythm patterns into services of worship. They are still a featured part of Moluccan Indonesian church practice. He sent Moluccan missionaries from his own major center, the small island of Ambon (or Amboina) in the southern Moluccas, to evangelize Irian Jaya New Guinea. The Minahassa peninsula in the Celebes (Sulawesi), where Kam's evangelism was effectively followed up by able successors, came to be called "a completely Christianized land," home for nearly half of all the Christians in the Dutch East Indies. The island of Ambon became a radiating center of indigenous evangelism spreading through the thousand islands of the Moluccas.[27]

But there were festering problems. In church structure, the Dutch missions were caught in an unwieldy, ambiguous mixture of church structures. On the one hand was the Protestant State Church of the Indies established by King William I of Holland near the beginning of the nineteenth century. On the other was an increasing number of independent missions that had inherited churches previously supported by the Dutch East Indies Company until its dissolution in 1798. Some of the missionaries continued to receive their salaries from the government. Others were directly under the jurisdiction and support of the missions. In 1854 the colonial government of Holland, which had inherited rule of the island from the defunct East India Company, sought to strengthen its control of the multiplying missions by requiring special permits for all missionaries at work in the colony, permits that could be canceled for any "disturbance of peace and order."[28]

On the whole, the spreading presence of new missions caused little confusion to the peace and order of the colony. With three thousand islands spread across the three thousand miles of the archipelago, it was easy to stake out stations of operation with more than enough room to

avoid abrasive contact. This was true not only of relations between the
Protestant groups, but also, usually, between Protestants and Catholics.

But at mid-century a deeper threat to Protestant missionary progress
arose, not from government control nor from sectarian strife over territorial rights. It has been described as "the conflict of creeds," a
disagreement about the very basics of the missionary enterprise, a confusion about its ultimate goal, and a shaking of its theological foundation.[29]
The result, as the century approached its sixth decade, was a premonition
of impending decline.

In 1858, the respected elder missionary J. Voorhoeve, who for twenty-
two years had served as treasurer of the old NZG, approached his board
for permission to resign. His reason was a shock: "It is no longer possible
for [me] to cooperate with many of those who preached a gospel different
from the Gospel of Jesus Christ."[30] Christian missions in the Indonesian archipelago had survived two and a half disheartening centuries
of obstacles without and within. Now halfway through the nineteenth
century and seemingly on the verge of a missionary breakthrough, an internal doctrinal dispute, deep-rooted and electrically controversial, arose
to threaten a critical breakdown of missionary momentum.[31]

How the Christian mission would fall or fail in the face of this theological "shaking of the foundations" will occupy much of the story not
only for the next forty years to 1900 but also into the twentieth century —
which must wait for chapter 28 to be told.

Indonesia Chronology (1797–1892)

1797	Netherlands Missionary Society (NZG) founded.
1798	Rule by Dutch East Indies Company ends. Taken over by the colonial government of Holland.
1800	65,000 to 200,000 Protestants in Amboina, Ceram, and Timor.
1808	Roman Catholics allowed to renew mission work.
1816	Revival of Dutch power.
1820	William I decrees union of Protestant churches.
1830	Culture system — government control of agriculture.
	Bible and tract distribution of British and Foreign Bible Societies brings growth in Eastern Java.
1834	Samuel Munson and Henry Lyman killed by Bataks.
1854	Colonial Government requires permits for missionaries.
1858	J. Voorhoeve resigns from NZG for theological reasons.
1887	About 80,000 Indonesian Christians reported in the islands.[32]

1860	Abolition of slavery; influenced by W. R. van Hoevell.
1881	Murder of missionary ends missionary residence in Bali.
	Liberal reforms replace privatization of land.
1890	Royal Dutch Oil Company (Shell) begins to develop oil production in Sumatra.
1892	Schism: *Hervormde* Church (Dutch Reformed, "liberal" or "high"), with its Netherlands Missionary Society (NZG) and *Gereformeerde* Church (Dutch Reformed "orthodox" or "low"), with the Netherlands Missionary Union. [33]

NOTES

1. Bruce Grant, *Indonesia* (Harmondsworth, U.K.: Penguin Books, 1967), 20.

2. There were no eyewitnesses to any cannibalism, and the report has been questioned. But Chinese travelers and traders had long described the Bataks as cannibals. See the most reliable first reports in William Thompson, *Memoirs of the Rev. Samuel Munson and the Rev. Henry Lyman* (New York: D. Appleton, 1839), passim, and 179–195. Cf. Newcomb, *A Cyclopedia of Missions*, 480.

3. On the eve of World War I it would number thirty thousand Batak adherents, fourteen thousand of whom had been baptized in the year 1913 (Robinson, *History of Christian Missions*, 260).

4. Herbert Feith, *The Decline of Constitutional Democracy in Indonesia* (Ithaca, N.Y.: Cornell University Press, 1962), cited by Grant, *Indonesia*, 21.

5. See above chap. 10.

6. Grant, *Indonesia*, 17–19.

7. See Latourette, *A History of the Expansion of Christianity*, 5:275; Grant, *Indonesia*, 20.

8. David Bentley-Taylor, *The Weathercock's Reward: Christian Progress in Muslim Java* (London: Overseas Missionary Fellowship, 1967), 16–17. This negative attitude toward Christian missions was more typical of Java, with its Muslim population, than of other parts of the islands. For supporting evidence, see Rauws et al., *The Netherlands Indies*, 34–35, 37; Latourette, *A History of the Expansion of Christianity*, 5:277. But cf. Vlekke, *Nusantara*, 132.

9. See vol. 1 of this work, chap. 10.

10. Latourette, *A History of the Expansion of Christianity*, 5:277; Vandenbosch, *The Dutch East Indies*, 46–49. Another reason for slow growth on Java is given by Philip van Akkeren: too long a period of missionary tutelage without self-government (*Sri and Christ: A Study of the Indigenous Church in East Java* [London: Lutterworth, 1970]). But that will be discussed in more detail in vol. 3.

11. A. Cabaton, *Java, Sumatra, and the Other Islands of the Dutch East Indies* (New York: Charles Scribner's Sons, 1911), 26–27, 140, 258. The population of Java in 1910 was 30 million; of the whole archipelago 36 million. The largest island, Sumatra, had only 3 million people then.

12. See, in addition to earlier report cited above, James W. Gould, *Americans in Sumatra* (The Hague: Martinus Nijhoff, 1961), 112–116; and Rauws et al., *The Netherlands Indies*, 80–81.

13. Lyman and Munson were not the first in that area. During a brief period of British rule (1811–1824), the English Baptist Society sent three missionaries to Sumatra. One of them, Richard Burton, translated "almost half the King James Bible" into a Batak script, and another, Nathaniel Ward, sought to treat victims of a cholera epidemic sweeping the island. Both safely reached a number of inland Batak villages and were politely received. They preached to large crowds but were not invited back, and when the region was returned to the Dutch that same year they never returned. See Richard Burton and Nathaniel Ward, "Report of a Journey into Batak Country in the Year 1824," in *TRAS* 1 (1827), 485–513.

14. Thompson, *Memoirs of the Rev. Samuel Munson and the Rev. Henry Lyman*, 178–193.

15. On the Batak church see Paul B. Pedersen, *Batak Blood and Protestant Soul: The Development of Batak National Churches in North Sumatra* (Grand Rapids, Mich.: William B. Eerdmans, 1970). For its present numerical ranking in Indonesia, see Patrick Johnstone, ed., *OW, 1993* (Grand Rapids, Mich.: Zondervan: Grand Rapids, 1993), 292–293.

16. Pedersen, *Batak Blood and Protestant Soul*, 52.

17. One condition of the union was that one of the ministers in Batavia would always be a Lutheran. Vandenbosch, *The Dutch East Indies*, 40; Vlekke, *Nusantara*, 282–283; Richter, *Die evangelische Mission in Niederandisch-Indien*, 19.

18. Rauws et al., *The Netherlands Indies*, 46, 49–50; Latourette, *A History of the Expansion of Christianity*, 5:278.

19. Rauws et al., *The Netherlands Indies*, 45–49.

20. Rauws et al., *The Netherlands Indies*, 49–55. The Dutch name of the Netherlands Missionary Society (NZG) is Nederlandsch Zendeling Genoorschap. The full English title of the church, the Protestant Church in the Dutch East and West Indies, included the West Indies in the Caribbean.

21. The first of the new missions was the Netherlands Missionary Union (Nederlandsche Zendings-Vereeniging, NZV) formed in Java in 1858. It prohibited membership to any who denied the deity of Jesus Christ. In its founding it was influenced by association with the Plymouth Brethren, but established a close relationship with the evangelical wing of the Dutch Reformed Church. Another was the Dutch Reformed Missionary Union (Nederlandsche Gereformeerde Zendingsvereeniging, ZGK) in 1860/1861, strictly Calvinistic and organizationally soon associated with the Christian Reformed Church. For more on the confusing proliferation of missions with similar names, see Rauws et al., *The Netherlands Indies*, 44–75, 109ff., 158; and Latourette, *A History of the Expansion of Christianity*, 5:282–284. Among other major Protestant missions were the Rhenish Missionary Society (RM), Missions of the Reformed Churches (ZGK), etc. See also the acronym chart (Rauws et al., *The Netherlands Indies*, 158).

22. On Kam, see I. H. Enklaar, *Joseph Kam, "Apostel der Mollukken"* (The Hague: Boekencentrum N.V., 1963).

23. Lovett, *The History of the London Missionary Society*, 1:105.

24. Enklaar, *Joseph Kam*, 12–74, and passim.

25. Munson, the martyr at the hands of the Bataks in 1833, had already noted that Muslims in the East Indies were not nearly so hostile — "so bigoted," as he put it — as elsewhere in Asia (Thompson, *Memoirs of the Rev. Samuel Munson and the Rev. Henry Lyman*, 78–79).

26. Enklaar, *Joseph Kam*, 46–47. William Carey wrote to his son, "I am afraid [Kam's] ideas of the nature of Christianity are very defective...I hope you keep on good terms with him, but you must carry on a work entirely separated from him, if you ever hope to be useful." Young Carey left the islands; it was Kam who was immensely "useful."

27. Enklaar, *Joseph Kam*, passim; Rauws et al., *The Netherlands Indies*, 38–49, 51; "Altar and Throne," 357–361; Pattiasina, "An Observation of the Historical Background of the Moluccan Protestant Church," 22–26; and Warneck, *Outline of a History of Protestant Missions*, 130. The organizers of the church in Minahassa, following Kam's evangelistic journeys, were J. H. Riedel and J. G. Schwartz, who began work there in 1831 after training in a missionary school in Germany founded on Moravian principles (Julius Richter, *A History of Protestant Missions in the Near East* [New York: Fleming H. Revell, 1910], 117, 130, 287). His successor in Ambon was B. N. J. Roskott, who translated the New Testament into the Malay dialect (Pattiasina, "An Observation of the Historical Background of the Moluccan Protestant Church," 26; Rauws et al., *The Netherlands Indies*, 172).

28. Rauws et al., *The Netherlands Indies*, 124. See the list of missions on 158.

29. Rauws et al., *The Netherlands Indies*, 58.

30. Rauws et al., *The Netherlands Indies*, 58, 66.

31. Kipp, *The Early Years of a Dutch Colonial Mission*, 28ff.

32. Rauws et al., *The Netherlands Indies*, 58.

33. Rauws et al., *The Netherlands Indies*, 51.

Chapter 19

The West and the Ancient Churches
of the Middle East (1800–1860)

I have heard a certain man [Wycliffe]... say that there were three causes
for [the pagans and Saracens] not wishing to be converted to the faith
of Jesus Christ: firstly, the diversity and contradiction of opinion among
Christians in various sects and on various subjects; secondly, the evil lives
of the Christians; and thirdly, the ill-faith of the Christians.

— Thos. Gascoigne, 1450[1]

They [the Nestorians] were... far more simple and scriptural in their religious beliefs and practices than any other Oriental sects of Christians,
acknowledging the Bible, in theory, at least, as the only rule of faith,
and rejecting all image and picture-worship... They were the "Protestants
of Asia."   — Justin Perkins, 1835[2]

EVER since Luther thundered against the Turkish military threat to
Western Christianity in the sixteenth century, and the Turks twice threatened Vienna — the second time as late as 1683 — Western Protestants
had been painfully slow to pursue a worldwide mission. As for the
Middle East, they regarded it more as impermeable enemy territory
than mission opportunity. Rome, on the other hand, as early as 1551,
was quick to recognize the tiny remaining islands of ancient Nestorianism and Syrian Christianity in the sea of Islamic Asia, as well as the
larger church of Armenian Orthodox Christians, as possible allies of a
Christian recovery in the lands of its origins. For the next two and a
half centuries popes remained in touch with the patriarchs of these suppressed Christian bodies, and the patriarchs drifted in and out of union
with Rome, as we have seen.[3] But to the Protestants the discovery of
the Nestorian Christians in Asia came as an almost unanticipated and
happy surprise.

The Nestorians of Persia (1800–1870)

One of the most dramatic moments in the history of Protestant missions
in West Asia occurred in 1834. It was the arrival in Persia (now Iran)
of Justin Perkins (1805–1869), the first resident Protestant missionary

to the Nestorians. So cordial was the welcome, and so delighted were he and his medical colleague, Dr. Asahel Grant, to find Christians there who treasured the Scriptures, accepted the authority of the Bible without question, and reverenced no statues of saints, that he wrote home that they had found "the Protestants of Asia," survivors of the ancient Church of the East, the Nestorians.

> They were very artless and simple, welcoming us with open arms and hearts to our labors. They were also far more simple and scriptural in their religious beliefs and practices than any other Oriental sects of Christians, acknowledging the Bible, in theory at least, as the only rule of faith, and rejecting all image and picture-worship, confession to priests, the doctrine of purgatory, etc., with hearty indignation. They were thus, in their deeply fallen state, still entitled to the honorable epithet ... *the Protestants of Asia.*[4]

Americans were not the first Protestants in West Asia, and Perkins was not the first American missionary there. Almost a hundred years earlier the Moravians had tried and failed to establish a mission in Persia from 1747 to 1750.[5] A half century later, in 1811, the incandescent Henry Martyn, from Cambridge University, who had declared on reaching India, "Now let me burn out for God,"[6] pushed on into Persia in a heroic attempt to present his Persian translation of the New Testament[7] to the Muslim shah in Teheran. He died as he wished, "burned out for God" with a raging fever, after barely a year in Asia, his mission unfulfilled. He never saw the shah, but the light lit by his death was to burn far brighter than the shah's celebrated 178-carat "Sea of Light" diamond (the Deryai-Noor). Martyn's translation finally did reach the Persian court thanks to the British ambassador, and the shah was so impressed with its "clear and luminous style" that he promised to read it "from the beginning to the end."[8] Published and circulated throughout the Middle East, it prepared the way for the American missionaries who came some two decades later. The first Americans were two clergymen, Eli Smith and H. G. O. Dwight, who explored Nestorian territory on Persia's northwestern border for the American Board of Foreign Missions in 1830.[9] But it was Perkins, four years later, in 1834, serving under the same mission as the explorers Smith and Dwight, who was the pioneer of a continuing Protestant presence in Persia.[10] He settled in Urmia (Orumiyeh, Ooroomiah), capital of Persian Azerbaijan, and his almost instant, unexpected welcome from non-Roman, non-Greek Orthodox Christians led him to believe he had found pre-Reformation Protestants.[11]

He was wrong. What he had found were not Protestants, but one of the last major pockets in West Asia of the Nestorians, the ancient Church of the East, which, as the missionaries knew from earlier reports, was once famous for its missionary passion throughout Asia. On closer acquaintance, moreover, he was compelled to modify his first impressions. His reports home are both sympathetic and blunt. The ancient glory, he wrote, had departed. In one of his more discouraged moments he described the old church as "a pitiful skeleton...[in] a valley of dry bones."[12] It was almost fatally weakened by centuries of persecution, spiritually starved by isolation and ignorance of its own Scriptures, and, unlike their abstinent Muslim neighbors, publicly addicted to alcohol.[13] Yet at the same time, he praised the tenacity with which the Nestorian clung to their old, historic faith, and would speak of how deeply touched he was by their eagerness for Christian fellowship, their thirst for learning and instruction, and, except for the lapses into drunkenness, their moral superiority to the Muslim culture around them.[14] In fact, he concluded, despite threats of death against proselytizing, the Nestorians could well be the missionaries of the future to Persia's Muslim millions.[15]

Mr. and Mrs. Perkins quickly won their confidence. They lived in a mud house where barley grew out of the damp mud mixed with straw from which their sleeping room was constructed. In two months Perkins started a school in the basement, the first of its kind in Central Asia, a Protestant "seminary" to train "pious teachers and preachers." Starting with seven students it soon had forty or fifty, including priests, many deacons and even some bishops.

For the next thirty-six years, translating the Bible, preaching two or three times on Sundays, Perkins lived, talked, and almost looked like a native in his great two-foot-high sheepskin hat.[16] So popular did he become that sometimes when he approached a village the people would march out en masse and bring him in to the sound of drums and trumpets.[17]

Urmia, which called itself the birthplace of Zoroaster, was at that time a fair-sized city of about twenty thousand, mostly Muslim but with a considerable Nestorian community. About two hundred of the three hundred villages on the fertile plain surrounding the city high above the great salt lake of Urmia were Muslim, and one hundred were Nestorian.[18] The great plain, sometimes called "Persia's Paradise," was rich with peach, pear, apricot, and plum trees. Forty miles farther west in the wild, bare mountains of Turkish Kurdistan, rising in places to twelve thousand feet above sea level, at Kudhannis (also spelled Kudshanes, Kudshannis, and Qudaanes) was the village residence of the Nestorian patriarch, Abraham Mar Shimon, who had recently moved out of Urmia and was represented in the city by a bishop.[19] Urmia was the center of just one of the scattered Nestorian enclaves driven from the old homeland of the ancient Church of the East where Syria, Turkey, modern Iraq, and Persia meet between the two great rivers, the Tigris and Euphrates. Far away, south and west on the Tigris near Mosul was another Nestorian patriarch, Mar Elias, and the relationship between the two heads of the Nestorians was ambiguous, for Nestorian Christians seemed content to accept either patriarch, depending perhaps on which was nearest.[20] In

1843 Kurdish attacks and massacres drove Mar Shimon out of the Urmia area to Mosul on the Tigris for safety.[21]

It is difficult to say just how many Nestorians were left in West Asia when the Protestants reached them. Perkins's estimate was 150,000, but Eli Smith after his earlier trip of exploration in 1833 reported only about 70,000 in Persia and Kurdistan. A reasonable estimate might be 125,000.[22]

Perkins had been studying old Syriac, the language of the Nestorian liturgy, but was dismayed to find that the scattered groups of Nestorians were almost entirely illiterate and could not read their own sacred texts. Of all the 150,000 or so surviving Nestorians that Perkins reported in West Asia, he said that not more than forty men and "one lone woman [Helena], the sister of the Assyrian patriarch"[23] could read the Syrian sacred books. But to his surprise, as he listened to the illiterate peasants in their impoverished hillside villages he suddenly realized that they were speaking in none of the common languages of the Middle East — Turkish, Persian, Arabic — but in a tongue that sounded to Perkins strikingly like those old Syriac texts. It was in fact a modern variation of the Syriac, never yet reduced to writing, and different enough from ancient Syriac to make readings of their ancient literature incomprehensible.

He was soon excitedly reporting to his mission board that spoken Nestorian Syriac was not a dead language, extinct for a thousand years, but the spoken language of a brave, long-forgotten, and long-persecuted but still surviving Christian community.[24] So with the help of Abraham, one of the Nestorian priests, he set out to reduce their spoken dialect to writing. When the people first heard the priest read the Lord's Prayer from the written translation, they giggled to hear the book talking their own language.[25]

The wise use of Nestorian Persian helpers was characteristic of the mission.[26] Within two years Perkins was joined by three more American men, but he had eight local Nestorians as full-time helpers, including three bishops and two priests.[27] The arrival of the first printing press in Urmia in 1840 introduced the Bible, beginning with the Psalms, to an ever spreading circle of readers avidly appreciative of Christian literature.[28] Some of the titles illustrate the basic themes of the Protestant evangelistic and scriptural approach to their mission: *On the Necessity of a New Heart* in 1841, "the first book ever printed in the spoken language of the Nestorians" in Urmia, and *The Psalms* in classic Syriac the same year. Others soon followed: *The Four Gospels* in Urmian Aramaic, *The Acts and Epistles* in classic Syriac, *The Faith of the Protestants*, in both classic Syriac and Urmian Aramaic, and *Twenty-Two Plain Reasons for Not Being a Roman Catholic*. In 1845 Perkins completed his translation of the complete New Testament into the spoken Aramaic, and it was published the next year.[29]

Within two months of his arrival in Urmia, as noted above, Perkins had enrolled seven Nestorian boys in a little school, "a seminary for males," for training "pious teachers and preachers." Perkins recruited as its principal native teacher Yohannon, the Nestorian priest, a gifted but strikingly unprepossessing thirty-year-old whom he described as a "ragged, crosseyed cripple" and one-time drunkard but with a sharp mind and a gift for languages.[30] Enrollment at the seminary climbed from seven to more than forty in less than a decade, including bishops, priests, and deacons. By 1862, under the direction of one of Perkins's colleagues, "the sainted Stoddard," the school had graduated over a hundred students, sixty of whom had become preachers.[31] The city's Muslims were so jealous, they demanded that the missionaries, Christians though they might be, open a school for Muslims, and Asahel Grant, M.D.,[32] who with his wife had just joined the Perkinses, was somewhat reluctantly persuaded to add the education of Muslims to his extremely crowded medical schedule.[33]

Just as surprising, considering the oppressive prejudice against freedom of education for women in Muslim lands, was the daring move of the doctor's good wife, Judith Grant. In an amazingly short time, in 1838, she gathered four Nestorian girls together for Persia's first "female seminary." She died a few months later, only twenty-five years old,[34] but the little school became famous later as the "Fidelia Fiske Seminary," so named for a young recruit from Mt. Holyoke College who joined the mission in 1843 and revived and rebuilt the school. The remarkable Miss Fidelia Fiske has been called "one of the greatest missionaries of modern times," the pioneering crusader for women's rights in Persia.[35]

The Nestorian-Protestant Schism (1846–1870)

From the beginning, the policy of the American Board (ABCFM) in entering the Middle East had been clearly stated and willingly accepted by its pioneering missionaries: its stated purpose was to evangelize the Muslim world through a reform of the ancient Christian churches of the East, and not to form a separate Protestant Church. This commitment to avoid proselytizing and to accept the Christian integrity of the Eastern churches was characteristic of all the early nineteenth-century Protestant missions in West Asia.

That is how the little mission in Urmia began its happy discovery of "fellow Protestants." The missionaries faithfully attended Nestorian masses. They accepted the authority and the ordination of its bishops, priests, and clergy, and welcomed their assistance as teachers in the mission schools and translators of the Scriptures. But before ten years had passed, it was becoming increasingly apparent that the Puritan simplicities of Congregational worship and order were not easily yoked with the long, unintelligible liturgies and high authoritarianism of the Nestorian hierarchies. The two traditions began to drift apart, at first almost unconsciously when the missionaries, after enduring a Nestorian mass in language that most Nestorians did not understand, sought to refresh their spirits at home with a simple celebration of the Lord's Supper in their own familiar language. A second break was from authoritarian order to Pietist ardor.[36] The missionaries had been raised in the warming evangelical environment of eighteenth-century New England's Great Awakenings (1725–1760 and 1787–1825), and remembering Calvin's motto, "Pietas et Scientia" were eager to see their schools do more than educate. To literacy and academic progress they longed to add spiritual experience and growth. The Bible was given a prominent place in the teaching, and the teachers set higher moral standards than those to which the students had been exposed. Daily prayers for forgiveness of sin and for personal conversion brought revival. A whole series of revivals followed, beginning in the schools. Three-fourths of the pupils in the seminary and two bishops were converted during the course of ten revivals in the fifteen years from 1846 to 1861. From the schools the revivals spread out to the villages and the churches.[37]

But not all were converted; revival also brought division. The distinction between the converted and the unconverted in an ancient church where all were considered members by baptism puzzled the villagers and enormously complicated life in the church. The higher ecclesiastics, particularly the patriarch in Khudannis, Abraham Mar Shimon V, regarded the enthusiasm of so many for the new, exciting ways as a threat to the church's authority over its people. He found more congenial the high regard for tradition in the short-lived American Episcopal mission to the Eastern churches (1839–1850) and criticized Congregational American separatism from the Nestorian hierarchy and considered fellowship between Anglicans and the American evangelicals to be "unnatural."[38] Mid-nineteenth-century Persian Nestorians were passionately attached to the forms of their historic faith, which had preserved their very identity through so many tortured years. So when authority and tradition collided with education, renewal, and changed lives, the result was another unintended step of separation between a welcomed but reform-minded mission and the old, old church.[39]

An open break came near in 1848 when the Nestorian patriarch "threw off the mask," as the prominent missionary statesman of the Urmian Mission's American Board in Boston put it. For the first time Patriarch Abraham Mar Shimon V publicly opposed the "reformers," the Protestants.[40] He denounced the American mission to the Russian embassy, nominal protectors of the mission in the absence of diplomatic relations between the United States and Persia. He next proceeded to order the schools broken up and tried to withdraw all native assistants from the foreign mission. But when his servants went so far as to fall upon the mission's closest friend in the Nestorian hierarchy, Bishop Yohannon of Urmia, and beat him severely, the people rebelled and the government intervened. Even the Muslims refused to join in any attack on the schools, and the shah's son, governor of the province, ordered an end to the unprovoked violence.[41]

The unhappy drift toward separation, however, was not to be stopped, though Justin Perkins, the pioneer, opposed separation until he died in 1869. The formal break was to come not in Persia with the Persian Nestorians, but with the other ancient Eastern churches (Greek, Jacobite, and Armenian); and not in Persia but on the other side of the border, in Turkey, to which we now turn.

Turkey (West Asia)

To Westerners at that time, the Ottoman Empire of the Turks was in some ways the least attractive of the four great Muslim empires that have ruled vast parts of Asia: Arab, Persian, Mongol, and Turk. Arabs, Persians, and even the Mongols in India produced great civilizations, treasures of art, architecture, and poetry. But the Turks, as Julius Richter claims with some justification, produced wealth for the few and a "mailed fist" for the many. Hitherto this survey of Asian Christian history has, with some exceptions, arbitrarily excluded West Asia and Asia Minor, partly because the region is rooted historically more to Greco-Roman Europe than to the Asian heartland, and also because to do it justice would require a shift of focus into Western church history and spread the story too thin.[42] But insofar as the Turks brought Asia Minor back into Asia — though they ruled it from a conquered corner of Europe — a brief overview is necessary. In the first four centuries of Turkish conquest (1280–1683) it was the Turks who attacked and Europe that was kept desperately on the defensive, on the very edge of disaster. The West lost Constantinople, its last living link with the old Roman empire, in 1453. Turks overran the Balkans, advanced to the gates of Vienna, took Crete, stabbed into the Ukraine, and attacked Poland. Then the tide turned, and for the next two centuries it was the Turks who retreated. In 1683 a mighty Ottoman army tried and failed for the second time to take Vienna and reeled back in utter rout toward Asia. Within thirty-five years they had been driven out of Hungary, Croatia, much of Serbia, and Transylvania. By 1800 their empire was in full decline, facing the advance of fresh new imperial powers from the north and west, Russia, Britain, and soon a resurgent France.

At the beginning of the nineteenth century, the politics of Western diplomacy and trade was becoming as important and almost as violent a force in the affairs of the region as Christian unity and disunity, or interfaith rivalries. As the two dominant Eastern empires, Ottoman Turkey and Qajar (Kajar) dynasty Persia, declined, three Western empires, Russia, Britain, and France opened what has been aptly described as "a battle of wits and espionage" for control of the Middle East and Central Asia.[43] It was not yet fueled by greed for oil; that came a century and a half later.

What the Western powers wanted was land and commerce, and the resulting tangle of wars between the five empires — three Christian and two Muslim — shook Asia not only in the Middle East but all around its periphery from the Crimea and Egypt to Afghanistan and India with even greater effect than the gentler competitive efforts of their citizens from rival segments of Christendom to reach the hearts and minds of the region's people.

This was the situation when the pioneers of the American Board came to Turkey in 1820, fifteen years before their counterparts in Persia opened work in Urmia. Unlike Persia, where Christians were very few and almost all of them were Nestorian, about one-third of the population of Turkey in Asia was Christian, and the Nestorians were one of the smallest and most isolated of the Christian enclaves in the empire. Each of the seven different Christian communities in the Ottoman Empire was a "nation within the nation"; their members were not Turkish citizens but wards of the Turkish Empire. Each church — Greek Orthodox, Armenian, Nestorian, Jacobite (Antiochene Orthodox), and Catholic Uniate (Maronite, Armenian, and Antiochene or "Greek") — jealously preserved its own identity, believing that to be its only hope of survival in the vast sea of Islam. It was a pattern even older than Islam: semi-autonomous, socially disadvantaged, and politically powerless non-Muslim religious ghettoes that were a throwback to the *millets* (or *melets*) of the Sassanid dynasty in fifth-century Zoroastrian Persia.[44]

The largest of the Christian communities in Asian Turkey was Armenian Orthodox, sometimes called Gregorian, and often described as Monophysite.[45] The second largest group was Greek Orthodox, found in Asia mostly along the coast of Asia Minor. The others were much smaller. The ancient Antiochene Orthodox community (Jacobite) was placed by the Ottoman Empire under the authority of the Armenian Orthodox patriarch of Constantinople, and its church was centered in Syria, which had been ruled by Turkey since the sixteenth century.[46] The non-Roman Nestorians have been described above. Four other Christian groups had established relations with Rome as uniate churches recognizing the authority of the pope: Maronites, Antiochene Rite Catholics,[47] Chaldaean Rite Catholics or Nestorian/Assyrian Catholics, and Armenian Rite Catholics.[48] Each, usually, had its own patriarch.

When the first Protestant missionaries arrived, they found that almost four centuries before, shortly after the Turks captured Constantinople in 1453, only two of these Christian patriarchs, the Greek and Armenian Orthodox, had been given legal status as the political heads of recognized religious minorities or "nations."[49] The Greek patriarch had pride of location in the imperial capital, Constantinople, and the higher title, "Ecumenical Patriarch." But in Asia the Armenian patriarch was the more powerful, not only as patriarch of the largest ethnic religious minority in the empire's huge Asian territories, but because for the first decades of the century all the other heads of non-Muslim, non-Greek Orthodox minorities were placed by Turkish law under his authority and could legally approach the government only through him. Not until 1831 were the Armenian Catholics given political status, and in 1844 the Antiochene Catholic. As late as 1848 the patriarchs of the Nestorians were still seeking recognition.[50] It was therefore to a legally unrecognized patriarch, Mar Shimon of Kudshannis[51] in the outermost mountains of eastern Turkey, that the independent Nestorians of Persian Urmia owed allegiance, as we have described earlier, though two-thirds of his Nestorian followers were in Turkey, and only one-third in Persia.[52]

An estimate in 1858 put the population of Turkey in Asia (Asia Minor, Syria, Palestine, Iraq, and Kurdistan) at 15 million, of which some 12 million were Muslim and 3.5 million were Christian. Of the Christians, 2 million were Armenian Orthodox, 1 million were Greek Orthodox, 260,000 Roman Catholic (Maronite and two Uniate churches), 240,000 Antiochene Orthodox, 60,000 independent Nestorian, and 2,000 Protestant.[53]

Armenian Orthodox (Gregorian)	2 million
Greek Orthodox	1 million
Antiochene Orthodox (Jacobite)	240,000
Independent Nestorian (Kurdistan)	60,000
Maronite	180,000
Uniate Nestorian (RC Chaldaeans)	40,000
Uniate Antiochene (RC Jacobites)	40,000 to 50,000

The three Western empires, Russia, Great Britain, and France, challenged declining Turkey in the nineteenth century, but were divided in their loyalties and relationship to these Christian communities. Russia, greatly sympathizing with the Greek Orthodox church, fought successfully on the side of Greek independence in the Greco-Turkish war of 1821–1831.[54] Britain intervened diplomatically but vigorously to protect the rights of the Nestorians and Armenians. France, recovering from the revolution and Waterloo, protected the interests of Roman Catholic missions. The American mission, from its beginnings in 1820 at Smyrna, felt more kinship with the Nestorians, and sought friendly relations with the Armenians.[55]

The relationship of the Christian missions to these long repressed and isolated Eastern churches developed in much the same pattern as on the Persian side of the border, but with one great difference. In Persia independent Nestorians were the dominant Christian minority whereas in Turkey they were very nearly the smallest, the most isolated and least powerful politically. At first the Eastern churches, with the exception of those related to Rome, and to a lesser extent the Greek Orthodox,[56] welcomed the coming of the Protestants, and the Protestant missions in turn came with the announced intention of honoring the ecclesiastical integrity of the ancient churches, which they hoped to revitalize.[57] Friction, however, soon developed, sometimes between missionaries and the hierarchy, and sometimes between the hierarchy and reform-minded elements in their own churches who had been stimulated by contacts with the missions.[58] Perhaps inevitably, a third step followed: withdrawal of approval by the patriarchal hierarchies of the Eastern churches, resentful of criticism of their traditions and fearful of loss of government recognition of their ancient ethnic religious rights, which finally forced the separation of the Protestants from the ancient churches.

The first regularly formed Protestant congregation in the Middle East in Asia was established for converted Nestorians at Diarbekir in Turkish Kurdistan in 1855 with 158 members.[59] An independent presbytery was organized in 1862.[60] The American Board went to considerable pains to justify so quick a reversal of their original ancillary and non-separatist policy after only twenty years of mission in the Middle East.[61] It broke apart the Protestants' two major missionary fellowships there, putting Anglicans and American Episcopalians in the difficult position of defending patriarchal persecution of the dissidents, and American Congregationalists in the equally difficult position of defending schism. George P. Badger, a Tractarian Anglican, was so openly hostile as to try to prevent the Muslim Sultan from extending to the reformers the hard-won rights of freedom of religion granted to Catholics and the Orthodox in Turkey.[62]

The Armenians

Among the oldest organized Christian communities in the world are the Armenians. A very ancient Indo-European people, they have been Christians ever since at least the fourth century, and probably before. Tradition claims as their founders the apostles Thaddaeus and Bartholomew. But their proudest claim is that they gave to the world the first authenticated Christian king in history, Tiridates (Trdat) III. The great Parthian missionary Gregory the Illuminator, while still only a lay evangelist, converted the Armenian king in 301. That is an earlier conversion than that of the Roman Constantine's (313), and is more credibly documented than the debatable conversion of Edessa's King Abgar (about 200).[63]

Recognizing the authority of the Scriptures, even before they had produced a written translation of the Bible into their own language in 433, the Armenians had appointed an order of translators to transmit orally to the worshipers in their own language the Greek or Syriac readings in the services.[64] By this time Armenians were spread widely from their home base between the Black Sea and the Caucasus, and were scattered in large groups across West Asia from Constantinople in Europe to the Turkish border with Persia and beyond. At the time of the great church divisions of fifth-century Christianity, when Nestorians in Syria and Persia, and Copts in Egypt, and even the Greek Orthodox and the Roman Catholics began to drift apart, the Armenians were too busy fighting for their lives against their many enemies to pay much attention to the great Council of Chalcedon, which has ever since defined Orthodox, Catholic Christian doctrine for the West. Like the Copts in Egypt and the Jacobites in Lebanon, the Armenians chose a Monophysite flavor for their Orthodoxy. The difference centered about the Monophysite insistence on the "one, united nature" of the person of Jesus Christ in the relationship of the divine to the human in his incarnation. Chalcedon settled the issue for the West: Christ is one *person* with "two *natures*, divine and human, different yet united," "indissoluble, yet without confusion."[65] The Armenians developed a mild compromise. As one of their eleventh-century writers put it: "if 'One Nature' is said for the indissoluble and indivisible union, and not for the confusion, and 'Two Natures' is said as being unconfused, immutable and indivisible, both are within the bounds of orthodoxy."[66]

Never did Armenia succeed in becoming a united, completely independent nation.[67] Instead, since the seventh century, the Armenian churches battled constantly and bravely for their theological ecclesiastical and ethnic independence against Persian Zoroastrians, Greek Orthodox, Roman Catholics, and finally in what must have seemed to be a final, doomed clash against the combined oppressions of Arabic and Turkish Islam.[68] But after twelve hundred years of struggle against all odds, another encounter changed Armenian history in ways that were, paradoxically, both bruising and liberating. This was the arrival in the Muslim "Middle East" of American Protestants.

The first Protestant mission to the Armenians was opened at Constantinople by the American Board of Commissioners for Foreign Missions in 1831. William Goodell, its pioneer, moved the mission into its first step toward a difficult separation from the Armenian patriarchate. In 1836 he began to hold public Protestant worship services in the capital. Hitherto the Protestants had held Bible studies in their homes. That same year the group of twelve Armenian Christians who were most closely associated with the missionaries ("evangelical" Armenians, as they began to be called) organized themselves into a "Union of the Pious."[69]

Alarmed at the threat of loss of control over the Armenian community, forces in the hierarchy at Constantinople[70] attempted to withdraw Armenians from missionary influence. But when the movement kept growing to number about five hundred "evangelicals" by 1839,[71] the frustrated antireform faction overreacted. They turned to persecution.[72] Even the patriarch Stepan protested the resort to violence. He was called "Stepan the Dove" because of his gentleness toward all, high or low, and for the zealots his approach was too passive. They forced him from office for being too kind to Protestants. Under his fanatical successor, Hagopos, the first years of persecution of the reformers by the hierarchy began.[73] National and ecclesiastical politics had triumphed. In fact, though, it must be said that there was politics at work on both sides. On the reformers' side the politics was international. In different ways Christian Russia, Britain, and France sometimes directly, sometimes indirectly, brought pressure to bear on the Turkish government for religious freedom for all Christians.

Russia did it by territorial expansion and annexation. Ever since the beginning of the century the Russians had been moving across Turkey's eastern border. By 1829 their protectorate had become outright annexation. The consequences for the Armenian community were immense. The patriarchate of Constantinople remained completely under Turkish control; but holy Echmiadzin, on the ancient patriarchal seat, was a thousand formidable miles away to the east and had been absorbed, along with the rest of eastern Armenia, as a protectorate of expanding Russia, taking at least a third of all the Armenians in Asia beyond the control of interference from Constantinople whether by a Muslim government or a Christian patriarchate in Constantinople. The Christian czar north of the Caucasian mountain range, which traditionally separated Russia from Persia and Turkey, was proving himself more powerful than a Turkish sultan or a Persian shah in the small mountain fiefdoms of Armenia, Georgia, and Azerbaijan. Christians in the east, in Armenia and Georgia, rejoiced, but were wise to be apprehensive.[74]

In the west, too, the situation improved temporarily for the Armenians. The persecution of 1839–1840 in Turkey abruptly ceased with the death of the Sultan Mahmud and the recall of the gentle Stepan to the patriarchate. But in 1843 the public execution of a young Armenian accused of apostasy from Islam in Constantinople in 1843 was a premonition of trouble to come. Conversion by a Muslim was legally punishable by death. But so strongly did the British ambassador, Lord Canning, protest the execution of a Christian convert that in 1844, supported by his French and German colleagues, he wrung from the sultan a written decree of freedom of religion for all subjects of the empire of "whatever religion or sect."[75] The relief was short-lived. Two years later, in 1846, a far more serious blow than Muslim violence fell upon the Protestants: excommunication. The patriarchate was in turmoil. Stepan, the friendly patriarch, was driven by intrigue from his position, recalled, but within a year resigned again, and after a troubled interlude, a fiercely antireformist, Bishop Matthew (Matteos Choohajian) became patriarch — all between 1839 and 1844.[76] The new patriarch discovered that there were eight thousand evangelical "prodigals" on record in Constantinople,[77] and beginning in January 1846, in the next six months he launched three blistering anathemas of excommunication against those who had joined the dissidents — "deceivers and blasphemers against the Church, and followers of the corrupt new sect":

whoever has [such] a son...or a brother, or a partner...and gives him bread, or assists him in making money, or has intercourse with him as a friend...give[s] bread to Judas...[They] are enemies of the holy faith of Christianity and destroyers of the holy orthodox Church of the Armenians ...Wherefore, their houses and shops also are accursed; and whoever goes to visit them, we shall learn, and make them public to the holy Church by terrible anathemas.[78]

The rhetoric was violent but no more devastating than the practical consequences of excommunication. In Muslim Turkey it stripped them of the civil rights that protected members of the government-recognized religious minorities.[79] It was the beginning of a second wave of persecution and violence.

In the next few years of imprisonment and kidnappings that followed, about half of those who had left the Old Church to turn Protestant were forced to recant.[80] Most painful was the fact that the harassers and persecutors were fellow Christians in the Old Church, not Muslims. An Armenian historian points to the irony of the situation: "freedom of conscience in religious matters decreed by a Muhammedan Government, was not granted by the Armenian Apostolic Church on grounds that national [Armenian] solidarity would be endangered."[81]

The resentment of the traditionalists against proselytizing and schism was understandable, but the violence was inexcusable. This was the breaking point. The evangelicals, unable in principle to surrender their right to evangelize and reform, came to the reluctant conclusion that unity within the old tradition was becoming impossible and separation inevitable.[82]

The final act of separation was inevitable. On July 1, 1846, at Constantinople "the first native [Protestant] church in Turkey came into being." It recorded forty communicant members; all but three were men. They met in the home of H. G. O. Dwight, but chose as their first pastor Apissoghom Khachadoorian. Besides the charter members the larger evangelical community numbered about a thousand, and three other churches.[83] Other separations quickly followed in several cities of Turkish Asia, including the important port of Trebizond on the Black Sea, Nicomedia (now, under its modern name of Izmit), and Adabazar.[84]

A year later (1847), over Patriarch Matteo's protests, and encouraged by a sympathetic British embassy, the Sultanate granted the seceders the religious rights of a recognized minority, a Protestant *millet* (or *melet*), with freedom of belief and worship.[85] It called itself the Armenian Evangelical Church though the official name given it by the government was the Protestant Church. When sporadic persecution of the reformers continued, the government in 1850 acceded to their request for a more specific edict, confirming the full civil rights not only of Armenian Protestants but of all Protestants in Turkey. It ordered an end to religious persecution of any kind against them,[86] and Lord Stratford, the

British ambassador, declared with emotion that this marked "the first time in Turkey" that the pure gospel was to be freed from the shackles of oppression and superstition.[87]

Armenian Protestants in Turkey in 1850 numbered only five native pastors and one native preacher, eight churches (two of them in Constantinople), a membership of about 240, with perhaps 1,000 adherents all told, and 38 American missionaries.[88] Three years later, a worldwide survey of Protestant missions reported that the number of adherents had doubled, to 2,012 (345 in Constantinople), churches had almost doubled to 15 (3 in Constantinople). One of the most encouraging features of the growth was that the number of Armenian Protestant pastors had increased from 5 to 17, with 40 native assistant preachers.[89] By 1855 there were 54 missionaries (including 3 single women), 13 Armenian pastors and preachers, and 64 Armenian lay assistants. There were 23 Armenian Protestant churches, the largest of which was not in Constantinople on the European side of the empire but in Syria at Aintab, north of Aleppo. More than a thousand worshipers crowded into it on a Sunday.[90]

The victory of the evangelical Armenians in securing not just for themselves but for all minorities the right of religious freedom was a remarkable achievement indeed, but it must not be overstated. The loss of only two thousand "restless dissidents" was a comparatively small setback to the continuing overwhelming strength of Old Armenian Orthodoxy. The Old Church had outlasted twelve hundred years of wars and persecutions. It still had more than a million members. It would survive. But the rest of the century was not kind to the Old Church. Disputes between its two great centers of Armenian Orthodoxy, Echmiadzin in the Persian east and Constantinople (Istanbul) in Turkey's European capital, kept the church in divisive internal turmoil. Roman Catholic missions were intruding with increasing strength from Europe. Russia was chipping away from Ottoman Turkey significant Armenian centers in the east.

Most inescapable of all these threatening shadows was the never benevolent, absolute power to intervene in church affairs of a despotic Muslim Empire over its religious minorities. Against this there was no appeal. Not until the adoption in 1860 of a conciliar-centered constitution under the ecclesiastical authority of the patriarch did the church begin to effect its own necessary administrative reforms.[91] Before another half century had scarcely passed, as we shall see, "absolute power" would bring "absolute corruption," and the victims would be the Armenians.

The Maronites

Third largest of the Christian minorities in the Ottoman Empire, after the Greek and Armenian Orthodox, were the Maronites. They were an ancient Christian community tracing back to the eighth century when they had settled in the mountains of Lebanon. Their distinguishing theological divergence from Orthodoxy was their belief that though the incarnate Jesus was a union of two natures, divine and human, his will — that is, his center of volition — remained single and focused.[92] In the eleventh century the Maronites of the Lebanon mountains gladly joined the Crusaders as Christian allies, and temporarily may have abandoned or deemphasized their doctrinal deviation, but if so, their acceptance of papal supremacy was short-lived.[93] Not until the thirteenth century did Rome begin actively to negotiate ecclesiastical relations with the sect. Negotiations continued very sporadically for another three hundred years until, after a council in 1596, the Maronite patriarch submitted to Rome, accepting changes in liturgy and doctrine, but insisting on retention of the Syriac rite and language, which was granted. The Maronites are the oldest of the Uniate churches of Eastern Christianity.[94]

Turkish Islam, under pressure from Britain and France, had approved a measure of religious freedom for Christians of all the major communities in Lebanon — Greek Orthodox, Armenian Orthodox, Catholic Uniate, and Protestant — but had not reckoned on a long-smoldering interfaith conflict peculiar to the two major religious groups of the Lebanese mountains, the Catholic Maronites and the Druzes. Both were ancient, isolated sectarian movements, and had long been considered heretical — the Maronites by Catholic and Orthodox Christianity, and the Druzes by orthodox Islam. The Maronites had recently made peace with Rome, but the Druzes still awaited the return of their eleventh-century messiah, al-Hakim, the strangely mystic ruler of Fatimid Egypt, who had died or mysteriously disappeared in A.D. 1021.[95]

The first half of the nineteenth century, 1808 to 1860, saw increasing friction between Lebanese Maronites and the sectarian Islamic Druzes. The two communities had been on reasonably friendly terms until two Lebanese Druze princes angered the Druzes by converting to Roman Catholic Christianity in 1756. The Maronites of the northern mountain region began to outnumber the Druzes of southern Lebanon, while Bashir Shihabi II, prince of Lebanon intermittently from 1788 to 1842, broke with the Druze aristocracy in 1819–1820, destroyed the feudal power of the Druze aristocracy, and seized power for himself. He was born a Maronite, but married a Druze, and pragmatically posed sometimes as Christian and sometimes as Muslim. He quickly became the overpowering figure of the first half of the nineteenth century in Lebanon, playing Egypt against Turkey, and France against them both.[96]

Whatever his real convictions may have been, the wily prince followed a policy often considered characteristic of the Druzes by their enemies, namely to hide in whatever religion was dominant at the moment: "to be a Christian among Christians, a Muslim among Muslims, and a Druze among the Druzes."[97] In 1832 Egypt took Lebanon from the Turks, controlling it for eight years, during which Bashir Shihabi II exploited their presence to break the power of the Druze aristocracy. For a while, in this period of nominal Egyptian rule and near autonomy in Lebanon, the Maronite patriarch, supported politically by Bashir, was close to being the "temporal and spiritual pope in Mt. Lebanon."[98] But Egypt, though more than a match for Ottoman Turkey, could not stand against the power of expanding European influence. In 1840 a consortium of the great Western powers drove the Egyptians out of Syria (which then included Lebanon) and restored the region to Turkish rule.

The result, however, was not peace but more war. In 1842 the Druze rebelled unsuccessfully against the Turkish empire and were suppressed. The Maronites, on the other hand, prospered. They were richer, better educated, and more numerous. By 1850 they outnumbered Lebanon's Druze population 160,000 to 27,000, and skillfully used the support of post-Napoleonic and still Catholic France as their trump card in negotiations with both the Druzes and Constantinople.[99] Turkey, alarmed at the rise of violence between the two religious communities, fearful of losing control, and prodded by the European powers, issued an edict of religious freedom, unusually liberal in a Muslim empire. It not only guaranteed Christians full religious liberty, but contained a clause that favored the small Protestant movement by, in effect, abolishing the civil power of the Christian patriarchs of the older churches.[100] As a result, neither the major Christian communities nor the Druzes were satisfied, and a full-fledged civil war among the rival religions erupted in 1860, culminating in horrible massacres of Christians in Lebanon and Damascus.

Protestants, as the weakest of the minorities, were the most vulnerable. They complained that the Maronites, though Christians, were more hostile than the non-Christian Druzes, but all suffered. It was estimated that eleven thousand Christians were massacred, another four thousand "perished of destitution," and three thousand Christian homes had been destroyed.[101] The ultimate winners were the Maronites. The rise of French influence in Asia Minor after the Crimean War favored the Catholic-connected Maronites and (to anticipate) eventually established Maronite supremacy in Lebanon for most of the next hundred years.[102]

Protestants in Syria

The early work of the Protestants in the Ottoman Empire, notably, that of ABCFM,[103] was based in the area around Constantinople, in Europe, which is beyond the scope of this volume. But mention must also be made of Protestant missions in Turkish Asia, Syria, which were centered after 1823 in what is now Lebanon at Beirut.[104] Within five years, assisted by an Armenian bishop and a highly literate Armenian priest, the ABCFM had established schools with about seven hundred pupils in the Beirut area, and had blazed a trail for women's rights by opening the first girls' school in all that part of the fiercely Muslim Middle East.[105]

On January 2, 1827, the bishop, Dionysius Garabed, and the priest, Gregory Wortabet (or Wartabed), were "solemnly received" into the communion and fellowship of the mission church, together with their wives, and a European Roman Catholic "lady of distinction."[106] The missionaries realized the significance of the event, marking, as it did, an ecclesiastical break between the mission and the Eastern churches, but they may not have fully anticipated the extent of its consequences.

The response was swift and furious. Within two weeks the Maronite patriarch excommunicated all who associated with the Protestants and flung an anathema at the missionaries.[107] Soon thereafter occurred an event that accelerated the chasm opening up between the ancient churches and the Americans who had arrived with the determination not to destroy the Eastern churches but to revitalize them. The death of their first martyr at the hands of Christians, not Muslims, quickly cooled the good intentions. Asad es Shidiak (1797–1830), an honors graduate from the Roman Catholic Maronite "college" in the mountains of Lebanon, was entrusted by the Maronite patriarch with the task of preparing an answer to Protestant charges against Catholic doctrines. His investigations required careful reading of the Scriptures which, to his own surprise, instead of refuting the charges, led him to join the Protestants. The angry patriarch lured him back to the convent and had him imprisoned, beaten, and chained. He died in prison three years later — from fever, said the Maronites, from starvation and mistreatment according to the Protestants.[108]

From that time on, so far did the breach continue to widen between the Protestants and the older churches that at the request of the Arab converts themselves, the Arab Christians in Beirut in 1848 organized an indigenous Protestant church, separate from the mission. It had sixteen native members (four Armenians, four Maronites, four uniate Catholic Greeks, three Druzes, and one Jacobite Syrian).[109] The explosive controversies between the powerful Maronites and the little community of Protestants inevitably froze the early attempts of the Protestants to keep open the Christian schools mentioned above. Enrollment dropped sharply and in 1833 the girls' school was suspended temporarily.[110] But by 1860, the American mission was able to report a network of free elementary schools enrolling 1,020 students (743 boys, 277 girls) including the girls' school relocated to Mt. Lebanon, two high schools, and a seminary, or college, founded in 1846. It was a small beginning, but out of it was to grow one of the most impressive contributions of American Protantism to the Middle East, a famous university, the American University of Beirut, and an equally significant advance in the education of women, Beirut College for Women.[111]

Not so impressive was the growth of the church in Syria. Despite a handful of able indigenous leaders who soon outnumbered the ten American missionaries, an estimate of the religions of Syria (Lebanon) in 1860 failed even to mention the Protestants. Their numbers were too small to count. Out of a total population in Syria/Lebanon of 1.5 million there were: 750,000 Sunni Muslims, 200,000 Maronites, 200,000 Nusairiyeh (a secret sect, akin to the Druzes, perhaps the survivors of ninth-century Carmathians), 150,000 Greek Orthodox, 80,000 Shi'ite (Metawileh) Muslims, 50,000 Greek Catholic, 50,000 Druzes, and 30,000 Jews.[112]

NOTES

1. R. W. Southern, *Western Views of Islam in the Middle Ages* (Cambridge, Mass.: Harvard University Press, 1962), quoting Thomas Gascoigne, *Loci e Libro Veritatum* (Oxford: Clarendon Press, 1881).

2. Justin Perkins, *Historical Sketch of the Mission to the Nestorians; and of the Assyrian Mission by Thomas Laurie* (New York: John A. Gray, 1862).

3. See above chap. 9. Here, as in volume 1, space and focus regrettably limit proper attention to the Greek and Russian churches of West Asia, which arguably belong more to the history of Western Christianity than to Asia. But some attention must begin to be given to Armenian Christianity, Eastern in origin and independent in theology, and cut off from its Western connections by the fall of Constantinople to the Turks in 1453.

4. Perkins, *Historical Sketch of the Mission to the Nestorians*, 9; and Asahel Grant's account written in 1841, *The Nestorians; or the Lost Tribes* (New York: Harper & Brothers, 1841), 17. Cf. Tracy, *History of the American Missions to the Heathen*, 262; and Rufus Anderson, *History of the Missions of the American Board of Commissioners for Foreign Missions to the Oriental Churches*, 2 vols. (Boston: Congregational Publishing Society, 1872) [hereafter *Missions to the Oriental Churches*], 1:172–173. On Grant's pioneering medical mission, see Rufus Anderson, *Missions to the Oriental Churches*, 2:175–195; John Elder, *History of the American Presbyterian Mission to Iran (1834–1960)* (Teheran: Literature Committee of the Church Council of Iran, 1960), 7, 19ff.

5. Richter, *A History of Protestant Missions in the Near East*, 92.

6. In Wilberforce, *Journal and Letters of Henry Martyn*, entry for May 17, 1806, 330. Cf. his entry for September 4, 1806, "I can see no fit emblem of my soul, but the burning bush" (*Journal and Letters*, 359); and "For the many that come to Bethlehem there be few that go on to Calvary" (Padwick, *Henry Martyn*, 150); and May 21, 1811, "Suffering the will of God is as necessary a part of spiritual discipline as doing, and much more trying" (George Smith, *Henry Martyn*, 339).

7. An imperfect Persian translation had been begun in Calcutta by Aga Sabat, an Arab Muslim with ten years residence in Persia, and to a lesser extent an Indian Muslim, Mirza Fitrat (or Fitrut). Martyn first helped them, then undertook a complete revision, which he took to Persia and again painstakingly revised (George Smith, *Henry Martyn*, 225–237, 417–438). See also Vivienne Stacey, *Life*

of Henry Martyn (Hyderabad: Henry Martyn Institute of Islamic Studies, 1980), 54–70.

8. George Smith, *Henry Martyn*, 483–491. Smith includes a translation of Shah Fateh Ali Khan's letter of acceptance (486f.). Pope Pius VII, however, prohibited its use by Catholics, warning that "the Holy Scriptures in the vulgar tongue, [produce] more injury than good" (491).

9. See Eli Smith, *Researches of the Rev. E. Smith and Rev. H. G. O. Dwight in Armenia with a Visit to the Nestorian and Chaldaean Christians of Oormiah and Salmas,* 2 vols. (Boston: Crocker and Brewster, 1833). Vol. 1 describes the Armenians; 2:201–265, the Nestorians; and thereafter again the Armenians.

10. On the American mission to Iran, Rufus Anderson, *Missions to the Oriental Churches*; Elder, *History of the American Presbyterian Mission to Iran*; and in German, Peter Kawerau, *Amerika und die orientalischen Kirchen: Ursprung und Anfang der amerikanischen Mission unter den Nationalkirchen Westasiens* (Berlin: W. de Gruyter, 1958). See also Richter, *A History of Protestant Missions in the Near East*.

11. Joseph, *The Nestorians and Their Muslim Neighbors*, 45.

12. Perkins, *Historical Sketch of the Mission to the Nestorians*, 8, 58–59.

13. Justin Perkins, *Missionary Life in Persia* (Boston: American Tract Society, 1961), 38–39. William R. Stocking, who arrived in 1837 and was influential in the first revival in Urmia (1846), was of the opinion that "spiritual death, rather than theological error, was the calamity of the Nestorians." Rufus Anderson, *Missions to the Oriental Churches*, 1:182, 197; and see Elder, *History of the American Presbyterian Mission to Iran*, 8–10.

14. Richter, *A History of Protestant Missions in the Near East*, 295; Eli Smith, *Researches of the Rev. E. Smith and Rev. H. G. O. Dwight in Armenia*, 2:298ff.; see also Perkins, *Historical Sketch of the Mission to the Nestorians*, 9; and Grant, *Nestorians*, 17.

15. Perkins, *Historical Sketch of the Mission to the Nestorians*, 8–9, 26.

16. Perkins, *Missionary Life in Persia*, 42–44; Perkins, *Historical Sketch of the Mission to the Nestorians*, 5, 8–10; Elder, *History of the American Presbyterian Mission to Iran*, 10–13; Rufus Anderson, *Missions to the Oriental Churches*, 1:170–173, 178–179, 332–333; 2:148, 321–322.

17. Perkins, *Missionary Life in Persia*, 42.

18. So wrote Samuel Rhea in 1851. Dwight W. Marsh, *The Tennesseean of Koordistan and Persia, Being Scenes and Incidents from the Life of Samuel Audley Rhea* (Philadelphia: Presbyterian Board of Publication, 1869), 55.

19. The patriarch's full title was Abraham Mar Shimon XIX (1825–1861), succeeding Nonah Mar Shimon XVIII (1785–1825). The patriarchal village was Kudshanes (Qudshanis, Kochanis, etc.). See Malech's uneven *History of the Syrian Nation*, and the better documented Donald Attwater, *Christian Churches of the East*, 2:172–173; and Aubrey A. Vine, *The Nestorian Churches*, 176.

20. Tracy, *History of the American Missions to the Heathen*, 262.

21. Newcomb, *A Cyclopedia of Missions*, 560–561. For four years Mar Shimon remained in Mosul, gradually distancing himself from the evangelical American missionaries there. In 1847 he moved to Urmia in Persia for two years, but when he there began to denounce the growing American mission in Persia, his own brothers, Deacon Isaac and Deacon Dunka, remonstrated with him, and in 1849, his power greatly diminished, he crossed the Turkish border back to his initial residence at Kudhannis.

22. Perkins, *Historical Sketch of the Mission to the Nestorians,* 5; Eli Smith, *Researches of the Rev. E. Smith and Rev. H. G. O. Dwight in Armenia,* 2:218–219. Estimates about the number of Nestorians in West Asia at the time vary widely: perhaps between 100,000 and 150,000 in an area from Urmia west about three hundred miles, and then south another three hundred miles along the Tigris River valley to Mosul, Arbela, and Kirkuk in modern Iraq (see Rufus Anderson, *Missions to the Oriental Churches,* 1:172–175; cf. Richter, *A History of Protestant Missions in the Near East,* 292ff.).

23. The Nestorian (Assyrian) patriarch was Mar Shimon; his wife was named Helena. Perkins, *Historical Sketch of the Mission to the Nestorians,* 10, See also Rufus Anderson, *Missions to the Oriental Churches,* 1:172; and Elder, *History of the American Presbyterian Mission to Iran,* 8. Estimates of the rate of literacy among the Nestorians varies as widely as of the total number of Nestorians. Perkins mentions the sole literate woman (*Historical Sketch of the Mission to the Nestorians,* 11); Rufus Anderson, *Missions to the Oriental Churches,* 1:172, writes of "about 40 intelligent Nestorians"; Richter's figure is not more than 20 or 30 men (*A History of Protestant Missions in the Near East,* 8), and Elder repeats Anderson's "about 40 men" (*History of the American Presbyterian Mission to Iran,* 1:8).

24. The most thorough study of the American missionaries' communication breakthrough from the classical to the colloquial Aramaic in Urmia is H. L. Murre-van den Berg, "From a Spoken to a Written Language: The Introduction and Development of Literary Urmia Aramaic in the Nineteenth Century" (PhD diss., University of Leiden, 1964).

25. Rufus Anderson, *Missions to the Oriental Churches,* 1:178. On the varieties of the vernacular, see Murre-van den Berg, "From a Spoken to a Written Language," 74–78, 321ff.

26. Murre-van den Berg, "From a Spoken to a Written Language," 79–83; Rufus Anderson, *Missions to the Oriental Churches,* 1:178

27. Rufus Anderson, *Missions to the Oriental Churches,* 1:173, 178, 182–183.

28. Murre-van den Berg, "From a Spoken to a Written Language," 83–85.

29. Murre-van den Berg, "From a Spoken to a Written Language," 83–85. On the date of completion of the New Testament translation, see Rufus Anderson, *Missions to the Oriental Churches,* 1:361.

30. See "Priest Yohannon," in Justin Perkins, *Nestorian Biography: Being Sketches of Pious Nestorians* (Boston: Massachusetts Sabbath School Society, 1857), 1–21.

31. Perkins, *Missionary Life in Persia,* 43; Perkins, *Historical Sketch of the Mission to the Nestorians,* 10.

32. On Asahel Grant, M.D., see Rufus Anderson, *Missions to the Oriental Churches,* 1:176, 186–195, 198ff., 206ff., 221. See Grant's own account of his travels, evangelism, and pioneering medical work in *The Nestorians,* 1–117. After four years in Urmia (1835–1839), he was assigned to the Nestorians across the Turkish/Persia border in Mosul, especially in the wild Kurdistan mountains north of that city.

33. Rufus Anderson, *Missions to the Oriental Churches,* 1:179. On Grant's pioneering medical mission, see Rufus Anderson, *Missions to the Oriental Churches,* 1:175–195; Elder, *History of the American Presbyterian Mission to Iran,* 7, 19ff.

34. Rufus Anderson, *Missions to the Oriental Churches,* 1:138–185.

35. Elder, *History of the American Presbyterian Mission to Iran*, 13–17; Rufus Anderson, *Missions to the Oriental Churches*, 1:317–318, 327, 347–348; 2:381–383.

36. Any who studied under John Mackay of Princeton will recognize the debt owed him in the phrasing of this sentence.

37. On the revivals, see Perkins, *Missionary Life in Persia*, 118–122, 129–136, 144–182. On the prominent role of women converts, see also Fidelia Fiske, "Sarah, Daughter of Priest Eshoo," "Blind Martha," and "Hoimer, the Wife of Naser," in Perkins, *Nestorian Biography*, 25–40, 43–51, 153–160.

38. The chief advocate of the Episcopal mission on the missionary side was Horatio Southgate, who had withdrawn from Andover Newton Seminary to leave the Congregationalists and turn Episcopal. On the Episcopal mission and its policies, see Horatio Southgate, *Narrative of a Visit to the Syrian Jacobite Church of Mesopotamia and the Character and Prospects of the Eastern Churches* (New York: Dana, 1856), 14–15, 19, 179ff., 198–199, 204–207, 228–231. See also P. E. Shaw, *American Contacts with the Eastern Churches 1820–1870* (Chicago: American Society of Church History, 1937), 35–70; and George Percy Badger, *The Nestorians and Their Rituals*, 2 vols. (London: John Masters, 1852), 1:xv, 6–11, 248, 367–368.

39. Perkins, *Missionary Life in Persia*, 123–125. The patriarch openly preferred the non-"converting" high Anglican mission of "the Pusey-ites" to the revival-minded Americans. His brother, however, Deacon Isaac, repented and participated in the revivals (176–177, 206–207).

40. Rufus Anderson, *Missions to the Oriental Churches*, 1:337ff.

41. Rufus Anderson, *Missions to the Oriental Churches*, 1:338–342.

42. For much the same reasons, the four-volume *EAH* limited its scope to a similar limitation of the term "Asia," xii.

43. Waterfield, *Christians in Persia*, 87n.

44. See vol. 1 of this work, 157, 221. On the *millet* system in the Ottoman Empire, see Benjamin Braude and Bernard Lewis, *Christians and Jews in the Ottoman Empire*, 2 vols. (New York and London: Holmes & Meier Publishers, 1982), 1:141–169, 261–285, 319–333; Avedis K. Sanjian, *Armenian Communities in Syria under Ottoman Dominion* (Cambridge, Mass.: Harvard University Press, 1965), 31–45; and Shaw, *American Contacts with the Eastern Churches.*

45. Armenians today prefer not to be called Monophysite. They have always accepted both the perfect deity of Christ and his perfect humanity, but differ theologically from Eastern Orthodoxy only in objecting to the use of the term "two natures" to the one person, the incarnate Jesus Christ, which, they would say, separates too much the divine and the human in Jesus. See vol. 1 of this work, chap. 12, 248ff.

46. See Joseph, *Muslim-Christian Relations and Inter-Christian Rivalries in the Middle East*, 29.

47. The Antiochene Rite uniate church is often called "Catholic Syrian," and sometimes "Catholic Jacobite." See Attwater, *The Catholic Eastern Churches*, 163–179.

48. Rome established the Armenian uniate patriarchate in 1742, with residence near Beirut; French diplomacy secured its recognition as a *millet* ("nation," or recognized and protected religious minority) in 1830. See Attwater, *Catholic Eastern Churches*, 205–209.

49. The Greek Orthodox patriarch was recognized in 1454 as uniting Eastern Orthodoxy under one head for the first time since the golden years of the Byzantine Empire. The loss of the support of a Christian state was at least partly offset by the advantage of independence from state religious control. The Armenian patriarch was recognized as head of an Armenian *millet* in 1461. See Kemal H. Karpat, "Millets and Nationality," in Braude and Lewis, *Christians and Jews in the Ottoman Empire*, 145–146.

50. Attwater, *The Christian Churches of the East*, and Joseph, *The Nestorians and their Muslim Neighbors*, 34, citing A. Carleton, "The Millet System" (PhD diss., Hartford Theological Seminary, 1936), 95, 137–140. See also Hagop Barsoumian, "The Dual Rule of the Armenian *Amira* Class within the Ottoman Government," in Braude and Lewis, *Christian and Jews in the Ottoman Empire*, 171–184; and Ormanian, *The Church of Armenia*, 77–78.

51. Abraham Mar Shimon XIX (Ormanian, *History of the Syrian Nation*, 315).

52. On the statistical imbalance of Nestorians between Turkey and Persia, see Perkins, *Historical Sketch of the Mission to the Nestorians*, 5. Cf. Richter, *A History of Protestant Missions in the Near East*, 105, 293, who notes that by 1910 Turkish Asia Minor, including Armenia and Kurdistan, had 10 million Muslims and 2.5 million Christians.

53. These figures are adjusted from two sources: Newcomb, *A Cyclopedia of Missions*, 751–752; and — for Uniate Nestorians, Uniate Jacobites, and independent Nestorians — Thomas Laurie in Perkins, *Historical Sketch of the Mission to the Nestorians*, 28, citing *MH*, 1857, 55. But Newcomb lists, 640,000 Roman Catholics total.

54. The Greek War of Independence (1821–1831) freed southern Greece from Turkish Muslim rule, but fairly large Greek Orthodox communities remained in the north and in Asia along the coast of Asia Minor. Most of the Muslim population in southern Greece was resettled to the north.

55. Tracy, *History of the American Missions to the Heathen*, 94, 98–99, 116ff., 130–131. The first missionaries were Pliny Fisk and Levi Parsons, in Smyrna. Mr. and Mrs. William Goodell and Mr. and Mrs. Isaac Bird reached Beirut in 1823, and the next year opened a small school there with six pupils which in eight months had grown to fifty, the small beginning of an educational enterprise that was to become famous throughout the Middle East (Rufus Anderson, *Missions to the Oriental Churches*, 1:40–44). See also Joseph, *Muslim Christian Relations in the Middle East*, 85–86; and Braude and Lewis, *Christians and Jews in the Ottoman Empire*, 1:179–180, 404.

56. See Tracy, *History of the American Missions to the Heathen*, 117–118, 131, 169–170, 202; Isaac Bird, *Bible Work in Bible Lands; or Events in the History of the Syrian Mission* (Philadelphia: Presbyterian Board of Publication, 1872), 137–138; and Richter, *A History of Protestant Missions in the Near East*, 187–192. On relations with the Greek Orthodox, see Rufus Anderson, *Missions to the Oriental Churches*, 2:279–314; and Bird, *Bible Work in Bible Lands*, 142–147.

57. See H. G. O. Dwight, *Christianity Revived in the East, or, A Narrative of the Work of God among the Armenians of Turkey* (New York: Baker and Scribner, 1850), 1–18.

58. On Armenian reform and Protestant missions from the reformers' perspective, see Arpee, *The Armenian Awakening*, 108–197; Rufus Anderson, *Missions to the Eastern Churches*, 90–140; and Dwight, *Christianity Revived in the East*, 23, 29, 35–36, and passim. For balance and critical analysis, see Shaw, *American Contacts*

with the Eastern Churches, 86–94; and Hagop A. Chakmakjian, *Armenian Christology and Evangelization of Islam* (Leiden: E. J. Brill, 1965), 111–135.

59. Elder, *History of the American Presbyterian Mission to Iran*, 22–23; Rufus Anderson, *Missions to the Oriental Churches*, 1:98–101. In Turkey's capital, Constantinople (Istanbul), a Protestant church was established in 1846, but Istanbul is in Europe.

60. Elder, *History of the American Presbyterian Mission to Iran*, 22–23.

61. For example, in 1841 American Protestant Episcopal policy advised respect for the ancient ecclesiastical authorities and avoidance of offensive intrusion within the jurisdiction of our Episcopal brethren, "not keeping aloof from the Eastern churches, but . . . by a wise and active interference in their behalf . . . to save them from schism and ruin" (see Southgate, *Narrative of a Visit to the Syrian Jacobite Church of Mesopotamia*, 14–15, 19). On early American Congregational policy, see Rufus Anderson, *Missions to the Oriental Churches*, 1:viii–x. But most consistently averse to separatist Protestant denominationalism were the Anglicans; see A. J. Maclean and William Henry Browne, *The Catholicos of the East and His People: [The] Eastern Syrian Christians of Kurdistan and Northern Persia (Known also as Nestorians* (London: SPCK, 1892), vii–ix. For a justification of Protestant missions to the Eastern churches, see Richter, *A History of Protestant Missions in the Near East*, 66ff. See also Shaw, *American Contacts with the Eastern Churches*, 22ff., 38ff., 189–195.

62. Badger, *The Nestorians and Their Rituals*, 1:xivf., 6–11; cf. Shaw, *American Contacts with the Eastern Churches*, 94–99.

63. On the tradition of Abgar VIII's Christianity, see vol. 1 of this work, 56ff. On Tiridates III and Gregory the Illuminator, see Ormanian, *The Church of Armenia*, 5–16; and in more popular style, Hagop Nersoyan, *A History of the Armenian Church, with Thirty-Five Stories* (New York: Armenian Church of North America, 1963), 20–43.

64. Ormanian, *The Church of Armenia*, 16, 18; Nersoyan, *A History of the Armenian Church*, 83–88.

65. See vol. 1 of this work, 169–170, 180, 191–192, 198ff.

66. St. Nerses the Gracious, cited by Archbishop Mesrob Ashjian, *Armenian Church Patristic and Other Essays* (New York: The Armenian Prelacy, 1994), 179. See the archbishop's discussion of the Armenians and Chalcedon on 172–181.

67. Even the crusader kingdom of Lesser Armenia in Cilicia in the thirteenth and fourteenth centuries represented only one part of the Armenian community.

68. On the Armenians and the *melet* system, see Ashjian, *Armenian Church Patristic and Other Essays*, 227–251; and Sanjian, *The Armenian Communities in Syria under Ottoman Dominion*, 31–45.

69. Or "Pietistic Union." See Giragos H. Chopourian, *The Armenian Evangelical Reformation: Causes and Effects* (New York: Armenian Missionary Association of America, 1972), 44, 65–72.

70. A subordinate administrative patriarchate for Armenian civil affairs under the Turkish government had been established in the capital in 1461 as a second patriarchate to balance the civil power granted to the Greek Orthodox Patriarch of Constantinople for the Greek community. The traditional patriarchate remained in Echmidzian in Asia Minor (Ormanian, *The Church of Armenia*, 76–77).

71. Arpee, *Armenian Awakening*, 10, 99–100. Cf. Dwight, *Christianity Revived*, 73.

72. Historians on both sides, Old Church (Gregorian) and reformers (Evangelicals) debate the severity of the "persecution." Chopourian, *Armenian Evangelical Reformation*, 92–93) evenhandedly summarizes the debate. He cites for Old Church arguments, Avedis Berberian, *History of Armenians* (in Armenian, 1871); Puzant Yeghiayan, *The Separation of the Armenian Catholic and Evangelical Denominations* (in Armenian, 1971); and Horatio Southgate, an early ABCFM missionary who became an Episcopalian and the American Episcopal bishop in Constantinople, *State of Christianity in Turkey* (1856). But he concludes, agreeing with Archbishop Maghak'ia Ormanian, *The Church of Armenia* (1955) and with the Protestant missionaries, that the persecution was more than harassment.

73. Chopourian, *The Armenian Evangelical Reformation*, 1, 43–45, 62, 66–75, 99. Cf. Arpee, *The Armenian Awakening*, 100ff.; Dwight, *Christianity Revived*, 77ff.; and Ormanian, *The Church of Armenia*, 84–94.

74. On Russian policy in the Middle East as it affected the churches, see Arpee, *History of Armenian Christianity*, 293–294; and Richter, *A History of Protestant Missions in the Near East*, 153–155. Russia had annexed Transcaucasia, including the patriarchal seat of Echmiadzin in 1800, and announced a protectorate over the Armenians. Two wars (Russo-Turkish in 1828–1829 and Crimea against England and France in 1853–1856) strengthened her control in the east. But in 1880, as we shall see, a Russianizing policy dictated from Moscow blotted out all rights of separate identity for the Armenians.

75. Chopourian, *Armenian Evangelical Reformation*, 113–114.

76. On the turbulence in the patriarchate at Constantinople, see the quick survey and chronology in Chopourian, *Armenian Evangelical Reformation*, 62–63, 156.

77. Chopourian, *Armenian Evangelical Reformation*, 78.

78. The full text of the second anathema, which includes this portion, is given in Dwight, *Christianity Revived in the East*, app. B, 170–171; and in Chopourian, *Armenian Evangelical Reformation*, 147. For the background events of the three anathemas, see Dwight, *Christianity Revived in the East*, 135–136, and Chopourian, *Armenian Evangelical Reformation*, 87ff.

79. Dwight, *Christianity Revived*, 135ff. Cf. Chopourian, *Armenian Evangelical Reformation*, 113.

80. Dwight, *Christianity Revived*, 144–154. Cf. Shaw, *American Contacts with the Eastern Churches*, 87. Protestant schools were closed, and missionary literature was confiscated.

81. Chopourian, *Armenian Evangelical Reformation*, 114. Chopourian elsewhere (77) cites a list of eight reasons suggested by Kevork-Mesrob (*History of the Nestorian Church* [1914], 518–519) for the rise of persecution by the hierarchy: the Armenian-Catholic conflict, fanatical zeal, the Amiras, the similar actions by the Greek Orthodox, encouragement by the sultanate, anger at European interference, extreme positions of some missionaries and reformers, and "the dark ignorance" of most of the Armenian community. Chopourian adds as two more fundamental reasons the increasing strength of the Protestants and a growing realization of basic theological differences between traditionalists and reformers (Chopourian, *Armenian Evangelical Reformation*, 77 n. 1).

82. Arpee, *The Armenian Awakening*, 163–171. A second, more detailed decree of toleration was issued in 1856. See Rufus Anderson, *Missions to the Oriental Churches*, 2:31–42, for the full text.

83. Dwight, *Christianity Revived*, 256; Chopourian, *Armenian Evangelical Reformation*, 91–92.

84. Arpee, *The Armenian Awakening*, 136–137.

85. This 1847 Protestant *millet* was the second separated from the jurisdiction of the Armenian Patriarch. The first was Catholic in 1830. On the *millet* system in the Ottoman Empire, see Ashjian, *Armenian Church Patristic and Other Essays*, 227–251; and Shaw, *American Contacts with the Eastern Churches*, 89–90. Chopourian, *Armenian Evangelical Reformation*, 117–123, deals with great sensitivity on the positive and negative consequences of the separation.

86. The full text is given by Rufus Anderson, *Missions to the Oriental Churches*, 2:4–7.

87. Rufus Anderson, *Missions to the Oriental Churches*, 2:4–7. Cf. Arpee, *The Armenian Awakening*, 138–142.

88. Arpee, *The Armenian Awakening*, 146. Cf. Chopourian's figures for 1846, 1872, and 1914 in *Armenian Evangelical Awakening*, 92.

89. The statistics are for 1853, but were published in 1858 in Newcomb, *A Cyclopedia of Missions*, 152, in its article "Armenians," which may, however, include some Protestants other than Armenians.

90. Rufus Anderson, *Missions to the Oriental Churches*, 2:26–27. If there were only two thousand Armenian Protestant adherents in Turkey in 1853, but eleven hundred in Aintab alone in 1855, the total number of Armenian evangelical adherents might well have been more than three thousand by 1860. Cf. the statistics for 1853 in Newcomb, *Cyclopedia of Missions*, 152. For a chronological listing of Evangelical Protestant churches organized in the empire between 1846 and 1856, see Arpee, *History of Armenian Christianity*, 269–270. The fastest-growing field in the mid-1850s was around Aintab in northern Syria. See Rufus Anderson, *Missions to the Oriental Churches*, 1:362–363, 421–426; 2:12–16, 46–47, 86, 223–224, 243–245.

91. Ormanian, *The Church of Armenia*, 89–94.

92. On the Maronites and the "single will" doctrine, called Monothelitism, see Matti Moosa, *The Maronites in History* (Syracuse: Syracuse University Press, 1986), 195–216.

93. See vol. 1 of this work, 389–390.

94. See Moosa, *The Maronites in History*, 217–278. Uniate churches, as we have noted, are those who accept the sovereignty of the pope and the Roman Catholic sacraments of baptism and marriage, but not the Latin liturgies, retaining their own languages for worship. The Uniate churches in Asia include the Antiochene Rite (Maronites, Syrian Jacobite Uniates, and the Malankarese church in India) and the Chaldaean Rite (Armenian Uniates, Chaldaean Nestorian Uniates, and the Malabar Uniates in India). To these might be added, in Africa, the Alexandrine Rite (the Coptic Uniates of Egypt and the Ethiopian Uniates).

95. See vol. 1 of this work, 383, 387; for the subsequent history of the Druze faith, see Nejla M. Abu-Izzeddin, *The Druzes: A New Study of Their History, Faith and Society* (Leiden: E. J. Brill, 1984), 3, 74ff., 101ff., 179ff., 198ff.; and Kais M. Firro, *A History of the Druzes*, vol. 9 *Handbuch der Orientalistik, erste abteilung, der Nahe und der Mittlere Osten* (Leiden: E. J. Brill, 1992), 1–53.

96. Abu-Izzeddin, *The Druzes*, 207ff. Prominent Druze families even donated land to the Maronites for building churches. See also Moosa, *The Maronites in History*, 283ff. Cf. C. H. Churchill, *The Druzes and the Maronites under the Turkish Rule from 1840 to 1860* (London: B. Quaritch, 1862; reprint, New York: Arno Press, 1973), 25–30.

97. Pierre Dib, *Histoire de L'Eglise Maronite*, vol. 2 *L'Eglise Maronite* (Beirut: Editions "La Sagesse," 1962), 2:173. Cf. Firro, *A History of the Druzes*, 22. Dib attributes the saying to Bap. Poujoulat; Firro to J. al-Halabi, an eighteenth-century Christian describing the Druze faith. On his power in religious circles, see Bird, *Bible Work in Bible Lands*, 68–69.

98. Firro, *A History of the Druzes*, 80, quoting A. A. Paton, *The Modern Syrians 1841–43, by An Oriental Student* (London: Longmans, Brown, Green and Longmans, 1844).

99. On the rise and fluctuating fortunes of the Lebanese Christian population, wealth, education and political power in this period, see Firro, *A History of the Druzes*, 115ff. Cf. Dib, *L'Eglise Maronite*, 2:345ff., 401ff., 427ff., 464–465.

100. The edict was the *Hatt-I-Humayun* of February 18, 1856. It granted security of life, property, and worship to Christians, but deprived them of some of their political power. See Dib, *L'Eglise Maronite*, 2:448–449, and Firro, *A History of the Druzes*, 118.

101. See Churchill's passionate description of the war between the minority religions in *The Druzes and the Maronites*, 219. More dispassionate is A. D. Aqiqi, *Lebanon in the Last Years of Feudalism, 1840–1868*, trans. Malcolm H. Kerr (Beirut: Catholic Press, 1959), 36, 106–116. The best summary of the civil war is in Firro, *A History of the Druzes*, 119–126.

102. Latourette, *A History of the Expansion of Christianity*, 6:48.

103. Anglicans, who criticized the Congregationalists and Presbyterians of the ABCFM for proselytizing converts from the ancient churches and chose a path of mutual ecclesiastical recognition rather than evangelism, succeeded in neither receiving recognition nor in evangelizing at this period. See Shaw, *American Contacts with the Eastern Churches*, 35–71. The most effective Anglican contributions to mid-Eastern Christianity was through the publications of the British and Foreign Bible Society, founded in 1804. See Canton, *A History of the British and Foreign Bible Society:* Arabic (1:103, 133–134, 377), Armenian (1:140–141), Turkish (1:157, 203, 332, 388–392), Armenian and Syriac (1:396–397), Syriac and Arabic (1:377), Arabic (2:102, 470), Armenian (2:8, 11, 21, 278–279, 288); Turkish (2:290, 471), Syriac (2:10, 106, 378, 471).

104. ABCFM missionaries entered the Near East at Constantinople in 1819, but it was William Goodell and Frank King who opened regular residential work in Beirut in 1823.

105. Rufus Anderson, *Missions to the Oriental Churches*, 1:107–108; Richter, *A History of Protestant Missions in the Near East*, 186; John Wortabet, *Researches into the Religions of Syria: or Sketches, Historical and Doctrinal of Its Religious Sects* (London: James Nisbet, 1860), 364.

106. Rufus Anderson, *Missions to the Oriental Churches*, 1:41–51; 224–227; and Tracy, *History of American Missions to the Heathen*, 130–131, 168, 179, 225–226. See also Dwight, *Christianity Revived in the East*, 11–12. On education for women, see also Rufus Anderson, *Missions to the Oriental Churches*, 1:44, 107–108; and Dwight, *Christianity Revived in the East*, 46–47, 143–144, 244. A school for Armenian girls

was established in Smyrna in 1836. In 1845 a "female seminary" was opened in Constantinople, meeting in the Goodell home, and Miss Lovell, just arrived from America for that purpose, was put in charge. On Archbishop Dionysius Carabet and Gregory Wortabed, see Bird, *Bible Work in Bible Lands*, 212–215, 286–290.

107. Bird, *Bible Work in Bible Lands*, 132ff., 159ff.; Rufus Anderson, *Missions to the Oriental Churches*, 1:48–51.

108. Rufus Anderson, *Missions to the Oriental Churches*, 1:44, 52–71.

109. Rufus Anderson, *Missions to the Oriental Churches*, 1:261–269, 368–369; Newcomb, *A Cyclopedia of Missions*, 741.

110. Rufus Anderson, *Missions to the Oriental Churches*, 1:107–108; Tracy, *History of the American Missions to the Heathen*, 109–110, 178.

111. Wortabet, *Researches into the Religions of Syria*, 384–388.

112. Wortabet, *Researches into the Religions of Syria*, ix, 421n. He has chapters on all the above religious bodies, and on the Protestants who, in 1860, counted fifteen missionaries (ten of them ABCFM), but numbers of church members too small to count.

Chapter 20

Calamity in the Middle East (1860–1900)

The primitive and unvarying tradition of this [Armenian] Church acknowledges as original founders the apostles St. Thomas and St. Bartholomew, whom she designates *the First Illuminators of Armenia.*
— Maghak'ia Ormanian (1912)[1]

The heroism of the Armenians, both Gregorians and Protestants, was admirable. "Death rather than deny our faith" was their motto. Twenty-five Protestant ministers and 175 Gregorian priests were massacred [in 1895], often after unspeakable tortures. — J. Richter (1910)[2]

For four hundred years the Turks had dominated the Middle East. They had carried Asia into Europe. Then in four short decades, the last forty years of the nineteenth century, the Ottoman Empire collapsed, and Islam once again lost control of the Mediterranean to Western Christian military power. But in Asia, with few exceptions, it lost neither lands nor people. The Middle East remained Muslim. Islamic power had been dangerously weakened, but in defeat it turned fiercely against its vulnerable Christian minorities, and most brutally against the Armenians.

The Decline of the Turks

Turkish decline had begun early in the nineteenth century. In 1826 the famed Janissary Corps revolted. Originally composed of young Bulgars, Bosnians, and Serbs four to eight years old, torn from their Christian homes in the Balkans, they were forcibly converted and rigidly trained

403

for single-minded celibacy, the Muslim faith, and war. For three centuries the Janissaries were the very heart of the Turkish military elite. But when the sultan, after a series of humiliating defeats, ordered a remodeling of the army along Western lines, they mutinied. The sultan's response was a bloody massacre that wiped out the entire corps. His attempted reforms, however, proved ineffective, and Turkish military power never recovered.

Next came a crumbling of the government infrastructure. The basic feudal foundations of landholdings on which the whole administrative support of the sultanate rested fell in 1858. The sultanate survived but only as nominally sovereign, and the Western powers — Russian, British, French, and finally German — turned his capital, Constantinople, into a theater for foreign embassies jostling each other for control of West Asia.

A nearly final blow occurred in 1874. The empire's finances collapsed. Turkey's ablest sultan in decades was murdered (Abdul Aziz, 1861–1876); his successor, Murad V (1876), was insane; and the next successor (Abdul Hamid II, 1876–1909) massacred Armenians, lost control of the Balkans, and was deposed in favor of the weakest sultan of them all, Muhammad V (1909–1915), contemptuously known as "the sick man of Europe." The overall situation of the Christian minorities in those last volatile decades of the empire did not significantly change, except for one catastrophic factor: appalling and inhumane persecutions.

Christians were as much a minority at the end of the century as at its beginning despite the great hopes of the new arrivals, the Protestants, who had come in the 1830s. Their mission schools achieved remarkable prestige, but there was no corresponding growth of the region's divided churches. Arnold Toynbee has described much of Asia's response to Western Christian missions as a ready acceptance of Christian missionary education primarily for the sake of acquiring the West's superior technology, but an equally forthright rejection of its evangelism as religious interference and colonialism in disguise.[3] The Middle East for better or for worse was still married to Islam.

Those nineteenth-century Protestant pioneers in Turkey and Persia, however, did come close to a breakthrough. They dreamed of rescuing dying empires and revitalizing ancient churches. Had they succeeded, it would have been the most significant missionary accomplishment in all the "great century" of Christian missions. It could have given the Christian faith an entrance into the mind of Islam, the largest single religious block impeding the worldwide progress of the Christian faith. In 1900 Islam was the faith of 12.4 percent of the world's population; Christians were 34.4 percent. A hundred years later, in 2000 (as we shall see in another volume) Muslims would be about 20 percent, but Christians were 33 percent.[4] A Christian breakthrough in the 1800s revitalizing the ancient churches of the East and giving pause to what was then a declining

Islam might well have rewritten the troubled story of Muslim-Christian relations in Asia.

The "Mountain Nestorians" (1860–1900)

In Muslim West Asia, let us look first once more at the ancient Church of the East, the Nestorians. No longer were they the dominant Christian force in Asia, a position they never recovered after the Mongolians turned Muslim late in the thirteenth and fourteenth centuries. In West Asia they still survived in fragile communities but were to be found almost entirely in western Persia (Iran) and along Turkey's eastern borders, far weaker and insecure than their distant counterparts, the Thomas Christians of southern India.

The startling discovery by the early American Protestant missionaries in West Asia, described earlier, of Christian villages hidden for centuries in the mountains of Kurdistan and Azerbaijan,[5] was barely forty years old when the euphoria of a Christian reunion East and West, began to fade. Years of increasing tension between the "ancient church" of the surviving Nestorians and the "converted" church of the American missionaries finally led to a formal break between the old and new. It was a parting of the ways between "old Nestorians," with their bishops and not very clearly understood traditions, and the "new Nestorians," with their mission schools and revivals.

This division of the Nestorians is sometimes called the schism of 1870, but the separation was never that clearly defined. As early as 1854 converted Nestorians began to attend the Lord's Supper with the missionaries in their homes without altogether forsaking the mass in the old churches. The next year, 1855, the first evangelical congregations were formed, numbering about 158 members. A presbytery was organized in 1862, and in 1870 the American Board (Congregationalist) decided to turn over to the Presbyterians its work among the Nestorians in Persia. It was the Presbyterians, recognizing the inevitable, who reluctantly surrendered a generation of cooperation with the Nestorian hierarchy for ecclesiastical independence as the "Reformed" Nestorian Church. One missionary wrote in 1871: "The old church is a fossil. It is the grave of piety and the Christian effort. Hence our Christians to live at all they have been compelled to leave it. In part they have been driven out, in part they have left it, and now the separation is complete."[6]

On the Persian side of the border, as they gradually separated, many of the Old Church leaders joined the new church. The seceders included a brother of a former Old Church patriarch, three bishops, seventy priests, and many deacons, but the most enthusiastically "Protestant" Nestorians were the women. In 1884 a joyful celebration was held in Urmia marking the fiftieth anniversary of Protestant work. High school students lined the roads to greet the participants. The Muslim governor attended. Most remarkable was the reaction of the Muslims. One official asked, "What are those women doing there with books in their hands?" "They are reading and singing," he was told. "Impossible," he said. So all the women who could read were asked to rise. Six hundred stood up. The record adds, "Fifty years ago not one woman would have responded."[7]

One of the last acts of the retiring ABCFM mission as it passed its responsibilities in Iran to the Presbyterians was to organize, in 1870, a seminary for the training of a pastorate and other Christian workers. In the process, its missionary president, the Rev. Joseph G. Cochran, transferred his church membership from Congregational to Presbyterian. Ten years later the seminary took the name of Urmia College.[8] At the fiftieth anniversary celebrations in 1884, visitors from America were met while still twelve miles from the city and escorted in procession by cheering believers, and even the Muslim governor sent a squad of soldiers to escort them into the city as an expression of official respect. The Protestants by then had formed four presbyteries, with twenty-five organized churches and forty-eight other meeting places, and reported thirty-six ordained ministers, thirty licentiates, a communicant membership of twenty-three hundred, and six thousand adherents.[9]

Entering the new century, average attendance at the Protestant meetings had risen to three thousand, which was encouraging, but there was a downside. After more than sixty years, the Protestant form of Persian Nestorianism, whether in the churches or the mission schools, was still heavily dependent on American financial support.[10] It was not prepared for the persecutions that were already breaking upon Christians across the border in Turkey in the 1890s.

The Armenians and Their Massacre

Unlike the Nestorians who were vulnerable under Muslim rule because of their weakness, the Armenians were vulnerable because of their strength. This was particularly true in Turkey where their cultural status was actually higher than that of the Turks as a whole, and their financial acumen gave them enviable visibility.[11] In general, the eastern Armenians found better treatment in Persia than in Turkey, but were caught agonizingly in tricornered wars between Turkey, Persia, and Russia. In the Turkish empire in 1860, the Armenians were the strongest of all the Christian minority communities.

Virtually all Armenians, despite intermittent jurisdictional disputes, were ineradicably and ethnically Christian, proud of their sixteen hundred years of unbroken Christian tradition stretching back to the founding of their church in A.D. 302 under its first patriarch, Gregory the Illuminator (ca. A.D. 240–332). Tiridates III (converted in A.D. 301) was the first reliably documented Christian king in the world.[12] But they were divided geographically, politically, and ecclesiastically.

Geographically and politically (but not ethnically) the Armenians in Turkish Asia Minor were Turkish, but farther east in the Persian Empire they were Persian. The dividing line was the shifting Turkish/Persian border from the eastern end of the Black Sea down to the tip of the Red Sea. Ecclesiastically also the Armenians had been divided ever since the traumatic fall of Constantinople (Istanbul) in 1453 to the Turks. Here too the division was east and west. The patriarchate in the east remained in ancient Echmiadzin (or Etchmiadzin), near Armenia's modern capital Yerevan, which for much of its later history was under Persian rule. After 1828 it became increasingly dominated by Russia. But, as noted in the preceding chapter, the conquering Turks, for obvious purposes of control of their non-Muslim religious minorities, created a new patriarchate of Constantinople (the old name) in their new capital (renamed Istanbul).[13]

The eastern patriarch in Echmiadzin retained his ancient title of "supreme patriarch." Politically, however, Constantinople became the more powerful. Both patriarchs possessed authority over about the same number of Armenians — more than a million and a half in each area. At the beginning of World War I, for example, it was estimated that the total number including Turkey, Persia, and Russia, totaled about 3.4 million Armenian Christians.[14] In the east the mix of Christian churches differed markedly from western Turkey and its southern provinces of Syria and Lebanon. In the west the dominant churches were Maronite and Greek Orthodox, with a small Protestant minority, but to the east the Armenian Orthodox were stronger, with smaller minorities of Jacobites (Antioch Orthodox), Uniate Monophysites (Jacobites converted to Roman Catholicism), and the "almost exterminated" Nestorians. In eastern Turkey Protestants were an even smaller but more progressive minority, and Protestant mission work was based in Mosul on the Turkish side, and Urmia across the border in Persia.[15]

Apart from its own internal rivalries and divisions, the Old Armenian Orthodox Church was weakened by the secession of three small schismatic minorities, Armenian Catholics,[16] Armenian Jacobites (Antiochene),[17] and Armenian Protestants (Evangelicals). Of these schisms, the Armenian Catholic minority was strongest in Lebanon, where it was aided by growing French power in the region, and in Cilicia.

As for the Armenian Protestants, the Evangelical Armenian Church was always only a tiny reform-minded minority within the larger, close-knit Armenian ethnic community. It was small but growing. In 1840 a charter of rights granted by the sultan neutralized for a time the power the Old Church Armenian clergy and aristocratic bureaucracy had to harass the protesting young evangelical reformers. In 1844 the government granted recognition to the Protestants as a legal minority community with its own rights. A few years later, in 1850, Protestants were raised to the same status as all other Christian communities of the Ottoman Empire, old or new, and in 1854 Turkey conceded the right of all Christians to testify in court on as equal a basis of credibility as Muslims.[18]

A promising Armenian Protestant center had grown up at Harpoot, east of the Euphrates and north of Urfa (Sanliurfa or old Edessa). This was the region from which twelve hundred years earlier the old Syrian Christianity of the Church of the East (Nestorian) had sent the first Christian missionary to China.[19] The evangelical Armenian church in Harpoot in 1860 had just received its first native pastor, and a network of small schools including a theological school for training evangelists was thriving. In Diarbekir, farther east, entire areas of the city that were once Turkish Muslim had become Christian — Armenian Orthodox, Jacobite, and Protestant.[20]

A translation of the Bible into Turkish using Armenian characters and as spoken by Armenians was in much demand.[21] The missionaries credited Armenian respect for the Bible, which their ancestors had translated into their language as early as 433,[22] for a series of revivals and encouraging evangelical growth in eastern Turkey. "The Armenians," wrote one of them, "accept a declaration of the Bible as ultimate." Comparing this unquestioning respect for biblical authority with unflattering Protestant ascription of Catholic neglect of Scripture in the vernacular, the Protestant missionaries began to write triumphantly of "hundreds and thousands of the dear Protestant brothers and sisters of this land — God's lights in the midst of surrounding darkness, God's witnesses even where Satan dwelleth."[23]

There was justification for their enthusiasm. They could point to results: between five thousand and ten thousand communicant members and a community of forty thousand Armenian Protestants at the time. By 1895 they had organized a remarkable educational network of eight colleges, five seminaries, and forty-four high schools with boarding students.[24] Thirty years later all such triumphalism vanished. An ominous turn of events in Ottoman Turkey cast its shadow over any prospect for the peaceful existence of any religious minorities in the militantly Muslim Middle East.

The period from 1894 to the end of World War I could well be called the darkest in all of Armenia's long history, but the troubles began earlier. Even the rapid expansion into the region by military power from the Christian West only temporarily eased their plight. Russia had been intermittently advancing into Armenian sections of eastern Turkey for fifty years. In 1878 she occupied part of Turkish Armenia and exacted a promise of government protection for persecuted Christian minorities, especially the Armenians. Large numbers of Armenians chose to migrate into Russia, where they prospered and began to hope for the restoration of an independent Armenian nation, a hope soon dashed first by renewed persecution in Turkey, and then by broken promises in czarist Russia.[25]

This situation presented the far northeastern half of old Armenia, which had been Russian or under Russian protection since the early 1800s, with tragedy of an unexpected sort — not massacre by Muslims but suppression and denationalization by a Christian power, Russia. In 1885 all Armenian schools were closed, five hundred of them; Armenian newspapers were closed; the name "Armenia" was condemned. In 1903 the Russian government confiscated all the property of the Armenian Church, touching off a rebellion that did not end until in 1906 when the government relented and restored to the church its property.[26] But not independence for Armenia.

In Turkey, full disaster did not break upon the Armenians until the 1890s. In 1894 the fanatical sultan Abdul Hamid II loosed his Kurdish irregulars to slaughter Armenians in retaliation against supposed secret conspiracies plotting rebellion. Massacre followed massacre, spreading eastward for the next two years from Constantinople to Trebizond and Diarbekir. It was described by observers as "organized tyranny" against the Armenians, indeed against all Christians.

The whole world was shocked. Atrocities, tortures, burnings, hackings, strangulations, and wild looting continued month after month until one weeping survivor reported, "We have been robbed of everything; they have not left us a rag wherewith to wipe away our tears." Later investigations revealed that 88,243 Armenians were murdered, 10,000 of them evangelical Protestants; 500,000 lost all they possessed; 2,493 villages were looted; 568 churches were destroyed; and 282 other churches were turned into mosques; 175 Armenian priests were martyred, as were 25 Protestant ministers. The old Armenian Archimandrite John Papizian refused to turn Muslim. His hands were cut off, then his arms at the elbows, then he was beheaded.[27]

In two terrible intervals of genocidal terror — the first from 1894 to 1895 at the end of the nineteenth century, and the second during World War I from 1915 to 1918 — all Armenians suffered, whether Old Armenian, Protestant, or Catholic.[28] The barbaric horrors of those two periods rank close to the savageries of Tamerlane, "scourge of God and the terror of the world," in the fourteenth century, though on a smaller scale.[29]

The Ottoman Empire was dying, and in those years of its despair it seemed to be determined that its non-Muslim Christian Armenians would die with it. The passion of Ottoman imperialism turned its hatred from a Christian West too strong to resist, and vented itself in fury against Christian minorities so vulnerable to accusations of collaboration with the enemy. In the next two decades nearly half of all the Armenians in Turkey were killed, about a million out of 2.2 million. "The organized murder of the Armenian race" is how Arnold Toynbee described it.[30] "Armenian blood flowed in rivers everywhere . . . 1,200 Armenians were burnt alive in the Orthodox cathedral at Urfa at Christmas 1895." Urfa was Old Edessa, mother of the Syrian branch of Asian Christianity that

had been the first to reach China in the seventh century.[31] Another observer wrote with emotion, "They marched them off into the desert"
to die. They "drowned them in batches, tied together, every night in
the Euphrates River. Women with child were forced to march with the
convoys and give birth to their babies on the road." The documented
reports of the atrocities stretch on and on.[32] The voice of the Christians
was silenced, save for pleas for mercy.

The comparative numerical strength of the religions in what is now
Turkey in 1900 is given as follows in the *Encyclopedia of World Christianity* (1982):[33] Muslim, 10,978,000 (77.3 percent); Christian, 3,092,000
(21.8 percent) — of whom, Orthodox, 2,950,000 (20.8 percent), Roman
Catholic, 74,500 (0.5 percent), Protestant, 66,000 (0.4 percent) — Jewish
80,000 (0.6 percent); Shamanist 50,000 (0.4 percent).

Lebanon

Lebanon was different. In 1860, following the great massacres of Maronites by the Druses (or Druzes) and the intervention of the French,[34]
Turkey yielded to French pressures and made Greater Syria, including
Lebanon, into an autonomous province with a Christian governor, an
astounding development in a Muslim empire. Maronites remained the
dominant Christian presence well into the twentieth century, and as a result, though the Eastern churches always remained divided, sometimes
bitterly and self-defeatingly divided, the resulting freedom for Christian
life and witness opened the door to a new burst of Christian activity in
the region, especially noticeable among the smallest sector of the Christian community, the Protestants. In fact, so close was the tie between the
French and the Maronites that early in World War I when Turkey found
itself at war with France, the Ottoman Empire asserted military control
in Lebanon, repealing briefly all the privileges of the Maronite Church,
and of all the other Christian churches as well, considering them guilty
by association with the Allied powers. Conversely, Turkey's defeat at the
end of the war brought a complete reversal. The Treaty of Paris in 1920,
influenced by the strong Maronite Patriarch Elias Huwayyik, granted
independence to Lebanon, and separation from Syria under a French
mandate, to the immense satisfaction, needless to say, of the Maronites.[35]

Perhaps it was the Protestant connection with the most powerful
emerging Western powers in that area that made the Muslim sultanate
hesitant to discriminate against the Protestants and their new churches.
A whole series of government edicts in the last half of the century, beginning in 1856, established liberty of conscience, right of acquisition of
property by foreigners, and the right of Christians to hold positions of
civil authority.[36]

The newcomers, the Protestants, made the most of the advantage of the new liberties. Because of their ambiguous relations with the jealous older ecclesiastical institutions, and the ever present undercurrent of Muslim hostility to any Christian religious presence, the Protestants chose the path of education as the most viable preparation for Christian evangelism.

In 1863 Daniel Bliss (1823–1916) opened the Syrian Protestant College with sixteen students in three small rooms. He had great dreams for his little school. It stands, he said, "to lay the foundations of a Christian literature through which the millions of Asia, the Barbary States of Egypt and Central Africa might be reached and blessed."[37] His dream was prophetic. It did indeed reach millions. Out of it grew a world-famous university, the American University of Beirut, the crowning accomplishment of American mission in the Middle East, proud and beautiful on its campus overlooking the Mediterranean Sea. In ten years the little college added a four-year school of medicine, at a time when medical education in America was designed for three years' study only. In Lebanon, at least, at the end of the century, prospects for Christian mission seemed far brighter than anywhere else in the Middle East. How far that might have been the result of Western control of the region after World War I, and how far it was the result of strong Christian minorities in all four branches of the faith (Catholic, Eastern Orthodox, Armenian, and to a lesser extent Protestant), would await the judgment of another century. Not so well known but just as important was the pioneering work of Protestant missions in the Middle East in insisting on education for women. The first missionaries found Syrian women purposely kept illiterate. A common saying that they encountered was, "One might as well try to teach a cat to read as a girl."[38] But almost on arrival the Protestants started a girls' school in Beirut in 1835, though for the next thirty years it was only intermittently able to operate. For many years the American School for Girls, founded in Tripoli in 1872, was the only boarding school for girls in northern Lebanon.[39]

The most effective early program for women's education began not with the Americans but with the British. In 1860, the same year that the Protestant Syrian College for men was founded by the American Board, an English missionary, a widow of some wealth, Mrs. J. Bowen Thompson, arrived in Beirut and began at her own cost to organize a network of Christian girls' schools that by 1902 had grown to twenty-six schools with more than four thousand pupils. To this she added a string of free medical dispensaries in memory of her late husband, a medical missionary. By 1902 the combined project numbered twenty-six schools and four dispensaries.[40]

Lebanon was the only territory in Asia other than the Philippines which in 1900 could claim a majority of Christians in its population (77 percent in a population of 410,000). The comparative statistics were: Christians, 317,000 (77.4 percent), of whom Roman Catholic, 317,400 (74.0 percent), Orthodox, 12,300 (2.9 percent), Protestants, 3,100 (0.5 percent); Muslims, 84,000 (20.6 percent); Jews 8,200 (2.0 percent).

It could not be said that at the end of the century Christian missions had yet made much of an impression on the Muslim world even in Lebanon where the concentration of Christians was greatest, or in Turkey where the number was largest. In 1900, as recorded by the *Christian World Encyclopedia,* the number of Christians, and their percentage of population, in the Middle East (West Asia) were as follows:[41]

Country	Population	Christians (including adherents)
Turkey	14,978,000	3,091,000 (21.8%)
Lebanon	410,000	371,000 (77.0%)
Syria	1,750,000	274,000 (15.7%)
Iraq	2,252,000	144,000 (6.4%)
Iran	9,700,000	116,000 (1.2%)
Jordan	250,000	14,000 (5.8%)
Kuwait	67,000	8,000 (0.5%)
Yemen, South	530,000	4,500 (0.8%)
Afghanistan	5,100,000	300 (0.0%)
Bahrain	65,000	200 (0.3%)
United Arab Emirates	50,000	50 (0.1%)
Saudi Arabia	2,730,000	50 (0.0%)
Oman	289,000	20 (0.0%)
Yemen, North	2,000,000	0 (0.0%)
TOTAL	40,171,000	4,642,500 (11.0%)

NOTES

1. Ormanian, *The Church of Armenia.*

2. Richter, *A History of Protestant Missions in the Near East,* 143.

3. See Arnold Toynbee, *Christianity among the Religions of the World* (New York: Scribner's, 1957), 49–51; and *The World and the West,* 54–61, 67ff.

4. See the updating of world Christian statistics by David Barrett in "Status of Global Mission, 2001," *IBMR* (January 2001): 25.

5. For the earlier nineteenth-century years of the Middle Eastern Nestorians see chap. 19 above.

6. Letter of 1871 quoted by Elder, *History of the American Presbyterian Mission to Iran,* 22.

7. Elder, *History of the American Presbyterian Mission to Iran,* 45.

8. In 1881 Urmia College counted five students in the theology course, five in medicine, fifteen in academic fine arts, and sixteen in an entering class. Six of the forty-one students were Muslim, but in 1904, to avoid confusion and friction and charges of proselytizing, a separate school for Muslims was formed. In 1913 the school for Muslims was merged with the College as the American School for Boys. See Andrew Judson Brown, *One Hundred Years: A History of the Foreign*

Missionary Work of the Presbyterian Church in the U.S.A. (New York: Fleming H. Revell, 1937), 492.

9. Elder, *History of the American Presbyterian Mission to Iran,* 42–47.

10. Elder, *History of the American Presbyterian Mission to Iran,* 23; and Richter, *A History of Protestant Missions in the Near East,* 304. By 1907, of the 25,000 or so Nestorians, the "Reformed Church" counted 2,658 communicant members and about 5,000 adherents, mostly on the Urmia plain. The Presbyterians by then also reported sixty-three village schools, with some 1,666 pupils.

11. See K. V. Sarkissian, "The Armenian Church," in Arberry, *Religion in the Middle East,* 1:486–488; and Charles Issawi, "The Transformation of the Economic Position of the *Millets* in the 19th Century," in Braude and Lewis, *Christians and Jews in the Ottoman Empire,* 1:261–285.

12. Ormanian, *The Church of Armenia,* 8–13.

13. On the two major patriarchates, omitting minor and temporary rivals, see Kevork B. Bardakjan, "The Rise of the Armenian Patriarchate of Constantinople," Braude and Lewis, *Christians and Jews in the Ottoman Empire,* 1:89–100; and on Echmiadzin, Ormanian, *The Church of Armenia,* 8–13, 37ff., 56–59, 72–73.

14. The patriarch of Constantinople's authority included in actual practice the tiny symbolic Armenian Patriarchate of Jerusalem, and the Catholicates of Cilicia, in southern Asia Minor, and Agthamar, near Van, a total of 1,776,000 Armenian Christians. The eastern patriarch ("supreme catholicos" of Echmiadzin) ruled 1,696,000, in Persia and Russia. See the statistical tables for "before the first world war" in Ormanian, *Church of Armenia,* 206ff.

15. Rufus Anderson, *Missions to the Oriental Churches,* 2:78–106. In Syria and in what is now called Iraq the "Nestorians" came to prefer to be called Assyrians. Mosul is ancient Assyrian Nineveh, and the language was Syrian Arabi, liturgically Syriac.

16. In 1830 Rome instituted a primatial archbishopric in Constantinople, which was elevated to a patriarchate in 1884. G. C. Anawati, "The Roman Catholic Church," in Arberry, *Religion in the Middle East,* 1:373–374; Braude and Lewis, *Christians and Jews in the Ottoman Empire,* 1:180.

17. Joseph, *Muslim-Christian Relations and Inter-Christian Rivalries in the Middle East,* 29–30, 161 n. 83. Jacobites in Turkey were placed by the Turkish government under the authority of the Armenian patriarch of Constantinople.

18. Rufus Anderson, *Missions to the Oriental Churches,* 2:8–10, lists the several stages of expanding liberties.

19. See vol. 1 of this work, 200ff. and 288ff., on Edessa and the seventh-century mission to China.

20. Rufus Anderson, *Missions to the Oriental Churches,* 2:275, 465–469; 105, 256ff.

21. Rufus Anderson, *Missions to the Oriental Churches,* 2:67–78.

22. On the Armenian Bible, Ormanian, *The Church of Armenia,* 16–19; and Nersoyan, *A History of the Armenian Church,* 89–96.

23. Rufus Anderson, *Missions to the Oriental Churches,* 2:59–77.

24. Rufus Anderson, *Missions to the Oriental Churches,* 2:59–77. In 1914 the figures for Armenian Protestantism in Asian (Cilician) Armenia were 13,891 communicant members, and a community of 50,000 (Chopourian, *Armenian Evangelical Reformation,* 92).

25. Sarkissian, "The Armenian Church," 1:482–492; Richter, *A History of Protestant Missions in the Near East*, 136–155; and Ormanian, *The Church of Armenia*, 72–73.

26. Richter, *A History of Protestant Missions in the Near East*, 176–180.

27. Richter, *A History of Protestant Missions in the Near East*, 135–153, esp. 140, 143, 145.

28. Equally tragic but smaller massacres occurred in 1905, 1908–1909, and 1920. Arberry, *Religion in the Middle East*, 1:480, 491; 2:497, 499, 521, 531.

29. See vol. 1 of this work, 480–487.

30. This figure is for Armenians in Turkey alone. Ormanian, *The Church of Armenia*, 76. See Arnold J. Toynbee, *Armenian Atrocities: The Murder of a Nation* (London and New York: Hodder & Stoughton, 1915), 186.

31. See vol. 1 of this work, 56ff.

32. See Viscount James Bryce, *The Treatment of Armenians in the Ottoman Empire 1915–16* (London: Causton & Sons, 1916), xxv, 26ff., 102ff., and passim.

33. Barrett, ed., *World Christian Encyclopedia*, 1982, 680.

34. See chap. 19.

35. Moosa, *The Maronites in History*, 187.

36. The edict of 1856, *Hatt-I-Humayun*, "the most important Turkish edict of the 19th century," was issued under Sultan Abdul Mejid (1839–1861). Cf. Firro, *A History of the Druzes*, 118; Dib, *L'Eglise Maronite*, 2:450f.

37. The college was built upon the foundation of a Christian Academy founded in 1843 near Beirut in the little village of Abeih, near "the cradle of Christian education" in Greater Syria. On the American University, Beirut, see Frederick J. Bliss, *Reminiscences of Daniel Bliss* (New York: Fleming H. Revell, 1920), 171 and passim; and Eileen Flower [Moffett], "Christian Education in Lebanon, A Moslem Frontier," MRE thesis, Princeton Theological Seminary, 1955, 22–51. The prominent names in its early growth were Daniel Bliss, D. Stuart Dodge, and John J. Phelps.

38. Richter, *A History of Protestant Missions in the Near East*, 191.

39. Flower [Moffett], "Christian Education in Lebanon," 56–61.

40. Richter, *A History of Protestant Missions in the Near East*, 203–204.

41. Barrett, ed. *World Christian Encyclopedia*, 1982. The list excludes Israel, which did not then exist as a nation, but figures for 1900 for the area now containing Israel were 29,700 Christian adherents in a population of 170,000. Of that number, 20,000 were Orthodox, 9,000 Roman Catholic, and 700 Protestant (500 of them Anglican) (p. 399).

Chapter 21

Advance in India (1860–1900)

The three main channels through which modern ideas have found their
way to India, are British rule, English education and Christian missions.
— S. Natarajan[1]

The real founder of the Church in Travancore was not Ringeltaube, but
Vedamanikam. In Kistna it was not Darling, but Venkayya. In Sialkot it
was not Gordon but Ditt. — Bishop Pickett[2]

Every diocese should have its own seminary for the training of a native
clergy. — Pope Leo XIII, 1893[3]

IT was becoming apparent to many in India as the nineteenth century
passed the halfway mark that momentum in the Christian communities
was not with the St. Thomas Christians who could claim that they had
been there for nearly 1800 hundred years, nor with the Roman Catholics
who had been there for the last 450 consecutive years. The St. Thomas
Christians, as we have seen,[4] had been split apart by the coming of the
Catholics, and were also crippled by their own internal divisions. Indian
Catholicism had been in decline for seventy years — some say longer —
and was uncharacteristically divided itself as the Portuguese hierarchy
of the *padroado* in Goa fought against direct papal control through apostolic vicars.[5] One historian of the Catholics in the Bombay area describes
the whole 130 years from 1720 to 1850 as the "long, dark days."[6]

For Protestants it was the beginning of the good years. One sign of
better days occurred in 1858. When the government of India was taken
from the hands of the East India Company and British India became
a crown colony, India's Protestant missionaries found they had gained
a strong supporter at the highest level, India's new empress, Queen
Victoria, Defender of the Faith.

The Syrian Thomas Christians of Kerala:
Strife and Division

The Protestants brought reform, which was good; they also brought
more church division, which was not. Claudius Buchanan, earlier in the

century, was the first Protestant to study the Syrian Christians exten-
sively. He quoted with relish their reaction to the first Catholics who
had reached them in the sixteenth century: " '[Your] Churches,' said the
Portuguese, 'belong to the Pope.' 'Who is the Pope?' said the Syrians of
Kerala, 'We never heard of him.' "[7] Before long, however, non-Catholic
Syrian Christians were saying much the same thing to the Protestants,
"We have St. Thomas. Who are Luther and Calvin and the bishop of
Canterbury?"

To some the Protestants were like a breath of fresh Christian air; to
others they were more of "a mixed bag of blessings and curses,"[8] and in
southwest India where almost all the Syrian Christians lived, the last half
of the century ended in ecclesiastical chaos. The ancient church of the
Thomas Christians was left shattered into four major groups (Roman
Syrian, Orthodox Syrian (Jacobite), Mar Thoma Syrian, and Anglican
Syrian), not counting several smaller ones of which the Nestorian Syrians were the most noteworthy. The Nestorians were what remained of
the ancient Church of the East in India, which kept its ancient ties to
Mesopotamia, not to Antioch or Rome.

The two largest divisions were Roman Syrian and Orthodox Syrian,
the latter recognizing the patriarch of Antioch, not the bishop of Rome,
as head of the church. By the end of the nineteenth century there were
about twice as many Roman Catholic Christians as there were Orthodox (Jacobite). But two newer divisions, Anglican and Mar Thoma, had
emerged. The story of the Roman Catholic majority is more appropriately
told later in this chapter in connection with the rest of Indian Roman
Catholicism.

The second largest, the Syrian Orthodox (Jacobite) Church represented
the majority of the traditionally Nestorian Thomas Christians who broke
away from Rome in the Coonen Cross revolt of 1653.[9] For some time
they had wavered between their older Nestorian tradition and a new
connection introduced in 1665 through the Jacobite Orthodox Patriarch
then at Diyarbakir in Turkey, but they gradually turned Orthodox, and in
the early nineteenth century Indian Syrian Orthodoxy entered 150 years
of turmoil.

The beginning of the trouble was closely related to the rising spread
of Anglicanism in British India. It started slowly in 1806 with a friendly
encounter between the English missionaries and the Thomas Christians,
and turned sour partly due to overzealous lack of sensitivity among a
few younger missionaries toward the ancient Syrian traditions. A contributing factor was a not altogether unjustified suspicion on the part of
the metropolitan, the head of Indian Syrian Orthodoxy, that the vigorous
and confident newly arrived Westerners would undermine his authority.
Rash action by one of the missionaries precipitated the break. The Syrian
Christian community had graciously shared with the mission the privilege of guarding ancient copper plates bearing the royal charter of their

history and identity. The Indian metropolitan held one key to the room containing the treasure; a missionary held the other. Hearing a rumor that the metropolitan was about to move the plates, the impetuous young missionary took them himself for safekeeping. The insult could not be recalled, not even by later apologies from the (Anglican) Church Missionary Society. Mission and church separated, with a minority leaving Indian Jacobitism for mission Anglicanism. The first independent Anglican church was formed in 1836; the first Anglican diocese in the area was organized in 1879.[10]

But within the Syrian Indian community, two serious sources of friction remained. For the traditionalists the issue of episcopal primacy in the church as an Indian metropolitanate was fundamental. For the younger leaders, however, the sore point was the issue of reforms urgently needed to keep up with changing times. Both these factors led to schisms.

The Reform Movement and the Mar Thoma Syrian Church

The first English missionaries in Kerala, as noted above, came under instructions "not to pull down the ancient church and build another, but to remove the rubbish and to repair the decaying places."[11] For a while they taught effectively at the Orthodox Old Seminary in Kottayam, which the Syrian church had started in 1815. They were there to reaffirm and reform, but not to proselyte. Nevertheless, perhaps without realizing it, simply by translating the Bible and the Anglican Prayer Book into the Malayalam vernacular instead of Syriac, and by confronting Roman Catholics and Orthodox with a new hierarchy neither Catholic nor Orthodox but tracing itself back to St. Thomas, they loosened the mortar of the old church's already crumbling structure. The Protestants had paved the way for schism, but not many Indian leaders chose to leave the old church peaceably with the Anglican missionaries.[12]

The most ardent of the young reformers chose to stay and fight. What they wanted was the old Syrian church but with certain reforms and adaptations learned from the Anglicans, especially a semiautonomous Indian clergy and a liturgy in Malayalam, the local language, not in either Latin or Syriac. Their efforts were foiled by the old church hierarchy, and in the end some gave up all hope of reform from within and left the old church to make a new and independent beginning.

Their great leader was a Jacobite priest, Abraham Malpan of Maramon (1796–1846), teacher of the Syriac Bible at the Syrian seminary in Kottayam, who stood firmly for the authority of Scripture over creeds, for translating the Bible and the liturgy from Syriac into the local language, Malayalam, and against processions for wooden images and prayers for the dead.[13] But when he proposed these changes to his superior in 1837, the Orthodox metropolitan, Dionysius IV (1825–1855), angrily excommunicated him.[14] Abraham then sent his nephew, Mathew, to Syria to plead his case before a higher power, the patriarch of Antioch. Mathew, who was a scion of an old Thomas Christian family that had produced nine metropolitans all named Mar Thoma (or Thomas),[15] not only presented the issues convincingly, he persuaded the patriarch to consecrate him as a metropolitan of Malankara (Malabar) with the title Mathew Mar Athanasius, and send him back better armed to carry out a program of reform.[16] Not surprisingly Mar Dionysius IV refused to recognize him when he returned in 1843, but Mathew found support from the Anglican missionaries and from the Travancore colonial government, which ruled in his favor in 1852. He presided over the Jacobite community until 1875, naming as his successor his cousin Thomas, the son of the revered founder of the Mar Thoma Syrian church, Abraham Malpan.[17]

That schism, however, between Jacobite Orthodox and the Protestant-leaning Mar Thoma Syrian reformers was not yet complete. It was a tangled struggle between the two lines of ecclesiastical power: reformers against traditionalists, whether the traditionalists were patriarchs in Syria or metropolitans in India. It eventually involved the local Indian government, two patriarchs of Antioch, and even the archbishop of Canterbury, who wisely advised Antioch to grant more autonomy to the Indian churches. But it was essentially Indian reform versus Antiochene authority that led to final schism in 1888–1889, when a pivotal court case awarded church property and ecclesiastical authority to Antioch.[18] The Mar Thoma reformists lost their church buildings and seminary; the Syrian Orthodox traditionalists (Jacobites as they were known) kept the property but lost the most actively evangelistic wing of their church, and before long divided again, as described below, still debating within themselves the extent of the authority of Antioch.

Meanwhile the Mar Thoma Church, the church of the reformists, started building its own churches and a seminary. One of its high priorities was mission to non-Christians, and before the newly named church was a year old it had organized the Mar Thoma Evangelistic Association and was soon bringing into the hitherto rather upper-class Syrian Christian community, which was not officially in the class system at all, a growing stream of people who found in the church not only a new faith but more freedom to rise above the old caste boundaries.

The growth was nourished by a series of revivals extending throughout the later decades of the nineteenth century and on into the twentieth century.[19] The high point of the year for the Mar Thoma Church is still today the Maramon Convention of the Evangelistic Association. Attendance soars above forty thousand to as high as eighty thousand, making it the largest regular annual gathering of Christians anywhere in the world.[20]

The Continuing Syrian Orthodox Church (Jacobites)

For the Orthodox loyalists, dissension did not end when the reformists left. Rivalry in the Indian Jacobite hierarchy for the title of metropolitan (equivalent to archbishop) of the Syrian Church in India was nothing new. It had played its abrasive part in the seventeenth-century schism with Rome, and exploded again in the closing half of the nineteenth century in the Mar Thoma Church schism.

In 1875 a patriarchal visit to the Malabar coast by the Orthodox Jacobite Patriarch Peter III of Antioch failed to satisfy the Mar Thoma reformers, and only temporarily confirmed the authority of the patriarchate over Indian Orthodoxy,[21] but it did lay the legal grounds for establishing, in 1888–1889, Syrian Orthodox ownership of church property in India, as we saw above. The court victory, however, was far from decisive, for in less than twenty years, in 1910, the Jacobite Patriarchate itself split in angry competition for the imperial favor of the Turkish sultan whose political power was weakening but who still ruled his country's religious minorities with the arbitrary willfulness of an absolute sovereign.[22]

Some of the subsequent history of the schism should be added here, though it spills over into the next century. Lacking firm direction in their home base, the confused and quarreling Jacobites in far-off India broke apart into two sections. One came to be known as the "Patriarchal" party, following a new Jacobite patriarch who had been installed in Antioch by the Turkish sultan and had visited India in 1909 to restore order and authority in the church. He abruptly excommunicated the presiding Indian metropolitan, Mar Dionysios VI (Vattasseril Geevarghese).[23] whom he suspected of loyalty to the former patriarch deposed by the sultan. Then he consecrated a new metropolitan, Cyril. But Dionysios did not fade away quietly. He was restored to his Metropolitanate as head of the church when the former patriarch, who had been deposed by the sultan, visited India in 1912 and promptly voided the excommunication of Dionysios VI, who was still popular with many. He went even farther and created, or reestablished, a "Catholicate of the East" for his branch of Indian Jacobites, making him the superior of a number of new metropolitans whom he consecrated. This time it was Cyril who was excommunicated. But both men had a following, and the result was schism: Metropolitan Cyril as head of the patriarchal party; Catholicos Dionysios VI as head of the Catholicos party.[24] It was the Catholicos party which eventually outnumbered the patriarchal about six to one, and after years of litigation finally in 1958 won the recognition of the Supreme Court at Delhi.[25]

In that year the two factions — the larger Orthodox Syrian Church of Malabar led by its Indian Catholicos, and the smaller Antiochene (or Jacobite) Syrian Orthodox Church led by its patriarch in Antioch through his metropolitan in India — reached a final agreement to recognize each other without demanding organizational unity — the Catholicos acknowledging only the spiritual supremacy of the patriarch.

Mass Movements:
Outreach to Outcastes (Dalits) and Tribals

Elsewhere in India, however, and for the rest of the nineteenth century, momentum remained with the Protestants. The Protestant advance took as its most visible form a wave of mass conversions to the Christian faith in the last forty years of the nineteenth century and marked this period as a critical turning point in the history of Indian Christianity. Significantly, the mass movements began not with the missionaries but under Indian Christian leadership, and they centered not among the elite of Indian society but among the lowest of the low, the "outcastes" (better called *dalits*, the "oppressed").[26] They were an important part of the beginnings of a shift from mission to Indian church leadership, though that developed only gradually and would take another hundred years to implement.

The roots of these nineteenth-century Christian mass movements with their foreshadowing of today's missionary "option for the poor" and "people movements" can be traced as far back as Francis Xavier's sixteenth-century Roman Catholic mission to the depressed fisherfolk on India's Cape Comorin coast.[27] Somewhat similar was a group movement that about 1818, three hundred years later, brought into the Protestant churches the low-caste palm-wine carriers, "toddy-drawers," of the Nadars of Tamilnadu. It was led by a converted *dalit*, baptized as Vedamanikam. Pickett calls this "the first of the mass movements."[28] Some thirty years later another such movement in Telugu country in Andhra Pradesh began with the conversion in 1849 of Venkayya, the leader of a robber band, by M. L. Darling of the Church Missionary Society. Venkayya, who must have been a most persuasive character, soon converted his relatives and neighbors, beginning a flood of new believers that snowballed until by 1901 there were twenty-nine thousand Christians in his district, and by 1911 close to fifty thousand.[29]

Two factors deserve notice, for they became the marks of the movement. The first was rapid church growth. From 1814 to 1818 the number of converts shot up from six hundred to three thousand, and the next year the London Missionary Society built for the Tamilnadu *dalits* "perhaps the second largest church in India" at Nagercoil. The other noteworthy characteristic of the movement was that the growth began with a *dalit*, Vedamanikam, leading his fellow *dalits* to Christ, not with the missionary, Ringeltaube.[30] But it is dangerous to generalize even about these two marks of the movements, rapid growth and native unordained Indian initiative. The bursts of growth occurred in too many various forms and in too many different contexts to allow of oversimple characterization.

For example, another of the early beginnings of the great Indian mass movements traces neither to a *dalit* nor to a missionary, but to the ministry of a revivalist Catholic priest in Germany, Johannes Gossner, who was associated with the Bavarian "Awakened Brethren," a group that was placed under suspension by the Inquisition a few years after Gossner had joined it. Twenty or so years later, in 1824, Gossner left the Roman communion to become a low-church Lutheran. He was befriended by the philosopher Schleiermacher whose background was also Pietist, though it was Mrs. Schleiermacher who was most impressed by the evangelist. Gossner was never to leave Europe for the mission field, but his life-long Pietist passion for combining the disciplines of Christian work and the practice of fervent prayer led him to form in 1836 what was popularly called the Gossner mission, one of the early examples of what later became known in America as nondenominational "faith missions." The much larger, better organized, and better known Basel mission, organized earlier in Switzerland, had somewhat similar characteristics. It adopted a Presbyterian form of church order; the Gossner mission remained Lutheran; the Gossner mission was short-lived, the Basel mission is still active worldwide, but both were independent of state and church control and support.[31]

Gossner's overseas mission began when four young Lutheran craftsmen who had been rejected for seminary as too uneducated for theological study came to Gossner with a plea to help them become missionaries. Beyond their lack of training, which was evident, he discerned an overflowing zeal for missionary evangelism overseas, and felt moved to accept them for private tutoring. Others joined them, studying every evening after work. One group went to Australia, but India became the centerpiece of the mission when in two years, 1838–1840, Gossner sent twenty missionaries there. They went unordained and with no financial guarantees, but usually with one ordained man accompanying them. In 1844 or 1845 four of them, dreaming of entering forbidden Tibet, chanced to meet a group of tribesmen in Calcutta from the hills in Chota Nagpur (now Jarkhand State), a fifteen-days journey to the west. They were from a tribal group then called "Kols" (now considered a pejorative term), and technically they were not *dalits*; they were aboriginal tribespeople who had never been in the caste system. To orthodox Hindus, they were simply rude, primitive savages, much given to drunkenness but devoted to music. To the unsophisticated young German craftsmen, however, who had suffered under European class prejudices, they seemed charmingly unspoiled and friendly. Immediately they abandoned their plans for Tibet and embarked on a journey of faith into the wild hills of Chota Nagpur. For five years there were no converts; then suddenly a rush of conversions. Gossner, in Germany, rejoiced, "We will have them all, every one of them." Then came the difficulties: missionary dissension and disorganization; the Great Sepoy rebellion of 1857, which drove the missionaries out of the hills, burned the station, and persecuted the believers; and then in 1858 the death of the founder, Johannes Gossner, who had "prayed mission-stations into being, and missionaries into faith." Nevertheless, despite the succession of disasters, by 1860 the returning missionaries could count more than ten thousand Chota Nagpuri Christians, all without an effective missionary organization or an assured flow of income.[32]

By the end of the century the Gossner mission, though it had generously turned control over part of its mission work and personnel to the Anglican Society for the Propagation of the Gospel,[33] was still operating in Chota Nagpur in 1902 and counted 51,557 baptized Christians, 46 missionaries, and 300 native helpers.[34] The secret of the success, humanly speaking, was the enthusiastic witness of unordained Christians, missionary and Indian, and, as the missionaries unfailingly pointed out, prayer. Of the 141 missionaries sent out by the Gossner mission only 15 were ordained clergymen.[35]

Not until the 1860s and 1870s, after India had become a British crown colony, did the mass movements begin to attract national attention. Azariah of Dornakal, a generation later in 1930, wrote:

> There were [in 1860] about a million Indian Christians. Nearly a third of them belonged to the old Syrian church on the Malabar coast that claims to have been established by the Apostle Thomas. Nearly two-thirds were Roman Catholics, the fruit of three and a half centuries of Missionary effort, and a few were connected with various Protestant churches. But during the last seventy years the million Christians have increased to about five millions.[36]

Part of the momentum for this fivefold increase was a pivotal missionary decision: to choose an emphasis on mission to the poor rather than a mission strategy aimed primarily at the rich, the educated, and the powerful. The choice was not easy, nor was it absolute. Evangelism and education for all, rich or poor, remained as mission priorities. But though many feared that a Christian option for the poor would only further alienate the elite in already caste-segregated India, most nineteenth-century Protestant missions in India determined to accept that risk, and adapted their mission policies to the challenge of the masses of "untouchables" knocking at their doors. It was a wise choice, not only in terms of Christian integrity, but also, as it turned out, of numerical church growth.

The largest of the mass movements occurred in what is now the state of Andhra Pradesh, spreading first among the Telugu-speaking people north of Madras. For nearly thirty years American Baptists had tried and failed to evangelize the area. After thirty years only one lone missionary was left, with not more than some thirty Christians to report. For Baptists that was failure; they grow fast, and were even then rejoicing at their amazing success in Burma. So the Home Board was about to close the mission when a young missionary candidate, John Clough (1836–1910), volunteered to give it another try. He reached India in 1865 and gathered the thirty converts to begin to pray for at least a hundred new believers within another year. Their prayers apparently were not answered. Two Brahman youths did profess to want to become Christians, but their families forcibly prevented them from being baptized. Then suddenly in 1866 a letter came from a man in an outlying village asking for a missionary to come out and baptize him, but there was a downside. He was an outcaste; he would never be accepted into the city's better-class Christian community. His name was Yerraguntla Periah, a Madiga, a leather worker, a *dalit* — poor, ignorant, and despised. There were no Madigas in the mission's church in Nellore.

But, as Clough later wrote:

> [The issue] was not open to us to debate . . . We were bound to receive every-one who believed in Jesus Christ. Thus was I wheeled around from dealing with the Brahmans, who stood at the top of the social ladder in India, way over to the other extreme — the outcaste, whom no one wanted.

The Baptist mission took as their text on the matter 1 Corinthians 1:26–29: "God hath chosen the foolish things of the world to confound the wise; and God hath chosen the weak things of the world to confound the things which are mighty." Therefore, to make the critical step of conversion more simple, they decided to require of their converts only three changes of lifestyle in their public social life in the villages: "do not work on Sunday; do not eat carrion; do not worship idols."[37]

This made sense to Periah, who was a very uncommon *dalit*. Though illiterate he had joined a reformed yoga sect that repudiated caste, and he won respect as a guru. When he discovered that yoga did not satisfy his soul he made his first contact with missionaries, and Christian faith changed his life. Even before baptism in 1866 he had begun to evangelize others, twenty or thirty in his village. With his guru staff he would trudge from village to village, eating with anyone who invited him but respecting the right of the higher castes to avoid him. He insisted on self-support and refused any regular subsidy from the mission, but would discuss theology and evangelistic policies for hours with the missionaries. Reports filtered back to mission headquarters that converts were coming in by the tens at first, then, after 1869 by the hundreds, and after 1878 by the thousands.[38]

The famine of 1876–1879 in Telugu territory brought a similar rush of conversions into the Lutheran churches there. Between 1871 and 1881 the number of Telugu Protestant believers of all denominations jumped fivefold from fifteen thousand to seventy-seven thousand.[39] A million people were starving, and the Lutheran missionaries voluntarily suspended much of their evangelistic efforts to join in emergency relief work. Thousands died, but thousands of survivors, impressed by the demonstration of love by the foreigners, asked to join the church. Compassion itself is a powerful evangelist. Critics denigrated the converts as "rice Christians," and even the missionaries were aware of the danger. Surveys, however, proved that the mass conversions, usually by family and village groups, strengthened rather than weakened the spiritual commitment of the converted.[40]

Meanwhile other accessions to the Christian faith were occurring in India, not as a nationally unified movement, but each with its own characteristics and isolated one from another by geographical location, denominational divisions, and sometimes by social caste boundaries even within the *dalit* outcaste communities.[41] In the far south, great numbers of the Nadars, toddy-carrier *dalits*, flocked to the Anglicans of the CMS to ask for admission to the church. By the end of the century Nadars, no longer despised, had become the backbone of the largest Anglican diocese in the country, Tinnevelly. Not even a dispute between two Anglican missions in the area, the CMS and the more high-church Society for the Propagation of the Gospel in Foreign Parts (SPG), seemed to slow the growth. Once considered low caste, the contagious evangelistic enthusiasm and self-reliant ways of the new converts won them ever-increasing community respect and social approval.[42]

Another such movement occurred among the leather-working Chuhras far to the north in the Punjab. The Chuhras were sweepers, scavengers, servants, and farm laborers. Their leader into a new life was another outcaste, "a dark little man, lame of one leg," named Ditt. He made his scant livelihood by buying and selling hides, which made him socially "unclean." Baptized by a United Presbyterian missionary, Samuel Martin in 1873, Ditt accepted the sacrament only on condition that he need not stay with the mission for training but be allowed to return immediately to tell the good news to his depressed-class people in his own village.[43] His first two converts were his wife and daughter; the next year four more; then house by house, village by village, "the religious wave rolled onward," and in 1877, only four years after his own conversion, Ditt had propelled the whole United Presbyterian mission into a decision to devote its "special attention" not to the rich but to the poor.[44]

From there the movement leaped beyond the borders of the United Presbyterians into Scottish Presbyterian territory, and Anglican, Methodist, Salvation Army, and Catholic areas. Fortunately the Protestant groups in the Punjab had managed to negotiate comity agreements with each other, dividing the area into noncompetitive geographical zones, and the growth continued. Figures from the 1911 census, reported by

John Webster, indicate that of the 164,000 Indian Christians in the Punjab at that time, about 93,000 were Presbyterian, 29,000 were Anglican, 18,000 were Salvation Army, and nearly 8,500 were Roman Catholic.[45]

Advance to the Northeast: Mission to the Tribes

Meanwhile, far north on the high eastern frontier where India borders China in territory then often vaguely called "Assam," another movement of Protestant conversions was emerging. Baptist missionaries among the tribal "headhunters" of the mountains reported sparks of response to the preaching of the faith where least expected. The whole area is now divided into the seven small northern states of what is known as Northeast India.[46] A glance at a modern map of India gives the impression that the frontier states are now almost completely cut off from the rest of India by the newly made Muslim country of Bangladesh. They seem to be left dangling at the edge of the map about to fall into Burma and slip down into the Indian Ocean. But nineteenth-century Britain's imperial process of unifying India brought the isolated frontiers closer to the center politically if not geographically. In 1858 Queen Victoria abruptly transferred authority over India from the British East India Company to the crown, and hitherto independent native states were gradually absorbed into her empire. Many expected that as the trend continued, the religion of the Hindu majority in the northeast plains would eventually replace the primitive forms of animistic beliefs prevailing among the hill people.[47] But surprisingly, to anticipate a little, three of the seven states (Meghalaya, Nagaland, and Mizoram) are now predominantly Christian, and a fourth (Manipur) is more than a third Christian. How did this happen? Much of the explanation belongs to the next century, but the nineteenth-century beginnings are an example of the power of people movements, the voluntary acceptance of the Christian faith by whole communities rather than by separating individual converts from their village family structures.[48]

As so often in Asian church history it all began not with a Western missionary, but an Asian, and in the early years it was in no way a mass people's movement. In 1813, the first Protestant missionary to make his way into the "headhunter hills" and stay long enough to make a convert was an Indian, Krishna Chandra Pal. He was William Carey's first baptized Hindu convert,[49] and his misson to the unreached frontier made him, in effect, the first foreign missionary of the Serampore mission, for the Hill tribes were then about as far from British Calcutta culturally as "the end of the world." He went as to "a far country." In fact Krishna Pal used those very words to explain to the Serampore missionaries his call to go farther:

> As I lay musing one night, I thought to myself... Mr. Carey is much engaged at Calcutta, Mr. Marshman in the School, and Mr. Ward in the Printing Office. Bengal is a large country; how shall the people know Christ? I would go to the end of the world to make His love known.[50]

Krishna Pal established himself near Guwahati (Gauhati), the largest city in Assam, in a smaller town at the edge of the Khasi/Jaintia Hills of what is now Meghalaya.[51] There he faced the uncertainties of a mission to a tribal culture which, though primitive, at least had "no distinctions of caste." He stayed about eight months and before returning to Serampore happily reported that he had baptized seven men, including two Khasi from the Hills and one from Assam.[52]

Efforts to continue the work Pal had started failed. The Serampore mission translated and printed the Bible into Assamese (the New Testament in 1819, the Old Testament in 1833), but it used Bengali characters and the Assamese could not understand it, nor of course could the tribals in the hills.[53] A Baptist school opened in Guwahati but closed within a year. A Baptist church was organized there also, but the Indian converts disappeared and the church dwindled from twelve members to four, who were all European. When the Serampore mission rejoined the British Baptists in 1837, the work in the Hills was abandoned.[54]

The Christian mission in the Hills did not end there, though; it was only the beginning. The mission came to life again in the 1840s when two new, enthusiastic groups entered the field: the American Baptists and the Welsh Calvinistic Methodists, who later changed their name to Welsh Presbyterian.

The Baptists came by riverboat from India up the long, fertile valley of the Brahmaputra River in 1836. It took the two pioneer couples (the Nathan Browns and the Oliver Cutters) four months to reach their goal, Sadiya, a small settlement on the edge of nowhere three hundred miles upriver from Guwahati at the northeast tip of Assam. They established a mission and managed to stay four years, but here too it seemed to end in failure. They had to leave reluctantly without baptizing a single convert after a violent tribal attack on the British garrison in Sadiya killed the commander and terrorized the town.[55]

But they did not abandon the Northeast. They found temporary refuge with a colleague, Miles Bronson, who had left Sadiya earlier to begin promising work in Jaipur farther south. He was well received by the local chief and even managed to start a school of twenty young men, all related to the chief. It was there with Bronson in Jaipur that effective Baptist work began in 1841, and the mission baptized its first convert, a young Assamese named Nidhi Levi (or Nidhiram).[56] That same year, though, for practical reasons the Baptists soon moved their center west to the larger town of Guwahati in Central Assam. Four years later they organized the Baptist Church of Assam as a combination of three widely separated but established churches, with plans to start a mission school at each church.[57] At one of them, the school/orphanage at Nagaon, the first of a series of small revivals broke out in 1847, and the first women were baptized, among them the one soon to be married to Nidhi, the first Christian convert.[58] It was a foretaste of what was to come, but the future was long in coming.

The next two decades were difficult, dangerous, and disappointing. Twenty years after the first baptism, and twenty-five years after the beginning of the American Baptist mission, there were, in 1861, only three small churches reporting a combined membership of fifty-four. More alarming was the fact that they had lost thirty-one members in just the last ten years.[59]

Farther south, the year 1841, which saw the Baptists organize, also marked the coming of another new mission to the frontier. It was confusingly named Welsh Calvinist Methodists' Foreign Mission, though it was theologically and organizationally more Presbyterian than Methodist and later changed the name accordingly.[60] The pioneers, Mr. and Mrs. Thomas Jones, settled in an area in the southern part of the Khasi Hills around Cherrapunji. But their first two decades, like that of the Baptists in the north, were extremely difficult. It might have been blamed on the weather. Cherrapunji has the reputation of being the wettest place in the world — thirty feet of rain annually. Mr. Jones wrote that "Most of my time is occupied in saving our goods from being ruined by the rain."[61] The gospel was preached, but there were no converts for four years. New recruits arrived, but the deaths of two missionaries, including Mrs. Thomas Jones, within a year and a half of each other dampened the joy the missionaries felt at the baptisms of their first two converts in 1845. The most devastating blow of all came about a year later. The mission's pioneer, Thomas Jones, was charged with injudicious conduct and was asked to leave the mission. He soon died after unsuccessfully trying to support himself in India in some business ventures. That left only one missionary couple on the field.[62] The only substantially encouraging bit of progress seemed to be the opening of a number of small mission schools, but even this aroused such violent opposition that there was some talk in Wales of closing the mission.[63]

It was not closed, and the number of baptisms continued slowly to rise for a few years,[64] then suddenly it dropped. The Great Indian Mutiny (the Sepoy Rebellion) of 1857–1858 was a disaster not only to British rule, but to the mission. In 1861 American Baptists in the north and Welsh Presbyterians in the south could together report only 116 communicant members in all the northeast frontier.[65]

A turning point came in the 1860s. Failure gave way to a series of the first real breakthroughs of the Christian message into the wider life and culture of the Hills. In the next forty years these two missions, the American Baptists and Welsh Presbyterian, reported that total membership had risen to nearly 24,000, about 8,000 Baptists and 15,600 Presbyterians in Northeast India by 1900.[66]

The year that marked a change for the better was 1867, when the missionaries began to report what looked to them, after the long drought, like a mass movement. Again the catalyst was native Indian, not a missionary but not a lay evangelist either. He was an Assamese convert, Kandura R. Smith, the ordained pastor of the first Baptist church in Guwahati, the son of a blind fisherman. Smith was a man of some standing in the community, for he had left a government position for the pastorate at less than half the salary. In 1863 he had baptized two converts from among the Garo tribals, Omed and Ramkhe. Four years later, he sent them back into the Garo Hills to take the faith to their kinsmen. Omed became "not only the first person of the North East to be ordained, but was also the first to baptize others." Within ten years the number of baptized converts had reached four hundred, and the mission organized a Baptist "association."[67]

In very much the same way, the gospel came in power to the Naga Hills, but with a difference. Though the evangelist was not a missionary, neither was he of the same tribal group as his hearers. In the 1870s an Assamese, named Godhula, was the first to evangelize the Nagas of the Naga Hills, and in 1872 he brought back nine converts to the mission station for baptism; within four years there were enough converts to form a Naga church.[68] It is noteworthy how missionaries and Assamese evangelists responded to the shock when their pioneer, Godhula, left the work under a cloud and drifted away from the faith. The missionaries did not lose faith in the converts. One missionary said, "I have always found it to advantage never to question the motive of a native Christian. Never drive a man into a corner."[69] The converts grieved but refused to be discouraged. A Khasia evangelist, when asked, "What would you do if all the missionaries also left?" replied, "We wish them to stay, but while the missionaries remain we stand by God's grace, and if they go we will stand by God's grace."[70] By 1900 half of the Baptists were Garos, 40 percent were tribals on the plains, and another 10 percent were in Nagaland.[71]

The Welsh "Methodist" Presbyterian pattern in what is now southern Mehgalaya was similar. By 1867 they had planted and organized enough churches, ten, to form a presbytery. In 1887 they established their first seminary, and they ordained the first four Khasi ministers in 1890.[72] F. S. Downs describes that presbytery as the first modern "comprehensively representative organization" in the Khasi Hills. By 1895 the church had grown into four presbyteries with nearly two hundred churches and decided the time had come to form a central Assembly of the Presbyterian Church. Presbyteries and Assembly, says Downs, became "primary agents of Khasi-Jaintia solidarity."[73]

One of the major factors in the growth of the church was the extraordinary courage of the tribal converts. Among the Khasis the heir to the royal chieftainship of Cherrapunji, U Borsing, became a Christian. Six months later the *raja* died, and U Borsing was named his successor, but only on condition that he renounce his conversion. He refused; another took his place. Not only had he lost his throne, but all his worldly possessions as well. His only response was, "I can throw off my cloak or my turban, but the covenant I have made with God I can no wise cast away."[74]

Not all the Protestant ventures in the last half of the century in the Northeast were so successful. The most volatile mission was the dream of an English millionaire in Leeds named Robert Arthington (1823–1900), an ardent evangelical Quaker. He "dressed shabbily, ate frugally and lived in penury...[he] had no love of money as such." But he had a burning heartfelt passion for mission to the unreached on the far frontiers, and had the wealth to quickstart an independent mission of his own. Money, however, without an adequate mission plan as to how it should be used brought failure. He had come to the conclusion from his study of the Bible that once the gospel had been preached to all people, Christ would come again to end the world in final victory. Therefore, to hasten the process, he demanded that any missionaries he supported must not establish permanent residence, but must go out two-by-two, abstain from liquor, not marry, not bother to learn the local language, and move on quickly after preaching through interpreters.[75] Except for the commonsense warning against strong drink, his "preach and pass on" methods made little immediate and lasting missionary impact. But neither were they a complete failure. The Arthington mission had sent some of the first missionaries to strategic areas in the hills. They made converts and prepared the way, particularly in Mizoram and Manipur, and when the mission in the Northeast began to dissolve in the 1890s, it amicably turned over its beginnings in Manipur to the American Baptists, and in Mizoram to the Welsh Calvinists (Presbyterian).[76]

Arthington's mission lasted only ten years. But before he died in 1900, he left a will that shows how much he had learned from his venture. The restrictions are gone. He left his estate of almost a million English pounds half to the British Baptist Mission and two-fifths to the London Missionary Society, with only one word of advice, saying in effect: mission to the unreached frontier is the primary challenge of mission anywhere. In summary, he advises, first find the unreached areas; put Luke, John, and Acts into the people's language; teach a small group how to read the gospel; then let one tribe evangelize another, and keep visiting each tribe until a church emerges.[77]

It would be anticipating the future to characterize the quickening beginnings of church growth in this period as a people movement, that is, conversion of whole communities, rather than by mass conversion.[78] As the nineteenth century was closing in 1901 the Christian population of the Northeast Territories was little more than 1 percent of the total population of India, which could scarcely be called a mass movement. But rapid growth was beginning, particularly in Meghalaya between what is now Bangladesh and Assam.[79] About 70 percent of the membership of the whole Christian community in the Northeast territories was in little Meghalaya, about twenty-four thousand out of thirty-six thousand Christians.[80]

Among the reasons for the growth, as Frederick Downs has analyzed them, were: first, linguistic adaptation of Christian literature to the native tribal languages instead of Bengali Indian, especially in Assam.[81] Similarly effective in making evangelism credible was a second reason, a sincere compassion for the poor so actively expressed by the Christian missionaries.[82] Another factor, sometimes obscured by the obvious injustices of foreign rule, was the beneficent side of British justice. British administrators in tribal territories were unusually supportive of the mission. One of them, chief commissioner Francis Jenkins in Assam, not only welcomed the American Baptists but virtually ran some of their schools for them when they were absent.[83] Just as important to the tribal peoples, the British principle of equal protection under the law, even when used to stabilize the country by isolating the restless tribes from the rest of India, was seen by many among the Northeast minorities as a protection against absorption into the oppressive features of the Hindu caste system.[84] Finally, as the nineteenth century neared its end, an evangelical awakening began to spread like the wind around the world from the green valleys of Wales to the green hills of Northeast India. There were stirrings in the hills in the 1860s and 1870s,[85] but the major quickenings of revival carry us past the turn of the century beyond the limits of this volume into the next hundred years.[86]

Rapid Catholic Growth in Chota Nagpur

Roman Catholics in the nineteenth century, preoccupied with their own divisions after the rites controversy and friction over Portuguese control of the Indian church, had lost some of Xavier's pioneering zeal for converting the lower fringes of India's social caste system. But in the 1880s one of the most astounding bursts of growth Catholic India had ever seen occurred in Chota Nagpur (in modern Bihar and Andhra Pradesh, south of the Ganges and east of Bengal). In four years, under the inspired leadership of the Belgian Jesuit, Constant Lievens, "the apostle of Chota Nagpur," more than 65,000 people entered the church. They were tribal people, not *dalits* but outside the Hindu caste system. It was the reentry of the revived Jesuit order which, beginning in 1885, triggered this mass movement among a number of northern aboriginal tribes. Lievens won the total confidence of the tribals when he courageously championed their claims to lands where once they had freely roamed and worked until robber landowners displaced and slowly enslaved them. Within three years he had baptized 16,000, and another 40,000 were clamoring to be Christian. Not much more than a decade or so after Lievens died of overwork, in 1910 Jesuits could count more than 150,000 of the tribal "outcastes" as members of the church.[87] Not the least significant aspect of this Catholic mass movement is the fact that in the next forty years or so, the administration of their Chota Nagpur mission "was almost the first in India to go more or less completely native."[88]

Mission Cooperation, Division, and Christian Unity

In that period of astonishing growth after mid-century, Christian missions in India seriously confronted a crippling handicap within their own ranks: internal Christian disputes and divisions.

CATHOLIC-PROTESTANT RELATIONSHIPS

While Protestants were just beginning to take steps to avoid open competition as the mass movements spread, they found it much more difficult to bridge their differences with the Catholics. In the Punjab when Catholic missioners welcomed disgruntled Protestants into their fold, the exasperated Protestants muttered in protest about "the Jesuit peril."[89] They claimed that Catholics were more ready to convert Protestants than Muslims or Hindus,[90] but the charges cut both ways. After all, the Catholics had been in India first.

In one instance, at least, there was a brief show of magnanimity. And there were encouraging examples of mutual trust and forbearance. During the great famine of 1876–1878, the Baptist missionaries in Telugu country, north of Madras, mounted a heroic famine relief effort during which they were besieged by thousands of requests for baptism. Fearing that hunger rather than faith was often likely to be the motive for the sudden interest in Christianity, the Baptists deferred all baptisms for the first fifteen months of the famine. Finally a friendly Catholic missionary in the area, a priest who had generously resisted the temptation to proselyte, told John Clough that in good conscience he could no longer withhold the sacrament from whose who sincerely requested it. "If you don't, we will," the priest said. That was enough to jar the Baptists out of their hesitation. Within six months they baptized 9,606 converts. On one memorable day between sunrise and sunset, July 3, 1878, Clough, with the *dalit* Periah, the man who had started it all, and other Indian evangelists, baptized 2,222 new believers.[91]

THE GOA SCHISM AMONG ROMAN CATHOLICS

Protestants were used to interdenominational rivalries, as we have seen above, but in India at mid-century even the Catholics were facing schism.

It centered about the consequences of the declining authority of the Portuguese *padroado*, and the resurgent power of the papacy. Since 1514 the Portuguese crown had enjoyed by what in hindsight may have been too generous a transfer to Portugal of rights inherently belonging not to the state but to the church: the rights of mission and church administration (*padroado*) in all Portugal's overseas territories. In India this ecclesiastical power was centered in Goa, under its royal appointee, the archbishop of Goa.

But outside Goa, all India was falling to British rule, and the Catholic missionary orders in British territories felt circumscribed and handicapped by their failing Portuguese connection. The result was a paralyzing split in Catholicism in India between Portuguese royal *padroado* and Rome's papal power represented by the vicariates and the Propaganda. It was a tug of war between a fading empire, on the one hand, which desperately wanted to retain the aura of power that a sixteenth-century papal grant of authority had given it to appoint its own bishops in colonial territories, and on the other, a papacy which recognized that Portugal no longer had the means or will to promote Christian missions at its past levels of support. The controversy reached its height in 1833 when fruitless negotiations between the Vatican and Portugal ended in an impasse. Only then did Pope Gregory XVI begin to break Portugal's ecclesiastical control by establishing vicariates responsible directly to Rome, not to Portugal or Goa. The angry king of Portugal promptly broke diplomatic relations with the pope.[92] This rancorous, often violent, division (the "Goan Schism of 1838–1858"),[93] was not completely resolved even in an agreement reached in 1886.

In that year a papal concordat divided India into seven archdioceses nominally presided over by Portugal's archbishop of Goa with the title of patriarch of the East Indies, and Portugal retained patronage over most of the west coast bishoprics.[94] But still there was friction. The new papal bishops in the east coast vicariates of Madras, Calcutta, and the Coromandel Coast were deeply resented by bishops and priests still loyal to Portugal. Some of the bitterest internecine Catholic confrontations broke out in the far south in Madurai between "Padroadists" in Goa defending Portugal's waning power of exclusive patronage (*padroado*), and "Propagandists" in Madurai supporting the more independent vicariates of the pope's Society for the Propagation of the Faith.[95] Not until 1886 was peace restored, and the powers of the Portuguese *padroado* were finally virtually ended by two Concordats.[96]

Estimates of the number of Catholics in India at that time vary, but the best figure seems to be about 1.64 million Catholics, of whom some 1 million were in territory under jurisdiction of the Vatican's Congregation de Propaganda Fide, and about half a million still acknowledged the claims of the Portuguese *padroado*.[97]

Meanwhile, in the 1860s and 1870s hundreds of dissatisfied Indian Catholics had sought peace by joining Lutheran or Anglican churches.[98] Conversely, in that same period, in times of Protestant strife, discontented Protestants were also seceding to the Catholics by the hundreds.[99] At the end of the century friction between Catholics and Protestants was still so intense that one respected researcher could write regretfully:

> one section of the foreign population, devoted to the interests of religion and often men of the most self-denying life, the Romanists, are in some sections a more serious foe than any European or native opponent. "The Jesuit advance in India" is a very real problem.[100]

PROTESTANT APPROACHES TO UNITY AND COOPERATION

How could the Protestants offer peace? At mid-century they were only beginning the long process of healing their own embarrassing denominational divisions. To the women belong considerable credit for leading the way toward interdenominational cooperation in India. In 1851–1852 Lady Mary Jane Kinnaird had become vitally concerned about mission work among women in India. It was "an age when the Church of England despised Dissenters and Dissenters distrusted Anglicans," but Church of Scotland though she was, Lady Kinnaird urgently requested the secretary of the Anglican Church Missionary Society, the distinguished Henry Venn, to allow the formation of a missionary organization for women missionaries in India representing otherwise separated church groups working there. Women work best with women in India, and all true believers, she insisted, can work together. Venn could not resist. It was called the Zenana Bible and Medical Mission.[101]

Encouraged by this example, and beginning in Calcutta in 1855, for the next twenty years a series of six General Missionary Conferences called representatives from a wide range of Protestant societies to meet together, first regionally, then nationally, to survey the damage caused by intermission rivalries, and to consider ways of peaceful cooperation.[102] But the divisions within the denominations themselves were often more troubling. It was the Presbyterians, challenged by the *dalit* mass movement of the Chuhras in the Punjab, who took the first effective steps toward mending the ruptures within the Presbyterian fold, divisions that the missionaries had brought with them from Britain, Holland, and America. A Presbyterian missionary in northern India, J. H. Macphail, was the catalyst, shaming his colleagues with this challenge: "How can you ask Christians in Gujarat, in the Punjab, to call themselves 'Irish...'? And others in the Central Provinces to name themselves Scottish Original Seceders, when they have never been in Scotland, are in no sense original, and don't know a thing about seceding?"[103]

It was more than embarrassment, however, that moved the dour Scots and fiery Irish missions to consider uniting their efforts. There were deep roots of agreement among almost all Protestant missionaries of the last half of the nineteenth century that smoothed the path to interdenominational cooperation in mission and gave hope to some that the Western splintering of denominations need not be perpetuated on the mission field. The missionary movement was born in the great nineteenth-century revivals that motivated more than one generation of the converted to volunteer to reach the ends of the world with the good news of salvation. In the closing decades of the century, as Sundkler points out, Moody's sermons and Sankey's *Sacred Songs and Solos* had prepared the home churches in Britain and America for working together.[104]

In three great organizational forward moves the Presbyterians joined hands in India. In 1875 they formed the Presbyterian Alliance of India and began to hold regular all-India Presbyterian conferences. In 1901 they organized the first inter-Presbyterian union, the South India United Church, which joined a Dutch Reformed presbytery in Arcot with a Scottish United Free presbytery there. And in 1904 all India's Presbyterians united to form the Presbyterian Church in India.[105]

In South India alone around 1900, a map of the denominational divisions there would display a crazy-quilt pattern of Protestant rivalries: 45 different missionary organizations, 10 or more denominations, and a total of about 500,000 Protestant total membership. The five largest Protestant communities in the south were Baptists (178,000), Anglicans (155,000), Congregational (96,000), Lutheran (48,000), Presbyterian (14,000), and Methodist (10,000).[106] Catholics in South India were three times larger (1,463,000), and the "Thomas" Syrian Christians in the west on the Malabar coast (not included in the above figures) numbered 925,000, but were divided roughly three ways — Roman Catholic, Orthodox, and Reformed.[107]

Developing a National Christian Leadership

In the training of a national leadership for the church in India, the Christian missions in India, both Catholic and Protestant, made some of their most significant forward steps in the latter half of the nineteenth century.

PROTESTANT MOVES TOWARD INDIAN LEADERSHIP

Among the Protestants, Indian leaders had already proved their mettle in the mass movements, but lack of training and education were still a serious handicap to the formation of a permanent core of recognized national Protestant leadership. A basic framework had been laid for such training in the emerging network of Protestant mission schools, most of them still at the high school level. But toward the end of the nineteenth century a few had reached the college level, though it is difficult to determine which are tertiary-level colleges. Richter concludes that in 1901 there were some forty such colleges, the most notable of which were three Scottish Presbyterian mission schools:[108] William Miller's Madras Christian College, the largest and most famous mission school in India at that time;[109] Duff's college in Calcutta;[110] and John Wilson's College near Bombay.[111] Out of such schools, which began to have a widening impact on Indian society and politics, came a cadre of remarkable Indian Christians equipped not only for leadership in the church but eager to apply it to raising the level of politics and society in the nation at large.

A major step in this direction was taken by a group meeting as Christian Indians in 1895 formed a Native Christian Association in Madras "with a view to mutual support and edification, and the advancement of social interests." S. Satthianadhan's keynote address pointed with some pride to progress but added a warning. He described in detail how the Indian Protestant community had risen from small numbers and little social importance to a "a recognized position of local influence and conscious strength." Then he said:

> I, for one, attribute all the progress, social, moral and intellectual, to the leaven of Christianity...Take away Christianity and substitute anything else, and our progress will prove a sham. We dare not look to mere civilization as worthy to be trusted with the moral, or even with the physical well-being of our community...Let us make it clear that there has not been in us a mere exchange of one creed for another, but that there has been a radical change of life.[112]

For the more specific purpose of training for the ordained ministry, some of the first theological seminaries grew out of schools for catechists at the high school level. One of the earliest specifically formed as a theological school was the Anglican (CMS) Theological Seminary at Madras formed in 1835. All instruction was in Tamil, not English. Less than forty years later the CMS had 83 ordained Indian priests in its mission territories in India. In all India at that time there were only "225 ordained native agents"; by 1900 the number was 893. "These 900...Hindu clergy are the glory and crown of Indian missions," adds Richter.[113]

CATHOLIC TRAINING OF INDIGENOUS PRIESTS

As for the Catholics, for three hundred years the training of native Catholic priests had languished despite the founding of two seminaries as early as 1540–1541, one in Goa developed by the Jesuits, and a Franciscan seminary near Cochin to provide training for St. Thomas Christians who had already for centuries enjoyed the benefits of an indigenous priesthood.[114] Catholics ordained their first Goan Indian priest in 1558. But a hundred years later in Goa, at the very heart of Portuguese Catholic India, fifty-four of its eighty-five parishes were still in the hands of ordained foreign missionaries, while only twenty-one were led by native

Goan priests. Even the powerful Sacred Congregation for the Propagation of the Faith (the Propaganda), which had been specifically charged in 1630 with the task of encouraging the ordination of native priests, proved ineffective against the power of Portuguese control and racial prejudice.[115]

To find an exception to this pattern, historians must reach back to the seventeenth century. In 1637 Pope Urban VII had appointed an Indian Brahman, Matteo de Castro, who was ordained and granted a doctorate and was consecrated bishop in Rome, as "the first apostolic vicar to India," "the first missionary of the Propaganda in the East." De Castro was assigned to Bijapur, which was then in Muslim territory outside Portuguese control. He was the earliest and one of the most controversial Indian advocates of the cause of Indian Christian leadership, never missing a chance to attack the Jesuits and the Portuguese for their Western arrogance toward his countrymen. Twelve years earlier, in 1625, he had traveled all the way to Rome to protest the refusal of the archbishop of Goa to ordain him or any other Brahman to the priesthood, vigorously defending the fitness of Indian Christians for that dignity.[116]

A turning point occurred in 1835 at Goa, historically the center of Catholicism in India. In that year Portugal, caught up in the fluctuating waves of secularization and democracy that swept Europe after the French Revolution, suppressed its old missionary religious orders both at home and abroad. This forced a transfer of responsibility for training Indian priests from the orders to the "secular" hierarchy of diocesan bishops and priests. It was high time. Already by then the number of European missionaries in those decades of Catholic decline had fallen so sharply, that when the decree was issued, out of about three missionaries in the orders in Goa only sixteen were Europeans, who nevertheless were still being given precedence in leadership and in leadership training.[117]

In 1845 Propaganda issued instructions for more emphasis on education with an important injunction that Catholic schools must be caste-blind and open to all, from Brahmans to outcastes.[118] The Jesuits established several colleges of high academic standard, but gave no religious instruction to non-Christians and reported few converts, except for some conversions of Brahmans at St. Joseph's College in Trichinopoly.[119] The 1850s saw the formation of a trend toward organizing a number of seminaries intentionally directed toward the education of Indian clergy at varying academic levels, rising decade by decade.

But not until the end of the century did the matter begin to receive the attention it deserved. The nineteenth century closed with a final climax under the energetic leadership of Pope Leo XIII (1878–1903), "the working man's pope," and "the Thomist pope" who not only promoted better relations between the church and modernizing society in the West, but promoted reform and reorganization in the church's overseas missions.

In a series of decisions in the 1880s and 1890s, he gave Indian Catholicism a new face. In 1890 he granted to Belgian Jesuits the authority and support to organize a pontifical seminary in South Asia with the academic capacity to match the best of anything in Europe. They chose a location in Kandy, Ceylon. Sixteen years later it reported 86 students from about half of all the dioceses in India and Ceylon, and by 1914 it pointed with some pride to the fact that 113 of its graduated students had been ordained.[120]

Women in Mission

Rufus Anderson, the greatest general secretary the American Board of Commissioners ever had, was opposed to appointing women as missionaries throughout all his long and effective career. As he was retiring in 1866, however, he sensed a turning of the tide, and said to his successor, "I cannot recommend bringing the women into this work; but you are a young man, go and do it if you can."[121] It was the women themselves, however, who turned the tide. Missionary wives in their letters home had long been movingly describing the tragedy of women in Asia, and particularly in India.[122] One writer's capsule summary of the lot of Asian women was an unforgettable three phrases: "unwelcomed at birth, unhonored in life, unwept in death."[123] To Christian women in the West this challenge had to be answered. It was evangelistic. Women missionaries were the only Christian witness allowed into the *zenanas*, the women's quarters of half the homes of India. It was an educational challenge. Women founded most of the only schools for females on the entire subcontinent. It was a medical challenge. India's culture not only segregated by caste, but in general also drew a highly restrictive line between the sexes. Male doctors could not minister effectively to half the country's population; they could not even touch the sick women.

So women, many of them single, began to come to the mission field by the hundreds. Between 1860 and 1900 at least forty-one Women's Boards of Foreign Missions had been organized in America alone.[124] In just the one country of India the number of women in Protestant missions shot up two and a half times from 479 to 1174 in twenty years (1881–1900).[125]

MEDICAL WORK FOR WOMEN

Women physicians were only a small segment of the missionary personnel, but that part was in itself enough to produce a "renaissance of medical missions" in India. It began in 1870 with the appointment of one woman, an American Methodist, Dr. Clara Swain, "the first woman physician with a diploma who ever set foot in Asia." Within a few months she had begun a medical class, enrolling fourteen girls from the Methodist orphanage and three married women. The nawab of Rampur came to visit, and remarked, "[I] did not know that girls could learn so much."[126] Later, called to the court of Rajputana as personal physician to the rani, she accepted because she saw it as an open door to promoting Christian work for women. It did not at all hurt her campaign of quiet insistence on female rights and Christian freedom that it was during her eleven years of an unmistakable Christian medical presence at the court that the Hindu dynasty of Rajputani produced its first natural-born male heir to the throne in a hundred years. For lack of sons, previous successors had been adopted. Dr. Swain claimed no credit, of course, but soon the court secretary appeared to ask her if she wanted a church built. She said no; it would be enough if for the time being she could hold a Christian service on her veranda open to all who wanted to hear her read a sermon and pray.[127]

About the same time a Scottish medical missionary from Kashmir made a suggestion that surprised the governing committee of the recently formed Zenana Bible Mission. The mission's goal was to promote evangelism and education for Indian women, sequestered and isolated as they were in the women's quarters of India's homes. Dr. Elmslie said, in effect, "The quickest way to break the barriers into the *zenanas* is by neither evangelism nor education but by healing the sick. Then education and evangelism will follow." He urged the committee to organize "female medical missions." The committee was impressed but uncertain. Even in Britain in the 1870s a medical career was considered "indecent" for proper British women, but faced with so great a need the committee approved and women volunteered.

The first to be sent abroad were Lucy Leighton and Mrs. Crawfurd, a Scots widow. Neither was a qualified doctor, but private medical training had made them the nearest thing to a woman physician that could be found. Miss Leighton died on the long voyage out; Mrs. Crawfurd reached Bombay and died of heat and exhaustion within three months.

Still the volunteers came. The first to survive was Elizabeth Bielby, a trained nurse. She lasted almost a year in Lucknow, capital of Oudh, then was forced to return to England in 1877, her health wrecked. Undaunted and determined to go back to India, she heard of a full-length medical course hitherto not opened to women, but India came first, as did India's women, whose need for medical care was greater than her need for more education. She went back to Lucknow in 1878 determined that when her furlough was due, she would finish the medical course. "A little knowledge is insufficient," she wrote, "and without a medical education no one should undertake the duties of a medical missionary." She opened a small hospital, more like a clinic, with her sister Alice as nurse. Alice died in three months.[128] As for Elizabeth, the people said, "Miss Bielby is a messenger direct from heaven." Word about her reached the maharajah of Puna, two hundred miles south of Lucknow, who begged her to come and heal his critically ill wife. Treatment was successful, and Miss Bielby was due to leave for furlough in England, but the maharani pressed her for a parting promise: "I want you to tell our Queen, and the Prince and Princess of Wales, and the men and women of England, what the women in our zenanas suffer when they are sick." And the maharani gave her a message, enclosed in a locket, to give to the queen in person, "not to send it through another." Miss Bielby knew it would be impossible — an unknown missionary before Queen Victoria. But three months later, a very surprised young missionary found herself giving the locket to the great queen at Windsor Castle, and the queen was saying, "We had no idea it was as bad as this, something must be done for these poor creatures."[129] Elizabeth Bielby, now fully qualified, returned to India to work as an independent missionary in the new women's hospital at Lahore.

Twenty years later another woman came to India who was to lift the role of women in medicine to new heights. She was Ida Scudder, born in India, daughter of a medical missionary but in no way intending to become a missionary herself. Fresh out of Northfield Young Ladies' Seminary and not yet twenty years old, she came back to India only because her mother was very ill and needed her. Few who saw her step off the ship rather reluctantly in 1890 would have believed that one day she would be known around the world simply as "Dr. Ida," and that in her own lifetime (1870–1960), the medical work she started at Vellore would be described as "the greatest medical center in all Asia, supported by forty Protestant denominations in more than ten different countries."[130] What turned her into a missionary was the day three years later when three different Hindu men came to the Scudders' door to plead with her to save the lives of their desperately sick wives. My father is the doctor, she said, not I. But he is a man, they said, and each one in anguish confessed that he would rather have his wife die than be tended by a male doctor. The wives died. But from that day in 1893 and for the next fifty-seven years Ida Scudder knew she had felt the call of God and must do something for India's women.[131] She returned to America to study medicine, and in 1900 returned as what she had never intended to be, a missionary. In 1900 at Vellore, a small city of about forty thousand people not far from Madras, she opened her first hospital, a hospital for women.

EDUCATIONAL WORK FOR WOMEN

Until at least the middle of the nineteenth century, Indian opposition to education for women was so violent that educated upper-class Hindus were obliged to organize in secret to try to educate the women in their own families.[132] Even the British Indian government opposed it up to as late as 1849.[133] But by the end of the century, the literacy rate for Christian women in India was higher than that for non-Christian men. What had made the difference?

Much of the credit goes to the quiet determination of women missionaries, single and married,[134] who in that same half century began to overtake and outnumber men in Protestant missions.[135] The beginnings were not conspicuous, as we saw earlier in the work of two pioneers of women's education: wise, warm hearted Hannah Marshman, wife of William Carey's colleague Joshua Marshman; and Mary Alice Cooke, who in 1820 was perhaps the first intentionally single woman Protestant missionary sent to Asia.[136] But the work did not blossom until the 1860s and 1870s. By then the women carried with them to the foreign field the memory of their own struggle in the West for equal rights in education. It was no coincidence that the book which the first woman medical missionary, Dr. Clara Swain, used in her weekly public worship on the veranda at the court in Rajasthan was a book of sermons by the revivalist and educator, Charles Finney, one of the principal leaders in the founding of Oberlin College, the first college in America to admit women to a full coeducational degree.[137]

Protestant women missionaries on the field were far less hesitant in respect to the role of women in mission than the mission boards in the West that had sent them out, or for that matter most Western colleges and universities. As late as 1859, England's great Church Missionary Society was refusing to send women candidates to the field, or, equally unwise, shielding their constituencies from knowing that a few had already been sent. In America, as noted above, Rufus Anderson, one of the most enlightened missionary statesmen of his age, was opposed to sending unmarried women out as missionaries.[138]

But the early missionary women had soon discovered how much they were needed. They were appalled to find, for example, that "only 400 girls [were] able to read in the whole of India."[139] The numbers may be wrong, but other estimates are not far different. Ninety years or so later, according to the census of 1901, out of the country's 150 million Indian women and girls, still barely 105,000 (one in 144) could read and write, and census officials believed that public shame alone kept the figures reported from being lower.[140] The tyranny of caste and gender prejudice prohibited male teachers from giving personal instruction to females outside the family under ten or twelve years of age.

At the beginning of Protestant work in India, as we noted above,[141] the missionary women had tried to do something about this problem. Hannah Marshman, wife of Joshua Marshman of the Serampore Trio, opened a little, short-lived Baptist school for girls in Calcutta in 1812.[142] A few years later, also in Calcutta, Mary Alice Cook (or Cooke), watched in tears as a little girl begged the teachers at the boys' school to let her learn with the boys, only to be turned away day after day for months. Miss Cook took direct action. She gathered fifteen girls around her and began to teach them. Within less than five years, by 1826, to the astonishment of the whole city, the enterprise had mushroomed into a network of thirty schools with six hundred girls, and a supporting women's organization delightfully named "Ladies' Society for Female Native Education in Calcutta and Vicinity."[143] Later Miss Cook (by then Mrs. I. Wilson) left the Anglican Church Missionary Society and entered the Plymouth Brethren to work for interdenominational education for women.[144]

These early beginnings were a struggle against the angry opposition of Hindu traditionalists. Not until the 1870s and 1880s as more single women missionaries joined the missions, did Christian insistence on the right to educate girls begin to make its difficult way into public approval. In 1870, on the same ship that brought Clara Swain to India as its first woman doctor, another strong-minded Methodist came to India, Isabella Thoburn (1840–1901). What Dr. Swain did for medical missions, Miss Thoburn did even more effectively as the champion for women's rights in education. Her own brother, already in India, was not sure that single women belonged on the mission field, except perhaps as secretaries. Isabella gently but firmly set him straight. "I did not come to be a copyist," she said. She had come, as she wrote, because "we must have trained Christian women to work with us," and "We need strong-minded women at the top, in order to lift up the great mass of ignorance below."[145] Her brother James, who became the first resident Methodist bishop in India, ruefully admitted later: "I had to reconsider ... and once for all accept the fact that a Christian woman sent out into the field was a Christian missionary, and that her time was as precious, her work as important, and her rights as sacred as those of the more conventional missionaries of the other sex."[146]

It did not take Isabella Thoburn long to win most of the rest of the mission to the same enlightened view. Within two months of her arrival she had opened a school for girls — six girls, two of them the daughters of the pastor. Their brother was posted as guard at the door in case of violent protest, but he was not needed. In another two months enrollment reached seventeen. The primary school became a high school in 1884, and the high school led to the foundation of Lucknow Christian College (now the Women's College of Lucknow University), the first Christian college for women in North India. Isabella Thoburn, with the help of a gift from the mother of one of the high school's first graduates, Shorat Chuckerbutty, threw all her energies into promoting a college for girls, and Lucknow Women's College, the first in northern India, was opened to classes in 1894.[147]

At this point the missionaries must share credit with Hindu reform movements, which since at least 1814 had been critically appraising traditional Hinduism as hopelessly reactionary, and were also promoting education for women, due partly to Christian influences. Most notable was the Brahmo Samaj of Ram Mohun Roy (1774–1833),[148] sometimes called "the Erasmus of India," a friend and admirer of Alexander Duff. In the absence of a Christian girls' college in the Punjab, Shorat Chuckerbutty entered Brahmo Samaj–related Bethune College and after graduation returned to become one of Lucknow College's earliest teachers.[149] Another of Isabella Thoburn's pupils, Lilivati Singh, addressed one of the earliest ecumenical world missionary conferences, New York 1900, and so impressed Benjamin Harrison, former president of the United States, that he declared, "If Christian missions had done nothing more than make a Miss Singh out of a Hindu girl, they had repaid all the money put into them."[150]

By 1891 591,000 of India's women were literate, and the influence of the Christian faith is strikingly evident in the literacy percentage of females recorded then for India's three major religions: for Muslims only three of every ten thousand (.003 percent), for Hindus four out of every thousand (0.4 percent), and for Christians seventeen of every hundred (17 percent).[151] In fact, within a few decades the literacy rate for Christian Indian women was higher than for non-Christian Indian men.[152]

Clouds on the Horizon:
Growing Hindu Reaction and Missionary Doubts

In 1861 the publication of two books, one by a British civil servant, and one by an Indian intellectual (*pandit*), marked a change that was to affect the history of Christian missions in India for the next century and a half.[153] The Britisher was John Muir (1810–1882). He was not a missionary but a civil servant of the East India Company, who apparently studied for a year under William Carey in Calcutta and is described as a "quasi-evangelical," strongly supportive of Christian missions. The Indian was Nilakantha (later Nehemiah) Goreh or Gore (1825–1885), scion of a prominent Brahmin family who held hereditary rights as counselor to the ruler of Bundelkhand, and a major contributor to the emphatic anti-Christian, antimissionary response by Hindu leaders against the intrusive presence of the foreign missionaries. Four years later, Goreh, the emphatic anti-Christian Hindu, was a baptized Christian, and Muir, the mission-minded Christian, was publishing his doubts about traditional Christianity.[154]

With Muir, whose Christian enthusiasm for lay evangelism quite surpassed his reputation as an administrator in the East India Company,[155] the loosening of his evangelistic zeal began about twenty years earlier. In 1844 a short-term appointment as principal of the Benares Sanskrit College slowly turned the evangelist into the teacher. He did not lose faith; he still sharply criticized Hinduism, but increasing interest in religious Sanskrit literature, and with Hindus who resisted evangelism, tempered his enthusiasm for quick conversions. But by 1849 his loss of any sense of urgency in the propagation of the gospel suggested a step toward the slippery slope of universalism.[156] But the final chapter of Muir's gradual loss of missionary momentum did not become apparent until after he left India in the 1850s for Scotland, where he endowed a chair of Sanskrit studies at the University of Edinburgh and fell in love with German biblical criticism. His last writings, in the 1870s, abandoned the Bible as superior to the ancient Sanskrit classics either as divine revelation or as a moral standard. In 1879 he wrote, "Are not even the literatures, whether sacred or profane, of all countries, more or less, disfigured by something repugnant to the moral sense?"[157]

The most dramatic answer to that question came in the form of the conversion of a Hindu pundit who had reacted most angrily to the anti-Hindu arguments of the early Muir. He was Nehemiah Goreh, who, however, had already made a step of religious transition within Hinduism. Goreh had turned from the cult of Siva, the sensuous "Destroyer" and patron of yoga, to the worship of Vishnu, "the Preserver," who also appears as Krishna the divine teacher.[158] These were the two most popular Hindu sects, each claiming that its god was the supreme deity in a much-diluted, semi-monotheistic way. The change of sectarian loyalty was an academic decision for Goreh, not an emotional impulse. It was based on careful research as to which claim was supported by the earliest Sanskrit Scriptures. Still, any thought of Christianity was out of the question. To him, that was a religion for simple-minded foreigners to whose proselytizing the best response would be expulsion from India, or isolation into a Christian ghetto.[159]

Nevertheless, it was not closely reasoned defense of the Christian faith and criticisms of weaknesses in Hindu religion that led Goreh to conversion. He had already studied Muir's writings and dismissed them as one-sided, dull, and inadequate. It was a personal encounter with a Calvinist evangelist, William Smith of the Church Missionary Society, a linguist who knew his Hinduism as well as his theology, that answered Goreh's doubts and changed the Brahman pundit's life.[160] His most serious doubts were about the doctrine of salvation through Christ alone, the justice of an innocent man suffering for the guilty, the miracles of Christ and the apostles, and the character of a God who would create souls, some of whom, as he knew, would end up in Hell.[161]

But four years later he was baptized, and could characterize his former beliefs as "a manifest poison," "depraving the human intellect."[162] Not all his doubts were resolved, and he continued to wrestle with the tensions between faith and reason. But he became a devout Anglo-Catholic, admitting modestly, as he wrote in 1888, "that it is not by going through a regular process of reason that men renounce one religion and embrace another, though such was certainly the case with me, and that is the very reason why my faith in Christianity is so poor."[163]

The story of this unexpected reversal of faith in the lives of two men, a missionary and a Hindu, in mid-nineteenth-century India is a premonitory shadow of Western religious decline and Eastern Christian growth. It would spread almost imperceptibly at first, but in the next 150 years it would be unmistakably one of the most critical factors in the modern history of the Christian church.

An Overview of Christianity in India, 1850–1900

What then were the results of this half-century of Christianity in India? Was it a period of advance or decline? The answer, of course, depends on what constitutes Christian advance. The usual answer is a resort to statistics, which can sometimes be misleading. But because the alternatives involve trying to measure the immeasurable, a preliminary look at the statistics is not out of place.

A few generalizations are inescapable. As the century ended India's Christian community numbered an estimated 2,735,000.[164] Within that community, the largest single unit was Roman Catholic, with almost 1,900,000 members in 1901. That represents an encouraging increase over their 1800 total of perhaps 800,000, but Catholics had still not recovered from their high of between 2 and 2.5 million in 1700, two hundred years earlier.[165] In terms of church growth, however, the most remarkable feature of the century was the rapid rise of the Protestants from about 20,000 in 1800[166] to over a million in 1900.

How much of that was due to the prestige of a Protestant British constitutional monarchy, or almost a century of slow Catholic growth or Protestant missionary zeal, or the West's economic and cultural challenge to India's seemingly outdated native Hinduism is debatable. But whatever the reasons, at the dawn of the twentieth century the Protestant/Anglican presence was beginning to dominate the Christian segment of the subcontinent. It was still considerably smaller in numbers than the Roman Catholics, but in its influence and prestige and growth Protestantism appeared to many non-Christian Indians to be the wave of the future in a British India.[167]

Protestant advance became most impressive in the last half of the century, 1851 to 1901. It was increasing at the rate of an average of 54 percent every ten years.[168] In fifty years India's counted Christians had risen from about 1,270,000 to 2,700,000 — Protestants from only 91,000 to 1,290,000; Catholics (including Syro-Malabar) from 1 million to 1,920,000; and Syrian Orthodox from 180,000 to 250,000.[169] Protestants had multiplied fourteen-fold; Catholics had nearly doubled.

Such statistics would be cause for most of the missions to rejoice except for one unavoidable, sobering comparison. In that same fifty years, the population of India had increased by over 100 million from about 150 million to more than 255 million. Comparing the statistics in 1851 and 1901 in terms of growth proportional to population instead of in number of members, though the Christian churches — Protestant, Catholics, and Orthodox all together — might point proudly to a gain of about half a million converts, that would make hardly a blip on the screen of the country's population. While the missions were converting half a million, India's predivision population had increased by 105 million.[170] True, the Christian percentage had increased from 0.8 percent to 1.1 percent, indicating that growth in the Christian community was higher than population growth, but the odds were still forbidding: 1 Indian Christian to every 94 non-Christians.[171]

In the number of missionaries also, Protestants in India were growing faster than the others. Statistics 1800 (1799) listed 150 Protestant foreign missionaries; by 1851 there were 339, but the figure is misleading. Had missionary wives been included, as they should have been for they had labored as faithfully as their husbands and had probably suffered more, the numbers would be nearer 300 and 6000, respectively.[172] By 1901 growth was almost exploding. If the report is correct, the number of American and European Protestant missionaries had leaped startlingly from 339 to 16,218, probably including the wives.[173] In contrast, the Catholic missions were still recovering from a long drought. In the three-year period from 1871 to 1873 there were a reported 733 foreign priests in India and 353 Indian priests, a total of 1,086. The missionaries were alarmed that their numbers were no longer growing.[174] A belated encouragement was a growing force of Catholic Sisterhoods and an anticipation of promised new recruits both male and female.[175]

A key to measuring success in the global Christian mission rests not merely in the number of missionaries and the number of church members. The most important measure in so many ways is the changing proportion of leadership in the church passing year by year from the missionaries to national church leaders, ordained and unordained.

In India in 1901 progress toward an Indian church for India was barely beginning. Modak reported Protestant growth from 7 native ministers in 1820 to 158 in 1845, and 4,185 in 1897. An increase from 158 to 4,185 Indian pastors in fifty-two years is worth commendation. But the sixteen or seventeen thousand foreign missionaries far outnumbered them. So when Stephen Neill, in his highly appreciated 1964 overall summary of Christian missions, commented on the leap in Protestant membership growth in the half century with a blunt charge that the Protestant missionaries were "singularly blind" to the changes from missionary to national leadership demanded by such a rapid explosion of success,[176] he was partly wrong but painfully right.

The Catholics had a longer history of attention to the problem. In 1851 they reported 1,126 foreign priests in All-India (including Burma and Ceylon), rising in 1901 to 2,615, but counting lay brothers and sisters the total number of missionaries rose from 1,206 to 1,732.[177] Nevertheless, they too had postponed three hundred years of argument and delayed full training of a native ministry. As early as 1630 the Vatican's missionary arm, the Propaganda Fide, had issued a decree on the need for native clergy.[178] Again 150 years later in 1787 the Propaganda restated the policy that "parish priests should preferably be nationals" of their own country.[179] But despite the protests of a few who took the call seriously, as late as 1862 "out of 18 vicariates, six had not even a single Indian priest," reports one recent Catholic study, which stated flatly that the apostolic vicars had been "negligent."[180]

Seven years later, two energetic popes shook the church into action. Decades of postrevolutionary disasters, including loss of its papal states in Italy, moved Pius IX to call a general Council, Vatican I, the first in three hundred years since the Council of Trent. His successor, Leo XIII (1878–1903), in three critical years at the end of the century, took the church a global step further, and reorganized its overseas missions. In India in 1886 a new Concordat with Portugal was the beginning of a process that was eventually to end that kingdom's crippling *padroado* stranglehold on missions in that subcontinent. That same year he established a Latin hierarchy under the Vatican's Propaganda Fide. The next year, 1887, Kerala's Catholic Syro-Malabar St. Thomas Christians in Southwest India were freed from both the *padroado* and the Latin vicariates and granted two apostolic vicariates of their own. In 1897 another Syrian apostolic vicar was added, finally recognizing the unique significance of indigenous leadership for Indian Catholicism.[181] A. J. Urumpackal sums up the importance of the lesson to be learned: "The evangelization of India by foreign bishops and missionaries was a system of the past and was not the ideal."[182]

But what of the less measurable yet more important and enduring results? The social impact of the Christian faith in the nineteenth century is almost as obvious as the numerical growth of church membership, but its direct linkage to Christianity is not as indisputably measurable. Such factors as foreign rule, Westernization, economics, and secularization were also involved. But the role of Christian missions in India's social changes is too well attested to be ignored. Christians, both Indian and missionary, led in the fight against widow-burning,[183] exploitation of laborers on the indigo plantations,[184] and caste barriers,[185] and they were more active, proportionate to their percentage of the population, than either Hindus or Muslims in the early years of the movement for Indian national independence.[186] Most troubling was the caste barrier. K. N. Subramanyam observes about nineteenth-century missions in India that "the only region in which Christians found high caste converts was in Bengal," and more were found in the Protestant community than among Catholics.[187]

The greatest Christian growth India had ever seen occurred in the last half of the nineteenth century and the beginning of the twentieth. Proportionately, most of it was Protestant. In the single decade of 1861–1872, the number of Protestants increased 61 percent while Catholic growth was 12 percent.[188]

How would the next century in India compare to the "great century," the nineteenth? In 1900, the estimate of the comparative numerical strength of the major religions in India's population of 229,900,000 according to David Barrett et al., eds., *World Christian Encyclopedia*, 2001, was as follows:[189]

	1900	2000
Hindu	184,028,000 (80.0%)	755,000,000 (74.5%)
Muslim	31,522,000 (8.7%)	123,000,000 (12.1%)
Tribal religions	6,670,000 (2.9%)	35,000,000 (3.4%)
Christians	3,820,000 (1.7%)	62,000,000 (6.2%)
Roman Catholic	1,920,000 (0.8%)	16,000,000 (1.5%)
Protestant (PIA)	1,200,000 (0.5%)	40,000,000 (5.0%)
Orthodox, Syrian	650,000 (0.3%)	3,000,000 (0.3%)
Sikh	2,180,000 (1.0%)	22,000,000 (2.2%)
Buddhist	200,000 (0.1%)	7,000,000 (0.7%)
Jain	1,320,000 (0.6%)	4,000,000 (0.4%)

As the century ended, Christian missions from abroad had barely made a scratch on the surface of the great subcontinent. But a few years earlier, in 1886, the evangelist Dwight L. Moody called more than a hundred college students together for a summer Bible study conference. Among those attending were two sons of India missionaries: Robert Wilder of Princeton and John Forman of Yale. Together with two others, Robert E. Speer of Princeton and John R. Mott of Cornell, they became the driving force of a student movement, the Student Volunteers for Foreign Missions, which in the next twenty years swept thousands of young Americans into overseas missionary service. A surprising number came to India, as we shall see. But the person who would stand out early and most clearly as a change agent for the future of Christianity in India was an Indian, Azariah of Dornakal.

India Chronology (1857–1900)

1857–1858	Great Sepoy Mutiny in Britain's India Army (which was 80 percent Indian).
1857	Mass movement among Kols of Chota Nagpur (now, Jharkhand) begins under lay Indian evangelists of the Gossner Mission.
1858	East India Company taken over by British crown.
1860	Mass movement of Nadars in Cape Comorin (now, Kanyakumari) and Travancore [site of the "first of the mass movements," 1818/1819, in LMS territory, Charles Meade, Vedamanikam]; also Evangelical Lutherans in Chota Nagpur among Oraons, Mundas.
1862	End of Moghul Empire.

1867	Mass movement among Santals (Bihar, Orissa) under Santal Mission (funded by Indians).
1869	Segment of Gossner Mission turns Anglican, mass movement continues. Also Baptists and CMS in Telugu area.
1870	Mass movement of Chuhras in Punjab, Andrew Gordon, United Presbyterian; Ditt.
1871	Mass movement among Mazhabi Sikh and Sweepers, Methodist Ep.
1877	Queen Victoria assumes title of Empress of India.
1878	New Diocese of Lahore (CMS).
1879	Mass movements in Tinnevelly; Anglicans divide Madras into two dioceses, Travancore and Cochin.
1880	Zenana Bible and Medical Mission, women's auxiliaries in mission (1828 — Mrs. I. Wilson, CMS, Darbyite, interdenominational).
1881	Church of England Zenana Missionary Society (CMS).
1885	Upper Burma annexed with Lower Burma to form British Burma; Jesuits enter Chota Nagpur; mass movement among tribals.
1886	First National Congress, mainly Hindu.
1891	Mass movement in Assam: first missionary visit to Mizoram (Lushai Hills), William Williams, Welsh Presbyterian.

NOTES

1. S. Natarajan, *A Century of Social Reform in India* (London: Asia Publishing House, 1959), 5.

2. J. Waskom Pickett, *Christian Mass Movements in India* (New York and Cincinnati: Abingdon Press, 1933), 56. Cf. the statement of Sundararaj Manickam citing J. J. Ellis: "the real 'father' of the Trichinopoly Mass Movement and the founder of the Church in the Mass Movement area is...not the missionary Ellis, but the semi-literate old headman of P. K. Palayam, Abraham *alias* Alagan (Sundararaj Manickam, *The Social Setting of Christian Conversion in South India: The Impact of the Wesleyan Methodist Missionaries on the Trichy-Tanjore Diocese* [Wiesbaden: Franz Steiner Verlag, 1977], 101).

3. Pope Leo XIII, in his encyclical *Ad Extremis*, 1893. The English translation of the encyclical ("On Seminaries for Native Clergy") is in Carlen, *The Papal Encyclicals*, 2:307–309.

4. Vol. 1, chap. 1 of this work.

5. See the *St. Thomas Christian Encyclopaedia of India*, 2:50, 54, 76, 79, 82ff.

6. Gense, *The Church at the Gateway of India, 1720–1850*, 1–110.

7. Claudius Buchanan, *Christian Researches in Asia* (London: Cadell and Davies, 1814), 106–150. It was Buchanan, first of the evangelical chaplains, who in 1806 found among the St. Thomas Christians the Peshitto manuscript of the Bible, "the only complete ancient MS of the Syriac Bible in Europe, except one at Milan." It is now at Cambridge University (Stock, *History of the Church Missionary Society*, 1:232). Buchanan reported a shorter, earlier visit by Dr. Kerr, senior Anglican chaplain at Madras (*Christian Researches in Asia*, 146ff.). Ten years later the first resident Protestant missionary arrived, Thomas Norton of the CMS (*St. Thomas Christian Encyclopaedia*, 2:94–95).

8. Paul Verghese [Paulos Gregorios], "The Syrian Orthodox Church," in *St. Thomas Christian Encyclopedia*, 2:76–78.

9. The Syrian Orthodox were called Jacobite after a sixth-century bishop, Jacob Bardaeus, who saved Monophysite Orthodoxy in Syria from impending extinction. See Moffett, *A History of Christianity in Asia*, 1:244–246.

10. P. Cheriyan, *The Malabar Syrians and the Church Missionary Society 1816–1840* (Kottayam, India : Church Missionary Society's Press, 1935), 106–111; Cyril Bruce Firth, *Introduction to Indian Church History* (Madras: Christian Literature Society, 1961), 161–168; D. Daniel, *The Orthodox Church of India*, 150–153. Cf. Leslie Brown, *The Indian Christians of St. Thomas*, 138ff.

11. Quoted by F. E. Keay, *A History of the Syrian Church in India*, rev. ed. (Madras: SPCK in India, 1952), 60.

12. *St. Thomas Christian Encyclopaedia of India*, 2:89, 95; D. Daniel, *The Orthodox Church of India*, 144–145.

13. For a full description of the twenty-three reforms proposed by Abraham Malpan, see Kuruvilla, *History of the Mar Thoma Church and its Doctrines*, 14–18. For a recent, broader theological and sociological reappraisal of Abraham Malpan, see M. M. Thomas, *Towards an Evangelical Social Gospel: A New Look at the Reformation of Abraham Malpan* (Madras: Christian Literature Society, 1977). And for an argument that Malpan's Malayalam liturgy was more radically Protestant than the more moderate 1872 rite, and the revised twentieth-century Mar Thoma liturgies, see Philip Tovey, "Abraham Malpan and the Amended Syrian Liturgy of CMS," in *ICHR* 29, no. 1 (1995): 38–55.

14. D. Daniel, *The Orthodox Church of India*, 88–89.

15. Mathew was from the Pakulomottam (or Pakalomottam) family, which produced nine metropolitans from 1665 to 1816. D. Daniel, *The Orthodox Church of India*, 66ff.; I. Daniel, *The Malabar Church and Other Orthodox Churches* (Haripad, Travancore, India : Suvarna Bharathi Press, 1950); Kuruvilla, *History of the Mar Thoma Church*, 18; and Susan Visvanathan, *The Christians of Kerala: History, Belief and Ritual among the Yakoba* (Madras: Oxford University Press, 1993), 46.

16. On Mathew Mar Athanasius (or Athanasios), who was metropolitan from 1842 to 1877, see L. Brown, *The Indian Christians of St. Thomas*, 141–148; and John R. K. Fenwick, *The Malabar Independent Syrian Church: A Brief Account of the Thozhiyur Metropolitical See* (Bramcote, Nottingham, U.K.: Grove Books, 1992), 25–31, 61. Also Tisserant, *Eastern Christianity in India*, 147–152.

17. D. Daniel, *The Orthodox Church in India*, 89–90; Paulos Mar Gregorios, *The Indian Orthodox Church* (Delhi and Kottayam: Sophia Press, 1982), 35–36. Fenwick, *The Malabar Independent Syrian Church*, 27–28; Tisserant, *Eastern Christianity in India*, 148ff.

18. On the court cases and issues, see the helpful summary in Firth, *An Introduction to Indian Church History*, 168–175; and in more detail, Visvanathan, *Christians of Kerala*, 24–32, 43ff.; and cf. Fenwick, *The Malabar Independent Indian Church*, 29–34; and Paul Verghese, "The Syrian Orthodox Church," 2:76–77. Tisserant, writing from a Roman Catholic point of view, gives a balanced treatment of the schism (*Eastern Christianity in India*, 147–155).

19. On the revivals and evangelism see Stock, *History of the Church Missionary Society*, 3:179–184; K. T. Joy, *The Mar Thoma Church: A Study of Its Growth and Contribution* (Kottayam, Kerala, India: Good Shepherd Press, 1986), 92–100.

20. T. V. Philip, in *St. Thomas Christian Encyclopedia*, 2:89ff.; Alexander Mar Thoma Metropolitan, *The Mar Thoma Church: Heritage and Mission*, 2nd rev. ed. (Tiruvalla India: Ashram Press, 1986), 60–61; V. Titus Varghese and P. P. Philip, *Glimpses of the History of the Christian Churches in India* (Madras: Christian Literature Society, 1983), 117–119; Joy, *The Mar Thoma Church*, 60ff.

21. Selected from D. Daniel, *The Orthodox Church of India*, 602ff.; and L. Brown, *Indian Christians of St. Thomas*, 145ff.

22. On the disputes over the patriarchate and their effect in India, see Leslie Brown, *Indian Christians of St Thomas*, 151–154 and footnotes. Cf. Tisserant, *Eastern Christianity in India*, 151–155.

23. Dionysios (or Dionysius) VI (Vattasseril Geevarghese) was metropolitan 1908/1909–1934/1935, not counting his temporary deposition (D. Daniel, *The Orthodox Church of India*, 181); cf. I. Daniel, *The Malabar Church and Other Orthodox Churches*, 15, 87, who spells the first name Vattaseril.

24. D. Daniel, *The Orthodox Church of India*, 109–128; Varghese and Philip, *Glimpses of the History of the Christian Churches in India*, 96–100; Leslie Brown, *Indian Christians of St. Thomas*, 153–154.

25. D. Daniel, *The Orthodox Church of India*, 165, 181; Varghese and Philip, *Glimpses*, 98ff.

26. India's outcastes have been known by many names: *harijans*, depressed classes, and even tribal aboriginals who are not strictly speaking outcastes, but the preferred term now is *dalit* (the oppressed). The best history on the subject is Webster, *A History of the Dalit Christians in India*. At several points its analysis differs from the classic early treatment by Bishop Pickett, *Christian Mass Movements in India*, which is still immensely valuable for its firsthand, detailed reports of a nationwide research study in the early 1930s of India's mass movements. See also Duncan B. Forrester's careful analysis of the issues in *Caste and Christianity: Attitudes and Policies on Caste of Anglo-Saxon Protestant Missions in India* (London: Curzon Press, and Atlantic Highlands, N.J.: Humanities Press, 1980).

27. See chap. 1.

28. Pickett, *Christian Mass Movements*, 38–41.

29. Gibbs, *The Anglican Church in India*; and Pickett, *Christian Mass Movements*, 49–50.

30. There were stirrings of this movement as early as 1802. Hugald Grafe, *The History of Christianity in Tamilnadu from 1800 to 1975* (Bangalore and Erlangen: Church History Association of India, 1990), 27ff., 80–97; Pickett, *Christian Mass Movements*, 38–41, 56; Lovett, *The History of the London Missionary Society*, 2:31–32. Vedamanikam was a Saivite in doctrine, but as a Sambavar by caste he was of lower social stature than the Nadars he led. As for the missionary, Charles Mead of the LMS, under whom Vedamanikam worked after Ringeltaube left, it

is sad to report that when much later Mead married a *dalit*, it was an act that in those days, 1856, "destroyed at a stroke his influence and usefulness" (Lovett, *The History of the London Missionary Society*, 2:167).

31. On Gossner and his Chota Nagpur mission, see Walter Holsten, *Johannes Evangelista Gossner: Glaube und Gemeinde* (Göttingen: Vandenhoeck & Ruprecht, 1949), 226–287, and passim; William Fleming Stevenson, *Praying and Winning: Being Some Account of What Men Can Do When in Earnest* (New York: Thomas Whittaker, [1882?]). On his connection with the Schleiermachers, and his loose ties to Lutheran denominationalism, see Stevenson, *Praying and Winning*, 297–300. On the "faith mission" pattern, in which Gossner followed the model of the earlier Basel mission (which sent out its first missionaries in 1821), see Paul Jenkins, *A Short History of the Basel Mission* (Basel: Basel Mission, 1989); and the standard German history, Wilhelm Schlatter, *Geschichte der Basler Mission 1815–1915*, 3 vols. (Basel: Basler Missionsbuchhandlung, 1916).

32. The Chota Nagpur (or Jarkhand) tribals were from a diverse group of tribes (Mundas, Orauns, Santhals, and Larka Hos) beyond the pale of the Hindu caste system principally in the state of what is now Jarkhand, and the neighboring states of Uttar Pradesh, Bihar, and Orissa. In the 1870s and 1880s they constituted about a third of the population of Chota Nagpur — 1.3 million "Kols" to 2.7 million Hindus. Stevenson, *Praying and Winning*, passim; Chatterton, *History of the Church of England in India*, 282–286; and F. S. Downs, letter, June 15, 2001.

33. See Chatterton, *History of the Church of England in India*, 282–297.

34. "Germany: Gossner Missionary Society," *The Encyclopedia of Missions*, 2nd ed. (New York and London: Funk & Wagnalls, 1904), 731. For an extended analysis of the ups and downs of the Gossner Mission, 1845–1885, from a Roman Catholic viewpoint, see Fidelis de Sa, *Crisis in Chota Nagpur: The Judicial Conflict between Jesuit Missionaries and British Government Officials 1889–1890* (Bangalore: Redemptorist Publication, 1975), 72–110.

35. Stevenson, *Praying and Winning*, 306.

36. V. S. Azariah and Henry Whitehead, *Christ in the Indian Villages*, 2nd ed. (London: Student Christian Movement Press, 1930), 18.

37. John E. Clough, *Social Christianity in the Orient: The Story of a Man, A Mission and a Movement* (New York: Macmillan, 1914), 84, 159.

38. Periah became a guru in a *rajayoga* sect before conversion. He was baptized with his wife in 1866. Clough, *Social Christianity in the Orient*, 72–381 (on Periah, 87–88, 92–108; on the decision to focus on mission and education for Madigas at the cost of excluding the higher castes, 118–135; on rapid growth, 138–158, 304, 317ff.; on the social revolution that followed, 159–184; on self-support, 105, 346–364). See also David Downie, *The Lone Star: The History of the Telugu Mission of the American Baptist Missionary Union* (Philadelphia: American Baptist Publication Society, 1893), 44ff., 77–134; Pickett, *Christian Mass Movements*, 47–49; and Webster, *History of the Dalit Christians*, 40–41, 52–53.

39. Richter, *A History of Missions in India*, 219.

40. Martin Luther Dolbeer, *A History of Lutheranism in the Andra Desa (The Telugu Territory of India) 1842–1920* (New York: Board of Foreign Missions, the United Lutheran Church of America, 1959), 143–249, 296–300. See also J. Waskom Pickett, *Christ's Way to India's Heart: Present-Day Mass Movements to Christianity,*

rev. ed. (New York: Friendship Press, 1938), 33–34, 50ff.; and Pickett, *Christian Mass Movements in India*, 332.

41. Forrester, *Caste and Christianity*, 79–80.

42. Chatterton, *A History of the Church of England in India*, 308–311; Pickett, *Christian Mass Movements*, 28, 38; and Grafe, *The History of Christianity in Tamilnadu*, 44–45. By the early twentieth century, if not before, Nadars (sometimes called Shanars) were not considered *dalits*. As early as 1810–1818 the smaller movement, described above, of Nadars into the church in Congregational (LMS mission) territory, was led by Vedamanikam, who was a Sambavar by caste, lower than the Nadars (Forrester, *Christianity and Caste*, 80; and Webster, *History of Dalit Christians*, 199). Nineteenth-century writings on India do not consistently distinguish between the fourth caste, Sudras, with their many subdivisions, and the so-called "fifth caste" of outcastes or untouchables, the *dalits*.

43. Andrew Gordon, *Our India Mission: A Thirty Year's History (1855–1885) of the India Mission of the United Presbyterian Church of North America* (Philadelphia: Andrew Gordon, 1886), 421–432; Webster, *History of the Dalit Christians*, 44–49; Pickett, *Mass Movements*, 42–47.

44. The full name is United Presbyterian Church in North America. In 1958 it united with the Presbyterian Church in the U.S.A. ("northern") as the United Presbyterian Church. For more on Ditt and the Punjab mass movement, see Frederick and Margaret Stock, *People Movements in the Punjab* (Pasadena, Calif.: William Carey Library, 1975), 64–67, 80–71; on the United Presbyterian India Mission policies, see 18–25, 77ff.

45. In round numbers. See Andrew Gordon, *Our India Mission*, 421–463; Webster, *History of the Dalit Christians*, 38, 44–49; Pickett, *Christian Mass Movements*, 42–45.

46. Assam, Manipur, Meghalaya, Mizoram [Harvest of the Hills], Nagaland, Tripura and, jutting into China, Arunchal Pradesh.

47. On the influence of both British administration and Christian mission on the development of tribal identities, see Frederick S. Downs, *History of Christianity in India*, vol. 5, part 5: *North East India in the Nineteenth and Twentieth Centuries* (Bangalore: Church History Association of India, 1992), 2–8, 15–23; and Frederick S. Downs, *Essays on Christianity in North-East India* (New Delhi: Indus Publishing Co., 1994), 34–35, 159ff., 199–207.

48. See Downs, *Essays on Christianity in North-East India*, 39–51, on Jesuit visits to the area as early as 1626, and a possible Catholic community in western Assam in 1682, which did not survive.

49. On the Serampore mission see chap. 12 above.

50. John Hughes Morris, *The History of the Welsh Calvinistic Methodists' Foreign Mission, to the End of the Year 1904* (Carnarvon, Wales: C. M. Book Room, 1910), 70.

51. Pandu, near Guwahati, was where Krishna Pal centered his mission. It was under British protection but in the kingdom of Cherrapunji (Downs, *History of Christianity in India*, 5/5:66). The Khasi Hills are in eastern Meghalaya; the Jaintia Hills are west; and Cherrapunji is south on what is now the Bangladesh border.

52. Morris, *History of the Welsh Calvinistic Methodists' Foreign Mission*, 70–71. Krishna Pal's converts at Pandu were examined and baptized by a Mr. Smith from Chattak.

53. A. K. Gurney, "The Bible in Assamese," in *The Assam Mission of the American Baptist Missionary Union: Papers and Discussion, 1886* (Calcutta: J. E. Thomas Baptist Mission Press, 1887). In 1886 the Assamese were still without a complete Bible in their language.

54. The Serampore mission had separated from the British Baptist mission in 1827 and rejoined it ten years later (Morris, *History of the Welsh Calvinistic Methodists' Foreign Mission*, 70–76; and F. S. Downs, "Early Christian Contacts with North East India," in *ICHR* 5, no. 1 [December 1971]: 70–77). See also Victor Hugo Sword, *Baptists in Assam: A Century of Missionary Service, 1836–1936* (Chicago: Conference Press, 1935).

55. Downs, "Early Christian Contacts," 69–77; Frederick S. Downs, "The Establishment of the American Baptist Assam Mission, 1836–1841," *ICHR* 6, no. 1 (June 1972): 71–78.

56. Sword, *Baptists in Assam*, 59–66. On Nidhi Levi Farwell, see Downs, *Essays on Christianity in North-East India*, 161–163, and *History of Christianity in India*, 5/5:70, 188.

57. Sword, *Baptists in Assam*, 73–82.

58. Sword, *Baptists in Assam*, 74.

59. Downs, *History of Christianity in India*, 5:1, 70–71; cf. his *Essays on Christianity in North-East India*, 52–53.

60. To avoid confusion I use the later name, Presbyterian. On the formation of the Welsh Missionary Society in 1795, its early relations with the independent London Missionary Society, and its change of name and connection from Methodist to Presbyterian, see Morris, *History of the Welsh Calvinistic Methodists' Foreign Mission*, 25–37; and Downs, *History of Christianity in India*, 5/5:68 n. 13.

61. Morris, *History of the Welsh Calvinistic Methodists' Foreign Mission*, 77–78.

62. Morris, *History of the Welsh Calvinistic Methodists' Foreign Mission*, 95–98.

63. Morris, *History of the Welsh Calvinistic Methodists' Foreign Mission*, 80–82, 84–89, 98, 101–108.

64. Morris, *History of the Welsh Calvinistic Methodists' Foreign Mission*, 90–94, 120–121.

65. Morris, *History of the Welsh Calvinistic Methodists' Foreign Mission*, 182, 144–146; and Downs, *History of Christianity in India*, 5/5:71. Baptists listed fifty-four (presumably adult baptized) members in 3 churches; Welsh Presbyterians 62 communicants, and 158 total membership in 16 churches and preaching stations.

66. For the Baptist statistics see Downs, *History of Christianity in India*, 5/5:77; for the Welsh Presbyterian, see Morris, *History of the Welsh Calvinistic Methodists' Foreign Mission*, 197. Downs notes the puzzling discrepancy with the government census report of 35,969 Christians in the Northeast.

67. F. S. Downs, "Origins of Christianity in the Garo Hills of Meghalaya," *ICHR* 6, no. 2, 82–86; Downs, *History of Christianity in India*, 5/5:78–80; Downs, *Essays on Christianity in North-East India*, 54–55, 155–159. A Baptist association is somewhat similar to a Presbyterian presbytery.

68. *The Assam Mission of the American Baptist Missionary Union, 1886*, 80–83; 223–226. Miles Bronson had planned such a mission but was unable to implement it. W. E. Clark sent Godhula to the Nagas, and sadly, thirteen years later saw him give up the work and fall into reprehensible behavior. Notwithstanding the scandal, the Naga churches kept growing under a faithful unordained Assamese

evangelist Zilla, who was able to report seventy-nine baptized Naga Christians to the Baptist mission in 1886.

69. *The Assam Mission of the American Baptist Missionary Union, 1886,* 131.

70. *The Assam Mission of the American Baptist Missionary Union, 1886,* 217.

71. Downs, *Essays on Christianity in North-East India,* 54–55.

72. Morris, *History of the Welsh Calvinistic Methodists' Foreign Mission,* 151–154, 179.

73. Downs, *Essays on Christianity in North-East India,* 35.

74. Morris, *History of the Welsh Calvinistic Methodists' Foreign Mission,* 164–166.

75. A. M. Chirgwin, *Arthington's Million: The Romance of the Arthington Trust* (London: Livingstone Press, [1936]), 74–82. The Arthington mission's original name was the Indian Aborigines Mission. Only two of his missionaries (J. H. Lorrain and F. W. Savidge, both English Baptists) of the thirteen missionaries sent out remained with the mission for more than about three years, and those two left in four, but returned to serve eventually under the British Baptist Mission. Arthington turned over the part of his mission started in 1893 among the Mizos in the Lushai Hills (now Mizoram, at that time part of Assam) to the Welsh Calvinists (1895–1898) (J. M. Lloyd, *History of the Church in Mizoram* [Harvest of the Hills] [Aizawl, Mizoram: Synod Publication Board, 1991], 25–39). His missionary in Manipur, William Pettigrew, resigned in 1896 to join the American Baptists (Downs, *History of Christianity in India,* 5/5:84–85). Pettigrew has the distinction of being the only missionary allowed to reside in Manipur until after World War I (Downs, *History of Christianity in India,* 5/5:83–84).

76. Downs, *History of Christianity in India,* 5/5:83–85.

77. Chirgwin, *Arthington's Million,* 32ff., 146–151.

78. On the principle of people movements see Donald McGavran's seminal studies, *Bridges of God: A Study in the Strategy of Mission* (New York: Friendship Press, 1955); *Understanding Church Growth,* 3rd ed., rev. and ed. Peter Wagner (Grand Rapids, Mich.: William B. Eerdmans, 1970), and *Ethnic Realities and the Church: Lessons from India* (Pasadena, Calif.: William Carey Library, 1979).

79. Downs, *History of Christianity in India,* 5/5:9, citing the census of 1901. By mid-century (1951) the proportion of Christians in the Northeast to total Indian Christian population had increased from 1.23 percent to 7.8 percent.

80. Downs, *History of Christianity in India,* 5/5:80. But note the discrepancy mentioned above in n. 66.

81. The "primary initiators and movers" in the effort to preserve Assamese as the official language of Assam were the two Baptist pioneers Nathan Brown and Miles Bronson, and Anandaram Dhekiyal Phukan, the first and only high-ranking Assamese scholar to publicly oppose the mandate of the British administration to use Bengali in the public schools of Assam in this period. Downs, *Essays on Christianity in North-East India,* 71ff., 81–141. On Phukan, see 25ff.

82. Downs, *History of Christianity in India,* 5/5:13–23.

83. Downs, *History of Christianity in India,* 5/5:33–63.

84. Downs, *History of Christianity in India,* 5/5:15–23; 176–180.

85. Church growth rose rapidly as early as 1867 in the Garo Hills of Meghalaya led by Garo evangelists, not the missionaries, and in Upper Assam in the 1870s by Assamese evangelists. Downs, "Origins of Christianity in the Garo

Hills," and *History of Christianity in India*, 5/5:79ff.; and Lloyd, *History of the Church in Mizoram*, 86ff.

86. For a brief comparison with late twentieth-century statistics see Johnstone, *OW*, 280, 285–286, 289.

87. Sa, *Crisis in Chota Nagpur*, vii–x, 111–319; Subramanyam, *The Catholic Community in India*, 51–56. Cf. statistics of growth in Sa, 315 n. 134, 319, and in Subramanyam, 56. For critical evaluations of Lievens' work, pro and con, see Sa, *Crisis in Chota Nagpur*, 315–337.

88. Sa, *Crisis in Chota Nagpur*; Subramanyam, *The Catholic Community in India*, 52–57. See also Sa, *Crisis in Chota Nagpur*, 328, and 72ff., 110 n. 221, who suggests that in his training and use of Indian leadership Lievens may have been following the methods of the German Lutherans of the Gossner mission in Chota Nagpur.

89. Sa, *Crisis in Chota Nagpur*. See also the Protestant criticism of Catholic schools in *Report of the First Decennial General Missionary Conference, Allahabad, 1872–73*, 475. On the rapid Catholic growth in Chota Nagpur, see Sa, *Crisis in Chota Nagpur*, 132–147, 327–328; and H. C. Permalil and E. R. Hambye, *Christianity in India: A History in Ecumenical Perspective* (Alleppey, India: Prakasam Publications, 1972), 254–255.

90. Webster, *History of the Dalit Christians*, 49; cf. Grafe, *History of Christianity in Tamilnadu*, 45; Sa, *Crisis in Chota Nagpur*, 103ff. Sa's book deals with the Jesuits and Lutheran missions in Chota Nagpur among Mundas and Oraons.

91. Clough, *Social Christianity in the Orient*, 269–290; Downie, *The Lone Star*, 111.

92. Hull, *Bombay Mission History*, 1:231ff.

93. See Hull, *Bombay Mission History*, 1:236–255 and passim; Perumalil and Hambye, *Christianity in India*, 1:156–165; 2:1–21, 170–201 (refers to Concordats of 1859, 1886).

94. There were three vicariates under the Propaganda in the early nineteenth century: Verapoly (Malabar), Pondicherry, and Bombay (including the Tibetan-Hindustan). After Portugal abolished the religious missionary orders in its territories in 1833, Rome added four more vicariates for non-Portuguese India: Calcutta, Madras, Ceylon, and Madurai. The seven episcopal dioceses of 1886 were Goa, Bombay, Agra, Calcutta, Madras, Verapoly, and Pondicherry. See the maps and text in Hull, *Bombay Mission History*, 1:1–xv; 2:1–21, 170–201; also Launay, *Histoire des missions de l'Inde*, 4:559–564; and the concise summary in Latourette, *A History of the Expansion of Christianity*, 6:74–77.

95. The new vicariates were Madras (1833), Bengal (1834), and the Coromandel Coast excluding Madras (1870), replacing the old Pondicherry vicariate. The earlier vicariates were Bijapur, or the vicariate of the Great Moghul, in 1637, which in 1720 became the vicariate of Bombay; and Malabar in 1657. See Hull, *Bombay Mission History*, 1:43–51, 214–237, 271–276, and passim.

96. Hull, *Bombay Mission History*, 1:291–293; 2:180–231, 435–438.

97. Hull, *Bombay Mission History*, 2:193ff., 232–238.

98. Sa, *Crisis in Chota Nagpur*, 313ff., 325ff.; Grafe, *History of Christianity in Tamilnadu*, 114, 116.

99. Kaj Baago, " 'Sheepstealing' in the 19th Century," in *Bulletin of the Church History Association of India* (November 1966): 31–36; Sa, *Crisis in Chota Nagpur*, 103, 118; Grafe, *History of Christianity in Tamilnadu*, 116–117.

100. Harlan P. Beach, ed., *A Geography and Atlas of Protestant Missions*, vol. 1 (New York: Student Volunteer Movement for Foreign Missions, 1901, 1903), 362. But he did add, "Local opposition from Hindus is far more common than Catholic interference." He attributed Catholic success to "its policy of tolerating among its converts the customs of caste and social observances" (363). See also Baago, "Sheepstealing," 25–26; Pickett, *Christian Mass Movements*, 255; Grafe, *History of Christianity in Tamilnadu*, 117–118.

101. J. C. Pollock, *Shadows Fall Apart: The Story of the Zenana Bible and Medical Mission* (London: Hodder & Stoughton, 1958), 17–21, 194. In 1957 the society changed its name to Bible and Medical Missionary Fellowship. See also Gaius J. Slosser, *Christian Unity: Its History and Challenge in All Communions, in All Lands* (London: Kegan, Paul, Trench, Trubner, 1929), 123.

102. The six conferences were Calcutta (1855) for Bengal; Benares (1857) for the Northwest; Ootacamund (1858) for South India, Liverpool in England (1860) for both missionaries and officers of English Societies; Lahore (1862–1863) for the Punjab; and Allahabad (1872–1873) for Northern India (Rufus Anderson, *History of the Missions of the American Board of Commissioners in India*, 264–265).

103. J. H. Macphail, *Conference* (May 1904), 22, quoted by Bengt Sundkler, *The Church of South India: The Movement toward Unity* (London: Lutterworth Press, 1954), 36.

104. Sundkler, *The Church in South India*, 20.

105. Sundkler, *The Church in South India*, 36–39. The South India United Church (Southern Presbyterian) joined the union, becoming officially Presbyterian again, but expressed the hope for a more inclusive union.

106. Richter, *A History of Missions in India*, 444–447. Richter's "*south* India" is roughly the east coast (Madras Presidency). The *all-India* Syrian Christian statistics were: Roman Catholic Uniate 500,000, Jacobite Syrian Orthodox 300,000, and Reformed (Mar Thoma) 125,000. Cf. the *all-India* (including Burma) 1901 census figures in *The Statesman's Year-Book, 1903*, 141–142: total Christians 2,923,241; Roman Catholics 1,202,039, Syrian Roman Uniate 322,586; Protestant 1,023,606 (Baptist 220,863, Anglican 453,612, Lutheran 155,455, Other 157,847); excluding Burma the Baptist number would be about 140,000.

107. Richter, *A History of Missions in India*, 445.

108. Richter, *A History of Missions in India*, 318–319. See also Latourette, *A History of the Expansion of Christianity*, 6:189–190, for a brief analysis of Protestant mission school education in India.

109. Richter, *A History of Missions in India*, 319; *Our Church's Work in India: The Story of the Missions of the United Free Church of Scotland in Bengal, Santalia, Bombay, Rajputana, and Madras* (Edinburgh: Oliphant, Anderson & Ferrier, n.d.), 389.

110. *Our Church's Work in India*, 29ff. The college remained under the Church of Scotland after the Disruption of 1843, and its name was changed first to the General Assembly's Institution, and then to the Scottish Churches College (Latourette, *A History of the Expansion of Christianity*, 6:145).

111. *Our Church's Work in India* (Maratha), 30–31.

112. "Korea," *ChHB* 18 (December 1895): 270.

113. Richter, *A History of Missions in India*, 422ff. In 1900 there were 893 Protestant ordained Indian pastors. "These 900 Hindu clergy are the glory and the crown of Indian missions," adds Richter (427).

114. Schurhammer, *Francis Xavier*, 2:240–243, 273–276; Moraes, *A History of Christianity in India*, 1:228.

115. Carlos Merces de Melo, *The Recruitment and Formation of the Native Clergy in India (16th–19th century): An Historico-Canonical Study* (Lisbon: Agencia Geral do Ultramar, 1955), 163–177; Alex Paul Urumpackal, *Vocations in India*, vol. 1, *The Religious Woman*, vol. 2, *The Clergy* (Kottayam, Kerala, India: Oriental Institute of Religious Studies, 1986, 1988), 2:242, 320. The Propaganda's decree was issued in 1630, reminding the hierarchy in India of the example of the disciples, and the greater influence Indian clergy, well acquainted with Indian custom and languages, might have upon their own people.

116. Ghesquière, *Mathieu de Castro*, 25–57, 106–117; Melo, *The Recruitment and Formation of the Native Clergy in India*, 2:215–220, 227–235, 238–244, 251–252; Urumpackal, *Vocations in India*, 2:239 n. 14. Back in India, de Castro was not altogether unprejudiced and arrogant himself and exercised his new power as a bishop vigorously. He started a seminary in Bijapur and too hastily ordained so many new Indian priests that he barely escaped censure by the Inquisition and in effect set back rather than advanced the cause of native Indian leadership.

117. Melo, *The Recruitment and Formation of the Native Clergy in India*, 163–177.

118. C. Becker, *Indisches Kastenwesen und Christliche Mission* (Aachen: Xaverius Verlag, 1921), 103.

119. Latourette, *A History of the Expansion of Christianity*, 6:94.

120. Latourette, *A History of the Expansion of Christianity*, 6:94, citing J.-B. Van der Aa, *Lettres de Kandy: Souvenir du Seminaire Pontifical 1906*; and *Catalogus Magistrorum et Alumnorum Pontificii Colegii Kandiensis A.D. MCMXXXII.*

121. Quoted by R. Pierce Beaver, *All Loves Excelling: American Protestant Women in World Mission* (Grand Rapids, Mich.: William B. Eerdmans, 1968), 85.

122. See for example, Mrs. Marcus B. Fuller, *The Wrongs of Indian Womanhood* (New York: Fleming H. Revell, 1900).

123. W. E. Oldham, "Isabella Thoburn," in *Effective Workers in Needy Fields*, ed. W. F. McDowell et al. (New York: Student Volunteer Movement for Foreign Missions, 1902), 91. For an Indian analysis of India's enforced "female decadence," as the missionaries described it, see Abhijit Dutta, "Position of Women and Female Education," in *Nineteenth Century Bengal Society and Christian Missionaries* (Calcutta: Minerva Associates, 1992), chap. 5, 120–142. See also Pollock, *Shadows Fall Apart*, 11–15 and passim.

124. Beaver, *All Loves Excelling*, 86ff.

125. Richter, *A History of Missions in India*, 220. Even more dramatic was a sudden overall increase in the total number of missionaries, due largely to the inclusion of women at last, both wives and single women, as recognized missionaries: the total recorded in 1851 had been 339; in 1890, 857, but in 1900, only ten years, later it had jumped to 3,836 (Beach, *A Geography and Atlas of Protestant Missions*, 1:381).

126. Dr. Clara Swain (1834–1910) reached India in 1870 (not 1857 as Richter records). In 1884 she received the urgent appeal to treat the Rani of Rajputana. As for the invitation to stay at the court, she hesitated, but "the more I prayed," she wrote, "the more I saw the hand of the Lord in it all, and I accepted . . . on condition that [she and her Indian] companion be allowed to work among the people as Christian women." Clara A. Swain, *A Glimpse of India* (New York: James Pott,

1909; reprint, New York and London: Garland Publishing, Inc., 1987), 159–335, esp. 163. Cf. Hollister, *The Centenary of the Methodist Church in Southern Asia*, 74–77; Mrs. J. T. Gracey, *Women's Medical Work in Foreign Lands* (Boston: Women's Foreign Mission Society of the Methodist Episcopal Church, 1888), 39; and Richter, *A History of Missions in India*, 349–352.

127. Swain, *A Glimpse of India*, 272–281.

128. Pollock, *Shadows Fall Apart*, 33–44.

129. Pollock, *Shadows Fall Apart*, 35–44, 63–66. In 1884 Queen Victoria kept her promise and told the wife of the new British viceroy of India, Lord Duffield to "do something" about the medical plight of India's women, and in 1885 Lady Duffield founded the "National Association for supplying Female Medical aid to the Women of India." By 1887 six "lady doctors" were serving under it. Under other funding, Miss Bielby's old Lucknow hospital was rebuilt and reopened in 1890 as the Lady Kinnaird Memorial Hospital.

130. Dorothy Clarke Wilson, *Dr. Ida: The Story of Dr. Ida Scudder of Vellore* (New York: McGraw-Hill, 1959), 3.

131. Wilson, *Dr. Ida*, 32–43.

132. One unexpected result was the formation about 1842 of "a secret society" of high-caste, educated Hindus, not Christians, who, observing the missionary schools, were "privately instructing their young daughters and other female relatives." One of Alexander Duff's early converts, the high Brahmin Krishna Mohun Banerjea, cast out by his family for his efforts toward Hindu reform, had acquaintances in that secret society, and became a powerful advocate of women's education (George Smith, *The Life of Alexander Duff*, 194–195, 81–87).

133. Richter, *A History of Missions in India*, 337–338.

134. On the reluctance to appoint women, and especially single women, for full missionary service, see, among other references: Beaver, *All Loves Excelling*, 31ff., 43ff., 50ff., 59ff. and passim; Stock, *History of the Church Missionary Society*, 1:124–125; 2:397–399; 3:367–373; Lovett, *The History of the London Missionary Society*, 2:235–241; Robert Stewart, *Life and Work in India: The Conditions, Methods, Difficulties, Results, Future Prospects and Reflex Influence of Missionary Labor in India, especially in the Punjab Mission of the United Presbyterian Church of North America* (Philadelphia: Pearl Publishing Co, 1896), 284–288; Sherring, *History of Protestant Missions in India*, 436 n. 1; Evelyn C. Gedge, ed., *Women in Modern India: Fifteen Papers by Indian Women Writers* (Bombay: D. B. Taraporewala, 1929), 63–77.

135. See the statistics in Beaver, *All Loves Excelling*, 107–108, assembled from Mrs. L. H. Daggett, *Historical Sketches of Woman's Missionary Societies in America and England* (Boston: L. H. Daggett, 1883); James Dennis, *Centennial Survey of Foreign Missions* (New York: Fleming H. Revell, 1902); Beach, *Geography and Atlas of Protestant Mission*, vol. 2; J. S. Dennis, H. P. Beach, and C. H. Fahs, eds., *World Atlas of Christian Missions* (New York: Student Volunteer Movement for Foreign Missions, 1911).

136. Beaver, *All Loves Excelling*, 60; Richter, *A History of Missions in India*, 334–335.

137. On the Oberlin connection with female education, see Robert Samuel Fletcher, *A History of Oberlin College from Its Foundation through the Civil War*, 2 vols. (Oberlin, Ohio: Oberlin College, 1943), 1:369–377. Oberlin in 1834 was first in America to give women access "to all the instructive facilities which hitherto have unreasonably distinguished the leading sex from theirs," acting against

the advice of Lyman Beecher who warned, "If you live in a powder house you blow up once in a while." See also Swain, *A Glimpse of India*, 279, as mentioned above.

138. Stock, *History of the Church Missionary Society*, 3:397–399. On some American parallels, see Beaver, *All Loves Excelling*, 62ff., 85ff., 98ff.

139. Richter, *A History of Missions in India*, 334. The year given for that figure is 1819.

140. According to the India census of 1901, reports Richter, the female population of India was about 150 million; 13 girls of every 1,000 were married below the age of five, 102 between five and ten years of age, and 423 between ten and fifteen; and only one women in 144 could read and write, which would mean 105,000 out of India's 150 million (Richter, *A History of Missions in India*, 329–331, and 330 n. 1). But compare his statistics on 310. The difference may be a distinction between the ability to read and the ability to write.

141. See chap. 12 above.

142. Richter, *A History of Missions in India*, 334.

143. Miss Cook (or Cooke, later Mrs. Isaac Wilson of the Church Missionary Society) reached India in 1821, sent out by the British and Foreign Bible Society to work for the Calcutta School Society. But when she found that not only was the society antagonistic toward a schoolmistress who was interested only in teaching girls, but also that one-third of the trustees were Hindus opposed to the teaching of Christianity in the Calcutta schools, she turned to the Church Missionary Society and began her own remarkable work. See Stock, *The History of the Church Missionary Society*, 1:199–200, 228, 283, 317; 2:161, 162; 3:138; and Richter, *A History of Missions in India*, 334–336, 340.

144. Stock, *The History of the Church Missionary Society*, 1:317.

145. J. M. Thoburn, *Life of Isabella Thoburn* (New York: Eaton and Mains, 1903; reprint, New York: Garland Press, 1987), 32, 181ff.; and Oldham, "Isabella Thoburn," 93–97.

146. Oldham, "Isabella Thoburn," 98; J. N. Hollister, *The Centenary of the Methodist Church in Southern Asia*, 71. On J. M. Thoburn, who in 1888 became Methodism's first resident bishop in India, see Hollister, 15, 123, 134ff., 176–177. On the role of women in other missions, see, for example: United Presbyterian N.A. in the Punjab (R. Stewart, *Life and Work in India* [Philadelphia, 1896], 131ff.).

147. Oldham, "Isabella Thoburn," 106–107.

148. Natarajan, *A Century of Social Reform in India*, 8, 26–40. But Natarajan's observation that "by 1862 the principle of equal education for men and women had been fully accepted in Western India" (40) is a little too optimistically sweeping. Bethune College was not founded until 1869, though its roots stretched back to a "Native Female School" started twenty years earlier at his own expense by a British government official. See Richter, *A History of Missions in India*, 338, 376. Cf. Neill, *A History of Christianity in India*, 2:165–166.

149. Hollister, *The Centenary of the Methodist Church in Southern Asia*, 78–81. Shorat Chuckerbutty, because there was as yet no college for women in the Punjab, graduated from Bethune College in Calcutta. See also Gerald H. Anderson, ed., *Biographical Dictionary of Christian Mission* (New York and London: Macmillan Reference USA/Simon & Schuster, 1998), 664.

150. W. F. McDowell et al., *Effective Workers in Needy Fields* (New York: Student Volunteer Movement for Foreign Missions, 1902), 102, 109–114.

151. Beach, *A Geography and Atlas of Protestant Missions,* 378, citing Sir William Wilson Hunter, *The Indian Empire: Its History, People and Products* (London: Trubner, 1892 edition).

152. Latourette, *A History of the Expansion of Christianity,* 6:200.

153. For the following paragraphs I am deeply dependent upon an outstanding PhD dissertation by Richard Fox Young, *Resistant Hinduism: Sanskrit Sources on Anti-Christian Apologetics in Early Nineteenth-Century India* (Vienna: Institute of Indology of the University of Vienna, 1981).

154. Young, *Resistant Hinduism,* on Muir, 49–61; on Gore, 101–103; and on both, 166–172. "The irony is striking," writes Young, "whereas the challenger became less and less orthodox in his Christian faith, the convert became more and more so in his" (172). Young's book has best documented and most fully presented the facts of this surprising and almost forgotten double turn-about of leading actors in early Christian-Hindu debate.

155. See Young, *Resistant Hinduism,* 49–53; Muir's dual role as active but unofficial supporter of Christian missions and as a mid-level official in the British East India Company was not uncommon at that period, in which an unusual number of company officers openly and evangelically supported the missionary enterprise in India. Many of them had been influenced at university by the famous Charles Simeon of King's College and Holy Trinity Church, Cambridge, who helped to found the Church Missionary Society.

156. Young, *Resistant Hinduism,* 57–60. Alexander Duff, more famous as an educator in India than Muir, could not allow Muir the teacher to take the urgency of divine judgment on false religions out of the missionary motive, and had earlier raised sharp objections to some of Muir's statements (59).

157. Quoted by Young, *Resistant Hinduism,* 166–169, citing on 169 John Muir, *Metrical Translations from Sanskrit Writers* (London: Trübner, 1879).

158. Some have loosely referred to a Hindu trinity of Supreme Gods: Brahma the Creator, Siva the Destroyer, and Vishnu the Preserver, but Brahma, identified with the caste system, was elitist; the other two were popular, and theistically sectarian. A well-written introduction to Hindu religion is A. L. Basham, ed., *A Cultural History of India* (London: Oxford University Press, 1975).

159. Young, *Resistant Hinduism,* 102–103.

160. Young, *Resistant Hinduism,* 102–108, 169–172.

161. Young, *Resistant Hinduism,* 104ff. Goreh also was critical of Christian condemnation of idolatry as ignoring the fact that it was not the idol which wise men revere, but what it symbolizes. And he defended the doctrine of transmigration of souls as more just to sinners than the Christian doctrine of salvation for believers alone.

162. Quoted by Young, *Resistant Hinduism,* 170. I have followed Young extensively but very selectively. His two-hundred-page published dissertation is carefully balanced and convincingly documented and is not to be blamed for inevitable distortions due to the unavoidable need for abbreviation.

163. Young, *Resistant Hinduism,* 171–172.

164. This total of 2.7 million excludes a category of "secret" and therefore uncountable but noticeable Christians. Barrett et al., eds., *World Christian Encyclopedia,* 2001. National totals here combine the separate statistics for India and Pakistan to adjust to the pre-1947 united India of 1900. And compare Catholic statistics for 1851–1921 in *India and Its Missions,* by the Capuchin Mission Unit

of the Catholic Students' Mission Crusade, 2 vols. (New York: Macmillan, 1923), 1: appendix tables 1, 2; and 2: tables 1 to 3, 5; citing *Die katholischen missionen* 40 (1912): 201; 41 (1913): 116; and 50 (1922): 195.

165. Latourette, *A History of the Expansion of Christianity*, 6:73, n. 20.

166. Richter, *A History of Missions in India*, 127. The use of the term "Protestant" in this volume usually refers to Protestants, Independents, and Anglicans (PIA).

167. See Latourette's comments on Protestant advance in this period (*A History of the Expansion of Christianity*, 6:194–195).

168. In 1851 the Protestant community had numbered only 91,000, Roman Catholics roughly 1 million, and non-Catholic Syrian Orthodox about 180,000 — a total of perhaps 1,270,000 (0.8 percent) of India's population of about 150 million (Richter, *A History of Missions in India*, 409; see his critical analysis of the statistics in his Appendix N, 442–449).

169. Statistics for this period have a high margin of error, and as far as possible exclude Burma and Ceylon. Figures for 1851 are adapted from estimates in Sherring, *History of Protestant Missions in India*, 431–432, 441–443; *The Year Book of Missions in India, Burma and Ceylon, 1912*, ed. J. P. Jones (Madras: Christian Literature Society for India, 1912), 157; and a reference to average Catholic rate of growth in South India between 1850 and 1861 (Launay, *Histoire des missions de l'Inde*, 3:69). Figures for 1900 are adapted from Barrett et al., eds., *World Christian Encyclopedia*, 2001, 360, 542, for India and Pakistan as undivided before 1947. For Catholic statistics 1851–1900, see Students' Missions Crusade, Capuchin unit, *India and Its Missions*, appendices 1–3.

170. These numbers are only approximate. Population figures vary partly due to different definitions of the borders of "India" in this period.

171. Using different figures, C. H. Robinson estimated the ratio as 1 in 111 (*History of Christian Missions*, 119).

172. S. Modak, *Directory of Protestant Indian Christians* (Ahmednagarh, India: Bombay Education Society Press, 1900), 2 vols., 1:vi; 2:appendix 19; and see *Report of the First Decennial General Missionary Conference, Allahabad, 1872–73*, 321–322.

173. Robinson, *History of Christian Missions*, 494. 16,218 looked at first like an error. Modak's *Indian Christian Directory*, vol. 2, appendix, 15, reported only 2,797 male Protestant missionaries in India in 1899. But four pages later (19) in another report, "Progress of Protestant Missions," it listed for 1897 6,576 "missionaries men," and 3,982 "unmarried women." Adding wives could bring the total to more than 17,000 if every missionary man had a wife. Further statistics were 4,185 native ministers, 67,754 "other native helpers," 1,448,861 native communicants, plus 447,165 native disciples or catechumens.

174. Capuchin Mission Unit, *India and its Missions*, 2: appendix table 1; and *Report of the First Decennial General Missionary Conference, Allahabad, 1872–73*, 533.

175. Barrett et al., eds.,*World Christian Encyclopedia*, 2001, 1:360. For a loose comparison, see Catholic figures (including Burma and Ceylon) for 1908 (Capuchin Mission Unit, *India and Its Missions*, 2: appendix table 3); and for 1913, which reported 1,268 European priests, 400 European lay Brothers, and 2,000 European Sisters (*Atlas Hierarchicus*, 1913, cited by C. H. Robinson, *History of Christian Missions*, 492).

176. Neill, *History of Christian Missions*, 365. He estimated the number of full-time Protestant Indian workers in 1858 at 2,400.

177. By 1909, distinguishing between European and Indian clergy, there were 1,136 European and 1,320 Indian priests, 562 Brothers, and 3,314 Sisters.

178. See Melo, *Recruitment and Formation of National Clergy in India*, 212–236.

179. Even earlier, in 1630, the Propaganda had issued a decree on the need for native clergy. See Melo, *Recruitment and Formation of National Clergy in India*, 215 and passim; and Kenneth Ballhatchet, *Caste, Class, and Catholicism in India 1789–1914* (Richmond, Surrey, U.K.: Curzon Press, 1998), 11, 67, 76.

180. Urumpackal, *Vocations in India*, 2:320.

181. Urumpackal, *Vocations in India*, 2:235–220.

182. Urumpackal, *Vocations in India*, 2:250.

183. E. J. Thompson, *Suttee*, 60ff., 141; Fuller, *The Wrongs of Indian Womanhood*, 50, 53, 135, 190, 193.

184. Dutta, *Christian Missionaries on the Indigo Question in Bengal*.

185. Forrester, *Caste and Christianity*, and "Indian Christian Attitudes to Caste in the Twentieth Century," in *ICHR* (Bangalore) 9, no. 1 (June 1975): 3–22.

186. G. A. Oddie, "Indians and the National Congress, 1885–1910," in *ICHR* (Bangalore) 2, no. 1 (June 1968): 45–54. Thirty-five to forty of the seven hundred registered delegates at the Madras meeting of the National Congress were Christians, and Indian Christians alone made up 2.5 percent of the attendance, in spite of the fact that Christians accounted for less than 0.79 percent of the population.

187. Subramanyam, *The Catholic Community in India*, 49; and see Sherring, *History of Protestant Missions in India*, 110, 355ff.

188. *Report of the First Decennial General Missionary Conference, Allahabad, 1872–73*, 535. In two decades, 1852 to 1872, the Catholic community's increase was from 695,656 to 808,034, an increase of 19 percent; Protestants in that period (1850–1871) grew from 91,092 to 224,258, an increase of 146 percent (*Report of the First Decennial General Missionary Conference, Allahabad, 1872–73*, 518, 533).

189. Barrett et al., eds., *World Christian Encyclopedia*, 2001, 1:360. The figures are for total adherents (or affiliated, as distinct from professing members) and include an estimate of 1,150,000 crypto-Christians, or secret Christians, who for social or political reasons keep their attachment to the faith private. The number of professing Christians is given as 2,670,000 (1.2 percent).

Chapter 22

China's Christians
at the Empire's End (1860–1900)

If I had a thousand pounds, China should have it. If I had a thousand lives,
China should have them. No! not *China*, but *Christ*.
— J. Hudson Taylor (1860)

The European nations have gone beyond the bounds of proper international intercourse with China whenever it was in their interest to do
so, and have refused to go beyond them when it was to China's interest
that they should do so. — Robert E. Speer[1]

The women who ventured alone overseas in ever-increasing numbers at
the turn of the century took their place with their more rebellious sisters
[at home] to constitute one of the most significant female generations in
American history. — Jane Hunter[2]

IN 1860 China was a wounded giant, stumbling toward the fall of
its two-thousand-year empire. Fifty some years later its last emperor,
a five-year-old boy, would be forced from his throne and China would
begin its first flawed experiments with democracy. But that, too, would
self-destruct in another fifty years. China was moving unknowingly but
irresistibly toward the most radical revolution in its history.

Chinese Christianity, like the country itself, approached the midpoint
of the century weak, wounded, and harassed. Catholics had lost perhaps
a third of their membership, and were stunned and wary after 150 years
of persecution.[3] Protestants were barely getting started. Their missionaries were not allowed to live outside the mud flats of Guangzhou until
1842.[4] They had not been able to organize a church until 1845. In 1860
they still occupied only a few scattered beachheads in the treaty ports,
and in all China they could count only 351 Chinese Protestant church
members.[5] The nineteenth century was later to be called "the great century of Protestant missions"; but with more than half of it gone, it did
not look like it yet in China.

However, the history of Christianity is full of instances in which times
of turbulent change opened doors for the progress of the gospel. Who
could have foretold that before the end of the nineteenth century the

Catholics, recently persecuted nearly out of sight if not out of existence, would once again be spread throughout all the provinces of the empire and beyond the Great Wall, doubling their membership of baptized Chinese in fifty years?[6] Or that the Protestants, who had established not one organized Chinese congregation until almost the middle of the century, by its end would be growing faster than the Catholics, and making a deeper, wider public impact upon Chinese politics and culture than even the Jesuits in their seventeenth-century glory days?[7]

What triggered such dramatic new developments in the oldest empire in the world? Regrettably, the first answer to that question cannot be an easy, "It was a miracle." Marvelous though the nineteenth century story of Christian missions proved to be, the first and most obvious answer, historians must say, is that the empire fell not because of the disturbing arrival of foreign missionaries, but for two more fundamental reasons. One was its own incompetence and the corrosive internal rebellions that bad government invariably ignites. The second was the trauma of two ugly, unforgivable little Western imperialist wars which were forced upon it from the outside, the Opium Wars of 1839–1842 and 1856–1860.[8] These were the principal inflammatory factors that, at mid-century, propelled China from its past into the future. To the Chinese they will always be remembered as a national humiliation, not a liberating step into the future. Insofar as the missions became associated in the Chinese mind, however peripherally, with the humiliation of the Opium Wars, it should not have been too surprising that the century ended in 1900 not with a massive turn toward Christianity, but with the short, sharp, anti-Christian, anti-Western explosion of the Boxer Rebellion.

From a missionary perspective, another surprise in the closing decades of the nineteenth century was to find that by 1900 a newcomer had become the largest Protestant missionary society in China, the China Inland Mission. The CIM, as it was widely known, had been an organized presence in China for only thirty-four years. Its greatest strength was pioneer evangelism, and not the least of its virtues was that it had always opposed the opium trade.[9] But so also had the other Christian missions. "Unanimously and actively" the missionaries were solidly against that deadly, narcotic evil.[10]

Hudson Taylor and the China Inland Mission[11]

Some old China hands had dismissed this new mission, when its first boatload of volunteers arrived in 1866, as a dubious upstart, doomed to failure. It was overloaded with single women, they said.[12] It was ridiculed as "the pigtail mission" for having its missionaries adopt Chinese ways of dress and hairstyle.[13] It had no organized, committed support from any of the world's major Protestant denominations. Its activity concentrated on areas of China where the number of Christians were fewest and the churches most scattered. How had it so quickly outstripped the rest of the 67 Protestant missions then in China? By 1900 more than a fourth of the 2,785 Protestant missionaries in China[14] were connected to this preaching, praying, nondenominational missionary society, almost as many as there were foreign Roman Catholic priests then in China.[15] The entry into China of this "faith mission," as such societies came to be called, was a foreshadowing of changing times in Protestant missions. The influence of this form of missionary agency has in no way been limited to China. But its best-known model has been the China Inland Mission.

This is how it started. One Sunday in 1865 a young missionary, who had been sent home from China so sick that he was advised not to think of returning if he wanted to remain alive, suddenly and uncharacteristically decided not to go to church that morning. Instead he went for a long walk by the sea to sort out his thoughts. His name was Hudson Taylor (1832–1905),[16] and ever since leaving China he had been haunted by a dread vision which not even his medical studies could wipe from his mind, a vision of millions of lost souls dying in China without the assurance of salvation in Christ. In all of China, with its swarming population of some 250 or 300 million people, there were in 1865 only ninety-one Protestant missionaries.[17] Suddenly the thought of comfortable English Christians sitting in a respectable English church singing hymns about their own salvation without a thought of the unreached was more than he could bear. So instead of joining his friends at worship, he walked by the sea and came to an unexpected conclusion. Whether it meant death or not, he resolved to return to China. He described the experience later: "I wandered out on the sands alone, in great spiritual agony, and there the Lord conquered my unbelief, and I surrendered myself for this service."[18]

Knowing his weakness, he began by praying for twenty-four "willing, skilful" missionaries to join him, two for each of China's eleven inland provinces which were still not effectively entered by Protestant missionaries, and two more for Mongolia. Two days later he walked into a bank, and with ten pounds opened an account for the China Inland Mission, a society that existed only in his prayers. Only ten pounds, but as he said later, it was enough; it was ten pounds "and all the promises of God."[19]

The next year he left England once more for China convinced that God was answering his prayers. Already he had recruited sixteen volunteers — a married couple, five single men, and nine unmarried women — to accompany him and his wife, Maria, as the first eighteen members of the China Inland Mission (CIM).[20]

That simple pattern of faith, prayer, and thanksgiving for answered prayer was to be repeated throughout the rest of Hudson Taylor's missionary life. It became the molding policy of the CIM, a pattern he had learned as much from his early friend, George Muller of Bristol, and from the "open" Brethren (who are sometimes misleadingly called "Plymouth" Brethren), as from his own personal and family background in the Wesleyan Methodist revivals.[21] Out of the revivals came the controlling theological foundations not only of the China Inland Mission but of most nineteenth-century Protestant missions: the lostness of the lost without Christ, and the good news of life eternal for as many as will believe in Him; the radical dehumanizing nature of sin, and the free gift of saving grace to those who repent and confess their sins; the authority of Scripture, and the importance of the experience of conversion. This was the missionary message.

Eighteen missionaries sailed with the Taylors to China in 1866, the founding party of the China Inland Mission.[22] In 1881, fifteen years later, the work was growing so rapidly that Taylor began to pray for seventy new workers in three years — forty-two men and twenty-eight women — though there were less than a hundred then in the entire mission. And the prayer was answered, forty-six of them coming in the last twelve months of the third year.[23] But two years later Taylor was praying again, this time for a hundred more missionaries, and by the end of the next year there *were* a hundred, either on their way or already in China. The magnitude of that achievement becomes evident when compared with the overall growth of the number of Protestant missionaries in China in those years. In one year, 1887, the CIM brought a hundred new missionaries; in the twenty-two previous years since the first CIM band of eighteen reached China, the total *Protestant* missionary community had increased by only five hundred, *including* the CIM's hundred.[24]

Still Taylor was not satisfied. In 1889, he began to pray for an impossible one thousand new recruits in the next five years. After eighty years of Protestant work there are less than forty thousand Protestant Chinese communicants, he pointed out. How else are China's 250 million or more people to be reached unless we have more evangelists? He issued a call for a thousand new men, but not for the CIM alone. This time he widened his concern to include any Protestant societies from any denominations willing to send and support missionaries for China. Anglicans, Presbyterians in Scotland, Ireland, and America, Methodists, Baptists, Congregationalists — each could at least send a hundred, he urged enthusiastically.[25] Taylor was never antidenominational. It is sometimes forgotten that Maria Taylor's brother-in-law, John Shaw Burdon, was the Anglican bishop of Victoria in Hong Kong (Xiangang in Pinyin).[26]

Nor did his call for a thousand *men* indicate a prejudice against women missionaries. In fact the China Inland Mission is a primary instance of an emerging, widening stream of missionary vision that did much to transform the nineteenth century into what has been called "the great century" of Protestant mission history. As the foremost example of the independent, "faith mission" missionary society, it broke barriers between denominations, between nations, between Western and national leadership in the churches, and between the roles of men and women in mission.

From its beginnings the China Inland Mission appointed as many or more women to mission as men. In the first pioneering group sailing to China in 1868, women including wives outnumbered men eleven to seven.[27] His wife, Maria Dyer Taylor, was fluent in Chinese and in Ningbo had quickly proved the value of women working with women.[28] In 1879 newly married Emily Snow King became the first foreign woman to penetrate into China's mountainous far west, into Gangsu province where the Silk Road enters China from Mongolia.[29] But it was not until the next year, 1880, when the mission daringly began to thrust unmarried women without European male escort into the unreached interior, that its emerging policy of equal treatment for women, hitherto quietly unpublicized, hit the wider foreign community in China "like a bombshell." Even some friends of the mission were shocked. The two pioneers were Jane Kidd and Elizabeth Wilson.[30]

On the vexing problem of interracial marriage the CIM also took a stand well ahead of the Western conventions of the time. As early as 1878 one of its young missionaries, George Parker, fell in love with a Chinese girl enrolled in one of the mission schools and asked permission to marry her. His mother in England was in tears; her father, an opium addict, objected, hoping for payment for his permission; and some of the missionaries felt it would set a bad example. But love and compassion prevailed, and in 1880 Shao Mianzi became the first Asian member of the mission.[31]

But very early the CIM had wisely begun to bring talented Chinese colleagues into the mission. By that same year, 1880, the number of Chinese colleagues in the mission outnumbered the foreign missionaries about 100 to 96.[32] The best known of them all was Xi Shongmo (ca. 1830–1896), "Pastor Hsi," a Chinese scholar and drug addict who was converted by a British Methodist missionary, David Hill, in 1879 as the four horrible years of "the great famine" were ending. Pastor Hsi worked with the CIM in such an independent but capable way that in 1886 Hudson Taylor ordained him as the first Protestant pastor in Shanxi and superintendent for the mission over a wide area. Remembering his deliverance from opium ("It is not the man that eats the opium, but the opium that eats the man") he established more than forty rehabilitation refuges for curing victims of the deadly habit.[33] The record of his enlarging relationships in the CIM community is one of the best early examples of a transition from missionary to Chinese leadership.

Like most Protestant mission societies of the nineteenth century the China Inland Mission was evangelical, but at the same time more ecumenical in a Christian way, like the eighteenth-century "awakenings" from which the nineteenth-century missionary movement arose. Taylor was reared in a warmly Methodist home; was touched by a revival at the age of nine and was converted, he wrote, at the age of seventeen.[34] Contrary to later critics of "faith mission" procedures and attitudes, the China Inland Mission was neither antidenominational nor separatist. About the year 1890, he wrote in answer to such criticism:

> Though a Baptist myself, as the head of a pan-denominational mission I have for twenty years [refused to give] instruction on this point [denominational preference]... We have six organized Presbyterian churches [in North Anhui and Zhejiang]...four episcopal stations [in Sichuan], four Methodist stations [in Kunming].[35]

The CIM was independent, international, and nondenominational, welcoming as members Anglicans, Baptists, Presbyterians, Methodists, Brethren, and Congregationalists, and Finns, Swedes, Germans, Americans, Britishers — and as many others as accepted its principles into its missionary fellowship without regard to national and denominational affiliation.

Even before the formation of the CIM, while Taylor was in China in the 1850s under the ill-fated China Evangelistic Society, he had formed a fast friendship with John L. Nevius, an American Presbyterian fresh out of Princeton Theological Seminary, whose opinions and later practical emphasis on self-support and native leadership in the Chinese churches encouraged Taylor as he came to similar convictions on missionary strategy. Taylor, at that time still a bachelor, may even have saved Nevius's life on one occasion by insisting on replacing the married Nevius who was bravely nursing a colleague dying of the dreaded, highly contagious smallpox.[36]

In the 1880s and 1890s the China Inland Mission took a further step toward cooperation across denominational barriers and gave organizational form to interdenominational cooperation by welcoming compatible "associate missions" into its fellowship and under its direction. The earliest such arrangement was with the pioneer Quaker (Friends) missionary to China in 1883. The first official "marriage of two missions" took place the next year with the Bible Christian Mission (independent but predominantly Wesleyan Methodist).[37] Various European societies soon followed suit in fast succession. By 1911 there were nineteen associated missions under the CIM umbrella, from Sweden, Norway, Germany, Denmark, Finland, Poland and Czechoslovakia.[38] In 1895 an even more startling ecumenical event took place: a CIM missionary, William W. Cassels (1858–1925), superintendent of the mission's work in West China, with the approval of the archbishop of Canterbury was appointed and consecrated bishop of West China. He was only thirty-five years old and served for another thirty years.[39]

By then, on the eve of World War I, the total number of missionaries with the China Inland Mission had risen to more than a thousand as noted above. Hudson Taylor's death in 1905 did not end the growth. His influence continued. As one of his missionaries said at the bed of a Christian school girl, dying unafraid, "It is not death to die."[40]

The Roman Catholic Recovery

In their brave enthusiasm for breaking into the interior to reach the un-reached, Protestants sometimes forgot that the Roman Catholics were already there. By 1858, eight years before the first boatload of China Inland Mission volunteers landed in Shanghai, there were Roman Catholic priests and worshipers in all of China's eighteen provinces, Manchuria and even Mongolia.[41] Compared with India, however, Chinese Christianity was small and weak, only a third the size of India's Christian community. There were no known survivors of earlier Nestorian Christians in China; no Syrian Christians as in India. But the situation was improving.[42]

The most obvious measure of a rapid recovery of Catholic missions in China after nearly two centuries of decline[43] was a sudden, dramatic increase in the number of missionaries. By 1907 the figure had risen to 1,575. In the short space of forty years the number had grown fivefold. If laymen and laywomen (the Brothers and Sisters) are included, the total number of Catholic foreign missionaries in 1907 was 2,177.[44] The largest missions, in terms of Chinese Christians in their territory, were the Jesuits in Jiongnan, the Vincentians (Lazarists) in north Chihli (now Hebei), and the Paris Missionary Society in Guangdong.[45]

The size of the Chinese Catholic community rose proportionately more slowly than the number of missionaries but nevertheless registered a remarkably strong increase. In 1870 there were reported 404,000 Chinese Catholics;[46] by 1907 the number had risen more than threefold to 1,072,000, with another 424,000 catechumens, a total of barely under 1,500,000 Catholics. Seventy percent of the Catholics were in the north and east central provinces. But in the number of Catholics, Jiangsu province (including Shanghai) in east central China was second only to Chihli in the north (later Hebei), including Beijing and parts of Manchuria.[47]

Catholic growth, however, was not as robust as that of the Protestants in China in this period. The Jesuits, once dominant throughout China, were still recovering from their long suppression and did not reenter China until 1844. After 1858 all China was placed under the direction of the Congregation for the Propagation of the Faith.[48]

Deserving special mention is the pioneering Catholic expansion into Mongolia. Its founder was the Vincentian Joseph Gabet, who had spent ten years in Mongolia (1837–1848). With the better known Abbé E-.R. Huc, he made a famous trip of exploration of more than two thousand miles in 1844–1846 across some of the most remote and impenetrable parts of China through Mongolia and Gangsu province to Tibet. It took them a whole year and a half to reach Lhasa where their welcome was so unexpectedly warm that they began to explore the possibility of starting a Christian mission there in the very capital of Tibetan Buddhism. They even made a private chapel for themselves, wide open to visitors, in the residence freely provided for them by the Tibetan Regent. But after about two months, Chinese-Tibetan tensions and the openly political opposition of the Chinese ambassador forced them to leave lest they stir up persecution from China.[49] The beginning of an organized mission in Mongolia, however, must be credited to what might be called the China Inland Mission of Roman Catholicism, the Scheutveld Congregation of the Immaculate Heart of Mary. In the 1860s the Scheutvelders took over the pioneering thrust of the two Vincentians and established a mission which eventually numbered 169 missionaries penetrating into largely untouched Mongolia and Gangsu province along the Old Silk Road. Their reports were a surprise. At the turn of the century, the Catholic community in southwest Mongolia was more than doubling its membership.[50]

On the negative side was the taint of French patronage. After the Taiping rebellion, freedom of the missions from the bonds of the Portuguese *padroado* dropped them into the hands of imperial France. It was in no way a total dependence, and it had its benefits, as with treaty clauses establishing freedom of access and practice for Christian, particularly Catholic, missions. But it only confirmed the festering hatred of foreigners so characteristic of the Confucianist elite, and led all too soon to three decades of intermittent outbreaks of violence from 1870 to 1900.[51]

Just as important for the future of Catholicism in China, the missions set steadily to work after the cessation of persecution to build up their all-important cadre of ordained native Chinese leaders. In the mid-1700s there were only 15 Chinese priests. Fifty years later, in 1800, the number had doubled, but still stood at only some 33. When the Treaty of Nanjing in 1844 began to open China to greater freedom for Christian worship and outreach, there were 130. From that time on the increase in the number of Chinese priests in the empire mounted steadily upward: from the 33 in 1800 to 157 in 1865, 320 in 1886, 470 in 1900, and the numbers were still rising.[52]

Among Catholic women, the rise in the number of female orders, both foreign and Chinese, was still more rapid. The first such European order, Daughters of St. Vincent de Paul, reached Macao in 1847, and the Sisters of St. Paul de Chartres arrived in Hong Kong in 1848.[53] Only gradually, and often against opposition from within, not just from outside the church, did they admit Chinese women to the Sisterhoods. But a movement in far western China long before — a hundred years earlier — had beaten the European women orders to the mission.

The first known clearly documented instances of individual Catholic women taking vows of celibacy for Christ occurred in the far western province of Sichuan (Szechwan) early in the eighteenth century, but family opposition was usually so intense that organization of what were known as Christian Virgins did not appear until the first Institute of Christian Virgins was formed and regulated by a Dominican apostolic vicar, Luigi Maggi, in 1744. The vows of chastity were in most cases at first temporary, and persecutions and social antagonisms slowed the growth. But by about 1800, transformed from personal pursuit of piety into service as lay evangelists and teachers — "though it was not necessary for Christian Virgins to learn how to write" — they were playing an important part in making the province the "most flourishing" Christian area in mid-nineteenth-century China.[54] Then, after the disruptions of the Taiping rebellion, the movement spread. In Shanghai in 1855 a Congregation (or Association) exclusively of Chinese-born women was formed in Shanghai, calling itself the Presentation Association; another was organized in Kirin, Manchuria, in 1858: the Sisters of the Sacred Heart of Mary. By 1900 there were at least ten such indigenous organizations of Chinese women's orders.[55]

The contribution of women both European and Chinese was an immediate expansion of compassionate Christian outreach through schools, orphanages, and hospitals to a huge, basic segment of Chinese society hitherto somewhat off limits to the male orders. However, the introduction of well-established European Sisterhoods may actually have slowed the development of the more indigenous associations of Chinese Sisters.[56] Single women missionaries could be accepted and excused as a curious facet of Western society, but it was much more difficult for Chinese families to accept so unnatural a pattern for their own daughters. Those who sought to devote themselves completely to the service of the church walked a very difficult and lonely path.

To make it more difficult, China's Catholic Christianity still lacked a central, cohesive administrative structure within the empire, a weakness usually found more commonly in Protestant missions than Catholic. At mid-century, in 1856 China had eleven vicariates, but no episcopal dioceses. The last two of the original dioceses, Nanjing and Macao, because of their controversial ecclesiastical linkage to Portuguese Macao, had been suppressed that year in favor of vicariates directly answerable to Rome.[57]

An attempt was made in 1879 to furnish a greater sense of national Catholic unity by the formation of five regional synods that were to meet together every five years, but it proved only marginally successful. Each vicariate and each of the Catholic mission societies worked independently, with little communication on plans and strategy. They reported directly to Rome, not to each other, partly due to the vast distances of China's geography, and partly as a result of the *padroado* controversy, alluded to above, which set the Portuguese crown represented by the king's appointed archbishop in Macao against the authority of the Vatican in Rome. What was needed was the creation of an archdiocese in China, not in colonial Macao, as the seat of Catholic authority in the empire.[58]

That goal, however, was not reached until after the First World War. Despite the increase in Chinese Catholic clergy and Chinese membership, Roman Catholicism was still foreign controlled and visibly dependent on the support of foreign powers as defined by the "unequal treaties." French intervention in favor of the Catholic missions was proving to be a mixed blessing, contributing as much to waves of anti-Christian, nationalist reaction, as to the furtherance of the Christian faith. As one of the best of historians of missions in China described the situation shortly before World War I, the Roman Catholic Church "was having little if any appreciable effect upon the life of the country as a whole."[59]

Protestant Progress toward National Influence

While the Roman Catholics continued to dominate the Christian map of China in terms of number of missionaries, churches, and converts, and the China Inland Mission was leading the way in expanding the outer frontiers of Protestant Christianity in China, it would be a mistake to underestimate the momentum of the older Protestant missions in China.

Thirty-eight years after the arrival of their pioneer missionary, Robert Morrison, in 1807, Protestants had still been unable to establish a single, fully organized Chinese Protestant congregation. The first to do so were the American Presbyterians in Ningbo in 1845, and then only after the Opium War of 1842/1843 had opened Ningbo as a treaty port.[60] In the next sixty years Protestants made up for their slow start. They not only planted Chinese churches out to the far borders of the empire, but also played a significant role in transforming China as it had not been changed in all the previous sixteen hundred years of Christian missions to East Asia.

When the Protestant missions in China held their first General Missionary Council in 1877 there were 473 missionaries, half of whom were women. There were 29 organized Protestant mission societies at work in the empire. The American Presbyterians (North) were the largest, with the newer China Inland Mission already a close second. The only other society with 50 missionaries or more was the American Board of Commissioners for Foreign Missions (ABCFM), mostly Congregational, the first foreign mission society formed in the United States. The London Missionary Society, the oldest Protestant mission in China, had more than 40 missionaries. Five other societies had more than 20 missionaries: the American Methodists (North), the Church Missionary Society (CMS, Anglican), and the English Wesleyans.[61]

Evangelism always remained the first priority of the Protestant missions throughout the nineteenth century. One of the leading Protestant missionaries of those times, Griffith John (1831–1912),[62] defined his motive for mission in these words at the 1877 Missionary Conference:

> As missionaries we believe we are in China in obedience to the command of our Lord; and the purpose of our mission is to disciple, or make Christians of this great nation...We are here, not to develop the resources of the country, nor for the advancement of commerce, nor for the mere promotion of civilization; but to do battle with the powers of darkness, to save men from sin, and conquer China for Christ.[63]

It is important to balance this emphasis on evangelism by what Griffith also said strongly at this same conference about the more broadly social forms of missionary witness. In the quotation above he was speaking on the work of the Holy Spirit in mission as fundamental, but he does not deprecate the human factor. He regarded medical missions and the production of Christian literature as indispensable.[64] Attacking the opium trade, he said that the connection of opium traffic with Western trade in China "speaks more eloquently and convincingly to the Chinese mind *against* Christianity...than the missionary does or can do *for* it."[65] And on the "unequal treaties" forced on China after the Opium Wars, while approving the religious toleration clauses, he warned against seeking special privileges for missionaries, and carefully distinguished between demanding *religious* freedom and seeking *political* advantage.[66]

As a practical fact, the priority given to evangelism and church growth by conversion to the Christian faith proved to have important social consequences in addition to the purely spiritual. Church growth by conversion furnished a visible, organized Chinese base for mission: a Chinese church. Without that, it was agreed, foreign missions could never make an effective impact upon the nation as a whole. The greater visible proportional growth of Chinese Protestantism compared to Catholicism in China in the latter decades of the century is one reason for the slowly but steadily increasing role of Protestants in the public arena, particularly in the establishment of schools and hospitals.

Numerical growth also explains why in this period the foreign Protestant *missions* were more prominent in the modernization and reform of China than the Chinese *church*. For a considerable number of years the missions grew faster than the church, and foreigners were more noticeable. In 1876 Protestant male missionaries already outnumbered the foreign Catholic priests 301 to 254. In half a century the number of Protestant missionaries had grown from 1 in 1807, to 81 in 1858, to 473 counting both men and women in 1876, and to 1,324 in 1893.[67]

Compared to the increase of missionaries, the growth of the Chinese Protestant church was relatively slower, but impressive nevertheless. In

1840 there were only about 40 baptized Chinese Protestants communicant members.[68] By 1877 there was encouraging growth to 13,500, but a tiny community compared to 400,000 Chinese Catholics. The number rose to 112,800 reported in 1899, and (to anticipate) when Protestants celebrated a century in China in 1907 they reported a baptized community of 178,000 and perhaps another 100,000 not yet baptized adherents. This was still less than a third the number of Chinese Catholics that year, 950,000.[69]

The Roman Catholic community was three hundred years older. It was larger; it was tested by persecutions; and it was far better informed on Chinese history and culture. But the Protestants were growing faster and in these years were with surprising rapidity becoming an unmistakable Christian presence in the modernization of the old empire. It was the mainline Protestant denominations, however, not the independent missions, which became a greater influence in the political and cultural transformation of nineteenth-century China. The independents, eager to reach the unreached, were farther from the centers of social power. It is difficult to single out any one denominational missionary as typical. In 1877 at the first strategic General Conference of the Protestant Missionaries of China, among the ninety-three Protestant missionaries assembled, male and female, outlines of transdenominational leadership began to emerge. Hudson Taylor was there, and Alexander Williamson of the Scottish National Bible Society, but most belonged to denominational societies. Some of the names were already well-recognized and respected, others soon would be — J. V. N. Talmage, Dutch Reformed;[70] Calvin Mateer, Presbyterian;[71] Young J. Allen, Methodist;[72] John L. Nevius, Presbyterian;[73] Hunter Corbett, Presbyterian;[74] and W. A. P. Martin, Presbyterian.[75] But perhaps the widest known missionary within and outside of Christian circles in those years was Timothy Richard, a Baptist.

TIMOTHY RICHARD AND SOCIAL SERVICE

The independent-minded Richard was a Welsh Baptist, notable in the last quarter of the nineteenth century as much for the controversies he stirred up as for his contributions to progress in mission expansion and national development. He was sent to China in 1869 by the English Baptist Missionary Society, which was better known for its connection to William Carey in India. In China, however, Richard was more famous than Carey, or for that matter at that time, than Hudson Taylor. It is interesting to note that Richard, a child of the Welsh revivals, volunteered first to join Hudson Taylor's strongly evangelical China Inland Mission, which, as was its generous habit, advised him to begin by seeking service with his own denominational mission.[76] Timothy Richard and Hudson Taylor are more often portrayed as opposites than colleagues — Taylor the passionate evangelist, and Richard the social activist who became famous for feeding the starving in the great famine of 1876–1877, the worst famine in Chinese history.[77] He became a trusted confidante of government viceroys and radical reformers alike, admired by Confucianists for his contributions to the improvement of China's educational system, and by Buddhists for his appreciation of "the truth in all religions." He wrote:

> There was a time when every religion considered itself true and every other false … the time is now come to say that there shall be only *One religion* in the future, and that one will contain what is truest and best in all past religions which reveal the Divine in them.[78]

For such statements Richard came to be criticized as a "syncretist" by members of his own mission. His words suggested a synthesizing of different truths. Actually, at his worst he was only marginally syncretistic, and at best a firmly committed Baptist Christian to the end. It was not to embrace the Buddhists that Richard, in 1891, left the Baptist mission, but to throw his great energies after twenty years of evangelistic and educational leadership into a program pioneered by Alexander Williamson (1829–1890), the first overseas agent of the National Bible Society of Scotland,[79] which eventually became The Christian Literature Society for China.[80] And he would speak, like Taylor, of converting "China's unreached millions." In 1890 Taylor, speaking to a full third of all the Protestant missionaries in China at the 1890 General Mission Conference in Shanghai, electrified them with a plea for one thousand evangelists to reach China's unsaved millions.[81] Twenty years later Richard also spoke of "conversion by the millions" at the World Missionary Conference, Edinburgh, 1910. But China's millions, Richard said, could most quickly be reached through Christian literature, expounding Christian truth through books to challenge the Chinese mind.[82]

Timothy Richard first caught the attention of the missionary community in China by his evangelistic successes in Shandong and Shanxi. He developed his own highly effective church planting method, a combination of four emphases. First, but not most important was adaptation to Chinese ways — described as "clothing Christian ideas in Chinese dress," like the great seventeenth-century Jesuit Matthew Ricci, and also curiously parallel to Hudson Taylor's "pigtail mission," the CIM.

Richard's second priority was the training of Chinese leadership through group Bible study for self-reliance in church planting. This began simply with Bible memorization. He noted, parenthetically, that those who memorized from John's gospel became "lovable mystics," while those who memorized from Ephesians became "strong Calvinists, sure of their election to do great things for God." In this aspect of his training methods he was much like his friend, the American Presbyterian John Nevius, whose "Nevius method" was later worked out in Manchuria and was carried into Korea with far-reaching consequences, as we shall see later. In this period he also developed a third strategy:

"seek the most worthy," choosing the best among his converts to convert others. Finally, and surely the most important secret, humanly speaking, of what deserves to be called success in mission, was simply that he loved the Chinese. His biographer, with great insight, observed that Richard did not "have to 'try' to love them, he simply did so."[83]

It was human compassion, visible to all in his labors to save the starving, which gave China what became a model of famine relief organization for the whole nation, and which brought Timothy Richard the kind of fame for which he never asked. He spent forty-five years in China. He was an evangelist, a relief worker, reformer, educator, respected by the last real emperor of China, and trusted as an advisor by the Chinese Christian who became the first president of the Chinese Republic. He died in England in 1919. "Had he died in China," wrote his biographer, W. E. Soothill, then professor of Chinese at Oxford, "his funeral would have been the greatest of any foreigner who has ever lived in that land."[84]

BISHOP SCHERESCHEWSKY AND BIBLE TRANSLATION

One unforgettable fragment of the rich human mosaic that Protestant missionaries spread across China was the ministry of an Episcopal Jewish bishop, Samuel Isaac Joseph Schereschewsky (1831–1906), the fourth Jewish Christian in the history of the Anglican Communion to become a bishop. He was converted through the influence of Christian Jews who invited him to celebrate Passover with them in New York shortly after he arrived as an immigrant from Europe, and in 1859 he went to China representing the Domestic and Foreign Missionary Society of the Protestant Episcopal Church of the United States.[85] In seminary a classmate had told him that he couldn't get into China. He replied, "I'd give my life if I could but oil the hinges of the door." Seventeen years later in 1877 he was consecrated bishop of China. Two years after his consecration he opened one of the first schools intentionally founded as a college, St. John's, in Shanghai. It became famous for high-level instruction in science and Western languages, particularly English.[86]

Schereschewsky's greatest achievements were in linguistics and Bible translation in order to open the eyes of a China whose whole culture rested on written foundations to a book which he firmly believed was God's Word to the whole world. Max Müller, the famous Indologist, is said to have remarked that Schereschewsky was "one of the six most learned Orientalists in the world." He spoke thirteen languages and could read twenty. In Chinese he mastered between nine and ten thousand characters.[87] This led him naturally to Bible translation, and supported by the American Bible Society he worked at it tirelessly, concentrating first on revising and improving translations in standard, literary Mandarin, sometimes called "classical, or antique Wenli," the language of the elite. But he soon felt that a greater need was for a translation into "modern, or easy Wenli," a "Bible for the poor."[88]

But no sooner had he offered to resign from his office in order to have time for translation (an offer quickly refused)[89] than he was felled by a stroke and was forced to leave China in 1881, unable to write or even put on his own glasses, and barely able to make himself understood. It was in this impossible state, however, that the man proved his mettle. He resolved to finish the project he had planned seven years earlier in China, a Bible in the language of the people. He will always be best and most warmly remembered for his "one-finger Bible." He found he could type with one finger. So using that finger, and when the finger failed, taking a stick in his hand to hammer at the keys, one at a time, he worked eight or nine hours a day at a new translation of the entire Bible in "easy Wenli." It took him six years. But its success was phenomenal. By 1900 it had become "the Bible of the common people in two-thirds of China," and as his version of Mandarin Chinese spread to Korea, Indochina, and even Japan, it was "the language of literature among one-fourth of the human race."[90]

A RISING TIDE FOR WOMEN

At the trail-blazing Moody conference for college students at Mount Hermon, New York, which launched the Student Volunteer Movement for Foreign Missions in 1886, the challenge was all-inclusive: "All should go, and go to all." The participants, however, were all men. Robert Wilder's sister Grace in Princeton, was as eager for mission service as he, and wistfully sent him off to the exclusively male conference for which she had been praying.[91] As it turned out, however, no such incidents of discrimination could keep the women from overseas mission. Grace Wilder went to India.[92] She was one of the stream of nearly two thousand volunteers who answered the missionary call and went overseas in the next two decades. More than half of them were women.[93]

But it was not the Student Volunteer Movement which paved the way for women in mission. The pioneers were the independent, nondenominational missions. In China, as we observed earlier, it was the China Inland Mission. On Hudson Taylor's first boatload of eighteen adult volunteers in 1866, women outnumbered men eleven to seven, and single women outnumbered bachelors eight to five.[94] Baptists, Methodists, and Presbyterians, along with almost all the other denominations, were still reluctant to grant women full missionary status in their missions. As late as 1889 thirty-nine out of the sixty-eight presbyteries of the Presbyterian Church U.S. responded to the formation of women's mission boards by voting against recognition of any mission organizations above the local church level.[95] But Hudson Taylor of the China Inland Mission not only actively recruited single women missionaries; he told his married missionary men, "Unless you intend your wife to be a true missionary, not merely a wife, home-maker, and friend, do not join us."[96]

Taylor took a further pioneering organizational step in 1889 when he created a woman's department of the China Inland Mission and chose as its director in London a strong-willed English woman, Henrietta Soltau, who refused to let ill health and a home assignment to dim her passion for mission service in China, though she herself was never able to make more than one strenuous visit there. Neither did she allow her roots in the Plymouth Brethren movement (not by coincidence called "Brethren," for they rigidly opposed a public role for women in the assemblies) to keep her from guiding some 547 women to an active, public mission with the China Inland Mission, where she found the same firm theological and biblical foundations but with a broader openness to missionary cooperation.[97]

Among the denominations, in England the Church Missionary Society, and in America the Baptists and Methodists had taken a leading role in promoting the work of women in mission. But no name has won wider recognition for overseas service than Charlotte (Lottie) Moon (1840–1912),[98] the Southern Baptist icon of a missionary heroine. She was only four feet three inches in height, but in the next century Southern Baptist "Lottie Moon" missionary offerings "largely paved the way for the growth of the largest missionary force of any evangelical or Protestant denomination."[99]

Lottie Moon went to China in 1873. At college, after some time of reaction against the revival religion of her Virginia Baptists, she had been "reconverted" during a campus revival and was baptized. She felt drawn to the call of foreign missionary service, but Southern Baptists in the 1860s "had appointed only one unmarried woman as a missionary and had vowed never to do it again."[100] Times change, and about fifteen years later she was on her way to China. She was a born evangelist, learned the village Chinese, lived and chatted with the village women. But after about twelve years in the mission center, more and more irked at the way the men were unable to agree with each other on mission policy,[101] she packed her things and moved out into the country, the only Christian, apparently, in the town of Pingtu. In a letter home she wrote with some asperity: "What women want who come to China is freedom to do the largest possible work... What women have a right to demand is perfect equality."[102] In another letter home, which had consequences far beyond anything she might have imagined, she suggested that Southern Baptist women take up a Christmas offering to send more women to China.

Lottie Moon died after nearly forty years in China principally because she had starved herself in order to give away her salary and most of her food to the hundreds around her in the Shandong famine of 1911 who had less than she. Her life was a challenging model for the Chinese Christians around her, both men and women. She not only started a school for training women church workers, she became an admired model for the Chinese male evangelists who worked with her. By the time she left China, her disciples in Pingtu were baptizing five hundred converts a year, and one of her students, by then a leading Chinese evangelist, is said to have baptized ten thousand people.

She left an estate of only about $250. But as her fellow Baptists would say, her Lord took what little she had left and as with the loaves and fishes worked a miracle. Remember that little Christmas letter she wrote home suggesting a Christmas offering? The Southern Baptist "Lottie Moon" Christmas offering in 1992 alone was more than $80 million.[103]

It would sadden her heart, though, to think that she would be remembered only for the money. There is a monument in Pingtu to Lottie Moon. It says nothing about money, and nothing about baptisms either, for that matter. It simply says, under her Chinese name as a missionary, "How she loved us."[104]

The Protestant Christian Educational Network

In all the missions, evangelism remained the highest priority. But the constant querying of the critics of the missionary enterprise by such recurring questions as: "Why tell the Chinese what to believe, when they already have three of the greatest of the world's religions"; or "Why start schools in a country with one of the greatest heritages of education in the world"; and "Why advocate reforming a governmental system that has lasted longer than any of your Western ones" — to these questions the Christian missionaries would simply say, "Because we want to share with you the things we hold most dear in our lives, and let you decide for yourselves whether they are good or bad for you."

In further response to such questions, particularly among the older missions as the nineteenth century neared its end and moved into the next century, the message of the twentieth-century missionary perceptibly broadened. Evangelism did not lose its priority, but rather was supported and enriched by wide-ranging programs of higher education, social reform, and scientific enlightenment.[105]

Timothy Richard was only one of many outstanding missionaries through whom the major Protestant missions became an influence in China's wrenching transition from absolute, imperial monarchy into the modern world of reform, revolution, and technology. He led in the establishment of a university for Shanxi province, accepting indemnity money for the Boxer atrocities only on condition that it be designated for a provincial university. He refused its presidency and promoted a fellow Baptist for the position. But perhaps because of its government sponsorship, it never became the effectively Christian university that its founders had planned, and passed into the hands of the Shanxi government in ten years.[106]

The substantive history of the Christian colleges in China begins only in the 1880s. Virtually all of them began not as colleges but as primary schools growing up into high schools (sometimes named "colleges"), and in time, some of the high schools rose into what we would today call colleges.[107] None of the Christian schools gave what would now be considered a full college-level education until after 1900.[108] Moreover, the missionaries made no attempt to disguise the fact that their goal in Christian education was not merely the education of the Chinese but the evangelization of China. In fact the first little primary school destined one day to become a college was started in Ningbo in 1844 by the American Presbyterians even before they organized their first Chinese church. Fifty years later, the primary school had become Hangchow Presbyterian College, and finally Hangchow Christian University.[109]

Some of the many colleges which the Protestants planted earned national prestige. St. John's College in Shanghai grew out of two boarding schools. It was founded as a college in 1879 by the American Episcopalian Bishop, Samuel Schereschewsky, to introduce "our Christian religion and Christian civilization" to China's educated elite.[110] Nanjing University opened as a small school, meeting in the home of the Methodist missionary John C. Ferguson in 1889, and blossomed into a major center for the introduction of Western learning in central China.[111] Further educational expansion by the missions moves past the century mark but should be mentioned here. Shantung Christian University (later Cheeloo University), founded in 1904 by American Presbyterians and English Baptists, won attention for its mathematics and Western science, and claimed to be "the first institution in China to offer work of collegiate grade."[112] Yenching University in Beijing, "the strongest, the largest, and the best endowed," arose in 1919, with J. Leighton Stuart as president, and Henry W. Luce, vice president, out of a series of unions of smaller Christian schools and universities (Presbyterian, Methodist, and Congregational).[113]

Education in such upper-level mission colleges was in both English and Chinese. They were the nineteenth-century parallels of the early Jesuits in China, the indispensable conduits of a revolutionary movement of human thought and technology from west to east around the world that, in the case of China, has been inadequately described as "the modernization" of the Chinese empire. It is no accident that so many of the leaders of that movement learned their lessons from the Christian schools, and the missions and the Chinese church.

Another early advocate of a wider dimension of outreach to the Chinese mind was William A. P. Martin (1827–1916),[114] whose sixty-six years of service in China (1850–1816) included not only long service as a Presbyterian missionary, but also imperial government appointments as, for example, dean of the Imperial University in Beijing (1869–1895) with special oversight of its science department, for which he has been called the "founder of modern state education in China."[115] His influence continued well into the next century and after the revolution of 1911/1912. In the new Republic of China he was one of the organizers of the International Reform Bureau, which promoted high moral standards and a new Chinese war on opium.[116]

A Chinese Church for the Chinese

In 1856 John Van Nest Talmage (1819–1892), of the American (Dutch) Reformed mission in China,[117] reported to his board that an evangelistic revival had led to a growing number of converts and a community that now numbered 121 church members in three organized churches in the Xiamen area. He asked permission to organize a *classis*, or presbytery. Since the one English Presbyterian missionary there had been cooperating with the American mission so closely that their Chinese converts assumed that all the missionaries were working in one church, Talmage proposed to organize a united Chinese presbytery, independent of either the American or the English home churches. In England the Presbyterians had no objection, but the American Dutch Reformed Synod rejected as premature the radical suggestion that a mission-founded church be set free from the parental supervision of its planters. The Dutch Reformed Synod ordered the Chinese churches of its mission to be organized under the authority of the Synod of Albany, New York.[118]

Talmage was indignant. The Xiamen missionaries ignored the ruling and organized the missionaries, the Chinese pastors, and ordained elders into a presbytery (classis) which they named in Chinese "A Great Meeting of Elders," a very attractive name in a Chinese cultural setting. The American Synod was not impressed and adamantly reaffirmed its earlier ruling. But never one to give up, Talmage argued his way to eventual victory. An example reveals his tenacity, his passion, and his humor:

> Let us suppose that one of the brethren feels himself aggrieved by the decision of the Classis of Amoy and appeals to the Synod of Albany, and thence to the General Synod... [I]n order that the appeal may be properly prosecuted... the appellant and the representative of the Classis should be present in these higher courts... Is the waste of time of a year or more nothing. And where shall the thousands of dollars of necessary expense come from. Now supposing this appellant to be a Chinese brother... He cannot speak, read, or write a word of English. Not a member of the Synod can speak, read or write a word of his language, except it be the brother prosecuting him... I ask, is it possible for him thus to obtain justice?[119]

Talmage stood fast for three basic principles: the unity of the Church — "in Christ Jesus there is no distinction of nationalities"; the right of the infant church in China to make its own decisions in China; and the indispensable knowledge of Chinese laws and customs, which in difficult cases will always give the advantage to those on the field, missionaries and Chinese, over those who must judge from afar.[120]

The counterargument at the American Synod was, "A 'self-regulating Classis'...is against every law, principle, canon, example and precedent in our books."[121] That argument prevailed, the ruling was reaffirmed, but with unexpected results. When the missionaries heard that the Synod had again rejected their request, the entire Reformed mission in Xiamen (Amoy) replied that it could not in good conscience follow the Synod's action and separate the Chinese Reformed and Presbyterian churches into two denominations. Therefore, "if the Synod is determined that such an organization must be effected, we can see no other way than to recall us and send hither men who see clearly their way to do that which to us seems wrong." Facing an impasse, the next meeting of the Synod in New York in 1864 accepted the church union already accomplished in Xiamen.[122] It was the first concrete step taken in China by two different denominations toward their ultimate goal: national Chinese churches no longer dependent, under God, on foreign missions or foreign support.

But it was a union engineered by two missions, and missionaries were still in charge. It did not prevent further years of mounting tension in the clash of cultures between East and West in the empire. It would take the rest of the century for the church to struggle through bitter anti-Christian movements and the climactic terrors of the Boxer Rebellion (1899–1900) before it could move from the defensive and begin seriously to become Chinese.

The Chinese Backlash[123]

Western writers on China differ widely between those who emphasize the basic "extreme tolerance" of the Chinese toward all religions,[124] and those who assert the direct opposite, that China has been "the most intolerant and the most bitterly persecuting government that the world has ever seen."[125] The truth is that China is too vast and her history too long for easy judgments; it has been both tolerant and persecuting.

The last forty years of the century are a classic example of the paradox. On the one hand, after the Opium Wars China bitterly resented the West's forced entry into China; on the other hand it sent students to study in the West, but only intermittently, until after 1900.[126] The same years saw an exhilarating growth of the number of foreign missionaries in China, paralleled by a slower steady growth of the number of converts in the Chinese churches; but they also exposed both missions and churches to shattering waves of anti-Christian, antiforeign propaganda, which rose to a horrifying climax in the Boxer Rebellion of 1899/1900.

The Opium Wars in the 1840s and 1850s left China inwardly enraged at its own humiliation, helpless to prevent self-styled Christian nations from imposing the curse of the drug traffic on a country that was trying to rid itself of addiction.[127] Guilt by association inevitably tarred the Christian missions with the sins of the Christian nations from which they had come. Prince Kung, brother of the emperor and ally of the empress-dowager Cixi (Tzü Hsi), was quoted as saying to the British minister, Sir Rutherford Alcock: "Take away your opium and your missionaries and you will be welcome."[128] Most non-Christian Chinese, said one observant missionary, "regarded the missionary as the vanguard of foreign armies."[129] Ever since the disastrous Taiping Rebellion, most Chinese found it difficult to distinguish the semi-Christianity of the Taiping rebels from the faith of the missionaries, and as a result lived with the perception that Christianity was the seventh column of invasion and the handmaiden of rebellion.

It is not surprising, therefore, to find that fast though the church might be growing in China, it was faced and sometimes outpaced by a rising storm of Chinese protest against all things foreign, including Christianity.[130] Protestants evangelized with less support from their related foreign governments — especially Great Britain and the United States — than Catholics received from France,[131] which was one reason for their greater popularity and influence in China in this period. But neither the Protestants nor the Catholics escaped criticism as being irritatingly and perhaps dangerously foreign.

Among the intellectual elite, protests were relatively mild and urbane. Viceroy Li Hongzhang was for twenty-five years the most influential government official in the empire, holding such titles as imperial tutor and grand secretary of state, in addition to being governor general of several key provinces. He wrote politely but loftily in 1886 that England did not need Confucius, and China did not need Jesus Christ, for "the teachings of Confucius and the doctrines of Jesus appear to be on one exalted plane, conceived and promulgated for the betterment of all mankind."[132]

But violence was in the air. The first notable incident of antiforeign violence occurred in 1862 in the southern inland province of Guizhou (Kweichow). Led by an arrogant, partly discredited official whose eleven concubines scandalized the missionaries, a mob stole images from the Catholic cathedral in the provincial capital. A few months later four Catholic seminarians were publicly beheaded, and other executions followed. Only grudgingly, under strong French pressure, was the responsible official removed from office and sent into exile.[133]

There was nothing new either in the accusations rumored against the missionaries, or in the outbreak of xenophobic riots. China has always been suspicious of foreigners, though missionaries often remarked at its general religious tolerance.[134] Traces of antiforeign sentiment stretch back for centuries,[135] and its reappearance in the nineteenth century after the provocations of the foreign wars and threats to Chinese sovereignty are remarkable as much for their comparative rarity as for their occasional severity.[136]

Y. C. Wang traces three stages of Chinese reaction to the West in the latter part of the nineteenth century. In the first stage, 1840–1860, Chinese intellectuals sharply rejected Western thought, including Christianity. In the second stage, 1860–1895, the attitude softened to a mixture of resentment and admiration. The third stage, 1895–1925 — after the empire's defeat by Japan, and the humiliating collapse of the anti-Western Boxer Rebellion — was a complete reversal of their earlier rejection and was marked, states Wang, by a feeling of national remorse and acceptance of Western superiority.[137]

The first stage was marked by literary attacks ranging from the obscene and vitriolic, such as invective against "the incarnate pig," Jesus Christ,[138] to reasonable complaints against the unjustified invasion of Chinese sovereignty during and after the Opium Wars. The unequal treaties that ended the wars granted foreigners special legal rights and provoked widespread resentment against missionary interference in legal cases on behalf of their converts, most noticeably by Catholic missionaries.[139] This was the background to the climax of tragedy, the Boxer Rebellion.

The Boxer Rebellion of 1899–1901[140]

Early in 1899 missionaries first noticed and reported to the Western world the disturbing actions of a band of hostile, turbaned rebels, the "Boxers," who were attacking towns and villages in various places under the slogan "Exalt the Dynasty; Destroy the Foreigners."[141] And it was the missionaries who many, both in China and the West, were quick to blame for the violent uprising.[142] But then and since it has been made very clear that the rebellion was basically antiforeign and only tangentially antimissionary.[143]

The chilling sequence of events leading up to the great uprising had already begun four years earlier in 1895 with a massacre of eleven missionaries, mostly Irish at Hueshan, on the southeast coast near Fuzhou. All but one of the nine adults were women, seven of them single women, and two infants. They belonged to two Anglican missions, The Church Missionary Society and the Church of England Zenana Society, the latter of which worked among women secluded in the women's quarters of Chinese homes. In August, a shouting mob of members of a secret anti-Manchu, anti-Christian society called the Vegetable Eaters stormed the missionary cottages. Three of the children were gathering flowers and thought the drums meant a procession, but seeing the spears and the look on the people's faces tried to run. They were seized by the hair, dragged to the cottage, and beaten. Three survived, but the six-year-old boy and the baby died. All in all, nine of the party were hacked, beaten, and burned to death. The only survivors were three of the children, one man who providentially lived five minutes away from the cottage, and one of the single women who was so cut and beaten she almost bled to death.[144]

All through the next four years the tensions mounted: drought and famine, loss of control by the central government, rural instability, German intrusion into Shandong province — "all producing a whirlwind of antiforeignism not very secretly encouraged by the empress dowager and her court."[145] The next few years were times of mounting tensions. The explosion came in 1899. One example perhaps will best catch in miniature the suddenness with which the movement turned against the missionaries. The following brief excerpts are from letters written by Eva Jane Price, who was killed in 1900 with her husband, Charles, and her seven-year-old daughter in remote Shanxi (Shansi) province west of Beijing over the mountains, a province almost as large as all of New England.

> Jan. 15, 1899. Did Charlie tell you about our happy Christmas day. You may wonder how I managed to entertain seventy-six [Chinese] women and children but I had open house all day...They were delighted with everything until it came to going downstairs. Some of them sat down and shuffled from one step to the other. It gave me a good chance to point out the disadvantage of the poor little [bound feet]...

> Dec. 6, 1899. There are five women here now breaking off opium and there are four babies besides...Teaching women is very uphill and discouraging work and opium sots are among the worst. But if Christ gave His very life-blood for them...I ought to be glad to do something, especially because He suffered it all for me as well as for them.

> Feb. 14, 1900. Do you hear of the trouble the Christians are having in two provinces just east of us? There is a native secret society called the "Boxers" who say they are going to overthrow the Protestant religion in China. They are persecuting the Catholics too.

> June 29, 1900. Last Sunday the most distressing rumors came that all the foreigners in Peking had been killed...Last eve we sat out in the court as usual trying to be brave. I went in about eight to help Florence [her daughter, seven years old] get ready for bed. Just as we finished Miss Eldred...called out, "They have come."

> June 30, 1900. So far we are safe, but living in a suspense that cannot be imagined...If we are to be murdered, one can but pray that it may come quickly...the heart refuses to act properly and knees and legs shake in spite of all effort to be brave and quiet, trusting in God. We do trust in him. "Fear not, it is all right.'" This is our witness...If we die, we die in peace!
>   Ever yours lovingly,
>   (Signed) Chas., Eva, Florence[146]

Not until September did the State Department confirm the tragic ending: ten missionaries and three children at Fenchou-fu and nearby Taiku had all been killed by a military escort while told they were being taken to safety over the mountains to the coast.[147]

A preliminary listing in the year 1901 records 135 adult Protestant missionaries and 53 children as victims of the Boxer cyclone, but others were discovered later and the total may never be known.[148] The Prices were among 102 adults and 41 children who were killed in the inland province of Shanxi alone.[149] It was the inland missions that suffered the heaviest casualties, the China Inland Mission and the Christian Missionary Alliance. The latter had only started the work in Mongolia seven years earlier, in 1893. Twenty-eight of their thirty-eight missionaries were killed and 14 of their children.[150] One of the worst of the massacres was south of Beijing at Baoding where 15 missionaries were killed in twenty-four hours;[151] a week earlier Miss Coombs, farther west in Taiyuan, was burned to death by a mob while trying to save 2 Chinese children; and a week later in the same place, by order of the vindictive provincial governor, 10 men, 14 women, and 9 children were all killed in one mad frenzy.[152]

The Roman Catholics were attacked even more fiercely than Protestants, though the number of their missionary martyrs was smaller. The list, probably incomplete, names 5 bishops, 31 European priests, 9 European sisters and 2 Marists.[153] The number of missionaries killed was fewer, but they lost tragically more of their Chinese converts than the Protestants — an estimated 30,000, compared to only 1,912 Protestant Chinese.[154] This was despite the fact that their greater numbers and larger concentration in parish and mission centers gave the Catholics the opportunity better to defend themselves, as in the heroic defense of the Beitang Cathedral in Beijing, and in Shanxi and Hebei (then Chihli).[155] In Mongolia, where 100 missionaries of the Immaculate Heart of Mary ministered to as many as 40,000 converts, their apostolic vicar, Bishop Hamer, was tortured, his fingers and toes were cut off and he was carted bleeding from village to village until he died. Eight of his missionary colleagues in Mongolia and three thousand native Christians were also killed.[156] Even the recently revived Russian Orthodox Mission in China lost about half of its some 7,000 communicant members.[157]

Much as the missionaries had suffered, they knew that the greater heroism and deeper suffering was that of the Chinese Christians. Something of the Chinese side of the heroism is told by the story of two survivors, who risked their lives trying to protect their foreign friends. Fei (or Fay) Chi Ho, a young colleague of the martyred Charles and Eva Price, was a teacher in the little mission school in Fenchou-fu. When the Boxers attacked he tried in vain to save the missionaries and barely escaped with his own life, only to find after a fearful trip across the mountains that his home had been reduced to rubble and both his parents had been killed.[158] The women were most vulnerable to the Boxer attacks because their bound feet made it impossible to run away. A Bible woman, Mrs. Ch'iang, mother of a Christian Chinese college student, was caught unable to hobble fast enough as she fled on her aching bound feet. They caught her crawling from a yard to find food and "struck her with swords until she was 'literally minced.' "[159] It has been said that the Boxer massacres "produced more Protestant martyrs than all the previous decades of the Protestant church's existence in China."[160]

It also produced more Christians. Despite a temporary pause, church growth increased rather than diminishing. In 1800 there were 202,000 baptized Roman Catholics in the empire. In 1897 the number had more than doubled to 532,448. For Protestants the increase was yet more phenomenal: from 1 baptized Chinese believer in 1814 to 112,808 communicant members in 1899 and a total Protestant community of more than 200,000.[161]

Such numbers are small in China. What could not yet be measured was the revolutionary impact of half a century of Christian schools and hospitals on a culture fast losing confidence in ancient Confucian patterns. And what was yet to come was the discovery of the incrementally increasing power of visibly changed lives in growing churches of Chinese Christians to survive the kind of violent dynastic changes that in former times had wiped the Christian faith out of its intermittent appearances in China.

The tragedies of the Boxer Rebellion were a grim ending to a troubled century in China. A better conclusion would be to point out that the storm clouds of its last months should not be allowed to obscure the fact that in retrospect the nineteenth century was precisely what it has been called: a "great century" of Christian expansion in China. But in some ways, the next century was even greater. In the twentieth century, as we shall see in another volume, Christianity in China faced tests and tribulations greater than the Boxer Rebellion, and surprisingly emerged with the greatest surge of numerical growth in its entire thirteen hundred years of history.

The *World Christian Encyclopedia*, 2001, estimated the comparative strength of Christianity in China's population of 472 million in 1900 as 1,670,000, less than one-half of 1 percent of the most populous country in the world. In relation to the traditional Chinese relations, however, it was fourth, but only a distant fourth. The table below is for 1900 compared with 2000. It is important to note that the growth since 1949 has occurred as a result of Chinese agency, not under the agency of foreign missioners:[162]

	1900	2000
Chinese folk religions	376,300,000 (79.7%)	360,000,000 (28.5%)
Buddhist	60,000,000 (12.7%)	106,000,000 (8.4%)
Muslims	24,000,000 (5.1%)	19,000,000 (1.5%)
Christians (professing)	1,670,000 (0.4%)	89,000,000 (7.1%)
Roman Catholic	1,200,000 (0.2%)	7,000,000 (0.6%)
Protestant (PIA)	436,000 (0.1%)	71,000,000 (6.0%)
Orthodox	34,000	
[double count: -800,000]		

NOTES

1. Robert E. Speer, *Mission and Politics in China: The Situation in China, A Record of Cause and Effect* (New York: Fleming H. Revell, 1900), 9.

2. Jane Hunter, *The Gospel of Gentility: American Women Missionaries in China* (New Haven, Conn.: Yale University Press, 1984), xvi.

3. On the anti-Christian decrees and persecutions of the eighteenth and early nineteenth centuries, see above chap. 5 and chap. 8. For greater detail see De Groot, *Sectarianism and Religious Persecution in China*, 271–275, 329ff., and passim; and Latourette, *History of Christian Missions in China*, 171–180.

4. See William C. Hunter, *The "Fan Kwae" [foreign devils] at Canton before Treaty Days 1825–1844, by An Old Resident* (London: Kegan Paul, Trench, 1882).

5. Newcomb, *A Cyclopedia of Missions*, 294.

6. Cf. Latourette, *A History of Christian Missions in China*, 182–183, and 329. His careful estimate is about 200,000 Roman Catholics as the persecutions abated in 1840, and about 500,000 by 1890. Louvet (*Les missions catholiques aux XIXme siècle*, 25, 175) gives a figure of 187,000 Catholics in 1800, 330,000 in 1850, and 601,400 in 1890.

7. See chap. 5 above.

8. Of the two Opium Wars, one missionary, S. Wells Williams, in *The Middle Kingdom: A Survey of the Geography, Government, Education, Social Life, Arts and History of the Chinese Empire*, 2 vols., rev. ed. (London: W. H. Allen, 1883), 2:463, wrote that in the first war the strong country, Britain, forced "the weaker [country, China] to pay for the opium within its borders against all its laws, thus paralyzing the little moral power its feeble government could exert to protect its subjects." And of the second war, another missionary, W. A. P. Martin, wrote that "it was marked by the pursuit of the most petty, private and even unjustifiable ends" (*A Cycle of Cathay, China North and South, with Personal Reminiscences* [Edinburgh and London: Anderson and Ferrier, 1896], 143–191).

9. On the China Inland Mission and its opposition to the opium trade, see A. J. Broomhall, *Hudson Taylor and China's Open Century*, vol. 7: *It Is Not Death to Die* (London: Hodder & Stoughton & Overseas Missionary Fellowship, 1989). Hudson Taylor did not mince words. Here is an example: "England is morally responsible for every ounce of opium now produced in China, as well as that imported from abroad" (cited by Broomhall from *National Righteousness* 1, no. 7 [1891]).

10. Latourette, *A History of Christian Missions in China,* 457–458, 462–463, who writes emphatically, "whatever weight the missionaries had was cast unanimously and actively against the evil" as noted above in chap. 13. On early missionary opposition to the opium trade, see "Chinese Edicts against the Opium Traffic," *ChRep* 5 (1836): 297–305; 8 (1839/1840): 310–317.

11. It is easy to confuse references to the vast amount of literature on the China Inland Mission — too many books, authors, and editors with the names Taylor and Broomhall. Each of Broomhall's splendid seven volumes of *Hudson Taylor and China's Open Century,* appear under different titles, which I will identify by volume number and title.

12. On the question of women as missionaries, see A. J. Broomhall, *Hudson Taylor and China's Open Century,* vol. 4: *Survivors' Pact,* 47–48, 227, 264ff.; vol. 6: *Assault on the Nine,* 232–251, 346, 348.

13. On the criticisms see, for example, Broomhall, *Hudson Taylor and China's Open Century,* vol. 4: *Survivors' Pact,* 225–226, 263–264, 287–292; vol. 5: *Refiner's Fire,* 144ff. On the policy of dressing in Chinese clothes and shaving the men's heads to the "pigtail," see vol. 4: *Survivors' Pact,* 225–227, 229–230, 232, 354–358, 382; vol. 5: *Refiner's Fire,* 143, 147, 194, 296–297; vol. 6: *Assault on the Nine,* 126, 134, 183, 315. On the later transition from Chinese to foreign dress among CIM missionaries, see vol. 6: *Assault on the Nine,* 296–297, 355–356, 368; 6:74, 423. Hudson Taylor said in 1880 of a new arrival, "He would be useful in Chejiang [Zhejiang, a coastal province] in foreign clothes, but ten times as useful in Chinese clothes upcountry" (6: *Assault on the Nine,* 315).

14. The 1900 statistics are from Beach, *Geography and Atlas of Protestant Missions,* 1:276. By 1913 the CIM reported 1,040 missionaries, including 240 in the European-associated missions that had placed their personnel under the direction of the CIM (*China and the Gospel: An Illustrated Report of the CIM, 1913* (London and Philadelphia: CIM, 1913), 140, 154.

15. The percentage of CIM missionaries in the total Protestant missionary community was 28 percent, taking a median figure between the 850 total members and associates reported in January 1906 (*ChM,* 77), and the 763 in 1905 (Henry Otis Dwight, ed. *Blue Book of Missions for 1905* [New York: Funk and Wagnalls, 1905], 49). The total number of Protestant missionaries in China, 2,708, comes from the *Blue Book,* which also reports 876 foreign Catholic priests as missionaries in China at that time (48).

16. Dr. and Mrs. Howard Taylor, *Hudson Taylor in Early Years: The Growth of a Soul* (New York: Hodder & Stoughton, George H. Doran, 1912), facing 89. Hudson Taylor's first years in China (1854–1860) were under Charles Gützlaff's Hong Kong–based, short-lived Chinese Evangelization Society, and though disillusioned by that society's lack of organization, he often referred to Gützlaff as "the grandfather of the China Inland Mission." The best sources on Hudson Taylor — in addition to the seven volumes mentioned above by Broomhall, *Hudson Taylor* — are Dr. and Mrs. Howard Taylor's, *Hudson Taylor in Early Years* (New York: Hodder & Stoughton, George H. Doran, 1912), and *Hudson Taylor and the China Inland Mission: The Growth of a Work of God* (London and Philadelphia: China Inland Mission, 1920). The best short biography is Marshall Broomhall, *Hudson Taylor: The Man Who Believed God* (London and Philadelphia: China Inland Mission, 1929). For historical background, see A. J. Broomhall's volume of *Hudson Taylor and China's Open Century,* vol. 1: *Barbarians at the Gates,* a panoramic

survey focusing on the political, cultural, and missionary background in China from 1800 to 1851.

17. J. Hudson Taylor, *China's Spiritual Needs and Claims* (London: Morgan and Scott, 1884), 9–16.

18. Quoted by M. Broomhall, *Hudson Taylor: The Man Who Believed God* (London and Philadelphia: China Inland Mission, 1929), 117. For the sources, see A. J. Broomhall, *Hudson Taylor and China's Open Century*, vol. 3: *If I Had a Thousand Lives*, appendix 4, 454–455. Cf. Taylors, *Hudson Taylor*, 2:33.

19. M. Broomhall, *Hudson Taylor*, 118, 119; Taylors, *Hudson Taylor*, 2:33.

20. Taylors, *Hudson Taylor*, 2:70–83; M. Broomhall, *Hudson Taylor*, 107.

21. Taylors, *Hudson Taylor*, 1:90, 112–113, 400; 2:60, 161–162. On Muller, see A. T. Pierson, *George Muller of Bristol* (New York: Baker & Taylor, 1899), 108–109, 440. On the "Plymouth" Brethren and Taylor and the CIM, see A. J. Broomhall, *Hudson Taylor and China's Open Century*, vol. 3: *If I Had a Thousand Lives*, appendix 2, 447–450. Cf. F. R. Coad, *A History of the Brethren Movement, Its Origins, Its Worldwide Development and Its Significance for the Present Day* (Exeter: Paternoster Press, 1968), 53, 76, 166–167, 179.

22. A. J. Broomhall, *Hudson Taylor and China's Open Century*, vol. 4: *Survivors' Pact*, 171–208. The Taylor children were also in the party.

23. A. J. Broomhall, *Hudson Taylor and China's Open Century*, vol. 6: *Assault on the Nine*, 299–300, 307–308, 322, 347–348, and 424 n. 327; Taylors, *Hudson Taylor*, 2:356, 358ff., 369, 378.

24. A. J. Broomhall, *Hudson Taylor and China's Open Century*, vol. 6: *Assault on the Nine*, 427ff., vol. 7: *It Is Not Death to Die*, 39–62; Taylors, *Hudson Taylor*, 2:419–433; Leslie Lyall, *A Passion for the Impossible: A Continuing Story of the Mission Hudson Taylor Began* (London: OMF Books, 1976), 58–59. The addition of the 100 new missionaries in one year brought the number of CIM missionaries to 225.

25. J. Hudson Taylor, "To Every Creature," in *ChM* (December 1889): 171–173. In that year, 1889, the CIM reported that it had 363 missionaries in China, and 144 native pastors, evangelists, preachers, and colporteurs (181).

26. A. J. Broomhall, *Hudson Taylor and China's Open Century*, vol. 6: *Assault on the Nine*, 216.

27. Single women outnumbered bachelors nine to five (A. J. Broomhall, *Hudson Taylor and China's Open Century*, vol. 4: *Survivors' Pact*, 148–150, 155, 172).

28. A. J. Broomhall, *Hudson Taylor and China's Open Century*, vol. 3: *If I Had a Thousand Lives*, 33, 255, 328, 426.

29. A. J. Broomhall, *Hudson Taylor and China's Open Century*, vol. 6: *Assault on the Nine*, 235–237.

30. A. J. Broomhall, *Hudson Taylor and China's Open Century*, vol. 6: *Assault on the Nine*, 239–250, 348, 397–398.

31. A. J. Broomhall, *Hudson Taylor and China's Open Century*, vol. 6: *Assault on the Nine*, 74, 247–248.

32. A. J. Broomhall, *Hudson Taylor and China's Open Century*, vol. 6: *Assault on the Nine*, 300.

33. Mrs. Howard Taylor (Geraldine Guinness), *Pastor Hsi, One of China's Scholars* (1900), 5th ed. (Philadelphia: China Inland Mission, 1905), esp. 93ff., 153–172, with many reprints; and its sequel, *Pastor Hsi, One of China's Christians* (1903; revised 7th ed., New York: Fleming H. Revell, 1905), esp. 181–185, 349–359. A recent

revised edition combines and shortens the two as *Pastor Hsi: A Struggle for Chinese Christianity* (Singapore: Overseas Missionary Fellowship, 1997), esp. 248–293.

34. Taylors, *Hudson Taylor*, 2:53, 66–67.

35. A. J. Broomhall, *Hudson Taylor and China's Open Century*, vol. 7: *It Is Not Death to Die*, 156; Cf. Taylors, *Hudson Taylor*, 2:416, n. 1.

36. A. J. Broomhall, *Hudson Taylor and China's Open Century*, vol. 3: *If I Had a Thousand Lives*, 100–101, 116, 132; 7:606–607, appendix 4. Nevius was later to become famous for what is called the "Nevius Method" of missionary work (based in part on the writings of Rufus Anderson and Henry Venn), which insisted on an early loosening of foreign missionary controls, and an insistence on the self-reliance of converts, and the organizing of self-supporting churches. There are parallels here to CIM policies, but the most spectacular success of the "Nevius Method" proved to be in Korea (see below chap. 24).

37. A. J. Broomhall, *Hudson Taylor and China's Open Century*, vol. 7: *It Is Not Death to Die*, 118ff.

38. A. J. Broomhall, *Hudson Taylor and China's Open Century*, vol. 7: *It Is Not Death to Die*, 120–126, 614, appendix 5.

39. Marshall Broomhall, *W. W. Cassels: First Bishop in Western China* (London and Philadelphia: China Inland Mission, 1926).

40. A. J. Broomhall, *Hudson Taylor and China's Open Century*, vol. 6: *Assault on the Nine*, 295. "It Is Not Death to Die" is the title of the last of A. J. Broomhall's *Hudson Taylor and China's Open Century* (to 1912 with concluding footnote to 1989). My footnotes attest my indebtedness to it.

41. A possible exception may have been Gangsu (Kansu), and perhaps Anhwei (Anhui). L.-E. Louvet, *Les missions catholiques au XIXme siècle*, 164–165; cf. Latourette, *A History of Christian Missions in China*, 240, 315, 318, 361, 390–391; and *China and the Gospel: Report of the C.I.M., 1913*, 144, 151. Anhwei was assigned to the Jesuits by 1856, and was entered by the CIM thirteen years later in 1869; French Vincentians itinerated in Gangsu before the 1860s, but residential mission was not established, under the Belgian Scheutvelt Fathers, until 1878, two years after it was entered by the CIM in 1876.

42. But even that was an improvement since 1800 when India had four to five times as many Christians as China. Louvet's massive survey of 1898 (*Les missions catholiques aux XIXme siècle*, 150, 175, 218–234) gives estimates of 986,000 Catholics in India (including Goa and Ceylon) in 1850, and a generous 330,000 for China. He reckoned the ratio of Catholics to population in 1896, about fifty years later, in India at 1/140; and in China at 1/750. Cf. Latourette, *A History of the Expansion of Christianity*, 6:253–256.

43. See chap. 8 above.

44. Bertram Wolferstan, *The Catholic Church in China, 1860–1907* (London: Sands, 1909), 453; cf. 1913 figures in Carolus Streit, *Atlas Hierarchicus* (Paderborn: Typographiae Bonifacianae, 1913), 214.

45. Jiongnan reported 259,101 members and catechumens; Hebei, 127,000; Guangdong, 60,000 members. Wolferstan, *The Catholic Church in China*, 450–452.

46. *Records of the General Conference of the Protestant Missionaries of China, Shanghai, 1877* (Shanghai: Presbyterian Mission Press, 1878), 488.

47. The exact figures reported in 1907 were 1,071,920 members, 424,321 catechumens, a total of 1,496,241. Guangdong province (including Guangzhou) was the fourth most Catholic province. See Wolferstan, *The Catholic Church in China*,

450–453. Cf. 1914 figures in "A Survey of Roman Catholic Missions," *IRM* 4 (1914): 461–468.

48. H. Jedin and John Dolan, *History of the Church*, vol. 8: *The Church in the Age of Liberalism*, ed. R. Aubert, trans. Margit Resch (New York: Crossroad, 1980), 8:187–188.

49. Abbé E. Huc, *Souvenirs d'un voyage dans la Tartare, le Thibet et la Chine pendant les annés 1844, 1845, 1846* (Lille: Maison du Bon Livre, 1900; Paris, 1950), and innumerable editions and translations including English (*Travels in Tartary, Tibet and China*, 2 vols. [London, 1928]). See also Huc's *Christianity in China, Tartary, and Thibet* (London: Longman, Brown, Green Longmans & Roberts, 1857). On Gabet's leading role, see Jedin and Dolan, *History of the Church*, 8:190, nn. 73, 74, 75.

50. Schmidlin, *Catholic Mission History*, 575, n. 34; 620. The Scheutveld Fathers were founded by Verbiest in Belgium in 1862. European Catholic missionaries had preached in Mongolia in the 1830s, and Mongolia was made a separate missionary vicariate in 1840; the Vincentians, who reported two thousand Christians among the Chinese immigrants into Mongolia and the building of their first church in Mongolia in 1838 (*APF*, 1840), 1:39–40), turned the field over to the Scheut Fathers in 1864. Mongolia was divided into three vicariates in 1883. See also Latourette, *A History of Christian Missions in China*, 538. Jedin and Dolan, *History of the Church*, 8:190.

51. Louis Tsing-sing Wei, *La politique missionaire de la France en Chine, 1842–1856* (Paris, 1960). Only Macao remained under Portuguese control, both politically and ecclesiastically.

52. Despite the terrors of the Boxer Rebellion, there were 521 Chinese priests in 1910. See D'Elia, *Catholic Missions in China*, 72.

53. Jedin and Dolan, *History of the Church*, 8:190–191.

54. See Robert Entenmann's research, "Christian Virgins in Eighteenth-Century Sichuan," in Daniel H. Bays, ed., *Christianity in China from the Eighteenth Century to the Present* (Stanford, Calif.: Stanford University Press, 1996), 180–193. The quotes are from 192–193. See also Entenmann's chapter "Catholics and Society in Eighteenth-Century Sichuan," 8–23.

55. Entenmann notes what may have been even earlier instances (1704–1747) of Chinese women taking the vow of celibacy as a Christian calling (Entenmann, "Christian Virgins in Eighteeenth-Century Sichuan," 182–184). For a full listing of the later, more organized nineteenth-century Chinese sisterhoods, see D'Elia, *Catholic Missions in China*, 74–75.

56. See Eric O. Hanson, *Catholic Politics in China and Korea* (Maryknoll, N.Y.: Orbis Books, 1980).

57. Johannes Beckmann, *Die katholische Missionsmethode in China in neuester Zeit, 1842–1931* (Immensee, Switzerland: Druck der Calendaria A.-G., 1931), 26–27.

58. See Schmidlin, *Catholic Mission History*, 615; and Latourette, *A History of Christian Missions in China*, 241–242, 345ff.

59. Latourette, *History of Christian Missions in China*, 565.

60. The first organized Protestant church in China seems to have been founded by the American Presbyterians (north) in Ningbo. See Latourette, *History of Christian Missions in China*, 248, citing J. C. Garritt, ed., *Jubilee Papers of the*

Central Presbyterian Mission, 1844–1894 (Shanghai, Presbyterian Mission, 1895), 1–3.

61. *Records of the General Conference of the Protestant Missionaries of China, Shanghai, 1877.*

62. On Griffith John and his work, see R. Wardlaw Thompson, *Griffith John: The Story of Fifty Years in China* (New York: A. C. Armstrong & Son, 1906).

63. Griffith John was speaking on the work of the Holy Spirit in missions. For the full address, see *Records of the General Conference of the Protestant Missionaries of China, Shanghai, 1877*, 32–44.

64. *Records of the General Conference of the Protestant Missionaries of China, 1877*, 12–13, 130ff.

65. *Records of the General Conference of the Protestant Missionaries of China, 1877*, 365.

66. *Records of the General Conference of the Protestant Missionaries of China, 1877*, 415–416.

67. On the statistics, see Latourette, *History of Christian Missions in China*, 52; and *China Mission Handbook* (Shanghai: American Presbyterian Mission Press, 1896), 325.

68. Latourette, *History of Christian Missions in China*, 226.

69. *Records of the General Conference of the Protestant Missionaries of China, 1877*, 487, 488; and D. MacGillivray, ed., *A Century of Protestant Missions in China, 1807–1907, Being the Centenary Conference Historical Volume* (Shanghai: American Presbyterian Press, 1907), 673–677. Catholic statistics are for the year 1870 and 1905, and the Protestant for 1876/1877 and 1905. Catholic and Catholic "community" includes all baptized, including infants; Protestant "communicant" refers only to adults baptized and admitted to full membership. The statistics also do not include Catholic foreign sisterhoods or laybrothers in China. Statistics such as these should be used with caution to compare differently organized church bodies.

70. On Talmage, see James E. Good, *Famous Missionaries of the Reformed Church* (Philadelphia: Sunday School Board of the Reformed Church, 1903).

71. On Mateer, see Daniel W. Fisher, *Calvin Wilson Mateer Forty-Five Years a Missionary in Shantung, China* (Philadelphia: Westminster Press, 1911); and for a more recent perspective, Irwin Hyatt, *Our Ordered Lives Confess: Three Nineteenth-Century American Missionaries in East Shantung* (Cambridge: Harvard University Press, 1976), 139–233.

72. On Allen, see Warren A. Chandler, *Young J. Allen: "The Man Who Seeded China"* (Nashville, Cokesbury Press, 1931); and more recently Adrian A. Bennett, *Missionary Journalist in China: Young J. Allen and His Magazines 1860–1883* (Athens: University of Georgia Press, 1983).

73. On Nevius, see Helen S. C. Nevius, *The Life of John Livingston Nevius, for Forty Years a Missionary in China* (New York: Fleming H. Revell, 1895).

74. On Corbett, see James R. E. Craighead, *Hunter Corbett: Fifty-Six Years a Missionary in China* (New York: Fleming H. Revell, 1921); and John J. Heeren, *On the Shantung Front* (New York: Board of Foreign Missions, Presbyterian U.S.A., 1940), 49, 60–61, 100ff. and passim.

75. On Martin, see Ralph Covell, *W. A. P. Martin, Pioneer of Progress in China* (Washington, D.C.: Christian University Press, 1978); and Jonathan Spence, *To Change China: Western Advisers in China, 1620–1960*, reprint of 1969 ed. (New York:

Penguin Books, 1980), 129–140. Martin, a Calvinistic Presbyterian, favored the Taiping rebels against the idolatrous empire, and when the revolution failed, adopted a top-down approach to evangelizing the nation, hoping to open China's mind to Christian faith by way of Western science, and living to see the empire fall and to serve the New China. See Martin, *A Cycle of Cathay.*

76. E. W. Price Evans, *Timothy Richard* (London: Carey Press, 1945), 18–19, 77; W. E. Soothill, *Timothy Richard of China* (London: Seeley, Service, 1924). See also A. J. Broomhall, *Hudson Taylor and China's Open Century,* vol. 7: *It is Not Death to Die,* 527.

77. Paul Richard Bohr, *Famine in China and the Missionary: Timothy Richard as Relief Administrator and Advocate of Reform, 1876–1884* (Cambridge, Mass. Harvard University East Asian Research Center, 1972). In contrasting Hudson Taylor and Timothy Richard, it is well not to exaggerate the differences. Taylor, the evangelist, was neither narrow nor intolerant nor antidenominational, and Richard, the social activist, was dismissed from his denomination. Evangelistic Taylor wrote anti-opium tracts, and activist Richard gave prime importance to the devotional life of Christians, translating for his converts parts of Jeremy Taylor's *Holy Living and Dying* (London: Charles Baldwyn, 1824). See A. J. Broomhall, *Hudson Taylor and China's Open Century,* vol. 7: *It Is Not Death to Die,* 72; and Soothill, *Timothy Richard,* 77.

78. Timothy Richard, *The New Testament of Higher Buddhism* (Edinburgh: T & T Clark, 1910), 142.

79. Williamson came to China first under the London Missionary Society in 1855; was sent home ill in 1857 and returned in 1863 for the Scottish Bible Society to evangelize and distribute Christian literature throughout North China, Manchuria, and Mongolia and to the Korean border. He was a convener of the first national, interdenominational Protestant missionary conference in Shanghai in 1877 (Latourette, *History of the Christian Missions in China,* 381, 398, 438, 440).

80. Soothill, *Timothy Richard,* 77.

81. A. J. Broomhall, *Hudson Taylor and China's Open Century,* vol. 7: *It Is Not Death to Die,* 136–137.

82. Timothy Richard, *Forty-Five Years in China, Reminiscences* (New York: Frederick A. Stokes, 1916), 332; Soothill, *Timothy Richard,* 291.

83. On these four principles of Timothy Richard's mission methods (adaptation, training, Chinese leadership, and Christian love), see Soothill, *Timothy Richard,* 67–70, 76, 92–93. But compare these with his five principles of mission to other religions, in "How a Few Men May Make a Million Converts" in the *ChRec* 32 (1901): 267–280. His five principles were: (1) the Christian message must be presented as "from the Gods or from God," (2) it must be considered essential to the salvation of the soul and "the true well-being of man," (3) it is superior to their old religions, (4) it can be approved by the government and by China's "devout leaders of the people," and (5) it commends itself to the human conscience. This was also the gist of his address to the Edinburgh World Missionary Conference, 1910, which did not receive as much of a response as, perhaps, he hoped.

84. Soothill, *Timothy Richard,* 19. On his brief meetings with Sun Yat-sen, who became president of the first Chinese republic, the "United Provinces of China," in 1911, see Soothill, *Timothy Richard,* 302ff.

85. Irenee Weber, *The Jewish Bishop and the Chinese Bible: S. I. J. Schereschewsky, 1831–1906* (Leiden: Brill, 1999); James Arthur Muller, *Apostle of China: Samuel Isaac Joseph Schereschewsky* (New York: Morehouse Publishing Co., 1937), 70ff., 111, 178, 250ff. and passim. He was born in Russian Lithuania and baptized by immersion as a Baptist in 1884, but joined the Presbyterian Church for two years, and then found his spiritual home as an Episcopalian in 1858. See the chronological table of Schereschewsky's life (260–262).

86. See Mary Lamberton, *St. John's University, Shanghai, 1879–1951* (New York: United Board for Christian Colleges in China, 1955). When ill health forced Schereschewsky to retire, his successor F. L. Hawks Pott for fifty-two years proved to be one of the ablest academic administrators in China (Jessie G. Lutz, *China and the Christian Colleges, 1850–1950* [Ithaca, N.Y.: Cornell University Press, 1971], 32–33, 274).

87. Muller, *Apostle of China*, 213.

88. Muller, *Apostle of China*, 64–68, 83–94. The phrase "poor man's Bible" was actually first used to describe his work in literary Chinese, not easy Wenli, because, as he himself said, he had always "made it a rule to use nothing but intelligible language." Unlike most Protestant translators, he preferred to use *Tianzhu* (Lord of Heaven), the long-established Roman Catholic word for God, not the two more common Protestant terms for God: *Shin* ("too indefinite"), and not *Shangti* (too closely associated with the "chief deity in the Chinese pantheon").

89. Muller, *Apostle of China*, 166–167, 195–200.

90. Muller, *Apostle of China*, 201–208. See also Jost O. Zetzsche, *The Bible in China: The History of the Union Version* (Sangt Augustin: Monumenta Serica Institution, 1999).

91. Robert Wilder, in *Student Mission Power: Report of the First International Convention of the Student Volunteer Movement, 1891* (Pasadena, Calif.: William Carey Library, 1979), 162–163. On Grace Wilder, see Eileen F. Moffett, "Grace Wilder, Vision 1887," unpublished manuscript, 1989. Robert Wilder paid this tribute to his sister at the first SVM convention, "God alone knows how much those meetings...owed their success to my sister's prayers." By the time of the 1891 convention 6,000 had volunteered for foreign mission, and 350 had already sailed.

92. See Latourette, *A History of the Expansion of Christianity*, 4:95–98.

93. Michael Parker, *The Kingdom of Character: The Student Volunteer Movement for Foreign Missions (1886–1926)* (Lanham, Md.: American Society of Missiology and University Press of America, 1998), 50, 54–55.

94. A. J. Broomhall, *Hudson Taylor and China's Open Century*, vol. 6: *Assault on the Nine*, 74, 245–246.

95. Beaver, *All Loves Excelling*, 101, 102.

96. Hyatt, *Our Ordered Lives Confess*, 235.

97. Ruth A. Tucker, *Guardians of the Great Commission: The Story of Women in Modern Missions* (Grand Rapids, Mich.: Zondervan, 1988), 111–114.

98. There are three major biographies of Lottie Moon. The traditionally pious *Lottie Moon* by Una Roberts Lawrence (Nashville: SS Board of Southern Baptist Convention, 1929) gives her too much of a halo but also proves she comes nearer than most to deserving one; Hyatt, *Our Ordered Lives Confess*, 93–136, reacts too far the other way and occasionally finds fault where there was no fault, but also reveals that even the best of saints have weaknesses. The most recent biography is Catherine B. Allen, *The New Lottie Moon Story* (Nashville: Broadman Press, 1980),

which strikes a substantial, well-researched balance. For an effective, incisive analysis of the three biographies and a concise portrait of Lottie Moon, see Alan Neely, "Saints Who Sometimes Were" in *MIS* 27 (October 1999): 447–455.

99. Catherine B. Allen, "Charlotte (Lottie) Moon," in *Mission Legacies: Biographical Studies of Leaders of the Modern Missionary Movement*, ed. G. H. Anderson et al. (Maryknoll, N.Y.: Orbis Books, 1994), 205–215. See also her biography of Miss Moon, *The New Lottie Moon Story*, and Hyatt, *Our Ordered Lives Confess*, 133.

100. Catherine B. Allen, "Charlotte (Lottie) Moon," 206; Hyatt, *Our Ordered Lives Confess*, 94–97.

101. On the rift between J. B. Hartwell and T. P. Crawford in Tengchou station, see Hyatt, *Our Ordered Lives Confess*, 12–14, 19–20, 60–61.

102. Hyatt, *Our Ordered Lives Confess*, 104–105. See Ruth A. Tucker and Walter Liefeld, *Daughters of the Church: Women and Ministry from New Testament Times to the Present* (Grand Rapids, Mich.: Zondervan, 1987), 303.

103. Catherine B. Allen, "Charlotte (Lottie) Moon," 205ff.; Hyatt, *Our Ordered Lives Confess*, 130, 133.

104. Catherine B. Allen, "Charlotte (Lottie) Moon," 210–214.

105. Irwin T. Hyatt, "Protestant Missions in China: The Institutionalization of Good Works" in *American Missionaries in China*, ed. Kwang-Ching Liu (Cambridge, Mass: Harvard University Press, 1966), 93–126. See also P. W. Pitcher, "Education a Factor in Evangelization," *ChRec* 23 (1892): 164–166.

106. Soothill, *Timothy Richard*, 253–258.

107. The best book on the history of Christian higher education in China is Lutz, *China and the Christian Colleges*. On the early stages, see 27–49.

108. Lutz, *China and the Christian Colleges*, 33.

109. Clarence B. Day, *Hangchow University: A Brief History* (New York: United Board for Christian Colleges in China, 1955), 1–11. The Presbyterians (northern) moved into Ningbo with characteristic vigor. Their first missionary, Dr. Divie Bethune McCartee, M.D., arrived in 1844 and almost immediately opened a hospital, a small clinic. Two married couples joined him in a few months: the Richard Q. Ways and the Coles. Way was a minister and Richard Cole a printer. Way opened the little boys' school in 1844 or 1845, and Cole set up a printing press in 1845. In 1846 Mrs. Richard Cole started a girls' boarding school. In 1847 they organized a Presbyterian church — all done, of course, "decently and in order." See Speer, *A Missionary Pioneer in the Far East*, 75, 83, 89–92.

110. Lutz, *China and the Christian Colleges*, 32–33, 55ff. On Schereschewsky and St. John's, see Latourette, *History of the Christians Missions in China*, 267, 368; and MacGillivray, *A Century of Protestant Missions in China*, 298ff.

111. MacGillivray, *A Century of Protestant Mission in China*, 443; Latourette, *History of the Christian Missions in China*, 629–630; Lutz, *China and the Christian Colleges*, 91–92, 109–110; and see John C. Ferguson, "Higher Education in China," in the *ChRec* 23 (1892): 152–157.

112. Lutz, *China and the Christian Colleges*, 28–29, citing William M. Decker, "The Foundations and Growth of Shantung Christian University, 1864–1917," MA thesis, Columbia University, 1948.

113. Stuart was later to become American ambassador to China in the 1940s, and Luce, whose son Henry R. Luce founded *Time* and *Life*, magazines, was for a number of years Yenching's vice president. From 1920 to 1928 the university was named Peking University, not to be confused with the earlier Methodist Peking

University, which was one of its roots. See Lutz, *China and the Christian Colleges,* 29ff., 121–123; Latourette, *History of Christian Missions in China,* 622–646. For a list of "higher grade" Protestant schools in 1914, see *ChMYB, 1915,* 401–402.

114. On Martin, see especially his own partly autobiographical *A Cycle of Cathay,* and Covell, *W. A. P. Martin*; and Peter Duus's monograph, "Science and Salvation in China: The Life and Work of W. A. P. Martin," in *American Missionaries in China,* ed. Kwang-Ching Liu (Cambridge, Mass.: Harvard University Press, 1966), 11–41.

115. Covell, *W. A. P. Martin,* 189, citing Robert E. Lewis, *The Educational Conquest of the Far East* (New York: Fleming H. Revell, 1903).

116. Covell, *W. A. P. Martin,* 264; and Lutz, *China and the Christian Colleges,* 44–49.

117. On Talmage, see J. G. Fagg, *Forty Years in South China: The Life of Rev. John Van Nest Talmage* (New York: A. D. F. Randolph, 1894); and a short biography in Good, *Famous Missionaries of the Reformed Church,* 235–243. Talmage, a graduate of New Brunswick Seminary, established residence in China in 1850, and made an important literary contribution by using the English alphabet to transliterate colloquial Chinese.

118. Fagg, *Forty Years in South China,* 173–188; Good, *Famous Missionaries of the Reformed Church,* 236–241.

119. Fagg, *Forty Years in South China,* 210.

120. Fagg, *Forty Years in South China,* 181, 192ff.

121. Fagg, *Forty Years in South China,* 199.

122. Fagg, *Forty Years in South China,* 218–223.

123. Some of the best sources on the anti-Christian movement of this period are: Paul A. Cohen, *China and Christianity: The Missionary Movement and the Growth of Chinese Antiforeignism, 1860–1870* (Cambridge, Mass.: Harvard University Press, 1963); Edmund S. Wehrle, *Britain, China, and the Antimissionary Riots, 1890–1900* (Minneapolis: University of Minnesota Press, 1966); and Paul A. Varg, *Missionaries, Chinese, and Diplomats: The American Protestant Missionary Movement in China, 1890–1952* (Princeton, N.J.: Princeton University Press, 1958). All three are well-researched and seek to be fair, but tilt to a secular bias. Their bibliographies and footnotes, however, open up a wealth of valuable source materials in English and Chinese. For a more Christian perspective see Latourette, *History of Christian Missions in China,* 466–475, 495–501, and missionary sources that are cited below.

124. The phrase "extremely tolerant" occurs in one of the best articles written in this period on Chinese antiforeignism, and should not be quoted out of context, John Ross of Manchuria, a Scottish Presbyterian, "The Riots and Their Lessons," in *ChRec* 23 (August 1892): 380–386. The complete sentence is: "As far as religion is concerned, the Chinese are not only 'reasonable' but extremely tolerant, till the professed religion assume, or is believed to assume, a political aspect" (381). Ross traces the beginnings of the association of Christianity with antigovernment conspiracies to the sixteenth- and seventeenth-century rites controversy, and especially the recent nineteenth-century Opium Wars.

125. This is G. N. Steiger's capsule summary of the thesis of J. J. M. de Groot's *Sectarianism and Religious Persecution in China,* with which Steiger disagrees (George Nye Steiger, *China and the Occident: The Origin and Development of the Boxer Movement* [New Haven, Conn.: Yale University Press, 1927], 12, n. 7).

126. Y. C. Wang, *Chinese Intellectuals and the West, 1872–1949* (Chapel Hill: University of North Carolina Press, 1966), 42ff.

127. On the opium trade and opium addiction in Qing dynasty China, see the brilliant study by Jonathan Spence in *Chinese Roundabout*, 228–256.

128. W. A. P. Martin, *A Cycle of Cathay*, 449. The words may be apocryphal, but see *Records of the Missionary Conference, Shanghai, 1890*, 573. On the trade in opium, effects of addiction, missionary condemnation of it, and Chinese attitudes toward it, see 85–90; *Records of the General Conference of the Protestant Missionaries of China, 1877*, essay by A. E. Moule, 352–367; and Thompson, *Griffith John*, 35, 38, 95, 405–408.

129. John Ross, "The Riots and Their Lessons," 381.

130. The most detailed study of one brief period of antimissionary protest and its earlier historical background in China is Cohen, *China and Christianity*. Well-documented but one-sided.

131. See Latourette, *History of Christian Missions in China*, 306–313, 473–476.

132. William Francis Mannix, ed., *Memoirs of Li Hung Chang* (Boston and New York: Houghton Mifflin, 1913), 40.

133. Cohen, *China and Christianity*, 114–123.

134. S. Wells Williams, the American Congregational missionary wrote in 1883, "The complete separation of the state religion from the worship of the common people accounts for the remarkable freedom of belief on religious topics" (*The Middle Kingdom*, 2:221).

135. On the Chinese anti-Christian tradition, see Cohen, *China and Christianity*, 1–60, 262ff. Cohen, in a note (285) finds a trace of antiforeign bias as far back as Confucius, who said, "The study of strange doctrines is dangerous indeed" (Bk. 2, ch. 16 of the *Lun-yü*).

136. On Chinese tolerance, see Alexander Michie, *China and Christianity* (Boston: Knight and Millet, 1900), 1–13, 56, n. 1, and 82, n. 1, citing John Ross of Manchuria.

137. Wang, *Chinese Intellectuals and the West*, 234ff.

138. See the pamphlet illustrations collected and reproduced in Cohen, *China and the Christians*, between 140 and 141.

139. On Catholic interference, see Latourette, *History of Christian Missions in China*, 309ff.; on Protestant interference, 421ff.

140. On the history and origins of the Boxers, see Joseph Esherick, *The Origins of the Boxer Uprising* (Berkeley: University of California Press, 1987); Immanuel C. Y. Hsü, *The Rise of Modern China* (New York: Oxford University Press, 1970), 493–501; Paul Cohen, "Christian Missions and Their Impact to 1900," in the *Cambridge History of China*, 15 vols., ed. Dennis Twitchett and John K. Fairbank (Cambridge: Cambridge University Press, 1978–), 10:543–590. Also Steiger, *China and the Occident*; Victor Purcell, *The Boxer Uprising: A Background Study* (Cambridge: Cambridge University Press, 1963); Chester C. Tan, *The Boxer Catastrophe* (New York: Columbia University Press, 1955). For an earlier survey of the immense bibliography of the subject of U.S. policies relating to the rebellion, see John M. H. Lindbeck, "American China Missionaries and the Policies of the United States in China, 1898–1901" (PhD diss., Yale University, 1948). And for authentic, moving accounts of the suffering and casualties read Nat Brandt, *Massacre in Shansi* (Syracuse, N.Y.: Syracuse University Press, 1994).

141. First to call attention to the uprising were Dr. H. D. Porter of the ABCFM, and the Jesuit Remy Isoré. See Steiger, *China and the Occident*, 131ff.

142. For a more dogmatic example see Paul H. Clements, who wrote in 1915, "The fault lies largely with Christianity" (*The Boxer Rebellion: A Political and Diplomatic Review* [New York: Columbia University Press, 1915], 74); and, with more moderation, Wen Ch'ing (Lim Boon-keng), *The Chinese Crisis from Within*, ed. G. M. Reith (London, 1901).

143. In defense of the missionaries, see, for example, Latourette, *A History of Christian Missions in China*, 507–508, 843; Purcell, *The Boxer Uprising*, 121–138; A. J. Brown, *New Forces in Old China* (New York: Fleming H. Revell, 1904), 249ff.

144. S. F. Harris, *A Century of Missionary Martyrs* (London: James Nisbet, 1897), 108–143.

145. Daniel H. Bays, personal comment, June 2001.

146. Citations from the annotated letters of the Charles Price family, missionaries of the American Board of Commissioners for Foreign Missions (Congregational), are taken by permission from Eva Jane Price, *China Journal 1889–1900: An American Family during the Boxer Rebellion: An American Missionary Family During the Boxer Rebellion, with the Letters and Diaries of Eva Jane Price and Her Family*, introductory notes and annotations by R. H. Felsing (New York: Charles Scribner's Sons, 1989), 206–243.

147. For other well-researched, well-written examples, see Brandt, *Massacre in Shansi*. One will suffice. Annie Gould, a shy, recent graduate of Mount Holyoke, who admitted that she had difficulty standing pain, died in the massacre at Baoding, south of Beijing in which thirty-three foreign missionaries were killed. The Boxers "trussed her like a pig being carried to slaughter." They carried her through the streets, hanging hands and feet tied to a pole, then placed her in a file of other missionaries. All were tied together with ropes around their necks and slowly walked to a corner of the city wall. One little girl, untied, trotted along beside her mother. There they first speared the little girl through the body, and the rest were beheaded one by one. Their bodies were thrown in a pit, their heads carried away (159–164, 210–213). Cf. Isaac Ketler, *The Tragedy of Paotingfu* (New York: Fleming H. Revell, 1902).

148. Arthur H. Smith, *China in Convulsion*, 2 vols. (New York: Fleming H. Revell, 1901), 2:648–649, citing a list by J. W. Stevenson of the China Inland Mission, which suffered the heaviest casualties, 58 adults, 21 children; next was the Christian and Missionary Alliance, 21 adults, 15 children; and third was the American Board to which the Prices belonged, 13 adults, 5 children. See also *ChRec* 31 (1900): 458–463 and passim; Ketler, *The Tragedy of Paotingfu*; Robert C. Forsyth, *The China Martyrs of 1900: A Complete Roll of the Christian Heroes Martyred in China in 1900, with Narratives of Survivors* (New York: Fleming H. Revell, 1904); Marshall Broomhall, *Martyred Missionaries of the China Inland Mission* (London: Morgan & Scott and CIM, 1901); and A. J. Broomhall, *Hudson Taylor and China's Open Century*, 7:291–456, together with summarizing chronology and statistics of the martyrdoms, 615–624, and Harris, *A Century of Christian Martyrs*, 109–143.

149. Forsyth, *The China Martyrs of 1900*, 486.

150. M. Broomhall, *Martyred Missionaries of the China Inland Mission*, xxvi, 328; Forsyth, *The China Martyrs of 1900*, 80–84; Latourette, *A History of the Expansion of Christianity*, 6:338–339.

151. Ketler, *The Tragedy of Paotingfu*.

152. Ketler, *The Tragedy of Paotingfu*; Forsyth, *The China Martyrs of 1900*, 26ff., 30–42, 499–501, and passim.

153. Latourette, *History of Christian Missions in China*, 512. On the Boxers against the Catholics in Shantung, see Jacobus J. A. Mathias Kuepers, *China und die katholische Mission in Sud-Shantung 1882–1900: die Geschichte einer konfrontation* (Steyl: Missiehaus, 1974). See also Latourette, *History of Christian Missions in China*, 508–513.

154. Latourette, *A History of Christian Missions in China*, 513, 517.

155. A. Favier, *The Heart of Pekin: Bishop A. Favier's Diary of the Siege*, ed. J. Freri (Boston, 1901), and Latourette, *History of Christian Missions in China*, 510–511.

156. Latourette, *History of Christian Missions in China*, 510–511.

157. Eugene Smirnoff, *A Short Account of the Historical Development and Present Position of Russian Orthodox Missions* (London: Rivingtons, 1903; reprint Welshpool, Powys, U.K: Stylite Publishing, 1986), 75–76. The Russian Mission had struggled, usually in vain, to maintain a much interrupted presence in China since 1714, but with no resident bishop until after the Boxer Rebellion. See also Latourette, *History of Christian Missions in China*, 486–487, 518.

158. Luella Miner, *China's Book of Martyrs: A Record of Heroic Martyrdoms and Marvelous Deliverances of Chinese Christians during the Summer of 1900* (Philadelphia: Westminster Press, 1903), 114–136; and Forsyth, *The China Martyrs of 1900*, 346–411. For more on the Chinese martyrs, see A. H. Smith, *China in Convulsion*, 2:652–660; A. J. Brown, *New Forces in Old China*, 274–279.

159. Brandt, *Massacre in Shansi*, 212. Her son at the mission college, North China College, Chang Ch'iang-Hsiang, miraculously survived two massacres (204–206, 248–249, 282).

160. Forsyth, *The China Martyrs of 1900*, 346, 348.

161. On the statistics, cf. *Records of the General Conference of the Protestant Missionaries of China (1877)*, 480–488; Latourette, *History of Christian Missions in China*, 182, 329; *China Mission Handbook 1897*; Louvet, *Les missions catholiques au XIXme siècle*, 175; and *Les Missiones Catholicae cura S. Congregationis de Propaganda Fide* (Rome, 1927), 377. A rough attempt herewith to correlate and chart the reported growth may be of interest, but remember the estimates vary widely.

	Protestants (communicants)	Catholics (baptized)
1800	0	202,000
1814	1	
1847	9	
1850		330,000
1853	351	
1865	3,132	
1870		404,500
1877	13,515	
1890	37,287	
1897	55,093	532,448
1899	112,808	

162. Barrett, ed., *World Christian Encyclopedia*, 1982, 231. China Christian statistics have an exceedingly large margin of error. The figure of nearly 80 million is a maximum estimate. Compare a government estimate of 25 million; and in Patrick Johnstone, ed., *OW, 2000* (Minneapolis: Bethany House, 2001), 184, an estimate of about 50 million Chinese Christians.

Chapter 23

Christianity Reappears in Japan (1859–1900)

> Where is the statue of the Virgin Mary?
> — A hidden Christian to Father Petitjean, 1865[1]

> We are hated by magistrates and priests, but we have planted the standard of truth here and will nevermore retreat.
> — Joseph Hardy Neesima, 1876[2]

IN 1639, as described in an earlier chapter,[3] the Tokugawa shogunate climaxed its fierce offensive against the Christian faith in Japan by sealing its national borders against the whole outside world in general,[4] and against Christianity in particular. Japan feared Christianity as a threat to the inner unity of the nation, and suspected that Christian missionaries were the spearhead of Western imperialism intruding from without. Two centuries later, in 1853, Tokugawa shoguns still ruled Japan, but the persecuted Roman Catholic community had disappeared. The shogunate itself, however, was also about to disappear. Suddenly in the summer of 1853 Japan's tight seal of security was broken open and the world again forced its way in. Four black naval vessels intruded uninvited into Tokyo (then Edo) Bay. They were American ships led by the pride of the U.S. Navy, a smoke-belching sail-and-steam side-wheeler under the command of Commodore Matthew C. Perry. Perry carried a letter from President Fillmore to the emperor of Japan, asking for the opening of one or two Japanese ports on the sea route from San Francisco to Shanghai. Open Japan? The shock was felt throughout the close-guarded islands. It divided the shogunate council into two factions. One resisted any change; the other, impressed as much by new Western technology as by the size of the ships' guns, argued that change was inevitable. In the end, in little more than a decade the reformers had won, the shogunate withered away, and Japan had a ruling emperor again, the emperor Meiji (1868–1912).

The Catholic Recovery

The Roman Catholics, eager to find out if any descendants of the early Christians had survived, had reestablished a Japan mission on Okinawa as early as 1846. Okinawa was then technically Chinese, with its own local "king," but was actually ruled from Japan by the daimyo of Satsuma.[5] It was another thirteen years, however — more than three hundred years after the arrival of the great Francis Xavier — that the first Catholic missionary of the modern period legally entered Japan. He was Father Prudence Girard, who came from Okinawa to Edo (Tokyo) in September 1859 as interpreter to French diplomats following up on the successful initiatives of the Perry expeditions. Girard came as the appointed head of the Japan mission of the Paris Missionary Society (*Missions Etrangères de Paris*) to which Rome now gave responsibility for the evangelization of Japan.[6] Within a few months a colleague, Eugène-Emmanuel Mermet, opened a little chapel in the northernmost treaty port, Hakodate. It was the first Christian house of worship in Japan since 1614.[7]

But it was in the far south that amazing things began to happen. In 1863 Roman Catholic priests reentered Nagasaki, which 250 years before had been the great center of Jesuit missions in Japan. Two years later they built a church, but no Japanese attended the dedication ceremony, for public worship had been prohibited by the police. Four weeks later, in March 1865, as Father Bernard Petitjean was looking at his new church he saw a group of about twelve or fifteen people standing in front of the closed door in a very silent and respectful way. He went at once and opened the door of the church, and the Japanese followed him in. He knelt to pray, and a woman stood near and whispered to him, "All of us have the same heart as you." "Where do you come from?" asked the astonished priest. "From Urakami," they said. "Nearly everyone there has the same heart." Another woman asked, "Where is the statue of the Holy Mary?" Another said, "We celebrate the Feast of Our Lord on the 25th day of the Cold Month." When they found that the priest had the same feast days, and the same statues, and was unmarried (the three marks they associated with true priests) they took him into their confidence. Very quietly at first, for fear of persecution, the missionary made contact with hundreds of secret Christians, then with thousands as the word spread that the Fathers had returned.[8] A year after the emergence of the hidden Christians, Father Petitjean in 1866 was made apostolic vicar of Japan.[9]

Communities of these descendants of the sixteenth- and seventeenth-century Japanese Christians were found in Urukami, the Gote Islands, and around Nagasaki. Some of them were only barely discernible as Christian. The years of persecution and isolation had diluted their faith with many superstitious practices. And not all of them were willing to return to the church and accept the authority of the French priests. Of the thirty thousand or so identified surviving "hidden Christians," only ten thousand to fourteen thousand rejoined the Roman Catholic Church. Some estimate that perhaps ten times that many preferred to keep to their mixture of Christianity with folk superstitions and refused communion with the French priests.[10]

The reappearance suddenly of so many secret Christians invigorated the Catholics and produced an immediate surge of growth. But it alarmed the Japanese authorities. Christianity was still officially a forbidden religion and persecution soon fell once more upon Father Petitjean's rediscovered Christians. In October 1866 he had been made bishop of Japan, and the very next year the persecutions began. For years the hidden Christians had all registered at Buddhist temples, hiding their Christian connections. Their worship centered on a communal meal and the veneration of their "holy objects," such as "holy water" for baptism and exorcism, and straw whips symbolizing flagellation, and paper crosses and holy pictures and medallions — all of them capable of concealment in various ways for fear of persecution.[11] They had accepted Buddhist funerals as a necessity, though after the Buddhist funeral they would often dig up the body and secretly give it a Christian funeral. Now they were told by the priests that it was not right even outwardly to accept Buddhist religious rites. In 1867 the Christians of Urakami notified the mayor that they would no longer allow Buddhist priests to bury their dead. The mayor was willing to help them, but the Buddhists, enraged, sent armed bands into their chapels, carried away about sixty Christian prisoners, and destroyed the chapels. The shogunate, sensitive alike to public opinion against Christianity and to pressure from the Western consulates for religious freedom, evaded taking any official stand on the problem and looked the other way.[12]

Never again did Roman Catholic Christianity in Japan experience the spectacular growth of those first few years of discovery of its "hidden Christians."

The Beginnings of Protestant Missions (1853–1872)

It was the good fortune of the early Protestant missions to ride in with the first waves of the momentous changes that the Perry expedition helped to bring through the guarded ports to the long-forbidden shores of Japan. One of Perry's interpreters was a China missionary, the ordained Congregationalist S. Wells Williams, sometimes described as "America's first orientalist."[13] Three days after anchoring, on July 11, 1853, the first open Protestant service ever held in modern Japan was observed on board Perry's ship in Tokyo Bay.[14] A few years later, one of the marines in his expedition, Jonathan Goble, who is described as "a religious man," became the first Baptist missionary in Japan, and published the first Japanese translation of a book in the Bible since the reopening of the country, the Gospel of Matthew. Some remember him for a very different achievement. He invented the *jinrikisha*, the ubiquitous two-wheeled "taxi" of Japan for the next hundred years.[15]

In 1856 the first American consul general, Townsend Harris, arrived to attempt to add commercial trading rights to the terms of the treaty. During the extended negotiations, in which Harris sought to include a clause of religious toleration, S. Wells Williams, the China missionary who had been Commodore Perry's interpreter, hopefully revisited Japan only to be told that the country would not admit foreigners unless "opium and Christianity could be kept out."[16] But Harris, a former Sunday school teacher, kept pressing against the legal restrictions on Christianity. He rigidly and pointedly kept the Sabbath, and began to read Episcopal services in his home in a loud voice that could be clearly heard through the paper windows, describing it with satisfaction as "the first blow . . . struck against the cruel persecution of Christianity by the Japanese." It was reported on one occasion that six Japanese Christians had attended the service. Harris's expressed concern for religious freedom was rewarded with a clause in the treaty of 1858 allowing Americans "free exercise of their religion," and the right to erect churches. It did not however, authorize the "preaching" of the Christian faith to the Japanese.[17]

It was not until July 1859 that Japan at last formally opened three treaty ports to nondiplomat foreigners — Kanagawa in central Japan, Nagasaki in the south, and Hakodate in the north — and almost at once the first Protestant missionaries stepped ashore. In fact the first arrivals, John Liggins and Channing Moore Williams, American Episcopalians, reached Nagasaki before the ports were actually opened.[18] The next arrival a few months later in Kanagawa was a Presbyterian, Dr. James Hepburn, M.D. (1815–1911). Before the year 1859 ended he was joined there by three American Dutch Reformed missionaries, including one who was to become probably the most influential of all the pioneers, G. H. F. Verbeck (1830–1898), later president of the school in Tokyo which developed into Japan's most prestigious institution of learning, the Imperial University.[19] In 1861 another American Dutch Reformed missionary arrived, James H. Ballagh, the greatest of the early evangelists, who in 1872 was asked to be the first pastor of the first Protestant church in Japan.[20]

For the first ten years of Protestant missions, these three denominations — Episcopal, Presbyterian, American Dutch Reformed — plus a small contingent of Free Baptists — were the only ones working in Japan. Historians have often noted the ability and character of that first generation of Protestant missionaries to Japan. They combined "to a remarkable degree a high order of talent with breadth of experience and achievement prior to their arrival."[21]

THE PLANTING OF THE PROTESTANT CHURCHES

Those beginning years were tense and difficult. Only very unwillingly had the Japanese admitted foreigners once again into their country,[22] and though the Protestants were destined to become the major Christian force in Japan in this period, their early years showed little signs of promise. They found a good number of young men eager to study English, and in this way made important contacts with some of the future leaders of Japan, but few of their students seemed willing to become Christian. Beginnings were also made in the translation of the Bible, and in medical and educational work. But after thirteen years of Protestant missionary work, in early 1872 only ten Japanese had been baptized as Protestants.[23]

The first convert was Mototaka Yano (Yano Ryu), a physician and Ballagh's teacher, baptized in 1864; two more, including the leading advisor of the daimyo of Hizen, were baptized by Verbeck in 1866.[24] It was Ballagh also, as noted above, who organized the first Protestant church in Japan in March 1872. This followed a week of prayer by the missionaries, followed by a similar week of prayer for Japanese students, during which about half a dozen of the thirty students attending fell to their knees praying with great emotion, "tears streaming down their faces." All told, eleven of the students were converted and around them Ballagh organized what he called, nondenominationally, the Church of Christ in Japan (*Nihon Kirisuto Kyokai*), though it was Presbyterian and Reformed in organization.[25] Its first meeting place was the clinic of the Presbyterian medical missionary, Dr. J. C. Hepburn. Its first pastor was J. H. Ballagh, of the Dutch Reformed Mission, and its first elder was Yoshiyasu Ogawa, of the samurai class, who five years later was ordained as one of the first Japanese Presbyterian ministers.[26] The congregation took as its simple creed the brief statement of faith of the World Evangelical Alliance, adding these words: "Our Church is not partial to any [denomination], believing only in the name of Christ in whom all are one, and believing that all who take the Bible as their guide, diligently studying it, are Christ's servants and our brothers."[27]

The Russian Orthodox Church in Japan

The Russian Orthodox Church's pioneer missionary, Ivan Kasatkin (known by his monastic name as Father Nikolai), landed on the northern island of Hokkaido in 1861, only a little more than a year later than the first Protestant missionaries in the south. But not for about seven years was he able to baptize his first two converts in 1868. Perseverance brought him his eventual success, but not without setbacks.[28] Most notable among his early converts was a schoolteacher with a little knowledge of Western medicine, Chiba Takusaburo. He had turned from Pure Land Buddhism to Orthodoxy and followed Father Nikolai from Sendai to Tokyo, but eventually turned Catholic and ended in the semirevolutionary Freedom and People's Rights (*jiyu-minken*) Movement.[29] Shifting loyalties in new converts was not uncommon in that uncertain period of Japan's second encounter with the bewildering West.

Two points distinguished Nikolai's methods from that of the Roman Catholics. He managed to keep the Orthodox Church in Japan semi-autonomous, united with the Russian church only through the bishop, and therefore free from its Russian politics. Second, he emphasized from the beginning the inclusion of lay Japanese leaders from each congregation into the working supervision of the church along with the European missionaries. In 1875, the first Great Synod of the Japanese Orthodox Mission ordained its first two Japanese priests, Paul Sawabe and John Sakai.[30] By 1900 there were 376 ordained Japanese priests, and a total membership of 25,700.[31]

The Meiji Restoration (1868–1900)

On January 3, 1868, a coup d'état deposed the shogunate and restored the emperor once again as ruler of Japan after almost three hundred years as a puppet, a powerless symbol of national identity. The 222nd emperor, known as Meiji, had succeeded to the throne in 1867 as a boy only sixteen years old and therefore dependent upon older court advisors, but he reigned for forty-three years, quickly showing a strong will of his own. He preferred the more reform minded of his advisors and outlived them all.

At first the restoration of imperial rule only worsened the situation for Japanese Christians, for in April an Imperial Rescript reaffirmed the Edict of 1614 against the "detestable sect of the Christians," and proclaimed a revival of the national faith, Shinto. Some of the most powerful figures behind the "restoration" were nationalistic Shintoists.[32] Four thousand Christians were ordered torn from their homes and sent as prisoners to the courts of the daimyo leaders of the coup. Persecutions lasted for five years, including torture to force recantations of the foreign faith. Buddhists were also placed under restrictions.[33]

Not until 1873 were the last anti-Christian edicts gradually lifted. Two years earlier in late 1871 the first Japanese mission to the United States and Europe had left Japan to negotiate clauses on commerce and religion in the foreign treaties of the 1850s. It reported back that friendly communication would be impossible as long as Christians were being persecuted. Reluctantly, and still anxious to preserve the accepted Shinto principle of unity of church and state, the government in 1873 began to remove the public notices of the edict against Christianity.[34] Persecuted Catholics recently exiled began to return, more than three thousand from one town near Nagasaki.[35] The samurai were ordered to relinquish their swords and pensions, and Westerners began to pour through Japan's open ports. However, inland travel and residence by missionaries was still technically forbidden though only loosely enforced.[36]

Buddhism as well was freed from its restrictions, and from that time on began to be actively promoted as a sister national religion of Shinto. But the promotion had its flip side: as a dual state-religion Buddhism now came under government control. The more Shinto the government became, the less power the Buddhists retained.[37] Christians were never more than intermittently effective rivals in Japanese culture to either Shinto or Buddhism. Moreover, the state's anti-Christian edicts were only slowly withdrawn, perhaps, as K. M. Panikkar has suggested, to give the government time to erect a strong dam against the rise of Christianity as a political factor.[38] Not until the end of the century was complete freedom of religion obtained, and free access for foreign residence outside the seaports.[39]

Mission Activities during the Period of Tolerance (1872–1890)

THE CATHOLICS

Catholic growth in the last decades of the century was mildly encouraging but short-lived. In contrast to Protestantism, which early established an appeal among the displaced but still respected samurai class, Catholics were for some years associated with the large number of former hidden Christians who still suffered from centuries of enmity and ostracism, and as Drummond notes, were regarded as "the poorest, most ignorant, lowest of the Christian sects."[40] At the end of the year in 1873 the Roman Church reported fifteen thousand believers, almost all of whom were the "rediscovered" Christians of the offshore islands. There were three churches (Yokohama, Nagasaki, and Kobe), two seminaries with seventy students, seven schools, two bishops, and twenty-nine missionaries. During that year it had baptized only 120 adult pagans.[41] It was in the 1870s that the first nuns of three French Catholic women's congregations reached Japan,[42] adding to the French dominance of the missions at that time.[43] In 1891, the bishop of Tokyo, Peter Osouf, was elevated to the rank of metropolitan (archbishop), heading what was now a proper hierarchy with three suffragan bishoprics, Osaka, Nagasaki, and Hakodate. One historian remarks that Catholics in Japan were prematurely rejoicing that "the golden age of the [modern] Japanese mission seemed now to have dawned."[44] But a harsher reality lay ahead.

THE PROTESTANTS: PROGRESS AND DIVISIONS (1872–1890)

If 1864, the year of the first convert, was the year of beginnings for the Japanese Protestant churches, 1872 became a major turning point, not without tensions, in their development. Only very unwillingly had the Japanese admitted foreigners once again into their country. In March 1872 Japan's first little Protestant church was organized. A few months later the old edict boards against Christianity were taken down from the street corners. And in September the first General Convention of Protestant Missionaries in Japan was held in Yokohama to plan for the future.

The period of preparation was over. Ten converts had been won. The church had been planted. Official opposition was lifted. The time for the building of the church had come. Twenty-one missionaries attended the conference and issued a document calling upon the various Protestant societies at work in Japan to seek unity in name and organization and methods of evangelization for the church now forming in Japan.[45]

But unity proved easier to plan than to achieve. The next seventy years (1872–1942) were to prove that organizational Christian unity was the dream of only a minority among Protestants. Their community as the century ended followed not the ideals of the first Japanese congregations — one Church of Christ for Japan — but the traditional denominational patterns of the West.

In 1873 there were fifty-three Protestant, Catholic, and Orthodox missionaries at work in Japan.[46] Though they lacked the unity of the Catholics, and had no sudden inflow of restored hidden Christians, the Protestants slowly but steadily gained on the older faith in national influence, and to a lesser extent in numbers. By 1883 there were ninety-three Protestant congregations, all but two of which were related to Western denominations. By 1889 there were almost forty thousand Protestant Christians, most of them in five major denominations: Presbyterian and Reformed with about ten thousand communicant members; Congregationalists also ten thousand, Methodists five thousand, Episcopalians four thousand, and Baptists one thousand.[47]

THE PRESBYTERIANS AND REFORMED[48]

Some of the first steps toward uniting the Protestant missionary effort in Japan were taken by the Presbyterians. Protestant missions were only twenty years old when, in October 1877, the three Presbyterian missions — Presbyterian Church in the U.S.A., United Presbyterian Church of Scotland, and the old Dutch Reformed Church in America, which had learned its lessons in Xiamen, China[49] — threw off their mission labels and formed what they called not the Presbyterian Church of Japan, but the Church of *Christ* in Japan (*Nippon Kirisuto Itchi Kyokai*), in the hope that other non-Presbyterian churches might be willing to unite in the union. It was the first instance of a union of Presbyterian churches to form a single national church on the mission field. But it was denominationally open-ended, ecumenical.[50]

The three missions also united their theological education program under the name of the Japanese church, transferring the theological class begun by S. R. Brown, the Reformed missionary at Yokohama, to a united seminary at Tokyo and giving it the name of Union Theological School. One of its earliest graduates was Uemura Masahisa, of the Yokohama

Band, who was to become the powerful pastor of the "citadel" Presby-terian church in Tokyo.[51] The creed adopted by the united church was a "book of confessions" which included the Westminster Confession, the Canons of the Synod of Dort, the Shorter Catechism, and the Heidel-berg Catechism. The union brought together nine churches: four from the Japan Christian Church (Reformed), and five from the Presbytery of Japan which had been organized in 1873 as a presbytery of the Synod of China. Its first General Assembly was held in 1881.[52]

> It was the Presbyterians, also, who established the first institutionalized Christian school in Japan. Mr. and Mrs. Christopher Carrothers, only months after reaching Tokyo in 1869 started a small school, mostly boys of course in those days. But they included a few girls the first year until the pressure of oriental social custom soon dictated that Mrs. Carrothers separate the girls into a school of their own.[53]

THE CONGREGATIONALISTS (NIPPON KUMIAI KYOKAI)[54]

Though the Congregationalists (now, in America, the United Church of Christ) organized their churches a little later than the Reformed and Presbyterian, they grew even faster. In five years, from 1883 to 1889, the churches associated with their American Board of Commissioners for Foreign Missions increased from only a thousand members to ten thou-sand. In 1885 they formed a loose federation, a General Conference of "associated churches" to which the missionaries were attached as cor-responding members only, with no control over local churches, which were expected to be self-supporting.[55]

From the beginning, Japanese leadership was outstanding in this church. Sawayama Paul, who founded the Naniwa Church in Osaka in 1878, became their "apostle of self-support." Even more influential — probably the most internationally respected Christian in Japan — was Niijima Jo (Joseph Neesima), who gained fame as founder in 1875 of the greatest of the early Christian schools, Doshisha, as a completely Japa-nese institution. It became a university in 1890. It was at Doshisha that a group of students, converted by L. L. Janes, formed themselves into the "Kumamoto Band" from which came some of the greatest leaders of the early church in Japan, as we shall see.[56]

THE METHODISTS[57]

One reason that the Methodists did not match the growth of the Presbyterians/Reformed and the Congregationalists in Japan was that some of their most outstanding converts separated themselves from the denomination to form independent congregations. The greatest of these was Kanzo Uchimura (1861–1930),[58] a pupil of Col. W. S. Clark, founder of the Imperial University in Sapporo on the far northern island of Hokkaido. It called itself the Sapporo Band, and formed a church that in 1883, stressing its Japanese ethnicity, chose to leave the more foreign-related Methodists to become independent. Uchimura went on to become the founder of the famous *Mukyokai* ("No Church") movement.[59]

Uchimura was not uncritical of Japan. In 1890, as a teacher in the new government academy in Tokyo, when the Imperial Rescript on Education was first presented in a ceremony replete with overtones of the emperor's divinity, he alone of the sixty professors and more than one thousand students present refused to bow. He was forced to resign, though some fellow Christians convinced him to agree that such a bow was not necessarily an act of worship. He opposed the Sino-Japanese War and the Russo-Japanese War, and earned an immense but largely unpopular reputation for independence and lack of patriotism. He was, however, anything but anti-Japanese. He rejected charges of independence. "Do not talk about independence. Talk about God," he wrote.[60] In 1893, as mentioned above, he had led seven members of the Sapporo Band out of the Methodist Church to form a "Japanese" church, and in 1901 gave his movement the name Mukyokai, or "No-Church." The best-remembered statement of his ideals are in the form of a short poem:

I love two J's and no third; one is Jesus and the other is Japan.
I do not know which I love more, Jesus or Japan.
I am hated by my countrymen for Jesus' sake and I am
   disliked by foreign missionaries for Japan's sake...
For Jesus' sake I cannot own any other God than His Father as my God
   and
   Father; and for Japan's sake I cannot accept any faith which comes in
   the name of
   foreigners. Come salvation, come death; I cannot disown Jesus and
   Japan...
O Jesus, thou art the Sun of my soul, the savior dear;
   I have given my all to thee!
O Japan, Land of lands, for thee we give Our hearts, our prayers, our
   service free...[61]

THE EPISCOPALIANS (NIPPON SEIKYOKAI)[62]

American Protestant Episcopalians were the first Protestant missionaries to enter Japan back at the beginnings of non-Catholic missions in 1859, but its first years were extremely tentative. All but one of its first handful of missionaries lasted only about a year, and the one survivor, C. M. Williams, who after six years had just baptized his first convert, was called back to America for two more years. He had been elected bishop of all China and Japan, and his new enormously enlarged duties left Japan with only one baptized convert, and one missionary, the Rev. G. Ensor, newly arrived in 1869, and not an American Protestant Episcopalian but an Anglican of the Church Missionary Society (CMS).

When Williams returned on a visit (his permanent residence was changed to China), he found Japan locked into the first stages of the great Meiji revolution, which would change Japan and change Christian missions in Japan in ways impossible then to predict.[63] Some signs pointed to chances for improvement, but the new government reaffirmed its prohibition of the "evil sect called Christian," and an early incident seemed to promise trouble. A convert of Ensor, the English missionary in Nagasaki, was seized on a minor complaint and promised liberty only if he would renounce his Christian faith. He refused and suddenly found himself in an iron cage with an iron collar around his neck and carted off to prison in Tokyo. It took the efforts of the American minister, Townsend Harris, to win his release.[64] If it was all a mistake, it was a frightening one.

The Episcopalian Church in Japan was reorganized in 1887 as a union of the Anglican and American Episcopalian mission churches. From the beginning it was supported by generous foreign subsidies. Generalizations are dangerous, but it is possible that this weakened its growth rather than strengthening it. Another problem the Episcopalians faced was the division of their bishop's administrative responsibilities between China and Japan, which hampered his relations with the two countries' governments and with Korea during and after the Sino-Japanese War of 1894–1895.[65]

THE BAPTISTS[66]

Unlike other parts of Asia, such as India and Burma where Baptists pioneered and grew, the Baptist beginnings in Japan were precarious beginnings, as were those of the Episcopalians. The first Baptist, Jonathan Goble, and his loyal wife nearly starved for lack of home support. In Japan he alienated missionaries and Japanese alike with his "uncontrollable temper."[67] That same year, 1860, the Southern Baptist Convention sent two married couples and a bachelor to Japan. The two couples vanished with their ship at sea en route to Japan, and the bachelor, C. H. Toy, turned Unitarian and became a professor at Harvard Divinity School. Efforts to reestablish the mission were ended until after the Civil War in America.[68] By 1889 Baptists had yet to produce an outstanding Japanese leader.[69]

The above five societies were joined in the next two decades by a host of other Protestant missions. The Plymouth Brethren came in 1888, and a German society, the Evangelical Protestant Mission, in 1885, which in spite of its name brought European liberal theology for the first time to Japan in any significant way. By 1889 Protestants in Japan had 249 churches, of which 92 were self-supporting; 25,514 members, 451 missionaries, and 14 theological seminaries with 287 students. The growth in church membership was spectacular, as noted above: from less than 1,000 in 1872 to almost 40,000 in 1888/1889.[70]

Especially impressive, and one reason for the growth, was the success of Protestant emphasis on education. In the last three decades of the century, the Japanese imperial government brought in more than 5,000 salaried Westerners including about 1,200 teachers to prepare the country for dealing with the outside world.[71] At least two of the government teachers, C. L. Clark and L. L. Janes, proved to be as effective evangelists as any missionary.[72] By 1889, in addition to the seminaries, 101 other Christian schools had been founded with 9,672 students.[73] Mission schools have been given much credit for bringing to Japan not only a Christian worldview but also the highly prized products of Western civilization and technology. Their advanced knowledge of science and history caught the attention of the nation. As early as 1883 the Methodist missionary, R. S. Maclay, observed a little too triumphantly, "The success with which the efforts of Christian missionaries in Japan have been crowned has probably never been surpassed in the history of Protestant Missions."[74] His rhetoric may have been a little too triumphant, but the growth was indeed. In the next five years, 1882–1887, "full membership" rose from 5,000 to 36,000.[75]

At the same time, however, Japanese Christians were becoming increasingly sensitive about foreign leadership of the church. The two most notable critics, blending appreciation of the witness of the missionaries with searching analysis of their weaknesses, were Uchimura, already mentioned, who had left the Methodists to form a fully Japanese church, and Uemura Masahisa, the leading Japanese figure in the Presbyterian/Reformed tradition, who instead of leaving the denomination, sought to enlarge its boundaries.[76]

The missionaries were not unaware of the problem, and of the irreplaceable factor of native Japanese leadership in the church. When asked why Protestants were proving so successful — even without rediscovered "hidden Christians" to swell their numbers — they gave as a primary reason the leadership quality of so many of their early converts. This should head the following list of explanations that are often given for the burst of Protestant growth in this period.

Japanese Christians Take the Initiative

But even more important than the above social and political factors for the growth of Christianity in Japan was the zeal and quality of the Japanese converts. Thirty percent of the early Japanese Christians were from the samurai class, though samurai were only 5 percent of the population as a whole. From the beginning, Japanese Christianity was an upper-middle-class, urban movement — samurai, students, and intellectuals. Yet despite their fairly high social status, the first Japanese Christians were fervent and evangelistic witnesses to Jesus Christ. One group of converts informed the missionaries that they were not yet ready to be organized as a church because some of their number still did not know how to preach.[77] Japanese Christians even began to make their mark on the political level. In the first general election held after the Meiji Restoration of the empire, nine pro-Christian candidates were elected to the National Assembly of 1890 (the Diet).[78]

Japanese students, usually from samurai background, were the most open social group in the nation to Christian evangelism, and they became electric proponents of the Christian faith. They gave the Protestant movement its first outstanding national leaders. Famous for this were what later were called the Student Christian "Bands." "Vitally important nuclei in the growth of the Protestant church" is how one historian of Japanese Christianity describes them.[79]

The first of them, the Yokohama Band, in 1872 was composed of the students of Samuel R. Brown.[80] From them came the impetus toward the founding of the first Japanese Protestant church, and it was this Band that produced such leaders as Masahisa Uemura, defender of orthodoxy;[81] Ibuka Kajinosuke, first Japanese president of Meiji Gakuin; and Yoichi Honda,[82] who was the first Japanese bishop of the Methodist Church.

The second group, the Kumamoto Band in the south, looked to a nonmissionary, government-imported teacher, L. L. Janes, a West Point graduate, as their leader. In 1876, he persuaded the suspicious non-Christian founders of a newly formed government school that the only way to teach the students westward learning was to use the New Testament as a textbook. Within five years he had become so admired that forty of them in 1875 climbed to the top of a nearby mountain and pledged themselves to follow Jesus Christ and work for a free Japan. This was the group that produced Jo Niishima (Joseph Hardy Neesima), who went to America for further education and later founded the first, and perhaps most famous, of Japan's Christian universities, Doshisha University in the old capital, Kyoto.[83]

But the most Japanese Christian of them all, Kanzo Uchimura, came from the third and northernmost of the Bands, the Sapporo Band on the island of Hokkaido. As mentioned above, he was introduced to the Bible by William S. Clark, who like Janes was a retired U.S. Army officer and zealous Christian teacher recruited by the Japanese government to teach in a non-Christian school. Baptized by the Methodists, he was revered as the founder of the strongly Japanese "No-Church" movement (*Mukyokai*).

Women in Mission

In Japan, with its tightly male-controlled culture, opportunities for women in the missions opened very slowly. But American culture in that period was not exactly wide open to them either. One of the first volunteers for Japan was told by her mission board that she had better look to Africa, as "it was too early to send ladies to Japan."[84] A first attempt by a single woman, Jane Conovan, in 1863, failed, and she left Japan for a more open situation in Shanghai. The first single woman successfully to begin sustained service in Japan was Mary E. Kidder, who in 1869 took over a little girls' school started a year or two earlier by Mrs. Hepburn of the Reformed Church Mission and built it up into what later became Ferris Seminary. Miss Kidder received such a welcome, not only from mothers, that enrollment jumped from less than six to twenty-two in two years, and the non-Christian governor was so impressed that he sent her a present, "a pretty closed carriage drawn by coolies," saying it is too far for her to walk to school. That same year, 1872, the first student in the school to ask for baptism was baptized with her mother and younger brother. But the beginnings were precarious. Publicly to become a Christian was still not easy. Other girls' schools were opened by the Christian missions — first in Kobe, Osaka, and Tokyo — but when one brave girl asked to be baptized she was disowned by her wealthy family.[85] Yet the little Ferris Seminary of Mrs. Hepburn and Mary Kidder has been described as "the mustard seed of women's education in Japan," and Richard Drummond adds that "within twenty-five years of its beginning a million and a half Japanese girls were receiving instruction in public or private schools."[86]

But not even by 1900 did women yet receive the recognition they deserved. Counting the wives, they outnumbered male missionaries 457 to 245, and the single women alone outnumbered the men. At the all-Japan missionary conference in Tokyo in 1900, one missionary wife, Mrs. G. P. Pierson, plaintively remarked, "I am only a missionary wife — not even called missionary in my own right."[87] On a more positive note the Conference was reminded by a single woman missionary, Miss J. E. Dudley of the ABCFM, that twenty-five years earlier, in 1875, there were "scarcely a score of Protestant women in Japan," but now (1900) there are nearly twenty thousand. And the old pioneer James Ballagh (American Dutch Reformed), stood to support her with the ringing affirmation that "The great evangelizing agency in Japan is Christian women."[88]

The Identification of Christianity with Western Civilization

To many Japanese, Christianity appeared to be the "wave of the future" and the channel for scientific and technical advance. Some began to believe that Christianity was the religion of all advanced peoples, and if Japan did not become Christian it would remain underdeveloped.[89] One prominent Japanese, Fukuzawa Yukichi, a distinguished educator and "leader of the liberal thought of the day," though he resisted becoming a Christian himself, went so far as to advocate the adoption of Christianity as the national religion of Japan.[90] In a world that he sensed would be dominated by the Christian West he felt that a non-Christian nation would be at a disadvantage. Fukuzawa was so influential in the 1880s as an authority on everything Western that for a while "all foreign works were popularly known as ... 'Fukuzawa books.' "[91]

The disestablishment of the old religions in Japan in the early 1870s[92] ended the privileged position that first Buddhism and later Shinto had enjoyed. It was only a temporary disestablishment as later history would soon reveal, and was not even officially published until 1884.[93] But this separation of the older religions from a favored relationship to the government gave Japanese Christians true freedom of choice for the first time in the matter of religious faith.

MISSIONARY PROTESTS AGAINST THE "UNEQUAL TREATIES"

After 1883, as Japan sought equality in treaty relations with the West, the Protestant missionaries publicly supported the Japanese side of this emotional issue, an act that surprised many of their critics and deeply impressed the general public. Such a repudiation of foreign designs against Japan's sovereignty in its own territory took away some of the stigma of colonialism from the foreign missions and supported the argument of some Japanese that the only factor that kept Japan as a second-rate nation was its status as a non-Christian country.[94]

BIBLE TRANSLATION AND DISTRIBUTION

Many other reasons might be added to this short list of important factors in the short twenty years of Japanese Protestantism's first rare and most important period of rapid growth. But there is one that may be more important then most. In almost every Asian mission field, a vital factor in the arsenal of Protestant missionary methods was the emphasis placed on putting the Scriptures quickly into the hands of the people. Japan was no exception. While the linguists were still polishing their skills, Jonathan Goble the Baptist, rejected by the chosen translators for his lack of proper academic training, produced his own readable though imperfect translation of the Gospel of Matthew in 1871 and immediately began to peddle copies along with other tracts through the streets of Tokyo. They sold with amazing rapidity.[95] The first acceptable translations of complete New Testament books, however, were begun by Dr. Hepburn, whose translation of Matthew was published in 1873.[96] The entire New Testament was first published in 1879, and the Old Testament in 1883.[97] Catholic translations lagged behind: a translation of the New Testament by Emil Raguet appeared in 1910, but a Catholic translation of the whole Old Testament was not completed apparently until as late as 1959.[98] All the missions were not only active in Bible classes and teaching, they were united in welcoming the supportive role of the Bible Societies — British and Foreign, American, Basle and Scottish. In 1891 there were 57,894 copies of the Bible, either entire or in portions, in circulation in Japan.[99]

MEDICAL WORK

Compared with other fields in Asia, in Japan medical missions did not play the same prominent pioneering role in opening up the country to the advance of Christianity as might have been expected. Two of the first six pioneer Protestants to enter Japan in 1859 were physicians, Dr. James C. Hepburn, a Presbyterian, and Dr. D. B. Simmons, of the American Reformed Mission. There was not a single hospital in Japan, and disease was everywhere, especially among the poor.[100] The need was so great that Dr. Hepburn opened a small dispensary in a rented Buddhist temple. It was crowded out with patients within a few months, but the government, alarmed at its popularity forced it to close,[101] and Dr. Hepburn turned his immense energies to the language study and translation of the Scriptures for which he is justly famous.[102]

Two other doctors, therefore, proved to be more prominent than Dr. Hepburn — Dr. John Cutting Berry in Kobe and Dr. Wallace Taylor in Osaka, both of the ABCFM. Dr. Berry developed his little dispensary which he had started in Kobe in 1872 into a class for ten students and won the critically important permission of the government to teach them Anatomy by dissection at a "hospital" in the Hiogo prefecture near Kobe. A building was built in 1873. Two years later classes in Chemistry, Physiology, and Materia Medica had been added at the hospital.[103] In 1886 a yet more advanced hospital was established at Osaka, merging with a Training School for Nurses there, with Dr. Berry as superintendent.

Already, however, even the mission doctors were questioning whether Christian medical institutions had a future in Japan. By 1883 Dr. Hepburn was still occasionally prescribing medicines but his heart was with the Bible translators, and he told the second General Conference of Protestant missionaries in Japan at Osaka that "Japan at the present day [is] not a field for medical missions." Once it was a necessity. "But now the Japanese physician [is] crowding out the foreign physician."[104]

In the next decade as the century was ending, those Japanese physicians were going more to Germany for advanced study than to England or the United States. What this meant for the missions was that Japanese Protestants who had been almost entirely related to the English-speaking missions were discovering a different face in Western Christianity. The earliest German mission had not even arrived yet when Dr. Hepburn made his pessimistic statement, but the Germans were coming. Two years later, in 1885 the first missionary to Japan of the German/Swiss Allgemeine Evangelisch Protestantische Missions Verein (General Evangelical Protestant Missionary Union) reached Japan under the protectorate of the grand duke of Saxe-Weimar. This mission was different, soon becoming better known for bringing German liberalism ("scientific theology and philosophy") into Japan than for its evangelism. In 1897 though it still had only five missionaries (two married couples and a bache-lor),[105] its less theologically radical but sympathetic affinity with the goals of the American Unitarian Mission, which had entered Japan in 1888, had already begun to create early ripples of discord and division in the Protestants' innocent missionary Garden of Eden in Japan.[106]

The Period of Reaction (1890–1900)

In the three decades from 1859 to 1889 the church had grown so re-markably that many missionaries predicted that Japan would soon be a Christian nation.[107] Over the years there have been many such pre-dictions for too many countries, and rarely are they ever fulfilled. The same proved true in Japan, where such early hopes remain disappoint-ingly unrealized. Beginning in 1890 new and unforeseen obstacles began to check the progress of the Christian faith, affecting both the Catholic and Protestant missions.

Complicating Japan's love affair with Western technology was an industrial revolution and all the accompanying cycles of advance and depression of modern economic and commercial structures. The first depression began in 1890 and added fuel to an often violent reaction against things Western, particularly among intellectuals. Christianity, with its appearance of progress and well-being at a time when Japan was suffering, was resented and even blamed for the depression. More-over, for all its growth in numbers, not all was well with the Japanese churches.

It is true that the number of Protestant churches increased from 93 in 1882 to 297 in 1891, and church communicant membership from 4,032 to 31,334 in those same nine years. The revivals and prayer meetings of the 1880s faded. In 1889, for example, 5,677 new members had been added to the Protestant churches. In 1890 only 1,199 additions were recorded. Some new converts left the church, and the sale of Bibles fell off. In some Christian schools, enrollment dropped as much as 50 percent.[108] In the theological seminaries the number of students plummeted from 316 in 1891 to only 98 in 1900.[109]

In numbers at least, Roman Catholics also increased.[110] But after 1890 the rate of advance, which is more significant than the numbers, slowed discouragingly. Why the sudden change in the fortunes of the church? The major reasons for the setback seem to have been a cooling of Japanese enthusiasm for Western civilization, and an exploding fire of Japanese nationalism lit by the unexpectedly easy defeat of the Chinese Empire by the little island nation which she had always despised. The Sino-Chinese War of 1894–1895 turned upside down two thousand years of history in East Asia. And in a newly confident Japan, just as the Tokugawa shoguns in seventeenth-century Japan had wanted Portuguese trade without the foreign religion of the Catholic Portuguese missionaries, so now at the end of the nineteenth century the Japanese felt they could learn Western scientific techniques without the Protestant missionary teachers. The Christian faith began to lose its practical appeal.

At the same time, Buddhism and Shinto were regaining popularity as more properly Japanese religions.[111] Adding to Japan's growing sense of resentment against the West was the failure of the treaty negotiations. Ever since 1865 Japan's relations with the West had been governed by a series of "unequal treaties," reluctantly accepted by the emperor. The special rights of extraterritoriality granted to foreigners robbed Japan of control over its own ports. All through the 1880s and into the 1890s Japan sought unsuccessfully to regain equal rights with the Western nations, but it was not until 1899 that at last it freed itself from the stigma of the unequal treaties.[112]

Through it all, however, direct persecution was almost unknown, although in some areas Buddhist rowdies harassed the Christians. But the initial, spontaneous popular appeal of the new religion from the West had been lost, and Christianity in Japan never regained its former rate of growth. Nevertheless, the church did continue to grow, though at a slower pace, and more missionary societies arrived to assume their share in the evangelization of Japan: American Lutherans in 1892, the Salvation Army in 1895, and Seventh-day Adventists in 1896, among others.

As the century ended, statistics from the larger missions then in Japan reported that the Presbyterian/Reformed group had the largest number of total Japanese Christians (10,789), barely ahead of the Congregationalists (10,214); Anglican/Protestant Episcopalian missions had the most missionaries, male and female including wives (182), which was only two more than the Presbyterian/Reformed (180). But the Methodists had more Japanese ordained ministers (99), compared to the Presbyterian/Reformed (81) in second place.[113]

In the Catholic missions also, decline, not progress, was already becoming evident. Foreign priests numbered 106 in 1900, and there were 32 ordained Japanese priests.[114] The population of Japan in 1900 was about 44 million.[115] The ratio of the 106 Catholic foreign ordained missionaries to population was therefore barely 1 to 415,000 Japanese. If the 152 unordained foreign Brothers and Sisters are added, the total of 258 foreign missionaries makes the ratio just under 1 to 289,000. Adding total Catholic membership in 1900 of 54,600 brings the ratio down to about 1 Japanese Catholic in every 800 Japanese.[116]

But as elsewhere in most of Asia, Christians were a tiny minority, 430,000 (1 percent) in a 1900 population of 44,825,000. The comparative table of Japan's religious spectrum lists Buddhism with eighty times as many followers as Christians.[117]

1900	
Total Population	44,825,000
Buddhists	35,660,000 (79.6%)
Shinto	6,720,000 (15.0%)
New religions	2,000,000 (4.5%)
Christian Total	430,000 (1.0%)
Protestants (PIA)	96,000 (0.8%)
Roman Catholic	55,000 (0.1%)
Orthodox	26,000

If we are to take a look forward to see what occurred in the following century, by the year 2000 the total Japanese population was 122 million. Of that number 70 million were estimated to be Buddhist; 4 million Shintoist; and 33 million followers of "new religions." There were 4.6 million Christians, or 3.6 percent of the total population. They were comprised of 1.7 million Protestants, five hundred thousand Catholics, twenty-six thousand Orthodox, and seven thousand "marginally" or "nominally" Christian.

NOTES

1. See below, n. 8.

2. Joseph Hardy Neesima, letter, June 6, 1876. Quoted in Arthur Sherburne Hardy, *Life and Letters of Joseph Hardy Neesima* (Boston and New York: Houghton Mifflin, 1892), 203–204.

3. Chap. 4 above.

4. The exception was one Dutch trading vessel a year allowed in Nagasaki, through which Western science and learning seeped into Japan. Fairly close relations with China also continued. See William E. Griffis, *The Japanese Nation in Evolution* (New York: Thomas Y. Crowell, 1907), 285–295.

5. The apostolic vicariate of Japan was erected in 1846. Its first apostolic vicar was Theodore-Auguste Forcade, who in 1846, though not allowed to set foot on shore, was the "first Catholic missionary of the 19th century to enter Nagasaki Bay." Francisque Marnas, *La religion de Jésus ressuscitée au Japon dans la seconde moitié du XIXe siècle*, 2 vols. (Paris: Delhomme et Briguet, 1896), 1:156ff.

6. Jennes, *History of the Catholic Church in Japan*, 204–211. Xavier's entry was not officially legal, so Girard's was perhaps the first officially legal entry in 245 years.

7. Jennes, *History of the Catholic Church in Japan*, 209, 211.

8. The best sources on the hidden Christians is Marnas, *La religion de Jésus ressuscitée au Japon*, 1:487–494ff., 503–504, 533–544; and more recently Stephen Turnbull, *The Kakure Kirishitan of Japan: A Study of Their [the hidden Christians] Development, Beliefs and Rituals to the Present Day* (Richmond, Surrey, U.K.: Curzon Press/Japan Library, 1998); Ann M. Harrington, *Japan's Hidden Christians/* (Chicago: Loyola University Press, 1993). Cf. Laures, *The Catholic Church in Japan*, 194–201, 208–215.

9. On Petitjean see J. B. Chaillet, *Mgr. Petitjean, 1829–1884, et la résurrection catholique du Japon au XIXe siècle* (Montceau-les-mines, 1919), 163; Jennes, *History of the Catholic Church in Japan,* 220.

10. See Harrington, *Japan's Hidden Christians,* 35–95. As reconstructed by contacts with the thirty thousand or more underground Christians who began to emerge after the 1850s, some details of their survival in hiding have been pieced together, such as the office of itinerant "baptizer," rotation of meeting places from home to home to avoid detection, the weaving of implicitly Christian details into required Buddhist temple funerals, and perhaps most important of all, the retention of a summarized Bible story handed down orally, and only much later written down in several versions in the 1820s, the *Tenchi Hajimari No Koto* ("The Beginnings of Heaven and Earth"). On the survival and organization of the hidden Christians outside Catholicism, see Turnbull, *The Kakure Christians of Japan,* 55–81. See also Jennes, *History of the Catholic Church in Japan,* 216–217; Latourette, *A History of the Expansion of Christianity,* 6:375–376.

11. Turnbull, *The Kakure Kirishitan of Japan,* 82–110, 156–173. Turnbull's study is based on his observations of the modern, separated hidden Christians (Kakure Kirishitan) who did not rejoin the Catholic Church. His working definition of the Kakure faith is that it is a form of Christianity directly related to sixteenth-century Catholicism, influenced by contact with Japanese religion, isolated from European Christianity, and emphasizing ritual over doctrine — concluding that it is syncretistic but not "illegitimate syncretism" (9–18).

12. Marnas, *La religion de Jesus ressuscitée au Japon,* 1:574ff., 2:19–75; Jennes, *History of the Catholic Church in Japan,* 223–224.

13. William Harlan Hale, "When Perry Unlocked the 'Gate of the Sun,'" *American Heritage* 9, no. 3 (April 1958): 94.

14. Drummond, *A History of Christianity in Japan,* 143.

15. Goble published his "pure Baptist" Matthew, a year before Brown and Hepburn published a translation of Mark and John. For a full, lively account of his independent ways, see F. Calvin Parker, *Jonathan Goble of Japan: Marine, Missionary, Maverick* (Lanham, Md.: University Press of America, 1990); and cf. Otis Cary, *History of Christianity in Japan,* vol. 2 (New York: Fleming H. Revell, 1909), 51–52, 65; G. Verbeck, "History of Protestant Missions," in *Proceedings of the General Conference of Protestant Missionaries in Japan, Osaka, 1883* (Yokohama, Japan: R. Meiklejohn, 1883), 26, 42.

16. F. W. Williams, "Journal of S. Wells Williams. Perry Expedition," in *ASJT* 37, part 11 (1910); Otis Cary, *History of Christianity in Japan,* 40.

17. Otis Cary, *History of Christianity in Japan,* 36–40. On Townsend Harris's negotiations and the treaties, see also Sansom, *The Western World and Japan,* 285–291; Herbert H. Gowen, *Five Foreigners in Japan* (New York: Fleming H. Revell, 1936), 260–271.

18. H. Ritter, *A History of Protestant Missions in Japan,* trans. G. E. Albrecht, rev. D. C. Greene (Tokyo: Methodist Publishing House, 1898), 8–9. On the treaty negotiations, a good summary is Sansom, *The Western World and Japan,* 275–281.

19. On Verbeck see Good, *Famous Missionaries of the Reformed Church,* 249–261.

20. Ritter, *A History of Protestant Missions in Japan.* See also Ballagh's sermon at the second General Missionary Conference of Missionaries of Japan, Osaka, 1883. *Proceedings of the General Conference of Protestant Missionaries of Japan, Osaka, 1883* (Yokohama: R. Meiklejohn, 1883), 1–20.

21. Drummond, *A History of Christianity in Japan,* 146.

22. Verbeck comments on the hatred of foreigners and Christians, "all inter-course with them was conducted under strict surveillance . . . we were regarded as persons who had come to seduce the masses of the people from their loyalty to the 'God-country' and corrupt their morals" ("History of Protestant Missions," in *Proceedings of the General Conference of Protestant Missionaries in Japan, Osaka, 1883,* 30–31.

23. Latourette, *A History of the Expansion of Christianity,* 6:385.

24. Verbeck, "History of Protestant Missions," 51. Verbeck baptized a con-verted Buddhist priest in 1868. On Yano's name cf. Drummond, *A History of Christianity in Japan,* 159; and Tomonobu Yanagita, *Short History of Christianity in Japan* (Sendai, Japan: Seisho Tosho Kankokai, 1957), 34.

25. G. Verbeck, "History of Protestant Missions," in *Proceedings of the General Conference of Protestant Missionaries in Japan, Osaka, 1883,* 52–53.

26. Otis Cary, *History of Christianity in Japan,* 130–131. The church's first dea-con also elected on that day was a Mr. Nimura who had been baptized by George Ensor of the Anglican CMS mission (Verbeck, "History" in *Proceedings of the General Conference of Protestant Missionaries in Japan, Osaka, 1883,* 53).

27. It was at the suggestion of Dr. Hepburn that the little group of Japanese, with their connections to American Dutch Reformed, Northern Presbyterian, and Anglican mission roots, chose to be nonsectarian. See Verbeck, "History of Protestant Missions," 52–53; Otis Cary, *History of Christianity in Japan,* 2:62, 76–77, 99, 130–131. A. J. Brown is in error in crediting the organization of this church to Samuel Brown who was, however, the teacher of several of the young men and who in 1862 had formed the first (American) Protestant (Dutch Reformed) Church in Japan, one of whose members may have been a Japanese (Otis Cary, *History of Christianity in Japan,* 2:57; cf. A. J. Brown, *One Hundred Years,* 696).

28. The best short summary of the Orthodox Mission in Japan is in Drum-mond, *A History of Christianity in Japan,* 339–359. For other reference see sections of general studies on Russian Orthdox Missions such as Serge Bolshakoff, *The For-eign Missions of the Russian Orthodox Church* (London: SPCK, 1943); and Smirnoff, *A Short Account.*

29. M. B. Jansen, *Making of Modern Japan* (Cambridge, Mass.: Harvard University Press, Belknap Press, 2000), 383–384.

30. Jansen, *Making of Modern Japan.*

31. *Proceedings of the General Conference of Protestant Missionaries in Japan, Tokyo, 1900* (Tokyo: Methodist Publishing House, 1901), 1005.

32. Jansen, *The Making of Modern Japan,* 350–354, 371–372; and J. Van Hecken, *The Catholic Church in Japan since 1859,* trans. and rev. J. Van Hoydonck (Tokyo: Herder Agency, Enderle Bookstore, 1963), 17. Notable among the Shintoists were Saigo Takamori of Satsuma and Goto Shojiro of Tosa.

33. Otis Cary, *History of Christianity in Japan,* 1:306–332; Jennes, *History of the Catholic Church in Japan,* 223–228. For an overall view of the Shinto revival and anti-Christian, anti-Buddhist character of the first years of the Meiji Restoration, see Jansen, *The Making of Modern Japan,* 350–355.

34. Jansen, *The Making of Modern Japan,* 355–361. Central in the treaty dis-cussions was a Japanese insistence on preserving the unity of the state and the foreign powers' pressure for freedom of commerce and religion (Drummond, *A History of Christianity in Japan,* 162–166).

35. Jennes, *History of the Catholic Church in Japan*, 228–229.

36. The first Japanese mission to the United States and Europe left in late 1871 to negotiate clauses on commerce and religion in the foreign treaties. Japan insisted on unity of state and religion; the foreign powers pressed for freedom of religion; proscription was abrogated in 1873. Drummond, *A History of Christianity in Japan*, 162–163.

37. Jennes, *History of the Catholic Church in Japan*, 229–232; Latourette, *A History of the Expansion of Christianity*, 6:377.

38. Panikkar, *Asia and Western Dominance*, 392.

39. Schmidlin, *Catholic Mission History*, 629.

40. Drummond, *A History of Christianity in Japan*, 316.

41. See Jennes, *History of the Catholic Church in Japan*, 231–233.

42. The women's societies were St. Maur, the Holy Infant Jesus of Chauffaille, and St. Paul of Chartres (Latourette, *A History of the Expansion of Christianity*, 6:377; and Jennes, *History of the Catholic Church in Japan*, 231).

43. On French missions see Schmidlin, *Catholic Mission History*, 567–569.

44. Schmidlin, *Catholic Mission History*, 629–630.

45. See Otis Cary, *History of Christianity in Japan*, 2:78–79.

46. John King Fairbank, Edwin O. Reischauer, and Albert M. Craig, *East Asia: The Modern Transformation* (Boston: Houghton Mifflin, 1965), 270. There were seventeen Roman Catholic priests, and eleven more arrived before the year was out (Drummond, *A History of Christianity in Japan*, 306; cf. Van Hecken, *Catholic Church in Japan since 1859*, 72–73.)

47. Tetsunao Yamamori, *Church Growth in Japan, 1859–1939* (Pasadena, Calif.: William Carey Library, 1974), 155–162. Cf. Winburn T. Thomas, *Protestant Beginnings in Japan: The First Three Decades, 1859–1889* (Tokyo and Rutland, Vt.: Charles E. Tuttle, 1959), 105, 139ff.; 73, 101; 48, 73, 101, 145; 91, 148–149; 71, 75.

48. For a short summary of the Presbyterian/Reformed group in 1900, see *Proceedings of the General Conference of Protestant Missionaries in Japan, Tokyo, 1900*, 885–897.

49. See above chap. 22.

50. W. Thomas, *Protestant Beginnings in Japan*, 105, 139ff.; A. J. Brown, *One Hundred Years*, 734.

51. Drummond, *A History of Christianity in Japan*, 166, 210.

52. Drummond, *A History of Christianity in Japan*, 177.

53. Verbeck, "History of Protestant Missions," 45; see also Otis Cary, *History of Christian Missions in Japan*, 2:68.

54. On the Congregationalists (ABCFM) in 1900, see *Proceedings of the General Conference of Protestant Missionaries in Japan, Tokyo, 1900*, 912–914.

55. W. Thomas, *Protestant Beginnings in Japan*, 146.

56. Hardy, *Life and Letters of Joseph Hardy Neesima*. See also Otis Cary, *History of Christianity in Japan*, 2:114ff.; and W. Thomas, *Protestant Beginnings in Japan*, 48, 73, 101, 146.

57. For a short additional summary on the Methodists in 1900 see *Proceedings of the General Conference of Protestant Missionaries in Japan, Tokyo, 1900*, 915–918.

58. The family name is Uchimura, which in the Orient is written first.

59. Kanzo Uchimura, *The Diary of a Japanese Convert* (New York: Fleming H. Revell, 1895). See also Raymond P. Jennings, *Jesus, Japan, and Kanzo Uchimura: A Study of the View of the Church of Kanzo Uchimura and Its Significance for Japanese*

Christianity (Tokyo: Kyoo Bun Kwan, Christian Literature Society, 1958); and Otis Cary, *History of Christianity in Japan*, 2:124–125.

60. See Ishida Takeshi, in *Culture and Religion in Japanese-American Relations: Essays of Uchimura Kanzo*, ed. Ray Moore (Ann Arbor: University of Michigan, 1981), 10–11, 14.

61. Uchimura wrote this in 1926. Quoted from Jennings, *Jesus, Japan, and Kanzo Uchimura*, 1–2.

62. For a short summary on the Episcopalians in 1900, see A. C. Shaw, in *Proceedings of the General Conference of Protestant Missionaries in Japan, Tokyo, 1900*, 879–884.

63. Henry St. George Tucker, *History of the Episcopal Church in Japan* (New York and London : Charles Scribner's Sons, 1938), 74–85.

64. Tucker, *History of the Episcopal Church in Japan*, 86, 87.

65. W. Thomas, *Protestant Beginnings in Japan*, 91, 148–149.

66. W. Thomas, *Protestant Beginnings in Japan*, 898–912, for a summary.

67. Otis Cary, *History of Christianity in Japan*, 52. Goble began his work in Japan under the American Baptist Free Mission Society in 1860.

68. Edwin B. Dozier, *A Golden Milestone in Japan* (Nashville: Broadman Press, 1940), 46; Otis Cary, *History of Christianity in Japan*, 2:52.

69. Dozier, *Golden Milestone in Japan*, 47–54.

70. Yamamori, *Church Growth in Japan*, 155–162.

71. Griffis, *Japanese Nation in Evolution*, 336–346; Laures, *Catholic Church in Japan*, 225–226.

72. W. S. Clark became famous as the moving spirit behind the Sapporo Band, and L. L. Janes for his connection with the Kumamoto Band.

73. Latourette, *A History of the Expansion of Christianity*, 6:391, 395–396.

74. *Proceedings of the General Conference of Protestant Missionaries, Osaka, 1883*, 138; cf. Latourette, *A History of the Expansion of Christianity*, 6:391–392.

75. *Proceedings of the General Conference of Protestant Missionaries, Tokyo, 1900*, 988–989.

76. On Uemura (family name first as Uemura Masahisa in Japanese, and often reversed as Masahisa Uemura in English), see Drummond, *A History of Christianity in Japan*, 208–220; Norimichi Ebizawa, "A Great Church Leader in Japan," in *Japanese Witnesses for Christ*, ed. Norimichi Ebizawa (New York: Association Press, 1957), 37–50; and Charles W. Iglehart, *A Century of Protestant Christianity in Japan* (Tokyo: Charles Tuttle, 1959), 50, 56, 80, 98, 111, 123, 140, 151, 155; Carl Michalson, *Japanese Contributions to Christian Theology* (Philadelphia: Westminster Press, 1960), 174, n. 26.

77. W. Thomas, *Protestant Beginnings in Japan*, 169–170; Yamamori, *Church Growth in Japan*, 44–45.

78. Nine pro-Christians out of a total of 826 seems small (1 percent), but is highly significant comparing the size of the Protestant community, 25,500, to the number of qualified voters, 42 million (0.06 percent). Yanagita, *A Short History*, 46; statistics from Langer, *Encyclopedia of World History*, 891; and Latourette, *A History of the Expansion of Christianity*, 6:391.

79. Drummond, *A History of Christianity in Japan*, 166–173.

80. On Brown, see William Elliot Griffis, *A Maker of the New Orient: Samuel Robbins Brown, Pioneer Educator in China, America, and Japan, the Story of His Life and Work* (New York: Fleming H. Revell, 1902).

81. For a short biographical sketch of Uemura, see Ebizawa, "A Great Church Leader in Japan," in *Japanese Witnesses for Christ*, chap. 3, 37–50.

82. On Honda, see Ebizawa, "Founder of the Methodist Church in Japan," in *Japanese Witnesses for Christ*, chap. 2, 30–36.

83. On Neesima (also spelled Neeshima and Niijima), in addition to sources mentioned above, see Ebizawa, "Joseph Neeshima, Founder of the First Christian University in Japan," in *Japanese Witnesses for Christ*, chap. 1, 17–29; and Drummond, *A History of Christianity in Japan*, 169–170.

84. *Proceedings of the General Conference of Protestant Missionaries, Tokyo, 1900*. 145. And for more detail on women's work in that period, 129–147, 256–272, 289–305. Two other early physicians, John C. Berry, and Wallace Taylor, both of the ABCFM, had similar success that by the end of the century was fading. On Berry, see Ritter, *History of Protestant Missions in Japan*, 74, 180, 283.

85. *Proceedings of the General Conference of Protestant Missionaries, Tokyo, 1900*, 130–136.

86. Drummond, *A History of Christianity in Japan*, 152.

87. *Proceedings of the General Conference of Protestant Missionaries, Tokyo, 1900*, 145.

88. *Proceedings of the General Conference of Protestant Missionaries, Tokyo, 1900*, 139 and 144–145.

89. Yamamori, *Church Growth in Japan*, 42–43. See also Edwin O. Reischauer, *The United States and Japan*, rev. ed. (New York: Viking Press, 1950), 136.

90. In 1881 Fukuzawa was publishing articles against Christianity; in 1884 he surprisingly and abruptly changed course and published the essay, "The Adoption of the Foreign Religion Is Necessary," perhaps more to catch the nation's attention than to suggest it seriously. Impressed by the Unitarianism of the American A. M. Knapp, who introduced himself as an envoy not a missionary, and who spurned conversion in favor of dialogue, Fukuzawa welcomed Unitarian missionaries into the faculty of his university, Keio. Though Unitarianism failed to establish organizational strength within Japanese Christianity, its open opposition to the message of the more traditional missions significantly weakened their evangelistic effectiveness. Jansen, *The Making of Modern Japan*, 321–322, 408, 462; Otis Cary, *History of Christianity in Japan*, 2:172–174, 199, citing the *Japan Weekly Mail*, July 12, 1884, and a second article January 24, 1885; and Drummond, *A History of Christianity in Japan*, 78–79. See also Sansom, *The Western World and Japan*, 469–470, 475–476.

91. Jansen, *The Making of Modern Japan*, 404, 460; Sansom, *The Western World and Japan*, 427–431.

92. Buddhism was disestablished in 1871; the effort to win recognition of Shinto as the national religion failed in 1872, and the edicts against Christianity were removed in 1873. See Jansen, *The Making of Modern Japan*, 350–355; Sansom, *The Western World and Japan*, 469–470.

93. Otis Cary, *History of Christianity in Japan*, 2:177ff.; Jansen, *The Making of Modern Japan*, 393–395.

94. Drummond, *A History of Christianity in Japan*, 191; Iglehart, *A Century of Protestant Christianity in Japan*, 66–67.

95. Otis Cary, *History of Christianity in Japan*, 2:84–85, 149. The first Protestant attempt to translate the Bible into Japanese was made outside Japan by the indefatigable China evangelist, Karl Gützlaff, who had briefly visited Japan in 1837,

with a ship unsuccessfully trying to return shipwrecked Japanese sailors from Macao. Two of them became Christian, "the first fruits of the Church of Christ in Japan," and helped with a flawed translation of Genesis, the four Gospels, and the Epistles of John (14–16).

96. Verbeck, "History of Protestant Missions in Japan," 41–44, 94–98*. Pages 89*–186* in Verbeck's history are starred as a later addition, the page numbering being reduplicated without asterisk after 186* in the *Proceedings* of the Osaka Conference, 1883. His "History" was reprinted with minor corrections in the *Proceedings* of the Tokyo Conference, 1900, 740–797, with an added section on the Baptists by John L. Dearing, 898–914 and other supplements, 915ff.

97. The Protestant translation of the New Testament was completed in 1879; its principal translators were J. C. Hepburn, S. R. Brown, D. C. Greene, and R. S. Maclay. See Verbeck, "History of Protestant Missions in Japan," 41–44, 114–117; Otis Cary, *History of Christianity in Japan*, 148–149. Nida, *The Book of a Thousand Tongues*, 485, lists the following chronology of publication: first portion in 1857, first New Testament in 1879, first complete Bible in 1883.

98. Drummond, *A History of Christianity in Japan*, 313, 316, 331.

99. See papers on Bible study, translating and distribution, *Proceedings of the General Conference of Protestant Missionaries, Tokyo, 1900*, 216–234, 503–537; *A Handbook of Foreign Missions, Containing an Account of the Principal Protestant Missionary Societies in Great Britain with Notice of Those on the Continent and in America; also an Appendix on Roman Catholic Missions* (London: Religious Tract Society, 1888), 313–324; Ritter, *History of Protestant Missions in Japan*, 83–85, 224–228; James S. Dennis, *Foreign Missions after a Century* (New York: Fleming H. Revell, 1893), 70–71.

100. Drummond, *A History of Christianity in Japan*, 149.

101. Verbeck, "History," in *Proceedings of the General Conference of the Protestant Missionaries, Osaka, 1883*, 44; Drummond, *A History of Christianity in Japan*, 148–149.

102. On his translation work, see *Proceedings of the General Conference of Protestant Missionaries, Tokyo, 1900*, 439–441.

103. Verbeck, "History," in *Proceedings of the General Conference of Protestant Missionaries, Osaka, 1883*, 63, 74–75.

104. *Proceedings of the General Conference of Protestant Missionaries, Osaka, 1883*, 321. The citation is the printed summary of his remarks. See also Theodore Palm's paper at the same conference on "The Position of Medical Missions" (310–321). See the similar sentiment of Dr. J. C. Berry on 323; and for a counter-view, the remarks of the Rev. T. S. Tyng on 324.

105. Ritter, *History of Protestant Missions in Japan*, 203–215. Ritter himself had connections with the German/Swiss mission, and the quoted phrase characterizing it is his own (see iv, 214).

106. Ritter, *History of Protestant Missions in Japan*, 150, 204ff., 318–321; and note Dr. J. D. Davis's opening address to the Tokyo, 1900, all-Japan missionary conference warning against the stripping away of the fundamentals of Christian faith by German theologians and American Unitarians (*Proceedings of the General Conference of Protestant Missionaries, Tokyo, 1900*, 54–57).

107. Ritter, *History of Protestant Missions in Japan*, 127–128; and see Drummond, *A History of Christianity in Japan*, 192; Dennis, *Foreign Missions after a Century*, 71–72.

108. W. Thomas, *Protestant Beginnings in Japan*, 183ff.

109. Latourette, *A History of the Expansion of Christianity*, 6:396.

110. This compares with a Roman Catholic community of 25,633 in 1881 increasing to 40,684 in 1891; and Russian Orthodox from 7,611 to 17,000 in 1890. See Latourette, *A History of the Expansion of Christianity*, 6:390, 396, 380; Yamamori, *Church Growth in Japan*, 155–162; and Spae, *Catholicism in Japan*, 46.

111. Jansen, *The Making of Modern Japan*, 354.

112. See Yamamori, *Church Growth in Japan*, 64–85; W. Thomas, *Protestant Beginnings in Japan*, 182–206.

113. *Proceedings of the General Conference of Protestant Missionaries, Tokyo, 1900,* 986ff. The totals are: Protestant membership 43,275, missionaries 723, Japanese ordained ministers 306. The full table contains much more detail. It would add to the total missionary column: 144 Methodists, 64 Congregationalists, and 60 Baptists. For ordained Japanese ministers, 44 Anglican/Episcopalian, 38 Congregational, and 8 Baptist. Also in other categories: Single women missionaries (Anglican/Episcopalian 72, Presbyterian/Reformed 57, Methodist 49, Congregational 26, Baptist 18); Unordained Japanese "ministers amd helpers" (Anglican/Episcopalian 137, Presbyterian/Reformed 109, Methodists 85, Congregational 51, Baptists 43).

114. *Proceedings of the General Conference of Protestant Missionaries, Tokyo, 1900,* 1005. Ritter, *History of Protestant Missions in Japan*, 359, for statistics as of 1896.

115. Beach, *Geography and Atlas of Protestant Missions*, 208. The statistic is for 1898.

116. *Proceedings of the General Conference Protestant Missionaries, Tokyo, 1900,* 1005.

117. Barrett, ed., *World Christian Encyclopedia*, 1982, 419–420. The figures for Protestants are for professing Christians, and include Anglicans and Japanese indigenous. Comparative statistics for the world religions are calculated by total community and are generally higher than those reported from within each religious grouping.

Chapter 24

Protestants and New Beginnings in Korea (1865–1905)

The [Korean] Church has always been one jump ahead of the missionaries.
— Archibald Campbell[1]

I was born in a heathen land, I was brought up in a heathen society . . . I discovered the utter impossibility of living a truly sinless life by any human help . . . I desire to be baptized for the hope that I may . . . God willing, live a useful life for myself and my brethren, [and] . . . may, when night comes have no need of seeking salvation at the gate of death, as many do . . .

I believe that God is love. Christ is the Saviour.
— Yun Tchi-Ho, 1887[2]

PROTESTANTS did not establish permanent missions in Korea until 1884. They were later to attribute the timing of their entry to providence. Earlier attempts had failed, for after the devastating Japanese invasion of the sixteenth century, the Manchu conquests of the seventeenth century, and Western intrusions into Asia in the nineteenth century, Korea had turned against all foreign contacts. It was known in the West as the Hermit Nation. But in 1882 the reclusive kingdom signed its first treaty with a Western country, the United States. So two years later when the first resident Protestant missionary arrived to stay, missionaries found themselves called upon to play a significant role in the opening up of Korea to the world.

They entered a country shaken to its roots by sudden, bewildering change, and about to be buffeted by four radical, transforming revolutions. The first was the fall of a decadent, 500-year monarchy, the Yi dynasty (1864–1910).[3] That first phase is the subject of this chapter. But looking ahead, in the next century history would still not be kind to the peninsula. The second phase was the humiliation of thirty-five years of paralyzing Japanese colonialism (1910–1945). The third was a change for the better, a brief period of euphoria as Korea recovered her independence, thanks to the defeat of Japan in World War II (1945–1950). But the fourth phase (1950–2000) was a volatile mixture of positives and negatives both political and ecclesiastic. It brought the crippling trauma of the cruel division of the country into a North and South. And it saw the growing Christian community confronted by an embarrassing explosion of church schisms. But through it all there ran inextinguishable sunbursts of unprecedentedly rapid church growth, the beginnings of which we shall now describe.

Robert J. Thomas, the First Protestant Martyr

The first serious attempt to start Protestant work in Korea traces back to the summers of 1865 and 1866, just as the great persecution of Catholics was about to break upon them. The pioneer Protestant who led the way was a Welsh Congregationalist, Robert Jermain Thomas (1839–1866), a prickly independent, eager to penetrate unreached parts of the world for the gospel. He was often at odds with the mission board under which he had come to China three years earlier, the famous London Missionary Society, which had sent Moffat and Livingstone to Africa and Robert Morrison to China. City life in Shanghai and the society of its large foreign population bored him. He longed to get out and "live among the Chinese," he said. "Send me to Mongolia," he wrote. Anywhere but Shanghai! But before the board could reply — it took a year for letters to go from Shanghai to London and back — he took off for Korea. He had met two refugees from Korea who said they were Christians and had rosaries and saints' medals to prove it. They didn't know the difference between Catholic and Protestant. Quickly he persuaded the agent of the National Bible Society of Scotland in China to send him with Chinese Bibles to explore the possibilities of a Protestant mission to the Hermit Kingdom. That was in August 1865, and he managed to spend two and a half months along Korea's west coast, dressing in Korean clothes most of the time and learning Korean with the help of friendly Roman Catholics.[4]

Back in China he discovered he had been reinstated by the London Missionary Society with the tempting offer of an appointment as teacher in charge of the Anglo-Chinese School in Beijing. But Korea was too much on his mind, and in the fateful year of 1866 he sailed again for Korea, this time on the *General Sherman,* an American schooner loaded with glass and tinplate and lured by hope of trade with the forbidden kingdom. The intruders nosed their way into the mouth of the Taitong River below the old northern capital, Pyengyang (Pyongyang). Deceived by a combination of exceptionally high tides and a summer flood, the ship rounded a bend and came within sight of the city. It never came back down to the sea again.

Not for two years was the outside world able to discover what had happened to its crew of twenty-three men (four Westerners, nineteen Chinese and Malay sailors) and one missionary. Thomas had been told that there were only eleven Catholic missionaries in Korea, and that no

Buddhist temples were allowed inside Korea's towns and cities. This convinced him that Korea presented an unusual opportunity for propagating Christianity. True or not, he could not have come at a worse time. The year 1866 was in the time of the great persecution of Catholics described in an earlier chapter.[5] Later a French gunboat brought back rumors that all aboard the *General Sherman* were killed.

The full truth of the affair is difficult to determine. On the way upriver it appears that a group of Korean Roman Catholics boarded the ship asking for help and that Thomas tried to comfort them, explaining that though he was not Catholic, like them he was a Christian. He gave them some Christian books and a silver coin stamped with the likeness of Queen Victoria. They went away convinced that he was secretly a French priest, for had he not given them a medal with the image of the Virgin Mary?[6]

The end of the story was pure tragedy. The American ship had intruded into waters forbidden to foreign commerce; its officers rashly seized and held a police magistrate sent to warn them off; they arrogantly demanded an audience with the governor; the vessel grounded in the mud as the tide went out; it was set afire by fire arrows and blazing pine boats which were floated against its sides. Thomas did not escape; all were killed. Eyewitnesses told different stories of his death. Some said he died on the ship in the flames, but the most widely accepted account is that he was killed by a soldier on the shore to whom he offered a Chinese Bible as the man hesitated before striking him. Thus died the first Protestant martyr in Korea, and it was almost twenty more years before any Protestants again penetrated the closely guarded peninsula.[7]

Earlier Protestant Attempts to Enter Korea

Thomas was not the first Protestant in Korea. Earlier contacts, however, had been either accidental or peripheral. Three hundred years earlier, as we saw in a previous chapter, some Dutch sailors had been shipwrecked on an island off Korea's southern coast. They were Protestants but not missionaries; all they wanted was to get out of Korea.[8] A more effective Protestant contact was a brief, passing landing in 1833 by the indefatigable Prussian Lutheran, Karl Gützlaff of China, who came as interpreter on a British trading vessel. When it paused for a week on an island off the west coast, he took the opportunity to translate the Lord's Prayer into Korean from the Chinese characters in the text of the Chinese Bible. Also, with the work ethic of a typical Protestant he endeavored to persuade the islanders to plant potatoes as an alternative to rice.[9] But no traces of his efforts survived in closed Korea. It took a Korean to make the first lasting Protestant impact on the country.

THE KOREAN INITIATIVE: SUH SANG-YUN

With the Protestants as with the Catholics a century earlier, intentional permanent mission in Korea began with a Korean, not a foreign missionary. And it began with that Korean risking his life to carry portions of the Bible in the Korean language into his own tightly closed homeland. His name was Suh Sang-Yun (1848–1926) and the Bible portion he brought with him was the Gospel of Luke, which had just been translated into Korean by Scottish missionaries across the border in Manchuria. There were then a reported twelve thousand Korean Catholics and no Korean Protestants in the country's population of about 10.5 million people.[10]

Suh Sang-Yun[11] was a *ginseng* peddler who, like several other such traders crossing the Chinese border, found help at the Scottish mission in Mukden (Shenyang) when their goods were stolen or when they fell sick. Two of the Presbyterian missionaries there, John Ross and John McIntyre, began to employ some of the better educated among them to help them in a project which Ross had undertaken: a translation of the New Testament for the large number of Koreans living along the border on both sides of the Yalu River. Some became Christians as they read and translated. The first convert was Lee (Yi) Ung-Ch'an in 1876, who became the first known baptized Korean Protestant.[12] But it was Suh Sang-Yun, baptized two years later, who is better known in Korea as the pioneer Korean evangelist. After assisting in the translation of the Gospel of Luke in 1883 Suh carried copies of the printed text back to his home village on Korea's west coast just north of the 38th Parallel. With Luke as his textbook, he gathered a group of believers into a house church, and that small Christian fellowship in the village of Sorai, without the benefit of ordained leadership but eager to practice their newfound faith, is justly called the cradle of Korean Protestant Christianity.[13] This was a whole year before the arrival of the first resident Western missionaries. Later, in 1889, when the first clergyman missionary, Horace G. Underwood, visited the far north on the Korea side of the Yalu River, he found thirty-three men ready for baptism who had in large part been converted and instructed by Suh Sang-Yun and his brother.[14]

THE AMERICAN MISSIONARIES ARRIVE

About a year after Suh planted the church in his home village, the first resident American missionary, Dr. Horace N. Allen, M.D. (1858–1932), made his way from China to Korea like the martyr R. J. Thomas, but with happier results. Korea was changing after a century of hunting down and persecuting Catholics but the first decade of Protestant foreign missions (1884–1894) was shadowed by the ever present danger of a return to hostility, and intermittent outbursts against foreigners.

Dr. Allen was a tall, balding, red-haired Presbyterian medical doctor from Akron, Ohio.[15] He had found it difficult to work with his missionary colleagues in China, and hoped to find more freedom of action in a

Korea as yet unclaimed by any Protestants. Despite the country's ban on foreign missionaries,[16] he negotiated an arrangement with the recently opened (1882) American legation to serve as its medical officer. A brilliant man and active Christian, but "not overly enthusiastic either about medicine or missions,"[17] Allen resigned from the Korea Presbyterian mission after only three years in anguish over shattered relationships with missionary colleagues. Invited to move into a career as a diplomat in the American foreign service, he soon rose to the highest position in the American legation in Seoul, that of U.S. minister to Korea. As missionary and then diplomat, he not only opened the door into closed Korea for Protestant missions, but also gave Korea its first Western hospital, and was a major factor in bringing steam railroads, streetcars, and waterworks to the country.

Organized Protestant mission in Korea began with Allen's hospital. Only about three months after his arrival, a brief, bloody attempted coup by young reformers came close to overthrowing the ruling political conservatives. The conservative leader, Prince Min Yong-Ik, a nephew of the queen, was attacked by assassins.[18] Dr. Allen was rushed across the city from the legation in a sedan chair to save the dying man. The prince amazingly recovered, and the king rewarded the missionary physician by granting him permission to open "a royal hospital," the first legally permitted public building under Christian control in Korea.[19] A colleague wrote of Dr. Allen in 1914 that "it is impossible to write a history of Korean Christianity and omit his name."[20] From the beginning, medical work remained critically important. Three of the first five Protestant missionaries in Korea were doctors.[21]

THE FIRST PROTESTANT CLERGYMEN

On Easter Sunday 1885, four months after Dr. Allen's dramatic medical rescue of the prince, the first Protestant clergymen arrived in Korea, a Presbyterian and a Methodist. The Presbyterian, Horace G. Underwood (1859–1916),[22] a bachelor, was a vigorous evangelist and linguist, destined to found the most prestigious Christian university in Korea, now Yonsei University. His brother John, of Underwood typewriter fame, is said to have remarked, "Horace went to Korea to make Christians; I stayed home to help him by making typewriters." It was his typewriter business that generously supported some of the earliest Presbyterian work in Korea. The Methodist, Henry G. Appenzeller (1858–1902),[23] came with his wife, and the couple were temporarily sent back to Japan. Korea was not yet open to foreign women outside the Western legations.

While Dr. Allen was winning a foothold for Protestants by his medical skills, the foreign Roman Catholic priests, not yet fully recovered from the shocks of a whole century of persecution, were still masking their public presence by dressing in Korean clothes. The Protestants were also uneasily aware that the edict prohibiting propagation of foreign religion had not been withdrawn, and were undecided about how far to test the law.[24] Allen, who was usually impatient and sometimes irascible, was nevertheless sensitive to the intricacies of international diplomacy. He urged his missionary colleagues to be cautious, and the American diplomatic community fully agreed.[25] But Underwood was so eager to evangelize that with some hesitation he ecumenically hired a Catholic Korean teacher as tutor, and was the first of the Protestant missionaries to acquire the ability to use the language fluently.[26] Within little more than a year, in July 1886, he had baptized his first Korean convert, Noh (or Ro) Tohsa.[27] By way of contrast, in China the pioneer Protestant Robert Morrison had toiled for seven years without a convert.

Appenzeller, the Methodist, also chafed at Allen's advice to go slow and dismissed his caution as an exaggerated fear that simply to try to start the work would cripple it.[28] Just one year after landing in 1885 he baptized the first Methodist convert, a Japanese resident in Korea; the next year he baptized the first woman in Korea to be baptized by a Protestant missionary.[29]

Incidentally, the baptism of women in Korea presented an unexpected problem, as an incident occurring a few years later illustrates, when the Methodist doctor, W. B. Scranton, who was also an ordained minister, was for the first time asked to baptize a Korean woman. It stands as a unique event, a minor triumph of missionary ingenuity in adapting Christian church practice to a native culture. Church services by then were customarily divided, with men on one side of a long central curtain and women on the other. The problem was, how could a male evangelist publicly baptize a female Korean in a culture that forbade physical contact between the sexes after the age of seven outside the family? Dr. Scranton was up to the challenge. He cut a hole in the curtain, asked the woman to put her head against the hole, and baptized the top of her head,[30] thankful that she was not a Baptist. Methodists in 1886 reported one probationer, one hundred adherents, and "one hospital overflowing."[31]

The first two organized churches in Korea opened in 1887 only a few months apart. One was Presbyterian, one Methodist, and for the next hundred years and more the Presbyterians and the Methodists formed the foundational infrastructure for a Protestant advance in Korea that had no equal anywhere else in Asia.[32] "First Church in Korea" was the headline in a church publication announcing that the Presbyterian pioneer H. G. Underwood had ordained two elders and organized a Presbyterian church with fourteen members in September 1887.[33] A month later H. G. Appenzeller organized the first Korean Methodist church.[34]

It was agreed, however, that because of government restrictions, the chief avenue of evangelistic approach to the Korean people would remain the medical hospital with its high favor in the royal family. Dr. Allen had already been appointed physician to the king, and the only doctors on the field were men. But the culture's strict separation of men and women made it imperative that a woman physician be found for the hospital who might be called to minister to the queen, a strong-minded, politically powerful woman. The hospital needed a woman, and both the Presbyterian and Methodist missions raced to be the first to find one. Annie Ellers, with two years completed in medical school, was persuaded to interrupt her M.D. course temporarily and hurry to Korea. She arrived in the summer of 1886 and was received as a doctor. Within three months Miss Ellers had successfully treated her first two patients, the Queen of Korea, and the wife of the Chinese ambassador, Yuan Shih-Kai, later to be president of the first Republic of China.[35] The unaccustomed sight of a foreign woman treating royalty startled the capital and attracted the pleased attention of the whole country, much as Dr. Allen's earlier lifesaving service to Prince Min had first opened the door to Christian work.

If Miss Ellers expected to find in the Presbyterian mission community a foretaste of the Kingdom of God, she was quickly disillusioned. There were three men in the mission: Allen the pioneer, Underwood the bachelor clergyman, and Dr. John W. Heron, who had turned down a medical professorship in America to come out to Korea as a doctor, and had been appointed before Dr. Allen but arrived later. All three were in their twenties, inexperienced and strong-minded. Miss Ellers had barely unpacked when two of them, Underwood and Heron, abruptly but temporarily resigned from the mission. "Unreconcilable differences" with Dr. Allen was given as the reason. Three months later, in 1887 after about three years as a missionary, Dr. Allen resigned to take a position with the Korean government. The whole mission seemed to have collapsed.[36]

It took another year to put it back together again, but two years later once again Dr. Allen resigned, deciding that he preferred the life of a diplomat to the uncertainties and frictions of life as a missionary. That settled, however, it should be noted that for the next fifteen years he was the most faithful and loyal friend any of the Korea missions could have asked for. Those first three years had been a disaster for the Presbyterians despite the ameliorating presence of Miss Ellers, but by 1890 they had not only recovered but had begun an unrivaled wave of church growth that in a few years was to carry them to a position of primary influence in Korean Christianity.

The first breakthrough into Korea's life and culture had been medical in the form of Dr. Allen's Royal Hospital. The second was in education, and in this the Methodists led the field. After only two years in Korea, Henry G. Appenzeller, the Methodist pioneer, opened the first legally recognized Christian school in Korea. He received royal endorsement for his Paichai (or Paejae) Boys School in 1887 despite its un-Confucian policy of student self-support and its strong Christian flavor. Appenzeller was insistent on the latter. "I want the students who come here to get converted," he said, and his first baptized Korean convert was a Paichai student.[37]

Most revolutionary of the Protestant educational innovations, however, was not a boys' school, but a school for girls, and it owed its beginnings to a strong, determined Methodist, Mrs. Mary F. Scranton, widowed mother of the first Methodist doctor, W. B. Scranton. Like her male colleagues, she too wasted no time in getting started, and within a year of arrival had begun work on a building for a "Girls' School and Home." But students were hard to find. One Confucian scholar was impressed by the regally Victorian bearing and full black dress and hat of the elder Mrs. Scranton, but when she suggested that he send his daughter to school, he protested like the typical Confucian that he was, "Can cows read?" Mrs. Scranton was forced to open the school with only one student, the concubine of a palace official who hoped that if she could learn English she might become interpreter to the queen.[38] The queen indeed granted the school her royal approval, sending it a name, Ewha [Pear Blossom] Institute. Who would have guessed that after so inauspicious a beginning the school would one day develop into the largest women's university in the world, Ewha Women's University?[39]

The gospel of those early Korea missionaries rejected an all too easy separation of the spiritual and the social in the Christian faith. Firmly orthodox in their theology and fervently committed to evangelism, they were equally and compassionately convinced of their Christian duty to meet the challenges of the day-to-day needs of the people whom they had come to serve. Protestant missions, which began with medicine for all and education for women as well as men even in a male-dominated Confucian culture, were more than willing to go further and exert a constantly broadening influence on Korea's rigidly structured social patterns. But in so doing, the missionaries posed a direct challenge to their own Western compatriots, foreign traders eager to exploit a newly opened market. Most of Dr. Allen's introduction of Western industrial and technological advances were made after he had left the mission for diplomatic service, but Underwood imported kerosene and agricultural tools, and Samuel A. Moffett, who joined the group in 1890 and pioneered a permanent move away from the treaty ports into the restricted Korean north, sponsored a timber concession on the Yalu River. When the traders complained of unfair rivalry, and demanded that the missionaries mind their own business, the missionaries replied that they took no profit for themselves and were only preparing their converts to deal with the new world of commerce and industry that was flooding in on them.[40] This did not lessen their focus on the priority of personal conversion and church planting. Rather it augmented and supported evangelism, making the faith easier to believe. It was in 1890 that this balance between faith and action began to be written into the mission policies of the two missions: Presbyterian and Methodist. Its clearest statement was one adopted by the northern Presbyterians at their annual meeting in that year, "the most business-like and forward looking one the Presbyterians had had."[41]

THE NEVIUS PLAN

Harmony had been restored. Dr. Allen had resigned again, without rancor, retaining in his rising diplomatic career an almost patriarchal concern for the well-being of the missions. The highlight of a meeting of the mission in the spring of 1890 had been the invited presence of a veteran China missionary, John L. Nevius, who urged the newly born mission not to make the mistake he said that some had made in China of retaining missionary control over the native converts and their churches too long. Instead, he advised, train them from the beginning not only in Bible classes but also in the practice of self-government, self-support, and self-propagation.[42] It might have seemed foolishly premature to plan a strategy of independence of a national church when there was only one tiny organized Presbyterian congregation to plan for, and a total Protestant community of little more than 300 adherents (Presbyterian and Methodist) of whom only 103 were adult Presbyterian communicant members.[43] But Nevius warned the Presbyterians, if you don't teach self-support at the beginning, it will all too soon be too late.[44] Known as the "Nevius Plan" in Korea, and as the "Three-Self Plan" elsewhere, this was adopted by the Presbyterian mission at a time when in all Korea it could count barely a hundred communicant church members, no ordained Korean pastors and only one organized congregation. Premature or not, the Nevius method proved to be one of the primary factors in the resulting numerical dominance of Presbyterianism in Korean Christianity, as we shall see.

Those ten years from 1884 to 1894 were the days of beginnings. Missionary residence was still limited to the treaty ports, Seoul (including Inchon) in the center, Pusan in the south, and a limited presence in Wonsan in the northeast. The Protestant missionaries were described as "all bunched in the foreign settlement" around the American and British legations in the capital. Some were already criticizing the image of the mission thus created in the minds of the people as a foreign community of wealth and nobility, accentuated by the missionaries' frequent access to the palace. There were two little organized churches, both in the capital, one Presbyterian, one Methodist. Growth was increasing, but only very slowly.[45] By 1894, Presbyterians could report only 52 communicants — with perhaps another 100 scattered in the north as a result of the ravages of the 1894–1895 war between China and Japan, the two empires which had conveniently chosen to fight each other in the helpless little kingdom that was caught between them.[46] Methodists in 1894 recorded 75 communicant members.[47]

The Foreign Wars; Korea Loses Its Independence

The year 1894 was a turning point in Korean history. It marked the beginning of the end of a five-hundred-year-old Korean dynasty. Japanese soldiers poured into the Korean peninsula to challenge China's traditional cultural and political dominance of the small kingdom. Ever since the seventeenth-century Mongol invasions of Kublai Khan, Chinese ascendancy was an accepted fact in Northeast Asia.[48] But China no longer had a Kublai Khan, only a puppet emperor ruled by a tyrant, the Empress Dowager. A new sun was rising in the east, Japan, but China, the sleeping giant, was unaware that the world had changed overnight. Her awakening was short and almost fatal, the Sino-Japanese War of 1894–1895. China surrendered in less than a year, and was forced to recognize Korean independence, losing the island of Formosa (Taiwan) to the Japanese at the same time. Korea's mortally wounded five-hundred-year-old Yi dynasty was left to struggle against rebellions within and expanding Asian imperialism from without. Five months after the end of the war, a mob organized by the victorious Japanese swept into the Korean palace, and murdered the powerful, pro-Chinese Korean queen, Queen Min.[49] In all but name Japan controlled the peninsula for the next fifty years until the end of World War II in 1945.

National disasters may either breed hatred and despair or turn a nation from self-pity to a search for deeper foundations than nationalism for strength and hope. In the case of Korea, despair and hope were mingled. The natural anticolonialist reaction to her loss of independence focused the country's anger not against Western but against Asian imperialists and thereby saved Christian missions in that small, oppressed nation from the stigma of guilt by association which for four hundred years of Western expansion had handicapped the spread of the gospel elsewhere across Asia. The result was a rare opportunity for friendly relations between the Koreans and the missionaries, and for the presentation of the gospel of the cross as a message of hope in the face of defeat. From that time on, the most marked feature of Korean Christianity has clearly been its amazingly rapid growth.

Beginnings of Massive Church Growth[50]

Evidence of multiple conversions does not begin to appear on the charts until 1895 and 1896, that is to say, immediately following the close of the Sino-Japanese War. Presbyterians and Methodists, the two larger Protestant denominations in Korea, had never in their first ten years on the peninsula (1884 to 1894) been able to report more than about 225 communicant member converts.[51]

The two little churches in Seoul, founded in 1887, had barely started to grow when the "Baby Riots" of 1888 brought a pause. In its first year the Presbyterian congregation founded by H. G. Underwood had more than tripled in numbers, from about 14 to 50, and he wrote, "Wherever the seed is sown it seems to take root."[52] Then the ugly rumors spread that the foreigners were stealing Korean children and eating them, and grinding them up in the new hospital to make medicine, and gouging out their eyes to use in their cameras.[53] Church attendance dropped, and new inquirers were few.[54]

The earliest reports of the kind of impressive, sustained rapid growth of the church that became the hallmark of Protestantism in Korea came from the Presbyterians in the north. Robert E. Speer, secretary of their New York Board of Foreign Missions, reported on his visit to Korea in 1897, "In the North the church has spread and penetrated as we saw nothing to surpass anywhere else in the world."[55] It was occurring in the northwest, in territory pioneered by Samuel A. Moffett (1864–1939).[56] Moffett was the first permanently resident Protestant missionary in Korea's northern "forbidden interior," the Korea outside the treaty ports.[57] Long-term Christian presence there was still officially outlawed. Though the anti-Christian edicts were by then only intermittently enforced, in his first three a half years he made six trips into the north to try to open the old capital Pyengyang as a mission station, and time after time he was driven out or threatened.[58] The city was reputed to be the wickedest city in Korea, famed for its tiger hunters, stone fights, and child prostitutes. In 1893 he was stoned on the street in front of the magistrate's office trying to win release for two imprisoned Korean evangelists, one of whom was his trusted colleague, Han Suk-Chin.[59]

In 1892 Moffett was joined in Pyengyang by a Methodist missionary doctor, William J. Hall (1860–1895),[60] and the two tried repeatedly to establish right of residence in the city by buying houses in the name of their Korean assistants.[61] In 1893, Moffett managed to stay in the city for all of seven months, and with two Presbyterian colleagues, William Swallen and Graham Lee, joining him, opened the old northern capital as a residential mission station. He was able to baptize his first eight converts in 1894 and gather them into communicant membership in a little house church, his home. Elated, and believing that at last a mission base in the north had been secured, he reported to his home Board, "There is a church started here."[62]

The joy was cut short by war. In June Chinese troops poured south to protect Korea against Japanese troops advancing north, and people were fleeing from the city by the hundreds. The great land battle of the Sino-Japanese War was fought in Pyengyang. Fifteen days after the battle Moffett returned with two other missionaries. He found the city devastated, his house in ruins, the stench of unburied dead bodies over-powering, and fear of cholera paralyzing the people. Then suddenly, to the missionaries' surprise, the people, non-Christians joining the Christians, greeted as friends and saviors the foreigners they had formerly tried to drive out of the city. They crowded into the hastily restored Moffett house, which served also as the Presbyterian church.[63] By October 1895 he reported 73 baptized communicants, 195 catechumens (probationers), 4 informally organized congregations, and meeting places in 7 substations around Pyengyang.[64] But Methodist work in the north suffered a severe blow when the greatly loved Dr. Hall died the next month, leaving only a handful of Methodist converts without reliable leadership in the war-torn, ravaged city.[65]

For the Presbyterians, however, the end of the war marked the beginning of what came to be called a "wildfire" of church growth.[66] Moffett ventured two reasons for the growth. The first was "the earnest and faithful work of the Korean lay evangelists," men like Han Suk-Chin and Suh Sang-Yun. The other was the limited and "judicious" use of foreign money — only so much as not to endanger progress toward self-support.[67] The Presbyterian Mission Board in New York, upon receiving his report, added a third reason: the missionaries had learned how to identify with the Korean people. Noting that Moffett had lived alone in one Korean house for two months in Pyengyang, the Board wrote, "Moffett has the true secret of missionary success," and quoted from his report: "I am situated ... as I have long wished to be, in direct contact with the people, living in the midst of them, meeting them every day and all day, entering into their lives and having them enter into mine."[68]

Korean Leadership Training for the Ministry

In the beginning, and for the first few decades, it was inevitable that the church would be governed by missionaries. The Presbyterian Church organized in Seoul by Underwood in 1887 was naturally under his care, and by 1890 was governed by a session composed of the three ordained Presbyterian missionaries then in Seoul: Underwood, Moffett, and Gifford.[69] Appenzeller, as the first ordained Methodist clergyman and founder of the first Methodist congregation, likewise led its first public services for Koreans.[70]

But the missionaries gave credit to their indispensable Korean evangelists for the rapid growth of Korean Protestant Christianity.[71] Training them for more advanced leadership of the growing number of organized churches developed out of the Bible class movement, which was a key element in the Nevius Plan, officially adopted by the Presbyterians in 1891.[72] Large winter classes were held in central locations every winter for all church members who could attend. In addition to laying the foundations for a biblically literate church membership, the classes drew attention to the brightest students as potential candidates for future leadership. This led to a further refinement in the Christian education process. Summer theological classes for those who showed promise for the ministry were begun in the south by H. G. Underwood, and in the north by S. A. Moffett.[73] But not until the first year of the new century was the training organized into Korea's first Protestant theological seminary.

By 1895 the trickle of converts won during the first ten years of Protestant work began in the north to turn into a flood. By 1900 60 percent of the Presbyterian communicant membership was concentrated in the northern provinces.[74] The training of leaders for the growing church developed into a two-pronged program, academic and ecclesiastical, but both with an evangelistically motivated base. On the academic side, Soongsil Academy, founded in 1897/1898 by Dr. William M. Baird as a class for young men in Pyengyang where the church was growing fastest, developed into a Christian college. In 1900 the academy began to raise its academic standards and added upper-level courses to become in 1908 Korea's first modern degree-granting college (now Soongsil University in Seoul).[75]

On the ecclesiastical side the summer theological classes grew into a seminary. In 1901 up north in Pyengyang where the church was growing fastest, S. A. Moffett invited two elders to come to his home for regular study at a higher level than simple Bible classes, and with a more specifically theological concentration than in the mission's emerging academies and college. In 1903 the theological curriculum was reorganized and chartered for a three-months-a-year schedule for five years, with assigned reading and practical ministerial experience for the other nine months. The fledgling Presbyterian Theological Seminary of Korea graduated its first class of seven out of an enrollment of seventy-five in 1907.[76]

Some have suggested that the separation of theological training from full college-level education was a mistake.[77] But it made sense to make the seminary fit the church rather than to ask the church to fit the seminary. Presbyterian congregations were springing up rapidly and needed trained leaders immediately. Eight years of full-time high school and college was too much to ask of their evangelists and elders before their church could have an ordained pastor. A gradual academic upgrading of the seminary curriculum seemed better, and the success of this Presbyterian mission policy in the next ninety years would seem to prove its wisdom.[78]

The Methodists in Korea were already well structured for training an indigenous pastorate. Their "class meeting" tradition of organizing small groups under lay leaders paved the way for leadership development. They ordained two Koreans as deacons in 1901, a first step toward ordination to full ministry. Deacons had the right to baptize and perform marriages but not to administer communion.[79] Presbyterians did not ordain deacons; neither had they yet ordained any Korean ministers;[80] and both denominations relied heavily on Korean evangelists, called "helpers" or "assistants." The northern Methodists, a little slower in moving to a fully ordained ministry, did not open their first seminary until 1907 in Seoul in the same year that the Presbyterians graduated their first class of seminarians.[81]

A number of outstanding Korean Christian leaders made their mark in those early years. The most nationally prominent was the first Southern Methodist Korean convert, Yun Tchi-Ho (later Baron Yun, 1864–1945), who was won to Christ and baptized in Shanghai while attending Young J. Allen's Anglo-Chinese College in 1887. His written request for baptism was eloquent. It read in part:

> I had not heard of God before I came to Shanghai — For
> I was born in a heathen land,
> I was brought up in a heathen society,
> I was taught in heathen literature.
> I continued in sin even after [hearing of God] — For
> sensual gratifications were preferred to sober and godly life
> ... I discovered the utter impossibility of living a truly sinless life by any
>   human help ...
> I desire to be baptized, for the hope —
> That I may ... God willing, live a useful life for myself and my brethren.
>   And that —
> I may when night comes have no need of seeking for salvation at the gate
>   of death, as many do ...
> I believe that —
> God is love.
> Christ is the Savior.
> If the prophecies concerning this ... world have been so literally fulfilled,
>   those concerning the future world must be true. [March 23, 1887][82]

Yun Tchi-Ho was the scion of a high aristocratic Korean family. Already at age seventeen his linguistic ability (he eventually was fluent in five languages) won him an appointment as interpreter for the first American minister to Korea, General Foote. Further study in China, at the Southern Methodist academy, the "Anglo-Chinese College" in Shanghai, led to his conversion, mentioned above, and gave him the opportunity for study at Emory College and Vanderbilt University. After his conversion and further education in America, his urgent pleas on behalf of mission to his homeland resulted in the establishment of the Southern Methodist mission in Korea. Some years after his return to his homeland in 1895, in 1904 he established not far north of Seoul what is now Kaesong the Anglo-Korean Academy, a Korean counterpart of the Anglo-Chinese college in Shanghai.[83]

First Steps from Mission Council to Korean Church

Very early, the Presbyterian USA Korea Mission (unofficially known as Northern Presbyterian) had moved faster than other denominations to coordinate their work with later arriving missions.[84] In 1890, as we have seen, they adopted what is known as "the Nevius Plan." Its goal was even more important than its mission strategy; its aim was a Korean church for Korea, a "self-governing, self-supporting, self-propagating" Korean church. When Australian Presbyterians, Southern Presbyterians, and Canadian Presbyterians also began work in Korea,[85] two needs quickly became obvious. One was the need for unity above the congregational level among the Korean Presbyterian churches. The other was the practical advantage of working together amicably and consistently with other Protestant denominations in a country as small as Korea. Their first priority was Presbyterian unity. Beginning in 1893, they formed what soon came to be called the Presbyterian Council.[86]

From the beginning the Presbyterian Council made very clear that it did not intend to repeat in Korea the divisions of its home denominations. The organizing constitution stated its goal emphatically: "to carry on all our native work with a view to the organization of but one native Presbyterian Church in Korea."[87] To this end in 1893 it enlarged the principles of the Nevius Plan, adopted in 1890, to include ten further specific recommendations on missionary methods. Four or five of them provide a sense of the whole:

Begin with the working classes rather than the higher.

Emphasize the conversion of women and the training of Christian girls, since mothers exercise so important an influence over future generations.

Establish elementary schools in country towns to produce future native teachers and ministers.

Produce a clearer Korean version of the Bible.

Train evangelists to replace missionary public evangelism.[88]

By permission of its home denominations in the West, the Council served for the next fourteen years (1893–1907) as an unofficial presbytery, authorized to examine candidates for membership, to form church sessions and district councils with similar power, and to license local Korean leaders "elected by the people or appointed by the missionary . . . to lead the Sabbath service." Until 1901 it was all missionary, but then began to invite elders and "helpers" (Korean lay preachers) to become members, holding its meetings in bilingual language sessions, Korean and English. The first such joint meeting of the Council recorded twenty-four missionaries, three Korean elders, and six Korean evangelists ("helpers").[89] Though it did not have anything but advisory power over the missions as such, it was the controlling body of all Korean Presbyterian congregations until 1907.

Interdenominational Cooperation

For the first six years of Protestant missions in Korea, the Presbyterians and Methodists were the only effective Protestant voice in the country. But in 1890 others began to arrive — Anglicans led by Bishop Charles John Corfe in 1890,[90] followed by Baptists in 1895.[91] The next year Southern Methodists established a mission at the urging of the young Korean aristocrat mentioned above, Yun Tchi-Ho, who had been converted in a mission school in China and then while studying in America became an eloquent advocate of foreign missions in churches and on college campuses. Three more Protestant missions entered the country in the first decade of the twentieth-century — the Seventh-day Adventists, the Oriental Missionary Society (OMS), and the Salvation Army.[92]

Bishop Corfe, devoutly Anglo-Catholic, organized his Church of England Mission like a missionary order with a touch of shipboard discipline acquired from his days in the British Navy. Anglican missionaries were celibate, poor within reason, highly literate, and constant in prayer. He wrote to an association of friends of the mission about the priority of prayer over finances in mission: "You have felt as keenly as I the superior value of a list of members who pray, over a list of members who pay." In missionary outreach to non-Christians, however, the Anglicans were somewhat delayed by their admirable determination to master the Korean language before they felt it proper to attempt to evangelize, lest they shame the gospel by clothing it in broken grammar.[93] This was a praiseworthy intention but it left them still studying while Presbyterians and Methodists, perhaps a bit too trusting that the Lord would make up for their mistakes, butchered the language for a while and talked and walked their way into the hearts of the people. In terms of churches and church members, Korea's Anglicans never quite caught up with the sudden surge of church growth, but their simple lifestyle was impressively Christian, their sensitivity to Korean culture was widely appreciated, and the graceful artistry of their Christian literature in the Korean language won them a significant following among the *literati*.

The early Baptists, who as mentioned reached Korea in 1895, had high hopes and a praiseworthy policy. One other denomination also entered the field in Korea in this last decade of the nineteenth century. A Canadian Baptist, Malcolm C. Fenwick, a fiery independent Baptist with a burning zeal to evangelize Korea, arrived in 1889. His first attempt failed, but back in America he formed the Corean Itinerant Mission and returned to Korea in 1895 in a valiant attempt to outdo the Nevius Method of self-support with complete reliance on new Korean converts rather than a foreign mission structure. It proved premature and ended when he died in 1935.[94]

Lest the crowding together of such a variety of missions — all calling themselves Protestants but with bewilderingly different labels (American, English, Australian, Canadian, Presbyterian, Methodist, Anglican, Baptist) — create confusion about the integrity of the gospel message, it began to seem to some that order must be made of the chaos. So, much as the Presbyterians had earlier seen the necessity of inter-Presbyterian cooperation, now conversations began across denominational lines between the missions to find ways of avoiding unseemly rivalry and geographical overlap. The first step toward cooperation was a comity agreement reached in 1892 between Presbyterians and Methodists. Despite some disapproval by the nonresident Methodist Bishop Foster, the two denominations approved joint occupation of towns of more than five thousand people, but in smaller towns agreed to respect the primary rights of the first missions to begin work in them. To be sure, the details of the agreement were easier to write than to implement. It would be fifteen more years before Methodists and Presbyterians could gradually redistrict the countryside and four thousand Methodists would suddenly become Presbyterians, while about the same number of Presbyterians awoke to find that they had become Methodists.[95]

The list of Protestant mission policies on which there was mutual agreement to cooperate ranged from Bible translation, a priority placed on work with the lower classes, the need for native leadership, the self-support principle of building churches, and a special emphasis on the conversion and training of Korean women.[96]

All these factors — disciplined missionary methods, emphasis on Scripture, training for indigenous ministerial leadership, steps toward cooperation — began to attract attention as possible reasons for the startling fact that in less than twenty years the newly arrived Protestants were growing disproportionately faster than the long-persecuted Korean Catholics.[97]

Why did the Protestants grow faster than the Catholics? Partly, of course, because statistically a small base requires fewer numbers to show a percentage rise. Another reasonable answer is that the Catholics were still in shock from one hundred years of persecution and were hesitant to evangelize publicly. A further reason, commonly advanced by the Protestants, was that they (the Protestants) were the first to give the Bible to the people in their own tongue. But an equally significant reason may be that the Protestants, particularly the Presbyterians, were more focused than the Catholics on the imperative of training and ordaining a Korean ministry in a Korean church. The next century would test the comparative effectiveness of their methods.

As the century ended, Protestant church growth was building up into what began to look to the missionaries like the beginnings of a tidal wave. In seven years, 1890 to 1897, the number of Korean Protestant communicant members had more than quadrupled: from 265 to 1,285 (Presbyterian and Methodist),[98] and the total number of adherents was approaching 5,000.[99] Marlin Nelson's table below reveals how quickly the number of adherents in Protestant churches accelerated in comparison to Catholic church growth in the years 1890 to 1910.[100] Protestant momentum appeared to be accelerating as the new century dawned.

Year	Roman Catholics	Protestants
1774	4,000	
1801	10,000	
1857	15,205	
1883	23,035	
1890	17,577	265
1897		4,899[101]
1900	42,441	18,081
1901		35,000 (25,000 Presb., 10,000 Meth.)
1910	73,517	167,352

Still, it is important to place this picture into context. In 1900, Korea's population reached 12 million (north and south), and Protestant growth in the three years since 1897 quadrupled again to nearly nineteen thousand adherents. But in the total spectrum of Korea's religions, Protestant resembled a ripple more than a tidal wave. There were almost twice as many Korean Catholics as Protestants, and the adherents' traditional religions far outnumbered the two tiny Christian flocks. Nevertheless, if one looks ahead at David Barrett's figures in the note below, the Christian percentage of the Korean population has risen from only 0.05 percent in 1900 to nearly 41 percent of the Korean population.[102] The optimists of 1900 seem to have been correct.

NOTES

1. Arch Campbell, *The Christ of the Korean Heart* (Columbus, Ohio: Falco Publishers, 1954), 100. For Roman Catholics in Korea in this period see chap. 14 above.

2. *GAL* (June 1887): 274–275.

3. The Yi dynasty had ruled Korea since 1392. Its name is pronounced Yee or Ee, and is sometimes transliterated Li or Lee.

4. See Samuel H. Moffett, "Thomas, First Protestant Martyr," *The Korea Herald*, April 22, 1973, 6.

5. See chap. 14 above, "The Catholic Century in Korea."

6. M. W. Oh, "The Two Visits of the Rev. R. J. Thomas to Korea," in *TRASK* 22 (1933). See also S. H. Moffett, "Thomas' Second Trip to Korea."

7. When Samuel A. Moffett, the pioneering missionary to establish residence in Pyengyang in 1892, formed a catechumen's class there the next year,

one of the candidates was a man who had received a Chinese New Testament from R. J. Thomas. See S. A. Moffett, "Early Days in Pyengyang," in *The Korea Mission Field* (Seoul) 21 (1925): 54; and Allen D. Clark, *A History of the Church in Korea* (Seoul: Christian Literature Society of Korea, 1971), 61–64.

8. See Ledyard, *The Dutch Come to Korea*, and chap. 6 above.

9. Gützlaff, *Journal of Three Voyages along the Coast of China*; and Paik, *The History of Protestant Missions in Korea*, 43–47. Apart from the group of Koreans in Manchuria, the most impressive but very temporary early Korean contact with Christianity outside Korea was by Yi Su-Jong (Rijutei) who as a student and political refugee in Japan translated the Gospel of Mark into Korean in 1884 (78–80). Other temporary missionary contacts with Korea and Koreans after Gützlaff and Thomas were made by Alexander Williamson of the National Bible Society of Scotland, Hunter Corbett and Calvin W. Mateer of the Presbyterian Mission in Shandong, China, Robert S. Maclay of the Methodist Mission in Japan, and Archdeacon J. R. Wolfe, an Anglican of the Church Missionary Society in Japan (51, 55–56, 77–90). On Gützlaff's work in China and Hong Kong, see above chap. 13.

10. On Korea's population, late-nineteenth-century contemporary sources vary widely — from 7 million to 15 million for the nation and from 150,000 to 400,000 for the capital city, Seoul. Cf. "The Country and People of Korea," in *GAL* 13, no. 6 (June 1887): 270–271, 273–277; J. R. Wolfe, "A Visit to Korea," *CMIR* (London), 10 NS (June 1885): 429; William Elliot Griffis, "Korea and Its Needs," *GAL* (August 1888): 371; and "Koreans at Home" (October 1889), cf. 433 (160,000 in Seoul), and 439 (300,000), the latter figure from an American secular magazine).

11. On Suh Sang-Yun (or So Sang-Yoon) see *The Christian Encyclopedia*, vol. 8 (in Korean) (Seoul: Christian Literature Press, 1983), 1003–1004; J. Ross, "The Christian Dawn in Korea," *MRW* NS, 3 (1890): 243, 247.

12. Three others were baptized about the same time, Paik Hong-Chun, Lee (Yi) Song-Ha, and Kim Chin-Ki. See the *Korean Repository* (Seoul) 2 (1891): 19–20; and Paik, *The History of Protestant Missions in Korea*, 51–55.

13. John Ross, "The Christian Dawn in Korea," 241–248; and Horace Grant Underwood (I), *The Call of Korea: Political-Social-Religious* (New York and London: Fleming H. Revell, 1908), 107, 135; Richard Baird, *William M. Baird of Korea: A Profile* (Oakland, Calif., private, 1968), 232.

14. Baird, *William M. Baird of Korea*, 232ff.

15. On Horace Allen, the primary sources are the Horace N. Allen Manuscripts, letters, diary, etc., in the New York Public Library. Many of his letters to his Mission Board are in the microfilm collection of the Presbyterian Historical Society, Philadelphia. The most important secondary source is the well-researched biography by Fred Harvey Harrington, *God, Mammon, and the Japanese: Dr. Horace N. Allen and Korean-American Relations, 1884–1905* (Madison: University of Wisconsin Press, 1944). On his relations with the mission and fellow missionaries, see Martha Huntley, *To Start a Work: The Foundations of Protestant Mission in Korea (1884–1919)* (Seoul: Presbyterian Church of Korea, 1987), 11–15, 29–30, 36–44, 106–118.

16. The royal decree of 1784 against Christianity had never been rescinded. See H. N. Allen, *A Chronological Index* (Seoul: Methodist Publishing House, 1901), 4. The foreign trade treaties of 1882–1883 negotiated by Western powers contained no freedom of religion clauses, and the State Department in 1884

refused to support such a request on behalf of "any single Christian sect in Korea to the exclusion of others." See George M. McCune and John A. Harrison, eds., *Korean-American Relations: Documents, 1883–1886* (Berkeley: University of California Press, 1951), 8.

17. Huntley, *To Start a Work*, 13, 15, 114–115, 122–123. She cites the quotation from a manuscript by George Heber Jones, "Rise of the Church in Korea," 3. See also Harrington, *God, Mammon, and the Japanese*, 78ff.

18. On the 1884 coup attempt, see Harold F. Cook, *Korea's 1884 Incident* (Seoul: Royal Asiatic Society, Korea Branch, 1972).

19. See Harrington, *God, Mammon, and the Japanese*, 45–50; Paik, *The History of Protestant Missions in Korea*, 1929 ed., 429–430.

20. Korea, as a small country, did not yet rate an embassy. Minister of the U.S. legation was the highest American diplomatic post in the country. A primary source on Dr. Allen is the *H. N. Allen Papers* (New York: New York Public Library). A well-written biography, stressing his diplomatic career more than his missionary service, is Harrington, *God, Mammon, and the Japanese*.

21. Drs. Allen, Heron, and Scranton.

22. On the first Horace Underwood, see *Rev. Underwood's Missionary Letters (1885, 1916)*, Korean trans. Kim In-Soo (Seoul: Presbyterian College and Theological Seminary, 2002); Lillias Horton Underwood, *Underwood of Korea: Being an Intimate Record of the Life and Work of the Rev. H. G. Underwood* (New York: Fleming H. Revell, 1918).

23. On Appenzeller, see Daniel M. Davies, *The Life and Thought of Henry Gerhard Appenzeller (1858–1902): Missionary in Korea* (Lewiston, N.Y.: E. Mellen Press, 1980); Everett N. Hunt Jr., *Protestant Pioneers in Korea* (Maryknoll, N.Y.: Orbis Books, 1980); William Elliot Griffis, *A Modern Pioneer in Korea: The Life Story of Henry G. Appenzeller* (New York: Fleming H. Revell, 1912); and Huntley, *To Start a Work*, 73–76, 91–92, 118–122.

24. See Paik, *The History of Protestant Missions in Korea*, 134–135.

25. Allen, manuscript, letter, May 7, 1885; Harrington, *God, Mammon, and the Japanese*, 79–80. See also Paik, *The History of Protestant Missions in Korea*, 110, 113–114, who cites a complaint from the Methodists, "Our [diplomatic] representatives here are more afraid we shall do [missionary] work than the Koreans themselves."

26. Huntley, *To Start a Work*, 107; L. H. Underwood, *Underwood of Korea*, 53.

27. H. G. Underwood, *Rev. Underwood's Missionary Letters*, 640–642, 752–753, 768–769, letter November 29, 1926, in *FM* 45, no. 5 (October 1886): 223–224; Huntley, *To Start a Work*, 82, 107; L. H. Underwood, *Underwood of Korea*, 53–54.

28. Cited by Huntley, *To Start a Work*, 91.

29. "The 69th Annual Report of the Methodist Episcopal Church, 1887," in *Woman's Work for Woman* (Philadelphia and New York, 1888), 312.

30. Mrs. M. W. Noble, "Autobiography of Mrs. Sam-Tok Chan," *Victorious Lives of Early Christians in Korea* (Seoul: Christian Literature Society of Korea, 1933), 31.

31. A probationer was baptized but not yet admitted to communicant membership; "adherent" included unbaptized attendants and inquirers at regular services. "68th Annual Report of the Missionary Society of the Methodist Episcopal Church for 1886" (New York, 1887), 265ff. Methodists in 1886 had "2 missionaries, 3 assistant missionaries" — i.e., wives — and 1 single woman missionary (Dr. Scranton's widowed mother).

32. The standard Protestant missionary histories are Paik, *The History of Protestant Missions in Korea*; Harry A. Rhodes, ed. *History of the Korea Mission, Presbyterian Church U.S.A., 1884–1934* (Seoul: Chosen Mission Presbyterian Church U.S.A., 1934); Charles D. Stokes, "History of Methodist Missions in Korea, 1885–1930" (PhD diss., Yale University, 1947); A. D. Clark, *A History of the Church in Korea*. For detail, accuracy, and readability an indispensable source is Huntley's *To Start a Work*.

33. That church became the present strong Saemoonan Presbyterian Church in the very center of Seoul. H. G. Underwood, Letter, in *ChHB* 3 (February 1888): 196; J. Ross, "The Christian Dawn in Korea," 247.

34. George Heber Jones, *Korea Quarter-Centennial Documents*, and "The Korea Mission of the Methodist Episcopal Church" (New York: Methodist Board of Foreign Missions, 1910), 24–25; A. D. Clark, *History of the Church in Korea*, 100.

35. Annie Ellers, Letter, July 25, 1886 (Moffett Collection); Huntley, *To Start a Work*, 98–105; Rhodes, *History of the Korea Mission*, 20–22, 114. In 1886 Ellers went to Korea under Presbyterian auspices. In 1887 Miss Ellers married the Rev. D. A. Bunker, who had come to Korea on the same boat as a teacher in the employment of the Korean government; in 1895 the Bunkers joined the Methodist mission, retiring in 1926.

36. On this first Presbyterian mission controversy, see H. G. Underwood, *Rev. Underwood's Missionary Letters*, 643–661; Huntley, *To Start a Work*, 106–118; Paik, *The History of Protestant Missions in Korea*, 110–111; Harrington, *God, Mammon, and the Japanese*, 72–84; L. H. Underwood, *Underwood of Korea*, 42ff.

37. Paichai Boys School, *Catalogue, 1888*; George Heber Jones, "Korea," *Korea Quarter-Centennial Documents*, 75–76; Griffis, *A Modern Pioneer in Korea*, 59. See also Paik, *The History of Protestant Missions in Korea*, 128–129, 229–233; Huntley, *To Start a Work*, 12–13; Charles A. Sauer, ed., *Within the Gate: Addresses delivered at the Fiftieth Anniversary of Korean Methodism* (Seoul: Korea Methodist News Service, 1934), 8.

38. "Woman's Work in Korea," *Korean Repository* 3, no. 1 (January 1896): 3–4.

39. Whether or not the concubine ever learned English we do not know. Ewha ("Pear Blossom") was the symbol of the Yi dynasty, for Yi (or E) means "pear."

40. See Yi Kyu-Tae, *The Modern Transformation of Korea* (Seoul: Sejong Publishing Co., 1970), 194ff.

41. Huntley, *To Start a Work*, 157; Rhodes, *History of the Korea Mission*, 86ff. For mission statistics, see 636ff. The quotation is from Huntley.

42. The mission then had seven members, Dr. and Mrs. Horace G. Underwood, Rev. and Mrs. D. L. Gifford, Mrs. J. W. Heron, Rev. Samuel A. Moffett, Miss Susan Doty (later Mrs. F. S. Miller). Rhodes, *History of the Korea Mission*, 625. Handwritten "Agenda, 1890 Meeting of the Korea Mission of the Presbyterian Church, U.S.A."; for the description quoted of the 1890 meeting see Huntley, *To Start a Work*, 157; and Rhodes, *History of the Korea Mission*, 625ff. For analysis of the Nevius Plan, see John L. Nevius, *Methods of Mission Work*, 2nd ed. (New York: Foreign Mission Library, 1895); and Rhodes, *History of the Korea Mission*, 86–90, 384–385; A. D. Clark, *A History of the Church in Korea*, 114. Cf. Paik, *The History of Protestant Missions in Korea*, 160, n. 281. For membership of the Presbyterian U.S.A. mission, see Rhodes, *History of the Korea Mission*, 625ff.

43. Methodists reported only nine communicants in 1890. Roy E. Shearer, *Wildfire: Church Growth in Korea* (Grand Rapids, Mich.: William B. Eerdmans, 1966), 224; Stokes, "History of Methodist Missions in Korea," xi.

44. On the Nevius Plan, see Nevius, *Methods of Mission Work*, Charles Allen Clark, *The Nevius Plan for Mission Work Illustrated in Korea* (Seoul: Christian Literature Society of Korea, 1938); Rhodes, *History of the Korea Mission*, 86–90, 374ff.

45. Eileen F. Moffett, ed., "S. A. Moffett Letters," November 9, and 23, 1892, in "Missionary Letters of Samuel A. Moffett of Korea, 1890–1939," Moffett Korea Collection, manuscript, Princeton Theological Seminary archives, Princeton, N.J.; H. G. Underwood, *Rev. Underwood's Missionary Letters*, 692.

46. Shearer, *Wildfire*, 222.

47. Shearer, *Wildfire*, 171.

48. See W. E. Henthorn, *Korea: The Mongol Invasions* (Leiden: E. J. Brill, 1963); and M. Frederick Nelson, *Korea and the Old Orders in East Asia* (Baton Rouge: Louisiana State University, 1946); and Deuchler, *Confucian Gentlemen and Barbarian Envoys*.

49. For confirmation of Japanese responsibility for the murder, see the recently translated report of the Russian ambassador in Korea at the time, edited by Gary Ledyard, "New Source Material from Russian Archives on the Assassination of Queen Min," Imperial Russian Legation, Seoul, 1895, Telegram 211, Appendix, VI.

50. The best studies of Korean Protestant church growth are Shearer, *Wildfire*; Alfred W. Wasson, *Church Growth in Korea* (New York: International Missionary Council, 1934); and Stokes, "History of Methodist Missions in Korea"; and for recent statistics and analysis, Marlin Nelson and Bong-Rin Ro, *Korean Church Growth Explosion* (Seoul: Asia Theological Association, 1983).

51. The figure of 225 communicants suggests a total Protestant community of between 300 and 400. Shearer, *Wildfire*, 47; Stokes, "History of Methodist Missions in Korea," appendix, xi.

52. See James Gale's 1888 letter in *MRW*, New Series, 2, no. 4 (April 1889); and Paik's citation of Underwood, *The History of Protestant Missions in Korea*, 140, 141.

53. L. H. Underwood, *Underwood of Korea*, 74–77; Paik, *The History of Protestant Missions in Korea*, 156–157; Huntley, *To Start a Work*, 132–133. Unlike China, where some missionaries were killed in similar riots fed by similar rumors, no foreigners in Korea were injured.

54. See Shearer, *Wildfire*, 47.

55. Robert E. Speer, *Report on the Mission in Korea of the Presbyterian Board of Foreign Missions* (New York: Board of Foreign Missions of the Presbyterian Church in the U.S.A., 1897), 6; and see W. M. Baird, letter, June 27, 1892; H. G. Underwood, letter, September 14, 1900; and Shearer, *Wildfire*, 50–51, particularly the dramatic chart on 51. For a detailed contemporary missionary report in 1896, see D. L. Gifford, *Every-Day Life in Korea* (New York: Fleming H. Revell, 1898), 208–229. Growth from 1895 to 1914 was not only markedly most rapid in the northwest, but also remained so up to 1936. For comparative Methodist statistics, see Stokes, "History of Methodist Missions in Korea," 147, 179.

56. On Samuel Austin Moffett, see the "Moffett Letters" in the Moffett Collection, Princeton, N.J.; Lee Jong-Hyeong, "Dr. Samuel Austin Moffett: His Life and Work in the Development of the Presbyterian Church in Korea, 1890–1936"

(PhD diss., Union Theological Seminary, Virginia, 1983); and Huntley, *To Start a Work*, 157–165, 175–176, 183–185, 247ff., and passim.

57. S. A. Moffett, "The Work of the Spirit in North Korea," *MRW* 18 (1893), 831–837. The interior was forbidden only to foreign residence, not to itinerant travel. The first treaty ports open to Western residence were Seoul (Inchon) in the center, Pusan in the south, and Wonsan in the northeast, in 1882 (Deuchler, *Korean Envoys and Western Barbarians*, 124).

58. His first visit was with the Methodist, Appenzeller, in 1890, and he tried to stay longer each time. S. H. Moffett, ed., *Samuel A. Moffett: First Letters from Korea, 1890–1891* (Seoul: Presbyterian Theological Seminary, 1975), 21–32, 41–47; and "Moffett Letters," March 17, September 6, 1982 (Moffett Collection, and Presbyterian Historical Society, Philadelphia).

59. S. A. Moffett, letter, July 30, 1894; and "A New Mission Station," *ChHB* (August 1893): 107. See also Gifford, *Every-Day Life in Korea*, 207–217; and Lee Jong-Hyeong, "Dr. Samuel Austin Moffett," 70–73.

60. Dr. Hall died in 1895 very soon after the end of the Sino-Japanese War. See Mrs. Rosetta Sherwood Hall, ed., *The Life of Rev. William James Hall, M.D.* (New York: Eaton and Mains, 1897).

61. Citing purchase of property by Japanese and Chinese in the city, they claimed that the "most favored nation clause" in Korea's foreign treaties permitted equal rights for the missionaries. On the property question, see "Moffett Letters," May 25, 1894; Lee Jong-Hyeong, "Dr. Samuel A. Moffett," 69–74; Paik, *The History of the Protestant Missions in Korea*, 211–212.

62. S. A. Moffett, letter, February 4, 1894; "The Work of the Spirit in North Korea," 831–837; and H. G. Underwood, "Korea Today," *MRW* 17 (1894): 661ff.

63. Graham Lee, letter, October 22, 1894; S. A. Moffett, "Evangelistic Work in Pyengyang and Vicinity," November 1, 1894 (Moffett Collection, and Presbyterian Historical Society, Philadelphia).

64. S. A. Moffett, "Pyengyang Report," October 1895 (Moffett Collection, and Presbyterian Historical Society, Philadelphia).

65. Paik, *The History of Protestant Missions in Korea*, 182–183, 213. Scandal had tarnished the reputation of the first native evangelist in the Methodist chapel (citing the [p. 202 of] *Annual Report of the Board of Foreign Missions of the Methodist Episcopal Church, 1892*, 286).

66. The title of Shearer's definitive work on early church growth in Korea is *Wildfire*.

67. S. A. Moffett, "Pyengyang Report."

68. *Fifty-Seventh Annual Report of the Board of Foreign Missions of the Presbyterian Church, U.S.A., 1894*, in *Presbyterian General Assembly, Reports of the Boards* (New York, 1894), 158–159. Shearer underlines the significance of such identification with the indigenous culture as a major factor in Protestant success in the northwest (*Wildfire*, 47).

69. Shearer, *Wildfire*, 86.

70. Paik, *The History of the Protestant Missions in Korea*, 10, dating the founding of the first Methodist church correctly as October 9, 1887, not 1886 as sometimes reported. The first episcopal visit to the Methodist church in Korea was made by Bishop H. W. Warren that same year.

71. S. A. Moffett wrote at the twenty-fifth anniversary of the mission in 1909, "While the missionaries set the example . . . to the Koreans is due the credit

for the great bulk of the evangelistic work and for the great ingatherings of souls." *Quarto Centennial Papers*, read before the Korea Mission of the Presbyterian Church in the U.S.A. at the annual meeting in Pyengyang, August 27, 1909, 26.

72. C. A. Clark, *The Nevius Method for Mission Work in Korea*, 86–95, gives the entire text of the Plan as adopted. Moffett, at the twenty-fifth anniversary celebration of the Northern Presbyterian Mission, reduced it to a sentence: "[The] two great principles [of the Nevius method] are the Bible Training Class and self-support." Twenty-five years later, it is said, that at the 50th Anniversary he amended the order of importance, saying in effect in answer to a question "What makes the Korean Church grow?" "For fifty years we have lifted up before these people the Word of God, and the Holy Spirit did the rest" (*Quarto Centennial Papers*, 18–22. See also A. D. Clark, *History of the Church in Korea*, 115–118).

73. On the Bible classes see C. A. Clark, *The Nevius Plan for Mission Work in Korea*, 34, 92–93, 99, 123–126, 220–222, 271–273.

74. See the dramatic graph of Presbyterian growth, 1895–1905, in Shearer, *Wildfire*, 51. Between 1896 and 1900 Presbyterians alone reported that communicant membership had shot up from 243 to 3,914. The north had only recently been opened to missionary residence, but already 60 percent (2,305) of their members was northern, mostly around Pyengyang. The next year the proportion rose to 67 percent, two-thirds, in the north, and 33 percent in the south (224–225).

75. The college graduated its first two students in 1908. On William M. Baird and his key role in the development of the Presbyterian missions' educational program, see Richard H. Baird, *William M. Baird of Korea*. On the academy and college, see 135–146; Huntley, *To Start a Work*, 268–270; and Paik, *The History of Protestant Missions in Korea*, 316–330.

76. Samuel A. Moffett, in *Catalogue of the Presbyterian Theological Seminary, 1916*, 8ff.; Rhodes, *History of the Korea Mission*, 162; Paik, *The History of Protestant Missions in Korea*, 291–292. The teaching in its first two decades was roughly post–high school level, not post-college. By 1918 it had become the largest Presbyterian seminary in the world (*The Christian Movement in Japan, 1919* [Tokyo, 1919], 345).

77. Paik, *The History of Protestant Missions in Korea*, 215–216, 304.

78. On the curriculum policy, see Samuel A. Moffett, "Historical Sketch," and passim, in *Catalogue of the Presbyterian Theological Seminary* (Seoul, 1916). Any study of the comparative growth of the Korean churches supports the importance of early training of national leaders.

79. See A. D. Clark, *History of the Church in Korea*, 106–107, 129–130; Stokes, "History of Methodist Missions in Korea," 111–112; Paik, *The History of Protestant Missions in Korea*, 306–307.

80. Presbyterians ordained the first Korean elders in 1900. There were two ordained elders in Pyengyang's central church in 1900; in 1903 there were only five ordained elders in the country. A. D. Clark, *History of the Church in Korea*, 133ff.; Korea Mission, Presbyterian Church USA, *The Fiftieth Anniversary Celebration of the Korea Mission of the Presbyterian Church in the USA* (Seoul: YMCA Press, 1934), 221.

81. A. D. Clark, *History of the Church in Korea*, 179–180.

82. *GAL* (June 1887): 274–275.

83. Donald N. Clark, "Yun Ch'i-Ho (1864–1945): Portrait of a Korean Intellectual in an Era of Transition," in *Occasional Papers on Korea*, no. 4, ed. James Palais and M. D. Lang (Seoul: National History Compilation Committee, 1975), and Yun Ch'i-Ho, *Yun Ch'i-Ho Ilgi*, vol. 2 (Seoul: National History Compilation Committee, 1975) contains the portions of his *Diary* written in English; and Paik, *The History of Protestant Missions in Korea*, 196–197, 393.

84. First had been the Northern Presbyterians (Presbyterian U.S.A.) in 1884, then the Australian Presbyterians (Victoria Mission) in 1888, the Southern Presbyterians (1892), and the Canadian Presbyterians in 1898. Canadian Presbyterians, however, had been working with the Americans as individuals for some time, notably James S. Gale (1888) and Dr. O. R. Avison and William Mackenzie (1893). See Speer, *Report on the Mission in Korea*, 10; and Paik, *The History of Protestant Missions in Korea*, 199–200, 276–277.

85. The first Canadian missionaries came as independents: J. S. Gale in 1888 for the Toronto Y.M.C.A. and joining the Northern Presbyterian Mission in 1892; Dr. R. A. Hardie who came in 1891 under the same auspices but who joined the Southern Methodists in 1898, and whose emphasis on prayer was one of the foundational catalysts of the great Korean Revival (1903–1907); and Malcolm C. Fenwick. On Gale, see Richard Rutt, *A Biography of James Scarth Gale* (Seoul: Royal Asiatic Society, Korea Branch, 1972); on Hardie, see Paik, *The History of Protestant Missions in Korea*, 190, 284, 332, 367–368, 373; on Fenwick, see below.

86. The Presbyterian Council was temporarily organized in 1889 as the United Council of the Missions of the American [Northern Presbyterian] and Victorian [Australian] Churches, but reorganized in 1893 to include the recently arrived American "Southern" Presbyterians as the Council of Missions Holding the Presbyterian Form of Government. In 1898 the Canadian Presbyterian Mission was added. The Council was usually referred to as the Presbyterian Council. Speer, *Report on the Mission in Korea*, 12–13; Rhodes, *History of the Korea Mission*, 385–386; A. D. Clark, *History of the Church in Korea*, 111, 134–140; Paik, *the History of Protestant Missions in Korea*, 198–199, 218–219, 276–277.

87. W. M. Baird, "Union of Presbyterian Missions in Korea," in *MRW*, New Series 6 (1893): 532.

88. C. C. Vinton, "Presbyterian Mission Work in Korea," *MRW* New Series 6 (1893): 671.

89. See A. D. Clark, *History of the Church in Korea*, 135–136, for a description of the alternating English and Korean language sessions.

90. See Bishop Charles John Corfe, *The Anglican Church in Korea* (Seoul: Seoul Press/Hodge, 1905); and the biography by Bishop H. H. Montgomery, *Charles John Corfe, Naval Chaplain, Bishop* (London: Society for the Propagation of the Gospel in Foreign Parts, 1927). See also Mark N. Trollope, *The Church in Korea* (London: A. R. Mowbray, 1915).

91. The first Baptist was Malcolm C. Fenwick (1889–1893, 1895–1935). See M. C. Fenwick, *The Church of Christ in Corea: A Pioneer Missionary's Own Story* (New York: Hodder & Stoughton; George H. Doran, 1911; Seoul: Baptist Publications, 1967, a reprint of the 1911 edition).

92. The dates of arrival were Adventists (1903), OMS (1907), and Salvation Army (1908). See Paik, *The History of Protestant Missions in Korea*, 303ff.; and A. D. Clark, *History of the Church in Korea*, 109ff.

93. The Anglican historian of the home mission Society wrote, "It was Bishop Corfe's wish that for the first five or six years of the Korea Mission the missionaries should refrain from attempting any direct evangelistic effort, and spend the time in quiet preparation, by study of the language, literature, habits, methods of thought, etc., of the people" (Pascoe, *Two Hundred Years of the S.P.G.*, 715.) Cf. Corfe, *The Anglican Church in Korea*, 1905, ii; also H. H. Montgomery, *Charles John Corfe*, 83, and 64, 70–73, 91.

94. A Baptist group from A. J. Gordon's Ella Thing Memorial Mission in Boston meged into Fenwick's mission for a short period in 1895. On Fenwick, see Fenwick, *The Church of Christ in Corea*.

95. See *The Fiftieth Anniversary Celebration of the Korea Mission, Presbyterian Church USA*, 93–97 and passim; and A. D. Clark, *History of the Church in Korea*, 112, 168–170.

96. Paik, *The History of Protestant Missions in Korea*, 191.

97. On the Catholics in this period, see above chap. 14.

98. Stokes, "History of Methodist Missions in Korea," xi, xiii, xv.

99. Wasson, *Church Growth in Korea*, 166. His figures are for "members and probationers."

100. Marlin Nelson, "A Critique of Korean Church Growth, 1975–1989," *Acts Theological Journal* (Seoul) 4 (1991): 86. On Presbyterian figures, see Shearer's suggestion of about a 3.6:1 ratio between communicant and noncommunicant membership in the Korean Presbyterian churches in 1898 (Shearer, *Wildfire*, 53, 224–225).

101. The 1897 figure is from Wasson, *Church Growth in Korea*, 166.

102. Barrett et al., eds., *World Christian Encyclopedia*, 2001, 662. The statistics (which include a double count of 2.5 million Christian adherents), are as follows:

	1900	2000
Total Population	8,000,000	46,800,000
Shaman (ethnorel.)	6,500,000 (81.3%)	7,300,000 (15.6%)
Buddhist	800,000 (10.0%)	7,200,000 (15.3%)
New Religionists	10,000 (0.1%)	7,200,000 (15.2%)
Confucianist	640,000 (8.0%)	5,200,000 (11.1%)
Total Christians	42,700 (0.5%)	19,100,000 (40.8%)
Roman Catholic	36,000 (0.5%)	3,700,000 (7.9%)
Protestants	19,000 (0.2%)	16,700,000 (35.7%)
Marginal		800,000 (1.8%)

Chapter 25

The Philippines (1860–1906)

The Aglipay schism is the most extraordinary in the whole history of religions. Not even the twelve apostles, with their tongues of fire, nor Mohammed with his armed legions ... did more in such a short period of time than what Monsignor Aglipay has accomplished for his Church.

— Manuel Lagasca, 1939[1]

I went down on my knees and prayed ... And it came to me this way ... (1) ... we could not give [the islands] back to Spain — that would be cowardly and dishonorable; (2) ... we could not turn them over to France or Germany — our commercial rivals ... (3) ... we could not leave them to themselves — they were unfit for self-government — and they would soon have anarchy and misrule worse than Spain's ... (4) ... there was nothing left but to take them ... and civilize and Christianize them ... as our fellowmen for whom Christ also died. And then I went to bed and went to sleep, and slept soundly.   — President William McKinley, 1903[2]

IT took only four hours of one great sea battle in Manila Bay to end nearly four centuries of Spanish rule in the Philippines. The transition, of course, took longer — four critical decades at the end of the nineteenth century, 1860–1900, and another decade at the beginning of the twentieth.

Seething beneath the surface of the transition years were island memories of 350 years of Spanish colonialism, from Magellan's landing in 1521[3] to the outbreak of the Philippine revolution. Two brief insurrections in 1872 and 1896 failed, but in 1898 the smoldering resentment of the Philippine people erupted into open flame. That same year Spain and the United States went to war over Cuba. In America the Philippine revolution went almost unnoticed. America's focus was on Cuba next door, not the faraway Philippines. But what happened at Manila Bay on that hot day in the Pacific in 1898 proved to be far more critical to the shaping of America's future as a world power than the little war in the Caribbean.

Admiral Dewey pushed his fleet at full speed from Hong Kong to Manila Bay — seven American ships against twelve Spanish. In four short hours of fighting (and three hours out for breakfast) all twelve Spanish ships had lowered their flags and were either sinking or afire.[4]

Spain had lost its empire in Asia. "Exit Spain; enter America," was how a Filipino historian summed it up,[5] and America's foreign relations in South and East Asia would never be the same.

The Spanish Friars under Pressure

Some blame Spain. For more than a hundred years after 1812 and beyond the end of the century, Spain, once the pillar of the church, was torn apart by antireligious violence after the pattern of the French Revolution. The Jesuits were expelled, the great orders and monasteries were dissolved and desecrated, and more than seventy thousand of their monks and religious were suppressed. Inevitably the collapse of their home base weakened the Spanish missions — Augustinians, Franciscans, Jesuits, and Dominicans — who for two hundred years had led in the evangelization of the islands. Others blame the Roman Catholic Church itself for its rigid authoritarian mission policies. Most would admit that the two, church and state, were inseparably responsible for the social injustices of the colonial period in the islands. The lines of power between colonial government and Catholic Church were drawn so closely that colonial power depended as much on the church as on the government; and the health and wealth of the church depended on the patronage of the government. Catholic power "was not simply spiritual, but economic and political as well."[6]

But in the rush to cast the burden of shame upon the church for the failure of Spanish colonialism, it might be wise to ask why is it that despite Catholic Spain's collapse, the Roman Catholic Church in the Philippines is still the largest single Christian community in all of Asia? And why did the anti-Spanish, anticlerical Philippine patriots of the failed revolution of 1896–1898 call their short-lived government the "most democratic Republic in Asia," the "first Christian Republic in the Orient"?[7] Why didn't they simply turn secular and atheistic like the later communists? To answer those questions, a balance must be found between the obvious and admitted injustices of Spanish ecclesiastic colonialism, and the equally inescapable positive credits owed to a heritage of more than three hundred years of Roman Catholic missions in the islands. "First of all," writes one historian of Philippine church history,

> [Spain and the missionaries] made of these islands one nation, fusing the various regions...into one people sharing a common national identity and a common faith. Secondly, despite all the obstacles...they succeeded in creating a Christian nation that eventually overthrew Spanish rule without rejecting the Christian faith.[8]

Catholic missions introduced to the islands books, printing, literature, Western science, medicine, music, architecture and technology.[9] At the end of the Spanish era, there were, in 1898, more than a thousand Catholic missionaries of the various mission orders in the Philippines.[10] Philippine Christians are still overwhelmingly Catholic. The population according to the census of 1903 was 7,635,000, of whom just under 7 million were at least nominally Catholic Christians.[11]

But beginning in the 1870s a strong undercurrent of nationalist agitation against the evils of colonial dictatorship blended into increasing resentment of the political power of the missions and their Spanish friars, and widened into attacks on the Spanish nature of the church. The intellectual and motivating leader of the nationalist revolt, Dr. Jose Rizal (1861–1896) is still revered as the country's "greatest genius." A child prodigy, he was reading the Spanish Bible at age five. He achieved fame as a poet, sculptor, philosopher, scientist, and patriot of the Philippine Revolution.[12] Raised a devout Catholic, he turned anticlerical with the revolution.

But not all the heroes of the revolution were anticlerical; they were more often simply anti-Spanish and pro-Philippine,[13] like the priest-martyrs of 1872 in the first of the rebellions. Best known among them was the Filipino priest Jose Burgos,[14] a curate at the Manila cathedral, who came to the hostile attention of the colonial powers when in 1864 he rose to defend the native clergy against Spanish discrimination in the church with an eloquent manifesto to the Spanish people. His arguments fell on deaf ears. Of 792 parishes in the islands in 1870, still only 181 were entrusted to Filipino clergy, and those were mainly small rural churches out in the countryside. Burgos found a powerful champion in the vigorous leader of Catholicism in the Philippines, the Spanish archbishop Gregorio Martinez, who ruled the church in the islands for thirteen years (1862–1875). When the Filipino priests were found guilty on the grounds that their criticisms were anti-Spanish, he refused the Spanish order to defrock them. But not even the archbishop could prevent the execution by strangling of three priests on charges of treason and sedition in 1872.[15] The death of the three Filipino priests was a spark for the buildup to revolution that followed. The archbishop's sympathetic support of the Filipino priests could not quiet the swelling anti-Spanish protests against discrimination and suppression. The result was a crippling, corrosive polarization between Spanish friars and Filipino priests — between the "regular" clergy (under Spanish monastic missionary orders), and the "secular" Philippine parish clergy under the authority of the archbishop.[16] When the sympathetic but weary archbishop resigned in 1875, his successor, Bernardino Nozaleda — after vacancies and an interim appointment[17] — proved to be an unpopular, violently pro-Spanish (and eventually anti-American) prelate.[18] Then the waves of anticlericalism spiraled upward from the countryside to the elite.

The grievances were many: arbitrary, dictatorial rule, centralization of government in Manila, absence of Filipino representation in the government process, confusion of functions between church and state.[19] The Spanish church was rich, the people were poor. In 1898 the Dominican, Recollect, and Augustinian missions owned 420,000 acres, including some of the best agricultural areas in the islands. They supervised 60,000 tenants, who were not apparently unpaid but nevertheless chafed and murmured at their serfdom.[20] The Spanish were arrogant; the Philippine clergy felt keenly their insults. One Spanish critic declared condescendingly, "Seven hundred and forty-eight *indio* priests...not only indicate a deviation in the choice of a profession as mistaken as it is censurable, but to my way of thinking, given the religious fanaticism of the Filipino people, constitute political dynamite." He suggested they were better put to work in industry or commerce than being taught theology and Latin.[21]

A third grievance was the perception that the Spanish missions, by their failure to train an indigenous clergy properly, were themselves responsible for the inadequacies they censured. As one of the best studies of the development of a Philippine native clergy describes it:

> The Filipino priest [was] neatly pinned between the horns of a dilemma. If he was incompetent, his incompetence proved that he could not be anything else; if he was competent, his competence proved that he was a rebel [anti-Spanish]. In either case the practical conclusion was the same, that is, that little effort need be expended on his formation.[22]

Popular indignation against the Spanish missioners and the widely disliked Archbishop Nozaleda overflowed into the streets. In 1888 the people paraded through Manila to present a "Petition," carefully loyal to Spain but bitterly anticlerical: "Long Live Spain! Long Live the Queen! Long Live the Army! Down with the Friars."[23] The national hero, Rizal, whose patriotism had begun to turn him away from the church, wrote:

> I wanted to hit the friars, but since they used religion not only as a shield but as a weapon, protection, castle, fort, and armor, etc., I was forced to attack their false and superstitious religion to fight the enemy who hid behind it...God should not be used as a shield and protector of abuses.[24]

There is a grim statistic that underlines the anti-Spanish ferocity of Philippine anger against the Spanish clergy. In the short two years of the Philippine-Spanish war, forty of the foreign friars were captured and killed by the revolutionists. A few were horribly tortured — run through with stakes, burned alive, cut to pieces in public.[25]

Catholics under the Americans

If the revolutionists expected the oppressive power of the Catholic Church to disappear with the coming of the Protestant Americans they were disappointed. The first American military governor, General E. S. Otis, was a Presbyterian; and the first civilian governor general, William H. Taft, later president of the United States, was a Unitarian, but some of the first actions of the American occupation seemed to favor the Spanish Catholic establishment. The terms of the surrender of Manila in 1898 had stipulated that its churches, Catholic of course, would be placed under the protection of the American army, not confiscated. So, to the anger of the Philippine parish priests and nationalists who had occupied them in hundreds of locations,[26] the incoming American government began to turn them over not to the nationalist hero Aglipay, and not to the independent Philippine parish priests who were serving in them, but to the hated Spanish Archbishop Nozaleda in Manila first,[27] and later throughout the islands. The independent Filipinos were aghast. How could the Americans do this to them? How could they force the victorious Filipino to return their churches and chapels to their defeated Spanish landlords, and of all people to Archbishop Nozaleda, "the synthesis of all the friars," as his outraged Philippine opponents cried. "He is not one friar, he is all of them."[28] And as further insult to the patriots, Nozaleda's American counterpart, an archbishop from New Orleans specially appointed by the Vatican, was received by the Americans with honor, and promptly proceeded to support the old Spanish hierarchy.[29]

When the military occupation was extended and hardened in 1900 into outright American annexation of the islands,[30] the war took an ugly turn. As John Smylie describes it, the Philippine reformers "turned against the Americans . . . for the same reason that [they] had opposed Spain. [They] wanted independence!"[31] Their hopes for self-rule and an American-style separation of church and state seemed doomed, so they took to the hills in a Philippine-American War of resistance. Public opinion in America about the annexation was at first divided, but in the presidential election of 1900 in which American expansion into the Philippines was a critical issue, it swung to the support of the Republican candidate, McKinley, an ardent Methodist who favored at least a temporary American rule over the islands.[32]

The second military governor, General Arthur MacArthur (whose son, famous World War II American army commander, would one day return to the Philippines) ended the revolutionists' war of resistance. His pledge of 1900 to disestablish the Roman Catholic Church somewhat placated the disappointed nationalist reformers and guaranteed to the islands the American constitutional right of freedom of religion, including "a complete separation of Church and State."[33]

The sudden fall of Spain as a colonial power was most sharply marked by the withdrawal of the Spanish friars from the Philippines. Of 1,104 foreign missionaries reported in 1896, by the end of 1903, only 246 were left, mostly in educational work, not in parish ministry. But it should be noted that where the churches had been under the care of Philippine priests the people still remained loyal Catholics.[34] Their anger was not against Rome but against Madrid.

Some of the anti-Spanish sentiment was transferred less angrily but still resentfully toward the Americans. After all, the Americans were also foreigners. And when Rome soon began to replace Spanish bishops with Americans instead of Filipinos, it was said that there was not a Filipino priest who did not condemn the appointments. Even the belated appointment of the first Filipino bishop, Jorge Barlin, did not quite quench the anger.[35]

To hasten the Spanish withdrawal, and to win popular approval, the American government agreed to buy more than forty thousand acres of the land owned by the Catholic missionary orders. The price seemed at that time exorbitant, over $7 million. It was gradually sold to Filipino tenants and others in long-term payments.[36]

The last Spanish bishop left the colony in 1904.[37] But more than one Protestant missionary concluded that in the end "the friars ... outwitted the American Government." America had won the war, they said, but the friars got the money, $20 million eventually.[38] The Roman Catholics were also to regain the favor of the people.

Protestant Missions and American Occupation

To Protestants the opening of the seven thousand islands of the archipelago and its 7 million people was an unanticipated gift of Providence. At the turn of the century, there was little collegial cordiality and reciprocal respect between the Catholic and Reformation branches of Christendom. To quote one prominent American missionary executive on the subject of Philippine Catholics in 1900, they "had no knowledge of the Bible, no real conception of Christianity, and were virtually non-Christians with a thin veneer of Romanism of the Spanish medieval type — a religion of forms and ceremonies with no relation to conduct."[39]

It is not surprising, therefore, to find that the first attempt to bring the Protestant faith into the islands was an effort to bring the Bible to the people. In Protestant missions, the first line of communication almost always was either Bible translation and distribution, or medical service. Nor was it surprising that the first missionary venture, in 1889, was made by two former Catholics who had newly discovered the Bible and had converted to Protestantism in Spain. One had been a Dominican priest, Manrique Alonzo Lallave, and the other a Baptist businessman named Castells. Lallave, ejected from the Dominican order in the early 1870s and relocated in Spain as a Protestant minister, translated the Gospel of Luke into the Philippine Pangasinan dialect, "the first Scripture portion ever to be printed in a Filipino tongue." Their project to distribute Bibles in Manila was quickly terminated by the Spanish authorities. Both suddenly and mysteriously fell desperately ill (by food poisoning, it was claimed) and Castells was deported.[40]

The first permanent Protestant presence was the YMCA which, with the support of the American army chaplains, was established in Manila in 1899.[41] Then came the rush of many Protestant mission agencies and missionaries. The pioneer in residential work was the Northern Presbyterian James B. Rodgers, who with his wife was transferred from Brazil in the justified expectation that fluency in Portuguese would facilitate communication in Spanish. Within a month of his arrival in early 1899 Rodgers preached his first Spanish sermon and organized the first Protestant Sunday school in the Philippines. There was only one criticism. When he prayed for peace, one of the twenty-two Filipinos present told him she would rather pray for Philippine independence than for peace.[42]

The first Protestant baptisms were by Rodgers in the private home of the Philippine "religious nationalists," Paulino and Nicolas Zamora, father and son. It is worth noting that a great uncle of Nicolas was one of the three Catholic martyrs of 1872, Jacinto Zamora. Of the nine baptized, seven chose to be Presbyterian including Paulino Zamora, and two asked permission to be Methodist, including his son, Nicolas Zamora, a sign of the close cooperation that developed between the various denominations in the islands.[43]

Even before the first missionaries were sent to the Philippines, a number of American mission boards — Northern Presbyterian, Methodist, and American Baptist — had discussed possible ways of avoiding friction. It was "the first time in history," one missionary executive asserted, that "before occupying a new field, the representatives of the various boards sat down cordially to plan the situation together, [and] pray over it."[44] But it was not until three years later, in 1901, that a union meeting of Protestant missionaries formed what they called the Evangelical Union and agreed upon an equitable division of territory and a common name, "Iglesia Evangelica" for the Philippine churches, allowing for the addition, if needed, of a denominational adjective in parentheses. They took as their models for missionary cooperation comity arrangements already worked out by the major Protestant missions in Japan and Korea.[45] Nevertheless, the Philippine Evangelical Union was weakened by the fact that for its first two decades its membership was limited to foreign missionaries.[46]

Nevertheless, for a moment a few years later, the drive for mission unity hovered on the brink of bringing together virtually all the Protestant work in the islands into one national church, the Evangelical Christian Church of the Philippine Islands. Frank Laubach, well known both for his extremely effective literacy programs and for his advocacy of cooperation in mission across denominational lines, wrote of the proposal, "organic unity fluttered so close that one could almost feel the beating of its wings."[47] But several factors impeded its implementation. One was the reluctance of the Baptists and Congregationalists to accept creedal formulations and any higher jurisdiction than the local congregation. Another weakness was the lack of Filipino voices in the planning and promotion of unity. A third was the sectarian irritation produced by the erection of geographical barriers between the denominations.[48]

Despite its flaws, the drive for comity was an important interdenominational step toward greater Protestant harmony and cooperation. The city of Manila was divided in half between Presbyterians and Methodists. The rest of the large island of Luzon was also divided about in half: the southern two-thirds was given to the Presbyterians, and most of the north to the Methodists. Panay Island was awarded to the Baptists, and Samar to the Presbyterians. The United Brethren and the Congregationalists were also assigned distinct fields, "so that in each place only one church would be developed and a united front be presented to the people." It was generally agreed that comity arrangements in the Philippines were more successfully initiated and carried out than in any other Protestant mission field. Only the Episcopalians and the Seventh-day Adventists found it impossible to join in the agreement.[49]

Thanks in great part to this initial spirit of mutual cooperation in mission, within the first three years of their missions (1900–1903) Protestants were able to report 45 churches planted and 4,000 members, and in the next fifteen years, by the time of the Philippine census in 1918, the number had grown to 594 churches with a membership of about 125,000.[50]

The Presbyterians, first on the field in residence, pioneered in medical work, higher education, and Protestant mission cooperation.[51] From the beginning they had called for the elimination of denominational rivalry in the race for church growth.[52] The Presbyterians also gave the Philippines their first Protestant medical missionary, Dr. J. Andrew Hall, in 1900, only a month after the arrival of Rodgers. The next year, 1901, they established the first Protestant school in the Philippines, Silliman Institute (now Silliman University), which was for years "the most influential Protestant institution of learning" in the islands.[53] A presbytery was formed in 1903. All four of its members were missionaries. Within a year they had ordained the first Filipino Presbyterian pastor, Monico Estrella (1853–1917).[54] The Methodists, however, became the largest of the Protestant Philippine denominations. Their mission policy focused on evangelistic meetings and Christian publications.[55] Nonresident Methodists had preceded even the Presbyterians. A Methodist army chaplain, for instance, held the first Protestant worship service in Manila, and a Methodist preacher-turned-businessman, together with a Methodist bishop from India, held the first evangelistic services as early as 1898.[56] Their first resident missionaries were three brave women who arrived in 1900 but were unable to stay more than a few months. It took the arrival of two clergymen and their wives shortly thereafter, followed by two bachelors,[57] to make possible in 1900 the organization of the first District Conference of Methodism in the Philippines with Bishop Frank Warne presiding only a week after dedicating the building of the first Methodist church building in Manila. It reported 220 probationers, 7 baptisms, and 7 Filipino workers, one of whom, Nicolas Zamora, had been ordained a few weeks earlier as the first ordained Filipino Protestant preacher.[58]

Less widely spread but very influential were American Episcopalians, due largely to the powerful presence of their bishop, Charles Henry Brent (1862–1929), the first Protestant Episcopal bishop in the Philippines.[59] For all his sixteen years in the Philippines (1901–1917) he advised against the Protestant temptation to proselyte Filipino Catholics, but to reach the unreached. He first established a strong Episcopalian urban presence in Manila. But a pioneering trip north among the primitive Igorots of northern Luzon along the unmapped valley of the Chico River in 1903 aroused his zeal for reaching the unreached. "If I were free to do so," he wrote, "I would not ask for a greater privilege than to give up my life for these people." The result was a notable Episcopal mission among people "who had just seven years earlier collected more than 70 human heads in an extravagant tribal war."[60] It was the same passion for witness where the gospel had not yet been carried that led Bishop Brent later to extended Episcopal mission in the other direction, to the far south where Muslim Moros of Mindanao and the Sulu archipelago were fiercely resistant to Western Christian penetration.[61] As Brent himself put it, all the Moro had learned from Western nations was "that we are able to kill him."[62]

Two other denominations deserve mention. The Baptists developed a policy of evangelism among targeted tribal groups which produced a promising initial response in the first decade of the century. But statistics record a failure to extend the range of their evangelistic outreach beyond the local into a national impact. Their graph of growth flattens out for the next fifty years.[63]

Almost invisible in this period was a little-known American mission that would in the coming decades become the largest of them all, the Seventh-day Adventists. They arrived in 1905 and must be mentioned.[64] As their name implies, their insistence on keeping the "sabbath" on Saturday instead of Sunday, and their emphasis on the second coming of Jesus Christ in a final millennium, distinguished them from other Protestant denominations,[65] but their growth rate in the islands proved to be the greatest of any one of the more mainstream missions.[66] Moreover, one of their separatist nationalist spin-offs was for a time even larger. A former Methodist, Felix Manalo, who had joined them in 1912, soon left them to start one of the most explosive of the indigenously Philippine independent churches, the Iglesia ni Cristo ("Church of Christ," *not* to be confused with the American Church of Christ).[67] Of this movement much more will be heard after World War II.

The Rise of the Independent Philippine Churches

The first, and for some time the largest example of a vigorous independent Philippine church movement was the Philippine Independent Church. It very soon quite eclipsed in scale the growth of the mission-connected Protestant churches. The independents were inheritors of a dream of Philippine independence that began to split them away from both the old church, Spanish Catholic, and the new churches, American Protestant. Their break-away climaxed in what is called "the schism of 1902," and beginnings are usually credited to or blamed on its first national leader, Aglipay, which is why it is popularly called the Aglipayan Church.

Father Gregorio Aglipay (1860–1940)[68] was a Filipino priest of the archdiocese of Manila, ordained in late 1889. His path toward schism traced to the clash of two competing loyalties in his own mind. The first loyalty was to his fellow Filipino clergy for whom he became a passionate advocate. That brought him into conflict with the Spanish-dominated hierarchy of the missionary orders, the friars. His second loyalty was to the Roman Catholic principle of the established unity of church and state. He dreamed of a Roman Catholic Church and a fully Philippine Catholic state. That produced his rebellion against the incoming American authorities who were not Catholic and did not grant Philippine independence, and who promoted the American Protestant principle of the separation of church and state. Aglipay thus found himself free from the Spanish colonists, but enmeshed by benevolent American protectionism, and at odds with those who seemed like his strongest possible allies, the Protestant missionaries. The latter welcomed his break with Spanish colonial Catholicism, but were not at all sympathetic with his reluctance to separate from Rome.[69]

Aglipay's first contacts with the Philippine revolution came when he was appointed as assistant (coadjutor) to the bishop of a large rural diocese north of Manila. When his Spanish bishop was captured in 1898 by the army of independence under General Emilio Aguinaldo, Aglipay seized the opportunity to strike a blow for national and ecclesiastical Filipino independence and "filled the vacuum" by appointing a Filipino diocesan priest to the position of "vicar general" of the province. His next step was to instruct the clergy to raise funds for the revolution. Not long thereafter Gen. Aguinaldo officially appointed Aglipay as military vicar general of the whole revolutionary army. From that time on, Aglipay began to take upon himself the role of successor to the colonial Spanish as the rightful head of free Philippine Catholics, always a

Filipino, still a Catholic, but Roman not Spanish Catholic.[70] He threw himself with enthusiasm into the appointment of Philippine priests to replace the Spaniards, though his authority to do so was not recognized by the Catholic hierarchy.[71] As late as 1901, some two years after the battle of Manila Bay, Aglipay was still fighting as a guerilla against the Americans in the mountains, with a price of fifty thousand pesos on his head. This "fanatical...Padre Aglipay," as one writer called him, was the last of the guerilla generals to surrender to the American army.[72]

But already before then, in 1899, when the Philippine war with Spain ended, and the revolutionists turned to war against the United States,[73] it was Rome who broke with Aglipay, not Aglipay with Rome. He was excommunicated on a charge of usurping the offices of a bishop without ecclesiastical consecration.[74] Not until 1902, however, did Aglipay finally make his own personal break with Rome and accept the position of supreme bishop of the schismatic Philippine Independent Church.

The original founder of that church probably was not Aglipay, who at the time still considered himself Roman Catholic, but Isabelo de los Reyes (1864–1938), who had turned bitterly anti-Catholic and launched an organized movement to separate from Rome, but who unlike Aglipay also repented and died as long ago he had begun, a Roman Catholic.[75] De los Reyes was a prolific journalist, a socialist, and founder of the first labor union in the Philippines.[76] Exiled for his violent denunciations of the oppression of the Philippine clergy by the Spanish friars, he returned to the islands in 1901 to organize an independent church, which he described as "a Christian Catholic Church which shall be Filipino in its personnel," and by September 1902 had persuaded the somewhat reluctant Aglipay to be its first bishop.[77]

Given the exhilarating release from three hundred years of Spanish dictatorship, and the heady prospect of Philippine independence, the immediate burst of enthusiastic response by Philippine priests and people should have come as no surprise. Almost all of the great island, Luzon, north of Manila rushed into the new church. That had been strong rebel territory. But Manila and the larger Luzon cities remained mostly Catholic. The middle islands, like Leyte and Samar, were little touched, but the great southern island of Mindanao went strongly Aglipayan. Statistics are widely variant. Aglipay himself in 1902 claimed 3 million adherents out of a total Philippine population of about 7 million. But taking the census of 1918 as reasonably reliable, which reported 1,417,000 Aglipayans out of a population of 10 million, it is not unreasonable to estimate that at its earlier height at the beginning of the twentieth century, probably a quarter of all the Catholics in the islands (1,600,000) left the Roman Catholic Church and joined the Philippine Independent Church.[78] Surprisingly, however, probably less than 100 Philippine priests joined the independents, out of a total of some 400 Philippine priests.[79] Tension between Ilocano nationalists under Aglipay and the Tagalog nationalists of Gen. Manuel Tinio may have slowed the movement toward schism.[80]

At any rate, the next decades were not easy for the new Philippine Independent Church. Theologically it veered to the left and turned Unitarian, perhaps influenced by the U.S. Governor William Howard Taft, a Unitarian, but more fundamentally by the increasingly unorthodox Isabelo de los Reyes.[81] This was unacceptably heretical to most Catholic priests, Filipino or foreign.[82] The Aglipay statement of doctrine of 1905 denies the trinity, and original sin, and as later expanded by de los Reyes it produced a "censored" Bible which omitted the trinity, the resurrection, and a doctrine of atonement whose Jesus Christ was of a special nature: "Although he had the appearance of a man He did not cease to be God, He was not a man as we are, but God with us."[83] The American Unitarian C. W. Wendte points to differences between American and Aglipayan unitarianism: the Aglipay form retains the priesthood and episcopate, baptism but without the trinitarian formula, and "Presbyterian" ordination.[84] He remarks that the Philippine Independent Church "is the only Church organized with more than twenty bishops, and hundreds of priests which holds modern science greater than the Bible and thus makes itself worthy of the twentieth century in which it has come into existence."[85] A further note should be added. The Aglipayan church is also the only church which in that same century recanted its Unitarianism and returned to trinitarian orthodoxy, but that came later.

Of more immediate effect on the Aglipayans than loss of orthodoxy was the loss of their church buildings. The magnificent cathedrals of the Spanish era, the hundreds of chapels and places of worship in all the islands were claimed as Catholic property by Rome, citing the text of the Treaty of Paris which ended the Spanish-American War. Beginning in 1906 the courts increasingly upheld the Vatican's rights.[86] This blow was almost fatal, for with the loss of their churches, as one historian has noted, "the tremendous boom in membership began to decline."[87] Nevertheless, before the twentieth century had ended, the Philippine Independent Church, founded by the priest–patriot general of guerillas Gregorio Aglipay, was the largest of the indigenous Philippine Christian communities, and claimed about as many members as all the Protestant mission–founded denominations combined.[88]

The statistics are hazy. In 1903 the leaders of the Aglipayan movement claimed that a quarter of the whole population of the islands (7,600,000) had joined them, and that barely 10 percent were attending Catholic mass.[89] But the figures reported in 1906 are probably more realistic: the four major Protestant churches in the Philippines (Methodist, Presbyterian, Episcopalian, and Baptist) seem to have had a total combined membership of less than 15,000 members (communicants, baptized, and inquirers or probationers); the Aglipayan Independent Church perhaps had fewer than 2 million members, but Roman Catholics were said to number about 7 million.[90] A more recent estimate for 1900 in the most recent edition of Barrett et al.'s *World Christian Encyclopedia*, 2001, compares the number of Christians with other religions in the islands in 1900 and 2000.[91] The statistics are as follows:

	1900	2000
Total Population	7 ,600,000	76,000,000
Total Christians	6,500,000 (86.2%)	68,000,000 (89.7%)
Catholic	5,980,000 (78.7%)	63,000,000 (82.4%)
Indigenous	1,000,000 (23.7%)	
Protestant (PIA)	100 (0%)	16,300,000 (24.7%)
Tribal religion	760,000 (10%)	2,000,000 (2.7%)
Muslim	266,000 (3.5%)	4,700,000 (6.2%)

Philippines Chronology (1860–1915)

1861	Royal decree transfers to Jesuits the Manila parishes of Filipino secular priests.
1862–1875	Pedro Pelaez, Jose Burgos, and Archbishop Martinez champion cause of Filipino priests.
1863	Spain establishes first public school system with Christian doctrine and church history in curriculum.
1868	Revolution in Spain liberalizes government in Philippines under De la Torre (1869–1871).
1872	Martyrdom of Burgos, Gomez, Zamora, "for treason."
	Rizal's "Propaganda Movement" for Philippine liberties.
1888	Protests against Spanish missionary orders.
1889	Lallave and Castells, converted Catholics, fail to establish Protestant work of Bible distribution.
1892	Philippine revolution: the *Katipunan society,* and Gen. Emilio Aguinaldo.
1893	The "Maura Law" reforms grant greater autonomy to the Filipino towns, too late.
1897	Gen. Aguinaldo, president of the Revolutionary Assembly.
1898	One archbishop (in Manila), four suffragan bishops (from Cebu, Nueva Segovia, Nueva Caceres, and Jaro).
1898	United States declares war on Spain over Cuba. Manila surrenders; Aguinaldo cooperates with the Americans.
	YMCA establishes first Protestant presence.
1899	Aguinaldo protests treaty terms; "First Philippine Republic."

1899   Gen. Arthur MacArthur defeats revolutionaries and ends guerilla war; Aguinaldo accepts American sovereignty in 1901.

1899   Presbyterians, Mr. and Mrs. James C. Rodgers, become first permanent Protestant missionaries.

1901   President McKinley reelected; American control established; Taft appointed first governor.

1903   Census data show population of 7,635,000, of whom 7 million (92 percent) are Christians.

1906   J. F. Smith, first American Roman Catholic governor general.

1909   U.S. authorities restore church property to Catholics.

1913   President Woodrow Wilson gives Filipinos control of their Assembly.

1916   Jones Act grants legislative authority to an All-Filipino Legislature, under U.S. governor general (1916–1935).

NOTES

1. M. Lagasca, *The Philippine Independent Church* (1939), preface, 5, quoted by Pedro S. Achútegui and Miguel A. Bernad, *Religious Revolution in the Philippines,* 4 vols. (Manila: Ateneo de Manila, 1960–1972), 1:210. Florid and exaggerated though the tribute may be, it catches something of the excitement of the movement's early growth.

2. Quoted, with annotation, by John E. Smylie, "Protestant Clergymen and America's World Role, 1865–1900" (ThD diss., Princeton Theological Seminary, 1959), 506. The language — "unfit for self-government" — is inexcusably patronizing, but not uncommon in that period. McKinley's motives were not unworthy; and the statistics may partly explain his judgment: in 1903 only 20 percent of the population could read and write in any language; in the election of 1912, only 1.45 percent of the voters were literate. See William Howard Taft's defense of American policy in the islands, in William Cameron Forbes, *The Philippine Islands,* 2 vols. (Boston and New York: Houghton Mifflin, 1928), 2:495–496.

3. For the early Spanish period, see above chap. 7.

4. George Dewey, *Autobiography of George Dewey* (New York, 1913), 195, 222; cited by Zaide, *Philippine Political and Cultural History,* 2:180ff.

5. Zaide, *Philippine Political and Cultural History,* 2:176ff.

6. Peter C. Gowing, "Disentanglement of Church and State," in *Studies in Philippine Church History,* ed. Gerald H. Anderson, 203–204; *NCE,* "Spain," 13:511–512; Schmidlin, *Catholic Mission History,* 634ff.

7. Zaide, *Philippine Political and Cultural History,* 2:195.

8. Bernad, *The Christianization of the Philippines,* 348.

9. See Zaide, *Philippine Political and Cultural History,* 89–105.

10. Dwight E. Stevenson, *Christianity in the Philippines: A Report on the Only Christian Nation in the Orient* (Lexington, Ky.: College of the Bible, 1955), 14.

11. Arthur Tuggy, *The Philippine Church: Growth in a Changing Society* (Grand Rapids, Mich.: William B. Eerdmans, 1971), 87. The census figures were 7,635,426 population; 6,987,686 "civilized" (i.e., Christianized), and 647,740 "wild" (i.e., Moslem or pagan tribal). Tuggy draws the conclusion that 92 percent were Christianized, 3 percent Muslim, and 5 percent pagan.

12. On Rizal see Camilo Osias, *José Rizal: Life and Times* (Manila, 1949); Eugene Hessel, *The Religious Thought of José Rizal,* rev. ed. (Quezon City, Philippines: New Day Publishing Co., 1983); Frank C. Laubach, *Rizal: Man and Martyr* (Manila: Community Publishers Inc., 1936).

13. The fullest treatment of the suppression of Filipino priests and their protest is John N. Schumacher, *Revolutionary Clergy: The Filipino Clergy and the Nationalist Movement, 1850–1903* (Quezon City, Philippines: Ateneo de Manila University Press, 1981).

14. On Burgos, see John N. Schumacher, *Father Jose Burgos: Priest and Nationalist* (Quezon City, Philippines: Ateneo de Manila University Press, 1972).

15. See Schumacher, *Father Jose Burgos,* 28–34, 249–259; Zaide, *Philippine Political and Cultural History,* 2:46–49; 112–115; and Achútegui and Bernad, *Religious Revolution in the Philippines,* 1:25–27.

16. Cesar Adib Majul, "Anticlericalism during the Reform Movement and the Philippine Revolution," in *Studies in Philippine Church History,* ed. Gerald H. Anderson, 152–171; Schumacher, *Revolutionary Clergy,* 20–32.

17. The interim archbishop was Pedro Payo, no more effective in defending his Filipino clergy than Martinez. See Schumacher, *Revolutionary Clergy,* 32; and the listing of bishops in Bernad, *The Christianization of the Philippines,* 361–364.

18. Schumacher, *Revolutionary Clergy,* 68–69, 92, 195–196, 211.

19. See the summary of the First [Schurman] Report of the Philippine Commission, 1900 (II,81) in Joseph R. Hayden, *The Philippines: A Study in National Development* (New York: Macmillan, 1942), 865–866.

20. Forbes, *The Philippine Islands,* 2:57–61; Majul, "Anticlericalism during the Reform Movement and the Philippine Revolution," 156–161. The Jesuits, who had less land, fewer missioners, and were heavily involved in education, were considered more supportive of the Filipino priests. Lewis Bliss Whittemore, *Struggle for Freedom: History of the Philippine Independent Church* (Greenwich, Conn.: Seabury Press, 1961), 103; Schumacher, *Revolutionary Clergy,* 276, n. 5.

21. De la Costa, "The Development of the Native Clergy in the Philippines," 99, citing Francisque Canamaque, *Las islas Filipinas* (Madrid, 1880), 63–65. One of the best collections of source material on the subject of the "disastrous failure to develop an adequate native clergy" is in John N. Schumacher, *Readings in Philippine Church History,* 2nd ed. (Quezon City, Philippines: Loyola School of Theology, Ateneo de Manila University, 1987), chap. 8, 193–230.

22. De la Costa, "The Development of the Native Clergy in the Philippines," 105.

23. Zaide, *Philippine Political and Cultural History,* 145.

24. Quoted by Majul, "Anticlericalism during the Reform Movement and the Philippine Revolution," 159. On the question of whether Rizal, before his execution six years later, 1896, returned to the Catholic faith, see Eugene A. Hessel, "Rizal's Retraction: A Note on the Debate," in the same volume, 133–151.

25. Frank Laubach, *The People of the Philippines: Their Religious Progress and Preparation for Spiritual Development in the Far East* (New York: George H. Doran,

1925), 113–114; Achútegui and Bernad, *Religious Revolution in the Philippines*, 1:44–50.

26. See Achútegui and Bernad, *Religious Revolution in the Philippines*, 1:79, 216–217, 233, 370ff.; Gowing, "Disentanglement of Church and State," 207–208.

27. Gowing, "Disentanglement of Church and State," 208.

28. Gowing, "Disentanglement of Church and State," 208; and Leon Ma. Guerrero, "Nozaleda and Pons," in *Studies in Philippine Church History*, ed. Gerald H. Anderson, 173.

29. Gowing, *Islands under the Cross*, 119–120. The New Orleans archbishop was Placido Chapelle, apostolic delegate.

30. For the rising stages of American interest and control (1873–1902), see the documents in Forbes, *The Philippine Islands*, 2:425–450.

31. Smylie, "Protestant Clergymen and America's World Role, 1865–1900," 477.

32. For a succinct overview of the annexation debate, pro and con, see Smylie, "Protestant Clergymen and America's World Role, 1865–1900," 476–489. For missionary and mission board perspectives, 489–532; and for the clergy in the United States, 533–556. On the Taft administration's efforts to promote Philippine civil leadership, see Taft's own statements quoted at length in Forbes, *The Philippine Islands*, 2:494–505. On McKinley, see also Tuggy, *The Philippine Church*, 80, 82–83.

33. Gowing, "The Disentanglement of Church and State," 209–218.

34. Latourette, *A History of the Expansion of Christianity*, 5:273; Laubach, *The People of the Philippines*, 113ff. See also Forbes, *The Philippine Islands*, 2:60. On the church property conflict, see Achútegui and Bernad, *Religious Revolution in the Philippines*, 1:313–338.

35. The replacements began in 1903; the last Spanish bishop left the country in 1904; and the first Filipino bishop, J. Barlin, was consecrated in 1906. On Barlin, see Schumacher, *Readings in Philippine Church History*, 320–321, 324, 343–344; Gowing, "The Disentanglement of Church and State," 216–218. Cf. Laubach, *The People of the Philippines*, 143.

36. On the land holdings of the Spanish religious orders, see Achútegui and Bernad, *Religious Revolution in the Philippines*, 1:146–152; Gowing, *Islands under the Cross*, 93–94, 115–117.

37. Gowing, "The Disentanglement of Church and State," 216–218.

38. Laubach, *The People of the Philippines*, 130–131.

39. A. J. Brown, *One Hundred Years*, 860.

40. T. Valentino Sitoy Jr., "Nineteenth-Century Evangelical Beginnings in the Philippines," *SEAJT* 9, no. 1 (October 1967): 49–53. Sitoy notes earlier attempts by the American and British Bible Societies to bring copies of the New Testament and Bible versions into the islands beginning as early as 1828 (42–45).

41. Kenton J. Clymer, *Protestant Missionaries in the Philippines, 1898–1916: An Inquiry into the American Colonial Mentality* (Urbana and Chicago: University of Illinois Press, 1986).

42. James B. Rodgers, *Forty Years in the Philippines* (New York: Board of Foreign Missions of the Presbyterian Church in the U.S.A., 1940), 32.

43. Rodgers, *Forty Years in the Philippines*, 31ff. On Nicolas Zamora, who became the outstanding early Philippine Methodist, and founder of a separate national denomination, La Iglesia Evangelica Metodista en las Islas Filipinas in

1909, see Richard L. Deats, "Nicolas Zamora: Religious Nationalist," in *Studies in Philippine Church History*, ed. Gerald H. Anderson (Ithaca, N.Y.: Cornell University Press, 1969), 325–336.

44. A. J. Brown, *One Hundred Years*, 868.

45. A. J. Brown, *One Hundred Years*, 862–867; T. Valentino Sitoy Jr., *Comity and Unity: Ardent Aspirations of Six Decades of Protestantism in the Philippines, 1901–1961* (Quezon City, Philippines: N.C.C. in the Philippines, 1989), 1–22; R. Pierce Beaver, *Ecumenical Beginnings in Protestant World Mission: A History of Comity* (New York: Thomas Nelson, 1962), 137–139. The Evangelical Union changed its name in 1929 to National Christian Council, in 1934 to Philippine Federation of Evangelical Churches, and again in 1947 to Philippine Federation of Christian Churches.

46. Gowing, *Islands under the Cross*, 157.

47. Laubach, *People of the Philippines*, 202–219 (quotation on 206). See also Sitoy, *Comity and Unity*, 56–64.

48. Gowing, *Islands under the Cross*, 157.

49. For the assigned geographical locations, which were followed until after World War II, see the map in Laubach, *People of the Philippines*, 203; Beaver, *Ecumenical Beginnings in Protestant World Mission*, 138–139. On the negotiations see Sitoy, *Comity and Unity*, map, vi, 14 f.; A. J. Brown, *One Hundred Years*, 864–869; Rodgers, *Forty Years in the Philippines*, 162ff.

50. Gowing, *Islands under the Cross*, 151. Membership grew to 630,000 by 1940.

51. James B. Rodgers, *Twenty Years of Presbyterian Work in the Philippines* (Manila: Christian Mission Press, 1919); A. J. Brown, *One Hundred Years*, 865, 871–874.

52. A. J. Brown, *One Hundred Years*, 871; Rodgers, *Twenty Years of Presbyterian Work in the Philippines*, 16.

53. A. J. Brown, *One Hundred Years*, 865, 884.

54. Sitoy, *Comity and Unity*, citing "The Evangelical Union," *Philippine Presbyterian* 12 (April 1921): 4; Rodgers, *Twenty Years of Presbyterian Work in the Philippines*, 8–11, 13.

55. Richard L. Deats, *The Story of Methodism in the Philippines* (Manila: Union Theological Seminary, 1964), 4, 9–10.

56. Deats, *The Story of Methodism in the Philippines*, 3–4; Hollister, *The Centenary of the Methodist Church in Southern Asia*, 222ff. The businessman/preacher was A. W. Prautch; the army chaplain was George Stull; the bishop, exploring possibilities for a permanent Methodist mission, was James M. Thoburn of India.

57. Deats, *The Story of Methodism in the Philippines*, 6, 7. The three Methodist pioneers were Dr. Annie Norton, and the Misses Julia Wisner and Margaret Cody in 1900; followed by Rev. and Mrs. Thomas Martin, Rev. and Mrs. Jesse McLaughlin, and W. A. Goodell and G. W. Fritz — all in 1900.

58. Deats, *The Story of Methodism in the Philippines*, 7–9; Tuggy, *The Philippine Church*, 100–103.

59. On Bishop Brent see Mark D. Norbeck, "The Legacy of Charles Henry Brent," in *IBMR* 20, no. 4 (1996): 163–168; Alexander C. Zabriskie, *Bishop Brent: Crusader for Christian Unity* (Philadelphia: Westminster Press, 1948); and Clymer, *Protestant Missionaries in the Philippines*, passim.

60. William Henry Scott, *Staunton of Sagada: Christian Civilizer*, reprint from *Historical Magazine of the Protestant Episcopal Church* 31, no. 4 (December 1962): 9.

61. Clymer, *Protestant Missionaries in the Philippines*, 17–18, 70–72.

62. Quoted by Clymer, *Protestant Missionaries in the Philippines 1898–1916*, 239, n. 34.

63. Tuggy, *The Philippine Church*, 108–114, 149.

64. Gowing, *Islands under the Cross*, 126; Arthur Whitefield Spaulding, *Origin and History of the Seventh-day Adventists*, 4 vols. (Washington D.C.: Review and Herald Publishing, 1962), 4:172.

65. See *Seventh-day Adventists Believe* (Washington, D.C.: General Conference of Seventh-day Adventists, 1988), 248ff., 332ff.

66. See Johnstone *OW 1993*, 448.

67. Albert J. Sanders, "An Appraisal of the *Iglesia ni Cristo*," in *Studies in Philippine Church History*, ed. Gerald H. Anderson, 350–365.

68. The standard sources on Aglipay and the Philippine Independent Church are Achútegui and Bernad, *Religious Revolution in the Philippines*; and Isacio R. Rodriguez, *Gregorio Aglipay y los Orígenes de la Iglesia Filipina Independiente, 1898–1917* (Madrid: Departamento de Misionología Española, 1960). Both are by Roman Catholic authors. Two important critical analyses of the sources, also by Catholics, are the well-documented chapter by Mary Dorita Clifford, "Iglesia Filipino Independiente," in *Studies in Philippine Church History*, ed. Gerald H. Anderson, 223–255; and the more recent careful study by Schumacher, *Revolutionary Clergy*. See also Francis H. Wise, "The History of the Philippine Independent Church (Iglesia Filipina Independiente): Analyzing It as a Social Movement" (MA thesis, University of the Philippines, 1965).

69. See Schumacher, *Revolutionary Clergy*, 194, 230–233.

70. Schumacher, *Revolutionary Clergy*, 98ff.; Achútegui and Bernad, *Religious Revolution in the Philippines*, 1:36–84. The provincial diocese was that of Nueva Segovia, with its seat in Vigan, home of the Catholic seminary of Vigan, from which Aglipay had graduated.

71. Gregorio Aglipay Cruz y Labayan in 1898 was irregularly given authority as ecclesiastical governor of a northern diocese by a Spanish bishop captured and held hostage by the revolutionists. His rank was raised by degrees by the revolutionists to independent national status. He was excommunicated in 1899 by a Philippine church court during the short Philippine-American war (Achútegui and Bernad, *Religious Revolution in the Philippines*, 1:69–103).

72. Schumacher, *Revolutionary Clergy*, 114; Whittemore, *Struggle for Freedom*, 89–90.

73. On the Philippine-American War compare the longtime standard by Julius W. Pratt, *Expansionists of 1895: Hawaii and the Spanish Islands* (Baltimore: Johns Hopkins, 1937), and Stuart C. Miller, *"Benevolent Assimilation": The American Conquest of the Philippines, 1899–1903* (New Haven, Conn.: Yale University Press, 1982).

74. Achútegui and Bernad, *Religious Revolution in the Philippines*, 85–103.

75. On de los Reyes's break with Rome, see Achútegui and Bernad, *Religious Revolution in the Philippines*, 1:179–192. On his return to the church in 1936, see 1:502–505. After his death in 1948, his sons strenuously but not convincingly denied that his renunciation of Aglipayanism was genuine (505–510).

76. In some ways the mind behind the independent church movement was neither Aglipay nor de los Reyes, but Apolinario Mabini, an advisor to Gen. Aguinaldo, whose *Manifesto* of 1899 proposed termination of Spanish ecclesiastical authority following the fall of Spanish colonialism, and called for Philippine

priests to organize a ruling council of their own. See Achútegui and Bernad, *Religious Revolution in the Philippines*, 1:104–109. On Isabelo de los Reyes, see the biographical sketch also in 1:164–180. Cf. Gowing, *Islands under the Cross*, 133–139.

77. Achútegui and Bernad, *Religious Revolution in the Philippines*, 1:181–209. Cf. the analysis of "Iglesia Filipina Independiente," 231–244.

78. The census of 1903 reported 7 million Christians in a population of 7,635,426 (Zaide, *Philippine Cultural and Political History*, 242). The estimate is by Peter Gowing writing for a Protestant survey (*Islands under the Cross*, 136), following Achútegui and Bernad's detailed analysis (*Religious Revolution in the Philippines*, 1:210–233, 443), which estimates 1.6 million broke with Rome out of a total of 6.3 million Catholics. Other estimates of the exodus vary from 2 million to an unbelievable figure of 5 million Aglipayans (1:443).

79. See Achútegui and Bernad, *Religious Revolution in the Philippines*, 1:231–232; Gowing, *Islands under the Cross*, 136. The former speaks of 36 priests turning Aglipayan, the latter estimates from 100 to 300.

80. On the Tagalog part in the revolution, see Schumacher, *Revolutionary Clergy*, 101, 124–134.

81. On the growth of unitarian theology in Aglipayanism, see Wise, "History of the Philippine Independent Church," 211–219, citing C. W. Wendte, *The Promotion of Unitarianism in Foreign Lands* (Boston: American Unitarian Association, 1912), 25–26; Achútegui and Bernad, *Religious Revolution in the Philippines*, 1:163, 263, 377: Whittemore, *Struggle for Freedom*, 141–145; and Gowing, *Islands under the Cross*, 139–140.

82. Achútegui and Bernad, *Religious Revolution in the Philippines*, 1:163, 269, 377; Whittemore, *Struggle for Freedom*, 140–144; Schumacher, *Revolutionary Priests*, 276.

83. The statement of 1905, and the personal revision of the Bible by de los Reyes, are quoted by Frank Laubach (citing P. H. P. Lerrigo, "A Bible of Philippine Manufacture"), *People of the Philippines*, 153–155.

84. Wendte, *The Promotion of Unitarianism in Foreign Lands*, 25–26, cited by Wise, "History of the Philippine Independent Church," 217.

85. Wendte, *Promotion of Unitarian Christianity in Foreign Lands*, as cited above by Wise.

86. The Vatican's rights were confirmed again in 1909.

87. Clifford, "Iglesia Filipino Independiente," 246–247. See also Laubach, *People of the Philippines*, 148–152.

88. Forbes, *The Philippine Islands*, 1:16, 2:66, citing *1918 Census*, 2:52. The 1918 census reported 7,790,937 Roman Catholics, 1,417,448 Aglipayans, and 124,573 Protestants, in a population of 10,314,000 (91 percent of which was Christian). The 1993 mission handbook, Johnstone, ed., *OW*, 448–449, lists total Protestant adherents of the mission founded churches as 4,966,000, and Philippine Independent Church as 4,800,000.

89. Schumacher, *Revolutionary Clergy*, 346.

90. Tuggy, *The Philippine Church*, 100–121, 128. Cf. Zaide, *Philippine Political and Cultural History*.

91. Barrett et al., eds., *World Christian Encyclopedia*, 2001, 594. A double count of 14.8 million persons should be subtracted from the Christian total, according to Barrett.

Chapter 26

Burma and Ceylon (1850–1900)

When it was announced...that no more funds were available for our support from America my heart sank within me...Brother Myat Keh and Brother Po Kway, however, said...the Lord would provide. Still I was very anxious...the salt jar was nearly empty. The next day [someone] came and filled it...the mats were getting old...and the [sisters brought new] mats...There was no lack...Before, we were not fully dependent on the churches...In a measure, we were sent and paid by the missionary...perhaps we put on airs. But after this we could not help loving our people and working for their souls.   — Thra Shwe Baw, Burma, ca. 1860 [1]

> Open a school and close a jail.
> — quoted by D. Kanagasabai Wilson,
> Ceylon, ca. 1900[2]

Burma:
Colonialism, Mission, and the Tribes

In 1811 the British refused Adoniram Judson entry into India and forced him to begin his mission in Burma instead. Thirteen years later the British moved into Burma, but by then the war with America was over and this time they rescued Judson from prison. Baptists in Burma not only preceded the British Empire but also stayed longer.[3] It is the church, not the empire on which "the sun never sets."

Judson died in 1850, just before the Second Anglo-Burma War of 1852–1853 divided Burma into a British south and a Burmese north, a north ruled by one of the best of its monarchs, King Mindon (1853–1878). That put an end to fifteen years of persecution under Mindon's two predecessors, one of whom is described as "drunken and insane," and the other, as "abandoned to pleasure." Mindon brought a measure of reform into a government that had degenerated under hopelessly corrupt governors and arrogant, irresponsible kings.[4] There followed for the Protestant missions a period of highly successful growth. And as in India a half century earlier, a Baptist had led the way. Judson was Burma's William Carey.

In 1850 almost all of Burma's eight thousand Baptists were in British territory in the southeast (Arakan), and the Karen southwest (Tenasserim).[5] The war once again opened the southern center of Burma to the Baptist missionaries who promptly moved back from their interim center across the bay in Tenasserim to which they had fled during the years

573

of government repression. They moved to Rangoon, Judson's last home, and with them they brought the Baptist Press, and later the Theological Seminary.[6]

Among their first actions in Rangoon was to call a Missionary Convention in 1853 to discuss mission policy for the next half century. Out of it developed three key decisions: the primacy of evangelism, the need for native pastors, and the importance of a new translation of the Bible with the intention of placing at least one copy of the Burmese Bible in every town and village where Burmese was spoken.[7]

THE BURMESE PREACHER-EVANGELISTS[8]

All were agreed that the first key, evangelism, would in the long run depend on the second: a determined effort to accelerate the training of a native Burmese clergy. The missionaries gratefully acknowledged their debt to the 11 Burmese pastors and 120 national preachers then on the rolls, who, as they put it: "had made the jungles ring with hymns and the praises of God, so that the missionaries, following in *their* footsteps, had found Christian churches already established." A goal was set: a Burmese ordained pastor for every church and Burmese evangelists to reach out to non-Christians lest the mission be reduced to Christians preaching to Christians without ever touching "the thousands who had not yet decided for Christ."[9]

In this period in the middle of the century the name of Saw (or Thra) Quala (b. ca. 1815) stands out. A Karen (of the Sgaw Karen tribe), he was the Baptists' second convert after Ko Tha Byu, the "apostle to the Karens."[10] When Francis Mason, linguist and pioneer to the "heartland" of the Karen tribes, was forced home by ill health in 1857, he decided to turn over the district, not to another missionary, but to his ablest helper, Saw Quala, in whom he had developed the utmost confidence. In the Karen, Saw, he astutely discerned a leader for a second stage of Christian outreach in Burma. Whereas Ko Tha Byu, the "apostle," had been indispensable and highly successful, he was nevertheless "wholly uneducated" and necessarily "under the eye of the missionary." Saw Quala, on the other hand, who had been converted by Ko Tha Byu, was trained and ordained, an independent missionary-evangelist in his own right, and entirely capable of taking charge of a whole district as his sole responsibility. He was, as Mason described him, "a specimen of . . . the advantages of education."[11]

Within two years of the time that Mason turned the district over to him, Saw Quala had increased the number of assistants working with him from 3 to 11; they had established 27 new churches; and had baptized 1,880 adult converts.[12] Quala wrote:

> I dare not rest, neither in the rains nor in the hot season. God has shown me my work and I stop not. I go hither and thither, up the mountains, down in

the valley, one night [or] two nights in [each place]. Some come to me from a distance . . . saying, "Teacher, thou sayest thou comest to exhort men and thou has never been to our streams . . . Dost thou not love us?" Then I feel unable to open my mouth . . . Brethren, teachers, teacheresses, pray for me.[13]

And he added in his journal, later, "When I think of my inability to do the work, I weep."[14]

Dr. Mason's commentary on this entry from Quala's journal is a tribute to the cultural sensitivity of several generations of nineteenth-century missionaries who have too easily and too often been dismissed as imperialists. He wrote:

Nothing could be easier than for me to hire an elephant or two, and finish the [work], nothing more gratifying than to baptize willing converts who give evidence of a change of heart, and to found new churches dedicated to our blessed Redeemer . . . I might baptize a thousand converts; but I am not willing to rob the natives of the honor of this work, which God has wrought through their instrumentality. Were I to baptize the converts, it would injure the influence of the native preachers with the people.[15]

Dr. Francis Mason also pioneered in answering the convention's second call — a request for a more usable translation of the Bible. Not only did Mason encourage the use of Karen evangelists, he, along with Jonathan Wade, made the significant decision to promote a version of the Bible in the Karen language to supplement what was already being done with the Bible in the national language, Burmese. The story is told that in 1831 on his first trip into Karen territory, an old man confronted him. "Where is our Book?" he asked, referring to the Karen legend referred to in a previous chapter.[16] "If you bring us our lost book, we will welcome you." Wade was quick to respond. It is said that he reduced the Karen language to writing even before he could speak it, and Dr. Mason against the advice of some that they should teach the use of Judson's Burmese Bible of 1823–1837, or at least produce a Roman phonetic transliteration, took Wade's adaptation of the Burmese alphabet to Karen sounds and threw himself into the arduous task of translating the Bible into Sgaw Karen. Thus did the Karens receive "their Book." The first printed portion was the Sermon on the Mount in 1837; the New Testament appeared in successive printing stages from 1843 to 1861, and the Old Testament in 1853.[17]

But the 1853 Convention was not always fellowship and light. It also brought into the open serious divisions of opinion between the field force of missionaries in the field and the Mission Board at home. This in turn contributed to the first schism in the mission in 1856. Six of the twenty or so missionary families left the American Baptist Mission to join a Baptist *Free* Mission Society because, they said, there were too many rules in the old mission that infringed on their rights as independent Baptists.[18]

THE THIRD ANGLO-BURMESE WAR AND BAPTIST GROWTH

In 1878 the good king Mindon died, leaving forty-six sons to fight over the succession. The winner was Thibaw, who unfortunately turned out to be a puppet in the hands of his unscrupulous queen Supayalat. It was she who persuaded him to clear his title to the throne by a massacre of about eighty of his brothers, sisters, uncles, and aunts. That did clear the title, but it also brought down on his head the disastrous Third Anglo-Burmese War of 1885–1886, and the annexation of all Upper Burma by Britain.

For the next fifty years (to 1937) Burma became the easternmost province of British India. But India and Burma is a mismatch. Burma is Buddhist. India is Hindu. Burma is more Mongol; India more Aryan. Burma leans to the practical; India to the philosophic. But the historian who remarks on those contrasts lets his metaphors run too far when he concludes, "[Burma] is as akin to India as iron ore is to buttered toast."[19] Despite the mismatch, and the irritations and humiliations of rule by a foreign power based in another country, the next years in Burma to the end of the century were a third stage of advance for Protestant missions. If the spreading conversions among the Karen tribes in south and central Burma were marks of the mid-century of Baptist mission in Lower Burma, the next stage was a quickening march to the north, into Upper Burma. One important aspect of the whole history of Christian expansion in Burma becomes more and more noticeable in each stage. The advance was almost entirely among the tribes, not among the ruling Burmese. In the first stage, even in the Judson era, as we have seen, the expansion was to the Karens. The second stage witnessed a notable shift of initiative. Whereas the earlier advance was by American missionaries to Karens, the second was Karen to Karens (Ko Tha Byu to his own people); and now the third advance was Karen to Kachins, from one tribe to another tribal group. Dominating each advance was not the colonial power, Britain, but first the Americans, then the tribal minorities.

The Kachin people form the largest group of highland tribes north of Mandalay. They live in the sharp ridges and valleys where an eastern extension of the Himalayas separates Burma from China, along a north-south equivalent of the Old Silk Road — a trade route from Southeast Asia up the rolling Irrawaddy River through the gorges, and over the mountains to China ("the Burma Road").[20] Their religion was "animism, pure and simple," with sacrifices of water-buffalo lashed to cross posts and beheaded.[21] After the Karens, the Kachin became the second major tribal group to turn Christian in what is often called a mass movement, but which might better be described in ethnic terms as a "people movement."[22]

The Baptists were a step ahead of the colonialists, beating the establishment of British military order in the Kachin hills by sixteen years.[23] It gave them time to prepare and as far as possible protect the tribes from the negative effects of foreign conquest, although in fact foreign rule proved to be no worse than the mistreatment of the tribes by Burma's own royal rulers. Before the war, in 1878, one of the first Baptist missionaries to the Kachins, S'Peh, himself a Karen, wrote, "I cannot walk about as freely as I wish. The Burmans have given out that they would massacre all the Kachins from fifteen years old and upwards."

The first Baptist pioneers[24] to the Kachins were a missionary, Josiah N. Cushing, and two, then three Karen missionaries from Bassein in the south — most importantly Bogolay (Thra Bo Gale) who stayed only briefly (but was the first Baptist missionary to enter a Kachin jungle village), and S'Peh (Thra Saw Pe), mentioned above, an ordained Baptist Karen who gathered the first converts. It is S'Peh who has been called "the first foreign missionary from America's first foreign mission field,"[25] a Karen missionary to the Kachins in the wild and still largely unconquered north. A letter he wrote in 1878 describes his difficulties and his courage. After his mention of the threats of massacre of all Kachin over the age of fifteen, he added: "I was a little afraid ... [But] I am ready to cast in my lot with these poor Kachins, to suffer with them, and to lead them with my whole heart to Christ."[26]

Illness and death cut short the work of a succession of missionary and Karen replacements until the arrival of the Rev. and Mrs. William Henry Roberts in 1879. In less than two years Mrs. Roberts was dead, but for the next forty years her husband worked tirelessly in the hills, and Roberts, who admitted he was no linguist, completed the first tentative translation of the Gospel of Matthew into Kachin. The year 1882 saw the first baptisms of the Kachin converts of Thra Saw Pe. But after four years of Baptist work in Bhamo, the center for reaching both the northern Shan[27] tribes and the Kachins, there were still all too few signs of success: one small Baptist church, and nineteen baptized believers. There was not a single Kachin teacher or preacher, and no Bible translation yet completed into their language.[28]

CHRISTIAN EDUCATION

The development of the Christian school system had been a second major priority of the first Annual Baptist Mission Conference of 1853, and was closely related to the other priorities adopted by that Conference — the training of national leadership for evangelism, and the translation of the Bible. All the teachers were chosen from the Christian community, and the aim was Christian instruction, not simply a replication of a secular education. But the most controversial question was whether the teaching should include the English language, or be limited to the vernacular. The temporary decision, reached with some protest, was to concentrate on the vernacular and drop instruction in English.[29]

The most revolutionary aspect of the development of Christian schools in Burma, as elsewhere in Asia, was education for women.[30] Ellen B. Mason was a pioneer in reaching the tribal women. She had come to Burma with her husband Francis in 1831. An early champion of women's rights, she was probably not unaware of a distressing Burmese proverb to the effect that a woman is no better than a dog. Years later the proverb was still in circulation and when one missionary challenged a Burman male to disavow it, the man took his cheroot out of his mouth and said, "Well, a woman *is* better than a female dog, but she is not better than a male."[31] By then (in the 1920s) he might have been joking, but to good Baptist women like Mrs. Mason a generation earlier it was no joke, and she set out to change things. So successful was she among the tribes that she was able to write in 1860:

> [S]ix years ago, not a Karen female could read a syllable. Now many hundreds can read and fifty young women are fitting themselves for teachers, twelve of whom have already branch schools upon the mountains. When the work was begun, the people ridiculed the proposition of instructing *girls* in books. Now the chiefs themselves select the girls, bring them down, feed them, clothe them, supply their books, and find them places for teaching ... When this work was begun, I had to support the men while clearing the ground for the school-house ... I had to measure out our own rice, meal by meal, to persuade them to stay over Sunday. The same chiefs [now] have supported themselves week after week to enjoy the privilege of coming in at night to study the word of God.[32]

Mrs. Mason continued to press with passion for more support for women's missionary outreach to women, dismissing the misconception of overwhelming missionary success in Burma with the reminder that among the 3 million women in British Burma, not more than thirty-six thousand have become Christian and were receiving Christian instruction. Moreover, she noted, all but one thousand of those women were Karen tribeswomen; only about a thousand were from the majority population (Burman or Talaing).[33] She not only overcame misconceptions at her church base in America, but was astoundingly successful in revolutionizing the position of women among the Karens. The difference was not missed by observers in Burma where only among the Karens, it was said, was there anything resembling an approach to equality of women with men. It was a great tragedy when shortly thereafter mental illness led Mrs. Mason into estrangement from the mission, and finally into open schism along with some followers.[34]

ROMAN CATHOLICISM IN BURMA (1850–1900)

After what a Catholic historian has described as a "timid" start of nearly three hundred years by a succession of Catholic orders since the fifteenth century,[35] there followed a less spectacular growth than that of the Baptists in Burma, but nevertheless a reasonable revival of Catholic missions during the seventy years from 1860 to the end of World War I.

The first half of the nineteenth century had seen little or no Catholic success. In 1825 the only Catholic priests left in the country were a native Burman and a Portuguese Indian. One of them died two years later.[36] In 1850, the future still looked bleak. Membership had stalled for a whole half century. It was five thousand in 1800, and was still five thousand in 1850.[37] The rise of radical secularism in Italy's wars of independence and unification (1848–1870) forced even the pope out of Rome in 1848, and Italian missionaries asked for the assignment of Burma to the French Missionary Society (Missions Etrangères de Paris). By 1862 the newly organized vicariate numbered one bishop, eleven missionaries, one native priest and about six thousand Christians.[38]

But within another thirty-four years by 1896 the number of bishops had tripled (3 apostolic vicars); the missionaries had more than quintupled to 62, and there were 325 churches or chapels. What was perhaps just as important, if not more so, two seminaries had been founded for training Burmese leadership, and there were more than ten times as many native priests (13). Best of all, the number of Catholics in Burma had increased nearly tenfold in forty-six years from a full stop at 5,000 in 1800, to 49,046 in 1896.[39]

Better yet, in the next four years, if the reported statistics are compatible, Roman Catholics ended the century with a flourish. In 1900 they reported a total membership of 70,000.[40] As with the Baptists, most of the growth was among the tribes, not the Buddhist Burmans, and there were still little more than a half as many Catholics in Burma as Protestants, but a better future seemed assured for the next millennium.

Modest success though all this was, it was nowhere near achieving a substantial numerical breakthrough into the majority culture of that overwhelmingly Buddhist nation. Christianity was still the lowest on the list of comparative religious statistics for 1900, though if we use David Barrett and associates' work and look forward a hundred years, we can see that the tiny flock would grow solidly but modestly in the twentieth century:[41]

	1900	2000
Total Population	10,450,000	46,100,000
Buddhists	10,055,000 (86.7%)	33,100,000 (72.7%)
Tribal religions	522,500 (5.0%)	5,700,000 (12.6%)
Muslims	338,000 (3.7%)	1,075,000 (2.4%)
Hindus	284,000 (2.7%)	893,000 (2.0%)
Christians	232,500 (2.2%)	3,773,000 (8.3%)
Protestants (PIA)	162,000 (1.3%)	3,100,000 (5.5%)
Roman Catholics	70,000 (0.7%)	590,000 (1.3%)

Burma Chronology (1824–1900)

1824	British Empire expands into Burma.
1825	Only two Catholic priests left in Burma (Western Brit. India).
1826	U Tha Aye, first Burmese ordained, first pastor of Burmese Baptist Church.
1830	Barnabites turn Burma over to papal jurisdiction.
1841	Apostolic vicar appointed to revive Catholic mission.
1855	Siam, British gain extraterritorial rights from Mongkut.
1856	Burma Baptist schism over Board infringement on missionary independence.
	Paris Foreign Mission Society assigned mandate for Burma mission.
1862	British gain trading rights in Burma.
1862	Catholic statistics in Burma: one bishop; eleven missionaries, one native priest, and six thousand Catholics.
1870	Second Baptist schism.
1877	First Anglican bishop in Burma.
1885	Third Anglo-Burmese War: Upper Burma loses independence to Britain. Burma administered as new province of India until 1897; final separation from India in 1935.
1893	American Baptists statistics in Burma: 139 missionaries, 610 native preachers, 550 churches, 30,000 communicants.
1896	Roman Catholic statistics: 3 apostolic vicars, 62 Western missionaries, 13 native priests, 325 churches or chapels, 49,046 adherents in a population of 9 million.

British Ceylon (1850–1900)

The second half of the nineteenth century should have been a happy ending to three hundred years of missionary effort in Ceylon. The nineteenth was "the great century" of Christian missions worldwide. The government of colonial Ceylon was British and Christian. Prominent Buddhists were turning Christian. The number of missionaries was rising for both Protestants and Catholics, and their schools, particularly the Anglican and Protestant, were becoming the most desirable on the island for upper-caste Sinhalese parents who wished their children to succeed in a world in which Westernization appeared to be the wave of the future. Everything pointed to an upbeat climax to usher in the twentieth century.

But in fact almost the direct opposite proved to be true. Halfway through the old century Christians in Ceylon saw the pendulum begin to swing the other way, and by 1900 Buddhism, which a good many missionaries had prematurely pronounced to be dying,[42] was emerging revitalized and stronger than at any time since the Portuguese occupation. In the next century, the 1900s, the social and religious bedrock choice of the culture would prove to be the old, familiar ways of the Buddhists, not the new Christianity of the missionaries.

THE BUDDHIST-CHRISTIAN DEBATES

A pivotal point in this clash of cultures was the great Panadura debate of 1873. It was also the most polemical, for unfortunately one of the ten rules accepted for the debate was that the Christian speakers should seek to prove Buddhism false, and the Buddhists likewise demonstrate the fallacy of Christian beliefs.[43] There were two major adversaries in this explicitly adversarial event. Representing Christianity was David Wickrametilleke de Silva (1817–1874), a convert from Buddhism with a reputation as a Pali scholar knowledgeable of the original texts of Theravada Buddhism.[44] His counterpart on the Buddhist side was Mohottivatte Gunananda, a militant anti-Christian monk and pamphleteer, whose oratory attracted thousands of hearers, and who used a somewhat limited knowledge of the rise of skeptical rationalism in Europe to impress the largely Buddhist audience with his attack on the credibility of the Christian Scriptures.[45]

Four thousand people, it is said, came to hear the ecclesiastical warriors face each other in the great debate of 1873, and two thousand more came the next day.[46] De Silva, speaking first, attacked a basic element of popular Buddhist teaching: that the human soul by meritorious actions in this life will be rewarded by a higher position in the next life of its reincarnation. But how can that be, he asked? The pure Buddhist teachings of your original texts, he said, say that the human being has no soul, and he proceeded to recite text after text of the Pali Scriptures to prove his point.[47]

Then Gunananda, his Buddhist opponent, rose in his impressive yellow robes. Richard F. Young describes the effect of his reply. He brushed aside the Christian speaker's reference to texts with a sneering intimation that de Silva knew so little about the ancient Pali texts that he could not even spell the words correctly. Then, using language his hearers understood, he deftly evaded the damage done by de Silva's argument that Buddhists deny the continuing existence of the soul because they teach that the soul is annihilated by its absorption into an undifferentiated *nirvana*. Gunananda switched the argument from the classical term for annihilation, a concept which to academic Buddhism was heresy, to urge his hearers to understand the soul as "cleaving to existence" as a continuing personal identity even in reincarnation.[48] The rest of his speech was a superficial broadside attack on the Christian Bible in which he described the Old Testament Jehovah as a bloodthirsty demon-god worshiped by blood sacrifices (a horrible sin in Buddhist eyes). Even worse was his caricature of the New Testament Jesus, as an evil impostor who caused the death of a hundred innocent children in Bethlehem, and "came to the world with the view of casting every one in hell."[49]

Both sides claimed victory in the debate. In hindsight, it is apparent that each side was talking past the other, convincing their own follow-ers about the mistakes of their adversaries by misinterpreting the basic premises of the other's religion. But as a debate the clear winner was probably the Buddhist, the spellbinding orator. His followers, who were in the large majority, were jubilant. They thought that at last the mis-sionaries had met their master, and it was enough for them that the old traditions could still prevail. In a sense, perhaps they were right. Given the momentum of tradition, and an innate resentment against foreign interference, the Buddhist revival of the nineteenth century so strength-ened Buddhist loyalties and cohesiveness that Christianity never again, not even in the next century, came near to challenging Buddhism as the religious foundation of Ceylon's culture.

PROTESTANT MISSIONS

Panadura 1873, however, may not have been as sharp a turning point as it may have seemed. True, it consolidated the country's solid support of Buddhism. But the Methodist Mission, whose missionaries, Ceylonese ministers, and particularly the lay converts who were the most zeal-ous organizers of the Christian/Buddhist debates, continued to grow. In fact, in the next twenty-seven years (1884–1900), Methodist membership (communicant and candidates) leaped by almost 80 percent from 2,069 to 3,169 in South Ceylon where the debates had been held.[50]

The largest of the non-Catholic missions, the Anglicans, had been the least involved in the debates, and in actual impact on Ceylonese soci-ety throughout the British period they remained the most dominant, though smaller in numbers than the Roman Catholics. Benefiting from British government connections and support, and from the high stan-dards of their educational network which was perceived as far superior and more likely to lead to advancement than the increasing number of Buddhist schools, Christian schools had a natural appeal to the educated and professional elite.[51]

Anglican growth remained relatively steady, as figures for their largest mission, the Church Missionary Society (CMS), reveal. In 1848 CMS had 10 missionaries, 3 native clergy, and 3,000 adherents, of whom 300 were communicants, and 3,000 in Christian schools.[52] In 1868 there were 11 missionaries, 7 native clergy, and 2,300 adherents, of whom 550 were communicants, and there were 3,200 in Christian schools.[53] By 1899 there were 57 missionaries, 23 native clergy, and 9,300 adherents, and 16,000 in their schools.[54]

The role of education as a means to win converts in Ceylon should be brought into relief at this point. In 1848, in the opinion of the historian of the Anglican mission who compiled the statistics quoted above, "the best work of the mission was in the schools," which were already then giving Christian education to more than three thousand children. Forty years later, in the northern district of Jaffa, he noted that two-thirds of the converts came from the schools.[55] Yet in 1899 he ended the Ceylon portion of his history on this optimistic note, "Few missions had at the end of fifty years been more scanty in results. Few missions have in thirty subsequent years presented more manifest signs of the working of the grace of God."[56]

But breaks in the pattern of growth — most noticeable from about 1865 to 1875 and again from 1883 to the death of the controversial Gunananda in 1890 — revealed the weakness of one-sided reliance on education apart from credible evangelism.[57] We have already referred to the negative effects of the Buddhist-Christian debates. Less noticeable but also damaging were the misunderstandings within and between the various Christian missions at work on the island.

The Ceylon Controversy of 1873 to 1882 in the Anglican Church in Ceylon is an example of an internal embarrassment.[58] It began as slowly festering friction between the "low-church" Anglican mission in Ceylon, the Church Missionary Society (CMS), and the island's "high-church" Anglican bishops. The CMS had reached Ceylon first, in 1817, before the arrival of resident bishops,[59] and they arrived with a reputation for operating independently from hierarchical control. More important, the CMS was — with the English Methodist mission[60] — one of the two strongest Protestant missions on the island. Nevertheless, in 1816 Ceylon had been placed under the supervision of the far-off bishop of Calcutta and in 1835, of the bishop of Madras. Ten years later Ceylon finally received a sincere "high-church" resident Anglican bishop, who did not look kindly on the independent ways of the "low-church" missionaries of the CMS.[61] The scene was set for conflict.

By the mid-1840s the controversy between the evangelical missionaries and the bishops over the management of the growing churches of the evangelists had become hopelessly entangled with an unexpected problem when 245,000 immigrant laborers were brought from Tamil areas of India in five years[62] for temporary work in the British coffee plantations that spread over thousands of miles in the hills of central Ceylon, formerly the kingdom of Kandy. Slavery had been abolished in Ceylon by the colonial government in 1844, but the new Tamil immigrants were treated almost as slaves. The death rate rose to an estimated 25 percent.[63] The Baptists were the first to mount a mission to them,[64] and the Anglicans a few years later formed what they called "the Tamil Coolie

Mission." Their intentions were good, but progress was obstructed for almost ten years by the controversy over who should be in charge of the operation — the "high-church" side (bishops, chaplains, and the Society for the Propagation of the Gospel), or the "low-church" side represented by the Church Missionary Society.[65]

The embarrassing affair dragged on for years and does no credit to British colonialism, nor to the missionaries, though both in different ways sought to deal with the problem.[66] The issue was resolved to the relief of both sides by a compromise in 1886,[67] partly because the Anglican Church in Ceylon had been disestablished five years earlier in 1881, and after forty-four years of state superintendence and financial support there was less to fight over.[68] Loss of government subsidies was actually more of a spur to greater missionary energy than a disadvantage. A few years later, the once-distrusted Bishop Copleston could smile at past rivalries and name one of his carriage horses "C.M.S." and the other "S.P.G" as he rode contentedly through the streets of Colombo.[69]

More concrete evidence of renewed Anglican vigor was the growth of the Anglican Church. Three years after the disestablishment the CMS reported that 1,700 of the Tamil laborers in the coffee plantations were enrolled as Christians in the mission.[70] In the twenty years from 1868 (the fiftieth year of the Ceylon mission) to 1888, the number of Anglican Ceylonese adherents had almost tripled, from 2,300 (including 550 communicants) to 6,500 (more than 2,000 communicants).[71]

With all the advantages of hindsight, critics of missions in Ceylon have branded the Anglican and Protestant missionaries in this period as too narrowly evangelistic, the bishops as too authoritarian, the coffee planters as too selfishly capitalistic, and the immigrants as too often drunk. There is some truth in every such criticism. But the century for Protestants ended with an upturn in mission relationships and encouraging growth in the churches of the major missions. Faith in salvation by Christ alone had been attacked but upheld. The British Empire was at its peak and the future for Protestantism in Ceylon, though never married to imperialism and often critical, seemed comparatively safe in its presence.

THE ROMAN CATHOLICS

Catholics in Ceylon entered the second half of the century with problems of their own, but also with new life. The first half closed with the vigorous, missionary reforms of a strong-willed, mission-minded pope, Gregory XVI, who ruled in Rome from 1831 to 1846.[72] In the second half of the century, the restoration he brought to Catholic missions worldwide after a devastatingly long drought was particularly effective in Ceylon. His extension of church discipline and missional accountability through apostolic vicariates directly under papal authority revitalized the Ceylonese Catholic missions and churches. In Gregory's fifteen years as pope, he is said to have appointed almost two hundred bishops around the world. His legacy in Ceylon is that three hundred years of Protestant rule, and some fifty years of an unexpected and upsetting Buddhist revival, could not displace the Catholic faith as the most enduring base for a Christian presence on the island, however much it may not have seemed to be dominant in a British colony.

For a while after the critical Christian/Buddhist debates in the 1860s and 1870s, Roman Catholics congratulated themselves that they had not been caught in the abrasive public confrontations that had so damaged hopes of further dialogue between the two parties.[73] They were persuaded that both the Protestants and the Buddhists had been weakened — the Protestants by their use and indiscriminate distribution of the Bible in imperfect Sinhalese, and the Buddhists by the vulnerability of their erroneous interpretations of true Christianity and the narrowness of their antiforeign rhetoric. But the rhetoric of their own Catholic tracts and publications was becoming as heatedly anti-Buddhist and as vulnerable to negative reaction as the language of the Protestant-Buddhist debates.[74]

The Catholic missions had also been weakened by internal friction, most notably by what is called "the Goan schism." Up to just before mid-century, in 1844, almost the only surviving Catholic missionaries were the Goan Oratorians, an order of Indian priests whose heroic sacrifices had saved the church in the seventeenth and eighteenth centuries. But isolation had weakened them emotionally and spiritually.[75] The arrival of new European priests for a reorganization of Catholic mission in Ceylon in 1849 into two distinct apostolic vicariates directly under the authority of the pope, not under the Portuguese archbishop of Goa, was a shock. To the Goan Oratorians it was perceived as a threat to their own proud position as an Asian priesthood for an Asian church.[76] But they had lost their moral credibility. In the half century of isolation from the larger church universal, the Oratorians had let slip the spiritual discipline that comes from connected committed responsibility within a broader world mission. One Catholic historian puts it very bluntly. He writes, "The Goanese Oratorians had clearly reached a state of decadence."[77] As the schism widened, the language grew angrily stronger.[78]

Catholics have survived worse schisms, and this one lasted only about forty years. In Ceylon they had the advantage of longer knowledge of local languages than the Protestants, and greater organizational unity after the reorganization of hierarchy under apostolic vicariates in 1855, 1883, and 1893. A concordat in 1886 decreed that primacy in Ceylon was not with the archbishop of Goa, but with the pope's apostolic vicars in the three vicariates into which Ceylon was then divided: Colombo in the south, Jaffna in the north, and Kandy in the high inland hills.[79]

But two years later, with the internal schism apparently ended,[80] trouble from outside the church fell upon it. An outburst of Buddhist protest exploded in the streets of Colombo. The Buddhists had ostentatiously built a large temple very close to the Catholic cathedral. And who should appear to provoke more trouble but Gunananda, the inflammatory Buddhist orator of the controversial Panadura debates of 1873, ten years earlier. This time he came to embarrass the Catholics, not the Protestants. He organized a Buddhist festival to parade a giant image of the Buddha past the cathedral just as Catholics in that Catholic neighborhood were celebrating Easter Sunday. Angry Catholics responded with violence. It was a volcanic eruption, wilder than any of the earlier Buddhist-Christian confrontations.[81] It was also a reminder that neither Protestant nor Catholic missions, even in a British-ruled colony, could any longer underestimate the depth of the Buddhist foundations of Sinhalese culture. The British colonial government quieted the tumult cautiously. From the beginning of British rule it had recognized the latent power of Ceylon's Buddhist culture and had followed a policy of careful tolerance, even to the extent of financial support of Buddhist schools, much to the displeasure of the missionaries, particularly Protestants who sometimes complained about "yellow-robed Buddhist priests" in prominent positions at government ceremonies.[82]

In Ceylon, the Oblates of Mary Immaculate (commonly called the OMIs) was the most influential and important Catholic order. The Oblates were founded in 1816 in France, and in Ceylon they led a strong renewal movement with a succession of outstanding apostolic vicars. Bishop Semeria in Jaffna (1856 to 1868) symbolized the rise of the Oblates to leadership in Ceylon. His first problem was a shortage of priests. Catholics had more church members, but Protestants had twice the number of missionaries. So on a trip to Europe he brought back the first Catholic women missionaries to Ceylon, six Sisters of the Holy Family.[83] He faced the fact the Catholic laity was uneducated, and began organizing catechetical training for children and adults.[84]

The greatest of the Oblate apostolic vicars in Ceylon, Bishop Christopher Bonjean, succeeded Bishop Semeria in Jaffna in 1868 and went on to become the bishop of the primary vicariate, Colombo, in 1883. Three years later, in another reorganization, he was elevated to head the hierarchy in Ceylon as the first archbishop of Colombo. From the beginning he impressed his peers by his vigorous efforts to increase the number of missionaries, and his insistent emphasis on a fourfold discipline of clergy formation: prayer, moral rectitude, common sense, and a thorough knowledge of the native religions and languages. Finding on arrival in Jaffna that there was only one indigenous Ceylonese diocesan priest, he organized a seminary to train parish priests, but was disappointed to find that the ordinands preferred to join the Oblate community rather than serve as diocesan parish priests. Nevertheless, under his insistent emphasis on piety linked to missionary outreach, the church slowly began to grow again in the north.[85]

More visibly successful was his vision for Catholic education. The breakthrough was the agreement he reached with the British colonial government in 1870 and 1871, which won government support for the financially impoverished, low-grade Catholic school system, allowing them to retain the right to appoint their own teachers and choose their own textbooks as long as they met government standards. The number of Catholic schools doubled in the next twelve years, from 50 to 108.[86]

The death of Archbishop Bonjean in 1892, and the arrival of Jesuit missionaries in Buddhist Kandy (erected as a new vicariate in 1893) marked the end of an era in Catholicism in Ceylon. But the old had laid the foundations for the future of the new. Decades of pleading by the old bishops for more missionaries had been answered and now at last there were almost enough workers for the unfinished task. The Catholic schools were rising fast to match the Anglican and Methodist networks' standards of modern education. There were still more than three times the number of Catholics as Protestants.

Had the century really been a success? Looking back at Ceylon a half century later, one Anglican historian entered a word of caution: "The task of the Church was growing harder: with a reviving nationalist spirit Buddhism was also becoming more militant, and any prestige enjoyed by Christianity as the religion of the country's rulers vanished away."[87]

It is difficult to argue that the nineteenth century was a great century for Christianity in Ceylon. Archbishop Bonjean never was able to see the achievement of his dream of an English seminary for training an indigenous clergy for the dominant Catholic community on the island.[88] The Hindu Tamils in the north and the Buddhist Ceylonese in the south did just that: build English schools to upgrade the educational level of their future leaders in a Westernizing world. A network of Hindu schools teaching in Tamil sparked a Hindu revival resulting in 1872 in the formation of what soon became Jaffna Hindu College, teaching in English in competition with similar Protestant, Catholic, and Buddhist educational rivals.[89] The Buddhists, strengthened by their far larger revival and rejoicing over the much-publicized conversion to Buddhism of two visitors from America — the theosophists Colonel Henry Steel Olcott (1832–1907), and Russia-born Madame Helena Blavatsky (1831–1891) — turned to Olcott to energize a reconstruction of their much-neglected school system. Olcott survived considerable controversy and has been credited with a major role in founding 3 colleges and 250 schools for the Ceylonese Buddhists to challenge the generally acknowledged superiority of the Christian schools.[90] The best-known Buddhist seminary was Ananda College.[91]

A glance at the statistics compiled by Barrett et al. in the table below is a rough measure of the relative strength of the religions of Ceylon in 1900, and offers a look ahead at what the next hundred years would bring.[92]

	1900	2000
Total Population	3,573,400	18,827,000
Buddhists	2,114,651 (59.2%)	12,878,763 (68.4%)
Hindus	828,000 (23.2%)	2,124,481 (11.3%)
Total Christians	378,859 (10.6%)	1,755,120 (9.3%)
Roman Catholics	295,859 (8.3%)	1,260,000 (6.7%)
Protestants (PIA)	83,000 (2.4%)	488,000 (2.6%)
Muslims	245,000 (6.9%)	1,694,603 (9.0%)

NOTES

1. Maung Shwe Wa, *Burma Baptist Chronicle*, 172–173, citing C. H. Carpenter, *Self-Support in Bassein* (Boston: Franklin Press, 1883), 242.

2. D. Kanagasabai Wilson, writing about the situation in Ceylon about 1900 in *The Christian Church in Sri Lanka: Her Problems and Her Influence* (Colombo: Study Centre for Religion and Society, 1975), 105.

3. The First Burmese War (1824–1826) took southwest and southeast Burma into the empire; the Second Burmese War (1852–1853) added south central Burma; and the Third Burmese War (1885) completed the incorporation of Burma into the British Empire.

4. Some early twentieth-century short histories of Burma include Stuart, *Burma through the Centuries*, 134ff., which contains the short descriptions quoted; and Sir George Scott, *Burma: A Handbook of Practical Commercial and Political Information* (London: Alexander Moring, 1906), 195ff.

5. See the statistics in Maung Shwe Wa, *Burma Baptist Chronicle*, 135.

6. Maung Shwe Wa, *Burma Baptist Chronicle*, 105ff., 143–166.

7. Maung Shwe Wa, *Burma Baptist Chronicle*, 144–149.

8. "Burmese" and "Burman" are often used interchangeably, but to avoid confusion I will use "Burmese" in the national sense as indicating all who are of Burmese citizenship, whether of the minority tribes or the Burman majority; and "Burman" in the ethnic sense as indicating nontribal Burmese of the ruling racial group. The Burman majority has for centuries been almost monolithically Buddhist; the tribal minorities were basically animist.

9. Maung Shwe Wa, *Burma Baptist Chronicle*, 144–149, citing *1853 Convention*, 49–51. Present at the convention were twenty missionaries and their wives, six Burmese assistants, one visiting missionary from Hong Kong, and two representatives sent by the home board, the American Baptist Missionary Union.

10. On Saw Quala see Francis Mason, "Saw Quala: The Second Karen Convert," serialized in *Baptist Missionary Magazine* 26 (1856): 1–5, 33–36, 65–70, 97–105, 127–135, 161–169, 262–266, 359–366, 385–390, 417–427, 449–456. The nominal prefix *Saw* (or *Sau*) means "young man"; *Ko* means "older brother," and *Thra* means "leader." On Ko Tha Byu see chap. 15 above, and Mason, *The Karen Apostle*.

11. Mason, "Saw Quala," 1–2, 4–5, 163.

12. Maung Shwe Wa, *Burma Baptist Chronicle*, 186ff.

13. Quoted by Mason, "Saw Quala," 187.

14. Francis Mason, "Letter," November 1857, in *Baptist Missionary Magazine* 38 (1858): 129–134, quotation p. 133.

15. Mason, "Letter," November 1857, 133–134.

16. See chap. 15.

17. Edward Norman Harris, *A Star in the East: An Account of American Baptist Missions to the Karens of Burma* (New York: Fleming H. Revell, 1920), 63–67; Maung Shwe Wa, *Burma Baptist Chronicle*, 124–216.

18. Despite general agreement on the primacy and methods of evangelism at the 1853 Convention, and considerable agreement on education in mission schools, differences surfaced on two points: whether to teach English in the schools, and the problem of remote control of the mission by the Home Board in America. Maung Shwe Wa, *Burma Baptist Chronicle*, 144–152.

19. I have lost the source of this vivid, debatable comparison, which reflects the exasperation of the British at tiny Burma's resistance through three Anglo-Burmese wars. Cf. Charles James Forbes Smith-Forbes, *British Burma and Its People* (London: John Murray, 1878), vi, 42ff.; Phayre, *History of Burma*, 5ff., 22.

20. On the Kachin tribes, their history and their religion, see Tegenfeldt, *A Century of Growth*, 1–54. Kachins call themselves *Jinghpaw*. See also Maung Shwe Wa, *Burma Baptist Chronicle*, 367ff.

21. Francis Kingdon Ward, *In Farthest Burma* (Philadelphia: Lippincott, 1921), 245, 248; and C. M. Enriquez, *A Burmese Arcady* (London: Seeley, Service, 1923), 93. For a more careful analysis of their religion see Tegenfeldt, *A Century of Growth*, 44–53.

22. This is the term popularized by Donald A. McGavran in his many writings to focus on the significance of the family and ethnic connections within each movement rather than on the numbers alone. See notably *The Bridges to God*.

23. Cushing and the Karen missionaries reached Bhamo in 1877; not until 1893 did the British have orderly control of the Kachin hills. See G. Scott, *Burma: A Handbook*, 206; and Tegenfeldt, *A Century of Growth*, 95.

24. Even before the American Baptists, French Roman Catholics had been in Bhamo since 1872 (see below); and the first Protestant missionaries, nonresidential, had been John W. Stevenson and Henry Soltau of the China Inland Mission in 1875. Tegenfeldt, *A Century of Growth*, 95, 313.

25. Randolph L. Howard, *Baptists in Burma* (Philadelphia: Judson Press, 1931), 80.

26. Howard, *Baptists in Burma*, 80–81, citing S'Peh's letter of January 11, 1878.

27. The Shan tribes in Burma's eastern bulge were ethnically Siamese (Thai), spilling over the border into Burma.

28. Tegenfeldt, *A Century of Growth*, 88–97, 113; Maung Shwe Wa, *Burma Baptist Chronicle*, 368ff.

29. Maung Shwe Wa, *Burma Baptist Chronicle*, 149–150.

30. The pioneer for schools for Burman girls was Susan Haswell, in Moulmein about the year 1850 (Howard, *Baptists in Burma*, 182ff.).

31. Howard, *Baptists in Burma*, 96.

32. Ellen B. Mason [Mrs. Francis Mason], *Tounghoo Women*, 2nd ed. (New York: Anson D. F. Randolph, 1860), iiif.

33. Mason, *Tounghoo Women*, 20. The Talaing are related to the Mon/Khmer (Cambodian) rulers of the Irrawaddy delta before the Burman conquest in the sixth century A.D.

34. Maung Shwe Wa, *Burma Baptist Chronicle*. Mrs. Mason fell ill in 1863, and led in some confusion the schism of 1870.

35. G. Cassock in Delacroix, *Histoire universelle des missions catholiques*, 3:488. The earlier orders were Franciscans (sixteenth century), Dominicans, Franciscans and Jesuits (sixteenth, seventeenth centuries), and Italian Barnabites (after 1721). By the second Anglo-Burmese War (1852) there were not more than five or six thousand Catholics in Burma. See Schmidlin, *Catholic Mission History*, 488; and Latourette, *A History of the Expansion of Christianity*, 6:225–227.

36. Latourette, *A History of the Expansion of Christianity*, 6:226–227. The mission was turned over by the Barnabites to the pope in 1830, and an apostolic vicar, Frederico Cao, came with two priests to revive the mission, which in 1841 reported 4,500 Catholics, widely scattered and still dwindling.

37. Louvet, *Les missions catholiques au XIXme siècle*, 160.

38. Cassock in Delacroix, *Histoire universelle des missions catholiques*, 3:32–33. Cf. Schmidlin, *Catholic Mission History*, 603–604.

39. Louvet, *Les missions catholiques au XIXme siècle*, 152.

40. Barrett, ed., *World Christian Encyclopedia*, 1982, 202.

41. Barrett, ed., *World Christian Encyclopedia*, 1982, 518. But compare Louvet's statistic for Burma in 1896 noted above as 49,200 Catholics.

42. The English Methodist Joseph Rippon, retiring to England in 1860 after ten years of debate with Buddhist leaders, told his hearers, "Buddhism is very strong but we have got it down. It is cowed" (Small, *A History of the Methodist Church in Ceylon*, 157).

43. Small, *History of the Methodist Church in Ceylon*, 574.

44. De Silva, after his conversion, became an ordained Methodist minister and assistant to Daniel Gogerly (1792–1862) who, to his credit, had in earlier debates discovered that if the missionaries were to criticize Buddhism they must first understand it. Gogerly had collected from many sources a treasured complete set of the original texts of the Theravada Buddhist *tipitaka*. It took the Buddhist scholars by complete surprise when the Christians began to use their own Hindu Scriptures against them to compare what the missionaries were quick to describe as corrupted contemporary Buddhist practice with the "pure" Buddhism of the ancient texts (see Young and Somaratna, *Vain Debates*, 44–45, 81–82).

45. For greater detail on Gunananda's background see Young and Somaratna, *Vain Debates*, 127–141.

46. Young and Somaratna, *Vain Debates*, 155–180, devotes a whole chapter to this debate, "Orators, Spectators, and Sherbet Vendors," from which I only venture to select some portions to summarize below.

47. Young and Somaratna, *Vain Debates*, 163; Small, *History of the Methodist Church in Ceylon*, 221.

48. On this closely reasoned argument, see Young and Somaratna, *Vain Debates*, 163–164.

49. See Young and Somaratna, *Vain Debates*, 165–168.

50. Small, *A History of the Methodist Church in Ceylon*, statistics, 662.

51. N. Abeyasingha, *The Radical Tradition: The Changing Shape of Theological Reflection in Sri Lanka* (Colombo: The Ecumenical Institute, 1985), 44–46, 52.

52. Stock, *History of the Church Missionary Society*, 2:280.

53. Stock, *History of the Church Missionary Society*, 3:297.

54. Stock, *History of the Church Missionary Society*, 4:258–261.

55. Stock, *History of the Church Missionary Society*, 2:280; 3:538–539.

56. Stock, *History of the Church Missionary Society,* 3:547.

57. Young and Somaratna, *Vain Debates,* 89, 115ff., 181ff., 215ff.; Abeyasingha, *The Radical Tradition,* 44–50.

58. See Stock, *History of the Church Missionary Society,* 3:201–216; Gibbs, *The Anglican Church in India,* 261–277; and Chatterton, *History of the Church of England in India,* 221–231.

59. The succession of Anglican bishops of Colombo in this period was: James Chapman (1845–1861), Piers C. Claughton (1862–1871), Hugh W. Jermyn (1871–1875), Reginald Stephen Copleston (1875–1902). See Gibbs, *The Anglican Church in India,* 413.

60. K. M. De Silva, *Social Policy and Missionary Organizations in Ceylon 1840–1855* (London: Longmans, for the Royal Commonwealth Society, 1965), 27.

61. Before the arrival of the first CMS missionaries in 1817/1818, the Anglican Church was represented not by a mission but by chaplains appointed by the government to serve the British community. See above chap. 16, and Tennent, *Christianity in Ceylon,* 79–80; Chatterton, *History of the Church in India,* 127–128; Latourette, *A History of the Expansion of Christianity,* 6:221. In 1865 the principle of "consensual compact" was adopted to emancipate the missions and churches in "self-governing colonies" from control in ecclesiastical matters by the crown through colonial governments, but it specifically excluded India and Ceylon as "unlikely to become self-governing colonies" (Gibbs, *The Anglican Church in India,* 155–156, 261).

62. Stock, *History of the Church Missionary Society,* 2:286–288, K. M. De Silva, *Social Policy and Missionary Organizations in Ceylon,* 235–269.

63. K. M. De Silva, *Social Policy and Missionary Organizations in Ceylon,* 235–269, 271–281, 299–300; Wilson, *The Christian Church in Sri Lanka,* 94–99. De Silva is highly critical of the inadequate missionary response to the problem; Wilson, a Methodist, is more appreciative of the long-term effectiveness of missionary pressures for justice. He quotes a phrase acknowledging the powerful influence of the Christian schools: "open a school and close a jail," adding that, "The work of the Mission schools was indeed the permanent foundation of the structure of the Tamil community that emerged slowly to freedom" (105). On "the rise and fall of coffee" in what was then Ceylon, see C. R. de Silva, *A History of Sri Lanka,* 160–164.

64. K. M. De Silva, *Social Policy and Missionary Organizations in Ceylon,* 270–273; cf. Wilson, *The Christian Church in Sri Lanka,* 99–105.

65. In essence the compromise was reached in 1882, but final negotiations continued. Stock, *History of the Church Missionary Society,* 3:198–216, 541–542; Gibbs, *The Anglican Church in India,* 261–277; and K. M. De Silva, *Social Policy and Missionary Organizations in Ceylon,* 270–281.

66. On the Ceylon colonial government's policy toward the Tamil immigrants, see De Silva, *Social Policy and Missionary Organizations in Ceylon,* 235–269. On the English Baptists who were the first missionaries to respond, see 270–273; and on the Anglicans, 273–281. Cf. the more sympathetic description of the response of the missionaries in Gibbs, *The Anglican Church in India,* 262–277; Stock, *History of the Church Missionary Society,* 3:201–277; and H. P. Thompson, *Into All Lands: The History of the Society for the Propagation of the Gospel in Foreign Parts 1701–1950* (London: SPCK, 1951), 192ff., 379ff., 636. Unfortunately for the SPG, Bishop Copleston directed that all his correspondence be destroyed upon his death.

67. In essence the compromise was reached in 1882, but final negotiations dragged on for four more years. Stock, *History of the Church Missionary Society*, 3:198–216, 541–652; Gibbs, *The Anglican Church in India*, 261–277; K. M. De Silva, *Social Policy and Missionary Organizations in Ceylon*, 270–281. De Silva is highly critical of the missionaries' inadequate response to Ceylon's "greatest social problem of the day" (287). Stock and Gibbs are more sympathetic to the missionaries.

68. It was English evangelicals who had earlier, in 1837, encouraged a major policy shift in the British government of Ceylon, a change from nominal establishment of the Anglican Church to active support of Anglican missionary work, which was publicly endorsed by an important statement from Governor Mackenzie, the secretary of state for the colonies (see C. R. de Silva, *Sri Lanka: A History*, 176–177).

69. Gibbs, *The Anglican Church in India*, 277.

70. *A Handbook of Foreign Missions*, 87.

71. Stock, *History of the Church Missionary Society*, 3:538–539.

72. On Gregory XVI and missions see chap. 8 above and note 63, p. 191, citing Claudia Carlen, ed., *The Papal Encyclicals*, 1:235–271.

73. The European Catholic missionaries did not have the language to take part in the debates (Boudens, *Catholic Missionaries in a British Colony*, 72; but cf. 75).

74. Young and Somaratna, *Vain Debates*, 180ff., 183, n. 402.

75. See above chap. 10.

76. The two vicariates were created in 1847 but were not implemented in Ceylon until 1849. See Boudens, *Catholic Missionaries in a British Colony*, 46–50, 59–65, 165.

77. Boudens, *Catholic Missionaries in a British Colony*, 58, comparing the Oratorians of the 1840s with their heroism in the 1600s and 1700s.

78. Boudens, *Catholic Missionaries in a British Colony*, 66.

79. See the useful line maps of the vicariates in Boudens, *Catholic Missionaries in a British Colony*, 174; and 146–149. An exception to the granting of authority in the three Ceylon vicariates to the apostolic vicars was the temporary right given to the displaced Portuguese archbishop of Goa to retain a symbolic continuing presence in a few very small areas.

80. The heritage of ill-will engendered by the Goan schism lingered for decades, and was actually not finally healed until about 1940, half a century later (Boudens, *Catholic Missionaries in a British Colony*, 59).

81. Boudens, *Catholic Missionaries in a British Colony*, 138; Young and Somaratna, *Vain Debates*, 188–197.

82. Stock, *History of the Christian Missionary Society*, 3:543. On the connection of the colonial government with Buddhism, see C. R. de Silva, *Sri Lanka: A History*, 177–180.

83. Boudens, *Catholic Missionaries in a British Colony*, 79–80, 89.

84. Boudens, *Catholic Missionaries in a British Colony*, 83.

85. Boudens, *Catholic Missionaries in a British Colony*, 111–116. The one secular priest then in the north was known by his baptismal name of Francis Xavier. He had been ordained in 1857. The first native Ceylonese graduate of the seminary Bonjean founded in Jaffna in 1871 to reach ordination to the priesthood was Saverimuttu Sandrasaga in 1876.

86. See Boudens, *Catholic Missionaries in a British Colony*, 116–117.

87. H. P. Thompson, *Into All Lands,* 636.

88. Boudens, *Catholic Missionaraies in a British Colony,* 140–143.

89. C. R. de Silva, *Sri Lanka: A History,* 180–183. By 1900 the percentage of Tamils in Ceylon (Sri Lanka), largely in the north, was approaching a quarter of the population of the country (3).

90. On Olcott, Blavatsky, and the "vague gnosticism" of their Theosophy in Ceylon, see Young and Somaratna, *Vain Debates,* 198–222. Among the controversies that arose was an angry rivalry that developed between Olcott and Gunananda, the charismatic defender of Buddhism in the Panadura debate. See also Boudens, *Catholic Missionaries in a British Colony,* 150–151; and *Encyclopaedia Britannica: Micropedia,* vol. 8, "Olcott."

91. *CE,* s.v. "Ceylon." The three primary seminaries were then St. Thomas College (Anglican), St. Joseph (Catholic), and Ananda College (Buddhist). But Jaffna College (Methodist) in the north, though not strictly speaking a seminary, should be added. It is said to have been, at its beginnings in 1834, the first school in oriental Asia to introduce modern Western education in English, and trained many of the early Methodist Ceylonese clergy (Small, *History of the Methodist Church in Ceylon,* 215–216, 319).

92. Barrett et al., eds., *World Christian Encyclopedia,* 2001, 695. The figures for the religions are total adherents, but for subtitled denominations they represent a tighter definition, "affiliates" (enrolled members). The category of "Protestant" includes Anglican, Protestant, and Independent, but excludes "marginal."

Chapter 27

Siam, Malaysia, and Vietnam (1860–1900)

Siam has not been disciplined by English or French guns, like China, but the country has been opened by missionaries.
— Ex-Regent Chao Phya Srisuriyawongse (ca. 1875)[1]

As I now look back...it is plain to me that the great lack of the mission all the way through has been the lack of well-trained helpers; and for this lack the mission is largely to blame. Those who are eager to accomplish the evangelization of the world within the present generation, should first of all lay hold of the present generation of Christians in every mission field. Fill these with enthusiasm...and we have a lever that will lift the world.
— Daniel McGilvary, 1912[2]

The sword had little to do with the spread of Islam [in South East Asia], nor did Arabs. Moslem traders and teachers came chiefly from southern India seeking profit...They had a new and strange learning; they claimed to heal sickness...and they married the daughters of communal chiefs.
— Kenneth P. Landon[3]

Siam (Thailand), Land of the Free

KINGS, MISSIONARIES, AND BUDDHISTS

In 1860 the king of Siam was Mongkut (who reigned from 1851 to 1868), the fourth ruler of the Chakri dynasty.[4] To most Western minds he is unforgettably known as the king in the musical, *The King and I*, but to historians he is Rama IV, "one of the great Asians of the nineteenth century,"[5] the reformer who opened up Siam to modernization[6] and the father of an even greater reformer, Chulalongkorn, Rama V (1868–1910). Chulalongkorn was Mongkut's ninth son but the first of the royal sons born of a royal queen. He was the greatest in a dynasty of poets and rulers who fought off Burma for a hundred years and was about to confront France and out-negotiate the British empire.[7] His dynasty still rules Thailand.

Siam in the 1860s was entering the period that would change its name to Thailand, meaning "the land of the free," for in its own language "Thai" means "free." The name change marks not a change from colony to independence, for Siam was never a colony, but rather an internal political transition from absolute Buddhist monarchy to a constitutionally democratic monarchy, a process that was finally completed in 1932.[8]

The immense popularity of *The King and I* has obscured the fact that the first tutors of nineteenth-century Siamese royalty were Protestant missionaries, not Anna Leonowens. While Mongkut was still "priest-prince" in the 1840s, he asked Jesse Casell, a Presbyterian in the Congregational Mission (ABCFM), to come into his temple grounds and teach him Western learning. Others, like Dr. Dan Bradley, a medical missionary, followed. Mongkut was "the first Asian monarch to understand, read, and write English."[9] A few years later when he became king he asked the three missions then in Siam (ABCFM, Baptist, and Presbyterian) to arrange for the missionary women to take turns every day except Sunday and holidays teaching the women of the court — thirty concubines, and the unmarried sisters of the king, and several nieces and court ladies.[10] Missionary influence in the highest circles of the Siamese court was a not insignificant factor in the nineteenth-century modernization of Siam.

After a few years the practice lapsed, but in the 1860s Mongkut revived it with a significant change of focus. Instead of part-time missionary teachers for the court women, he sent for a full-time governess to enlighten his considerable number of offspring in the palace, fifty-seven in all, including the all-important heir to the throne, Chulalongkorn. Mrs. Anna Leonowens arrived from Singapore in 1862. She came to a country where the cowrie shells which were still the legal currency were just being replaced with flat metal coins.[11] She was not a missionary. In fact her contract forbade her to teach the Christian religion. The missionaries highly respected her, though privately they wished she would appear more frequently at Sunday church services.[12]

It is not apparent what influence if any Mrs. Leonowens may actually have had in the remarkable reforms of King Mongkut and her one-time pupil, Chulalongkorn, who became king in 1868, the year after she left, and who reigned for the next forty highly critical years of the modernizing of Siam (1868–1910).[13] She claimed no credit for the reforms, but it is true that she did teach her royal pupils passages from the Bible, like the Sermon on the Mount, and that she found an interested audience among her charges for *Uncle Tom's Cabin*.[14] It is also true that she mentions the reforms with great satisfaction in her writings. She was proud that her one-time pupil, the new king, spoke out bravely against slavery, and that he soon freed his own personal slaves, saying, "I see no hope for our country until she is freed from the dark blot of slavery."[15]

Mrs. Leonowens also credited Chulalongkorn with edicts of religious toleration in 1870 and 1872, which is partly true. He risked the enmity of powerful forces by his personal advocacy of freedom of religion for the sincere followers of any faith, not an easy act for a very young king who bore the title Protector of the Buddhist Faith. But the first edict of toleration was actually issued by his then equally reform-minded regent,[16] and the second, in 1878, though quoting a royal letter, was written and proclaimed by Chulalongkorn's High Commissioner at the court of the autocratic, antimissionary vassal, the prince of Chiengmai.[17]

SLOW BEGINNINGS OF PROTESTANT MISSIONS

Not even a fair amount of Siamese tolerance made the propagation of the Christian faith easy in that thoroughly Buddhist land. After fifteen years without visible results, the pioneering American Board of Commissioners for Foreign Mission (largely Congregational) transferred its attention and missionary personnel to China in 1849.[18] The American Baptists, who had sent the first resident Protestant missionaries to the country in 1833, suspended mission to Siamese nationals after thirty-six years in order to concentrate on work with the ethnic Chinese in Siam.[19]

It was the Presbyterians who, though not the first in Siam, persevered. They had labored there for eighteen years with few volunteers and little success, but in 1858, though still without a single Siamese convert of their own, they formed a presbytery composed of their four ordained missionaries, all of them Americans. They named it the Presbytery of Siam.[20] So few Thai had been converted up to that time that when Nai Chune, a teacher in the school the missionaries had organized, applied for Christian baptism they found it difficult to believe that he was sincere and kept postponing the baptism for weeks. Only when the young man's constant persistence finally persuaded them that, in their words, "the miracle of converting grace had actually been wrought even in a Siamese" did they baptize him the next year.[21]

One missionary historian marks the year 1860 as the end of the "Pioneer Period" and the beginning of the "Period of Expansion."[22] Leading the modest expansion were the American Presbyterians, for after 1860 the other major Protestant missions, including a short-lived new one, an independent mission named the American Missionary Association,[23] all suffered sharp declines, as we have noted above. Even the Presbyterians were far from optimistic about their prospects, as their hesitancy to baptize Nai Chune revealed. For twenty years their history had been mainly the story of the labors of just three people, the Rev. and Mrs. Stephen Mattoon and Dr. S. R. House. But in 1860, the arrival of eight new enthusiastic young missionary recruits almost quadrupled the size of their mission and revived their spirits. Suddenly they numbered eleven and were emboldened to plan bravely for future expansion.[24]

Expansion, however, was not to be the future of Protestantism in Siam. Forty years later, in 1900, as the century ended, the total Protestant community in Siam numbered only 5,000 adherents; there were six times as many Roman Catholics; and the total Christian community was only six-tenths of 1 percent of the population.[25] Especially in the south was the progress slow. Even after the proclamation of religious toleration in 1870, the Presbyterians could report only 18 church members in Bangkok, and 20 in Petchaburi to the south on the Gulf of Siam.[26] In 1878

McFarland organized the first country church south of Bangkok where the Petchaburi River enters the Gulf of Siam (Thailand).[27] There were no legal infringements on evangelism, but the response was extremely slow. Communicant members in southern Siam rose from 15 in 1867, to 38 in 1872, and still only 148 in 1882.[28]

Western medicine and Western education became in practice, if not in theory, the most effective way of breaking down the barriers of religious differences into the hearts of the Siamese people. At times it seemed that Christian medical practice would finally open the door for evangelism. The first Protestant missionary in Siam had been a doctor, the indefatigable Karl Gützlaff, who was a doctor of medicine though he does not seem to have practiced medicine and is far better known as an evangelist and linguist in China than for his few months in Siam in 1828–1831.[29] The real medical pioneer, however, was Dan Beach Bradley, M.D., whose thirty-eight years of labor in Siam (1835–1873) laid enduring foundations not only for medical work, but for Protestant evangelism, Bible translation, and printing as well. Within days of his landing, he opened the first medical dispensary. In 1840 he was the first to introduce vaccination to Siam, using virus carried by a sailing ship which took nine months to reach Bangkok from America.[30]

The first mission hospital opened in Petchaburi about 1882, and was greatly expanded through the generosity of the king himself. About 1884 a breakthrough into national influence and recognition seemed to be imminent. The first government hospital to practice modern medicine was organized to treat soldiers in the Siamese army and high officials. To serve as its head, the king turned to Dr. Tien Hee (later called Phya Sarasin), a graduate of the Presbyterian mission boarding school who had completed medical training at New York University.[31] But the result in terms of the expansion of Christianity was minimal. The most effective medical missionary advances were in the north, as we shall see later.

A second hope for evangelistic outreach into the culture was centered in the development of a network of Christian schools. In 1852 the Presbyterian mission opened its first school, a day school for boys. In Siam only boys were formally educated, and training was Buddhist. But this school was most unusual in that its founder and head was not only not Buddhist, but was not even a man. An unusual woman indeed was Mrs. Stephen Mattoon, "always trying to make a better world for poor people" as the Siamese described her. She opened her little school for boys in a Peguan village near Bangkok on September 13, 1852.[32] It was the first in a long line of mission schools which began to make significant changes in the country's models for education. That same month, in Bangkok, a school for Chinese students was started in 1853 by a Chinese assistant of the mission, and "the first outstanding Protestant convert in Siam," Sinsaa Ki-eng Qua-Sean (d. 1859),[33] which later, changing its teaching language from Chinese to Thai, evolved into what is called Bangkok Christian College; ten schools also emerged in the region around Petchaburi, south of Bangkok (1865–1885), not to mention schools in Northern Siam which are noted later. By mid-1885 in southern Siam the mission reported two boarding schools for boys and two for girls, and eight day schools for both sexes. The boys' school in Bangkok reported "little religious interest" among the boys, but six conversions among the girls in the Bangkok school. Pupils in the schools farther south around Petchaburi, where there was a considerable community of Laos refugees from the north, were much more responsive to a Christian witness. In northern Siam, entered more recently, there was a small girls' school, and no school as yet for boys.[34]

Another near breakthrough into the national mind of Siam, after the acceptance of the medical breakthrough, came out of these small beginnings of Christian education. In 1878, in a land where education was traditionally almost entirely in the hands of Buddhist priests in Buddhist temples,[35] the Buddhist king, Chulalongkorn, made a surprising appointment. He asked a member of the Presbyterian mission, Samuel G. McFarland (1830–1897), to be the first head of the royal college which he intended to found, and superintendent of public education in Bangkok. The king's school was to be the first college-grade school in Siam. McFarland accepted the challenge as an unequalled and probably never to be repeated opening for shaping the minds of the future leaders of the country, but it was difficult to leave his boys' school in Petchaburi, and the little new church he had started on the Petchaburi River — the first country church in southern Siam. No restrictions were placed on his freedom for personal Christian witness, but he fretted lest the ten years he would spend in administration at the Royal College might be taking him from his "higher duties" as a missionary.[36]

Despite apparent breakthroughs in medicine and education, and despite the favorable treatment the mission received in high government circles, the church, which was the primary object of all the missionaries' endeavors, did not grow. Why? Statistics tell the story. In 1900 the two Presbyterian missions (South Siam and Northern Siam, or Laos) reported twenty-nine schools but only twenty-four small churches in the whole country.[37] There is no simple answer for the decline, but part of the problem was the strength that a national religion brings to the shaping of a national identity. And once accepted, any threat to that religion threatens the nation. In Buddhist Siam, the implicit threat was Christianity.

BUDDHIST REACTION

The overpowering presence of Buddhism, symbiotically intertwined with the strong national culture it had helped to create, was an almost impermeable wall against the penetration of other religions from foreign cultures. Like Islam in the Middle East, so was Buddhism in Southeast Asia — Burma, Ceylon, and Siam. King Mongkut, who radically shaped the modernization of Siamese national culture, called himself "the Luther of Buddhism," justifiably proud of his role in reformation of the country's state religion.[38] An example is related by a missionary from a later generation. He asked a young Siamese, "Are you a Christian?" "No," he replied, "I am a Thai."[39] It was as simple as that. Siam is Buddhist; I am Siamese, so I am not a Christian; I am a Buddhist.

In general, the nineteenth-century Protestant mission encounter with Siam took on the form of attack, not accommodation, though it was rarely as belligerent as the word "attack" suggests. Debate was usually friendly but unbending; differences were not denied but affirmed, and the missionaries were unshakably sure with a confidence and a rhetoric that must have seemed arrogant to people of other faiths that the only true way of salvation was through Jesus Christ alone. The call to missionary service in the nineteenth century was a clear and consistent challenge to carry the light of the gospel to lands, like Siam, "buried in the deepest shadows of heathenish night," to quote an early medical pioneer in Bangkok, Samuel R. House (1817–1898). House was a gentle but sometimes quick-tempered man with the heart of an evangelist, who hated to see suffering and pain and was widely loved for saving hundreds of lives in a cholera epidemic that killed more than thirty-five thousand. He almost contracted cholera himself. He also performed what may have been the first surgical operation under ether anesthesia in all of Asia.[40] To him, and to most missionaries of that period, saving the souls of the Siamese was even more important than saving their lives, but they were willing to risk their own lives to do both.

THE PROTESTANT PRINCIPLE,
THE BIBLE AS THE WORD OF GOD

Another possible reason also for the slow growth may well have been a failure in the Siam mission of sustained attention to Bible translation and distribution. Translating the Bible into the national languages and tribal dialects of all the world's bewildering variety of tongues has always been a highly significant distinguishing difference between imperial colonialist and Protestant missionary expansion from the West around the world.[41] Until recently it has also been a significant mark of contrasting priorities in Roman Catholic and Protestant mission policy. With Protestants, access to the Bible through translations was a supreme practical priority. For Roman Catholics, the first priority was to establish the church. Yet in Siam, it took the Protestants almost a hundred years to publish a complete Bible in the Thai language.

Not that they failed to approach the task, they just did not finish it. Karl Gützlaff, who entered Siam as the first Protestant missionary in 1828, made a rough translation of the whole Bible into Siamese by 1830. It was too imperfect to publish.[42] But using Gützlaff's preliminary attempt, later missionaries used a mission press sent by the American Board of Commissioners for Foreign Missionaries to print and distribute Scripture portions,[43] first in Siamese, then later (after 1891) in Lao (northern Thai) which though closely related linguistically to Siamese used completely different written characters.[44] Incidentally, it was the missionary printing of the Bible portions that first made writing more readable for the Thai themselves by separating the printed words instead of running them all together without spacing.[45] But the complete Siamese New Testament was not published until 1844, and the complete Bible not until as late as 1893,[46] sixty-six years after Gützlaff's first trial translations.

Nevertheless, though Protestants in Siam lagged in Bible translation and church growth, there were signs here and there of encouragement for the struggling mission. Among them was a growing appreciation of the indispensable role of women in missions.

WOMEN'S WORK FOR WOMEN

By 1900, as we have observed, more than half of the Protestants in world-wide foreign mission were women.[47] But for the first forty years of the Presbyterian mission in Siam, except for their unexpected welcome into the forbidden women's quarters of the royal court, recognition of their contribution to the work of the mission had been somewhat muted. It was a cultural weakness of the nineteenth-century Christian West to grant full missionary status only to men. But change was in the wind. The gentle doctor, Samuel House, sent his wife home alone on health leave in 1871. She recovered quickly and began to speak so fervently to the women in American churches on the plight of women in Siam that her husband wrote, "Don't step out of your sphere into the pulpit. If you unsex yourself I am not sure you will be welcomed back as warmly."[48] Undeterred, the missionary wives began to make friendships in high Siamese social circles, and won for themselves increasing freedom of action for a missionary approach to women at the other end of the social scale. Mrs. McFarland at Petchaburi, south of Bangkok, had already in 1865 begun to invite girls from less fortunate homes to come to the missionary women for informal education, limited largely to vocational training, in the hope that the girls, by learning how to earn a little money, could improve their status in family relationships. So successful was the experiment that Patchaburi, which means "diamond city," became known as "the sewing machine town."[49]

When Mrs. Samuel House returned to Siam after her health leave, she did much the same in Bangkok. The missionary women, encouraged by the eager response of their Siamese pupils, decided to enlarge the scope of their teaching from vocational to general education. In 1874 they turned the training sessions into the country's first girls' boarding school, the Wang Lang School.[50] Its early years were precarious, but an unusual event in 1888 suddenly catapulted the little girls' school into the center of national recognition. A royal prince, H.R.H. Prince Naradhip Prabandhu Bongs, startled the mission by asking to enroll his eldest daughter, Princess Barnbimbal, in the Christian school, opening the doors of that one-time school for vocational training to the highest of the elite to study beside girls of the lower classes for a first-class education, and all students, both high and low, were required to share in the daily housework — sweeping, washing dishes, making their own clothing — much to the shock of highborn parents, who nevertheless usually accepted it for their children as the price of keeping them in this strange, but prestigious Christian school. Daily Bible study was a part of the curriculum. Graduates of Wang Lang became much in demand as teachers throughout the country. Later the school was moved to a larger campus and was renamed Wattana Wittaya Academy, raising its curriculum to secondary (high school) level.[51]

To the women of the mission Siam thus owes the first Christian approach to the secluded women's quarters of the upper classes (*zenana* mission, as it was termed in India), as well as its first school for girls. It may even have been the first example of *zenana* mission not only in Siam but in all Asia, as Dr. House claimed in 1888.[52]

EXPANSION INTO NORTHERN SIAM

As it turned out, however, the fruitful edge of mission and church expansion was to be not in the south, in Bangkok and its presbytery of foreign missionaries, but in the north led by the decision of two missionary couples to break away from the capital area and head for the frontier among the unreached Lao tribes. One of the couples was delayed by illness, but in 1867, the Rev. Daniel McGilvary and his wife Sophia, the daughter of the veteran Dr. Dan Bradley, set off on the long, hot trip five hundred miles up the Menam River from Bangkok to Chiengmai. McGilvary's dream "was to see the whole [Thai] family [North and South] brought within reach of the Gospel message." The journey took three strenuous, difficult months, but the results in the next two years made it all worthwhile. Considering the excruciatingly small number of converts won in southern Siam in the preceding forty years of Protestant effort, they were surprised and gratified when in less than two years seven Laotian Thai converts asked for baptism. This was more than the mission in the capital, Bangkok, had accomplished in twenty years.[53]

Three of the first converts were people of some standing in the provincial capital. The first, Nan Inta, at one time a Buddhist abbot, and said to be related to royalty, came to McGilvary for medicine for a cold. McGilvary was no doctor but necessity had taught him to learn as much as he could from scientific and medical books. The former abbot was also interested in talking about religion. So once again in mission history, as with the Jesuits in seventeenth-century China,[54] it was an eclipse of the sun that startled an inquirer into believing the missionary. McGilvary not only told him that there would be an eclipse of the sun that month, and that it would not be swallowed by the dragon Rahu, but how and why and at exactly what hour it would occur. When it happened just as the missionary had predicted, Nan Inta began to read the Siamese translation of the Gospel of John very, very seriously. He was baptized in 1868. The second convert, Noi Sunya, was a native doctor from a nearby village who within four months would be martyred for his faith. But no premonitions of disaster clouded the enthusiasm of those first months, and wonder of wonders, two members of the royal family itself "showed serious interest in Christianity."[55]

How quickly the enthusiasm changed to mourning. "I have often wondered," Dr. McGilvary wrote later, "whether all foreign missions have as many and as rapid alternations of sunshine and shadow, as the Lao mission."[56] Suddenly in September 1869 Kawilorot, the prince of Chiengmai, turned cruelly against the missionaries. Blaming a failure of the rice crop on them, he asked the court in Bangkok to have the interfering foreigners removed. When this was refused, he vented his vengeance by seizing two of their recent converts, Nan Chai, an ex-Buddhist abbot, and Noi Sunya, the doctor of native medicine. They were publicly bound and beaten senseless, taken into the jungle and clubbed unmercifully. One managed to survive, and was killed with a thrust of a spear.[57] Only a few days before Nan Chai, the ex-abbot, had written for a missionary wife on a slip of paper as a specimen of the Lao language, "Nan Chai has become a disciple. He loves Jesus very much."[58]

The prince died within a year. "We forgot his treachery and cruelty," wrote McGilvary, "and thought only of his interesting human qualities ... taking tea with us, and ... the dry jokes that he so much enjoyed. He was a tender father ... a warm, though a fickle and inconstant friend ... In many respects he was a good ruler." Their forgiveness was immediate, but the work of the mission in the north did not recover from the shock, nor the converts from their fear of another outburst for the next fifteen to twenty years.[59] In fact, whether in the north or the south, the progress of Christian missions in Thailand would never match the growth, for example, of the Baptists among the tribes in neighboring Burma. There were never to be in Thailand the mass conversions as were occurring among the Burmese Karens, or among the *dalits*, the outcastes of India.

TRAINING FOR NATIONAL LEADERSHIP

In the south, after the proclamations of religious toleration in the 1870s, encouraging events did give promise of better days ahead for Siam. Though the mission was not very successful in its announced goal of training Siamese leadership for the church in these forty years from 1860 to 1900, it did at least organize itself for further advances. In 1883 it formed a second presbytery in the north — this one, like the 1853 presbytery, was also composed entirely of missionaries.[60] Daniel McGilvary, the pioneer in the north, proposed to the presbytery the formation of a small theological training class. The presbytery was enthusiastic — too enthusiastic, McGilvary thought. It drew up a plan for a large school, under a Board of Education, with regulations and curriculum "better suited to American conditions," he wrote, "than to those among the Lao churches." It included an unrealistically low level of financial support for the men to be enrolled. The evangelists themselves declined to consider it, and the experiment, declared McGilvary, "was killed by too much 'red tape.'"[61]

Undaunted, McGilvary continued to instruct and nurture evangelists one by one from among the converts, though this was most successful in the north. The organization of the second presbytery effectively also divided the mission, north and south, into two missions. A contrast between the two, north and south, has been sharply analyzed in Swanson's *Krischak Muang Nua: A History of the Church in Northern Thailand.* He portrays it essentially as a difference in mission priorities. The south emphasized the institutions, especially educational, but "the Laos [northern Thai] mission's primary commitment was to evangelism, that is, to the converting of large numbers of non-Christians."[62]

Outstanding among the trainees whom McGilvary gathered about him for mentoring in the north was Nan Ta, an "adopted son" of the persecuting Prince Kawilorot, the persecutor-prince. It was reported that Nan was associating with the missionaries and asking questions about Christianity, despite his relation to royalty. Apprised of his danger, he barely escaped across the border into Burma at the time of the 1869 martyrdoms, mentioned above. Only twenty-four years old then, and not yet a Christian, he wandered for nine years, always carrying a Siamese copy of the Gospel of Matthew given him by Dr. McGilvary. After the Toleration Edict of 1878 he returned at last to his wife, who contrary to Thai custom had providentially not married again, and to the nine-year-old daughter whom he had never seen. "The man did not have to become a Christian — he was one already," said the missionaries, and set him to studying the Gospel of Matthew.[63] He later, in 1889, became the first ordained northern Thai minister in the north, and was soon called to be the assistant pastor, then co-pastor of the "First Church" in Chiengmai, events which have been called "the first signs of an emergence of a pastoral leadership for the northern Thai church."[64]

Still, in 1894, sixty-six years after the first Presbyterian missionary reached Siam, there was only one ordained Thai minister, Nan Ta. Again the northern presbytery faced the problem, and again it came up with an answer that proved abortive. It decided to ordain six of the forty or fifty evangelists who had received training at a lower-level training school under Dr. W. C. Dodd at Lamphun (Lampoon) about thirty miles south of Chiengmai. In addition to the six they ordained to the ministry, they licensed three others as lay preachers. It was about the same time that the "three-self" missionary principles — self-support, self-government, self-propagation — of Henry Venn in England, and Rufus Anderson of the American Board of Commissioners for Foreign Missions, and John L. Nevius, the Presbyterian missionary in China, were beginning to reap dramatic results in Korea. The Siam mission, therefore, voted not only to ordain the men, but also to hold the Siamese churches responsible for their support as pastors. But what worked in Korea did not prove workable in northern Thailand, and the movement collapsed, not to be revived for another seventeen years.[65]

Among the many reasons for the apparent failure given at that time and since, the most prominent have been (1) that mission policy was mission centered, not Siamese church centered; (2) that it overemphasized territorial expansion; and (3) that as already mentioned it was too slow to promote the circulation of the Bible in Siamese.[66] As for the training of leadership the criticisms were that the evangelists were not yet adequately prepared for the nurture of emerging church congregations; that the actual training period was too short, generally about one month a year; and that the single-minded emphasis on evangelism and territorial expansion left widely spread and isolated congregations with neither the resources nor the leadership for spiritual growth or for developing a sense of community in their own villages or in a national church or in the social culture of their nation.[67] By 1900 there was still only one ordained Siamese minister.[68] Herbert Swanson, in his candid analysis of the history of this period, suggests seven patterns of late nineteenth-century Protestant missionary methods that may account for the slow growth, and are worth close consideration. His focus is on northern Thailand, but he finds the roots of the problem in the general mission policies of the largest Protestant group in the country, the Presbyterian mission, during the critical years from 1870 to 1890:

1. Alienation from Thai life and culture by the mission's confrontational approach to Buddhism as idolatry.

2. Separation of converts from family and friends by conversion.

3. Dependency on foreign money.

4. Presbyterian theological legalism.

5. One-sided emphasis on evangelism at the expense of Christian nurture.

6. Failure to develop local native leadership for the church.

7. Lack of missionary personnel and of continuity in missionary presence.[69]

ROMAN CATHOLIC MISSIONS

When Gützlaff, the first Protestant missionary, stepped ashore in Siam in 1828 he found that Roman Catholics had been intermittently at work there for three hundred years, since 1567 and perhaps even earlier.[70] But in the 1700s, the after-effects of the China rites controversy brought persecution of Christians to Buddhist Siam. As the missionaries to China had been expelled for refusal to honor Confucian rites, so now Siam expelled French priests for refusing to honor Buddhist state ceremonies. All missionaries were expelled in 1779, but were recalled by the king a few years later in the interests of establishing better trade relations with the West.[71] For the next four decades, Catholic missions in Siam were crippled by bitter rivalry between the fading Portuguese and the rising French in Southeast Asia. The stand-off ended only in 1834 with a settlement confirming the authority of the French apostolic vicar of Siam under the Vatican's mission board, the Congregation for the Propagation of the Faith (Propaganda Fide).[72] Nevertheless, when the Protestants arrived there was a significant community of Roman Catholics in the country. In 1811 the number reported was less than 3,000, mostly around Bangkok.[73] And for the country as a whole, the nineteenth century would show a tenfold increase in the number of Catholics, from 2,300 in 1800 to 24,600 in 1896.[74]

Two names stand out in the history of Siamese Catholicism in the rest of the nineteenth century, two apostolic vicars: Msgr. J.-B. Pallegoix, and Msgr. Jean-Louis Vey. Pallegoix, who had been coadjutor in Bangkok for three years, was named apostolic vicar of Eastern Siam (Bangkok) in 1841 when the vicariate was divided between Siam and Malaysia (Western Siam). He was already famous as a linguist in Siamese and Pali, and as a friend and tutor of King Mongkut (Rama IV) while the latter was still a monk. He was that remarkable king's "first important contact with western thought." Mongkut was so impressed that he may even have considered the possibility of starting a new religion for Siam, combining what he thought was best in Buddhism and science and perhaps Christianity.[75] But in 1846 Pallegoix's command of the language led him, perhaps overhastily and certainly too polemically, to publish a book in Siamese caustically critical of Buddhism as "not a religion in the true sense." He was accused of insulting Buddhist monks and nuns, and deriding any Buddhist who demands obedience to Buddhist principles as "out of his mind." The reaction was swift. The book was blocked from publication; the missionaries were warned. In 1849 when they still refused to attend royal Buddhist ceremonies, in this case a ceremony of offerings to Buddha to stop a cholera plague, King Rama III, Mongkut's brother, ordered eight French missionaries banished from the country.[76]

Relations between Buddhists and Catholics understandably turned sour. But Rama III died within two years, and was succeeded by his more tolerant brother, Mongkut. The priests were invited back in 1851, and a treaty with France in 1856 officially granted freedom of choice in religion to Siamese, and to the foreign priests freedom of travel and permission to build schools and hospitals. When Pallegoix retired in

1865 after twenty-five years in Siam, the measure of the recovery of Catholicism during his tenure can be seen in the annual statistical report for 1865 which records a church membership of eight thousand, almost tripling the number reported in 1811.

Jean-Louis Vey (1840–ca. 1909) was of peasant birth and had only one good eye, but proved to be a brilliant student, a wise administrator, and one of the most successful of Roman Catholic missionaries in Siam. He reached Bangkok in 1865, the year of Pallegoix's retirement, and almost at once was made director of the small seminary at Assumption in one of the Catholic enclaves made possible by the gradual extension of extraterritorial rights. These were at first granted only to French citizens in Siam, then to Asians in their employ in the 1880s, and then to full extraterritoriality in the 1890s.[77] Vey's further promotion was rapid. In 1875 he was consecrated bishop and appointed apostolic vicar of Siam.[78]

The great achievement of his vicariate was the expansion of the Roman Catholic Church north into Laos (Northern Siam). An attempt had been made earlier from Cambodia, in 1858, but all three of the missionaries who were sent died of "forest fever." Vey, in one of the first acts of his vicariate, sent the first successful mission north in 1876. In their first year Fathers Prodhomme and Perraux baptized forty Laotians (Northern Siamese).[79] Though Catholics had long preceded Protestants in the South, the Protestants had preceded them in the North. Mr. and Mrs. McGilvary had already reached Chiengmai ten years earlier, as noted above. But Catholics and Protestants were both rewarded by evidences of more rapid Christian growth in the north. By 1897, the number of Catholics there had grown in twenty years from forty to eight thousand or nine thousand, twice the number of Protestant church members, four thousand.[80] One result was that both Protestants and Catholics separated their missions, south (Siam) and north (Laos): the Protestants under two presbyteries in 1883,[81] the Catholics under two vicariates in 1899.[82]

Vey's episcopacy in Siam lasted for thirty-four years, from 1875 to 1909. The division of the vicariate brought a welcome focus on free Siam, where he was most at home, and freed him from some of the tensions that expanding French and British colonialism inflicted on much of the rest of the Malaysian and Indochinese peninsula. Five years after his consecration, "the first full-blooded Siamese to be ordained in the Roman Catholic Church was raised to the priesthood."[83] Vey is credited with more than doubling the number of Catholics in Siam from about 10,000 to 23,600, which is not a remarkable numerical increase when compared with other fields, but a considerable achievement in unresponsive Buddhist Siam. In other categories also the results were encouraging. The number of Catholic churches and chapels rose from twenty-two to fifty-seven. Even more significant was a reassuring rise in the number of native priests. It had more than tripled, from six to twenty-one, about one of every two missionaries.[84] The training of an indigenous priesthood was at the heart of Vey's strategy of mission, and his greatest achievement may well have been the building up of the seminary, started earlier by a predecessor in 1802 in Bangkok.[85]

An important part of Msgr. Vey's mission policy was his determination to maintain friendly relations with the reform-minded government of King Chulalongkorn. In a time of forceful, armed French intrusion into Siamese territory, he refused to become a pawn of the French colonialists. "We do not mix religion, the reign of God, with politics," he wrote. But at one critical point in 1893, when the encroaching French threatened a naval bombardment of defenseless Bangkok, he personally persuaded the French consul and the gunboat captains to negotiate a peaceful compromise. The king came to respect his advice, and on Chulalongkorn's visit to Europe in 1897 Vey arranged a highly successful audience for the king with Pope Leo XIII. On behalf of educational reform in Siam he built up the scattering of small Catholic schools into a network of forty-nine Catholic elementary schools, culminating in the founding of Assumption College for boys at the high school level in 1885, and a Convent school for girls the same year. The college, which was soon placed under the direction of the religious Brothers of St. Gabriel, had an enrollment ranging about 390, of whom about 15 a year were baptized and joined the church.[86] In 1898 the Catholic community comprised one bishop with 53 Western priests, 18 native priests, 90 sisters of 3 congregations, most of whom were native, and 29,200 Roman Catholics. They had founded a college and fifty-two schools about half of which were for boys and half for girls.[87]

As the century closed in 1900, the total Christian community in Thailand, both Catholic and Protestant, is estimated in the 2001 edition of the *World Christian Encyclopedia* as 35,000 out of a population of 6 million. The following are overall estimates for a comparison of the major religions in 1900 and what they would be in 2000:[88]

	1900	2000
Total Population	6,000,000	61,400,000
Buddhists	5,500,000 (90.8%)	52,400,000 (85.3%)
Chinese ethnic	240,000 (4.0%)	530,000 (0.9%)
Muslims	90,000 (1.5%)	4,200,000 (6.8%)
Total Christians	35,000 (0.6%)	1,400,000 (2.2%)
Roman Catholic	30,000 (0.5%)	255,000 (0.4%)
Protestants	5,000 (0.1%)	1,182,000 (1.8%)
Tribal religions	180,000 (3.0%)	1,300,000 (2.1%)

Malaysia and Singapore:
Colonialism, Islam, and the Church

Malaysia in 1860 was a tangle of small Muslim sultanates rapidly being absorbed by imperial-minded Britain-in-Asia. Britain had humbled India and defeated mighty China and saw little to block its expansion into the tropical Malay Peninsula and across the South China Sea to northern Borneo. From their colonial enclaves in the south, Penang, Singapore, and Malacca, the British moved north along the coast in 1867 to begin systematically extending, by negotiation or force, political control over the native states without entirely robbing them of a nominal independence. In 1896 Britain grouped four of the most important sultanates into the Federated Malay States. This brought all Malaysia effectively under the administration of a British resident general at its capital in Kuala Lumpur.[89]

To those planning Christian missions who were familiar with the history of Christian-Muslim relations, Malaysia was a stone wall at the outer edge of impermeable Islam. But some saw two possibilities for change. One was the supposed prestige that rule by Christian Britain might bring to Christian missionaries there. The other was the possibility that the peninsula was so far from the center of Muslim military and cultural centers in the Middle East that Islamic influence there would be greatly diluted.

On both counts the hope was illusory. On the first count, British diplomacy was politely but carefully neutral on religion in Muslim areas. On the second, if there was any dilution of Islamic evangelistic effectiveness, it could usually be attributed more to the persistence of local animistic traditions than to distance from the Middle East. In any case, for a century Islam had been almost irresistibly moving south and east in Asia. Many have described the reasons for its missionary success. Kenneth Landon graphically summarizes them in a chapter entitled "The Islamization of Southeast Asia," which I must compress because of space constraints:

> No religion ever made conversion easier than did Islam.... All one had to do was utter the two words of the confession of faith, "there is no God but Allah and...Muhammed is [his] Messenger..." The sword had little to do with [it], nor did Arabs. Moslem traders and teachers came chiefly from southern India...They were not zealots...nor were they missionaries...but teachers [and traders]...They claimed to heal sickness and drive away spirits...and they married the daughters of communal chiefs.[90]

For the rest of the nineteenth century and on into the twentieth century, Muslim traders in Southeast Asia proved to be more powerfully evangelistic than holy wars, and Muslim teachers found their way into rulers' palaces more easily than Christian missionaries.

PROTESTANT MISSIONS

Despite such obstacles, the Anglicans did establish a presence as early as about 1786.[91] But more than a hundred years later a visiting Anglican bishop expressed great disappointment. The Anglican Church in Malaysia, he wrote, seemed "left behind and out of sight by the Roman and Methodist Episcopal Missions . . . [whose] splendid establishments [were] conspicuous throughout these regions."[92] Northcott suggests that much of the reason for Anglican lack of progress may have been its close identification with the British government, and the fact that it not only began as an "exclusively white concern" but remained so until the 1930s.[93]

Nevertheless, one inestimable contribution to the future was made by the Anglican pioneers: a church liturgy and structure upon which a future for a church could stand. The first Anglican bishop, Chambers, was enthroned in Singapore in 1870. Just as important, and even more important for the growth of an indigenous Anglican community, was the appointment the next year of a Tamil catechist, Royapen Balavendrum, who in 1880 received ordination as a deacon, partially supported by the Society for the Propagation of the Gospel. It was Balavendrum who broke the Anglicans out of their expatriate Western ghetto into the equally expatriate but far more indigenous and fast-growing Indian community of the Straits Settlements. Some Tamils, however, seemed to find the warmhearted Methodists more congenial than high-church Anglicans.[94]

The most successful Protestant mission in Malaysia proved to be that of the American Methodists.[95] They came late to the peninsula, but they started strong with a strong leader, James Thoburn, whom we have already met as one of the great American missionaries to India.[96] In 1888 Thoburn became the first Methodist bishop of a diocese that included both his own India, and Malaysia, fifteen hundred miles away across the Bay of Bengal. One of the strengths of Methodism's worldwide missionary enterprise in those days when the world was not yet global was an episcopal structure that enabled it, when necessary, to initiate timely penetration and organizational support into unreached territory from within Asia, in this case India, rather than waiting for committee action from its faraway home boards in New York or London.[97] So in 1887, two years after Methodists in Asia had already established missionary residence in Malaysia, as we shall see below, one member of the Methodist mission board in New York, after some debate about irregular procedure, ended the debate by declaring, "I believe we have established a Mission [in Singapore] and did not know it." Two years later in 1889 recognition and financial support for a Malay mission was made official, and in 1892 the mission was elevated to become the Malay Mission Conference.[98] But to begin again with the beginnings, it was in 1885 that the first Methodist resident missionary reached Malaysia. The American Thoburn of India had planned the mission but it was an India-born Englishman, William F. Oldham (1854–1935), who established it. He was the son of an officer in Britain's India army and as a curious teenager growing up in India he was propelled toward conversion almost inadvertently while watching some "odd-looking American evangelists" preaching in a tent at a Methodist crusade in Poona.[99] This led him to Methodist schooling in America at Allegheny College and Boston University. On his return to India, Thoburn challenged him to consider a field of great missionary opportunity opening up in the new British colony at the tip of the Malay Peninsula, and swept Oldham and his wife away to Singapore.

Oldham's India background gave him his first opening for effective Christian witness. He spoke some Tamil, and was well received by the growing community of immigrant Tamil workers. But very wisely he soon appointed one of their own, a Tamil evangelist, Benjamin Pillai, as "missionary to the Tamils" in Singapore.[100] Later, Oldham's medical colleague, Dr. Benjamin West, who was as busy with evangelism as with medical work, found indispensable the assistance of another Tamil evangelist, an Indian appropriately named Simon Peter.[101]

Even more successful was the mission's first contact with the Chinese community in Malaysia through a chance invitation to Oldham to address a small group of the leading Chinese businessmen in Singapore. They had been meeting together regularly in what they called the "Celestial Reading Society" to improve their English. Oldham appropriately chose for his subject "Astronomy," and so impressed them with his eloquence and knowledge that he was asked to tutor some of them individually. Eventually, because they wanted their sons also to learn English, this led to the spread of a Methodist school network in the peninsula which two decades later numbered about eight thousand students, fourteen hundred of whom were in the Anglo-Chinese School that Oldham had founded in 1886 less than a year after his landing in Singapore.[102] The large community of expatriate Chinese proved to be the most receptive minority in the multi-cultured peninsula. "The Chinese," wrote Oldham, were "physically more robust than the Indian, and commercially more alert than the Malay, and of more independent and adventurous spirit than either."[103] The first Methodist Chinese Church was organized in Singapore in 1891.[104]

Another missionary recruit from the British armed forces was a young new arrival in 1887, the Englishman W. G. Shellabear, who brought with him an important reminder of the greatest and most difficult challenge of all in that Muslim peninsula, mission to Malays. Shellabear was able for a while to gather together a small Malay congregation, but like most such heroic efforts to reach Muslims it never fully survived. He never gave up, however, and devoted most of the rest of his life to a new translation of the Bible into Malay, winning great respect for his fluency in the language, writing for Malay Christians "some of the most exquisite hymns in any language."[105]

It was Oldham, also, who early recognized another challenge. "Any mission in the Orient," he wrote, "that touches only men cannot hope to make either rapid or permanent advance."[106] He asked the Home Board for more women missionaries. The reply was "We haven't the money for it." Whereupon, Mary Ninde, from deep in Minnesota, stood up at an executive committee meeting of the Board and said, "[If money is the problem] the women from frozen Minnesota will establish a mission at the equator, if it becomes necessary to wear calico dresses in order to do so." It so happened that at the same time another woman far from Minnesota, an Australian, Sophia Blackmore, who had been strongly moved by the Holiness Movement in Methodism, had just arrived in India looking to be a missionary. The timing was serendipitous, and Minnesota and Australia were soon united in mission by her appointment to Singapore.[107]

Sophia Blackmore (1857–1945) became a name to conjure with on the peninsula.[108] She was "the first Methodist [single] woman missionary in Malaysia and the longest tenured" (1887–1927). She was the pioneer in establishing women's education as a priority, and tirelessly walked the streets to save girls from the vicious grasp of slavery and prostitution. She laid the foundation for a school for training Bible women in the 1890s, and was astute in discerning the most able for advanced study as future leaders in indigenous work among women. For a while she even edited a simple paper for Malay readers.[109] What Oldham was to education for men in Malaysia, Sophia Blackmore was in the infinitely more difficult struggle for the education of women. An article of appreciation written eight years after she had retired from the field called the seven Methodist Girls' Schools in Singapore and Malaya, which all could trace their heritage back to Miss Blackmore's pioneering beginnings, "the Seven Wonders of Malaya."[110]

Nevertheless, as the century ended, though the prospects for some slow growth seemed reasonable, particularly in the field of education, there were no major breakthroughs into the mainstream of life in the Malay Peninsula. Even under British rule, the majority religion, Islam, remained almost untouched. Apart from the Methodists and some Chinese Christians, there was little expressed protest against the opium trade.[111] Church statistics for the region are hard to unscramble, and compared to the population of 2 million gave little reason for optimism. The Methodists, for example, the largest non-Western Protestant community, reported only three thousand members and probationers in twenty-four churches.[112] Anglicans were more numerous, but included many expatriates. Few, if any, were Malay.

ROMAN CATHOLIC PERSISTENCE

The largest Christian body in the Malay Peninsula in 1900 was Roman Catholic, but its history was also complex and troubled. There are reports of possible ancient Nestorian contacts,[113] and Portuguese Catholics had been in the Peninsula for three centuries. Protestant Holland expelled the Portuguese in 1641, but not even 150 years of Dutch military and trade dominance had been able to eradicate the Catholic communities the Portuguese had planted. Priests risked their lives to hold secret masses. The historian Roxborogh observes that Christians in Melaka [Malacca], the capital of the Muslim sultanate, were always "most religious when under siege."[114] Anti-Catholic repression eased after 1710 and a new Catholic church was built, but there was no resident bishop in Malaysia until after 1841 when an apostolic vicariate of the Malay Peninsula was created and given to the Paris Foreign Mission Society as an independent mission.[115]

Nor did Britain's advance down the Malay Peninsula uproot either Islam, or the Catholic minority communities where they still survived in the small sultanates. The church grew perceptibly faster among the Chinese ethnic group in Malaysia than among the Indian in the nineteenth century, and very little among the Malay. Baptismal records indicate that "Chinese Christians were growing more by conversions, and the Indians more from 'biological growth.'"[116]

The Treaty of Pangkor in 1874, despite its restrictions on Christian evangelism of Malays, greatly improved the ability of Catholic missions to revive and strengthen the roots planted in earlier centuries by the Portuguese, and by the Paris Foreign Mission Society, which in 1841 had been given authority as an apostolic vicariate over the whole Malay Peninsula. The French mission's Church of the Assumption in Penang "became in many ways the mother church" of a period of modest Catholic expansion, which was most effective among the Eurasian, Chinese, and Indian communities.[117]

David Barrett's statistics for Malaysia (including its components across the South China Sea in northern Borneo) in 1900 and 2000 show the following to be the estimated measurable results of Christian missions beginning and continuing in the period we are discussing:

	1900	2000
Total Population	2,100,000	23,244,000
Muslims	1,024,024 (49%)	10,600,000 (47.7%)
Chinese folk religion	522,000 (25%)	5,380,000 (24.1%)
Hindus	200,000 (10%)	1,630,000 (7.3%)
Tribal (ethnoreligious)	200,000 (10%)	760,000 (3.4%)
Buddhists	105,000 (5%)	1,480,000 (6.7%)
Total Christians	34,000 (1.5%)	1,850,000 (8.3%)
Roman Catholics	20,000 (0.9%)	720,000 (3.3%)
Protestants	12,000 (0.6%)[118]	1,040,000 (4.7%)

Indo-China (Annam and Tonkin — Vietnam)

Today's Vietnam (Annam and Tonkin) is the dominant member of the trio of three Buddhist or semi-Buddhist countries clustered on the eastern and southern edge of what was long called Indochina. With a population of about 80 million in the year 2000, Vietnam had eight times as many people as Cambodia, and almost sixteen times as many as Laos. Five hundred years ago the Khmer empire of Cambodia was the greatest power in Southeast Asia. But by 1860 the area had become a French colony of Indochina, and the favored religion was Roman Catholicism, as Anglicanism was in neighboring Malaysia and Singapore. But as Islam was never in danger of replacement on the Malay Peninsula by Christianity, Buddhism was never seriously threatened in Indochina.

In contrast to Malaysia, where the church barely survived centuries of persecution, the church in Vietnam (Annam or Cochinchina in the South, and Tonkin in the North) emerged from a hundred years of even bloodier massacres and martyrdoms, to become, after the Philippines, the church's strongest bastion in Southeast Asia. In what is now Vietnam, it entered the nineteenth century with 3 apostolic vicars, 15 missionaries, 119 indigenous priests, and over more than 300,000 Catholic believers. By 1850 the number of Catholics had increased to 465,000, and in 1896 Catholic statistics included 10 apostolic vicars, 270 missionaries, almost 400 indigenous priests, and a Catholic community of more than 700,000 in 2,886 churches and chapels, and 1,646 schools.[119]

But the statistics do not tell the story of the bravery and martyrdoms by which the church paid for such growth. So many French missionaries and native Christians were murdered in the two worst periods of persecution, 1822–1841 and 1848–1861, that one was named "the great persecution" and the other "the sinister years." In just four of those years, 1857–1861, 5 apostolic vicars, 9 French priests and 116 Annamese priests were martyred; about 10,000 leading local Catholics were imprisoned, and the total death was reported to be 40,000. Then it was that France, long eager for an excuse to absorb the kingdoms into its empire, in 1862 forced a treaty of peace which made the three eastern provinces of Cochinchina into a French colony, French Indochina, and promised its surviving Christians freedom of religion.[120] In 1863 King Norodom of Cambodia accepted a French protectorate; and in 1867 the French occupied the three western provinces, though Tonkin rebelled.

When persecutions continued, France finally annexed both north and south in 1886. Some dreamed of a great Christian empire in an Asia under France. Reality was not so grand. True, in the hundred years of the nineteenth century, despite the blood and slaughter, or perhaps because of it, the number of Catholics in Vietnam had tripled. Whole towns became Catholic. In 1893 France added Laos to its protectorate, and soon unified the area under a French governor general as Indochina. But French colonialism antagonized the patriots, and French colonists turned anticlerical as a secular reaction spread in France. More threatening was a spreading spirit of anti-Westernism among the Annamese *literati*, fueled with inflammatory tracts and proclamations.[121]

The real revolution, however, which changed the fate of Vietnam did not break out until 1946, some fifty years later. The estimates of Barrett et al. for the religions of Vietnam in 1900 and 2000 are as follows:[122]

	1900	2000
Total Population	11,000,000	79,800,000
Buddhists	7,600,000 (70%)	39,534,000 (49.5%)
Tribal (ethno) religions	2,200,000 (20%)	10,800,000 (13.5%)
New religions		9,000,000 (11.3%)
Christians	900,000 (8.2%)	6,600,000 (8.3%)
Catholics	900,000 (8.2%)	5,320,000 (6.7%)
Protestants (PIA)		1,200,000 (1.5%)
Chinese folk religions	200,000 (1.8%)	800,000 (1.0%)
Muslims	77,000 (0.7%)	570,000 (0.7%)

NOTES

1. The prince's warm approval of the missionaries is quoted in Backus, *Siam and Laos*, title page. The ex-regent's personal name was Luang Nai Sit. Like other members of the royal family, he was a friend of the pioneer missionary Dr. Dan Bradley and others and welcomed their contribution to the opening of Siam to the world. Cf. McFarland, *Historical Sketch of Protestant Missions in Siam*, 12ff., 63–65; Bradley, *Siam Then*, 40.

2. McGilvary, *A Half-Century among the Siamese and the Lao*, 287.

3. Kenneth P. Landon, *Southeast Asia: Crossroad of Religions* (Chicago: University of Chicago Press, 1947), 134–135.

4. The nineteenth- and early twentieth-century Chakri kings of Siam and their reigns were Rama I (1782–1809), Rama II (1809–1824), Rama III (1824–1851), Rama IV/Mongkut (1851–1868), Rama V/Chulalongkorn (1868–1910), Rama VI/Vajiravudh (1910–1925).

5. Abbot Low Moffat, *Mongkut, the King of Siam* (Ithaca, N.Y.: Cornell University Press, 1961).

6. Mongkut deserves to be remembered more for his social and political reforms than for his fictionalized portrait in Anna Leonowens's two volumes, or *The King and I*, or for a famous letter received by Abraham Lincoln in which he offered to send the American president elephants, more suitable for presidential transport than a mere horse carriage, an offer answered with dignified appreciation by Lincoln. On Mongkut's statecraft and reforms see Moffat, *Mongkut*, 24–40; on his toleration toward missionaries, 154–168; on his letters to American presidents, 74, 87–95.

7. Siam's first war with expanding Burma was in 1538. It fought off Western foreign colonialism throughout the last half of the nineteenth century, sometimes by territorial concessions, such as by ceding Laos and western Cambodia to France in the 1890s (see Syamananda, *History of Thailand*, 135ff.).

8. Only partial and brief interruptions have imperiled Siam's eight hundred years of independence. In the thirteenth century the Mongol advance of Kublai Khan drove the Thai south out of Kunming into the Indochinese peninsula, and for a time in the fourteenth century they were overshadowed by the Khmer of

Cambodia but outfought them. In 1569 Burma briefly captured the Siamese capital. In 1942 Thailand was temporarily occupied by the Japanese. But it is still "the land of the free." See Syamananda's *A History of Thailand*; and David K. Wyatt, *Thailand: A Short History* (New Haven, Conn.: Yale University Press, 1984). An important shorter survey emphasizing religious factors is in Landon's *Southeast Asia*, 100–133; 165, passim.

9. Syamananda, *A History of Thailand*, 119.

10. On the American missionary tutors, male and female, see McFarland, *Historical Sketch of Protestant Missions in Siam*, 19–20, 63, 211; Backus, *Siam and Laos*, 320–337, 370–372; and Moffat, *Mongkut*, 164–165. The first three women chosen were Mrs. Dan Bradley (BCFM), Mrs. Stephen Mattoon (Presbyterian), and Mrs. John Taylor Jones (Baptist).

11. McFarland, *Historical Sketch of Protestant Missions in Siam*, 63.

12. See Bradley, *Siam Then*, 101–104. Anna Leonowens tells her own story in *The Romance of the Harem* (Boston: James R. Osgood, 1873), and *The English Governess at the Siamese Court, Recollections* (Philadelphia: Porter & Coates, 1870).

13. On the negative reaction of modern Thai to "The King and I" image of the Mrs. Leonowens period, see Syamananda, *A History of Thailand*, 124.

14. Leonowens, *The Romance of the Harem*, 248–249. Her book is anecdotal, but believable.

15. On the emancipation of the slaves, see Syamananda, *A History of Thailand*, 172. Cf. Anna Leonowens on slavery in Siam in *The Romance of the Harem*, 14–64, 257–270, and on the proclamations of King Chulalongkorn, 264–270. The quotation attributed to the king is on pp. 267–268.

16. After 1873 the once reformist ex-regent turned more conservative and obstructed some of Chulalongkorn's reforms. See *New Encyclopaedia Britannica*, "Si Suriyawong," 15th ed. (1997), 10:774:1a.

17. Herbert Swanson's carefully documented *Krischak Muang Nua*, 28–29, analyzes the "myth" of the "edict of toleration," arguing for a more gradual development. The first edict, upon Chulalongkorn's coronation in 1868, applied only to subjects born during his reign and was issued by his regent. It was specifically extended to northern Siam in 1878 in a ruling issued and worded, with the king's permission, by the Siamese Commissioner in Chiengmai. Specifying Christianity in particular, it officially ended outright persecution in the north, though intermittent repressions continued. The full text of the edict is given by Wells, *History of Protestant Work in Thailand*, 60–62.

18. On the ABCFM in Siam, see McFarland, *Historical Sketch of Protestant Missions in Siam*, 10–26.

19. The American Baptists entered Siam from Burma in 1833, shortly after the London Missionary Society in 1828, and the first ABCFM missionary there, David Abeel in 1831, but in 1833 when the others had left, the Baptists remained as the first long-term residential Protestant mission in the country. By 1839, their first missionary, Rev. John Taylor Jones, had translated all the New Testament, except Hebrews and Revelation, into the Thai language. It was completed and published in 1844. But in 1868/1869 the Baptists suspended their ministry to the Siamese in order to concentrate on their more successful work with the Chinese in Siam. By 1871 they reported six churches and 418 members. The last Baptist missionary of this period left Siam in 1893 (McFarland, *Historical Sketch of Protestant Missions in Siam*, 10–34, 344–351; Swanson, *Krischak Muang Nua*, 3–5).

20. McFarland, *Historical Sketch of Protestant Missions in Siam*, 50. A typographical error reads the date as 1878 instead of the correct 1858.

21. Nai Chune died in 1877. See Backus, *Siam and Laos*, 380–381, 407–408. Cf. McFarland, *Historical Sketch of Protestant Missions in Siam*, 50, where a typographical error reads the date of the baptism as 1878.

22. McFarland's dates for the two periods are: 1828–1860, the Pioneer Period; and 1860–1928, the Period of Expansion, the latter date marking the one hundredth anniversary of Protestantism in Thailand. McFarland, *Historical Sketch of Protestant Missions in Siam*, 51, 296.

23. Dr. Dan Bradley, the Presbyterian pioneer of the Congregational Mission Board (ABCFM) in Siam, left that board when it ceased operation in Siam in 1849 and joined the new American Mission Association in 1850, serving independently until his death in 1873 (McFarland, *Historical Sketch of Protestant Missions in Siam*, 18–20).

24. McFarland, *Historical Sketch of Protestant Missions in Siam*, 51.

25. Barrett et al., eds., *World Christian Encyclopedia*, 2001, 664. In 1925 the figure was fourteen thousand total Christians in a population of about 9 million (Dennis, Beach and Fahs, *World Atlas of Christian Missions*, 77, 186).

26. Backus, *Siam and Laos*, 400.

27. Wells, *History of Protestant Work in Thailand*, 34.

28. See statistics in Backus, *Siam and Laos*, 389, 401, 410, 416.

29. McFarland, *Historical Sketch of Protestant Missions in Siam*, 3–5, 195.

30. On Dr. Bradley, see McFarland, *Historical Sketch of Protestant Missions in Siam*, 8, 12–18, 23–26, 195–196; Backus, *Siam and Laos*, 357.

31. Backus, *Siam and Laos*, 239–240; McFarland, *Historical Sketch of Protestant Missions in Siam*, 198.

32. Mrs. Mattoon was indeed an unusual woman. Her grandson, Norman Mattoon Thomas, was equally remarkable and tenacious — America's perennial socialist candidate for the presidency of the United States from 1924 to 1948. Her husband, Stephen, who spoke Thai "like a native," according to Townsend Harris of Japan, was the first U.S. consul in Siam (1856), and fretted because it distracted him from his "higher calling" as a missionary (Lucy Starling, *Dawn over Temple Roofs*, 92–93; and Symananda, *History of Thailand*, 121).

33. Ki-eng Qua-Sean was born in Xiamen, where he practiced Oriental medicine. He was converted under the teaching of ABCFM missionaries in 1844 on a visit to Bangkok. See S. S. Nuam Sresthidor, "Outstanding Men and Women of Siam," in McFarland, *Historical Sketch of Protestant Missions in Siam*, 288–289; and Wells, *History of Protestant Work in Thailand*, 25.

34. *Report*, Presbyterian (U.S.A.) Board of Foreign Missions, 1886, 112–116.

35. Syamananda, *A History of Thailand*, 128; see also "Education in Siam," chap. 19 in McFarland, *Historical Sketch of Protestant Missions in Siam*, 210. The Royal College was founded by Chulalongkorn in 1871 in the Grand Palace, "the first school in the accepted sense of the word [in Siam]." There was no government Department of Education until 1887.

36. McFarland, *Historical Sketch of Protestant Missions in Siam*, 99, 218–219; Wells, *History of Protestant Work in Thailand*, 34; A. J. Brown, *One Hundred Years*, 939.

37. *Report*, Presbyterian [USA] Board of Foreign Missions, 1901, 338.

38. Dennis, Beach, and Fahs, *World Atlas of Christian Missions*, 1925, 186.

39. Swanson, *Krischak Muang Nua*, 164.

40. The phrase quoted is from Dr. House's chap. 21 in Backus, *Siam and Laos,* 417. For more on Dr. House see Feltus, *Samuel Reynolds House of Siam,* esp. 65–90, 156–164; and E. B. McDaniel, "Medical Missions," in McFarland, *Historical Sketch of Protestant Missions in Siam,* 196. For adversarial anecdotal criticism of House, see Bradley, *Siam Then,* 175ff.

41. See Sanneh, *Translating the Message.*

42. See chap. 17 above ; Wells, *History of Protestant Work in Thailand,* 6–7.

43. The American Baptist Mission brought in a second press in 1836. McFarland, *Historical Sketch of Protestant Missions in Siam,* 16, 29, 38, 346, 378.

44. Wells, *History of Protestant Work in Thailand,* 84–85; McGilvary, *A Half Century among the Siamese and the Lao,* 222–223.

45. McFarland, *Historical Sketch of Protestant Missions in Siam,* 124–125, 250.

46. McFarland, *Historical Sketch of Protestant Missions in Siam,* 253ff. The first complete New Testament in Siamese was the work of the Baptist, Rev. John Taylor Jones.

47. From the United States alone, in 1900, there were 2,419 women mission-aries in the foreign field: 1,291 wives, 1,015 single women, and 113 women physicians (either single or married). See Dennis, *Centennial Survey of Foreign Mission,* 257.

48. Feltus, *Samuel Reynolds House of Siam,* 210.

49. McFarland, *Historical Sketch of Protestant Missions in Siam,* 94–95.

50. McFarland, *Historical Sketch of Protestant Missions in Siam,* 68–70. The Wang Lang School was known later as the Harriet M. House School, and locally as "Mem Cole's School" in honor of its long-term principal, Miss Edna S. Cole. In 1921 it was renamed Wattana Wittaya Academy. On the role of Mrs. House (Harriet Pettit House), who as early as 1858 had less formally initiated sewing classes for girls, see Feltus, *Samuel Reynolds House of Siam,* 205–216.

51. McFarland, *Historical Sketch of Protestant Missions in Siam,* 71–91. The move was in 1921.

52. Backus, *Siam and Laos,* 372, quoting Dr. Samuel House.

53. The second couple, the Jonathan Wilsons, were delayed for a year. McGil-vary, *A Half Century among the Siamese and the Lao,* 66–101; Swanson, *Krischak Muang Nua,* 8–12; McFarland, *Historical Sketch of Protestant Missions in Siam,* 58–59, 66, 113–118; Backus, *Siam and Laos,* 394.

54. See chap. 5 above.

55. McGilvary, *A Half Century among the Siamese and the Lao,* 96–101; Swanson, *Krischak Muang Nua,* 11; Wells, *History of Protestant Work in Thailand,* 54.

56. McGilvary, *A Half Century among the Siamese and the Lao,* 283.

57. McGilvary, *A Half Century among the Siamese and the Lao,* 96–99, 101–129; Wells, *History of Protestant Work in Thailand,* 55–58; Swanson, *Krischak Muanag Nua,* 12–15; Backus, *Siam and Laos,* 389–399. The first Laos convert was Nan Inta (394, 407).

58. McGilvary, *A Half Century among the Siamese and the Lao,* 117.

59. Swanson's chronology for Christianity in Thailand in that period dif-fers from McFarland's, mentioned above. Instead of two periods, "Pioneer — 1818–1860" and "Expansion — 1860–1928," which more correctly describes only southern Siam, Swanson divides the history in the north into three periods: "The Early Years — 1867–1869," "The Hard Years — 1870–1889," and "Expansion — 1889–1900" (Swanson, *Krischak Muang Nua,* ix, 22, 25).

60. McGilvary, *A Half Century among the Siamese and the Lao*, 257. With the formation of the second presbytery, the Presbyterian mission was also, in effect, divided into two separate missions, north and south, and remained so divided until the formation of the "National Christian Church in Siam" in 1934 (A. J. Brown, *One Hundred Years*, 961ff.).

61. McGilvary, *A Half Century among the Siamese and the Lao*, 259–262; McFarland, *Historical Sketch of Protestant Missions in Siam*, 226–227.

62. Swanson, *Krischak Muang Nua*, 104.

63. McGilvary, *A Half Century among the Siamese and the Lao*, 225–228; McFarland, *Historical Sketch of Protestant Missions in Siam*, 227–228. Nan Ta is not to be confused with Nan Inta, McGilvary's first convert. Both men became the early models of effective ordained native ministry in the north.

64. Swanson, *Krischak Muang Nua*, 95.

65. McFarland, *Historical Sketch of Protestant Missions in Siam*, 226–228.

66. Swanson, *Krischak Muang Nua*, iii–iv.

67. See Swanson, *Krischak Muang Nua*, iii–iv, 39ff., 90.

68. McFarland, *Historical Sketch of Protestant Missions in Siam*, 154, 217, 226–231.

69. Swanson, *Krischak Muang Nua*, 21ff.; cf. 164ff. But on Swanson's first point (the encounter of religions), cf. Presbyterianism in Korea only about two decades later, where drawing a sharp distinction between religious factors in the national culture and Christianity was one of the reasons given for rapid Christian growth.

70. See chap. 17; and *CE*, s.v. "Siam." A Franciscan, Bonferre, entered "the great kingdom of Pegua and Siam" in 1550 and preached for three years but without results. The apostolic vicariate of Siam was created in 1669; in 1841 it was divided into Eastern Siam (Bangkok) and Western Siam (Malacca); in 1899 Eastern Siam was divided into Bangkok (Eastern Siam), and Tharé (Laos). Launay, *Histoire de la mission de Siam*, for the earlier period; and the chart of the apostolic vicariates in the Indochina peninsula in S. Delacroix, *Histoire universelle des missions catholiques*, 3:246.

71. See above chap. 16.

72. The Portuguese claimed rights for all mission in Asia under its patronage (*padroado*) agreement with the Vatican. See above chap. 2. Chumsriphan, "Jean-Louis Vey," 129ff.

73. Launay, *Histoire de la mission de Siam*, 2:179–180.

74. Louvet, *Les missions catholiques au XXIXme siècle*, 160.

75. Launay, *Histoire générale de la Société des Missions Etrangères*, 3:115ff.; Latourette, *A History of the Expansion of Christianity*, 6:242; cf. Moffat, *Mongkut*, 15, 18–21, 180–181.

76. Chumsriphan, "Jean-Louis Vey," 132–133. Msgr. Pallegoix's book was titled "Pudcha Wischana" (Questions and Answers).

77. On French-Siamese relations and extraterritoriality, see Syamananda, *History of Thailand*, 139–141.

78. Chumsriphan, "Jean-Louis Vey," 138–141.

79. Chumsriphan, "Jean-Louis Vey," 142ff. The first Catholic center, Kengkol, was considered too far north, and was shifted east to Ubon in 1881.

80. Catholic figures from Chumsriphan, "Jean-Louis Vey"; Protestant from Swanson, *Krischak Muang Nua*, 170. Protestant figures for "church members" seem

to average about twice the number of "communicants." For example, Presbyterians, the only Protestant mission there, reported 1,841 communicant members in the north in 1894; by contrast Presbyterians in southern Siam reported only 325 communicants that year (*Presbyterian Board of Foreign Missions Annual Report, 1896*, 215, 208–209).

81. McGilvary, *A Half Century among the Siamese and the Lao*, 257.

82. Chumsriphan, "Jean-Louis Vey," 147–148. Vey remained as apostolic vicar of Siam, and Father Cruz was consecrated apostolic vicar of Laos.

83. Latourette, *A History of the Expansion of Christianity*, 6:243.

84. Chumsriphan, "Jean-Louis Vey," 151–152.

85. Chumsriphan, "Jean-Louis Vey," 165–167.

86. Chumsriphan, "Jean-Louis Vey," 152–163.

87. Latourette, *A History of the Expansion of Christianity*, 6:243.

88. Barrett et al., eds., *World Christian Encyclopedia*, 2001, 734. Statistics in 1900 for neighboring Laos, which was at times considered part of Thailand or Burma, were: Population 1,500,000; Buddhist 905,000 (60 percent); Tribal Chinese religions 580,000 (39 percent); and Christians 8,000 Roman Catholics (0.5 percent). There was no Protestant mission in Laos until about 1905 (*WCE*, 1981, 447).

89. The four states (Perak, Selangor, Negri Sembilan, and Pahang) added in 1874 to Penang (1786), Singapore (1819) and Malacca (1824) were technically independent of the British-controlled Straits Settlements. Situated as they were along the east coast of the Straits of Malacca they were important to complete British naval control of the Straits, the strategic entrance to the major trade route to East Asia. This effectively established an implicitly recognized boundary between "British" Malaysia, and Dutch Indochina (see Brian Harrison, *South-East Asia: A Short History* [London: Macmillan, 1955], 176ff., 204–205; and Barbara Watson Andaya and Leonard Y. Andaya, *A History of Malaysia* [London: Macmillan, 1982]).

90. Landon, *Southeast Asia*, 133–135.

91. Hunt, Hing, and Roxborogh, *Christianity in Malaysia*, 34ff.; and see above chap. 17.

92. Quoted by Michael S. Northcott, in Hunt, Hing, and Roxborogh, *Christianity in Malaysia*, pp. 50–51, citing *Singapore Diocese Annual Report* (May 1911), 15.

93. Northcott, in Hunt, Hing, and Roxborogh, *Christianity in Malaysia*, 35–50.

94. Northcott, in Hunt, Hing, and Roxborogh, *Christianity in Malaysia*, 39–40.

95. On Malaysian Methodism, see Theodore R. Doraisamy, *The March of Methodism in Singapore and Malaysia, 1885–1980* (Singapore: Methodist Book Room, 1982); Hunt, Hing, and Roxborogh, *Christianity in Malaysia*, 142–198.

96. See above chap. 21.

97. See Hwa Yung and Hunt, in Hunt, Hing, and Roxborogh, *Christianity in Malaysia*, 142–143; and Hollister, *The Centenary of the Methodist Church in Southern Asia*, 219–220.

98. Doraisamy, *The March of Methodism in Singapore and Malaysia*, 4–19; Hollister, *The Centenary of the Methodist Church in Southern Asia*, 219-221.

99. Poona is in northwestern India. The conversion was at a Taylor crusade during the four-year campaign in India of the independent Methodist Bishop William Taylor, a Methodist apostle of "self-supporting mission" who preached his fiery way around the world. The preacher who so impressed Oldham was

Daniel O. Fox (Doraisamy, *The March of Methodism in Singapore and Malaysia,* 3; see also William Taylor's irresistible autobiography).

100. Daraisamy, *The March of Methodism,* 9, 20–21, 33.

101. West was multi-talented, in medical work, evangelism, and education, planting churches and schools among both the Chinese and Tamil communities (Doraisamy, *The March of Methodism,* 14–15, 33). See also Hunt, Hing, and Roxborogh, *Christianity in Malaysia,* 150.

102. W. F. Oldham, *India, Malaysia and the Philippines* (New York: Eaton & Mains, 1914), 228–233; Doraisamy, *March of Methodism,* 8–9. In 1900, under Oldham and with the energetic help of Dr. B. F. West, enrollment in the Methodists' Anglo-Chinese School was 590, which was higher than in either of the earlier Western curriculum schools, the government's Raffles Institute, and the Catholic St. Joseph's Institution (Hwa Yung and Hunt, in Hunt, Hing, and Roxborogh, *Christianity in Malaysia,* 152). See also Hollister, *The Centenary of the Methodist Church in Southern Asia,* 217–218. By 1900 there were Methodist schools in Penang, Taiping, Ipoh, Teluk Anson, and Kuala Lumpur, almost always at the request of local residents (Hwa Yung and Hunt, in Hunt, Hing, and Roxborogh, *Christianity in Malaysia,* 161).

103. Oldham, *India, Malaysia and the Philippines,* 214.

104. Doraisamy, *The March of Methodism,* 14–17.

105. Oldham, *India, Malaysia and the Philippines,* 243–244; Doraisamy, *The March of Methodism,* 3. Hwa Yung and Hunt, in Hunt, Hing, and Roxborogh, *Christianity in Malaysia,* 150.

106. Oldham, *India, Malaysia and the Philippines,* 245.

107. There are several versions of the story. See Hollister, *The Centenary of the Methodist Church in Southern Asia,* 218; Theodore R. Doraisamy, ed., *Sophia Blackmore in Singapore* (Singapore: Methodist Church in Singapore, 1987), 5.

108. Oldham, *India, Malaysia and the Philippines,* 245–246; See Doraisamy, *Sophia Blackmore in Singapore,* which is a biography consisting largely of excerpts from her letters.

109. Hwa Yung and Hunt, in Hunt, Hing, and Roxborogh, *Christianity in Malaysia,* 152, 154, 164, 328; Doraisamy, *March of Methodism,* 24, 27.

110. Doraisamy, *Sophia Blackmore,* 66. He cites an article by Miss Thirza A. Bunce in *The Malaysia Message/Message,* Jubilee issue, 1935.

111. Hunt, Hing, and Roxborogh, *Christianity in Malaysia,* 347–348.

112. Hwa Yung and Hunt in Hunt, Hing, and Roxborogh, *Christianity in Malaysia,* 159. Given the irregular geographical, political, and ethnic division of colonial Malaysia, it is difficult to obtain comprehensible statistics for the region.

113. John Roxborogh, in Hunt, Hing, and Roxborogh, *Christianity in Malaysia,* 3–4.

114. John Roxborogh, in Hunt, Hing, and Roxborogh, *Christianity in Malaysia,* 6.

115. John Roxborogh, in Hunt, Hing, and Roxborogh, *Christianity in Malaysia,* 7–10. He cites, among others, R. Cardon, *Catholicism in the East and the Diocese of Malacca* (Singapore: Malaya Catholic Leader, 1938).

116. Hunt, Hing, and Roxborogh, *Christianity in Malaysia,* 15, citing Paul Decroix, *A Short History of the Catholic Church in Taiping 1897–1987.*

117. John Roxborogh, in Hunt, Hing, and Roxborogh, *Christianity in Malaysia*, 9–17. See also F. G. Lee, *The Catholic Church in Malaya*. By 1827 there may have been as many as twelve hundred Catholics in Penang (Roxborogh, 11).

118. Barrett, ed., *World Christian Encyclopedia*, 1982, 472. The Protestant statistics show ten thousand Anglicans, indicating a favorable effect of British rule; and two thousand others, slightly different from figures reported above.

119. Louvet, *Les missions catholiques au XIXme siècle*. 158–160. The 310,000 Catholics in what is now Vietnam were divided as follows: Cochin China 50,000, Western Tonkin 120,000, East Tonkin 140,000. Cf. Schmidlin, *Catholic Mission History*, 550–551. On the two important regional synods in the century — Cochin China, Cambodia, and Champa, 1841; and at the Vatican, 1880; and including the first regional Synod of Tonkin, 1900 — see Josef Metzler, *Die Synoden in Indochina 1625–1934* (Paderborn and Munich: Ferdinand Schoningh, 1984), 121–256.

120. Statistics differ. See Louvet, *Les missions catholiques au XIX siècle*, 158–160; Tran-Minh Tiét, *Histoire des Persécutions au Viet-Nam* (Paris: Editions "Transpacifique," 1955), 39–57, 69–96 — especially Louvet, *Les missions catholiques au XIX siècle*, 158; Tran-Minh, 87.

121. See Schmidlin, *Catholic Mission History*, 606–607.

122. Barrett et al., eds., *World Christian Encyclopedia*, 2001, 803. Estimates for Laos and Cambodia are uncertain.

Chapter 28

Indonesia (1860–1900)

Who must send missionaries? The organized institutionalized church. Whom must the church send? Her sons and daughters. What is the purpose...? Indeed, the conversion of the heathen, the salvation of souls and the increase of the church... Yet these are only means toward that ultimate goal which is the glory of God the Father.   — Abraham Kuyper, 1871.[1]

Protestant Renewal in a Dutch Colony

In the 1860s a young Dutch village preacher who had dabbled brilliantly in "modern" theology at the university[2] found that his first pastorate was changing his faith in a surprising way. He was not aware of the fact that the change would some day not only greatly affect the politics of late nineteenth-century Holland, but would also progressively alter the character of Dutch rule over the Indonesian archipelago. His talks with his rural congregation so moved the young Abraham Kuyper (1837–1920) that he turned again to the Calvinism of his childhood, embracing its firm orthodoxy but broadening it, like Calvin, with the challenge of its inseparable social and political implications. At the university he had been enthralled with the teachings of his mentor, Johannes H. Scholten, a "new theology" reinterpreting the Scriptures from the perspectives of the Biblical Criticism school of what was considered a more scientific examination of the Bible's documents. A fellow student said, "I really believe that Scholten is greater than Paul." But it was the pastorate, as a Dutch historian writes, which changed Kuyper, not by "an academic conversion but a religious one." Kuyper credits it to a growing admiration of the simple faith of the farmers and laborers in his congregation.[3] It brought him to a restored faith in the "whole gospel," a faith both social and spiritual, an integration of faith and life that soon swept him into Holland's tumultuous party politics as an "anti-revolutionary" in a revolutionary period. His position was a bold, forceful opposition to the new liberalism. In the church, in the early 1870s he outfought the liberals as the new young minister of the Amsterdam State Church, the country's most prestigious parish with 140,000 members (men, women, and children), more than half the population of the city.[4] In 1874, when he was somewhat unexpectedly elected to the Parliament by the Antirevolutionary Party, he proved to be as dominant in national politics as in the church. He rose like a rocket on a

622

program advocating state aid to religious schools and, most importantly for Christian missions, calling for a reform of Dutch colonial policies. His power spread, though not without intense opposition, and brought him political victory in 1900, and the office of prime minister in 1901.[5] His influence powerfully but indirectly brought a welcome infusion of ethical integrity to Holland's colonial policy, which in turn produced a refreshing surge of energy to the Dutch missionary outreach in the Indies.[6]

The man most directly responsible for the mid-century renewal of missionary advance in the archipelago was Ludwig Nommensen (1834–1918), who landed on Sumatra in 1862.[7] Sumatra was the largest of the islands though not its most heavily populated, and was non-Malay and non-Muslim. It was religiously animist, which in the history of Christian missions has almost invariably meant a far more receptive response to the Christian message than when the contact was with the more sophisticated cultures of the so-called higher regions, Islam, Hinduism, or Buddhism. Moreover, Nommensen was not a Dutchman like the colony's rulers. He was a German Pietist, born the year the martyrs, Munson and Lyman, had been murdered,[8] and he came under a German missionary society, the Rhenish Mission, which had been founded in 1828 as an interdenominational (Lutheran and Reformed) mission of Calvinists, Lutherans, and unaffiliated Pietists.[9]

Nommensen landed in 1862. A profound religious experience following a severe illness had led him to volunteer for missionary service and he was determined, like Munson and Lyman, to move inland. Prevented from doing so for several months, he practiced homeopathic medicine to win the confidence of Batak traders on the coast and threw himself into the study of their Batak language. Before the year was over he had not only managed to penetrate into the mountains beyond the limits of Dutch rule, but had confounded those who had warned him that he would be killed. He returned alive and well with reports of a most friendly reception.[10]

For the next fifty-six years until he died in 1918, Nommensen gradually overcame the tribesmen's fears of the Dutch. He won the friendship of hostile local *rajahs* and confronted the powerful *datu*-priests of the Batak high god, *Mula Djata Na Bolon*, with a bold, open defiance of the power of the ghosts and serpent demons of the underworld from which the priests claimed to protect the people.[11]

Nommensen baptized his first converts, four men, four women, and five children, in 1865, and that same day baptized his friend and protector, Rajah Pontus Lumbantobing, "the first person of authority in northern Batakland to accept Christianity."[12] Enlisting converted *rajahs* for assigned responsibilities in the organized congregations became an effective strategy for church planting and growth, giving a sign of tribal approval to the evangelists who were sent out after 1873 from the congregations into unreached areas.[13] In a parallel emphasis similar to the "three-self" policies of mission strategists like Rufus Anderson and Henry Venn, he insisted that "a teacher or pastor who was paid for by some outside source could only dull the edge of an independent Church."[14]

Though often frustrated by the opposition of the chief *rajah* of the old independent Batak dynasty who quite understandably associated Nommensen's presence with the Dutch invaders, Nommensen quietly managed to win the confidence of the lesser *rajahs* by the zeal with which he protested against the feared slave trade, and by his passionate counsel against blood violence between the tribes. He established a model "Christian village," complete with a medical clinic, for converts who had been driven out of their former villages for becoming Christian. "The spiritual and social were closely aligned in Nommensen's mind," comments Paul Pedersen, quoting one of his sayings: "When the spiritual message has been accepted, the people become more conscious of the social misery in which they have been living."[15]

The last chief *rajah* of the Bataks was displaced by the Dutch in 1883. In that critical time of transition the leaders of the Bataks began to look to Nommensen as the guide and spokesman. The church growth that followed was so rapid that his alarmed fellow missionaries feared that in his eagerness to baptize he must be lowering the gospel standards of church membership. Nommensen calmed them with the admonition that changing times demanded changing methods, and that they must learn how to fish not "with a hook but with a net."[16]

Events justified his method. To anticipate somewhat, by the time that Nommensen died in 1918 the church among the Bataks counted some 180,000 members, a seminary and 14 ordained Batak ministers or workers called *pendeta*, along with 78 teachers and 2,200 elders. The mission numbered 62 European missionaries and 13 missionary deaconesses.[17]

Schism and Friction within Protestant Missions

Nommensen's "net" had developed some holes. Mention was made above of J. Voorhoeve's resignation from the old Netherlands Missionary Society for theological reasons in 1858. The reasons were both theological and ecclesiastical. Influenced by friendship with a group of Plymouth Brethren (Darbyists), he rejected communion with his former society not only because it was not more forthright in defending the deity of Jesus Christ, but because its rigid Reformed ecclesiology of the denominational church could not be defended, he thought, on biblical grounds. The result was a major missiological split. He left the old Missionary Society (NZG) to help form a new Netherlands Missionary Union (NZV). It began a period of intense activity for new societies.

One observer called the year 1864 "the fatal year," the year that the old society, tired of dissension, formally decided to leave "everyone free to form his own opinion" on some key issues, and this of course was pounced on by the dissenters as an abdication of theological principle. A long, sad road of controversy was opening up between what is variously described as "modernists" and "orthodox," or between "liberals" and "conservatives," as the missions approached one of the early forks in that road.[18]

But not all the consequences were negative. The schisms were not as "fatal" as some had predicted. In fact, Dr. Rauws, writing in 1935 about the controversies, came to the conclusion "that the founding of new [missionary] societies has greatly advanced the Kingdom of God." Indonesia's three thousand miles of scattered islands were too much for the original Netherlands Missionary Society. Now it was able to concentrate on its thriving work in Minahassa, Middle East Java, and the Moluccas, and the new missions found more than enough of a challenge in the largest island, Sumatra, and South Celebes and the long stretch of islands from West Java to Timur, and even on to eastern New Guinea (Irian Jaya).[19]

Impact on Society

In the islands, as in the Western world at that time, the evangelical revivals brought with them an enlightening passion for social reform. In 1860, Holland abolished slavery in its colonies. Much of the credit for this belongs to a churchman who had been thrown out of the Indies for his eloquent protests against colonial abuses, especially the trade in slaves. Banished from the East Indies for his criticisms of colonialist trade practices, W. R. Baron van Hoevell, a product of the revivals in the Netherlands, entered politics and mounted a successful twelve-year campaign against the shame of slavery.[20] He paved the way for the political victories of the even more towering political figure, Abraham Kuyper, mentioned above, who in 1901 as minister of the Dutch government for five years inaugurated an "ethical christian" policy for Holland's foreign and domestic relations, strongly supportive of Christian missions.[21]

Another factor favoring the spread of Christianity was the repeal of the law forbidding the teaching of any religion in schools supported by government funds. Dutch colonial policy, still obsessed with trade, turned "fanatically neutral" as H. Kraemer has described it.[22] Put crassly, Protestant Holland put trade before religion. If religion hindered trade and if Christian teaching in mission schools turned Muslims against the Dutch, then education must be neutral. The solution was religious pluralism for society, and no religion of any kind in the schools.

But a counter-tide was rising in Holland. Fed by the evangelical revivals, Christian influence in Dutch politics in the 1890s[23] led to greater emphasis on education both at home and abroad, education not hostile to the Christian faith. In the islands, Christian schools sprang up in the villages. Where once the people in rural areas set schools afire to keep their children "from the painful necessity of education," mission schools began to supplement and support government encouragement of education.

Out of those same refreshing nineteenth-century revivals in Holland arose a renewal of missionary enthusiasm, together with a reaction against state control of Dutch missions, and criticism of the chilling secularizing effects that dependence on the government was exerting on the motivating energies and theological convictions that were basic to missionary commitment. In mid-century, 1858–1861, three new Dutch missionary societies were formed, less inclusive, less political, more evangelistic, and incisively theological: the Netherlands Missionary Union (NZV), the Utrecht Missionary Union (UZV) and the Dutch Reformed Missionary Association (NZG).[24]

By 1900 Protestants outnumbered the older Catholic community in the islands about two to one. This does not, however, represent a collapse of the original Portuguese Catholic community.

Roman Catholic Missions

It is true that after the shift from Portuguese colonialism to Dutch control in the archipelago Catholic Church membership was decimated. True but misleading, argues Herbert Feith. He makes the case that the impact of western colonialism was

> minimal in Indonesia for the first two hundred years — both under Portugal for the first hundred, and then for another hundred under the Dutch — and in fact favored neither Protestantism or Catholicism. He sees the intractable religious resistance and continuing military and trading power of the major Muslim states even under colonial pressure as more of an obstacle to missionary advance than foreign imperialism. The intrusion of both powers, by their contrast with the more familiar Asian religion of Islam may have served more to drive the area into Islam as a counter-Western balance than to convert it to Christianity.[25]

Things began to change for the better for Catholics in the nineteeenth century, but only temporarily. When the Dutch East India Company was dissolved in 1800 and Holland took back control of the government with a firmer hand, it recognized the rights of religious freedom for Catholics in 1807. This partially kept Catholic missions from too close a connection with the western colonialism which by then was politically and unmistakably Dutch. In 1826 Rome authorized an organization of the first apostolic prefecture, Batavia, and in 1845 appointed an apostolic vicar. About the same time the Dutch government began to grant subsidies to the Catholic Church somewhat like those it was giving to the Protestants.[26]

For the next half century, however, this gave to the Catholics only a partial, much restricted freedom, little more than a gesture toward impartiality. It represented a position of neutrality rather than promotion of religion. In its attempt to be fair it was virtually hostile to Christian evangelism and education.[27] A Dutch priest was appointed in 1807 to minister to the Dutch Catholic community in the capital, but only because for a brief period Holland had been defeated by France. Catholic missionaries were limited narrowly to the island of Java. Their base was strengthened by formation of an apostolic vicariate in 1842. But as late as 1854 the Dutch governor general still claimed the authority to appoint and locate Catholic priests anywhere in islands under Dutch control. Not until the Treaty of Lisbon in 1859 were the islands officially opened to Catholic missionaries, and in that same year Rome gave to the Jesuits ecclesiastical priority over the whole Dutch territory.

Meanwhile, the Dutch had been gradually extending their rule beyond the original trading ports. Invigorated by the freedom newly granted to Catholics, their missions made attempts to widen Catholic mission expansion north to Sumatra, the Celebes (Sulawesi) and most effectively after 1850 to the land-Dyak tribes beyond the shifting Dutch/British colonial boundaries in the hill forests of northern Borneo.[28] The Dyaks lived in villages of huts raised on poles and made of bamboo and palm leaves. They were "poor, proud, arrogant," intractably primitive, always armed with a large knife but not violently warlike. There was not a Christian among them. In 1886 Felix Westerwoudt (1861–1898) of the English Catholic missionary society (St. Joseph's of Mill Hill) ventured into the hills on a mission to these poorest of the poor. Within two years he had built a little wooden church but still had no congregation. He worked alone for five and a half years, then was joined by two Franciscan Sisters. Seven years later, gaunt and bloodied by constant attacks of river and swamp leeches, malaria and pneumonia, he died. He left no hundreds, much less thousands of Christian converts — perhaps only ten families, seventy people all told. But he had made an impression on the whole tribe. He had given them a chapel, a school, and a sense of personal and community identity deeper than tribal loyalty. He had taught them to read and write and grow coffee. He had given them hope. Even his death brought new life to the mission and for the next hundred years the Dyaks would still remember him as the founder of "Borneo's most promising mission."[29]

For the most part, however, outside Java it was only in a little "splay of islands," the Lesser Sundas at the far eastern end of the archipelago where Portuguese control had lingered longest, that the Catholics managed to retain a continuing, dominant presence. The Sundas became an enduring center of Indonesian Catholicism — a thousand miles from the capital in Batavia and only relatively safe from harassment. From Flores, the orchid isle, to Timor and its trace of tiny islets tailing off into the east toward New Guinea, it was the safest refuge the much persecuted Catholics could find.[30]

In this Catholic haven at the outer edge of the archipelago, the Jesuits opened a "college" in 1898, based on an active network of Catholic elementary schools for boys and girls. When the Jesuits were expelled during the catastrophic after-effects of the French Revolution, they transferred the work in Timor to the missionaries of the Society of the Divine Word in 1913 with results that exceeded all expectations.[31] In 1900 no one could have predicted that an independent East Timor — known as Portuguese Timor after the division of the island between the Dutch and Portuguese in 1859, and then an Indonesian province until after World War II — would be second only to the Philippines as the only other large area in Asia with Catholics making up a majority of its population.[32]

Conclusion

In 1900, the estimate of Christian numerical strength as compared to the other major religious bodies in that third most highly populated country in Asia (38,800,000 inhabitants) shows the Christian faith a distant fifth to the two majority religions of the islands. The largest of the two was not yet Islam, but a vast variety of tribal religions on the islands which had not yet been converted by the rising spread of Muslim rule. That faith would not predominate numerically until the twentieth century. Of the other three religions the strongest, at least numerically, would prove to be what are sometimes identified as the "new religions," indigenous animisms which in Indonesia, and mostly on Java, were syncretistically adapting elements of their tribal cultures to the increasingly persistent pressures of Muslim rule. The two smaller religions were Hinduism and Christianity. The former was rapidly declining except on Bali, but still outnumbered the Christians.[33]

The table below, adapted from Barrett et al., eds., *World Christian Encyclopedia*, 2001, demonstrates the changes in the religious situation in Indonesia at the end of our period in 1900 and shows how Christianity fared statistically a century later in the year 2000.

	1900	2000
Total Population	38,800,000	212,100,000
Tribal religions	17,700,000 (45.6%)	5,334,000 (2.5%)
Muslims	15,500,000 (40.0%)	116,105,000 (54.7%)
New religions	3,900,000 (10.0%)	46,234,000 (21.8%)
Hindus	780,000 (2.0%)	7,259,000 (3.4%)
Total Christians	540,000 (1.4%)	27,804,000 (13.1%)
Protestants (PIA)	470,000 (1.2%)	20,700,000 (9.7%)
Roman Catholics	56,000 (0.1%)	5,752,000 (2.7%)
Buddhists	200,000 (0.5%)	1,938,000 (0.9%)
Chinese folk religions	195,000 (0.5%)	3,000,000 (1.4%)[34]

NOTES

1. Summary of Kuyper's 1871 address to the Netherlands Reformed Missionary Society, in Frank Vanden Berg, *Abraham Kuyper* (Grand Rapids, Mich.: William B. Eerdmans, 1960), 66.

2. G. Puchinger, *Abraham Kuyper: His Early Journey of Faith* (Amsterdam: VU University Press, 1998), 11–16; Vanden Berg, *Abraham Kuyper*, 18–34.

3. Puchinger describes Kuyper's radical evangelical change as "three conversions": the first when he was ten years old, probably in a revival meeting; the second as he finished a doctoral dissertation on the Polish reformer Laski and John Calvin; and the third in his village pastorate. Puchinger, *Abraham Kuyper*, 11–12, 21–27; cf. Vanden Berg, *Abraham Kuyper*, 33–45.

4. See Vanden Berg, *Abraham Kuyper*, 55–78. On his theological base, R. E. L. Rodgers, *The Incarnation of the Antithesis, An Introduction to the Educational Thought and Practice of Abraham Kuyper* (Edinburgh: Pentland Press, 1992), 9–42; and Harry Fernhout, "Man, Faith and Religion in Bavinck, Kuyper and Dooyeweerd," ThM thesis, Institute for Christian Studies, Toronto, 1975.

5. For biographies of Kuyper in this period, see Vanden Berg, *Abraham Kuyper*, 765, and passim (1960), and P. Kasteel, *Abraham Kuyper* (Kampen: J. H. Kok, 1938), passim. On his educational policy, see Rodgers, *The Incarnation of the Antithesis*.

6. James E. McGoldrick, *Abraham Kuyper: God's Renaissance Man* (Auburn, Mass.: Evangelical Press, 2000), 185–186. For a short survey of Dutch colonialism in Asia, see Amry Vandenbosch, "The Dutch in the Far East," in *The Netherlands*, ed. Bartholomew Landheer (Berkeley: University of California Press, 1944), 333–345.

7. For biographies of Nommensen see Martin E. Lehmann, *A Biographical Study of Ingwer Ludwig Nommensen (1834–1918), Pioneer Missionary to the Bataks of Sumatra* (Lewiston, N.Y.: Edwin Mellen Press, 1996); Johannes Warneck, *Ludwig Ingwer Nommensen*, 4th ed. (Wuppertal-Barmen: Verlag des missionhauser, 1934); and Nellie de Waard, *Pioneer in Sumatra* (Chicago: Moody Press, 1962).

8. On the martyrs Munson and Lyman, see above chap. 18.

9. On the great Rhenish Mission see Alfred Bonn, *Ein Jahrhundert Rheinische Mission* (Barmen: Missionshaus, 1928). The prolific writer on missionary methods, Johannes Warneck, served under this mission as a missionary to the Bataks, and after 1920 as director of the whole mission. See his autobiography, *Werfet eure*

Netze aus (Berlin: M. Warneck, 1938), and *The Living Christ and Dying Heathenism: The Experience of a Missionary in Animistic Heathenism* (Grand Rapids, Mich.: Baker Book House, 1954).

10. M. E. Lehmann, *Nommensen*, 5–14, 80–91; J. Warneck, *50 Jahre Batakmission in Sumatra* (Berlin: Martin Warneck, 1911), 26ff., 49ff.

11. M. E. Lehmann, *Nommensen*, 119–131. On Batak religion, see Philip L. Tobing, *The Structure of the Toba-Batak Belief in the High God* (Amsterdam: Jacob van Campen, 1956). See also Pedersen, *Batak Blood and Protestant Soul*, 60.

12. M. E. Lehmann, *Nommensen*, 142–145, 168–170; Pedersen, *Batak Blood and Protestant Soul*, 56–59. Cf. J. Warneck, *50 Jahre Batakmission in Sumatra*, 63, 51–52; and Andar Lumbantobing, *Das Amt in der Batak-Kirche* (Wuppertal-Barmen: Rheinischen Missions-Gesellschaft, 1955), 26–27.

13. M. E. Lehmann, *Nommensen*, 193ff.

14. Theodor Müller-Krüger, *Sedjarah Geredja di Indonesia* (Djakarta, Indonesia: Badan Penerbit Kristen, 1959), quoted by Pedersen, *Batak Blood and Protestant Soul*, 66.

15. Pedersen, *Batak Blood and Protestant Soul*, 63.

16. Müller-Krüger, *Sedjarah Geredja di Indonesia*, 66, quoted by Pedersen, *Batak Blood and Protestant Soul*, 66.

17. Pedersen, *Batak Blood and Protestant Soul*, 66. Cf. M. E. Lehmann, *Nommensen*, 147.

18. Rauws et al., *The Netherlands Indies*, 58–71.

19. Rauws et al., *The Netherlands Indies*, 60.

20. Vlekke, *Nusantara*, 284, citing W. van Hoevell, *De emancipatie der slaven in Nederlandisch Indie* (Groningen, 1848). Van Hoevell, back home in Holland, spoke eloquently on behalf of the East Indians and urged that their welfare, not the traders' greed, should govern a Christian nation's colonial policies.

21. Vanden Berg, *Abraham Kuyper*, 87–88, 65–66, 190–191. And see Amy Kandenbusch, "Missions on the Island of Bali," *IRM* 23 (1934): 206–214. Cf. P. Kasteel, *Abraham Kuyper*.

22. Rauws et al., *The Netherlands Indies*, 79.

23. Latourette, *A History of the Expansion of Christianity*, 5:281. Vandenbosch, *Dutch East Indies*, 209–210, 214.

24. The first of the new societies, the Netherlands Missionary Union (Nederlandsche Zendings-Vereeniging, NZV) was formed in Java in 1858. It prohibited membership to any who denied the deity of Jesus Christ. In its founding it was influenced by association with the Plymouth Brethren, but established a close relationship with the evangelical wing of the Dutch Reformed Church. Another was the Dutch Reformed Missionary Association (Nederlandsche Gereformeerde Zendingsvereeniging, ZGK) in 1860/1861, strictly Calvinistic and organizationally soon associated with the Christian Reformed Church. The Utrecht Missionary Society (UZV), organized in 1859, was more exclusive theologically than the old Netherlands Missionary Society (NZG, 1797) from which the others had separated, but was more ecclesiastical than the "low church" Netherlands Missionary Union (NZV). For more on the confusing proliferation of missions with similar names, see Rauws et al., *The Netherlands Indies*, 44–75, 109ff.; and Latourette, *A History of the Expansion of Christianity*, 5:282–284. Among other major Protestant missions were the Rhenish Missionary Society (RM), and

various Missions of the Reformed Churches (ZGK), etc. See also the acronym chart (Rauws et al., *The Netherlands Indies*, 158).

25. See Herbert Feith, "Indonesia," in *Governments and Politics of Southeast Asia*, ed. George McT. Kahin (Ithaca, N.Y.: Cornell University Press, 1959), 159–162, citing J. C. Van Leur, "Indonesian Trade and Society," 113.

26. A major source in Dutch for this period is J. H. Van der Velden, *Die Roomsche-Katholike Missie in Netherlandsch Oost-Indie 1808–1908* (Nijmegen: L. C. G. Malmberg, 1908); and in German, Julius Richter, *Die evangelische Mission in Niederlandisch-Indien* (Gutersloh: C. Bertelsmann, 1931). See also Amry Vandenbosch, *The Dutch East Indies*, 63–66, 208–209.

27. Vandenbosch, *The Dutch East Indies*, 41ff., 208.

28. *New Catholic Encyclopedia*, 1967, vol. 7, "Indonesia," and Latourette, *A History of the Expansion of Christianity*, 5:294–295.

29. E. Westerwoudt van Rijckevorsel, *Felix Westerwoudt: Missioner in Borneo* (Maryknoll, N.Y.: Catholic Foreign Mission Society of America, 1924). In contrast to Catholic success, the hitherto dominant, more city-centered Anglican mission in that part of North Borneo (now Sarawak, East Malaysia) in the period 1880–1909 was suffering from temporary administrative confusion and a disappointing decline. See Graham Saunders, *Bishops and Brookes: The Anglican Mission and the Brooke Raj in Sarawak 1848–1941* (Singapore: Oxford University Press, 1992), 204–229.

30. Delacroix, *Histoire universelle des missions catholiques*, pl. vii; 377–382; *New Catholic Encyclopedia*, vol. 7, "Indonesia"; Rauws et al., *The Netherlands Indies*, 131–132; John Considine, *Across a World* (Toronto and New York: Longmans Green, 1942), 257–259.

31. Delacroix, *Histoire universelle des missions catholiques*, 382.

32. In 2000, the Philippines, much larger of course, had 62 million Roman Catholics, 82.4 percent of its population; Timor had only 800,000, but that was 89.9 percent of its population. In no other country in Asia are Roman Catholics in the majority, though Lebanon comes closest: 1.4 million Roman Catholics, 42.5 percent of the population (*World Christian Encyclopedia*, 2001).

33. Barrett, ed., *World Christian Encyclopedia*, 1982, 372–373.

34. Barrett et al., eds., *World Christian Encyclopedia*, 2001, 372. The double count would subtract about 150,000 from these figures.

Epilogue

Thinking Back
and Looking Ahead

One must think backward in order to live forward.

— Søren Kierkegaard

It was the best of times, it was the worst of times.

— Charles Dickens

In geographic extent, in movements issuing from it, and in its effect upon the [human] race, in the nineteenth century Christianity had a far larger place in human history than at any previous time.

— Kenneth Scott Latourette, 1943[1]

In our statistical reports...[native agents] are all still called "helpers," whereas...ought they not to be considered as the main force, with the missionary for their helper?   — S. H. Chester, 1900[2]

Thinking Back

The nineteenth century has been called "the great century" in the expansion of Christianity, but it did not begin that way.

It began with Roman Catholic missions still staggered by the suppression and expulsion of their most vigorous and famous missionary order, the Jesuits. It began with Dutch Protestants vigorously pursuing trade in their colonies but neglecting their missions. In India it began with British colonialists driving William Carey out of Calcutta into the interior where he was forced to take on superintendence of a failing indigo factory in order to support his family. In China it began with an empire which, fearing British imperial expansion, forbade permanent residence to Robert Morrison in 1807, and allowing Protestant missionaries little progress for the next forty years. There were still an estimated 300,000 Christians in China, including Macao, but another anti-Christian edict in 1811 drove out the missionaries and brought violent persecution upon the Chinese converts. There was no resident Protestant missionary at all in Japan until 1859. The first half of the nineteenth century in Asia was more of an attempt to recover from setbacks and shaky starts than of great missionary achievements.

632

The nineteenth century has also been called the great century of colonialism, the climax of three hundred years of intrusion into Asia by the strangers from the west. To return to the metaphor with which this volume began, they came by sea like three great tidal waves — first the Iberian, Spanish, and Portuguese in the 1500s; then the Dutch in the 1600s; and finally in the 1700s and 1800s the British. Like three great walls of water they washed over the eastern islands and crashed on the coasts of Asia in lethal, devastating waves. There was death in those invading seas. But seawater carries salt, and when the water recedes, the salt remains — and salt brings savor to the food of life.

If the colonists were like the water, the missionaries were the salt. Jesus described them as "the salt of the earth." But the fact that they came together, colonizers and missionaries, made it difficult for Asians to believe that the Western Christian missionaries who came in with the same waves were anything but the religious arm of imperial colonialism. And another hard fact must be factored into the metaphor, the fact that the salt left by a tidal wave kills the plants in the fields it covers, however much it may later add taste to the food on people's tables.

PATTERNS OF ADVANCE AND RECESSION
IN ASIAN CHRISTIAN HISTORY

By the end of the nineteenth century, most of Asia had concluded that Christianity and the colonial enterprise were inseparable. But nineteenth-century mission records, when examined at the beginning of the twenty-first century, also provide considerable evidence to ground belief that empire was a prickly companion of mission — sometimes helpful, sometimes hostile — and not the inseparable ally of the missionary as commonly pictured in mid- to late-twentieth-century writing on the subject. There was a difference between the two dynamics as they impinged on Asia, much like the difference between the water and the salt in the sea.

Only at almost the very height of the last imperial wave, the Anglo-Saxon wave, did the tide of Christian missions in Asia and Africa begin to turn in the new faith's favor. Catholic recovery followed a recession, and Protestants, rediscovering their sense of a missionary mandate, brought new life and unprecedented numbers to their missions. By 1900 for the first time in the history of Christianity, the expansion of the church could truly be called global. Protestants, like the Catholics before them, had finally circled the earth and approached the twentieth century with unbounded optimism under the banner "evangelize the world within our generation."

Was it too late? For about sixty generations Christians had been striving toward that goal, yet a rough outline of past missions to Asia, such as the one with which I portray in summary form the dynamics recounted in the present work, reveals that most advances were followed by a recession, and every recession was followed by an advance. Colonialism was certainly the context in which Christian mission in Asia took place from 1500 to 1900. But that may not be the main story when looked at, say, in another two centuries. Look again at the roller-coaster ride of Asian church history.

I. Beginnings to 1500 (volume 1 of this work)

   1. First advance (50–225 A.D.): The Syrian tradition
      Thomas to India (50 A.D.); Addai to Edessa (100 A.D.?)

   2. Second advance (225–900): The Old Silk Road
      Nestorians move across Asia from Persia (225)

   3. Armenians establish a Christian kingdom (300)
      Nestorians reach China (635–900)

   4. First recession (450–1000)
      The Great Schism of Christendom (451)
      The Muslim advance (622–1000)

   5. Third advance (1000–1350): Nestorian and Catholic
      Nestorians in Central Asia (1000); re-enter China (1200)
      Catholic contacts in Asia (1245–1346)

   6. Second recession (1270–1500)
      The last Christian crusade (1270–1291)
      Retreat of the Mongols (1260–1370)
      Islam converts Central Asia; Tamerlane (1330–1500)

II. Tidal Waves in Asia: 1500–1900 (volume 2 of this work)

   1. Fourth advance (1500–1750): Return of the West
      The Catholic wave, Portuguese and Spanish (sixteenth century)
      The Protestant wave
      Dutch (seventeenth century)
      Danish and Germans to India (early eighteenth century)

   2. Third recession (1750–1830): Catholic decline

   3. Fifth advance (1800–1900+): The Anglo-Saxon wave
      "The Great Century" of Protestant missions
      Catholic recovery

   4. Fourth recession or sixth advance? (1900–2000)

REFLECTIONS ON HISTORICAL PATTERNS

The empires are gone, but the church remains. What does this portend for the future? In 1500, the starting point of this volume, Portuguese cannon were threatening India, and Catholics were caught off balance by the discovery that there was already a strong Christian community there of Syrian descendants of the ancient Nestorian communities who attributed their conversion to St. Thomas as fervently as Catholics claimed spiritual descent from St. Peter. Their Syrian forebears had come to India without arms, and it is not surprising that they resisted Catholic newcomers who came with Christian words but different saints and in ships that carried guns.

Two and a half centuries later, in 1800, Western Christians, Catholic and Protestant, were still wrestling with the handicapping stigma of their association with imperial conquest. Yet, it was in that age of arrogant colonialism that Western Christian missions, Catholics and Protestants alike, achieved their greatest worldwide missionary successes since the conversion of Europe. There are perils in such success. Expansion in Europe in the fourth and ninth centuries was tainted by the coercive effect of connection with Christianized Roman imperialism. Mission expansion in Asia from the sixteenth to the end of the nineteenth century was similarly stained by its connection with Western colonialism.

So we must ask again, how "great" was the nineteenth century in Asian church history and its larger global context? The answer must be compressed into a series of sweeping and therefore debatable generalizations.

FIVE DEBATABLE GENERALIZATIONS

The first generalization is that if the measure of growth is the number of Christian adherents, the nineteenth century was a great success. Between 1800 and 1900 the global Christian community came close to tripling in size. While world population was increasing from about 900 million to 1.62 billion, the number of Christians in the world rose from about 200 million in 1810[3] to 558 million in 1900.[4] Measured in percentage of growth rate, world population grew 57 percent, and Christianity grew a remarkable 188 percent. A third of all the people in the world were Christians, with Catholics outnumbering Protestants in 1900 nearly two to one.[5]

From a wider chronological perspective, beginning with Catholic expansion in the sixteenth and seventeenth centuries, never had any religion expanded so globally as Christianity between 1500 and the early 1900s. The nearest parallel would be Islam from the seventh to the fifteenth centuries. But unlike Christianity, Muslim expansion was never global until the late twentieth century, and then it would still be only marginally represented outside certain well-defined geographical areas. The lasting impact of Muslim migration into Europe and the Americas would remain undetermined as the twenty-first century began.

While Asia's continental population was increasing 65 percent, from 980 million in 1800 to 1.6 billion in 1900,[6] the total Christian community in Asia, though it grew to an estimated 21 or 22 million in 1900[7] — was but a microscopic segment of the religious mosaic of a continent which by then contained more than half (57 percent) of all the people in the world. The Christian segment itself was split. Of the perhaps 20 million *Asian* Christians in 1900, 11 million were Catholic; 2.8 million were Protestant; 6.8 million were Orthodox. Those numbers need to be seen in comparison with Asia's 830 million adherents of other major faiths in

1900, including: 400 million Confucianists and "folk religionist worshippers"; 203 million Hindus; 200 million Muslims; 125 million Buddhists; 49 million Taoists and Shintoists.[8]

Add all the Christians together and in 1900 still they were little more than a scattering of sand along the beaches of Asia's then 950 million people. But they were not sand; they were "the salt of the earth," and on any plate or planet a little salt goes a long way

The second generalization is that the nineteenth century was a Protestant century, the golden century of Protestant missions. If this seems to conflict with the statistics above, which show Catholics as outnumbering Protestants two to one in Asia in 1900, one explanation is that in rate of growth, as distinct from numerical growth, Protestants, who had the mathematical advantage of a lower starting point, reached the year 1900 increasing far faster than their Roman Catholic counterparts. Admittedly, this makes nineteenth-century Christian missions sound like a not very cordial race between two wary competitors, but the irenic influence of the Second Vatican Council was sixty years in the future. Mission literature of the period still bristled with hurled epithets — "papists" in William Carey's *Inquiry*, and even more angrily, "heretics" in Ch. Dallet's *Controversial Catechism*.[9]

Protestants were on the march to claim the world, exuberant and prematurely confident, at times arrogant. The associate editor of the popular Protestant journal *MRW* wrote in 1895, "The Anglo-Saxon is the supreme colonizer, and civilizer, and Christianizer under the sun."[10] Such self-conceit was not uncommon then. But to balance the record, when similar claims of ethnic superiority had surfaced seven years earlier at the 1888 London Centennial Missions Conference, protesters from both America and Britain had the saving grace to remind the boasters that the West was not without its own sins — an exorbitantly profitable opium market for example, and the slave trade, and traffic in liquor and guns,[11] not to mention the "unequal treaties" that gave Westerners extraterritorial land rights in defeated or intimidated countries.

The nineteenth was the first century in which Protestants (with the brave exceptions of little Holland and the Danes and Moravians) ventured away from their comfortable home in the "Christian West" to meet the challenge of a world still largely unreached. For most of the nearly three hundred years since the Reformation, Protestant energies had been consumed by the struggle to survive in Europe after the break from the Roman Church. Now, breathing easier, they turned to their Bibles, and their Bibles turned them to the world, and in the next hundred years they almost overtook a three-hundred-year Catholic lead in the number of foreign missionaries worldwide.

The missionaries on the field were more apt to be openly critical of Western imperialism than people in their Protestant home churches. Mission archives often reveal how mixed were their attitudes, sometimes patronizing and arrogant toward the cultures they were trying to reach, sometimes honestly angry at barbarities and injustices, and sometimes superficially optimistic, reporting missionary triumphs while glossing over missionary failures.[12]

Yet, all in all, weaknesses and mistakes admitted, and strengths not unduly magnified, it was a Protestant century. The numbers were with the Catholics, growth was with the Protestants. Statistics for 1880–1885 show Protestants gaining adherents three times as fast as Catholics in East and South Asia (a 9 percent per year growth for Protestants and 3.5 percent for Catholics).[13] Nor did Protestant growth stop in 1900.

These beginnings of rapid Protestant growth made the last decades of the century a time of overflowing enthusiasm for foreign missions. A respected church historian, William Schaff, at the same 1888 London Conference reflected the prevailing mood in this confident analysis of mission history: "There are three epochs of missions in History — the apostolic, the medieval, and the modern. The result of the first was the conversion of the Roman Empire; the result of the second was a Christian Europe; and the result of the third will be the conversion of the whole world."[14]

Enthusiasm breeds its own heroes and heroines, and the churches in the West found in news from the mission fields its models of Christian courage and self-sacrifice. The most popular examples in Asia were Carey and Henry Martyn in India, Robert Morrison and Hudson Taylor in China, and Adoniram Judson in Burma. Lesser known to the American and British public were the Catholics, hundreds of them: the martyrs of Korea and of the Boxer Rebellion in China, and heroes who were not martyred, like Alexander of Rhodes in what is now Vietnam. It was typical that for most of the century fewer missionary heroines than heroes emerged in the popular press, but some of the most prominent became household words: "Ann of Ava" (Mrs. Judson Taylor) in Burma, "Dr. Ida" (Ida Scudder) of India, and later, Lottie Moon of China.

Protestants may have glamorized their heroes and heroines. But the proof that their strengths far outweighed the faults is in the legacy they left to history: a Protestant Christian community spread for the first time around the world.

The third generalization about the nineteenth century is that it was a century of evangelism. This was true of both Protestants and Catholics, but Protestant preaching was more urgent, more personal. Catholics stressed planting the church;[15] for Protestants the most important and immediate task was to make disciples, to lead the unbelieving to a personal faith in Jesus Christ. True to their roots in the Great Awakenings, and the Wesleyan revivals, Protestants believed that church membership does not guarantee salvation — personal knowledge of and commitment to Jesus as Lord do.

The ruling theology of missions in nineteenth-century Protestantism was a message revived and refired by Dwight L. Moody in the late 1800s.

Its authority came from the Bible. Its focus was unambiguous: Jesus is the only Savior. Critics describe it as "too narrowly soteriological," but its effects were more global than the narrowly Western theologies of the critics.[16] Its method was outlined in three stages: proclaim, persuade, and then organize a church.[17]

Young volunteers learned it in college. President Timothy Dwight told them at Yale in 1813 that if they had the will and the faith, it was reasonable to believe that with God's help the whole world could be brought to the Savior, perhaps "not far from the year 2000."[18] Charles Hodge at Princeton in 1856 told them, "There are now 800 million or 900 million human beings living on the earth... If they do not believe, they cannot be saved."[19] In 1900 the president of Columbia University, Seth Low, told organizers of the Ecumenical Missionary Conference in New York: "What can Christians do better, in such a time as this, than to bear their unshaken testimony to their belief that there is no other Name under heaven, whereby men must be saved, but the Name of Jesus Christ?"[20]

The response to this challenge was sudden and overwhelming. On college campuses all over America, in the space of only a year or two in the late 1880s and early 1890s, three thousand volunteers, including five hundred women, had signed pledges of missionary intent.[21] By the hundreds, then by thousands they went — "marching as to war," but to a gentle war. Their armor was the Gospel, the good news that Jesus Christ is "the Savior of the world."

Some have described their zeal and faith as "fundamentalism," which is partly true, for they sought to emphasize the fundamentals of the faith — which they understood as the uniqueness of Christ, the canon of Scripture, the central role of God's grace, the reality of sin, salvation by faith, and the mandate to make disciples. But when "fundamentalism" is improperly used to apply a twentieth-century term to a nineteenth-century situation, it becomes a category mistake that easily misleads the reader trying to understand what motivated the nineteenth-century missioner. The "fundamentalist" controversy takes its name from later pamphlets and controversy in America shortly before the outbreak of World War I.[22] What the earlier missionary pioneers were preaching was nineteenth-century, mainline Protestantism, the fundamentals held by virtually every Christian Church, but particularly emphasized in English-language Protestantism.

The message was so clear and simple that more sophisticated observers often missed its inner complexities and practical flexibility. They were therefore unduly surprised when the simple Gospel was received with joy. Alexander Duff, though he is remembered more as an advocate of advanced education in India than as an evangelist, kept the priorities straight: education, of course, "but the church that is no longer evangelistic will soon cease to be evangelical," he said.[23]

As the century progressed, America entered the international arena both in Christian mission and in nationally expanding political relationships. Its fresh enthusiasm for foreign missions and a growing sense of national identity added a sharper edge to questions of mission priorities and motive. Britons and Germans led the way in Protestant missionary outreach in the first half of the century, but as early as 1810 American involvement, both political and missionary, began to spread. As in Catholicism earlier, Western political expansion and Christian mission moved in tandem, and America, though less obviously, was no exception.

In 1811 America sent out its first missionaries. In 1812 it challenged the British Empire. In 1900 it defeated the Spanish Empire. And from the beginning it regarded itself popularly — though not constitutionally — as a Christian nation. In the process of thus forming a national identity, complex tensions grew between American traditional nationalism and Christian missionary internationalism. George Washington had warned, "Beware of foreign entanglements," but Jesus Christ had said, "Go ye into all the world." On the missionary side, America sent Adoniram and Ann Judson to Burma, Abeel and Bridgeman to Malacca, Peter Parker to China, Justin Perkins to the Nestorians in Persia, and James Ballagh to Japan.[24]

After the War of 1812 internationalism gathered momentum in American society, but the tensions only grew more complex.[25] In mission, the challenge was how to choose between two goals facing a Christian America: "Is the aim of the missionary to Christianize or to civilize?" it was asked. In the nineteenth century, Hutchison suggests, Protestant America chose the first answer: to Christianize. One of the contributing reasons for the choice, he goes on to imply, has been the example of two recent American Christian missions. One of them failed — the missionary effort to bring native American Indian culture into the American mainstream. This weakened Christian confidence in civilizing as an effective model for mission. The other example was the startling contrast presented by the initial evangelistic success of the American Protestant mission to Hawaii in the 1820s, which seemed to be God's seal of approval on direct proclamation of the gospel.[26]

A somewhat similar but not so apt parallel might be found in Asia. It would be to compare Catholic missions in India with Protestant missions in the South Pacific. This is unfair to Catholic missions. It builds on the unfavorable, but partly true perception, that a perceived Catholic decline in India in the early nineteenth century was due to the blighting shadow of Portuguese colonialism,[27] and in contrast, that the remarkable Protestant growth in the South Pacific islands under new and independent British and American mission societies vindicated a "Jesus-only" mission of evangelism unencumbered and undiluted by the trumpets and guns of imperialism.

More important, though, than comparison of isolated examples, the records of the Protestant missionaries themselves point to a more deeply rooted factor in the shaping of mission motives. To most missionaries, the choice of a goal was not to be dictated by the success or failure of a mission. The determining factor was not temporary results, but the overriding authority of Jesus Christ as given clearly through the Scriptures. This, they believed, was not a mandate to civilize, but a commission to proclaim, to make disciples, to evangelize. All else was secondary. If through lives transformed by conversion, the world was changed for the better, that was a consummation not only devoutly to be wished, but to be actively worked for, always mindful, however, that the future was not in human hands but in God's.[28] Francis Wayland, for almost twenty years president of Brown University, wrote in the 1850s: "The Son of God has left us with no directions for civilizing the heathen, and then Christianizing them. We are not commanded to teach schools in order to undermine paganism, and then, on its ruins, to build up Christianity."[29]

Nineteenth-century missionaries did build schools, and heal the sick, rescue slaves, and champion women's rights, but that is not why they went to the ends of the earth. They went, as they so often said, "to tell the world about the Lord Jesus Christ."

After the Civil War, another infusion of American personnel poured out across the seas. In the 1880s the infusion became a flood. The Moody revivals, the Student Volunteer Movement, and German Pietism poured streams of young missionaries to the coasts of Asia, and on into the unreached interior. In America foreign missions became a student movement.[30]

My fourth generalization is to venture the proposition that the nineteenth century was "a century of women in mission." Pierce Beaver rightly catches the sense of movement toward such a goal in the subtitle of one of his books on the role of women in mission, "The First Feminist Movement in North America." But it was a century of progress toward equality for women, not a century of equality achieved. And it was more apparent in Protestant missions than in Catholic societies.

In the 1800s Protestant women in America took their first steps toward that goal. Missionary wives (and unordained men) were still not classified as missionaries in many early statistics, and until the 1860s single women were rare in Protestant missions.[31] Their lives as missionary women were harder, their sacrifice was greater, and they died faster. Beaver sadly made note of the grave of an early China pioneer in Ningbo, surrounded by the graves of his seven wives, some widowed, some single women missionaries, whom he had married one by one, as one after another died so far from home.[32] In India William Carey's wife broke under the strain and lost her mind. Mrs. Harriet Newell, one of the first two American women foreign missionaries, was the first American foreign missionary, male or female, to die overseas.

By 1820 the Church Missionary Society, the "low-church" counterpart to the Anglican Society for the Propagation of the Gospel, first began to use the term "assistant missionary" for women. In 1822 in America a double wall was breached, the wall against single women, and the wall against black women. The American Board of Commissioners for Foreign Missions sent a single woman, who was also an African American born in slavery, Betsey Stockton, a Presbyterian of Princeton, New Jersey, as a missionary to Hawaii. It hesitated to call her officially a missionary, but emphatically noted that she was not a servant. She founded one of the first schools for the children of commoners in the islands.[33] Ten years later, a man finally stepped up to battle publicly for the cause of single women in mission. The Rev. David Abeel of the [Dutch] Reformed Church in America was on health leave from Malacca where he had been a missionary to the Chinese. He became aware of the prejudice of his mission board, the American Board of Commissioners for Foreign Missions (ABCFM), against the formation of "female agencies," as he called women's boards for mission, and raised a strong protest. His pamphlet, "Appeal to Christian Ladies in Behalf of Christian Education in China and Adjacent Countries," was one of the first significant public statements to call for a clearly defined role for women in mission.[34]

Independent voluntary societies were more receptive of women. From its beginnings in the 1860s, for example, the China Inland Mission granted equal status to its women missionaries. But for the most part the goal was not achieved in the nineteenth century. Among both Protestants and Catholics, it was not until women proved so indispensable and so numerous that they could no longer be treated as extras that the inequality of recognition began to lessen. A rollicking bit of doggerel, date and source unknown, may have exaggerated the injustice but was wickedly true enough to draw blood:

> In the field of Christian missions,
> In this bivouac of life,
> You will find the Christian soldier
> Represented by his wife.

Nevertheless, by 1900 women were a Protestant missionary majority worldwide. In the 249 Protestant mission societies reporting to the Ecumenical Missionary Conference in New York, women missionaries outnumbered men 6,772 to 6,259.[35] Irene H. Barnes paid tribute to them in 1896, "By the turn of the century the woman medical missionary was widely acclaimed as an icon of the mission movement, her office was seen to represent 'the noblest, and perhaps the divinest, calling for Christian womanhood.' "[36]

Women earned their place in modern mission history, however, not solely by weight of numbers. They earned it the hard way, as a story that should be better known illustrates well. Annie Taylor of Tibet was born of "wealthy but worldly" parents who tried to dissuade her from going off to China with the China Inland Mission. Nevertheless, she studied midwifery and dentistry to prepare for the mission field. In China, against advice, Annie Taylor twice entered forbidden Tibet alone. She dressed in native clothes, and lived for a while in a Tibetan monastery. Later she spent five months in a Tibetan village, but was forced to leave. She reached what she thought would be safety in the border kingdom of Sikkim, between Nepal and Bhutan, but was arrested, robbed, and left with no means of support. Twice she survived attempts to poison her. Turned loose, she stumbled toward India, walking twenty to thirty miles a day with no fire at night and often without food. When at last she struggled across the border she had nothing to show for her long ordeal except for the one Tibetan convert she had made, a young man escaping from an angry village chief and whose bleeding feet she had treated on the way. Only one convert, but, that, according to A. T. Pierson, made it all worthwhile.[37]

Women like Annie Taylor proved their worth to skeptical men and stubborn board executives at home. Long before they were given the vote in their missions or societies, their male colleagues had discovered the disconcerting fact that mission was only half effective without the help of women who could do what men could never do in Asian cultures. They could work directly, woman to woman, in situations where cultural barriers kept male missionary doctors away from treating women, and native husbands and fathers kept foreign evangelists away altogether from their wives and daughters. *Woman's Work for Woman*, a journal founded in 1871 in an America that was still wary about suffragettes, became the favorite missionary reading in many a home and congregation.

A fifth generalization about the nineteenth-century Protestant mission is that its characteristic mission structure was the "voluntary society."[38] Missionary efforts and bodies often evolved, at least partially, into church missionary societies, but they typically began as a movement of pietists and independents. This was challenged by a return to denominational dominance in organized mission societies, but the voluntary missionary ideal survived to see denominations wane in the twentieth century, while independent missions and specialized parachurch organizations were hailed by many as the wave of the future.

Not even William Carey, who is often termed the "father of Protestant foreign missions," could get all his fellow Baptists to become involved at the same time in any one thing, not even in a mission society. The church support of the Particular Baptists soon dried up, and the "church society" became a "voluntary society," and Carey was forced into complete independence.[39]

The earliest surviving Protestant voluntary mission organization was the renowned London Missionary Society (1795). It set the pattern for evangelical, ecumenical obedience to Christ as superseding dependence on denominational ecclesiastical control or government authority.[40] The independence was clear; the ecumenicity selective and vaguely negative. The founders declared as their fundamental principle: we will not "send Presbyterianism, Independency, Episcopacy, or any other form of Church order (about which there may be difference of opinion among serious persons), but the Glorious Gospel of the blessed God, to the heathen."[41] The rhetoric sounded dutifully cooperative, but perhaps lacked the fiber of creedal and ecclesiastical identity. The society eventually drifted into a denominational connection with British Congregationalism.[42] In the nineteenth century, however, its roster of missionary heroes is probably as illustrious as any society in Protestant history: Morrison in China, Chalmers in New Guinea, Livingstone and Moffat in Africa, and many more.

The first American missionary society was also independent, an interdenominational union of Congregationalists, Presbyterians, Dutch Reformed, and Baptists — the American Board of Commissioners for Foreign Missions (1810).[43] For years, even after the Baptists left to form their own denominational mission, the ABCFM was the flagship of American missions. Three of the most famous European mission societies were likewise independent: the Basel mission (1815), founded by the German Christian Fellowship, whose missionary seminary trained hundreds of overseas workers noted for their effective integration of evangelism and social service;[44] the Berlin Mission (1824), a Pietist branch of the Basel mission which began to send missionaries itself in 1833;[45] and the Rhenish Missionary Society (1828), which included Lutherans, Calvinists, and nonconfessional Pietists.[46] Even the renowned Church Mission Society of the English church was criticized by Anglican traditionalists for organizing too independently. Only after the CMS had operated for forty years of successful missionary outreach was it officially approved,[47] and then perhaps only because it appealed to high-church Anglicans as a parallel to plural missionary orders in Catholicism.

Roman Catholic Missions

But after all these generalizations about Protestants and the Protestant century, an important counterpoint must be made: even if momentum was with the Protestants, one should not underestimate what the Catholics achieved. Protestant missions were already forty years into their great century before the Catholics in 1832 began to recover from the discouraging eighteenth-century missionary decline brought about by waning fortunes of Portugal and Spain, the effects of the Napoleonic Wars on France, and the suppression of the Jesuits. One Catholic writer described what was left of Catholic missions in that disastrous period as "pitiful relics and ruins" in "a fallow field."[48]

By contrast, Protestants were multiplying in every direction. Their Ecumenical Missionary Conference in New York, 1900, was not as ecumenical as its title claimed. It was thoroughly evangelical and Protestant and missionary, and delegates spoke proudly of its spirit of Christian unity. But there were no Catholics, no Orthodox, and no leaders of the new indigenous churches forming across the seas among the delegates. For a broader view of the state of world Christian mission, that supposedly "ecumenical conference" might at least have appended a brief survey of Catholic missions, as did the *A Handbook of Foreign Missions* published in 1888 twelve years earlier for a world missionary conference in London. That *Handbook* frankly recognized that the largest missionary body in the world was still the Roman Catholic Church. Its statistics and a book published several years later, comparing Catholics and Protestants in India and China, and in areas adjacent to each in Asia made that clear:

	India	Adjacent	China	Adjacent
Roman Catholic adherents	1,282,000	674,000	482,000	77,000
Catholic foreign missionaries	996	342	472	416[49]
Protestant adherents (1893)	710,000		150,000	
Protestant foreign missionaries	998		1,296[50]	

Comparing worldwide Catholic mission statistics for 1800 and 1900 gives yet more proof of a remarkable Catholic recovery. In 1800, according to Louvet, one could count scarcely three hundred missionaries (Franciscan, Dominicans, Vincentians, and members of the Paris Mission Society) overseas. In 1900, in the male missionary orders alone there were twelve thousand ordained priests and five hundred lay Brothers, to which he adds an additional ten thousand "indigenous Sisters." His overall total was sixty thousand missionaries and apparently included European Sisters. In one century, the nineteenth, he estimated that the total number of new Catholic Christians in the mission fields (including England, Scotland, Holland, and the United States) had climbed from 5 million in 1800 to 25 million at the end of the century. There had been nothing like it since the time of the apostles, he exclaimed.[51]

In Asia as a continent, however, there was little ground in 1900 for Christian triumphalism, whether Catholic or Protestant. Asia had 980 million inhabitants out of a total world population of 1.6 billion.[52] As we remarked at the beginning of this volume, Asia is the home of all five of the world's major religions. But Christianity is by far the smallest religion in its home continent. Worldwide in 1900 there were perhaps 1.1 billion adherents of non-Christian religions (Muslim, Hindu, Buddhist, tribal, etc.), chiefly in Africa and Asia, and 558 million Christians, almost all in the West.[53]

Looking Ahead:
The Nineteenth Century as Prologue to the Present

In 1900 a wave of optimism was sweeping through the Christian churches. Given the remarkable recovery of Catholic missions, and expanding Protestant growth and vigor, would not the twentieth century turn out to be even greater than the "great century"? Or as has happened so often in the two-thousand-year story, would advance in mission be followed by another recession?

Perhaps a final optimistic generalization about what was unfolding may be stated as follows: *The nineteenth century was the beginning of the rise of* Asian *churches for Asia's millions.* That statement, however, can be made only in hindsight and in the light of what was happening as one century ended and a new century unfolded. In 1900, the West was still full of confidence that its culture was superior to all others. Few could foresee the day when a generation of Asian Christians would begin to fashion churches that were increasingly ecumenical and Asian.

The beginnings of this occurred in the nineteenth century, when observant missionaries started to face the fact that there could be no indigenous churches without indigenous leadership. And then, if that were true, they realized that inevitably the role of the foreign missionary would have to change.

Conferences of missionaries in India and China in the mid-1800s, in Japan after 1860, and in Korea after 1890 again and again repeated the call to evangelize, educate the laity, and find and train leaders from among them. By the time of the Ecumenical Missionary Conference in New York there was general agreement that, as one delegate phrased it, "the native agent is the center of all permanent work in mission."[54] Agreement on the goal, however, did not translate into agreement on how to reach it.

The missionary representatives from Asia at the conference differed markedly, for instance, over the viability of the "three-self" missionary principle (self-support, self-government, and self-propagation), which was advocated by two leading mission statesmen of the century, the Anglican Henry Venn, secretary of the CMS, and Rufus Anderson, a Congregationalist, the secretary of the ABCFM. The central premise of the principle called for training national leaders and reducing dependence on foreign funds. In Asia variations of the policy had proved effective at Harpoot, Syria, in the 1860s,[55] and in Burma with the Baptists,[56] and in an adapted form called the Nevius Method, named for the American Presbyterian John Nevius, had been most faithfully and successfully demonstrated by the recently arrived Presbyterian missions in Korea in the 1890s.

Two representatives from Korea, the Rev. H. G. Underwood and the medical missionary Dr. C. C. Vinton, strenuously urged the policy of disciplined, measured self-support in every department of missionary work — evangelistic, educational, and medical — as the key to the development of indigenous leadership. Statistics from Korea supported their case. Doctor Vinton told the assembly that six years after the policy had been adopted, "Where four years ago [1896] less than 800 baptized Christians were reported, in the present year the number reaches nearly 5,000."[57] Underwood cited the case of Suh Kyung-Jo, one of the earliest Korean converts, who later became one of the first seven to be ordained a minister. When a missionary guest offered him payment for teaching him Korean at home, Suh replied, "Well, you pay me just for what it costs for your board ... but I cannot take your money for preaching. If I take your money and go out and preach they will all laugh at me; I will lose my influence and the work will stop."[58]

The conference was impressed, but not swept off its feet. Critics reminded the Korea enthusiasts that other factors could explain growth in Korea. God's providence, not just the Nevius Method, surely had a hand in any growth; and Japan's recent defeat of China with methods learned from Western Christian nations might explain Korean willingness to listen so seriously to Western missionaries.[59] Two important American mission board secretaries, Presbyterian and Methodist, took a mediating role in the argument: F. F. Ellinwood, Northern Presbyterian, and Walter R. Lambert, Southern Methodist. They supported the policy but suggested that the key was the difference between "beginning right" and "beginning wrong," namely that self-support was remarkably effective if begun early, but if introduced too late was usually doomed. Dr. Ellinwood expressed the wise opinion that if a policy of dependence continues too long, it takes "a century to uproot the evils of a system of coddling."[60]

Enthusiasm was on the side of the three-self policy, and supporting statistics from the 1888 London Centenary Conference on Protestant Mission spoke well for the future of Protestant missions. As evidence, they cited what it meant if it were true as reported that of thirty-six thousand Protestant missionaries in the world in 1888, thirty thousand were native evangelists, then six thousand were foreign missionaries.[61] Most of the indigenous workers were undoubtedly still on foreign support. But on that critical point — the extent of the dependence — the statistics are not clear. What is clear is that few leaders in third-world churches were known by name outside their local national communities.

There were exceptions like Liang Fa, whose early tracts indirectly influenced the rise of the Taiping Rebellion; Pandita Ramabai of India; Joseph Niijima (Neesima) of Japan, the founder of Doshisha University; and Yun Tchi-Ho of Korea, who was an early supporter of the Student Volunteer Movement in America. But the nineteenth century was still primarily the century of the Western missionaries.

As the century drew to its close in 1900, the important all-Protestant missionary conference, often mentioned above, was held in New York in 1900.[62] To it came as many as two hundred thousand people to Carnegie Hall and city churches near it for the most ambitious celebration of worldwide mission in the history of the modern missionary movement to that date. It was said to be "the largest sustained formal religious event in the history of the Republic."[63] Two former presidents, Benjamin Harrison and William McKinley, and a future president, Theodore Roosevelt, then governor of New York, sat in the front row of the platform at the grand opening and addressed it.[64]

Statistics printed with the Conference Report help to explain the upbeat mood of the occasion. By 1900, in little more than a hundred years of Protestant missions, the total number of "native Christians" in their mission fields was said to have risen from almost none to 4.4 million. Communicant membership of the churches was 1.3 million. Protestant foreign missionaries had risen to a total of 15,460, and the number of ordained indigenous clergy to 4,053.[65]

A survey in 1895 by the editor of the *Missionary Review of the World* gives a revealing glimpse of how the great century of missions appeared to an observant Protestant in 1895. Looking back at the hundred years since William Carey, he described the world in biblical terms as an advancing Christendom marching against unbelieving Heathendom, but on a mission to persuade, not to conquer. And, best of all, the advance was no longer monolithically Western. He counted 11,450 Western Protestant missionaries, now outnumbered by 47,200 ordained and unordained native Christian workers, missionaries in their own countries. Adding the two figures together, he described the rise of a force of more than 55,000 Protestant missionaries on the mission field a "stupendous achievement." In their mission churches he estimated were 1 million communicant members, which together with some 2 to 3 million adherents formed, in his estimate, an overseas world community of 3 or 4 million.[66]

By itself that would mean little against the background of the huge mass of humanity that was and still is Asia. The metaphor of salt comes to mind again. It was character and quality, not the numbers of the converts that made the difference. Like the original disciples of Jesus of Nazareth, Asia's Christians came for the most part from the lower classes, but they were not ordinary. As in the first century, so in the nineteenth, young churches planted by missionaries were being built by their own leaders into the new rising churches of Asia, Africa, and Latin America.

Who could have predicted at the end of the nineteenth century that within eight short decades of the next century, the twentieth, Christians of the "mission fields" would outnumber Christians in the "sending" West; that in China, Christians would be the fastest-growing segment of the population; that there would be more Presbyterians in Korea than in the United States; that an emancipated Philippines would have Christian Filipino presidents; that a non-Christian president of India would claim with pride that the Christian "apostle to Asia," Thomas, had chosen to come to India; and that Japan would elect a descendant of a martyred Catholic saint to be its prime minister?

But there is a flip side to this rosy summary. Who would also have predicted in 1900 that only fourteen years later, in what some had over-confidently labeled "Christendom," the same "Christian" nations that had sent their missionaries around the world would fight in deadly war that would kill millions? Or that in the 1930s theologians would attack the very foundations of the Christian world mission, describing its Christology as "unexplained symbolism," and its emphasis on evangelism for conversion as narrow-minded evasion of a broader call to evangelism by "living and human service" as "preparation for world unity in civilization."[67]

In church history the good news, "the gospel," spreads out from the center. But that center is never geographic. It is personal; it is Jesus Christ as known through the Scriptures. His disciples pass on the good news; people listen and become Christians. They form churches, human centers, and these do become geographic. When one such human center falters, life flows outward to form new centers. Any look at the present indicates just such a faltering in the West, the old "Christendom." But where will the new centers appear? Any look into the future for new centers of Christianity will have to give serious attention to Asia, the continent where it all began, and which now may well become the primary emerging new center of Christian global mission in the twentieth century. But it is presumptuous to try to predict which, if any, will be the next "great century" in mission. With God "a thousand years is but as a day," and "the whole world is in his hands."

In 1895 Delavan Leonard concluded his review of "A Hundred Years of Missions" with a statement worthy of remembrance:

> All things considered, a most wonderful achievement [was] made in a single century . . . The [missionary] force is ridiculously impotent if standing alone, but is abundantly able, wholly adequate with the Great Captain to devise and lead . . . What more is needed . . . ? Go ye into all the world.[68]

Such was the faith and hope of that generation. "Jesus Christ is the way, the truth and the life"; he is the only "saviour of the world."

The nineteenth century was a century of faith, and for most Protestant missionaries that was the core from which their faith extended to all that Jesus Christ had said, and done, and would do for those to whom he came and for whom he died, saying "Go ye into all the world." So they went. For nineteenth-century Catholic missions the motivation was much the same and equally simple: obedience, but obedience with all the added nuances of two thousand years of tradition. In the century of faith, there was power in such simplicity. But would those sturdy nineteenth-century missionary foundations survive another hundred years in the complex, upsetting, fast-moving twentieth century within human memory? It is clear in 2004 that they did.

A quick look at what occurred in the twentieth century closes this epilogue on an upbeat note of hope for the twenty-first century. Statistics are not the best measure of faith, but they do measure survival. The table below is adapted from David Barrett's comparison of the global membership of the world's major religions in 1900 and 2000.[69] Look at the table. The church is still there, and still in mission, and still growing. And Adoniram Judson's brave phrase rang as true in the twentieth century as it did in the nineteenth: "The future is as bright as the promises of God."

But perhaps a quotation from a Western foreign missionary, however faithful and famous he may have been, is the wrong note on which to close. The fact is that at the end of the "great century" of foreign missions a better end for this volume would be a voice from an Asian Christian.

The voice is the voice of an almost forgotten man, an unnamed Baptist deacon in tribal Burma about fifty years after Judson. Christian Karens in the hills a hundred miles northeast of Rangoon were starving. A plague of rats had destroyed their harvest. Missionaries found their little church congregation reduced to eating the rats that had destroyed their rice crop. Formerly they had tried to poison the rats. Now the missionaries could do little to help but pray for them. They were about to leave when a Karen deacon brought them a gift, ten rupees (five dollars). He said, "This is from our church for [our] Ka-Khyen mission," a frontier mission to a tribe farther north. "No," said their foreign friends, "you must use this for yourselves. You are starving." The deacon shook his head. "Yes, but we can live on rats. The Ka-Khyen cannot live without the gospel."[70]

Jesus Christ was born in Asia. Some say that Christianity has failed in Asia. Not so. The numbers tell us otherwise. And the mounting chorus of voices from Asia's Christians should remind us in the doubting West that God never fails.

World Religious Statistics, 1900 and 2000

	1900	2000
Total World Population	1.6b	6b
Christians	558m	2b
Catholics	267m	1.1b
Protestants (PIA)*	141.5m	821m
Muslims	200m	1.2b
Hindus	203m	824m
Buddhists	127m	364m
Ethnoreligionists†	118m	231m
New Religionists	5.9m	103m
Non-Religious	3m	774m
Atheists	226,000	150m

*PIA = Protestant, Independent, Anglican
†Ethnoreligionists = folk or tribal religions

NOTES

1. Latourette, *A History of the Expansion of Christianity*, 5:1.

2. S. H. Chester, Secretary, Board of Foreign Mission, Presbyterian Church U.S., in *Ecumenical Missionary Conference, New York, 1900*, 2:255.

3. David Barrett estimates Christian and world population in 1800 as 208 million of 902 million (23.1 percent) (*Christian World Encyclopedia*, 1982). Barrett's table lists the chronology of growth thus:

1000: World population: 269m, among whom Christians are 50m (18.7%).
1500: World population: 425m, among whom Christians are 81m (19%).
1800: World population: 900m, among whom Christians are 208m (23.1%)
1900: World population: 1.62b, among whom Christians are 558m (34.4%).
2000: World population: 6.1b, among whom Christians are 1.9b (30%).

4. Barrett, in *IBMR* (January 2000): 25.

5. The percentage of all Christians (adherents) was estimated as 34.4 percent (Barrett, *IBMR* [January 1999]: 25). The figures were: Catholics 266 million, total Protestants 141 million, and Orthodox 103 million.

6. United Nations, Population Division, "World Population Growth from Year 0 to 2050" (online, 1999), p. 3 of 4. Asia's population in 1500 was estimated as 500 million; in 1750, 790 million; in 1800, 980 million; in 1850, 1.26 billion; in 1900, 1.65 billion; in 1910, 1.75 billion; in 1920, 1.86 billion; in 1930, 2.07 billion; in 1940, 2.30 billion; in 1950, 2.52 billion; 1960, 3.02 billion.

7. Barrett et al., eds., *World Christian Encyclopedia*, 2001, 13.

8. Figures are from Barrett et al., eds., *World Christian Encyclopedia*, 2001.

9. Ch. Dallet, *Controversial Catechism: Or Short Answers to the Objections of Protestants against the True Religion*, 5th ed. (Bangalore: Spectator Press, 1894).

10. Delavan L. Leonard, *A Hundred Years of Missions* (New York: Funk & Wagnalls, 1895), 131–132.

11. Thomas A. Askew, "The 1888 London Centenary Conference: Ecumenical Disappointment or American Missions Coming of Age?" (*IBMR* 18, no. 3 [July 1994]: 114–115). Much the same mixture of Western pride and rebuke of Western greed occurred at the New York Ecumenical Mission Conference in New York in 1900 (*Ecumenical Missionary Conference, New York, 1900*, 1:402, 405, 457; and 2/2:79; and passim).

12. A helpful book of essays on the problems of academic research and fair reporting of the Protestant missionary movement is Robert A. Bickers and Rosemary Seton, eds., *Missionary Encounters: Sources and Issues* (Richmond, Surrey, England: Curzon Press, 1996).

13. *A Handbook of Foreign Missions, 1888*, 334.

14. Quoted by Thomas Askew, "The 1988 Centenary Mission Conference," 114.

15. See, for example, Ernest Brandewie, *In the Light of the Word: Divine Word Missionaries of North America* (Maryknoll, N.Y.: Orbis Books, 2000), 153–154.

16. David Bosch, *Transforming Mission: Paradigm Shifts in Theology of Mission* (Maryknoll, N.Y.: Orbis Books, 1991) 281. He uses the phrase in a nonpejorative way to differentiate it from the broader range of interests in the evangelical philosophy of Jonathan Edwards.

17. For source material on the early emphasis on proclamation and conversion, see Corr, " 'The Field Is the World,' " 43–50, 260ff., 287ff., 290ff., 307–308. Corr's focus is on the American Board of Commissioners for Foreign Missions.

18. Timothy Dwight, *Sermon: Delivered in Boston, Sept. 10, 1813, before the American Board of Foreign Missions,* 2nd ed. (Boston: Samuel T. Armstrong, 1813), 27–28.

19. Charles Hodge, *Conference Papers, or, Analyses of Discourses, Doctrinal and Practical Delivered on Sabbath Afternoons to the Students of the Theological Seminary, Princeton, N.J.* (New York: Charles Scribner, 1879), 326–329.

20. *Ecumenical Missionary Conference, New York, 1900,* 1:14. President James B. Angell of the University of Michigan added his presence and support to the conference (1:47, 180, 320, 341; 11:370).

21. See *Student Mission Power*; Michael Parker, *The Kingdom of Character*; and Askew, "The 1888 London Centenary Conference," 116.

22. See the series named *The Fundamentals: A Testimony to the Truth* (Chicago: Testimony, 1910–).

23. *Ecumenical Missionary Conference, New York, 1900,* 2:329. Duff was quoted at the Conference by A. T. Pierson, editor of the *Missionary Review.*

24. Incomplete Protestant statistics in 1888 show the trend of increasing American participation. The American societies were younger and were growing faster. They had the larger number of Asian Protestant communicant church members (98,000), closely followed by the British, and with a lesser number the Germans (24,000). The numbers for adherents, as distinct from communicants, is: British societies (268,000), American (225,000) and European (80,000). The larger British number here is perhaps attributable to the prestige of British rule. But hasty conclusions should be avoided for the quoted statistics are neither totalled, nor coordinated (*A Handbook of Foreign Missions,* 12 and passim).

25. William R. Hutchison, *Errand to the World: American Protestant Thought and Foreign Missions* (Chicago: University of Chicago Press, 1987).

26. Hutchison, *Errand to the World.*

27. See above chap. 8.

28. Cf. Rufus Anderson, *Foreign Missions: Their Relations and Claims* (New York: Charles Scribner, 1869), 110–119.

29. Francis Wayland, *The Apostolic Ministry* (Rochester: Sage & Brother, 1853), 19, cited by Hutchison, *Errand to the World,* 84.

30. See *Student Mission Power.*

31. Pierce Beaver dates October 9, 1800, as marking the first step toward equality for American women in mission, the day that Mary Webb organized the interdenominational Boston Female Society of Missionary Purposes (*American Protestant Women in World Mission,* an updated and revised second edition of his *All Loves Excelling*). For a discussion of the relation between women in mission and feminism, see Ruth Tucker, *Guardians of the Great Commission,* 37–40.

32. Beaver, *All Loves Excelling,* 54ff.

33. Eileen F. Moffett, "Betsy Stockton, Pioneer American Missionary," in *IBMR* 19, no. 2 (April 1995): 71–76.

34. "Female Agency Among the Heathen" (London: Edward Suter, 1850), 261–265, as cited in Beaver, *American Protestant Women in World Mission,* 89–91. A quotation from Rufus Anderson, the outstanding secretary of the ABCFM, reflects the board's attitude toward formation of women's boards of mission. "In

a word, woman was made for man...," though it is unfair to judge him by this short quote taken out of context. See R. Pierce Beaver, ed., *To Advance the Gospel: Selections from the Writings of Rufus Anderson* (Grand Rapids, Mich.: William B. Eerdmans), 211, and cf. 15, 28–29, 199.

35. *Ecumenical Missionary Conference,* 2:424.

36. Irene H. Barnes, *Behind the Great Wall: The Story of the C.E.Z.M.S., Work and Workers in China* (London: Marshall Brothers: Church of England Zenana Missionary Society, 1896), cited by Rosemary Fitzgerald, in Bickers and Seton, *Missionary Encounters,* 176.

37. Arthur T. Pierson, *The Modern Mission Century: Viewed as a Cycle of Divine Working: A Review of the Missions of the Nineteenth Century with Reference to the Superintending Providence of God* (New York: Baker and Taylor, 1901), 191–193.

38. Ralph D. Winter and R. Pierce Beaver, *The Warp and the Woof: Organizing for Mission* (Pasadena, Calif.: William Carey Library, 1970). In the technical language of sophisticated sociology a "voluntary society" is called a "sodality"; a "church mission" is called a "modality." The sodality is formed within a larger community for a more focused task than the total community may be ready to attempt. The modality is the larger community — a nation, or tribe, or a Christian denomination. For Catholics papal mission would be a modality (a "church" mission); a missionary order, like the Jesuits, would be a sodality, a voluntary society.

39. See above, chap. 12.

40. Goodall, *History of the London Missionary Society.* In 1966 its name was changed to the Congregational Council for World Mission.

41. See Lovett, *The History of the London Missionary Society,* 1:28–29, 49–51.

42. See C. Sylvester Horne, *The Story of the L.M.S.,* 2nd ed. (London: London Missionary Society, 1895).

43. Strong, *The Story of the American Board: An Account of the First Hundred Years of the American Board of Commissioners for Foreign Missions* (Boston: Pilgrim Press, 1910); F. F. Goodsell, *You Shall Be My Witnesses* (Boston: American Board of Commissioners for Foreign Missions, 1959); Beaver, *To Advance the Gospel,* 64–68.

44. H. Witschi, *Geschichte der Basler Mission,* 5 vols., vols. 1–3 by Wilhelm Schlatter (Basel: Verlag der Basler Missionbuchhandlung, 1916); vol. 4 by Wilhelm Schlatter, revised by Hermann Witschi (Basel: Basileia Verlag, 1965); vol. 5 by H. Witschi (Basel: Basileia Verlag, 1970).

45. J. Richter, *Geschichte der Berliner Missionsgesellschaft* (Berlin: Berliner ev. Missionsgesellschaft, 1924).

46. Bonn, *Ein Jahrhundert Rheinische Mission.*

47. On the difficult relationship between the Society for the Propagation of the Gospel (high church), and the Church Missionary Society (low church), see M. E. Gibbs, *The Anglican Church in India,* 71–83, 121–125.

48. Schmidlin, *Catholic Mission History,* chap. 4, "Period of Decline, from the Second Half of the 17th to the Beginning of the 19th Century" (555), quoting Robert Streit, *Die Missionsliteratur des 19 Jahrhunderts* (1917).

49. *A Handbook of Foreign Missions,* 327–338, 341. The date for the statistics is 1886/1887. "Adjacent to India" includes Burma, Siam to Indochina and Malaysia; "around China" includes Korea, Japan, Manchuria, Mongolia, and Tibet. Not included in Asia are the Philippines, Indonesia, Central Asia, and the Middle East.

50. Leonard, *A Hundred Years of Missions*, 131–132.

51. Louvet, *Les missions catholiques au XIXme siècle*, 412ff.

52. Louvet, *Les missions catholiques au XIXme siècle*, 412ff. Cf. United Nations, *World Population Prospects*, 1998 revision (New York, by Internet), which estimates 1,650,000 population in 1900, 947 million of whom were in Asia.

53. Barrett, in *IBMR*, 25.

54. H. M. M. Hackett, former Anglican Church Missionary Society in India, in *Ecumenical Missionary Conference, New York, 1900*, 2:251; and see chaps. 23–25 on indigenization of missionary work, 2:251–324.

55. *Ecumenical Missionary Conference, New York, 1900*, 2:292ff.

56. *Ecumenical Missionary Conference, New York, 1900*, 2:297–299.

57. *Ecumenical Missionary Conference, New York, 1900*, 1:534ff.

58. *Ecumenical Missionary Conference, New York, 1900*, 2:306–307.

59. Arthur H. Erwin of India, in *Ecumenical Missionary Conference, New York, 1900*, 2:307–308. Other influential critics included R. M. Mateer of China.

60. *Ecumenical Missionary Conference, New York, 1900*, 2:321–324.

61. Askew, "The 1888 London Centenary Missionary Conference," 114.

62. *Ecumenical Missionary Conference, New York, 1900*.

63. Thomas A. Askew, "The Ecumenical Missionary Conference, New York, 1900: A Centennial Appraisal," unpublished manuscript, 1999, 1.

64. Former president Grover Cleveland, though not present, was an honorary member of the conference.

65. The statistics, prepared by James S. Dennis, were appended to the Report of the Conference (*Ecumenical Missionary Conference, New York, 1900*, 2: 424–431, with the most condensed summary on 427).

66. Leonard, *A Hundred Years of Missions*, 417. His statistics reported 11,450 Protestant missionaries, about 4,300 were ordained men, less than 1,000 were unordained men, 3,650 were wives and 2,575 were single women (his numbers do not quite add up). Of the 47,200 native workers, 4,200 were ordained, 43,000 were lay pastors, evangelists. teachers, etc. Cf. the more accurate figures of James S. Dennis five years later for the 1900 Ecumenical Missionary Conference in New York (*Ecumenical Missionary Conference, New York, 1900*, 2:242, as cited above).

67. See W. E. Hocking, *Re-Thinking Missions: A Layman's Inquiry* (New York: Fleming H. Revell, 1932), 52, 65; cf. Robert E. Speer, *"Re-Thinking Missions" Examined* (New York: Fleming H. Revell, 1933), reprinted from *MRW* (January 1933); Bosch, *Transforming Mission*, 321–327.

68. Leonard, *A Hundred Years of Mission*, 418.

69. Barrett, "Status of Global Mission, 2001," *IBMR* (January 2001): 25.

70. William F. Bainbridge, *Along the Lines of the Front: A General Survey of Baptist Home and Foreign Missions* (Philadelphia: American Baptist Publication Society, 1882), 180. The unnamed deacon was a Bassein Sgau Karen.

Bibliography

Abdullah, Munshi. *The Hikayat Abdullah*. Trans. and annotated by A. H. Hill. Vol. 28, Pt. 3 of the *Journal of the Malayan Branch of the Royal Asiatic Society*. Singapore: Malay Publishing House, 1955.

Abeel, David. *Journal of a Residence in China and the Neighboring Countries, from 1829 to 1833*. New York: Leavitt, Lord, 1834.

————. *The Missionary Conference at Jerusalem: Or an Exhibition of the Claims of the World to the Gospel*. New York: John S. Taylor, 1838.

Abeyasingha, Nihal. *The Radical Tradition: The Changing Shape of Theological Reflection in Sri Lanka*. Colombo: The Ecumenical Institute, 1985.

Abeyasinghe, Tikiri. *Portuguese Rule in Ceylon, 1594–1612*. Colombo: University of Ceylon, 1966.

Abu-Izzeddin, Nejla M. *The Druzes: A New Study of Their History, Faith and Society*. Leiden: E. J. Brill, 1984.

Achútegui, Pedro S., and Miguel A. Bernad. *Religious Revolution in the Philippines*. 4 vols. Manila: Ateneo de Manila, 1960–1972.

Adeney, David H. *China: Christian Students Face the Revolution*. London: Inter-Varsity Press, 1973.

Adhaw, S. M. *Pandita Ramabai*. Madras: Christian Literature Society, 1979.

Afzal, Cameron. "An Interview with William McElwee Miller." Typescript, 1985.

Aikawa, Takaaki, and Lynn Leavenworth. *The Mind of Japan: A Christian Perspective*. Valley Forge, Pa.: Judson Press, 1967.

Akkeren, Philip van. *Sri and Christ: A Study of the Indigenous Church in East Java*. London: Lutterworth, 1970.

Albaugh, Dana M. *Between Two Centuries: A Study of Four Baptist Mission Fields, Assam, South India, Bengal-Orissa and South China*. Philadelphia: Judson Press, 1935.

[Alexander of Rhodes]. *Voyages et missions du Père Alexandre de Rhodes*. New edition. Paris: Julien, Lanier, 1854.

Algra, A. *De Gereformeerde Kerken in Nederlands-Indie Indonesie (1877–1961)*. Franeker: T. Wever, [1967].

Allen, Catherine B. "Charlotte (Lottie) Moon." In *Mission Legacies: Biographical Studies of Leaders of the Modern Missionary Movement*, ed. G. H. Anderson et al., 205–215. Maryknoll, N.Y.: Orbis Books, 1994.

————. *The New Lottie Moon Story*. Nashville: Broadman Press, 1980.

Allen, Horace N. *A Chronological Index*. Seoul: Methodist Publishing House, 1901.

————. "The H. N. Allen Papers." New York Public Library.

Altholz, Josef L. *The Churches in the Nineteenth Century*. Indianapolis and New York: Bobbs-Merrill, 1967.

Alzona, Encarnacion. *A History of Education in the Philippines, 1565–1930*. Manila: University of the Philippines Press, 1932.

Amaladass, Anand, ed. *Jesuit Presence in Indian History*. Anand, India: Gujarat Sahitya Prakash, 1988.

Amaladass, Anand, and Francis X. Clooney, trans. and ed. *Preaching Wisdom to the Wise: Three Treatises by Roberto de Nobili, S.J., Missionary and Scholar in Seventeenth Century South India*. St. Louis: Institute of Jesuit Sources, 2000.

Amann, E. "Malabares (Rites)." *DTC* 9:1704–1746.

Ambedkar, Bhimrao Ramji. *The Untouchables: Who Were They, and Why They Became Untouchable*. New Delhi: Amrit Book Co., 1948.

American Missionaries and Social Change in China: Collision and Confluence. A Public International Symposium. Portland, Ore.: Northwest Regional China Council, 1994.

Ames, Michael M. "Westernization or Modernization: The Case of Sinhalese Buddhism." *Social Compass* 20 (1973): 139–170.

Andaya, Barbara Watson, and Leonard Y. Andaya. *A History of Malaysia*. London: Macmillan, 1982.

Anderson, Gerald H., ed. *Biographical Dictionary of Christian Missions*. New York and London: Macmillan Reference USA/Simon & Schuster, 1998.

―――, et al., eds. *Mission Legacies: Biographical Studies of Leaders of the Modern Missionary Movement*. Maryknoll, N.Y.: Orbis Books, 1994.

―――, ed. *Studies in Philippine Church History*. Ithaca, N.Y.: Cornell University Press, 1969.

Anderson, Robert K. *My Dear Redeemer's Praise: The Life of Luther Lisgar Young, Sometime Missionary in Korea and Japan*. Hansport, N.S., Canada: Lancelot Press, 1979.

Anderson, Rufus. *Foreign Missions: Their Relations and Claims*. New York: Charles Scribner, 1869.

―――. *History of the Missions of the American Board of Commissioners for Foreign Missions in India*. Boston: Congregational Publishing Society, 1875.

―――. *History of the Missions of the American Board of Commissioners for Foreign Missions to the Oriental Churches*. 2 vols. Boston: Congregational Publishing Society, 1872.

―――. "Missionary Schools." In *Biblical Repository [The American]* 12 (1838): 87–113.

Andrews, Charles Freer. *Sadhu Sundar Singh: A Personal Memoir*. London: Hodder & Stoughton, 1934.

Anesaki, Masaharu. "Prosecution of Kirishitans after the Shimabara Insurrection." *MN* 1, no. 2 (1938).

Annales Ecclesiasticos de Philipinas, 1574–1682. 2 vols. Ed. and trans. Ruperto C. Santos. Manila: Roman Catholic Archbishop of Manila, 1994.

Annals of the Propagation of the Faith (APF). Dublin. Before 1838 published as *Lettres Edifiantes*.

Appasamy, Aiyadurai J. *The Gospel and India's Heritage*. London: SPCK, 1942.

―――. *Sundar Singh: A Biography*. London: Lutterworth Press, 1958.

Appenzeller, H. G. See Daniel M. Davies. *Life and Thought of Henry Gerard Appenzeller* (1988); and Griffis, *A Modern Pioneer in Korea* (1912).

Apram, Mar. *Mar Abdisho Thondanat: A Biography*. Trichur, India: Mar Narsai Press, 1987.

Aqiqi, A. D. *Lebanon in the Last Years of Feudalism, 1840–1868*. Trans. Malcolm H. Kerr. Beirut: Catholic Press, 1959.

Aragón, J. Gayo. "The Controversy over Justification of Spanish Rule in the Philippines." In *Studies in Philippine Church History*, ed. Gerald H. Anderson. Ithaca, N.Y.: Cornell University Press, 1969.

Arai, Hakuseki. *Lessons from History: Arai Hakuseki's Tokushi Yoron.* Trans. with commentary Joyce Ackroyd. St. Lucia and New York: University of Queensland Press, 1982.

Aranas, Alfredo G. "A Note on Jesuits and the Philippine Language." *PS* 53 (1985): 221–226.

Arattukulam, Michael. *St. Francis Xavier on the Malabar Coast.* Booklet. Alleppey, India, 1968.

Arberry, A. J., ed. *Religion in the Middle East: Three Religions in Concord and Conflict.* 2 vols. Cambridge: Cambridge University Press, 1969.

Archivum S. Congregationis pro Gentium Evangelizatione seu de Propaganda Fide. Rome.

Armenia: A Continuing Tragedy. Geneva: WCC Commission of the Churches on International Affairs, 1984.

Arpee, Leon. *The Armenian Awakening: A History of the Armenian Church, 1820–1860.* Chicago and London: University of Chicago Press/T. Fisher Unwin, 1909.

———. *A Century of Armenian Protestantism 1846–1946.* New York: Armenian Missionary Association of America, 1946.

———. *A History of Armenian Christianity from the Beginning to Our Own Time.* New York: Armenian Missionary Association of America, 1946.

Ashjian, Mesrob. *Armenian Church Patristic and Other Essays.* New York: Armenian Prelacy, 1994.

Ashley-Brown, W. *On the Bombay Coast and Deccan: The Origin and History of the Bombay Diocese.* London: SPCK, 1937.

Asia Watch. *Freedom of Religion in China: January 1992.* New York and Washington, D.C.: Human Rights Watch, 1992.

Askew, Thomas A. "The Ecumenical Missionary Conference, New York, 1900: A Centennial Appraisal." Unpublished manuscript, 1999.

———. "The 1888 London Centenary Conference: Ecumenical Disappointment or American Missions Coming of Age?" *IBMR* 18, no. 3 (July 1994): 114–115.

The Assam Mission of the American Baptist Missionary Union: Papers and Discussion, 1886. Calcutta: J. W. Thomas Baptist Mission Press, 1887.

Athyal, Saphir, ed. *Church in Asia Today: Opportunities and Challenges.* Singapore: Asia Lausanne Committee for World Evangelization, 1996.

Atiya, A. S. *A History of Eastern Christianity.* London: Methuen, 1968.

Attwater, Donald. *The Christian Churches of the East.* Vol. 1: *Churches in Communion with Rome.* Vol. 2: *Churches Not in Communion with Rome.* Milwaukee: Bruce Publishing Co., 1961.

Attwater, Rachel. *Adam Schall: A Jesuit at the Court of China, 1592–1666.* London: Geoffrey Chapman, 1963.

Axtell, James. "Were Indian Conversions Bona Vide?" In *Christianity and Missions 1450–1800*, ed. J. S. Cummins. Brookfield, Vt.: Ashgate, 1997.

Azariah, Vedanayakam Samuel, and Henry Whitehead. *Christ in the Indian Villages.* 2nd ed. London: Student Christian Movement Press, 1930.

———. *India and the Christian Movement.* Madras: Christian Literature Society for India, 1936.

―――. See also Susan Billington Harper, *In the Shadow of the Mahatma: Bishop V. S. Azariah and the Travails of Christianity in British India*; Carol Graham, *Azariah of Dornakal*; and J. Z. Hodge, *Bishop Azariah of Dornakal*.

Baago, Kaj. "The First Independence Movement among Indian Christians." *ICHR* (Mysore City, India), 1, no. 1 (June 1967): 65–82.

―――. *A History of the National Christian Council of India, 1914–1964*. Mysore, India: Wesley Press, 1965.

―――. *Pioneers of Indigenous Christianity*. Bangalore: Christian Literature Society, 1969.

―――. "'Sheepstealing' in the 19th Century." *Bulletin of the Church History Association of India* (November 1966): 31–36.

Backus, Mary, ed. *Siam and Laos: As Seen by Our American Missionaries*. Philadelphia: Presbyterian Board of Publications, 1884.

Badger, George Percy. *The Nestorians and Their Rituals*. 2 vols. London: John Masters, 1852.

Badley, Brenton T., ed. *Visions and Victories in Hindustan: A Story of the Mission Stations of the Methodist Episcopal Church in Southern India*. Madras: Methodist Publishing House, 1931.

Bainbridge, William F. *Along the Lines at the Front: A General Survey of Baptist Home and Foreign Missions*. Philadelphia: American Baptist Publications Soc., 1882.

Baird, Richard. *William M. Baird of Korea: A Profile*. Oakland, Calif.: private, 1968.

Baird, William M. "Union of Presbyterian Missions in Korea." *MRW*, N.S. 6 (1893): 532.

Baker, Donald L. "The Martyrdom of Paul Yun: Western Religion and Eastern Ritual in 18th Century Korea." *TRASK* 54 (1979): 33–58.

Baker, Frances J. *The Story of the Woman's Foreign Missionary Society of the Methodist Episcopal Church 1869–1895*. Cincinnati/New York: Cranston & Curtis/Hunt & Eaton, 1896; reprint New York & London: Garland Publishing, Inc., 1987.

Baker, Richard Terrill. *Ten Thousand Years: The Story of Methodism's First Century in China*. New York: Methodist Church, Board of Missions, 1947.

Balasundra, Franklyn. *Contemporary Asian Christian Theology*. Bangalore: United Theological College and ISPCK, 1955.

Baldwin, Frank P., Jr. "The March First Movement: Korean Challenge and Japanese Response." PhD diss., Columbia University, 1969.

Balfour, Margaret I., and Ruth Young. *The Work of Medical Women in India*. Oxford: Oxford University Press, 1929.

Ballhatchet, Kenneth. *Caste, Class, and Catholicism in India 1789–1914*. Richmond, Surrey, U.K.: Curzon Press, 1998.

Bangert, William V. *A History of the Society of Jesus*. 2nd ed., rev. St. Louis: Institute of Jesuit Sources, 1986.

Barber, Benjamin Russel. *Kali Charan Banurji: Brahmin, Scholar, Saint*. Madras: Christian Literature Society for India and Calcutta: The National Council of Young Men's Christian Associations of India and Ceylon, 1912.

Barnes, Irene H. *Behind the Great Wall: The Story of the C.E.Z.M.S., Work and Workers in China*. London: Marshall Brothers: Church of England Zenana Missionary Society, 1896.

Barnett, Suzanne Wilson, and John King Fairbank, eds. *Christianity in China: Early Protestant Missionary Writings*. Cambridge, Mass.: Harvard University Press, 1985.

Barpujari, H. K. *The American Missionaries in India (1836–1900 A.D.)*. Guwahati, India: Spectrum Publications, 1986.

Barrett, David B. *Cosmos, Chaos and Gospel: A Chronology of World Evangelization*. Birmingham, Ala.: New Hope Press, 1987.

———. "Status of Global Mission, 2001." *IBMR* (January 2001): 25.

———, ed. *World Christian Encyclopedia*. New York: Oxford University Press, 1982.

———, George Vurian, and Todd Johnson, eds. *World Christian Encyclopedia*. 2nd ed. New York: Oxford University Press, 2001.

Basham, A. L., ed. *A Cultural History of India*. London: Oxford University Press, 1975.

Bates, M. Searle. *China in Change: An Approach to Understanding*. New York: Friendship Press, 1969.

———. *Gleanings from the Manuscripts of M. Searle Bates: The Protestant Endeavor in Chinese Society, 1890–1950*. Ed. Cynthia McLean. New York: The China Program, NCCC, USA, 1984.

Bauswein, Jean-Jacques, and Lukas Vischer. *The Reformed Family Worldwide: A Survey of Reformed Churches, Theological Schools, and International Organizations*. Grand Rapids, Mich.: William B. Eerdmans, 1999.

Bays, Daniel H., ed. *Christianity in China: From the Eighteenth Century to the Present*. Stanford, Calif.: Stanford University Press, 1996.

———. "The Early Years of the Oriental Missionary Society: Foreign Missionaries and Native Evangelists in Japan, 1901–1917," *FH* 31, no. 1 (Winter–Spring 1997): 15–27.

Beach, Harlan P., ed. *A Geography and Atlas of Protestant Missions*. 2 vols. New York: Student Volunteer Movement for Foreign Missions, 1901, 1903.

Beach, Harlan P., and Burton St. John, eds. *World Statistics of Christian Missions*. New York: Foreign Missions Conference of North America, 1916.

Bear, James Edwin, Jr. "The Mission Work of the Presbyterian Church in the United States in China, 1867–1952." 5 vols. Unpublished manuscript. Union Theological Seminary, Richmond, Va.

Beaver, R. Pierce. *All Loves Excelling: American Protestant Women in World Mission*. Grand Rapids, Mich.: William B. Eerdmans, 1968.

———. *American Protestant Women in World Mission*. Grand Rapids, Mich.: William B. Eerdmans, 1980.

———. *Ecumenical Beginnings in Protestant World Mission: A History of Comity*. New York: Thomas Nelson, 1962.

———. *The Gospel and Frontier Peoples: A Report of a Consultation, December 1972*. Pasadena: William Carey Library, 1973.

———, ed. *To Advance the Gospel: Selections from the Writings of Rufus Anderson*. Grand Rapids, Mich.: William B. Eerdmans, 1967.

Beck, James R. *Dorothy Carey: The Tragic and Untold Story of Mrs. William Carey*. Grand Rapids, Mich.: Baker Book House, 1992.

Becker, C. *History of the Catholic Missions in Northeast India (1890–1915)*. Trans. and ed. G. Stadler and S. Karotemprel. Shillong, India: Firma KLM Private Ltd., Sacred Heart College, 1980.

———. *Indisches Kastenwesen und Christliche Mission*. Aachen: Xaverius Verlag, 1921.

Beckmann, Johannes. *Die katholische Missionsmethode in China in neuester Zeit, 1842–1931*. Immensee, Switzerland: Druck der Calendaria A.-G., 1931.

Beltrami, G. *La Chiesa caldea nel secolo dell'Unione. Orientalia Christiana* 29, no. 83. Rome, 1933.

Bennett, Adrian A. *Missionary Journalist in China: Young J. Allen and His Magazines 1860–1883*. Athens: University of Georgia Press, 1983.

Bennett, J. W. *Ceylon and Its Capabilities*. Reprint of 1843 London ed. Rajagiriya, Sri Lanka: Trumpet Publishers, 1984.

Bentley-Taylor, David. *The Weathercock's Reward: Christian Progress in Muslim Java*. London: Overseas Missionary Fellowship, 1967.

Berkov, Robert. *Strong Man of China: The Story of Chiang Kai-Shek*. Boston: Houghton Mifflin Co., 1938.

Bernad, Miguel A. *The Christianization of the Philippines: Problems and Perspectives*. Manila: Filipiniana Book Club, 1972.

Bernard, Henri. *Les îles Philippines du grand archipel de la Chine*. Tientsin: La Procure de la Mission de Sienhsien, 1936.

Bernard-Maitre, Henri. *La sagesse chinoise et philosophie chrétienne*. Serie Culturelle des Hautes Etudes de Tientsin. Paris: Cathasia, 1935.

———, ed. *Lettres et Mémoires d'Adam Schall S.J.* See Adam Schall, *Historica Relatio*.

Bernoville, Gaetan de. *The Jesuits*. Abridged and trans. Kathleen Balfe. London: Burns, Oates, and Washbourne, 1937.

Berry, Mary Elizabeth. *Hideyoshi*. Cambridge: Harvard University Press, 1982.

Bertrand, J. *La Mission du Maduré d'après des documents inédits*. 4 vols. Paris: Poussielgue-Rusand, 1847–1854.

Bettray, P. Johannes. *Die Akkommodationsmethode des Matteo Ricci*. Rome: Gregorian University, 1955.

Beven, F. Lorenz, ed. *A History of the Diocese of Colombo: A Centenary Volume*. Colombo: The Times of Ceylon, 1946.

Bickers, Robert A., and Rosemary Seton, eds. *Missionary Encounters: Sources and Issues*. Richmond, Surrey, Eng.: Curzon Press, 1996.

Biermann, Benno M. *Die Anfange der Neueren Dominikanermission in China*. In *Missionswissenschaftliche Abhandlungen und Texte*, No. 10, ed. J. Schmidlin. Munster in Westfalen: Aschendorffschen Verlagsbuchhandlung, 1927.

Biernatzki, William E., Luke Jin-chang Im, and Anselm K. Kim. *Korean Catholicism in the 1970s: A Christian Community Comes of Age*. Maryknoll, N.Y.: Orbis Books, 1975.

Biographical Dictionary of Christian Missions. See under G. H. Anderson, ed.

Bird, Isaac. *Bible Work in Bible Lands; or Events in the History of the Syrian Mission*. Philadelphia: Presbyterian Board of Publication, 1872.

Blackmore, Sophia. *Sophia Blackmore in Singapore: Educational and Missionary Pioneer 1887–1927. Selections*. Ed. Theodore R. Doraisamy. Singapore: Methodist Church in Singapore, 1987.

Blair, Emma Helen, and James Alexander Robertson, eds. *The Philippine Islands 1493–1803: Explorations by Early Navigators, Descriptions of the Islands and Their Peoples, Their History and Records of the Catholic Missions*. 55 vols. Translated and annotated. Cleveland: Arthur H. Clark, 1903–1907.

Blair, William Newton. *Gold in Korea*. Topeka, Kans.: H. M. Ives, 1957.

———. *The Korea Pentecost and Other Experiences*. New York: Presbyterian Board of Foreign Missions, n.d. [1909].

Blanford, Carl E. *Chinese Churches in Thailand*. Bangkok: Suribayan Publishers, n.d. [1973].

Blaze, L. E. *A History of Ceylon*. Colombo: Christian Literature Society, 1900.

Bliss, Frederick J. *Reminiscences of Daniel Bliss*. New York: Fleming H. Revell, 1920.

Boal, Barbara M. *The Konds: Human Sacrifice and Religious Change*. Warminster, Wilts., England: Aris & Phillips, 1982.

Boardman, Eugene Powers. *Christian Influence upon the Ideology of the Taiping Rebellion 1851–1864*. Madison: University of Wisconsin Press, 1952.

Boardman, George Dana. See Alonzo King, *Memoir of George Dana Boardman*; and Joseph Chandler Robbins, *Boardman of Burma*.

Boetzelaer van Dubbledam, Carel Wessel Theodorus. *De Gereformeerde Kerken in Nederland en de Zending in Oost-Indie in Dagen der Oost-Indishe Compagnie*. Utrecht: B. den Boer, 1906.

Bohr, Paul Richard. *Famine in China and the Missionary: Timothy Richard as Relief Administrator and Advocate of Reform, 1876–1884*. Cambridge, Mass.: Harvard University East Asian Research Center, 1972.

————. "Liang Fa's Quest for Moral Power." In *Christianity in China: Early Protestant Missionary Writings*, ed. Suzanne Wilson Barnett and John King Fairbank, 36–37. Cambridge, Mass.: Harvard University Press, 1985.

Bolasco, Mario V. *Points of Departure: Essays on Christianity, Power and Social Change*. Manila: St. Scholastica's College, 1994.

Bolshakoff, Serge. *The Foreign Missions of the Russian Orthodox Church*. London: SPCK, 1943.

Bonn, Alfred. *Ein Jahrhundert Rheinische Mission*. Barmen: Missionshaus, 1928.

Boorman, Howard, ed. *Biographical Dictionary of Republican China*. 4 vols. New York: Columbia University Press, 1967–1971.

Boorstin, Daniel J. *The Discoverers*. New York: Random House, 1983.

Booth-Tucker, F. St. G. de L. See F. A. Mackenzie, *Booth-Tucker, Sadhu and Saint*.

Bornemann, Fritz. *Arnold Janssen: Founder of Three Missionary Congregations 1837–1909*. Trans. J. Vkogelgesang. Rome: Collegio del Verbo Divino, 1975.

————. *As Wine Poured Out: Blessed Joseph Freinademetz SVD Missionary in China*. Rome: Divine Word Missionaries, 1984.

Bosch, David J. "The Biblical Roots of Christian Mission." In *Toward the Twenty-First Century in Mission*, ed. J. Phillips and R. Coote, 176. Grand Rapids, Mich.: Eerdmans, 1993.

————. *Transforming Mission: Paradigm Shifts in Theology of Mission*. Maryknoll, N.Y.: Orbis Books, 1991.

Boudens, Robrecht. *The Catholic Church in Ceylon under Dutch Rule*. Rome: Officium Libri Catholici, 1957.

————. *Catholic Missionaries in a British Colony: Successes and Failures in Ceylon 1796–1893*. In *NRSM* 28 (1979): 1–181.

Bowring, John. *The Kingdom and People of Siam; with a Narrative of the Mission to that Country in 1855*. 2 vols. London: John W. Parker, 1857; reprint, New York: AMS, 1975.

Boxer, Charles R. *The Christian Century in Japan, 1549–1650*. Berkeley and Los Angeles: University of California Press; London: Cambridge University Press, 1951.

————. *Dutch Merchants and Mariners in Asia, 1602–1795*. London: Variorum Reprints, 1988.

————. *Fidalgos in the Far East 1550–1770*. London and New York: Oxford University Press, 1968.

———. "Portuguese and Dutch Colonial Rivalry, 1641–1661." *Studia* 2. Lisbon: Centro de Estudos Historicos Ultramarinos, July 1958.

———. *The Portuguese Seaborne Empire, 1415–1825.* London: Hutchinson, 1969.

———. "The Problem of the Native Clergy in the Portuguese and Spanish Empires from the Sixteenth to the Eighteenth Centuries." In *The Mission of the Church and the Propagation of the Faith.* Ed. G. J. Cuming, 85–105. Cambridge: Cambridge University Press, 1970.

Boyce, W. B., J. Mullins and E. B. Underhill. *The Missionary World, Being an Encyclopaedia of Christian Missions.* New York: Anson D. F. Randolph, [1872].

———. *Race Relations in the Portuguese Colonial Empire 1415–1825.* Oxford: Clarendon Press, 1963.

Brackney, William H. "The Legacy of Adoniram Judson." *IBMR* 22, no. 1 (July 1998): 122–127.

Bradley, William L. *Siam Then: The Foreign Colony in Bangkok before and after Anna.* Pasadena, Calif.: William Carey Library, 1981.

Braganza, Jose Vicente. *The Encounter: The Epic Story of the Christianization of the Philippines.* Manila: Catholic Trade School, 1965.

Braisted, Paul Judson. *Indian Nationalism and the Christian Colleges.* New York: Association Press, 1935.

Brand, Donald Vincent. "The Philippine Independent Church: A Social Movement." PhD diss., Cornell University, 1980.

Brandewie, Ernest. *In the Light of the Word: Divine Word Missionaries of North America.* Maryknoll, N.Y.: Orbis Books, 2000.

Brandt, Nat. *Massacre in Shansi.* Syracuse, N.Y.: Syracuse University Press, 1994.

———. *When Giants Walked the Earth: The Life and Times of Wilhelm Schmitz SVD.* Freiburg: University Press, 1990.

Braude, Benjamin, and Bernard Lewis, eds. *Christians and Jews in the Ottoman Empire.* 2 vols. New York and London: Holmes & Meier Publishers, 1982.

Breslin, Thomas A. *China, American Catholicism and the Missionary.* University Park and London: Pennsylvania State University Press, 1980.

Bridgman, Elijah C. "Brief Memoir of the Evangelist Leang A-Fa." *MH* 30 (October 1834): 353–357.

Bridgman, Eliza J., ed. *The Life and Labors of Elijah Coleman Bridgman.* New York, 1864.

Broderick, James. *The Progress of the Jesuits 1556–79.* London, 1946.

———. *St. Francis Xavier (1506–1552).* New York: Pellegrini & Cudahy, 1952.

Brohier, R. L. *Links between Sri Lanka and the Netherlands.* Colombo: Netherlands Alumni Association of Sri Lanka, 1978.

Broomhall, A. J. *Hudson Taylor and China's Open Century.* 7 vols.,: vol. 1: *Barbarians at the Gates;* vol. 2: *Over the Treaty Wall, 1850–57;* vol. 3: *If I Had a Thousand Lives, 1856–65;* vol. 4: *Survivors' Pact, 1865–67;* vol. 5: *Refiner's Fire, 1868–75;* vol. 6: *Assault on the Nine, 1875–87;* vol. 7: *It Is Not Death to Die, 1886–89.* London: Hodder & Stoughton & Overseas Missionary Fellowship [former CIM], 1981–1989.

———. *National Righteousness* 1, no. 7 (1891).

Broomhall, Marshall. *By Love Compelled.* London: Hodder& Stoughton, 1936.

———. *Hudson Taylor: The Man Who Believed God.* London and Philadelphia: China Inland Mission, 1929.

———. *The Jubilee Story of the China Inland Mission.* London: Morgan & Scott, 1915.

———. *Martyred Missionaries of the China Inland Mission*. London: Morgan & Scott and CIM, 1901.

———. *Present-Day Conditions in China*. New York: Fleming H. Revell, 1908.

———. *Robert Morrison, A Master-builder*. London: Student Christian Movement, 1924.

———. *W. W. Cassels: First Bishop in Western China*. London and Philadelphia: China Inland Mission, 1926.

Brou, A. "L'Abbé Jean-Baptiste Sidotti." *RHM* (Paris) 14 (1937): 367–379, 494–501; 15 (1938): 80–91.

———. "Missions goanaises et conversions forcées?" *RHM* 13 (1936): 32–43.

Brouillon, Nicolas. *Missions de Chine: Mémoire sur létat actuel de la Mission du Kiang-Nan, 1842*. Paris: Julien, Lanier, 1855.

Brouwer, Ruth Compton. *New Women for God: Canadian Presbyterian Women and India Missions, 1876–1914*. Toronto: University of Toronto Press, 1990.

Brown, Arthur Judson. *The Chinese Revolution*. New York: Student Volunteer Movement, 1912.

———. *The New Era in the Philippines*. New York: Fleming H. Revell, 1903.

———. *New Forces in Old China*. New York: Fleming H. Revell, 1904.

———. *One Hundred Years: A History of the Foreign Missionary Work of the Presbyterian Church in the U.S.A.* New York: Fleming H. Revell, 1937.

———. *Report of a Visitation of the [China, Korea, Philippine, Syria] Missions of the Presbyterian Church U.S.A, 1901–1902*. 4 reports published separately. New York: Presbyterian Board of Foreign Missions, 1901–1902.

Brown, David. *Memorial Sketches of the Rev. David Brown, with a Selection of His Sermons, Preached at Calcutta*. London: T. Cadell and W. Davies, 1816.

Brown, George Thompson. *Earthen Vessels and Transcendent Power: American Presbyterians in China, 1837–1952*. Maryknoll, N.Y.: Orbis Books, 1997.

———. *Mission to Korea*. Richmond, Va.: Presbyterian Church, U.S., Board of World Missions, 1962.

Brown, Leslie W. *The Indian Christians of St. Thomas: An Account of the Ancient Syrian Church of Malabar*. 2nd ed. Cambridge: Cambridge University Press, 1982.

Brumbaugh, T. T. "Reports of the Joint Deputation to Korea, January 9, 1947." Manuscript. Korea Commission, Far Eastern Joint Office, Foreign Missions Office of the Christian Churches of North America. January 9, 1948, 17.

Bryant, M. Darrol, and Durwood Foster. *A Time for Consideration: A Scholarly Appraisal of the Unification Church*. New York: E. Mellen, 1978.

———, ed. *Hermeneutics and Unification Theology*. New York: Rose of Sharon Press, 1980.

Bryce, James, Viscount Grey of Fallodon. *The Treatment of Armenians in the Ottoman Empire 1915–16*. London: Sir Joseph Causton & Sons, 1916.

Buchanan, Claudius. *Christian Researches in Asia*. London: Cadell and Davies, 1814.

Buijtenen, M. P. et al., eds. *Unitas Fratrum*. Utrecht, the Netherlands: Riksarchief in Utrecht, 1975.

Burkhardt, G. E. *Die Evangelische Mission in China und Japan. Zweite Auflage, ganzlich ungearbeiter und bis auf die Gegenwart fortgeführt von Dr. K. Grundemann*. Biefeld and Leipzig, 1880.

Burton, Margaret E. *The Education of Women in China*. New York: Fleming H. Revell, 1911.

Burton, Richard, and Nathaniel Ward. "Report of a Journey into Batak Country in the Year 1824." *TRAS* 1 (1827): 485–513.

Butterfield, Fox. *China: Alive in the Bitter Sea*. New York: Times Books, 1982.

Cabaton, A. *Java, Sumatra, and the Other Islands of the Dutch East Indies*. New York: Charles Scribner's Sons, 1911.

Caldarola, Carlo. *Christianity: The Japanese Way*. [Mukyokai]. Leiden: E. J. Brill, 1979.

Callery, J.-M., and Yvan. *History of the Insurrection in China; with Notices of the Christianity, Creed, and Proclamations of the Insurgents*. Trans. from the French by J. Oxenford. New York: Harper & Brothers, 1853.

The Cambridge History of China. Ed. Dennis Twichett and John K. Fairbank. 15 vols. Cambridge: Cambridge University Press, 1978–.

The Cambridge History of India. Vols. 4, 5. Ed. E. J. Rapson. Cambridge: Cambridge University Press, 1922.

The Cambridge History of Iran. Vols. 6, 7. Ed. W. B. Fisher. Cambridge: Cambridge University Press, 1968–1991.

The Cambridge History of Japan. Vols. 4, 5, 6. Ed. John W. Hall et al. Cambridge: Cambridge University Press, 1988.

Campbell, Arch. *The Christ of the Korean Heart*. Columbus, Ohio: Falco Publishers, 1954.

Campbell, William. *An Account of Missionary Success in the Island of Formosa*. 2 vols. Ed. with appendices by William Campbell. London: Trubner, 1889.

———. *Formosa under the Dutch, Described from Contemporary Records*. London: Kegan Paul, Trench, Trubner, 1903.

Camps, Arnulf. *Jerome Xavier S.J. and the Muslims of the Mogul Empire*. Schoneck-Beckenried, 1957.

———. *Studies in Asian Mission History, 1956–1998*. Leiden: Brill, 2000.

Cantlie, James, and C. Sheridan Jones. *Sun Yat Sen and the Awakening of China*. New York: Fleming H. Revell, 1912.

Canton, William. *A History of the British and Foreign Bible Society*. 5 vols. London: John Murray, 1904, 1910.

Capuchin Mission Unit of the Catholic Students' Mission Crusade. *India and Its Missions*. 2 vols. New York: Macmillan, 1923.

Cardon, R. *Catholicism in the East and the Diocese of Malacca*. Singapore: Malaya Catholic Leader, 1938.

Carey, Eustace. *Memoir of William Carey*. Boston: Gould, Kendall & Lincoln, 1836.

Carey, S. Pearce. *William Carey*. 8th ed., rev. and enlarged. London: Carey Press, 1934.

Carey, William. *An Enquiry into the Obligations of Christians to Use Means for the Conversion of the Heathens*. Leicester: Ann Ireland, 1792. Facsimile printings: London: Hodder & Stoughton, 1891; London: Henderson & Spalding, 1934; London: Carey Kingsgate Press, 1961.

———. *The Journal and Selected Letters of William Carey*. Macon, Ga.: Smyth & Helwys, 2000.

———. *Serampore Letters, Being the Unpublished Correspondence of William Carey and Others with John Williams, 1800–1816*. Ed. Leighton and Mornay Williams. New York: Fleming H. Revell, 1892.

————. See also S. Pearce Carey, *William Carey*; John Clark Marshman, *Life and Times of Carey, Marshman and Ward*; A. H. Oussoren, *William Carey*; George Smith, *Life of William Carey*.

Carlen, Claudia, ed. *The Papal Encyclicals*. 5 vols. London: Eyre & Spottiswoode, 1966.

Carleton, A. "The Millet System." PhD diss., Hartford Theological Seminary, 1936.

Carmichael, Amy Wilson. *Things As They Are: Mission Work in South India*. Chicago: Fleming H. Revell, 1904.

Carpenter, C. H. *Self-Support in Bassein*. Boston: Franklin Press, 1883.

Carson, Arthur L. *The Story of Philippine Education*. Quezon City, Philippines: New Day Publishers, 1978.

Carter, Terry G., ed. *The Journals and Letters of William Carey*. Macon, Ga.: Smyth & Helwys, 2000.

Cary, Frank. *History of Christianity in Japan*. Tokyo: Kyo Bun Kwan, 1959.

Cary, Otis. *A History of Christianity in Japan*. 2 vols. New York: Fleming H. Revell, 1909.

Castro, Matteo (or Mathieu) de. See Theodore Ghesquière, *Mathieu de Castro*.

The Catholic Church in Modern China: Perspectives. Ed. Edmond Tang and Jean-Paul Wiest. Maryknoll, N.Y.: Orbis Books, 1993.

The Catholic Church in the Philippines Today. Statistics and essays by I. Alonso, J. McGeough, R. de Argarate, J. B. Velasco. Manila: Historical Conservation Society, 1968.

Catholic Encyclopedia (CE). New York: Appleton, 1907–1922.

Caton, A. R. *The Key of Progress: A Survey of the Status and Conditions of Women in India*. London: Oxford University Press, 1930.

Cauthen, Baker J., et al. *Advance: A History of the Southern Baptist Foreign Missions*. Nashville: Broadman Press, 1970.

Chabrié, Robert. *Michael Boym, Jésuite Polonais et la Fin des Ming en Chine (1646–1662)*. Paris: P. Bossuet, 1933.

Chaillet, J. B. *Mgr. Petitjean, 1829–1884, et la résurrection catholique du Japon au XIXe siècle*. Montceau-les-mines, 1919.

Chakmakjian, Hagop A. *Armenian Christology and Evangelization of Islam*. Leiden: E. J. Brill, 1965.

Chaliha, Jaya, and E. Le Joly, compilers. *The Joy in Loving: A Guide to Daily Living with Mother Teresa*. New York: Viking Penguin, 1997.

Chandler, Warren A. *Young J. Allen: "The Man Who Seeded China."* Nashville: Cokesbury Press, 1931.

Chao, Jonathan T'ien-en. "The Chinese Indigenous Church Movement, 1919–1927." PhD diss., University of Pennsylvania, 1986.

————. *A History of the Church in China since 1949*. 2 vols. Grand Rapids, Mich.: Outreach Inc., 1995.

————. *Wise as Serpents, Harmless as Doves: Christians in China Tell Their Stories*. Pasadena, Calif.: William Carey Library, 1988.

Chapman, Priscilla. *Hindoo Female Education*. London: R. B. Seeley & W. Burnside, 1839.

Charbonnier, Jean. *Histoire des Chrétiens de Chine*. Paris: Desclée/Bégédis, 1992.

Chatterjee, S. K. [Saral Kumar Chatterji]. *Hannah Marshman: The First Woman Missionary in India*. Hooghly, India: S. S. Chatterjee, 1987.

Chatterton, Eyre. *A History of the Church of England in India since the Early Days of the East India Company.* London: SPCK, 1924.

——. *The Story of Fifty Years' Mission Work in Chota Nagpur.* London: SPCK, 1901.

——, ed. *A History of the Church in China since 1949: A Reader.* 2 vols. Grand Rapids, Mich.: Outreach Inc., 1995.

Chenchiah, Pandipeddi. *The Theology of Chenchiah: with Selections from his Writings.* Bangalore: Christian Institute for the Study of Religion and Society, 1966.

Cheng, J. C. *Chinese Sources for the Taiping Rebellion, 1850–1864.* Hong Kong: Hong Kong University Press, 1963.

Cheng, Nien. *Life and Death in Shanghai.* New York: Grove Press, 1986.

Chen-yuan. *Documents Concerning Kanghsi and the Roman Legate.* Peiping: Ku-kung po-wu-yuan, 1932.

Cheriyan, P. *The Malabar Syrians and the Church Missionary Society 1816–1840.* Kottayam, India: Church Missionary Society's Press, 1935.

China Against the World. Reprinted from *The North American Review.* N.A.R. Publishing Co., 1900.

China and Christianity: Historical and Future Encounters. Ed. James D. Whitehead, Y. M. Shaw, N. G. Girardot. Notre Dame, Ind.: University of Notre Dame, 1979.

China Centenary Missionary Conference Records . . . Shanghai, 1907. Shanghai/New York: American Tract Society, 1907.

China Inland Mission. *China and the Gospel: An Illustrated Report of the CIM, 1913.* London and Philadelphia: CIM, 1913.

China Mission Handbook. Shanghai: American Presbyterian Mission Press, 1896.

China Mission Year Book (ChMYB). Multi-volume, 1910– . Shanghai: Christian Literature Society for China. Name changed to *China Christian Year Book (CCYB)* in 1926.

The Chinese Church as Revealed in the National Christian Conference, 1922. Shanghai: National Christian Conference [Oriental Press], 1922.

Chirgwin, Arthur Mitchell. *Arthington's Million: The Romance of the Arthington Trust.* London: Livingstone Press, [1936].

Chirino, Pedro. *The Philippines in 1600 (Relación de las Islas Filipinas).* In Spanish with English translation by R. Echevarría. Manila: Historical Conservation Society, 1969.

Choi, Andreas. *L'erection du premier vicariat apostolique et les origines de Catholicisme en Corée.* Schoneck-Beckenried, Switzerland: NRSM, 1961.

Choi, Doug Sung. "The Roots of the Presbyterian Conflicts in Korea, 1910–1954, and the Predominance of Orthodoxy." PhD diss., University of California Santa Barbara, 1994.

Choi, Sung-il. "John Ross (1842–1915) and the Korean Protestant Church." PhD diss., Edinburgh University, 1992.

Chopourian, Giragos H. *The Armenian Evangelical Reformation: Causes and Effects.* New York: Armenian Missionary Association of America, 1972.

Chou, Sun-Ae. "A History of Presbyterian Women in Korea." Trans. Lee Kwang-Soon. Manuscript, photocopy, 1978.

Cho Young-Taek. "Cause of Schism in the Korean Presbyterian Church." In Korean. 1973.

Christensen, Torben, and William R. Hutchison, eds. *Missionary Ideologies in the Imperialist Era; 1180–1920.* Aarhus, Denmark/Cambridge, Mass.: Aros Publishers/Harvard Theological Review, 1984.

Christian and Missionary Alliance. *Missionary Atlas: A Manual of the Foreign Work of the Christian and Missionary Alliance. Historical and Descriptive.* Harrisburg, Pa.: Christian Publications, 1950.

The Christian Movement in China in a Period of National Transition: Three Papers [T. C. Chao, R. O. Hall, R. Scott] *Prepared for the Tambaram Meeting, Dec. 1938.* Mysore, India: International Missionary Council, 1938.

The Christian Movement in Japan. Tokyo, annually 1903–1927; thereafter name was changed to *The Japan Christian Year Book.* Various titles and publishers.

The Christian Occupation of China. Ed. M. T. Stauffer. Shanghai: China Continuation Committee, 1922.

Christie, Dugald. *Thirty Years in the Manchu Capital in and around Moukden in Peace and War.* New York: McBride & Nast, 1914.

Chu, Michael, ed. *The New China: A Catholic Response.* New York: Paulist Press, 1977.

Chumsriphan, Surachai. "The Great Role of Jean-Louis Vey, Apostolic Vicar of Siam (1875–1909) in the Church History of Thailand during the Reformation of King Rama V, the Great (1868–1910)." PhD diss., Gregorian University, Rome, 1990.

Chun, Sung C. *Schism and Unity in the Protestant Churches of Korea.* Seoul: Christian Literature Society of Korea, 1979.

Churchill, Charles Henry. *The Druzes and the Maronites under the Turkish Rule from 1840 to 1860.* New York: Arno Press, 1973; reprint of London: Quaritch, 1862 ed.

Cieslik, Hubert. "The Case of Christovão Ferreira." *MN* 29, no. 1 (1974): 1–54.

——. "The Great Martyrdom in Edo 1623." *MN* 10, no. 1/2 (1954): 1–44.

Clancy, Thomas H. *An Introduction to Jesuit Life: The Constitutions and History through 435 Years.* St. Louis: Institute of Jesuit Sources, 1976.

Clark, Allen D. *A History of the Church in Korea.* Seoul: Christian Literature Society of Korea, 1971.

——. "A Study of Religion and the State in the Japanese Empire with Particular Reference to the Shrine Problem in Korea." Thesis: Princeton Theological Seminary, 1939.

Clark, Charles Allen. *The Nevius Plan for Mission Work in Korea.* Seoul: Y.M.C.A. Press, 1937.

Clark, Donald N. "Yun Ch'i-Ho (1864–1945): Portrait of a Korean Intellectual in an Era of Transition." In *Occasional Papers on Korea.* No. 4. Ed. James B. Palais and M. D. Lang. Seoul: National History Compilation Committee, 1975.

Clarke, W. K. Lowther. *A History of the S.P.C.K.* London: SPCK, 1959.

Clement, Ernest W. *Christianity in Modern Japan.* (Philadelphia: American Baptist Publication Society, 1905.

——. *A Handbook of Modern Japan.* Chicago: A. C. McClurg, 1903.

Clement, J. *Memoir of Adoniram Judson: His Life and Missionary Labors.* Auburn, N.Y.: Derby and Miller, 1851.

Clements, Paul H. *The Boxer Rebellion: A Political and Diplomatic Review.* New York: Columbia University Press, 1915.

BIBLIOGRAPHY

Clifford, Mary Dorita. "Iglesia Filipino Independiente." *Studies in Philippine Church History*, ed. Gerald H. Anderson. Ithaca, N.Y.: Cornell University Press, 1969.

Clough, Emma Rauschenbusch. *Tales of a Telugu Pariah Tribe*. New York: Fleming H. Revell, 1899.

Clough, John E. *Social Christianity in the Orient: The Story of a Man, a Mission and a Movement*. New York: Macmillan, 1914.

Clymer, Kenton J. *Protestant Missionaries in the Philippines, 1898–1916: An Inquiry into the American Colonial Mentality*. Urbana and Chicago: University of Illinois Press, 1985.

Cnattingius, Hans. *Bishops and Societies: A Study of Anglican Colonial and Missionary Expansion 1698–1850*. London: SPCK, 1952.

Coad, F. R. *A History of the Brethren Movement, Its Origins, Its Worldwide Development and Its Significance for the Present Day*. Exeter: Paternoster Press, 1968.

Coalter, Milton J., et al. *The Re-forming Tradition: Presbyterians and Mainstream Protestantism*. Louisville: Westminster/John Knox Press, 1992.

Cochrane, Henry Park. *Among the Burmans: A Record of Fifteen Years*. New York: Fleming H. Revell, 1904.

Cochrane, Thomas. *Survey of the Missionary Occupation of China*. Shanghai: Christian Literature Society for China, 1913.

Codrington, H. W. *A Short History of Ceylon*. Rev. ed. London: Macmillan, 1939.

Cogswell, James A. *Until the Day Dawn: A History of the Work of the Japan Mission of the Presbyterian Church in the United States*. Atlanta: Board of World Missions, 1957.

Cohen, Paul A. *China and Christianity: The Missionary Movement and the Growth of Chinese Antiforeignism, 1860–1870*. Cambridge, Mass.: Harvard University Press, 1963.

———. "Christian Missions and Their Impact to 1900." In *Cambridge History of China*, ed. John K. Fairbank, 10:543–580. Cambridge: Cambridge University Press, 1978– .

Cokley, J. F. *The Church of the East and the Church of England: A History of the Archbishop of Canterbury's Assyrian Mission*. Oxford: Clarendon Press, 1992.

Coleridge, Henry James. *The Life and Letters of St. Francis Xavier*. 2 vols. 4th ed. London: Burns & Oates, 1886.

Conn, Harvey M. "Studies in the Theology of the Korean Presbyterian Church," I–IV. *Westminster Theological Journal* 29 (November 1966): 24–57; 30 (May 1966): 136–178; (November 1967): 24–49; and (May 1968): 135ff..

Conroy, Hilary. *The Japanese Seizure of Korea, 1868–1910: A Study of Realism and Idealism in International Relations*. Philadelphia: University of Pennsylvania Press, 1960.

Considine, John. *Across a World*. Toronto and New York: Longmans Green, 1942.

Continuation Committee Conferences in Asia, 1912–1913. Ed. John R. Mott. New York: Chairman, Continuation Committee, 1913.

Cook, Harold F. *Korea's 1884 Incident*. Seoul: Royal Asiatic Society, Korea Branch, 1972.

Cooley, Frank L. "Altar and Throne." PhD diss., Yale University, 1961.

———. *The Growing Seed: The Christian Church in Indonesia*. Jakarta, Indonesia: Dewan Gerega-gerega di Indonesia, 1981.

———. *Indonesia: Church and Society*. New York: Friendship Press, 1968.

Cooper, Michael. *Rodrigues the Interpreter: An Early Jesuit in Japan and China*. New York: Weatherhill, 1974.

————, trans. *This Island of Japan: João Rodrigues' Account of Sixteenth-Century Japan*. Tokyo and New York: Kodansha, 1973.

Corbett, Hunter. See James R. E. Craighead. *Hunter Corbett*; and J. J. Heeren. *On the Shantung Front*.

Corfe, Charles John. *The Anglican Church in Korea*. Seoul: Seoul Press/Hodge, 1905.

————. "Log-Book [1889–1897]." Manuscript copy.

————. See also H. H. Montgomery, *Charles John Corfe: Naval Chaplain–Bishop*.

Corr, Daniel Philip. " 'The Field Is the World': Proclaiming, Translating and Serving by the American Board of Commissioners for Foreign Missions." PhD diss., Fuller Theological Seminary, 1993.

Correia-Afonso, J. *Jesuit Letters and Indian History*. Bombay: Indian Historical Research Institute, 1955.

Cory, Ralph, trans. "Some Notes on Father Gregorio de Cespedes, Korea's First European Visitor." *TRASK* 27 (1937): 1–55.

Coughlin, Margaret M. "Strangers in the House: J. Lewis Shuck and Issachar Roberts, First American Baptist Missionaries to China." PhD diss., University of Virginia, 1972.

Coutts, Frederick. *The History of the Salvation Army*. Vols. 6, 7. London: Hodder & Stoughton, 1973, 1986.

Covell, Ralph R. *Confucius, the Buddha, and Christ: A History of the Gospel in Chinese*. Maryknoll, N.Y.: Orbis Books, 1986.

————. *Pentecost of the Hills in Taiwan*. Pasadena, Calif.: Hope Publishing House, 1998.

————. *W. A. P. Martin, Pioneer of Progress in China*. Washington, D.C.: Christian University Press, 1978.

Cox, F. A. *History of the Baptist Missionary Society from 1782 to 1842 to Which Is Added a Sketch of the General Baptist Mission*. 2 vols. London: T. Ward and G. & J. Dyer, 1842.

Cracknell, Kenneth. *Justice, Courtesy and Love: Theologians and Missionaries Encountering World Religions, 1846–1914*. London: Epworth Press, 1995.

Craighead, James R. E. *Hunter Corbett: Fifty-Six Years Missionary in China*. New York: Fleming H. Revell, 1921.

Crétineau-Joly, J. *Clément XIV et les Jésuites, ou histoire de la destruction des Jésuites*. Paris: Mellier Frères, 1848.

Cronin, Vincent. *A Pearl to India: The Life of Robert de Nobili*. London: Hart Davis, 1959.

————. *The Wise Man from the West*. London: R. Hart-Davis, 1955.

Crosbie, Philip. *March Till They Die*. Westminster, Md.: Newman Press, 1956.

Crouch, Archie R. *Christianity in China: A Scholar's Guide to Resources in the Libraries and Archives in the United States*. Armonk, N.Y.: M. E. Sharpe, 1989.

————. *Rising through the Dust: The Story of the Christian Church in China*. New York: Friendship Press, 1948.

Cummins, J. S. *A Question of Rites: Friar Domingo Navarrete and the Jesuits*. Aldershot, U.K., and Rutland, Vt.: Scolar Press, 1993.

———, ed. *Christianity and Missions, 1450–1800.* Brookfield, Vt.: Ashgate Publishing Co., 1997. No. 28 in "An Expanding World" series of collected essays.

———, ed. *The Travels and Controversies of Friar Domingo Navarrete 1618–1686.* Cambridge: Cambridge University Press, 1962.

Cynn, Hueng-Wo. *The Rebirth of Korea.* New York: Abingdon Press, 1920.

Daggett, Mrs. L. H. *Historical Sketches of Woman's Missionary Societies in America and England.* Boston: L. H. Daggett, 1883.

Dahmen, P. *Un Jésuite Brahme: Robert de Nobili.* Bruges: Museum Lessianum Sectio Missionaria, 1924.

Dallet, Ch. *Controversial Catechism: Or Short Answers to the Objections of Protestants against the True Religion.* 5th ed. Bangalore: Spectator Press, 1894.

———. *Histoire de l'église de Corée.* 2 vols. Paris: Librairie Victor Palmé, 1874; reprint, Seoul: Royal Asiatic Society, Korea Branch, 1975.

———. *Traditional Korea* (English translation of ethnographic introduction to 1874 French text of Dallet's *Histoire*). New Haven, Conn.: Human Relations Area Files, 1954.

Daniel, David. *The Orthodox Church of India: History and Faith.* 2nd ed. New Delhi: Rachel David, 1986.

Daniel, I. *The Malabar Church and Other Orthodox Churches.* Haripad, Travancore, India: Suvarna Bharathi Press, 1950.

Daniel, K. N. *Mar Thoma Church in Peril.* Tiruvalla, India: St. Joseph's Printing House, 1961.

da Silva, Cosme, O. M. *Fidalgos in the Kingdom of Kotte, Sri Lanka, 1505–1656: The Portuguese in Sri Lanka.* Colombo: Harwoods Publishers, 1990.

da Silva Rego, Antonio. *Documentacão para a historia das missões do Padroado portugues do Oriente.* Lisbon: Fundação Oriente, 1991.

da Trinidade, Paulo. See Trinidade, Paulo da.

Davey, Cyril J. *The Story of Sadhu Sundar Singh.* Chicago: Moody Press, 1963.

David, Immanuel. *Reformed Church in America Missionaries in South India, 1839–1938: An Analytical Study.* Bangalore: Asian Trading Company, 1986.

David, M. D. *Asia and Christianity.* Bombay: Himalaya Publishing House, 1985.

Davies, Daniel M. "Building a City on a Hill in Korea: The Work of Henry G. Appenzeller." In *Church History* 61, no. 4 (December 1992): 422–435.

———. *The Life and Thought of Henry Gerhard Appenzeller (1858–1902), Missionary in Korea.* Lewiston, N.Y.: E. Mellen Press, 1988.

Davies, Evan. *Memoir of the Rev. Samuel Dyer, Sixteen Years Missionary to the Chinese.* (London: J. Snow, 1846).

d'Avril, Adolphe. *La Chaldée Chrétienne.* Paris: Bureaux de l'Oeuvre des Ecoles Orient, 1892.

Day, Clarence B. *Hangchow University: A Brief History.* New York: United Board for Christian Colleges in China, 1955.

Dean, William. *The China Mission. Being a History of the Various Missions of All Denominations among the Chinese.* New York: Sheldon, and London: Trübner, 1859.

Deats, Richard L. *Nationalism and Christianity in the Philippines.* Dallas: Southern Methodist University Press, 1967.

———. "Nicolas Zamora: Religious Nationalist." In *Studies in Philippine Church History,* ed. Gerald H. Anderson. Ithaca, N.Y.: Cornell University Press, 1969.

———. *The Story of Methodism in the Philippines*. Manila: Union Theological Seminary, 1964.

Decennial Missionary Conference, India. *Report of the First Decennial General Missionary Conference, Allahabad, 1872–73*. London and Madras: Seeley, Jackson, and Halliday, 1873.

Decker, William M. "The Foundations and Growth of Shantung Christian University, 1864–1917." MA thesis, Columbia University, 1948.

De Groot, J. J. M. *Sectarianism and Religious Persecution in China: A Page in the History of Religions*. 2 vols. in 1. Amsterdam: Johannes Müller, 1903.

De Gruché, Kingston. *Dr. D. Duncan Main of Hangchow, who is known in China as Dr. Apricot of Heaven Below*. London: Marshall, Morgan & Scott, n.d.

De la Costa, Horacio. "The Development of the Native Clergy in the Philippines." In *Studies in Philippine Church History*, ed. Gerald H. Anderson. Ithaca, N.Y.: Cornell University Press, 1969.

———. "Episcopal Jurisdiction in the Philippines during the Spanish Regime." In *Studies in Philippine Church History*, ed. Gerald H. Anderson. Ithaca, N.Y.: Cornell University Press, 1969.

———. "Jesuit Education in the Philippines to 1768," *PS* 1 (1956).

———. *The Jesuits in the Philippines, 1581–1768*. Cambridge, Mass.: Harvard University Press, 1961.

Delacroix, Simon, ed. *Histoire universelle des missions catholiques*. 4 vols. Paris: Librairie Grund, 1957.

Delavignette, R. C. *Christianity and Colonialism*. Trans. J. R. Foster. New York: Hawthorn Books, 1964.

D'Elia, Paschal M. *The Catholic Missions in China: A Short Sketch of the History*. Shanghai: Commercial Press, 1941.

D'Elia, Pasquale M., ed. *Fonti Ricciane: Documenti originali concernenti Matteo Ricci e la storia delle prime relazioni tra l'Europa e la Cina (1579–1615)*. 3 vols. Rome: Libreria dello Stato, 1942–1949); referred to as D'Elia, *Fonti Ricianne*.

de Moidrey, Joseph. *La hiérarchie catholique en Chine, en Corée et au Japon (1307–1914)*. *Variétés Sinologiques*, no. 10. Shanghai: L'Orphélinat de T'ou-se-we, Zikawei, 1914.

Dennett, Tyler. *Americans in Eastern Asia: A Critical Study of the Policy of the United States with Reference to China, Japan and Korea in the 19th Century*. New York: Macmillan, 1922.

Dennis, James S. *Centennial Survey of Foreign Missions*. New York: Fleming H. Revell, 1902.

———. *Foreign Missions after a Century*. New York: Fleming H. Revell, 1893.

———. "Statistical Summary of Foreign Missions Throughout the World." In *Ecumenical Missionary Conference, New York, 1900*, 2:419–434. New York: American Tract Society, 1900.

de Silva, Chandra Richard. *Sri Lanka: A History*. New Delhi: Vikas Publishing House, 1987; reprint, 1994.

De Silva, K. M. *A History of Sri Lanka*. Delhi: Oxford University Press, 1981.

———. *Social Policy and Missionary Organizations in Ceylon 1840–1855*. London: Longmans, for the Royal Commonwealth Society, 1965.

de Souza, Teotonio R. See Souza.

de Soysa, Harold. See Soysa.

Deuchler, Martina. *Confucian Gentlemen and Barbarian Envoys.* Seattle and London: University of Washington Press, 1977.

Devanandan, Paul D. *Christian Concern in Hinduism.* Bangalore: Christian Institute for the Study of Religion and Society, 1961.

———. *The Gospel in Renascent Hinduism.* London: SCM Press, 1959.

———. *Paul D. Devanandan: A Selection.* Ed. Joachim Wietzke. Madras: CLS, 1983–1987.

de Waard, Nellie. *Pioneer in Sumatra.* Chicago: Moody Press, 1962.

Dewey, George. *Autobiography of George Dewey.* New York, 1913.

Dharmaraj, J. S. *Colonialism and Christian Mission: Postcolonial Reflection.* Delhi: ISPCK, 1993.

———. "Serampore Missions and Colonial Connections." *ICHR* (Delhi), 26 (June 1992): 21–35.

Diaz, Hector. *A Korean Theology: Chu-Kuo Yo-Ji: Essentials of the Lord's Teaching, by Chong Yak-jong Augustine, 1760–1801.* Immensee: NZM, 1992.

Dib, Pierre. *Histoire de L'Eglise Maronite.* 2 vols. Beirut: Editions "La Sagesse," 1962.

Didelot, Jean-Claude. *Missions Etrangères de Paris.* Le Sarment, France: Fayard, 1986.

Dolbeer, Martin Luther. *A History of Lutheranism in the Andhra Desa (The Telugu Territory of India) 1842–1920.* New York: Board of Foreign Missions, the United Lutheran Church in America, 1959.

Donovan, John F. *The Pagoda and the Cross: The Life of Bishop Ford of Maryknoll.* New York: Charles Scribner's Sons, 1967.

Don Peter, W. L. A. *Historical Gleanings.* Colombo: Arnold's International Printing House, 1990.

———. *Studies in Ceylon Church History.* Colombo: The Catholic Press, 1963.

———. *Xavier as Educator.* Delhi: Jesuit Educational Association of India, 1974.

Doraisamy, Theodore R. *The March of Methodism in Singapore and Malaysia, 1885–1980.* Singapore: Methodist Book Room, 1982.

Doraisawmy, Solomon. *Christianity in India: Unique and Universal Mission.* Madras, India: Christian Literature Society, 1986.

D'Orsey, Alex, J. D., comp. *Portuguese Discoveries, Dependencies and Missions in Asia and Africa.* London: H. Allen, 1893.

Downie, David. *The Lone Star: The History of the Telugu Mission of the American Baptist Missionary Union.* Philadelphia: American Baptist Publication Society, 1893.

Downs, Frederick S. "Early Christian Contacts with North East India." *ICHR* 5, no. 1 (December 1971): 69–77.

———. *Essays on Christianity in North-East India.* New Delhi: Indus Publishing Co., 1994.

———. "The Establishment of the American Baptist Assam Mission, 1836–1841." *ICHR* 6, no. 1 (June 1972): 71ff.

———. *North East India in the Nineteenth and Twentieth Centuries.* Vol. 5 part 5 of *History of Christianity in India.* Bangalore: Church History Association of India, 1992.

———. "Origins of Christianity in the Garo Hills of Meghalaya." *ICHR* 6, no. 2 (1972): 79–86.

Dozier, Edwin B. *A Golden Milestone in Japan.* Nashville: Broadman Press, 1940.

Drach, George, and Calvin F. Kuder. *The Telugu Mission of the General Council of the Evangelical Lutheran Church in North America.* Philadelphia: General Council Publishing House, 1914.

Drège, Jean-Pierre. "Les aventures de la typographie et les missionnaires protestants en Chine au XIXe siècle." *JA* 30 (1992): 279–309.

Drewery, Mary. *William Carey, Shoemaker and Missionary.* London: Hodder & Stoughton, 1978.

Dries, Angelyn. *The Missionary Movement in American Catholic History.* Maryknoll, N.Y.: Orbis Books, 1998.

Drummond, Richard H. *A History of Christianity in Japan.* Grand Rapids, Mich.: William B. Eerdmans, 1971.

D'Sa, M. *History of the Catholic Church in India.* 2 vols. Bombay, 1910, 1924.

Dubois, Abbé Jean Antoine. *Hindu Manners, Customs and Ceremonies.* Trans. from the author's later French Ms. and ed. with notes and biography by Henry K. Beauchamp. 3rd ed. Oxford: Clarendon Press, 1906.

———. *Letters on the State of Christianity in India, in which the Conversion of the Hindoos Is Considered as Impracticable.* Nine letters from 1815 to 1821. Ed. Sharda Paul. New Delhi: Associated Publishing House reprint, 1977.

Dufay, François. *En Chine l'etoile contre la croix.* Paris: Casterman, 1954.

Duff, Alexander. *India and India Missions: including Sketches of the Gigantic System of Hinduism Both in Theory and Practice.* Edinburgh: John Johnstone, 1840; reprint, New Delhi: Swati Publications, 1988.

———. See also William Paton, *Alexander Duff, Pioneer of Missionary Education;* George Smith, *The Life of Alexander Duff.*

Dunne, George H. *Generation of Giants: The First Jesuits in China.* London: Burns & Oates, and Notre Dame, Ind.: University of Notre Dame Press, 1962.

Dunne, Tad. *Spiritual Exercises for Today: A Contemporary Presentation of the Classic Spiritual Exercises of Ignatius Loyola.* San Francisco: Harper/San Francisco, 1990.

Dutta, Abhijit. *Christian Missionaries on the Indigo Question in Bengal 1855–1861.* Calcutta: Minerva Associates, 1989.

———. *Nineteenth-Century Bengal Society and Christian Missionaries.* Calcutta: Minerva Associates, 1992.

Duus, Peter. *The Abacus and the Sword: The Japanese Penetration of Korea, 1895–1910.* Berkeley: University of California Press, 1995.

———. "Science and Salvation in China: The Life and Work of W. A. P. Martin." In *American Missionaries in China,* ed. Kwang-Ching Liu, 11–41. Cambridge, Mass.: Harvard University Press, 1966.

Dwight, Henry G. O. *Blue Book of Missions for 1905.* New York: Funk and Wagnalls, 1905.

———. *Christianity Revived in the East, or, A Narrative of the Work of God among the Armenians of Turkey.* New York: Baker and Scribner, 1850.

Dwight, Timothy. *Sermon: Delivered in Boston, September 10, 1813, before the American Board of Foreign Missions.* 2nd ed. Boston: Samuel T. Armstrong, 1813.

Dyrness, William A. *Learning about Theology from the Third World.* Grand Rapids, Mich.: Zondervan, 1990.

Eberhard, Wolfram. *A History of China.* 3rd ed. Berkeley and Los Angeles: University of California Press, 1971.

Ebisawa, Arimichi. "Irmao Lourenco, the First Japanese Lay-Brother of the Society of Jesus, and His Letter." *MN* 5, no. 1 (1942): 225–233.

Ebizawa, Norimichi, ed. *Japanese Witnesses for Christ*. New York and London: Association Press/Lutterworth Press, 1957.

Ebright, Donald Fossett. *The National Missionary Society of India, 1904–1942*. Chicago: Ebright, 1944.

Ecumenical Missionary Conference, New York, 1900. 2 vols. New York: Religious Tract Society, 1900.

Eddy, Daniel C. *Christian Heroines*. Boston: Estes and Lauriat, 1881.

Eddy, George Sherwood. *Pathfinders of the World Missionary Crusade*. New York and Nashville: Abingdon-Cokesbury, 1945.

Edinburgh World Missionary Conference 1910. See *World Missionary Conference 1910*.

Edwards, Dwight W. *Yenching University*. New York: United Board for Christian Higher Education in Asia, 1959.

Egan, Eileen. *Such a Vision of the Street: Mother Teresa — The Spirit and the Work*. New York: Doubleday, 1985.

Elder, John. *History of the American Presbyterian Mission to Iran (1834–1960)*. Teheran: Literature Committee of the Church Council of Iran, 1960.

Eliade, Mircea, ed. *ERel*. New York: Macmillan, 1987.

Elison, George. *Deus Destroyed: The Image of Christianity in Early Modern Japan*. Harvard East Asian Monographs 141. Cambridge, Mass.: Harvard University Press, 1988; reprint of 1973 edition.

Ellsberg, Robert, ed. *Gandhi on Christianity*. Maryknoll, N.Y.: Orbis Books, 1991.

Elwood, Douglas J. *Churches and Sects in the Philippines*. Dumaguete City, Philippines: Silliman University, 1968.

Embree, Ainslie T. *Utopias in Conflict: Religion and Nationalism in Modern India*. Berkeley: University of California Press, 1990.

The Encyclopedia of Missions. 2nd ed. New York and London: Funk & Wagnalls, 1904.

Endo, Shusaku. *Silence*. Tokyo: Sophia University, 1969.

England, John C. *The Hidden History of Christianity in Asia: The Churches of the East before the Year 1500*. Delhi: ISPCK and CAA, 1996.

Enklaar, I. H. *Joseph Kam, "Apostel der Molukken."* The Hague: Boekencentrum N.V., 1963.

Enriquez, C. M. *A Burmese Arcady*. London: Seeley, Service, 1923.

Entenmann, Robert E. "Christian Virgins in Eighteenth-Century Sichuan," and "Catholics and Society in Eighteenth-Century Sichuan." In *Christianity in China from the Eighteenth Century to the Present*, ed. D. H. Bays, 180–193, and 8–23. Stanford, Calif.: Stanford University Press, 1966.

Esherick, Joseph. *The Origins of the Boxer Uprising*. Berkeley: University of California Press, 1987.

Evans, E. W. Price. *Timothy Richard*. London: Carey Press, 1945.

Evans, Rob, and Tosh Arai, eds. *The Church and Education in Asia*. Singapore: Christian Conference of Asia, 1980.

Ewing, James C. R. See R. E. Speer, *Sir James Ewing*.

Fagg, John Gerardus. *Forty Years in South China: The Life of Rev. John Van Nest Talmage*. New York: A. D. F. Randolph, 1894.

Fairbank, John K. *China: A New History*. Cambridge, Mass.: Harvard University Press, 1992.

————, ed. *The Missionary Enterprise in China and America.* Cambridge, Mass.: Harvard University Press, 1974.

Fairbank, John King, Edwin O. Reischauer, and Albert M. Craig, *East Asia: The Modern Transformation.* Boston: Houghton Mifflin, 1965.

Fasseur, Cornelius. *The Politics of Colonial Exploitation: Java, the Dutch, and the Cultivation System.* Trans. R. E. Elson and Ary Kaal. Ed. R. E. Elson. Ithaca, N.Y.: Southeast Asia Program, Cornell University, 1992.

Favier, A. *The Heart of Pekin: Bishop A. Favier's Diary of the Siege.* Ed. J. Freri. Boston, 1901.

Federal Council of the Churches of Christ in America. *The Korea Situation.* New York: Federal Council of Churches, 1919.

Fehrenbach, T. R. *This Kind of War.* New York: Macmillan, 1963.

Feith, Herbert. *The Decline of Constitutional Democracy in Indonesia.* Ithaca, N.Y.: Cornell University Press, 1962.

Feltus, George Haws. *Samuel Reynolds House of Siam, Pioneer Medical Missionary.* New York: Fleming H. Revell, 1924.

Fenger, J. Ferd. *History of the Tranquebar Mission.* An English translation of a German translation from the Danish original. Tranquebar, India: Evangelical Lutheran Mission Press, 1863.

Fenwick, John R. K. *The Malabar Independent Syrian Church: A Brief Account of the Thozhiyur Metropolitical See.* Bramcote, Nottingham, U.K.: Grove Books, 1992.

Fenwick, Malcolm C. *The Church of Christ in Corea: A Pioneer Missionary's Own Story.* New York: Hodder & Stoughton; George H. Doran, 1911; Seoul: Baptist Publications, 1967, a reprint of the 1911 edition.

Ferguson, D. W. "Philippus Baldaeus and His Book on Ceylon." *Ceylon Antiquary and Literary Register* (Colombo) 4 (1936): 304–310, 337–345, 386–394, 435–445.

Ferguson, John C. "Higher Education in China." *ChRec* 23 (1892): 152–157.

Fernandez, Gil G., ed. *Light Dawns over Asia: Adventism's Story in the Far Eastern Division 1888–1988.* Silang, Cavite, Philippines: Adventist International Institute of Advanced Studies, 1990.

Fernandez, Pablo. *History of the Church in the Philippines (1521–1898).* San Juan, Metro Manila: Life Today Publications, 1988.

Fernhout, Harry. "Man, Faith, and Religion in Bavinck, Kuyper and Dooyeweerd." ThM thesis, Institute for Christian Studies, 1975.

Fiedler, Klaus. *The Story of Faith Missions.* Oxford: Regnum Books International, 1994.

Fifty-Seventh Annual Report of the Board of Foreign Missions of the Presbyterian Church, U.S.A., 1894. Presbyterian General Assembly, Reports of the Boards. New York, 1894.

Findlay, G. G., and W. W. Holdsworth. *The History of the Wesleyan Methodist Missionary Society.* 5 vols. London: Epworth Press, 1921–1924.

Firro, Kais M. *A History of the Druzes.* Vol. 9 in *Handbuch der Orientalistik, erste abteilung, der Nahe und der Mittlere Osten.* Leiden: E. J. Brill, 1992.

Firth, Cyril Bruce. *An Introduction to Indian Church History.* Madras: Christian Literature Society, 1961.

Fischer, Edward. *Mission in Burma: The Columban Brothers' Forty-Three Years in Kachin Country.* New York: Seabury Press, 1980.

Fisher, Daniel W. *Calvin Wilson Mateer, Forty-Five Years a Missionary in Shantung, China.* Philadelphia: Westminster Press, 1911.

Fitch, George A. *My Eighty Years in China*. Taipei, Taiwan: Mei Ya Publications, 1967.

Fitzgerald, Charles P. *The Birth of Communist China*. Baltimore: Penguin Books, 1964.

———. *A Concise History of East Asia*. New York: Frederick A. Praeger, 1966.

Fleming, D. L. *A Contemporary Reading of the Spiritual Exercises: A Companion to St. Ignatius's Text*. 2nd ed., rev. St. Louis: Institute of Jesuit Sources, 1980.

Fletcher, Robert Samuel. *A History of Oberlin College from Its Foundation through the Civil War*. 2 vols. Oberlin, Ohio: Oberlin College, 1943.

Forbes, William Cameron. *The Philippine Islands*. 2 vols. Boston and New York: Houghton Mifflin, 1928.

Foreign Missions Conference of N.A. *Reports*. 1899–1905 (7th to 12th Conferences, 1899–1905). New York: Foreign Missions Library.

Forman, Charles W. "A History of Foreign Mission Theory." In *American Missions in Bicentennial Perspective*, ed. R. Pierce Beaver. South Pasadena, Calif.: William Carey Library, 1977.

Forrester, Duncan B. *Caste and Christianity: Attitudes and Policies on Caste of Anglo-Saxon Protestant Missions in India*. London: Curzon Press, and Atlantic Highlands, N.J.: Humanities Press, 1980.

———. "Indian Christian Attitudes to Caste in the Twentieth Century." *ICHR* (Bangalore) 9, no. 1 (June 1975): 3–22.

Forsyth, Robert Coventry, ed. *The China Martyrs of 1900: A Complete Roll of the Christian Heroes Martyred in China in 1900, with Narratives of Survivors*. New York: Fleming H. Revell, 1904.

Fortescue, Adrian. *The Lesser Eastern Churches*. London: Catholic Truth Society, 1913; reprint New York: AMS Press, 1972.

Foster, Arnold. *Christian Progress in China*. London: Religious Tract Society, 1889.

Foster, John. "The Christian Origins of the Taiping Rebellion." *IRM* 40, no. 1 (1951): 158.

Fridell, Elmer A. *Baptists in Thailand and the Philippines*. Philadelphia: Judson Press, 1956.

Frois, P. Luis. *Die Geschichte Japans (1549–1578). Nach der Handschrift der Ajuda-bibliotheck in Lissabon*. Trans. with commentary by G. Schurhammer and E. A. Voretzsch. Leipzig: Verlag der Asia Major, 1926.

Fujita, Neil S. *Japan's Encounter with Christianity: The Catholic Mission in Pre-Modern Japan*. New York: Paulist Press, 1991.

Fuller, Mrs. Marcus B. *The Wrongs of Indian Womanhood*. New York: Fleming H. Revell, 1900.

Fulop-Miller, Rene. *The Jesuits: A History of the Society of Jesus*. New York: Capricorn Books, 1930; reprint, 1963.

Fung, Raymond. *Households of God on China's Soil*. Maryknoll, N.Y.: Orbis Books, 1982.

Furber, H. *Rival Empires of Trade in the Orient*. Minneapolis: University of Minnesota Press, 1976.

Furnivall, John S. *Colonial Policy and Practice: A Comparative Study of Burma and Netherlands India*. Cambridge: Cambridge University Press, 1948.

Furuya, Yasuo C. *A History of Japanese Theology*. Grand Rapids, Mich.: William B. Eerdmans, 1997.

Gale, James. Letter, 1888. *MRW*, New Series, 2, no. 4 (April 1889).

Gallagher, Louis J. *China in the Sixteenth Century: The Journals of Matthew Ricci 1583–1610.* New York: Random House, 1953.

Galvao, Antonio (?). *Historia das Moluccas.* See Hubert Jacobs *A Treatise on the Moluccas.*

Gandhi, Mahatma. *The Message of Jesus Christ.* Bombay: Bharatiya Vidya Bhavam, 1965.

Ganss, G. E. *The Constitutions of the Society of Jesus.* St. Louis: Institute of Jesuit Sources, 1970.

Garnier, Albert J. *A Maker of Modern China.* London: The Carey Press, 1945.

Garrett, Shirley. *Social Reformers in Urban China: The Chinese Y.M.C.A. 1895–1926.* Cambridge, Mass.: Harvard University Press, 1970.

Garritt, J. C., ed. *Jubilee Papers of the Central Presbyterian Mission, 1844–1894.* Shanghai: Presbyterian Mission, 1895.

Garside, B. A. *Within the Four Seas: Memoirs of B. A. Garside.* New York: Frederick C. Bell, 1985.

Gascoigne, Thomas. *Loci e Libro Veritatum.* Oxford: Clarendon Press, 1881.

Geddes, Michael. *The History of the Church of Malabar.* London: S. Smith and B. Walford, 1694.

Gedge, Evelyn Clara, ed. *Women in Modern India: Fifteen Papers by Indian Women Writers.* Bombay: D. B. Taraporewala, 1929.

Genischen, D. H.-W. "Were the Reformers Indifferent to Missions?" *Student World* (Geneva) 53, nos. 1,2 (1960): 119–127.

Gense, J. H. *The Church at the Gateway of India, 1720–1850.* Bombay: St. Xavier's College, 1960.

George, V. C. *The Church in India before and after the Synod of Diamper.* Alleppey, India: Prakasam Publications, 1977.

Gerhard, Johann. *Loci Theologici.* 9 vols. Tubingae: Sumtibus Io. Georgii Cottae, 1762–1787.

Germann, W. *Ziegenbalg und Plutschau: Die Grundungsjahre der Trankebarschen Mission.* 2 parts. Erlangen: Andreas Deichert, 1868.

Germany, Charles H. *Protestant Theologies in Modern Germany: A History of Dominant Theological Currents from 1920 to 1960.* Tokyo: ISSR Press, 1965.

Gernan, Jacques. *China and the Christian Impact.* Cambridge: Cambridge University Press, 1985.

Gernet, Jacques. *China and the Christian Impact: A Conflict of Cultures.* Trans. Janet Lloyd. Cambridge: Cambridge University Press, 1986.

Ghesquière, Theodore. *Mathieu de Castro, premier vicaire apostolique aux Indes: Une création de la Propagande à ses débuts.* Louvain: Bureaux de la Revue, 1937.

Ghougassian, Vazken. *The Emergence of the Armenian Diocese of New Julfa in the Seventeenth Century.* Atlanta: Scholars Press, 1998.

Giamil, S. *Genuinae relationes inter sedem Apostolicam et Assyriorum orientalis seu Chaldaeorum ecclessiam.* Rome: Ermanno Loescher, 1902.

Gibbons, Herbert Adams. *The Blackest Page of Modern History: Armenian Events of 1915.* New York: G. P. Putnam's, 1916.

Gibbs, H. A. R., and J. H. Kramers, eds. *Shorter Encyclopedia of Islam.* Leiden: Brill, 1953.

Gibbs, M. E. *The Anglican Church in India, 1600–1970.* Delhi: ISPCK, 1972.

Gibson, J. Campbell. *Mission Problems and Mission Methods in South China.* New York: Fleming H. Revell, 1901.

Gifford, D. L. *Every Day Life in Korea.* New York: Fleming H. Revell, 1898.

Gih, Andrew. *China's Wonderful Reviving.* London, 1935.

Ginsel, W. A. *De Gereformeerde Kerk op Formosa of de lotgevallen eener handelskerk onder de Oost-Indische-Compagnie 1627–1662.* Leiden: P. J. Mulder, 1931.

Glover, R. H. *The Progress of Worldwide Missions.* New York: Harper, 1952.

Gnanapragasam, V. M. "Interfaith Dialogue of Early Christian Missionaries in Tamil Nadu." *ICHR* 27, no. 2 (December 1993): 121–129.

Gnolfo, G. *Un missionario assorino: Tomasso dei Conti Valguarnera, S.J.* Catania: Sicilgraf, 1974.

Gogerly, Daniel John. *Ceylon Buddhism: Being the Collected Writings of Daniel John Gogerly.* Colombo: Wesleyan Methodist Book Room, 1908.

Gogerly, George. *The Pioneers: A Narrative of Facts Connected with Early Christian Missions in Bengal, Chiefly Relating to the Operations of the London Missionary Society.* London: John Snow, 1871.

Goh, Moo-Song. "Western and Asian Portrayals of Robert Jermain Thomas (1839–1866)." Ph.D. diss., University of Birmingham, 1995.

Gonzalez-Balado, José Luis. *Stories of Mother Teresa.* Liguori, Mo.: Liguori Publications, 1983.

Good, James E. *Famous Missionaries of the Reformed Church in China.* Philadelphia: Sunday School Board of the Reformed Church, 1903.

Goodall, Norman. *A History of the London Missionary Society 1895–1945.* London and New York: Oxford University Press, 1954.

Goodrich, L. C., and Fang Chaoying. *Dictionary of Ming Biography, 1368–1644.* 2 vols. New York and London: Columbia University Press, 1976.

Goodsell, F. F. *You Shall Be My Witnesses.* Boston: American Board of Commissioners for Foreign Missions, 1959.

Gordon, Andrew. *Our India Mission: A Thirty Year's History (1855–1885) of the India Mission of the United Presbyterian Church of North America.* Philadelphia: Andrew Gordon, 1886.

Gordon, M. L. *An American Missionary in Japan.* Boston/New York: Houghton, Mifflin, 1893.

Goslinga, Adriaan. *Dr. Karl Gützlaff en het Nederlandsche Protestantisme in het midden der vorige eevw.* The Hague: Boekencentrum n.v., 1941.

Gould, James W. *Americans in Sumatra.* The Hague: Martinus Nijhoff, 1961.

Gouvea, Anthony de. *Jornado de Arcebispo da Goa Dom Frey: A. de Menezes.* Coimbra, 1606. Trans. into French by J.-B. de Glen as *Histoire orientale des grands progres de l'église catholique et romaine en la reduction des anciens chrestiens dits de S. Thomas.* Brussels, 1609.

Gowen, Herbert H. *Five Foreigners in Japan.* New York: Fleming H. Revell, 1936.

Gowing, Peter G. "Disentanglement of Church and State." In *Studies in Philippine Church History,* ed. Gerald H. Anderson. Ithaca, N.Y.: Cornell University Press, 1969.

———. *Islands under the Cross: The Story of the Church in the Philippines.* Manila: National Council of Churches in the Philippines, 1967.

Gracey, Mrs. J. T. *Women's Medical Work in Foreign Lands.* Boston: Women's Foreign Mission Society of the Methodist Episcopal Church, 1888.

Grafe, Hugald. *Tamilnadu in the Nineteenth and Twentieth Centuries.* Vol. 4, part 2 of *History of Christianity in India.* Bangalore and Erlangen: Church History Association of India, 1990.

Graham, Carol. *Azariah of Dornakal.* London: SCM Press, 1946.

Grant, Asahel. *The Nestorians; or the Lost Tribes.* New York: Harper & Brothers, 1841.

Grant, Bruce. *Indonesia.* Harmondsworth, U.K.: Penguin Books, 1967.

Gray, Arthur R., and Arthur M. Sherman. *The Story of the Church in China.* New York: The Domestic and Foreign Missionary Society [Episcopalian], 1913.

Grayson, James H. *Early Buddhism and Christianity: A Study in the Emplantation of Religion.* Leiden: Brill, 1985.

———. *John Ross, First Missionary to Korea.* In Korean. Seoul, 1892.

Gregorios, Paulos Mar. *The Indian Orthodox Church.* Delhi and Kottayam: Sophia Press, 1982.

Griffis, William Elliot. *Hepburn of Japan and His Wife and Helpmates.* Philadelphia: Westminster Press, 1913.

———. *The Japanese Nation in Evolution.* New York: Thomas Y. Crowell, 1907.

———. "Koreans at Home." *GAL* (October 1889): 433.

———. "Korea and Its Needs." *GAL* (August 1888): 371.

———. *A Maker of the New Orient: Samuel Robbins Brown, Pioneer Educator in China, America, and Japan, the Story of His Life and Work.* New York: Fleming H. Revell, 1902.

———. *A Modern Pioneer in Korea: The Life Story of Henry G. Appenzeller.* New York: Fleming H. Revell, 1912.

———. *Verbeck of Japan.* Chicago: Fleming H. Revell, 1900.

Grijalva, Joshua, compiler. *Ethnic Baptist History.* Miami: Meta Publishers, 1992.

Grimes, Cecil John. *Towards an Indian Church: The Growth of the Church of India in Constitution and Life.* London: SPCK, 1946.

Grousset, René. *Empire of the Steppes.* Trans. Naomi Walford. New Brunswick, N.J.: Rutgers University Press, 1970.

Grun, Bernard. *The Timetables of History.* New York: Simon & Schuster, 1972, 1987.

Guennou, Jean. *Missions Etrangères de Paris.* Paris: Sarment, Librairie Fayard, 1986.

Guerreiro, Fernão. *Jahangir and the Jesuits: With an Account of the Travels of Benedict Goes and the Mission to Pegu.* Trans. C. H. Payne. London: George Routledge, 1930.

Guerrero, Leon Ma. "Nozaleda and Pons." In *Studies in Philippines Church History,* ed. Gerald H. Anderson. Ithaca, N.Y.: Cornell University Press, 1969.

Guilday, Peter. "The Sacred Congregation de Propaganda Fide." *CHR* 6 (1920/1921): 478–494.

Gulbenkian, Roberto. "The Translation of the Four Gospels into Persian." *NRSM* 29 (1981): 1–91.

Gupta, K. P. *The Christian Missionaries in Bengal, 1793–1833.* Calcutta: Firma K. L. Mukhopadhyay, 1971.

Gurney, A. K. "The Bible in Assamese." *The Assam Mission of the Baptist Missionary Union: Papers and Discussions, 1886.* Calcutta: J. W. Thomas Baptist Mission Press, 1887.

Gutiérrez, David. *The Augustinians from the Protestant Reformation to the Peace of Westphalia 1518–1628.* Villanova, Pa.: Augustinian Historical Institute, Villanova University, 1979.

Gützlaff, Karl (Charles). Collection of copies of Gützlaff manuscript apparently written in his own hand, 1849. Edinburgh, University of Edinburgh, New

College, Centre for the Study of Christianity in the Non-Western World. 11 items.

———. *The Journal of Three Voyages along the Coast of China, in 1831, 1832, and 1833, With Notices of Korea, and the Loo-Choo Islands.* London: Fr. Westley and A. H. Davis, 1834.

Habig, Marion A. *In Journeyings Often: Franciscan Pioneers in the Orient.* New York: Franciscan Institute, 1953.

Hacker, J. H. *A Hundred Years in Travancore, 1806–1906: A History and Description of the Work of the London Missionary Society in Travancore, South India.* London: H. R. Allenson, 1908.

Hagspiel, Bruno. *Along the Mission Trail*, vol. 2: *In the Nederlands East Indies.* Techny, Ill.: Mission Press S.V.D., 1925.

Hakuseki, Arai. *Lessons from History: The Tokushi Yoron.* Trans. and commentary by Joyce Ackroyd. St. Lucia and New York: University of Queensland Press, 1982.

Haldane, Alexander. *Memoirs of the Lives of Robert Haldane of Airthrey and His Brother James Alexander Haldane.* New York: Robert Carter, 1853.

Hale, William Harlan. "When Perry Unlocked the 'Gate of the Sun.'" *American Heritage* 9, no. 3 (April 1958): 94.

Hall, Robert. *An Address to the Public on the Renewal of the Charter of the East-India Company.* London: Josiah Conder, 1813.

Hall, Mrs. Rosetta Sherwood, ed. *The Life of Rev. William James Hall, M.D.* New York: Eaton and Mains, 1897.

Hall, Thelma Wolfe. *I Give Myself: The Story of J. Louis Shuck and His Mission to the Chinese.* Richmond, Va.: private, 1983.

Hamberg, Theodore. *The Visions of Hung-Siu-tshuen and Origin of the Kwangsi Insurrection.* New York: Praeger Reprint, 1969, from original, Hong Kong, 1854.

Hambye, E. R. *Eighteenth Century.* Vol. 3 in *History of Christianity in India.* Bangalore: Church History Association of India, 1997.

A Handbook of Foreign Missions, Containing an Account of the Principal Protestant Missionary Societies in Great Britain with Notice of Those on the Continent and in America; also an Appendix on Roman Catholic Missions. London: Religious Tract Society, 1888.

Handbuch der Orientalistik. Vol. 8, section 2. *Religionsgeschichte des Orients in der Zeit der Weltreligionen.* Ed. Bertold Spuler. Leiden and Cologne: E. J. Brill, 1961.

Hanson, Eric O. *Catholic Politics in China and Korea.* Maryknoll, N.Y.: Orbis Books, 1980.

Hardy, Arthur Sherburne. *Life and Letters of Joseph Hardy Neesima.* Boston and New York: Houghton, Mifflin, 1892.

Harney, M. P. *The Jesuits in History.* New York: America Press, 1941.

Harper, Marvin Henry. "The Methodist Episcopal Church in India: A Study of Ecclesiastical Organization and Administration." Lucknow, India: Lucknow Publishing House, 1936. PhD diss., University of Chicago.

Harper, Susan Billington. *In the Shadow of the Mahatma: Bishop V. S. Azariah and the Travails of Christianity in British India.* Grand Rapids, Mich.: William B. Eerdmans, 2000.

Harrington, Ann M. *Japan's Hidden Christians.* Chicago: Loyola University Press, 1993.

Harrington, Fred Harvey. *God, Mammon, and the Japanese: Horace N. Allen and Korean-American Relations, 1884–1905.* Madison: University of Wisconsin Press, 1944.

Harris, Edward Norman. *A Star in the East: An Account of American Baptist Missions to the Karens of Burma.* New York: Fleming H. Revell, 1920.

Harris, Elizabeth J. "A Case of Distortion: The Evangelical Missionary Interpretation of Buddhism in 19th Century Sri Lanka." *Dialogue* (Ecumenical Institute for Study and Dialogue, Colombo) 21 (1994).

Harris, S. F. *A Century of Missionary Martyrs.* London: James Nisbet, 1897.

Harrison, Brian. *South-East Asia: A Short History.* London: Macmillan, 1955.

Havret, Henri. "La Stele Chretienne de Si-Ngan-Fou." *Variétés Sinologiques* no. 12 (Shanghai: Imprimerie de la Mission Catholique, 1897).

Harvey, G. E. *History of Burma.* New York and London: Longmans, Green and Co., 1925.

Hayden, Joseph Ralston. *The Philippines: A Study in National Development.* New York: Macmillan, 1942.

Heasman, K. E. *Evangelicals in Action: An Appraisal of Their Social Work in the Victorian Era.* London: G. Bles, 1962.

Hedlund, Roger E. "Carey: A Missiologist before Time." *ICHR* (Bangalore) 27, no. 2 (June 1993): 29–49.

———. *Evangelization and Church Growth: Issues from the Asian Context.* Mylapore, Madras, India: C.G.R.C. McGavran Institute, 1992.

———. *World Christianity.* Vol. 3, *South Asia.* Monrovia, Calif.: RC, Mission Advanced Research and Communication Center, 1980.

Heeren, John J. *On the Shantung Front.* New York: Board of Foreign Missions, Presbyterian U.S.A., 1940.

Heiar, James A. *The Church in the Philippines.* Philippines: Divine Word University Publications, 1980.

Heiler, Friedrich. *The Gospel of Sadhu Sundar Singh.* New York: Oxford University Press, 1927.

Henderson, Gregory. "Chong Ta-san: A Study in Korea's Intellectual History." *JAS* 16 (1957): 3.

Henrion, Matthieu. *Histoire générale des missions catholiques depuis le XIIIe siècle jusqu'a nos jours.* 2 vols. Paris: Gaume Frères, 1847.

Hensman, C. R. *Sun Yat-sen.* Naperville, Ill.: SCM Book Club, 1971.

Henthorn, W. E. *Korea: The Mongol Invasions.* Leiden: E. J. Brill, 1963.

Hepburn, James C. See William Elliot Griffis, *Hepburn of Japan.*

Hessel, Eugene. *The Religious Thought of José Rizal.* Rev. ed. Quezon City, Philippines: New Day Publishing Co., 1983.

Historiography of the Chinese Catholic Church: Nineteenth and Twentieth Centuries. Vol. 1, Louvain Chinese Studies. Ed. Jeroom Heyndrickx. Leuven: K. U. Leuven, Ferdinand Verbiest Foundation, 1994.

History of Christianity in India. 5 vols. Bangalore: Church History Association of India, 1982–1997. Vol. 1: *From the Beginning Up to the Middle of the Sixteenth Century,* by A. Mathias Mundadan (1984); vol. 2: *From the Middle of the Sixteenth Century to the End of the Seventeenth Century,* by Joseph Thekkedath (1982); vol. 3: *Eighteenth Century,* by E. R. Hambye (1997); vol. 4/2: *Talminadu in the Nineteenth and Twentieth Centuries,* by Hugald Grafe (1990); vol. 5/5: *North East India in the Nineteenth Century,* by Frederick S. Downs (1992).

Hminga, Chhangte Lal. *The Life and Witness of the Churches in Mizoram.* Serkawn, Mizoram, India: Literature Committee of the Baptist Church of Mizoram, 1987.

Ho, Ping-ti. *Studies on the Population of China, 1368–1953.* Cambridge, Mass.: Harvard University Press, 1959.

Hocking, William. *Re-Thinking Missions: A Laymen's Inquiry.* New York: Fleming H. Revell, 1932.

Hodge, Charles. *Conference Papers, or, Analyses of Discourses, Doctrinal and Practical Delivered on Sabbath Afternoons to the Students of the Theological Seminary, Princeton, N.J.* (New York: Charles Scribner, 1879), 326–329.

Hodge, J. Z. *Bishop Azariah of Dornakal.* Madras: Christian Literature Society for India, 1946.

Hoefer, Herbert E. *Churchless Christianity.* Madras: Asian Programme for Advancement of Training and Studies, India; and Gurukul Lutheran Theological College, 1991.

Hoffmann, Johannes B. *37 Jahre Missionar in Indian: Trostliche Erfahrungen beim Naturvolk der Mundas der Misserfolg in der Missionierung hoherer Kasten und seine Ursachen.* Innsbruck: Verlagsanstalt Tyrolia, 1923.

Hoffmann, Karl. "Das erste päpstliche Missionsinstitut." *ZMW* 12 (1922): 76–82. Much of this whole volume is on the "Propaganda," and its tercentennial anniversary.

Hollenweger, Walter J. *The Future of Mission and the Mission of the Church.* Birmingham, Eng.: Selly Oak Colleges, 1993.

Hollis, Christopher. *The Jesuits: A History.* London: Macmillan, 1968.

Hollis, Michael. *Paternalism and the Church: A Study of South Indian Church History.* New York and London: Oxford University Press, 1962.

Hollister, John N. *The Centenary of the Methodist Church in Southern Asia.* Lucknow, India: Lucknow Publishing House, 1956.

Holsten, Walter. *Johannes Evangelista Gossner: Glaube und Gemeinde.* Göttingen: Vandenhoeck & Ruprecht, 1949.

Holton, D. C. *Modern Japan and Shinto Nationalism: A Study of Present-Day Trends in Japanese Religions.* Chicago: University of Chicago Press, 1943.

Hong, Harold S., Won-Yong Ji, and Chung-Choon Kim, eds. *Korea Struggles for Christ: Memorial Symposium for the Eightieth Anniversary of Protestantism in Korea.* Seoul: Christian Literature Society of Korea, 1966.

Hopkins, Hugh Evan. *Charles Simeon of Cambridge.* Grand Rapids, Mich.: William B. Eerdmans, 1977.

Horne, C. Sylvester. *The Story of the L.M.S.* 2nd ed. London: London Missionary Society, 1895.

Hoskins, Mrs. Robert. *Clara A. Swain, M.D.: First Medical Missionary to the Women of the Orient.* Boston: Women's Foreign Missionary Society, Methodist Episcopal Church, 1912.

Hough, James. *The History of Christianity in India from the Commencement of the Christian Era.* 3 vols. London: R. B. Seeley and W. Burnside, 1839–1860.

Hourani, Albert. *A History of the Arab Peoples.* Cambridge, Mass.: Belknap Press of Harvard University Press, 1991.

House, Samuel R. See George Haws Feltus, *Samuel Reynolds House of Siam.*

Houtart, François. *Religion and Ideology in Sri Lanka.* Bangalore: St. Peter's Seminary, 1974.

Houtart, François, and Geneviève Lemercinier. *Size and Structure of the Catholic Church in India: The Indigenization of an Exogeneous Religious Institution in a Society in Transition.* Louvain-la-Neuve: Université Catholique de Louvain, 1982.

Howard, Randolph L. *Baptists in Burma.* Philadelphia: Judson Press, 1931.

Hsü, Immanuel C. Y. *The Rise of Modern China.* New York: Oxford University Press, 1970.

Hubbard, Ethel Daniels. *Ann of Ava.* New York: Missionary Education Movement, 1913.

Huber, Mary Taylor, and Nancy C. Lutkehaus. *Gendered Missions: Women and Men in Missionary Discourse and Practice.* Ann Arbor: University of Michigan Press, 2000.

Huc, Abbé. *Le Christianisme en Chine en Tartar ie et au Thibet.* 4 vols. Paris: Gaume Freres, 1857. English translation of first two volumes. *Christianity in China, Tartary and Thibet.* 2 vols. New York: P. J. Kenedy, 1897.

———. *Souvenirs d'un voyage dans la Tartare, le Thibet et la Chine pendant les annés 1844, 1845, 1846.* Lille: Masion du Bon Livre, 1900.

Hudson, D. Dennis. "The Conversion Account of H. A. Krishna Pillai." *ICHR* 2, no. 1 (June 1968): 15–43.

Hull, Ernest R. *Bombay Mission History and the Padroado Question.* 2 vols. Bombay: Examiner Press, 1927.

Hummel, Arthur, ed. *Eminent Chinese of the Ch'ing Period (1644–1912).* 2 vols. Washington, D.C.: U.S. Government Printing Office, 1943.

Hunsberger, George R. "Conversion and Community: Revisiting Lesslie Newbigin's Debate with M. M. Thomas." *IBMR* 22, no. 3 (July 1998): 112–117.

———. "The Missionary Significance of the Biblical Doctrine of Election as a Foundation for a Theology of Cultural Pluralism in the Missiology of J. E. Lesslie Newbigin." PhD diss., Princeton Theological Seminary, 1987.

Hunt, Bruce F. *For a Testimony.* London: Banner of Truth Trust, 1966.

———. "Korean Martyrs." in *RBM* 4, nos. 2, 3, 4 (October 1968–December 1968, February 1969).

———. *Out of Prison.* Philadelphia: Orthodox Presbyterian Church, 1942.

Hunt, Everett N., Jr. *Protestant Pioneers in Korea.* Maryknoll, N.Y.: Orbis Books, 1980.

Hunt, Michael H. *The Making of a Special Relationship: The United States and China to 1914.* New York: Columbia University Press, 1983.

Hunt, Robert, Lee Kam Hing, and John Roxborogh, eds. *Christianity in Malaysia: A Denominational History.* Selangor Darul Ehsan, Malaysia: Pelanduk Publications, 1992.

Hunter, Alan, and Don Bloomington. "Survey Article: Christianity in the People's Republic of China," *Religion* 20 (1990): 177–183.

Hunter, Jane. *The Gospel of Gentility: American Women Missionaries in China.* New Haven, Conn.: Yale University Press, 1984.

Hunter, William C. *The "Fan Kwae" [foreign devils] at Canton before Treaty Days 1825–1844, by An Old Resident.* London: Kegan Paul, Trench, 1882.

Huntley, Martha. *To Start a Work: The Foundations of Protestant Mission in Korea, 1884–1919.* Seoul: Presbyterian Church of Korea, 1987.

Hu Shih. *The Chinese Renaissance: The Haskell Lectures.* Chicago: University of Chicago Press, 1933.

Hutchinson, E. W. *Adventurers in Siam in the Seventeenth Century.* London: Royal Asiatic Society, 1940.

Hutchison, William R. *Errand to the World: American Protestant Thought and Foreign Missions.* Chicago: University of Chicago Press, 1987.

Hutton, J. H. *Caste in India: Its Nature, Function, and Origins.* Cambridge: Cambridge University Press, 1946.

Hyatt, Irwin T. *Our Ordered Lives Confess: Three Nineteenth-Century American Missionaries in East Shantung.* Cambridge: Harvard University Press, 1976.

————. "Protestant Missions in China: The Institutionalization of Good Works." In *American Missionaries in China,* ed. Kwang-Ching Liu, 93–126. Cambridge: Harvard University Press, 1966.

Iglehart, Charles W. *A Century of Protestant Christianity in Japan.* Tokyo: Charles E. Tuttle, 1959.

————. *Cross and Crisis in Japan.* New York: Friendship Press, 1957.

Imbrie, William M. *The Church of Christ in Japan: A Course of Lectures.* Philadelphia: Westminster Press, 1906.

Ingham, Kenneth. *Reformers in India, 1793–1833: An Account of the Work of Christian Missionaries on Behalf of Social Reform.* Cambridge: Cambridge University Press, 1956.

Interpretative Statistical Survey of the World Mission of the Christian Church. New York and London: International Missionary Council, 1938.

Iparaguirre, Ignatius. *Historia de la práctica de los Ejercicios Spirituales de San Ignacio Loyola.* 3 vols. Bilbao/Rome: Institutum Historicum Societatis Jesu.

Irudayaraj, Xavier, ed. *Emerging Dalit Theology.* Madras: Jesuit Theological Secretariate, 1990.

Isham, Mary. *Valorous Ventures: A Record of Sixty and Six Years of the Woman's Foreign Missionary Society, Methodist Episcopal Church.* Boston: WFMS, Methodist Episcopal Church, 1936.

Iskander ibn Yaq'ub Abkarius. *The Lebanon in Turmoil: Syria and the Powers in 1860.* Trans. with introduction and conclusion by J. F. Scheltema. New Haven, Conn.: Yale University Press, 1920.

Jackson, John. *Mary Reed, Missionary to Lepers.* 11th ed. London: Mission to Lepers, 1912.

Jacob, Plamthodathil S. *The Experiential Response of N. V. Tilak.* Madras: Christian Literature Society, 1979.

Jacobs, Hubert T. T., ed. and trans. *A Treatise on the Moluccas (c. 1544), Probably the Preliminary Version of Antonio Galvão's lost Historia das Moluccas.* St. Louis: Jesuit Historical Institute, 1971.

Janin, Père. *The Separated Eastern Churches.* London: Sands, 1933.

Jann, P. A. *Die catholischen Missionen in Indien, China und Japan. Ihre Organisation und das portugiesische Patronat von 15 bis in 18 Jahrhundert.* Paderborn, 1915.

Jansen, Marius B. *The Making of Modern Japan.* Cambridge, Mass.: Harvard University Press, Belknap Press, 2000.

Jansen, Marius B., and Gilbert Rozman, eds. *Japan in Transition from Tokugawa to Meiji.* Princeton, N.J.: Princeton University Press, 1986.

Jay, Robert R. *Religion and Politics in Rural Central Java.* Cultural Report Series No. 12. New Haven, Conn.: Yale University South East Asia Studies, 1963.

Jayaprakash, L. Joshi. *Evaluation of Indigenous Missions of India.* Kilpauk, Madras, India: Church Growth Research Centre, 1987.

Jedin, Hubert, and John Dolan, eds. *History of the Church*. 10 vols., New York: Crossroad, 1980–1981. Vol. 5: *Reformation and Counter Reformation*, ed. E. Iseloh et al., trans. P. Becker; vol. 6: *The Church in the Age of Absolutism and Enlightenment*, ed. W. Muhler et al., trans. G. J. Holt; vol. 7: *The Church between Revolution and Restoration*, ed. R. Aubert et al., trans. P. Becker; vol. 8: *The Church in the Age of Liberalism*, ed. R. Aubert, trans. Margit Resch; vol. 9: *The Church in the Industrial Age*, ed. R. Aubert et al., trans. Margit Resch.

Jeffery, Mary Pauline. *Dr. Ida: India. The Life Story of Ida S. Scudder*. New York: Fleming H. Revell, 1938.

Jeffrey, Robert. *The Indian Mission of the Irish Presbyterian Church: A History of Fifty Years of Work in Kathiawar and Gujarat*. London: Nisbet, 1890.

Jenkins, Paul. *A Short History of the Basel Mission*. Basel: Basel Mission, 1989.

Jenkins, R. C. *The Jesuits in China and the Legation of Cardinal De Tournon*. London: David Nutt, 1994.

Jennes, Joseph. *A History of the Catholic Church in Japan, from Its Beginnings to the Early Meiji Era (1549–1873)*. Tokyo: Committee of the Apostolate, 1959; reprint, Oriens Institute for Religious Research, 1973.

Jennings, Raymond P. *Jesus, Japan, and Kanzo Uchimura: A Study of the View of the Church of Kanzo Uchimura and Its Significance for Japanese Christianity*. Tokyo: Kyoo Bun Kwan, Christian Literature Society, 1958.

Ji, Won-Yong. *A History of Lutheranism in Korea: A Personal Account*. St. Louis: Concordia Seminary, 1988.

Johnstone, Patrick, ed. *OW, 1993*. Grand Rapids, Mich.: Zondervan, 1993.

———. *OW*. Minneapolis: Bethany House, 2001.

Jones, E. Stanley. *Mahatma Gandhi: An Interpretation*. New York: Abingdon-Cokesbury Press, 1948.

Jones, George Heber. "The Growth of the Church in the Mission Field: III, Presbyterian and Methodist Missions in Korea," *IRM* 1 (July 1912): 412–434.

———. *Korea Quarter-Centennial Documents* [Methodist]. "The Korea Mission of the Methodist Episcopal Church"; "Christian Medical Work"; "Education in Korea"; "Competent Witnesses..."; "The Korean Revival," etc. New York: Methodist Board of Foreign Missions, 1910.

Jones, J. P., ed. *The Year Book of Missions in India, Burma and Ceylon, 1912*. Madras: Christian Literature Society for India, 1912.

Joo, Seung Joong. "The Early Protestant Missionaries' Preaching in the Korean Church." ThM thesis, Columbia Theological Seminary, Decatur, Georgia, 1991.

Joseph, John Henry. *Muslim-Christian Relations and Inter-Christian Rivalries in the Middle East: The Case of the Jacobites in the Age of Transition*. Albany: State University of New York Press, 1983.

———. *The Nestorians and Their Muslim Neighbors: A Study of Western Influence on Their Relations*. Princeton, N.J.: Princeton University Press, 1961.

Joseph, K. V. "The Vicissitudes of Syrian Christians in the Maritime Trade of Pre-Modern Kerala," *ICHR* 23 (1989): 132–143.

Joy, K. T. *The Mar Thoma Church: A Study of Its Growth and Contribution*. Kottayam, Kerala, India: Good Shepherd Press, 1986.

Jubilee Sketches: An Outline of the Work of the Church Missionary Society in Ceylon. Colombo, 1869.

Judson, Edward. *The Life of Adoniram Judson*. New York: A. D. F. Randolph, 1883.

Judson, Emily [Chubbock]. *Memoir of Sarah B. Judson, Member of the American Mission to Burmah.* New York: L. Colby, 1849.

Juhanon, Mar Thoma. *Christianity in India and a Brief History of the Mar Thoma Syrian Church.* Revised ed. Madras: K. M. Cherian, 1968.

Jurji, Edward J. *The Middle East: Its Religion and Culture.* Philadelphia: Westminster Press, 1956.

Just, Mary. *Immortal Fire: A Journey through the Centuries with the Missionary Great.* St. Louis: Herder, 1951.

Justus, M. "Schwartz: A Missionary in Politics, 1750–1798." *ICHR* (Delhi) 26, no. 1 (1992): 35–49.

Kahin, George McT., ed. *Governments and Politics of Southeast Asia.* Ithaca, N.Y.: Cornell University Press, 1959.

Kandenbusch, Amy. "Missions on the Island of Bali," *IRM* 23 (1934): 206–214.

Kanjamala, Augustine. *Divine Word Missionaries (SVD) in India.* Pune, India: Isshvani Publications, n.d. [1988].

Kasteel, P. *Abraham Kuyper.* Kampen: J. H. Kok, 1938.

Kataoka Yakichi. "Life of Brother Lorenco." *Missionary Bulletin* 3 (Himeji and Tokyo, 1949): 12–25.

Kato, Genchi. *A Study of Shinto: The Religion of Japan.* London: Curzon Press, 1970; reprint of Tokyo ed., 1926.

Kawerau, Peter. *Amerika und die orientalischen Kirchen. Ursprung und Anfang der amerikanischen Mission unter den Nationalkirchen Westasiens.* Berlin: W. de Gruyter, 1958.

Kaye, John William. *Christianity in India: An Historical Narrative.* London: Smith, Elder, 1859.

Keay, F. E. *A History of the Syrian Church in India.* Rev. ed. Madras: SPCK, 1952.

Kemperman, Steve. *Lord of the Second Advent.* Ventura, Calif.: Regal Press, 1981.

Kerrison, Ray. *Bishop Walsh of Maryknoll: Prisoner of Red China.* New York: G. P. Putnam's Sons, 1962.

Ketler, Isaac C. *The Tragedy of Paotingfu.* New York: Fleming H. Revell, 1902.

Khan, Mumtaz Ali. *Seven Years of Change: A Study of Some Scheduled Castes in Bangalore District.* Madras: Christian Literature Society, 1979.

Kiang, Wen-Han. *The Chinese Student Movement.* Morningside Heights, N.Y.: King's Crown Press, 1948.

Kil, Chin-Kyong. *Yongke Kil Son Ju.* Biography of Rev. Kil Son-Ju. Seoul: Chongno Sojok, 1980.

Kim, Byong-Suh. "The Explosive Growth of the Korean Church Today: A Sociological Analysis." *IRM* 74 (January 1985): 59–72.

Kim, Chang-Seok Thaddaeus. *Lives of 103 Martyr Saints of Korea.* Seoul: Catholic Publishing House, 1984.

Kim, D. L., and Mindy Schrader. *The Korean War: An Assessment of the Historical Record, Conference Report.* Washington, D.C.: The Korea Society, 1955.

Kim, Joseph Chang-Mun, and John Jae-sun Chung, eds. *Catholic Korea: Yesterday and Today.* Seoul: Catholic Korea Publishing Co., 1964.

Kim, Kyoung Jae. *Christianity and the Encounter of Asian Religions: Methods of Correlation, Fusion of Horizons and Paradigm Shifts in the Korean Grafting Process.* Zoetermeer, Netherlands: Uitgeverij Boekcentrum, 1994.

Kim, Yang Sun. "History of the Korean Church in the Ten Years Since Liberation (1945–1955)." Trans. A. D. Clark. Mimeograph, 1955.

Kim, Yun Kuk. "The Korean Church Yesterday and Today." *Korean Affairs* (Seoul)
    1 (March/April 1962): 81–105.
Kincaid, Eugenio. See Alfred Patton, *The Hero Missionary.* New York: H. Dayton,
    1858.
King, Alonzo. *Memoir of George Dana Boardman.* Boston: Lincoln, Edmands, 1834.
Kinnear, Angus I. *The Story of Watchman Nee: Against the Tide.* Fort Washington,
    Pa.: Christian Literature Crusade, 1973.
Kipp, Rita Smith. *The Early Years of a Dutch Colonial Mission: The Karo Field.* Ann
    Arbor: University of Michigan Press, 1990.
Kipp, Rita Smith, and Susan Rodgers, eds. *Indonesian Religions in Transition.*
    Tucson: University of Arizona Press, 1987.
Klaveren, J. J. van. *The Dutch Colonial System in the East Indies.* Rotterdam:
    Benedictus, 1953.
Knowles, James D. *Memoir of Mrs. Ann H. Judson, Late Missionary to Burmah.*
    Boston: Lincoln & Edmands, 1829.
Knox, Robert. *An Historical Relation of Ceylon.* 2nd ed. Dehiwala, Ceylon: Tisara
    Prakasakayo, 1958; from the London, 1681, original.
Kojiki. See Donald L. Philippi.
Kollaparambil, Jacob. *The Archdeacon of All-India: An Historico-Juridical Study.*
    Rome: Lateran University, 1972.
————. *The Babylonian Origin of the Southists among the St. Thomas Christians.* Rome:
    Pont. Institutum Studiorum Orientalium, 1992.
Kono, Yoshi S. *Japanese Expansion on the Asian Continent.* Vol. 1. Berkeley:
    University of California Press, 1937.
Korea Mission, Presbyterian Church USA. *The Fiftieth Anniversary Celebration of
    the Korea Mission of the Presbyterian Church in the USA.* Seoul: YMCA Press,
    1934.
Korea Missions Prayer Calendar. See *Prayer Calendar.*
The Korean Situation. No. 1 and 2. New York: Federal Council of the Churches of
    Christ in America, 1919 and 1920.
Kottuppallil, George. *History of the Catholic Missions in Central Bengal 1855–1886.*
    Shillong, India: Vendrame Institute, 1988.
Kozaki, Hiromichi. *Reminiscences of Seventy Years: The Autobiography of a Japanese
    Pastor.* Trans. Nariaki Kozaki. Tokyo: Kyo Bun Kwan, n.d. [1933?].
Kpobi, David Nii Anum. *Mission in Chains: The Life, Theology and Ministry of the
    Ex-slave Jacobus E. J. Capitein (1717–1747).* Zoetermeer, Netherlands: Uitgeverij
    Boekcentrum, 1993.
Krahl, Joseph. *China Missions in Crisis: Bishop Laimbeckhoven and His Times, 1738–
    1787.* Rome: Gregorian University Press, 1964.
Kristof, Nicholas D., and Sheryl WuDunn. *China Wakes: The Struggle for the Soul
    of a Rising Power.* New York: Times Books, Random House, 1994.
Ku, Dae-Yol. *Korea under Colonialism: The March First Movement and Anglo-Japanese
    Relations.* Seoul: Royal Asiatic Society, Korea Branch, 1985.
Kuepers, Jacobus J. A. M. *China und die katholische Mission in Sud-Shantung 1882–
    1900: die Geschichte einer konfrontation.* Steyl: Missiehaus, 1974.
————. "The Dutch Reformed Church in Formosa 1627–1662: Mission in a
    Colonial Context." *NRSM/NZM* 27 (1978): 1–46.
Kuno, Y. S. *Japanese Expansion on the Asian Continent.* 2 vols. Berkeley and Los
    Angeles: University of California Press, 1937–1940.

Kuriakose, M. K. *History of Christianity in India: Source Materials*. Indian Theological Library, Serampore College. Madras: Christian Literature Society, 1982.

Kurian, V. Mathew. "Syrian Christians and the Political Economy of Kerala." *ICHR* 28 (December 1994): 91–104.

Kuruppu, D. J. B. *The Pearl of the Indian Ocean: A Handbook of Ceylon*. Colombo: Catholic Messenger Press, 1924.

Kuruvilla, K. K. *A History of the Mar Thoma Church and Its Doctrines*. Madras: Christian Literature Society for India, 1951.

Kwantes, Anne C. *Presbyterian Missionaries in the Philippines: Agents of Social Change 1898–1910*. Quezon City, Philippines: New Day Publishers, 1989.

Kyu-Tae, Yi. *The Modern Transformation of Korea*. Seoul: Sejong Publishing Co., 1970.

Labourt, M. J. "Notes sur les schismes de l'église Nestorienne du 16 au 19 siècle." *JAS* Series 10, vol. 11 (1908): 227–235.

Lach, Donald F. *Asia in the Making of Europe*. 3 vols. in 7 parts. Vol. 1: *The Century of Discovery*. Vol. 2: *A Century of Wonder* (Book 1: *The Visual Arts*; Book 2: *The Literary Arts*; Book 3: *The Scholarly Disciplines*). Vol. 3: *A Century of Advance* (Book 1: *Trade, Missions, Literature*; Book 2: *South Asia*; Book 3: *Southeast Asia*; Book 4: *East Asia*). Chicago: University of Chicago Press, 1965–1993.

———. *China in the Eyes of Europe: The Sixteenth Century*. Chicago: University of Chicago Press, 1965.

Lach, Donald F., and Carol Flaumenhaft, eds. *Asia on the Eve of Europe's Expansion*. Englewood Cliffs, N.J.: Prentice-Hall, 1965.

Lacouture, Jean. *Jesuits: A Multibiography*. Trans. J. Leggatt. Washington, D.C.: Crosspoint, 1995.

Laman, Gordon D. "Our Nagasaki Legacy: An Examination of the Period of Persecution of Christianity and Its Impact on Subsequent Christian Mission in Japan." *NAJT* (Tokyo) 28/29 (March/September 1982): 94–141.

Lambert, Tony. *The Resurrection of the Chinese Church*. London: Hodder & Stoughton, 1991.

Lamberton, Mary. *St. John's University, Shanghai, 1879–1951*. New York: United Board for Christian Colleges in China, 1955.

Lande, Aasulv. *Meiji Protestantism in History and Historiography: A Comparative Study of Japanese and Western Interpretations of Early Protestantism in Japan*. Vol. 58 in Studies in the Intercultural History of the Church. Frankfurt-am Main: Peter Lang, 1989.

Landon, Kenneth P. *Southeast Asia: Crossroad of Religions*. Chicago: University of Chicago Press, 1947.

Langer, William L. *An Encyclopedia of World History*. Rev. ed. Boston: Houghton Mifflin, 1948.

Latourette, Kenneth Scott. *The Chinese: Their History and Culture*. 2 vols. New York: Macmillan, 1941.

———. *A History of Christian Missions in China*. New York: Macmillan, 1929.

———. *A History of the Expansion of Christianity*. 7 vols. New York: Harper & Brothers, 1939.

Laubach, Frank Charles. *The People of the Philippines: Their Religious Progress and Preparation for Spiritual Development in the Far East*. New York: George H. Doran, 1925.

———. *Rizal: Man and Martyr.* Manila: Community Publishers Inc., 1936.

Launay, Adrien C. *Histoire de la mission de Cochinchine, 1658–1923 documents historiques.* 3 vols. Paris: Missions étrangères de Paris, 2000.

———. *Histoire de la mission de Siam 1662–1811.* 2 vols. Paris: Tequi, 1920.

———. *Histoire de la mission du Tonkin.* Paris: Missions étrangères de Paris, 2000.

———. *Histoire des missions de Chine. Mission du Kouang-Tong.* Paris: Anciennes Maisons Douniol et Retaux, 1917.

———. *Histoire des missions de l'Inde: Pondichéry, Maissour, Coimbatour.* 4 vols. Paris: Charles Douniol, 1898.

———. *Histoire générale de la Société des Missions-Etrangères.* 3 vols. Paris: Tequi, 1894.

———. *Journal d'André Ly, Prêtre Chinois, Missionaire et notaire apostolique, 1746– 1763.* 2nd ed. Hong Kong: Imprimerie de Nazareth, 1924.

Laures, Johannes. *The Catholic Church in Japan: A Short History.* Tokyo and Rutland, Vt.: Charles Tuttle, 1954.

———. *Kirishitan Bunko: A Manual of Books and Documents on the Early Christian Mission in Japan.* 3rd ed. Monumenta Nipponica Monographs no. 5. Tokyo: Sophia University, 1957.

———. "Koreas Erste Berührung mit dem Christentum." *ZMR* 40 (1956): 177– 189.

———. *Studies on Takayama Ukon.* In *Instituto Portugues de Hongkong, Seccão de Historia.* Macau: Imprensa Nacional, 1955.

———. *Two Japanese Christian Heroes: Justo Takayama Ukon and Gracia Hosokawa Tamako.* Rutland, Vt.: Bridgewater/Charles E. Tuttle, 1959.

Lautenschlager, Roy S. *On the Dragon Hills.* Philadelphia: Westminster Press, 1970.

Lawrence, Carl. *The Church in China: How It Survives and Prospers under Communism.* Minneapolis: Bethany House, 1985.

Lawrence, Una Roberts. *Lottie Moon.* Nashville: SS Board of Southern Baptist Convention, 1929.

Ledyard, Gary. *The Dutch Come to Korea.* Seoul: Royal Asiatic Society, Korea Branch, 1971.

Lee, Felix George. *The Catholic Church in Malaya.* Singapore: Eastern Universities Press, 1963.

Lee, Gabriel Gab-Soo. "Sociology of Conversion: Sociological Implications of Religious Conversion to Christianity in Korea." PhD diss., Fordham University, 1961.

Lee, Jong-Hyeong. "Dr. Samuel Austin Moffett: His Life and Work in the Development of the Presbyterian Church of Korea, 1890–1936." PhD diss., Richmond, Va.: Union Theological Seminary, 1983.

Lee, Kun Sam. *The Christian Confrontation with Shinto Nationalism: A Historical and Critical Study of Christianity and Shinto in Japan . . . (1868–1945).* Philadelphia: Presbyterian and Reformed Publishing Co., 1966.

Lee, Peter H., ed. *Sources of Korean Civilization.* Vol. 2. New York: Columbia University Press, 1996.

Lee, Robert. *Stranger in the Land: A Study of the Church in Japan.* London: Lutterworth Press, 1967.

Lee, Sang Hyun, ed. *Essays on Korean Heritage and Christianity.* Princeton Junction, N.J.: Association of Korean Christian Scholars in North America, 1984.

Lee, Seung-Joon. "A Study on the Historical Development of the Schisms of the Korean Presbyterian Church (1945–1981)." s.l.: n.d. [1989].

Lehmann, Arno. *Alte Briefe aus Indien: Unveroffentlichte Briefe von Bartolomaus Ziegenbalg 1706–1719*. Berlin: Evangelische Verlagsanstalt, 1957.

———. *It Began in Tranquebar: The Story of the Tranquebar Mission*. Madras: Christian Literature Society, 1956.

Lehmann, Jean-Pierre. *The Roots of Modern Japan*. New York: St. Martin's Press, 1982.

Lehmann, Martin E. *A Biographical Study of Ingwer Ludwig Nommensen (1834–1918), Pioneer Missionary to the Bataks of Sumatra*. Lewiston, N.Y.: Edwin Mellen Press, 1996.

Leibniz, Gottfried Wilhelm. *Discourse on the Natural Theology of the Chinese*. Translated, with introduction, notes, and commentary by Henry Rosemont Jr. and D. J. Cook. No. 4 in *Monographs of the Society for Asian and Comparative Philosophy*. Hawaii: University Press of Hawaii, 1977.

Le Joly, Edward. *Mother Teresa of Calcutta: A Biography*. New York: Harper & Row, 1977, 1983.

Leonard, Delavan L. *A Hundred Years of Missions*. New York: Funk & Wagnalls, 1895.

Leonowens, Anna. *The English Governess at the Siamese Court, Recollections*. Philadelphia: Porter & Coates, 1870.

———. *The Romance of the Harem*. Ed. with introduction by Susan Morgan. Charlottesville and London: University of Virginia Press, 1991.

Les ordres religieux: La Sociètè des Missions-Etrangères. Paris: Librairie Letouzey et Ané, 1923.

Lesourd, Paul. *Histoire des missions catholiques*. Paris: Librairie de l'Arc, 1937.

Lettres edifiantes et curieuses de Chine par des missionaires jésuites 1702–1776. Ed. J.-L. Vissière. Paris: Garnier-Flammarion, 1979.

Leung, Beatrice Kit-fun. *Sino-Vatican Relations: Problems of Conflicting Authority*. Cambridge: Cambridge University Press, 1992.

Leung, Beatrice, and John D. Young. *Christianity in China: Foundations for Dialogue*. Hong Kong: University of Hong Kong, 1993.

Levenson, Joseph R. *Confucian China and Its Modern Fate: A Trilogy*. 3 vols. in 1. Berkeley and Los Angeles: University of California Press, 1968.

———. "Confucian China and Taiping 'Heaven': Political Implications of Clashing Religious Concepts." *Comparative Studies in Society and History* 4 (July 1962): 436–453.

Lewis, Bernard. *The Jews of Islam*. Princeton, N.J.: Princeton University Press, 1984.

Lewis, C. B. *The Life of John Thomas, Surgeon of the Earl of Oxford, East Indiaman, and First Baptist Missionary to Bengal*. London: Macmillan, 1873.

Lewis, Robert E. *The Educational Conquest of the Far East*. New York: Fleming H. Revell, 1903.

Li, Hung Chang. *Memoirs of Li Hung Chang*. Ed. William F. Mannix. Boston/New York: Houghton Mifflin, 1913.

Li, Zhisui. *The Personal Life of Chairman Mao*. New York: Random House, 1994.

Liang Ch'i-ch'ao. *Intellectual Trends in the Ch'ing Period*. Trans. with introduction and notes by Immanuel C. Y. Hsü. Cambridge, Mass.: Harvard University Press, 1959.

Lindbeck, John M. H. "American China Missionaries and the Policies of the United States in China, 1898–1901." PhD diss., Yale University, 1948.

Liu, Kwang-Ching. *American Missionaries in China: Papers from Harvard Seminars.* Cambridge, Mass.: Harvard University Press, 1966.

Lloyd, J. Meirion. *History of the Church in Mizoram (Harvest of the Hills).* Aizawl, Mizoram: Synod Publication Board, 1991.

Lobley, Joseph Albert. *The Church and the Churches in Southern India: A Review of the Portuguese Missions.* Cambridge: Deighton, Bell, 1870.

Lodwick, Kathleen, comp. *The Chinese Recorder Index: A Guide to Christian Missions in Asia, 1867–1941.* Vol. 1. Wilmington, Del.: Scholarly Resources, 1986.

Lopez, Rafael, and Alfonso Felix Jr. *The Christianization of the Philippines: The Orders of Philip II and the Basic Reports and Letters of Legaspi, Urdaneta.* Manila: Historical Conservation Society, 1965.

Louvet, Louis-Eugène. *La Cochinchine religieuse.* 2 vols. Paris: Ernest Leroux, 1885.

———. *Journal d'André Ly, Prêtre Chinois, Missionaire et Notaire Apostolique, 1746–1763.* 2nd ed. Hong Kong: Imprimerie de Nazareth, 1924.

———. *Les missions catholiques au XIXme siècle.* Lille: Société de Saint Augustin, 1898.

———. *Les Missiones Catholicae cura S. Congregationis de Propaganda Fide.* Rome: S. C. Propaganda Fide, 1927.

Lovett, Richard. *The History of the London Missionary Society, 1795–1895.* 2 vols. London: Henry Frowde, 1899.

Lucas, Bernard. *Shall We Proselytise Hindus or Evangelise India.* London: Macmillan, 1914.

Lumbantobing, Andar. *Das Amt in der Batak-Kirche.* Wuppertal-Barmen: Rheinischen Missions-Gesellschaft, 1955.

Lutz, Jessie Gregory. *China and the Christian Colleges, 1850–1950.* Ithaca, N.Y.: Cornell University Press, 1971.

———. *Chinese Politics and Christian Missions: The Anti-Christian Movements of 1920–28.* Vol. 3. *The Church and the World Series.* Notre Dame, Ind.: Cross Cultural Publications, 1988.

———, ed. *Christian Missions in China: Evangelists of What?* Boston: D. C. Heath, 1965.

Lutz, Jessie G., and Rolland Ray Lutz. "The Invisible China Missionaries: The Basel Mission's Chinese Evangelists, 1847–1866." *Mission Studies* 24 12, no. 2 (1995): 204–227.

Ly, Andre. *Journal d'André Ly, Prêtre Chinois, Missionare et notaire apostolique, 1746–1763.* 2nd ed. Hong Kong: Imprimerie de Nazareth, 1924.

Lyall, Leslie T. *Come Wind, Come Weather.* Chicago: Moody Press, 1960.

———. *God Reigns in China.* London: Hodder & Stoughton, 1985.

———. *John Sung: A Biography.* London: China Inland Mission, 1954.

———. *New Spring in China.* London: Hodder & Stoughton, 1980.

———. *A Passion for the Impossible: A Continuing Story of the Mission Hudson Taylor Began.* London: Overseas Missionary Fellowship Books, 1976.

———. *Three of China's Mighty Men.* London: Overseas Missionary Fellowship Books, 1973.

Macartney, George. *An Authentic Account of an Embassy from the King of Great Britain to the Emperor of China.* Philadelphia: Robert Campbell, 1799.

MacGillivray, D., ed. *A Century of Protestant Missions in China, 1807–1907, Being the Centenary Conference Historical Volume.* Shanghai: American Presbyterian Mission Press, 1907.

MacInnis, Donald E. *Religion in China Today: Policy and Practice.* Maryknoll, N.Y.: Orbis Books, 1989.

Mackenzie, F. A. *Booth-Tucker, Sadhu and Saint.* London: Hodder & Stoughton, 1930.

Maclagan, Edward. *Jesuits and the Great Moghul.* London: Burns & Oates, 1932.

Maclean, Arthur John, and William Henry Browne. *The Catholicos of the East and His People: [The] Eastern Syrian Christians of Kurdistan and Northern Persia (Known also as Nestorians).* London: SPCK, 1892.

Macnicol, Nicol. *India in the Dark Wood.* London: Edinburgh House Press, 1930.

Madsen, Richard. *China's Catholics: Tragedy and Hope in an Emerging Civil Society.* Berkeley: University of California Press, 1998.

Main, Duncan. See K. De Gruché, *Dr. D. Duncan Main.*

Majul, Cesar Adib. "Anticlericalism during the Reform Movement and the Philippine Revolution." In *Studies in Philippine Church History,* ed. G. Anderson. Ithaca, N.Y.: Cornell University Press, 1969.

———. *Pandita Ramabai.* London: Student Christian Movement, 1926.

Majumdar, R. C., et al. *Advanced History of India.* London: Macmillan, 1946; reissued, New York: Macmillan, 1967.

Malalgoda, Kitsiri. *Buddhism in Sinhalese Society, 1750–1900: A Study of Religious Revival and Change.* Berkeley: University of California Press, 1976.

———. "The Buddhist-Christian Confrontation in Ceylon, 1800–1880." *Social Compass* (Louvain) 20 (1973): 171–200.

Malatesta, E. J., ed. *T'ien-chu Shih-i.* Trans. with notes by Douglas Lancashire and Peter Hu Kuo-chen. St. Louis: Institute of Jesuit Sources, 1985.

Malech, George David. *History of the Syrian Nation and the Old Evangelical-Apostolic Church of the East.* Minneapolis, 1910.

Manickam, Sundararaj. *The Social Setting of Christian Conversion in South India: The Impact of the Wesleyan Methodist Missionaries on the Trichy-Tanjore Diocese.* Wiesbaden: Franz Steiner Verlag, 1977. Beitrage zur Sudasien-Forschung, University Heidelberg, No. 33.

Mannix, William Francis, ed., *Memoirs of Li Hung Chang.* Boston and New York: Houghton Mifflin, 1913.

Marnas, Francisque. *La religion de Jésus (Iaso Ja-kyo) ressuscitée au Japon dans la seconde moitié du XIXe siècle.* 2 vols. Paris: Delhomme et Briguet, 1896.

Marsh, Dwight W. *The Tennesseean of Koordistan and Persia, Being Scenes and Incidents from the Life of Samuel Audley Rhea.* Philadelphia: Presbyterian Board of Publication, 1869.

Marshall, Harry Ignatius. *The Karen People of Burma: A Study in Anthropology and Ethnology.* Ohio State University Bulletin (Columbus), 26, no. 1 (April 1922).

Marshman, John Clark. *The Life and Times of Carey, Marshman, and Ward: Embracing the History of the Serampore Mission.* 2 vols. London: Longman, Brown, Green, Longmans, & Roberts, 1859.

Mar Thoma, Alexander, Metropolitan. *The Mar Thoma Church: Heritage and Mission.* Tiruvalla, India: Ashram Press, 1985.

Mar Thoma, Juhanon. *Christianity in India and the Mar Thoma Syrian Church.* Madras: Diocesan Press, 1952.

Martin, William Alexander Parsons [W.A.P]. *A Cycle of Cathay, or China North and South, with Personal Reminiscences.* Edinburgh and London: Anderson and Ferrier, 1896.

Martin, W. A. P. See Ralph Covell, *W. A. P. Martin.*

Marty, Martin, and R. Scott Appleby, eds. *Religion, Ethnicity and Self-Identity: Nations in Turmoil.* Hanover, N.H., and London: University Press of New England, 1997.

Martyn, Henry. *Journal and Letters of Henry Martyn.* Ed. and abridged S. Wilberforce. New York: M. W. Dodd, 1851.

Mason, Ellen. *Tounghoo Women.* 2nd ed. New York: Anson D. F. Randolph, 1860.

Mason, Francis. *The Karen Apostle, or, Memoir of Ko Tha-Byu, the First Karen Convert.* Rev. ed. Boston: Gould, Kendall and Lincoln, 1847.

———. "Letter," November 1857, in *Baptist Missionary Magazine* 38 (1858): 129–134.

———. "Saw Quala: The Second Karen Convert," serialized in *Baptist Missionary Magazine* 26 (1856): 1–5, 33–36, 65–70, 97–105, 127–135, 161–169, 262–266, 359–366, 385–390, 417–427, 449–456.

Massey, Ashish Kumar, and June Hedlund. "William Carey and the Making of Modern India." *ICHR* 27, no. 1 (June 1993): 7–18.

Mateer, Calvin Wilson. See D. W. Fisher, *Calvin Wilson Mateer.*

Mateer, Robert McCheyne. *Character-Building in China: The Life-Story of Julia Brown Mateer.* New York: Fleming H. Revell, 1912.

Mathew, A. *Christian Missions, Education and Nationalism: From Dominance to Compromise.* Shakti, Nagar, India: Anamika Prakashan, 1988.

Maung Shwe Wa. *Burma Baptist Chronicle.* Ed. Genevieve Sowards and Erville Sowards. Rangoon: Burma Baptist Convention, 1963.

Mayhew, Arthur. *Christianity and the Government of India: An Examination of the Christian Forces at Work in the Administration of India, 1600–1920.* London: Faber & Gwyer, 1929.

McCune, George M., and John A. Harrison, eds. *Korean-American Relations: Documents, 1883–1886.* Berkeley: University of California Press, 1951.

McCune, George M., and Horace H. Underwood. "The Korean Shrine Question: A Debate." *Presbyterian Tribune* 58 (January 20, 1938): 6–11.

McDonald, N. A. *Siam: Its Government, Manners, Customs, &c.* Philadelphia: Alfred Martin, 1871.

McDowell, W. F., et al. *Effective Workers in Needy Fields.* New York: Student Volunteer Movement for Foreign Missions, 1902.

McFarland, George Bradley, ed. *Historical Sketch of Protestant Missions in Siam, 1828–1928.* Bangkok: Bangkok Times Press, 1928.

McGavran, Donald A. *Bridges of God: A Study in the Strategy of Mission.* New York: Friendship Press, 1955.

———. *Ethnic Realities and the Church: Lessons from India.* Pasadena, Calif.: William Carey Library, 1979.

———. *Understanding Church Growth.* 3rd ed. Rev. and ed. C. Peter Wagner. Grand Rapids, Mich.: William B. Eerdmans, 1970.

McGee, Gary B. *This Gospel Shall Be Preached: History and Theology of Assemblies of God Foreign Missions.* 2 vols. Springfield, Mo.: Gospel Publishing House, 1986, 1989.

McGilvary, Daniel. *A Half Century among the Siamese and the Lao.* New York: Fleming H. Revell, 1912.

McGoldrick, James E. *Abraham Kuyper: God's Renaissance Man.* Auburn, Mass.: Evangelical Press, 2000.

McGovern, Melvin P. *Specimen Pages of Korean Moveable Type.* Los Angeles: Dawson's Book Shop, 1966.

McKenzie, F. A. *Korea's Fight for Freedom.* Seoul: Yonsei University Press, 1969; reprint of London, 1920 ed.

———. *The Tragedy of Korea.* Seoul: Yonsei University Press, 1969; reprint of London, 1908 ed.

McLeish, Alexander. *Burma: Christian Progress to the Invasion.* London and New York: World Dominion Press, 1942.

———. *A Christian Archipelago: Religion in the Philippines.* London and New York: World Dominion Press, 1941.

———. *Christian Progress in Burma.* London and New York: World Dominion Press, 1929.

———. *Sabang to Balikpapan: The Netherlands Indies.* London and New York: World Dominion Press, 1939.

McNeur, George Hunter. *China's First Preacher, Liang A-Fa 1789–1855.* Shanghai: Kwang Hsueh Publishing House, Oxford University Press, China Agency, 1934.

Meadows, Thomas Taylor. *The Chinese and Their Rebellions.* London: Smith, Elder, 1856.

Medhurst, William Henry. *China: Its State and Prospects.* Boston: Crocker & Brewster, 1838.

———. *Pamphlets Issued by the Chinese Insurgents in Nanking.* Shanghai, 1853.

Meersman, Achilles. *The Ancient Franciscan Provinces in India 1500–1835.* Bangalore: Christian Literature Society Press, 1971.

———. "Franciscan Bishops in India and Pakistan." *AFH* 72 (1979): 134–161.

———. *The Franciscans in the Indonesian Archipelago 1300–1775.* Louvain, Belgium: Nauwelaerts, 1967.

———. *The Friars Minor, or Franciscans in India 1291–1942.* Karachi: Rotti Press, 1943.

———. "Some Eighteenth-Century Statistics of the Archdiocese of Goa and of the Diocese of Cochin." *ICHR* 2, no. 1 (June 1968): 97–118.

Melo, Carlos Merces de. *The Recruitment and Formation of the Native Clergy in India (16th–19th century): An Historico-Canonical Study.* Lisbon: Agencia Geral do Ultramar, Divisão de Publicacões e Biblioteca, 1955.

Mércérian, Jean. *Histoire et institutions de l'église arménienne: Evolution nationale et doctrinale, spiritualité.* Beirut: Imprimerie Catholique, 1965.

Merwin, John Jennings. "The Oriental Missionary Society Holiness Church in Japan, 1901–1983." Diss. Fuller Theological Seminary, 1983.

Merwin, Wallace C. *Adventure in Unity: The Church of Christ in China.* Grand Rapids, Mich.: William B. Eerdmans, 1974.

Metzler, Josef. *Die Synoden in Indochina 1625–1934.* Paderborn and Munich: Ferdinand Schoningh, 1984.

Meyer, Milton W. *Southeast Asia: A Brief History.* Totowa, N.J.: Littlefield, Adams, 1971.

Michael, Franz H., with Chung-li Chan. *The Taiping Rebellion: History and Documents.* 3 vols. Seattle and London: University of Washington Press, 1966–1971.

Michalson, Carl. *Japanese Contributions to Christian Theology.* Philadelphia: Westminster Press, 1960.

Michie, Alexander. *China and Christianity.* Boston: Knight and Millet, 1900.

Middleton, Thomas C. *Religion and Education in the Philippines: A Review of the Commissions' Reports.* Philadelphia: Dolphin Press, 1903.

Miller, Stuart C. *"Benevolent Assimilation": The American Conquest of the Philippines, 1899–1903.* New Haven, Conn.: Yale University Press, 1982.

Miller, William McElwee. See Cameron Afzal, "An Interview with William McElwee Miller."

Milne, William. *A Retrospect of the First Ten Years of the Protestant Mission to China.* Malacca: Anglo-Chinese Press, 1820.

Min, Kyongbae. *Church History of Korea.* Seoul: Christian Literature Society of Korea, 1973.

Minamiki, George. *The Chinese Rites Controversy from Its Beginning to Modern Times.* Chicago: Loyola University Press, 1985.

Miner, Luella. *China's Book of Martyrs: A Record of Heroic Martyrdoms and Marvelous Deliverances of Chinese Christians during the Summer of 1900.* Philadelphia: Westminster Press, 1903.

———. ed. *Two Heroes of Cathay: An Autobiography and a Sketch.* New York: Fleming H. Revell, 1903.

Mingana, A. "The Early Spread of Christianity in India." Reprint from *BJRL* (Manchester) 10, no. 2 (July 1926).

Missionary Atlas: A Manual of the Foreign Work of the Christian and Missionary Alliance. Harrisburg, Pa.: Christian Publications, 1964.

Mission Problems in New Persia: A Report of the All-Persia Intermission Conference of 1926. For Private Circulation. Beirut: American Press, 1926.

Missionary Year-Book for 1889 of the Protestant Missionary Societies in Great Britain, the Continent of Europe, and America. London: Religious Tract Society, 1889.

Missions Advanced Research and Communication Center. *Status of Christianity Country Profile.* Monrovia, Calif.: World Vision. *Indonesia* (1973).

M'Laren, Mrs. Duncan. *The Story of Our Manchurian Mission.* Edinburgh: Offices of United Presbyterian Church, 1896.

Modak, S. *Directory of Protestant Indian Christians.* Ahmednagarh, India: Bombay Education Society Press, 1900.

Moffat, Abbot Low. *Mongkut, the King of Siam.* Ithaca, N.Y.: Cornell University Press, 1961.

Moffatt, Michael. *An Untouchable Community in South India: Structure and Consensus.* Princeton, N.J.: Princeton University Press, 1979.

Moffett, Eileen F. "Betsy Stockton, Pioneer American Missionary," in *IBMR* 19, no. 2 (April 1995): 71–76.

———. "Christian Education in Lebanon, A Moslem Frontier," MRE thesis, Princeton Theological Seminary, 1955, 22–51.

———. "Grace Wilder, Vision 1887." Unpublished manuscript, 1989.

———, ed. "Missionary Letters of Samuel A. Moffett of Korea, 1890–1939." Moffett Korea Collection, manuscript, Princeton Theological Seminary archives, Princeton, N.J.

Moffett, Samuel Austin. "Early Days in Pyengyang." *The Korea Mission Field* (Seoul) 21 (1925): 54.

———. "Evangelistic Work in Pyengyang and Vicinity." November 1, 1894 (Moffett Collection).

———. "Historical Sketch." In *Catalogue of the Presbyterian Theological Seminary.* Seoul, 1916.

———. "Lessons from Birth: 200 Years from William Carey," *Latin America Evangelist* (January–March 1992): 15–16.

———. "A New Mission Station." *ChHB* (August 1893): 107.

———. "Policy and Methods for the Evangelization of Korea." *ChRec* 37 (1906): 235–248.

———. "The Work of the Spirit in North Korea." *MRW* 18 (1893): 831–837.

———. See also Eileen Moffett, "Missionary Letters . . ."; and Lee Jong-Hyeong, "Dr. Samuel Austin Moffett: His Life and Work."

Moffett, Samuel A., and J. Edward Adams, eds. *Presentation of Difficulties which Have Arisen in the Chosen [Korea] Mission of the Presbyterian Church in the U.S.A. [The College Question].* Pyengyang, Korea: privately printed, 1918.

Moffett, Samuel Hugh. *The Christians of Korea.* New York: Friendship Press, 1962.

———. *A History of Christianity in Asia.* Vol. 1: *Beginnings to 1500.* San Francisco: HarperCollins, 1992; 2nd rev. ed., Maryknoll, N.Y.: Orbis Books, 1998.

———. "The Independence Movement and the Missionaries." *TRASK* 54 (Seoul, 1979).

———. "Thomas, First Protestant Martyr." *Korea Herald,* April 22, 1973.

———. "Thomas' Second Trip to Korea," *Korea Herald,* May 6, 1973.

———. , ed. *Samuel A. Moffett: First Letters from Korea, 1890–1891.* Seoul: Presbyterian Theological Seminary, 1975.

Monsen, Marie. *The Awakening: Revival in China, a Work of the Holy Spirit.* London: China Inland Mission, 1961.

Montgomery, Helen Barrett. *The King's Highway: A Study of the Present Conditions on the Foreign Field.* W. Medford, Mass.: Central Committee on the United Study of Foreign Missions, 1915.

Montgomery, H. H. *Charles John Corfe, Naval Chaplain, Bishop.* London: Society for the Propagation of the Gospel in Foreign Parts, 1927.

Montgomery, James H., and Donald A. McGavran. *The Discipling of a Nation.* Milpitas, Calif.: Global Church Growth Bulletin, 1980.

Monumenta Xaveriana. Madrid: Typis Agustine Avriel, 1899–1900.

Mooij, J. *Atlas der Protestantsche Kerk in Nederlandsch Oost-Indië in Dagen der Oost-Indishe Compagnie.* Weltevreden, Java: Martinus Nijhoff, 1925.

Moore, Ray A., ed. *Culture and Religion in Japanese-American Relations: Essays on Uchimura Kanzo, 1861–1930.* Ann Arbor: University of Michigan Press, 1981.

Moosa, Matti. *The Maronites in History.* Syracuse: Syracuse University Press, 1986.

Moraes, G. M. *A History of Christianity in India.* Vol. 1. *From Early Times to St. Francis Xavier: A.D. 52–1542.* Bombay: Manaktalas, 1964.

Moravian Church in America. "The Moravian Church: Its History, Faith and Ministry." Bethlehem, Pa.: Moravian Church in America, 1978, pamphlet.

Morgan, Bruce P. *Thai Buddhism and American Protestantism: In their Social, Cultural, and Historical Setting.* Chiengmai: Thailand Theological Seminary, 1966.

Morris, Ivan. *The Nobility of Failure.* New York: Noonday Press, 1975.

Morris, John Hughes. *The History of the Welsh Calvinistic Methodists' Foreign Mission, to the End of the Year 1904*. Carnarvon, Wales: C. M. Book Room, 1910.

Morrison, Elizabeth [Armstrong]. *Memoirs of the Life and Labours of Robert Morrison*. 2 vols. London: Longman, Orme, Brown, Green and Longman, 1839.

Morrison, Robert. *The Knowledge of Christ Supremely Excellent: The Means and Duty of Diffusing It among All Nations*. London: Francis Westley, 1825.

———. *A Parting Memorial: Consisting of Miscellaneous Discourses . . . , with Remarks on Missions*. London: W. Simpkins and R. Marshall, 1826.

———. "Respecting the Disposition and Policy of This Government toward Christianity" *ChRep* 6 (June 1837).

———. See also Marshall Broomhall, *Robert Morrison, A Master Builder*; Elizabeth Morrison, *Memoirs of the Life and Labours of Robert Morrison*. 2 vols.; Lindsay Ride, *Robert Morrison, The Scholar and the Man*.

Mott, John R. *The Present World Situation*. New York: Student Volunteer Movement for Foreign Missions, 1915.

———, ed. *The Continuation Committee Conferences in Asia, 1912–1913*. New York: Chairman, Continuation Committee, 1913.

Moule, Arthur Evans. "The First Arrival of the Jesuits at the Capital of China." *New China Review* 4 (1922): 480–488.

———. *Half a Century in China Recollections*. London: Hodder & Stoughton, 1911.

Muller, James Arthur. *Apostle of China: Samuel Isaac Joseph Schereschewsky, 1831–1906*. New York: Morehouse, 1937.

Müller-Krüger, Theodor. *Sedjarah Geredja di Indonesia*. Djakarta, Indonesia: Badan Penerbit Kristen, 1959.

Mullins, Mark R., and Richard Fox Young, eds. *Perspectives on Christianity in Korea and Japan: The Gospel and Culture in East Asia*. Lewiston, N.Y.: Edwin Mellen Press, 1995.

Mundadan, A. Mathias. *The Arrival of the Portuguese in India and the Thomas Christians under Mar Jacob, 1498–1552*. Bangalore: Dharmaram College, 1967.

———. *From the Beginning Up to the Middle of the Sixteenth Century*. Vol. 1 of *History of Christianity in India*. Bangalore: Church History Association of India, 1984.

———. *Indian Christians: Search for Identity and Struggle for Autonomy*. Bangalore: Dharmaram College, 1984.

———. "The Invalidity of the Synod of Diamper." *The ICHR* 1, no. 1 (June 1967): 9–28.

———. *Sixteenth-Century Traditions of St. Thomas Christians*. Bangalore: Dharmaram College, 1970.

Mungello, D. E. *Curious Land: Jesuit Accommodation and the Origins of Sinology*. Honolulu: University of Hawaii Press, 1985, 1989.

Murao, M. S., and W. H. Walton. *Japan and Christ: A Study in Religious Issues*. London: Church Missionary Society, 1928.

Murdoch, James, and Isoh Yamagata. *A History of Japan during the Century of Early Foreign Intercourse (1542–1651)*. 3 vols. Kobe, Japan: The Chronicle, 1903.

Murre-van den Berg, H. L. "From a Spoken to a Written Language: The Introduction and Development of Literary Urmia Aramaic in the Nineteenth Century." PhD diss., University of Leiden, 1964.

Nag, Kalidas, and Debhyoti Burman, eds. *The English Works of Raja Rommohun Roy.* 7 parts. Calcutta: Sadharan Brahmo Samaj, 1945–1958.

Nahm, Andrew C., ed. *Korea under Japanese Colonial Rule: Studies of the Policy and Techniques of Japanese Colonialism.* Lansing: Western Michigan University, 1973.

Natarajan, S. *A Century of Social Reform in India.* London: Asia Publishing House, 1959.

National Christian Conference. . . Shanghai, 1922. *The Chinese Church as Revealed in the National Christian Conference, Shanghai, 1922.* Shanghai: Oriental Press, 1922.

National Christian Council of China. *The Church in China Today.* Shanghai: NCCC, 1926.

———. *The National Christian Council: A Five Years' Review, 1922–1927.* Shanghai: NCCC, 1927.

National Council of the Churches of Christ U.S.A. *Documents of the Three-Self Movement: Source Materials for the Study of the Protestant Church in Communist China.* New York: NCCCUSA, 1963.

Navarrete, Domingo Fernandez. *The Travels and Controversies of Friar Domingo Navarrete, 1618–1686.* 2 vols. Ed. J. S. Cummins. Cambridge: Cambridge University Press, 1962.

NCE. New York: McGraw-Hill, 1967.

Nee, Watchman (Nee Shu-zu). *The Church and the Work.* 3 vols. New York: Christian Fellowship Publishers, 1982.

Needham, Joseph. *Chinese Astronomy and the Jesuit Mission: An Encounter of Cultures.* London: The China Society, 1958.

Neely, Alan. "Saints Who Sometimes Were." *MIS* 27 (October 1999): 447–455.

Neesima, Joseph Hardy. See Arthur Sherburne Hardy, *Life and Letters of Joseph Hardy Neesima.*

Neez, Msgr. *Documents sur le Clergé Tonkinois aus XVII et XVIII Siècles.* Paris: P. Tequi, 1925.

Neill, Stephen. *A History of Christianity in India.* Vol. 1: *The Beginnings to A.D. 1707.* Vol. 2: *1707–1858.* Cambridge: Cambridge University Press, 1984, 1985.

———. *History of Christian Missions.* New York: Penguin, 1964.

Nelson, M. Frederick. *Korea and the Old Orders in East Asia.* Baton Rouge: Louisiana State University Press, 1946.

Nelson, Marlin. "A Critique of Korean Church Growth, 1975–1989," *Acts Theological Journal* (Seoul) 4 (1991).

Nelson, Marlin, and Bong-Rin Ro. *Korean Church Growth Explosion.* Seoul: Asia Theological Association, 1983.

Nersoyan, Hagop. *A History of the Armenian Church, with Thirty-Five Stories.* New York: Armenian Church of North America, 1963.

Nevius, Helen S. Coan. *The Life of John Livingston Nevius, for Forty Years a Missionary in China.* New York: Fleming H. Revell, 1895.

Nevius, John L. *China and the Chinese: A General Description of the Country, Its Civilization, Religious and Social Institutions.* New York: Harper & Bros., 1872.

———. *Methods of Missionary Work.* 2nd ed. New York: Foreign Mission Library, 1895.

Newbigin, Lesslie. *Foolishness to the Greeks: Can the West Be Converted?* Grand Rapids, Mich.: William B. Eerdmans, 1966.

Newcomb, Harvey. *A Cyclopedia of Missions*. New York: Charles Scribner, 1858.

Newman, Elizabeth Mary. See C. E. Tyndale-Biscoe, *Elizabeth Mary Newman, 1855–1932: The Florence Nightingale of Kashmir*.

Newton, Ken. *Glimpses of India Church History*. Bombay: Gospel Literature Service, 1975.

Ng, Lee-ming. "Christianity and Social Change: The Case in China, 1920–1950." PhD diss., Princeton Theological Seminary, 1971.

Nicholls, Bruce John. *Contextualization: A Theology of Gospel and Culture*. Downers Grove, Ill., and Exeter, England: InterVarsity Press/Paternoster Press, 1979.

———. "Resurgent Hinduism and the Christian Faith: The Challenge of Religious Syncretism and the Biblical Basis for a Christian Apologetic with Special Reference to the Old Testament." Th.M. thesis, Princeton Theological Seminary, 1961.

Nicolson, John. "The Reverend Charles Gützlaff, The Opium War and General Gough." *MIS* 13 (July 1985): 352–361.

Nida, Eugene, ed. *The Book of a Thousand Tongues*. Rev. ed. New York: United Bible Societies, 1972.

Nielsen, Fredrik. *The History of the Papacy in the XIXth Century*. 2 vols. New York: E. P. Dutton, 1906.

Niijima, Jo. See Arthur Sherburne Hardy, *Life and Letters of Joseph Hardy Neesima*.

Nobili, Roberto de. *Preaching Wisdom to the Wise: Three Treatises by Roberto de Nobili in Dialogue with the Learned Hindus of South India*. Intro., annotated, and trans. Anand Amaladass and Francis X. Clooney. St. Louis: Institute of Jesuit Sources, 2000.

Noble, Mrs. M. W. *Victorious Lives of Early Christians in Korea*. Seoul: Christian Literature Society of Korea, 1933.

Norbeck, Mark D. "The Legacy of Charles Henry Brent." *IBMR* 20, no. 4 (1996): 163–168.

Northcott, Henry. *Glorious Company: One Hundred and Fifty Years Life and Work of the London Missionary Society 1795–1945*. London: Livingstone Press, 1945.

Notrott, L. *Die Gossnersche Mission unter den Kohls*. 2 vols. Halle: Richard Mühlmann, 1874, 1888.

Oddie, G. A. "Indian Christians and the National Congress, 1885–1910." *ICHR* 2, no. 1 (June 1968): 45–54.

Ogilvie, J. N. *The Apostles of India*. Baird Lectures. London: Hodder & Stoughton, 1915.

Oh, M. W. "The Two Visits of the Rev. R. J. Thomas to Korea." *TRASK* 22 (1933).

Oldham, William F. *India, Malaysia and the Philippines: A Practical Study*. New York: Eaton & Mains, 1914.

———. "Isabella Thoburn." In R. P. McDowell et al. *Effective Workers in Needy Fields*. New York: Student Volunteer Movement for Foreign Mission, 1902.

———. *Thoburn — Called of God*. New York: Methodist Book Concern, 1918.

Oliver, Robert T. *Syngman Rhee: The Man Behind the Myth*. New York: Dodd Mead, 1954.

———. *Verdict in Korea*. State College, Pa.: Bald Eagle Press, 1952.

One World A-Building. New York: Board of Foreign Missions, Presbyterian Church USA, 1946.

Ordres religieux, Les. See *Les ordres religieux*.

Oriente Cattolico: Cenni storia e statistiche. Città del Vaticano: Congregatio pro ecclesia Orientali, 1962.

Ormanian, Maghak'ia. *The Church of Armenia: Her History, Doctrine, Rule, Discipline, Literature, and Existing Condition.* 2nd rev. English ed. London: A. R. Mowbray, 1955.

Orr, J. Edwin. *Evangelical Awakenings in Eastern Asia.* Minneapolis: Bethany Fellowship Inc., 1975.

——. *The Fundamentals: A Testimony to the Truth.* 15 vols. Chicago: Testimony, 1910–.

——. "Why Campus Revivals Spark Missionary Advance." Compiled from his writings, in *The Christian Herald* (October 1982): 20–24, 73–75.

Osaka Conference of Protestant Missionaries of Japan, 1883. Yokohama, Japan: Meiklejohn, 1883.

Osias, Camilo. *José Rizal: Life and Times.* Manila, 1949.

Osias, Camilo, and Avelina Lorenzana. *Evangelical Christianity in the Philippines.* Dayton, Ohio: United Brethren Publishing House, 1931.

Otto, Joseph A. *Grundung dur Neuen Jesuitenmission durch General Pater Johann Philip Roothaan.* Freiburg im Breisgau: Herder, 1939.

Our Church's Work in India: The Story of the Missions of the United Free Church of Scotland in Bengal, Santalia, Bombay, Rajputana, and Madras. Edinburgh: Oliphant, Anderson & Ferrier, n.d. Various authors.

Oussoren, A. H. *William Carey, Especially His Missionary Principles.* Leiden: Sijthoff's Uitgeversmaatschappij, 1945.

Outerbridge, Leonard. *The Lost Churches of China.* Philadelphia: Westminster Press, 1952.

Pachuau, Lalsangkima. "Robert Arthington, Jr. and the Arthington Aborigines Mission." *ICHR* 28, no. 2 (December 1994): 105–123.

Padberg, John. *Jesuit Spirituality.* Chicago: Loyola University Press, 1990.

Padwick, Constance. *Henry Martyn, Confessor of the Faith.* London: Student Christian Movement, and New York: George H. Doran, 1922.

Pagés, Léon. *Histoire de la religion chrétienne au Japon depuis 1598 jusqu'a 1651.* Paris: Charles Douniol, 1869.

Paik, George (Nak-chun Paek). *The History of Protestant Missions in Korea, 1832–1910.* Seoul: Yonsei University, 1987.

Pak Ung-Kyu. "From Fear to Hope: The Shaping of Premillennialism in Korea." PhD diss., Westminster Seminary, Philadelphia, 1998.

Palais, James B. *Confucian Statecraft and Korean Institutions: Yu Hyongwon and the Late Choson Dynasty.* Seattle and London: University of Washington Press, 1996.

Panikkar, K. M. *Asia and Western Dominance: A Survey of the Vasco da Gama Epoch of Asian History, 1498–1945.* London: George Allen & Unwin, 1953.

Panikkar, Raymond. *The Unknown Christ of Hinduism.* London: Darton, Longman and Todd, 1964.

Papajian, Sarkis. *A Brief History of Armenia.* Fresno, Calif., private, 1974.

Parker, F. Calvin. *Jonathan Goble of Japan: Marine, Missionary, Maverick.* Lanham, Md.: University Press of America, 1990.

Parker, John. *Windows into China: The Jesuits and Their Books, 1580–1730.* Boston: Public Library of the City of Boston, 1978.

Parker, Michael. *The Kingdom of Character: The Student Volunteer Movement for Foreign Missions (1886–1926)*. Lanham, Md.: American Society of Missiology and University Press of America, 1998.

Pas, Julian F., ed. *The Turning of the Tide: Religion in China Today*. Hong Kong: Oxford University Press, 1989.

Pascoe, C. F. *Two Hundred Years of the S.P.G.: An Historical Account of the Society for the Propagation of the Gospel in Foreign Parts 1701–1900 (Based on a Digest of the Society's Records)*. London: SPG, 1901.

Paton, A. A. *The Modern Syrians 1841–43, by An Oriental Student*. London: Longmans, Brown, Green and Longmans, 1844.

Paton, D. M. *Christian Missions and the Judgment of God*. London: SCM Press, 1953.

Paton, William. *Alexander Duff, Pioneer of Missionary Education*. New York: H. Doran; London: Student Christian Movement, 1923.

Patterson, George N. *Christianity in Communist China*. Waco, Tex.: Word Books, 1969.

Pattiasina, Joseph Marcus. "An Observation of the Historical Background of the Moluccan Protestant Church and the Implications for Mission and Congregational Structures." DMiss diss., Fuller Theological Seminary, 1987.

Patton, Alfred S. *The Hero Missionary, or, A History of the Labors of the Rev. Eugenio Kincaid*. New York: H. Dayton, 1858.

Paulos, Mar Gregorios. *The Indian Orthodox Church: An Overview*. Delhi and Kottayam, India: Sophia Press, 1982.

Payne, C. H. *Akbar and the Jesuits: An Account of the Jesuit Missions to the Court of Akbar by Father Pierre du Jarric, SJ*. London: Routledge, 1926.

Pedersen, Paul B. *Batak Blood and Protestant Soul: The Development of National Batak Churches in North Sumatra*. Grand Rapids, Mich.: William B. Eerdmans, 1970.

Peiris, Edmund, and Achilles Meersman. *Early Christianity in Ceylon*. See Trinidade. *Conquista do Oriente*.

Pennell, Alice Maud. *Pennell of the Afghan Border, the Life of Theodore Leighton Pennell*. London: Seeley, Service, 1901.

Penny, Frank. *The Church in Madras, Being the History of the Ecclesiastical and Missionary Action of the East India Company in the Presidency of Madras in the Seventeenth and Eighteenth Centuries*. 3 vols. London: Smith, Elder, 1904–1922.

Perera, Simon G. *Catholic Negombo: A Brief Sketch of the Catholic Church in Negombo under the Portuguese and the Dutch*. Colombo: Catholic Union of Ceylon, 1924.

———. *Life of the Venerable Joseph Vaz*. Galle, Ceylon, 1953.

Perera, Simon G., ed. *The Oratorian Mission in Ceylon: Historical Documents relating to the Life and Labours of the Venerable Father Joseph Vaz, His Companions and Successors*. Colombo: Caxton Printing Works, 1936.

Perkins, Justin. *Historical Sketch of the Mission to the Nestorians; and of the Assyrian Mission by Thomas Laurie*. New York: John A. Gray, 1862.

———. *Missionary Life in Persia*. Boston: American Tract Society, 1861.

———. *Nestorian Biography: Being Sketches of Pious Nestorians*. Boston: Massachusetts Sabbath School Society, 1857.

Permalil, H. C., and E. R. Hambye. *Christianity in India: A History in Ecumenical Perspective*. Alleppey, India: Prakasam Publications, 1972.

Perniola, V. *The Catholic Church in Sri Lanka. The Dutch Period: Original Documents translated into English*. 3 vols. Vol. 1: 1658–1711. Vol. 2: 1712–1746. Vol. 3: 1747–1795. Dehiwala, Sri Lanka: Tisara Prakasakayo Ltd., 1983–1985.

Peter, W. L. A., Don, ed. *Franciscans and Sri Lanka*. Colombo: Evangel Press, 1983.

Pfister, Louis. *Notices Biographiques et Bibliographiques sur les Jésuites de l'Ancienne Mission de Chine*. 2 vols. Chang-hai, China: Mission Catholique de T'ou-se-we, 1932–1934.

Phadnis, Urmila. *Religion and Politics in Sri Lanka*. Columbia, Mo.: South Asia Books, 1976.

Phan, Peter C. *Mission and Catechesis: Alexandre de Rhodes and Inculturation in Seventeenth-Century Vietnam*. Maryknoll, N.Y.: Orbis Books, 1998.

Phayre, Arthur P. *History of Burma*. 1883; reprint, London: Susil Gupta, 1967.

Phelan, John Leddy. *The Hispanization of the Philippines: Spanish Aims and Filipino Responses, 1565–1700*. Madison: University of Wisconsin Press, 1967.

Philip, P. O. *Report on a Survey of Indigenous Christian Efforts in India, Burma, and Ceylon*. Poona, India: Scottish Mission Industries Co., 1928.

Philip, Robert. *The Life and Opinions of the Rev. William Milne, D.D., Missionary to China, Illustrated by Biographical Annals of Asiatic Missions from Primitive to Protestant Times*. Philadelphia: Herman Hooker, 1840.

Philippi, Donald L. *Kojiki: A Translation*. Princeton, N.J.: Princeton University Press, 1968.

Philips, C. H., ed. *Historians of India, Pakistan and Ceylon*, 3rd ed. Oxford: Oxford University Press, 1967.

Phillips, Godfrey. *The Untouchables' Quest: The Depressed Classes of India and Christianity*. New York: Friendship Press, 1936.

Phillips, James M. *From the Rising of the Sun: Christians and Society in Contemporary Japan*. Maryknoll, N.Y.: Orbis Books, 1981.

Pickett, Jarrell Waskom. *Christian Mass Movements in India*. New York and Cincinnati: Abingdon Press, 1933.

———. *Christ's Way to India's Heart: Present-Day Mass Movements to Christianity*. Rev. ed. New York: Friendship Press, 1938.

Pickett, J. W., A. L. Warnshuis, G. H. Singh, and D. A. McGavran. *Church Growth and Group Conversion*. Lucknow, India: Lucknow Publishing House, 1956.

Pieris, P. E. *Ceylon: The Portuguese Era. Being a History of the Island for the Period 1505–1658*. 2 vols. Colombo: Colombo Apothecaries Co., 1913; 2nd ed. vol. 2, 1983.

———. *Ceylon and the Hollanders, 1658 to 1796*. Tellippalai, Ceylon: American Ceylon Mission Press, 1918.

———, ed. *The Dutch Power in Ceylon (1602–1670)*. London: Curzon Press, 1929; new printing, 1973.

Pieris, P. E., and M. A. H. Fitzler. *Ceylon and Portugal*, Part 1. *Kings and Christians 1539–1552, from the Original Documents at Lisbon*. Leipzig: Verlag der Asia Major, 1927.

Pierson, Arthur T. *George Muller of Bristol*. New York: Baker & Taylor, 1899.

———. "How Will the Church Meet the Crisis?" *GAL* 12, no. 12 (December 1891): 539–541.

———. *The Modern Mission Century Viewed as a Cycle of Divine Viewing: A Review of the Missions of the Nineteenth Century with Reference to the Superintending Providence of God*. New York: Baker & Taylor, 1901.

Pigafetta, Antonio. *Magellan's Voyage around the World*. English trans. by James A. Robertson. In Emma Helen and James Alexander Robertson, eds. *The Philippine Islands 1493–1803: Explorations by Early Navigators, Descriptions of the*

Islands and Their Peoples, Their History and Records of the Catholic Missions. 55 vols. Translated and annotated. Cleveland: Arthur H. Clark, 1903–1907.

Pitcher, P. W. "Education a Factor in Evangelization." *ChRec* 23 (1892): 164–166.

Pluvier, Jan M. *A Handbook and Chart of Southeast Asian History.* Kuala Lumpur: Oxford University Press, 1967.

Podipara, Placid. *The Malabar Christians.* Alleppey, India: Prakasam Publications, 1972.

Poitras, Edward W. "The Legacy of Henry G. Appenzeller." *IBMR* (October 1994), 177–180.

Pollock, John Charles. *Hudson Taylor and Maria: Pioneers in China.* New York: McGraw-Hill, 1962.

———. *Shadows Fall Apart: The Story of the Zenana Bible and Medical Mission.* London: Hodder and Stoughton, 1958.

Popley, H. A. *K. T. Paul: Christian Leader.* 2nd ed. Madras: Christian Literature Society, 1987.

Porter, David. *Mother Teresa: The Early Years.* Grand Rapids, Mich.: William B. Eerdmans, 1986.

Pothacamury, Thomas. *The Church in Independent India.* World Horizon Reports, No. 22. Maryknoll, N.Y.: Maryknoll Publications, 1956.

Pothan, S. G. *The Syrian Christians of Kerala.* New York: Asia Publishing House, 1963.

Potts, E. Daniel. *British Baptist Missionaries in India 1793–1837: The History of Serampore and Its Missions.* Cambridge: Cambridge University Press, 1967.

Prakasar, S. Gnana. *A History of the Catholic Church in Ceylon.* Vol. 1: *Period of Beginnings, 1505–1602.* Colombo: Catholic Union of Ceylon, 1924.

Pratt, Julius W. *Expansionists of 1895: Hawaii and the Spanish Islands.* Baltimore: Johns Hopkins University Press, 1937.

Prayer Calendar of Christian Missions in Korea, and General Directory. Ed. Allen D. Clark et al. Seoul: Christian Literature Society, 1957–1987.

Presbyterian Church in the U.S.A. Board of Foreign Missions. *Annual Reports.* New York, 1838–.

Presbyterian Church in Korea. *1907 Minutes of the Fifteenth Annual Meeting of the Council of Presbyterian Mission in Korea and the First Annual Meeting of the Presbyterian Church in Korea.* Pyengyang, Korea, 1907.

"The Present Movement for Korean Independence in its Relation to the Missionary Work of the Presbyterian Churches: A Private Report Prepared for the Board of Foreign Missions by the Executive Committee of the Chosen Mission at Seoul, April 22nd–24th, 1919." Manuscript, photocopy, Moffett collection, Princeton.

Price, Eva Jane. *China Journal 1889–1900: An American Missionary Family during the Boxer Rebellion, with the Letters and Diaries of Eva Jane Price and Her Family,* introductory notes and annotations by R. H. Felsing. New York: Charles Scribner's Sons, 1989.

Priolkar, A. K. *The Goa Inquisition: Being a Quartercentenary Commemoration Study of the Inquisition in India.* Bombay: Bombay University Press, 1961.

Prior, John Mansford. *Church and Marriage in an Indonesian Village.* Vol. 55 in *Studies in the Intercultural History of Christianity.* Frankfurt am Main: Peter Lang, 1988.

Proceedings of the General Conference of Protestant Missionaries in Japan, Tokyo, 1900. Tokyo: Methodist Publishing House, 1901.

Proceedings of the General Conference of Protestant Missionaries of Japan, Osaka, 1883. Yokohama: R. Meiklejohn, 1883.

Proceedings of the South India Missionary Conference, Ootacamund, 1858. Madras: SPCK, 1858.

Pro Mundi Vita. *Thailand in Transition: The Church in a Buddhist Country.* Brussels: Pro Mundi Vita, Centrum Informations, [1973].

"Publications concerning Indian Missions." *ERev* 12 (April-June 1808): 151–181.

Puchinger, G. *Abraham Kuyper: His Early Journey of Faith.* Amsterdam: VU University Press, 1998.

Pulikkunnel, Joseph. "The Kerala Church Structure during the Pre-Diamper Period and the Changes That Have Taken Place Since Then." *Indian Journal of Theology* (Calcutta), 34, no. 1–3 (January–September 1985): 89–99.

Purcell, Victor. *The Boxer Uprising: A Background Study.* Cambridge: Cambridge University Press, 1963.

Puthenpurakal, J. *Mission in the Documents of the Catholic Church.* Shillong, India: Vendrame Institute Publications, Sacred Heart Theological College, 1997.

Quarto Centennial Papers, read before the Korea Mission of the Presbyterian Church in the U.S.A. at the annual meeting in Pyengyang, August 27, 1909.

Queyroz, Fernão de. *The Temporal and Spiritual Conquest of Ceylon.* 3 vols. Trans. S. G. Perera [from the 1688 original]. Colombo: A. C. Richards, Acting Government Printer, 1930.

Rafael, Vincente L. *Contracting Colonialism: Translation and Christian Conversion in Tagalog Society under Early Spanish Rule.* Ithaca, N.Y.: Cornell University Press, 1988.

Raj, Sunder. *The Confusion Called Conversion.* New Delhi: TRACI Publications, 1986.

Rajamanickam, S. *The First Oriental Scholar.* Tirunelveli, 1972.

———. "The Old Madurai Mission, A Chronological Table." *ICHR* 21 (1987): 130–133.

———. "Roberto de Nobili and Adaptation." *ICHR* 1 (1967): 83–91.

Rajapakse, Reginald L. "Christian Missions, Theosophy and Trade: A History of American Relations with Ceylon 1815–1915." PhD diss., University of Pennsylvania, 1973.

Ramabai, Pandita. *The Life and Letters of Pandita Ramabai.* Compiled by Sister Geraldine, ed. A. B. Shaw. Bombay: Maharashtra State Board for Literature and Culture, 1977.

———. See also S. M. Adhaw, *Pandita Ramabai.*

Ransom, C. W. *The Christian Minister in India: His Vocation and Training.* London: Lutterworth Press, 1945.

Rauws, Joh., H. Kraemer, F. J. F. van Hasselt, and N. A. C. Slotemaker de Bruïne. *The Netherlands Indies.* London and New York: World Dominion Press, 1935.

Records of the General Conference of the Protestant Missionaries of China, Shanghai, 1877. Shanghai: Presbyterian Mission Press, 1878.

Reed, Mary. See J. Jackson, *Mary Reed, Missionary to Lepers.*

Rees, D. Vaughan. *The "Jesus Family" in Communist China.* London: Paternoster Press, 1959.

Rees, Ronald. *China Faces the Storm: The Christian Church in China Today.* London: Edinburgh House, 1937.

Reichelt, G. Th. *Die Himalaya-Mission der Brüdergemeine.* Gutersloh: C. Bertelsmann, 1896.

Reischauer, Edwin O. *The United States and Japan.* 3rd rev. ed. Cambridge, Mass.:
Harvard University Press, 1965.

Religions and Communities of India. Ed. P. N. Chopra. New Delhi: Vision Books,
1982.

Retana, Wenceslao E. *Archivo del Bibliofilo Filipino.* 5 vols. Madrid, 1895–1905.

Rhodes, Alexandre de. *Voyages et missions du Père Alexandre de Rhodes de la Com-
pagnie de Jesus en la Chine et autres royaumes de l'Orient.* 1653. Ed. S. Cramoisy.
Reprint Paris: Julien, Lanier, 1854. In English. *Rhodes of Vietnam.* Trans.
S. Hertz. Westminster, Md.: Newman Press, 1966.

Rhodes, H. A., ed. *History of the Korea Mission, Presbyterian Church U.S.A., 1884–
1934.* Vol. 1. Seoul: Chosen Mission Presbyterian Church U.S.A., 1934.

———. and Archibald Campbell, Vol. 2. New York: Commission on Ecumenics
and Mission, Presbyterian Church, USA, 1965.

Ricci, Matteo. *China in the Sixteenth Century: The Journals of Matthew Ricci: 1583–
1610.* Trans. Louis J. Gallagher of Nicholas Trigault's Latin translation, *De
Christiana Expeditione apud Sinas,* 1615, of Ricci's diary and other writings.
New York: Random House, 1953.

———. *Fonti Ricciane: Documenti originali concernenti Matteo Ricci e la storia delle
prime relazioni tra l'Europa e la Cina (1579–1615).* 3 vols. Ed. Pasquale M. D'Elia.
Rome: Libreria dello Stato, 1942–1949; referred to as D'Elia, *Fonti Ricianne.*

———. *Opere storiche del P. Matteo Ricci.* Vol. 2: *Le Lettere dalla Cina, 1580–1610.*
Macerata, Italy: F. Giorgetti, 1911–1913.

———. *The True Meaning of the Lord of Heaven (T'ien-chu Shih-i).* Trans., with Chinese text, by D. Lancashire and P. Hu Kuo-chen. St. Louis: Institute of Jesuit
Sources, 1985.

Richard, H. L. *Christ-Bhakti: Narayan Vaman Tilak and Christian Work among Hindus.*
Delhi: ISPCK, 1991.

Richard, Timothy. *Forty-Five Years in China, Reminiscences.* New York: Frederick A.
Stokes, 1916.

———. *The New Testament of Higher Buddhism.* Edinburgh: T & T Clark, 1910.

———. See also E. W. Price Evans, *Timothy Richard;* W. E. Soothill, *Timothy Richard
of China.*

Richter, Julius. *Die Evangelische Mission in Niederlandisch-Indien, Fern- und Sudost-
Asien, Australien, Amerika.* 2 vols. in 1. Gutersloh: C. Bertelsmann, 1931, 1932.

———. *Geschichte der Berliner Missions-gesellschaft.* Berlin: Berliner ev. Missions-
gesellschaft, 1924.

———. *A History of Missions in India.* Trans. S. H. Moore. New York: Fleming H.
Revell, 1908.

———. *A History of Protestant Missions in the Near East.* New York: Fleming H.
Revell, 1910.

Ride, Lindsay. *Robert Morrison: The Scholar and the Man.* Hong Kong: Hong Kong
University Press, 1957.

Riemersma, Jelle C. *Religious Factors in Early Dutch Capitalism 1550–1660.* The
Hague/Paris: Mouton, 1967.

Rienstra, M. Howard, ed. and trans. *Jesuit Letters from China 1583–1584.* Minneapolis: University of Minnesota Press, 1986.

Rijckevorsel, E. Westerwoudt van. *Felix Westerwoudt: Missioner in Borneo*. Maryknoll, N.Y.: Catholic Foreign Mission Society of America, 1924.

Ritchie, Jefferson. "Historiography of the Korean Revival of 1907." Unpublished manuscript, 1988.

Ritter, H. *A History of Protestant Missions in Japan*. Trans. G. E. Albrecht. Rev. D. C. Greene. Tokyo: Methodist Publishing House, 1898.

Ro, Bong-Rin, and Marlin Nelson. *Korean Church Growth Explosion*. Revised and enlarged ed. Seoul: Word of Life Press, 1995.

Robbins, Joseph Chandler. *Boardman of Burma*. Philadelphia: The Judson Press, 1940.

Robert, Dana L. *American Women in Mission: A Social History of Their Thought and Practice*. Macon, Ga.: Mercer University Press, 1996.

———. *Evangelism at the Heart of Mission*. New York: General Board of Global Ministries, United Methodist Church, 1997.

Roberts, J. M. *The Triumph of the West*. Boston: Little, Brown, 1985.

Roberts, Walter N. *The Filipino Church: The Story of the Development of an Indigenous Evangelical Church in the Philippine Islands as Revealed in the Work of the Church of the United Brethren in Christ*. Dayton, Ohio: United Brethren in Christ, 1936.

Robinson, Charles Henry. *History of Christian Missions*. New York: Charles Scribner's Sons, 1915.

Rodgers, James B. *Forty Years in the Philippines*. New York: Board of Foreign Missions of the Presbyterian Church in the U.S.A., 1940.

———. *Twenty Years of Presbyterian Work in the Philippines*. Manila: Christian Mission Press, 1919.

Rodgers, R. E. L. *The Incarnation of the Antithesis: An Introduction to the Educational Thought and Practice of Abraham Kuyper*. Edinburgh: Pentland Press, 1992.

Rodriguez, Isacio R. *Gregorio Aglipay y los Orígenes de la Iglesia Filipina Independiente, 1898–1917*. Madrid: Departamento de Misionología Española, 1960.

Rogier, J. L., R. Aubert, and M. D. Knowles. *Geschichte der Kirch*. 5 vols. Einsiedel and Zurich: Benziger Verlag, 1966.

Ronan, Charles E., and Bonnie B. C. Oh. *East Meets West: The Jesuits in China, 1582–1773*. Chicago: Loyola University Press, 1988.

Ronning, N. N. *Lars O. Skrefsrud, an Apostle to the Santals*. Minneapolis: Santal Mission in America, 1940.

Ross, Andrew C. "Alessandro Valignano." *MIS* 27, no. 4 (October 1999): 503–513.

———. *A Vision Betrayed: The Jesuits in Japan and China, 1542–1742*. Maryknoll, N.Y.: Orbis Books, 1994.

Ross, John. "The Christian Dawn in Korea." *MRW* NS, 3 (1890): 243, 247.

———. *Mission Methods in Manchuria*. New York: Fleming H. Revell, 1903.

———. *Old Wang: The First Chinese Evangelist in Manchuria*. London: Religious Tract Society, 1889.

———. "The Riots and Their Lessons." *ChRec* 23 (August 1892): 380–386.

———. See also Choi Sung-il, *John Ross*; James Grayson, *John Ross*.

Rosso, Antonio Sisto. *Apostolic Legations to China of the Eighteenth Century*. South Pasadena, Calif.: P. and Ione Perkins, 1948.

Rowbotham, Arnold J. *Missionary and Mandarin: The Jesuits at the Court of China*. Berkeley: University of California Press, 1942.

Roxborogh, John. *A Short Introduction to Malaysian Church History.* 2nd rev. ed. Kuala Lumpur: Malaysian Church History Study Group, 1989.

Rubinstein, Murray. *The Origins of the Anglo-American Missionary Movement in China 1807–1840.* Lanham, Md.: Scarecrow Press, 1996.

Ruiz de Medina, Juan. *The Catholic Church in Korea: Its Origins 1566–1784.* Trans. John Bridges. Rome: Istituto Storica, 1991.

Rutt, Richard. *A Biography of James Scarth Gale.* Seoul: Royal Asiatic Society, Korea Branch, 1972.

Ryang, J. S., ed. *Southern Methodism in Korea: Thirtieth Anniversary.* Seoul: Methodist Episcopal Church South, 1929.

Ryang, Key S. "Horace Grant Underwood (1851–1916) in Korea." *Journal of Modern Korean Studies* 3 (December 1987): 71–94.

Ryu, Tong-sik. *Hankuk chongkyo wa Kidokkyo (The Christian Faith and the Religions of Korea).* Seoul: Christian Literature Society, 1965. Cf. the translation by David Ross, "Gospel and Religion in Korea." Moffett collection, typescript manuscript, n.d.

Sa, Fidelis de. *Crisis in Chota Nagpur: The Judicial Conflict between Jesuit Missionaries and British Government Officials 1889–1890.* Bangalore: Redemptorist Publications, 1975.

Saeki, P. Yoshiro. *The Nestorian Documents and Relics in China.* 2nd ed. Tokyo: Maruzen, 1951.

Sahu, Dhirendra Kumar. *The Church of North India: A Historical and Systematic Theological Inquiry into an Ecumenical Ecclesiology.* Peter Lang: Frankfurt am Main, 1994.

Samartha, Stanley J. *Courage for Dialogue: Ecumenical Issues in Inter-religious Relationships.* Geneva: World Council of Churches, 1981.

———. *One Christ, Many Religions: Towards a Revised Christology.* Maryknoll, N.Y.: Orbis Books, 1994.

Sanders, Albert J. "An Appraisal of the *Iglesia ni Cristo.*" In *Studies in Philippine Church History,* ed. Gerald H. Anderson. Ithaca, N.Y.: Cornell University Press, 1969.

Sangma, Milton S. "Advent of the Pioneer Christian Missions in North-East India." *ICHR* 28, no. 1 (June 1994): 5–14.

Sangster, Margaret. *A Manual of Missions of the Reformed (Dutch) Church in America.* New York: Board of Publication, Reformed Church in America, 1877.

Sanjian, Avedis K. *The Armenian Communities in Syria under Ottoman Dominion.* Cambridge, Mass.: Harvard University Press, 1965.

Sanneh, Lamin O. *Translating the Message: The Missionary Impact on Culture.* Maryknoll, N.Y.: Orbis Books, 1989.

Sansom, George Bailey. *A History of Japan.* 3 vols. Stanford, Calif.: Stanford University Press, 1958–1963.

———. *Japan: A Short Cultural History.* Rev. ed. D. Appleton-Century Co., 1931, 1943.

———. *The Western World and Japan: A Study in the Interaction of European and Asiatic Cultures.* New York: Alfred A. Knopf, 1950.

Santiago, Luciano P. R. *The Hidden Light: The First Filipino Priests.* Quezon City, Philippines: New Day Publishers, 1987. Revised and enlarged from articles of same title in *PS* (Manila), 31 (1983): 129–188, and *Philippine Quarterly of Culture and Society* 12 (1984): 1–24, 128–181.

Sapsezian, Aharon. *Armenian Christianity: The Faith of a Nation.* Paramus, N.J.: Armenian Missionary Association of America, 1997.

Sarkissian, K. *A Brief Introduction to Armenian Christian Literature.* London: Faith Press, 1959.

Sauer, Charles A. *When the Wolves Came.* Seoul: Yonsei University, 1973.

———, ed. *Within the Gate: Addresses Delivered at the Fiftieth Anniversary of Korean Methodism.* Seoul: Korea Methodist News Service, 1934.

Saunders, Graham. *Bishops and Brookes: The Anglican Mission and the Brooke Raj in Sarawak 1848–1941.* Singapore: Oxford University Press, 1992.

Saverimuttu, P. Nicholas Hai Maria. *The Life and Times of Orazio Bettacchini, the First Vicar Apostolic of Jaffna, Ceylon (1810–1887).* Rome: Urbaniana University Press, 1980.

Schall, Adam [John Adam Schall von Bell]. *Historica Relatio eorum quae contigerunt occasione concertationis Calendarii Sinici facta a R. P. Joanne Adamo Schall.* Latin text ed. Henri Bernard, with French translation by P. Bornet (*Lettres et Mémoires d'Adam Schall*). Tientsin: Hautes Études, 1942.

Schereschewsky, Samuel I. J. See J. A. Muller, *Apostle of China.*

Schlatter, Wilhelm. *Geschichte der Basler Mission 1815–1915.* 3 vols. Basel: Basler Missionsbuchhandlung, 1916.

Schlyter, Herman. *Der China-Missionar Karl Gützlaff und Seine Heimatbasis.* Lund: C. W. K. Gleerup, 1976.

———. *Geschichte der Missionen in China von den altesten Zeiten bis auf Gützlaff, herausgegeben von dem Pommerschen Hauptverein für Evangel: Missionen in China.* Stettin, 1850.

———. *Karl Gützlaff als Missionar in China.* Lund: C. W. K. Gleerup, 1946.

Schmidlin, Joseph. *Catholic Mission History.* Techny, Ill.: Mission Press, 1933.

———. *Catholic Mission Theory.* Trans. Matthias Braun. Techny, Ill.: Mission Press, 1931.

———. "Die Gründung der Propagandakongregation (1622)." *ZMR* 12: (1922): 1–14.

———. "Gregor XVI als Missionspapst (1831–1846)." *ZMR* 21 (1931): 209–228.

———. *Katholische Missionsgeschichte.* Steyl. 1924. English translation, *Catholic Mission History*, M. Braun. Techny Ill.: Mission Press, 1933, updates and amplifies the original German edition.

Schneider, H. G. *Leh in Kaschmir. Eine Missionstat der Brüdergemeine.* Herrnhut: Missionsbuchhandlung, n.d.

———. *Ein Missionsfeld aus dem Westlichen Himalaya.* Gnadau, Germany: Unitats-Buchhandlung, 1880.

———. *Working and Waiting for Tibet: A Sketch of the Moravian Mission in the Western Himalayas.* London: Morgan & Scott, 1891.

Schreurs, Peter. *Caraga Antigua 1521–1910: The Hispanization and Christianization of Agusan, Surigao, and East Davao.* Cebu City, Philippines: University of San Carlos, 1989.

Schulze, Adolf, and S. H. Gapp. *World-Wide Moravian Missions.* Bethlehem, Pa.: Comenius Press, 1926.

Schumacher, John N., and H. De la Costa. *Church and State in the Philippine Experience: The Nineteenth and Twentieth Centuries.* Manila: Loyola Papers no. 3, 1976.

———. *Father Jose Burgos: Priest and Nationalist.* Quezon City, Philippines: Ateneo de Manila University Press, 1972.

———. *Readings in Philippine Church History.* 2nd ed. Quezon City, Philippines: Loyola School of Theology, Ateneo de Manila University, 1987.

———. *Revolutionary Clergy: The Filipino Clergy and the Nationalist Movement, 1850–1903.* Quezon City, Philippines: Ateneo de Manila University Press, 1981.

Schurhammer, Georg. *Francis Xavier: His Life and His Times.* Trans. M. J. Costelloe. Freiburg, 1955– . Originally published as *Franz Xaver: sein Leben und seine Zeit.* 4 vols. Rome: Jesuit Historical Institute, 1973– .

———. *The Malabar Church and Rome during the Early Portuguese Period and Before.* Trichinopoly, India, 1934.

———. *Orientalia.* Rome: Institutum Historicum Societatis Iesu, 1963.

———. *Xaveriana.* Lisbon: Centro de Estudos Historicos Ultramarinos, 1964.

Schurhammer, G., and E. A. Voretzsch. *Ceylon zur Zeit des Konigs Bhuvaneka Bahu und Franz Xavers 1539–1552.* 2 vols. Leipzig: Verlag der Asia Major, 1928 (Portuguese with German notes).

Schurhammer, G., and Josef Wicki. *Epistolae S. Francisci Xaverii.* Rome: MHSI, 1944.

Schütte, Josef Franz. *Valignano's Mission Principles for Japan.* Vol. 1: *From His Appointment as Visitor until His First Departure from Japan (1573–1582).* Part 1: *The Problem (1573–1582).* Part 2: *The Solution (1580–1582).* Trans. J. J. Coyne. St. Louis: Institute of Jesuit Sources, 1980, 1985.

Scott, Sir George. *Burma: A Handbook of Practical Commercial and Political Information.* London: Alexander Moring, 1906.

Scott, William Henry. *The Discovery of the Igorots: Spanish Contacts with the Pagans of Northern Luzon.* Quezon City, Philippines: New Day Publishers, 1974.

———. *Staunton of Sagada: Christian Civilizer.* Reprint from *Historical Magazine of the Protestant Episcopal Church* 31, no. 4 (December 1962).

Scudder, Ida S. See M. Pauline Jeffery, *Dr. Ida: India,* and Dorothy Clarke Wilson, *Dr. Ida: The Story of Dr. Ida Scudder of Vellore.*

Seamands, J. T. "Growth of the Methodist Church in South India." Diss., Asbury Theological Seminary, Wilmore, Ky., 1968.

Sebes, Joseph. *The Jesuits and the Sino-Russian Treaty of Nerchinsk (1689): The Diary of Thomas Pereira, S.J.* Rome: Institutum Historicum S.I., 1961.

Seth, Mesrovb Jacob. *Armenians in India: From the Earliest Times to the Present Day.* New Delhi and Madras: Asian Educational Services, 1992; first published by the author, Calcutta, 1937.

Seventh-day Adventist Encyclopedia. Vol. 10. 2nd ed., rev. Hagerstown, Md.: Herald and Review, 1996.

Seventh-day Adventists Believe. Washington, D.C.: General Conference of Seventh-day Adventists, 1988.

Sharma, Sri Ram. *The Religious Policy of the Mughal Emperors.* London: Asia Publishing House, 1962.

Shaw, P. E. *American Contacts with the Eastern Churches, 1820–1870.* Chicago: American Society of Church History, 1937.

Shearer, Roy E. "Animism and the Church in Korea." MA thesis, Fuller Theological Seminary, 1969.

———. *Wildfire: Church Growth in Korea.* Grand Rapids, Mich.: William B. Eerdmans, 1966.

Shenk, Wilbert R. *Henry Venn–Missionary Statesman*. Maryknoll, N.Y.: Orbis Books, 1983.

———. "Rufus Anderson and Henry Venn: A Special Relationship." *IRM* 5, no. 4 (October 1981): 168–172.

Sheridan, James E. *Chinese Warlord: The Career of Feng Yu-shiang*. Stanford, Calif.: Stanford University Press, 1966.

Sherring, M. A. *The History of Protestant Missions in India, 1706 to 1881*. 2nd rev. ed. London: Religious Tract Society, 1884.

Shetty, V. T. Rajashekar. *Dalit Movement in Karnataka*. Madras: Christian Literature Society, 1978.

Shiels, W. Eugene. *King and Church: The Rise and Fall of the Patronato Real*. Chicago: Loyola University Press, 1961.

Shoberl, Frederic. *Present State of Christianity and of Its Missionary Establishments for Its Propagation in All Parts of the World*. New York: J. & J. Harper, 1828.

Shortland, John R. *The Persecutions of Annam: A History of Christianity in Cochin China and Tongkin*. London: Burns & Oates, 1875.

Shourie, Arun. *Missionaries in India: Continuities, Changes, Dilemmas*. New Delhi: ASA Publications, 1994.

Shwe Wa, Maung. See Maung Shwe Wa.

Sieber, Godfrey. *The Benedictine Congregation of St. Ottilien*. St. Ottilien: EOS Verlag, 1992.

Sih, Paul K. T. *Decision for China: Communism or Christianity*. Chicago: Henry Regnery, 1959.

Silva, Cosme da. See da Silva, Cosme.

Silva, C. R. de. See de Silva, C. R.

Silva, K. M. de. See de Silva, K. M.

Simeon, Charles. *Memorial Sketches of the Rev. David Brown, with a Selection of His Sermons Preached at Calcutta*. London: T. Cadell & W. Davies, 1816.

Singh, K. S. *Birsa Munda and His Movement 1874–1901: A Study of a Millenarian Movement in Chotanagpur*. Calcutta: Oxford University Press, 1983.

Singh, Sadhu Sundar. *The Christian Witness of Sadhu Sundar Sing: A Collection of his Writings*. Ed. T. D. Francis. Madras: Christian Literature Society, 1989.

———. See also C. F. Andrews, *Sadhu Sundar Singh: A Personal Memoir*; A. J. Appasamy, *Sundar Singh*; Perumalla Surya Prakash, *The Preaching of Sadhu Sundar Singh*; Friedrich Heiler, *The Gospel of Sadhu Sundar Singh*.

Siregar, Susan Rodgers. *Adat, Islam and Christianity in a Batak Homeland*. Papers in International Studies, S. E. Asia Series No. 57. Athens: Ohio University Press, 1981.

Sitoy, T. Valentino, Jr. *Comity and Unity: Ardent Aspirations of Six Decades of Protestantism in the Philippines, 1901–1961*. Quezon City, Philippines: National Council of Churches of Christ in the Philippines, 1989.

———. *A History of Christianity in the Philippines: The Initial Encounter*. Vol. 1. Quezon City, Philippines: New Day Publishers, 1985.

———. "Nineteenth-Century Evangelical Beginnings in the Philippines." *SEAJT* 9, no. 1 (October 1967): 42–55.

"The 69th Annual Report of the Methodist Episcopal Church, 1887." In *Woman's Work for Woman* (Philadelphia and New York, 1888), 312.

Slosser, Gaius Jackson. *Christian Unity: Its History and Challenge in All Communions, in All Lands*. London: Kegan, Paul, Trench, Trubner, 1929.

Small, W. J. T., ed. *A History of the Methodist Church in Ceylon 1814–1964*. Colombo: Wesley Press, 1964.

Smalley, William A. *Translation as Mission: Bible Translation in the Modern Missionary Movement*. Macon, Ga.: Mercer University Press, 1991.

Smirnoff, Eugene. *A Short Account of the Historical Development and Present Position of Russian Orthodox Missions*. London: Rivingtons, 1903; reprint, Welshpool, Powys, U.K.: Stylite Publishing, 1986.

Smith, A. Christopher, "A Tale of Many Models: The Missiological Significance of the Serampore Trio." *MIS* 20. no. 4 (October 1992): 479–500.

———. "William Ward, Radical Reform, and Missions in the 1790s." *American Baptist Quarterly* 10, no. 3 (September 1991): 218–244.

Smith, Arthur H. *China in Convulsion*. 2 vols. New York: Fleming H. Revell, 1901.

———. *The Uplift of China*. New York: Eaton & Mains, 1907.

Smith, Eli. *Researches of the Rev. E. Smith and Rev. H. G. O. Dwight in Armenia with a Visit to the Nestorian and Chaldaean Christians of Oormiah and Salmas*. 2 vols. Boston: Crocker and Brewster, 1833.

Smith, George. *The Conversion of India: From Pantaenus to the Present Time, A.D. 193–1893*. New York: Fleming H. Revell, [1894].

———. *Henry Martyn, Saint and Scholar*. London: Religious Tract Society, 1892.

———. *The Life of Alexander Duff*. 2 vols. London: Hodder & Stoughton, 1879. 3rd ed. abridged and revised, 1899.

———. *The Life of William Carey, D.D., Shoemaker and Missionary*. London: John Murray, 1885.

———. *Short History of Christian Missions*. Edinburgh: T & T Clark, 1884.

Smith, Timothy Lawrence. *Called Unto Holiness*. St. Louis: Nazarene Publishing House, 1962.

Smith, V. A. *Akbar the Great Mogul 1542–1605*. Oxford: Clarendon Press, 1917.

Smith-Forbes, Charles James Forbes. *British Burma and Its People*. London: John Murray, 1878.

Smylie, John Edwin. "Protestant Clergymen and America's World Role, 1865–1900." ThD diss., Princeton Theological Seminary, 1959.

Snaitang, O. L. *Christianity and Social Change in Northeast India among the Khasi-Jainti Hill Tribes of Meghalaya*. Calcutta: Vendrame Institute, Shillong, 1993.

Soebadio, Haryati, and C. A. du Marchie Sarvaas, eds. *Dynamics of Indonesian History*. Amsterdam/New York and Oxford: North Holland Publishing Co., 1978.

Soedjatmoko, Mohammad Ali, G. J. Resink, and G. McT. Kahn, eds. *An Introduction to Indonesian Historiography*. Ithaca, N.Y.: Cornell University Press, 1965.

Song-yong, Yu. *Ching-bi-ro*. Hyon Am Press edition, 1969.

Soothill, W. E. *Timothy Richard of China*. London: Seeley, Service, 1924.

Southern, R. W. *Western Views of Islam in the Middle Ages*. Cambridge, Mass.: Harvard University Press, 1962.

Southgate, Horatio. *Narrative of a Visit to the Syrian Jacobite Church of Mesopotamia and the Character and Prospects of the Eastern Churches*. New York: Dana, 1858.

South India Missionary Conference, Ootacamund, 1858. *Report*. Madras: SPCK, 1858.

Souza, Teotonio R. de. "Spiritual Conquest of the East: A Critique of the Church Historiography of Portuguese Asia." *ICHR* 19, no. 1 (June 1985): 10–24.

Soysa, Harold de. *The Church of Ceylon: Her Faith and Mission.* Colombo: Daily News Press for the Church of Ceylon, 1945.

Spae, Joseph J. *Catholicism in Japan.* Tokyo: International Institute for the Study of Religions, 1963.

———. *Christianity Encounters Japan.* Tokyo: Oriens Institute for Religious Research, 1968.

Spaulding, Arthur Whitefield. *Origin and History of Seventh-day Adventists.* 4 vols. Washington, D.C.: Review and Herald Publishing Association, 1962.

Speer, Robert E. *Mission and Politics in China: The Situation in China, A Record of Cause and Effect.* New York: Fleming H. Revell, 1900.

———. *A Missionary Pioneer in the Far East: Divie Bethune McCartee.* New York: Fleming H. Revell, 1922.

———. *Report of Deputation Sent by the Board of Foreign Missions, Presbyterian Church U.S.A., 1915, to Visit the Missions in Siam and the Philippine Islands.* New York: Board of Foreign Missions, Presbyterian Church U.S.A., 1916.

———. *Report on the Mission in Korea of the Presbyterian Board of Foreign Missions, 1897.* New York: Board of Foreign Mission of the Presbyterian Church U.S.A., 1897.

———. *"Re-Thinking Missions" Examined.* New York: Fleming H. Revell, 1933; reprinted from *MRW* (January 1933).

———. *Sir James Ewing.* New York: Fleming H. Revell, 1928.

Spence, Jonathan D. *The China Watchers: Western Advisers in China, 1620–1960.* New York and Harmondsworth: Penguin Books, 1980.

———. *Chinese Roundabout: Essays in History and Culture.* New York and London: W. W. Norton, 1992.

———. *Emperor of China: Self-Portrait of K'ang-hsi.* New York: A. Knopf, 1974.

———. *The Memory Palace of Matteo Ricci.* New York: Viking Penguin, 1984.

———. *To Change China: Western Advisers in China, 1620–1960.* Reprint of 1969 ed. New York: Penguin Books, 1980.

Stacey, Vivienne. *Life of Henry Martyn.* Hyderabad: Henry Martyn Institute of Islamic Studies, 1980.

Stanley, Brian. *The Bible and the Flag: Protestant Missions and British Imperialism in the Nineteenth and Twentieth Centuries.* Leicester, Eng.: Apollos, 1990.

———. *The History of the Baptist Missionary Society 1792–1992.* Edinburgh: T & T Clark, 1992.

Starling, Lucy. *Dawn over Temple Roofs.* New York: World Horizons, 1960.

The Statesman's Year-Book. London: Macmillan, 1864– .

Steensgaard, Niels. *The Asian Trade Revolution of the Seventeenth Century: The East India Companies and the Decline of the Caravan Trade.* Chicago and London: University of Chicago Press, 1974.

Steiger, George Nye. *China and the Occident: The Origin and Development of the Boxer Movement.* New Haven, Conn.: Yale University Press, 1927.

Stevens, George B. *The Life, Letters and Journals of the Rev. and Hon. Peter Parker, M.D.* Boston and Chicago: Congregational Publishing Society, 1896.

Stevenson, Dwight E. *Christianity in the Philippines: A Report on the Only Christian Nation in the Orient.* Lexington, Ky.: College of the Bible, 1955.

Stevenson, William Fleming. *Praying and Winning: Being Some Account of What Men Can Do When in Earnest.* New York: Thomas Whittaker, [1882?].

Stewart, Robert. *Life and Work in India: The Conditions, Methods, Difficulties, Results, Future Prospects and Reflex Influence of Missionary Labor in India, especially in the Punjab Mission of the United Presbyterian Church of North America.* Philadelphia: Pearl Publishing Co., 1896.

Stirrat, R. L. *Power and Religiosity in a Post-Colonial Setting: Sinhala Catholics in Contemporary Sri Lanka.* Cambridge: Cambridge University Press, 1992.

Stock, Eugene. *Beginnings in India.* London: SPCK, 1917.

———. *An Heroic Bishop: the Life Story of French of Lahore.* 2nd ed. London: Hodder & Stoughton, 1914.

———. *The History of the Church Missionary Society: Its Environment, Its Men and Its Work.* 5 vols. London: Church Missionary Society, 1899, 1916.

Stock, Frederick and Margaret. *People Movements in the Punjab with Special Reference to the United Presbyterian Church.* Pasadena, Calif.: William Carey Library, 1975.

Stokes, Charles D. "History of Methodist Missions in Korea, 1885–1930." PhD diss., Yale University, 1947.

Streit, Carolus. *Atlas Hierarchicus.* Paderborn: Typographiae Bonifacianae, 1913.

Streit, P. Karl. *Katholischen Missionsatlas.* Steyl, Germany: Verlag der Missionsdruckerei, 1906.

Streit, Robert, and Johannes Dindinger. *Bibliotheca Missionum.* 10 vols. Munster and Aachen: Veröffentlichungen des Internationalen Instituts für missionswissenschaft Forschung, 1916–1939.

Strong, W. E. *The Story of the American Board: An Account of the First Hundred Years of the American Board of Commissioners for Foreign Missions.* Boston: Pilgrim Press, 1910.

St. Thomas Christian Encyclopaedia of India. 2 vols. Ed. G. Menachery. Trichur, India: St. Thomas Christian Encyclopaedia of India, 1973, 1982.

Stuart, John. *Burma through the Centuries.* London: Kegan, Paul, Trench, Trubner, 1925.

Student Mission Power: Report of the First International Convention of the Student Volunteer Movement, 1891. Pasadena, Calif.: William Carey Library, 1979.

Stueck, William. *The Korean War: An International History.* Princeton, N.J.: Princeton University Press, 1995.

Stults, Donald Leroy. *Developing an Asian Evangelical Theology.* Mandaluyong, Manila, Philippines: OMF Literature Inc., 1989.

Subramanyam, Ka Naa. *The Catholic Community in India.* Madras: Macmillan, 1970.

Sundkler, Bengt G. M. *The Church of South India: The Movement toward Unity.* London: Lutterworth Press, 1954.

Suria, Carlos. *History of the Catholic Church in Gujarat.* Anand, Gujarat, India: Gujarat Sahitya Prakash, 1990.

"A Survey of Roman Catholic Missions." *IRM* 4 (1915): 461–468.

Surya Prakash, Perumalla. *The Preaching of Sadhu Sundar Singh: A Homiletic Analysis of Independent Preaching and Personal Character.* Bangalore: Wordmakers, 1991.

Swain, Clara A. *A Glimpse of India.* New York: James Pott, 1909; reprint, New York and London: Garland Publishing, Inc., 1987.

———. See Mrs. Robert Hoskins, *Clara A. Swain, M.D., First Medical Missionary to the Women of the Orient.*

Swanson, Herbert R. *Krischak Muang Nua: A Study in Northern Thai Church History.* Bangkok: Chuan Printing Press, 1984.

———. *Towards a Clean Church: A Case Study in 19th Century Thai Church History.* Bangkok: Church of Christ in Thailand, 1991.

Sword, Victor H. *Baptists in Assam: A Century of Missionary Service, 1836–1936.* Chicago: Conference Press, 1935.

Syamananda, Rong. *A History of Thailand.* 3rd ed. Bangkok: Chulalongkorn University, 1977.

Syiemlieh, David. *A Brief History of the Catholic Church in Nagaland.* Shillong, India: Vendrame Institute Publications, 1990.

Sykes, P. M. *A History of Persia.* London: Macmillan, 1915.

Takeshi, Ishida. *Culture and Religion in Japanese-American Relations: Essays of Uchimura Kanzo.* Ed. Ray Moore. Ann Arbor: University of Michigan, 1981.

Talmage, John Van Nest. *A Prisoner of Christ Jesus in Korea.* Montreat, N.C.: desk-top printing slightly abridged from 1947 original manuscript, Presbyterian Historical Foundation.

———. See also John Gerardus Fagg, *Forty Years in South China: The Life of John Van Nest Talmage.*

Tan, Chester C. *The Boxer Catastrophe.* New York: Columbia University Press, 1955.

Tang, Edmond, and Jean-Paul Wiest, eds. *The Catholic Church in Modern China.* Maryknoll, N.Y.: Orbis Books, 1993.

Tarzian, Mary Mangigian. *The Armenian Minority Problem, 1914–1934.* Atlanta: Scholars Press, 1992.

Tassinari, R. "The End of Padre Sidotti: Some New Discoveries." *MN* 5, no. 1 (1942): 246–253.

Taylor, Dr. and Mrs. Howard. *Hudson Taylor and the China Inland Mission: The Growth of a Work of God.* London and Philadelphia: China Inland Mission, 1920.

———. *Hudson Taylor in Early Years: The Growth of a Soul.* New York: Hodder & Stoughton, George H. Doran, 1912.

Taylor, Hudson. See Marshall Broomhall, *Hudson Taylor, The Man Who Believed God,* and *By Love Compelled* (1936); A. J. Broomhall, *Hudson Taylor and China's Open Century,* 7 vols.; and J. C. Pollock, *Hudson Taylor and Maria.*

Taylor, Mrs. Howard (Geraldine Guinness). *Pastor Hsi,* 3 vols. 1. *Pastor Hsi: One of China's Scholars.* Philadelphia: China Inland Mission, 1900; 5th ed. 1905; 2. *Pastor Hsi: One of China's Christians.* New York: Fleming H. Revell, 1903; 7th ed., 1905; and 3. *Pastor Hsi: A Struggle for Chinese Christianity.* Singapore: Overseas Missionary Fellowship, 1997, combining and revising vols. 1 and 2.

Taylor, Jeremy. *Holy Living and Dying.* London: Charles Baldwyn, 1824.

Taylor, J. Hudson. *China's Spiritual Needs and Claims.* London: Morgan and Scott, 1884.

———. "To Every Creature," *ChM* (December 1889): 171–173.

Taylor, Richard. *Acknowledging the Lordship of Christ: Selected Writing of Richard W. Taylor.* Ed. Saral K. Chatterji. Bangalore/Delhi: Christian Institute for the Study of Religion/ISPCK, 1992.

Taylor, William. *Story of My Life.* New York: Eaton & Mains, 1895.

Tegenfeldt, Herman G. *A Century of Growth: The Kachin Baptist Church of Burma.* Pasadena, Calif.: William Carey Library, 1974.

Tennent, James Emerson. *Christianity in Ceylon*. London: John Murray, 1850; reprint, New Delhi: Asian Educational Services, 1998.

Thailand in Transition: The Church in a Buddhist Setting. Special Notes, No. 48. Brussels: Pro Mundi Vita, 1973.

Thayil, Thomas. "The Origin of the Latin Christians of Kerala." In the *St. Thomas Christian Encyclopaedia*, ed. G. Menachery. 2 vols. Trichur, India: St. Thomas Christian Encyclopaedia of India, 1973, 1982.

Thekkedath, Joseph. *From the Middle of the Sixteenth Century to the End of the Seventeenth Century*. Vol. 2 in *History of Christianity in India*. Bangalore: Church History Association of India, 1982.

———. *The Troubled Days of Francis Garcia, S.J., Archbishop of Cranganore (1641–1659)*. Rome: Università Gregoriana, 1972.

Theresa, Dominic A. S. "Vicars Apostolic and Missions under the Propaganda in the XVII and XVIII Centuries." In the *St. Thomas Christian Encyclopaedia of India*. Ed. G. Menachery, 1:27ff. 2 vols. Trichur, India: St. Thomas Christian Encyclopaedia of India, 1973, 1982.

Thoburn, Isabella. See J. M. Thoburn, *Life of Isabella Thoburn*.

Thoburn, James M. *India and Malaysia*. Cincinnati/New York: Cranston & Curts/Hunt & Eaton, 1893.

———. *Life of Isabella Thoburn*. Cincinnati: Jennings & Pye, 1903; reprint, New York and London: Garland Publishing Co. 1987.

———. *Light in the East*. Evanston, Ill.: Thomas Craven, 1894.

———. *My Missionary Apprenticeship*. New York: Phillips & Hunt, 1896.

Thomas, A. *Histoire de la mission de Pékin*. Part 1: *Depuis les origines jusqu'a l'arrivée des Lazaristes*, 1–464; Part 2: *Depuis l'arrivée des Lazaristes jusqu'a la revolte des Boxeurs*, 1:1–758. Paris: Louis-Michaud, 1923.

Thomas, Abraham Vazhayil. *Christians in Secular India*. Rutherford and Cranbury, N.J.: Fairleigh Dickinson University Press, 1974.

Thomas, George. *Christian Indians, and Indian Nationalism 1885–1950: An Interpretation in Historical and Theological Perspectives*. Vol. 22 in *Studien zur Interkulturellen Geschichte des Christianisme*. Frankfurt a.M: Peter D. Lang, 1979.

Thomas, M. M. *The Acknowledged Christ of the Indian Renaissance*. London: SCM, 1969.

———. *The Christian Response to the Asian Revolution*. London: SCM Press, 1966.

———. *Religion and the Revolt of the Oppressed*. Delhi: ISPCK, 1981.

———. *Towards an Evangelical Social Gospel: A New Look at the Reformation of Abraham Malpan*. Madras: Christian Literature Society, 1977.

Thomas, Paul Westwood and Paul William. *The Days of Our Pilgrimage: The History of the Pilgrim Holiness Movement*. Marion, Ind.: Wesley Press, 1976.

Thomas, P. J. *100 Indian Witnesses to Jesus Christ*. Bombay: Bombay Tract and Book Society, 1974.

Thomas, Winburn T. *Protestant Beginnings in Japan: The First Three Decades, 1859–1889*. Tokyo and Rutland, Vt.: C. E. Tuttle, 1959.

Thompson, Augustus C. *Moravian Missions: Twelve Lectures*. New York: Charles Scribner's Sons, 1882.

Thompson, Edward John. *Suttee: A Historical and Philosophical Enquiry into the Hindu Rite of Widow-Burning*. London: George Allen & Unwin, 1928.

Thompson, H. P. *Into All Lands: The History of the Society for the Propagation of the Gospel in Foreign Parts 1701–1950.* London: SPCK, 1951.

Thompson, R. Wardlaw. *Griffith John: The Story of Fifty Years in China.* New York: A. C. Armstrong & Son, 1906.

Thompson, William. *Memoirs of the Rev. Samuel Munson and the Rev. Henry Lyman.* New York: D. Appleton, 1839.

Thurston, Mrs. Lawrence, and Ruth M. Chester. *Ginling College.* New York: United Board for Christian Colleges in China, 1955.

Ting, K. H. *Christian Witness in China Today.* Kyoto, Japan: Doshisha University Press, 1985.

———. *No Longer Strangers: Selected Writings of K. H. Ting.* Ed. R. L. Whitehead. Maryknoll, N.Y.: Orbis Books, 1989.

Tisserant, Cardinal Eugene. *La Chaldée Chrétienne.* Paris: Bureaux de l'Oeuvre des Ecoles Orient, 1892.

———. *Eastern Christianity in India: A History of the Syro-Malabar Church from the Earliest Time to the Present Day.* Trans. E. R. Hambye. Westminster, Md.: Newman Press, 1957.

———. "L'Eglise Nestorienne." In *DTC* 9.

Tobing, Philip O. Lumban. *The Structure of the Toba-Batak Belief in the High God.* Amsterdam: Jacob van Campen, 1956.

Tong, Hollington K. *Christianity in Taiwan: A History.* Taipei: China Post, 1961.

Torbet, Robert G. *Venture of Faith: The Story of the American Baptist Foreign Missionary Society and the Woman's American Baptist Foreign Missionary Society 1814–1954.* Philadelphia: Judson Press, 1955.

Totman, Conrad. *Tokugawa Ieyasu: Shogun.* Union City, Calif.: Heian International Inc., 1983.

Tovey, Philip. "Abraham Malpan and the Amended Syrian Liturgy of CMS." *ICHR* 29, no. 1 (1995): 38–55.

Tow, Timothy. *Ting Li Mei: The First Chinese Evangelist.* Singapore: Far Eastern Bible College Press, 1988.

Towery, Britt F. *Churches of China: Taking Root Downward, Bearing Fruit Upward.* 3rd ed. Waco, Tex.: Baylor University, 1990.

Toynbee, Arnold J. *Armenian Atrocities: The Murder of a Nation.* London and New York: Hodder & Stoughton, 1915.

———. *Christianity among the Religions of the World.* New York: Scribner's, 1957.

———. *The World and the West.* New York: Oxford University Press, 1953.

Tracy, Joseph. *History of the American Board of Commissioners for Foreign Missions.* 2nd ed. New York: M. W. Dodd, 1842.

———. *History of the American Missions to the Heathen from Their Commencement to the Present Time.* Worcester, Mass.: Spooner & Howland, 1840.

Trager, Helen G. *Burma through Alien Eyes.* New York: Frederick A. Praeger, 1966.

Tran-Minh, Tiét. *Histoire des Persécutions au Viet-Nam.* Paris: Editions "Transpacifique," 1955.

Trigault, Nicholas, ed. See Matteo Ricci, *China in the Sixteenth Century.*

Trinidade, Paulo da. *Conquista do Oriente.* Trans. of vol. 3, ch. 1–56 by E. Peiris and A. Meersman as *Early Christianity in Ceylon.* Chilaw, Colombo: Edmund Pieris, 1972.

Trollope, Mark N. *The Church in Korea.* London: A. R. Mowbray, 1915.

Trowbridge, T. C. *Armenia and the Armenians*. Marash, Turkey: From *The New Englander*, January 1874.

Tuck, Patrick J. N. *French Catholic Missionaries and the Politics of Imperialism in Vietnam, 1857–1914*. Liverpool: Liverpool University Press, 1987.

Tucker, Henry St. George. *The History of the Episcopal Church in Japan*. New York and London: Charles Scribner's Sons, 1938.

Tucker, Ruth A. *Guardians of the Great Commission: The Story of Women in Modern Missions*. Grand Rapids, Mich.: Zondervan, 1988.

Tucker, Ruth A., and Walter Liefeld. *Daughters of the Church: Women and Ministry from New Testament Times to the Present*. Grand Rapids, Mich.: Zondervan, 1987.

Tuggy, Arthur Leonard. *The Philippine Church: Growth in a Changing Society*. Grand Rapids, Mich.: William B. Eerdmans, 1971.

Tuggy, Arthur Leonard, and Ralph Toliver. *Seeing the Church in the Philippines*. Manila: O.M.F. Publishers, 1972.

Turnbull, Stephen. *The Kakure Kirishitan of Japan: A Study of Their [the hidden Christians] Development, Beliefs and Rituals to the Present Day*. Richmond, Surrey, U.K.: Curzon Press/Japan Library, 1998.

Twitchett, Denis C., and John K. Fairbank, eds. *The Cambridge History of China*. Vols. 10–15. Cambridge: Cambridge University Press, 1978– .

Tyndale-Biscoe, C. E. *Elizabeth Mary Newman, 1855–1932: The Florence Nightingale of Kashmir*. London: Seeley, Service, n.d.

Uchimura, Kanzo. *The Diary of a Japanese Convert*. New York: Fleming H. Revell, and Tokyo: Keiseisha, 1895.

Underwood, Horace Grant. *The Call of Korea: Political-Social-Religious*. New York and London: Fleming H. Revell, 1908.

———. "Korea Today." *MRW* 17 (1894): 661ff.

———. Letter. *ChHB* 3 (February 1888): 196.

———. "An Outline History of the Korea Mission of the Presbyterian Church in U.S.A." In *Rev. Underwood's Missionary Letters*, 918–943.

———. *The Religions of Eastern Asia*. New York: Macmillan, 1910.

———. *Rev. Underwood's Missionary Letters (1885–1916)*. Trans. Kim In-Soo. Seoul: Presbyterian College and Theological Seminary, 2002. Letter November 29, 1926, *FM* 45, no. 5 (October 1886): 223–224.

———. See also Key S. Ryang, "Horace Grant Underwood (1851–1916) in Korea."

Underwood, Horace Horton. *Modern Education in Korea*. New York: International Press, 1926.

Underwood, Lillias H. *Fifteen Years Among the Top-Knots*. New York: American Tract Society, 1904.

———. *Underwood of Korea: Being an Intimate Record of the Life and Work of the Rev. H. G. Underwood*. New York: Fleming H. Revell, 1918.

United Nations, Population Division, "The World at Six Billion." 1991, by telnet.

———. "World Population Growth from Year 0 to 2050." 1999, by telnet.

Urumpackal, Alex Paul. *Vocations in India*. Vol. 1: *The Religious Women*. Vol. 2: *The Clergy*. Kottayam, Kerala, India: Oriental Institute of Religious Studies, 1986, 1988.

Uyttenbroeck, Thomas. *Early Franciscans in Japan*. Himeji, Japan: Committee of the Apostolate, 1959.

Vaidyan, Thomas. "The Mar Thoma Church: A Critical Study." *The Indian Journal of Theology* (Calcutta), 34, nos. 1–3 (1985).

Van Buskirk, James Dean. *Korea, Land of the Dawn.* New York: Friendship Press, 1968.

Vanden Berg, Frank. *Abraham Kuyper.* Grand Rapids, Mich.: William B. Eerdmans, 1960.

Vandenbosch, Amry. *The Dutch East Indies: Its Government, Problems, and Politics.* Berkeley: University of California Press, 1941.

———. "The Dutch in the Far East." In *The Netherlands,* ed. Bartholomew Landheer, 333–345. Berkeley: University of California Press, 1944.

———. "Missions on the Island of Bali." *IRM* 23 (1934): 205–214.

van Gulik, W. "Die Konsistorialakten über die Begründung des uniert-chaldäischen Patriarchates von Mosul unter Papst Julius III." In *Oriens Christianus.* Vol. 2. Rome, 1904.

Van Hecken, Joseph L. *The Catholic Church in Japan since 1859.* Trans. and rev. J. Van Hoydonck. Tokyo: Herder Agency, Enderle Bookstore, 1963.

Van Helsdingen, W. H., and H. Hoogenberk, eds. *Mission Interrupted: The Dutch in the East Indies and Their Work in the XXth Century.* Amsterdam and New York: Elsevier, 1945.

van Hoevell, W. R. *De emancipatie der slaven in Nederlandisch Indie.* Groningen: C. M. von Bolhuis Hoitsema, 1848.

Varg, Paul A. *Missionaries, Chinese, and Diplomats: The American Protestant Missionary Movement in China, 1890–1952.* Princeton, N.J.: Princeton University Press, 1958.

Varghese, V. Titus, and P. P. Philip. *Glimpses of the History of the Christian Churches in India.* Madras: Christian Literature Society, 1983.

Väth, Alfons. *Johann Adam Schall von Bell, S.J., Missionar in China, Kaiserlicher Astronom und Ratbeger am Hofe von Peking, 1592–1666.* Cologne: J. P. Bachem, 1933.

Vaulx, Bernard de. *Histoire des missions catholiques françaises.* Paris: Fayard, 1951.

———. *History of the Missions.* Vol. 99: *Twentieth Century Encyclopedia of Catholicism.* New York: Hawthorne Press, 1961.

Veer, Peter van der. *Religious Nationalism: Hindus and Muslims in India.* Berkeley: University of California Press, 1994.

Velden, J. H. Van der. *Die Roomsche-Katholike Missie in Netherlandsch Oost-Indie 1808–1908.* Nijmegen: L. C. G. Malmberg, 1908.

Venn, Henry. See Wilbert Shenk, *Henry Venn.*

Verbeck, Guido F., "History of Protestant Missions in Japan." In *Proceedings, General Conference of the Protestant Missions in Japan, Osaka, 1883.* Yokohama, Japan: R. Meiklejohn, 1883; and *Proceedings, General Conference…,* 1900. Tokyo: Methodist Publishing House, 1901.

Verbiest, Ferdinand. *The Astronomia Europaea of Ferdinand Verbiest.* Dillingen, 1687. Latin text, Eng. trans., notes, commentary. Nettetal: Steyler Verlag, 1993.

Verkuyl, J. *Contemporary Missiology.* Grand Rapids, Mich.: William B. Eerdmans, 1978.

Vine, Aubrey R. *The Nestorian Churches: A Concise History of Nestorian Christianity in Asia from the Persian Schism to the Modern Assyrians.* London: Independent Press, 1937.

Vines, Charlotte E. *Indian Medical Sketches*. London: Church of England Zenana Medical Missionary Society, 1908.

Vinton, C. C. "Presbyterian Mission Work in Korea." *MRW* New Series, 6, no. 9 (September 1893): 671.

Visvanathan, Susan. *The Christians of Kerala: History, Belief and Ritual among the Yakoba*. Madras: Oxford University Press, 1993.

Vlekke, Bernard H. M. *Nusantara: A History of the East Indian Archipelago*. Cambridge, Mass.: Harvard University Press, 1945.

———. *The Story of the Dutch East Indies*. Cambridge, Mass.: Harvard University Press, 1946.

Von der Mehden, Fred R. *Religion and Modernization in Southeast Asia*. Syracuse, N.Y.: Syracuse University Press, 1986.

Von Oeyen, Robert R. *Philippine Evangelical and Independent Catholic Churches: An Historical Bibliography of Church Records and Source Material in the Manila Area*. Quezon City: Asian Center, University of the Philippines, 1970.

Vovelle, Michel. *The Revolution against the Church: From Reason to the Supreme Being*. Trans. A. José. Columbus: Ohio State University Press, 1991.

Wagner, Rudolf G. *Reenacting the Heavenly Vision: The Role of Religion in the Taiping Rebellion*. Berkeley: University of California Press, 1982.

Waldron, John D. *Pioneering Salvationists*. Compiled anthology. New York: Salvation Army, 1987.

Walker, F. Deaville. *William Carey: Missionary Pioneer and Statesman*. London: Student Christian Movement, 1926.

Walls, Andrew. "The American Dimension in the History of the Missionary Movement." In *Earthen Vessels: American Evangelicals and Foreign Missions 1880–1980*, ed. J. A. Carpenter and W. R. Shenk, 1–25. Grand Rapids, Mich.: Eerdmans, 1990.

Wallstrom, Timothy C. *The Creation of a Student Christian Movement to Evangelize the World: A History of the Student Volunteer Movement for Foreign Missions*. Pasadena: Calif.: William Carey Press, 1980.

Walsh, James A. *Observations in the Orient: The Account of a Journey to Catholic Mission Fields in Japan, Korea, Manchuria, China, Indo-China and the Philippines*. Ossining, N.Y.: Catholic Foreign Missionary Society of America, 1919.

Wang, Y. C. *Chinese Intellectuals and the West, 1872–1949*. Chapel Hill: University of North Carolina Press, 1966; reprint, Taiwan: Rainbow Bridge Book, 1966.

Wanless, Lillian Emery. *Wanless of India: Lancet of the Lord*. Boston: W. A. Wilde, 1944.

Wanless, William. *An American Doctor at Work in India*. New York: Fleming H. Revell, 1932.

Warburton, Stacy R. *Eastward! The Story of Adoniram Judson*. New York: Round Table Press, 1937.

Ward, Francis Kingdon. *In Farthest Burma*. Philadelphia: Lippincott, 1921.

Ward, William H. *A View of the History, Literature, and Mythology of the Hindoos: Including a minute Description of their Manners and Customs*. 2 vols. Serampore, India: Mission Press, 1815, 1818.

Warneck, Gustav. *Outline of a History of Protestant Missions from the Reformation to the Present Time*. Trans. G. Robson from the 7th German edition. New York: Fleming H. Revell, 1903.

Warneck, Johannes. *50 Jahre Batakmission in Sumatra*. Berlin: Martin Warneck, 1911.

———. *The Living Christ and Dying Heathenism: The Experience of a Missionary in Animistic Heathenism*. Grand Rapids, Mich.: Baker Book House, 1954.

———. *Ludwig Ingwer Nommensen*. 4th ed. Wuppertal-Barmen: Verlag des missionhauser, 1934.

———. *Werfet eure Netze aus*. Berlin: M. Warneck, 1938.

Wasson, Alfred W. *Church Growth in Korea*. New York: International Missionary Council, 1934. Studies in the World Mission of Christianity. *Occasional Papers*, No. 1.

Waterfield, R. E. *Christians in Persia*. London: George Allen & Unwin, 1973.

Watson, Hazel T. "Revival and Church Growth in Korea 1884–1910." MA thesis, Fuller Theological Seminary, 1969.

Wayland, Francis. *The Apostolic Ministry*. Rochester: Sage & Brother, 1853.

———. *A Memoir of the Life and Labors of the Rev. Adoniram Judson, D.D.* 2 vols. Boston: Phillips, Sampson, and Co., 1853.

Weber, Hans-Ruedi. *Asia and the Ecumenical Movement 1895–1961*. London: SCM Press, 1966.

Weber, Irenee. *The Jewish Bishop and the Chinese Bible: S. I. J. Schereschewsky*. Leiden: Brill, 1999.

Webster, John C. B. *A History of the Dalit Christians in India*. San Francisco: Mellen Research University Press, 1992.

Weems, Benjamin B. *Reform, Rebellion, and the Heavenly Way*. Tucson: University of Arizona Press, 1964.

Wehrle, Edmund S. *Britain, China, and the Antimissionary Riots, 1890–1900*. Minneapolis: University of Minnesota Press, 1966.

Wei, Louis Tsing-sing. *La politique missionnaire de la France en Chine (1842–1856)* (*Fa-kuo tui Hua ch'uan chiao cheng ts'e shang ho ch'uan chiao tzu yu*). Paris: Nouvelles Éditiones latines, 1960; Beijing, 1991.

Weldon, John. "A Sampling of the New Religions: Four Groups Described." In *IRM* 47, no. 268 (October 1978): 407–426.

Wells, Harold. "Korean Syncretism and Theologies of Interreligious Encounter: The Contribution of Kyoung Jae Kim." In *AJT* 12, no. 1 (April 1998): 56–76.

Wells, Kenneth E. *History of Protestant Work in Thailand, 1828–1958*. Bangkok: Church of Christ in Thailand, 1958.

Wen Ch'ing (Lim Boon-keng). *The Chinese Crisis from Within*. Ed. G. M. Reith. London, 1901.

Wendte, C. W. *The Promotion of Unitarianism in Foreign Lands*. Boston: American Unitarian Association, 1912.

Wessels, Cornelius. *Early Jesuit Travellers in Central Asia, 1603–1721*. The Hague: Martinus Nijhoff, 1924.

Wherry, E. M. *Woman in Missions: Papers and Addresses at the Woman's Congress of Missions, October 1893*. New York: American Tract Society, 1894.

Whisler, F. B., and I. C. Whisler. *India's Awakening*. Indianapolis: Publishing House of the Pentecostal Bands, n.d.

Whitehead, James D., Y. M. Shaw, N. J. Girardot, eds. *China and Christianity*. Notre Dame, Ind.: University of Notre Dame, 1979.

Whiteway, R. S. *The Rise of the Portuguese Power in India, 1497–1550*. London: A. Constable, 1889.

Whittemore, Lewis Bliss. *Struggle for Freedom: History of the Philippine Independent Church*. Greenwich, Conn.: Seabury Press, 1961.

Whyte, Bob. *Unfinished Encounter: China and Christianity*. Glasgow and London: William Collins Sons, 1988.

Wickeri, Philip L. "Christianity and the Taiping Rebellion: An Historical and Theological Study." MDiv thesis, Princeton Theological Seminary, 1974.

———. *Seeking the Common Ground: Protestant Christianity, the Three-Self Movement and China's United Front*. Maryknoll, N.Y.: Orbis Books, 1988.

Wicki, Josef (Iosephus). *Documenta Indica*, 14 vols., in *Monumenta Historica Societatis Iesu*. Rome: MHSI, 1948–1979.

———. "Early Jesuit Connections." In *St. Thomas Christian Encyclopaedia of India*, vol. 2.

Wiest, Jean-Paul. *Maryknoll in China: A History, 1918–1955*. Armonk, N.Y., and London: M. E. Sharpe, 1988.

Wietzke, Joachim, ed. *Paul D. Devanandan: A Selection*. See under Devanandan.

Wiggins, Arch R. *The History of the Salvation Army*. Vol. 5. London: Thomas Nelson, 1968.

Wilberforce, S., ed. *Journal and Letters of the Rev. Henry Martyn*. 1st American ed. New York: M. W. Dodd, 1851.

Wilbur, C. Martin. *The Student Volunteer Movement for Foreign Missions: Some Personal Reminiscences*. Pamphlet. New York, 1935.

———. *Sung Yat-sen, Frustrated Patriot*. New York: Columbia University Press, 1976.

Willeke, Bernward. "Biographical Data on the Early Franciscans in Japan (1584–1640)." *AFH* 83 (1990).

———. *Imperial Government and Catholic Missions in China During the Years 1784–1785*. St. Bonaventure, N.Y.: Franciscan Institute, 1948.

Williams, C. Peter. *The Ideal of the Self-Governing Church: A Study in Victorian Missionary Strategy*. Leiden: E. J. Brill, 1990.

Williams, F. W. "Journal of S. Wells Williams: Perry Expedition." *ASJT* 37, part 11 (1910).

Williams, S. Wells. *The Middle Kingdom: A Survey of the Geography, Government, Education, Social Life, Arts and History of the Chinese Empire*. 2 vols. Rev. ed. London: W. H. Allen, 1883.

Willis, Helen. *"Through Encouragement of the Scriptures": Ten Years in Communist Shanghai*. Hong Kong: Christian Book Room, 1963.

Wilson, D. Kanagasabai. *The Christian Church in Sri Lanka: Her Problems and Her Influence*. Colombo: Study Centre for Religion and Society, 1975.

Wilson, Dorothy Clarke. *Dr. Ida: The Story of Dr. Ida Scudder of Vellore*. New York: McGraw-Hill, 1959.

Wilson, K. *The Twice Alienated Culture of Dalit Christians*. Hyderabad, India: Booklinks Corp., 1982.

Winius, George Davison. *The Fatal History of Portuguese Ceylon: Transition to Dutch Rule*. Cambridge: Harvard University Press, 1971.

Winter, Ralph D., and R. Pierce Beaver. *The Warp and the Woof: Organizing for Mission*. Pasadena, Calif.: William Carey Library, 1970.

Wise, Francis H. "The History of the Philippine Independent Church (Iglesia Filipina Independiente): Analyzing It as a Social Movement." MA thesis, University of the Philippines, 1965.

Witschi, H. *Geschichte der Basler Mission.* 5 vols. Vols. 1–3 by Wilhelm Schlatter (Basel: Verlag der Basler Missionbuchhandlung, 1916); vol. 4 by Wilhelm Schlatter, revised by Hermann Witschi (Basel: Basileia Verlag, 1965); vol. 5 by H. Witschi (Basel: Basileia Verlag, 1970).

Wolfe, J. R. "A Visit to Korea." *CMIR* (London), 10 NS (June 1885): 429.

Wolferstan, Bertram. *The Catholic Church in China, 1860–1907.* London: Sands, 1909.

Wolpert, Stanley. *A New History of India.* 2nd ed. New York: Oxford University Press, 1982.

"Woman's Work in Korea." *Korean Repository* 3, no. 1 (January 1896): 3–4.

Wood, Robert D. *In These Mortal Hands: The Story of the Oriental Missionary Society. The First Fifty Years.* Greenwood, Ind.: OMS International, 1983.

Wood, W. A. R. *A History of Siam: from the Earliest Times to the Year 1781, with a Supplement.* London: T. Fisher Unwin, 1926.

Woodsmall, Ruth Frances. *Easter Women Today and Tomorrow.* Boston: Central Committee on the United Study of Foreign Missions, 1933.

World Atlas of Christian Missions. Ed. J. S. Dennis, Harlan Beach, Charles Fahs. New York: Student Volunteer Movement for Foreign Missions, 1911.

World Christian Encyclopedia. Ed. David R. Barrett. 1st ed. New York: Oxford University Press, 1982.

World Christian Encyclopedia. Ed. David R. Barrett, George Vurian, and Todd Johnson. 2nd ed. New York: Oxford University Press, 2001.

World Christian Handbook, 1949, 1952, 1957, 1962, 1968. Ed. K. G. Grubb. London: World Dominion Press.

World Missionary Conference 1910, Reports. 9 vols. Edinburgh, London, New York: Oliphant, Anderson & Ferrier/Fleming H. Revell, 1910.

Wortabet, John. *Researches into the Religions of Syria: or Sketches, Historical and Doctrinal of Its Religious Sects.* London: James Nisbet, 1860.

Wright, David (John). "Sea Power and Diplomacy in the Far East." *TRASK* (Seoul) 67 (1992).

Wright, Edward Reynolds, ed. *Korean Politics in Transition.* Seattle: University of Washington Press, 1975.

Wu, Chao-Kwang. *The International Aspect of the Missionary Movement in China.* Baltimore and London: Johns Hopkins Press/Oxford University Press, 1930.

Wyatt, David K. *Thailand: A Short History.* New Haven, Conn.: Yale University Press, 1984.

Wylie, Alexander. "The Bible in China." *The Bible Society Monthly Reporter.* August 1882.

———. *Memorials of Protestant Missionaries to the Chinese: Giving a List of Their Publications and Obituary Notices.* Shanghai: American Presbyterian Mission Press, 1867.

Wylie, Mrs. Macleod. *The Gospel in Burmah.* London: W. H. Dalton, 1859.

Xavier, Francis. See H. J. Coleridge, *The Life and Letters of St. Francis Xavier;* and G. Schurhammer, *Francis Xavier.*

Xing, Jun (Hsing Jun). *Baptized in the Fire of Revolution: The American Social Gospel and the YMC. in China: 1919–1937.* Bethlehem, Pa.: Lehigh University Press, 1996.

Yamamori, Tetsunao. *Church Growth in Japan, 1859–1939.* Pasadena, Calif.: William Carey Library, 1974.

Yamamoto, J. Isamu. *The Puppet Master: An Inquiry into Sun Myung Moon and the Unification Church.* Downers Grove, Ill.: InterVarsity Press, 1977.

Yanagita, Tomonobu. *A Short History of Christianity in Japan.* Sendai, Japan: Seisho Tosho Kankokai, 1957.

Yang, Nak-Heong. *Reformed Social Ethics and the Korean Church.* New York: Peter Lang, 1997.

Year Book of Missions for India, Burma and Ceylon, 1912. Ed. J. P. Jones. Madras: Christian Literature Society for India, 1912.

Yim, Hee Mo. *Unity Lost — Unity Regained in Korean Presbyterianism: A History of Divisions in Korea Presbyterians and the Role of the Means of Grace.* Frankfurt-am-Main: Peter Lang, 1996.

Yoo, Boo-Woong. *Korean Pentecostalism, Its History and Theology.* Frankfurt am Main/New York: Verlag Peter Lang, 1987.

Young, John D. *Confucianism and Christianity: The First Encounter.* Hong Kong: Hong Kong University Press, 1983.

Young, Kenneth T. "American Advisers in Thailand." In *Asia* no. 14 (Spring 1969): 1–31.

Young, Luther Lisgar. See Robert K. Anderson, *My Dear Redeemer's Praise: The Life of Luther Lisgar Young.*

Young, Richard Fox. *Resistant Hinduism: Sanskrit Sources on Anti-Christian Apologetics in Early Nineteenth-Century India.* Vienna: Institute of Indology of the University of Vienna, 1981.

Young, Richard Fox, and J. P. V. I. Somaratna. *Vain Debates: The Buddhist-Christian Controversies of Nineteenth-Century Ceylon.* Vienna: Institute of Indology, University of Vienna, 1996.

Yu, Chai-shin, ed. *The Founding of Catholic Tradition in Korea.* Mississauga, Ontario, Canada: Korean and Related Studies Press, 1996.

Yun Ch'i-Ho. *Yun Chi'-Ho's Diaries (Yun Ch'i-Ho Ilgi).* 5 vols. Seoul: National History Compilation Committee, 1974–1975. Containing English translations of some sections (1890–1902).

Zabriskie, Alexander C. *Bishop Brent: Crusader for Christian Unity.* Philadelphia: Westminster Press, 1948.

Zaide, Gregorio F. *Philippine Political and Cultural History.* 2 vols. Manila: Philippine Education Co., 1949.

Zetzsche, Jost O. *The Bible in China: The History of the Union Version.* Sangt Augustin: Monumenta Serica Institution, 1999.

Zeylanicus. *Ceylon between Orient and Occident.* London: Elek Books, 1970.

Zhang, John B. Shijiang. "Toward a Wider Reconciliation: A Cultural-Theological Reflection on the Division within the Church in China." *EAPR* 34, no. 1/2 (1997).

Index

725